AMERICAN GOVERNMENT
POWER & PURPOSE

THIRTEENTH EDITION

AMERICAN GOVERNMENT
POWER & PURPOSE

Theodore J. Lowi
Cornell University

Benjamin Ginsberg
The Johns Hopkins University

Kenneth A. Shepsle
Harvard University

Stephen Ansolabehere
Harvard University

W.W. NORTON
NEW YORK · LONDON

W. W. Norton & Company has been independent since its founding in 1923, when William Warder Norton and Mary D. Herter Norton first published lectures delivered at the People's Institute, the adult education division of New York City's Cooper Union. The firm soon expanded its program beyond the Institute, publishing books by celebrated academics from America and abroad. By mid-century, the two major pillars of Norton's publishing program—trade books and college texts—were firmly established. In the 1950s, the Norton family transferred control of the company to its employees, and today—with a staff of four hundred and a comparable number of trade, college, and professional titles published each year—W. W. Norton & Company stands as the largest and oldest publishing house owned wholly by its employees.

Editor: Lisa Camner McKay
Assistant Editor: Sarah Wolf
Project Editor: Christine D'Antonio
Media Editor: Toni Magyar
Associate Media Editor: Lorraine Klimowich
Media Editorial Assistants: Cara Folkman and Kathryn Young
Marketing Manager: Erin Brown
Production Manager: Vanessa Nuttry
Book Designer: Kiss Me I'm Polish LLC, New York
Design Director: Rubina Yeh
Composition: Jouve North America—Brattleboro, VT
Manufacturing: Quad Graphics, Taunton

Library of Congress Cataloging-in-Publication Data

American government : power & purpose / Theodore J. Lowi,
Cornell University, Benjamin Ginsberg, The John Hopkins University,
Kenneth A. Shepsle, Harvard University, Stephen Ansolabehere,
Harvard University. — Thirteenth edition.
       pages cm.
  Includes bibliographical references and index.
  ISBN 978-0-393-92244-8 (hardcover)
  1. United States—Politics and government.   I. Lowi, Theodore J.
JK276.L69 2013
320.473—dc23
                                                    2013039130

W. W. Norton & Company, Inc., 500 Fifth Avenue, New York, N.Y. 10110-0017
www.wwnorton.com

W. W. Norton & Company Ltd., Castle House, 75/76 Wells Street,
London W1T 3QT
1 2 3 4 5 6 7 8 9 10

For Our Families

Angele, Anna, and Jason Lowi
Sandy, Cindy, and Alex Ginsberg
Rise, Nilsa, and Seth Shepsle
Laurie Gould and Rebecca and
Julia Ansolabehere

Contents

2   Constructing a Government:
The Founding and the Constitution   32

7

The Presidency as an Institution 248

8 The Executive Branch: Bureaucracy in a Democracy 302

PART 3 DEMOCRATIC POLITICS

10 Public Opinion 392

11 Elections   446

13 Groups and Interests 558

Preface

This book was written for faculty and students who are looking for a little more than just "nuts and bolts" and who are drawn to an analytical perspective. No fact about American government is intrinsically difficult to grasp, and in an open society such as ours, facts abound. The philosophy of a free and open media in the United States makes information about the government that would be suppressed elsewhere readily available. The advent of the Internet and other new communication technologies has further expanded the opportunity to learn about our government. The ubiquity of information in our society is a great virtue. Common knowledge about the government gives our society a vocabulary that is widely shared among its citizens and enables us to communicate effectively with each other about politics. But it is also important to reach beyond that common vocabulary and develop a more sophisticated understanding of politics and government. The sheer quantity of facts in our society overwhelms us at times. In a 24/7 news cycle it can be hard to pick out what stories are important and to stay focused on them. The single most important task of the teacher of political science is to confront popular ideas and information and to choose from among them the small number of really significant concepts that help us make better sense of the world. This book aims to help instructors and students accomplish this task.

The analytical framework of this book is oriented around five principles that we use to help make sense of politics:

1. All political behavior has a purpose.

2. Institutions structure politics.

3. All politics is collective action.

4. Political outcomes are the products of individual preferences and institutional procedures.

5. How we got here matters.

This Thirteenth Edition continues our endeavor to make *American Government: Power and Purpose* the most authoritative and contemporary introductory text on the market. The approach of the book has not changed. Those who have used this book in the past are familiar with the narrative it presents about American government and politics—the storyline of how the U.S. government has evolved, how it operates, and the characters involved in the unfolding development of our polity. This book also presents an analytical approach to understanding American politics based on the five principles outlined on the previous page. We are guided by the belief that students of government need an analytical framework for understanding political phenomena—a framework rooted in some of the most important insights the discipline of political science has to offer and that encourages students to draw out the general lessons about collective action and collective decision making.

The major changes in this Thirteenth Edition are intended to deepen the text's analysis of how group politics intersects with the institutions and processes of American government. In addition, the book's organization has been tightened, while new section headings help guide students in their reading. The most significant changes include:

- **A new framework in Chapter 5 provides students with a simple but powerful way to analyze civil rights.** Significantly revised, Chapter 5 helps students to understand the contestation over civil rights in terms of *who* has a right and who does not, *what* they have a right to, and *how much* any individual is allowed to exercise that right.

- **Expanded coverage draws on exciting recent research to present students with an analytical perspective on race, gender, and group identity in American politics.** This expansion includes a new section on identity politics in Chapter 10, which analyzes how group identities influence individuals' political opinions and beliefs. Chapter 11 considers the implications of group politics in redistricting battles as well as demographic shifts in who votes and how people vote. Chapter 12 extends the discussion of the group basis of political party identification and allegiance.

- **Six new Analyzing the Evidence units written by expert researchers highlight the political science behind the information in the book,** while the remaining units have been updated with new data and analysis. Each unit poses an important question from political science and presents evidence that can be used to analyze the question. The six new units are:

"Advocacy and Representation for Marginalized Groups"
in Chapter 5
Contributed by Dara Z. Strolovitch, Princeton University

"Why Do Congresswomen Outperform Congressmen?"
in Chapter 6
Contributed by Chris Berry, University of Chicago

"Congressional Design and Control of the Bureaucracy"
in Chapter 8
Contributed by Sean Gailmard, University of California, Berkeley

"The Contact Hypothesis and Attitudes about Gay Rights"
in Chapter 10
Contributed by Patrick J. Egan, New York University

"Candidate Religion and Partisan Voting" in Chapter 12
Contributed by Geoffrey C. Layman, University of Notre Dame;
David E. Campbell, University of Notre Dame; John C. Green,
University of Akron; and Jeremiah J. Castle, University of Notre Dame

"Where Does Interest in the News Come From?" in Chapter 14
Contributed by Scott Althaus, University of Illinois, Urbana-Champaign,
and James Gimpel, University of Maryland, College Park

For the Thirteenth Edition we have profited greatly from the guidance of many
teachers who have used earlier editions and from the suggestions of numerous
thoughtful reviewers. We thank them by name in the Acknowledgments. We
recognize that there is no single best way to craft an introductory text, and we
are grateful for the advice we have received.

Theodore J. Lowi
Benjamin Ginsberg
Kenneth A. Shepsle
Stephen Ansolabehere

Acknowledgments

Our students at Cornell, Johns Hopkins, and Harvard have already been identified as an essential factor in the writing of this book. They have been our most immediate intellectual community, a hospitable one indeed. Another part of our community, perhaps a large suburb, is the discipline of political science itself. Our debt to the scholarship of our colleagues is scientifically measurable, probably to several decimal points, in the footnotes of each chapter. Despite many complaints that the field is too scientific or not scientific enough, political science is alive and well in the United States. Political science has never been at a loss for relevant literature, and without that literature, our job would have been impossible.

We are pleased to acknowledge our debt to the many colleagues who had a direct and active role in criticism and preparation of the manuscript. The First Edition was read and reviewed by Gary Bryner, Brigham Young University; James F. Herndon, Virginia Polytechnic Institute and State University; James W. Riddlesperger, Jr., Texas Christian University; John Schwarz, University of Arizona; Toni-Michelle Travis, George Mason University; and Lois Vietri, University of Maryland. We also want to reiterate our thanks to the four colleagues who allowed us the privilege of testing a trial edition of our book by using it as the major text in their introductory American Government courses: Gary Bryner, Brigham Young University; Allan J. Cigler, University of Kansas; Burnet V. Davis, Albion College; and Erwin A. Jaffe, California State University–Stanislaus.

For subsequent editions, we relied heavily on the thoughtful manuscript reviews we received from David Canon, University of Wisconsin; Russell Hanson, Indiana University; William Keech, Carnegie Mellon University; Donald Kettl, University of Wisconsin; Anne Khademian, University of Wisconsin; William McLauchlan, Purdue University; J. Roger Baker, Wittenburg University; James Lennertz, Lafayette College; Allan McBride, Grambling State University; Joseph Peek, Jr., Georgia State University; Grant

Neeley, Texas Tech University; Mark Graber, University of Maryland; John Gilmour, College of William and Mary; Victoria Farrar-Myers, University of Texas at Arlington; Timothy Boylan, Winthrop University; Robert Huckfeldt, University of California–Davis; Mark Joslyn, University of Kansas; Beth Leech, Rutgers University; and Charles Noble, California State University, Long Beach.

For the Eighth Edition, we benefited from the comments of Scott Ainsworth, University of Georgia; Thomas Brunell, Northern Arizona University; Daniel Carpenter, Harvard University; Brad Gomez, University of South Carolina; Paul Gronke, Reed College; Marc Hetherington, Bowdoin College; Gregory Huber, Yale University; Robert Lowry, Iowa State University; Anthony Nownes, University of Tennessee; Scott Adler, University of Colorado–Boulder; John Coleman, University of Wisconsin–Madison; Richard Conley, University of Florida; Keith Dougherty, University of Georgia; John Ferejohn, Stanford University; Douglas Harris, Loyola College; Brian Humes, University of Nebraska–Lincoln; Jeffrey Jenkins, Northwestern University; Paul Johnson, University of Kansas; Andrew Polsky, Hunter College–CUNY; Mark Richards, Grand Valley State University; Charles Shipan, University of Iowa; Craig Volden, Ohio State University; and Garry Young, George Washington University.

For the Ninth Edition, we were guided by the comments of John Baughman; Lawrence Baum, Ohio State University; Chris Cooper, Western Carolina State University; Charles Finochiaro, State University of New York–Buffalo; Lisa Garcia-Bellorda, University of California–Irvine; Sandy Gordon, New York University; Steven Greene, North Carolina State University; Richard Herrera, Arizona State University; Ben Highton, University of California–Davis; Trey Hood, University of Georgia; Andy Karch, University of Texas at Austin; Glen Krutz, University of Oklahoma; Paul Labedz, Valencia Community College; Brad Lockerbie, University of Georgia; Wendy Martinek, State University of New York–Binghamton; Nicholas Miller, University of Maryland Baltimore County; Russell Renka, Southeast Missouri State University; Debbie Schildkraut, Tufts University; Charles Shipan, University of Iowa; Chris Shortell, California State University, Northridge; John Sides, University of Texas at Austin; Sean Theriault, University of Texas at Austin; and Lynn Vavreck, University of California, Los Angeles.

For the Tenth Edition, we were grateful for the detailed comments of Christian Grose, Vanderbilt University; Kevin Esterling, University of California–Riverside; Martin Johnson, University of California–Riverside; Scott Meinke, Bucknell University; Jason MacDonald, Kent State University; Alan Wiseman, Ohio State University; Michelle Swers, Georgetown University; William Hixon, Lawrence University; Gregory Koger, University of Miami; and Renan Levine, University of Toronto.

For their advice on the Eleventh Edition, we thank Scott Ainsworth, University of Georgia; Bethany Albertson, University of Washington; Brian Arbour, John Jay College; James Battista, University at Buffalo, State University of New York; Lawrence Becker, California State University, Northridge; Damon Cann, Utah State University; Jamie Carson, University of Georgia; Suzanne Chod, Pennsylvania State University; Michael Crespin, University of Georgia; Ryan Emenaker, College of the Redwoods; Kevin Esterling, University of California–Riverside; Brad Gomez, Florida State University; Sanford Gordon, New York University; Christian Grose, Vanderbilt University; James Hanley, Adrian College; Ryan Hurl, University of Toronto; Josh Kaplan, University of Notre Dame; Wendy Martinek, Binghamton University; Will Miller, Southeast Missouri State University; Evan Parker-Stephen, Texas A&M University; Melody Rose, Portland State University; Eric Schickler, University of California–Berkeley; John Sides, George Washington University; and Lynn Vavreck, University of California–Los Angeles.

For the Twelfth Edition we looked to comments from John M. Aughenbaugh, Virginia Commonwealth University; Christopher Banks, Kent State University; Michael Berkman, Pennsylvania State University; Cynthia Bowling, Auburn University; Matthew Cahn, California State University, Northridge; Damon Cann, Utah State University; Tom Cioppa, Brookdale Community College; David Damore, University of Nevada, Las Vegas; Kevin Esterling, University of California–Riverside; Jessica Feezell, University of California–Santa Barbara; Charle J. Finocchiaro, University of South Carolina; Rodd Freitag, University of Wisconsin, Eau Claire; Kevin Jefferies, Alvin Community College; Nancy Jimeno, California State University, Fullerton; Gregory Koger, University of Miami; David E. Lewis, Vanderbilt University; Allison M. Martens, University of Louisville; Thomas M. Martin, Eastern Kentucky University; Michael Andrew McLatchy, Clarendon College; Ken Mulligan, Southern Illinois University, Carbondale; Geoffrey D. Peterson, University of Wisconsin, Eau Claire; Jesse Richman, Old Dominion University; Mark C. Rom, Georgetown University; Laura Schneider, Grand Valley State University; Scot Schraufnagel, Northern Illinois University; Ronald P. Seyb, Skidmore College; Martin S. Sheffer, Tidewater Community College; Charles R. Shipan, University of Michigan; Howard A. Smith, Florida Gulf Coast University; Michele Swers, Georgetown University; Charles Tien, Hunter College; Elizabeth Trentanelli, Gulf Coast State College; and Kenneth C. Williams, Michigan State University.

We also thank the reviewers who advised us on this Thirteenth Edition: Michael M. Binder, University of North Florida; Stephen Borrelli, The University of Alabama; Dan Cassino, Fairleigh Dickinson University; Jangsup Choi, Texas A&M University–Commerce; Martin Cohen, James Madison University; Jeff Colbert, Elon University; Richard S. Conley, University of Florida; Mark Croatti, American University; David Dulio, Oakland University; Andrew M. Essig, DeSales University; Kathleen Ferraiolo, James Madison University; Emily R. Gill, Bradley University; Brad T. Gomez, Florida State University; Paul N. Goren, University of Minnesota; Thomas Halper, Baruch College; Audrey A. Haynes, University of Georgia; Diane J. Heith, St. John's University; Ronald J. Hrebenar, The University of Utah; Ryan Hurl, University of Toronto Scarborough; Richard Jankowski, SUNY Fredonia; Kevin Jefferies, Alvin Community College; Timothy R. Johnson, University of Minnesota; Kenneth R. Mayer, University of Wisconsin–Madison; Mark McKenzie, Texas Tech University; Fiona Miller, University of Toronto Mississauga; Richard M. Pious, Barnard College; Tim Reynolds, Alvin Community College; Martin Saiz, California State University, Northridge; Dante Scala, University of New Hampshire; Sean M. Theriault,

University of Texas at Austin; J. Alejandro Tirado, Texas Tech University; Terri Towner, Oakland University; Nicholas Valentino, University of Michigan; Harold M. Waller, McGill University; and Jeffrey S. Worsham, West Virginia University.

An important contribution to recent editions was made by the authors of the Analyzing the Evidence units. We are grateful to the authors of the new Analyzing the Evidence units in the Thirteenth Edition, who are named in the Preface. In addition, Jenna Bednar, Jamie Carson, Andrea Campbell, Kevin Esterling, Beth Leech, David Lewis, Andrew D. Martin, Kenneth Mayer, Kevin M. Quinn, and Joseph Ura contributed to this feature in earlier editions, and much of their work is still reflected in this edition. We also thank Joe Williams, who provided valuable assistance in updating the data figures and tables throughout the book.

We would also like to thank our partners at W. W. Norton & Company, who have continued to apply their talents and energy to this textbook. The efforts of Erin Brown, Christine D'Antonio, Cara Folkman, Lorraine Klimowich, Toni Magyar, Lisa Camner McKay, Vanessa Nuttry, Sarah Wolf, and Kathryn Young kept the production of the Thirteenth Edition coherent and in focus. We also thank Roby Harrington, Steve Dunn, and Ann Shin, whose contributions to previous editions remain invaluable.

We are more than happy, however, to absolve all these contributors from any flaws, errors, and misjudgments that this book contains. We wish it could be free of all production errors, grammatical errors, misspellings, misquotes, missed citations, etc. From that standpoint, a book ought to try to be perfect. But substantively we have not tried to write a flawless book; we have not tried to write a book to please everyone. We have again tried to write an effective book, a book that cannot be taken lightly. Our goal was not to make every reader a political scientist. Our goal was to restore politics as a subject of vigorous and enjoyable discourse, releasing it from the bondage of the 30-second sound bite and the 30-page technical briefing. Every person can be knowledgeable because everything about politics is accessible. One does not have to be a television anchorperson to profit from political events. One does not have to be a philosopher to argue about the requisites of democracy, a lawyer to dispute constitutional interpretations, an economist to debate public policy. We will be very proud if our book contributes in a small way to the restoration of the ancient art of political controversy.

Theodore J. Lowi
Benjamin Ginsberg
Kenneth A. Shepsle
Stephen Ansolabehere

AMERICAN GOVERNMENT
POWER & PURPOSE

1

Five Principles of Politics

American government and politics are extraordinarily complex. The United States has many levels of government: federal, state, county, city, and town—to say nothing of a host of special and regional authorities. Each of these governments operates under its own rules and statutory authority and is related to the others in complex ways. In many nations, regional and local governments are appendages of the national government. This is not true in the United States. America's state and local governments possess a considerable measure of independence and authority. Each level of government, moreover, consists of an array of departments, agencies, offices, and bureaus, each with its own policies, jurisdiction, and responsibilities, and undertaking a variety of sometimes overlapping tasks. At times this complexity gets in the way of effective governance, as in the case of governmental response to emergencies. America's federal, state, and local public safety agencies seldom share information and frequently use incompatible communications equipment, so they are often not even able to speak to each other. For example, on September 11, 2001, New York City's police and fire departments could not effectively coordinate their responses to the terrorist attack on the World Trade Center because their communications systems were not linked. While communication has improved in the last decade, it is still the case that many security and policy agencies, ranging from the Central Intelligence Agency (CIA) to the National Security Agency (NSA) to the Department of Homeland Security (DHS) to the Federal Bureau of Investigation (FBI), possess separate computer operating systems and databases that inhibit cooperation through sharing.

The complexity of America's government is no accident. Complexity was one element of the Founders' grand constitutional design. The framers of the Constitution hoped that an elaborate division of power among institutions and between the states and the federal government would allow a variety of competing groups, forces, interests, and ideas to have access to arenas of decision making and a voice in public affairs—while preventing any single group or coalition from monopolizing power. One set of interests might be active and powerful in some states, other forces would be influential in the national legislature, and still other groups might prevail in the executive branch. The overall pattern would disperse power and opportunity, allowing many groups to achieve at least some of their political goals. In this way, America's political tradition associates complexity with liberty and political opportunity.

But although America's institutional complexity creates many avenues and possibilities for political action, its complexity also places a considerable burden on citizens who might wish to achieve something through political participation, for they may not be able to easily discern where particular policies are actually made, who the influential decision makers are, and what forms of political participation are most likely to be effective. This is one of the paradoxes of political life: In a dictatorship, lines of political authority may be simple, but opportunities to influence the use of power are few; in America, political opportunities are plentiful, but how they should be used is far from obvious. Indeed, precisely because America's institutional and political arrangements are so complex, many Americans are mystified by government. As we see in Chapter 10, many Americans have difficulty making sense of even the basic features of the Constitution.

If America's government seems complex, its politics can be utterly bewildering. Like the nation's governmental structure, its political processes have numerous components. For most Americans, the focal point of politics is the electoral process. As we see in Chapter 11, tens of millions of Americans participate in a host of national, state, and local elections, during which they listen to thousands of candidates debate a perplexing array of issues. Candidates inundate the media with promises, charges, and countercharges while an army

CORE OF THE ANALYSIS

➡️ Five principles of politics can help us think analytically about American government and make sense of the apparent chaos and complexity of the political world. These five principles are:

➡️ All political behavior has a purpose (rationality principle).

➡️ Institutions structure politics (institution principle).

➡️ All politics is collective action (collective action principle).

➡️ Political outcomes are the products of individual preferences and institutional procedures (policy principle).

➡️ How we got here matters (history principle).

of pundits and journalists, whom we also discuss in Chapters 10 and 14, adds its own clamor to the din.

Politics, however, does not end on Election Day. Indeed, given the growing tendency of losers to challenge election results in the courts, even elections do not end on Election Day. The most famous of these challenges, of course, was the resolution of the 2000 presidential election by the Supreme Court in *Bush v. Gore*. Long after the voters have spoken, political struggles continue in Congress, the executive branch, and the courts; they embroil political parties, interest groups, and the mass media. In some instances, the participants in political struggles and their goals seem fairly obvious. For example, it is no secret that businesses and upper-income wage earners strongly support programs of tax reduction, farmers support maintenance of agricultural subsidies, and labor unions oppose increasing the eligibility age for Social Security. Each of these forces has created or joined organized groups to advance its cause. We examine some of these groups in Chapter 13.

In other instances, though, the participants in political struggles and their goals are not so clear. Sometimes corporate groups hide behind environmental causes to surreptitiously promote their economic interests. Strong environmental requirements make it difficult for prospective competitors to enter their markets. Other times groups claiming to want to help the poor and downtrodden seek only to help themselves. And to make matters worse, many of the government's policies are made behind closed doors, away from the light of publicity. Ordinary citizens can hardly be blamed for failing to understand bureaucratic rule making and other obscure techniques of government.

MAKING SENSE OF GOVERNMENT AND POLITICS

Can we find order in the apparent chaos of politics? The answer is that we can, and doing so is the purpose of this text. Finding order in the apparent chaos of politics is precisely what political scientists do. The discipline of political science, and especially the study of American politics, is devoted to identifying patterns and regularities in all the noise and maneuvering of everyday political life. This is motivated by two fundamental questions: What do we observe? And why?

The first question makes clear that political science is an *empirical* enterprise. By this we mean that it aims to identify facts and patterns that are true in the world around us. What do voters decide when they enter the polling booth? What strategies and tactics do candidates employ to capture votes? What decisions do legislators make about how to vote on bills? What groups organize and put pressure on the institutions of government? How do the media report politics? What tools are available to the president to get what he or she wants in dealing with Congress? How have courts intervened in regulating political life? How do they come to the decisions they have made? These and many other questions have been explored by political science in an effort to observe and ascertain what is true about the political world and will be taken up in great detail in later chapters.

The second question—Why?—is the fundamental concern of science. We not only would like to know that something is true about the world. We also want to know why it is true. Knowing why something is true requires us to create a theory of how the world works. And a theory is constructed from basic principles. The remainder of this chapter will present a set of such basic principles. They will help us navigate the apparent chaos of politics and make sense of what we observe. In this way we not only describe politics, we analyze it.

There is a third type of question that is *normative* rather than empirical or analytical. Normative questions focus on "should" issues—What should the responsibilities of citizenship consist of? How should legislators vote on motions before them? How should judges judge and presidents lead? Political science grapples with all three types of questions. In this book we believe that answers to the empirical and analytical help us formulate answers to the normative.

One of the most important goals of this book is to help readers learn to analyze what they observe in American politics.[1] Analysis requires abstracting. For example, in political science, we are not much interested in an analysis that explains *only* why the Republicans gained congressional seats in the 2010 elections. Explanations that provide an account of a unique circumstance are the province in which pundits, journalists, and other commentators engage as soon as the polls close. You find them on television news programs as well as on the op-ed pages of newspapers. Rather, as political scientists, we seek a more general theory of voting choice that we can apply to particular instances—such as the 2010 elections.

In this chapter, we first discuss what we mean by *government* and *politics*. Then we introduce our five principles of politics. These principles are intentionally somewhat abstract, because we want them to apply to a wide range of circumstances. However, we provide concrete illustrations along the way, and in later chapters we apply the principles presented here more extensively to help us understand the specific features of politics and government in the United States. We conclude this chapter with a brief guide to analyzing evidence, something you will find useful as we examine empirical information throughout the rest of the book.

What Is Government?

Government is the term generally used to describe the formal political arrangements by which a land and its people are ruled. Government is composed of institutions and processes that rulers establish to strengthen and perpetuate their power or control over a land and its inhabitants. A government may be as simple as a tribal council that meets occasionally to advise the chief or as complex as

 government

The institutions and procedures through which a land and its people are ruled

---

1   For an entire book devoted to the issue of analysis, see Kenneth A. Shepsle, *Analyzing Politics: Rationality, Behavior, and Institutions*, 2nd ed. (New York: Norton, 2010).

---

autocracy ➡

A form of government in which a single individual rules

oligarchy ➡

A form of government in which a small group of landowners, military officers, or wealthy merchants controls most of the governing decisions

democracy ➡

A system of rule that permits citizens to play a significant part in the governmental process, usually through the selection of key public officials

constitutional government ➡

A system of rule in which formal and effective limits are placed on the powers of the government

authoritarian government ➡

A system of rule in which the government recognizes no formal limits but may nevertheless be restrained by the power of other social institutions

our own vast establishment, with its elaborate procedures, laws, governmental bodies, and bureaucracies. This more complex government is sometimes called the state, an abstract concept referring to the source of all public authority.

Forms of Government

Governments vary in their institutional structure, in their size, and in their modes of operation. Two questions are of special importance in determining how governments differ from each other: Who governs? And, how much government control is permitted?

In some nations political authority is vested in a single individual—a king or dictator, for example. This state of affairs is called an **autocracy**. When a small group of landowners, military officers, or wealthy merchants controls most of the governing decisions, the government is said to be an **oligarchy**. If more people participate and the populace is deemed to have some influence over decision making, the government is tending toward **democracy**.

Governments also vary considerably in terms of how they govern. In the United States and some other nations, governments are severely limited in terms of *what* they are permitted to control (they are restricted by substantive limits) as well as *how* they go about exercising that control (they are restricted by procedural limits). Governments that are so limited are called **constitutional** governments. In other nations, although the law imposes few real limits, a government is nevertheless kept in check by other political and social institutions that it is unable to control but must come to terms with, such as autonomous territories, an organized church, organized business groups, or organized labor unions. Such governments are generally called **authoritarian**. In a third, very small group of nations, including the Soviet Union under Joseph Stalin, Nazi Germany, and present-day North Korea, governments not only are free of legal limits but also seek to eliminate those organized social groupings that might challenge or limit their authority. These governments typically attempt to dominate or control every sphere of political, economic, and social life and, as a result, are called **totalitarian**.

Politics

In its broadest sense, the term *politics* refers to conflicts over the character, membership, and policies of any organization to which people belong. As Harold Lasswell, a famous political scientist, once put it, politics is the struggle over "who gets what, when, how."[2] Although politics is a phenomenon that can be found in any organization, in this book **politics** refers to conflicts and struggles over the leadership, structure, and policies of governments. But politics also involves collaboration and cooperation. The goal of politics, as we define it, is

---

2 Harold D. Lasswell, *Politics: Who Gets What, When, How* (1936; repr., New York: Meridian, 1958).

to have a share or a say in the composition of the government's leadership, how the government is organized, or what its policies are going to be.

Politics takes many forms. As they attempt to influence the policies and leadership of the government, individuals may run for office, vote, join political parties and movements, contribute money to candidates, lobby public officials, participate in demonstrations, write letters, talk to their friends and neighbors, go to court, and engage in numerous other activities. Some forms of politics are aimed at gaining power, some at influencing those in power, and others at bringing new people to power and throwing the old leaders out. Those in power use myriad means and strategies to try to achieve their goals. Power, in short, is a central focus of politics, but not always or only for its own sake. Power is sought for purposes—to elevate some and remove others, to introduce new policies, and to preserve old ones.

Even though it takes many forms, politics possesses an underlying logic that can be understood in terms of five simple principles:

1. All political behavior has a purpose.
2. Institutions structure politics.
3. All politics is collective action.
4. Political outcomes are the products of individual preferences, institutional procedures, and collective action.
5. How we got here matters.

Some of these principles may seem obvious or abstract. They prove useful, however, because they possess a distinct kernel of truth on the one hand, yet on the other hand are sufficiently general to help us understand politics in a wide variety of settings. Armed with these principles, we can perceive the order underlying the apparent chaos of political events and processes whenever and wherever they take place.

 totalitarian government

A system of rule in which the government recognizes no formal limits on its power and seeks to absorb or eliminate other social institutions that might challenge it

 politics

Conflict, struggle, cooperation, and collaboration over the leadership, structure, and policies of government

FIVE PRINCIPLES OF POLITICS

The Rationality Principle: All Political Behavior Has a Purpose

One compelling reason that governments do what they do is that they respond to what people want. All people have goals and their political behavior is guided by these goals. For many citizens, political behavior is as simple as reading a headline or an editorial in the newspaper while drinking their morning coffee or discussing the latest local political controversy with a neighbor over the back fence. Though political, these actions are normal routines of everyday life. Beyond these very basic acts, citizens' political behavior broadens to include still relatively modest activities, such as watching a political debate on television, arguing about politics with a coworker, signing a petition, or attending a city council meeting. These are understood to be explicitly political activities that require some forethought. Political behavior requiring even more premeditation and effort includes going to the polls and casting a vote in the November election (having first registered in a timely manner), contacting one's legislative representatives about a political issue, contributing time or money to a political campaign, or even running for local office.

Some of these acts require time, effort, financial resources, and resolve, whereas others place small, even insignificant, demands on a person. Nevertheless, all of them are done for specific reasons. They are not random; they are not entirely automatic or mechanical, even the smallest of them; they are purposeful. Sometimes they are engaged in for the sake of entertainment (reading the front page in the morning) or just to be sociable (chatting about politics with a neighbor, coworker, or family member). At other times, they take on considerable personal importance explicitly because of their political content—because an individual cares about, and wants to influence, an issue, a candidate, a party, or a cause. We will treat all of this political activity as purposeful, as having a goal. Indeed, our attempts to identify the goals of various political activities will help us understand them better.

We've just noted that many of the political activities of ordinary citizens are hard to distinguish from conventional everyday behavior—reading newspapers, watching television news, discussing politics, and so on. For the professional politician, on the other hand—the legislator, executive, judge, party leader, bureau chief, or agency head—nearly every act is explicitly political. The legislator's decision to introduce a particular piece of legislation, give a speech in the legislative chamber, move an amendment to a pending bill, vote for or against that bill, or accept a contribution from a particular group requires her careful attention. There are pitfalls and dangers, and the slightest miscalculation can have huge consequences. Introduce a bill that appears to be too pro-labor in the eyes of your constituents, for example, and before you know it you're charged with being in bed with the unions during the next election campaign. Give a speech against job quotas for minorities, and you risk your standing with the minority communities in your state or district. Accept campaign contributions from industries known to pollute, and environmentalists think you are no friend of the earth. Nearly every move a legislator makes is fraught with risks. And because of these risks, legislators think about their moves before they make them—sometimes carefully, sometimes not; sometimes correctly, sometimes not. But whatever actions they take or decide against taking, they make their choices with forethought, with deliberation, with calculation. Their actions are not knee-jerk but are, in a word, **instrumental**. Individuals think through the benefits and the costs of a decision, speculate about future effects, and weigh the risks of their decision. Making decisions is all about weighing probabilities of various events and determining the personal value of various outcomes.

To find examples of instrumental behavior, consider elected officials. Most politicians want to keep their positions or move up the political ladder to even more important positions. They like their jobs for a variety of reasons—salary, privileges, prestige, stepping-stones, and opportunities for accomplishment, to

instrumental

Done with purpose, sometimes with forethought, and even with calculation name just a few. So we can understand why politicians do what they do by thinking of their behavior as instrumental, with a goal of keeping their jobs. This is quite straightforward in regard to elected politicians. They often see no further than the next election and think mainly about how to prevail in that contest. To understand their routines and behaviors, it is essential to figure out who can help them win. "Retail" politics involves dealing directly with constituents, as when a politician helps an individual navigate a federal agency, find a misplaced Social Security check, or apply to a service academy. "Wholesale" politics involves appealing to collections of constituents, as when a legislator introduces a bill that would benefit a group that is active in his state or district (say, veterans), secures money for a bridge or public building in his hometown, or intervenes in an official proceeding on behalf of an interest group that will, in turn, contribute to the next campaign. Politicians may do any and all of these things because it is "right" or for ideological reasons. But we institute elections and provide incentives for politicians to help constituents as a means of winning elections, just in case their generosity of spirit and personal ideology are insufficient. Elections and electoral politics are thus premised on instrumental behavior by politicians.

Political scientists have found it useful to explain the behavior of elected politicians by treating the "electoral connection" as the principal motivation.[3] Elected politicians, in this view, base their behavior on the goal of maximizing votes at the next election, or maximizing their probability of winning. Of course, politicians seek other things as well—public policy objectives, power in their institution (for legislators, this includes acquiring committee chairs and party leadership posts), and ambition for higher office (members of the House may want to become senators, and senators may want the presidency).[4] Primary emphasis on the electoral motivation is premised on the fact that re-election is a necessary condition for pursuing any of the other objectives.[5]

But what about political actors who are not elected? What do they want? Consider a few examples:

- Agency heads and bureau chiefs, motivated by policy preferences and power, seek to maximize their budgets.

- Legislative committee chairs (who are elected to Congress but appointed to committees) are "turf minded," intent on maximizing their committee's policy jurisdiction and thus its power.

---

3 The classic statement of this premise is David R. Mayhew, *Congress: The Electoral Connection* (New Haven, CT: Yale University Press, 1974). Although nearly four decades old, this book remains a source of insight and wisdom.

4 The classic statement of this additional premise is Richard F. Fenno, *Congressmen in Committees* (Boston: Little, Brown, 1973), another book that remains relevant decades after its publication.

5 As Vince Lombardi, the famous coach of the Green Bay Packers football team, once said, "Winning isn't everything; it's the only thing."

- Voters cast ballots to influence the policies of government, with an eye to their own personal welfare as well as their conception of "what's best for the country."

- Justices, serving lifetime terms, maximize the prospects for their view of constitutional interpretation to prevail.[6]

In each of these instances, we can postulate motivations for political actors that seem to fit the political context in which they are found. These goals often have a strong element of self-interest, but they may be broadened out to incorporate "enlightened self-interest," including the welfare of others (such as their families), the entire society, or even all of humanity.

The Institution Principle: Institutions Structure Politics

institutions ➡️

The rules and procedures that provide incentives for political behavior, thereby shaping politics

In pursuing political goals, people—especially elected leaders and other government officials—confront certain recurring problems, and they develop routines and standard ways of addressing those problems. Routinized, structured relations are what we call institutions. **Institutions** are the rules and procedures that provide incentives for political behavior, thereby shaping politics. Institutions may discourage conflict, encourage coordination, enable bargaining, and thus facilitate decision making, cooperation, and collective action.

Institutions are part script and part scorecard. As scripts, they choreograph political activity. As scorecards, they list the players, their positions, what they want, what they know when they take actions, what they can do, and when they can do it. As a consequence, institutions *matter*. The U.S. Senate, for example, was one kind of legislative body when the institutional way in which its members were selected was election by state legislature; it became quite a different kind of legislative body when its members were popularly elected by a state's voters. Term limits, to take another example of how institutions matter, will affect the power of an incumbent mayor, governor, or president: A prohibition against running for re-election weakens an executive by removing the leverage she might otherwise have had if there were the possibility of securing another term in office.

Although the Constitution sets the broad framework for American political institutions, much adaptation and innovation takes place as the institutions themselves are bent to the various purposes of strategic political actors who want to win for their side and defeat the other side. Our focus here will be on the authority that institutions provide politicians for the pursuit of public policies.

---

6 For most political actors, self-interest motivates their behavior. The motivations or purposes of judges and justices have proved more difficult to ascertain in light of the fact that they typically enjoy lifetime appointments (and thus are not looking ahead to the next election or occasion for "contract renewal"). For an interesting discussion of judicial motivations by an eminent law professor and incumbent judge, see Richard Posner, "What Do Judges Maximize? (The Same Thing Everybody Else Does)," *Supreme Court Economic Review* 3 (1993): 1–41.

The discussion is divided into four broad subjects: jurisdiction, agenda and veto power, decisiveness, and delegation.

Jurisdiction.

A critical feature of an institution is the domain over which institutional members have the authority to make decisions. Political institutions are full of specialized **jurisdictions** over which individuals or subsets of members have authority. One feature of the U.S. Congress, for example, is the existence of "standing committees," whose jurisdictions are carefully defined by law. Most members of Congress become specialists in all aspects of the jurisdiction of their committees—and they often seek committee assignments based on the subjects in which they want to specialize. Committee members are granted specific authority within their jurisdiction to set the agenda of the larger parent chamber. For example, proposed legislation related to the military must pass through the Armed Services Committee before it can be voted on by the entire House or Senate. Thus, the politics of the legislative institution in the United States is affected by the way its jurisdiction-specific committees are structured. Similarly, a bureau or agency is established by law, and its jurisdiction—its scope of authority—is firmly fixed. For example, the Food and Drug Administration possesses well-defined authority to regulate the marketing of pharmaceuticals but is not permitted to regulate products falling outside its jurisdiction.

jurisdiction

The domain over which an institution or member of an institution has authority

Agenda Power and Veto Power.

Agenda power describes who determines what will be taken up for consideration in an institution. Those who exercise some form of agenda power are said to engage in gatekeeping. They determine which alternatives may pass through the gate onto the institution's agenda and which alternatives will have the gate slammed in their face. Gatekeeping, in other words, consists of the power to make proposals and the power to block proposals from being made. The ability to keep something off an institution's agenda should not be confused with **veto power**. Veto power is the ability to defeat something even if it does become part of the agenda. In the legislative process, for example, the president has no general gatekeeping authority—he has no agenda power and thus cannot force the legislature to take up a proposal—but does have (limited) veto power provided by the Constitution. Congress, on the other hand, controls its own agenda—its members can place matters on the legislative agenda. Congress cannot be prevented from passing a measure, but a presidential veto can prevent a measure from becoming the law of the land. Thus, when it comes to legislation, agenda power is vested in the legislature. Veto power is possessed both by the legislature and the president (the assent of each is required for a bill to become a law). We'll examine these processes in more detail in Chapters 6 and 7.

agenda power

The control over what a group will consider for discussion

veto power

The ability to defeat something even if it has made it on to the agenda of an institution

Decisiveness.

Another crucial feature of an institution is its rules for making decisions. It might sound like a straightforward task to lay out the rules for decision making, but in practice such rules often require a raft of conditions and qualifications. Every organization has rules of some sort, and the more an organization values participation by the broadest range of its members, the more it needs those rules: the requirement of participation must be balanced with the

decisiveness rules →

A specification of when a vote may be taken, the sequence in which votes on amendments occur, and how many supporters determine whether a motion passes or fails

delegation →

The transmission of authority to some other official or body for the latter's use (though often with the right of review and revision)

principal-agent relationship →

The relationship between a principal and his or her agent. This relationship may be affected by the fact that each is motivated by self-interest, yet their interests may not be well aligned

need to bring discussion and activity to a close at some point so that a decision can be made. This is why one of the motions that can be made on the floor of a legislature is to "move" the previous question, a motion to close the debate and move immediately to a vote.[7] In some legislatures, though, inaction seems to take precedence over action. In the U.S. House of Representatives, for example, a motion to adjourn (and thus not vote on a measure) takes precedence over a motion to move the previous question. In the U.S. Senate, to take another example, a supermajority (60 votes) is required to close debate and move to a vote. **Decisiveness rules** thus specify when votes may be taken and the sequence in which votes may occur, and—most important of all—how many individuals supporting a motion are sufficient for it to pass.

Delegation. A final aspect of institutional authority concerns delegation. Representative democracy is the quintessential instance of **delegation**. Citizens, through voting, delegate the authority to make decisions on their behalf to representatives—chiefly legislators and executives—rather than exercising political authority directly. We can think of our political representatives as our *agents*, just as we may think of professionals and craftspeople whose services we retain—doctors, lawyers, accountants, plumbers, mechanics, and so on—as agents whom we hire to act on our behalf. Why would those with authority, whom we will call *principals*, delegate some of their authority to agents? This has to do with the virtues of decentralization and of division and specialization of labor. The answer is that both principals and agents benefit from it. Principals benefit because they are able to off-load to experts and specialists tasks that they themselves are less capable of performing. Ordinary citizens, for example, are not so well versed in the tasks of governance as are professional politicians. Thus by delegating, citizens do not have to be specialists and can focus their energies on other things. This is the rationale for representative democracy. Agents benefit as well, since delegation means there is a demand for their services, which enables them to exercise authority and receive compensation for their efforts.

Examples of principals and agents abound in politics. Elected officials are agents for citizen-principals. Leaders are agents for their followers. Government bureaus—called *agencies* after all—serve as agents for elected principals in the executive and legislative branches.[8] Law clerks are agents for the judges who employ them. Lobbyists are agents of special interests. In short, the political world is replete with links between principals and agents.

The relationship between a principal and agent allows the former to delegate to the latter with gains for both, which may seem almost too good to be true. But there is a dark side to this **principal-agent relationship**. As the eighteenth-century economist Adam Smith noted in his classic work, *The Wealth of Nations*

---

7   For a general discussion of motions to close debate and get on with the decision, see Henry M. Robert, *Robert's Rules of Order* (1876), items III. 21 and VI. 38. *Robert's* has achieved the icon status and now exists in an enormous variety of forms and shapes.

8   Thus, elected officials are simultaneously agents of their constituents and principals for bureaucrats to whom they delegate authority to implement policy.

(1776), economic agents are not motivated by the welfare of their customers to grow vegetables, make shoes, or weave cloth; rather, they do those things out of their own self-interest. Thus a principal must take care when delegating to agents that those agents are properly motivated to serve the principal's interests, either by sharing his or her interests or by deriving something of value (reputation, compensation, and so on) for acting to advance those interests. The principal will need to have some instruments by which to monitor and validate what her agent is doing and then reward or punish the agent accordingly. Nevertheless, a principal will not bother to eliminate entirely the agent's prospective deviations from the principal's interests. The reason is **transaction costs**. The effort necessary to negotiate and then police every aspect of a principal-agent relationship becomes, at some point, more costly than it is worth. In sum, the upside of delegation consists of the assignment of activities to precisely those agents who possess a comparative advantage in performing them. The downside is the prospective misalignment of the goals of agents with the goals of principals and thus the possibility of agents marching to the beat of their own drummers. Delegation is a double-edged sword.

 transaction costs

The cost of clarifying each aspect of a principal-agent relationship and monitoring it to make sure arrangements are complied with

Characterizing institutions in terms of jurisdiction, agenda power, veto power, decisiveness, and delegation covers an immense amount of ground. Our purpose here has been to introduce the many ways collectivities arrange their business and routinize it, thereby enabling cooperation and facilitating political bargaining and decision making. A second purpose has been to highlight the potential diversity in institutional arrangements—there are so many ways to do things collectively. This diversity underscores the sophistication and intelligence of the framers of the U.S. Constitution in the institutional choices they made more than two centuries ago, as we discuss in the following chapter. Finally, we want to make clear that institutions not only make rules for governing but also present strategic opportunities for various political interests, depending on how the institutions are designed. As George Washington Plunkitt, the savvy and candid political boss of Tammany Hall, said of the institutional situations in which he found himself, "I seen my opportunities, and I took 'em."[9]

The Collective Action Principle: All Politics Is Collective Action

The third factor that helps explain why governments do what they do is that political action is collective. It involves building, combining, mixing, and amalgamating people's individual goals. This sometimes occurs in highly institutionalized settings—a committee, legislature, or bureaucracy, for example. However, it also occurs in less institutionalized settings—a campaign rally, a get-out-the-vote drive, or a civil rights march. Moreover, collective action can be difficult to orchestrate because the individuals involved in the decision-making process often

9   In the nineteenth century and well into the twentieth, Tammany Hall was the club that ran New York City's Democratic Party like a machine.

have different goals and preferences. The result is mixed motives for cooperation. Conflict is inevitable; the question is how it can be resolved. The most typical and widespread means of resolving collective dilemmas is bargaining among individuals. But when the number of parties involved is too large to engage in face-to-face bargaining, incentives must be provided to get everyone to act collectively.

Informal Bargaining. Political bargaining may be highly formal or entirely informal. Relations among neighbors, for example, are usually based on informal give-and-take. To present a personal example, one of this book's authors has a neighbor with whom he shares a hedge on their property line. First one takes responsibility for trimming the hedge and then the other, alternating from year to year. This arrangement (or bargain) is merely an understanding, not a legally binding agreement, and it was reached amicably and without much fuss or fanfare after a brief conversation. No organized effort—such as hiring lawyers, drafting an agreement, and having it signed, witnessed, notarized, filed at the county courthouse, and so on—was required to reach this bargain.

Bargaining in politics can be similarly informal and unstructured. Whether called horse trading, back-scratching, logrolling, or wheeling and dealing, it has much the same flavor as the casual, over-the-fence negotiation between neighbors that was just described. Deals will be struck depending on the preferences and beliefs of the participants. If preferences are too incompatible or beliefs too inconsistent with one another, then a deal simply may not be possible. If preferences and beliefs are not too far out of line, then there will be a range of possible bargaining outcomes, some of which slightly advantage one party, others of which advantage other parties. In short, there will be room for a compromise.

In fact, much of politics *is* informal, unstructured bargaining. First, many disputes subjected to bargaining are of sufficiently low impact that establishing elaborate formal machinery for dealing with them is just not worth the effort. Rules of thumb often develop as a benchmark—such as "split the difference" or "take turns" (the outcome of the hedge-trimming example just given). Second, repetition can contribute to successful cooperation. If a small group engages in bargaining today over one matter and tomorrow over another—as neighbors bargain over draining a swampy meadow one day, fixing a fence another, and trimming a hedge on still another occasion—then patterns develop. If one party constantly tries to extract maximal advantage, then the other parties will cease doing business with him or her. If, on the other hand, each party "gives a little to get a little," then a pattern of cooperation develops over time. It is the repetition of similar, mixed-motive occasions that allows this pattern to emerge without formal trappings. Many political circumstances are either amenable to informal rules of thumb like those mentioned or are repeated with sufficient frequency as to allow cooperative patterns to emerge.[10]

---

10 A wonderful description of how ranchers in Shasta County, California, organized their social lives and collective interactions in just this fashion is found in Robert C. Ellickson, *Order without Law: How Neighbors Settle Disputes* (Cambridge, MA: Harvard University Press, 1991).

Formal Bargaining. Other bargaining situations are governed by rules. The rules describe such things as who gets to make the first offer, how long the other parties have to consider it, whether other parties must take it or leave it or can make counteroffers, the method by which they convey their assent or rejection, what happens when all (or some decisive subset) of the others accept or reject it, what happens next if the proposal is rejected, and so on. It may be hard to imagine two neighbors deciding how to trim their common hedge under procedures as explicit and formal as these. It makes more sense, however, to imagine a bargaining session over wages and working conditions between labor and management at a large manufacturing plant proceeding in just this manner. The distinction suggests that some parties are more suited to formal proceedings, whereas others get on well enough without them. The same may be said about situations. A husband and wife are likely to divide household chores by informal bargaining, but this same couple would employ a formal procedure if they were dividing household assets in a divorce settlement.

Formal bargaining is often associated with events that take place in official institutions—legislatures, courts, party conventions, administrative and regulatory agencies. These are settings in which situations involving mixed motives arise over and over again. Year in and year out, legislatures pass statutes, approve executive budgets, and oversee the administrative branch of government. Courts administer justice, determine guilt or innocence, impose sentences, resolve differences between disputants, and render interpretive opinions about the meaning of the law. Party conventions nominate candidates and approve the platforms on which they base their campaigns. Administrative and regulatory agencies implement policy and make rulings about its applicability. All of these are instances of mixed-motive circumstances in which different parties have different goals; thus while gains from cooperation are possible, bargaining failures are also a definite possibility. In the spring of 2013, for instance, President Obama and the Democratic leadership in the Senate sought comprehensive gun control legislation—expanded background checks, a ban on assault weapons, and a reduction in the size of magazine clips—whereas most Republicans in the Senate, along with gun-owner interest groups like the National Rifle Association, opposed these extensions of federal control. Through a formalized legislative process—proposals, amendments, debate, and so on—gains from cooperation might have been possible. A compromise might have taken the form of expanded background checks but no further restrictions on assault weapons or magazines. With this compromise, the Democrats might have obtained some of the controls they sought while Republicans might have avoided blame for the failure of a policy that public opinion clearly supported. Such an amendment was proposed by two relatively conservative senators and ultimately supported by the Democratic side. However, the compromise did not obtain the necessary votes for passage, a bargaining failure in which the Senate Democrats and President Obama looked ineffectual and the Senate Republicans looked obstructionist. Each side wanted more, and as a consequence, each side ended up tarnished by the failure to agree.

Although it did not work in this particular situation, in general the formal bargaining that takes place through institutions is governed by rules that regularize proceedings both to maximize the prospects of reaching agreement and to guarantee that procedural wheels do not have to be reinvented each time a similar bargaining problem arises. This is our first application of the institution principle: institutions facilitate (but do not always succeed in producing) collective action.

Collective Dilemmas and Bargaining Failures. Even when gains are possible from collective action—when people share some common objective, for example—it still may not be feasible to arrive at a satisfactory conclusion. Let us take the simple example of two farmers interested in mending a piece of fence that separates their properties. For simplicity, suppose that Farmer Jones and Farmer Smith each value the mended fence at some positive level, V. Suppose further that the total cost (in terms of time or effort) to do this chore is c, a big enough cost to make the job not worth the effort if a farmer had to do it all by himself. For example, if each farmer values the mended fence at $700, but the cost to repair it on his own is $1,000, the net benefit to one farmer repairing it alone ($700 minus $1,000) is less than zero—and thus not an attractive option. If they shared the cost equally, their net benefit would each be $V-c/2$, in our example, $700 minus $500—a positive net benefit of $200 to both. If one of the farmers, however, could off-load the entire project on his neighbor, then he would not have to bear any of the cost and would enjoy the mended fence valued by him at V ($700). The situation is displayed in Figure 1.1. Each row gives the options available to Jones and each column the options available to Smith. The lower-left entry in each cell of the figure is the payoff to Jones if he selects the row option and Smith selects the column option; the upper-right entry in each cell is Smith's payoff. Thus if both choose to mend the fence (the upper-left cell), then they each enjoy a (positive) net benefit of $V-c/2$. If, on the other hand, Jones takes on the job, but Smith does not—this is the upper-right cell of the figure—then Jones pays the full price and receives $V-c$ (which is negative) and Smith gets the full value, V. The other two cells are filled in according to this logic.

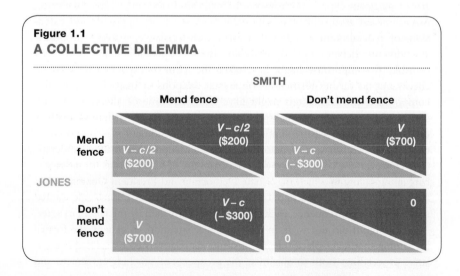

Figure 1.1
A COLLECTIVE DILEMMA

Consider now how Jones might think about this problem. On the one hand, if Smith chooses to mend the fence (left column in the figure), then Jones gets $V-c/2$ if he does too, but he does even better, V, if he lets Smith do the whole job. On the other hand, if Smith chooses not to mend the fence (right column in the figure), then Jones gets $V-c$ if he goes ahead and does the job himself (this is negative) but gets zero if he too does not take up the task. Putting these together, Jones realizes that *no matter what Smith does, Jones is better off not mending the fence.* Following the same logic, Smith will arrive at the same conclusion. So, each chooses "don't mend fence," and each gets a payoff of zero, even though both would have been better off if both had chosen "mend the fence."

This is a famous dilemma in social science.[11] It is a dilemma because the two individuals actually share a common goal—mending the fence—but each person's individual rationality causes both of them to do worse than they needed to. Had they only "suspended" their rationality and contributed to the common objective, then each would have been better served than when both are behaving in a fully rational manner. Even if the two farmers sat down and tried to overcome this dilemma, the dilemma still persists, as each has a rational temptation to defect from a bargain in which both agree to mend the fence. Moreover, each is nervous that the other will defect, given the incentives of the situation, and so feels compelled to defect himself.

The broad point of this example is that bargaining, even with common values and objectives, is no guarantee that a positive outcome will occur. We encounter dilemmas and bargaining failures like the one facing the two farmers frequently in politics. We will also discover that people have invented some methods that partially mitigate bargaining failures.

Collective Action, Free Riders, Public Goods, and the Commons.
The idea of political bargaining suggests an intimate kind of politics, involving face-to-face relations, negotiation, compromise, give-and-take, and so on. Such bargaining results from the combination of mixed motives and small numbers. When the numbers of individuals or other actors become large, bargaining may no longer be practical. If 100 people own property bordering a swampy meadow, how does this community solve the swamp's mosquito problem? How does the community secure the benefits that arise from cooperation? In short, what happens if a simple face-to-face interaction, possibly amenable to bargaining, now requires coordination among a large number of people?

In the swamp meadow example, everyone shares some common value—eliminating the mosquito habitat—but they may disagree on other matters. Some may want to use pesticides in the meadow, while others are concerned about the environmental impact. And there are bound to be disagreements over how to pay for the project. A collective action problem arises, as in this example, when there is something to be gained if the group can cooperate and assure one another that no one will get away with bearing less than their fair share of the

---

11 In another context, it is known as the prisoner's dilemma. We encounter it again in Chapter 13 when we discuss interest groups.

effort. Face-to-face bargaining, however, is made impractical by sheer numbers. The issue, then, is how to accomplish some common objective among a large number of interested parties.

Groups of individuals intent on **collective action** will ordinarily establish some decision-making procedures—relatively formal arrangements by which to resolve differences, coordinate the group to pursue a course of action, and sanction slackers, if necessary. Workers in a manufacturing plant, for example, may attempt to form a union. Or, to take another example, like-minded citizens may organize a political party. Most groups will also require a leadership structure, which is necessary even if all the members of the group are in agreement about how to proceed. This structure is necessary to deal with a phenomenon known as **free riding**. Imagine that each owner of land bordering a swamp wants the area cleared of mosquitoes. If one or a few owners were to clear the swamp alone, their actions would benefit all the other owners as well, without any efforts on the part of these others. They would be free riders, enjoying the benefit of others' efforts without contributing themselves. (The same issue faced farmers Smith and Jones in the fence-mending problem described earlier.) It is this prospect of free riding that risks undermining collective action. A leadership structure will have to be in place to threaten and, if necessary, inflict punishments to discourage individuals from reneging on the individual contributions required to enable the group to pursue its common goals.

Another way to think about this is to describe a commonly shared goal—in the present example a mosquito-free meadow—as a public good. A **public good** is a benefit that others cannot be denied from enjoying, once it has been provided. Once the meadow is mosquito free, it will constitute a benefit to *all* the members of the group, even those who have not contributed to its provision. More generally, a public good is one that can be "consumed" by individuals without using it up, and for which there are no means at hand to exclude individuals easily. A classic example is a lighthouse. Once it is erected, it aids all ships, and there is no simple way to charge a ship for its use. Another classic example is national defense. It protects taxpayers and tax avoiders alike. A third example is clean air. Once enough people restrict their polluting, the air is cleansed and may be enjoyed even by those who have not restricted their polluting. (Imagine owners of hybrid vehicles whose reduced pollution makes for cleaner air enjoyed even by those whose automobiles produce lots of noxious exhaust.) Because public goods have these properties, it is easy for some members of a group to free ride on the efforts shouldered by others. And as a result, it may be difficult to get anyone to provide it in the first place. Collective action is required, and this in turn often requires leaders (or governments) with the capacity to induce all to contribute to its provision.

One of the most notorious collective action problems involves too much of a good thing. Known as the **tragedy of the commons**, this type of problem reveals how unbridled self-interest can have damaging collective consequences. A political party's reputation, for example, can be seen as something that benefits all politicians affiliated with the party. This collective reputation is not irreparably harmed if one legislator in the party pushes her advantage

---

collective action

The pooling of resources and the coordination of effort and activity by a group of people (often a large one) to achieve common goals

free riding

Enjoying the benefits of some good or action while letting others bear the costs

public good

A good that, first, may be enjoyed by anyone if it is provided and, second, may not be denied to anyone once it has been provided

tragedy of the commons

The idea that a common-access facility, owned by no one because it is available to everyone, will be overutilized by getting approval for a minor amendment helpful to a special interest in her district. But if lots of party members do it, the party comes to be known as the champion of special interests, and its reputation is tarnished. A pool of resources is not much depleted if someone takes a little of it. But it does become depleted if lots of people take from it—a forest is lost a pine tree at a time; an oil reserve declines a barrel at a time; the atmosphere is polluted a particle at a time. The party's reputation, the forest, the oil reserve, and the atmosphere are all *commons*.[12] The problem to which they are vulnerable is *overgrazing*—a common resource that is irreparably depleted by individual actions.[13]

To summarize, individuals try to accomplish goals not only as individuals but also as members of larger collectivities (families, friendship groups, clubs, associations, and political parties) and even larger categories (economic classes, ethnic groups, and nationalities). The rationality principle covers individual initiative. The collective action principle describes the paradoxes encountered, the obstacles that must be overcome, and the incentives necessary for individuals to work with others to coordinate their energies, accomplish collective purposes, and secure the dividends of cooperation. Much of politics is about doing this or failing to do this. The institution principle discussed previously takes this argument to its logical conclusion, focusing on collective activities that are regularized because they are both important and frequently occurring. Institutions do the public's business while relieving communities of having to reinvent collective action each time it is required. Thus we have a rationale for government.

The Policy Principle: Political Outcomes Are the Products of Individual Preferences and Institutional Procedures

At the end of the day, we are interested in the results of politics—the collective decisions that emerge from the political process. A Nebraska farmer, for example, cares about how public laws and rulings affect his welfare and that of his family, friends, and neighbors. He cares about how export policies affect the prices his crops and livestock products earn in international markets and how monetary policy influences inflation and, as a result, the cost of purchasing fuel, feed, seed, and fertilizer; about the funding of public and private research and development efforts in agriculture and their effect on the quality and reliability of the scientific information he obtains; and about the affordability of the state

12 The original meaning is of a pasture on which cows graze to the point of damaging the land. A most insightful discussion of "commons problems," of which these are examples, is Elinor Ostrom, *Governing the Commons: The Evolution of Institutions for Collective Action* (New York: Cambridge University Press, 1990).

13 The classic statement is Garrett Hardin, "The Tragedy of the Commons," *Science* 162 (1968): 1243–8.

university, where he hopes to educate his children. He also cares, eventually, about inheritance laws and their effect on his ability to pass his farm on to his kids without Uncle Sam taking a huge chunk of it in estate taxes. As students of American politics, we need to consider the link between individual goals, institutional arrangements, collective action, and policy outcomes. How do all of these leave their marks on policy? What biases, predilections, and tendencies manifest themselves in public decisions?

The linchpin is the motivations of political actors. As we saw in our discussion of the rationality principle, their ambitions—ideological, personal, electoral, and institutional—provide politicians with the incentives to craft policies in particular ways. In fact, most policies make sense only as reflections of individual politicians' interests, goals, and beliefs. Examples include:

Personal interests: Congressman X is an enthusiastic supporter of subsidizing home heating oil (but opposes regulation to keep its price down) because some of his friends own heating-oil distributorships.[14]

Electoral ambitions: Senator Y, a well-known political moderate, has lately been introducing very conservative amendments to bills dealing with the economy to appeal to more conservative financial donors, who might then contribute to her budding presidential campaign.

Institutional ambitions: Representative Z has promised his vote and given a rousing speech on the House floor supporting a particular amendment because he knows it is near and dear to his party leader. He hopes his support will earn him her endorsement next year for an assignment to the prestigious Appropriations Committee.

These examples illustrate how policies are politically crafted according to both institutional procedures and individual aspirations. The procedures, as we saw in a previous discussion, are a series of chutes and ladders that shape, channel, filter, and prune the alternatives from which policy choices are ultimately made. The politicians who populate these institutions, as we have just noted, are driven both by private objectives and by public purposes, pursuing their own private interests while working on behalf of their conception of the public interest.

Because the institutional features of the American political system are complex and policy change requires success at every step, change is often impossibly difficult, meaning the status quo usually prevails. A long list of players must be satisfied with the change, or it won't happen. Most of these politicians will need some form of "compensation" to provide their endorsement and support.

---

14 These friends would benefit from people having the financial means to buy home heating oil but would not want the price they charge for the oil restricted.

Majorities are usually built by legislators drafting bills so as to spread the benefits to enough members of the legislature to get the requisite number of votes for that particular bill. Derisively, this is called pork-barrel legislation. It can be better understood by remembering that the overwhelming proportion of pork-barrel projects that are distributed to build policy majorities are justified to voters as valuable additions to the public good of the various districts. What may be pork to the critic is actual bridges, roads, and post offices.

Elaborate institutional arrangements, complicated policy processes, and intricate political motivations make for a highly combustible mixture. The policies that emerge are inevitably lacking in the neatness that citizens desire. But policies in the United States today are sloppy and slapdash for a clear reason: the tendency to spread the benefits broadly is the result when political ambition comes up against a decentralized political system.

The History Principle: How We Got Here Matters

There is one more aspect of our analysis that is important: we must ask how we have gotten where we are. How did we get the institutions and policies that are in place? By what series of steps? When by choice and when by accident? Every question and problem we confront has a history. History will not tell the same story for every institution. Nevertheless, without history, we have neither a sense of causation nor a full sense of how institutions are related to one another. In explaining the answer to why governments do what they do, we must turn to history to see what choices were available to political actors at a given time, what consequences resulted from those choices and what consequences might have flowed from the paths not chosen.

Imagine a tree growing from the bottom of the page. Its trunk grows upward from some root ball at the bottom, dividing into branches that continue to grow upward, further dividing into smaller branches. Imagine a path through this tree, from its very roots at the bottom of the page to the end of one of the highest branches at the top of the page. There are many such paths, from the one point at the bottom to many possible points at the top. If instead of a tree this were a time diagram, then the root ball at the bottom would represent some specific beginning point and all of the top-branch endings would represent some terminal time. Each path is now a possible history, the delineation of movement from some specific beginning to some concluding time. Alternative histories, like paths through trees, entail irreversibilities. Once one starts down a historical path (or up a tree), one cannot always retrace one's steps.[15] Once things happen, they cannot always un-happen. Some futures are foreclosed by the choices people have already made or, if not literally foreclosed, then made extremely unlikely.

---

15 Clearly with tree climbing this is not literally true, or once we started climbing a tree, we would never get down! So the tree analogy is not perfect here.

path dependency

The idea that certain possibilities are made more or less likely because of the historical path taken

It is in this sense that we explain a current situation at least in part by describing the historical path by which we arrived at it. Some scholars use the term **path dependency** to suggest that some possibilities are more or less likely because of events that occurred and choices that were made earlier in history. Both the status quo and the path from it significantly delimit future possibilities. For example, in the early 1990s, President Clinton formulated the "Don't Ask, Don't Tell" policy for the treatment of gay men and lesbians in the military: the military could not ask about a soldier's sexual orientation, and gay men and lesbians could serve so long as they did not reveal their sexual orientation. This move made it virtually impossible to return to the old status quo (in which gay men and lesbians could not serve at all). On the other hand, the path chosen by the Clinton administration also made it very difficult to propose an even more enlightened policy in which gay and lesbian Americans in the military were not prevented from asserting their identity (a change that was not to happen for two decades).

Three factors that help to explain why history often matters in political life are rules and procedures, loyalties and alliances, and historically conditioned points of view. As for the first of these factors, rules and procedures, choices made during one point in time continue to have important consequences for years, decades, or even centuries. For example, America's single-member-district plurality voting rules, established in the eighteenth century, continue to shape the nation's party system today.[16] Those voting rules, as we shall see in Chapter 12, help explain why the United States has a two-party system rather than the multi-party systems found in many other Western democracies. Thus a set of choices made 200 years ago affects party politics today.

A second way in which history often matters in politics is through the persistence of loyalties and alliances. Many of the political alliances that are important in American politics today are products of events that took place decades ago. For example, Jewish voters are among the Democratic Party's most loyal supporters, consistently giving 80 or 90 percent of their votes to Democratic presidential candidates. Yet on the basis of economic interest, Jews, one of the wealthier social groups in America, might be expected to vote for the Republicans. In recent years, moreover, the GOP has been a stronger supporter of Israel than the Democrats. Why, then, do Jews overwhelmingly support the Democrats? Part of the answer has to do with history. In the late nineteenth and early twentieth centuries, Jews suffered considerable discrimination in the United States. In the 1930s, though, under the leadership of Franklin Delano Roosevelt, the Democratic Party was one vehicle through which Jews in America began their climb to the success they enjoy today. This historical experience continues to shape Jewish political identity. Similar historical experiences help to explain the political loyalties of African Americans, Cuban Americans, and others.

16 Single-member districts are arrangements in which one legislator is selected from each district. (Other electoral systems select multiple members from each district.) A plurality voting rule declares that the one legislator selected in a district is the one with the most votes (not necessarily a majority).

A third factor explaining why history matters is the fact that past events and experiences shape current viewpoints and perspectives. For example, many Americans now in their sixties and seventies viewed events during the war in Iraq through the lens of the Vietnam War. Those influenced by the memory of Vietnam often see U.S. military involvement in a third world country as likely to lead to a quagmire of costs and casualties. Interestingly, in the 1960s, many older Americans viewed events in Vietnam through the lens of the 1930s, when the Western democracies were slow to resist Adolf Hitler's Germany. Thus to those influenced by events of the 1930s and World War II, failure to respond strongly to aggression was seen as a form of appeasement that would only encourage hostile powers to use force against American interests. Both groups saw the world through perspectives that they had learned from their own histories.

CONCLUSION

This introductory chapter has asked much of the reader. We have set the stage for an analytical treatment of the phenomena that constitute American politics. This analytical approach requires attention to *argument* and *evidence*. To construct an argument about some facet of American politics—why were young voters attracted to Barack Obama in 2008 or Ronald Reagan in 1980? Why do incumbent legislators in the House and Senate have so much success in securing re-election? Why does the president dominate media attention?—we can draw on a set of five principles. The linchpin is the rationality principle, emphasizing individual goal seeking as a key explanation for behavioral patterns. But politics is a collective undertaking, and it is often structured by political arrangements, so we also focus on collective action and the institutions in which such action takes place (collective action principle, institution principle). The combination of goal-seeking individuals engaging in collective activity in institutional contexts provides leverage for understanding why governments govern as they do—making laws, passing budgets, implementing policies, rendering judicial judgments (policy principle). But we could not make entire sense of these activities without an appreciation of the broader historical path (history principle). These five principles, then, are tools of analysis. They are also tools of discovery, permitting the interested observer to uncover new ideas about why politics works as it does.

Arguments may be tight or loose, compelling or questionable, persuasive or dubious. To know if an argument truly contributes to our understanding of the real world around us, we need to look at evidence. In the study of American politics, much of this evidence takes the form of quantitative data, and much of it is easily accessible on websites. How to make sense of such evidence is what political scientists do in their workaday world. In the Analyzing the Evidence unit beginning on page 26, we provide a brief glimpse of how to go about this task. We hope it proves helpful in allowing you to think analytically about political information as we move through the remaining chapters of the book.

Drawing on the lesson of the history principle, we begin in the remaining chapters of Part 1 by setting the historical stage. With analytical principles and strategies for analyzing evidence in hand, we are in a position to understand what influenced and inspired the founding generation more than two centuries ago to create a national government and a federal political system, while preserving individual rights and liberties.

For Further Reading

Selections highlighted in red are included in *Readings in American Politics: Analysis and Perspectives*, Third Edition.

Bianco, William T. *American Politics: Strategy and Choice*. New York: Norton, 2001.

Dahl, Robert A. *Who Governs? Democracy and Power in an American City*. New Haven, CT: Yale University Press, 1961.

Downs, Anthony. *An Economic Theory of Democracy*. New York: Harper & Row, 1957.

Ellickson, Robert C. *Order without Law: How Neighbors Settle Disputes*. Cambridge, MA: Harvard University Press, 1991.

Hardin, Garrett, "The Tragedy of the Commons," *Science* 162 (1968): 1243–8.

Hindmoor, Andrew. *Rational Choice*. New York: Palgrave-Macmillan, 2006.

Kiewiet, D. Roderick, and Mathew McCubbins. *The Logic of Delegation*. Chicago: University of Chicago Press, 1991.

Mayhew, David R. *Congress: The Electoral Connection*. New Haven, CT: Yale University Press, 1974.

Mueller, Dennis. *Public Choice III*. New York: Cambridge, 2003.

Olson, Mancur, Jr. *The Logic of Collective Action: Public Goods and the Theory of Groups*. 1965. Reprinted with new preface and appendix. Cambridge, MA: Harvard University Press, 1971.

Putnam, Robert D. *Making Democracy Work: Civic Traditions in Modern Italy*. Princeton, NJ: Princeton University Press, 1993.

Riker, William H. *Liberalism against Populism: A Confrontation between the Theory of Democracy and the Theory of Social Choice.* San Francisco: Freeman, 1982.

Shepsle, Kenneth A. *Analyzing Politics: Rationality, Behavior, and Institutions.* 2nd ed. New York: Norton, 2010.

Shepsle, Kenneth A. "Rational Choice Institutionalism," in R. A. W. Rhodes, Sarah A. Binder, and Bert A. Rockman, eds. *The Oxford Handbook of Political Institutions.* New York: Oxford University Press, 2006, pp. 23–39.

How Do Political Scientists Know What They Know?

The five principles introduced in this chapter provide a foundation for understanding and explaining political life. However, to make and test arguments about politics, we need more than just an analytical framework; we also need empirical evidence. Political scientists study facts about politics and analyze and interpret these facts to assess different arguments and claims. Typically, we study data, systematically collecting facts and information, and examining the structure of data to see whether they are consistent, or not, with a given line of thinking.

Consider one of the most basic questions about voting: Why do people vote the way they do? In elections, Americans face two main alternatives in the form of the Democratic Party and the Republican Party. These parties have distinctive policy priorities, notably in the important area of economic policy. Since at least the 1930s, the Democratic Party has favored economic policies that redistribute income to poorer segments of society; Republicans, on the other hand, favor lower taxes and little or no redistribution. It is often argued that people vote according to their economic self-interest: people choose the candidate from the party that maximizes their income. On reflection, however, we can see that other factors may also affect voting decisions, including the candidates' personal qualities, important noneconomic issues, and even candidates' appearance or habits. Which factor best explains vote choice?

Table A Vote Cast for President, 2012

VOTE CAST	NUMBER
BARACK OBAMA (Democrat)	65,907,213
MITT ROMNEY (Republican)	60,931,767
Other candidates	2,196,907
Did not vote	90,073,191

What Are Data? Data are systematic measurements or observations that are collected as a source of information about a theoretically defined concept or idea. In our example there is a political behavior that we want to explain, *vote choice*. Vote choice is a general concept, and we can define it before we ever observe an election. The first step in collecting data is to represent the concept that we are interested in as a variable. A variable defines all possible outcomes of a concept that could occur and assigns them a unique label or value. Vote choice, for instance, may take four possible values or outcomes: vote for the Democratic Party candidate, vote for the Republican Party candidate, vote for another party or candidate, or don't vote.

The second step in collecting data is to measure the behavior of interest. This requires the

We might, for instance, conduct in-depth interviews with a dozen or so people about how they decided to vote. However, we often require more evidence to support a given claim; a small number of people might not be sufficiently representative.

Censuses and random sample surveys allow social scientists to collect information systematically on a large number of cases. These means of collecting data are staples of social sciences. With a census we observe all individuals in the population at a given moment. Every 10 years, the United States conducts a comprehensive enumeration of all people living in the country, including information on families, education levels, income, race and ethnicity, commuting, housing, and employment. An election is a census, as it is a comprehensive count of all votes cast in a given election. So we can measure a variable such as vote choice by taking count of all electoral votes and nonvotes in the voting-eligible population (Table A).

A survey, on the other hand, consists of a study of a relatively small subset of individuals. We call this subset a sample. We can measure a variable for those individuals in the sample, and extrapolate patterns from the sample to the entire population. One of the most important social science research projects of the second half of the twentieth century is the American National Election Study, or ANES. The ANES is a national survey that has been conducted during every presidential election and most midterm congressional elections since 1948 to gauge how people voted and to understand why. In recent years, the ANES has used a sample of 2,000 Americans to make inferences about the entire voting population of over 100 million. Today, most of the information used by public policy makers, businesses, and academic researchers, including estimates of variables like unemployment and inflation, television and radio ratings, and most demographics of the population, are measured using surveys.

Summarizing Data. Communicating the information in a census or survey requires tools for summarizing data. First, we compute the frequency with which each value of a variable occurs. Frequency may be either the *number of times* that a specific behavior or value of a variable occurs or the percent of the observations in which it occurs.

Second, we construct a graph or statistic that summarizes the frequencies of all values of the variable. The distribution of a variable expresses how often each of the values of the variable occurs. A bar chart displays all possible values of a variable on one axis, usually the horizontal axis; the heights of the bars equal the frequency or *percent* of cases observed for each value (Figure A).

Vote Cast for President, 2012

Figure A VOTE (%)

Mitt Romney (Republican)	Barack Obama (Democrat)	Other	Did not vote
28	30	1	41

Figure B

Mitt Romney (Republican) 28%
Barack Obama (Democrat) 30%
Other 1%
Did not vote 41%

Figure C Party Identification, 1952–2012

PERCENTAGE

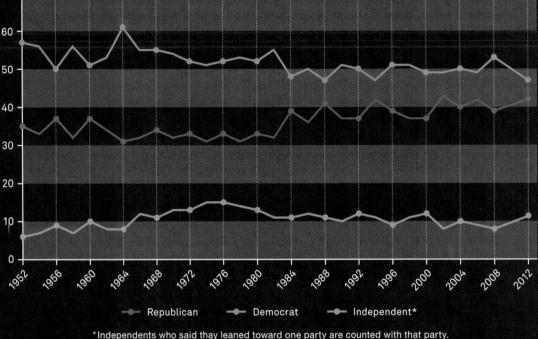

—•— Republican   —•— Democrat   —•— Independent*

*Independents who said thay leaned toward one party are counted with that party.

In a pie chart, the frequency for each value is depicted as a share of the whole (Figure B). A line graph is often used to show frequency over time (Figure C).

The distribution of income in the United States offers a somewhat different example. This variable takes a range of values, from the smallest household income to the largest household income. For ease of presentation, we can organize this variable into categories. In Figure D, the first category is "less than $10,000," the second category is "$10,000 to $19,999," and so forth up to the top category, "$200,000 or more." All possible income levels are covered in this classification.

Variables such as income can also be characterized with statistics, such as the median or mean. In this example, the median is the value of household income such that half of all households have incomes below the value and half have income above it. Fifty percent of all cases have income above the median value, and 50 percent have income below it; thus the median is also called the 50th percentile. The median household income in the United States in 2011 was $50,054, meaning that half of all households have income below that value and half have income above that amount. The mean is the average value for the variable. In the case of household income, the mean equals the sum of all households' incomes divided by the number of households. Personal income received by households totaled approximately $8.4 trillion in 2011, and there were 121 million households. So the average household income was $69,677.

Figure D Distribution of Household Income in the United States, 2011

PERCENTAGE OF ALL HOUSEHOLDS

HOUSEHOLD INCOME (U.S. DOLLARS)

Why do the median and mean differ? In calculating the median, every household is equal. We merely count the percent above and below a certain income level. The mean value weights households according to their incomes; consequently, a household with $200,000 income contributes 10 times as much to the calculation of the mean as a household with $20,000. If there were only a small difference in income among households, the mean would be very close to the median. The difference between the median income and the mean income thus provides a way to measure inequality. Only about one-third of households had income above the mean value of $69,677.

Testing Arguments Using Data. Let's return to the idea discussed at the beginning of the section: that people vote their economic self-interest. Is this claim correct?

To test this idea, we need to formulate a hypothesis. In the social sciences, hypotheses often take the form of stating a relationship between two variables, such as income and vote choice.

To test the hypothesis that people vote their economic self-interest, we want to know to what extent voting decisions match up with individuals' income levels. As stated earlier, in the United States today, the Republican Party generally favors lower income taxes and less income redistribution, and the Democratic Party favors higher income taxes and more income redistribution. We therefore want to know if people in high-income households vote Republican more often than people in low-income households. The difference we observe in vote choice between high- and low-income groups is considered to be the effect of income on vote choice.

To see whether the effect of income on the vote is indeed large, we can use the data in Table B to examine the actual voting behavior of different sorts of individuals. The national exit polls in 2012 reveal that 63 percent of voters with income less than $30,000 chose the Democratic candidate, Barack Obama. By comparison, 46 percent of those with income over $100,000 chose Barack Obama. This large difference (17 percentage points) reveals that income is associated with vote choice, but it is not absolutely determinative: not every person of high income voted Republican in this election, and not everyone in low-income groups voted Democrat.

Table B Vote by Level of Income

INCOME	OBAMA	ROMNEY
Under $30,000	63%	37%
$30,000–$49,999	57%	43%
$50,000–$99,999	48%	52%
$100,000 or more	46%	54%

As we explore alternative arguments about what determines vote choice, we can make many different comparisons—men versus women, college graduates versus high school graduates, and so forth. Our goal is to find which, if any, of these potential explanations best accounts for the variation in vote choice. Throughout this book, we will consider other political outcomes besides voter behavior, such as the support by members of Congress for different types of legislation and how often the executive succeeds in passing legislation.

Many times we will look for a relationship or association between two variables to see if the predictions from an argument hold true, and if they do, we take that as evidence supporting the argument. A relationship or association between two variables, sometimes called a correlation, should not be taken to mean that one of the variables caused the other to occur. Causation is more difficult to establish. A correlation between two variables X (say X is a measure of education) and Y (say Y is a measure of income) is consistent with a theory that education increases one's earning power. From a simple correlation, however, one cannot tell whether many years of education caused high income or high income led to many years of education. It is also possible that some other variable, say high intelligence, caused both many years of education and high income.

Social scientists design experiments and carefully controlled comparisons in order to measure causal relationships. Observing simple associations and correlations, though, is not the final step in verifying our arguments, ideas, or theories about how politics works.

Be a Savvy Consumer of Quantitative Data. Beyond the figures and tables in this book, which reflect data from sources that we consider reliable and accurate, you will undoubtedly encounter other data about politics in the news and elsewhere. Before you take such data—and whatever argument they seem to support—at face value, it is worth asking a few questions about how the data were gathered and presented.

➡ What is the source of the data? Is it a respected source like a government office or a major mainstream news organization, which may be relied upon to gather and report data accurately? Or are they from a source that is likely to have a goal other than accurate presentation of the data, like an interest group, a campaign, or an entertainment website?

➡ When were the data collected and how? What is the date (or date range) for the data? Are the data from a census or sample, and how large is the sample?

➡ What is being measured? For example, in a poll showing support for a candidate, is it the percent of all Americans? The percentage of likely voters? The percentage of Democrats or Republicans?

➡ Why are the data presented a certain way? Is this the best way to present these data? Does it distort the data in any way? What relationships and patterns do we observe in the data?

Thinking through the questions above can help you better understand the information in the data figures and tables found throughout this book as well as in other academic writing and in the news. In each of the chapters to follow, you will find an Analyzing the Evidence unit, highlighting arguments and evidence on some of the subjects of that chapter. Many of these sections discuss how political scientists use the basic methodology discussed above to test arguments about American politics.

SOURCES:
Table A U.S. Census Bureau, "The Diversifying Electorate—Voting Rates by Race and Hispanic Origin in 2012 (and Other Recent Elections)," May 2013, www.census.gov/prod/2013pubs/p20-568.pdf (Note: the estimates presented in this report may differ from those based on administrative data or exit polls); CNN, "Election 2012: Results," December 10, 2012, www.cnn.com/election/2012/results/main; Susan Page, "Voter Turnout Higher in Swing States Than Elsewhere," *USA Today*, December 23, 2012, www.usatoday.com/story/news/politics/2012/12/23/voter-turnout-swing-states/1787693/; United States Election Project, "2012 General Election Turnout Rates," March 25, 2013, http://elections.gmu.edu/Turnout_2012G.html (all accessed 6/19/13).
Table B "President Exit Polls," *New York Times*, http://elections.nytimes.com/2012/results/president/exit-polls (accessed 6/19/13); and "Exit Polls 2012: How the Vote Has Shifted," *Washington Post*, November 6, 2012, www.washingtonpost.com/wp-srv/special/politics/2012-exit-polls/table.html (accessed 6/19/13).
Figure C Jeffrey M. Jones, "In U.S., Democrats Re-Establish Lead in Party Affiliation," January 9, 2013, www.gallup.com/poll/159740/democrats-establish-lead-party-affiliation.aspx (accessed 6/19/13); and RTT News, "Poll Shows Democrats Retake Lead in Party Affiliation in 2012," January 9, 2013, www.rttnews.com/2034821/poll-shows-democrats-retake-lead-in-party-affiliation-in-2012.aspx (accessed 6/19/13).
Figure D Linda Levine, "The Distribution of Household Income and the Middle Class," Congressional Research Service, November 13, 2012, http://assets.opencrs.com/rpts/RS20811_20121113.pdf, p. 2.

2

Constructing a Government: The Founding and the Constitution

To really understand the character of the American Founding and the meaning of the American Constitution, it is essential to look beyond myths and rhetoric. Our first principle of politics is that all political behavior has a purpose. The men and women who became revolutionaries were guided by a number of purposes. Most of the nation's Founders, though highly educated, were not political theorists. They were, rather, hardheaded and pragmatic in their commitments and activities. Although their interests were not identical, they did agree that a relationship of political and economic dependence on a colonial power, one that did not treat them as full-fledged citizens of the empire, was intolerable. The decision to break away from Britain in 1776 and, over the succeeding decade, fashion institutions of self-governance was the consequence.

Many of those most active in the initial days of the Revolution felt backed into a corner, their decisions forced. For years, the imperial center in London, preoccupied by wars with France that had spread across several continents, had left the colonists to their own devices. These were years in which the colonists enjoyed an immense amount of local control and home rule. These institutional arrangements suited merchants, farmers, and planters in the separate colonies. Local control under the mild direction of colonial governors left colonists to tend to their own business for the most part. But suddenly, as the war with France drew to a close in the 1760s, the British presence became more onerous and more intrusive. This historical experience incited collective action. In reaction to English attempts to extract tax revenues to pay for the troops that were being sent to defend the colonial frontier, protests erupted throughout the colonies against the infamous Stamp Act of 1765. This act required that all printed and legal documents, including newspapers, pamphlets, advertisements, notes and bonds, leases, deeds, and licenses, be printed on official paper stamped and sold by English officials. To show their displeasure with the act, the colonists held mass meetings, participated in parades, lit bonfires, and conducted other demonstrations throughout the spring and summer of 1765. In Boston, for example, a stamp agent was hanged and burned in effigy, leading to his resignation. Later the home of the lieutenant governor was sacked because of a rumor that he supported the Stamp Act. By November 1765, business was proceeding and newspapers were being published without stamps; in March 1766, Parliament repealed the detested law. Through their protest, the nonimportation agreements that the colonists subsequently adopted, and the Stamp Act Congress that met in October 1765, the colonists took the first steps down a path that ultimately would lead to war and the establishment of a new nation.

This is where we begin our story in the present chapter. We first assess the political backdrop of the American Revolution. From the history principle we can understand how nearly a century of relatively light-handed colonial administration by London produced a set of expectations among the colonists that later British actions unmistakably violated. Then we examine the Constitution that ultimately emerged—after a rather bumpy experience in self-government just after the Revolution—as the basis for America's government. This document is the quintessential institutional arrangement that structures political relationships, facilitates collective action, and encourages peaceful conflict resolution. We conclude with a reflection on the Founding period by

CORE OF THE ANALYSIS

 The framers of the Constitution, although guided by underlying values, also had conflicting goals and interests.

 The first attempt at a new arrangement for self-government relied on institutions that were too weak to achieve collective action on behalf of the nation.

 The conflicting interests of the Founders were eventually accommodated through a complex set of rules and procedures set forth in the Constitution, which divided power among three branches of the federal government and between states and the federal government.

 The Constitution not only provides a framework for government but also often guides the policy process, even to this day.

emphasizing a lesson to be learned from the Founding that continues to be important throughout American history. The lesson is that politics, as James Madison said in the *Federalist Papers*, generally involves struggles among conflicting interests. In 1776, the main conflict was between pro-Revolutionary and anti-Revolutionary forces. In 1787, the major struggle was between the Federalists and the Antifederalists. Today the struggle is between the Democratic and Republican parties, each representing competing economic, social, and sectional interests. Often political ideas are the weapons developed by competing interests to further their own causes. The New England merchants who cried "no taxation without representation" cared more about lower taxes than expanded representation. Yet today representation is one of the foundations of American democracy.

As we try to understand American politics, we see that institutions matter a good deal. In fact, institutions matter in two ways. First, the institution principle tells us that institutions shape politics and affect the results of political conflicts—who wins and who loses. Second, the policy principle tells us that institutional procedures (coupled with individual preferences) help to determine policy outcomes—what the government can and cannot do. In the United States, no set of institutions is more important than the Constitution. What are the basic rules embodied in the Constitution? What significance have constitutional precepts had for American life? These are key questions addressed in this chapter. Of course, the history principle suggests that the Constitution itself was affected by the events of the colonial and founding periods. So, let us first turn to the events that preceded and shaped America's basic law.

THE FIRST FOUNDING: INTERESTS AND CONFLICTS

Competing ideals often reflect competing interests, and so it was in Revolutionary America. The American Revolution and the Constitution were outgrowths and expressions of a struggle among economic and political forces within the colonies. Five sectors of society had interests that were important in colonial politics: (1) the New England merchants; (2) the southern planters; (3) the "royalists"—holders of royal lands, offices, and patents (licenses to engage in a profession or business activity); (4) shopkeepers, artisans, and laborers; and (5) small farmers. Throughout the eighteenth century, these groups were in conflict over issues of taxation, trade, and commerce. For the most part, however, the southern planters, the New England merchants, and the royal officeholders and patent holders—groups that together made up the colonial elite—were able to maintain a political alliance that held in check the more radical forces representing shopkeepers, laborers, and small farmers. After 1750, however, by seriously threatening the interests of New England merchants and southern planters, British tax and trade policies split the colonial elite. This split permitted radical forces to expand their political influence and set into motion a chain of events that culminated in the American Revolution.[1]

British Taxes and Colonial Interests

Beginning in the 1750s, the debts and other financial problems faced by the British government forced it to search for new revenue sources. This search rather quickly led to the Crown's North American colonies, which on the whole paid remarkably little in taxes to the mother country. The British government reasoned that a sizable fraction of its debt was, in fact, attributable to the expenses it had incurred in defense of the colonies during the recent French and Indian War, as well as to the continuing protection from Indian attacks that British forces were giving the colonists and to the protection that the British navy was providing for colonial shipping. Thus during the 1760s, Britain sought to impose new, though relatively modest, taxes on the colonists.

Like most governments of the period, the British regime had at its disposal only limited ways to collect revenues. The income tax, which in the twentieth century became the single most important source of government revenue, had not yet been developed. For the most part in the mid-eighteenth century, governments relied on tariffs, duties, and other taxes on commerce, and it was to such taxes, including the Stamp Act, that the British turned during the 1760s. British interests (revenue) and institutions (Parliament and colonial administration) combined to produce a plausible solution to an existing problem, as suggested by the policy principle.[2]

The colonists were accustomed to managing their own affairs and were resentful of British meddling. Moreover, the Stamp Act and other taxes on commerce, such as the Sugar Act of 1764, which taxed sugar, molasses, and other commodities, most heavily affected the two groups in colonial society whose commercial interests and activities were most extensive: the New England merchants and southern planters. Because their interests coincided, these two groups were able to quickly engage in collective action to address these problems. Under the famous slogan "no taxation without representation," the merchants and planters together purposefully organized opposition to the new taxes. In the course of the struggle against British tax measures, the planters and merchants

---

1   The social makeup of colonial America and some of the social conflicts that divided colonial society are discussed in Jackson Turner Main, *The Social Structure of Revolutionary America* (Princeton, NJ: Princeton University Press, 1965).

2   Parliament also enacted the Proclamation of 1763 as part of the British settlement with the Native Americans. This withdrew the right of colonists to settle lands west of the Allegheny Mountains, preserving them for native populations. Among others, the families of George Washington and Benjamin Franklin had speculated on these lands and thus faced serious financial loss. See Norman Schofield, *Architects of Political Change: Constitutional Quandaries and Social Choice Theory* (New York: Cambridge University Press, 2006), chap. 3. A compact version is found in Norman Schofield, "Evolution of the Constitution," *British Journal of Political Science* 32 (2002): 1–23.

broke with their royalist allies and turned to their former adversaries—the shop-keepers, small farmers, laborers, and artisans—for help. With the assistance of these groups, the merchants and planters organized demonstrations and boycotts of British goods that ultimately forced the Crown to rescind most of its new taxes. It was in the context of this unrest that a confrontation between colonists and British soldiers in front of the Boston customs house on the night of March 5, 1770, resulted in what came to be known as the Boston Massacre. Nervous British soldiers opened fire on the mob surrounding them, killing five colonists and wounding eight others. News of this event quickly spread throughout the colonies and was used by radicals to fan anti-British sentiment.

From the perspective of the merchants and planters, however, the British government's decision to eliminate most of the hated taxes meant a victorious end to their struggle with the mother country. They were eager to end the unrest they had helped arouse, and they supported the British government's efforts to restore order. Indeed, most respectable Bostonians supported the actions of the British soldiers involved in the Boston Massacre. In their subsequent trial, the soldiers were defended by John Adams, a pillar of Boston society and a future president of the United States. Adams asserted that the soldiers' actions were entirely justified, provoked by a "motley rabble of saucy boys, negroes and mulattoes, Irish teagues and outlandish Jack tars." All but two of the soldiers were acquitted.[3]

Despite the efforts of the British government and the better-to-do strata of colonial society, it proved difficult to bring an end to the political strife. The more radical forces representing shopkeepers, artisans, laborers, and small farmers, who had been mobilized and energized by the struggle over taxes, continued to agitate for political and social change within the colonies. These "radicals" were generally individuals from the middling classes who had some education and often an intellectual skill but little political influence. Their radicalism consisted of the idea that people like themselves were just as fit to govern as members of the colonial elite. Led by individuals such as Samuel Adams, a cousin of John Adams, these radicals asserted that British power supported an unjust political and social structure within the colonies, and they began to advocate an end to British rule.[4] That the British revenue-raising policies backfired so dramatically was a result of their greatly underestimating colonial resistance. Although the policies seemed rational and sensible before the fact, they appeared mistaken after the fact and were rescinded. The rationality principle only requires people to do the best they can at the time they act. There are bound to be uncertainties that can only imperfectly be taken into account and thus necessitate subsequent adaptation. So the British attempts to raise revenue and then to adapt this strategy in the face of the resulting unrest were rational, but it proved difficult to undo the damage caused by their initial misreading of the situation.

3   Quoted in George B. Tindall and David E. Shi, *America: A Narrative History,* 8th ed. (New York: Norton, 2010), p. 202.

4   For a discussion of events leading up to the Revolution, see Charles M. Andrews, *The Colonial Background of the American Revolution: Four Essays in American Colonial History* (New Haven, CT: Yale University Press, 1924).

Organizing resistance to the British authorities required widespread support. Collective action, as noted, may emerge spontaneously in certain circumstances, but the colonists' campaign against the British imperial power in late eighteenth-century America was a series of encounters, maneuvers, and ultimately, confrontations that required planning, coalition building, bargaining, compromising, and coordinating—all elements of the give-and-take of politics. Conflicts among the colonists had to be resolved by bargaining, persuasion, and even force. Cooperation needed cultivation and encouragement. Leadership was clearly a necessary ingredient.

Political Strife and the Radicalizing of the Colonists

The political strife within the colonies was the background for the events of 1773–74. In 1773, the British government granted the politically powerful East India Company a monopoly on the export of tea from Britain, eliminating a lucrative form of trade for colonial merchants. To add to the injury, the East India Company sought to sell the tea directly in the colonies instead of working through the colonial merchants. Tea was an extremely important commodity in the 1770s, and these British actions posed a mortal threat to the New England merchants. The merchants once again called on their radical adversaries for support. The most dramatic result was the Boston Tea Party of 1773, led by Samuel Adams. Today's "Tea Party" protestors are generally conservatives opposing taxes and regulation. The Tea Party protestors of 1773 were radicals hoping to undermine the authority of the British government.

The Boston Tea Party was of decisive importance in American history. The merchants had hoped to force the British government to rescind the Tea Act, but they did not support any demands beyond this one. They certainly did not seek independence from Britain. Samuel Adams and the other radicals, however, hoped to provoke the British government to take actions that would alienate its colonial supporters and pave the way for a rebellion. This was precisely the purpose of the Boston Tea Party, and it succeeded. By dumping the East India Company's tea into Boston Harbor, Adams and his followers goaded the British into enacting a number of harsh reprisals. Within five months of the incident in Boston, the British Parliament had passed a series of acts that closed the port of Boston to commerce, changed the provincial government of Massachusetts, provided for the removal of accused persons to Britain for trial, and added new restrictions upon movement to the West from the southern colonies—further alienating the southern planters who depended on access to new western lands. These acts of retaliation confirmed the worst criticisms of England and helped radicalize Americans and move them toward collective resistance to British rule.[5]

The choice of this course of action by British politicians looks puzzling in retrospect, but at the time it appeared reasonable to those who prevailed in

5   For an intriguing take on the role of dense population networks in cities that promoted collective action against the British, see Edward L. Glaeser, "Revolution of Urban Rebels," *Boston Globe*, July 4, 2008, Section A.

Parliament that a show of force was required. The toleration of lawlessness and the making of concessions, they felt, would only egg on the more radical elements in the colonies to take additional liberties and demand further concessions. The British, in effect, drew a line in the sand. Their repressive reactions became a clear point around which dissatisfied colonists could rally. Radicals such as Samuel Adams had been agitating for more violent measures to deal with Britain. But ultimately they needed Britain's political repression to create widespread support for independence.[6]

Thus the Boston Tea Party set into motion a cycle of provocations and retaliations that in 1774 resulted in the convening of the First Continental Congress, an assembly consisting of delegates from all parts of the colonies, which called for a total boycott of British goods and, under the prodding of the radicals, began to consider the possibility of independence from British rule. The eventual result was the Declaration of Independence.

The Declaration of Independence

In 1776, the Second Continental Congress appointed a committee consisting of Thomas Jefferson of Virginia, Benjamin Franklin of Pennsylvania, Roger Sherman of Connecticut, John Adams of Massachusetts, and Robert Livingston of New York to draft a statement of American independence from British rule. The Declaration of Independence was written by Jefferson, who drew many of his ideas from the thoughts of the British philosopher John Locke, whose work was widely read in the colonies. Adopted by the Second Continental Congress, the Declaration was an extraordinary document in both philosophical and political terms. Philosophically, the Declaration was remarkable for its assertion—derived from Locke—that certain rights, called "unalienable rights"—including life, liberty, and the pursuit of happiness—could not be abridged by governments. In the world of 1776, a world in which some kings still claimed to rule by divine right, this was a dramatic statement. Politically, the Declaration was remarkable because, despite the different interests that divided the colonists along economic, regional, and philosophical lines, it identified and focused on problems, grievances, aspirations, and principles that might unify the various colonial groups. The Declaration was an attempt to identify and articulate a history and a set of principles that might help to forge national unity.[7]

The Declaration of Independence, however, was not a blueprint for governance. Often, scholars compare and contrast the Declaration and the Constitution and call the former a more radical or even libertarian document and

---

6   For an extensive discussion of how misunderstandings and incorrect beliefs caused the situation to spin out of control, see Jack N. Rakove, Andrew R. Rutten, and Barry R. Weingast, "Ideas, Interest, and Credible Commitments in the American Revolution," 2008, http://ssrn.com/abstract=1153515 (accessed 2/3/09).

7   A "biography" of the Declaration is found in Pauline Maier, *American Scripture: Making the Declaration of Independence* (New York: Knopf, 1997).

the latter a more conservative text. Both the Declaration and the Constitution, however, share some common philosophical underpinnings. Both derive from John Locke the idea that the purpose of government is the protection of life, liberty, and property. The Declaration uses these ideas as a justification for overthrowing a monarchical government. The Constitution, on the other hand, seeks to create a government that will guarantee the achievement of these goals. Thus, America's founding documents share philosophical underpinnings but apply these to different purposes.

The Revolutionary War

In 1775, even before formally declaring their independence, the colonies had begun to fight the British, most notably at Lexington and Concord, Massachusetts, where colonial militias acquitted themselves against trained British soldiers. Nevertheless, the task of defeating Britain, then the world's premier military power, seemed impossible. To maintain their hold on the colonies, the British sent a huge expeditionary force composed of British regulars and German mercenaries along with artillery and equipment. To face this force, the colonists relied on inexperienced and lightly armed militias. To make matters worse, the colonists were hardly united in their opposition to British rule. Many colonists saw themselves as loyal British subjects and refused to take up arms against the king. Thousands, indeed, took up arms *for* the king and joined pro-British militia forces.

The war was brutal and bloody with tens of thousands of casualties among the colonists, among British troops, and among the Native Americans who fought on both sides of the conflict. Eventually the revolutionary armies prevailed mainly because the cost to England of fighting a war thousands of miles from home became too great. Colonial militias prevented British forces from acquiring enough food and supplies locally. As a result, these had to be brought from Europe at enormous expense. As is often the case in asymmetric conflicts today, colonial forces did not have to defeat the British—they needed only to prevent the British from defeating them until Britain's will and ability to fight waned. Thus, with the eventual help of Britain's enemy, France, the colonists fought until Britain decided it had had enough of a seemingly endless colonial war. The war ended with the signing of the Treaty of Paris, which officially granted the 13 American colonies their independence.

The Articles of Confederation

Having declared their independence, the colonies needed to establish a governmental structure—a set of institutions through which to govern. In November 1777, the Continental Congress adopted the **Articles of Confederation and Perpetual Union**—the United States' first written constitution. Although it was not ratified by all the states until 1781, it was the country's operative constitution for almost 12 years, until March 1789.

Articles of Confederation and Perpetual Union

America's first written constitution. Adopted by the Continental Congress in 1777, the Articles of Confederation and Perpetual Union were the formal basis for America's national government until 1789, when they were superseded by the Constitution

The Articles of Confederation formed a constitution concerned primarily with limiting the powers of the central government. The central government, first of all, was based entirely in Congress. Because it was not intended to be a powerful government, it was given no executive branch. Execution of its laws was to be left to the individual states. Second, Congress had little power. Its members were not much more than delegates or messengers from the state legislatures. They were chosen by the state legislatures, their salaries were paid out of the state treasuries, and they were subject to immediate recall by state authorities. In addition, each state, regardless of its size, had only a single vote. Furthermore, amendments to the Articles required the unanimous agreement of the 13 states.

Congress was given the power to declare war and make peace, to make treaties and alliances, to coin or borrow money, and to regulate trade with Native Americans. It could also appoint the senior officers of the United States Army. But it could not levy taxes or regulate commerce among the states. Moreover, the army officers it appointed had no army to serve in because the nation's armed forces were composed of the state militias. An especially dysfunctional aspect of the Articles of Confederation was that the central government could not prevent one state from discriminating against other states in the quest for foreign commerce.

In brief, the relationship between Congress and the states under the Articles of Confederation was much like the contemporary relationship between the United Nations and its member states, a relationship in which virtually all governmental powers are retained by the states. It was properly called a confederation because, as provided under Article II, "each state retains its sovereignty, freedom, and independence, and every power, jurisdiction, and right, which is not by this Confederation expressly delegated to the United States, in Congress assembled." Not only was there no executive but there was also no judicial authority and no other means of enforcing Congress's will. If there were to be any enforcement at all, it would be done for Congress by the states.[8] In essence, each state was an independent nation-state. All told, the Articles of Confederation were an inadequate institutional basis for collective action.

THE SECOND FOUNDING: FROM COMPROMISE TO CONSTITUTION

Institutional arrangements, devised to accomplish various collective purposes by creating routines and processes, aren't always well suited to these tasks. The Declaration of Independence and the Articles of Confederation were not sufficient to hold the nation together as an independent and effective nation-state. Almost from the moment of armistice with the British in 1783, moves were afoot to reform and strengthen the Articles of Confederation.

8   See Merrill Jensen, *The Articles of Confederation* (Madison: University of Wisconsin Press, 1963).

International Standing, Economic Difficulties, and Balance of Power

There was a special concern for the country's international position. Competition among the states for foreign commerce allowed the European powers to play the states against one another, creating confusion on both sides of the Atlantic. At one point during the winter of 1786–87, John Adams, a leader in the struggle for independence, was sent to negotiate a new treaty with the British, one that would cover disputes left over from the war. The British government responded that because the United States under the Articles of Confederation was unable to enforce existing treaties, it would negotiate with each of the 13 states separately. Moreover, absent the protection of the British navy, American shipping—upon which the New England states depended—was easy prey for pirates and predator nations. The government under the Articles could offer no help.

At the same time, well-to-do Americans—in particular the New England merchants and southern planters—were troubled by the influence that populist forces exercised in the Continental Congress and in the governments of several of the states. The colonists' victory in the Revolutionary War not only had meant the end of British rule but also had significantly changed the balance of political power within the new states. As a result of the Revolution, one key segment of the colonial elite—the royal land, office, and patent holders—was stripped of its economic and political privileges. In fact, many of these individuals, along with tens of thousands of other colonists who considered themselves loyal British subjects, had left for Canada after the British surrender. And as the pre-Revolutionary elite was weakened, the pre-Revolutionary radicals were now better organized than ever before and were the controlling forces in such states as Pennsylvania and Rhode Island, where they pursued economic and political policies that struck terror in the hearts of the pre-Revolutionary political establishment. In Rhode Island, for example, between 1783 and 1785 a legislature dominated by representatives of small farmers, artisans, and shopkeepers had instituted economic policies, including drastic currency inflation, that frightened businessmen and property owners throughout the country. Of course, the central government under the Articles of Confederation was powerless to intervene. Commerce within the states stagnated and several of the states borrowed money just to finance the debts they had acquired during the Revolutionary War. Americans were facing their first, but not last, debt crisis.

The Annapolis Convention

The continuation of international weakness and domestic economic turmoil led many Americans to consider whether their newly adopted form of government might not already require revision. Experiments in governance don't always work out. After nearly a decade under the Articles, in the fall of 1786, many state leaders accepted an invitation from the Virginia legislature to attend a conference of representatives of all the states. Delegates from five states actually attended.

This conference, held in Annapolis, Maryland, was the first step toward the second founding. One positive result of the Annapolis Convention was a carefully worded resolution calling on Congress to send commissioners to Philadelphia at a later time "to devise such further provisions as shall appear to them necessary to render the Constitution of the Federal Government adequate to the exigencies of the Union."[9] This resolution was drafted by Alexander Hamilton, a 34-year-old New York lawyer who had played a significant role in the Revolution as George Washington's secretary and would play a still more significant role in framing the Constitution and forming the new government in the 1790s. But the resolution did not necessarily imply any desire to do more than improve and reform the Articles of Confederation.

Shays's Rebellion

It is possible that the Constitutional Convention of 1787 in Philadelphia would never have taken place at all except for a single event that occurred soon after the Annapolis Convention: Shays's Rebellion. Like the Boston Tea Party, this was a focal event. It concentrated attention, coordinated beliefs, produced widespread fear and apprehension, and thus convinced waverers that something was broken and needed fixing. In short, it prompted collective action by providing politicians who had long been convinced that the Articles were flawed and insufficient with just the ammunition they needed to convince a much broader public of these facts.[10]

Daniel Shays, a former army captain, led a mob of farmers in a rebellion against the government of Massachusetts in 1787. The purpose of the rebellion was to prevent foreclosures on their debt-ridden land by keeping the county courts of western Massachusetts from sitting until after the next election. The state militia dispersed the mob, but for several days Shays and his followers terrified the state government by attempting to capture the federal arsenal at Springfield, provoking an appeal to Congress to help restore order. Within a few days, the state government regained control and captured 14 of the rebels (all were eventually pardoned). Later that year, a newly elected Massachusetts legislature granted some of the farmers' demands. Although the incident ended peacefully, its effects lingered and spread.

This episode showed that Congress under the Confederation had been unable to act decisively in a time of crisis. This inadequacy provided critics of the Articles of Confederation with precisely the evidence they needed to push Hamilton's Annapolis resolution through the Congress. Thus the states were asked to send representatives to Philadelphia to discuss constitutional revision. Delegates were eventually sent by every state except Rhode Island.

9 Quoted in Samuel Eliot Morison, Henry Steele Commager, and William E. Leuchtenburg, *The Growth of the American Republic*, 6th ed. (New York: Oxford University Press, 1969), I: 244.

10 For an easy-to-read argument that supports this view, see Keith L. Dougherty, *Collective Action under the Articles of Confederation* (New York: Cambridge University Press, 2001).

The Constitutional Convention

In May 1787, 29 of a total of 73 delegates selected by the state governments convened in Philadelphia, with political strife, international embarrassment, national weakness, and local rebellion fixed in their minds. Recognizing that these issues were symptoms of fundamental flaws in the Articles of Confederation, the delegates soon abandoned the plan to revise the Articles and committed themselves to a second founding—a second and ultimately successful attempt to create a legitimate and effective national system. This effort occupied the convention for the next five months. Americans had learned a good deal from what many saw as the shortcomings of the Articles of Confederation. They learned, for example, that executive power was a necessary component of effective government. They also learned that without an army or navy the government could not protect its citizens' interests. Demonstrating once again that history matters, Americans' experiences under the Articles helped shape the new Constitution.

A Marriage of Interest and Ideals. For years, scholars have disagreed about the motives of the Founders in Philadelphia. Among the most controversial views of the framers' motives is the "economic" interpretation put forward by the historian Charles Beard and his disciples.[11] According to Beard's account, America's Founders were a collection of securities speculators and property owners whose only aim was personal enrichment. From this perspective, the Constitution's lofty principles were little more than sophisticated masks behind which the most venal interests sought to enrich themselves. Although Beard's arguments are extreme in their exclusive emphasis on economics, there is some foundation for them. Northern economic interests feared debtor revolts, while southern planters feared slave revolts. Capital investment and its protection were weak under the Articles not only because of potential rebellions but also because of inflated currencies, limited credit markets, and outstanding public debt. Also, manufacturers needed protection from foreign competition, and exporters (primarily of southern cotton) needed the security of safe passage for their cargoes on the high seas.

Contrary to Beard's approach is the view that the framers of the Constitution were concerned with philosophical and ethical ideas. Indeed, the framers sought to devise a system of government consistent with the dominant philosophical and moral values of the day.[12]

Lurking in the background was a generalized suspicion of distant central government. As the historian Joseph Ellis observed, this was the "core argument used to discredit the authority of Parliament and the British monarch . . . an obsessive suspicion of any centralized political power that operated in faraway

---

11 Charles A. Beard, *An Economic Interpretation of the Constitution of the United States* (New York: Macmillan, 1913).

12 For an analytical treatment, see Schofield, *Architects of Political Change*, chap. 4.

places."[13] But in fact, these interests and ideals belong together: the Founders' interests were reinforced by their principles. The convention that drafted the U.S. Constitution was chiefly organized by the New England merchants and southern planters. Although the delegates representing these groups did not all hope to profit personally from an increase in the value of their securities, as Beard would have it, they did hope to benefit in the broadest political and economic sense by breaking the power of their radical foes and establishing a system of government more compatible with their long-term economic and political interests. Thus the framers—in line with the rationality principle—sought to create a new government capable of promoting commerce and protecting property from radical state legislatures. They also sought to liberate the national government from the power of individual states and their sometimes venal and corrupt local politicians. At the same time, they hoped to fashion a government less susceptible than the existing state and national regimes to populist forces hostile to the interests of the commercial and propertied classes. These highly educated but practically experienced politicians were instrumentally motivated by both interests and ideals. The Constitutional Convention was a grand exercise in rationality and collective action.

The Great Compromise. The proponents of a new government fired their opening shot on May 29, 1787, when Edmund Randolph of Virginia offered a resolution that proposed corrections and enlargements in the Articles of Confederation. The proposal, which showed the strong influence of James Madison, was not a simple motion. It provided for virtually every aspect of a new government. Randolph later admitted it was intended to be an alternative draft constitution, and it did in fact serve as the framework for what ultimately became the Constitution.[14]

This proposal, known as the Virginia Plan, provided for a system of representation in the national legislature based on the population of each state, the proportion of each state's revenue contribution, or both. (Randolph also proposed a second branch of the legislature, but it was to be elected by the members of the first branch.) Because the states varied enormously in size and wealth, the Virginia Plan was thought to be heavily biased in favor of the large states that would have greater representation in the proposed system.

While the convention was debating the Virginia Plan, additional delegates arriving in Philadelphia were beginning to mount opposition to it. Their resolution, introduced by William Paterson of New Jersey and known as the New Jersey Plan, did not oppose the Virginia Plan point for point. Instead, it concentrated on specific weaknesses in the Articles of Confederation, in the spirit

---

13 Joseph Ellis, *Founding Brothers: The Revolutionary Generation* (New York: Knopf, 2000), p. 7.

14 There is no verbatim record of the debates, but Madison was present during virtually all of the deliberations and kept full notes on them. Madison's notes, along with the somewhat less complete records kept by several other participants in the convention, are available in a four-volume set. See Max Farrand, ed., *The Records of the Federal Convention of 1787*, rev. ed., 4 vols. (New Haven, CT: Yale University Press, 1966).

of revision rather than radical replacement of that document. However, their opposition to the Virginia Plan's scheme of representation was sufficient to send its proposals back to the committee to be worked into a common document. In particular, delegates from the less populous states, which included Delaware, New Jersey, Connecticut, and New York, asserted that the more populous states, such as Virginia, Pennsylvania, North Carolina, and Massachusetts, would dominate the new government if representation were to be determined by population. The smaller states argued that each state should be equally represented in the new regime regardless of its population.

The issue of representation was one that threatened to wreck the entire constitutional enterprise. Delegates conferred, factions maneuvered, and tempers flared. James Wilson of Pennsylvania told the small-state delegates that if they wanted to disrupt the Union they should go ahead. The separation could, he said, "never happen on better grounds." Small-state delegates were equally blunt. Gunning Bedford of Delaware declared that the small states might look elsewhere for friends if they were forced. "The large states," he said, "dare not dissolve the confederation. If they do the small ones will find some foreign ally of more honor and good faith, who will take them by the hand and do them justice." These sentiments were widely shared. The Union, as Oliver Ellsworth of Connecticut put it, was "on the verge of dissolution, scarcely held together by the strength of a hair." Convention delegates, acting as agents for the interests of their respective states, bargained, cajoled, and made attempts at persuasion in the rational pursuit of a result they would prefer.

The outcome of this debate was the **Great Compromise**, also known as the Connecticut Compromise. Under the terms of this compromise, in the first chamber of Congress—the House of Representatives—the members would be apportioned according to the number of inhabitants in each state. This, of course, was what delegates from the large states had sought. But in the second chamber—the Senate—each state would have an equal vote regardless of its size; this was to deal with the concerns of the small states. This compromise was not immediately satisfactory to all the delegates. Indeed, two of the most vocal supporters of the small-state faction, John Lansing and Robert Yates of New York, were so incensed by the concession that their colleagues had made to the large-state forces that they stormed out of the convention.

In the end, however, both sets of forces preferred compromise to the breakup of the Union, and the plan was accepted. The Analyzing the Evidence unit for this chapter explores, in more detail, the states' conflicting interests and how these shaped the eventual compromise.

 Great Compromise

An agreement reached at the Constitutional Convention of 1787 that gave each state an equal number of senators regardless of its population but linked representation in the House of Representatives to population

The Question of Slavery: The Three-Fifths Compromise.

Many of the conflicts that emerged during the Constitutional Convention were reflections of the fundamental differences between the slave and nonslave states, differences that pitted the southern planters and New England merchants against each other. This was the first premonition of a conflict that would almost destroy the Republic in later years.

Over 90 percent of all slaves resided in five states—Georgia, Maryland, North Carolina, South Carolina, and Virginia—where they accounted for 30 percent of

Voting at the Constitutional Convention

Under the Articles of Confederation, there was a unicameral Congress in which each state delegation received a single vote regardless of state population. So Virginia, with roughly 700,000 people, had the same share of votes as Rhode Island, with a population closer to 70,000. Among the issues considered by the framers at the Constitutional Convention, one of the most contentious involved how representation in the Congress would work under the new Constitution.

The larger states supported the Virginia Plan—because under this plan at least one of the chambers of Congress would be elected with representation proportional to population, giving the more populous states more of a voice in the national government. Given that the smaller, less populous states were poised to lose representation if votes in Congress were based on population, delegates from those states proposed the New Jersey Plan, which called for the creation of a unicameral legislature with one vote per state. Moreover, many of the delegates from the smaller states threatened to leave the Convention if the Virginia Plan were ratified. In an attempt to prevent the smaller states from departing, Roger Sherman proposed the Connecticut Compromise.

Representation in the First Congress

👤 = 30,000 people
👤 Free population
👤 Slave population

States*/Population**	VOTE ON VIRGINIA PLAN	VOTE ON CONNECTICUT COMPROMISE
VIRGINIA 747,550	YES	NO
PENNSYLVANIA 433,611	YES	NO
MASSACHUSETTS 378,556	YES	—
NEW YORK 340,241	NO	—
MARYLAND 319,728	—	YES
NORTH CAROLINA 395,005	YES	YES
SOUTH CAROLINA 249,073	YES	NO
CONNECTICUT 237,655	YES	YES
NEW JERSEY 184,139	NO	YES
GEORGIA 82,548	YES	NO
NEW HAMPSHIRE 141,899	—	—
DELAWARE 59,096	NO	YES
RHODE ISLAND 69,112	—	—

* Maryland's delegates were split equally and thus did not vote. Delegates from New Hampshire never attended at the same time as those from New York, hence their lack of participation. Rhode Island did not send any delegates to attend the Convention.

** Population data are based on the 1790 census and therefore are only approximate with respect to populations in 1787.

This plan called for a bicameral legislature, with representation based on population in the lower house and equal representation of states in the upper house. Although the Virginia Plan received more votes on first consideration, ultimately the Connecticut Compromise was adopted by a 5–4 vote to preserve a union with all 13 original members.

Representation in the First Congress

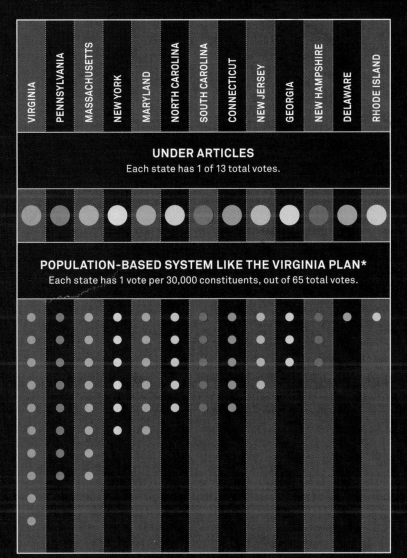

| VIRGINIA | PENNSYLVANIA | MASSACHUSETTS | NEW YORK | MARYLAND | NORTH CAROLINA | SOUTH CAROLINA | CONNECTICUT | NEW JERSEY | GEORGIA | NEW HAMPSHIRE | DELAWARE | RHODE ISLAND |

UNDER ARTICLES
Each state has 1 of 13 total votes.

POPULATION-BASED SYSTEM LIKE THE VIRGINIA PLAN*
Each state has 1 vote per 30,000 constituents, out of 65 total votes.

If we consider the number of representatives in Congress that each state would receive under the various plans, it becomes clear why individual states voted the way they did. Under the articles and the proposed New Jersey Plan, even the smallest states had 1 out of 13 votes in the Congress.

Under a population-based system like the Virginia Plan, the smaller states would lose voting power in the Congress. For example, in a population-based system with one representative per 30,000 people, Delaware would only have 1 out of 65 votes—significantly less voting power than the 1 out of 13 these states enjoyed under the articles and other arrangements that would give each state equal representation in Congress.

* Note that the framers calculated the number of representatives per state using population estimates. The first census was not taken until 1790.

SOURCES:
Keith L. Dougherty and Jac C. Heckelman, "A Pivotal Voter from a Pivotal State: Roger Sherman at the Constitutional Convention," *American Political Science Review 100* (May 2006): 297–302.
Clinton L. Rossiter, *1787: The Grand Convention* (New York: Macmillan Publishing Company, 1996).

the total population. In some places, slaves outnumbered nonslaves by as much as 10 to 1. If the Constitution were to embody any principle of national supremacy, some basic decisions would have to be made about the place of slavery in the general scheme.

Northerners and southerners eventually reached agreement through the **Three-Fifths Compromise**. The seats in the House of Representatives would be apportioned according to a "population" in which five slaves would count as three people. The slaves would not be allowed to vote, of course, but the number of representatives would be apportioned accordingly. This arrangement was supported by the slave states, which included some of the biggest and some of the smallest states at that time. It was also accepted by many delegates from nonslave states who strongly supported the principle of property representation, whether that property was expressed in slaves or in land, money, or stocks. The concern exhibited by most delegates was over how much slaves would count toward a state's representation rather than whether the institution of slavery would continue.

The issue of slavery was the most difficult one faced by the framers, and it nearly destroyed the Union. Although some delegates believed slavery to be morally wrong, an evil and oppressive institution that made a mockery of the ideals and values espoused in the Constitution, morality was not the issue that caused the framers to support or oppose the Three-Fifths Compromise. Whatever they thought of the institution of slavery, most delegates from the northern states opposed counting slaves in the distribution of congressional seats. Wilson of Pennsylvania, for example, argued that if slaves were citizens, they should be treated and counted like other citizens. If, on the other hand, they were property, then why should not other forms of property be counted toward the apportionment of Congress? But southern delegates made it clear that if the northerners refused to give in, they would never agree to the new government. Even southerners such as Edmund Randolph of Virginia, who conceded that slavery was immoral, insisted on including slaves in the allocation of congressional seats. This conflict between the southern and northern delegates was so divisive that many came to question the possibility of creating and maintaining a union of the two. Pierce Butler of South Carolina declared that the North and the South were as different as Russia and Turkey. Eventually the North and the South compromised on the issue of slavery and representation. Indeed, northerners even agreed to permit a continuation of the odious slave trade to keep the South in the Union. But in due course, Butler proved to be correct, and a bloody war was fought when the disparate interests of the North and the South could no longer be reconciled.

Three-Fifths Compromise →

An agreement reached at the Constitutional Convention of 1787 stipulating that for purposes of the apportionment of congressional seats, every slave would be counted as three-fifths of a person

THE CONSTITUTION

The political significance of the Great Compromise and the Three-Fifths Compromise was to reinforce the unity of the mercantile and planter forces that sought to create a new government. The Great Compromise reassured those who feared that the importance of their own local or regional influence would be reduced by the new governmental framework. The Three-Fifths Compromise temporarily defused the rivalry between the merchants and the planters. Their unity secured, members of the alliance supporting the establishment of a new government moved to fashion a constitutional framework consistent with their economic and political interests.

The framers of the Constitution understood that well-designed institutions make it easier to achieve collective goals. They understood also that the institutions they built could affect political outcomes for decades, if not centuries, to come. Accordingly, the framers took great care to construct institutions that over time would help the nation accomplish what they viewed as important political purposes.

In particular, the framers sought first a new government that would be strong enough to promote commerce and protect property from radical state legislatures such as Rhode Island's. This goal became the basis for national control over commerce and finance, as well as for both the establishment of national judicial supremacy and the effort to construct a strong presidency. Second, the framers sought to prevent what they saw as the threat posed by the "excessive democracy" of the state and national governments under the Articles of Confederation. Here again the framers' historical experience mattered. This goal led to such constitutional principles as **bicameralism** (division of the Congress into two chambers), checks and balances, staggered terms of office, and indirect election (selection of the president by an electoral college rather than directly by the voters). Third, the framers, lacking the power to force the states or the public at large to accept the new form of government, sought to identify principles that would help secure support. This goal became the basis for the constitutional provision for direct popular election of representatives and, subsequently, the basis for the addition of the Bill of Rights to the Constitution. Finally, the framers wanted to be certain that the government they created did not use its power to pose even more of a threat to its citizens' liberties and property rights than did the radical state legislatures they feared and despised. To prevent the new government from abusing its power, the framers incorporated into the Constitution such principles as the separation of powers and federalism.

 bicameralism

The division of a legislative assembly into two chambers, or houses

The framers provided us with a grand lesson in purposive behavior. They came to Philadelphia united by a common distaste for government under the Articles and animated by the agitation following Shays's Rebellion. They didn't always agree on what it was they disliked about the Articles. They certainly didn't agree on how to proceed—hence the necessity for the historic compromises we have just described. But they did believe that the acts of fostering commerce and protecting property could be served better by a set of institutional arrangements other than that provided by the Articles. They agreed that the institutional arrangements of government mattered for their lives and for those of their fellow citizens. They believed that both too much democracy and too much governmental power were threats to the common good, and they felt compelled to find instruments and principles that weighed against them. Let us assess the major provisions of the Constitution's seven articles to see how each relates to these objectives.

The Legislative Branch

The first seven sections of Article I of the Constitution provide for a Congress consisting of two chambers—a House of Representatives and a Senate. Members of the House of Representatives are given two-year terms of office and are to be elected directly by the people. Members of the Senate are to be appointed by the state legislatures (this provision was changed in 1913 by the Seventeenth Amendment, which instituted direct election of senators) for six-year terms. These terms, moreover, are staggered so that the appointments of one-third of the senators expire every two years. The Constitution assigns somewhat different tasks to the House and the Senate. Though the approval of each body is required for the enactment of a law, the Senate alone is given the power to ratify treaties and approve presidential appointments. The House, on the other hand, is given the sole power to originate revenue bills.

The character of the legislative branch is directly related to the framers' major goals. The House of Representatives was designed to be directly responsible to the people, to encourage popular consent for the new Constitution, and to help enhance the power of the new government. At the same time, to guard against "excessive democracy," the power of the House of Representatives was checked by the Senate, whose members are to be appointed rather than elected directly by the people and are to serve long (six-year) terms. The purpose of this provision, according to Alexander Hamilton, was to avoid "an unqualified complaisance to every sudden breeze of passion, or to every transient impulse which the people may receive."[15] Staggered terms of service in the Senate, moreover, were intended to make that body even more resistant to popular pressure. Because only one-third of the senators would be selected at any given time, the composition of the institution would be protected from changes in popular preferences transmitted by the state legislatures. This would prevent what James Madison called "mutability in the public councils arising from a rapid succession of new members."[16] Thus the structure of the legislative branch was designed to contribute to governmental power, promote popular consent for the new government, and at the same time place limits on the popular political currents that many of the framers saw as a radical threat to the economic and social order.

The issues of power and consent are important throughout the Constitution. Section 8 of Article I lists the specific powers of Congress, which include the authority to collect taxes, borrow money, regulate commerce, declare war, and maintain an army and navy. By granting it these powers, the framers indicated clearly that they intended the new government to be far more influential than its predecessor. At the same time, by defining the new government's most important powers as belonging to Congress, the framers sought to promote popular acceptance of this critical change by reassuring

---

15 Alexander Hamilton, James Madison, and John Jay, *The Federalist Papers*, Clinton Rossiter, ed. (New York: New American Library, 1961), no. 71.

16 *The Federalist*, no. 62.

citizens that their views would be fully represented whenever the government exercised its new powers.

As a further guarantee to the people that the new government would pose no threat to them, the Constitution implies that any powers not listed are not granted at all. This is the doctrine of **expressed powers**. The Constitution grants only those powers specifically expressed in its text. No new powers can be seized on by the national government without a constitutional amendment. In the absence of such an amendment, any power not enumerated is conceived to be "reserved" to the states (or the people). But the framers intended to create an active and powerful government, so they also included the **necessary and proper clause**, sometimes known as the elastic clause, which signifies that the enumerated powers are meant to be a source of strength to the national government, not a limitation on it—that the government may employ means "necessary and proper" to implement the expressed powers. As we will see, the question of what powers can or cannot be exercised by the federal government is still debated in our time. For example, opponents of the 2010 Affordable Care Act (Obamacare) said the federal government lacked the power to require Americans to purchase health insurance. The Supreme Court upheld major provisions of the law, but the debate continues.[17]

expressed powers

The powers enumerated in the Constitution that are granted to the federal government

necessary and proper clause

Article I, Section 8, of the Constitution, which enumerates the powers of Congress and provides Congress with the authority to make all laws "necessary and proper" to carry them out; also referred to as the elastic clause

The Executive Branch

The Constitution provides for the establishment of the presidency in Article II. As Alexander Hamilton commented, the presidential article was aimed toward creating "energy in the Executive." It did so in an effort to overcome the natural stalemate that was built into both the bicameral legislature and the separation of powers among the legislative, executive, and judicial branches. The Constitution afforded the president a measure of independence from the people and from the other branches of government, particularly Congress.

Some of the framers had argued for a plural executive or executive council in order to avoid the evils that many associated with a monarch. In *Federalist 70*, however, Hamilton argued that "energy" required a single rather than a plural executive. While abuse of power should be guarded against by checks and balances and other devices, energy also required that the executive should be provided with "competent powers" to direct the nation's business.[18] These would include the unconditional power to accept ambassadors from other countries; this provision amounts to the power to "recognize" other countries. The president is also given the power to negotiate treaties, although their acceptance requires the approval of the Senate. The president is given the unconditional right to grant reprieves and pardons, except in cases of impeachment. And the president is provided with the power to appoint major departmental personnel, convene Congress in a special session, and veto congressional enactments.

17 *National Federation of Independent Business v. Sebelius*, 567 U.S. ____ (2012).

18 *The Federalist*, no. 70.

(The veto power is formidable, but it is not absolute because Congress can override it by a two-thirds vote.)[19]

The framers hoped to create a presidency that would make the federal government, rather than the states, the agency capable of timely and decisive action to deal with public issues and problems. This goal is the meaning of the "energy" that Hamilton hoped to impart to the executive branch.[20] At the same time, however, the framers sought to help the president withstand (excessively) democratic pressures by making the office subject to indirect rather than direct election (through selection by a separate electoral college). The extent to which the framers' hopes were realized is the topic of Chapter 7.

The Judicial Branch

In establishing the judicial branch in Article III, the Constitution reflects the framers' preoccupations with enhancing the power of the national government and checking radical democratic impulses while guarding against potential interference with liberty and property from the new national government itself.

Under the provisions of Article III, the framers created a court that was to be literally a supreme court of the United States and not merely the highest court of the national government. The most important expression of this intention was granting the Supreme Court the power to resolve any conflicts that might emerge between federal and state laws. In particular, the Supreme Court was given the right to determine whether a power was exclusive to the federal government, concurrent with the states, or exclusive to the states. The significance of this was noted by Justice Oliver Wendell Holmes, Jr., who observed, "I do not think the United States would come to an end if we lost our power to declare an act of Congress void. I do think the union would be imperilled if we could not make that declaration as to the laws of the several states."[21]

In addition, the Supreme Court was assigned jurisdiction over controversies between citizens of different states. The long-term significance of this provision was that as the country developed a national economy, it came to rely increasingly on the federal judiciary, rather than the state courts, for the resolution of disputes.

Judges were given lifetime appointments to protect them from popular politics and interference by the other branches. To further safeguard judicial independence, the Constitution also prohibited Congress from reducing the

---

19 A modern description of executive-legislature relations is "The president proposes; the Congress disposes." The president may propose to the legislature when the subject is a treaty or a major departmental appointment or a federal judge or justice, which must be approved by the Senate; then the president is a legislative "agenda setter." When, however, it is a proposed law or budget, it is a "suggestion" that the legislature may choose to ignore altogether. Such proposals are then said to be "dead on arrival" because Congress marches to the beat of its own drummer.

20 *The Federalist*, no. 70.

21 Oliver Wendell Holmes, Jr., *Collected Legal Papers* (New York: Harcourt, Brace, 1920), pp. 295–6.

---

salary of any sitting judge. This did not mean, however, that the judiciary would remain totally impartial to political considerations or to the other branches, for the president appoints the judges and the Senate approves the appointments. Congress also has the power to create inferior (lower) courts, change the jurisdiction of the federal courts, add or subtract federal judges, and even change the size of the Supreme Court.

No direct mention is made of **judicial review**—the power of the courts to render the final decision when a conflict of interpretation of the Constitution or of laws arises between the courts and Congress, the courts and the executive branch, or the courts and the states. Scholars generally feel that judicial review is implicit in the very existence of a written constitution and in the power given directly to the federal courts over "all Cases . . . arising under this Constitution, the Laws of the United States, and Treaties made, or which shall be made, under their Authority" (Article III, Section 2). The Supreme Court eventually assumed the power of judicial review. Its assumption of this power, as we see in Chapter 9, was based not on the Constitution itself but on the politics of later decades and the membership of the Court.

 judicial review

The power of the courts to declare actions of the legislative and executive branches invalid or unconstitutional. The Supreme Court asserted this power in *Marbury v. Madison* (1803)

National Unity and Power

Various provisions in the Constitution address the framers' concern with national unity and power, including Article IV's provisions for comity (reciprocity) among states and among the citizens of all states.

Each state is prohibited from discriminating against the citizens of other states in favor of its own citizens, with the Supreme Court charged with deciding in each case whether a state has discriminated against goods or people from another state. The Constitution restricts the power of the states in favor of ensuring that the national government holds enough power to give the country a free-flowing national economy.

The framers' concern with national supremacy was also expressed in Article VI in the **supremacy clause**, which provides that national laws and treaties "shall be the supreme Law of the Land." This means that all laws made under the "Authority of the United States" are superior to all laws adopted by any state or any other subdivision and the states are expected to respect all treaties made under that authority. This provision was a direct effort to keep the states from dealing separately with foreign nations or businesses. The supremacy clause also binds the officials of all state and local, as well as federal, governments to take an oath of office to support the national Constitution. This means that every action taken by the U.S. Congress must be applied within each state as though the action were, in fact, state law.

 supremacy clause

A clause of Article VI of the Constitution that states that all laws passed by the national government and all treaties are the supreme laws of the land and superior to all laws adopted by any state or any subdivision

Amending the Constitution

The Constitution establishes procedures for its own revision in Article V. Its provisions are so difficult that Americans have availed themselves of the amending process only 17 times since 1791, when the first 10 amendments were adopted.

Many other amendments have been proposed in Congress, but fewer than 40 of them have come even close to fulfilling the Constitution's requirement of a two-thirds vote in Congress, and only a fraction have gotten anywhere near adoption by three-fourths of the states. The Constitution can also be amended by a constitutional convention. Occasionally proponents of particular measures, such as a balanced-budget amendment, have called for a constitutional convention to consider their proposals. Whatever the purpose for which it was called, however, such a convention would presumably have the authority to revise America's entire system of government.

It should be noted that any body of rules, including a national constitution, must balance the need to respond flexibly to changes on the one hand with the caution not to be too flexible on the other. An inflexible body of rules is one that cannot accommodate major change. It risks being rebelled against, a circumstance in which the slate is wiped clean and new rules are designed—or ignored altogether. Too much flexibility, however, is disastrous. It invites those who lose in normal everyday politics to replay battles at the constitutional level. If institutional change is too easy to accomplish, the stability of the political system becomes threatened. This means, as stated in the institution principle, that the institutional arrangements characterized in a constitution should structure politics by providing a framework, not rigidly specify political outcomes explicitly. There is no magic formula to tell us whether a document has the right degree of flexibility. The only answer is that a constitution must pass the test of time. The fact that our constitution has survived for more than two centuries should be taken as a point in its favor.

Ratifying the Constitution

The rules for ratification of the Constitution of 1787 are set forth in Article VII of the Constitution. This provision actually violated the amendment provisions of the Articles of Confederation. For one thing, it adopts a nine-state rule in place of the unanimity required by the Articles. For another, it provides for ratification to occur in special state conventions called for that purpose rather than in the state legislatures. All the states except Rhode Island eventually did set up state conventions to ratify the Constitution.

Constitutional Limits on the National Government's Power

As we have indicated, although the framers sought to create a powerful national government, they also wanted to guard against possible misuse of that power. To that end, the framers incorporated two key principles into the Constitution: the **separation of powers** and **federalism** (see Chapter 3). A third set of limitations, in the form of the **Bill of Rights**, was added to the Constitution to help

---

separation of powers

The division of governmental power among several institutions that must cooperate in decision making

---

federalism

The system of government in which a constitution divides power between a central government and regional governments

---

Bill of Rights

The first 10 amendments to the U.S. Constitution, adopted in 1791. The Bill of Rights ensures certain rights and liberties to the people

---

secure its ratification when opponents of the document charged that it paid insufficient attention to citizens' rights.

The Separation of Powers. No principle of politics was more widely shared at the time of the 1787 Founding than the principle that power must be used to balance power. The French political theorist Baron de la Brède et de Montesquieu (1689–1755) believed that this balance was an indispensable defense against tyranny. His writings, especially his major work, *The Spirit of the Laws*, "were taken as political gospel" at the Philadelphia convention. Although the principle of the separation of powers was not explicitly stated in the Constitution, the entire structure of the national government was built precisely on Article I, the legislature; Article II, the executive; and Article III, the judiciary (Figure 2.1).

However, separation of powers is nothing but mere words on parchment without a method to maintain the separation. The method became known by the popular label **checks and balances**. Each branch is given not only its own powers but also some power over the other two branches. Among the most familiar checks and balances are the president's veto as a power over Congress

◀ checks and balances

The mechanisms through which each branch of government is able to participate in and influence the activities of the other branches

Figure 2.1
THE SEPARATION OF POWERS

LEGISLATIVE	EXECUTIVE	JUDICIAL
Passes federal laws	Enforces laws	Reviews lower-court decisions
Controls federal appropriations	Serves as commander in chief of armed forces	Decides constitutionality of laws
Approves treaties and presidential appointments	Makes foreign treaties	Decides cases involving disputes between states
Regulates interstate commerce	Nominates Supreme Court justices and federal court judges	
Establishes lower-court system	Pardons those convicted in federal court	

and Congress's power over the president through its control of appointments to high executive posts and to the judiciary. Congress also has power over the president with its control of appropriations and (by the Senate) the right of approval of treaties. The judiciary was assumed to have the power of judicial review over the other two branches.

Another important feature of the separation of powers is the principle of giving each of the branches a distinctly different constituency. Theorists such as Montesquieu called this a "mixed regime," with the president chosen indirectly by electors, the House by popular vote, the Senate (originally) by state legislature, and the judiciary by presidential appointment. By these means, the occupants of each branch would tend to develop very different outlooks on how to govern, different definitions of the public interest, and different alliances with private interests.

Federalism. Compared with the confederation principle of the Articles of Confederation, federalism was a step toward greater centralization of power. The delegates agreed that they needed to place more power at the national level, without completely undermining the power of the state governments. Thus they devised a system of two sovereigns—the states and the nation—with the hope that competition between the two would be an effective limitation on the power of both.

The Bill of Rights. Late in the Philadelphia convention, a motion was made to include a bill of rights in the Constitution. After a brief debate, in which hardly a word was said in its favor and only one speech was made against it, the motion to include it was almost unanimously turned down. Most delegates sincerely believed that because the federal government was already limited to its expressed powers, any further protection of citizens was not needed. The delegates argued that the states should adopt bills of rights because their greater powers needed greater limitations. But almost immediately after the Constitution was ratified, there was a movement to adopt a national bill of rights. This is why the Bill of Rights, adopted in 1791, makes up the first 10 amendments to the Constitution and is not incorporated into the body of it. We have a good deal more to say about the Bill of Rights in Chapter 4.

THE FIGHT FOR RATIFICATION: FEDERALISTS VERSUS ANTIFEDERALISTS

The first hurdle faced by the new Constitution was ratification by state conventions of delegates elected by the people of each state. This struggle for ratification was carried out in 13 separate campaigns. Each was influenced by local as well as national considerations. Two sides faced off throughout the states,

Table 2.1

FEDERALISTS VERSUS ANTIFEDERALISTS

	FEDERALISTS	ANTIFEDERALISTS
Who were they?	Property owners, creditors, merchants	Small farmers, frontiersmen, debtors, shopkeepers
What did they believe?	Elites are best fit to govern and "excessive democracy" is dangerous	Government should be close to the people and the concentration of power in the hands of the elites is dangerous
What system of government did they favor?	Strong national government; believed in "filtration" so that only elites would obtain governmental power	Retention of power by state governments and protection of individual rights
Who were their leaders?	Alexander Hamilton, James Madison, George Washington	Patrick Henry, George Mason, Elbridge Gerry, George Clinton

however, calling themselves Federalists and Antifederalists (Table 2.1).[22] The Federalists supported the Constitution and preferred a strong national government. The Antifederalists opposed the Constitution and preferred a decentralized federal government; they took their name by default, in reaction to their better-organized opponents. The Federalists were united in their support of the Constitution, whereas the Antifederalists were divided in what they believed the alternative to the Constitution should be.

During the struggle over ratification of the proposed Constitution, Americans argued about great political issues and ideals. How much power should the national government be given? What safeguards were most likely to prevent the abuse of power? What institutional arrangements could best ensure adequate representation for all Americans? Was tyranny to be feared more from the many or from the few?

---

22 An excellent analysis of the ratification campaigns—based on a quantitative assessment of the campaigners' own words as found in campaign documents, pamphlets, tracts, public letters, and the eighteenth-century equivalent of op-ed pieces (such as the individual essays that make up the *Federalist Papers*)—is William H. Riker, *The Strategy of Rhetoric: Campaigning for the American Constitution* (New Haven, CT: Yale University Press, 1996).

In political life, of course, ideals—and values—are seldom completely divorced from some set of interests. In 1787, Americans were divided along economic, regional, and political lines. These divisions inevitably influenced their attitudes toward the profound political questions of the day. Many well-to-do merchants and planters, as we saw earlier, favored the creation of a stronger central government that would have the capacity to protect property, promote commerce, and keep some of the more radical state legislatures in check. At the same time, many powerful state leaders, such as Governor George Clinton of New York, feared that strengthening the national government would reduce their own influence and status. Each of these interests, of course, justified its position with an appeal to basic values.

Ideas are often important weapons in political warfare, and seeing how and by whom they are wielded can illuminate their otherwise obscure implications. Even if an idea is invented and initially brandished to serve an interest, however, once it has been articulated, it can take on a life of its own and prove to have implications that transcend the narrow interests it was created to serve. For example, some opponents of the Constitution who criticized the absence of a bill of rights in the initial document did so simply with the hope of blocking the document's ratification. Yet the bill of rights that was added to the Constitution has proved for over two centuries to be a bulwark of civil liberty in the United States.

As this example shows, truly great political ideas transcend the interests that initially set them forth. The first step in understanding a political value is understanding why and by whom it is espoused. The second step is understanding the full implications of the idea itself—implications that may go far beyond the interests that launched it. Whatever the underlying clash of interests that may have guided them, the Federalists and the Antifederalists presented important alternative visions of America.

During the ratification struggle, thousands of essays, speeches, pamphlets, and letters were presented in support of and in opposition to the proposed Constitution. The best-known pieces supporting ratification of the Constitution were the 85 essays written under the name Publius by Alexander Hamilton, James Madison, and John Jay between the fall of 1787 and the spring of 1788. The *Federalist Papers*, as they are collectively known today, defended the principles of the Constitution and sought to dispel fears of a national authority. The Antifederalists published essays of their own, arguing that the new Constitution betrayed the Revolution and was a step toward monarchy. Among the best of the Antifederalist works were the essays, usually attributed to New York Supreme Court justice Robert Yates, that were written under the name Brutus and published in the *New York Journal* at the same time the *Federalist Papers* appeared. The Antifederalist view was also ably presented in pamphlets and letters written by a former delegate to the Continental Congress and future U.S. senator, Richard Henry Lee of Virginia, using the pen name the Federal Farmer. These essays highlight the major differences of opinion between Federalists and Antifederalists. Federalists appealed to basic principles of government in support of their nationalist vision. Antifederalists cited equally fundamental precepts to support their vision of a looser confederacy of small republics.

The two sides engaged in what was almost certainly the very first nation-wide political campaign in the history of the world. Though each side was itself only loosely organized, they did address their collective action problem—a rudimentary form of coordination and cooperation was manifest. This was especially evident in the division of labor among Hamilton, Madison, and Jay as they alternately wrote under the Publius pseudonym on different aspects of the newly drafted Constitution in an effort to effect its ratification in the state of New York.

Representation

One major area of contention between the two sides was the question of representation. The Antifederalists asserted that representatives must be "a true picture of the people, . . . [possessing] the knowledge of their circumstances and their wants."[23] This could be achieved, argued the Antifederalists, only in small, relatively homogeneous republics such as the existing states. In their view, the size and extent of the entire nation precluded the construction of a truly representative form of government.

The absence of true representation, moreover, would mean that the people would lack confidence in and attachment to the national government and would refuse to obey its laws voluntarily. As a result, according to the Antifederalists, the national government described by the Constitution would be compelled to resort to force to secure popular compliance. The Federal Farmer averred that laws of the remote federal government could be "in many cases disregarded, unless a multitude of officers and military force be continually kept in view, and employed to enforce the execution of the laws, and to make the government feared and respected."[24]

Federalists, for their part, did not long for pure democracy and saw no reason that representatives should be precisely like those they represented. In their view, government must be representative *of* the people but must also have a measure of autonomy *from* the people. Their ideal government was to be constructed such that it would be capable of serving the long-term public interest even if doing so conflicted with the public's current preference. In more contemporary terms, Federalists sought representatives who were *trustees*, whereas Antifederalists sought *delegates*.

Federalists also dismissed the Antifederalist claim that the distance between representatives and constituents in the proposed national government would lead to popular disaffection and compel the government to use force to secure obedience. Federalists replied that the system of representation they proposed

23 Melancton Smith, quoted in Herbert J. Storing, *What the Anti-Federalists Were For: The Political Thought of the Opponents of the Constitution* (Chicago: University of Chicago Press, 1981), p. 17.

24 "Letters from the Federal Farmer," no. 2, in Herbert Storing, ed., *The Complete Anti-Federalist,* 7 vols. (Chicago: University of Chicago Press, 1981).

was more likely to produce effective government. In Hamilton's words, there would be "a probability that the general government will be better administered than the particular governments."[25] Competent government, in turn, should inspire popular trust and confidence more effectively than simple social proximity between rulers and ruled.

The Threat of Tyranny

tyranny

Oppressive government that employs the cruel and unjust use of power and authority

A second important issue dividing Federalists and Antifederalists was the threat of **tyranny**—unjust rule by the group in power. Both opponents and defenders of the Constitution frequently affirmed their fear of tyrannical rule. Each side, however, had a different view of the most likely source of tyranny and, hence, of the way in which the threat was to be forestalled.

From the Antifederalist perspective, the great danger was the tendency of all governments—including republican governments—to become gradually more and more "aristocratic" in character, with a small number of individuals in positions of authority using their stations to gain more and more power over the general citizenry. In essence, the few would use their power to tyrannize the many. For this reason, Antifederalists were sharply critical of those features of the Constitution that divorced governmental institutions from direct responsibility to the people—institutions such as the Senate, the executive, and the federal judiciary.

The Federalists, too, recognized the threat of tyranny. They were not naive about the motives and purposes of individuals and took them to be no less opportunistic and self-interested than the Antifederalists did. But the Federalists believed that the danger particularly associated with republican governments was not aristocracy but, instead, majority tyranny. The Federalists were concerned that a popular majority, "united and actuated by some common impulse of passion, or of interest, adverse to the rights of other citizens," would endeavor to "trample on the rules of justice."[26] From the Federalist perspective, it was precisely those features of the Constitution attacked as potential sources of tyranny by the Antifederalists that offered the best hope of averting the threat of oppression. The size and extent of the nation, for instance, were for the Federalists a bulwark against tyranny. In Madison's famous formulation, reflecting the logic of the collective action principle,

> The smaller the society, the fewer probably will be the distinct parties and interests . . . the more frequently will a majority be found of the same party; and the smaller the number of individuals composing a majority, and the smaller the compass within which they are placed, the more easily will they concert and execute their plans of oppression. Extend the sphere, and you take in a greater variety of parties and interests; you make it less probable that a

25 *The Federalist,* no. 27.

26 *The Federalist,* no. 10.

majority of the whole will have a common motive to invade the rights of other citizens; or if such a common motive exists, it will be more difficult for all who feel it to discover their own strength, and to act in unison with each other.[27]

The Federalists understood that, in a democracy, temporary majorities could abuse their power. The Federalists' misgivings about majority rule were reflected in the constitutional structure. The indirect election of senators, the indirect election of the president, the judicial branch's insulation from the people, the separation of powers, the president's veto power, the bicameral design of Congress, and the federal system were all means to curb majority tyranny. These features of the Constitution suggest, following the institution principle, the framers' awareness of the problems of majority rule and the need for institutional safeguards. Except for the indirect election of senators (which was changed in 1913), these aspects of the constitutional structure remain in place today.[28] In essence, the Federalists sought to place limits on collective action in order to protect liberty. We shall return to this idea in Chapters 4 and 5.

To some extent, the Federalists were influenced by an understanding of history that differed from that of the Antifederalists. Federalists believed that colonial history, to say nothing of the history of the Greeks, showed that republican governments were often endangered by mob rule. The Antifederalists, by contrast, thought that history revealed the dangers of aristocratic conspiracies against popular liberties. History matters, but it is always subject to interpretation.

Governmental Power

A third major difference between Federalists and Antifederalists was the issue of governmental power. Both the opponents and the proponents of the Constitution agreed on the principle of limited government. They differed, however, on the fundamentally important question of how to place limits on governmental action. Antifederalists favored limiting and enumerating the powers granted to the national government in relation to both the states and the people at large. To them, the powers given the national government ought to be "confined to certain defined national objects."[29] Otherwise, the national government would "swallow up all the power of the state governments."[30]

---

27 *The Federalist,* no. 10.

28 A classic development of this theme is found in James M. Buchanan and Gordon Tullock, *The Calculus of Consent: Logical Foundations of Constitutional Democracy* (Ann Arbor: University of Michigan Press, 1962). For a review of the voting paradox and a case study of how it applies today, see Kenneth A. Shepsle, *Analyzing Politics: Rationality, Behavior and Institutions,* 2nd ed. (New York: Norton, 2010), pp. 53–89.

29 "Essays of Brutus," no. 7.

30 "Essays of Brutus," no. 6.

Antifederalists bitterly attacked the supremacy clause and the necessary and proper clause of the Constitution as unlimited and dangerous grants of power to the national government.[31]

Antifederalists also demanded that a bill of rights be added to the Constitution to place limits on the government's exercise of power over the citizenry. "There are certain things," wrote Brutus, "which rulers should be absolutely prohibited from doing, because if they should do them, they would work an injury, not a benefit to the people."[32] Similarly, the Federal Farmer maintained that "there are certain unalienable and fundamental rights, which in forming the social compact . . . ought to be explicitly ascertained and fixed."[33]

Federalists favored the construction of a government with broad powers. They wanted a government that had the capacity to defend the nation against foreign foes, guard against domestic strife and insurrection, promote commerce, and expand the nation's economy. Hamilton pointed out that these goals could not be achieved without allowing the government to exercise the necessary power. Federalists acknowledged, of course, that every power could be abused but argued that the way to prevent misuse of power was not by depriving the government of the powers needed to achieve national goals. Instead, they argued that the threat of abuse of power would be mitigated by the Constitution's internal checks and controls. As Madison put it,

> The power surrendered by the people is first divided between two distinct governments, and then the portion allotted to each subdivided among distinct and separate departments. Hence a double security arises to the rights of the people. The different governments will control each other, at the same time that each will be controlled by itself.[34]

The Federalists' concern with avoiding unwarranted limits on governmental power led them to oppose a bill of rights, which they saw as nothing more than a set of unnecessary restrictions on the federal government. For the Federalists, the issue was one of national versus state power, not substantive rights as such. They feared that a bill of rights would weaken the federal government relative to the states.

The Federalists acknowledged that abuse of power remained a possibility but felt that the risk had to be taken because of the goals to be achieved. "The very idea of power included a possibility of doing harm," said the Federalist John Rutledge during South Carolina's ratification debates. "If the gentleman would show the power that could do no harm," Rutledge continued, "he would at once discover it to be a power that could do no good."[35]

---

31 Storing, *What the Anti-Federalists Were For,* p. 28.

32 "Essays of Brutus," no. 9.

33 "Letters from the Federal Farmer," no. 2.

34 *The Federalist,* no. 51.

35 Quoted in Storing, *What the Anti-Federalists Were For,* p. 30.

CHANGING THE INSTITUTIONAL FRAMEWORK: CONSTITUTIONAL AMENDMENT

The Constitution has endured for more than two centuries as the framework of government. But it has not endured without change. Without change, the Constitution might have become merely a sacred relic, stored under glass.

Amendments: Many Are Called, Few Are Chosen

The need for change was recognized by the framers of the Constitution, and the provisions for the amendments were incorporated into Article V. Since 1791, when the first 10 amendments, the Bill of Rights, were added, only 17 amendments have been adopted. And two of them—Prohibition and its repeal—cancel each other out, so that for all practical purposes only 15 amendments have been added to the Constitution since 1791, despite vast changes in American society and its economy.

Four methods of amendment are provided for in Article V:

1. Passage in House and Senate by two-thirds vote; then ratification by majority vote of the legislatures of three-fourths (now 38) of the states.

2. Passage in House and Senate by two-thirds vote; then ratification by conventions called for that purpose in three-fourths of the states.

3. Passage in a national convention called by Congress in response to petitions by two-thirds (now 34) of the states; ratification by majority vote of the legislatures of three-fourths of the states.

4. Passage in a national convention, as in method 3; then ratification by conventions called for that purpose in three-fourths of the states.

(Figure 2.2 illustrates each of these methods.) Because no amendment has ever been proposed by national convention, however, routes 3 and 4 have never been employed. And route 2 has been employed only once (for the Twenty-First Amendment, which repealed the Eighteenth, or Prohibition, Amendment). Thus route 1 has been used for all the others.

The Twenty-Seven Amendments

The Constitution and its amendments are reproduced at the end of this book. Most of the Constitution's 27 amendments share a common characteristic: all but two are concerned with the structure or composition of government. This is consistent with the dictionary, which defines *constitution* as the "makeup or

Figure 2.2
ROUTES OF AMENDMENT

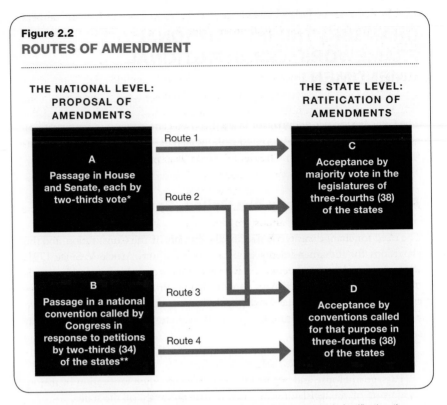

THE NATIONAL LEVEL: PROPOSAL OF AMENDMENTS

THE STATE LEVEL: RATIFICATION OF AMENDMENTS

A Passage in House and Senate, each by two-thirds vote*

B Passage in a national convention called by Congress in response to petitions by two-thirds (34) of the states**

Route 1
Route 2
Route 3
Route 4

C Acceptance by majority vote in the legislatures of three-fourths (38) of the states

D Acceptance by conventions called for that purpose in three-fourths (38) of the states

* In each amendment proposal, Congress has the power to choose the method of ratification, the time limit for consideration by the states, and other conditions of ratification.

** This method of proposal has never been employed. Thus amendment routes 3 and 4 have never been attempted.

composition of a thing." And it is consistent with the concept of a constitution as higher law because the whole point and purpose of a higher law is to establish a framework within which government and the process of making ordinary law can take place. Even those who would have preferred more changes in the Constitution would have had to agree that there is great wisdom in this principle. A constitution ought to enable legislation and public policies to take place, but it should not determine what that legislation or those public policies ought to be.

The purpose of the 10 amendments in the Bill of Rights was basically structural: to give each of the three branches clearer and more restricted boundaries. The First Amendment clarifies the jurisdiction of Congress. Although the powers of Congress under Article I, Section 8, do not justify laws regulating religion, speech, and the like, the First Amendment makes this limitation explicit: "Congress shall make no law . . ." The Second, Third, and Fourth Amendments similarly spell out limits on the executive branch. Such limits were seen as a necessity given the abuses of executive power Americans had endured under British rule.

The Fifth, Sixth, Seventh, and Eighth Amendments contain some of the most important safeguards for individual citizens against the arbitrary exercise of governmental power. And these amendments sought to accomplish their goal by defining the judicial branch more concretely and clearly than had been done in Article III of the Constitution. Table 2.2 analyzes the 10 amendments included in the Bill of Rights.

Five of the 17 amendments adopted since 1791 are directly concerned with expansion of the electorate (Table 2.3). These occasional efforts to expand the electorate were made necessary by the fact that the Founders were unable to establish a national electorate with uniform voting qualifications. Stalemated on that issue, the delegates decided to evade it by providing in the final draft of Article I, Section 2, that eligibility to vote in a national election would be the same as "the Qualifications requisite for Electors of the most numerous Branch of the State Legislature." Article I, Section 4, added that Congress could alter state regulations as to the "Times, Places and Manner of holding Elections for Senators and Representatives." Nevertheless, this meant that any important expansion of the American electorate would almost certainly require a constitutional amendment.

Six more amendments are also electoral in nature, although not concerned directly with voting rights and the expansion of the electorate. These six amendments are concerned with the elective offices themselves (the Twentieth, Twenty-Second, and Twenty-Fifth) or with the relationship between elective offices and the electorate (the Twelfth, Fourteenth, and Seventeenth; Table 2.4).

Table 2.2
THE BILL OF RIGHTS: ANALYSIS OF ITS PROVISIONS

AMENDMENT	PURPOSE
I	Limits on Congress: Congress is not to make any law establishing a religion or abridging the freedom of speech, press, or assembly or the right to petition the government.
II, III, IV	Limits on the executive: The executive branch is not to infringe on the right of people to keep arms (II), is not to arbitrarily take houses for use by a militia (III), and is not to engage in the search or seizure of evidence without a court warrant swearing to a belief in the probable existence of a crime (IV).
V, VI, VII, VIII	Limits on the courts: The courts are not to hold trials for serious offenses without provision for a grand jury (V), a petit (trial) jury (VII), a speedy trial (VI), presentation of charges, and confrontation of hostile witnesses (VI). Individuals may not be compelled to testify against themselves (V) and are immune from trial more than once for the same offense (V). Neither bail nor punishment can be excessive (VIII), and no property can be taken without just compensation (V).
IX, X	Limits on the national government: All rights not enumerated are reserved to the states or the people.

Table 2.3

AMENDING THE CONSTITUTION TO EXPAND THE ELECTORATE

AMENDMENT	PURPOSE	YEAR PROPOSED	YEAR ADOPTED
XIV	Provided, in Section 1, a national definition of citizenship	1866	1868
XV	Extended voting rights to all races	1869	1870
XIX	Extended voting rights to women	1919	1920
XXIII	Extended voting rights to residents of the District of Columbia	1960	1961
XXIV	Extended voting rights to all classes by abolition of poll taxes	1962	1964
XXVI	Extended voting rights to citizens ages 18 and over	1971	1971

Another five amendments have sought to expand or limit the powers of the national and state governments (Table 2.5).[36] The Eleventh Amendment protects the states from suits by private individuals and takes away from the federal courts any power to hear suits by private individuals of one state (or a foreign country) against another state. Three other amendments in Table 2.5 are obviously designed to reduce state power (the Thirteenth), reduce state power and expand national power (the Fourteenth), and expand national power (the Sixteenth). The Twenty-Seventh puts a limit on Congress's ability to raise its own salary.

The two missing amendments underscore the meaning of the rest: the Eighteenth, or Prohibition, Amendment and the Twenty-First, its repeal. They represent the only instance in which the country tried to *legislate* by constitutional

---

36 The Fourteenth Amendment is included in this table as well as in Table 2.3 because it not only seeks to define citizenship but also *seems* to intend that this definition of citizenship include, along with the right to vote, all the rights of the Bill of Rights, regardless of the state in which the citizen resides. A great deal more will be said about this in Chapter 4.

Table 2.4

AMENDING THE CONSTITUTION TO CHANGE THE RELATIONSHIP BETWEEN THE ELECTED OFFICES AND THE ELECTORATE

AMENDMENT	PURPOSE	YEAR PROPOSED	YEAR ADOPTED
XII	Provided a separate ballot for the vice president in the electoral college	1803	1804
XIV	Penalized states for depriving freed slaves of the right to vote	1866	1868
XVII	Provided for the direct election of senators	1912	1913
XX	Shortened the time between elections and inauguration of the new president and Congress	1932	1933
XXII	Limited the presidential term	1947	1951
XXV	Provided for presidential succession in case of disability	1965	1967

amendment. In other words, the Eighteenth is the only amendment that was designed to deal directly with a substantive social problem. And it was the only amendment ever to have been repealed. Two other amendments—the Thirteenth, which abolished slavery, and the Sixteenth, which established the power to levy an income tax—can be said to have had the effect of legislation. But the purpose of the Thirteenth Amendment was to restrict the power of the states by forever forbidding them to treat any human being as property. As for the Sixteenth Amendment, it is certainly true that income-tax legislation followed immediately; nevertheless, the amendment concerns itself strictly with establishing the power of Congress to enact such legislation. The legislation came later.

For those whose hopes for change center on the Constitution, it must be emphasized that the amendment route to social change is, and always will be, extremely limited. This is "path dependency," as captured in the history principle, with a vengeance. The status quo—the original Constitution—and the arduousness of its amendment process provide durability on the one hand and constrain the prospects for change on the other. Through a constitution it is

Table 2.5

**AMENDING THE CONSTITUTION TO EXPAND OR
LIMIT THE POWER OF GOVERNMENT**

AMENDMENT	PURPOSE	YEAR PROPOSED	YEAR ADOPTED
XI	Limited the jurisdiction of federal courts over suits involving the states	1794	1795
XIII	Eliminated slavery and the rights of states to allow property in the form of persons	1865*	1865
XIV	Established due process of law in state courts for all persons; later used to apply the entire Bill of Rights to the states	1866	1868
XVI	Established the national power to tax income	1909	1913
XXVII	Limited Congress's power to raise its own salary	1789	1992

*The Thirteenth Amendment was proposed on January 31, 1865, and adopted less than a year later, on December 6, 1865.

possible to establish a working structure of government, and through a consti-tution it is possible to establish basic rights of citizens by placing limitations and obligations on the powers of that government. Once these structures have been accomplished, the real problem is how to extend rights to those people who do not already enjoy them.

REFLECTIONS ON THE FOUNDING:
IDEALS OR INTERESTS?

At the start of this chapter, we stressed the need to look beyond the myths and rhetoric of the Founding era to analyze the goals of the Founders, their struggle to resolve their conflicts and reach their collective goals, and the institutions that resulted from their endeavor. The story of the Founding—the initial decision of Britain's New World colonies to chart a separate course (the Declaration of

Independence), a successful revolution and the creation of a confederation of states with a weak central government (the Articles of Confederation), and the re-creation of an entirely elaborated new body of institutional arrangements (the Constitution), what Seymour Martin Lipset called the "first new nation"[37]—is a chronicle of purposeful collective action leading to the creation of a unique political scaffolding for governance.

The revolutionary generation, the politicians of the Articles years, and those who met in Philadelphia to create a new nation were rational actors with specific goals and purposes in mind. Northern merchants and manufacturers wanted property protection and security, unfettered opportunities to trade in domestic and international markets, and the financial security of sound currency, low taxes, and limited public debt. Southern planters also wanted property protection (with some of that property human in form), low tariffs to enable them to obtain manufactured goods cheaply, and access to international markets for their products and for slaves. Small farmers, tradesmen, and artisans wanted easy credit, relief from onerous taxes, and permissive policies toward debt. Independence, loose federation, and finally a new nation with a central government capable of effective action were the goals, at different times, toward which the economic and political purposes of many of these groups pointed.

To orchestrate a revolution, organize a confederation, or draft a constitution requires a large variety of collective actions. Behaviors of many must be coordinated, participation must be induced, efforts must be focused on common objectives, and free riding must be discouraged. During the Founding period, political leaders facilitated this process. Jefferson and Adams brought the colonies to the point of separating from the motherland; Washington was pivotal in the revolutionary phase; a variety of politicians came together to bargain over the directions to be taken by the Confederation, often without success; Madison, Hamilton, Washington, and ultimately Franklin presided over the drafting of the Constitution. In sum, collective action, coordinated by motivated leadership, paved the historical path from colony to new nation.

We've also seen that new institutions were needed to organize the new government successfully. Colonial institutions were satisfactory for 150 years, especially in a context in which the mother country was preoccupied with events elsewhere. Independence and self-governance became institutional objectives when the burdens of colonialism began to weigh heavily on the economic circumstances and political freedoms of the colonists. Over a 15-year period (roughly 1775–90), the Founders experimented with and ultimately crafted a political order that, in most of its aspects, has survived more than two centuries. The final product of the Constitutional Convention has to be considered an extraordinary victory for the groups that had most forcefully called for the creation of a new system of government to replace the Articles of Confederation. Antifederalist criticisms forced the Constitution's proponents to accept the addition of a bill of rights designed to limit the powers of the national government. In general, however, it was the Federalist vision of America that

---

37 Seymour Martin Lipset, *The First New Nation* (New York: Norton, 1979).

triumphed. The Constitution adopted in 1789 created the framework for a powerful national government that has defended the nation's interests, promoted its commerce, and maintained national unity in the years since.

Though the Constitution was the product of a particular set of political forces, the form of government it established has a significance that goes far beyond the interests of its authors. As we have observed, political ideals often take on lives of their own. The great political values incorporated into the Constitution continue, more than two centuries later, to shape our political lives in ways that the framers may not have anticipated. For example, when they empowered Congress to regulate commerce among the states in Article I, Section 8, of the Constitution, they could hardly have anticipated that this provision would become the basis for many of the federal government's regulatory activities in areas as diverse as the environment and civil rights.

Two great constitutional notions, federalism and civil liberties, will be discussed in Chapters 3 and 4, respectively. As we close our discussion of the Founding and move on to an examination of federalism, it is worth reflecting on the Antifederalists. Although they were defeated in 1789, the Antifederalists present us with an important picture of a road not taken, an America that might have been. Would we have been worse off as a people if we had been governed by a confederacy of small republics linked by a national administration with severely limited powers? Were the Antifederalists correct in predicting that a government given great power in the hope that it might do good would, through "insensible progress," inevitably come to serve the interests of the few at the expense of the many? More than two centuries of government under the federal Constitution are not necessarily enough to definitively answer these questions. Only time will tell.

For Further Reading

Selections highlighted in red are included in *Readings in American Politics: Analysis and Perspectives*, Third Edition.

Allison, Robert. *The American Revolution: A Concise History.* New York: Oxford University Press, 2011.

Amar, Akhil Reed. *America's Constitution: A Biography.* New York: Random House, 2005.

Bailyn, Bernard. *The Ideological Origins of the American Revolution.* Cambridge, MA: Harvard University Press, 1967.

Beard, Charles A. *An Economic Interpretation of the Constitution of the United States.* New York: Macmillan, 1913.

Beeman, Richard. *Plain, Honest Men: The Making of the American Constitution.* New York: Random House, 2010.

Breyer, Stephen. *Active Liberty: Interpreting Our Democratic Constitution*. New York: Knopf, 2005.

Chernow, Ron. *Alexander Hamilton*. New York: Penguin, 2004.

Dahl, Robert. *How Democratic Is the American Constitution?* 2nd ed. New Haven, CT: Yale University Press, 2003.

Ellis, Joseph. *Founding Brothers: The Revolutionary Generation*. New York: Knopf, 2000.

Ellis, Joseph. *His Excellency, George Washington*. New York: Knopf, 2004.

Farrand, Max, ed. *The Records of the Federal Convention of 1787*. Rev. ed., 4 vols. New Haven, CT: Yale University Press, 1966.

Glaeser, Edward C. "Revolution of Urban Rebels." *Boston Globe*, July 4, 2008, Section A.

Hamilton, Alexander, James Madison, and John Jay. *The Federalist Papers*, no. 10 and no. 51. Clinton Rossiter, ed. New York: New American Library, 1961.

Keller, Morton. *America's Three Regimes: A New Political History*. New York: Oxford University Press, 2007.

Lutz, Donald. *Colonial Origins of the American Constitution*. New York: Liberty Fund, 2010.

Maier, Pauline. *American Scripture: Making the Declaration of Independence*. New York: Knopf, 1997.

Newton, Michael. *Angry Mobs and Founding Fathers: The Fight for Control of the American Revolution*. New York: Eleftheria, 2011.

Riker, William H. *The Strategy of Rhetoric: Campaigning for the American Constitution*. New Haven, CT: Yale University Press, 1996.

Storing, Herbert J., ed. *The Complete Anti-Federalist*. 7 vols. Chicago: University of Chicago Press, 1981.

3

Federalism and the Separation of Powers

The great achievement of American politics in the eighteenth century was the fashioning of an effective constitutional structure of political institutions. Although it is an imperfect and continuously evolving work in progress, this structure of law and political practice has served its people well for more than two centuries by managing conflict, providing inducements for bargaining and cooperation, and facilitating collective action. It has had at least one major failure: the cruel practice of slavery, which ended only after a destructive civil war. But the basic configuration of institutions first formulated in Philadelphia in 1787 survived that tragedy and has otherwise stood the test of time.

Two of America's most important institutional features are federalism and the separation of powers. Federalism seeks to limit government by dividing it into two levels, national and state, each with sufficient independence to compete with the other, thereby restraining the power of both.[1] The separation of powers seeks to limit the power of the national government by dividing government against itself—by giving the legislative, executive, and judicial branches separate functions, thus forcing them to share power.

In Chapter 1 we observed that institutions organize political life. Institutions, however, take many forms and can choreograph collective action in a variety of ways. One important way in which political institutions vary is the manner in which they distribute decision, agenda, and veto powers. The institutions

---

1 The notion that federalism requires separate spheres or jurisdictions in which lower and higher levels of government are uniquely decisive is developed fully in William H. Riker, *Federalism: Origin, Operation, Significance* (Boston: Little, Brown, 1964). This American version of federalism is applied to the emerging federal arrangements in the People's Republic of China during the 1990s in a paper by Barry R. Weingast, "The Economic Role of Political Institutions: Market-Preserving Federalism and Economic Development," *Journal of Law, Economic, and Organization* 11 (1995): 1–32.

established by authoritarian regimes are usually designed to concentrate power in the hands of a small group of leaders who determine what will be considered, make the final decisions, and seek to block the actions of others. In democratic states, in contrast, political institutions are usually designed to allow a variety of groups to participate in decision making and provide at least a measure of agenda and veto power to a number of actors.

In the United States, the framers of the Constitution created institutions that would widely disperse involvement in decision making, including agenda-setting power and veto power. Federalism assigns agenda-setting power, decision-making power, and veto powers to the federal government and to each of the 50 states. The separation of powers gives several federal institutions a degree of control over the agenda, the power to affect decisions, and the ability to block the actions of the others. The framers feared that concentrating power in a small number of hands would threaten citizens' liberties, and they were surely correct. Yet, although the constitutional dispersion of power among federal institutions and between the federal government and the states may well protect our liberties, it often seems to make it impossible to get anything done collectively. This lack of decisiveness sometimes appears to negate the most important reason for building institutions in the first place.

Since the adoption of the Constitution, ambitious politicians have developed a variety of strategies for overcoming the many impediments to policy change that inevitably arise in our federal system of separated powers. Most commonly, those seeking to promote a new program may try to find ways of dispersing the program's benefits so that other politicians controlling institutional veto powers will be persuaded that it is in their interest to go along. Thus, federalism and the separation of powers have given rise to the federal pork

CORE OF THE ANALYSIS

 Two of the most important institutional features of America's government are federalism and the separation of powers.

 Federalism assigns agenda-setting, decision-making, and veto powers to the federal government and the 50 states.

 The apportionment of powers between the federal government and the states has shifted over time.

 The separation of powers delineates the authority of the executive branch, Congress, and the courts, giving each a degree of control over the agenda, the power to affect decisions, and the ability to block the actions of the others.

barrel, to the defense subcontracting system, and to grants-in-aid and other forms of policy that reflect the dispersion of decision, agenda, and veto powers. For example, if the executive branch hopes to win congressional support for a new weapons system, it generally sees to it that portions of the new system are subcontracted to firms in as many congressional districts as possible. In this way, dispersion of benefits helps to overcome the separation of powers between the executive and legislative branches. Similarly, as we see below, federal officials often secure state cooperation with national programs by offering the states funding, called grants-in-aid, in exchange for their compliance. These programs help to overcome the limitations of federalism. Thus, consistent with our discussion of the five principles of politics in Chapter 1, America's public policies are shaped by the institutional arrangements through which individual efforts must flow.

However, institutions are not carved in stone. Once created, they are subject to revision and modification as competing forces seek new decision rules that will give them an advantage, and as the leaders of institutions seek to strengthen their own power and expand their own jurisdictions at the expense of other institutions. In recent decades, the presidency has increased in power relative to Congress, and the federal government has grown in jurisdiction relative to the states. Nevertheless, these two core institutional features, federalism and the separation of powers, remain at the heart of the American system of government. Let us examine these features and assess their consequences for American government.

WHO DOES WHAT? FEDERALISM AND INSTITUTIONAL JURISDICTIONS

federalism

The system of government in which a constitution divides power between a central government and regional governments

sovereignty

Supreme and independent political authority

Federalism can be defined as the division of powers and functions between the national government and the state governments. Federalism limits national and state power by creating two levels of government—the national government and the state governments, each with a large measure of **sovereignty** and thus the ability to restrain the power of the other. As we saw in Chapter 2, the states existed as individual colonies before independence, and for nearly 13 years they were virtually autonomous units under the Articles of Confederation. In effect, the states had retained too much power relative to the national government, a problem that led directly to the Annapolis Convention in 1786 and to the Constitutional Convention in 1787. Under the Articles, disorder within states was beyond the reach of the national government (see Shays's Rebellion, discussed in Chapter 2), and conflicts of interest between states were not manageable. For example, states were making their own trade agreements with foreign countries and companies, which could then play off one state against another for special advantages. Some states adopted trade tariffs and further barriers to foreign commerce that were contrary to the interests of other states.[2] Tax and other barriers were also being erected between the states.[3] But even after the ratification of the Constitution, the states continued to be more important than the national government. For nearly a century and a half, virtually all of the fundamental policies governing the lives of Americans were made by the state legislatures, not by Congress.

Why Keep the States: The Importance of History. Many of the Constitution's framers, particularly Alexander Hamilton, had hoped to create something close to a unitary national government and to circumscribe severely the power of the individual states. The fact that the framers established a federal system in which the states retained significant powers is an illustration of the importance of history. Each of the states had a well-established set of governmental institutions staffed by legislators, judges, and executive officials who had no desire to see their power and autonomy submerged in a new national government. New York's governor George Clinton, for example, opposed the idea of a stronger national government mainly because he enjoyed his position as the chief executive of what amounted to an important independent nation. At the same time, citizens identified with their own states. The people of North America were not Americans. Instead, they had already had several generations to become Virginians, New Yorkers, Pennsylvanians, and so on. Well-established popular identification with the 13 states was another reason that even the most nationalistic of the framers was forced to accept the idea that the states would continue as important entities. In a sense, the framers were faced by the same historically given realities faced today by advocates of a stronger European Union (EU). The nations of Europe have historically distinct identities, well-entrenched governments, and loyal citizens. Given the force of history, uniting these nations is no easy matter. Like America's Founders, the architects of the EU, bowing to history, have generally sought to erect the new regime on federal foundations.

Federalism in the Constitution: Who Decides What

American federalism recognized two sovereigns in the original Constitution and reinforced the principle in the Bill of Rights by granting a few expressed powers to the national government and reserving the rest to the states. Thus, the Constitution defined the jurisdiction of each level of government.

The Powers of the National Government. As we saw in Chapter 2, the expressed powers granted to the national government are found in Article I,

---

2 For a good treatment of these conflicts of interest between states, see Forrest McDonald, *E Pluribus Unum: The Formation of the American Republic, 1776–1790* (Boston: Houghton Mifflin, 1965), chap. 7, esp. pp. 319–38.

3 See David M. O'Brien, *Constitutional Law and Politics*, 3rd ed. (New York: Norton, 1997), I: 602–3.

implied powers

Powers derived from the necessary and proper clause (Article I, Section 8) of the Constitution. Such powers are not specifically expressed but are implied through the expansive interpretation of delegated powers

reserved powers

Powers, derived from the Tenth Amendment to the Constitution, that are not specifically delegated to the national government or denied to the states; these powers are reserved to the states

eminent domain

The right of the government to take private property for public use, with reasonable compensation awarded for the property

police power

The power reserved to the government to regulate the health, safety, and morals of its citizens

Section 8, of the Constitution. These 17 powers include the powers to collect taxes, coin money, declare war, and regulate commerce (which became a very important power for the national government). Article I, Section 8, also contains an important source of power for the national government: the **implied powers** that enable Congress "to make all Laws which shall be necessary and proper for carrying into Execution the foregoing Powers." Not until several decades after the Founding did the Supreme Court allow Congress to exercise the power granted in this necessary and proper clause, but as we see later in this chapter, this doctrine allowed the national government to expand considerably the scope of its authority, although the process was a slow one. In addition to these expressed and implied powers, the Constitution affirms the power of the national government in the supremacy clause (Article VI), which makes all national laws and treaties "the supreme Law of the Land."

The Powers of State Governments. One way in which the framers sought to preserve a strong role for the states was through the Tenth Amendment to the Constitution. The Tenth Amendment presents a decision rule, or general principle governing decisions, stating that the powers the Constitution does not delegate to the national government or deny to the states are "reserved to the States respectively, or to the people." The Antifederalists, who feared that a strong central government would encroach on individual liberty, repeatedly pressed for such an amendment as a way of limiting national power. Federalists agreed to the amendment because they did not think it would do much harm, given the powers the Constitution already granted to the national government. The Tenth Amendment is also called the **reserved powers** amendment because it aims to reserve powers to the states.

The most fundamental power retained by the states is that of coercion—the power to develop and enforce criminal codes, administer health and safety rules, and regulate the family via marriage and divorce laws. The states have the power to regulate individuals' livelihoods: if you're a doctor or a lawyer or a plumber or a barber, you must be licensed by the state. Even more fundamental, the states have the power to define private property: private property exists because state laws against trespass define who is and who is not entitled to use a piece of property. If you own a car, your ownership isn't worth much unless the state is willing to enforce your right to possession by making it a crime for anyone else to drive your car without your permission. Similarly, your "ownership" of a house or piece of land means that the state will enforce your possession by prohibiting others from occupying the property against your will. At the same time, however, under its power of **eminent domain**, the state may seize your property for virtually anything it deems to be a public purpose. If the state chooses to seize your property, it is required by its own constitution and the federal Constitution to compensate you for your loss. The decision to take the property, though, is well within the recognized powers of the states.

A state's authority to regulate these fundamental matters is commonly referred to as the **police power** of the state and encompasses the state's power to regulate the health, safety, welfare, and morals of its citizens. Policing is what states do—they coerce you in the name of the community in order to maintain public order. And this was exactly the type of power the Founders intended the states to exercise.

In some areas, the states share **concurrent powers** with the national government: they retain and share some power to regulate commerce and affect the currency—for example, by chartering banks, granting or denying corporate charters, and regulating the quality of products or the conditions of labor. This issue of concurrent versus exclusive power has come up from time to time in our history, but wherever there has been a direct conflict of laws between the federal and the state levels, the issue has most often been resolved in favor of national supremacy.

States' Obligations to One Another. The Constitution also creates obligations among the states. These obligations, spelled out in Article IV, were intended to promote national unity. By requiring the states to recognize actions taken in other states as legal and proper, the framers aimed to make the states less like independent countries and more like parts of a single nation. Article IV, Section 1, calls for "Full Faith and Credit" among states, meaning that each state is normally expected to honor the "public Acts, Records, and Proceedings" that take place in any other state. So, for example, if two people are married in Texas—marriage being regulated by state law—Missouri must recognize that marriage even though the couple was not married under Missouri state law.

This **full faith and credit clause** has recently become entangled in the controversy over same-sex marriage. In 14 states (as of October 2013), individuals of the same sex may marry. A number of other states, though, have passed "defense of marriage acts" that define marriage as a union only between a man and a woman. Eager to show its disapproval of same-sex marriage, Congress passed the federal Defense of Marriage Act (DOMA) in 1996, declaring that states will *not* have to recognize a same-sex marriage legally contracted in another state. DOMA also barred same-sex couples from receiving federal health, tax, social security, and other benefits available to heterosexual couples. In June 2013, the Supreme Court invalidated this section of the law, ruling that in states where same-sex marriage is legal, same-sex married couples are entitled to federal benefits.[4] The case was decided on equal protection grounds (to be discussed in Chapter 5). The ruling, however, is also likely to compel states to recognize same-sex marriages performed in other states.

Article IV, Section 2, known as the comity clause, also seeks to promote national unity. It provides that citizens enjoying the **privileges and immunities** of one state should be entitled to similar treatment in other states. What this clause has come to mean is that a state cannot discriminate against someone from another state or give special privileges to its own residents. For example, in the 1970s, when Alaska passed a law that gave residents preference over nonresidents in obtaining work on the state's oil and gas pipelines, the Supreme Court ruled the law illegal because it discriminated against citizens of other states.[5]

concurrent powers

The authority possessed by *both* state and national governments, such as the power to levy taxes

full faith and credit clause

The provision in Article IV, Section 1, of the Constitution requiring that each state normally honors the public acts and judicial decisions that take place in another state

privileges and immunities

The provision in Article IV, Section 2, of the Constitution stating that a state cannot discriminate against someone from another state or give its own residents special privileges

----

4 *United States v. Windsor*, 570 U.S. ____ (2013).

5 *Hicklin v. Orbeck*, 437 U.S. 518 (1978).

This clause also regulates criminal justice among the states by requiring states to return fugitives to the states from which they have fled. Thus in 1952, when an inmate escaped from an Alabama prison and sought to avoid being returned to Alabama on the grounds that he was being subjected to "cruel and unusual punishment" there, the Supreme Court ruled that he must be returned, according to Article IV, Section 2.[6] This example highlights the difference between the obligations among states and those among different countries. Recently France refused to return an American fugitive because he might be subject to the death penalty, which does not exist in France.[7] The Constitution clearly forbids states from doing something similar.

Limitations on the States. Although most of the truly coercive powers of government are reserved to the states, the Constitution does impose some significant limitations. As discussed in the previous section, states cannot discriminate against denizens of other states, and states must extradite alleged criminals to the state with jurisdiction. Another potential limit on states is in a clause in Article I, Section 10, that provides that "no State shall, without the Consent of Congress, . . . enter into any Agreement or Compact with another State." Compacts are a way for two or more states to reach a legally binding agreement about how to solve a problem that crosses state lines. In the early years of the Republic, states turned to compacts primarily to settle border disputes. Today with the support of the federal government they are used for a wide range of issues but are especially important in regulating the distribution of river water, addressing environmental concerns, and operating transportation systems that cross state lines.[8] A well-known contemporary example is the Port of New York Authority (now the Port Authority of New York and New Jersey), a compact formed between New York and New Jersey in 1921. Without it, such public works as the bridge connecting Brooklyn and Staten Island, the bridges connecting New Jersey and Staten Island, the Lincoln Tunnel, the George Washington Bridge, and the expansion and integration of the three major airports could not have been financed or completed.[9]

The federal government has occasionally blocked a proposed interstate compact, thus limiting state action in certain spheres. In 1939, for example, President Franklin Delano Roosevelt vetoed a bill that would have granted consent in advance to states to enter into compacts relating to fishing in the Atlantic Ocean. Roosevelt considered the advance authorization to be too vague. In 2001, Congress refused to allow the renewal of a compact among the several

6 *Sweeney v. Woodall,* 344 U.S. 86 (1953).

7 Marlise Simons, "France Won't Extradite American Convicted of Murder," *New York Times,* December 5, 1997, p. A9.

8 Patricia S. Florestano, "Past and Present Utilization of Interstate Compacts in the United States," *Publius* (Fall 1994): 13–26.

9 A good discussion of the status of the New York Port Authority in politics is found in Wallace Sayre and Herbert Kaufman, *Governing New York City—Politics in the Metropolis* (New York: Russell Sage Foundation, 1960), chap. 9.

New England states that regulated milk prices. The New England compact has been opposed by Midwestern dairy farmers. More often than it prohibits compacts, however, Congresss attaches conditions to its approval of proposed interstate compacts. For example, when it approved the compact among Virginia, Maryland, and the District of Columbia establishing the Washington Metropolitan Transit Authority in 1960, Congress set a number of conditions including requiring the publication of specified data and information by the Authority.[10]

Local Government and the Constitution. Local government, including counties, cities, and towns, occupies a peculiar but very important place in the American system. In fact, the status of American local government is probably unique in world experience. First, it must be pointed out that local government has no status in the American Constitution. *State* legislatures created local governments, and *state* constitutions and laws permit local governments to take on some of the responsibilities of the state governments. Most states amended their own constitutions to give their larger cities **home rule**—a guarantee of noninterference in various areas of local affairs. But local governments enjoy no such recognition in the Constitution. Local governments have always been mere conveniences of the states.[11]

 home rule

The power delegated by the state to a local unit of government to manage its own affairs

Local governments became administratively important in the early years of the Republic because the states possessed little administrative capability. They relied on local governments—cities and counties—to implement the laws of the state. Local government was an alternative to a statewide bureaucracy. Today, local governments and state bureaucracies both compete and cooperate with one another. Take, for example, the relationship between state and county police forces, which usually involve a mix of collegiality and rivalry.

The Slow Growth of the National Government's Power

Before the 1930s, America's federal system could have been characterized as one of **dual federalism**, a two-layered system—national and state—in which the states and their local principalities did most of the governing. That is, the jurisdiction of the states was greater than that of the federal government. We refer to it as the traditional system precisely because almost nothing about our pattern of government changed during two-thirds of our history. That is, of

 dual federalism

The system of government that prevailed in the United States from 1789 to 1937 in which fundamental governmental powers were shared between the federal and state governments, with the states exercising the most important powers

10 John R. Koza, Barry Fadem, Mark Grueskin, Michael Mandell, Robert Richie, and Joseph Zimmerman, *Every Vote Equal*, 3rd ed. (Los Altos, CA: National Popular Vote Press, 2011), chap. 5.

11 A good discussion of the constitutional position of local governments is in York Y. Willbern, *The Withering Away of the City* (Bloomington: Indiana University Press, 1971). For more on the structure and theory of federalism, see Thomas R. Dye, *American Federalism: Competition among Governments* (Lexington, MA: Lexington Books, 1990), chap. 1; and Martha Derthick, "Up-to-Date in Kansas City: Reflections on American Federalism," *PS: Political Science and Politics* 25 (December 1992): 671–5.

course, with the exception of the four years of the Civil War, after which we returned to the traditional system.

But there was more to dual federalism than merely the existence of two tiers. The two tiers were functionally quite different from each another. There have been debates in every generation over how to divide responsibilities between the two tiers. As we have seen in this chapter, the Constitution delegated a list of specific powers to the national government and reserved all the rest to the states. That left a lot of room for interpretation, however, because of the final, "elastic" clause of Article I, Section 8. The three formal words *necessary and proper* amounted to an invitation to struggle over the distribution of powers between national and state governments. We confront this struggle throughout the book. However, the most remarkable aspect of the history of American federalism is that federalism remained dual for nearly two-thirds of that history, with the national government remaining steadfastly within a "strict construction" of Article I, Section 8.

The Supreme Court has at times acted as arbiter in the debate over the distribution of powers between national and state governments. The first and most important case favoring national power was *McCulloch v. Maryland*.[12] The issue was whether Congress had the power to charter a bank, in particular the Bank of the United States (created by Congress in 1791 over Thomas Jefferson's constitutional opposition), because no express power to create banks was found anywhere in Article I, Section 8. Chief Justice John Marshall, speaking for the Supreme Court, answered that such a power could be "implied" from the other specific powers in Article I, Section 8, specifically the commerce clause, plus the final clause enabling Congress "to make all Laws which shall be necessary and proper for carrying into Execution the foregoing Powers." Thus the Court created the potential for significant increases in national governmental power by creating a decision rule that favored the national government over the states. Essentially, Marshall's ruling said that if a goal was allowed in the Constitution and Congress's chosen means to achieve the goal was not prohibited by the Constitution, Congress could act.

A second question of national power also arose in *McCulloch v. Maryland*: the question of whether Maryland's attempt to tax the bank was constitutional. Once again Marshall and the Supreme Court took the side of the national government, arguing that a legislature representing all the people (Congress) could not be taxed out of business by a state legislature (Maryland) representing only a small portion of the American people. This opinion was accompanied by Marshall's immortal dictum that "the power to tax is the power to destroy." It was also in this case that the Supreme Court recognized and reinforced the supremacy clause: whenever a state law conflicts with a federal law, the state law should be deemed invalid because "the Laws of the United States . . . shall be the supreme Law of the Land." (The concept of federal supremacy was introduced in Chapter 2 and will come up again in Chapter 9.)

This nationalistic interpretation of the Constitution was reinforced by another major case, that of *Gibbons v. Ogden* in 1824. The important but

---

12 *McCulloch v. Maryland*, 4 Wheaton 316 (1819).

relatively narrow issue was whether the state of New York could grant a monopoly to Robert Fulton's steamboat company to operate an exclusive service between New York and New Jersey. Aaron Ogden had secured his license from Fulton's company, whereas Thomas Gibbons, a former partner of Ogden's, had secured a competing license from the U.S. government. Chief Justice Marshall argued that Gibbons could not be kept from competing because the state of New York did not have the power to grant this particular monopoly affecting other states' interests. At issue was the **commerce clause** in Article 1, Section 8 of the Constitution, which delegates to Congress the power "to regulate Commerce with foreign nations, and *among the several States* and with Indian tribes" [emphasis added]. In his decision, Marshall insisted that the definition of the commerce clause was "comprehensive" but added that the comprehensiveness was limited "to that commerce which concerns more states than one." This opinion gave rise to what later came to be called interstate commerce.[13]

Despite the Supreme Court's expansive reading of national power in the early years of the Republic, between the 1820s and the 1930s federal power grew slowly if at all. During the Jacksonian period, a states' rights coalition developed in the Congress. Among the most important members of this coalition were state party leaders who often had themselves appointed to the Senate where they jealously guarded the powers of the states they ruled. Of course, the senators and members of the House from the southern states had a particular reason to support states' rights. So long as the states were powerful and the federal government weak, the South's "peculiar institution" of slavery could not be threatened.

Aside from the interruption of the Civil War, the states' rights coalition dominated Congress, affected presidential nominations—a matter also controlled by the state party leaders—and influenced judicial appointments, which required senatorial acquiescence, as well. Indeed, the Supreme Court turned sharply away from the nationalistic jurisprudence of John Marshall in favor of a states' rights interpretation of the Constitution. One area in which this interpretation was particularly noticeable was in cases concerning the commerce clause. For many years, any effort by the federal government to regulate commerce in such areas as fraud, the production of impure goods, the use of child labor, or the existence of dangerous working conditions or long hours was declared unconstitutional by the Supreme Court as a violation of the concept of interstate commerce. Regulation in these areas would mean the federal government was entering the factory and the workplace, areas inherently local because the goods produced there had not yet passed into commerce and crossed state lines. Rather, the Court held that regulation of these areas constituted police power, a power reserved to the states. No one questioned the power of the national government to regulate certain kinds of businesses, such as railroads, gas pipelines, and waterway transportation, because they intrinsically involved interstate

 commerce clause

The clause found in Article I, Section 8, of the Constitution, which delegates to Congress the power "to regulate Commerce with foreign Nations, and among the several States, and with the Indian Tribes." This clause was interpreted by the Supreme Court to favor national power over the economy

---

13 *Gibbons v. Ogden*, 9 Wheaton 1 (1824).

commerce.[14] But well into the twentieth century, most other efforts by Congress to regulate commerce were blocked by the Supreme Court's interpretation of federalism, with the concept of interstate commerce as the primary barrier.

For example, in the 1918 case of *Hammer v. Dagenhart*, the Supreme Court struck down a statute prohibiting the interstate shipment of goods manufactured with the use of child labor. Congress had been careful to avoid outlawing the production of such goods, which took place within states and only prohibited their interstate shipment. The Court, however, declared that the intent of Congress had been to outlaw the manufacture of the products in question and declared that the statutory language was merely a ruse.[15]

After his election in 1932, President Franklin Delano Roosevelt was eager to expand the power of the national government. His "New Deal" depended on governmental power to regulate the economy and to intervene in every facet of American society. Roosevelt's efforts provoked sharp conflicts between the president and the federal judiciary. After making a host of new judicial appointments and threatening to expand the size of the Supreme Court, Roosevelt was able to bend the judiciary to his will. Beginning in the late 1930s, the Supreme Court issued a series of decisions converting the commerce clause from a barrier to a source of national power.

Among the most important of these cases was *National Labor Relations Board v. Jones & Loughlin Steel Company*.[16] At issue was the National Labor Relations Act, known as the Wagner Act, which prohibited corporations from interfering with the efforts of employees to organize into unions, to bargain collectively over wages and working conditions, and to go on strike and engage in picketing. The newly formed National Labor Relations Board (NLRB) had ordered Jones & Loughlin to reinstate workers fired because of their union activities. The appeal reached the Supreme Court because the steel company had made a constitutional issue over the fact that its manufacturing activities were local and therefore beyond the government's reach. The Supreme Court rejected this argument, declaring that a large corporation with subsidiaries and suppliers in many states was inherently involved in interstate commerce and hence subject to congressional regulation. In other decisions, the Court upheld minimum wage laws, the Social Security Act and, in the case of *Wickard v. Filburn*, federal rules controlling how much of any given commodity local farmers might grow.[17]

After 1937, the Supreme Court threw out the old distinction between interstate and intrastate commerce. The Court began to refuse even to review appeals challenging acts of Congress that protected the rights of employees to

---

14 In *Wabash, St. Louis, and Pacific Railway Company v. Illinois,* 118 U.S. 557 (1886), the Supreme Court struck down a state law prohibiting rate discrimination by a railroad; in response, Congress passed the Interstate Commerce Act of 1887, creating the Interstate Commerce Commission (ICC), the first federal regulatory agency.

15 *Hammer v. Dagenhart,* 247 U.S. 251 (1918).

16 *National Labor Relations Board v. Jones & Loughlin Steel Company,* 301 U.S. 1 (1937).

17 *Wickard v. Filburn,* 317 U.S. 111 (1942).

organize and engage in collective bargaining, regulated the amount of farmland in cultivation, extended low-interest credit to small businesses and farmers, and restricted the activities of corporations dealing in the stock market, as well as many other laws that contributed to the construction of the "regulatory state" and the "welfare state."

Cooperative Federalism and Grants-in-Aid: Institutions Shape Policies

Roosevelt was able to overcome judicial resistance to expansive New Deal programs. Congress, however, forced him to recognize the continuing importance of the states by crafting a number of programs in such a way as to encourage the states to pursue nationally set goals while leaving them some leeway to administer programs according to local values and needs.

If the traditional system of two sovereigns performing highly different functions can be called dual federalism, the system that prevailed after the 1930s could be called **cooperative federalism**, which generally refers to supportive relations, sometimes partnerships, between the national government and the state and local governments. It comes in the form of federal subsidization of special state and local activities; these subsidies are called **grants-in-aid**. But make no mistake about it: although many of these state and local programs would not exist without the federal grant-in-aid, the grant-in-aid is also an important form of federal influence. (Another form of federal influence, the mandate, is covered in the next section.) Thus, the shift from dual federalism to cooperative federalism was a subtle but important institutional change. The system of a dual federalism left decision, agenda, and veto powers in the realm of domestic policy firmly in the hands of the states. The system of cooperative federalism that emerged in the 1930s gave the federal government far greater control over the domestic political agenda. Under the regime of dual federalism, for example, corporations mainly concerned themselves with state regulation of their business. Most firms hardly even bothered to lobby in Washington. With the emergence of cooperative federalism and a greater federal role in the nation's economy, hardly any firm could afford not to lobby in Washington.

A grant-in-aid is really a kind of bribe, or a "carrot," whereby Congress appropriates money for state and local governments with the condition that the money be spent for a particular purpose as defined by Congress. Congress uses grants-in-aid because it does not have the political or constitutional power to command local governments to do its bidding. Federalism gives the states the power to veto many national government efforts. For example, some states have threatened to opt out of the federal No Child Left Behind education law and thus veto it in their own jurisdictions. When you can't command, a monetary inducement becomes a viable alternative. For instance, the nationwide speed limit of 55 miles per hour was not imposed on drivers by an act of Congress. Instead, Congress bribed the state legislatures by threatening to withdraw the federal highway grants-in-aid if the states did not set that speed limit. In the early 1990s, Congress began to ease up on the states, permitting them, under

 cooperative federalism

A type of federalism existing since the New Deal era, in which grants-in-aid have been used strategically to encourage states and localities (without commanding them) to pursue nationally defined goals. Also known as intergovernmental cooperation

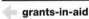 **grants-in-aid**

A general term for funds given by Congress to state and local governments

certain conditions, to go back to the 65-mile-per-hour (or higher) limit without losing their highway grants. The grant-in-aid is one more example of the fact that institutions shape policies. America's constitutional system gives the states de facto vetoes over many potential national government programs. As a result, the central government has learned to craft policies likely to elicit the states' cooperation.

This approach came to be applied to cities as well. Congress set national goals, such as public housing and assistance to the unemployed, and provided grants-in-aid to meet them. World War II temporarily stopped the distribution of these grants. But after the war, Congress resumed the provision of grants for urban development and school lunches. The value of such **categorical grants-in-aid** increased from $2.3 billion in 1950 to over $450 billion in 2008 (Figure 3.1). Sometimes Congress requires the state or local government to match the national contribution dollar for dollar, but for some programs, such as the interstate highway system, the congressional grant-in-aid provides a significant percentage of the cost.

For the most part, the categorical grants created before the 1960s simply helped the states perform their traditional functions, such as educating and

categorical grants-in-aid

Funds given by Congress to states and localities and that are earmarked by law for specific categories, such as education or crime prevention

ANALYZING THE EVIDENCE

Federal grants-in-aid began to expand dramatically during the 1960s. What political trends might explain this expansion? What are the ramifications of this trend for individuals and for states?

Figure 3.1

THE HISTORICAL TREND OF FEDERAL GRANTS-IN-AID

NOTE: Excludes outlays for national defense, international affairs, and net interest.
SOURCE: Office of Management and Budget, *Budget of the U.S. Government, Fiscal Year 2013*, www.whitehouse.gov/omb/budget/historicals (accessed 10/4/12).

policing.[18] In the 1960s, however, the national role expanded, and the number of categorical grants increased dramatically. For example, during the 89th Congress (1965–66) alone, the number of categorical grant-in-aid programs grew from 221 to 379.[19] The grants authorized during the 1960s announced national purposes much more strongly than did earlier grants. Central to that national purpose was the need to provide opportunities to the poor.

Many of the categorical grants enacted during the 1960s were **project grants**, which require state and local governments to submit proposals to federal agencies. In contrast to the older **formula grants**, which used a formula (composed of such elements as need and state and local capacities) to distribute funds, the new project grants made funding available on a competitive basis. Federal agencies would give grants to the proposals they judged to be the best. In this way, the national government acquired substantial control over which state and local governments got money, how much they got, and how they spent it.

The political scientist Morton Grodzins characterized the shift to post–New Deal cooperative federalism as a move from "layer cake federalism" to "marble cake federalism,"[20] in which the line distinguishing intergovernmental cooperation and sharing has blurred, making it difficult to say where the national government ends and the state and local governments begin. Figure 3.2 demonstrates the basis of the marble cake idea. In the late 1970s, federal aid contributed 25 to 30 percent of the operating budgets of all the state and local governments in the country (Figure 3.3). In 2010, federal aid accounted for more than 35 percent of state and local budgets. This increase was temporary, resulting from the Obama administration's $787 billion stimulus package designed to help state and local governments weather the 2008–10 recession. Briefly, however, federal aid became the single largest source of state revenue, exceeding sales and property tax revenues for the first time in U.S. history.

 project grants

Grant programs in which state and local governments submit proposals to federal agencies and for which funding is provided on a competitive basis

 formula grants

Grants-in-aid in which a formula is used to determine the amount of federal funds a state or local government will receive

Regulated Federalism and National Standards

Developments from the 1960s to the present have moved well beyond cooperative federalism to what might be called regulated federalism.[21] Regulated federalism is an important new decision rule, enhancing the national government's

---

18 Kenneth T. Palmer, "The Evolution of Grant Policies," in *The Changing Politics of Federal Grants,* Lawrence D. Brown, James W. Fossett, and Kenneth T. Palmer, eds. (Washington, DC: Brookings Institution, 1984), p. 15.

19 Palmer, "Grant Policies," p. 6.

20 Morton Grodzins, "The Federal System," in *Goals for Americans,* ed. President's Commission on National Goals (Englewood Cliffs, NJ: Prentice-Hall, 1960), p. 265. In a marble cake, the white cake is distinguishable from the chocolate cake, but the two are streaked rather than arranged in distinct layers.

21 The concept and the best discussion of this modern phenomenon are found in Donald F. Kettl, *The Regulation of American Federalism* (1983; repr., Baltimore: Johns Hopkins University Press, 1987), esp. pp. 33–41.

Figure 3.2
FOUR VIEWS OF FEDERALISM

DUAL FEDERALISM

National Government

State Governments

Layer Cake

COOPERATIVE FEDERALISM

Cooperation on some policies

National Government

State Governments

Marble Cake

REGULATED FEDERALISM

RECIPE

National Standards

Conditional Grants

Unfunded Mandates

Preemption

National government mandates the recipe.

State governments are mandated to provide the ingredients.

National government determines policies; state governments pay for and administer them.

NEW FEDERALISM

RECIPE

Policies

Laws

State governments provide the recipe.

National government provides the ingredients.

Revenue sharing →

Devolution of power →

Block grants →

State governments have more flexibility to make policy and administer programs.

power. In some areas, the national government actually regulates the states by threatening to withhold grant money unless state and local governments conform to national standards. The most notable instances of this kind of regulated federalism are in the areas of civil rights, poverty programs, and environmental protection. This focus reflects a general shift in federal regulation away from the oversight and control of strictly economic activities toward "social regulation"—intervention on behalf of individual rights and liberties, environmental protection, workplace safety, and so on. In these instances, the national government provides grant-in-aid financing but sets conditions the states must meet to keep the grants (see again Figure 3.2). The national government refers to these policies as "setting national standards." Important examples include the Asbestos Hazard Emergency Act of 1986, which requires school districts to inspect for asbestos hazards and remove them from school buildings when necessary, and the Americans with Disabilities Act of 1990, which requires all state and local governments to promote access for the disabled to all government buildings. The net effect of these national standards is that state and local policies are

Figure 3.3
THE RISE, DECLINE, AND RECOVERY OF FEDERAL AID

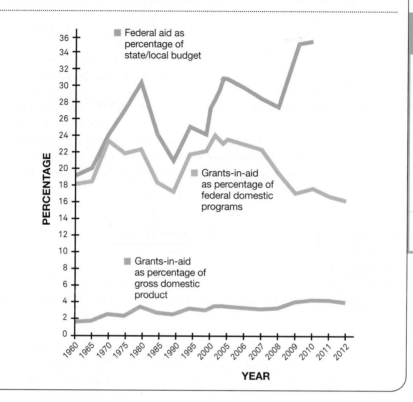

■ Federal aid as percentage of state/local budget

■ Grants-in-aid as percentage of federal domestic programs

■ Grants-in-aid as percentage of gross domestic product

YEAR

NOTE: Data for 2012 are estimated.
SOURCES: U.S. Census, www.census.gov/estimate/summary_report (accessed 10/4/12), and Office of Management and Budget, www.whitehouse.gov/omb/budget/historicals (accessed 10/4/12).

ANALYZING THE EVIDENCE

The extent to which state and local governments rely upon federal funding has varied a great deal over time. What difference does it make if the states are fiscally dependent upon the federal government?

more uniform from coast to coast. National regulations and standards provide coordination across states and localities and solve collective action problems.

However, there are a number of other programs in which the national government engages in regulated federalism by imposing national standards on the states without providing any funding at all. These have come to be called **unfunded mandates**.[22] These burdens became a major part of the rallying cry that produced the Republican Congress elected in 1994 and its Contract with America. One of the first measures adopted by the Republican 104th Congress

◀ unfunded mandates

National standards or programs imposed on state and local governments by the federal government without accompanying funding or reimbursement

22 John J. DiIulio and Donald F. Kettl report that in 1980 there were 36 laws that could be categorized as unfunded mandates. And despite the concerted opposition of the administrations of Ronald Reagan and George H. W. Bush, another 27 laws qualifying as unfunded mandates were adopted between 1982 and 1991. See John DiIulio, Jr., and Donald F. Kettl, *Fine Print: The Contract with America, Devolution, and the Administrative Realities of American Federalism* (Washington, DC: Brookings Institution, 1995), p. 41.

in 1995 was an act to limit unfunded mandates: the Unfunded Mandates Reform Act (UMRA). UMRA was considered a triumph of lobbying efforts by state and local governments, and it was "hailed as both symbol and substance of a renewed congressional commitment to federalism."[23] Under this law, any mandate with an uncompensated state and local cost estimated at greater than $50 million a year, as determined by the Congressional Budget Office, can be stopped by a point of order raised on the House or Senate floor. This so-called stop, look, and listen requirement forced Congress to take positive action to own up to a mandate and its potential costs.

The effect of UMRA has not been revolutionary. UMRA does not prevent members of Congress from passing unfunded mandates; it only makes them think twice before they do. Moreover, the act exempts several areas from coverage. And states must still enforce antidiscrimination laws and meet other requirements in order to receive federal assistance. On the other hand, UMRA is a serious effort to move the national-state relationship a bit further toward the state side.

New Federalism and the National-State Tug-of-War

Federalism in the United States can be understood in part as a tug-of-war between those seeking more uniform national standards and those seeking more room for variability from state to state. Presidents Richard Nixon and Ronald Reagan called their efforts to reverse the trend toward national standards and reestablish traditional policy making and implementation the "new federalism." They helped craft national policies whose purpose was to return more discretion to the states. Examples of these policies include Nixon's revenue sharing and Reagan's **block grants**, which consolidated a number of categorical grants into one larger category, leaving the state (or local) government more discretion to decide how to use the money.

block grants

Federal funds given to state governments to pay for goods, services, or programs, with relatively few restrictions on how the funds may be spent

President Barack Obama, on the other hand, seemed to believe firmly in regulated federalism. In 2009, Obama proposed a record-shattering $3 trillion national budget that included hundreds of millions of dollars in grants to the states for public works and infrastructural improvements as part of his plan to stimulate the nation's faltering economy. Obama told the state governors that he would be watching to see that they spent the money wisely and in a manner consistent with the federal government's purposes. Once again, the national government seemed to view the states as administrative arms more than independent laboratories.

This same idea seemed manifest in the Obama administration's new health care reform law. Under the law, every state is required to establish an insurance exchange where individuals in need of health insurance can shop for the best rate. The law also required states to expand their Medicaid programs, adding as many as 15 million Americans to the Medicaid rolls. A number of states were concerned that the costs of the new program would fall on their already strained budgets, and 12 state attorneys general brought suit in federal courts charging

23 Paul Posner, "Unfunded Mandate Reform: How Is It Working?" *Rockefeller Institute Bulletin* (1998): 35.

that the program's mandates violate the Tenth Amendment. Following conflicting rulings in the lower federal courts, the Supreme Court considered the issue in 2012 and upheld major provisions of the legislation, although the Court ruled that the federal government cannot require that Medicaid rolls be expanded. The Analyzing the Evidence unit on the next page looks at how health care policy varies across the states.

The Supreme Court as Referee. The courts establish the decision rules that determine the relationship between federal and state power. For much of the nineteenth century, federal power remained limited. The Tenth Amendment was used to bolster arguments about **states' rights**, which in their extreme version claimed that the states did not have to submit to national laws when they believed the national government had exceeded its authority. Arguments in favor of states' rights were voiced less often after the Civil War. But the Supreme Court continued to use the Tenth Amendment to strike down laws that it thought exceeded national power, including the Civil Rights Act passed in 1875.

In the early twentieth century, however, the Tenth Amendment appeared to lose its force. Reformers began to press for national regulations to limit the power of large corporations and to preserve the health and welfare of citizens. The Supreme Court approved some of these laws, but it struck down others, including a law combating child labor. The Court stated that the law violated the Tenth Amendment because only states should have the power to regulate conditions of employment. By the late 1930s, however, the Supreme Court had approved such an expansion of federal power that the Tenth Amendment appeared irrelevant. In fact, in 1941, Justice Harlan Fiske Stone declared that the Tenth Amendment was simply a "truism," that it had no real meaning.[24]

Recent years have seen a revival of interest in the Tenth Amendment and important Supreme Court decisions limiting federal power. Much of the renewed interest stems from conservatives who believe that a strong federal government encroaches on individual liberties and so power should be returned to the states through the process of devolution. In 1996, the Republican presidential candidate, Bob Dole, carried a copy of the Tenth Amendment with him to read at rallies.[25] Around the same time, the Eleventh Amendment concept of **state sovereign immunity** was revived by the Court. This legal doctrine holds that states are immune from lawsuits by private individuals or groups claiming that the state violated a statute enacted by Congress.

The Supreme Court's ruling in *United States v. Lopez* in 1995 fueled further interest in the Tenth Amendment. In that case, the Court, stating that Congress had exceeded its authority under the commerce clause, struck down a federal law that barred handguns near schools.[26] It was the first time since the New Deal that the Court had limited congressional powers in this way. The Court further limited the power of the federal government over the states in a 1996 ruling based

states' rights

The principle that states should oppose increases in the authority of the national government. This view was most popular before the Civil War

state sovereign immunity

A legal doctrine holding that states cannot be sued for violating an act of Congress

24 *United States v. Darby,* 312 U.S. 100 (1941).

25 W. John Moore, "Pleading the 10th," *National Journal,* July 29, 1995, p. 1940.

26 *United States v. Lopez,* 514 U.S. 549 (1995).

Health Care Policy and the States

Contributed by
Jenna Bednar
University of Michigan

Responsibility for health care policy and poverty relief is entangled in the 2010 Patient Protection and Affordable Care Act (ACA), an attempt by Congress to standardize access to health care nationally, as well as to contain costs. The primary federalism question in the ACA is what level of government, state or federal, should set Medicaid eligibility criteria. Medicaid is a program to provide health care coverage to the poor and is jointly financed by the federal and state governments. The states set Medicaid eligibility requirements, prescribing an income threshold above which a resident is ineligible to receive Medicaid-funded benefits. States set widely varying thresholds for Medicaid eligibility. The ACA addresses that variation by prescribing a federal minimum income threshold.

The first map below shows the 2013 Medicaid eligibility thresholds for working parents of Medicaid-eligible children. (In almost all states, limited-income adults without dependent children are not eligible for Medicaid benefits.) The thresholds are expressed as a percentage of the federal poverty level (FPL), which in 2013 was $23,550 for a family of four. A Minnesota family could earn up to $50,633 (215% of FPL) and the parents would still qualify for Medicaid benefits, while the same family living in Texas would be ineligible if they earned more than $5,888 (25% of FPL). The second map shows the percentage of limited-income adults who lacked health insurance in each state in 2011.

Medicaid Eligibility Thresholds and Percentage Uninsured*

MEDICAID ELIGIBILITY
Threshold, working adults with dependent children, as percent of FPL

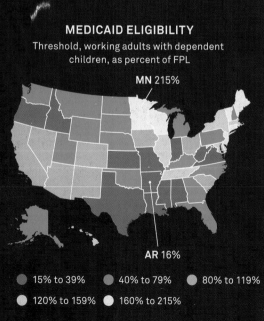

MN 215%

AR 16%

- 15% to 39%
- 40% to 79%
- 80% to 119%
- 120% to 159%
- 160% to 215%

UNINSURED
Percentage uninsured, 2011

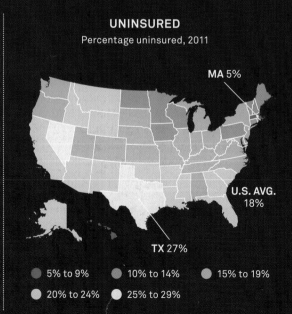

MA 5%

U.S. AVG. 18%

TX 27%

- 5% to 9%
- 10% to 14%
- 15% to 19%
- 20% to 24%
- 25% to 29%

Rules as of January 1, 2013; FPL criteria from 2013

When public policy is decentralized in a federal system, not only can states set policy according to their own preferences and capacity, as demonstrated by the variation in Medicaid eligibility, but states may innovate to improve policy. For example, in 2006 Massachusetts enacted a law that required residents to obtain insurance but subsidized or offered free coverage for the poor. In the graph below, we see the proportion of the non-elderly Massachusetts adult population without health insurance compared with the proportion of non-elderly adults without health insurance nationwide. Although Massachusetts already had a far lower rate of uninsured than the national average, the introduction of health policy reform further reduced the percentage of uninsured at a time when the national average was increasing.

The ACA is modeled on the Massachusetts plan. Two aspects have been politically controversial: the requirement that all individuals obtain insurance and the standardization of Medicaid eligibility to 133% of FPL, or $31,322 for a family of four (2013). If states comply with the ACA prescription, access to Medicaid benefits will expand considerably, including extending coverage to all limited-income adults regardless of whether they have dependent children, a population that currently lacks access to Medicaid. However, it does so by centralizing authority, reducing the states' control over health care policy and poverty relief.

Although the federal government will pay the lion's share of the costs of the expanded Medicare coverage through at least 2020, many states were unhappy with the dictum from the central government, and 26 states joined lawsuits to challenge Congress's authority. In 2012 the Supreme Court ruled that states cannot be required to conform their Medicaid eligibility thresholds to the national minimum. As of June 2013, 21 states have indicated that they will not raise their Medicaid eligibility thresholds to meet the ACA minimum. Ultimately, the fate of health care responsibility will rest with the American public, as they grow to accept or reject the arguments made on both sides.[1]

Percentage of Population without Health Insurance**

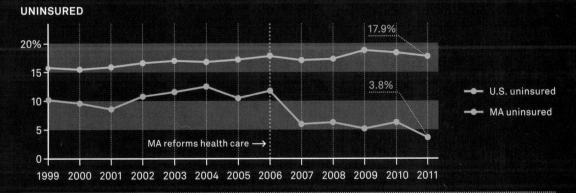

1 Data and analysis for this unit are from the following sources: 2013 FPL data from the U.S. Department of Health and Human Services, Federal Register Volume 77, Number 57 (Friday, March 23, 2012); *National Federation of Independent Business v. Sebelius,* 567 U.S. __ (2012); Kaiser Family Foundation, "Status of State Action on the Medicaid Expansion Decision, as of June 20, 2013," http://kff.org/medicaid/state-indicator/state-activity-around-expanding-medicaid-under-the-affordable-care-act/; as well as legislative analysis by the author.

* SOURCE: Kaiser Family Foundation, "Adult Income Eligibility Limits at Application as a Percent of the Federal Poverty Level (FPL)." January 2013, http://kff.org/medicaid/state-indicator/income-eligibility-low-income-adults/; and "Health Insurance Coverage of the Non-Elderly 0-64," http://kff.org/other/state-indicator/nonelderly-0-64/#.

** SOURCE: Compiled from U.S. Census Bureau, Current Population Survey, 2012 Annual Social and Economic Supplement, Health Insurance, Table HI05 (2011, 2010), Table HI A-6.

on the Eleventh Amendment. That ruling prevented Seminole Indians from suing the state of Florida in federal court. A 1988 law had given Indian tribes the right to sue a state in federal court if the state did not negotiate in good faith issues related to gambling casinos on tribal land. The Supreme Court's ruling appeared to signal a much broader limitation on national power by raising new questions about whether individuals can sue a state if it fails to uphold federal law.[27]

Another significant decision involving the relationship between the federal government and state governments was the 1997 case of *Printz v. United States*, in which the Court struck down a key provision of the Brady bill, enacted by Congress in 1993 to regulate gun sales. Under the terms of the act, state and local law enforcement officers were required to conduct background checks on prospective gun purchasers. The Court held that the federal government cannot require states to administer or enforce federal regulatory programs.[28] Because the states bear administrative responsibility for a variety of other federal programs, this decision could have far-reaching consequences. Finally, in another major ruling from the 1996–97 term, in *City of Boerne v. Flores*, the Court ruled that Congress had gone too far in restricting the power of the states to enact regulations they deemed necessary for the protection of public health, safety, or welfare (see Chapter 4).[29] These rulings signal a move toward a much more restricted federal government.

This trend continued with the 2006 *Gonzales v. Oregon* case. The *Gonzales* case involved Oregon's physician-assisted suicide law, which permitted doctors to prescribe lethal doses of medication for terminally ill patients who requested help ending their lives. In 2001, then U.S. attorney general John Ashcroft issued an order declaring that any physician involved in such a procedure would be prosecuted for violating the federal Controlled Substances Act. The state of Oregon joined several physicians and patients in a suit against Ashcroft's order. Eventually, the U.S. Supreme Court ruled that the federal government could not overrule state laws determining how drugs should be used so long as the drugs were not prohibited by federal law.[30]

In 2012, however, the Court gave indication that it would once again underline the importance of national power in the nation-state tug-of-war. In addition to the "Obamacare" decision cited earlier, the Supreme Court struck down portions of an Arizona immigration law, declaring that immigration was a federal, not a state, matter.[31] And in its 2013 decision in the case of *Arizona v. Inter Tribal Council of Arizona, Inc.,* the Supreme Court struck down an Arizona law requiring individuals to show documentation of citizenship when registering to vote. The Court ruled that this requirement was preempted by the federal National Voter Registration Act requiring states to use the official federal voter registration form.[32]

---

27 *Seminole Tribe v. Florida*, 517 U.S. 44 (1996).

28 *Printz v. United States*, 521 U.S. 898 (1997).

29 *City of Boerne v. Flores*, 521 U.S. 507 (1997).

30 *Gonzales v. Oregon*, 546 U.S. 243 (2006).

31 *Arizona v. United States*, 567 U.S. ____ (2012).

32 *Arizona et. al. v. Inter Tribal Council of Arizona, Inc.,* 570 U.S. ____ (2013).

Of course, shifting interpretations of the Constitution often reflect underlying struggles for political power and nowhere is this more true than in the realm of federalism. Generally speaking, those political forces that control the national government advocate a jurisprudence of nationalism. Those uncertain of their ability to retain control of the commanding heights of Capitol Hill and the White House but more sure of their hold on at least some states support respect for state power and remind Americans of the wisdom of the Tenth Amendment. Thus, the Marshall Court reflected the nationalistic spirit of America's founders. Marshall's successor, Chief Justice Roger Taney, gave us the most extreme denationalizing period, virtually inventing the concept of states' rights, as slavery and its expansion were endangering the Union. Franklin Delano Roosevelt created a court that would advance his efforts to strengthen the powers of the federal government. In recent decades, Republicans, who control a majority of the states, have expressed respect for states' rights while Democrats, with more power at the national level, have sought to increase the power of the federal government. This is reflected in the fact that the Burger Court (1969–96) and the Rehnquist Court (1986–2005) were more sympathetic to the powers of the states, whereas the Roberts Court (2005–present) has generally supported national power. How different institutional forms will influence decision, agenda, and veto powers is a matter of political principle—and political interest.

THE SEPARATION OF POWERS

As we noted at the beginning of this chapter, the separation of powers gives several different federal institutions the ability to influence the nation's agenda, to affect decisions, and to prevent the other institutions from taking action—dividing agenda, decision, and veto power. This arrangement may be cumbersome, but the Constitution's framers saw it as an essential means of protecting liberty.

In his discussion of the separation of powers, James Madison quoted the originator of the idea, the French political thinker Baron de Montesquieu: "There can be no liberty where the legislative and executive powers are united in the same person . . . [or] if the power of judging be not separated from the legislative and executive powers."[33] Using this same reasoning, many of Madison's contemporaries argued that there was not *enough* separation among the three branches, and Madison had to backtrack to insist that complete separation was not required:

> Unless these departments [branches] be so far connected and blended as to give to each a constitutional control over the others, the degree of separation

---

33 Alexander Hamilton, James Madison, and John Jay, *The Federalist Papers*, Clinton L. Rossiter, ed. (New York: New American Library, 1961), no. 47, p. 302.

which the maxim requires, as essential to a free government, can never in practice be duly maintained.[34]

This is the secret of how Americans have made the separation of powers effective: they have made it self-enforcing by giving each branch of government the means to participate in, and partially or temporarily obstruct, the workings of the other branches.

Checks and Balances: A System of Mutual Vetoes

The means by which each branch of government interacts with the others is known informally as checks and balances. This arrangement gives each branch agenda and veto power, under a decision that requires all the branches to agree on national policies (Figure 3.4). The best-known examples are the presidential power to veto legislation passed by Congress; the power of Congress to override the veto by a two-thirds majority vote; the power of Congress to impeach the president; the power of the Senate to approve presidential appointments; the power of the president to appoint the members of the Supreme Court and the other federal judges with Senate approval; and the power of the Supreme Court to engage in judicial review (discussed below). The framers sought to guarantee that the three branches would in fact use the checks and balances as weapons against each other by giving each branch a different political constituency: direct, popular election of the members of the House and indirect election of senators (until the Seventeenth Amendment, adopted in 1913); indirect election of the president (still in effect, at least formally); and appointment of federal judges for life. All things considered, the best characterization of the separation-of-powers principle in action is, as we said in Chapter 2, "separated institutions sharing power."[35]

Legislative Supremacy

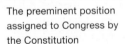

legislative supremacy

The preeminent position assigned to Congress by the Constitution

Although each branch was to be given adequate means to compete with the other branches, it is also clear that within the system of separated powers the framers provided for **legislative supremacy** by making Congress the preeminent branch. Legislative supremacy made the provision of checks and balances in the other two branches all the more important.

The most important indication of the intention of legislative supremacy was made by the framers when they decided to place the provisions for national powers in Article I, the legislative article, and to treat the powers of the national government as powers of Congress. In a system based on the "rule of law," the

---

34 *The Federalist*, no. 48, p. 308.

35 Richard E. Neustadt, *Presidential Power and the Modern Presidents: The Politics of Leadership from Roosevelt to Reagan* (1960; rev. ed., New York: Free Press, 1990), p. 33.

Figure 3.4
CHECKS AND BALANCES

LEGISLATIVE

EXECUTIVE OVER LEGISLATIVE

President can veto acts of Congress

President can call a special session of Congress

President carries out, and thereby interprets, laws passed by Congress

Vice president casts tiebreaking vote in the Senate

JUDICIAL OVER LEGISLATIVE

Court can declare laws unconstitutional

Chief justice presides over Senate during hearing to impeach the president

LEGISLATIVE OVER EXECUTIVE

Congress can override presidential veto

Congress can impeach and remove president

Senate can reject president's appointments and refuse to ratify treaties

Congress can conduct investigations into president's actions

Congress can refuse to pass laws or provide funding that president requests

LEGISLATIVE OVER JUDICIAL

Congress can change size of federal court system and number of Supreme Court justices

Congress can propose constitutional amendments

Congress can reject Supreme Court nominees

Congress can impeach and remove federal judges

Congress can amend court jurisdictions

Congress controls appropriations

JUDICIAL OVER EXECUTIVE

Court can declare executive actions unconstitutional

Court has the power to issue warrants

Chief justice presides over impeachment of president

EXECUTIVE

JUDICIAL

EXECUTIVE OVER JUDICIAL

President nominates Supreme Court justices

President nominates federal judges

President can pardon those convicted in federal court

President can refuse to enforce the courts' decisions

power to make the laws is the supreme power. Section 8 provides in part that "*Congress* shall have Power To lay and collect Taxes . . . ; To borrow Money . . . ; To regulate Commerce" [emphasis added]. The Founders also provided for legislative supremacy in their decision to give Congress the sole power over appropriations and to give the House of Representatives the power to initiate all revenue bills. Madison recognized legislative supremacy as part and parcel of the separation of powers:

> It is not possible to give to each department an equal power of self-defense. In republican government, the legislative authority necessarily predominates. The remedy for this inconveniency is to divide the legislature into different branches; and to render them, by different modes of election and different principles of action, as little connected with each other as the nature of their common functions and their common dependence on the society will admit.[36]

In other words, Congress was so likely to dominate the other branches that it would have to be divided against itself, into House and Senate. One almost could say that the Constitution provided for four branches, not three.

Although "presidential government" gradually supplanted legislative supremacy after 1937, the relative power position of the executive and legislative branches since that time has varied. The degree of conflict between the president and Congress has changed with the rise and fall of political parties, and it has been especially tense during periods of **divided government**, when one party controls the White House and another controls Congress, as has been the case almost continuously since 1969.

divided government ➡

The condition in American government in which the presidency is controlled by one party while the opposing party controls one or both houses of Congress

Checks and Balances: The Rationality Principle at Work

The framers' idea that the president and Congress would check and balance each other rests, in part, on an application of the rationality principle. The framers assumed that each branch would seek to maintain or even expand its power and would resist what the framers called "encroachments" on its prerogatives by the other branch. This idea certainly seems consistent with the behavior of presidents and congressional leaders. At least since the Nixon administration, presidents and members of Congress have battled almost constantly over institutional prerogatives. For example, what culminated in the Watergate struggle between Congress and President Richard Nixon began when Nixon sought to implement a reorganization of the executive branch that would have increased presidential control and reduced congressional oversight powers.[37] After Nixon's resignation, Congress enacted several pieces of legislation, including the

---

36 *The Federalist*, no. 51, p. 322.

37 Benjamin Ginsberg and Martin Shefter, *Politics by Other Means*, 3rd ed. (New York: Norton, 2002), chap. 1.

War Powers Act, to delimit presidential power. When he took office, President Ronald Reagan worked to undo Congress's efforts and to bolster the power of the White House. Reagan had a good deal of success, particularly in undermining the War Powers Act, though Congress ultimately put a stop to his efforts through investigations into presidential wrongdoing in the so-called Iran-Contra affair. During the Clinton era, Congress impeached the president but failed to convict him. During President George W. Bush's second term in office, Congress and the president battled constantly over the president's frequent refusals to disclose information to Congress on the basis of **executive privilege** and his assertions that only the White House was competent to manage the nation's security. "I am the decider," the president famously averred. During his first months in office, President Obama had little reason to clash with Congress. Both houses were controlled by Democrats, and the Democratic leadership was eager to cooperate with the new president. However, this "honeymoon" between Obama and Congress ended when the GOP took control of the House of Representatives in 2010 and fought the president, particularly on taxes and the federal budget. In 2011, Congress forced the president to agree to spending cuts to end an impending crisis over the nation's debt ceiling (see Chapter 15).

Though each institution has registered success and failures in this struggle, over time, the president has generally possessed an advantage. The president is a unitary actor, whereas Congress, as a collective decision maker, suffers from collective action problems (see Chapter 13). That is, each member of Congress may have individual interests that are inconsistent with the collective interests of Congress as a whole. For example, when Congress initially registered its support for President Bush's plan to use force in Iraq in 2003, members were uneasy about the fact that the president was asserting that he actually did not need congressional approval—that he was the only decider. The president was using the war to underline claims of institutional power, but few members of Congress thought it would be politically safe to express that viewpoint when the public was clamoring for action. These considerations help explain why, over time, the powers of the presidency have grown and those of Congress diminished.[38] We will return to this topic in Chapter 7.

 executive privilege

The claim that confidential communications between the president and the president's close advisers should not be revealed without the consent of the president

The Role of the Supreme Court: Establishing Decision Rules

The role of the judicial branch in the separation of powers has depended on the power of judicial review (see Chapter 9), a power not provided for in the Constitution but asserted by Chief Justice Marshall in 1803:

> If a law be in opposition to the Constitution; if both the law and the Constitution apply to a particular case, so that the Court must either decide that

---

38 Matthew Crenson and Benjamin Ginsberg, *Presidential Power: Unchecked and Unbalanced* (New York: Norton, 2007).

case conformable to the law, disregarding the Constitution, or conformable to the Constitution, disregarding the law; the Court must determine which of these conflicting rules governs the case: This is of the very essence of judicial duty.[39]

Marshall's decision was an extremely important assertion of judicial power and has been the basis of the judiciary's influence in American life ever since. In effect, Marshall declared that whenever there was doubt or disagreement about which rule should apply in a particular case, the Court would decide. In this way, Marshall made the Court the arbiter of all future debates between Congress and the president and between the federal and state governments.

In terms of numbers of cases, judicial review of the constitutionality of acts of the president or Congress is relatively rare. For example, there were no Supreme Court reviews of congressional acts in the 50 plus years between *Marbury v. Madison* (1803) and *Dred Scott v. Sandford* (1857). In the century or so between the Civil War and 1970, 84 acts of Congress were held unconstitutional (in whole or in part), but there were long periods of complete Supreme Court deference to Congress, punctuated by flurries of judicial review during times of social upheaval. The most significant of these was 1935–36, when 12 acts of Congress were invalidated, blocking virtually the entire New Deal program.[40] Then, after 1935, when the Court made its great reversals, no significant acts were voided until 1983, when the Court declared unconstitutional the legislative veto, a practice in which Congress authorized the president to take action but reserved the right to rescind presidential actions with which it disagreed.[41] Another decision, in 1986, struck down the Gramm-Rudman Act of 1985, which mandated a balanced budget. That act, the Court held, delegated too much power to the comptroller general, a congressional official, to direct the president to reduce the budget.[42] The Supreme Court became much more activist (that is, less deferential to Congress) after the elevation of Justice William H. Rehnquist to the position of chief justice in 1986.[43] All of the cases in Table 3.1 altered some aspect of federalism by declaring unconstitutional all or an important portion of an act of Congress, and the end of this episode of judicial activism against Congress is not over. Between 1995 and 2002, at

---

39 *Marbury v. Madison*, 1 Cranch 137 (1803).

40 The Supreme Court struck down eight out of ten New Deal statutes. For example, in *Panama Refining Company v. Ryan*, 293 U.S. 388 (1935), the Court ruled that a section of the National Industrial Recovery Act of 1933 was an invalid delegation of legislative power to the executive branch. And in *Schechter Poultry Corporation v. United States*, 295 U.S. 495 (1935), the Court found the National Industrial Recovery Act itself to be invalid for the same reason.

41 *Immigration and Naturalization Service v. Chadha*, 462 U.S. 919 (1983).

42 *Bowsher v. Synar*, 478 U.S. 714 (1986).

43 Cass R. Sunstein, "Taking Over the Courts," *New York Times*, November 9, 2002, p. A19.

Table 3.1

A NEW FEDERAL SYSTEM? THE CASE RECORD, 1995–2006

CASE	DATE	COURT HOLDING
United States v. Lopez, 514 U.S. 549	**1995**	Voids federal law barring handguns near schools: it is beyond Congress's power to regulate commerce.
Seminole Tribe v. Florida, 517 U.S. 44	**1996**	Voids federal law giving tribes the right to sue a state in federal court: "sovereign immunity" requires a state's permission to be sued.
Printz v. United States, 521 U.S. 898	**1997**	Voids key provision of Brady law requiring states to make background checks on gun purchases: as an "unfunded mandate," it violated state sovereignty under the Tenth Amendment.
City of Boerne v. Flores, 521 U.S. 507	**1997**	Restricts Congress's power under the Fourteenth Amendment to regulate city zoning and health and welfare policies to "remedy" rights: Congress may not expand those rights.
Alden v. Maine, 527 U.S. 706	**1999**	Declares states "immune" from suits by their *own* employees for overtime pay under the Fair Labor Standards Act of 1938. (See also the *Seminole* case.)
United States v. Morrison, 529 U.S. 598	**2000**	Extends *Seminole* case by invalidating Violence against Women Act: states may not be sued by individuals for failing to enforce federal laws.
Gonzales v. Oregon, 546 U.S. 243	**2006**	Upholds state assisted-suicide law over attorney general's objection.

least 26 acts or parts of acts of Congress were struck down on constitutional grounds.[44]

Since the New Deal period, the Court has been far more deferential toward the president, with only five significant confrontations. One was the so-called steel seizure case of 1952, in which the Court refused to permit President Harry Truman to use "emergency powers" to force workers back into the steel mills during the Korean War.[45] A second case was *United States v. Nixon*, in which the Court declared unconstitutional President Nixon's refusal to respond to a subpoena to make available the infamous White House tapes as evidence in a criminal prosecution. The Court argued that although executive privilege did protect confidentiality of communications to and from the president, this protection did not extend to data in presidential files or tapes linked to criminal prosecutions.[46] During the heat of the Clinton scandal, the Supreme Court rejected the claim that the pressures and obligations of the office of president were so demanding that all litigation "but the most exceptional cases" should be deferred until the end of the president's term.[47] But of far greater importance, the Supreme Court struck down the Line Item Veto Act of 1996 on the grounds that it violated Article I, Section 7, which prescribes procedures for congressional enactment, and presidential acceptance or veto, of statutes. The line item veto allowed the president to veto specific items in spending and tax bills without vetoing the entire bill. The Court held that any such change in the procedures of adopting laws would have to be made by amendment to the Constitution, not by legislation.[48]

The fifth confrontation came after the September 11, 2001, terrorist attacks. But because of the terrorism scare, it was the least restrictive of the five. In *Rasul v. Bush,* decided in 2004, the Court held that the estimated 650 "enemy combatants" detained without formal charges at the U.S. Naval Station at Guantánamo Bay, Cuba, had the right to seek release through a **writ of *habeas corpus***.[49] However, in Section 7 of the 2006 Military Commissions Act, Congress declared that enemy combatants held at Guantánamo Bay could not avail themselves of the right of *habeas corpus*. Then, in 2008, the Supreme Court responded by striking down Section 7 and affirming that the Guantánamo detainees had the right to challenge their detentions in federal court.[50] The Court noted that *habeas corpus* was among the most fundamental constitutional rights and was included in the Constitution even before the Bill of Rights was added.

writ of *habeas corpus*

A court order demanding that an individual in custody be brought into court and shown the cause for detention. *Habeas corpus* is guaranteed by the Constitution and can be suspended only in cases of rebellion or invasion

---

44 Sunstein, "Taking Over the Courts."

45 *Youngstown Sheet and Tube Company v. Sawyer,* 343 U.S. 579 (1952).

46 *United States v. Nixon,* 418 U.S. 683 (1974).

47 *Clinton v. Jones,* 520 U.S. 681 (1997).

48 *Clinton v. City of New York,* 524 U.S. 417 (1998).

49 *Rasul v. Bush,* 542 U.S. 466 (2004).

50 *Boumediene v. Bush,* 553 U.S. 723 (2008).

FEDERALISM AND THE SEPARATION OF POWERS: COLLECTIVE ACTION OR STALEMATE?

Institutions are designed to solve collective action problems, but the solutions can take many different forms. The framers of the American Constitution believed that agenda, decision, and veto powers should be dispersed among many different institutions. And because history matters and the 13 existing states already possessed considerable autonomy when the Constitution was drafted, the framers had little choice but to relinquish a considerable measure of agenda, decision, and veto powers to them as well. The result was our federal system of separated powers.

Critics of the American constitutional framework have often pointed to this dispersion of governmental power as a source of weakness and incoherence in America's policy-making processes. Because of federalism, America's national government is often unable to accomplish what might be a matter of course in most nations. For example, in the case of *United States v. Lopez*, cited earlier, the Supreme Court invalidated a federal statute prohibiting the possession of firearms near schools, saying that it was an unconstitutional encroachment on the sovereignty of the states. In a country with a unitary system of government, this statute would not face this type of hurdle.

Because of the separation of powers, Congress often finds itself stymied by the president—or the president by Congress—in efforts to bring about changes in policy. The president possesses a veto over congressional action. Congress can, by legislation, seek to limit the powers of the executive. In 2008, for example, Congress attempted to express its displeasure with the president's conduct in the war on terrorism by enacting legislation outlawing a number of harsh methods authorized by the president for the interrogation of terrorist suspects. The president responded with a veto. In 2011, the newly elected Republican House of Representatives promised to repeal the president's recently enacted health care program. The Senate, still controlled by the Democrats, disagreed, and the president promised to veto any bill that threatened what he viewed as the major achievement of his first term in office. In the meantime, legal challenges to the new law eventually led to a Supreme Court decision upholding main provisions of the new legislation. The dispersion of power among different institutions of government ensures that collective action will be difficult, though not impossible.

At times, however, stalemate between Congress and the president may become so severe that the government is virtually paralyzed. In 2013, for example, conservative Republicans in the House of Representatives launched a major political attack on the Obama administration. The GOP refused to allow a vote on any continuing resolution (CR) to extend the government's spending authority that contained funding for the Affordable Care Act (ACA), the president's signature health care program. Senate Democrats and the president said they would not accept a CR that did not provide funding for the ACA. Without a CR, much of the government's spending authority lapsed, and thus most federal agencies were forced to close in a "government shutdown." Republicans also threatened to refuse to raise the nation's debt limit, reducing the government's borrowing power and forcing still further cuts in government programs, to say nothing of posing a serious threat to the federal government's credit worthiness. In this situation, a partial shutdown of the federal government was the result when Congress and the president both hoped to gain political advantage from the politics of stalemate. After a tense 16 days, Republicans and Democrats agreed to a spending bill and a new debt ceiling that would continue government operations for at least three more months.

Thus the separation of powers has real political consequences. The framers, though, did not want to make collective action too easy. They thought it was important to provide checks and balances that would protect the nation from the tyrannical actions of a small number of leaders, as well as from precipitous and thoughtless actions on the part of larger groups—the framers called this latter possibility "majority tyranny." The framers believed that well-constructed institutions should diminish the likelihood of inappropriate and unwise collective action, even at the cost of occasional stalemate. In recent years, the U.S. government often has been criticized more for what it *has* done, especially with regard to the wars in Iraq and Afghanistan, than what it *has not* done. Many Americans believe that Congress should have done more to thwart presidential war policies and hope the judiciary will do more to delimit presidential war powers in the future. The framers likely would have understood this desire to check the executive branch. Stalemate is not always the worst collective outcome.

For Further Reading

Selections highlighted in red are included in *Readings in American Politics: Analysis and Perspectives*, Third Edition.

Bednar, Jenna. *The Robust Federation*. New York: Cambridge University Press, 2008.

Campbell, Tom. *Separation of Powers in Practice*. Palo Alto, CA: Stanford University Press, 2004.

Crenson, Matthew, and Benjamin Ginsberg. *Presidential Power: Unchecked and Unbalanced*. New York: Norton, 2007.

Ferejohn, John A., and Barry R. Weingast, eds. *The New Federalism: Can the States Be Trusted?* Stanford, CA: Hoover Institution Press, 1997.

Fisher, Louis. *Constitutional Conflicts between Congress and the President*. 7th ed. Lawrence: University of Kansas Press, 2007.

Hamilton, Alexander, James Madison, and John Jay. *The Federalist Papers*, no. 39. Clinton Rossiter, ed. New York: New American Library, 1961.

Karmis, Dimitrios, and Wayne Norman. *Theories of Federalism: A Reader*. New York: Palgrave, Macmillan, 2005.

LaCroix, Alison L. *The Ideological Origins of American Federalism*. Cambridge, MA: Harvard University Press, 2010.

Noonan, John T. *Narrowing the Nation's Power: The Supreme Court Sides with the States*. Berkeley: University of California Press, 2002.

Posner, Richard. *Not a Suicide Pact: The Constitution in a Time of National Emergency*. New York: Oxford University Press, 2006.

Riker, William H. *Federalism: Origin, Operation, Significance*. Boston: Little, Brown, 1964.

Robertson, David. *Federalism and the Making of America*. New York: Routledge, 2011.

Samuels, David, and Matthew Shugart, *Presidents, Parties and Prime Ministers: How the Separation of Powers Affects Party Organization and Behavior*. New York: Cambridge University Press, 2010.

Smith, Rogers M. *Civic Ideals: Conflicting Visions of Citizenship in U.S. History*. New Haven, CT: Yale University Press, 1997.

Van Horn, Carol E. *The State of the States*. 4th ed. Washington, DC: CQ Press, 2004.

Winston, Pamela. *Welfare Policymaking in the States: The Devil in Devolution*. Washington, DC: Georgetown University Press, 2002.

4

Civil Liberties

Institutions are designed to solve collective action problems, and in the United States among the most important constitutional instruments created for this purpose are civil liberties and civil rights. To "solve," however, does not mean simply to facilitate collective action. Instead, the constitutional principles of civil liberties and civil rights presented in the Bill of Rights also *regulate* collective action. Civil liberties are limitations or restrictions on collective action. In effect, the concept of civil liberties defines certain spheres of activity, such as speech or worship, in which the government's authority to interfere with individual conduct is limited. Civil rights are the rules determining who may participate or be represented in collective decision-making processes, as well as regulating the ways in which the government can and cannot treat its citizens. Thus, generally speaking, civil liberties limit collective action by restricting the government's jurisdiction. Civil rights, on the other hand (as we will see in Chapter 5), regulate collective action by establishing important decision rules for the government's conduct.

Jurisdiction over civil liberties and civil rights issues is primarily exercised by the courts, which have developed myriad decision rules and procedures designed to resolve controversies in these realms. The U.S. Supreme Court, in particular, asserts a good deal of agenda and veto power when it comes to the interpretation of constitutional principles, and we will examine many Supreme Court decisions in this chapter and in Chapter 5. The Supreme Court's jurisdiction over constitutional issues is derived from Article III of the Constitution, from statutes, and from prior decisions of the Court itself. But consistent with the concept of checks and balances, other actors—particularly the U.S. Congress—also claim agenda and veto power in these realms. Congress's jurisdiction stems from Article II of the Constitution, which gives Congress the power to make the laws, and from its role in the process of amending the Constitution, as defined in Article V.

In their rulings, the courts are heavily influenced by history. Every court decision recites the history of prior court decisions relating to the principles at hand. This use of history is called *precedent*. When courts issue their decisions, they constantly refer to the opinions of prior courts to justify their interpretations, logic, and ultimate findings. Seldom will a court depart from established precedent. Even the Supreme Court is always careful to justify its decisions by pointing to numerous precedents and will seldom overturn established legal principles. Because the job of a court is to apply rather than to make the law, history in the form of precedent is an important factor limiting judicial discretion.

As we observed in our discussion of federalism and the separation of powers, institutional principles are not carved in stone. Over the past century, a number of civil liberties have been strengthened, placing greater limits on collective action. In the realm of civil rights, as Chapter 5 will show, African Americans and others who were once excluded from participation in many collective processes have won the right to be included. In both areas, change came as a result of political struggles and was punctuated by battles within and between Congress and the courts. With these considerations in mind, let us examine the character and evolution of civil liberties in America, to be followed by a discussion of civil rights in the next chapter.

ORIGINS OF THE BILL OF RIGHTS

When the first Congress under the new Constitution met in late April 1789 (having been delayed since March 4 by the lack of a quorum because of bad winter roads), the most important item of business was consideration of a proposal to

CORE OF THE ANALYSIS

➡ Civil liberties are rules that limit the government's authority to interfere in certain spheres of activity. They restrict the government's jurisdiction in areas such as free speech and religion.

➡ Americans' most important civil liberties are found in the Constitution's Bill of Rights—which might have been called the Bill of Liberties.

➡ Originally, the limits in the Bill of Rights applied only to the federal government. It took a series of Supreme Court decisions in the twentieth century to apply these limits to the states as well.

➡ Today's conception of civil liberties has been shaped by their historical development and their interpretation by key political actors, especially the Supreme Court.

add a bill of rights to the Constitution. Such a proposal by the Virginia delegate George Mason had been turned down with little debate in the waning days of the Constitutional Convention in September 1787 because of arguments by Alexander Hamilton and other Federalists that a bill of rights was irrelevant in a constitution providing the national government with only delegated powers. How could the national government abuse powers not given to it in the first place? Hamilton was also concerned that a bill of rights would weaken the new government by limiting its jurisdiction even before it had an opportunity to organize itself. But when the Constitution was submitted to the states for ratification, Antifederalists, most of whom had *not* been delegates in Philadelphia, picked up on the argument of Thomas Jefferson (who also had not been a delegate) that the omission of a bill of rights was a major imperfection of the new Constitution. Whatever the merits of Hamilton's or Jefferson's positions, to gain ratification, the Federalists in Massachusetts, South Carolina, New Hampshire, Virginia, and New York made an "unwritten but unequivocal pledge" to add a bill of rights and a promise to confirm (in what became the Tenth Amendment) the understanding that all powers not delegated to the national government or explicitly prohibited to the states were reserved to the states or to the people.[1]

James Madison, who had been a delegate to the Philadelphia convention and later became a member of Congress, may still have believed privately that a bill of rights was not needed. But in 1789, recognizing the urgency of obtaining the Antifederalists' support for the Constitution and the new government, he fought for a bill of rights, arguing that the ideals it embodied would acquire "the character of fundamental maxims of free Government, and as they become incorporated with the national sentiment, counteract the impulses of interest and passion."[2]

"After much discussion and manipulation . . . at the delicate prompting of Washington and under the masterful prodding of Madison," the House adopted 17 amendments; the Senate adopted 12 of these. Ten of the amendments were ratified by the necessary three-fourths of the states, making them part of the Constitution on December 15, 1791—from the start, these 10 were called the Bill of Rights.[3]

civil liberties ⇨

The protections of citizens from improper governmental action

Civil liberties can be defined as protections of citizens from improper governmental action. When adopted in 1791, the Bill of Rights was seen as guaranteeing a private sphere of personal liberty free of governmental restrictions. As Jefferson had put it, a bill of rights "is what people are entitled to against every government on earth." In this sense, we could call the Bill of Rights a bill of

---

1   Clinton L. Rossiter, *1787: The Grand Convention* (New York: Norton, 1987), p. 302.

2   Quoted in Milton Konvitz, "The Bill of Rights: Amendments I–X," in *An American Primer,* 2 vols., Daniel J. Boorstin, ed. (Chicago: University of Chicago Press, 1966), I: 159.

3   Rossiter, *1787,* p. 303, where he also reports that "in 1941 the States of Connecticut, Massachusetts, and Georgia celebrated the sesquicentennial of the Bill of Rights by giving their hitherto withheld and unneeded assent."

liberties because the amendments focus on what government must *not* do. For example (with emphasis added):

1. "Congress shall make *no* law . . ." (I)

2. "The right . . . to . . . bear Arms, shall *not* be infringed." (II)

3. "*No* Soldier shall . . . be quartered . . ." (III)

4. "*No* Warrants shall issue, but upon probable cause . . ." (IV)

5. "*No* person shall be held to answer . . . unless on a presentment or indictment of a Grand Jury . . ." (V)

6. "Excessive bail shall not be required . . . *nor* cruel and unusual punishments inflicted." (VIII)

Thus the Bill of Rights is a series of "thou shalt nots"—restraints addressed to government, limiting its jurisdiction. Some of these restraints are *substantive*, putting limits on *what* the government shall and shall not have the power to do, such as establishing a state religion, quartering troops in private homes without consent, or seizing private property without just compensation. Other restraints are procedural, dealing with how the government is supposed to act. For example, even though the government has the substantive power to declare certain acts to be crimes and to arrest and imprison persons who violate its criminal laws, it may not do so except by fairly meticulous observance of procedures designed to protect the accused. The best-known procedural rule is that a person is presumed innocent until proven guilty. This rule does not question the government's power to punish someone for committing a crime; it questions only the way the government determines who committed the crime. Substantive and procedural restraints together identify the realm of civil liberties. While the distinction between liberties and rights seems clear in theory, in practice several provisions of the Bill of Rights assert both a liberty and right. Proponents of the Bill of Rights wished to make it clear that their enumeration of rights and liberties should not be deemed exhaustive. Americans might be entitled to other constitutional protections not formally included in the Bill of Rights. This concern was addressed by the Ninth Amendment, which declares that the enumeration in the Constitution of some rights "shall not be construed" to mean that the people do not retain others rights as well.

NATIONALIZING THE BILL OF RIGHTS

The First Amendment provides that "Congress shall make no law respecting an establishment of religion . . . or abridging the freedom of speech, or of the press; or the right of . . . [assembly and petition]." But this is the only amendment in the Bill of Rights that addresses itself exclusively to the national government. For example, the Second Amendment provides that "the right of the people to keep and bear Arms, shall not be infringed." The Fifth Amendment says, among other things, that *no person* "shall . . . be twice put in jeopardy of life or limb" for the same crime, that *no person* "shall be compelled in any criminal case to be a witness against himself," that *no person* shall "be deprived of life, liberty, or property, without due process of law," and that private property cannot be taken "without just compensation."[4] Because the First Amendment is the only part of the Bill of Rights that is explicit in its intention to put limits on the national government, a fundamental question inevitably arises: Do the remaining amendments of the Bill of Rights put limits on state governments, or do they put them only on the national government?

Dual Citizenship

The question of whether the Bill of Rights also limits state governments was settled in 1833 in a way that may seem odd to Americans today. The 1833 case was *Barron v. Baltimore*, and the facts were simple. In paving its streets, the city of Baltimore had disposed of so much sand and gravel in the water near John Barron's wharf that the value of the wharf for commercial purposes was virtually destroyed. Barron brought the city into court on the grounds that it had, under the Fifth Amendment, unconstitutionally deprived him of his property.

Here Chief Justice Marshall, in one of the most significant Supreme Court decisions ever handed down, said:

> The Constitution was ordained and established by the people of the United States for themselves, for their own government, and not for the government of individual States. Each State established a constitution for itself, and in that constitution provided such limitations and restrictions on the powers of its particular government as its judgment dictated. . . . If these propositions be correct, *the fifth amendment must be understood as restraining the power of the General Government, not as applicable to the States.*[5] [Emphasis added]

In other words, if an agency of the *national* government had deprived Barron of his property, there would have been little doubt about Barron's winning his case. But if the constitution of the state of Maryland contained no such provision protecting citizens of Maryland from such action, then Barron had no legal leg to stand on against Baltimore, an agency of the state of Maryland.

---

4   It would be useful at this point to review all the provisions of the Bill of Rights to confirm this distinction between the wording of the First Amendment and the wording of the rest (see the Appendix). The emphasis in the examples is not in the original. For a spirited and enlightening essay on the extent to which the entire Bill of Rights is about equality, see Martha Minow, "Equality and the Bill of Rights," in *The Constitution of Rights: Human Dignity and American Values,* Michael J. Meyer and William A. Parent, eds. (Ithaca, NY: Cornell University Press, 1992), pp. 118–28.

5   *Barron v. Mayor and City of Baltimore,* 32 U.S. 243 (1833).

Barron v. Baltimore confirmed "dual citizenship"—that is, that each American was a citizen of the national government and separately a citizen of one of the states. This meant that the Bill of Rights did not apply to decisions or procedures of state (or local) governments. Even slavery could continue because the Bill of Rights could not protect anyone from state laws treating people as property. In fact, the Bill of Rights did not become a vital instrument for the extension of civil liberties for anyone until after a bloody civil war and the revolutionary Fourteenth Amendment intervened. And even so, nearly another century would pass before the Bill of Rights would truly come into its own. This is a case where America's history has truly mattered. America's states predated the creation of the federal government. The states joined the Union voluntarily, retaining many of their sovereign powers. In many other nations, subnational governments were created by and for the administrative convenience of the central government. In the United States, the nationalization of governmental powers has proceeded slowly and in fits and starts.

The Fourteenth Amendment

From a constitutional standpoint, the defeat of the South in the Civil War settled one question and raised another. It probably settled forever the question of whether secession was an option for any state. After 1865, there was to be more "united" than "states" to the United States. But this left unanswered just how much the states were obliged to obey the Constitution and, in particular, the Bill of Rights. Just reading the words of the Fourteenth Amendment, anyone might think it was almost perfectly designed to impose the Bill of Rights on the states and thereby reverse *Barron v. Baltimore*. The very first words of the Fourteenth Amendment point in that direction:

> All persons born or naturalized in the United States, and subject to the jurisdiction thereof, are citizens of the United States and of the State wherein they reside.

This provides for a single national citizenship, and at a minimum that means civil liberties should not vary drastically from state to state. That would seem to be the spirit of the Fourteenth Amendment: to nationalize the Bill of Rights by nationalizing the definition of citizenship.

This interpretation of the Fourteenth Amendment is reinforced by the next clause of the amendment:

> No State shall make or enforce any law which shall abridge the privileges or immunities of citizens of the United States; nor shall any State deprive any person of life, liberty, or property, without due process of law.

All of this sounds like an effort to extend the Bill of Rights in its entirety to citizens wherever they might reside. But this was not to be the Supreme Court's interpretation for nearly a century. Within five years of ratification of the Fourteenth

Amendment in 1868, the Court was making decisions as though the amendment had never been adopted. The shadow of *Barron* grew longer and longer. In an important 1873 decision known as the *Slaughter House Cases*, the Supreme Court determined that the federal government was under no obligation to protect the "privileges and immunities" of citizens of a particular state against arbitrary actions by that state's government. The Court argued that the framers of the Fourteenth Amendment could not have intended to incorporate the entire Bill of Rights.[6] Yet when the Civil Rights Act of 1875 attempted to protect blacks from discriminatory treatment by proprietors of hotels, theaters, and other public accommodations, the Supreme Court disregarded its own primary argument in the previous case. This time the Court distinguished between state action and private action, declaring that the Fourteenth Amendment applied only to discriminatory actions by state officials, "operating under cover of law," and not to discrimination against blacks by private individuals, even though these private individuals were companies offering services to the public.[7] Thus the Court held that the Civil Rights Act of 1875 was unconstitutional. Such narrow interpretations raised the inevitable question of whether the Fourteenth Amendment had incorporated any of the Bill of Rights. The Fourteenth Amendment remained shadowy until the mid-twentieth century. The shadow was *Barron v. Baltimore* and the Court's unwillingness to "nationalize" civil liberties—that is, to interpret the civil liberties expressed in the Bill of Rights as imposing limitations not only on the federal government but also on the states.

It was not until the very end of the nineteenth century that the Supreme Court began to nationalize the Bill of Rights by incorporating its civil liberties provisions into the Fourteenth Amendment. Incorporation can be seen as an expansion of the power and authority of the federal government and an erosion of the autonomy of the individual states. Thus, it is no accident that the major periods of incorporation were the 1930s and the 1960s, when Congress and the president sought to enhance federal power vis-à-vis the states and encouraged the courts, through the appointment process and in other ways, to facilitate the effort. During the 1930s, most First Amendment limitations were imposed on the actions of the states; during the 1960s, the states were compelled to adhere to many of the remaining provisions of the Bill of Rights.

Table 4.1 outlines the major steps in the process of incorporation. The only change in civil liberties during the first 60 years after the adoption of the Fourteenth Amendment came in 1897, when the Supreme Court held that the due process clause of the Fourteenth Amendment did in fact prohibit states from taking property for a public use without just compensation.[8] This effectively overruled *Barron* because it meant that a citizen of Maryland, or any state, was henceforth protected from a "public taking" of property even if the state

---

6   *The Slaughter House Cases,* 83 U.S. 36 (1873).

7   *The Civil Rights Cases,* 109 U.S. 3 (1883).

8   *Chicago, Burlington, and Quincy Railroad Company v. Chicago,* 166 U.S. 226 (1897).

Table 4.1

INCORPORATION OF THE BILL OF RIGHTS
INTO THE FOURTEENTH AMENDMENT

SELECTED PROVISIONS AND AMENDMENTS	DATE "INCORPORATED"	KEY CASES
Eminent domain (V)	1897	Chicago, Burlington, and Quincy Railroad v. Chicago
Freedom of speech (I)	1925	Gitlow v. New York
Freedom of the press (I)	1931	Near v. Minnesota ex rel. Olson
Free exercise of religion (I)	1934	Hamilton v. Regents of the University of California
Freedom of assembly (I)	1939	Hague v. Committee for Industrial Organization
Freedom from unnecessary search and seizure (IV)	1949	Wolf v. Colorado
Freedom from warrantless search and seizure ("exclusionary rule") (IV)	1961	Mapp v. Ohio
Freedom from cruel and unusual punishment (VIII)	1962	Robinson v. California
Right to counsel in any criminal trial (VI)	1963	Gideon v. Wainwright
Right against self-incrimination and forced confessions (V)	1964	Malloy v. Hogan Escobedo v. Illinois
Right to privacy (III, IV, and V)	1965	Griswold v. Connecticut
Right to remain silent (V)	1966	Miranda v. Arizona
Right against double jeopardy (V)	1969	Benton v. Maryland
Right to bear arms (II)	2010	McDonald v. Chicago

constitution did not provide such protection. The power of public agencies to seize private property is called eminent domain. According to the Fifth Amendment, private owners must be paid "just compensation" by the government if it decides that it needs their property. In a broader sense, however, *Barron* still cast a shadow because the Supreme Court had "incorporated" into the Fourteenth Amendment only the property protection provision of the Fifth Amendment and no other clause, let alone the other amendments of the Bill of Rights. In other words, although due process applied to the taking of life and liberty as well as property, only property was incorporated into the Fourteenth Amendment as a limitation on state power.

No further expansion of civil liberties through incorporation occurred until 1925, when the Supreme Court held that freedom of speech is "among the fundamental personal rights and 'liberties' protected by the due process clause of the Fourteenth Amendment from impairment by the states."[9] In 1931, the Court added freedom of the press to that short list of civil rights protected by the Bill of Rights from state action; in 1934, it added freedom of religion; and in 1939, it added freedom of assembly.[10] But that was as far as the Court was willing to go. This one-by-one application of the provisions of the Bill of Rights is known as *selective incorporation*, as distinguished from the notion of "total incorporation" advocated by some scholars. Total incorporation is the idea that all of the provisions of the Bill of Rights were applied to the states by the Fourteenth Amendment. As late as 1937, the Supreme Court was still loath to nationalize civil liberties beyond the First Amendment. In fact, the Court in that year took one of its most extreme turns backward toward *Barron v. Baltimore*.

The state of Connecticut had indicted a man named Frank Palko for first-degree murder, but a lower court found him guilty of only second-degree murder and sentenced him to life in prison. Unhappy with the verdict, the state of Connecticut appealed the conviction to its highest court, won the appeal, got a new trial, and succeeded in getting Palko convicted of first-degree murder. Palko appealed to the Supreme Court on what seemed an open-and-shut case of double jeopardy—being tried twice for the same crime. Yet though a majority of the Court agreed that this could indeed be considered a case of double jeopardy, the justices decided that double jeopardy was *not* one of the provisions of the Bill of Rights incorporated into the Fourteenth Amendment as a restriction on the powers of the states. Justice Benjamin Cardozo, considered one of the ablest Supreme Court justices of the twentieth century, rejected the argument made by Palko's lawyer that "whatever is forbidden by the Fifth Amendment is forbidden by the Fourteenth also." Cardozo responded tersely, "There is no such general rule." Palko was eventually executed for the crime—because he lived in the state of Connecticut rather than in a state whose constitution included a guarantee against double jeopardy.

---

9 *Gitlow v. New York*, 268 U.S. 652 (1925).

10 *Near v. Minnesota ex rel. Olson*, 283 U.S. 697 (1931); *Hague v. Committee for Industrial Organization*, 307 U.S. 496 (1939).

Cases like *Palko* extended the shadow of *Barron* into its second century, despite adoption of the Fourteenth Amendment. The Constitution, as interpreted by the Supreme Court, left standing the framework in which the states had the power to determine their own law on a number of fundamental issues. It left states with the power to pass laws segregating the races—and 13 states chose to exercise that power. The constitutional framework also left states with the power to engage in searches and seizures without a warrant, indict accused persons without benefit of a grand jury, deprive persons of trial by jury, force persons to testify against themselves, deprive accused persons of their right to confront adverse witnesses, and as we have seen, prosecute accused persons more than once for the same crime.[11] All of these were implicitly identified in the *Palko* case as "not incorporated" into the Fourteenth Amendment as limitations on the powers of the states.

The Constitutional Revolution in Civil Liberties

For more than 30 years after the *Palko* case, the nineteenth-century framework was sustained, but signs of change came after 1954, in *Brown v. Board of Education*, when the Supreme Court overturned the infamous *Plessy v. Ferguson*.[12] *Plessy* was a civil rights case involving the "equal protection" clause of the Fourteenth Amendment but was not an issue of applying the Bill of Rights to the states. (We will discuss *Plessy*'s significance for civil rights in the next chapter.) Nevertheless, *Brown* indicated clearly that the Supreme Court was going to be expansive about civil liberties because in that case the Court effectively promised that it was actively going to subject the states and all actions affecting civil rights and civil liberties to **strict scrutiny**. In retrospect, one could say that this constitutional revolution was given a jump-start by the *Brown* decision,[13] even though the results were not apparent until after 1961, when the number of incorporated civil liberties increased (see Table 4.1).

As with the federalism revolution, the constitutional revolution in civil liberties was a movement toward nationalization. But the two revolutions required opposite motions on the part of the Supreme Court. In the area of commerce (the first revolution), the Court had to decide to assume a passive role by not interfering as Congress expanded the meaning of the commerce clause of Article I, Section 8. This expansion has been so extensive that the national government can now constitutionally reach a single farmer growing 20 acres of wheat or a small restaurant selling barbecue to local "whites only" without the farmer's

 strict scrutiny

The most stringent standard of judicial review of a government's actions in which the government must show that the law serves a "compelling state interest"

---

11 *Palko v. Connecticut,* 302 U.S. 319 (1937), was explicitly reversed in *Benton v. Maryland,* 395 U.S. 784 (1969), in which the Court said that double jeopardy was in fact incorporated into the Fourteenth Amendment as a restriction on the states.

12 *Brown v. Board of Education,* 347 U.S. 483 (1954); *Plessy v. Ferguson,* 163 U.S. 537 (1896).

13 The first constitutional revolution began with *National Labor Relations Board v. Jones and Laughlin Steel Corporation,* 301 U.S. 1 (1937).

or the restaurant's being anywhere near interstate commerce routes. In the second revolution, involving the Bill of Rights and the Fourteenth Amendment rather than the commerce clause, the Court had to assume an active role, which required close review not of Congress but of the laws of state legislatures and the decisions of state courts to apply a single national Fourteenth Amendment standard to the rights and liberties of all citizens.

Table 4.1 shows that until 1961, only the First Amendment had been fully and clearly incorporated into the Fourteenth Amendment.[14] After 1961, several other important provisions of the Bill of Rights were incorporated. Of the cases that expanded the Fourteenth Amendment's reach, among the most famous (partly because it became the subject of a best-selling book and a popular movie) is *Gideon v. Wainwright*, which established the right to counsel in a criminal trial.[15] In *Mapp v. Ohio*, the Court held that evidence obtained in violation of the Fourth Amendment ban on unreasonable searches and seizures would be excluded from trial.[16] This "exclusionary rule" was particularly irksome to police and prosecutors because it meant that patently guilty defendants sometimes got to go free because the evidence that clearly damned them could not be used. In *Miranda*, the Court's ruling required that arrested persons be informed of the rights to remain silent and have counsel present during interrogation.[17] This is the basis of the **Miranda rule** of reading persons their rights, which is familiar to most Americans from movies and TV police shows. By 1969, in *Benton v. Maryland*, the Supreme Court had come full circle regarding the rights of the criminally accused, explicitly reversing the *Palko* ruling and thereby incorporating double jeopardy.

Beginning in the mid-1950s, the Court expanded another important area of civil liberties: rights to privacy. In 1958, the Supreme Court recognized "privacy in one's association" in its decision to prevent the state of Alabama from using the membership list of the National Association for the Advancement of Colored People (NAACP) in its investigations.[18] As we see later in this chapter, legal questions about the right to privacy have come to the fore in more recent cases concerning birth control, abortion, homosexuality, and assisted suicide.

Miranda rule

The convention derived from the Supreme Court's 1966 ruling in the case of *Miranda v. Arizona* whereby persons under arrest must be informed of their legal rights, including their right to counsel, before undergoing police interrogation

---

14 The one exception was the right to a public trial (the Sixth Amendment), but the 1948 case did not mention the right to a public trial as such; it was cited in a 1968 case as establishing the right to a public trial as part of the Fourteenth Amendment. The 1948 case was *In re Oliver*, 333 U.S. 257, where the issue was put more generally as "due process," and public trial itself was not mentioned. Later opinions, such as *Duncan v. Louisiana*, 391 U.S. 145 (1968), cited the *Oliver* case as the precedent for incorporating public trials as part of the Fourteenth Amendment.

15 Anthony Lewis, *Gideon's Trumpet* (New York: Random House, 1964); *Gideon v. Wainwright*, 372 U.S. 335 (1963).

16 *Mapp v. Ohio*, 367 U.S. 643 (1961).

17 *Miranda v. Arizona*, 384 U.S. 436 (1966).

18 *NAACP v. Alabama*, 357 U.S. 449 (1958).

THE BILL OF RIGHTS TODAY

Since liberty requires restraining the power of government, the general status of civil liberties can never be considered fixed and permanent.[19] Though the Court adheres to law and precedent, every provision in the Bill of Rights is subject to interpretation, and in any dispute involving a clause of the Bill of Rights, interpretations will always be shaped by the interpreter's interest in the outcome. As we have seen, the Court continuously reminds everyone that if it has the power to expand the Bill of Rights, it also has the power to contract it.[20]

One good way to examine the Bill of Rights today is the simplest way: to take the provisions one at a time. Some of these provisions are settled areas of law, and some are not. Any one of them could be reinterpreted by the Court at some point.

The First Amendment and Freedom of Religion

> Congress shall make no law respecting an establishment of religion, or prohibiting the free exercise thereof; or abridging the freedom of speech, or of the press; or the right of the people peaceably to assemble, and to petition the Government for a redress of grievances.

The Bill of Rights begins by guaranteeing freedom of religion, and the First Amendment provides for that freedom in two distinct clauses: "Congress shall make no law [1] respecting an establishment of religion, or [2] prohibiting the free exercise thereof." The first clause is called the establishment clause, and the second is called the free exercise clause. Let us examine the meaning of each clause.

Separation between Church and State. The **establishment clause** and the idea of "no law" regarding the establishment of religion could be interpreted in several possible ways. One interpretation, which probably reflects the views of many of the First Amendment's authors, is that the government is prohibited from establishing an official church. Official state churches, such as the Church of England, were common in the eighteenth century and were viewed by many Americans as inconsistent with a republican form of government. Indeed, many American colonists had fled Europe to escape persecution for having rejected state-sponsored churches. A second possible interpretation is the "nonpreferentialist" or "accommodationist" view, which holds that the

 establishment clause

The First Amendment clause that says, "Congress shall make no law respecting an establishment of religion." This law means that a wall of separation exists between church and state

---

19 This section is taken from Benjamin Ginsberg, Theodore J. Lowi, Margaret Weir, and Caroline J. Tolbert, *We the People: An Introduction to American Politics,* 9th ed. (New York: Norton, 2013).

20 For a lively and readable treatment of the possibilities of restricting provisions of the Bill of Rights without actually reversing prior decisions, see David G. Savage, *Turning Right: The Making of the Rehnquist Supreme Court* (New York: Wiley, 1992).

government may not take sides among competing religions but is not prohibited from providing assistance to religious institutions or ideas so long as it shows no favoritism. The United States accommodates religious beliefs in a variety of ways, from the reference to God on U.S. currency to the prayer that begins every session of Congress. These forms of establishment have never been struck down by the courts.

The third view regarding religious establishment, which for many years dominated Supreme Court decision making in this realm, is the idea of a "wall of separation" between church and state that cannot be breached by the government. The concept of a wall of separation was Jefferson's own formulation, and it has figured in many Supreme Court cases arising under the establishment clause. For two centuries, Jefferson's words have had a powerful impact on our understanding of the proper relationship between church and state in America.

Despite the absolute sound of the phrase *wall of separation*, there is ample room to disagree on how high the wall is or of what materials it is composed. For example, the Court has been consistently strict in cases of school prayer, striking down such practices as Bible reading,[21] nondenominational prayer,[22] a moment of silence for meditation, and pregame prayer at public sporting events.[23] In each of these cases, the Court reasoned that school-sponsored observations, even of an apparently nondenominational character, are highly suggestive of school sponsorship and therefore violate the prohibition against establishment of religion. On the other hand, the Court has been quite permissive (and some would say inconsistent) about the public display of religious symbols, such as city-sponsored Nativity scenes in commercial or municipal areas.[24] And although the Court has consistently disapproved of government-financed support for religious schools, even when the purpose has been purely educational and secular, it has permitted certain direct aid to students of such schools in the form of busing, for example. In 1971, after 30 years of cases involving religious schools, the Court attempted to specify some criteria to guide its decisions and those of lower courts, indicating, for example, in a decision invalidating state payments for the teaching of secular subjects in parochial schools, circumstances under which the Court might allow certain financial assistance. The case was *Lemon v. Kurtzman*; in its decision, the Supreme Court established three criteria to guide future cases, in what came to be called the **Lemon** test. The Court held that government aid to religious schools would be accepted as constitutional if (1) it had a secular purpose, (2) its effect was neither to advance nor to inhibit religion, and (3) it did not entangle government and religious institutions in one another's affairs.[25]

Lemon test

Rule articulated in *Lemon v. Kurtzman* according to which governmental action in respect to religion is permissible if it is secular in purpose, does not lead to "excessive entanglement" with religion, and neither promotes nor inhibits the practice of religion

21 *Abington School District v. Schempp*, 374 U.S. 203 (1963).

22 *Engel v. Vitale*, 370 U.S. 421 (1962).

23 *Wallace v. Jaffree*, 472 U.S. 38 (1985).

24 *Lynch v. Donnelly*, 465 U.S. 668 (1984).

25 *Lemon v. Kurtzman*, 403 U.S. 602 (1971). The *Lemon* test is still good law, but as recently as the 1994 Court term, four justices urged that it be abandoned. Here is a settled area of law that may become unsettled.

Although these restrictions make the *Lemon* test a hard test to pass, imaginative authorities have found ways to do so, and the Supreme Court has demonstrated a willingness to let them, perhaps moving toward a more accommodationist view of the establishment clause. In 1995, for example, the Court narrowly ruled that a student religious group at the University of Virginia could not be denied student activities funds merely because it was a religious group espousing a particular viewpoint about a deity. The Court called the denial "viewpoint discrimination" and declared that it violated the free speech rights of the group.[26] This led two years later to a new, more conservative approach to the separation of church and state. In 1997, the Court accepted the practice of sending public school teachers into parochial schools to provide remedial education to disadvantaged children.[27]

In 2004, the question of whether the phrase *under God* in the Pledge of Allegiance violates the establishment clause was brought before the Court. Written in 1892, the pledge had been used in schools without any religious references. But in 1954, in the midst of the Cold War, Congress voted to change the pledge, in response to the "godless Communism" of the Soviet Union. The conversion was made by adding two key words, so that the revised version read, "I pledge allegiance to the flag of the United States of America and to the Republic for which it stands, one nation *under God*, indivisible, with liberty and justice for all" [emphasis added].

Ever since the change was made, there has been a constant murmuring of discontent from those who object to an officially sanctioned profession of belief in a deity as a violation of the religious freedom clause of the First Amendment. In 2003, Michael Newdow, the father of a kindergarten student in a California elementary school, forced the issue to the surface when he brought suit against the local school district. Newdow, an atheist, argued that the reference to God turned the daily recitation of the pledge into a religious exercise. A federal court ruled that although students were not required to recite the pledge at all, having to stand and listen to others say "under God" still violated the First Amendment's establishment clause. The case was appealed to the Supreme Court, and on June 14, 2004—50 years to the day after the adoption of "under God" in the pledge—the Court ruled that Newdow lacked a sufficient personal stake in the case to bring the complaint.[28] This inconclusive decision by the Court left "under God" in the pledge while keeping the issue alive for possible resolution in a future case.

In two cases in 2005, the Supreme Court ruled, also inconclusively, on government-sponsored displays of religious symbols. Both cases involved displays of the Ten Commandments. In *Van Orden v. Perry*, the Court said in a 5–4 decision that a display of the Ten Commandments in the Texas state capital did

26 *Rosenberger v. University of Virginia*, 515 U.S. 819 (1995).

27 *Agostini v. Felton*, 521 U.S. 203 (1997). The case being overruled was *Aguilar v. Felton*, 473 U.S. 402 (1985).

28 *Elk Grove Unified School District v. Newdow*, 542 U.S. 1 (2004).

not violate the Constitution.[29] However, in *McCreary v. ACLU*, decided at the same time and also by a 5–4 margin, the Court determined that a display of the Ten Commandments inside two Kentucky court houses was unconstitutional.[30] Justice Breyer, the swing vote in the two cases, intimated that the difference had been the purpose of the displays. Most legal observers, though, could see little difference between the two and assume that the Court will provide further clarification in future cases.

free exercise clause

The First Amendment clause that protects a citizen's right to believe and practice whatever religion he or she chooses

Free Exercise of Religion.
The **free exercise clause** protects the right to believe and practice whatever religion one chooses; it also protects the right to be a nonbeliever. Generally speaking, problems arise under the free exercise clause not because the government specifically decides to interfere with religion. Rather, they arise because generally applicable secular laws happen to intrude on the beliefs of one or another group. The precedent-setting case involving free exercise was *West Virginia State Board of Education v. Barnette* (1943), which involved the children of a family of Jehovah's Witnesses who refused to salute and pledge allegiance to the American flag on the grounds that their religious faith did not permit it. Three years earlier, the Court had upheld such a requirement and had permitted schools to expel students for refusing to salute the flag. But the entry of the United States into a war to defend democracy coupled with the ugly treatment to which the Jehovah's Witnesses' children had been subjected induced the Court to reverse itself and endorse the free exercise of religion even when it may be offensive to the beliefs of the majority.[31]

Although the Supreme Court has been fairly consistent and strict in protecting the free exercise of religious belief, it has taken pains to distinguish between religious beliefs and *actions* based on those beliefs. In one case, for example, two Native Americans had been fired from their jobs for smoking peyote, an illegal drug. They claimed they had been fired from their jobs illegally because smoking peyote was a religious sacrament protected by the free exercise clause. The Court disagreed with their claim in an important 1990 decision.[32] The Court said that the state's duty to prevent the use of dangerous drugs should be given more weight than the claimed religious exercise. Congress, however, supported the religious claim and went on to engage in an unusual controversy with the Court, involving the separation of powers as well as the proper application of the separation of church and state. Congress literally reversed the Court's 1990 decision with the enactment of the Religious Freedom Restoration Act (RFRA) of 1993, which forbids any federal agency or state government to restrict a person's free exercise of religion unless the federal agency or state government

29 *Van Orden v. Perry*, 545 U.S. 677 (2005).

30 *McCreary v. ACLU*, 545 U.S. 844 (2005).

31 *West Virginia State Board of Education v. Barnette*, 319 U.S. 624 (1943). The case it reversed was *Minersville School District v. Gobitus*, 310 U.S. 586 (1940).

32 *Employment Division v. Smith*, 494 U.S. 872 (1990).

demonstrates that its action "furthers a compelling government interest" and "is the least restrictive means of furthering that compelling governmental interest." One of the first applications of the RFRA was to a case brought by St. Peter's Catholic Church against the city of Boerne, Texas, which had denied permission to the church to enlarge its building because the building had been declared a historic landmark. The case went to federal court on the argument that the city had violated the church's religious freedom as guaranteed by Congress in the RFRA. The Supreme Court declared the RFRA unconstitutional, but on grounds rarely utilized, if not unique to this case: Congress had violated the separation-of-powers principle, infringing on the powers of the judiciary by going so far beyond its lawmaking powers that it ended up actually expanding the scope of religious rights rather than just enforcing them. The Court thereby implied that questions requiring a balancing of religious claims against public policy claims were reserved strictly to the judiciary.[33]

The *City of Boerne* case did settle some matters of constitutional controversy over the religious exercise and the establishment clauses of the First Amendment, but it left a lot more unsettled. What about the refusal of some Amish parents to send their children to school beyond eighth grade because of their belief that exposing their children to "modern values" undermines their religious commitment? In this example, the Court decided in favor of the Amish and endorsed a very strong interpretation of the protection of free exercise.[34] Or, what if free exercise of religion clashes with other values such as nondiscrimination? A 2010 case involved a public law school in California that denied the use of school funds and facilities to a Christian student group that excluded gays and non-Christians. In a 5–4 ruling, the Court said the school was acting to prevent discrimination, not interfering with the student group's right to exercise its religion.[35]

The First Amendment and Freedom of Speech and the Press

> Congress shall make no law . . . abridging the freedom of speech, or of the press.

Because democracy depends on an open political process and politics is basically talk, freedom of speech and freedom of the press are considered critical. For this reason, they were given a prominence in the Bill of Rights equal to that of freedom of religion. In 1938, freedom of speech (which in all important respects includes freedom of the press) was given extraordinary constitutional status when the Supreme Court established that any legislation that attempts

---

33 *City of Boerne v. Flores,* 521 U.S. 507 (1997).

34 *Wisconsin v. Yoder,* 406 U.S. 205 (1972).

35 *Christian Legal Society v. Martinez,* 561 U.S. ____ (2010).

to restrict these fundamental freedoms "is to be subjected to a more exacting judicial scrutiny . . . than are most other types of legislation."[36]

The Court was saying that the democratic political process must be protected at almost any cost. This higher standard of judicial review came to be called *preferred position*. Preferred position implies that speech—at least some kinds of speech—will be protected almost absolutely. In 2011, for example, the Supreme Court ruled 8–1 that the Westboro Baptist Church, a tiny Kansas institution, had a First Amendment right to picket the funerals of American soldiers killed in action while displaying signs reading "Thank God for Dead Soldiers." Members of the church believe that these deaths represent divine punishment for America's tolerance of homosexuality and other matters. In his opinion, Chief Justice Roberts wrote, "As a nation we have chosen to protect even hurtful speech on public issues to ensure that we do not stifle public debate."[37] But, even though we do protect many types of speech with which most Americans strongly disagree, it turns out that only some types of speech are fully protected against restrictions. Many forms of speech are less than absolutely protected— even though they are entitled to a preferred position.

Political Speech. Political speech was the activity of greatest concern to the framers of the Constitution, even though they found it the most difficult provision to observe. Within seven years of the ratification of the Bill of Rights, Congress adopted the infamous Alien and Sedition Acts, which, among other things, made it a crime to say or publish anything that might tend to defame or bring into disrepute the government of the United States. Quite clearly, the acts' intentions were to criminalize the very conduct given absolute protection by the First Amendment. Fifteen violators, including several newspaper editors, were indicted, and a few were convicted before the relevant portions of the acts were allowed to expire.

The first modern free speech case arose immediately after World War I. It involved persons who had been convicted under the federal Espionage Acts of 1917 for opposing American involvement in the war. The Supreme Court upheld the act and refused to protect the speech rights of the defendants on the grounds that their activities—appeals to draftees to resist the draft—constituted a **"clear and present danger"** to security.[38] This is the first and most famous test of when government intervention or censorship can be permitted, though it is no longer used by courts.

It was only after the 1920s that real progress toward a genuinely effective First Amendment was made. Since then, political speech has been consistently protected by the courts even when it has been deemed "insulting" or

clear and present danger ⇨

The criterion formerly used to determine whether speech is protected or unprotected, based on its capacity to present a "clear and present danger" to society

---

36 *United States v. Carolene Products Company*, 304 U.S. 144 (1938), 384. This footnote is one of the Court's most important doctrines. See Alfred H. Kelly, Winfred A. Harbison, and Herman Belz, *The American Constitution: Its Origins and Development*, 7th ed., 2 vols. (New York: Norton, 1991), II: 519–23.

37 *Snyder v. Phelps*, 562 U.S. ____ (2011).

38 *Schenck v. United States*, 249 U.S. 47 (1919).

"outrageous." Here is the way the Supreme Court put it in one of its most important statements on the subject:

> The constitutional guarantees of free speech and free press do not permit a State to forbid or proscribe advocacy of the use of force or of law violation *except where such advocacy is directed to inciting or producing imminent lawless action and is likely to incite or produce such action.*[39] [Emphasis added]

This statement was made in the case of a Ku Klux Klan leader, Charles Brandenburg, who had been arrested and convicted of advocating "revengent" action against the president, Congress, and the Supreme Court, among others, if they continued "to suppress the white, Caucasian race." Although Brandenburg was not carrying a weapon, some members of his audience were. Nevertheless, the Supreme Court reversed the state courts and freed Brandenburg while declaring Ohio's Criminal Syndicalism Act unconstitutional because it punished persons who "advocate, or teach the duty, necessity, or propriety [of violence] as a means of accomplishing industrial or political reform" or who publish materials or "voluntarily assemble . . . to teach or advocate the doctrines of criminal syndicalism." The Supreme Court argued that the statute did not distinguish "mere advocacy" from "incitement to imminent lawless action." It would be difficult to go much further in protecting freedom of speech. Typically, the federal courts will strike down restrictions on speech if they are deemed to be "overbroad," "vague," or lacking "neutrality" in terms of the content of the speech, for example, if a statute prohibited the views of the political left but not the political right, or vice versa.

Another area of recent expansion of political speech—the participation of wealthy persons and corporations in political campaigns—was opened up in 1976 with the Supreme Court's decision in *Buckley v. Valeo.*[40] Campaign finance reform laws of the early 1970s, arising out of the Watergate scandal, sought to put severe limits on campaign spending, and a number of important provisions were declared unconstitutional on the basis of a new principle that spending money by or on behalf of candidates is a form of speech protected by the First Amendment. The issue came up again in 2003, after passage of a new and still more severe campaign finance law, the Bipartisan Campaign Reform Act (BCRA; 2002). This time, in *McConnell v. Federal Election Commission*, the majority seriously reduced the area of speech protected by the *Buckley v. Valeo* decision by holding that Congress was well within its power to put limits on the amounts individuals could spend, plus severe limits on the amounts of "soft money" that could be spent by corporations and their PACs and limits on issue advertising prior to Election Day. The Court argued that "the selling of access . . . has given rise to the appearance of undue influence [that justifies] regulations impinging on First Amendment rights . . . in order to curb corruption or the

---

39 *Brandenburg v. Ohio,* 395 U.S. 444 (1969).

40 *Buckley v. Valeo,* 424 U.S. 1 (1976).

appearance of corruption."[41] This decision was the anomaly, however. In 2007, in the case of *Federal Election Commission v. Wisconsin Right to Life*, the Supreme Court struck down a key portion of BCRA, finding that the act's limitations on political advertising violated the First Amendment's guarantee of free speech.[42] In 2008, in the case of *Davis v. Federal Election Commission*, the Supreme Court struck down another element of BCRA, the so-called millionaire's amendment, which had increased contribution limits for opponents of self-funded, wealthy candidates.[43] And, in *Citizens United v. Federal Election Commission*, in 2010, the Court ruled that corporate funding of independent election ads could not be limited under the First Amendment.[44] In these decisions, the Court took the view that limits on political spending amounted to limits on free speech.

Symbolic Speech, Speech Plus, and the Rights of Assembly and Petition.

The First Amendment treats the freedoms of assembly and petition as equal to the freedoms of religion and political speech. Freedom of assembly and freedom of petition are closely associated with speech but go beyond it to speech associated with action. Since at least 1931, the Supreme Court has sought to protect actions that are designed to send a political message. (Usually the purpose of a symbolic act is not only to send a direct message but also to draw a crowd—to do something spectacular in order to draw spectators to the action and thus strengthen the message.) Generally speaking, state and federal governments may enact reasonable regulations governing the time, place, and manner of speech so long as they do not discriminate against particular messages or messengers. A limitation on political parades after 7 P.M., for example, must apply to *all* parades. Thus the Court held unconstitutional a California statute making it a felony to display a red flag "as a sign, symbol or emblem of opposition to organized government."[45] This ordinance seemed to be aimed at one particular political view.

Although today there are limits on how far one can go with actions that symbolically convey a message, the protection of such action is very broad. Thus although the Court upheld a federal statute making it a crime to burn draft cards to protest the Vietnam War on the grounds that the government had a compelling interest in preserving draft cards as part of the conduct of the war itself, it considered the wearing of black armbands to school a protected form of assembly. In these sorts of cases, a court will often use the standard it articulated in the draft card case, *United States v. O'Brien*, and now known as the "*O'Brien* test."[46] Under the terms of the *O'Brien* test, a statute restricting

---

41 *McConnell v. Federal Election Commission*, 540 U.S. 93 (2003).

42 *Federal Election Commission v. Wisconsin Right to Life*, 551 U.S. 449 (2007).

43 *Davis v. Federal Election Commission*, 554 U.S. 724 (2008).

44 *Citizens United v. Federal Election Commission*, 558 U.S. 310 (2010).

45 *Stromberg v. California*, 283 U.S. 359 (1931).

46 *United States v. O'Brien*, 391 U.S. 367 (1968).

expressive or symbolic speech must be justified by a compelling government interest and be narrowly tailored toward achieving that interest.

Another example is the burning of the American flag as a symbol of protest. In 1984, at a political rally held during the Republican National Convention in Dallas, a political protester burned an American flag in violation of a Texas statute that prohibited desecration of a venerated object. In a 5–4 decision, the Supreme Court declared the Texas law unconstitutional on the grounds that flag burning is expressive conduct protected by the First Amendment.[47] Congress reacted immediately with a proposal for a constitutional amendment reversing the Court's decision, and when the amendment failed to receive the necessary two-thirds majority in the Senate, Congress passed the Flag Protection Act of 1989. Protesters promptly violated this act, and their prosecution moved quickly into the federal district court, which declared the new law unconstitutional. The Supreme Court, in another 5–4 decision, affirmed the lower court's decision.[48] In 2003, the Supreme Court struck down a Virginia cross-burning statute, ruling that states could make cross burning a crime as long as the statute required prosecutors to prove that the act of setting fire to the cross was intended to intimidate. Justice Sandra Day O'Connor wrote for the majority that the First Amendment permits the government to forbid cross burning as a "particularly virulent form of intimidation" but not when the act was "a form of symbolic expression."[49] This decision will almost inevitably become a more generalized First Amendment protection of any conduct, including flag burning, that can be shown to be a form of symbolic expression.

Closer to the original intent of the assembly and petition clause is the category of **speech plus**—following speech with physical activity such as picketing, distributing leaflets, and other forms of peaceful demonstration or assembly. Such assemblies are consistently protected by courts under the First Amendment; state and local laws regulating such activities are closely scrutinized and frequently overturned. But the same assembly on private property is quite another matter and can in many circumstances be regulated. For example, the directors of a shopping center can lawfully prohibit an assembly protesting a war or supporting a ban on abortion. Assemblies in public areas can also be restricted under some circumstances, especially when the assembly or demonstration jeopardizes the health, safety, or rights of others. This condition was the basis of the Supreme Court's decision to uphold a lower-court order restricting the access that abortion protesters had to the entrances of abortion clinics.[50]

 speech plus

Speech accompanied by activities such as sit-ins, picketing, and demonstrations. Protection of this form of speech under the First Amendment is conditional, and restrictions imposed by state or local authorities are acceptable if properly balanced by considerations of public order

47 *Texas v. Johnson*, 491 U.S. 397 (1989).

48 *United States v. Eichman*, 496 U.S. 310 (1990).

49 *Virginia v. Black*, 538 U.S. 343 (2003).

50 For a good general discussion of "speech plus," see Louis Fisher, *American Constitutional Law* (New York: McGraw-Hill, 1990), pp. 544–6. The case upholding the buffer zone against the abortion protesters is *Madsen v. Women's Health Center*, 512 U.S. 753 (1994).

Freedom of the Press. For all practical purposes, freedom of speech implies and includes freedom of the press. With the exception of the broadcast media, which are subject to federal regulation, the press is protected under the doctrine prohibiting **prior restraint**. Beginning with the landmark 1931 case of *Near v. Minnesota*,[51] the Supreme Court has held that except under the most extraordinary circumstances, the First Amendment prohibits government agencies from seeking to prevent newspapers or magazines from publishing whatever they wish. Indeed, in the case of *New York Times v. United States*, the so-called Pentagon Papers case, the Supreme Court ruled that the government could not even block publication of secret Defense Department documents furnished to the *New York Times* by an opponent of the Vietnam War who had obtained the documents illegally.[52] In a 1990 case, however, the Supreme Court upheld a lower-court order restraining the Cable News Network (CNN) from broadcasting tapes of conversations between the former Panamanian dictator Manuel Noriega and his lawyer, supposedly recorded by the American government. By a vote of 7–2, the Court held that CNN could be restrained from broadcasting the tapes until the trial court in the Noriega case had listened to the tapes and decided whether their broadcast would violate Noriega's right to a fair trial.[53]

Libel and Slander. Some speech is not protected at all. If a written statement is made in "reckless disregard of the truth" and is considered damaging to the victim because it is "malicious, scandalous, and defamatory," it can be punished as **libel**. If an oral statement of such nature is made, it can be punished as **slander**.

Today most libel suits involve freedom of the press, and the realm of free press is enormous. Historically, newspapers were subject to the law of libel, which provided that newspapers that printed false and malicious stories could be compelled to pay damages to those they defamed. In recent years, however, American courts have greatly narrowed the meaning of libel and made it extremely difficult, particularly for politicians or other public figures, to win a libel case against a newspaper. In the important case of *New York Times v. Sullivan*, the Court held that to be deemed libelous a story about a public official not only had to be untrue but also had to result from "actual malice" or "reckless disregard" for the truth.[54] In other words, the newspaper had to *deliberately* print false and malicious material. In practice, it is nearly impossible to prove that a paper deliberately printed maliciously false information, and it is especially difficult for a politician or other public figure to win a libel case. Essentially, the print media have been able to publish anything they want about a public figure. The courts have generally been more sympathetic to libel and slander claims made by private individuals.

prior restraint

An effort by a government agency to block the publication of material it deems libelous or harmful in some other way: censorship. In the United States, the courts forbid prior restraint except under the most extraordinary circumstances

libel

A written statement made in "reckless disregard of the truth" and considered damaging to a victim because it is "malicious, scandalous, and defamatory"

slander

An oral statement made in "reckless disregard of the truth" and considered damaging to a victim because it is "malicious, scandalous, and defamatory"

---

51 *Near v. Minnesota ex rel. Olson*, 283 U.S. 697 (1931).

52 *New York Times v. United States*, 403 U.S. 713 (1971).

53 *Cable News Network v. Noriega*, 498 U.S. 976 (1990).

54 *New York Times v. Sullivan*, 376 U.S. 254 (1964).

In at least one recent case, however, the Court has opened up the possibility of public officials' filing libel suits against the press. In 1985, the Court held that the press was immune from libel only when the printed material was "a matter of public concern." In other words, in future cases a newspaper would have to show that the public official was engaged in activities that were indeed *public*. This new principle has made the press more vulnerable to libel suits, but it still leaves an enormous realm of freedom for the press. For example, the late Reverend Jerry Falwell, a cofounder of the Moral Majority, lost his libel suit against *Hustler* magazine even though the magazine had published a cartoon depicting Falwell having drunken intercourse with his mother in an outhouse. A unanimous Supreme Court rejected a jury verdict in favor of damages for "emotional distress" on the grounds that parodies, no matter how outrageous, are protected because "outrageousness" is too subjective a test and thus would interfere with the free flow of ideas protected by the First Amendment.[55]

Obscenity and Pornography. If libel and slander cases can be difficult because of the problem of determining the truth of statements and whether those statements are malicious and damaging, cases involving pornography and obscenity can be even stickier. It is easy to say that pornography and obscenity fall outside the realm of protected speech, but it is impossible to draw a clear line defining where protection ends and unprotected speech begins. Not until 1957 did the Supreme Court confront this problem, and it did so with a definition of obscenity that may have caused more confusion than it cleared up. Justice William Brennan, in writing the Court's opinion, defined obscenity as speech or writing that appeals to the "prurient interest"—that is, books, magazines, films, and other material whose purpose is to excite lust as this appears "to the average person, applying contemporary community standards." Even so, Brennan added, the work should be judged obscene only when it is "utterly without redeeming social importance."[56] Brennan's definition, instead of clarifying the Court's view, caused more confusion. In 1964, Justice Potter Stewart confessed that although he found pornography impossible to define, "I know it when I see it."[57]

All attempts by the courts to define pornography and obscenity have proved impractical because each instance required courts to screen thousands of pages of print material or feet of film alleged to be pornographic. The vague and impractical standards that had been developed meant ultimately that almost nothing could be banned on the grounds that it was pornographic and obscene. An effort was made to strengthen the restrictions in 1973, when the Supreme Court expressed its willingness to define pornography as a work that as a whole is deemed prurient by the "average person" according to "community standards," depicts sexual conduct "in a patently offensive way," and lacks "serious

---

55 *Hustler Magazine v. Falwell,* 485 U.S. 46 (1988).

56 *Roth v. United States,* 354 U.S. 476 (1957).

57 Concurring opinion in *Jacobellis v. Ohio,* 378 U.S. 184 (1964).

literary, artistic, political, or scientific value." This definition meant that pornography would be determined by local rather than national standards. Thus a local bookseller might be prosecuted for selling a volume that was a best-seller nationally but was deemed pornographic locally.[58] This new definition of standards did not help much either, and not long after 1973 the Court again began to review all such community antipornography laws, reversing most of them. This area of free speech is far from settled.

In recent years, the battle against obscene speech has focused on pornography on the Internet. Opponents of this form of expression argue that it should be banned because of the easy access children have to the Internet. The first major effort to regulate the content of the Internet occurred on February 1, 1996, when the 104th Congress passed major telecommunications legislation. Attached to the Telecommunications Act was an amendment, called the Communications Decency Act (CDA), that was designed to regulate the online transmission of obscene material. The constitutionality of the CDA was immediately challenged in court by a coalition of interests led by the American Civil Liberties Union (ACLU). In the 1997 Supreme Court case of *Reno v. ACLU*, the Court struck down the CDA, ruling that it suppressed speech that "adults have a constitutional right to receive."[59] Congress again tried to limit children's access to Internet pornography with the 2001 Children's Internet Protection Act, which required public libraries to install antipornography filters on all library computers with Internet access. The law was challenged, and in 2003 the Court upheld it, asserting that its provisions did not violate library patrons' First Amendment rights.[60] In 2003, Congress enacted the Prosecutorial Remedies and Other Tools to End the Exploitation of Children Today (PROTECT) Act, which outlawed efforts to sell child pornography via the Internet. The Supreme Court upheld this act in the 2008 case of *United States v. Williams*, in which the majority said that criminalizing efforts to pander child pornography did not violate free-speech guarantees.[61]

In 2000, the Supreme Court also extended the highest degree of First Amendment protection to cable (not broadcast) television. In *United States v. Playboy Entertainment Group*, the Court struck down a portion of the Telecommunications Act of 1996 that required cable TV companies to limit the broadcast of sexually explicit programming to late-night hours. In its decision, the Court noted that the law already provided parents with the means to restrict access to sexually explicit cable channels through various blocking devices. Moreover, such programming could come into the home only if parents decided to purchase such channels in the first place.[62]

----

58 *Miller v. California*, 413 U.S. 15 (1973).

59 *Reno v. ACLU*, 521 U.S. 844 (1997).

60 *United States v. American Library Association*, 539 U.S. 194 (2003).

61 *United States v. Williams*, 553 U.S. 385 (2008).

62 *United States v. Playboy Entertainment Group, Inc.*, 529 U.S. 803 (2000).

Fighting Words. Speech can also lose its protected position when it moves toward the sphere of action. "Expressive speech," for example, is protected until it moves from the symbolic realm to the realm of actual conduct—to direct incitement of damaging conduct with the use of so-called **fighting words**. In 1942, the Supreme Court upheld the arrest and conviction of a man who had violated a state law forbidding the use of offensive language in public. He had called the arresting officer a "goddamned racketeer" and "a damn Fascist." When his case reached the Supreme Court, the arrest was upheld on the grounds that the First Amendment provides no protection for such offensive language because such words "are no essential part of any exposition of ideas."[63] This case was reaffirmed in a much more famous and more important case decided at the height of the Cold War, when the Supreme Court held that

 fighting words

Speech that directly incites damaging conduct

> there is no substantial public interest in permitting certain kinds of utterances: the lewd and obscene, the profane, the libelous, and the insulting or "fighting" words—those which by their very utterance inflict injury or tend to incite an immediate breach of the peace.[64]

Since that time, however, the Supreme Court has reversed almost every conviction based on arguments that the speaker had used "fighting words" in a political context. (Abusive language outside a political context is unlikely to be considered protected speech.) But again, this is not an absolutely settled area. In recent years, the increased activism of minority and women's groups has prompted a movement against words that might be construed as offensive to members of a particular group. This movement has come to be called, derisively, political correctness, or PC. In response to this movement, many organizations have attempted to impose codes of etiquette that acknowledge these enhanced sensitivities. These efforts to formalize the restraints on the use of certain words in public are causing great concern over their possible infringement on freedom of speech. But how should we determine what words are "fighting words" and therefore fall outside the protections of the freedom of speech?

Student Speech. One category of conditionally protected speech is the free speech of high school students in public schools. In 1986, the Supreme Court backed away from a broad protection of student free speech rights by upholding the punishment of a high school student for making a sexually suggestive speech. The Court opinion held that such speech interfered with the school's goal of teaching students the limits of socially acceptable behavior.[65] Two years later the

---

63 *Chaplinsky v. State of New Hampshire,* 315 U.S. 568 (1942).

64 *Dennis v. United States,* 341 U.S. 494 (1951), which upheld the infamous Smith Act of 1940, which provided criminal penalties for those who "willfully and knowingly conspire to teach and advocate the forceful and violent overthrow and destruction of the government."

65 *Bethel School District No. 403 v. Fraser,* 478 U.S. 675 (1986).

Supreme Court took another conservative step by restricting students' speech and press rights even further, defining them as part of the educational process and not to be treated with the same standard as adult speech in a regular public forum.[66] An even more recent case involving high school students is the 2007 case of *Morse v. Frederick*.[67] This case dealt with the policies of Juneau-Douglas High School in Juneau, Alaska. In 2002, the Olympic torch relay passed Juneau on its way to Salt Lake City for the opening of the Winter Olympics. As the torch passed Juneau-Douglas High, a senior, Joseph Frederick, unfurled a banner that read, "Bong Hits 4 Jesus." The school's principal promptly suspended Frederick, who then brought suit for reinstatement, alleging that his free speech rights had been violated. Like most of America's public schools, Juneau-Douglas High prohibits assemblies or expressions on school grounds that advocate illegal drug use. Schools say that some federal aid is contingent on this policy. Civil libertarians, of course, see such policies as restricting students' right to free speech—a right that has been recognized by the Supreme Court since a 1969 case in which it said an Iowa public school could not prohibit students from wearing antiwar armbands. Unfortunately for Frederick, today's Supreme Court has a much more conservative cast than its 1969 counterpart. Speaking for the Court's majority, Chief Justice Roberts said that the First Amendment did not require schools to permit students to advocate illegal drug use.

In addition, scores of universities have attempted to develop speech codes to suppress utterances deemed to be racial or ethnic slurs. What these universities often find, however, is that the codes may produce more problems than they solve. Speech codes at public universities have been struck down by federal judges as unconstitutional infringements of speech. Such concerns are not limited to universities, although universities have probably moved furthest toward efforts to formalize "politically correct" speech guidelines. Similar developments have taken place in large corporations, both public and private, in which many successful complaints and lawsuits have been brought, alleging that the words of employers or their supervisors create a "hostile or abusive working environment." The Supreme Court has held that "sexual harassment" that creates a "hostile working environment" includes "unwelcome sexual advances, requests for sexual favors, and other *verbal* or physical conduct of a sexual nature"[68] [emphasis added]. A fundamental free speech issue is involved in these regulations of hostile speech.

Hate Speech. Many jurisdictions have drafted ordinances banning forms of expression designed to assert hatred toward one or another group, be they African Americans, Jews, Muslims, or others. Such ordinances seldom pass constitutional muster. The leading Supreme Court case in this realm is the 1992 decision in *R.A.V. v. City of St. Paul*.[69] Here, a white teenager was arrested for burning a cross on the lawn of a black family in violation of a municipal ordinance that

---

66 *Hazelwood School District v. Kuhlmeier,* 484 U.S. 260 (1988).

67 *Morse v. Frederick,* 551 U.S. 393 (2007).

68 *Meritor Savings Bank v. Vinson,* 477 U.S. 57 (1986).

69 *R.A.V. v. City of St. Paul,* 506 U.S. 377 (1992).

banned cross burning. The Court ruled that such an ordinance must be *content neutral*, that is, not prohibiting actions directed at some groups but not others. The statute in question prohibited only cross burning—typically an expression of hatred of African Americans. Since a statute banning all forms of hateful expression would be deemed overly broad, the *R.A.V.* standard may suggest that virtually all hate speech is constitutionally protected. In the 1993 case of *Wisconsin v. Mitchell*, however, the Court ruled that a state can consider whether a crime was motivated by bias against a minority group. So-called hate crimes can be more severely punished than similar acts committed for other reasons.[70] The Court distinguished this judgment from the *R.A.V.* decision by noting that *R.A.V.* was concerned with expression, whereas the Wisconsin ordinance in question in the *Mitchell* case was aimed at violent action.

Commercial Speech. Commercial speech, such as newspaper or television advertising, does not have full First Amendment protection because it cannot be considered political speech. Initially considered to be entirely outside the protection of the First Amendment, commercial speech has made gains during the twentieth century. Some commercial speech is still unprotected and therefore regulated. For example, the regulation of false and misleading advertising by the Federal Trade Commission is an old and well-established power of the federal government. The Supreme Court long ago approved the constitutionality of laws prohibiting the electronic media from carrying cigarette advertising.[71] The Court has upheld a state-university ban on Tupperware parties in college dormitories.[72] It has upheld city ordinances prohibiting the posting of all signs on public property (as long as the ban is total, so that there is no hint of censorship).[73] And the Supreme Court, in a heated 5–4 decision written by Chief Justice William Rehnquist, upheld Puerto Rico's statute restricting gambling advertising aimed at residents of Puerto Rico.[74]

However, the gains far outweigh the losses in the effort to expand the protection commercial speech enjoys under the First Amendment. As the scholar Louis Fisher explains, "In part, this reflects the growing appreciation that commercial speech is part of the free flow of information necessary for informed choice and democratic participation."[75] For example, the Court in 1975 struck down a state statute making it a misdemeanor to sell or circulate newspapers encouraging abortions; the Court ruled that the statute infringed on constitutionally protected speech and the right of the reader to make informed choices.[76]

---

70 *Wisconsin v. Mitchell*, 508 U.S. 476 (1993).

71 *Capital Broadcasting Company v. Acting Attorney General*, 405 U.S. 1000 (1972).

72 *Board of Trustees, State University of New York v. Fox*, 492 U.S. 469 (1989).

73 *City Council v. Taxpayers for Vincent*, 466 U.S. 789 (1984).

74 *Posadas de Puerto Rico Associates v. Tourism Company of Puerto Rico*, 478 U.S. 328 (1986).

75 Fisher, *American Constitutional Law*, p. 546.

76 *Bigelow v. Virginia*, 421 U.S. 809 (1975).

On a similar basis, the Court reversed its own earlier decisions upholding laws that prohibited dentists and other professionals from advertising their services. For the Court, medical-service advertising was a matter of health that could be advanced by the free flow of information.[77] In a 1983 case, the Supreme Court struck down a congressional statute that prohibited the unsolicited mailing of advertisements for contraceptives. In 1996, the Court struck down Rhode Island laws and regulations banning the advertisement of liquor prices as a violation of the First Amendment.[78] And in a 2001 case, the Court ruled that a Massachusetts ban on all cigarette advertising violated the First Amendment right of the tobacco industry to advertise its products to adult consumers.[79] These instances of commercial speech are significant in themselves, but they are all the more significant because they indicate the breadth and depth of the freedom existing today to direct appeals broadly to a large public, whether to sell goods and services or to mobilize people for political purposes.

The Second Amendment and the Right to Bear Arms

A well regulated Militia, being necessary to the security of a free State, the right of the people to keep and bear Arms, shall not be infringed.

The point and purpose of the Second Amendment is the provision for militias; they were to be the backing of the government for the maintenance of local public order. *Militia* was understood at the time of the Founding to be a military or police resource for state governments, and militias were specifically distinguished from armies and troops, which came within the sole constitutional jurisdiction of Congress. Some individuals, though, have always argued that the Second Amendment also establishes an individual right to bear arms. In its 2008 decision in the case of *District of Columbia v. Heller*, the Supreme Court ruled that the federal government could not prohibit individuals from owning guns for self-defense in their homes.[80] The case involved a District of Columbia ordinance that made it virtually impossible for residents to possess firearms legally. The District of Columbia is an entity of the federal government, and the Court did not indicate that its ruling applied to state firearms laws. However, in the 2010 case of *McDonald v. Chicago*, the Court struck down a Chicago firearms ordinance and applied the Second Amendment to the states as well.[81]

---

77 *Virginia State Board of Pharmacy v. Virginia Citizens Consumer Council*, 425 U.S. 748 (1976). Later cases restored the rights of lawyers to advertise their services.

78 *44 Liquormart, Inc., and Peoples Super Liquor Stores, Inc., Petitioners v. Rhode Island and Rhode Island Liquor Stores Association*, 517 U.S. 484 (1996).

79 *Lorillard Tobacco v. Reilly*, 533 U.S. 525 (2001).

80 *District of Columbia v. Heller*, 554 U.S. 570 (2008).

81 *McDonald v. Chicago*, 561 U.S. 3025 (2010).

Rights of the Criminally Accused

Except for the First Amendment, most of the battle to apply the Bill of Rights to the states was fought over the various protections granted to individuals who are accused of a crime, who are suspects in the commission of a crime, or who are brought before the court as a witness to a crime. The Bill of Rights entitles every American to **due process** of law. The concept of due process of law means that the government must respect all the legal rights to which every individual is entitled. The Fourth, Fifth, Sixth, and Eighth Amendments, taken together, are the essence of the due process of law, even though this fundamental concept does not appear until the very last words of the Fifth Amendment. In the next sections, we look at specific cases that illuminate the dynamics of this important constitutional issue. The procedural safeguards that we will discuss may seem remote to most law-abiding citizens, but they help define the limits of governmental action against the personal liberty of every citizen. Many Americans believe that "legal technicalities" are responsible for setting many criminals free. In many cases, that is absolutely true. In fact, setting defendants free is the very purpose of the requirements that constitute due process. One of America's traditional and most strongly held juridical values is that "it is far worse to convict an innocent man than to let a guilty man go free."[82] In civil suits, verdicts rest on "the preponderance of the evidence"; in criminal cases, guilt has to be proved "beyond a reasonable doubt"—a far higher standard. The provisions for due process in the Bill of Rights were added in order to improve the probability that the standard of reasonable doubt will be respected.

 due process

Proceeding according to law and with adequate protection for individual rights

The Fourth Amendment and Searches and Seizures

> The right of the people to be secure in their persons, houses, papers, and effects, against unreasonable searches and seizures, shall not be violated, and no Warrants shall issue, but upon probable cause, supported by Oath or affirmation, and particularly describing the place to be searched, and the persons or things to be seized.

The purpose of the Fourth Amendment is to guarantee the security of citizens against unreasonable (that is, improper) searches and seizures. In 1990, the Supreme Court summarized its understanding of the Fourth Amendment brilliantly and succinctly: "A search compromises the individual interest in privacy; a seizure deprives the individual of dominion over his or her person or property."[83] But how are we to define what is reasonable and what is unreasonable?

---

82 *In re Winship*, 397 U.S. 358 (1970). An outstanding treatment of due process in issues involving the Fourth through Seventh Amendments is found in Fisher, *American Constitutional Law*, chap. 13.

83 *Horton v. California*, 496 U.S. 128 (1990).

exclusionary rule

The ability of courts
to exclude evidence
obtained in violation of
the Fourth Amendment

The 1961 case of *Mapp v. Ohio* illustrates the beauty and the agony of one of the most important of the procedures that have grown out of the Fourth Amendment—the **exclusionary rule**, which prohibits evidence obtained during an illegal search from being introduced in a trial. Dollree (Dolly) Mapp was "a Cleveland woman of questionable reputation" (by some accounts), the ex-wife of one prominent boxer, and the fiancée of an even more famous one. Acting on a tip that Dolly Mapp was harboring a suspect in a bombing incident, several policemen forcibly entered her house, claiming they had a warrant to look for the suspect. The police did not find the suspect but did find some materials connected to the local numbers racket (an illegal gambling operation) and a quantity of "obscene materials," which were in violation of an Ohio law banning possession of such materials. Although the warrant was never produced, the evidence that had been seized was admitted by a court, and Mapp was charged and convicted of illegal possession of obscene materials.

By the time Mapp's appeal reached the Supreme Court, the issue of obscene materials had faded into obscurity, and the question before the Court was whether any evidence produced under the circumstances of the search of her home was admissible. The Court's opinion affirmed the exclusionary rule: under the Fourth Amendment (applied to the states through the Fourteenth Amendment), "all evidence obtained by searches and seizures in violation of the Constitution . . . is inadmissible." This means that even people who are clearly guilty of the crime of which they are accused must not be convicted if the only evidence for their conviction was obtained illegally. This idea was expressed by Supreme Court Justice Benjamin Cardozo nearly a century ago when he wrote that "the criminal is to go free because the constable has blundered."

The exclusionary rule is the most severe restraint ever imposed by the Constitution and the courts on the behavior of the police. The exclusionary rule is a dramatic restriction because it rules out precisely the evidence that produces a conviction; it frees those people who are *known* to have committed the crime of which they have been accused. Because it works so dramatically in favor of persons known to have committed a crime, the Court has since softened the application of the rule. In recent years, the federal courts have relied on a discretionary use of the exclusionary rule, whereby they make a judgment as to the "nature and quality of the intrusion." It is thus difficult to know ahead of time whether a defendant will or will not be protected from an illegal search under the Fourth Amendment.[84]

Another recent issue involving the Fourth Amendment is the controversy over mandatory drug testing. Such testing is most widely used on public employees, and in an important case the Supreme Court upheld the U.S. Customs Service's drug-testing program for its employees.[85] That same year the Court approved drug and alcohol tests for railroad workers if the workers were involved in a serious accident.[86] After Court approvals of those two cases in 1989, more

---

84 For a good discussion of the issue, see Fisher, *American Constitutional Law*, pp. 884–9.

85 *National Treasury Employees Union v. Von Raab*, 489 U.S. 656 (1989).

86 *Skinner v. Railroad Labor Executives Association*, 489 U.S. 602 (1989).

than 40 federal agencies initiated mandatory employee drug tests. The practice of drug testing was reinforced by a presidential executive order widely touted as the "campaign for a drug-free federal workplace." These growing practices gave rise to public appeals against the general practice of "suspicionless testing" of employees. Regardless of any need to limit the spread of drug abuse, doing so by testing public employees seemed patently unconstitutional, in violation of the Fourth Amendment. A 1995 case, in which the Court upheld a public school district's policy requiring that all students participating in interscholastic sports submit to random drug tests, surely contributed to the efforts of federal, state, and local agencies to initiate random and suspicionless drug and alcohol testing.[87] The most recent cases suggest, however, that the Court is beginning to consider limits on the "war" against drugs. In a decisive 8–1 decision, the Court applied the Fourth Amendment as a shield against "state action that diminishes personal privacy" when the officials in question are not performing high-risk or safety-sensitive tasks.[88] Using random and suspicionless drug testing as a symbol to fight drug use was, in the Court's opinion, carrying the exceptions to the Fourth Amendment too far.

More recently, the Court found it unconstitutional for police to use trained dogs in roadblocks set up to look for drugs in cars. Unlike drunk-driving roadblocks, where public safety is directly involved, narcotics roadblocks "cannot escape the Fourth Amendment's requirement that searches be based on suspicion of individual wrongdoing."[89] The Court also ruled that the police may not use thermal-imaging devices to detect suspicious patterns of heat emerging from private homes without obtaining the usual search warrant.[90] In 2012, the Court held that GPS tracking (such as attaching a GPS device to a vehicle to track its movements) also constitutes a search under the Fourth Amendment and therefore requires a warrant.[91]

The Fifth Amendment

> No person shall be held to answer for a capital, or otherwise infamous crime, unless on a presentment or indictment of a Grand Jury, except in cases arising in the land or naval forces, or in the Militia, when in actual service in time of War or public danger; nor shall any person be subject for the same offense to be twice put in jeopardy of life or limb; nor shall be compelled in any criminal case to be a witness against himself, nor be deprived of life, liberty, or property, without due process of law; nor shall private property be taken for public use, without just compensation.

87 *Vernonia School District v. Acton,* 515 U.S. 646 (1995).

88 *Chandler et al. v. Miller, Governor of Georgia et al.,* 520 U.S. 305 (1997).

89 *Indianapolis v. Edmund,* 531 U.S. 32 (2000).

90 *Kyllo v. United States,* 533 U.S. 27 (2001).

91 *United States v. Jones,* 565 U.S. ____ (2012).

Grand Juries. The first clause of the Fifth Amendment, the right to have a **grand jury** determine whether a trial is warranted, is considered "the oldest institution known to the Constitution."[92] Grand juries play an important role in federal criminal cases. However, the provision for a grand jury is the one important civil liberties provision of the Bill of Rights that was not incorporated by the Fourteenth Amendment to apply to state criminal prosecutions. Thus some states operate without grand juries. In such states, the prosecuting attorney simply files a "bill of information" affirming that there is sufficient evidence available to justify a trial. If the accused person is to be held in custody, the prosecutor must take the available information before a judge to determine whether the evidence shows probable cause.

Double Jeopardy. "Nor shall any person be subject for the same offense to be twice put in jeopardy of life or limb" is the constitutional protection from **double jeopardy**, or being tried more than once for the same crime. The protection from double jeopardy was at the heart of the *Palko* case in 1937, which, as we saw earlier in this chapter, also helped establish the principle of selective incorporation of the Bill of Rights. It took another 30 years for the Court to nationalize the constitutional protection against double jeopardy.

Self-Incrimination. Perhaps the most significant liberty found in the Fifth Amendment, and the one most familiar to many Americans who watch television crime shows, is the guarantee that no citizen "shall be compelled in any criminal case to be a witness against himself." The most famous case concerning self-incrimination is one of such importance that Chief Justice Earl Warren assessed its results as going "to the very root of our concepts of American criminal jurisprudence." Twenty-three-year-old Ernesto Miranda was sentenced to between 20 and 30 years in prison for the kidnapping and rape of an 18-year-old woman. The woman had identified him in a police lineup and, after two hours of questioning, Miranda confessed, subsequently signing a statement that his confession had been made voluntarily, without threats or promises of immunity. These confessions were admitted into evidence, served as the basis for Miranda's conviction, and also served as the basis of the appeal of his conviction all the way to the Supreme Court. In one of the most intensely and widely criticized decisions ever handed down by the Supreme Court, Ernesto Miranda's case produced the rules the police must follow before questioning an arrested criminal suspect.

The reading of a person's "Miranda rights" has become a standard scene in every police station and on virtually every dramatization of police action on television and in the movies. *Miranda* advanced the civil liberties of accused persons not only by expanding the scope of the Fifth Amendment clause covering coerced confessions and self-incrimination but also by confirming the right to counsel. The Supreme Court under Warren Burger and William Rehnquist considerably softened the Miranda restrictions, making the job of the police a little easier, but

---

92 E. S. Corwin and Jack Peltason, *Understanding the Constitution* (New York: Wadsworth, 2007), p. 286.

the Miranda rule still stands as a protection against egregious police abuses of arrested persons. The Supreme Court reaffirmed Miranda in *Dickerson v. United States*.[93] However, in the 2010 case of *Berghuis v. Thompkins*, the Supreme Court did introduce an important qualification to the *Miranda* rule, saying in a 5–4 decision that statements made by suspects who did not expressly waive their rights (usually by signing a form) could still be used against them.[94] The dissenting justices expressed the fear that this decision would open the way for police abuses.

Eminent Domain. Another fundamental clause of the Fifth Amendment is the "takings clause," which extends to each citizen a protection against the taking of private property "without just compensation." Although this part of the amendment is not specifically concerned with protecting persons accused of crimes, it is nevertheless a fundamentally important instance where the government and the citizen are adversaries. As discussed earlier in this chapter, the power of any government to take private property for a public use is called eminent domain. This power is essential to the very concept of sovereignty. The Fifth Amendment neither invented eminent domain nor took it away; its purpose was to put limits on that inherent power through procedures that require a demonstration of a public purpose and the provision of fair payment for the seizure of someone's property. This provision is now universally observed in all American principalities, but it has not always been meticulously observed.

The first modern case confronting the issue of public use involved a mom-and-pop grocery store in a rundown neighborhood on the southwest side of the District of Columbia. In carrying out a vast urban-redevelopment program in the 1950s, the city government of Washington, D.C., took the property as one of a large number of privately owned lots to be cleared for new housing and business construction. The owner of the grocery store and his successors, after his death, took the government to court on the grounds that taking property from one private owner and eventually turning that property back, in altered form, to another private owner was an unconstitutional use of eminent domain. The store owners lost their case, though they received cash compensation for their property. The Supreme Court's argument was a curious but very important one: that "public interest" can mean virtually anything a legislature says it means. In other words, since the overall slum clearance and redevelopment project was in the public interest, according to the legislature, the eventual transfers of property that were going to take place were justified.[95] In 1984 and again in 2005 the Supreme Court reaffirmed that decision.[96]

---

93 *Dickerson v. United States,* 530 U.S. 428 (2000).

94 *Berghuis v. Thompkins,* 560 U.S. ____ (2010).

95 *Berman v. Parker,* 348 U.S. 26 (1954). For a thorough analysis of the case, see Benjamin Ginsberg, "*Berman v. Parker*: Congress, the Court, and the Public Purpose," *Polity* 4 (1971): 48–75.

96 *Hawaii Housing Authority v. Midkiff,* 469 U.S. 2321 (1984), and *Kelo v. City of New London,* 545 U.S. 469 (2005).

The Sixth Amendment and the Right to Counsel

> In all criminal prosecutions, the accused shall enjoy the right to a speedy and public trial, by an impartial jury of the State and district wherein the crime shall have been committed, which district shall have been previously ascertained by law, and to be informed of the nature and cause of the accusation; to be confronted with the witnesses against him; to have compulsory process for obtaining witnesses in his favor, and to have the Assistance of Counsel for his defense.

Like the exclusionary rule of the Fourth Amendment and the self-incrimination clause of the Fifth Amendment, the "right to counsel" provision of the Sixth Amendment is notable for freeing defendants who seem to the public to be patently guilty as charged. Other provisions of the Sixth Amendment, such as the right to a speedy trial and the right to confront witnesses before an impartial jury, are less controversial in nature.

Gideon v. Wainwright is the perfect case study because it involved a disreputable person who seemed patently guilty of the crime for which he was convicted. In and out of jails for most of his 51 years, Clarence Earl Gideon received a five-year sentence for breaking into and entering a poolroom in Panama City, Florida. While serving time in jail, Gideon became a fairly well-qualified "jail-house lawyer," made his own appeal on a handwritten petition, and eventually won the landmark ruling on the right to counsel in all felony cases.[97] *Gideon* was decided in 1963, and the following year, in *Escobedo v. Illinois*, the Supreme Court ruled that suspects had a right to counsel during police interrogations, not just when their cases reached trial.[98]

The right to counsel has been expanded during the past few decades. For example, although at first the right to counsel was met by judges' assigning lawyers from the community as a formal public obligation, most states and cities have now created an office of public defender whose state-employed professional defense lawyers typically provide poor defendants with much better legal representation. And although these defendants cannot choose their private defense attorneys, they do have the right to appeal a conviction on the grounds that the counsel provided by the state was deficient. For example, in 2003 the Supreme Court overturned the death sentence of a Maryland death-row inmate, holding that the defense lawyer had failed to fully inform the jury of the defendant's history of "horrendous childhood abuse."[99] Moreover, the right to counsel extends beyond serious crimes to any trial, with or without a jury, that holds the possibility of imprisonment.[100]

---

97 For a full account of the story of the trial and release of Clarence Earl Gideon, see Lewis, *Gideon's Trumpet.*

98 *Escobedo v. Illinois*, 378 U.S. 478 (1964).

99 *Wiggins v. Smith*, 539 U.S. 510 (2003).

100 For further discussion of these issues, see Corwin and Peltason, *Understanding the Constitution*, pp. 319–23.

The Eighth Amendment and Cruel and Unusual Punishment

The Eighth Amendment prohibits "excessive bail," "excessive fines," and "cruel and unusual punishment." Virtually all the debate over Eighth Amendment issues focuses on the last clause of the amendment: the protection from "cruel and unusual punishment." One of the greatest challenges in interpreting this provision consistently is that what is considered "cruel and unusual" varies from culture to culture and from generation to generation. And unfortunately, it also varies by class and race.

By far the biggest issue in the inconsistency of class and race as constituting cruel and unusual punishment arises over the death penalty. In 1972, the Supreme Court overturned several state death penalty laws not because they were cruel and unusual but because they were being applied in a capricious manner.[101] Very soon after that decision, a majority of states revised their capital-punishment provisions to provide clear standards.[102] Since 1976, the Court has consistently upheld state laws providing for capital punishment, although it also continues to review numerous death penalty appeals each year.

Between 1976 and 2012, states executed 1,317 people. Most of those executions occurred in southern states, with Texas leading the way at 491. As of 2002, 38 states had adopted some form of capital punishment, a move approved of by about three-quarters of all Americans. (See the Analyzing the Evidence unit on the following page.)

Although virtually all criminal conduct is regulated by the states, Congress has also jumped on the bandwagon, imposing capital punishment for more than 50 federal crimes. Despite the seeming popularity of the death penalty, the debate has become, if anything, more intense. In 1997, for example, the American Bar Association passed a resolution calling for a halt to the death penalty until concerns about its fairness—that is, whether its application violates the principle of equality—and concerns about ensuring due process are addressed. In 2000, the governor of Illinois imposed a moratorium on the death penalty and created a commission to review the capital punishment system. After a two-year study by the commission, Illinois adopted a number of reforms, including a ban on executions of the mentally handicapped. In June 2002, the Supreme Court banned all executions of mentally handicapped defendants, a decision that could move 200 or more people off death row.[103] In 2008, the Court issued a number of death penalty opinions, declaring that death was too harsh a penalty for a child rapist[104] and invalidating a death sentence for a black defendant where the prosecutor had improperly excluded African Americans from the jury.[105] In a

---

101 *Furman v. Georgia*, 408 U.S. 238 (1972).

102 *Gregg v. Georgia*, 428 U.S. 153 (1976).

103 *Atkins v. Virginia*, 534 U.S. 304 (2002).

104 *Kennedy v. Louisiana*, 554 U.S. 407 (2008).

105 *Snyder v. Louisiana*, 552 U.S. 472 (2008).

Evaluating
the Death Penalty

Contributed by
Joseph Ura
Texas A&M University

Statistical analysis of the relationship between the availability of the death penalty as a punishment and murder rates produces mixed evidence of the deterrent effect of the death penalty. In general, analysis of national crime data indicates that there is a negative relationship between the use of the death penalty and the murder rate over the last half-century. That is, as the number of executions goes down the rate of murders nationwide goes up, and vice versa. In contrast, analysis that compares murder rates in states with the death penalty to states without it often finds that states that continue to utilize the death penalty have crime rates that are comparable to states that do not utilize the death penalty.

Evaluating the effectiveness of the death penalty deterrent presents substantial challenges for social science. The association between the use of the death penalty and crime rates over time is complicated by the close association between the number of executions and other law enforcement and penal policy changes. For example, increasing numbers of executions during the 1980s and 1990s were part of a larger trend of sending greater numbers of convicted criminals to prison for longer periods of time. Likewise, it is difficult to simply compare crime rates in death penalty states and non–death penalty states, since the comparisons are complicated by economic, social, and demographic differences among states which are associated with variance in state crime rates.

Executions and the Murder Rate

NUMBER OF
EXECUTIONS

MURDER RATE
(PER 100,000)

- Number of executions   - Murder rate

Over time, there is a reasonably strong negative relationship between the annual number of executions and the murder rate. Murder rates in the United States began to rise dramatically around 1967 and remained high until the mid-1990s. The sharp rise and subsequent decline in the murder rate corresponds to periods of declining and then increasing use of the death penalty. This aggregate correlation supports claims that the use of the death penalty deters potential murders.

SOURCE: Bureau of Justice Statistics, *FBI Uniform Crime Report.*

Incarceration and the Murder Rate

INCARCERATION RATE
(PER 100,000)

MURDER RATE
(PER 100,000)

- ● Incarceration rate
- ● Murder rate

The increased use of the death penalty in the United States during the 1990s was part of a larger trend of increased utilization of the criminal justice system. The rate of incarceration in the United States grew steadily through the 1980s before jumping dramatically during the 1990s. The growth of the penal population in the United States was also coincident with other policy changes designed to reduce crime, including a dramatic increase in the number of police officers, and changes in the American criminal landscape, such as stabilization of the market for illegal drugs. It is therefore difficult to pinpoint the effects of a single causal force out of several reinforcing developments that occurred at more or less the same time.

SOURCE: Sourcebook of Criminal Justice Statistics, www.albany.edu/sourcebook (accessed 5/20/13).

Executions and the Murder Rate per State, 2010

DEATH PENALTY

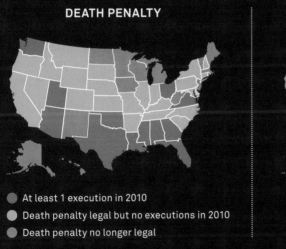

- ● At least 1 execution in 2010
- ● Death penalty legal but no executions in 2010
- ● Death penalty no longer legal

MURDER RATE
(per 100,000)

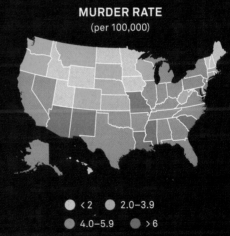

- ● < 2
- ● 2.0–3.9
- ● 4.0–5.9
- ● > 6

Across states, the relationship between the use of the death penalty and murder rates provides little evidence of a deterrent effect. In 2010, the murder rate in the 14 states that had abolished the death penalty completely was 4.3 per 100,000 people. Among the states that allow the death penalty but did not carry out an execution in 2010, the murder rate averaged 4.6 per 100,000 people. And, in the 11 states that conducted at least one execution, the murder rate averaged 5.4 per 100,000 people. The 2010 data pattern is typical, which challenges the idea that criminals are deterred from committing murder by the availability of the death penalty.

SOURCE: Bureau of Justice Statistics, *FBI Uniform Crime Report*.

decision that received worldwide attention, the Court ruled that the International Court of Justice had no authority to order a Texas court to reopen a death penalty case involving a foreign national.[106]

Many death penalty supporters praise its deterrent effects on other would-be criminals. Although studies of capital crimes usually fail to demonstrate any direct deterrent effect, the punishment's failure to act as a deterrent may be due to the lengthy delays—typically years and even decades—between convictions and executions. A system that eliminates undue delays would surely enhance deterrence. And deterring even one murder or other heinous crime, proponents argue, is more than ample justification for such laws. Beyond that argument, the death penalty is seen as a proper expression of retribution, echoed in the biblical phrase "an eye for an eye." If the world applauded the execution of Nazis after World War II, for example, how could it deny the right of society to execute a serial killer?

Constitutional objections to the death penalty often invoke the Eighth Amendment's protection against punishments that are "cruel and unusual." Yet the death penalty can hardly be considered a violation of this protection, say supporters, since it was commonly used in the eighteenth century and was supported by most early American leaders. And although the poor, men, blacks, and Latinos are more likely than others to find themselves sitting on death row, this fact reflects the painful reality that these categories of individuals are more likely to commit crimes.

Death penalty opponents are quick to point out that the death penalty has not been proved to deter crime, either in the United States or abroad. In fact, America is the only Western nation that still executes criminals. The fact that American states execute criminals debases rather than elevates society by extolling vengeance. If the government is to serve as an example of proper behavior, say foes, it has no business sanctioning killing when incarceration will similarly protect society. As for the Constitution, most of the Founders surely supported the death penalty. But, foes note, they also countenanced slavery and lived at a time when society was both less informed about, and more indifferent to, the human condition. Modern Americans' greater civility should be reflected in how the society defines individual rights.

Furthermore, according to death penalty foes, execution is expensive—more expensive than life imprisonment—precisely because the government must make every effort to ensure that it is not executing an innocent person. Curtailing legal appeals would make the possibility of a mistake too great. And although most Americans do support the death penalty, people also support life without the possibility of parole as an alternative. Race also intrudes in death penalty cases: people of color (who are more likely to face economic deprivation) are disproportionately more likely to be sentenced to death, whereas whites charged with identical crimes are less likely to be given the ultimate punishment. Finally, according to opponents, a life sentence may be a worse punishment than the death penalty.

---

106 *Medellin v. Texas*, 552 U.S. 491 (2005).

The Right to Privacy

Some of the people all of the time and all of the people some of the time would just like to be left alone, to have their own private domain into which no one—friends, family, government, church, or employer—has the right to enter without permission.

Many Jehovah's Witnesses felt that way in the 1930s. They risked serious punishment in 1940 by telling their children not to salute the flag or say the Pledge of Allegiance in school because of their understanding of the first commandment's prohibition of the worship of "graven images." As noted in our discussion of the free exercise of religion, they lost their appeal, the children were expelled, and the parents were punished. However, the Supreme Court later concluded that the 1940 decision had been "wrongly decided." These two cases arose under the freedom of religion provisions of the First Amendment, but they were also the first cases to confront the possibility of another right that is not mentioned anywhere in the Constitution or the Bill of Rights: the right to be left alone. When the Court began to take a more activist role in the mid-1950s and 1960s, the idea of a **right to privacy** was revived. In 1958, the Supreme Court recognized "privacy in one's association" in its decision to prevent the state of Alabama from using the membership list of the NAACP in the state's investigations. The Constitution does not specifically mention a right to privacy, but recall that the Ninth Amendment declares that the rights enumerated by the Constitution are not an exhaustive list.

 right to privacy

The right to be left alone, which has been interpreted by the Supreme Court to entail individual access to birth control and abortions

Birth Control. The sphere of privacy was drawn in earnest in 1965, when the Court ruled that a Connecticut statute forbidding the use of contraceptives violated the right of marital privacy. Estelle Griswold, the executive director of the Planned Parenthood League of Connecticut, was arrested by the state of Connecticut for providing information, instruction, and medical advice about contraception to married couples. She and her associates were found guilty as accessories to the crime and fined $100 each. The Supreme Court reversed the lower-court's decisions and declared the Connecticut law unconstitutional because it violated "a right of privacy older than the Bill of Rights—older than our political parties, older than our school system." Justice William O. Douglas, author of the majority decision in the *Griswold* case, argued that this right of privacy is also grounded in the Constitution because it fits into a "zone of privacy" created by a combination of the Third, Fourth, and Fifth Amendments. A concurring opinion, written by Justice Arthur Goldberg, attempted to strengthen Douglas's argument by adding that "the concept of liberty . . . embraces the right of marital privacy though that right is not mentioned explicitly in the Constitution [and] is supported by numerous decisions of this Court . . . and *by the language and history of the Ninth Amendment*"[107] [emphasis added].

---

107 *Griswold v. Connecticut*, 381 U.S. 479 (1965), and *Griswold v. Connecticut*, concurring opinion. In 1972, in *Eisenstadt v. Baird*, 405 U.S. 438 (1972), the Court extended the privacy right to unmarried women.

Abortion. The right to privacy was confirmed and extended in 1973 in the most important of all privacy decisions and one of the most important Supreme Court decisions in American history: *Roe v. Wade*. This decision established a woman's right to seek an abortion and prohibited states from making abortion a criminal act.[108] The Burger Court's decision in *Roe* took a revolutionary step toward establishing the right to privacy. It is important to emphasize that the preference for privacy rights and for their extension to include the rights of women to control their own bodies was not something invented by the Supreme Court in a vacuum. Most states did not regulate abortions in any fashion until the 1840s, at which time only 6 of the 26 states had any regulations governing abortion at all. In addition, many states had begun to ease their abortion restrictions well before the 1973 *Roe* decision, although in recent years a number of states have reinstated some restrictions on the procedure.

By extending the umbrella of privacy, this sweeping ruling dramatically changed abortion practices in America. In addition, it galvanized and nationalized the abortion debate. Groups opposed to abortion, such as the National Right to Life Committee, organized to fight the new liberal standard, while abortion rights groups sought to maintain that protection. In recent years, the legal standard shifted against abortion rights supporters in three key Supreme Court cases.

In *Webster v. Reproductive Health Services*, the Court narrowly upheld (by a 5–4 majority) the constitutionality of restrictions on the use of public medical facilities for abortion.[109] And in the 1992 case of *Planned Parenthood v. Casey*, another 5–4 majority of the Court upheld *Roe* but narrowed its scope, refusing to invalidate a Pennsylvania law that significantly limits freedom of choice. The Court's decision defined the right to an abortion as a "limited or qualified" right subject to regulation by the states as long as the regulation does not constitute an "undue burden."[110] More recently, the Court had another opportunity to rule on what constitutes an undue burden. In the 2000 case of *Stenberg v. Carhart*, the Court, by a vote of 5–4, struck down Nebraska's ban on partial-birth abortions because the law had the "effect of placing a substantial obstacle in the path of a woman seeking an abortion."[111] In 2007, however, the Supreme Court upheld a federal ban on partial-birth abortions, essentially overturning the earlier decision.[112]

Homosexuality. In the last two decades, the right to be left alone began to include the privacy rights of gay men and lesbians. One morning in Atlanta in the mid-1980s, Michael Hardwick was arrested by a police officer who discovered him in bed with another man. The officer had come to serve a warrant for Hardwick's arrest for failure to appear in court to answer charges of drinking in

---

108 *Roe v. Wade,* 410 U.S. 113 (1973).

109 *Webster v. Reproductive Health Services,* 492 U.S. 490 (1989), which upheld a Missouri law that restricted the use of public medical facilities for abortion. The decision opened the way for other states to limit the availability of abortion.

110 *Planned Parenthood v. Casey,* 505 U.S. 833 (1992).

111 *Stenberg v. Carhart,* 530 U.S. 914 (2000).

112 *Gonzales v. Carhart,* 550 U.S. 124 (2007).

public. One of Hardwick's unknowing housemates invited the officer to look in Hardwick's room, where he found Hardwick and another man engaging in "consensual sexual behavior." Hardwick was then arrested under Georgia's laws against heterosexual and homosexual sodomy. Hardwick filed a lawsuit against the state, challenging the constitutionality of the Georgia law, and won his case in the federal court of appeals. The state of Georgia, in an unusual move, appealed the court's decision to the Supreme Court. The majority of the Court reversed the lower-court decision, holding against Hardwick on the grounds that "the federal Constitution confers [no] fundamental right upon homosexuals to engage in sodomy" and that there was therefore no basis to invalidate "the laws of the many states that still make such conduct illegal and have done so for a very long time."[113]

Seventeen years later, and to most everyone's surprise, the Court overturned *Bowers v. Hardwick* with a dramatic pronouncement that gays are "entitled to respect for their private lives" as a matter of constitutional due process. With *Lawrence v. Texas*, state legislatures no longer had the authority to make private sexual behavior a crime.[114] Drawing from the tradition of negative liberty, the Court maintained, "In our tradition the State is not omnipresent in the home. And there are other spheres of our lives and existence outside the home, where the State should not be a dominant presence." Explicitly encompassing lesbians and gay men within the umbrella of privacy, the Court concluded that the "petitioners are entitled to respect for their private lives. The State cannot demean their existence or control their destiny by making their private sexual conduct a crime." This decision added substance to the Ninth Amendment "right of privacy."

The Right to Die. Another area ripe for further litigation and public discourse is the so-called right to die. A number of highly publicized physician-assisted suicides in the 1990s focused attention on whether people have a right to choose their own death and receive assistance in carrying it out. Can this become part of the privacy right, or is it a new substantive right? In the 2006 case of *Gonzales v. Oregon*, the Supreme Court upheld an Oregon law that allowed doctors to use drugs to facilitate the deaths of terminally ill patients who requested such assistance.[115] This decision is not a definitive ruling on the right-to-die question, but it does suggest that the Court is not hostile to the idea.

CIVIL LIBERTIES AND COLLECTIVE ACTION

Constitutional guarantees of civil rights and civil liberties often seem clear in the abstract, but they inevitably produce thousands of complex questions and controversies every year when they are applied to concrete cases. Every government

---

113 *Bowers v. Hardwick,* 478 U.S. 186 (1986).

114 *Lawrence and Garner v. Texas,* 539 U.S. 558 (2003).

115 *Gonzales v. Oregon,* 546 U.S. 243 (2006).

agency, for example, is constitutionally required to respect Americans' civil liberties. The government, though, is also obligated to protect the public's health and safety. This duty is sometimes called the "police power" and is exercised by the federal government and the governments of the states. Suppose that Congress enacts a law allowing national security agencies to sift through millions of phone calls searching for evidence of terrorist plots. Is such a law an unjustified intrusion on civil liberties or a necessary and legitimate effort to prevent bloodshed? In 2008, the Supreme Court declined to hear a case brought by a civil liberties group that wanted to halt a large-scale federal wiretapping program aimed at identifying possible terrorist communications. This action let stand a lower-court ruling that had allowed the program to continue. These concerns surfaced again in the summer of 2013, when a National Security Agency (NSA) contract employee released details of Operation PRISM, an elaborate NSA eavesdropping effort that resulted in the agency accessing the phone and e-mail records of millions of Americans. Civil libertarians charged that NSA had violated the law and the Constitution. President Obama and NSA officials answered that some inadvertent violations of the relevant statutes might have occurred, but that the agency's actions were needed to protect American security. As these examples suggest, the precise character of constitutional limitations on collective action is always open to debate however much we may agree on the basic principles. As part of that debate, we sift through our history to identify similar situations in the past and to determine whether the decisions made then still apply to the present. We call this the history principle; the courts call it precedent.

Civil liberties are also important examples of our collective action principle. Liberties are limitations on collective action. They identify spheres of individual autonomy into which the nation as a whole, acting through its government, is not permitted to intrude. If not for civil liberties, collective action would quickly become tyranny.

For Further Reading

Selections highlighted in red are included in *Readings in American Politics: Analysis and Perspectives*, **Third Edition.**

Ackerman, Bruce. *Before the Next Attack: Preserving Civil Liberties in an Age of Terrorism.* New Haven, CT: Yale University Press, 2006.

District of Columbia v. Heller, 554 U.S. 570, 2008.

Dworkin, Ronald. *Justice in Robes.* Cambridge, MA: Belknap Press, 2006.

Koppelman, Andrew M. *Same Sex, Different States: When Same-Sex Marriage Crosses State Lines.* New Haven, CT: Yale University Press, 2006.

Levy, Leonard W. *Freedom of Speech and Press in Early America: Legacy of Suppression.* New York: Harper & Row, 1963.

Lewis, Anthony. *Freedom for the Thought That We Hate: A Biography of the First Amendment*. New York: Basic Books, 2010.

Lewis, Anthony. *Gideon's Trumpet*. New York: Random House, 1964.

O'Brien, David. *Constitutional Law and Politics: Civil Rights and Civil Liberties*. 9th ed. New York: Norton, 2014.

Rosenberg, Gerald N. *The Hollow Hope: Can Courts Bring About Social Change?* Chicago: University of Chicago Press, 1991.

Walker, Samuel. *Presidents and Civil Liberties from Wilson to Obama*. New York: Cambridge University Press, 2012.

5

Civil Rights

Chapter Outline

- What Are Civil Rights?

- The Struggle for Civil Rights

- The Politics of Rights

- Affirmative Action

- Civil Liberties and Civil Rights: Regulating Collective Action

civil rights

The legal or moral claims that citizens are entitled to make on the government

As we observed in Chapter 4, civil liberties limit what people are allowed to do freely in society. They amount to restrictions on government, and as such they restrain the collective decision making of the people as expressed through the decisions of Congress. **Civil rights**, the topic of this chapter, also shape collective action and collective decision making, but in a very different way. Civil rights regulate *who* can participate in the political process and civil society and *how* they can participate. They determine such things as who can vote, who can serve in office, who can have a trial or serve on juries, and when and how we can petition the government to take action. The scope of civil rights is vast, stretching well beyond voting. Civil rights also define how people are treated in employment, education, and other aspects of American society.

In some nations, citizens have few, if any, civil rights. They have no right to vote, no right to stand for office, and no right to be judged by their peers if accused of a crime. America, on the other hand, began life as a nation with a number of civil rights guaranteed in both the federal and state constitutions. The federal Constitution provided such rights as representation in Congress (Article I, Section 2), established who can serve in Congress and become president, and guaranteed the privilege of habeas corpus for all people (Article I, Section 9). The Bill of Rights defined civil rights further, especially the right of all persons to due process of the laws, guaranteed in the Fifth Amendment.

America's early conception of civil rights was much narrower than it is today. Originally, the U.S. Constitution did not guarantee a general right to vote; it left voting and many other civil rights to the states. The Founders' initial rules permitted widely disparate treatment of different categories of individuals, including women, members of minority racial and ethnic groups, owners of property, and others. One way in which states limited civil rights was by linking those rights to property ownership. At the same time, states often put restrictions on who could own property. For instance, women were often not allowed to inherit property or could not own property in their own name if they were married.

In addition, women were denied the right to vote and their access to education was limited. Members of minority racial and ethnic groups also faced many forms of legally sanctioned discrimination, preventing them from voting, owning property, or securing employment. Over the 225 years since the adoption of the Constitution, there has been a tremendous expansion of civil rights to different groups of people and to different spheres of civil life.

The greatest restrictions on civil rights at the time of the American Constitution were on black people. Only 5 of the 13 original states were free states in 1789. The other 8 states permitted slavery, and slaves came almost entirely from Africa or the Caribbean. Those slaves possessed virtually no civil rights. The Constitution banned the importation of slaves after 1808, but permitted the practice of slavery to continue. Immediately prior to the Civil War, roughly 4 million African Americans were slaves in the southern states where they were the backbone of the agricultural economy of the region. Slavery was by that time prohibited in most of the Northern states, and the issue of whether or not slavery should be allowed in America's western territories bitterly divided the nation. In the 1857 case of *Dred Scott v. Sandford*, involving the fate of a former slave, the Supreme Court ruled that a former slave was not a citizen under Missouri law (the state in question), could not bring suit in court, and was merely his master's personal property. Moreover, said the Court, slavery could not be excluded from the territories.[1] This decision inflamed sectional divisions, infuriated antislavery groups in the North, and helped to provoke the Civil War.

In the aftermath of the Civil War, Congress adopted the Thirteenth, Fourteenth, and Fifteenth amendments to the Constitution to protect civil rights that had been violated by the practice of slavery. The Thirteenth Amendment prohibited slavery and involuntary servitude in the United States. The Fifteenth extended the right to vote to blacks, stating, "The right of citizens of the United States to vote shall not be denied or abridged by the United States or by any State on account of race, color, or previous condition of servitude." The Fourteenth

CORE OF THE ANALYSIS

 Civil rights are rules that govern collective decision-making processes and outcomes. They curb the power of majorities to exclude or harm individuals on the basis of factors such as race, gender, or ethnic background.

 Today's conception of civil rights has been shaped by the historical development of these ideas and their interpretation by key political actors, especially the Supreme Court.

1   *Dred Scott v. Sandford*, 60 U.S. 393 (1857).

Amendment asserted the idea of civil rights much more broadly for all citizens of the United States. Section 1 of the amendment states:

> All persons born or naturalized in the United States, and subject to the jurisdiction thereof, are citizens of the United States and of the State wherein they reside. No State shall make or enforce any law which shall abridge the privileges or immunities of citizens of the United States; nor shall any State deprive any person of life, liberty, or property, without due process of law; nor deny to any person within its jurisdiction the equal protection of the laws.

equal protection clause

The provision of the Fourteenth Amendment guaranteeing citizens "the equal protection of the laws." This clause has been the basis for the civil rights of African Americans, women, and other groups

The last clause of this section, called the **equal protection clause**, has transformed civil rights in the United States, as it creates the foundation for asserting equal civil rights for all persons. These words launched a century of political movements and legal efforts to press for racial equality. African Americans' quest for civil rights in turn inspired many other groups—including members of other racial and ethnic groups, women, people with disabilities, and gay men and lesbians—to seek new laws and constitutional guarantees of their civil rights. Their struggles were aided by the simplicity of the equal protection clause, which offers its guarantee to any person. Although the Thirteenth, Fourteenth, and Fifteenth amendments were ratified in the context of the Civil War, the Fourteenth Amendment in particular has, over time, been the basis for the expansion of civil rights to many groups in American society.

Under the Constitution today, no American may be excluded from participation or representation in collective decision-making processes or treated adversely by decision makers on account of such factors as race, gender, or ethnic background. Legislative actions and legal decrees, however, have rarely been sufficient to guarantee civil rights. As we see in this chapter, the enforcement of this guarantee was hard-won, and debates over the extent of the government's responsibility in ensuring equal protection persist. The reason is that the definition of civil rights depends not only on what laws are passed or the interpretation of the words of the Constitution but on the behavior of people in society. How can we understand historical patterns of discrimination? Are there political divisions between whites and racial and ethnic minorities such that a majority of the white population opposes the preferred candidates of a majority of the black or Hispanic populations? Is there evidence of intentional discrimination in election administration, employment, housing, and other activities?

WHAT ARE CIVIL RIGHTS?

Civil rights are the rules the government must follow with regard to the treatment of individuals when collective decisions are made. Some civil rights concern who can be involved in collective decisions and how. Other civil rights concern how people are treated in civil society, including who has access to public facilities, such as schools and public hospitals. Increasingly, civil rights have extended to private spheres of life, including the right to work, the right to marry, and whether clubs and organizations can exclude people on the basis of gender or race. Even when no legal right currently exists, civil rights are asserted as a matter of justice or morality. When there is a demand for new civil rights, society must decide whether and how rights should be extended.

Civil rights can be thought of in terms of three features: who, what, and how much. Who has a right and who does not? A right to what? And how much is any individual allowed to exercise that right?

Consider the right to vote. The "what," of course, is the vote. The "who" concerns which persons are allowed to vote. Today in the United States all citizens 18 years of age and older are eligible to vote. There are additional criteria for voting imposed by states, such as requirements in some states that voters show photo IDs or prohibiting voting by ex-felons. The "how much" concerns whether that right can be exercised equally—whether some people's votes count more than others or whether the election laws create greater obstacles for some people and make it easier for other people. For instance, until the mid-1960s, the California State Senate had one senator from Los Angeles County, with 6 million people, and one senator from Inyo County, with 14,000 people. The votes of the 14,000 people translated into the same amount of representation in the California state senate as the votes of the 6 million people. The U.S. Supreme Court ruled that arrangements such as that violated the equal protection clause and hence the civil rights of those in the more populous counties.

In the course of American history, two principles have emerged that answer "who" enjoys civil rights and "how much." First, civil rights ought to be universal—that is, all persons should enjoy civil rights. Second, civil rights ought to be equal—that is, all people who enjoy a civil right ought to be allowed an equal ability or opportunity to practice that right.

Before these principles emerged, however, some of the most profound political debates and deepest divisions in American society concerned *who* has civil rights. At the time of the Founding, most states granted voting rights exclusively to white male property owners. In 1787, the constitutions and laws of many states also imposed religious criteria, forbidding Catholics or Jews from voting, standing for office, and engaging in other public activities. Over the subsequent two centuries, there has been a dramatic expansion of the civil rights of all persons in the United States.

In the United States today, civil rights are guaranteed to all U.S. citizens. One of the first acts of Congress was the Naturalization Act of 1790, which provided the rules for granting citizenship to immigrants. Today, any person born in the United States is automatically a citizen (such people are called natural born citizens). In addition, legal immigrants to the United States can become citizens through a process of "naturalization." Generally speaking, naturalization requires that the immigrant has resided in the United States as a legal resident for at least five years, has demonstrated the ability to read, write, and speak English, has passed a basic U.S. civics and history test, and is of good moral standing.[2]

---

2 www.uscis.gov/naturalization

Citizens can live in the country and travel to other countries with all of the privileges and protections of the United States. In addition, citizens who are age 18 or older can vote. Only citizens can serve in Congress. Only a natural-born citizen can be president of the United States. Age is also a basic criterion for civil rights in the United States. Until 1971, the voting age in most U.S. states was 21, but in reaction to the draft during the Vietnam War, in which men 18 and older could be conscripted into the military, the Constitution was amended to set the voting age at 18. The Constitution also creates age criteria for running for office: you must be at least 25 years of age to serve in the U.S. House; 30 years of age to serve in the Senate, and 35 years of age to serve as president. Today, the largest groups of people not allowed to participate in American elections are those who are underage and those who are not citizens.

Interestingly, citizenship has not always been a requirement for voting in the United States. At the beginning of the nineteenth century, many states and cities allowed noncitizens to vote. In reaction to the influx of immigrants from Germany and other countries of central Europe, most states imposed citizenship requirements for voting. Even as late as the 1920s, however, there remained some municipalities in which noncitizens could vote in local elections.

The *what* of civil rights covers a wide range of fundamental rights. Perhaps the most basic civil right in any country is the right to be in the country. For much of the first century of the United States, there were virtually no restrictions on who could enter the country. In 1875, Congress passed the Page Act, which prohibited some immigrants as "undesirable." The act was introduced by Senator Horace Page to "end the danger of cheap Chinese labor and immoral Chinese women."[3] A series of subsequent acts have further defined who may enter the country, how, and for how long, including a system of quotas on immigrants from each country that lasted from 1924 to 1966. Today, U.S. immigration law requires that persons who wish to reside in the United States permanently acquire "lawful permanent resident" status (the "green card") through family- or employment-based sponsorship. The law does place some limits on the number of green cards that can be approved in a year. Problems arise, however, for people who have illegally entered the country or who have stayed beyond the term allowed for temporary visitors. As discussed later, the management of the right to be in the country remains one of the central debates over civil rights.

Political rights are also civil rights. These include the right to vote, the right to run for office, and the right to association. Indeed, much of the historical struggle over civil rights has concerned the expansion of political rights, which are today enjoyed by nearly all adult citizens.

Another class of civil rights are legal rights. The right of *habeas corpus*—the right to be presented before a court if you are accused of a crime—is one of the most basic and oldest civil rights, dating back at least to the Magna Carta,

---

3   George Anthony Peffer, "Forbidden Families: Emigration Experiences of Chinese Women under the Page Law, 1875–1882," *Journal of American Ethnic History* 6. 1 (Fall 1986): 28–46. p. 28.

the charter of liberties in England that was adopted in 1215. It is treated as a fundamental civil right granted to any person in the United States or its territories. One of the most powerful rights in the Constitution is the right to due process of law. The Fifth Amendment states that "No person shall . . . be deprived of life, liberty, or property without the Due Process of Law." That is, the federal government must respect the legal rights that are owed a person; the government cannot harm a person without following the exact course of the law. Later, the Fourteenth Amendment extended due process to state governments as well. The right to due process of law in the Constitution applies to all persons, not just certain types of people. Consequently, due process provides the foundation for the assertion of many specific types of rights and the expansion of rights beyond those favored in a particular state or federal law.

Less obvious are rights to other aspects of civil society. Do you have a right to own property? Do you have a right to education? Do you have a right to a job or to a minimum standard of living or to have access to medical care? Do you have the right to serve in the military, or not to serve in the military in the case of a draft? Do you have a right to marriage, even if you are gay or lesbian?

A wide range of economic and civil activities are, in fact, governed by civil rights. We have a right to due compensation if the government takes our property. We have the right to access to public schools, and public hospitals cannot turn away people at their emergency rooms. Answers vary as to whether one has a right to employment or to form a union at work to bargain for better wages and benefits. In some states it is exceedingly hard to form a union. In other states and in some industries, one has to be a member of a union in order to practice a trade.

Medical practice today, for instance, raises increasingly complicated questions about the right to work. An immigrant who is a medical doctor, trained and licensed in a foreign country, must still go through the American medical training and licensing procedure in order to practice in the United States. This is a restriction on the right of these people to work.

The question of *how much* individuals can exercise or assert their civil rights is perhaps the subtlest of the three dimensions. The guiding principle is that of equality. Americans adhere to a belief in equality, even when it is difficult to impose in practice. The Declaration of Independence begins with the proposition that "all men are created equal." The Constitution establishes the House of Representatives to represent all people (not just citizens, voters, or other subgroups). Perhaps most importantly, the Fourteenth Amendment to the Constitution establishes the right to equal protection of the laws for all persons. Like the due process clause, equal protection applies regardless of one's race, gender, wealth, residency, or citizenship.

The equal protection clause in the Fourteenth Amendment has been instrumental in asserting broad and equal rights for all persons in the United States. The Fourteenth Amendment applies to all persons and to all laws. One of the first ordinances struck down by the U.S. Supreme Court under the Fourteenth Amendment pertained to discrimination in labor laws, construction permits, and business licenses against Chinese legal residents.[4] In the case of *Patsone v. Pennsylvania*, the Court struck down limits on noncitizens' abilities to develop natural resources—in this case the right of an Italian immigrant for having a shotgun for purposes of hunting.[5] And in a string of decisions from 1962 to 1968, the Supreme Court ruled that the equal protection clause means that all people have equal voting rights: one person's vote cannot have greater say in collective decision making of the country than another person's.

What civil rights we enjoy and who has them is itself a political decision. The Constitution sets forth a small number of civil rights. The Bill of Rights created a larger number of legal rights. But, many of the civil rights we enjoy now were not specified explicitly in the Constitution, and instead were left to Congress and the states to determine. In other words, most of the civil rights we enjoy today are the result of legislation, litigation, and administration that took place after the country was founded. And getting government action requires collective action by those affected.

THE STRUGGLE FOR CIVIL RIGHTS

Who has what civil rights is a source of contention precisely because those who have civil rights, such as the right to vote, are asked to extend those rights to those who do not. White male property owners had disproportionate political power in 1790 because they had voting rights while no one else did. In order to expand voting rights to other groups, those who had power had to decide to remove property qualifications, extend voting rights to women and blacks, and remove other restrictions, such as age and religion. Needless to say, the expansion of voting rights has not always gone smoothly. Indeed, democracy can be a barrier to the creation of civil rights.

Consider the case of noncitizen voting rights. The first constitution of New York state, adopted in 1777, allowed all male inhabitants the right to vote. This meant that noncitizens and blacks could vote, a right they enjoyed for over 40 years. The state then experienced a backlash against the growing numbers of European immigrants and black migrants, who were settling in the city of New York. A popular vote authorized a convention to revise the state's constitution, which was rewritten so as to exclude these groups. The second constitution, adopted in 1821, restricted voting rights to male citizens and removed property qualifications for whites but not for blacks.[6] The majority of the people in the

---

4   *Yick Wo v. Hopkins*, 118 U.S. 356 (1886).

5   *Patsone v. Pennsylvania*, 232 U.S. 138 (1914).

6   For text of the first constitution see http://en.wikisource.org/wiki/New_York
    _Constitution_of_1777. For text of the second constitution see http://en.wikisource
    .org/wiki/New_York_Constitution_of_1821.

state of New York—who were white citizens—feared the growing power of immigrants, blacks, and city dwellers, and rather than lose power, they decided to take away the rights of immigrant and black populations. This situation, of course, is precisely what James Madison feared when he wrote *Federalist Paper* no. 10 during the debate over the Constitution—that a tyranny of the majority would take away the rights of the minority.[7]

American history is littered with stories akin to the 1821 New York constitution. Throughout American history, legislatures have restricted voting rights to the "right people" using poll taxes, literacy tests, registration, and redistricting. Even today, courts, legislatures, and executive branch departments have determined that some states have imposed new election laws with the effect of disenfranchising poorer people, minorities, elderly people, and students.[8] Although we might find such restrictions objectionable, they are not irrational from the point of view of those in power, who seek to safeguard their own position and interests by limiting the size of the group that can participate in collective decision making.

More amazing, then, is the fact that Americans have chosen to expand civil rights more than they have chosen to restrict them. Civil rights in legal, political, and civil society have expanded steadily over time. The initial expansions have not always come through the ballot or through the legislatures. Often it is the courts—the least democratic branch of government—that insist on the creation or expansion of civil rights. But, as we will learn in Chapter 9, the courts cannot act alone. They need the concurrence of the people and the support of the legislature and the executive to define and protect civil rights. Often, as was the case with property qualifications and women's suffrage, a public consensus emerges to change our Constitution and our laws and to expand our conception of civil rights. At other times, legal decisions can serve as the first step in a broader change in the consensus in American society, as the courts insist that democracy respect rights even when the instinct of the people runs to the contrary. However, it can take decades, even centuries, to change political cultures and to give political power and other civil rights to those who are powerless.

The Right to Vote

Voting is one of the most basic civic acts in American society; it is the backbone of our representative democracy. But the right to vote (and indeed most civil rights) is not automatic or even expressly guaranteed in our Constitution. Rather, the Constitution left the power to run elections up to the states, and the

---

7   *The Federalist*, no. 10.

8   The Department of Justice prevailed in its challenge to voter identification laws in Texas in 2012 because the procedures made getting an appropriate form of identification costly and that, the DC District Court concluded, would make it more difficult for poor people to vote. That in turn would have a disparate effect on blacks and Hispanics because higher proportions of those groups are very low income.

states carried over the suffrage rules from their colonial charters. In most states that meant that only white men with property had the right to vote; in some, only Protestants had that right. These restrictions have, from the beginning of the United States, been a source of political conflict. The right to suffrage and other civil rights cut to the core of what democracy means. Is America a democracy of all people? Can a democracy be legitimate if participation is restricted to less than half of the population? Those who have been excluded have struggled to gain the right to vote, and those who benefit from restrictions on the franchise have tried to maintain the restrictions. Over the past two centuries, legislatures and courts have defined and redefined who does and does not have this basic right. This willingness to fight over the right to vote demonstrates how significant a right it is.

Religious restrictions on the right to vote were the first to go. Article 1 of the Constitution prohibits religious tests as a qualification for "any office or Public Trust under the United States." The last religious test for civic participation was eliminated in 1825 when Maryland dropped its prohibition on Jews serving in public office.[9]

Property qualifications fell next. At the time of the Founding, most states required some form of property ownership as a criterion for voting or running for office. The states inherited this practice from Britain, where land created social title and status as well as wealth and where democracy was still a practice of the landed elite.[10] Throughout the first half of the nineteenth century, the American states began to shed the requirement that people hold property in order to vote or stand for office, especially as the economy became more industrial and less agricultural, with large numbers of people moving to cities for work. These new city denizens were less likely to own their own property. By 1850, property qualifications were eliminated as a requirement for voting and running for office. Even still, many states (for example, Wisconsin and Texas) had poll taxes well into the twentieth century. Voters would have to pay a nominal amount, such as $2, every time they voted. Poll taxes abridged the civil rights of poor people, and they were often administered so as to discriminate against black people. The Twenty-Fourth Amendment to the Constitution eliminated poll taxes in 1964.

The restrictions on the right to vote based on religion and property were removed with relatively little protest. The struggle to extend the right to vote to women and to racial and ethnic minorities, however, proved much more contentious, fueling two of the greatest struggles in American political history. The protection of the right to vote as well as other civil rights of blacks

---

9 An Act for the Relief of Jews in Maryland, Passed February 26, 1825, Archives of Maryland, Vol. 3183, p. 1670, February 26, 1825.

10 Throughout the nineteenth century and into the twentieth century the United Kingdom changed the voting requirements in England, Scotland, and Wales, most significantly dropping property requirements in the 1832 and 1867 Reform acts. For an excellent history of the politics of electoral reform in nineteenth-century England, see Charles Seymour, *Electoral Reform in England and Wales* (New Haven, CT: Yale University Press, 1915).

and other racial and ethnic minorities remains a struggle today, and the legal guarantee of those rights came only recently, with the passage of the Civil Rights Act (1964) and the Voting Rights Act (1965). The conflict over race runs so deep in U.S. politics that we will discuss that matter separately. Suffice it to say here that the Voting Rights Act remains an important, yet controversial, tool in fighting discrimination against blacks, Hispanics, and Asians in the administration of elections, and legal cases continue to find evidence of significant discrimination even today.[11]

Women's Suffrage. At the beginning of the 1800s, few municipalities granted women voting rights. New Jersey explicitly granted women the right to vote in 1790, but the legislature removed that right in 1807. It took an entire century of agitation and activism, of protest and political maneuvering, to guarantee women's voting rights. In the decades prior to the Civil War, attitudes about women's civil rights began to change. The changes came in part because of practical problems of maintaining property, inheritance, and settlement in new states and territories. The United States adapted laws of inheritance and property from Britain, which granted men control over all property, and those laws proved problematic in a country of settlers, rather than established families and classes. It is no coincidence that many of the newer states, such as Indiana and Kentucky, were the first ones to give women economic rights. At about that time, American women began to organize and engage in collective action to advance their political and social rights, including the right to vote. In 1848, women and men attending the Seneca Falls Convention issued the "Declaration of Sentiments and Resolutions," asserting that women were entitled to rights in every way equal to those of men. Present at the Seneca Falls meeting in 1848 were the people who would lead the movement for women's civil rights—Elizabeth Cady Stanton, Lucretia Mott, Mary Ann McClintock, and the abolitionist leader Frederick Douglass.

In 1869, the National Women's Suffrage Association (NWSA) was formed in New York, and it immediately began an effort to amend the U.S. Constitution to allow women to vote. By the 1880s, the issue of voting rights for women was the subject of mass meetings, parades, and protests, and as of 1917, NWSA had 2 million members. The change in laws to extend suffrage to women began in the western states and territories. In 1869, Wyoming (still a territory then) was the first to extend women the right to vote, followed by Colorado in 1893 and Utah in 1895. In 1916, Montana became the first state to elect a woman to the U.S. Congress. At last, New York, the home of the women's suffrage movement, passed a law granting suffrage to women. By 1918, all of the western states and territories plus Michigan and New York had granted women full suffrage. Once a critical mass of states had granted women the right to vote, it was only a matter of time before Congress changed federal law. In 1919, Congress passed the

---

11 In *State of Texas v. Holder*, the U.S. District Court of the District of Columbia found that the state had intentionally discriminated against blacks and Hispanics in drawing its district lines. Memorandum Opinion, Civil Action No. 11-1303, August 28, 2012.

Nineteenth Amendment granting women the right to vote in federal elections.[12] Two months later, the amendment was ratified by the states, and women across the United States voted in the presidential election of 1920.

The Right to Vote for Black Americans. The struggle to extend full voting rights to racial minorities, especially blacks, cuts to even deeper divisions in American society. It took a full century after the Civil War for Congress to guarantee minorities' voting rights with the Voting Rights Act of 1965, and the battle to protect minority voting rights continues today.

The Fifteenth Amendment to the Constitution gives blacks voting rights, and during the decade of Reconstruction the federal government enforced those rights. With the withdrawal of federal troops from the South, however, state legislatures and local governments in the South (and elsewhere) began to enact practices that excluded blacks from elections or weakened their political power. In many states, blacks were excluded from primary elections, a practice called the White Primary. Poll taxes, literacy tests, registration list purges, and other tactics were used to keep blacks from voting.[13] District and municipal boundaries were drawn to place blacks in jurisdictions in which they had little or no impact on the election of representatives or the approval of public expenditures.[14]

Blacks had little hope of changing state law because the state legislatures had written the laws and/or state legislators had benefited electorally from them. Congress was also reluctant to pass federal legislation to enforce the Fifteenth Amendment. At last the Supreme Court intervened. It struck down the White Primary in the *Smith v. Allwright* case in 1944, in which it asserted the power of the federal government to intervene in the states' conduct of elections in order to protect the voting rights of blacks.[15] The Court acted again in 1961 in the *Gomillion v. Lightfoot* case, this time ruling that state and local governments could not draw the boundaries of election districts so as to discriminate against blacks.[16] At last Congress itself intervened with the Voting Rights Act, sweeping aside a large number of state laws and practices that were used to discriminate against blacks. That act has been amended several times to expand who is covered, including Hispanics (1975) and language groups (1982), and what sorts of activities are prohibited, most notably racially discriminatory districting.

The fight over minority voting rights, however, continues. New administrative procedures, such as laws requiring that people show a government-issued photo ID, and legislative district maps, drawn every 10 years, are subject to intense scrutiny and debate. There are frequent allegations that these practices

---

12 Woman Suffrage, *Collier's New Encyclopedia*, 1921 edition. http://en.wikisource.org /wiki/Collier%27s_New_Encyclopedia_%281921%29/Woman_suffrage.

13 V. O. Key, *Southern Politics in State and Nation* (New York: Alfred A. Knopf, 1949).

14 Bernard Taper, *Gomillion v. Lightfoot: The Tuskegee Gerrymander Case* (New York: McGraw-Hill, 1962).

15 *Smith v. Allwright,* 321 U.S. 649 (1944).

16 *Gomillion v. Lightfoot,* 364 U.S. 339 (1960).

affect minorities' voting rights adversely and even embody intentional discrimination. Disputes over these laws often end up in federal courts. For their part the courts must examine not only the circumstances in which the laws were passed but they must also examine the electoral behavior in the state or area and assess the likely impact of the rules on minority voters. Since the 1982 amendments to the Voting Rights Act, this has required consultation with social scientists to develop measures of how blacks, Hispanics, and whites vote, and the likely effects of these laws on the ability of minorities to elect their preferred candidates. We discuss how political scientists address these concerns in Chapters 10 and 11. Since the 1960s, the courts—and not the legislatures—have become the arena in which minorities, poor people, city dwellers, and many others can argue for the protection of their voting rights.

In 2013 the Supreme Court declared unconstitutional an important section of the Voting Rights Act in the case of *Shelby County v. Holder*. This section— Section 4(b)—obligated jurisdictions in Alabama, Alaska, Arizona, Georgia, Louisiana, Mississippi, South Carolina, and Texas, as well as municipalities and counties in other states, to obtain approval of any change in election administration procedures from the Department of Justice or the Federal District Court in the District of Columbia—a procedure called *preclearance*. Congress had originally used a formula for determining which states needed to obtain preclearance based on the turnout of minorities relative to the turnout of whites. The Supreme Court ruled that the states no longer fit with the facts, as the ratio of minority turnout to white turnout in Alabama was similar to that in Massachusetts. The *Shelby County* case did not gut the Voting Rights Act, however, as other parts of the act still hold. The decision shifts the legal battles to those other sections.[17] It also puts the question of preclearance back on Congress's agenda.

Racial Discrimination in the Nineteenth and Twentieth Centuries

The Supreme Court was initially no more ready to enforce the civil rights aspects of the Fourteenth Amendment than it was to enforce the civil liberties provisions. The Court declared the Civil Rights Act of 1875—a key piece of reconstruction legislation written to enforce the new Constitutional provisions—to be unconstitutional on the grounds that it sought to protect blacks from discrimination by *private* businesses. The Civil Rights Act of 1875, sometimes called the Force Act, guaranteed blacks equal treatment in public accommodations, such as public transportation, and prohibited states and local governments from excluding blacks from jury service. According to the Court, the Fourteenth Amendment was intended to protect individuals from discrimination only in the case of actions by *public* officials of state and local governments. This decision gutted much of the legislation needed to make the provisions in the Thirteenth, Fourteenth, and Fifteenth amendments a reality.

---

17 *Shelby County v. Holder*, 570 U. S. ____ (2013).

***Plessy v. Ferguson*: "Separate but Equal."** In 1896, the Court went still further, in the infamous case of *Plessy v. Ferguson*. It upheld a Louisiana statute that required segregation of the races on trolleys and other public carriers (and, by implication, in all public facilities, including schools). Homer Plessy, a man defined as "one-eighth black," had violated a Louisiana law that provided for "equal but separate accommodations" on trains and a $25 fine for any white passenger who sat in a car reserved for blacks or any black passenger who sat in a car reserved for whites. The Supreme Court held that the Fourteenth Amendment's "equal protection of the laws" was not violated by racial distinction as long as the law applied to both races equally. Many people generally pretended that blacks were treated equally as long as some accommodation existed. The Court said that although

> the object of the [Fourteenth] Amendment was undoubtedly to enforce the absolute equality of the two races before the law, . . . it could not have intended to abolish distinctions based on color, or to enforce social, as distinguished from political, equality, or a commingling of the two races upon terms unsatisfactory to either.[18]

What the Court was saying in effect was that the use of race as a criterion of exclusion in public matters was not unreasonable. This was the origin of the **"separate but equal" rule**, which was not reversed until 1954.

Challenging "Separate but Equal." The Supreme Court had begun to change its position on racial discrimination before World War II by defining more strictly the criterion of equal facilities in the "separate but equal" rule. Notably, in 1938, the Court rejected Missouri's policy of paying qualified blacks' tuition to out-of-state law schools rather than admitting them to the University of Missouri Law School.[19]

After the war, modest progress resumed. In 1950, the Court rejected Texas's claim that its new "law school for Negroes" afforded education equal to that of the all-white University of Texas Law School; without confronting the "separate but equal" principle itself, the Court's decision anticipated *Brown v. Board of Education* by opening the question of whether any segregated facility could be truly equal.[20] The same was true in 1944, when the Supreme Court struck down the southern practice of "white primaries," which legally excluded blacks from participation in the process of nominating candidates. Here the Court simply recognized that primaries could no longer be regarded as the private affairs of the parties but were an integral aspect of the electoral process. This decision made parties "an agency of the State," and any practice of discrimination

---

"separate but equal" rule

→

The doctrine that public accommodations could be segregated by race but still be equal

---

18 *Plessy v. Ferguson,* 163 U.S. 537 (1896). The sole dissent to this decision came from Justice John Marshall Harlan, who wrote, "Our constitution is colorblind, and neither knows nor tolerates classes among citizens."

19 *Missouri ex rel. Gaines v. Canada,* 305 U.S. 337 (1938).

20 *Sweatt v. Painter,* 339 U.S. 629 (1950).

against blacks was therefore "state action within the meaning of the Fifteenth Amendment."[21] The most important pre-1954 decision was probably *Shelley v. Kraemer*, in which the Court ruled against the widespread practice of "restrictive covenants," whereby the seller of a home added a clause to the sales contract requiring the buyers to agree not to sell their home to any nonwhite, non-Christian, and so on.[22] The Court ruled that although private persons could sign such restrictive covenants, they could not be judicially enforced because the Fourteenth Amendment prohibits any organ of the state, including the courts, from denying equal protection of its laws.

However, none of these pre-1954 cases confronted head-on the principle of "separate but equal" as such and its legal and constitutional support for racial discrimination. Each victory by the Legal Defense Fund of the NAACP was celebrated for itself and was seen, it was hoped, as a trend, but each was still a small victory, not a leading case. The massive effort by the southern states to resist direct desegregation and to prevent further legal actions by making a show of equalizing the quality of white and black schools convinced the NAACP that the Supreme Court was not ready for a full confrontation with the constitutional principle sustaining segregation. Congress meanwhile remained unwilling to take on the issue of racial segregation in the South, especially given the power of Southern Democrats inside the U.S. Senate, as we discuss in the next chapter. Thus, even though the NAACP doubted the readiness of the courts to tackle segregation, the leadership of the organization saw the courts as its only hope. In 1952, the NAACP brought cases in South Carolina, Virginia, Kansas, Delaware, and the District of Columbia, arguing that the principle of segregation itself was unconstitutional. The strategy was to file suits simultaneously in different federal districts so that inconsistent results between any two states would more quickly lead to Supreme Court acceptance of at least one appeal.[23] The Kansas case became the focal point. It seemed to be ahead of the pack in its district court, and it had the special advantage of being located in a state outside the Deep South.[24]

Oliver Brown, the father of three girls, lived "across the tracks" in a low-income, racially mixed Topeka neighborhood. Every school-day morning, Linda Brown took a school bus to the Monroe School for black children, about a mile

21 *Smith v. Allwright,* 321 U.S. 649 (1944).

22 *Shelley v. Kraemer,* 334 U.S. 1 (1948).

23 The best reviews of strategies, tactics, and goals is found in John Hope Franklin, *From Slavery to Freedom: A History of Negro Americans,* 4th ed. (New York: Knopf, 1974), chap. 22; and Richard Kluger, *Simple Justice: The History of* Brown v. Board of Education *and Black America's Struggle for Equality* (New York: Vintage, 1977), chaps. 21 and 22.

24 The District of Columbia case came up too, but because the District of Columbia is not a state, the case did not directly involve the Fourteenth Amendment and its equal protection clause. It confronted the Court on the same grounds, however: that segregation is inherently unequal. Its victory in effect was incorporation in reverse, with equal protection moving from the Fourteenth Amendment to become part of the Bill of Rights. See *Bolling v. Sharpe,* 347 U.S. 497 (1954).

away. In September 1950, Oliver Brown took Linda to the all-white Sumner School, which was closer to home, to enter her in the third grade, in defiance of state law and local segregation rules. When they were refused, Brown took his case to the NAACP, and soon thereafter *Brown v. Board of Education* was born. In mid-1953, the Court announced that the several cases on their way up would be reargued within the context of a set of questions having to do with the intent of the Fourteenth Amendment. Almost exactly a year later, the Court responded to those questions in one of the most important decisions in its history.

In deciding the case, the Court, to the surprise of many, basically rejected as inconclusive all the learned arguments about the intent and the history of the Fourteenth Amendment and committed itself to considering only the *consequences* of segregation:

> Does segregation of children in public schools solely on the basis of race, even though the physical facilities and other "tangible" factors may be equal, deprive the children of the minority group of equal educational opportunities? We believe that it does. . . . We conclude that, in the field of public education, the doctrine of "separate but equal" has no place. Separate educational facilities are inherently unequal.[25]

The *Brown* decision altered the constitutional framework protecting civil rights in two fundamental respects. First, after *Brown*, the states would no longer have the power to use race as a criterion of discrimination in law. Second, the national government would from then on have the constitutional basis for extending its power (hitherto in doubt, as we saw earlier) to intervene with strict regulatory policies against the discriminatory actions of state or local governments, school boards, employers, and many others in the private sector.

de jure segregation

Racial segregation that is a direct result of law or official policy

de facto segregation

Racial segregation that is not a direct result of law or government policy but is, instead, a reflection of residential patterns, income distributions, or other social factors

Civil Rights after *Brown v. Board of Education*. Although *Brown v. Board of Education* withdrew all constitutional authority to use race as a criterion of exclusion, this historic decision was merely a small first step in establishing equal civil rights for blacks. First, most states refused to cooperate until sued, and many ingenious schemes were employed to delay obedience (such as paying the tuition of white students to attend newly created "private" academies). Second, even as southern school boards began to cooperate by eliminating their legally enforced **de jure segregation**, extensive actual **de facto segregation** remained in the North and the South as a consequence of racially segregated housing, which was not affected by the 1954 *Brown* principles. Third, discrimination in employment, public accommodations, juries, voting, and other areas of social and economic activity was not directly touched by *Brown*.

A decade of frustration following *Brown* made it fairly obvious that adjudication alone would not succeed. The goal of equal protection required positive, or affirmative, action by Congress and administrative agencies. And given massive southern resistance and generally negative national public opinion toward racial

---

25 *Brown v. Board of Education*, 347 U.S. 483 (1954).

integration, progress would not be made through courts, Congress, or agencies without intense, well-organized support. The number of peaceful civil rights demonstrations for voting rights and public accommodations increased greatly during the first 14 years following *Brown*.[26]

Organized civil rights demonstrations began to mount slowly but surely after *Brown v. Board of Education*. In an impressive demonstration of collective political action, hundreds of thousands of Americans, both black and white, exercised their right to peaceably assemble and petition the government for a redress of grievances, demanding that the civil rights guaranteed to white Americans now be recognized and protected for black Americans too. By the 1960s, the many organizations that made up the civil rights movement had accumulated experience and built networks capable of launching massive direct-action campaigns against southern segregationists. The Southern Christian Leadership Conference, the Student Nonviolent Coordinating Committee, and many other organizations had built a movement that stretched across the South. That movement used the media to attract nationwide attention and support. In the massive March on Washington in 1963, the Reverend Martin Luther King, Jr., staked out the movement's moral claims in his "I Have a Dream" speech. Also in the 1960s, images of protesters being beaten, attacked by police dogs, and set on with fire hoses did much to win broad sympathy for the cause of black civil rights and discredit state and local governments in the South. In this way, the movement created intense pressure for a reluctant federal government to take more assertive steps to defend black civil rights.

Why Fight for Civil Rights? Collective Action and Selective Benefits.

One of the tenets of our five principles of politics from Chapter 1 is that individuals have little incentive to participate in mass-action politics. After all, what possible difference could one person make by taking part in a civil rights protest? Participation is costly in terms of time, and in the case of civil rights marchers even one's health or life was endangered. The risks outweighed the potential benefits, yet hundreds of thousands of people *did* participate. Why?

Even though little scholarly attention has been paid by those who apply this perspective to the civil rights movements,[27] a general answer is available. Most rational analysis takes behavior to be *instrumental*—motivated by and directed toward some purpose or objective. But behavior may also be *experiential*. People do things, on this account, because they like doing them—they feel good inside, they feel free of guilt, they take pleasure in the activity for its own sake. We maintain that this second view of behavior is entirely compatible with rational accounts. Instrumental behavior may be thought of as *investment activity*, whereas experiential behavior may be thought of as *consumption activity*. With the latter, it is the behavior itself that generates utility, rather than the consequences produced by the behavior. To take a specific illustration of collective action, many

---

26 Jonathan D. Casper, *The Politics of Civil Liberties* (New York: Harper & Row, 1972), p. 90.

27 One notable exception is Dennis Chong, *Collective Action and the Civil Rights Movement* (Chicago: University of Chicago Press, 1991).

CAUSE AND EFFECT IN THE CIVIL RIGHTS MOVEMENT

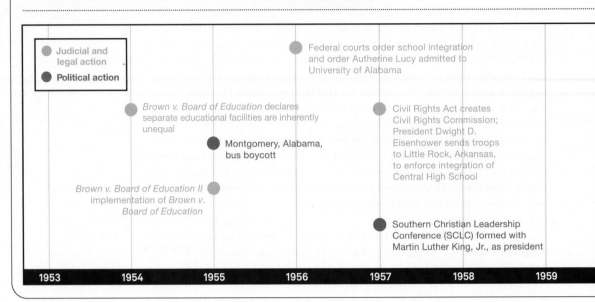

Judicial and
legal action

Political action

Federal courts order school integration
and order Autherine Lucy admitted to
University of Alabama

Brown v. Board of Education declares
separate educational facilities are inherently
unequal

Montgomery, Alabama,
bus boycott

Civil Rights Act creates
Civil Rights Commission;
President Dwight D.
Eisenhower sends troops
to Little Rock, Arkansas,
to enforce integration of
Central High School

Brown v. Board of Education II
implementation of *Brown v.
Board of Education*

Southern Christian Leadership
Conference (SCLC) formed with
Martin Luther King, Jr., as president

| 1953 | 1954 | 1955 | 1956 | 1957 | 1958 | 1959 |

people certainly attended the 1963 March on Washington because they cared about civil rights. But it is unlikely that many deluded themselves into thinking their individual participation made a large difference to the fate of the civil rights legislation they supported through the march. Rather, they attended because they wanted to be part of a social movement, hear Martin Luther King, Jr., speak, and identify with the hundreds of thousands of others who felt the same way. Also—and this should not be minimized—many participated because they anticipated that the march would be fun, an adventure of sorts.

So experiential behavior is consumption-oriented activity predicated on the belief that the activity in question is fulfilling, apart from its consequences. Individuals are bound to be animated both by the consumption value of a particular behavior and by its instrumental value, the rational (investment) explanation that we have used throughout this book. To insist on only one of these complementary forms of rationality while excluding the other is to provide but a partial explanation.

Opportunity in Education

Education has been the focus of some of the most important battles over civil rights. An important reason is that Americans believe that everyone should have an equal chance to succeed in life. That commitment to equality is underscored by the centrality of public education in the United States. Since the early nineteenth century American communities and states have provided

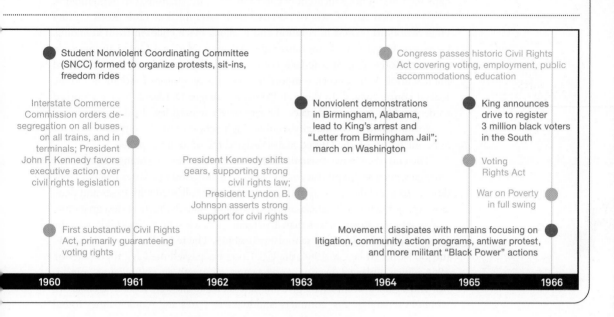

Student Nonviolent Coordinating Committee (SNCC) formed to organize protests, sit-ins, freedom rides

Interstate Commerce Commission orders de-segregation on all buses, on all trains, and in terminals; President John F. Kennedy favors executive action over civil rights legislation

First substantive Civil Rights Act, primarily guaranteeing voting rights

President Kennedy shifts gears, supporting strong civil rights law; President Lyndon B. Johnson asserts strong support for civil rights

Nonviolent demonstrations in Birmingham, Alabama, lead to King's arrest and "Letter from Birmingham Jail"; march on Washington

Movement dissipates with remains focusing on litigation, community action programs, antiwar protest, and more militant "Black Power" actions

Congress passes historic Civil Rights Act covering voting, employment, public accommodations, education

King announces drive to register 3 million black voters in the South

Voting Rights Act

War on Poverty in full swing

| 1960 | 1961 | 1962 | 1963 | 1964 | 1965 | 1966 |

public education to all persons. That has been essential to help immigrants join our society—to help them learn English, learn our society's values, and learn skills necessary to gain employment. Universal access to public education has also helped produce one of the most efficient and productive workforces in the world. Leaving large segments of our population uneducated is potentially bad for the economy, and it is certainly bad for those people. Grossly unequal opportunities for children to receive education will likely mean grossly unequal opportunities for individuals to have a good job, to participate in politics, and to realize their potential.

Those inequities in educational opportunities were painfully obvious in the 1950s. Poverty rates of blacks far exceeded those of whites. Equal access to quality education, it was thought, would reduce and perhaps eliminate those inequities over the course of a generation.

School Desegregation, Phase One. Although the District of Columbia and some of the school districts in the border states began to respond almost immediately to court-ordered desegregation, the states of the Deep South responded with a carefully planned delaying tactic known as *massive resistance*. Southern politicians stood shoulder to shoulder to declare that the Supreme Court's decisions and orders were without effect. The legislatures in these states enacted statutes ordering school districts to maintain segregated schools and state superintendents to terminate state funding wherever there was racial mixing in the classroom.

Most of these plans were tested in the federal courts and struck down as unconstitutional.[28] But southern resistance was not confined to legislation. Perhaps the most serious incident occurred in 1957, in Arkansas. On September 4, 1957—the first day of school—a large mob assembled at Little Rock Central High School to protest integration and to block black children from attending. Governor Orval Faubus mobilized the Arkansas National Guard to intercede against enforcement of a federal court order to integrate Little Rock's Central High School. A three-week standoff between the governor of Arkansas and the federal courts ensued. In the end, President Dwight D. Eisenhower was forced to deploy U.S. troops and place the city under martial law. Faubus responded by closing all four of the city's public high schools. In December 1959, the Supreme Court of the United States ordered the schools reopened.

The end of massive resistance, however, became the beginning of still other strategies, such as "pupil placement" laws.[29] As the southern states invented new devices to avoid desegregation, the federal courts followed with cases and decisions quashing them. That cat-and-mouse game stalled efforts at desegregation. Ten years after *Brown,* fewer than 1 percent of black school-age children in the Deep South were attending schools with whites. The federal courts could not do the job alone. At last, in 1964, the U.S. Congress passed the Civil Rights Act of 1964, which outlawed discrimination against racial, ethnic, and religious minorities and against women. To give the law teeth, it allowed federal agencies to withhold federal grants, contracts, and loans to states and municipalities found to discriminate or obstruct the implementation of the law.

It is important to observe here the mutual dependence of the courts and the legislatures—not only do the legislatures need constitutional authority to act but the courts also need legislative and political assistance, through the power of the purse, the power to organize administrative agencies to implement court orders, and the ability to focus political support. Consequently, even as Congress finally moved into the field of school desegregation (and other areas of equal protection), the courts continued to exercise their powers, not only by issuing court orders against recalcitrant school districts but also by extending and reinterpreting aspects of the equal protection clause to support legislative and administrative actions.

School Desegregation: Busing and Beyond. The most important judicial extension of civil rights in education after 1954 was probably the *Swann* decision of 1971, which held that state-imposed desegregation could be brought

---

28 The two most important cases were *Cooper v. Aaron*, 358 U.S. 1 (1958), which required Little Rock, Arkansas, to desegregate, and *Griffin v. Prince Edward County School Board*, 377 U.S. 218 (1964), which forced all the schools of that Virginia county to reopen after they had been closed for five years to avoid desegregation.

29 *Shuttlesworth v. Birmingham Board of Education*, 358 U.S. 101 (1958), upheld a pupil placement plan purporting to assign pupils on various bases, with no mention of race. This case interpreted *Brown* to mean that school districts must stop explicit racial discrimination but were under no obligation to take positive steps to desegregate. For a while, black parents were doomed to case-by-case approaches.

about by busing children across school districts even where relatively long distances were involved. But the decision went beyond that, adding that under certain limited circumstances even racial quotas could be used as the "starting point in shaping a remedy to correct past constitutional violations" and that the pairing or grouping of schools and the reorganizing of school attendance zones would also be acceptable (Figure 5.1).[30]

Three years later, however, the *Swann* case was severely restricted when the Supreme Court determined that only cities found guilty of deliberate and de jure racial segregation (segregation in law) would have to desegregate their schools. This decision was handed down in the 1974 case of *Milliken v. Bradley*, involving the city of Detroit and its suburbs.[31] The *Milliken* ruling had the effect of

Figure 5.1

PERCENTAGE OF SOUTHERN BLACK CHILDREN ATTENDING SCHOOL WITH WHITES, 1955–73

ANALYZING THE EVIDENCE

What happened in 1964 that accounts for the upward trend beginning in 1965?

NOTE: Dashed line indicates missing data.
SOURCE: Gerald N. Rosenberg, *The Hollow Hope: Can Courts Bring About Social Change?* (Chicago: University of Chicago Press, 1991), pp. 50–51.

30 *Swann v. Charlotte-Mecklenburg Board of Education*, 402 U.S. 1 (1971).

31 *Milliken v. Bradley*, 418 U.S. 717 (1974).

exempting most northern states and cities from busing because school segregation in northern cities is generally de facto (segregation in fact), resulting from segregated housing and thousands of acts of private discrimination against blacks and other minorities.

Additional progress in the desegregation of schools is likely to be extremely slow unless the Supreme Court decides to permit federal action against de facto segregation and the various kinds of private schools and academies that have sprung up for the purpose of avoiding integration. The prospects for further school integration diminished with a series of Supreme Court decisions handed down in the 1990s. In 1995, for example, in *Missouri v. Jenkins*, the Court signaled to the lower courts that they should "disengage from desegregation efforts."[32] This is a direct and explicit threat to the main basis of the holding in the original 1954 *Brown v. Board of Education* decision. In 2007, the Court went further, declaring unconstitutional programs put in place by the Louisville and Seattle school districts that used race as a determining factor in admissions in order to achieve racial diversity. Provocatively, Chief Justice John Roberts quoted the counsel for Oliver Brown in his decision for the majority, writing, "We have one fundamental contention which we will seek to develop in the course of this argument, and that contention is that no state has any authority under the equal protection clause of the Fourteenth Amendment to use race as a factor in affording educational opportunities among its citizens."[33]

Women and Education. Women have also suffered from unequal access to education. Throughout the nineteenth century, relatively few colleges and professional schools admitted women. (Oberlin College was the first to do so.) Even as late as the 1960s, elite universities such as Harvard and Yale did not admit women, and even at colleges that did admit women, women had many fewer opportunities to participate in programs, clubs, and athletics. Congress took an initial step to remedy these inequities with the Civil Rights Act of 1964, but the most significant federal legislation to guarantee women equal access to education is the 1972 Education Act. Title IX of this act forbids gender discrimination in education. The Education Act provided the nudge that many schools needed. By the mid-1970s most universities had become fully coed. But enforcing equality was more difficult.

The Education Act of 1972 provided fairly weak enforcement provisions, but it has proven an effective tool for litigation. Perhaps the most significant step came in 1992, when the Court decided in *Franklin v. Gwinnett County Public Schools* that violations of Title IX of the 1972 Education Act could be remedied with monetary damages.[34] The Court's 1992 ruling opened the door for further legal action in the area of education and led to stronger enforcement against

---

32 *Missouri v. Jenkins*, 515 U.S.70 (1995). The quotation is from David M. O'Brien, *Supreme Court Watch 1996* (New York: Norton, 1996), p. 220.

33 *Parents Involved in Community Schools v. Seattle School District No. 1*, 551 U.S. 701 (2007).

34 *Franklin v. Gwinnett County Public Schools*, 503 U.S. 60 (1992).

---

sexual harassment, gender inequities in resources (such as lab space, research support for faculty, and athletics), and gender inequities in compensation. In the two years after the *Franklin* case, complaints to the Education Department's Office for Civil Rights about unequal treatment of women's athletic programs nearly tripled. In several high-profile legal cases, some prominent universities have been ordered to create more women's sports programs; many other colleges and universities have begun to add more women's programs in order to avoid potential litigation.[35]

In 1996, the Supreme Court made another important decision about gender and education by putting an end to all-male schools supported by public funds. It ruled that the Virginia Military Institute's policy of not admitting women was unconstitutional.[36] Along with the Citadel, an all-male military college in South Carolina, Virginia Military Institute (VMI) had never admitted women. It argued that the unique educational experience it offered, including intense physical training and the harsh treatment of freshmen, would be destroyed if women were admitted. The Court, however, ruled that the male-only policy denied "substantial equality" to women. Two days after the Court's ruling, the Citadel announced that it would accept women. VMI considered becoming a private institution in order to remain all male, but in September 1996 the school board finally voted to admit women. The legal decisions may have removed formal barriers to entry, but the experience of the female cadets at these schools has not been easy. The first female cadet at the Citadel, Shannon Faulkner, won admission in 1995 under a federal court order but quit after four days. Although four women were admitted to the Citadel after the Supreme Court decision, two of them quit several months later. They charged harassment by male students, including attempts to set the female cadets on fire.[37]

THE POLITICS OF RIGHTS

The Nineteenth Amendment, *Brown v. Board of Education*, the Civil Rights Acts, and the Voting Rights Act were the signal achievements of the civil rights movements of women and blacks. They helped redefine the meaning of civil rights in America not just for those groups but for all people. The civil rights movements of women and of blacks became models for other groups of people to press civil rights claims, and the strategies of the NWSA and the NAACP have been widely mimicked (see the Analyzing the Evidence unit). The principles behind equality in voting and in education have since

---

35 Jennifer Halperin, "Women Step Up to Bat," *Illinois Issues 21* (September 1995): 11–14.

36 *United States v. Virginia,* 518 U.S. 515 (1996).

37 Judith Havemann, "Two Women Quit Citadel over Alleged Harassment," *Washington Post,* January 13, 1997, p. A1.

Advocacy and Representation for Marginalized Groups

Contributed by
Dara Z. Strolovitch
Princeton University

Historically, women, people of color, and low-income people have faced institutional barriers to participating in collective political processes. When formal avenues of participation, such as voting, are closed, these groups have turned to advocacy organizations as a means to offset this paucity of legislative representation. Indeed, for many years, national advocacy organizations offered some of the only political voice and visibility available to groups such as African Americans in the South and women of all races, who were denied formal voting rights until well into the twentieth century. Long before most women could vote, for example, the National American Woman Suffrage Association mounted protests and lobbied legislators.

The extension of certain formally recognized civil rights to women, people of color, and low-income people has not ended the need for advocacy organizations, however, and the second half of the twentieth century witnessed an explosion in the number of organizations representing these groups. By speaking for marginalized populations on the national political stage, such organizations provide a crucial bridge between the often unheard political voices of underrepresented groups and government institutions, helping to reduce racial, gender, and sex-based discrimination and to create new resources and opportunities for low-income people.

Number of National Women's, People of Color, and Economic Justice Organizations Founded by Decade, 1850–2000

NUMBER

DECADE FOUNDED

SOURCES: The 2000 Survey of Social and Economic Justice Advocacy, Dara Z. Strolovitch, *Affirmative Advocacy: Race, Class, and Gender in Interest Group Politics* (Chicago: University of Chicago Press, 2007); and the 2007 Study of Public Interest Advocacy in the New Millennium, Dara Z. Strolovitch, "Affirmative Advocacy in Hard Times," in *Nonprofit Advocacy*, Steven Smith, Yutaka Tsujinaka, and Robert Pekkanen, eds. (Baltimore: Johns Hopkins Press, forthcoming).

But while the proliferation of advocacy organizations is a striking feature of contemporary American politics, the extent to which these groups have leveled the representational playing field is unclear. First, the growth in the number of social and economic justice organizations has been vastly outpaced by increased numbers of business and professional organizations, and organizations that represent marginalized groups constitute only a modest proportion of the larger interest group universe.

Interests Represented by Organizations in Washington

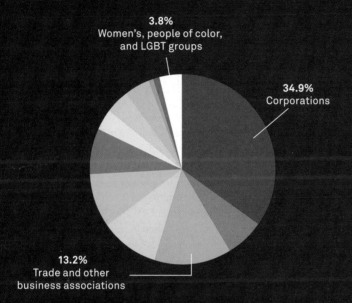

3.8%
Women's, people of color, and LGBT groups

34.9%
Corporations

13.2%
Trade and other business associations

INTERESTS

- Women's, people of color, and LGBT groups = 3.8%
- Unions = 1%
- Poverty/social welfare = **0.8%**
- Public interest = **4.6%**
- Education = **4.2%**
- Health = **3.5%**
- Foreign = **7.8%**
- Other/unknown = **9.1%**
- State and local governments = **10.4%**
- Trade and other business associations = **13.2%**
- Occupational associations = **6.8%**
- Corporations = **34.9%**

Kay Lehman Schlozman and her coauthors collected data about the nearly 12,000 organizations with representatives in Washington, D.C. Over a third of these organizations represent corporations, while labor unions account for 1 percent, social welfare organizations for 0.8 percent, and groups speaking for women, people of color, and LGBT people together account for a mere 3.8 percent.

SOURCE: Kay Lehman Schlozman, Sidney Verba, and Henry E. Brady, *The Unheavenly Chorus: Unequal Political Voice and the Broken Promise of American Democracy* (Princeton, NJ: Princeton University Press, 2012), p. 321.

Advocacy organizations that represent women, people of color, and low-income people have also been criticized for focusing on the needs of the more advantaged members of the marginalized constituencies. Research confirms the validity of this criticism: a survey of 286 organizations found that women's and African American groups, for example, were much more active on affirmative action in higher education than they were on the welfare reform legislation that passed in 1996, which had major implications for low-income women and people of color.[1] Although advocacy organizations can fall short, however, many take deliberate steps to more effectively represent disadvantaged constituents.

1 Dara Z. Strolovitch, *Affirmative Advocacy: Race, Class, and Gender in Interest Group Politics* (Chicago: University of Chicago Press, 2007).

been applied to many other areas, including employment, housing, immigration, access to public facilities, and athletics. With the push for rights in these spheres, there has also been a push back. Just how far do civil rights extend?

Outlawing Discrimination in Employment

The federal courts and the Justice Department entered the arena of discrimination in employment through Title VII of the Civil Rights Act of 1964, which outlaws job discrimination by all private and public employers, including government agencies (such as fire and police departments), that employ more than 15 workers. We have already seen that the Supreme Court gave "interstate commerce" such a broad definition that Congress had the constitutional authority to ban discrimination by virtually any local employers.[38] Title VII makes it unlawful to discriminate in employment on the basis of color, religion, sex, or national origin, as well as race.

A potential difficulty with Title VII is that the complaining party has to show that deliberate discrimination was the cause of the failure to get a job or a training opportunity. Of course, rarely does an employer explicitly admit discrimination on the basis of race, sex, or any other illegal reason. Recognizing the rarity of such an admission, the courts have allowed aggrieved parties (the plaintiffs) to make their case if they can show that an employer's hiring practices had the *effect* of exclusion. A leading case in 1971 involved a class action by several black employees in North Carolina attempting to show with statistical evidence that blacks had been relegated to one department of the Duke Power Company, which involved the least desirable of manual labor jobs, and that they had been kept out of contention for the better jobs because the employer had added high school education and passing grades on specially prepared aptitude tests as qualifications for those jobs. The Supreme Court held that although the statistical evidence did not prove intentional discrimination and the requirements were race neutral in appearance, their effects were sufficient to shift the burden of justification to the employer to show that the requirements were a "business necessity" that bore "a demonstrable relationship to successful performance."[39] The ruling in this case was subsequently applied to other hiring, promotion, and training programs.[40] In recent years, though, the Supreme Court has placed a number of limits on employment discrimination suits. In 2007, for example, in the case of *Ledbetter v. Goodyear Tire and Rubber Co.* the Court said that a complaint of gender discrimination must be brought within 180 days of the time the

---

38 See especially *Katzenbach v. McClung*, 379 U.S. 294 (1964).

39 *Griggs v. Duke Power Company*, 401 U.S. 424 (1971). See also Allan P. Sindler, *Bakke, DeFunis, and Minority Admissions: The Quest for Equal Opportunity* (New York: Longman, 1978), pp. 180–9.

40 For a good treatment of these issues, see Charles O. Gregory and Harold A. Katz, *Labor and the Law*, 3rd ed. (New York: Norton, 1979), chap. 17.

discrimination was alleged to have occurred.[41] This blocks suits based on events that might have taken place in the past. In 2009, Congress enacted the Ledbetter Fair Pay Act to overturn the Court's decision and give workers more time to file pay discrimination claims. And in a pair of important 2008 decisions, the Court helped individuals who sought to bring employment discrimination complaints by declaring that employers were barred from retaliating against them.[42] Fear of retaliation is a powerful force discouraging employees from seeking to assert their legal rights.

Women and Gender Discrimination

Although women succeeded in gaining voting and property rights long ago, women continue to suffer discrimination in a variety of forms, particularly in the realm of employment. Here, women benefited from the civil rights movement and, especially, from Title VII. Title VII not only provided a valuable tool for the growing women's movement in the 1960s and 1970s but in many ways the law actually fostered the movement's growth.[43] The National Organization for Women's (NOW) first major campaign involved picketing the Equal Employment Opportunity Commission (EEOC) for its refusal to ban sex-segregated employment advertisements.

Building on these victories and the growth of the women's movement, women's rights activists sought an equal rights amendment (ERA) to the Constitution. The proposed amendment was short: its substantive passage stated that "equality of rights under the law shall not be denied or abridged by the United States or by any State on account of sex." The amendment's supporters believed that such a sweeping guarantee of equal rights was a necessary tool for ending all discrimination against women and for making gender roles more equal. Opponents charged that it would be socially disruptive and would introduce changes—such as coed restrooms—that most Americans did not want. The amendment easily passed Congress in 1972 and won quick approval in many state legislatures but fell three states short of the 38 needed to ratify the amendment by the 1982 deadline for its ratification.[44]

Despite the failure of the ERA, gender discrimination expanded dramatically as an area of civil rights law. In the 1970s, the conservative Burger Court helped to establish gender discrimination as a major and highly visible civil

41 *Ledbetter v. Goodyear Tire and Rubber Co.*, 550 U.S. 618 (2007).

42 *CBOC West v. Humphries*, 553 U.S. 442 (2008); *Gomez-Perez v. Potter*, 553 U.S. 474 (2008).

43 Material in this and subsequent sections is adapted from Benjamin Ginsberg, Theodore J. Lowi, Margaret Weir, and Caroline J. Tolbert, *We the People: An Introduction to American Politics*, 9th ed. (New York: Norton, 2013).

44 See Jane J. Mansbridge, *Why We Lost the ERA* (Chicago: University of Chicago Press, 1986); and Gilbert Steiner, *Constitutional Inequality* (Washington, DC: Brookings Institution, 1985).

intermediate scrutiny

The test used by the Supreme Court in gender discrimination cases. Intermediate scrutiny places the burden of proof partially on the government and partially on the challengers to show that the law in question is constitutional

rights issue. Although the Burger Court refused to treat gender discrimination as equivalent to racial discrimination,[45] it did make it easier for plaintiffs to file and win suits on the basis of gender discrimination by applying an "intermediate" level of review to these cases.[46] This **intermediate scrutiny** is midway between traditional rules of evidence, which put the burden of proof on the plaintiff, and the doctrine of strict scrutiny, which requires the defendant to show not only that a particular classification is reasonable but also that there is a need or compelling interest for it. Intermediate scrutiny shifts the burden of proof partially onto the defendant, rather than leaving it entirely on the plaintiff.

Elevated awareness of sexual harassment as a form of gender discrimination has also advanced the cause of women's civil rights. Courts began to find sexual harassment a form of sex discrimination during the late 1970s. In 1986, the Supreme Court recognized two forms of sexual harassment—the quid pro quo type, which involves sexual extortion, and the hostile-environment type, which involves sexual intimidation.[47] In its decision the Court said that sexual harassment may be legally actionable even if the employee did not suffer tangible economic or job-related losses in relation to it. And in 1993, the Court said that sexual harassment may be legally actionable even if the employee did not suffer tangible psychological costs as a result of it.[48] In two 1998 cases, the Court further strengthened the law when it said that whether or not sexual harassment results in economic harm to the employee, an employer is liable for the harassment if it was committed by someone with authority over the employee—by a supervisor, for example. But the Court also said that an employer may defend itself by showing that it had a sexual harassment prevention and grievance policy in effect.[49]

The development of gender discrimination as an important part of the civil rights struggle has coincided with the rise of women's politics as a discrete movement in American politics. As with the struggle for racial equality, the relationship between changes in government policies and political action suggests that changes in government policies to a great degree produce political action. Today the existence of a powerful women's movement derives in large measure from the enactment of Title VII of the Civil Rights Act of 1964 and from the Burger Court's vital steps in applying that law to the protection of women. The recognition of women's civil rights has become an issue that in many ways transcends the usual distinctions of American political debate. In the heavily partisan debate over the federal crime bill enacted in 1994, for instance, the section

---

45 See *Frontiero v. Richardson*, 411 U.S. 677 (1973).

46 See *Craig v. Boren*, 423 U.S. 1047 (1976).

47 *Meritor Savings Bank v. Vinson*, 477 U.S. 57 (1986).

48 *Harris v. Forklift Systems*, 510 U.S. 17 (1993).

49 *Burlington Industries v. Ellerth*, 524 U.S. 742 (1998); *Faragher v. City of Boca Raton*, 524 U.S. 775 (1998).

of the bill that enjoyed the widest support was the Violence against Women Act, whose most important feature was that it defined gender-biased violent crimes as a matter of civil rights and created a civil rights remedy for women who have been the victims of such crimes. But since the Supreme Court ruled key provisions of the act unconstitutional in 2000, the struggle for women's rights will likely remain part of the political debate.

Latinos

The labels "Latino" and "Hispanic" encompass a wide range of groups with diverse national origins, distinctive cultural identities, and particular experiences. For example, the early political experiences of Mexican Americans were shaped by race and region. In 1898, Mexican Americans were given formal political rights, including the right to vote. In many places, however, and especially in Texas, Mexican Americans were segregated and prevented from voting by such means as the white primary and the poll tax.[50]

The earliest independent Mexican American political organizations, the League of United Latin American Citizens (LULAC) and the American GI Forum, worked to stem discrimination against Mexican Americans in the years after World War II. By the late 1950s, the first Mexican American had been elected to Congress, and four others followed in the 1960s. In the late 1960s, a new kind of Mexican American political movement was born. Inspired by the black civil rights movement, Mexican American students launched boycotts of high school classes in Los Angeles, Denver, and San Antonio. Students in colleges and universities across California joined in as well. Among their demands were bilingual education, an end to discrimination, and greater cultural recognition. In Crystal City, Texas, which had been dominated by Anglo politicians despite a population that was overwhelmingly Mexican American, the newly formed La Raza Unida Party took over the city government.[51]

Discrimination against Mexican Americans and other Latinos in the Southwest was pervasive prior to World War II, with segregated schools common in Texas and California along with housing and employment restrictions. In 1947, LULAC won an important court victory in the case of *Mendez v. Westminster*, which overturned an Orange County, California, policy of school segregation aimed at Mexican Americans.[52] The *Mendez* case was an important precedent

---

50 New Mexico had a different history because not many Anglos settled there initially. (*Anglo* is the term for a non-Hispanic white of European background.) Mexican Americans had considerable power in territorial legislatures between 1865 and 1912. See Lawrence H. Fuchs, *The American Kaleidoscope* (Hanover, NH: University Press of New England, 1990), pp. 239–40.

51 On the La Raza Unida Party, see Carlos Muñoz, Jr., and Mario Barrera, "La Raza Unida Party and the Chicano Student Movement in California," in *Latinos and the Political System*, F. Chris Garcia, ed. (Notre Dame, IN: University of Notre Dame Press, 1988), pp. 213–35.

52 *Mendez v. Westminster*, 161 F.2d. 744 (Ninth Cir. 1947).

for *Brown v. Board of Education* and is now recognized as a major landmark in the civil rights struggle.

In recent years, Latino political strategy has developed along two tracks. One is a traditional ethnic-group path of voter registration and voting along ethnic lines, because Hispanic voter registration typically lags far behind the rates at which whites and even blacks are registered to vote. This strategy is helped by the enormous growth of the Latino population resulting in part from immigration. The second is a legal strategy using the various civil rights laws designed to ensure fair access to the political system. The Mexican American Legal Defense and Education Fund (MALDEF) has played a key role in designing and pursuing the latter strategy.

Asian Americans

The early Asian experience in the United States was shaped by a series of naturalization laws dating back to 1790, the first of which declared that only white aliens were eligible for citizenship. Chinese immigrants had begun arriving in California in the 1850s, drawn by the boom of the gold rush. They were immediately met with hostility. The virulent antagonism toward Chinese immigrants in California led Congress in 1870 to declare Chinese immigrants ineligible for citizenship. In 1882, the first Chinese Exclusion Act suspended the entry of Chinese laborers.

At the time of the Exclusion Act, the Chinese community was composed predominantly of single male laborers, with few women and children. The few Chinese children in San Francisco were initially denied entry to the public schools; only after parents of American-born Chinese children pressed legal action were the children allowed to attend public school. Even then, however, they were made to attend a separate Chinese school. American-born Chinese children could not be denied citizenship, however; this right was confirmed by the Supreme Court in 1898, when it ruled in *United States v. Wong Kim Ark* that anyone born in the United States was entitled to full citizenship.[53] Still, new Chinese immigrants were barred from the United States until 1943; China by then had become a key wartime ally, and Congress repealed the Chinese Exclusion Act and permitted Chinese residents to become citizens.

Immigration climbed rapidly after the 1965 Immigration and Nationality Services Act, which lifted discriminatory quotas. In spite of this and other developments, limited English proficiency barred many Asian Americans and Latinos from full participation in American life. Two developments in the 1970s, however, established rights for language minorities. In 1974, the Supreme Court ruled in *Lau v. Nichols*, a suit filed on behalf of Chinese students in San Francisco, that school districts have to provide education for students whose English is limited.[54] It did not mandate bilingual education, but it

---

53 *United States v. Wong Kim Ark,* 169 U.S. 649 (1898).

54 *Lau v. Nichols,* 414 U.S. 563 (1974).

established a duty to provide instruction that students could understand. The 1970 amendments to the Voting Rights Act of 1965 permanently outlawed literacy tests as a prerequisite to register to vote and mandated bilingual ballots or oral assistance for those who speak Spanish, Chinese, Japanese, Korean, Native American languages, or Eskimo languages.

Immigration and Rights

From its very beginning the United States has struggled to define the rights of immigrants and the notion of citizenship. Waves of immigration have led to legislation restricting who can come to the United States legally. These regulations have included quotas, visas, and other controls on how long people can reside in the United States and what privileges they enjoy while here. Today we live in a period of unusually high immigration to the United States, especially from Mexico and Latin America, but also from Asia. Approximately one in eight persons in the United States today was born in another country. Such a high level of immigration has led to efforts to stem the influx of people to the country. It has also led to contentious questions as to whether immigrants should enjoy the same civil rights as citizens, such as the right to vote and equal access to education, or whether immigrants should enjoy a narrower set of rights. This question gets to the question of *what rights*, as described earlier in the chapter.

Asian Americans, Latinos, and other groups have been concerned about the impact of immigration laws on their civil rights. Many Asian American and Latino organizations opposed the Immigration Reform and Control Act of 1986 because it imposes sanctions on employers who hire undocumented workers. Such sanctions, they feared, would lead employers to discriminate against Latinos and Asian Americans. These suspicions were confirmed in a 1990 report by the General Accounting Office that found employer sanctions had created a "widespread pattern of discrimination" against Latinos and others who appear foreign.[55] Organizations such as MALDEF and the Asian Law Caucus monitor and challenge such discrimination. These groups have turned their attention to the rights of legal and illegal immigrants as anti-immigrant sentiment has grown in recent years.

The Supreme Court has ruled that illegal immigrants are eligible for education and medical care but can be denied other social benefits; legal immigrants, however, are to be treated much the same as citizens. But growing immigration—including an estimated 300,000 illegal immigrants per year—and mounting economic insecurity have undermined these practices. Groups of voters across the country now strongly support drawing a sharper line between immigrants and citizens. Not surprisingly, the movement to deny benefits to noncitizens began in California, which experienced sharp economic

---

55 Dick Kirschten, "Not Black and White," *National Journal*, March 2, 1991, p. 497.

distress in the early 1990s and has the highest levels of immigration of any state. In 1994, Californians voted in favor of Proposition 187, which denied illegal immigrants all services except emergency medical care. Supporters of the measure hoped to discourage illegal immigration and pressure illegal immigrants already in the country to leave. Opponents contended that denying basic services to illegal immigrants risked creating a subclass of residents in the United States whose lack of education and poor health would threaten all Americans. In 1994 and 1997, a federal court declared most of Proposition 187 unconstitutional, affirming previous rulings that illegal immigrants should be granted public education.

The question of the rights of illegal immigrants points to an even tougher problem. Congress has the power to deny public benefits to this group, but doing so would go against long-standing traditions in American political culture. Legal immigrants have traditionally enjoyed most of the rights and obligations of citizens (such as paying taxes). The Constitution begins with "We the People of the United States"; likewise, the Bill of Rights refers to the rights of *people*, not the rights of citizens. But even as Congress continues to debate immigration policy, several states, led by Arizona, have enacted their own laws aimed at identifying and deporting illegal immigrants within their borders. Immigration continues to be a divisive issue in American politics.

Americans with Disabilities

The concept of rights for people with disabilities began to emerge in the 1970s as the civil rights model spread to other groups. The seed was planted in a little-noticed provision of the 1973 Rehabilitation Act that outlawed discrimination against individuals on the basis of disabilities. As in many other cases, the law itself helped give rise to the movement demanding rights.[56] Modeling itself on the NAACP's Legal Defense Fund, the disability movement founded a Disability Rights Education and Defense Fund to press its legal claims. The movement achieved its greatest success with the passage of the Americans with Disabilities Act (ADA) of 1990, which guarantees people with disabilities equal employment rights and access to public businesses. Claims of discrimination in violation of this act are considered by the EEOC. The impact of the law has been far-reaching as businesses and public facilities have installed ramps, elevators, and other devices to meet its requirements.[57]

---

56 See the discussion in Robert A. Katzmann, *Institutional Disability: The Saga of Transportation Policy for the Disabled* (Washington, DC: Brookings Institution, 1986).

57 For example, after pressure from the Justice Department, one of the nation's largest rental car companies agreed to make special hand controls available to any customer requesting them. See "Avis Agrees to Equip Cars for Disabled," *Los Angeles Times*, September 2, 1994, p. D1.

Gay Men and Lesbians

In less than 50 years, the gay rights movement has become one of the largest civil rights movements in contemporary America. Beginning with street protests in the 1960s, it has grown into a well-financed and sophisticated lobby. The Human Rights Campaign is the primary national political action committee that raises and distributes campaign money to further the gay rights agenda. It provides campaign financing and volunteers to work for candidates endorsed by the group. The movement has also formed legal rights organizations, including the Lambda Legal Defense and Education Fund.

The 1990s proved something of a watershed moment in the fight for gay rights, witnessing both the first national anti-gay laws and the first declaration by the Supreme Court protecting the civil rights of gay men and women. In 1993, President Bill Clinton confronted the question of whether gays should be allowed to serve in the military. As a candidate, Clinton had said he favored lifting the ban on gays in the military. The issue set off a huge controversy in the first months of his presidency. After nearly a year of deliberation, the administration enunciated a compromise: its "Don't Ask, Don't Tell" policy, which allowed gay men and lesbians to serve in the military as long as they did not openly proclaim their sexual orientation or engage in homosexual activity. Two years later, the gay rights movement experienced a further setback when Clinton signed the Defense of Marriage Act (DOMA), which recognized a marriage as the union of one man and one woman for the purposes of the application of federal laws, such as taxes and benefits.

As in the case of other civil rights movements, it was the Supreme Court that took a major step in protecting gay men and lesbians from discrimination. This marked an important departure from its earlier jurisprudence. The first gay rights case that the Court decided, *Bowers v. Hardwick* (1986), ruled against a right to privacy that would protect consensual homosexual activity. After the *Bowers* decision, the gay rights movement sought suitable legal cases to test the constitutionality of discrimination against gay men and lesbians, much as the civil rights movement had done in the late 1940s and 1950s.[58] As one advocate put it, "Lesbians and gay men are looking for their *Brown v. Board of Education*."[59] Among the cases tested were those stemming from local ordinances restricting gay rights (including the right to marry), job discrimination, and family law issues such as adoption and parental rights. In 1996, in *Romer v. Evans*, the Supreme Court explicitly extended fundamental civil rights protections to gay men and lesbians by declaring unconstitutional a 1992 amendment to the Colorado state constitution that prohibited local governments from passing ordinances to protect gay rights.[60] The decision's forceful language highlighted

---

58 *Bowers v. Hardwick*, 478 U.S. 186 (1986).

59 Quoted in Joan Biskupic, "Gay Rights Activists Seek a Supreme Court Test Case," *Washington Post*, December 19, 1993, p. A1.

60 *Romer v. Evans*, 517 U.S. 620 (1996).

the connection between gay rights and civil rights as it declared discrimination against gay people unconstitutional.

Finally, in *Lawrence v. Texas* (2003), the Court overturned *Bowers* and struck down a Texas statute criminalizing certain intimate sexual conduct between consenting partners of the same sex.[61] A victory for lesbians and gay men every bit as significant as *Roe v. Wade* was for women, *Lawrence v. Texas* extends at least one aspect of civil liberties to sexual minorities: the right to privacy. However, this decision by itself does not undo the various exclusions that deprive lesbians and gay men of full civil rights.

Another important victory occurred in 2010, when Congress finally repealed Don't Ask, Don't Tell. In 2008, then-candidate Barack Obama promised to repeal the act should he be elected. When he did not do so in the first months of his administration, he was roundly criticized by gay rights activities. After a lengthy study by the Defense Department of the possible consequences of allowing openly gay men and women to serve, Congress voted for the repeal of Don't Ask, Don't Tell.

The focal point for the assertion of gay rights has now become the right to marry. Unlike women and blacks who fought for equal treatment in education, employment, and voting, gay rights activists have targeted marital rights. In part this is symbolic, as same-sex couples seek social and legal recognition of their relationships as equally valid as those of opposite-sex couples. And in part it is economic, as federal and state laws treat married couples differently for such economic policies as taxes, inheritance, and benefits.

The first changes to the right to marry occurred at the state level, much like the contests for women's suffrage in the late nineteenth century. In 2004, the Supreme Judicial Court of Massachusetts ruled that under the state's constitution, same-sex couples were entitled to marry. The state senate then requested the court to rule on whether a civil-union statute (avoiding the word *marriage*) would, as it did in Vermont, satisfy the court's ruling, in response to which the court ruled negatively, asserting that civil unions are too much like the "separate but equal" doctrine that maintained legalized racial segregation from 1896 to 1954. As of October 2013, legislatures, courts, and voters in California, Connecticut, Delaware, Iowa, Maine, Maryland, Massachusetts, Minnesota, New Hampshire, New Jersey, New York, Rhode Island, Vermont, Washington state, and the District of Columbia had legalized same-sex marriage. In addition, another three states provided for civil unions for same-sex couples. However, as with the women's suffrage movement a century earlier, there has been strong push back against these changes. In November 2004, voters in 11 states approved bans on same-sex marriage. As of 2013, 35 states limit marriage to opposite-sex couples.

The discrepancy between some state laws, which recognized same-sex marriage, and the federal law under DOMA, which did not, ultimately proved to be the act's undoing. The nation's laws extend to everyone equally; that is the meaning

---

61 *Lawrence and Garner v. Texas,* 539 U.S. 558 (2003).

of equal protection under the Fifth and Fourteenth amendments. Edith Windsor and Thea Speyer were a same-sex couple who resided in New York but were lawfully married elsewhere. In 2009, Speyer died, leaving her estate to Windsor. Windsor sought the exemption afforded to surviving spouses from federal estate taxes, but under DOMA she was prevented from that benefit. In 2013 the Supreme Court ruled DOMA unconstitutional "as a depravation of liberty of the person protected by the Fifth Amendment."[62]

AFFIRMATIVE ACTION

In the past 50 years, the politics of rights not only spread to increasing numbers of groups in society but also expanded its goal. The relatively narrow goal of equalizing opportunity by eliminating discriminatory barriers evolved into the far broader goal of **affirmative action**—compensatory action to overcome the consequences of past discrimination and encourage greater diversity. In 1965, President Lyndon Johnson attempted to inaugurate affirmative action by executive orders directing agency heads and personnel officers to pursue vigorously a policy of minority employment in the federal civil service and in companies doing business with the national government. But affirmative action did not become a prominent goal until the 1970s.

The Supreme Court and the Burden of Proof

As this movement spread, it began to divide civil rights activists and their supporters. The whole issue of qualification versus minority preference was addressed in the case of Allan Bakke. Bakke, a white man with no minority affiliation, brought suit against the University of California Medical School at Davis on the grounds that in denying him admission the school had discriminated against him on the basis of his race (that year the school had reserved 16 of 100 available slots for minority applicants). He argued that his grades and test scores had ranked him well above many students who had been accepted at the school and that the only possible explanation for his rejection was that the others were black or Hispanic and he was white. In 1978, Bakke won his case before the Supreme Court and was admitted to the medical school, but he did not succeed in getting affirmative action declared unconstitutional. The Court rejected the procedures at the University of California because its medical school had used both a quota and a separate admissions system for minorities. The Court agreed with Bakke's argument that racial

 affirmative action

A policy or program designed to redress historic injustices committed against specific groups by making special efforts to provide members of these groups with access to educational and employment opportunities

---

62 *United States v. Windsor*, 570 U.S. ____ (2013). That same day the Court also cleared the way for legalization of gay marriage in California in the case *Hollingsworth v. Perry*, 570 U.S. ____ (2013).

---

categorizations are suspect categories that place a severe burden of proof on those using them to show a "compelling public purpose." The Court went on to say that achieving "a diverse student body" was such a public purpose, but the method of a rigid quota of student slots assigned on the basis of race was incompatible with the equal protection clause. Thus the Court permitted universities (and other schools, training programs, and hiring authorities) to continue to take minority status into consideration but limited severely the use of quotas to situations in which previous discrimination had been shown and the quotas were used more as a guideline for social diversity than as a mathematically defined ratio.[63]

For nearly a decade after *Bakke*, the Supreme Court was tentative and permissive about efforts by corporations and governments to experiment with affirmative action programs in employment.[64] But in 1989, the Court returned to the *Bakke* position, ruling that any "rigid numerical quota" is suspect. In *Wards Cove v. Atonio*, the Court further weakened affirmative action by easing the way for employers to prefer white men, holding that the burden of proof of unlawful discrimination should be shifted from the defendant (the employer) to the plaintiff (the person claiming to be the victim of discrimination).[65] This decision virtually overruled the Court's prior holding.[66] That same year, the Court ruled that any affirmative action program already approved by federal courts could be challenged by individuals (usually white men) who alleged that the program discriminated against them.[67]

In 1995, the Supreme Court's ruling in *Adarand Constructors v. Pena* further weakened affirmative action. This decision stated that race-based policies, such as preferences given by the government to minority contractors, must survive strict scrutiny, placing the burden on the government to show that such affirmative action programs serve a compelling government interest and are narrowly tailored to address identifiable past discrimination.[68]

Other developments in the courts and the states also worked to restrict affirmative action in important ways. One of the most significant was the *Hopwood* case, in which white students challenged admissions practices at the University of Texas Law School, charging that the school's affirmative action program discriminated against whites. Critics of affirmative action have asserted that the practice amounts to "reverse discrimination," in which the rights of the majority are actively curtailed through race-conscious policies. In 1996, a federal court ruling on the case (the U.S. Court of Appeals for the Fifth Circuit) stated that

---

63 *Regents of the University of California v. Bakke*, 438 U.S. 265 (1978).

64 *United Steelworkers of America v. Weber*, 443 U.S. 193 (1979); and *Fullilove v. Klutznick*, 448 U.S. 448 (1980).

65 *Wards Cove Packing Company v. Atonio*, 490 U.S. 642 (1989).

66 *Griggs v. Duke Power Company*, 401 U.S. 424 (1971).

67 *Martin v. Wilks*, 490 U.S. 755 (1989).

68 *Adarand Constructors v. Pena*, 515 U.S. 200 (1995).

race could never be considered in granting admissions and scholarships at state colleges and universities.[69] This decision effectively rolled back the use of affirmative action permitted by the 1978 *Bakke* case. In *Bakke*, as noted earlier, the Supreme Court had outlawed quotas but said that race could be used as one factor among many in admissions decisions. Many universities and colleges have since justified affirmative action as a way of promoting racial diversity among their student bodies. What was new in the *Hopwood* decision was the ruling that race could *never* be used as a factor in admissions decisions, even to promote diversity. In 1996, the Supreme Court refused to hear a challenge to the *Hopwood* case. This meant that its ruling remains in effect in the states covered by the Fifth Circuit—Texas, Louisiana, and Mississippi—but does not apply to the rest of the country.

This betwixt-and-between status of affirmative action was where things stood in 2003, when the Supreme Court took two cases against the University of Michigan that would clarify legal policy on affirmative action. The first suit, *Gratz v. Bollinger*, alleged that by using a point-based ranking system that automatically awarded 20 points (out of 150) to African American, Latino, and Native American applicants, the university's undergraduate admissions policy discriminated unconstitutionally against white students with otherwise equal or superior academic qualifications. The Supreme Court agreed, 6–3, arguing that something tantamount to a quota was involved because undergraduate admissions lacked the necessary "individualized consideration," employing instead a "mechanical one," based too much on the favorable minority points.[70] The Court's ruling in *Gratz v. Bollinger* was not surprising, given *Bakke*'s holding against quotas and recent decisions calling for strict scrutiny of all racial classifications, even those that are intended to remedy past discrimination or promote future equality.

The second case, *Grutter v. Bollinger*, broke new ground. Barbara Grutter sued the University of Michigan Law School on the grounds that it had discriminated in a race-conscious way against white applicants with grades and law boards equal or superior to those of minority applicants. A precarious vote of 5–4 aligned the majority of the Supreme Court with Justice Lewis Powell's opinion in *Bakke* for the first time. In *Bakke*, Powell had argued that diversity in education is a compelling state interest and that constitutionally, race could be considered a positive factor in admissions decisions. In *Grutter*, the Court reiterated Powell's holding and, applying strict scrutiny to the law school's policy, found that its admissions process was narrowly tailored to the school's compelling state interest in diversity because it gave a "highly individualized, holistic review of each applicant's file," in which race counted but was not used in a "mechanical way."[71]

---

69 *Hopwood v. State of Texas*, 78 F.3d 932 (Fifth Cir. 1996).

70 *Gratz v. Bollinger*, 539 U.S. 244 (2003).

71 *Grutter v. Bollinger*, 539 U.S. 306 (2003).

Throughout the 1990s, federal courts, including the Supreme Court, had subjected public affirmative action programs to strict scrutiny to invalidate them. *Adarand Constructors v. Pena* (1995) definitively established the Supreme Court's view that constitutionally permissible use of race must serve a compelling state interest. Between *Korematsu v. United States* (1944)[72] and *Grutter*, no consideration of race had survived strict scrutiny. Such affirmative action plans that had survived constitutional review did so before 1995, under a lower standard of review, one reserved for policies intended to remedy racial injustice. For affirmative action to survive under the post-1995 judicial paradigm, the Court needed to find that sometimes racial categories can be deployed to serve a compelling state interest. That the Court found exactly this in *Grutter* puts affirmative action on stronger ground—at least if its specific procedures pass the Supreme Court's muster and until the Court's majority changes. But the subject of affirmative action clearly has not yet been fully settled. In the 2009 case *Ricci v. DeStefano*, the Court ruled that New Haven, Connecticut, officials had discriminated against white firefighters when they threw out a promotions exam because no nonwhite candidate received a high enough score for promotion.[73] The Court said that employers must show "a strong basis in evidence" under Title VII of the Civil Rights Act and may not rely simply on a test's outcome to show racial discrimination. Most recently, in *Fisher v. University of Texas*, the Supreme Court upheld the principles stated in *Grutter* and *Bakke*, that universities, municipalities, and other agencies can engage affirmative action but those programs are subject to strict scrutiny by the courts.[74]

Referenda on Affirmative Action

The courts have not been the only center of action: challenges to affirmative action have also emerged in state and local politics, in the form of ballot initiatives or referendums that ask voters to decide the issue. One of the most significant state actions was the passage of the California Civil Rights Initiative, also known as Proposition 209, in 1996. Proposition 209 outlawed affirmative action programs in the state and local governments of California, thus prohibiting state and local governments from using race or gender preferences in their decisions about hiring, contracting, and university admissions. The political battle over Proposition 209 was heated, and supporters and defenders took to the streets and airwaves to make their case. When the referendum was held, the measure passed with 54 percent of the vote, including 27 percent of the black vote, 30 percent of the Latino vote, and 45 percent of the Asian

72 *Korematsu v. United States*, 323 U.S. 214 (1944).

73 *Ricci v. DeStefano*, 129 S.Ct. 2658 (2009).

74 *Fisher v. University of Texas*, 570 U.S. ____ (2013).

American vote.[75] In 1997, the Supreme Court refused to hear a challenge to the new law.

Many observers predicted that the success of California's ban on affirmative action would provoke similar movements in states and localities across the country. But the political factors that contributed to the success of Proposition 209 in California may not exist in many other states. Winning a controversial state referendum takes leadership and lots of money. The popular California Republican governor Pete Wilson led with a strong anti-affirmative action stand (favoring Proposition 209), and his campaign had a lot of money for advertising. But similar conditions did not exist elsewhere. Few prominent Republican leaders in other states were willing to come forward to lead the anti-affirmative action campaign. Moreover, the outcome of any referendum, especially a complicated and controversial one, depends greatly on how the issue is drafted and placed on the ballot. California's Proposition 209 was framed as a civil rights initiative: "The state shall not discriminate against, or grant preferential treatment to, any individual or group on the basis of race, sex, color, ethnicity, or national origin." Different wording can produce quite different outcomes, as a 1997 vote on affirmative action in Houston revealed. There the ballot initiative asked voters whether they wanted to ban affirmative action in city contracting and hiring, not whether they wanted to end preferential treatment. In that city, 55 percent of voters decided in favor of affirmative action.[76]

CIVIL LIBERTIES AND CIVIL RIGHTS: REGULATING COLLECTIVE ACTION

Over the past century, America has strengthened its citizens' liberties and expanded their rights. Both civil liberties and civil rights are solutions to collective action problems. Strengthening the former means imposing more restrictions on some forms of collective action. Expanding the later means allowing more individuals to take part in collective decision making and imposing restrictions on the sorts of decisions that can be reached.

Institutions help to solve collective action problems, but no particular solution is carved in stone. Contending political forces continually seek to change the institutional rules to serve their particular purposes. In the United States today, for example, some groups argue the need for additional rights

---

75 Michael A. Fletcher, "Opponents of Affirmative Action Heartened by Court Decision," *Washington Post*, April 13, 1997, p. A21.

76 See Sam Howe Verhovek, "Houston Vote Underlined Complexity of Rights Issue," *New York Times*, November 6, 1997, p. A1.

for gay men and lesbians, immigrants, and others who have often faced political, social, and economic discrimination. Opponents of this idea assert that the expansion of civil rights to include such matters as same-sex marriage or social and educational benefits for illegal immigrants is inappropriate. The outcomes of this and other struggles over liberties and rights are never certain. Institutions matter, but exactly how they will matter in the years to come is always subject to change.

For Further Reading

Selections highlighted in red are included in *Readings in American Politics: Analysis and Perspectives*, Third Edition.

Baer, Judith, and Leslie Goldstein. *The Constitutional and Legal Rights of Women.* Los Angeles: Roxbury, 2006.

Brown v. Board of Education of Topeka, 347 U.S. 483, 1954.

Dawson, Michael. *Not in Our Lifetimes: The Future of Black Politics.* Chicago: University of Chicago Press, 2011.

Garrow, David J. *Bearing the Cross: Martin Luther King, Jr., and the Southern Christian Leadership Conference: A Personal Portrait.* New York: Morrow, 1986.

Gerstmann, Evan. *Same-Sex Marriage and the Constitution.* New York: Cambridge University Press, 2004.

Glendon, Mary Ann. *Rights Talk: The Impoverishment of Political Discourse.* New York: Free Press, 1991.

Jackson, Thomas. *From Civil Rights to Human Rights.* Philadelphia: University of Pennsylvania Press, 2006.

Klarman, Michael. *From Jim Crow to Civil Rights: The Supreme Court and the Struggle for Racial Equality.* New York: Oxford University Press, 2004.

Lewis, Anthony. *Gideon's Trumpet.* New York: Random House, 1964.

Meltsner, Michael. *The Making of a Civil Rights Lawyer.* Charlottesville: University of Virginia Press, 2006.

O'Brien, David. *Constitutional Law and Politics: Civil Rights and Civil Liberties.* 9th ed. New York: Norton, 2014.

Sugrue, Thomas. *Sweet Land of Liberty: The Forgotten Struggle for Civil Rights in the North.* New York: Random House, 2009.

Tushnet, Mark, and Michael Olivas. *Colored Men and Hombres Aqui:* Hernandez v. Texas *and the Emergence of Mexican American Lawyering.* Houston: Arte Publico Press, 2006.

Yoshino, Kenji. *Covering: The Hidden Assault on Our Civil Rights.* New York: Random House, 2007.

6

Congress:
The First Branch

The U.S. Congress is the "first branch" of government under Article I of our Constitution and is also among the world's most important representative bodies. Most of the world's representative bodies only represent—that is, their governmental functions consist mainly of affirming and legitimating the national leadership's decisions. The U.S. Congress is one of the few national representative bodies that actually possesses powers of governance. For example, the U.S. Congress never accedes to the president's budget proposals without making major changes, whereas both the British House of Commons and the Japanese Diet always accept the budget exactly as proposed by the government.

This unique status of the American Congress provides an illustration of the institution principle. In the separation-of-powers regime institutionalized by the U.S. Constitution, the American executive cannot govern alone. The legislature, in particular, actively participates. In Richard Neustadt's memorable phrase, the executive and the legislature in the United States are "separated institutions sharing power."[1] In parliamentary regimes, such as Britain or Japan, in contrast, the executive controls its majority in parliament. These different institutional arrangements give different powers to different players. In the American case, the institutional arrangements were intended to give Congress a great deal of power relative to the president.

Congress controls a formidable battery of powers that it uses to shape policies and, when necessary, defend its prerogatives against the executive branch. Congress has vast authority over the two most important powers given to any government: the power of force (control over the nation's military forces) and the power over money. Specifically, according to Article I, Section 8, Congress can "lay and collect Taxes," deal with indebtedness and bankruptcy, impose

---

1   Richard E. Neustadt, *Presidential Power: The Politics of Leadership* (New York: Wiley, 1960), p. 42.

duties, borrow and coin money, and generally control the nation's purse strings. It also may "provide for the common Defence and general Welfare," regulate interstate commerce, undertake public works, acquire and control federal lands, promote science and "useful Arts" (pertaining mostly to patents and copyrights), and regulate the militia.

In the realm of foreign policy, Congress has the power to declare war, deal with piracy, regulate foreign commerce, and raise and regulate the armed forces and military installations. These powers over war and the military are supreme— even the president, as commander in chief of the military, must obey the laws and orders of Congress *if* Congress chooses to assert its constitutional authority. (In the past century, Congress has usually ceded this authority to the president.) Further, the Senate has the power to approve treaties (by a two-thirds vote) and the appointment of ambassadors. Capping these powers, Congress is charged to make laws "which shall be necessary and proper for carrying into Execution the foregoing Powers, and all other Powers vested by this Constitution in the Government of the United States, or in any Department or Officer thereof."

If it seems to you that many of these powers, especially those having to do with war and spending, actually belong to the president, that is because modern presidents do exercise great authority in these areas. The modern presidency is a more powerful institution than it was two centuries ago, and much of that power has come from Congress, either because Congress has delegated the power to the president by law or because Congress has simply allowed, or even

CORE OF THE ANALYSIS

 Members of Congress, like all politicians, are ambitious and thus eager to serve the interests of their constituents in order to improve their chances of re-election.

 Congress is the most important representative institution of American government. In many ways, Congress works because its system of representation harnesses individual legislators' ambitions and puts them to use.

 The internal organization of Congress solves the collective action problems that arise due to the many and varied goals of individual legislators.

 Rules matter in the legislative process, and the process through which a bill becomes a law affects which proposed bills succeed and in what form.

urged, presidents to be more active in these areas.[2] As we noted in Chapter 1, institutions evolve over time, as the various players seek to adapt them to their purposes. This helps explain why today the executive branch seems like a more important branch of government than Congress. Still, the constitutional powers of Congress remain intact in the document. As we shall see, congressional power cannot be separated from congressional representation. Indeed, there is a reciprocal relationship between the two. Without its array of powers, Congress could do little to represent effectively the views and interests of its constituents. At the same time, the power of Congress is ultimately a function of its capacity to represent important groups and forces in American society effectively. All five principles of politics from Chapter 1 are important to our understanding of the institutional structure of the contemporary Congress.

We begin our discussion with a brief consideration of representation. Then we examine the institutional structure of the contemporary Congress and the manner in which congressional powers are organized and employed. Throughout, we point out the connections between these two aspects—the ways in which representation affects congressional operations (especially through "the electoral connection") and the ways in which congressional institutions enhance or diminish representation (especially Congress's division-of-labor and specialization-of-labor committee system).

REPRESENTATION

constituency

The district making up the area from which an official is elected

delegate

A representative who votes according to the preferences of his or her constituency

trustee

A representative who votes based on what he or she thinks is best for his or her constituency

Congress is the most important representative institution in American government. Each member's primary responsibility is to the district, to her **constituency**, not to the congressional leadership, a party, or even Congress itself. Yet the task of representation is not a simple one. Views about what constitutes fair and effective representation differ, and constituents can make very different kinds of demands on their representatives. Members of Congress must consider these diverse views and demands as they represent their districts (Figure 6.1).

Legislators generally vary in the weight they give to personal priorities and to the desires of their campaign contributors and past supporters. Some see themselves as perfect agents of others: they have been elected to do the bidding of those who sent them to the legislature, and they act as **delegates**. Others see themselves as having been selected by their fellow citizens to do what they think is "right," and they act as **trustees**. Most legislators are a mix of these two types. And all, one way

2   On the issue of congressional delegation to the executive, two valuable sources are D. Roderick Kiewiet and Mathew D. McCubbins, *The Logic of Delegation: Congressional Parties and the Appropriations Process* (Chicago: University of Chicago Press, 1991), and David Epstein and Sharyn O'Halloran, *Delegating Powers: A Transaction Cost Politics Approach to Policy Making under Separate Powers* (New York: Cambridge University Press, 1999).

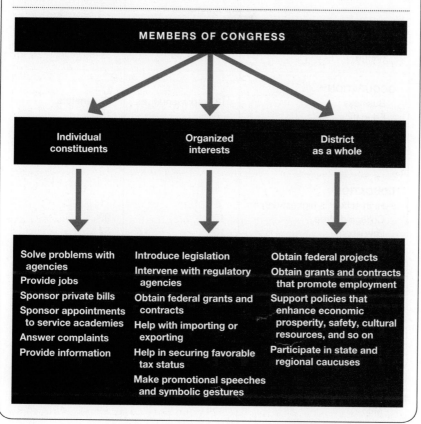

Figure 6.1

HOW MEMBERS OF CONGRESS REPRESENT THEIR DISTRICTS

MEMBERS OF CONGRESS

Individual constituents	Organized interests	District as a whole
Solve problems with agencies	Introduce legislation	Obtain federal projects
Provide jobs	Intervene with regulatory agencies	Obtain grants and contracts that promote employment
Sponsor private bills	Obtain federal grants and contracts	Support policies that enhance economic prosperity, safety, cultural resources, and so on
Sponsor appointments to service academies	Help with importing or exporting	
Answer complaints	Help in securing favorable tax status	Participate in state and regional caucuses
Provide information	Make promotional speeches and symbolic gestures	

or another, need to survive the next election in order to pursue whatever role they formulate for themselves. Rational agents necessarily must focus on survival.

Legislators not only represent others; they may be representative *of* others as well. The latter is especially salient today when it comes to gender and race, where descriptive representation is symbolically significant at the very least. Descriptive characteristics permit women members and representatives drawn from minority groups to serve and draw support from those with whom they share an identity, both inside their formal constituency and in the nation at large. (See Table 6.1 for a summary of demographic characteristics of members of Congress.) Descriptive representation for African American and Hispanic minorities has been facilitated by the process of drawing new district boundaries within states every 10 years following the decennial census of the population. Districts have been created—so-called majority minority districts—with racial or ethnic minorities in the majority.

As we discussed in Chapter 1, one person might be trusted to speak for another if the two are formally bound together so that the representative is in some way

Table 6.1

DEMOGRAPHIC SUMMARY OF MEMBERS OF CONGRESS

	HOUSE	SENATE
AGE*		
Average	57 years	62 years
Range	30–89 years	39–89 years
OCCUPATION**		
Business	187 representatives	27 senators
Education	77	15
Law	156	55
Public service/politics	184	42
Previous military experience	87	18
EDUCATION†		
High school is highest degree	21	1
College degree	405	99
Law degree	169	57
PhD	20	0
MD	22	3
RELIGION††		
Protestant	247	52
Catholic	136	27
Jewish	22	11
Mormon	8	7
GENDER		
Women	77	20
Men	358	80
RACE/ETHNICITY		
African American	40	2
Hispanic/Latino	34	4
Asian/Pacific Islander	12	1
CONGRESSIONAL SERVICE		
Number serving in first term	75	14
Average length of service	9.1 years	10.2 years
	(4.6 terms)	(1.7 terms)

*Age at time of election (November 6, 2012).

**Most members list more than one occupation.

†Education categories are not exclusive (e.g., a representative with a law degree might also be counted as having a college degree).

††Ninety-eight percent of members cite a specific religious affiliation. Other affiliations not listed here include Buddhist, Muslim, Hindu, Orthodox Christian, and Unitarian.

SOURCE: Jennifer E. Manning, "Membership of the 113th Congress: A Profile," Congressional Research Service, April 11, 2013.

accountable to those he purports to represent. If representatives can somehow be punished or held to account for failing to speak properly for their constituents, then we know they have an incentive to provide good representation even if their own backgrounds, views, and interests differ from those of the people they represent. This idea is called **agency representation**—the sort of representation that takes place when constituents have the power to hire and fire their representatives (who act as their agents). Frequent competitive elections are an important means by which constituents hold their representatives to account and keep them responsive to their own views and preferences. The idea of a representative as agent is similar to the relationship between lawyer and client. True, the relationship between the member of Congress and as many as 700,000 "clients" in the district or that between the senator and possibly millions of clients in the state is very different from that of the lawyer and client. But the criteria of performance are comparable.

We would expect at the very least that each representative will constantly be seeking to discover the interests of the constituency and will be speaking for those interests in Congress and other centers of government.[3] We expect this because we believe that members of Congress, like politicians everywhere, are ambitious. For many, this ambition is satisfied simply by maintaining a hold on their present office and advancing up the rungs of power in that body. Some, however, may be looking ahead to the next level—to higher legislative office, as when a representative seeks a Senate seat, or to an executive office, as when a legislator returns home to run for the state's governorship, or at the highest level, when a legislator seeks the presidency.[4] This means that members of Congress may not only be concerned with their present *geographic* constituency. They may want to appeal to a different geographic constituency, for instance, or seek support from a broader gender, ethnic, or racial community. We shall return to this topic shortly in a discussion of elections. But we can say here that in each of these cases the legislator is eager to serve the interests of constituents, either to enhance her prospects of contract renewal at the next election or to improve the chances of moving to another level. In short, the agency conception of representation works in proportion to the ambition of politicians (as "agents") and the capacity of constituents (as "principals") to reward or punish on the basis of the legislator's performance and reputation.[5]

 agency representation

The type of representation according to which representatives are held accountable to their constituents if they fail to represent them properly. That is, constituents have the power to hire and fire their representatives

---

3   The classic description of interactions between politicians and "the folks back home" is given by Richard F. Fenno, Jr., *Home Style: House Members in Their Districts* (Boston: Little, Brown, 1978). Essays elaborating on Fenno's classic are found in Morris P. Fiorina and David W. Rohde, eds., *Home Style and Washington Work* (Ann Arbor: University of Michigan Press, 1989).

4   For more on political careers generally, see John R. Hibbing, "Legislative Careers: Why and How We Should Study Them," *Legislative Studies Quarterly* 24 (1999): 149–71. See also Cherie D. Maestas, Sarah Lutton, L. Sandy Maisel, and Walter J. Stone, "When to Risk It? Institutions, Ambitions, and the Decision to Run for the U.S. House," *American Political Science Review* 100, no. 2 (May 2006): 195–208.

5   Constituents aren't a legislative agent's only principals. He may also be beholden to party leaders and special interests, as well as to members and committees in the chamber. See Forrest Maltzman, *Competing Principals* (Ann Arbor: University of Michigan Press, 1997).

House and Senate: Differences in Representation

The framers of the Constitution provided for a **bicameral legislature**—a legislative body consisting of two chambers. As we saw in Chapter 2, the framers intended each of these chambers, the House and the Senate, to represent a different constituency. Members of the House were to be "close to the people," elected by popular vote every two years. Because they saw the House as the institution closest to the people, the framers gave it a special power. All **money bills**, that is, bills authorizing new taxes or authorizing the government to spend money for any purpose, were required to originate in the House of Representatives. Until the Seventeenth Amendment (1913) provided for direct popular election of senators, members of the Senate were appointed by state legislatures for six-year terms, were to represent the elite members of society, and were to be attuned more to the interests of property than to those of the population. Today members of both the House and the Senate are elected directly by the people. The 435 members of the House are elected from districts apportioned according to population; the 100 members of the Senate are elected by state, with two senators from each. Senators continue to have longer terms in office and usually represent much larger and more diverse constituencies than do their counterparts in the House of Representatives (Table 6.2).

The House and the Senate play different roles in the legislative process. In essence, the Senate is the more deliberative of the two bodies: it is the forum in which any and all ideas can receive a thorough public airing. The House is the more centralized and the more organized of the two bodies: it is better equipped to play a routine role in the governmental process. In part, this difference stems from the different rules governing the two bodies. These rules give House leaders more control over the legislative process and provide for House members to specialize in certain legislative areas. The rules of the much smaller, more freewheeling Senate give its leadership relatively little power and discourage specialization. This is the institution principle at work. The two legislative chambers are organized in very different ways, reflecting not only their differences in size

Table 6.2

DIFFERENCES BETWEEN THE HOUSE AND THE SENATE

	HOUSE	SENATE
Minimum age of member	25 years	30 years
Length of U.S. citizenship	At least 7 years	At least 9 years
Length of term	2 years	6 years (staggered)
Number per state	Depends on population: approx. 1 per 30,000 in 1789; approx. 1 per 700,000 today	2 per state
Constituency	Tends to be local	Is both local and national

but also their differences in electoral rhythm, constituencies, and roles. House members specialize, their specialized activities take place mainly in committees, and deliberations by the full House take place mainly in response to committee proposals. The institution is organized to facilitate expeditious consideration of committee bills. The Senate does many of the same things. But senators are less specialized, partly because of their more heterogeneous constituencies, and therefore involve themselves in many more areas of policy. Senate proceedings permit wider participation and more open-ended deliberation.

Both formal and informal factors also contribute to the differences between the two chambers of Congress. Differences in the length of terms and the requirements for holding office specified by the Constitution generate differences in how the members of each body develop their constituencies and exercise their powers of office. The result is that members of the House more effectively and more frequently serve as the agents of well-organized local interests with specific legislative agendas—for instance, used-car dealers seeking relief from regulation, labor unions seeking more favorable legislation, or farmers looking for higher subsidies. The small size and relative homogeneity of their constituencies and the frequency with which they must seek re-election make House members more attuned than senators to the legislative needs of local interest groups. This is what the framers intended when they drafted the Constitution—namely, that the House of Representatives would be "the people's house" and that its members would reflect and represent public opinion in a timely manner.

Senators, on the other hand, serve larger and more heterogeneous constituencies. As a result, they are somewhat better able than members of the House to serve as the agents of groups and interests organized on a statewide or national basis. Moreover, with longer terms in office, senators have the luxury of considering "new ideas" or seeking to bring together new coalitions of interests, rather than simply serving existing ones. This, too, was the intent of the Constitution's drafters—that the Senate should provide a balance to the more responsive House, with its narrower and more homogeneous constituencies. The Senate was said to be the saucer that cools the tea, bringing deliberation, debate, inclusiveness, calm, and caution to policy formulation.

For much of the late twentieth century, the House exhibited more intense partisanship and ideological division than the Senate. Because of their diverse constituencies, senators tended to be more inclined to seek compromise positions that offended as few voters and interest groups as possible. Members of the House, in contrast, with their party's domination in more homogeneous districts, were less inclined to seek compromises and more willing to stick to their partisan and ideological guns. For instance, the House divided almost exactly along partisan lines on the 1998 vote to impeach President Bill Clinton. In the Senate, by contrast, 10 Republicans joined Democrats to acquit Clinton of obstruction of justice charges, and in a separate vote five Republicans joined Democrats to acquit Clinton of perjury.[6] However, beginning with

---

6   Eric Pianin and Guy Gugliotta, "The Bipartisan Challenge: Senate's Search for Accord Marks Contrast to House," *Washington Post*, January 8, 1999, p. 1.

the presidency of George W. Bush, even the Senate grew more partisan and polarized—especially on social issues and the war in Iraq.[7] During Barack Obama's presidency, many of the president's initiatives dealing with the economic crisis, health care, gay rights, financial rescues, and most other areas received virtually no Republican support.

The Electoral System

In light of their role as agents of various constituencies in their states and districts and the importance of elections as a mechanism by which principals (constituents) reward and punish their agents, representatives are very much influenced by electoral considerations. Three factors related to the American electoral system affect who gets elected and what she does once in office. The first set of issues concerns who decides to run for office and which candidates have an edge over others. The second issue is the advantage incumbents have in winning re-election. Finally, the way congressional district lines are drawn can greatly affect the outcome of an election. Let us examine more closely the impact of these considerations on who serves in Congress.

Running for Office. Voters' choices are restricted from the start by who decides to run for office. In the past, decisions about who would run for a particular elected office were made by local party officials. A person who had a record of service to the party, or who was owed a favor, or whose "turn" had come up might be nominated by party leaders for an office.[8] Today few party organizations have the power to slate candidates in that way. Instead, the decision to run for Congress is a more personal choice. One of the most

---

7 On the confirmation of Supreme Court nominations, however, even in an atmosphere of elevated partisanship, moderates from both parties in the Senate have prevented partisan extremism from dominating. Chief Justice John Roberts, Justice Samuel Alito, Justice Sonia Sotomayor, and Justice Elena Kagan were all approved with at least some support from both parties. However, lower-court judicial nominees were blocked frequently during the Bush administration and the Obama administration, leaving many vacant seats on the federal bench.

8 In the nineteenth century, it was often considered an *obligation*, not an honor, to serve in Congress. The real political action was back home in the state capital or a big city, not in Washington. So the practice of "rotation" was devised, according to which a promising local politician would do a tour of duty in Washington before being slated for an important local office. This is not to say that electoral incentives—the so-called electoral connection, in which a legislator's behavior was motivated by the desire to retain the seat for himself or his party—was absent in nineteenth-century America. See, for example, Jamie L. Carson and Erik J. Engstrom, "Assessing the Electoral Connection Evidence from the Early United States," *American Journal of Political Science* 49 (2005): 746–57. See also William T. Bianco, David B. Spence, and John D. Wilkerson, "The Electoral Connection in the Early Congress: The Case of the Compensation Act of 1816," *American Journal of Political Science* 40 (1996): 145–71.

important factors determining who runs for office is a person's ambition.[9] A potential candidate may also assess whether he can attract enough money to mount a credible campaign. The ability to raise money depends on connections to other politicians, interest groups, and the national party organization. Wealthy individuals may finance their own races. In 2000, for example, the New Jersey Democrat and former investment banker Jon Corzine spent more than $60 million of his own money to win a U.S. Senate seat. (In 2005, he spent a similar amount of money to win the governorship of New Jersey. But money isn't everything. Despite his wealth, Corzine lost this post four years later.) One of the biggest spenders in the 2012 election was Elizabeth Warren who, though not wealthy herself, raised $50 million in her successful campaign for a Senate seat representing Massachusetts.

Features distinctive to each congressional district also affect the field of candidates. Among them is the range of other political opportunities that may lure potential candidates away. In addition, the way the congressional district overlaps state legislative boundaries may affect a candidate's decision to run. A state-level representative or senator who is considering a run for the U.S. Congress is more likely to assess her prospects favorably if the state district largely coincides with the congressional district (because the voters will already know her). For similar reasons, U.S. representatives from small states, whose congressional districts cover a large portion of the state, are far more likely to run for statewide office than members of Congress from large states. For example, John Thune was elected as the lone representative from South Dakota in 1996. His constituency thus completely overlapped those of Senators Tim Johnson and Tom Daschle. In 2002, Thune challenged Johnson, losing by barely 500 votes. In 2004, he defeated Daschle, then the Democratic leader in the Senate. For any candidate, decisions about running must be made early because once money has been committed to declared candidates, it is harder for new candidates to break into a race. Thus the outcome of a November election is partially determined many months earlier, when decisions to run are finalized.[10]

Incumbency. **Incumbency** plays a very important role in the American electoral system and in the kind of representation citizens get in Washington. Once in office, members of Congress are typically eager to remain in office and make politics a career. Over the course of the twentieth century, Congress developed into a professional legislature, a legislature whose members serve full time for multiple terms (Figure 6.2).[11] The career ambitions of members of Congress are

 incumbency

Holding the political office for which one is running

---

9   See Linda L. Fowler and Robert D. McClure, *Political Ambition: Who Decides to Run for Congress* (New Haven, CT: Yale University Press, 1989), and Alan Ehrenhalt, *The United States of Ambition: Politicians, Power, and the Pursuit of Office* (New York: Times Books, 1991).

10 On the thesis of "strategic candidacy," see Gary C. Jacobson, *The Politics of Congressional Elections*, 8th ed. (New York: Pearson Longman, 2012).

11 Nelson W. Polsby, "The Institutionalization of the U.S. House of Representatives," *American Political Science Review* 62, no. 1 (March 1968): 144–68.

Figure 6.2

AVERAGE TURNOVER IN THE HOUSE OF REPRESENTATIVES

NOTE: Average turnover is the percent of new members in the House averaged over five House elections in a decade. In the period 1790–2012, the mean turnover was 30.7.
SOURCE: Based on John Swain, Stephen A. Borelli, Brian C. Reed, and Sean F. Evans, "A New Look at Turnover in the U.S. House of Representatives, 1789–1998," *American Politics Quarterly* 28 (2000): 435–57, plus author updates.

helped by an array of tools that they can use to stack the deck in favor of their re-election. These tools have been created by incumbent legislators themselves to aid their own cause—the rationality principle at work once again. Through effective use of this arsenal of weapons, an incumbent establishes a reputation for competence, imagination, and responsiveness—the attributes most principals look for in an agent.

Perhaps the most important advantage of incumbency is the opportunity legislators have to serve on legislative committees. Especially in the House, but often in the Senate as well, incumbent legislators are able to burnish their policy credentials, to develop expertise and, critically, to be in a position to help constituents, either through affecting the legislative agenda or interceding with the bureaucracy. It is here—on committees—that incumbents establish a track record of accomplishments that compares favorably with the mere promises of electoral challengers. This advantage is especially powerful when a legislator's committees deal with issues central to the lives of his constituents. (And, party leaders in Congress are adept at matching their members to the "right" committees—yet another example of the rationality principle at work.) Finally, the advantage of committee membership is cumulative: continuous service on a committee not only enhances a legislator's policy credentials and expertise but also positions her for committee leadership posts.

The opportunity to help constituents is a clear advantage that committee membership gives incumbents. But helping constituents—and thus gaining support in the district—goes beyond the particular committees in which a member serves. In establishing an attractive political reputation and a "personal" relationship with his constituents, well over a quarter of a representative's time and nearly two-thirds of the time of his staff members is devoted to constituency service (termed **casework**). This service is not merely a matter of writing and mailing letters. It includes talking to constituents, providing them with minor services, introducing special bills for them, and attempting to influence decisions by agencies and regulatory commissions on their behalf. Indeed, one might think of the member's legislative staff and office operation as a congressional enterprise, much like a firm, with the member himself or herself as the chief executive officer.[12]

One very direct way in which incumbent members of Congress serve as the agents of their constituencies is through **patronage**. Patronage refers to a variety of forms of direct services and benefits that members provide for their districts. One of the most important forms of patronage is **pork-barrel legislation**. Through pork-barrel legislation, representatives seek to capture federal projects and federal funds for their districts (or states in the case of senators) and thus "bring home the bacon."

A common form of pork barreling is the earmark, the practice through which members of Congress insert language into otherwise pork-free bills that provides special benefits for their own constituents.[13] For example, among the more outrageous earmarks in a 2005 transportation bill was a bridge in Alaska that cost more than $10 million and connected the mainland to an island on which no one lives (the so-called bridge to nowhere). This earmark proved so embarrassing to the Republicans once they began receiving adverse publicity that they rescinded the appropriation.

By 2010 House Republicans had sworn off earmarks altogether and their partisan colleagues in the Senate, though less enthusiastically, seemed willing to go along. In one of the last actions taken by the 111th Congress—the lame-duck session following the November 2010 elections—a spending bill funding government operations through March 2011 was stripped of nearly all earmarks.

 casework

An effort by members of Congress to gain the trust and support of constituents by providing personal services. One important type of casework consists of helping constituents obtain favorable treatment from the federal bureaucracy

 patronage

The resources available to higher officials, usually opportunities to make partisan appointments to offices and confer grants, licenses, or special favors to supporters

 pork-barrel legislation

The appropriations made by legislative bodies for local projects that often are not needed but are created so that local representatives can carry their home district in the next election

---

12 For more on the congressional office as an enterprise that processes the casework demands of constituents, see Robert H. Salisbury and Kenneth A. Shepsle, "Congressman as Enterprise," *Legislative Studies Quarterly* 6 (1981): 559–76.

13 For a study of academic earmarking, see James D. Savage, *Funding Science in America: Congress, Universities, and the Politics of the Academic Pork Barrel* (New York: Cambridge University Press, 1999). For a general study of pork-barrel activity, see the excellent book by Diana Evans, *Greasing the Wheels: Using Pork Barrel Projects to Build Majority Coalitions in Congress* (New York: Cambridge University Press, 2004).

Pork-barrel activities by incumbent legislators bring a number of our principles from Chapter 1 into play. Incumbent legislators engage in the practice because it furthers their electoral objectives (the rationality principle). They succeed to the degree that they are able to join with fellow legislators in exchanging support for one another's projects (the collective action principle). These efforts are facilitated by institutional procedures: amendments to appropriations bills, omnibus legislation, and opportunities to insert special provisions into bills (the institution principle). And they decidedly influence the mix and location of spending by the federal government (the policy principle). From time to time, as with the "bridge to nowhere," the practice becomes so egregious that Congress establishes procedures to restrict the activity, thereby constraining the actions of members of Congress in the future (the history principle). In the most recent Congress any earmark inserted in a bill must be accompanied by the name of the sponsoring legislator. For those earmarks popular in the district and not noticeably embarrassing to colleagues, a member would not object to her association. The practice, however, will discourage more outrageous efforts.

Finally we should note that all of these incumbent benefits are publicized though another incumbency advantage—the franking privilege. Under a law enacted by the 1st Congress in 1789, members of Congress may send mail to their constituents free of charge to keep them informed of governmental business and public affairs. Under current law, members receive an average of about $100,000 in free postage for mailings to their constituents. There is a great variety of franked mail. Some target special groups on issues of direct interest to them—for example, news about minimum wage legislation sent to union households in the district. Most common of all are "your congressman at work" newsletters, which are sent to households in an entire district on a regular basis.

Members may not use these funds to send mail outside their districts, however, or to send mass mailings within 90 days of a primary or general election. Despite the restrictions, the franking privilege provides incumbents with a valuable resource for publicizing their activities and making themselves visible to voters.

The incumbency advantage is evident in the high rates of re-election among congressional incumbents: over 90 percent for House members and nearly 90 percent for members of the Senate in recent years (Figure 6.3).[14] In the 2010 elections, dozens of incumbent Democrats lost their seats to Republican challengers in the House, but still a majority of all incumbents (from both parties) who ran held on to their seats—nearly 80 percent of Democrats and more than 98 percent of Republicans. In 2012, 91 percent of those incumbents running

---

14 Norman J. Ornstein, Thomas E. Mann, and Michael J. Malbin, *Vital Statistics on Congress, 1995–1996* (Washington, DC: CQ Press, 1996), pp. 60–1 (see also subsequent editions); Robert S. Erickson and Gerald C. Wright, "Voters, Candidates, and Issues in Congressional Elections," in *Congress Reconsidered*, 8th ed., Lawrence C. Dodd and Bruce I. Oppenheimer, eds. (Washington, DC: CQ Press, 2005), pp. 77–106; and John R. Alford and David W. Brady, "Personal and Partisan Advantage in U.S. Congressional Elections, 1846–1990," in *Congress Reconsidered*, 5th ed., Lawrence C. Dodd and Bruce I. Oppeheimer, eds. (Washington, DC: CQ Press, 1993), pp. 141–57.

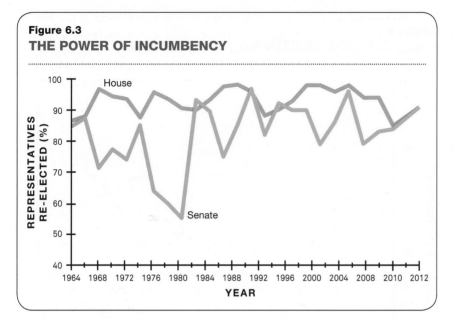

Figure 6.3

THE POWER OF INCUMBENCY

SOURCES: Center for Responsive Politics, www.opensecrets.org/bigpicture/reelect.php?cycle=2010, and author updates.

for re-election in each chamber won. In the Senate, 10 of the 33 incumbents left the body, but 21 of the 23 running for re-election were successful; in the House 39 members retired, 13 lost primaries, and 27 lost in the general election, leaving 356 of 396 successful.

An additional incumbency advantage is in fund-raising. With their "brand name," incumbents are in a position to raise campaign funds throughout their term, often in such quantities as to overwhelm prospective challengers. Members of Congress almost always are able to outspend their challengers (Figure 6.4).[15] Over the past quarter-century, and despite many campaign finance regulations that were meant to level the playing field, the gap between incumbent and challenger spending has grown. Members of the majority party in the House and Senate are particularly attractive to donors who want access to those in power.[16]

Incumbency can help a candidate by discouraging potential opponents, not only because of an incumbent's war-chest advantages but also because challengers fear that the incumbent has simply brought too many benefits to the district or is too well liked or too well known.[17] Challengers may also decide that a district's partisan leanings are too unfavorable. The incumbency advantage is

15 Stephen Ansolabehere and James Snyder, "Campaign War Chests and Congressional Elections," *Business and Politics* 2 (2000): 9–34.

16 Gary W. Cox and Eric Magar, "How Much Is Majority Status in the U.S. Congress Worth?" *American Political Science Review* 93, no. 2 (June 1999): 299–309.

17 Kenneth Bickers and Robert Stein, "The Electoral Dynamics of the Federal Pork Barrel," *American Journal of Political Science* 40 (1996): 1300–26.

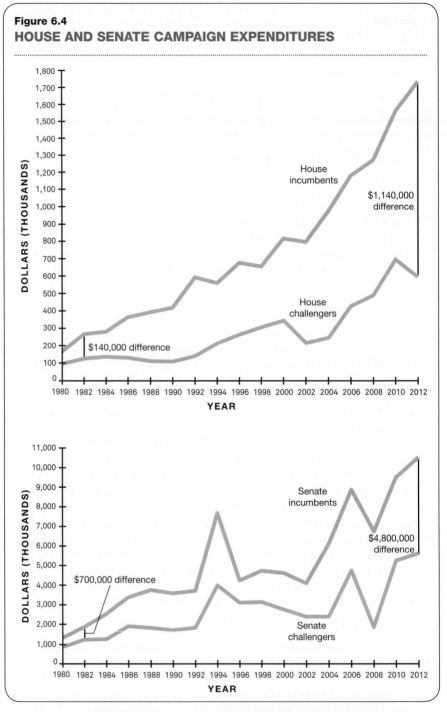

Figure 6.4

HOUSE AND SENATE CAMPAIGN EXPENDITURES

SOURCES: Norman J. Ornstein, Thomas E. Mann, and Michael J. Malbin, *Vital Statistics on Congress, 2001–2002* (Washington, DC: American Enterprise Institute, 2002), pp. 87, 93; and Campaign Finance Institute, www.cfinst.org (accessed 8/8/11).

evident in what is called sophomore surge—the tendency for candidates to win a higher percentage of the vote when seeking their second term in office than they won in their initial election victory. The advantage of incumbency tends to preserve the status quo in Congress by discouraging potentially strong challengers from running.

When incumbents do face strong challengers, however, the incumbents are often defeated.[18] The reason is that strong challengers are willing to throw their hat into the ring only when they believe the incumbent is weak, out of touch, too preoccupied with national affairs, or plagued by scandal or declining capabilities. Indeed, incumbents afflicted in any of these ways may choose to retire voluntarily (strategic retirement) instead of facing the high probability of defeat. Another source of incumbent vulnerability is the unpopularity of their party label. In 2006, Senator Lincoln Chafee (R-R.I.) illustrated the latter. Despite a personal popularity rating of 62 percent in the polls, he was defeated as many Rhode Islanders signaled their displeasure with the Bush administration and the Republican Congress.

The role of incumbency also has implications for the social composition of Congress. For example, the incumbency advantage makes it harder for women to increase their numbers in Congress because most incumbents are men. Female candidates who run for open seats (for which there are no incumbents) are just as likely to win as male candidates but they have to wait until a seat opens up.[19] (See the Analyzing the Evidence unit for further discussion of the election of women to Congress.) Supporters of term limits argue that such limits are the best way to get new faces into Congress. They believe that the incumbency advantage and the tendency of many legislators to view politics as a career mean that very little turnover will occur in Congress unless limits are imposed on the number of terms a legislator can serve.

But the tendency toward the status quo is not absolute. In 1992, an exceptionally high retirement rate among members of the House created more open seats and brought new faces into Congress.[20] In 1994, a large number of open seats combined with an unprecedented mobilization of Republican voters to shift control of Congress to the Republican Party. In 2006, the reverse happened. The Democrats needed to gain 15 seats to capture the House, and they won double that number; in the Senate, they captured the six Republican seats they needed to win control of that chamber. The election in 2010 saw another reversal as Republicans easily exceeded the gains required to capture the House

---

18 Jacobson, *The Politics of Congressional Elections.*

19 See Barbara C. Burrell, *A Woman's Place Is in the House: Campaigning for Congress in the Feminist Era* (Ann Arbor: University of Michigan Press, 1994); and David Broder, "Key to Women's Political Parity: Running," *Washington Post*, September 8, 1994, p. A17.

20 The reason for the high voluntary retirement rate that year is interesting. Congress had passed a reform making it impossible for members to pocket money left in their office accounts when they retired. The last year in which pocketing this money was permitted was 1992, and a number of members took that opportunity to retire, some enriching themselves by hundreds of thousands of dollars.

Why Do Congresswomen Outperform Congressmen?

CHAPTER | 06

Contributed by
Chris Berry
University of Chicago

The 97 women sworn into the U.S. Congress in January 2013 made history as the largest number ever elected. Despite this achievement, women are still substantially underrepresented in elected offices. As the charts show, women have never held more than 20 percent of the seats in either the House of Representatives or the Senate.

Share of Seats Held by Women

HOUSE ■ Women ■ Men

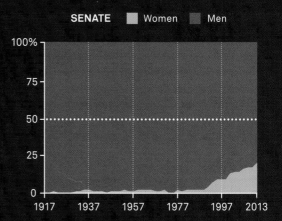

SENATE ■ Women ■ Men

Why are women underrepresented in elected office? One reason is continued discrimination by voters against female candidates. According to a Gallup survey, 11 percent of respondents reported that they would not vote for a female candidate, and another 11 percent would vote for a female "only with reservations." This is a significant hurdle for female politicians to overcome.

Would You Vote for a Candidate Who Was...?

SOURCE: USA Today / Gallup Poll, February 9–11 and March 2–4, 2007 (N=1,011).

■ Completely comfortable voting for

■ Would vote for with reservations

■ Would not vote for

When women confront voter bias, only the most talented, politically ambitious females will attempt to run for office, and voters will elect only the most highly capable women. Because of one or both of these factors, the women who *win* a seat will be higher performing than their male colleagues, on average. That individuals facing discrimination must perform better in order to succeed is familiar from the history of minorities in professional sports. A leading example is Jackie Robinson, the first African American to play major league baseball and one of the best players of all time. Researchers have dubbed this phenomenon "The Jackie (and Jill) Robinson Effect."

To measure a legislator's performance on the job, we can look at constituency services, which includes bringing home federal projects, and legislating, which means writing bills and shepherding them through the lawmaking process. The chart below provides evidence that congresswomen outperform congressmen on both dimensions. For each activity, the performance of men is normalized to 1 and the score for women indicates the percentage by which women outperform the men. For example, the score of 1.09 for women in the first bar indicates that a district receives on average 9 percent more spending in the years when a woman represents it. This is equivalent to roughly $50 million per year. Congresswomen also sponsor and cosponsor more bills than congressmen do, and they obtain more cosponsors on their own legislation.

These results are consistent with the idea that women outperform men in logrolling, coalition building, and other deal-making activities that are essential to being a successful legislator. Note, however, that the argument is not that women are innately more talented or harder working than men but that the process by which women are selected into office means that those *who are elected* have to work harder or be more capable. Over time, if voter prejudice against women were eliminated, women's observed performance advantage should evaporate as well.

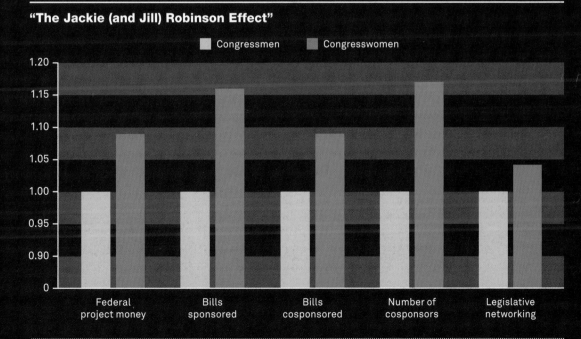

"The Jackie (and Jill) Robinson Effect"

SOURCE: Sarah F. Anzia and Christopher R. Berry, "The Jackie (and Jill) Robinson Effect: Why Do Congresswomen Outperform Congressmen?" *American Journal of Political Science,* 55, no. 3 (2011): 478–93.

and barely fell short of capturing the Senate. As these elections suggest, the advantages of incumbency, always considerable, are not necessarily decisive.

Congressional Districts. The final factor that affects who wins a seat in Congress is the way congressional districts are drawn. Every 10 years, state legislatures must redraw congressional districts to reflect population changes. In 1929, Congress enacted a law fixing the total number of congressional seats at 435. As a result, when states with fast-growing populations gain districts, they do so at the expense of states with slower population growth. In recent decades, this has meant that the nation's growth areas in the South and West have gained congressional seats at the expense of the Northeast and the Midwest (Figure 6.5). After the 2010 census, for example, Texas gained four seats and Florida two, whereas New York and Ohio lost two each. Redrawing congressional districts is a highly political process: in most states, districts are shaped to create an advantage for the majority party in the state legislature, which controls the redistricting process (subject to a possible veto by the governor who may be of a different party). In this complex process, those charged with drawing districts use sophisticated computer technologies to come up with the most favorable district boundaries. Redistricting can create open seats and may pit incumbents of the same party against each other, ensuring that one of them will lose. Redistricting can also give an advantage to one party by clustering voters with some ideological or sociological characteristics in a single district or by separating those voters into two or more districts. **Gerrymandering** can have a major effect on the outcome of congressional elections. Before 1980, for example, California's House seats had been almost evenly divided between the two parties. After the 1980 census, a redistricting effort controlled by the Democrats, who held both houses of the state legislature as well as the governorship, resulted in Democrats' taking control of two-thirds of the state's seats in the U.S. House of Representatives.[21] Another more recent case benefited the Republicans. The 2002 congressional election was the first one under the redistricting required by the 2000 census. In 2003, the Texas legislature, controlled by the Republicans, set to work drawing up a *new* set of congressional districts. Ordinarily this exercise is performed once per decade, after the constitutionally required census. But, argued the Texas Republicans, nothing prohibits a state from doing it more frequently. Democrats in the Texas state legislature were furious and twice staged walkouts, even fleeing across the border to Oklahoma to avoid a posse of Texas Rangers sent to retrieve them. These walkouts delayed proceedings by making it difficult to assemble enough legislators to meet the minimum requirements to do legislative business. Finally, however, the Republicans prevailed, redrawing the federal districts in a way that was very favorable to them. In the next election in 2004, the Republicans gained five seats in Texas, defeating four Democratic incumbents,

gerrymandering

The apportionment of voters in districts in such a way as to give unfair advantage to one political party

---

21 David Butler and Bruce Cain, *Congressional Redistricting: Comparative and Theoretical Perspectives* (New York: Macmillan, 1992).

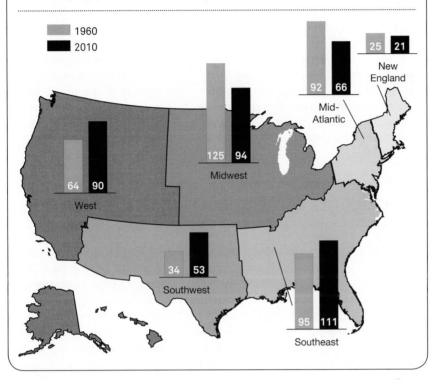

Figure 6.5

APPORTIONMENT OF HOUSE SEATS BY REGION, 1960 AND 2010

- 1960
- 2010

New England
25 | 21

Mid-Atlantic
92 | 66

Midwest
125 | 94

West
64 | 90

Southwest
34 | 53

Southeast
95 | 111

SOURCE: U.S. Census Bureau, Congressional Apportionment, 2010 Census Briefs, Table 1, www
.census.gov/prod/cen2010/briefs/c2010br-08.pdf (accessed 2/16/13).

in part as a result of their redistricting maneuver.[22] Examples such as these explain why the two national parties invest substantial resources in state legislative and gubernatorial contests during the electoral cycle that precedes the year in which congressional district boundaries will be redrawn. The Analyzing the Evidence unit in Chapter 11 takes a closer look at redistricting and its ramifications.

As we see in Chapter 11, since the passage of the 1982 amendments to the 1965 Voting Rights Act, race has become a major—and controversial—consideration in drawing voting districts. These amendments, which encouraged the creation of districts in which members of racial minorities have decisive majorities, have greatly increased the number of minority representatives in

22 In late 2004, the U.S. Supreme Court ordered a lower federal court to reconsider the "extra" Texas redistricting plan. This case worked its way back to the Supreme Court. In June 2006, the Court ruled that the Texas legislature was within its rights to redistrict more than once per decade; however, it also ruled that some of the particular decisions about district boundaries violated the rights of Latino voters.

Congress. Among the most fervent supporters of the new minority districts were white Republicans, who used the opportunity to create more districts dominated by white Republican voters.[23]

These developments raise thorny questions about representation. Some analysts argue that although the system may grant minorities greater descriptive representation (also called sociological representation), it has made it more difficult for them to win substantive policy goals.[24] There is no doubt that descriptive representation has grown. After the 2012 election the House is more female and minority than ever in its history, though this is primarily a Democratic Party affair.[25] But, especially regarding minorities, the creation of a growing number of minority-majority districts has meant that minority voter proportions in other districts have become diluted, opening up the possibility that representatives from these districts will be less responsive to minority policy concerns.

PROBLEMS OF LEGISLATIVE ORGANIZATION

The U.S. Congress is not only a representative assembly. It is also a legislative body. For Americans, representation and legislation go hand in hand. Yet governing is a challenge. It is extraordinarily difficult for a large, representative assembly to formulate, enact, and implement laws. Just the internal complexities of conducting business within Congress—the legislative process—are daunting. In addition, many individuals and institutions have the capacity to influence the legislative process. Because successful legislation requires the confluence of so many distinct factors, it is little wonder that most of the thousands of bills considered by Congress each year are defeated long before they reach the president.

The supporters of legislative proposals often feel that the formal rules of the congressional process are deliberately designed to prevent their own deserving proposals from ever seeing the light of day. But these rules allow Congress to play an important role in lawmaking. If it wants to be more than a rubber stamp for the executive branch, which many other representative assemblies around the world are limited to, a national legislature such as Congress must develop a division of labor, set an agenda, maintain order through rules and procedures, and place limits on discussion. If it wants to accomplish these tasks in a representative setting in which a veritable diversity of political preferences exists, then it must

---

23 David Lublin, *The Paradox of Representation: Racial Gerrymandering and Minority Interests in Congress* (Princeton, NJ: Princeton University Press, 1997).

24 Lani Guinier, *The Tyranny of the Majority: Fundamental Fairness in Representative Democracy* (New York: Free Press, 1995). See also David Epstein and Sharyn O'Halloran, "Measuring the Electoral and Policy Impact of Majority-Minority Voting Districts," *American Journal of Political Science* 42 (1999): 367–95.

25 The Democratic Caucus in 2013 is 53 percent female and minority, whereas the Republican Conference is 90 percent white male.

find the ways and means to allow cooperation despite the variety of interests and coalitions and to make compromises despite conflicts. We will first take up the general issues that face any legislature or decision-making group possessing diverse preferences: the problems of cooperation, coalitions, and compromises.

Cooperation in Congress

A number of factors make cooperation difficult in Congress. A popularly elected legislative assembly—the Boston City Council, the Kansas state legislature, the U.S. Congress, the French National Assembly, or the European Parliament—consists of politicians who harbor a variety of political objectives. Because they got where they are by winning an election and many hope to stay where they are or possibly advance their political careers, these politicians are intimately aware of whom they must please to do so:

- Because campaigns are expensive propositions, most politicians are eager to please those who can supply resources for the next campaign—campaign donors, PACs, important endorsers, party officials, volunteer activists.

- The most recent campaign—one that the politicians won—provides them with information about just how their victory was secured. It is sometimes quite difficult to sort out the myriad factors, but at the very least the politicians have a good sense of what categories of voters supported them and may be prepared to support them again if performance is adequate.

- Many politicians not only aim to please campaign contributors and voters but also have an agenda of their own. Whether for private gain or public good, politicians come to the legislature with policy goals of personal importance.

Congress consists of a heterogeneous group of legislators, and the specific public policies that they want to pursue are thus many and varied. They may be considered from two perspectives. First, owing to their different constituencies, legislators will give priority to different realms of public policy. A Cape Cod congressman will be interested in shipping, fishing, coastal preservation, harbor development, tourism, and shipbuilding. An inner-city Philadelphia congresswoman may not care much at all about those issues, focusing instead on welfare reform, civil rights policy, aid to inner-city school systems, and job-retraining programs. Montana's sole member of Congress is probably not interested in coastal preservation or inner-city schools but rather in ranching, agriculture, mining, and public land use. Evidently, Congress encompasses a mélange of legislative priorities.

Second, the opinions its members hold on any given issue are diverse. Although interest in environmental protection, for example, ranges from high among those who count many Sierra Club members among their constituents to low among those who have other fish to fry, once environmental protection is on the agenda there is a broad range of preferences for specific initiatives. Some want pollution discharges carefully monitored and regulated by a relatively powerful watchdog agency. Others believe that more decentralized and less intrusive means, such as marketable pollution permits, are the way to go—so-called cap-and-trade policies. Still others think the entire issue is overblown, that any proposed cure is worse than the disease, and that the country would be best served by leaving well enough alone.

Diversity in both priorities and preferences among legislators is sufficiently abundant that the view of no group of legislators predominates. Legislative consensus must be built—this is what legislative politics is all about. Each legislator clamors to get his priority issue the attention he believes it deserves or to make sure his position on a given issue prevails. But neither effort is likely to succeed on its own merits. Support must be assembled, deals consummated, and promises and threats used. In short, legislators intent on achieving their objectives must cooperate, coalesce, and compromise. And these activities are facilitated by rules and procedures. This system leads to the division and specialization of legislative work, the regularization of procedures, and the creation of agenda power. All of these organizational features of Congress arise as part of a governance structure to allow for cooperation and coalition building—activities that yield compromise policies.

Underlying Problems and Challenges

Before we can understand why Congress selects particular ways to institutionalize its practices, we need a finer appreciation of other underlying problems with which legislators must grapple. Then we can consider how the U.S. Congress deals with these problems.

Matching Influence and Interest. Legislatures are highly egalitarian institutions. Each legislator has one vote on any issue coming before the body. Whereas a consumer has a cash budget that she may allocate in any way she wishes to categories of consumer goods, a legislator is not given a vote budget in quite the same sense. Instead, his budget of votes is "dedicated"—one vote for each motion before the assembly. He cannot aggregate the votes in his possession and cast all or some large fraction of them for a motion on a subject near and dear to his heart (or the hearts of his constituents). This is a source of frustration because, as we have noted, the premise of instrumental behavior dictates that legislators would, if they could, concentrate whatever resources they commanded on those subjects of highest priority to them. The egalitarian arrangement thus forces legislators to make deals with one another—"I'll support you on this motion if you support me on a future motion."

Information. Legislators do not vote for outcomes directly but, rather, for instruments (or policies) whose effects produce outcomes. Thus legislators, to vote intelligently, must know the connection between the instruments they vote for and the effects they desire. In short, they must have information and knowledge about how the world works.

Few legislators—indeed, few people in general—know how the world works in very many policy domains except in the most superficial of ways. Nearly everyone in the legislature would benefit from the production of valuable information, at the very least information that would allow all of them to eliminate policy instruments that make very little difference in solving social problems or even make matters worse. Producing such information, however, is not a trivial matter. Simply to digest the knowledge that is being produced outside the legislature by knowledge-industry specialists (academics, scientists, journalists, interest groups) is a taxing task. Clearly institutional arrangements that provide incentives to some legislators to produce, evaluate, and disseminate this knowledge for others will permit public resources to be used more effectively. Because legislatures are in competition with other branches of government—particularly the executive—legislators need to meet certain informational requirements just to keep up with the competition.

Compliance. The legislature is not the only game in town. The promulgation of public policies is a joint undertaking in which judges, executives, bureaucrats, and others participate alongside legislators. If the legislature develops no means with which to monitor what happens after a bill becomes law, then it risks seeing public policies implemented in ways other than those it intended when the law was passed. But it is just not practical for all 435 representatives and all 100 senators to march down to this or that agency on Pennsylvania Avenue to ensure appropriate implementation by the executive bureaucracy. Compliance will not just happen, and like the production and dissemination of reliable information at the policy-formulation stage, the need for oversight of the executive bureaucracy is but an extension of the cooperation that produced legislation in the first place. It, too, must be institutionalized.

What we have suggested in this abstract discussion about legislative institutions and practices is that Congress is a place in which different kinds of representatives congregate and try to accomplish goals so that they may reap the support of their respective constituents back home. This very diversity is problematic—it requires cooperation, coalitions, and compromise. In addition, there is a mismatch of influence and interest (owing to one person, one vote), information about the effectiveness of alternative policies is in short supply, and the legislature must worry about how its product—public laws—gets treated by the other branches of government. These are the problems that legislatures, including the U.S. Congress, devise institutional arrangements to solve or at least mitigate. This is where the rationality principle and institution principle join forces.

THE ORGANIZATION OF CONGRESS

We now examine the organization of Congress and the legislative process, particularly the basic building blocks of congressional organization: political parties, the committee system, congressional staff, the caucuses, and the

party caucus, or party conference

A normally closed meeting of a political or legislative group to select candidates or leaders, plan strategy, or make decisions regarding legislative matters

Speaker of the House

The chief presiding officer of the House of Representatives. The Speaker is elected at the beginning of every Congress on a straight party vote. He or she is the most important party and House leader

majority leader

The elected leader of the party holding a majority of the seats in the House of Representatives or the Senate. In the House, the majority leader is subordinate in the party hierarchy to the Speaker

minority leader

The elected leader of the party holding less than a majority of the seats in the House or Senate

parliamentary rules of the House and Senate. Each of these factors plays a key role in the organization of Congress and in the process through which Congress formulates and enacts laws. We also look at powers Congress has in addition to lawmaking and explore the future role of Congress in relation to the powers of the executive.

Party Leadership and Organization in the House and the Senate

One significant aspect of legislative life is not even part of the *official* organization: political parties. The legislative parties—primarily Democratic and Republican in modern times but numerous others over the course of American history—are organizations that foster cooperation, coalitions, and compromise. They are the vehicles of collective action, both for legislators sharing common policy objectives inside the legislature and for those very same legislators as candidates in periodic election contests back home.[26] In short, political parties in Congress are the fundamental building blocks from which policy coalitions are fashioned to pass legislation and monitor its implementation, thereby providing a track record on which members build electoral support.

Every two years at the start of a new Congress, the members of each party gather to elect their House leaders. This gathering is called the **party caucus** by the Democrats and the **party conference** by the Republicans. The elected leader of the majority party is later proposed to the whole House and is automatically elected to the position of **Speaker of the House**, with voting along straight party lines. The House majority caucus (or conference) also elects a **majority leader**. The minority party goes through the same process and selects the **minority leader**. Both parties also elect "whips," who line up party members on important votes and relay voting intentions to the party leaders.

In December 2006, in the wake of the November elections, the Democrats become the majority party in both chambers. In the House, they selected Nancy Pelosi of California as Speaker, Steny Hoyer of Maryland as majority leader, and James Clyburn of South Carolina as whip. The Republicans, who had in the previous Congress made John Boehner of Ohio their majority leader, kept him on as minority leader, as well as Roy Blunt of Missouri as minority whip. In 2008, Republicans chose Eric Cantor of Virgina to replace Blunt as

26 For a historically grounded analysis of the development of political parties as well as a treatment of their general contemporary significance, see John H. Aldrich, *Why Parties? The Origin and Transformation of Political Parties in America* (Chicago: University of Chicago Press, 1995). For an analysis of the parties in the legislative process, see Gary W. Cox and Mathew D. McCubbins, *Legislative Leviathan: Party Government in the House*, 2nd ed. (Berkeley: University of California Press, 2006). See also their *Setting the Agenda: Responsible Party Government in the U.S. House of Representatives* (New York: Cambridge University Press, 2005). A provocative essay questioning the role of parties is Keith Krehbiel, "Where's the Party?" *British Journal of Political Science* 23 (1993): 235–66.

whip, but otherwise the leadership from both parties remained the same. In 2010 there was another reversal of fortune as the Republicans stormed back into the majority. Both parties kept their top leaders: Boehner and Cantor as Speaker and majority leader, respectively, and Pelosi and Hoyer as their minority counterparts. As the 2012 elections continued Republican control of the House, the leadership remained the same.

At one time, party leaders strictly controlled committee assignments, using them to enforce party discipline. Today representatives often expect to receive the assignments they want and resent leadership efforts to control assignments. The leadership's best opportunities to use committee assignments as rewards and punishments come when more than one member seeks a seat on a committee.

Generally representatives seek assignments that will allow them to influence decisions of special importance to their districts. Representatives from farm districts, for example, may request seats on the Agriculture Committee.[27] This is one method by which the egalitarian allocation of power in the legislature is overcome. Even though each legislator has just one vote on each issue in the full chamber, she, by serving on the right committees, is able to acquire extra influence in areas important to her constituents. Seats on powerful committees such as Ways and Means, which is responsible for tax legislation, and Energy and Commerce, responsible for health, energy, and regulatory policy, are especially popular.

We now turn to the Senate, where the president pro tempore, a position designated in the Constitution, exercises mainly ceremonial leadership. Usually the majority party designates the member with the greatest seniority to serve in this capacity. Real power is in the hands of the majority and minority leaders, each elected by party caucus. Together they control the Senate's calendar, or agenda, for legislation. In addition, the senators from each party elect a whip.

The 2002 elections gave the Republican Party a one-seat majority in the Senate. In the 2004 election, they gained an additional four seats, for a 55-to-45 majority. Republicans re-elected Bill Frist of Tennessee as majority leader, while Democrats replaced the recently defeated Tom Daschle of South Dakota with Harry Reid of Nevada as the minority leader. After their six-seat gain in the 2006 election, the Democrats named Reid majority leader. The Republicans elected Mitch McConnell of Kentucky to the post of minority leader. Both were re-elected to these positions after the 2008, 2010, and 2012 elections.

Party leaders reach outside their respective chambers in an effort to augment their power and enhance prospects for their party programs. One important external strategy involves fund-raising. In recent years, congressional leaders have established their own political action committees. Interest groups are

---

27 For an extensive discussion of the committee-assignment process in the U.S. House, see Kenneth A. Shepsle, *The Giant Jigsaw Puzzle: Democratic Committee Assignments in the Modern House* (Chicago: University of Chicago Press, 1978); and Scott A. Frisch and Sean Q. Kelly, *Committee Assignment Politics in the U.S. House of Representatives* (Norman: University of Oklahoma Press, 2006). See also E. Scott Adler, *Why Congressional Reforms Fail: Reelection and the House Committee System* (Chicago: University of Chicago Press, 2002).

usually eager to contribute to these "leadership PACs" in order to curry favor with powerful members of Congress. The leaders, in turn, use the funds to support the various campaigns of their party's candidates and thereby create a sense of obligation and loyalty among those they help.[28]

In addition to the tasks of organizing Congress, congressional party leaders set the legislative agenda. Not only do the party leaders have considerable sway over Congress's agenda in the large but they also regulate the fine-grained deliberation over specific items on the agenda. This aspect of agenda setting is multifaceted. At the outset, for example, a bill is initially filed with the clerk of the House as a legislative proposal. The Speaker of the House then determines which committee has jurisdiction over it. Indeed, since the mid-1970s, the Speaker has been given additional bill-assignment powers, known as multiple referral, permitting him to assign different parts of a bill to different committees or the same parts sequentially or simultaneously to several committees.[29] The steering and agenda setting by party leaders work, however, within an institutional framework consisting of structures and procedures.

Having described some of the powers of party leaders, we might pause and ask an even more basic question: Why do members allow themselves to be governed by powerful party leaders? Leaders, after all, are elected by their rank-and-file members, and in their respective party caucuses the rank and file determine how powerful they will permit their leaders to be. Indeed, the power of party leaders has ebbed and flowed over time. From the end of World War II until as late as the 1970s, for example, when the Democrats were the majority party most of the time, party leaders were relatively weak. Speaker of the House Sam Rayburn (D-Tex.), to give one example, was beloved by his followers and was quite successful at persuading members to toe the party line during the 1940s and 1950s. But persuasion was just about the only tool at his disposal. Later party leaders possessed more potent tools. Jim Wright (D-Tex.), for example, who served as Speaker in the 1980s, was provided with considerable power over committee assignments and chaired most of the party committees that formulated policy objectives for the Democrats. Why did party leaders become more powerful?

---

28 Rank-and-file members, especially those from safe districts who face limited electoral challenges, have also created their own PACs, which enable them to contribute to their party and its candidates. See Eric S. Heberlig, "Congressional Parties, Fundraising, and Committee Ambition," *Political Research Quarterly* 56 (2003): 151–61.

29 For a historical look, see David W. Rohde and Kenneth A. Shepsle, "Leaders and Followers in the House of Representatives: Reflections on Woodrow Wilson's *Congressional Government*," *Congress and the Presidency* 14 (1987): 111–33. An analysis of the House leadership is Eric Schickler and Kathryn Pearson, "The House Leadership in an Era of Partisan Warfare," in *Congress Reconsidered*, 8th ed., pp. 207–26. A companion piece on the Senate is C. Lawrence Evans and Daniel Lipinski, "Obstruction and Leadership in the U.S. Senate," in *Congress Reconsidered*, 8th ed., pp. 227–48. An update is Kathryn Pearson and Eric Schickler, "The Transition to Democratic Leadership in a Polarized House," in *Congress Reconsidered*, 9th ed., Lawrence C. Dodd and Bruce I. Oppenheimer, eds. (Washington, DC: CQ Press, 2008), pp. 165–89.

The political scientists John Aldrich and David Rohde have sought to understand these ebbs and flows in the power of a party over its members, or what they call "conditional party government." They suggest that the institutional strength of party leaders is conditional; it depends on particular circumstances. The circumstance they emphasize is the degree to which party members share policy goals. If the rank and file are relatively homogeneous in this respect, they will endow their leaders with considerable power to prosecute the shared agenda. If, on the other hand, party members are heterogeneous in their goals, they will be less disposed to empower a leader (indeed, they will be suspicious of any exercise of power by a leader). Thus the Democratic Party of the 1940s and 1950s, with its northern liberal wing and its southern conservative wing, was heterogeneous in the extreme and provided its leaders with few power resources. The effects of the Voting Rights Act of 1965, one of which was that formerly Democratic constituencies in the South started electing Republicans, began to be felt in the 1970s, reducing the diversity in the Democratic ranks and thus rendering the party more homogeneous. Under this changed circumstance, Democratic Party legislators, who were more focused than before on moderate and liberal goals, were prepared to empower their leaders.[30]

The Committee System: The Core of Congress

If the system of leadership in each party and chamber constitutes the first set of organizational arrangements in the U.S. Congress, then the committee system provides it with a second set of organizational structures. But these are more a division-of-labor and specialization-of-labor system than the hierarchy-of-power system that determines leadership arrangements.

Congress began as a relatively unspecialized assembly, with each legislator participating equally in every step of the legislative process in all realms of policy. By the time of the War of 1812, if not earlier, Congress had begun employing a system of specialists—the committee system—because members with different interests and talents wished to play disproportionate roles in some areas of policy making while ceding influence in areas in which they

---

30 A now-classic treatment of the ebbs and flows of parties and their leaders in the modern era is David W. Rohde, *Parties and Leaders in the Post-Reform House* (Chicago: University of Chicago Press, 1991). For a more historical perspective, see David W. Rohde, John H. Aldrich, and Mark M. Berger, "The Historical Variability in Conditional Party Government, 1877–1986," in *Party, Process, and Political Change in Congress: New Perspectives on the History of Congress*, David W. Brady and Mathew D. McCubbins, eds. (Palo Alto, CA: Stanford University Press, 2002), pp. 17–35. For a development of the analytical argument, see David W. Rohde and John H. Aldrich, "The Logic of Conditional Party Government: Revisiting the Electoral Connection," in *Congress Reconsidered*, 7th ed., Lawrence C. Dodd and Bruce I. Oppenheimer, eds. (Washington, DC: CQ Press, 2001), pp. 265–92. A complementary theoretical perspective is offered by the political scientists Gary Cox and Mathew McCubbins in both *Legislative Leviathan* and *Setting the Agenda*.

were less interested.[31] If, Rip van Winkle–like, a congressman had fallen asleep in 1805 and woke up in 1825, he would have found himself in an entirely transformed legislative world. The legislative chambers in the beginning of that period consisted of bodies of generalists. By the end of the period, in policy area after policy area, the legislative agenda was dominated by groups of specialists serving on standing committees. If, on the other hand, our legislator had fallen asleep in 1825 and awoke a *century* later, the legislature would not seem so very different. In short, organizational decisions in the first quarter of the nineteenth century affected legislative activity over a long horizon. This is the history principle at work.

The congressional committee system consists of a set of standing committees, each with its own jurisdiction, membership, and authority to act. Each **standing committee** is given a permanent status by the official rules, with a fixed membership, officers, rules, a staff, offices, and above all, a jurisdiction that is recognized by all other committees and, usually, the leadership as well (Table 6.3). The jurisdiction of each standing committee is defined by the subject matter of legislation. Except for the Rules Committee in the House and the Rules and Administration Committee in the Senate, all the important committees receive proposals for legislation and process them into official bills. The House Rules Committee decides the order in which bills come up for a vote and determines the rules that govern the length of debate and opportunity for amendments. The Senate Rules Committee focuses more on administrative matters—managing Senate buildings, the Government Printing Office, the Senate library, and other services—but also on substantive matters including corrupt practices, presidential succession, and the regulation of federal elections. The jurisdictions of the standing committees usually parallel those of the major departments or agencies in the executive branch. There are important exceptions—Appropriations and Rules in both chambers, for example—but by and large the division of labor is self-consciously designed to parallel executive-branch organization.

Jurisdiction. The world of policy is partitioned into policy jurisdictions, which become the responsibility of committees. The members of the Armed Services Committee, for example, become specialists in all aspects of military affairs, the subject matter defining their committee's jurisdiction. Legislators tend to have disproportionate influence in their respective committee jurisdictions, not only because they have become the most knowledgeable members of the legislature in that area of policy but also because they are given the opportunity to exercise various forms of agenda power, a subject we develop further in the next section.

Dividing up institutional activities among jurisdictions, thereby encouraging participants to specialize, has its advantages. But it has its costs, too. If the Armed Services Committee of the House of Representatives had no restraints, its members would undoubtedly shower their districts with military facilities and

---

standing committee ➡

A permanent legislative committee that considers legislation within its designated subject area; the basic unit of deliberation in the House and Senate

---

31 The story of the evolution of the standing committee system in the House and the Senate in the early part of the nineteenth century is told in Gerald Gamm and Kenneth A. Shepsle, "Emergence of Legislative Institutions: Standing Committees in the House and Senate, 1810–1825," *Legislative Studies Quarterly* 14 (1989): 39–66.

Table 6.3

STANDING COMMITTEES OF CONGRESS, 2013*

HOUSE COMMITTEES	
Agriculture	Intelligence
Appropriations	Judiciary
Armed Services	Natural Resources
Budget	Oversight and Government Reform
Education and the Workforce	Rules
Energy and Commerce	Science, Space, and Technology
Ethics	Small Business
Financial Services	Transportation and Infrastructure
Foreign Affairs	Veterans' Affairs
Homeland Security	Ways and Means
House Administration	

SENATE COMMITTEES	
Agriculture, Nutrition, and Forestry	Finance
Appropriations	Foreign Relations
Armed Services	Health, Education, Labor, and Pensions
Banking, Housing, and Urban Affairs	Homeland Security and Governmental Affairs
Budget	Judiciary
Commerce, Science, and Transportation	Rules and Administration
Energy and Natural Resources	Small Business and Entrepreneurship
Environment and Public Works	Veterans' Affairs

* These were the committees in the 113th Congress (2013–14). Committee names and jurisdictions change over time, as does the number of committees.

contracts. In short, the delegation of authority and resources to specialist sub-units exploits the advantages of the division and specialization of labor but risks jeopardizing the collective objectives of the group as a whole. The monitoring of committee activities thus goes hand in hand with delegation.

Sometimes new issues arise that fit neatly into no jurisdiction. Some, such as the issue of energy supplies that emerged during the 1970s, are so multifaceted that bits and pieces of them are spread across many committee jurisdictions. Other issues, such as the regulation of tobacco products, fall into the gray area claimed by several committees. In this case in the House, the Energy and Commerce Committee, with its traditional claim on health-related issues, fought with the Agriculture Committee, whose traditional domain includes crops such as tobacco, for jurisdiction over this issue. Still others, like Homeland Security, arise at a time of crisis, overlap with the jurisdictions of other committees, and take time to sort out turf responsibilities. Turf battles between committees of Congress are notorious.[32] These battles involve committee chairs, the Office of the Parliamentarian, the political leadership of the chamber, and from time to time, select committees appointed to realign committee jurisdictions.

Authority. Committees may be thought of as agents of the parent body to which jurisdiction-specific authority is provisionally delegated. In this section, we describe committee authority in terms of gatekeeping and after-the-fact authority.

gatekeeping authority

The right and power to decide if a change in policy will be considered

Normally any member of the legislature can submit a bill calling for changes in some policy area. Almost automatically this bill is assigned to the committee of jurisdiction, and very nearly always, there it languishes. In a typical session in the House of Representatives, about 8,000 bills are submitted, fewer than 1,000 of which are acted on by the appropriate committee of jurisdiction. In effect, then, although any member is entitled to make proposals, committees get to decide whether to open the gates and allow the bill to be voted on by the full chamber. Related to **gatekeeping authority** is a committee's **proposal power**. After a bill is referred to a committee, the committee may take no further action on it, amend the legislation in any way, or even write its own legislation before bringing the bill to the floor for a vote. Committees, then, are lords of their jurisdictional domains, setting the table, so to speak, for their parent chamber.[33]

proposal power

The capacity to bring a proposal before the full legislature

---

32 An outstanding description and analysis of these battles is found in David C. King, "The Nature of Congressional Committee Jurisdictions," *American Political Science Review* 88, no. 1 (March 1994): 48–63. See also King's *Turf Wars: How Congressional Committees Claim Jurisdiction* (Chicago: University of Chicago Press, 1997).

33 This setup clearly gives committee members extraordinary power in their respective jurisdictions, allowing them to push policy into line with their own preferences—but only up to a point. If the abuse of their agenda power becomes excessive, the parent body has structural and procedural remedies available to counteract the committee's actions—such as stacking the committee with more compliant members, deposing a particularly obstreperous committee chair, or removing policies from a committee's jurisdiction. These are the clubs behind the door that only rarely have to be employed; their mere presence suffices to keep committees from the more outrageous forms of advantage taking.

A committee also has responsibilities for bargaining with the other chamber and for conducting oversight, or **after-the-fact authority**. Because the U.S. Congress is bicameral, once one chamber passes a bill, the bill must be considered by the other chamber. If the other chamber passes a bill different from the one passed in the first chamber and the first chamber refuses to accept the changes made, then the two chambers ordinarily meet in a **conference committee**, in which representatives from each chamber hammer out a compromise. In the great majority of cases, conferees are drawn from the committees that had original jurisdiction over the bill.[34] The committee's effective authority to represent its chamber in conference-committee proceedings constitutes the first manifestation of after-the-fact power that complements its before-the-fact gatekeeping and proposal powers.

A second manifestation of after-the-fact committee authority consists of the committee's primacy in legislative **oversight** of policy implementation by the executive bureaucracy. Even after a bill becomes a law, it is not always (indeed, it is rarely) self-implementing. Executive agents—bureaucrats in the career civil service, commissioners in regulatory agencies, political appointees in the executive branch—march to their own drummers. Unless legislative actors hold their feet to the fire, they may not do precisely what the law requires (especially in light of the fact that statutes are often vague and ambiguous). Congressional committees are continuously watchful of the manner in which legislation is implemented and administered. They play this after-the-fact role by allocating staff and resources to track what the executive branch is doing and, from time to time, holding oversight hearings in which particular policies and programs are given intense scrutiny. This, in turn, gives congressional committees an additional source of leverage over policy in their jurisdictions. Oversight is discussed further in Chapter 8 on the bureaucracy.

Subcommittees. The standing committees of the U.S. House are divided into about 100 even more specialized subcommittees. These subcommittees serve their full committees in precisely the same manner as the full committees serve the parent chamber. Thus, in their narrow jurisdictions they have gatekeeping, proposal, interchamber bargaining, and oversight powers. For a bill on wheat to be taken up by the full Agriculture Committee, for example, it first has to clear the subcommittee on General Farm Commodities. All of the issues involving assignments, jurisdictions, and authority that we discussed earlier regarding full committees apply at the subcommittee level as well.

Hierarchy. At the committee level, the mantle of leadership falls on the committee chair. She, together with the party leaders, determines the committee's agenda and then coordinates the committee's staff, investigatory resources, and subcommittee structure.[35] This coordination includes scheduling hearings,

 after-the-fact authority

The authority to follow up on the fate of a proposal once it has been approved by the full chamber

 conference committee

A joint committee created to work out a compromise for House and Senate versions of a piece of legislation

 oversight

The effort by Congress, through hearings, investigations, and other techniques, to exercise control over the activities of executive agencies

---

34 See Kenneth A. Shepsle and Barry R. Weingast, "The Institutional Foundations of Committee Power," *American Political Science Review* 81, no. 1 (March 1987): 85–104.

35 Because subcommittee chairs do essentially the same things in their narrower jurisdictions, we won't provide a separate discussion of them.

"marking up" bills—that is, transforming legislative drafts into final versions—and scripting the process by which a bill goes from committee to floor proceedings to final passage. For many years, Congress followed a rigid **seniority** rule for the selection of committee chairs. The benefits of this rule are twofold. First, the chair will be occupied by someone knowledgeable in the committee's jurisdiction, familiar with interest-group and executive-branch players, and politically experienced. Second, the larger institution will be spared divisive leadership contests that reduce the legislative process to efforts in vote grubbing. There are costs, however: senior individuals may be unenergetic, out of touch, even senile.

The U.S. House operated according to a strict seniority principle from about 1910 (and, informally, even earlier) until the mid-1970s, when most members felt that the burdens of this arrangement were beginning to outweigh its advantages. Committee chairs are now elected by the majority-party members of the full legislature, though there remains a presumption (which may be rebutted) that the most senior committee member will normally assume the chair.[36]

Decisiveness on Committees. When a committee goes about its business, its chair exercises agenda power, as noted. But she is not a dictator. Any proposal made to the committee by the chair must ultimately secure the support of a committee majority. In this setting, who is *decisive*? That is, whose vote is necessary and sufficient for a motion to pass? The answer is provided by the *median-voter theorem*. This theorem can be stated as follows: (1) if the alternatives under consideration can be represented as points on a line, (2) if individuals have a most-preferred point, and (3) if their preferences decrease steadily for points farther away, then the most-preferred point of the median (middle) voter can defeat any other point in a majority contest.

In Figure 6.6 we have a five-person committee that must choose a point on the line ranging from 0 to 100. Each member has a favorite point, represented by the peak of his curve, and his preferences decline steadily as points farther and farther away are considered. The median-voter theorem asserts that the favorite point of member 3 can beat any other point in a majority contest. A majority comprising members 3, 4, and 5 prefers 3's favorite to any point to its left; a majority comprising members 1, 2, and 3 prefers 3's favorite to any point to its right; therefore 3's favorite can prevail against *any* point. We will discuss the median-voter theorem again in Chapter 11 in the context of elections.

Monitoring Committees. If unchecked, committees might easily take advantage of their authority. Indeed, what prevents committees from exploiting their before-the-fact proposal power and their after-the-fact bargaining and oversight authority? As we saw in Chapter 1, in our discussion of the principal-agent problem, principals must be certain that agents are properly motivated to

---

36 Beginning with the Republican takeover of the House in 1995, committee chairs have been term limited. After three terms, a chair must step down. It appears that party leaders exert more authority today in the appointment of new chairs.

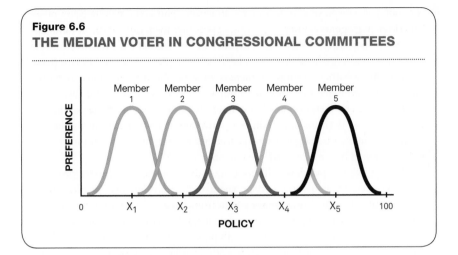

Figure 6.6

THE MEDIAN VOTER IN CONGRESSIONAL COMMITTEES

serve the principal's interests, either by actually sharing the principal's interests themselves or by deriving something of value (reputation, compensation, and so on) for acting to advance those interests. Alternatively, the principal will need to have some instruments by which to monitor and validate what her agent is doing, rewarding or punishing the agent accordingly.

Consider again the example of congressional committees. The House or Senate delegates responsibility to its Committee on Agriculture to recommend legislative policy in the field of agriculture. Not surprisingly, legislators from farm districts are most eager to get onto this committee, and for the most part their wishes are accommodated. The Committee on Agriculture, consequently, is composed mainly of farm legislators. And nonfarm legislators are relieved at not having to spend their time on issues of little material interest to them or their constituents. In effecting this delegation, however, the parent legislature is putting itself in the hands of its farm colleagues, benefiting from their expertise on farm-related matters, to be sure, but laying itself open to the danger of planting the fox squarely in the henhouse. The Committee on Agriculture becomes not only a collection of specialists but also a collection of advocates for farm interests. How can the parent body know for certain, therefore, that a recommendation from that committee is not more a reflection of its advocacy than a reflection of its expertise? This is the risk inherent in delegation in principal-agent relationships.

And it is for this reason that the parent legislature maintains a variety of tools and instruments to protect itself from being exploited by its agents. First, it does not allow committees to make final decisions on policy; it allows only recommendations, which the parent legislature retains the authority to accept, amend, or reject. A committee has agenda power, but it is not by itself decisive. Second, the parent body relies on the committee's concern for its own reputation. Making a recommendation on a piece of legislation is not a one-shot action; the committee knows it will return to the parent body time and time again with legislative recommendations, and it will not want to tarnish its reputation for expertise by too much advocacy. Third, the parent body relies on competing agents—interest groups, expert members not on the committee, legislative specialists in the other chamber of the legislature, executive-branch specialists, and even academics—to keep its own agents honest. Fourth, party leaders, through their control of plenary time on the floor, monitor committee products to make sure they are compatible with party goals. Finally, in the House there is an institutional club behind the door—the discharge petition. A committee that is sitting on a bill, not permitting it to be taken up by the full chamber, can be discharged of responsibility for the bill if a petition to that effect is signed by a majority of the chamber.

Nevertheless, a principal will not bother to eliminate *entirely* these prospective deviations from his interests by agents who have interests of their own. A principal will suffer some **agency loss** from having delegated authority to a "hired hand"; therefore, nearly all principal-agent relationships will be imperfect in some respects from the principal's perspective. The Committee on Agriculture, for example, cannot get away with spending huge proportions of the federal budget on agricultural subsidies to farmers. But it can insert small items into agriculture bills from time to time—an experimental grain-to-fuel conversion project in an important legislator's state or district, for example, or special funds to the U.S. trade representative to give priority to agriculture-related trade issues. The parent body, as we suggested, will find it worth its while to keep an eye on the Agriculture Committee, but it won't be worth its while to take action on every instance of indulgence by the committee. The transaction cost of monitoring and overseeing committee performance gets excessive if perfection is the objective.

Thus we see the institution principle providing some guidance on how a group of legislators organizes itself for business. The legislators take advantage of the division and specialization of labor, dividing themselves into specialized subgroups (committees and subcommittees) and thus enjoying the benefits of expertise from these subunits. But they also guard against the subunits' going off half-cocked in pursuit of their own narrower interests. The parent legislature in effect uses institutional arrangements to regulate and oversee its subunits' activities.

Committee Reform. Over the years, Congress has reformed its organizational structure and operating procedures. Most changes have been made to improve efficiency, but some reforms have also represented a response to political considerations. In the 1970s, a series of reforms substantially altered the organization of power in Congress. Among the most important changes put into place at that time were the election of committee chairs, an increase in the number of subcommittees, greater autonomy for subcommittee chairs, the opening of most committee deliberations to the public, and a system of multiple referral of bills that allowed several committees to consider one bill at the same time. One of the driving impulses behind these reforms was an effort to reduce the power of committee chairs.

As a consequence of those reforms, power became more fragmented, making it harder to reach agreement on legislation. In 1995, the Republican

agency loss

The difference between what a principal would like an agent to do and the agent's performance leadership of the 104th Congress sought to concentrate more authority in the party leadership. One of the ways the House achieved this was by abandoning the principle of seniority in the selection of a number of committee chairs, appointing them instead according to their loyalty to the party. This move tied committee chairs more closely to the leadership. In addition, the Republican leadership eliminated 25 of the House's 115 subcommittees and gave committee chairs more power over their subcommittees. The result was an unusually cohesive congressional majority, which pushed forward a common agenda. House Republicans also agreed to impose a three-term limit on committee and subcommittee heads. As a result, all the chairs were replaced in 2001, in many instances by the most senior Republican committee member, but the net result was a redistribution of power in the House of Representatives. Since 2001 some of the earlier practices have slowly begun to reassert themselves. Speaker Nancy Pelosi and the Democratic majority in 2007 observed seniority in the appointment of nearly all committee chairs. But it is not automatic, and committee chairs are on notice that significant deviations from a party policy consensus will not be tolerated. For example, in 2009 a newly enlarged Democratic majority replaced John Dingell (D-Mich.), a fixture in the House for half a century, as chair of the Commerce and Energy Committee with Henry Waxman (D-Calif.), a less senior member of the committee.

The role of committees in the legislative process was evident during Obama's first term. In the midst of the financial crisis, taxing and spending committees played major roles in shepherding a stimulus package and a rescue of the auto industry through both chambers, as well as follow-up monitoring of the earlier rescue of banks and other financial players. During this period, the banking committees produced major regulatory reforms for their industry. At the same time, the health committees produced what ultimately became Obama's health care policy. In all these activities, Speaker Pelosi and Majority Leader Reid conducted and choreographed. The legislative record of the 111th Congress was testimony both to an efficient division- and specialization-of-labor committee system *and* to authoritative and strong party leadership.

The Staff System: Staffers and Agencies

A congressional institution ranking just below committees and parties in importance is the staff system. Every member of Congress employs a large number of staff members, whose tasks include handling constituency requests and, to a large and growing extent, dealing with legislative details and the activities of administrative agencies. Increasingly, staffers bear the primary responsibility for formulating and drafting proposals, organizing hearings, dealing with administrative agencies, and negotiating with lobbyists. Indeed, legislators typically deal with each other through staff members rather than through direct, personal contact. Representatives and senators together employ nearly 11,000 staffers in their Washington and home offices. In addition to the personal staffs of individual senators and representatives, Congress also employs roughly 2,000 committee staffers. These individuals make up the permanent staff, who often stay regardless of turnover in Congress and are attached to every House and Senate committee. They are responsible for organizing and administering the committee's work, doing research, scheduling, organizing hearings, and drafting legislation.

Not only does Congress employ personal and committee staffs, but it has also established three **staff agencies** designed to provide the legislative branch with resources and expertise independent of the executive branch. These agencies enhance Congress's capacity to oversee administrative agencies and evaluate presidential programs and proposals. They are the Congressional Research Service, which performs research for legislators who wish to know the facts and competing arguments relevant to policy proposals or other legislative business; the Government Accountability Office, through which Congress can investigate the financial and administrative affairs of any government agency or program; and the Congressional Budget Office, which assesses the economic implications and likely costs of proposed federal programs, such as the Bush administration rescue packages for the failing financial system in 2008 and Barack Obama's stimulus package in 2009.

staff agencies

The agencies responsible for providing Congress with independent expertise, administration, and oversight capability

Informal Organization: The Caucuses

In addition to the official organization of Congress, an unofficial organizational structure also exists: the caucuses, formally known as legislative service organizations (LSOs). A **congressional caucus** is a group of senators or representatives who share certain opinions, interests, or social characteristics. There are ideological caucuses such as the liberal Democratic Study Group and the conservative Democratic Forum. There are also a large number of caucuses composed of legislators representing particular economic or policy interests, such as the Travel and Tourism Caucus, the Steel Caucus, the Mushroom Caucus, and the Concerned Senators for the Arts. Legislators who share common backgrounds or social characteristics have organized such caucuses as the Congressional Black Caucus, the Congressional Caucus for Women's Issues, and the Hispanic Caucus. All these caucuses seek to advance the interests of the groups they represent by promoting legislation, encouraging Congress to hold hearings, and pressing administrative agencies for favorable treatment.

congressional caucus

An association of members of Congress based on party, interest, or social characteristics such as gender or race

RULES OF LAWMAKING:
HOW A BILL BECOMES A LAW

The institutional structure of Congress is one key factor that helps shape the legislative process. A second and equally important set of factors is made up of the rules of congressional procedure. These rules govern all the procedures from introducing a bill through submitting it to the president for signing.

Not only do these regulations influence the fate of every bill, but they also help determine the distribution of power in Congress.[37]

Committee Deliberation

Even if a member of Congress, the White House, or a federal agency has spent months developing and drafting a piece of legislation, it does not become a bill until a senator or a representative officially submits it to the clerk of the House or Senate and it is referred to the appropriate committee for deliberation. No floor action on any bill can take place until the committee with jurisdiction over it has taken all the time it needs to deliberate.[38] During the course of its deliberations, the committee typically refers the bill to one of its subcommittees, which may hold hearings, listen to expert testimony, and amend the proposed legislation before referring it to the full committee for its consideration. The full committee may accept the recommendation of the subcommittee or hold its own hearings and prepare its own amendments. Even more frequently, the committee and subcommittee may do little or nothing with a bill and simply allow it to die in committee.

Once a bill's assigned committee or committees in the House of Representatives have acted affirmatively, the whole bill or various parts of it are transmitted to the Rules Committee, which determines the specific rules under which the legislation will be considered by the full House. Together with the Speaker, it influences when debate will be scheduled, for how long, what amendments will be in order, and the order in which they will be considered. The Speaker also rules on all procedural points of order and points of information raised during the debate. A bill's supporters generally prefer what is called a **closed rule**, which puts severe limits on floor debate and amendments. Opponents of a bill usually prefer an **open rule**, which permits potentially damaging floor debate and makes it easier to add amendments that may cripple the bill or weaken its chances of passing.

Debate

A bill that passes in committee and clears the Rules Committee is then scheduled for debate by the full House. Party control of the agenda is reinforced by the rule giving the Speaker of the House and the majority leader of the Senate

 closed rule

The provision by the House Rules Committee that prohibits the introduction of amendments during debate

 open rule

The provision by the House Rules Committee that permits floor debate and the addition of amendments to a bill

---

37 We should emphasize, although we don't mean to confuse the reader, that a legislature "suspends" its rules as often as it follows them. There are unorthodox ways to proceed in order to avoid procedural logjams, and the House and, especially, the Senate frequently resort to these unorthodox ways. See Barbara Sinclair, *Unorthodox Lawmaking: New Legislative Processes in the U.S. Congress*, 3rd ed. (Washington, DC: CQ Press, 2007).

38 A bill can be pulled from a committee by a discharge petition, but this is an extreme measure and is resorted to only rarely. Other parliamentary tricks may also be attempted, but it is fair to say that most of the time at least it is the committee of jurisdiction that influences the course of a bill.

the power of recognition during debate on a bill. Usually the chair knows the purpose for which a member intends to speak well in advance of the occasion. Spontaneous efforts to gain recognition are often foiled. For example, the Speaker may ask, "For what purpose does the member rise?" before deciding whether to grant recognition. In general, the party leadership in the House has total control over debate. In the Senate, each member has substantial power to block the close of debate. A House majority can override opposition, whereas it takes an extraordinary majority (60 votes) to close debate in the Senate. In recent years, with partisanship in both chambers on the rise, prolonging debate, using procedural delays, and generally dragging one's feet have been potent tools for the minority to frustrate the majority.

In the House, virtually all of the time allotted by the Rules Committee for debate on a given bill is controlled by the bill's sponsor and its leading opponent. These two participants are, by rule and tradition, granted the power to allocate most of the debate time in small amounts to members who are seeking to speak for or against the measure.

In the Senate, other than the power of recognition, the leadership has much less control over floor debate. Indeed, the Senate is unique among the world's legislative bodies for its commitment to unlimited debate. Once given the floor, a senator may speak for as long as she wishes unless an extraordinary majority votes to end debate. On a number of memorable occasions, senators have used this right to prevent action on legislation they opposed. Through this tactic, called the **filibuster**, small minorities or even one individual in the Senate can force the majority to give in to his demands. During the 1950s and 1960s, for example, opponents of civil rights legislation often sought to block its passage by adopting the filibuster. Sixty votes are needed to end a filibuster. This procedure is called **cloture**.

It should be noted that the modern filibuster is used mostly as a "threat." An indication by a senator that she intends to filibuster is often sufficient to induce the majority leader to move on to another topic rather than waste the Senate's valuable plenary time. In the 112th Congress, Minority Leader McConnell used the filibuster threat repeatedly to thwart Obama administration proposals. On practically any matter the upper chamber has effectively become the "60-vote Senate" because 60 votes are needed to end debate and allow a bill to come to a vote.

Although it is the best known, the filibuster is not the only technique used to block Senate action. Under Senate rules, members have a virtually unlimited ability to propose amendments to a pending bill. Each amendment must be voted on before the bill can come to a final vote. The introduction of new amendments can be stopped only by unanimous consent. This, in effect, can permit a determined minority to filibuster by amendment, indefinitely delaying the passage of a bill.

Senators can also place "holds," or stalling devices, on bills to delay debate. Senators place holds on bills when they fear that openly opposing them will be unpopular. Because holds are kept secret, the senators placing the holds do not have to take public responsibility for their actions.[39]

filibuster

A tactic used by members of the Senate to prevent action on legislation they oppose by continuously holding the floor and speaking until the majority backs down. Once given the floor, senators have unlimited time to speak, and it requires a cloture vote of three-fifths of the Senate to end a filibuster

cloture

A rule allowing a supermajority of the members of a legislative body to set a time limit on debate over a given bill

---

39 This and other features of the Senate rules came under intense scrutiny in the 112th Congress (2011–12) and remain on the reform agenda today.

Once a bill is debated on the floor of the House and the Senate, the leaders schedule it for a vote on the floor of each chamber. By then, congressional leaders know what the vote will be; leaders do not bring legislation to the floor unless they are fairly certain it is going to pass. As a consequence, it is unusual for the leadership to lose a bill on the floor. On rare occasions, however, the last moments of the floor vote can be dramatic, as each party's leadership puts its whip organization into action to make sure wavering members vote with the party. In October 2008, a massive Treasury-sponsored plan to rescue failing financial institutions was defeated in the House *despite* the support of the leadership of both parties. Because the vote came just before the 2008 elections, members were afraid to buck strong constituency opposition to the rescue plan. (A modified version passed a week later, though still with substantial and vocal opposition.) In 2010 the stimulus package proposed by the Obama administration to pump money into an economy deep in recession passed in both chambers. In the House, it passed easily—246 to 183—the only uncertainty being whether there would be any Republicans supporting it; there weren't. In the Senate, there was genuine excitement; the critical vote there was 60 to 40, just enough to close down a prospective filibuster and allow for final passage.

Conference Committee: Reconciling House and Senate Versions of a Bill

Getting a bill out of committee and through both of the houses of Congress is no guarantee that it will be enacted. Frequently bills that began with similar provisions in both chambers emerge with little resemblance to one another. Alternatively, a bill may be passed by one chamber but undergo substantial revision in the other chamber. If the differences cannot be worked out by passing the revised version back to the other chamber and having it accept any changes, a conference committee composed of the senior members of the committees or subcommittees that initiated the bills may be required to iron out differences. Sometimes members or leaders will let objectionable provisions pass on the floor with the idea that they will be eliminated in conference. Conference agreement requires majority support from each of the two delegations. Legislation that emerges successfully from a conference committee is more often a compromise than a clear victory of one set of forces over another.

When a bill comes out of conference, it faces one more hurdle. Before it can be sent to the president for signing, the House-Senate conference report must be approved on the floor of each chamber. It must be voted up or down; no amendments are in order. Usually such approval is given quickly. Occasionally, however, a bill's opponents use the report as one last opportunity to defeat a piece of legislation.

Presidential Action

Once adopted by the House and the Senate, a bill goes to the president, who may choose to sign the bill into law or **veto** it (Figure 6.7). The veto is the president's constitutional power to reject a piece of legislation. To veto a bill, the president

 veto

The president's constitutional power to turn down acts of Congress within 10 days of their passage while Congress is in session. A presidential veto may be overridden by a two-thirds vote of each house of Congress

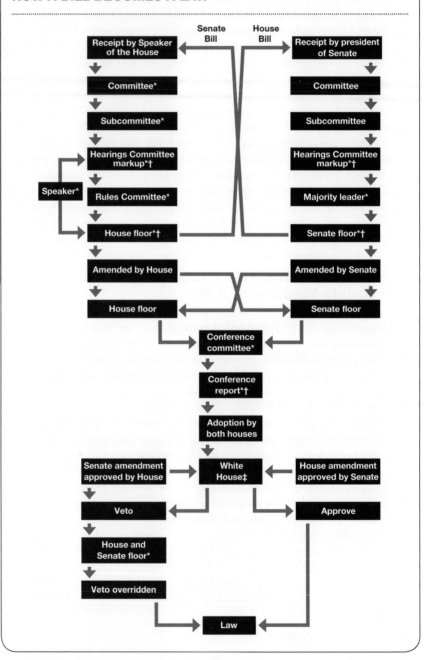

Figure 6.7
HOW A BILL BECOMES A LAW

* Points at which the bill can be amended.
† Points at which the bill can die.
‡ If the president neither signs nor vetoes the bill within 10 days, it automatically becomes law.

returns it within 10 days to the house of Congress in which it originated, along with objections to it. If Congress adjourns during the 10-day period and the president has taken no action, the bill is also considered to have been vetoed—by means of the **pocket veto**. The possibility of a presidential veto affects the willingness of members of Congress to push for different pieces of legislation at different times. If they think a proposal is likely to be vetoed, they might shelve it for a later time. Alternatively, the sponsors of a popular bill opposed by the president might push for passage to force the president to pay the political costs of vetoing it.[40] During the entire first term of President George W. Bush (2001–05), not one bill was vetoed. In the next two years, the president vetoed a single bill. But in the 110th Congress (2007–08), the Republican president faced a Congress controlled by the Democrats. The president vetoed 11 bills, and four of his vetoes were overridden. In President Obama's first term, he vetoed only two bills, a Department of Defense funding resolution and a minor bill on notaries. This low veto rate reflects the fact that Obama's party controlled at least one chamber of Congress during his first term.

A presidential veto may be overridden by a two-thirds vote in both the House and the Senate. A veto override says much about the support that a president can expect from Congress, and it can deliver a stinging blow to the executive branch. In 2007, a popular pork-barrel bill, the Water Resources Development Act, was vetoed by President Bush. His message to Congress, in part, stated:

> I am returning herewith without my approval H.R. 1495, the "Water Resources Development Act of 2007."
>
> This bill lacks fiscal discipline. I fully support funding for water resources projects that will yield high economic and environmental returns to the Nation and each year my budget has proposed reasonable and responsible funding. . . . However, this authorization bill makes promises to local communities that the Congress does not have a track record of keeping. The House of Representatives took a $15 billion bill into negotiations with a $14 billion bill from the Senate and instead of splitting the difference, emerged with a Washington compromise that costs over $23 billion. This is not fiscally responsible. . . . The bill's excessive authorization for over 900 projects and programs exacerbates the massive backlog of ongoing Corps construction projects, which will require an additional $38 billion in future appropriations to complete.[41]

Despite his opposition, both houses overwhelmingly overrode his veto. Presidents will often back down from their threat to veto a bill if they believe Congress will override the veto. On the other hand, congressional proponents will often modify or withdraw entirely a bill that the president threatens to veto.

 pocket veto

A veto that is effected when Congress adjourns during the time a president has to approve a bill and the president takes no action on it

40 John B. Gilmour, *Strategic Disagreement: Stalemate in American Politics* (Pittsburgh, PA: University of Pittsburgh Press, 1995).

41 *Congressional Record*, at 2007 H12458.

These strategic interactions between the legislature and the executive branch are taken up in the next chapter.

Procedures in Congress: Regular and Unorthodox

We have noted that although there is a regular procedure in each chamber, it is often abandoned, and an abnormal, or unorthodox, procedure is devised. The treatment of appropriations bills in the period leading up to the November 2004 election provides an excellent example.

According to its regular procedure, the House passes 13 separate appropriations bills after each one has passed through an appropriations process, beginning with a subcommittee hearing, followed by full Appropriations Committee deliberations, and concluding with passage by the full House. These 13 measures are then transmitted to the Senate, which subjects each of them to its own regular appropriations process. Each of the bills (13 in all) now has a House version and a Senate version. Thirteen separate conference committees are set up to compromise on the differences between each pair. The 13 compromised versions are then sent back to each chamber for final approval. And in principle, though rarely in practice, this entire process is completed before October 1, the day on which the new fiscal year begins.

But 2004 was an election year, and members up for re-election really did not want to remind the voters that the appropriations bills they were passing were going to produce the largest deficit in history. So an unorthodox procedure was invented. Different versions of the appropriations bill to fund the legislative branch passed the House and the Senate through the normal process and was sent to conference. During the conference, the other 12 bills were tacked on, making a single appropriations bill. This omnibus bill was sent to each chamber for a single up-or-down vote. In voting for the omnibus measure, a member was "innoculated" against local objections from constituents. He could respond, "I know, I know. The omnibus bill is not ideal. But what was I to do? Defeating it would have shut the government down."

Even more unorthodox was the final passage of President Obama's health care bill in 2010. The House initially passed a health care bill in November 2009 with no Republican support and much grumbling from some Democrats who were unhappy with various aspects. But the Senate was the real battleground. A Senate version of the health care bill passed on Christmas Eve 2009. Upon their return after the holiday recess, Democratic leaders in the House and Senate plotted how to combine the two versions. But there was a shock that disrupted their plans—on January 19, 2010, Scott Brown, a Republican, won the Massachusetts Senate seat that had been temporarily held by a Democrat after the death of Ted Kennedy (a Democrat and strong supporter of health care reform). The Senate had been filibuster-proof with 60 Democrats but was now no longer since the number of Democratic senators dropped below the magic cloture threshold. So any further vote in the Senate, which would be necessary to approve changes to the bill, could now be blocked by the Republican minority. What was to be done?

The Democrats took an unusual route. Speaker Pelosi and the Democratic leadership convinced Democrats in the House to support the Senate version of the bill, passing it 219 to 212. The identical bill was thus passed by both chambers, and no further vote was needed in the Senate. House Democrats were not happy with the Senate version, but they were placated by the promise of a second bill in which their concerns would be addressed. The second bill employed the so-called reconciliation procedure, a relatively arcane method that requires only a simple majority in each chamber. Thus a filibuster was avoided in the Senate. On March 26, the Senate passed this second bill, 56 to 43, the House passed it, 220 to 207, and the way was clear for Obama to sign health care reform into law.

Before leaving this topic, it is worth noting that normal and abnormal procedures involve either the conventional or the creative application of existing rules. Each chamber, however, is granted by the Constitution the privilege of formulating its own rules of procedure. So from time to time, the House or the Senate will change its rules of procedure. At other times, a dominant coalition in a chamber will threaten to do this unless it is allowed its way under the existing rules. Here we see the confluence of the rationality principle and the institution principle as rational legislators seek to (re)arrange their chamber's institutional procedures in order to accomplish particular purposes or realize particular goals.

This phenomenon was dramatically illustrated in May 2005. Even though Republicans were in the majority in the Senate, President Bush's judicial nominations were threatened by a filibuster by Democratic senators. (The Senate must formally approve a president's nominations to the federal judiciary.) In the face of nominations whose approval looked vulnerable to a blocking action by the minority party, Bill Frist, the Senate majority leader, unveiled what came to be known as the *nuclear option*. It entailed a clever parliamentary maneuver in which debate could be brought to a close not by securing the 60 votes normally required (which the Republicans did not control) but by a simple majority. This would be executed by formally requesting the president of the Senate (Vice President Dick Cheney) to end debate without a cloture vote because the issue before the Senate was the constitutional one of "advising and consenting" on a presidential judicial nomination. It was expected that any such move on the part of the Republicans would be followed by the Democrats' appealing any ruling by the Senate president to end debate. But that ruling required only a majority vote to be sustained. In this manner, the Republicans could end-run the practice of unlimited debate that normally prevails in the Senate, on constitutional issues at least. The nuclear option was never implemented, however. The very threat of it induced a number of moderate senators to agree to support a motion to end debate (thereby producing the 60 needed votes) and bring a presidential nominee forward for a final vote. These senators were willing to accommodate a vote so long as the president and the Republican majority did not abuse this concession by bringing forward "extremist" nominees.[42] With fortunes reversed in 2011—a Democratic president and a

---

42 For a model of the judicial confirmation process, see David W. Rohde and Kenneth A. Shepsle, "Advising and Consenting in the 60-Vote Senate: Strategic Appointments to the Supreme Court," *Journal of Politics* 69 (2007): 664–77.

filibuster-inclined Senate Republican minority—it was Democrats who clamored for a nuclear option and a similar deal between Senate Democrats and Republicans concerning Obama's appointees was reached.

The Distributive Tendency in Congress

To pass a policy, it is necessary to authorize the policy—that is, to provide statutory authority to a government agency to implement the legislation—and then provide appropriations to fund the implementation. The list of politicians whose consent is required in these processes is extraordinarily long. At a minimum, it includes majorities of the relevant committee and subcommittee of each chamber (almost certainly including their chairs), the Appropriations Committee and the appropriate subcommittee in each chamber (including their chairs), the House Rules Committee, chamber majorities (including leaders of the majority party), and the president. Some of the legislators may go along without requiring much for their states or districts on the assumption that their turn will come on another bill. But most of these politicians will need some form of "compensation" in order to provide their support.

With so many hurdles to clear before a legislative initiative can become a law, the benefits must be spread broadly. It is as though a bill had to travel on a toll road past a number of tollbooths, each one housing a collector with her hand out for payment. On rare occasions, the required toll takes the form of a personal bribe—a contract to a firm run by a congressman's brother, a job for a senator's daughter, a boondoggle "military inspection" trip to a Pacific isle for a legislator and his companion. Occasionally there is a wink-and-a-nod understanding, usually given by the majority leader or committee chair, that support from a legislator today will result in reciprocal support for legislation of interest to her down the road. Most frequently features of the bill are drafted initially or revised so as to be more inclusive, spreading the benefits widely among beneficiaries. This is the **distributive tendency**.

distributive tendency

The tendency of Congress to spread the benefits of a policy over a wide range of members' districts

The distributive tendency is part of the American system of representative democracy. Legislators, in advocating the interests of their constituents, are eager to advertise their ability to deliver for their state or district. They maneuver to put themselves in a position to claim credit for good things that happen there and duck blame for bad things. This is the way they earn trust back home, deter strong challengers in upcoming elections, and defeat those who do run against them. It means that legislators must take advantage of every opportunity that presents itself. In some instances, the results may seem bizarre. In April 2003, for example, Senator Thad Cochran (R-Miss.) was able to insert into the bill funding the war in Iraq language that provided $250 million for "disaster relief" for southern catfish farmers.[43] Most Americans would never have guessed that driving Saddam Hussein from power would have an effect on catfish farming in Mississippi.

----

43 Dan Morgan, "War Funding Bill's Extra Riders," *Washington Post*, April 8, 2003, p. A4.

This system, which is practiced in Washington and most state capitals, means that political pork gets spread around; it is not controlled by a small clique of politicians or concentrated in a small number of states or districts. But it also means that public authority and appropriations do not go where they are most needed. The most impoverished cities do not get much money as appropriate because some of the available money must be diverted to buy political support. The neediest individuals often do not get tax relief, health care, or occupational subsidies for reasons unrelated to philosophy or policy grounds. It is the distributive tendency at work. And it is one of the unintended consequences of the separation of powers and multiple veto points.[44] As the policy principle suggests, rationality combines with institutional practices to leave their marks on the shape of policy.[45]

HOW CONGRESS DECIDES

What determines the kinds of legislation that Congress ultimately produces? The process of creating a legislative agenda, drawing up a list of possible measures, and deciding among them is very complex. In this process, a variety of influences from inside and outside government play important roles. External influences include a legislator's constituency and various interest groups. Influences from inside government include party leadership, congressional colleagues, and the president. Let us examine each of these influences individually and then consider how they interact to produce congressional policy decisions.

Constituency

Because members of Congress want to be re-elected, the views of their constituents have a key influence on the decisions legislators make. Yet constituency influence is not so straightforward as we might think. In fact, most constituents do not even know what policies their representatives support. The number of citizens who *do* pay attention to such matters—the attentive public—is usually very small. Nonetheless, members of Congress spend a lot of time worrying about what their constituents think because these representatives realize that their choices may be scrutinized in a future election and used as ammunition by an opposing candidate. Because of this possibility, members of Congress try

---

44 See George Tsebelis, *Veto Players: How Political Institutions Work* (Princeton, NJ: Princeton University Press, 2002).

45 Since the 2010 elections, involving major Republican gains across the boards, there has been an antispending sentiment in the air in Washington. Earmarks, another name for pork-barrel projects, have been targeted. Legislators are of mixed minds about eliminating earmarks—they love being on record against spending but hate losing *their* earmarks.

to anticipate their constituents' policy views.[46] Legislators are more likely to be influenced by those views if they think voters will take them into account during elections. In this way, constituents may affect congressional policy choices even when there is little direct evidence of their awareness of those choices.[47]

Interest Groups

Interest groups are another important external influence on the policies that Congress produces. When members of Congress are making voting decisions, interest groups that have some connection to constituents in the districts of particular members are most likely to be influential. For this reason, interest groups with the ability to mobilize followers in many congressional districts may be especially influential in Congress. The small-business lobby, for example, played an important role in defeating President Clinton's proposal for comprehensive health care reform in 1993–94. The mobilization of networks of small businesses across the country meant that virtually every member of Congress had to take their views into account. In 2009, the Obama administration brought small business groups and the insurance industry to the table on health care very early in the process precisely because of this.

In addition to mobilizing voters, interest groups contribute money. In the 2012 electoral cycle, interest groups and PACs gave many millions of dollars in campaign contributions to incumbent legislators and challengers. What does this money buy? A popular conception is that campaign contributions buy legislative votes. In this view, legislators vote for whichever proposal favors the bulk of their contributors. Although the vote-buying hypothesis makes for good campaign rhetoric, it has little factual support. Empirical studies by political scientists show little evidence that contributions from large PACs influence legislative voting patterns.[48]

----

46 See John W. Kingdon, *Congressmen's Voting Decisions* (New York: Harper & Row, 1973), chap. 3; and R. Douglas Arnold, *The Logic of Congressional Action* (New Haven, CT: Yale University Press, 1990). See also Joshua Clinton, "Representation in Congress: Constituents and Roll Calls in the 106th House," *Journal of Politics* 68 (2006): 397–409.

47 Interest groups from the state or district (which we discuss later) can be useful to legislators in this respect when they provide information concerning the significance of particular issues for various constituency groups. In effect, they provide legislators with heads-up signals and wake-up calls. See Kenneth W. Kollman, *Outside Lobbying: Public Opinion and Interest Group Strategies* (Princeton, NJ: Princeton University Press, 1998).

48 See Janet M. Grenke, "PACs and the Congressional Supermarket: The Currency Is Complex," *American Journal of Political Science* 33, no. 1 (February 1989): 1–24. More generally, see Jacobson, *The Politics of Congressional Elections*. For a view that interest groups spend too little, not too much, money, see Stephen Ansolabehere, John de Figueiredo, and James Snyder, "Why Is There So Little Money in U.S. Politics?" *Journal of Economic Perspectives* 17 (2003): 105–30.

If contributions don't buy votes, what do they buy? Our claim is that campaign contributions influence legislative behavior in ways that are difficult for the public to observe and political scientists to measure. The institutional structure of Congress provides opportunities for interest groups to influence legislation outside the public eye, which legislators and contributors prefer.

Committee proposal power enables legislators, if they are on the relevant committee, to introduce legislation that favors contributing groups. Gatekeeping power enables committee members to block legislation that harms contributing groups. The fact that certain provisions are *excluded* from a bill is as much an indicator of PAC influence as the fact that certain provisions are *included*. The difference is that it is hard to measure what you don't see. Committee oversight powers enable members to intervene in bureaucratic decision making on behalf of contributing groups.

The point here is that voting on the floor, the alleged object of campaign contributions according to the vote-buying hypothesis, is a highly visible, highly public act, one that could get a legislator in trouble with his broader electoral constituency. The committee system, on the other hand, provides loads of opportunities for legislators to deliver "services" to PAC contributors and other donors who are more subtle and better hidden from public view. Thus we suggest that the most appropriate places to look for traces of campaign-contribution influence on the legislative process are in the manner in which committees deliberate, mark up proposals, and block legislation from the floor; outside public view, these are the primary arenas for interest-group influence.[49]

Interest groups mobilize voters and contribute campaign finance, but that's not all they do. They also convey information. While it is true that legislators become specialists, acquire expertise, and hire expert staff to assist them, much specialized knowledge, especially about how various aspects of policy will affect local constituencies, is possessed by lobbyists. Informational lobbying is a very important inside-the-beltway activity. Interest group expenditures on lobbying dwarf money given in campaign contributions.[50]

Party Discipline

In both the House and the Senate, party leaders have a good deal of influence over the behavior of their party members. This influence, sometimes called party discipline, was once so powerful that it dominated the lawmaking process. Let us define as a **party vote** a vote on which 50 percent or more of the members of one party take one position while at least 50 percent of the members of

 party vote

A roll-call vote in the House or Senate in which at least 50 percent of the members of one party take a particular position and are opposed by at least 50 percent of the members of the other party. Party votes are less common today than they were in the nineteenth century

---

49 A complementary effect of campaign contributions is not to buy votes that would otherwise be unavailable to a contributor. It is, rather, to increase the likelihood that legislators *already sympathetic* will be re-elected. Interest groups thus primarily support their friends with contributions rather than attempting to convert opponents to their cause.

50 See Sven E. Feldmann and Morten Bennedsen, "Informational Lobbying and Political Contributions," *Journal of Public Economics* 90 (2006): 631–56.

roll-call votes

Votes in which each legislator's yes or no vote is recorded

the other party take the opposing position. At the beginning of the twentieth century, most **roll-call votes** in the House of Representatives were party votes. The frequency of party votes declined through most of the twentieth century as legislative parties grew more ideologically diverse. Democrats included liberals from the big cities and conservatives from the South. Republicans included conservatives from the Midwest and West and moderates from the Northeast. The tail end of this decline in party voting can be observed in Figure 6.8 between 1955 and 1970. Beginning in the 1970s, however, legislative parties grew more homogeneous and more polarized. Conservative southern districts began electing Republicans, and liberal northeastern districts began sending Democrats to Congress. The data shown in the figure reflect this, with party votes ticking upward from the 1970s onward. Some of this change is the result of the intense partisan struggles that began during the administrations of Ronald Reagan and George H. W. Bush. Straight party-line voting was also seen briefly in the 103rd Congress (1993–94) after Bill Clinton's election in 1992. The situation soon gave way, however, to the many long-term factors working against party discipline in Congress, as seen in the decline in party voting over the rest of the 1990s.[51] Since the election of George W. Bush, accompanied by Republican

ANALYZING THE EVIDENCE

Party voting increased in the 1970s, peaked in the mid-1990s, and has remained fairly high since then. What contributes to party voting?

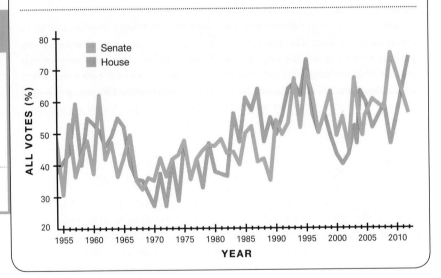

Figure 6.8
PARTY UNITY SCORES BY CHAMBER

NOTE: The scores represent the percentage of recorded votes on which the majority of one party voted against the majority of the other party.

SOURCE: Voteview, http://pooleandrosenthal.com/party_unity.htm (accessed 6/27/11); and ftp://voteview.com/partyunity_house_senate_1-112.dat (accessed 6/11/13).

51 There were fluctuations during George W. Bush's presidency—declines in party voting following September 11 and then surges and declines in subsequent years (see Figure 6.8).

congressional control, party voting again ticked upward. And in the first Obama administration, party voting in both chambers was strong—Republican votes supporting Obama initiatives were quite rare. In the last Congress of Obama's first term (the 112th), the Senate minority leader announced his main objective was to defeat Obama in the 2012 election and kept the Republican troops unified in opposition on almost every Senate vote of importance. Hence: gridlock.[52]

To some extent, party divisions are based on ideology and background. Republican members of Congress are more likely than Democrats to be drawn from rural or suburban areas. Democrats are likely to be more liberal on economic and social questions than their Republican colleagues. This ideological gap has been especially pronounced since 1980 (Figure 6.9).[53] Ideological differences certainly help explain roll-call divisions between the two parties.[54] Ideology and background, however, are only part of the explanation of party unity. The other part has to do with party organization and leadership. Although party organization has weakened since the beginning of the twentieth century, today's party leaders still have some resources at their disposal: (1) committee assignments, (2) access to the floor, (3) the whip system, (4) logrolling, and (5) the presidency. These resources are regularly used and are often effective in securing the support of party members.[55]

Committee Assignments. Leaders can create debts among members by helping them get favorable committee assignments. These assignments are made early in the congressional careers of most members and ordinarily cannot be taken from them if they later balk at party discipline. Nevertheless, if the leadership goes out of its way to get the right assignment for a member, the effort is likely to create a bond of obligation that can be called on without any other payments or favors.

---

52 One of the hidden consequences of polarization between the parties is what is *not* voted on. In the Senate, especially, the majority leader often pulls from the floor those bills on which unified minority opposition would otherwise sink the measure.

53 This figure is slightly misleading in showing Southern Democrats becoming more liberal. It is true, but for a nonobvious reason: there are fewer and fewer Southern Democrats, with the ones remaining most likely to be urban and/or minority legislators.

54 Keith T. Poole and Howard Rosenthal, *Congress: A Political-Economic History of Roll Call Voting* (New York: Oxford University Press, 1997). As a result, it is hard to sort out the effects of party and ideology. On this latter issue, see Krehbiel, "Where's the Party?"

55 Legislative leaders may behave in ways that enhance their reputation for being willing to punish party members who stray from the party line. The problem of developing such a credible reputation is analyzed in Randall Calvert, "Reputation and Legislative Leadership," *Public Choice* 55 (1987): 81–120; and is summarized in Kenneth A. Shepsle, *Analyzing Politics: Rationality, Behavior, Institutions*, 2nd ed. (New York: Norton, 2010), pp. 460–8.

Figure 6.9

THE WIDENING IDEOLOGICAL GAP BETWEEN THE PARTIES

HOUSE OF REPRESENTATIVES

SENATE

SOURCE: Voteview, Party Polarization: 1879–2012, http://pooleandrosenthal.com/politicalpolarization
.asp (accessed 6/11/13).

In 2005, the Republicans removed several members from the House Ethics Committee because of their participation, in the previous Congress, in investigating the House Republican leader, Tom DeLay. Inasmuch as the Ethics Committee is seen as a bipartisan watchdog, these actions were regarded as muscle-flexing responses by the Republican leadership. Bipartisan or not, the leadership seemed to be saying, as noted earlier, that some lines should not be crossed. In a bold move at the end of the 112th Congress, as the nation approached an end-of-the-year set of tax and spending deadlines, Speaker Boehner removed several recalcitrant Republicans from the Budget Committee.

Access to the Floor. The most important everyday resource available to the parties is control over access to the floor. With thousands of bills awaiting passage and most members clamoring for access to influence a bill or publicize themselves, floor time is precious. In the Senate, the leadership allows ranking committee members to influence the allocation of floor time—who will speak for how long. In the House, the Speaker, as head of the majority party (in consultation with the minority leader), allocates large blocks of floor time. Thus floor time is allocated in both houses of Congress by the majority and minority leaders. More important, the Speaker of the House and the majority leader in the Senate possess the power of recognition. Although this power may not appear to be substantial, it is a formidable authority and can be used to stymie a piece of legislation completely or to frustrate a member's attempts to speak on a particular issue. Because the power is significant, members of Congress usually attempt to stay on good terms with the Speaker and the majority leader to ensure that they will continue to be recognized.[56]

The Whip System. Some influence accrues to party leaders through the **whip system**, which is primarily a communications network. Between 12 and 20 assistant and regional whips are selected by geographic zones to operate at the direction of the majority or minority leader and the whip. They take polls of all the members to learn their intentions on specific bills. This information enables the leaders to know if they have enough support to allow a vote and whether the vote is so close that they need to put pressure on a few swing votes. Leaders also use the whip system to convey their wishes and plans to the members, but only in very close votes do they exert pressure on a member. In those instances, the Speaker or a lieutenant will go to a few party members who have indicated they will switch if their votes are essential. The whip system helps the leaders limit the practice of pressuring members to a few times per session. It helps maintain party unity in both houses of Congress, but it is particularly critical in the House of Representatives because of the large number of legislators whose positions and votes must always be accounted for.

Logrolling. An agreement between two or more members of Congress who have nothing in common except the need for mutual support is called **logrolling**. The agreement states, in effect, "You support me on bill X, and I'll support you on a bill of your choice." Because party leaders are the center of the communications networks in the two chambers, they can help members create large logrolling coalitions. Hundreds of logrolling deals are made each year, and although there are no official records, it would be a poor party leader whose

 whip system

A communications network in each house of Congress. Whips poll the membership to learn their intentions on specific legislative issues and assist the majority and minority leaders in various tasks

 logrolling

A legislative practice wherein reciprocal agreements are made between legislators, usually in voting for or against a bill. In contrast to bargaining, logrolling unites parties that have nothing in common but their desire to exchange support

---

56 A recent analysis of how floor time is allocated is found in Cox and McCubbins, *Setting the Agenda*.

whips did not know who owed what to whom.[57] In some instances, logrolling produces strange alliances. A seemingly unlikely alliance emerged in Congress in June 1994, when 119 mainly conservative senators and representatives from oil-producing states met with President Clinton to suggest that they might be willing to support the president's health care proposals in exchange for his support for a number of tax breaks for the oil industry. Senator J. Bennett Johnston of Louisiana, a leader of the oil-state representatives, contended that the issues of health care and oil production were closely related because both "affected the long-term economic security of the nation." Ironically, the oil-producing groups that promoted this alliance are generally among the most conservative forces in the nation. When asked what he thought of the president's health care proposal, George Alcorn, a leading industry lobbyist involved in the logrolling effort, dismissed Clinton's plan as "socialized medicine." Another alliance of strange bedfellows was the 1994 "corn for porn" logroll in which liberal urbanites supported farm programs in exchange for rural support for National Endowment for the Arts funding (at a time when many conservatives thought that the art produced by some NEA grantees bordered on the pornographic). Good logrolling, it would seem, is not hampered by minor ideological concerns.[58] In this case, the rationality principle (exemplified by a willingness to support a policy to which one is opposed in exchange for reciprocal support for a policy one cares passionately about) and the institution principle (in which the separation of powers allows the president and legislators to cut deals) work in unusual ways to produce policy outcomes.

The Presidency. Of all the influences that maintain the clarity of party lines in Congress, the influence of the presidency is probably the most important. Indeed, it is a touchstone of party discipline in Congress. Since the late 1940s, under President Harry Truman, presidents each year have identified a number of bills to be considered part of their administration's program. By the mid-1950s, both parties in Congress began to look to the president for these proposals, which became the most significant part of Congress's agenda. The president's support is a criterion for party loyalty, and party leaders are able to use it to rally some members.

---

57 For an analysis of the formal problems that logrolling (or vote trading) both solves and creates, see Shepsle, *Analyzing Politics*, pp. 374–6. It is argued there that logrolling cannot be the entire solution to the problem of assembling majority coalitions out of the diverse preferences found in any political party. The reason is that although party leaders can try to keep track of who owes what to whom, the bookkeeping is imperfect and highly complex at best. Nevertheless, if anyone is positioned to orchestrate a system of logrolling, it is the party leaders. And of all those who have tried to facilitate such "cooperation," Robert Byrd (D-W. Va.), who served as both majority whip and majority leader in the Senate, was the acknowledged master. For an insightful analysis of the ways party leaders build majority coalitions through the strategic use of pork-barrel projects, see Evans, *Greasing the Wheels*.

58 Allen R. Meyerson, "Oil-Patch Congressmen Seek Deal with Clinton," *New York Times*, June 14, 1994, p. D2.

Weighing Diverse Influences

Clearly many factors affect congressional decisions. But at various points in the decision-making process, some are likely to be more influential than others. For example, interest groups may be more effective at the committee stage, when their expertise is especially valued and their visibility is less obvious. Because committees play a key role in deciding what legislation reaches the floor of the House or the Senate, interest groups can often put a halt to bills they dislike, or they can ensure that the options that do reach the floor are those that the group's members support.

Once legislation reaches the floor and members of Congress are deciding among alternatives, constituent opinion will become more important. Legislators are also influenced very much by other legislators: many of their assessments about the substance and politics of legislation come from fellow members of Congress.

The influence of the external and internal forces described in the preceding section also varies according to the kind of issue being considered. On policies of great importance to powerful interest groups—farm subsidies, for example—those groups are likely to have considerable influence. On other issues, members of Congress may be less attentive to narrow interest groups and more willing to consider what they see as the general interest.

Finally, the mix of influences varies according to the historical moment. The Republicans' 1994 electoral victory allowed their party to control both houses of Congress for the first time in 40 years. That fact, combined with an unusually assertive Republican leadership, meant that party leaders became especially important in decision making. The willingness of moderate Republicans to support measures they had once opposed indicated the unusual importance of party leadership in this period. As the House Democratic minority leader, Richard Gephardt, put it, "When you've been in the desert forty years, your instinct is to help Moses."[59]

BEYOND LEGISLATION: ADDITIONAL CONGRESSIONAL POWERS

In addition to the power to make the law, Congress has at its disposal an array of other instruments through which it can influence the process of government.

Advice and Consent: Special Senate Powers

The Constitution has given the Senate a special power, one that is not based on lawmaking: the president has the power to make treaties and appoint top executive officers, ambassadors, and federal judges—but only "with the Advice and

---

59 Quoted in David Broder, "At 6 Months, House GOP Juggernaut Still Cohesive," *Washington Post*, July 17, 1995, p. A1.

Consent of the Senate" (Article II, Section 2). For treaties, two-thirds of those senators present must concur; for appointments, a majority is required.

The power to approve or reject presidential requests also involves the power to set conditions. The Senate only occasionally exercises its power to reject treaties and appointments. Only nine Supreme Court nominees have been rejected by the Senate during the past century, while most have been approved.[60]

More common than the Senate rejection of presidential appointees is a senatorial "hold" on an appointment. By Senate tradition, any member may place an indefinite hold on the confirmation of a mid- or lower-level presidential appointment. The hold may be a signal of a senator's willingness to filibuster a nomination, but it is typically used by senators trying to wring concessions from the White House on matters having nothing to do with the appointment in question. After Bush came to power in January 2001, the Democrats in the Senate actively scrutinized judicial nominations. Senate Democrats prevented final confirmation votes on a dozen especially conservative nominees, a matter about which President Bush frequently complained during the 2004 re-election campaign. Of course, Republicans had done exactly the same thing to many judicial nominations in the preceding Clinton administration and continued the practice in the Obama administration.

Judicial nomination politics loomed large during Bush's second term. During the summer of 2005, Justice Sandra Day O'Connor announced her retirement. Bush nominated John Roberts, a sitting federal judge, as her replacement. Before he could be confirmed, Chief Justice William Rehnquist died. President Bush withdrew Roberts's nomination and then renominated him to replace Rehnquist as chief justice, which the Senate confirmed. Bush then turned to O'Connor's replacement. His initial nominee, presidential confidante and White House Counsel Harriet Miers, was forced to withdraw amid charges of cronyism and lack of experience. Bush then nominated Samuel Alito, a federal appeals court judge with a substantial track record and solidly conservative credentials.

During his first term in office, President Obama had the opportunity to name two new justices when David Souter and John Paul Stevens announced their retirements. To replace Souter, Obama chose federal appeals court judge Sonia Sotomayor, the first Hispanic to serve on the Supreme Court. To take Stevens's place, Obama named Solicitor General Elena Kagan. Republicans grumbled that both nominees were too liberal but made only token objections since Sotomayor and Kagan would be replacing liberal justices and so would not change the balance of power on the Court.

Senatorial advice and consent is also required on treaties. Thus, at the end of the first Congress of the Obama presidency—one featuring frequent

---

60 Of President George W. Bush's three nominees, however, although two were confirmed, one nominee withdrew because of a concern that she could not succeed.

obstruction from Republicans—it was surprising that they joined Democrats in consenting to the New Start treaty with Russia to reduce nuclear arsenals. Most presidents make every effort to take potential Senate opposition into account in treaty negotiations and will frequently resort to **executive agreements** with foreign powers instead of treaties. The Supreme Court has held that such agreements are equivalent to treaties, but they do not need Senate approval.[61] In the past, presidents sometimes concluded secret agreements without informing Congress of the agreements' contents or even their existence. For example, American involvement in the Vietnam War grew in part out of a series of secret arrangements made between American presidents and the South Vietnamese during the 1950s and 1960s. Congress did not even learn of the existence of these agreements until 1969. In 1972, Congress passed the Case Act, which requires that the president inform Congress of any executive agreement within 60 days of its having been reached. This provides Congress with the opportunity to cancel agreements that it opposes. In addition, Congress can limit the president's ability to conduct foreign policy through executive agreement by refusing to appropriate the funds needed to implement an agreement. In this way, for example, Congress can modify or even cancel executive agreements to provide economic or military assistance to foreign governments.

> **executive agreement**
>
> An agreement between the president and another country that has the force of a treaty but does not require the Senate's "advice and consent"

Impeachment

The Constitution, in Article II, Section 4, also grants Congress the power of **impeachment** over the president, vice president, and other executive officials. Impeachment means charging a government official (president or otherwise) with "Treason, Bribery, or other high Crimes and Misdemeanors" and bringing her before Congress to determine guilt. Impeachment is thus like a criminal indictment, in which the House of Representatives acts like a grand jury, voting (by simple majority) on whether the accused ought to be impeached. If a majority of the House votes to impeach, the impeachment trial is held in the Senate, which acts like a trial jury by voting whether to convict and forcibly remove the person from office (this vote requires a two-thirds majority).

Controversy over Congress's impeachment power has arisen over the grounds for impeachment, especially the meaning of "high Crimes and Misdemeanors." A strict reading of the Constitution suggests that the only impeachable offense is an actual crime. But a more commonly agreed on

> **impeachment**
>
> The charging of a government official (president or otherwise) with "Treason, Bribery, or other high Crimes and Misdemeanors" and bringing him or her before Congress to determine guilt

---

61 *United States v. Pink*, 315 U.S. 203 (1942). For a good discussion of the problem, see James W. Davis, *The American Presidency: A New Perspective* (New York: Harper & Row, 1987), chap. 8. A recent analysis is found in William G. Howell, *Power without Persuasion: The Politics of Direct Presidential Action* (Princeton, NJ: Princeton University Press, 2003).

definition is that "an impeachable offense is whatever the majority of the House of Representatives considers it to be at a given moment in history."[62] In other words, impeachment, especially impeachment of a president, is a political decision.

The United States came closest to impeaching and convicting a president in 1867. Andrew Johnson, a southern Democrat who had battled a congressional Republican majority over Reconstruction, was impeached by the House but saved from conviction by one vote in the Senate. At the height of the Watergate scandal in 1974, the House started impeachment proceedings against President Richard Nixon, but Nixon resigned before the House could proceed. The possibility of impeachment arose again in 1998, when President Clinton was accused of lying under oath and obstructing justice in the investigation into his sexual affair with White House intern Monica Lewinsky. In October 1998, the House voted to impeach the president. At the conclusion of the Senate trial in 1999, Democrats, joined by a handful of Republicans, acquitted the president of both charges.

POWER AND REPRESENTATION

Because they feared both executive and legislative tyranny, the framers of the Constitution pitted Congress and the president against each other. And as the history principle suggests, this has provided us with a legacy of interbranch competition. During the first century of American government, Congress was the dominant institution. American foreign and domestic policy was formulated and implemented by Congress, and generally the most powerful figures in American government were the Speaker of the House and the leaders of the Senate—not the president. During the nineteenth century, Congress—not the president—dominated press coverage on "the affairs of government."[63] The War of 1812 was planned and fought by Congress; President Madison's resolve against the war dissolved under relentless pressure from congressional warhawks led by Speaker of the House Henry Clay. The great sectional compromises before the Civil War were formulated in Congress without much intervention from the executive branch. Even during the Civil War, a period of extraordinary presidential leadership, a joint congressional committee on the conduct of the war played a role in formulating war plans and campaign tactics—and even had a hand in the promotion of officers. After the Civil

---

62 Carroll J. Doherty, "Impeachment: How It Would Work," *Congressional Quarterly Weekly Report*, January 31, 1998, p. 222.

63 Samuel Kernell and Gary C. Jacobson, "Congress and the Presidency as News in the Nineteenth Century," *Journal of Politics* 49 (1987): 1016–35.

War, when President Andrew Johnson sought to interfere with congressional plans for Reconstruction, he was summarily impeached, saved from conviction by only one vote. Subsequent presidents understood the moral and did not attempt to thwart Congress.

This congressional preeminence began to diminish at the beginning of the twentieth century, so that by the 1960s the executive had become, at least temporarily, the dominant branch of American government. The major domestic policy initiatives of the twentieth century—Franklin Delano Roosevelt's New Deal, Harry Truman's Fair Deal, John F. Kennedy's New Frontier, and Lyndon Johnson's Great Society—all included some congressional involvement but were essentially developed, introduced, and implemented by the executive. In the area of foreign policy, although Congress continued to be influential during the twentieth century, the focus of decision-making power clearly moved into the executive branch. The War of 1812 may have been a congressional war, but in the twentieth century American entry into World War I, World War II, Korea, Vietnam, Iraq, Afghanistan, and a host of lesser conflicts was essentially a presidential—not a congressional—decision. In the last 40 years, there has been a good deal of resurgence of congressional power vis-à-vis the executive. This has occurred mainly because Congress has sought to represent many important political forces, such as the civil rights, women's, environmental, consumer, and peace movements, which in turn became constituencies for congressional power. It also has been helped along by the creation of congressional agencies, especially the Congressional Budget Office, the Congressional Research Service, and the Government Accountability Office, to provide the legislature with informational support independent of the executive branch. During the mid-1990s, Congress became more receptive to a variety of new conservative political forces, including groups on the social and religious right as well as more traditional economic conservatives. After Republicans won control of both houses in the 1994 elections, Congress took the lead in developing programs and policies supported by these groups. These efforts won Congress the support of conservative forces in its battles for power against a Democratic White House.

To herald the new accessibility of Congress, Republican leaders instituted a number of reforms designed to eliminate many of the practices that they had long criticized as examples of Democratic arrogance. Republican leaders reduced the number of committees and subcommittees, eliminated funding of the various unofficial caucuses, imposed term limits on committee chairs, eliminated the practice of proxy voting, reduced committee staffs by one-third, ended Congress's exemption from the labor, health, and civil rights laws that it imposed on the rest of the nation, and prohibited members from receiving most gifts. With these reforms, Republicans hoped to make Congress both more effective and more representative. Term limits and bans on gifts were seen as increasing the responsiveness of Congress to new political forces and to the American people in general. Simplification of the committee structure was seen as making Congress more efficient and thus potentially more effective and more powerful. To some extent, unfortunately, the various reforms worked at cross-purposes. Simplification of the committee structure and elimination of funding for the caucuses increased the power of the leadership, thereby muting the effectiveness of more representative elements. In another instance, when term limits for committee and subcommittee chairs were finally imposed in 2001, the result was confusion because experienced leaders were forced to step down, spreading power around in a more representative manner but diminishing committee effectiveness. This is the dilemma of congressional reform. Efficiency and representation are often competing principles in our system of government, and we must be wary of gaining one at the expense of the other. In the next chapter, we turn to the second branch of American government, the presidency, to view this dilemma from a somewhat different angle.

CONCLUSION

Our discussion in this chapter has been both descriptive and analytical. The Constitution sets the stage by describing Congress's role in politics. The U.S. Congress is a two-chamber legislature with the authority to develop and pass legislation (with the concurrence of the president) on the one hand, and the power to oversee policy implementation by the president and executive bureaucracy on the other hand. It is present at the creation, so to speak, and has a continuing responsibility after a law is crafted. Each chamber keeps an eye on the other chamber and ultimately must come to terms with that other chamber on joint legislative products that are sent on to the president for his signature. But each chamber has a life of its own as well. Each is organized by its majority party, itself possessing an organizational structure of leaders and followers. For efficiency reasons, and to accommodate the career and policy ambitions of its members, committee systems in the House and Senate allow for the division and specialization of labor; each of these committees is a "little legislature"[64] with committee leaders and a subcommittee structure. In addition to pursuing substantive policy objectives through legislation by authorizing new programs and reauthorizing existing ones, the two chambers have a special role to play in the financial realm—raising revenue from taxes and appropriating monies to fund authorized programs. In addition, the Constitution gives the Senate further responsibilities, including the approval of treaties and the confirmation of federal judges, Supreme Court justices, and high administrative officers.

In analytical terms, the U.S. Congress is an institutional arrangement. First, in light of the rationality principle, it arranges itself in accordance with the policy and career ambitions of its members. These goals encompass

64 The classic statement is George Goodwin, *The Little Legislatures* (Amherst: University of Massachusetts Press, 1970).

re-election, the achievement of personal policy objectives, and the attainment of influence and position inside the legislative chamber. Politicians are ambitious for themselves, their party, and their constituencies. To accomplish at least some of the personal objectives of 435 individuals in one chamber and 100 in the other, politicians must engage in bargaining, coordination, and cooperation. These activities are orchestrated by institutional rules, structures, and procedures, the effects of which are found in the policies ultimately produced. It should be noted that, given the size of majorities required in each chamber to produce results, policy benefits must be distributed widely in what we called the *distributive tendency*. The resulting product isn't always pretty; there are occasional "bridges to nowhere" and other undesirable pork-barrel projects. But this is what it takes to accomplish goals in a diverse, multiperson, elected body. Over the course of more than two centuries, each chamber has created ways of doing business, reformed them, and sometimes engineered entirely new ways of conducting its affairs. The history of what has gone before channels this institutional engineering.

The two chambers of the American legislature do not operate in a vacuum. In front of them are the president, the executive bureaucracy, and the courts, which jointly participate in lawmaking and its implementation. Behind them is public opinion, which ultimately renders judgment on their efforts by rewarding or punishing individuals through elections. In the next three chapters we take up the presidency, the executive branch, and the court system. In Part 3 we explore public opinion and elections.

For Further Reading

Selections highlighted in red are included in *Readings in American Politics: Analysis and Perspectives*, Third Edition.

Adler, E. Scott. *Why Congressional Reforms Fail: Reelection and the House Committee System*. Chicago: University of Chicago Press, 2002.

Aldrich, John H., and David W. Rohde. "The Republican Revolution and the House Appropriations Committee," *Journal of Politics* 62 (2000): 1–33.

Binder, Sarah. *Stalemate: Causes and Consequences of Legislative Gridlock*. Washington, DC: Brookings Institution, 2003.

Binder, Sarah, and Paul Quirk, eds. *Institutions of Democracy: The Legislative Branch*. New York: Oxford University Press, 2004.

Brady, David W., and Mathew D. McCubbins, eds. *Party, Process, and Political Change in Congress: New Perspectives on the History of Congress*. Palo Alto, CA: Stanford University Press, 2002 (vol. 1); 2007 (vol. 2).

Brady, David W., and Craig Volden. *Revolving Gridlock: Politics and Policy from Carter to Bush.* 2nd ed. Boulder, CO: Westview Press, 2005.

Cox, Gary W. *Legislative Leviathan: Party Government in the House.* 2nd ed. Berkeley: University of California Press, 2006.

Cox, Gary W., and Jonathon Katz. *Elbridge Gerry's Salamander: The Electoral Consequences of the Reapportionment Revolution.* Cambridge, UK: Cambridge University Press, 2002.

Cox, Gary W., and Mathew D. McCubbins. *Setting the Agenda: Responsible Party Government in the U.S. House of Representatives.* New York: Cambridge University Press, 2005.

Fenno, Richard F., Jr. *Home Style: House Members in Their Districts.* Boston: Little, Brown, 1978.

Fiorina, Morris P. *Congress: Keystone of the Washington Establishment.* 2nd ed. New Haven, CT: Yale University Press, 1989.

Frisch, Scott A., and Sean Q. Kelly. *Committee Assignment Politics in the U.S. House of Representatives.* Norman: University of Oklahoma Press, 2006.

Gamm, Gerald, and Kenneth A. Shepsle. "Emergence of Legislative Institutions: Standing Committees in the House and the Senate, 1810–1825," *Legislative Studies Quarterly* 14 (1989): 39–66.

Harbridge, Laurel, and Neil Malhotra. "Electoral Incentives and Partisan Conflict in Congress: Evidence from Survey Experiments," *American Journal of Political Science* 55 (2011): 494–510.

Jacobson, Gary C. *The Politics of Congressional Elections.* 8th ed. New York: Longman, 2012.

Krehbiel, Keith. *Pivotal Politics: A Theory of U.S. Lawmaking.* Chicago: University of Chicago Press, 1998.

Mayhew, David R. *Congress: The Electoral Connection.* New Haven, CT: Yale University Press, 1974.

Rohde, David W. *Parties and Leaders in the Post-Reform House.* Chicago: University of Chicago Press, 1991.

Smith, Steven S., and Christopher J. Deering. *Committees in Congress.* 3rd ed. Washington, DC: CQ Press, 1997.

Stewart, Charles H. *Analyzing Congress.* 2nd ed. New York: Norton, 2012.

Wawro, Gregory, and Eric Schickler. *Filibuster: Obstruction and Lawmaking in the United States Senate.* Princeton, NJ: Princeton University Press, 2006.

7

The Presidency as an Institution

Chapter Outline

- The Constitutional Origins and Powers of the Presidency

- The Rise of Presidential Government

- Presidential Government

- Presidential Power: Myths and Realities

America's last eight presidents have left office under political clouds and, in five cases, sooner than they wanted. Lyndon Johnson did not run for re-election in 1968 after the Vietnam War turned large segments of his own party against him. As the Watergate scandal unfolded and the House prepared to vote impeachment, Richard Nixon chose to resign in 1974 to avoid almost certain conviction. Nixon's appointed successor, Gerald Ford, was defeated for election to a full term in 1976. Jimmy Carter, who ousted Ford, was, himself, denied re-election by Ronald Reagan. Reagan won re-election to a second term but left office with a reputation damaged by the Iran-Contra scandal. Reagan's successor, George H. W. Bush, was defeated for re-election by Bill Clinton. Clinton served two full terms but only after surviving an impeachment and numerous scandals. Clinton's successor, George W. Bush, will be remembered as the least popular president in the history of opinion polling. Barack Obama, elected in 2008 as a popular successor to Bush, won re-election in a bruising campaign in 2012, despite presiding over four years of economic sluggishness and indifferent international performance.

Yet even as our presidents have limped out of the White House or struggled to remain there, the presidency as an institution has grown in power and prominence. Indeed, over the past century, the presidency has become America's most powerful institution in the realms of foreign and military policy and, arguably, in arenas of domestic policy as well. One reason that presidential power has grown despite the difficulties presidents have faced has to do with the character of the presidency as an institution. The presidency is America's only political institution characterized by unitary rather than collective decision-making processes. Members of Congress and the judiciary must deliberate, compromise, and vote before reaching decisions. The president may wish to seek advice from many sources but, in the end, exercises the powers of the office on his own authority. As former president George W. Bush once said, "I am the decider."

Unitary "deciders" are usually better able to accrue power than collective decision makers. To begin with, the unitary decider usually sees a direct relationship between the power of the institution and the ability to achieve whatever political goals she might have. Presidents Reagan and Clinton, for example, worked diligently and successfully to expand the president's power of regulatory review (discussed later in the chapter), so that they could use the bureaucratic rule-making process to achieve their policy goals without the need for congressional approval. For members of collective decision-making bodies such as Congress, on the other hand, the situation is not so simple. Members of Congress are often confronted with collective action problems and motivated to put their immediate political interests ahead of the long-term power of the institution. For example, in October 2008, Congress responded to enormous political pressure for quick action to deal with the nation's financial crisis by giving the executive branch unprecedented new economic powers. Several years later, President Obama used this new economic authority to promote new rules to refinance federally guaranteed mortgages and to ease repayment schedules for federal student loans. Few congressional lawmakers considered how their votes would affect the long-term balance of power between the legislative and

CORE OF THE ANALYSIS

➡ The Constitution endows the president with a limited number of expressed powers. Other presidential powers are delegated by Congress or claimed by presidents without specific statutory authority.

➡ Over time, the presidency has accumulated more and more power relative to the other institutions of government, partly because the president doesn't face the same collective action problems as Congress.

➡ Presidents can broaden their powers through successful execution of the law.

➡ Presidential power can also be enhanced through strategic interactions with other political actors, and through a president's ability to build popular support.

➡ Historic events requiring bold action and leadership by the president, such as the Great Depression, can also contribute to the president's power.

executive branches. Typically, as one observer put it in an earlier context, few members are prepared to "speak up for the institutional interests of Congress."[1]

At the same time, collective decision makers often feel pressure to cede power to unitary deciders when expeditious action seems of paramount importance. During times of crisis, when a quick response is needed and the public is impatient with constitutional limitations on collective action, Congress and the judiciary typically accede to presidential demands for new executive powers to deal expeditiously with the emergency.

Hence, the character of the presidency as an institution—the fact that the president is a unitary decider—helps to explain why the presidency has gained in power over time at the expense of other institutions, particularly Congress. Of course, the fact that the president is a unitary decider, coupled with the growth of presidential power, also helps to explain why presidents usually become quite unpopular over the course of their terms. Unlike members of Congress and other participants in collective decision making, presidents cannot escape responsibility for their decisions and are invariably blamed when things go wrong. The problem with being the decider in more and more policy spheres is that presidents have opportunities to make more mistakes and generate more opposition. Thus, ironically, the growing power of the presidency as an institution is one reason that so many of our recent presidents have seen their own popularity fade after a few years in office. President Obama, for instance, entered office with over 60 percent approval; this dropped to just 38 percent in October 2011. Approval has hovered near 50 percent for Obama's second term.

Our focus in this chapter is on the development of the institutional character of the presidency, the power of the presidency, and the relationship between the two. The chapter concerns itself with three major topics. First, we review the constitutional origins and powers of the presidency. Second, we review the history of the American presidency to see how the office has evolved from its original status under the Constitution. Third, we assess the means by which presidents can enhance their own ability to govern.

THE CONSTITUTIONAL ORIGINS AND POWERS OF THE PRESIDENCY

The presidency as an institution was established by Article II of the Constitution. Article II begins by asserting, "The executive Power shall be vested in a President of the United States of America." It goes on to describe the qualifications for the office (one must be a natural-born citizen, at least thirty-five years of age, and a resident of the United States for at least 14 years), the manner in which the president is to be chosen, and the basic powers of the presidency. By

---

1 Robert G. Kaiser, "Congress-s-s-s: That Great Hissing Sound You Hear Is Congress Giving Up Its Clout," *Washington Post*, March 14, 2004, p. B1.

vesting the executive power in a single president, the framers were emphatically rejecting proposals for various forms of collective leadership. Some delegates to the Constitutional Convention had argued in favor of a multiheaded executive or an "executive council" to avoid undue concentration of power in the hands of one individual. Most of the framers, however, hoped the president would be capable of taking quick and decisive action. The framers thought a unitary executive would be more energetic than some form of collective leadership. They believed that a powerful executive would help protect the nation's interests vis-à-vis other nations and promote the federal government's interests relative to the states. In other words, the framers opted for a decider rather than a deliberative body.

Immediately following the first sentence of Article II, Section 1, of the Constitution, the manner in which the president is to be chosen is defined. This is an odd sequence, and it says something about the difficulty the delegates were having over how to provide great power of action to the executive and at the same time balance that power with limitations. This reflected the twin struggles deeply etched in the memories of the founding generation—against the powerful executive authority of King George III and the dismal low energy of the government under the Articles of Confederation. There was disagreement between those delegates who wanted the president to be selected by, and thus responsible to, Congress and those delegates who preferred that the president be elected directly by the people. Direct popular election would create a more independent and more powerful presidency. With the adoption of a scheme of indirect election through an electoral college, in which the electors would be selected by the state legislatures (and close elections would be resolved in the House of Representatives), the framers hoped to achieve a "republican" solution: a strong president responsible to state and national legislators rather than directly responsible to the electorate. This indirect method of electing the president dampened the power of most presidents in the nineteenth century by denying them a political base of support and legitimacy independent of Congress and the state legislatures.

The presidency was strengthened somewhat in the 1830s with the introduction of the national convention system of nominating presidential candidates. Until then, candidates had been nominated by their party's congressional delegates. The convention system was seen as a victory for democracy over the congressional elite, giving the presidency a base of power independent of Congress. This additional independence did not immediately transform the presidency into the office we recognize today, but the national convention did begin to open the presidency to larger social forces and newly organized interests in society.

Whereas Article II, Section 1, explains how the president is to be chosen, Sections 2 and 3 outline the powers and duties of the president. These two sections identify two sources of presidential power. One source is the specific language of the Constitution. For example, the president is specifically authorized to make treaties, grant pardons, and nominate judges and other public officials. These clearly defined powers are called the **expressed powers** of the office and cannot be revoked by Congress or any other agency without an amendment to

 expressed powers

The powers enumerated in the Constitution that are granted to the federal government

the Constitution. Other expressed powers include the power to receive ambassadors and to command the military forces of the United States.

The second source of presidential power lies in the declaration in Article II that the president "shall take Care that the Laws be faithfully executed." Because the laws are enacted by Congress, this language implies that Congress is to delegate to the president the power to implement or execute its will. Powers given to the president by Congress are called **delegated powers**. In principle, Congress delegates to the president only the power to identify or develop the means through which to carry out its decisions. So, for example, if Congress determines that air quality should be improved, it might delegate to a bureaucratic agency in the executive branch the power to identify the best means of bringing about such an improvement, as well as the power to implement the cleanup process. In practice, of course, decisions about how to clean the air are likely to have an enormous effect on businesses, organizations, and individuals throughout the nation. As it delegates power to the executive, Congress substantially enhances the importance of the presidency and the executive branch. In most cases, Congress delegates power to bureaucratic agencies in the executive branch rather than to the president. As we shall see, however, contemporary presidents have found ways to capture a good deal of this delegated power for themselves.

Presidents have claimed a third source of institutional power beyond expressed and delegated powers. These are powers that are not specified in the Constitution or the law but are said to stem from "the rights, duties and obligations of the presidency."[2] They are referred to as the **inherent powers** of the presidency and are most often asserted by presidents in times of war or national emergency. For example, after the fall of Fort Sumter and the outbreak of the Civil War, President Lincoln issued a series of executive orders, although he had no clear legal basis for doing so. Without even calling Congress into session, Lincoln combined the state militias into a 90-day national volunteer force, called for 40,000 new volunteers, enlarged the regular army and navy, diverted $2 million in unspent appropriations to military needs, instituted censorship of the U.S. mail, ordered a blockade of southern ports, suspended the writ of *habeas corpus* in the border states, and ordered military police to arrest individuals whom he deemed to be guilty of engaging in or even contemplating treasonous actions.[3] Lincoln asserted that these extraordinary measures were justified by the

delegated powers

Constitutional powers assigned to one government agency but exercised by another agency with the express permission of the first

inherent powers

Powers claimed by a president that are not expressed in the Constitution but are inferred from it

---

2   In the case of *In re Neagle*, 135 U.S. 1 (1890), David Neagle, a deputy U.S. marshal, had been authorized by the president to protect a Supreme Court justice whose life had been threatened by an angry litigant. When the litigant attempted to carry out his threat, Neagle shot and killed him. Neagle was then arrested by local authorities and tried for murder. His defense was that his act was "done in pursuance of a law of the United States." Although the law was not an act of Congress, the Supreme Court declared that it was an executive order of the president and that the protection of a federal judge was a reasonable extension of the president's power to "take Care that the Laws be faithfully executed."

3   James G. Randall, *Constitutional Problems under Lincoln* (New York: Appleton, 1926), chap. 1.

president's inherent power to protect the nation.[4] Subsequent presidents, including Franklin Delano Roosevelt and George W. Bush, have had similar views.

Expressed Powers

The president's expressed powers, as defined by Article II, Sections 2 and 3, fall into several categories:

1. *Military.* Article II, Section 2, provides for the power as "Commander in Chief of the Army and Navy of the United States, and of the Militia of the several States, when called into the actual Service of the United States."

2. *Judicial.* Article II, Section 2, provides the "Power to grant Reprieves and Pardons for Offences against the United States, except in Cases of Impeachment."

3. *Diplomatic.* Article II, Section 2, provides the "Power, by and with the Advice and Consent of the Senate, to make Treaties." Article II, Section 3, provides the power to "receive Ambassadors and other public Ministers."

4. *Executive.* Article II, Section 3, authorizes the president to see to it that all the laws are faithfully executed. Section 2 gives the chief executive power to appoint, remove, and supervise all executive officers and appoint all federal judges.

5. *Legislative.* Article I, Section 7, and Article II, Section 3, give the president the power to participate authoritatively in the legislative process.

Military Power. The president's military powers are among the most important of the powers exercised by the chief executive. The position of **commander in chief** makes the president the highest military authority in the United States, with control of the entire defense establishment. The president is also head of the nation's intelligence network, which includes not only the Central Intelligence Agency (CIA) but also the National Security Council (NSC), the National Security Agency (NSA), the Federal Bureau of Investigation (FBI), and a host of less well-known but very powerful international and domestic security agencies.

commander in chief

The power of the president as commander of the national military and the state national guard units (when called into service)

Domestic Defense Power. The president's military powers extend into the domestic sphere. Article IV, Section 4, provides that "the United States shall . . . [protect] every State . . . against Invasion . . . and . . . domestic Violence." Congress has made this an explicit presidential power through statutes directing the president as commander in chief to discharge these

---

4   E. S. Corwin, *The President: Office and Powers,* 4th ed. (New York: New York University Press, 1957), p. 229.

obligations.[5] The Constitution restrains the president's use of domestic force by providing that a state legislature (or governor when the legislature is not in session) must request federal troops before the president can send them into the state to provide public order. Yet this proviso is not absolute. First, presidents are not obligated to deploy national troops merely because a state legislature or governor makes such a request. And more important, the president may deploy troops in a state or city without a specific request from a state legislature or governor if the president considers it necessary to maintain an essential national service during an emergency, enforce a federal judicial order, or protect federally guaranteed civil rights.

One historic example of the unilateral use of presidential emergency power to protect the states against domestic disorder, even when the states do not request it, was the decision by President Dwight Eisenhower in 1957 to send troops into Little Rock, Arkansas, against the wishes of the state of Arkansas in order to enforce court orders to integrate Little Rock's Central High School. As we saw in Chapter 5, the governor, Orval Faubus, had posted the Arkansas National Guard at the entrance of the school to prevent the court-ordered admission of nine black students. After an effort to negotiate with the governor failed, President Eisenhower reluctantly sent 1,000 paratroopers to Little Rock; they stood watch while the black students took their places in the all-white classrooms. This case makes quite clear that the president does not have to wait for a request by a state legislature or a governor before acting as a domestic commander in chief.[6] More recently, President George W. Bush sent various military units to the Gulf Coast in response to Hurricanes Katrina and Rita in 2005, and, in 2010, President Obama sent Coast Guard and teams from other agencies to participate in the rescue and cleanup following the BP *Deepwater Horizon* explosion and oil spill in the Gulf of Mexico. In most instances of domestic disorder—whether a result of human or natural events—presidents tend to exercise unilateral power by declaring a "state of emergency," thereby making available federal grants, insurance, and direct assistance.

Military emergencies have typically also led to expansion of the domestic powers of the executive branch. This was true during World Wars I and II and was the case during the "war on terrorism" as well. Within a month of the September 11 attacks, the White House had drafted, and Congress had enacted, the USA PATRIOT Act, expanding the power of government agencies to engage in domestic surveillance, including electronic surveillance, and restricting judicial review of such efforts. The following year Congress created the Department of Homeland Security, combining offices of 22 federal agencies into one huge new cabinet department that would be responsible for protecting the nation from attack.

---

5   These statutes are contained mainly in Title 10 of the United States Code, Sections 331, 332, and 333.

6   A now classic study covering all aspects of the domestic use of the military is that of Adam Yarmolinsky, *The Military Establishment* (New York: Harper & Row, 1971).

Judicial Power. The presidential power to grant **reprieves**, **pardons**, and **amnesties** involves the power of life and death over all individuals who may be a threat to the security of the United States. Presidents may use this power on behalf of a particular individual, as did Gerald Ford when he pardoned Richard Nixon in 1974 "for all offenses against the United States which he . . . has committed or may have committed." Or they may use it on a large scale, as Andrew Johnson did in 1868 when he gave full amnesty to all Southerners who had participated in the "Late Rebellion" and as Jimmy Carter did in 1977 when he declared an amnesty for all Vietnam War draft evaders. President Clinton issued a number of controversial pardons during his last weeks in office.

Diplomatic Power. The president is America's "head of state," its chief representative in dealings with other nations. As head of state, the president has the power to make treaties for the United States (with the advice and consent of the Senate). When President George Washington received Edmond Genet ("Citizen Genet") as the formal emissary of the revolutionary government of France in 1793 and had his cabinet officers and Congress back his decision, he established a greatly expanded interpretation of the power to "receive Ambassadors and other public Ministers," extending it to the power to "recognize" other countries. That power gives the president the almost unconditional authority to review the claims of any new ruling group to determine whether it indeed controls the territory and population of its country and therefore can, in the president's opinion, legitimately commit it to treaties and other agreements.

In recent years, presidents have expanded the practice of using executive agreements instead of treaties to establish relations with other countries.[7] An **executive agreement** is like a treaty because it is a contract between two countries, but an executive agreement does not require approval by the Senate. (A treaty does require a two-thirds vote of approval by the Senate.) Ordinarily executive agreements are used to carry out commitments already made in treaties or to arrange for matters well below the level of policy. But when presidents have found it expedient to use an executive agreement in place of a treaty, Congress has typically acquiesced.

Executive Power. The most important basis of the president's power as chief executive is found in Article II, Section 3, which stipulates that the president must see that all the laws are faithfully executed, and Section 2, which provides that the president will appoint and supervise all executive officers and appoint all federal judges (with Senate approval). The power to appoint the principal executive officers and to require each of them to report to the president on subjects relating to the duties of their departments makes the president the true chief executive officer of the nation. In this manner, the Constitution focuses executive power and legal responsibility on the president. The famous sign on

 reprieve

Cancellation or postponement of a punishment

 pardon

Forgiveness of a crime and cancellation of relevant penalty

 amnesty

A pardon extended to a group of persons

 executive agreement

An agreement between the president and another country that has the force of a treaty but does not require the Senate's "advice and consent"

---

7 In *United States v. Pink,* 315 U.S. 203 (1942), the Supreme Court confirmed that an executive agreement is the legal equivalent of a treaty despite the absence of Senate approval.

President Truman's desk, "The buck stops here," was not merely an assertion of Truman's personal sense of responsibility but was in fact evidence of his recognition of the legal and constitutional responsibility of the president.

The president's executive power is not absolute, however, as many presidential appointments, including ambassadors, cabinet officers and other high-level administrators, and federal judges, are subject to majority approval by the Senate. In this, the Senate has *not* acquiesced, often refusing to confirm presidential nominees or holding them hostage by failing even to bring them up for an up-or-down vote. This pattern is particularly evident in the confirmation process for federal judges. Table 7.1 shows, for Bush's last Congress and Obama's first, that the former had a confirmation success rate of about two-thirds, while the latter's was less than half.

The George W. Bush administration, supported by conservative scholars, argued that Article II of the Constitution vests all executive power in the president, who, by implication, is in full control of the executive branch. This idea is called the theory of the unitary executive. The theory is often disputed in principle, but presidents often act as though they believe it. The theory of the unitary executive is controversial in part because it denies Congress a significant role in managing the bureaucracy, concentrating this authority instead in the hands of the executive. This undermines the view of the American separation of powers system that executive and legislature are two branches "sharing powers."[8]

executive privilege ⇨

The claim that confidential communications between the president and the president's close advisers should not be revealed without the consent of the president

Another component of the president's power as chief executive is **executive privilege**. Executive privilege is the claim that confidential communications between a president and close advisers should not be revealed without the consent of the president. Presidents have made this claim ever since George Washington refused a request from the House of Representatives to deliver documents concerning negotiations of an important treaty. Washington refused (successfully) on the grounds that, first, the House was not constitutionally

Table 7.1

NOMINATIONS TO FEDERAL COURTS

PRESIDENT	CONGRESS	NOMINATIONS	CONFIRMED	WITHDRAWN	EXPIRED
George W. Bush	110th	104	68	6	30
Barack Obama	111th	113	62	1	50

SOURCE: Library of Congress, http://thomas.loc.gov/ (accessed 9/25/13).

8   For a famous statement of this, see Richard E. Neustadt, *Presidential Power* (1960; rev. ed. New York: Free Press, 1980).

part of the treaty-making process and, second, that diplomatic negotiations required secrecy.

Executive privilege became a popular part of the checks-and-balances counterpoint between the president and Congress, and presidents have usually had the upper hand when invoking it. Although many presidents have claimed executive privilege, the concept was not tested in the courts until the 1974 Watergate affair, during which President Nixon refused congressional demands that he turn over secret White House tapes that congressional investigators thought would establish Nixon's complicity in illegal activities. In *United States v. Nixon*, the Supreme Court ordered Nixon to turn over the tapes.[9] The president complied with the order and resigned from office to avoid impeachment and conviction. *United States v. Nixon* is often seen as a blow to presidential power, but in actuality the Court's ruling recognized for the first time the validity of a claim of executive privilege, although it held that it did not apply in this instance. Subsequent presidents have cited *United States v. Nixon* in support of their claims of executive privilege. For example, the administration of George W. Bush invoked executive privilege when it refused to give Congress documents relating to the president's decision to make use of warrantless wiretaps in the so-called CIA leak case, in which the identity of a CIA operative was revealed after her husband criticized the administration. The Bush administration also invoked executive privilege when it refused to obey congressional subpoenas demanding materials pertaining to the firing of a number of assistant U.S. attorneys.[10] More recently, in June 2012, the Obama administration appealed to executive privilege in refusing to comply with a subpoena from the House of Representatives for documents related to operation "Fast and Furious," a Justice Department drug-trafficking program.

Legislative Power. The president plays a role not only in the administration of government but also in the legislative process. Two constitutional provisions are the primary sources of the president's power in the legislative arena. The first of these is the provision in Article II, Section 3, providing that the president "shall from time to time give to the Congress Information of the State of the Union, and recommend to their Consideration such Measures as he shall judge necessary and expedient." The second of the president's legislative powers is of course the veto power assigned by Article I, Section 7.[11]

---

9 *United States v. Nixon*, 418 U.S. 683 (1974).

10 A recent extension of executive power by President George W. Bush is the "signing statement," which is discussed later in this chapter.

11 There is a third source of presidential power implied in the provision for faithful execution of the laws. This is the president's power to impound funds—that is, to refuse to spend money Congress has appropriated for certain purposes. One author referred to this as a "retroactive veto power" (Robert E. Goosetree, "The Power of the President to Impound Appropriated Funds," *American University Law Review*, January 1962).

Delivering a State of the Union address might not appear to be of any great import. It is a mere obligation on the part of the president to make recommendations for Congress's consideration. But as political and social conditions favored an increasingly prominent role for presidents, each president, especially since Franklin Delano Roosevelt, has relied on this provision to become the primary initiator of proposals for legislative action in Congress and the principal source for public awareness of national issues, as well as the most important single individual participant in legislative decisions. Few today doubt that the president, together with the executive branch as a whole, is the primary source of many important congressional actions.

The **veto** is the president's constitutional power to turn down acts of Congress (Figure 7.1). It alone makes the president the most important single legislative leader.[12] No bill vetoed by the president can become law unless both the House and Senate override the veto by a two-thirds vote. In the case of a **pocket veto**, Congress does not have the option of overriding the veto but must reintroduce the bill in the next session. A pocket veto can occur when the president is presented with a bill during the last 10 days of a legislative session. Usually if a president does not sign a bill within 10 days, it automatically becomes law. But this is true only while Congress is in session. If a president chooses not to sign a bill presented within the last 10 days that Congress is in session, then the 10-day limit expires while Congress is out of session, and instead of becoming law, the bill is considered vetoed. In 1996, a new power was added to the president's lineup—the **line-item veto**—giving the president the power to strike specific spending items from appropriations bills passed by Congress unless they were reenacted by a two-thirds vote of both the House and the Senate. In 1997, President Clinton used this power 11 times to strike 82 items from the federal budget. But in 1998 the Supreme Court ruled that the Constitution does not authorize the line-item veto.[13] Only a constitutional amendment would give this power to the president.

The Games Presidents Play: The Veto. Use of the veto varies according to the political situation that each president confronts. George W. Bush vetoed no bill during his first term, a period in which his party controlled both houses of Congress. He vetoed only one bill during the first two years of his second term, another period during which Congress was controlled by his party.[14] In the

veto ➡

The president's constitutional power to turn down acts of Congress within 10 days of their passage while Congress is in session. A presidential veto may be overridden by a two-thirds vote of each house of Congress

pocket veto ➡

A veto that is effected when Congress adjourns during the time a president has to approve a bill and the president takes no action on it

line-item veto ➡

The power of the executive to veto specific provisions (lines) of a bill passed by the legislature

12 For more on the veto, see Chapter 6. Also see Robert J. Spitzer, *The Presidential Veto: Touchstone of the American Presidency* (Albany: State University of New York Press, 1988), and Charles M. Cameron, *Veto Bargaining: Presidents and the Politics of Negative Power* (New York: Cambridge University Press, 2000).

13 *Clinton v. City of New York*, 524 U.S. 417 (1998).

14 A caveat: President George W. Bush, as observed in an earlier footnote, relied on signing statements as something of a substitute for the veto. Had the Supreme Court declared the maneuver unconstitutional, the president would have been forced to face squarely the decision to use the power of the veto.

Figure 7.1
THE VETO PROCESS

Bill passes Congress. → **Bill is presented to the president.**

Bill is reviewed by:
- special assistants
- Office of Management and Budget party
- relevant department head
- key legislative leaders in president's party
- key lobbyists close to president
- Justice Department

If no action is taken after 10 working days while Congress is in session . . .

Bill dies (pocket veto).

If no action is taken after 10 working days while Congress is in recess . . .

If bill is acceptable to the president . . .

President signs the bill, usually in a public ceremony in the presence of key sponsors and supporters. Pens used become souvenirs.

Bill becomes law and is given a legal designation (e.g., PL-111-999).*

If a veto is recommended, the bill goes to . . .

- Staff assistants
- Relevant department head
- Speech writers

Bill is vetoed.

Veto is overridden.

Bill is returned to Congress. Override requires two-thirds vote of both houses.

Bill lives.

Bill dies.

Congress fails to override veto.

*PL stands for "public law"; 111 is the Congress (e.g., the 111th Congress was in session in 2009–11); 999 is the number of the law.

---

last two years of his second term, with Congress controlled by the Democrats, he vetoed 11 bills. In President Obama's first term, with Democratic control of both the House and the Senate in the first two years, he vetoed only two bills. He vetoed no bills in the second two years, after the Democrats lost their House majority and had their Senate majority pared down, but this was mainly because the Republican strategy of obstruction, especially in the Senate, produced very little legislative product.[15] In general, presidents have used the veto to equalize or perhaps upset the balance of power with Congress. While the simple power to reject or accept legislation in its entirety might seem like a crude tool for making sure that legislation adheres to a president's preferences, the politics surrounding the veto is complicated, and it is rare that vetoes are used simply as bullets to kill legislation. Instead, vetoes are usually part of an intricate bargaining process between the president and Congress, involving threats of vetoes, the repassage of legislation, and second vetoes.[16]

The fact that presidents rarely veto legislation does not mean that vetoes and veto bargaining have an insignificant influence over the policy process. The fact that presidents vetoed only several hundred of the more than 20,000 public bills that Congress sent to them between 1945 and 2010 belies the centrality of the veto to presidential power. Many of these bills were insignificant and not worth the veto effort. Thus it is important to separate "significant" legislation, for which vetoes frequently occur, from insignificant legislation.[17] Vetoes can also be effective—even though they are rarely employed—because individuals will condition their actions on the basis of how they think others will respond.[18] With respect to vetoes, this means that members of Congress will alter the content of a bill to make it more to a president's liking in order to discourage a veto. Thus the veto power can be influential even when the veto pen rests in its inkwell.[19]

Rhetoric and reputation take on particular importance when vetoes become part of a bargaining process. Bargaining between Congress and the president is strategic and an example of the rationality principle in action. The president tries to influence legislators' beliefs about what they must do to keep the president from using the veto power. The key to veto bargaining is uncertainty. Members of Congress are often unsure about the president's policy preferences and therefore don't know which bills the president is willing to sign. When the policy preferences of the president and Congress diverge, as they typically do in a divided government, the president tries to convince Congress that his preferences are more extreme than they really are in order to get Congress to enact legislation that is closer to what he really wants. If members of Congress knew the president's preferences ahead of time, they would pass a bill that was close to what *they* wanted, subject to minimally satisfying the president. Through strategic use of the veto and veto threats, a president tries to shape Congress's beliefs about his policy preferences in order to gain greater concessions from Congress. Reputation is central to presidential effectiveness in this

---

15 For the complete list of presidential vetoes, see www.senate.gov/reference/Legislation/Vetoes/vetoCounts.htm.

16 Charles M. Cameron, *Veto Bargaining*. See also David W. Rohde and Dennis Simon, "Presidential Vetoes and Congressional Response: A Study of Institutional Conflict," *American Journal of Political Science* 29 (1985): 397–427.

17 David R. Mayhew, *Divided We Govern: Party Control, Lawmaking, and Investigations, 1946–1990* (New Haven, CT: Yale University Press, 1991).

18 Jack H. Nagel, *The Descriptive Analysis of Power* (New Haven, CT: Yale University Press, 1975).

19 See Rohde and Simon, "Presidential Vetoes and Congressional Response."

process.[20] By influencing congressional beliefs, the president is building a policy reputation that will affect future congressional behavior.

During the first year of his presidency, Barack Obama threatened to veto a defense spending bill that contained $369 billion in funding for the production of the F-22 fighter as well as a congressional resolution that would have blocked the release of about $350 billion in economic stimulus funds. After meeting with the president, members of Congress agreed to release the stimulus funds. On the issue of the F-22, however, Congress was reluctant to concede. Nevertheless, on July 21, 2009, with the backing of Defense Secretary Robert Gates and former Republican presidential nominee John McCain, Obama's position was sustained by a vote in the Senate, stripping funds for the F-22 from a defense appropriations measure. The House, which had previously voted to appropriate the funds, followed the Senate's lead on July 30, agreeing to eliminate the funds.

What about the relationship between mass public support for the president and the use of the veto? At least for the modern presidency, a crucial resource for the president in negotiating with Congress has been public approval as measured by opinion polls.[21] In some situations, members of Congress pass a bill not because they want to change policy but because they want to force the president to veto a popular bill that he disagrees with in order to hurt his approval ratings.[22] The key is that the public, uncertain of the president's policy preferences, uses information implied by vetoes to reassess what it knows about his preferences. As a result, vetoes may come at a price to the president. A president must, according to the rationality principle, weigh the advantages of using the veto or threatening to do so—to gain concessions from Congress—against the hit he may take in his popularity. The president may be reluctant to use the veto or the threat of a veto to gain concessions from Congress if it will hurt him in the polls. But in some cases, the president will take a hit in his approval ratings by vetoing a bill that is drastically inconsistent with his policies.[23]

Delegated Powers

Many of the powers exercised by the president and the executive branch are not set forth in the Constitution but are the products of congressional statutes and resolutions. Over the past three-quarters of a century, Congress has voluntarily

---

20 Neustadt, *Presidential Power*.

21 Theodore J. Lowi, *The Personal President: Power Invested, Promise Unfulfilled* (Ithaca, NY: Cornell University Press, 1985).

22 Timothy Groseclose and Nolan McCarty, "The Politics of Blame: Bargaining before an Audience," *American Journal of Political Science* 45 (2001): 100–19.

23 For a study of the ways presidents involve and mobilize mass public opinion on behalf of policies they pursue, see Brandice Canes-Wrone, *Who Leads Whom? Presidents, Policy, and the Public* (Chicago: University of Chicago Press, 2006). Also see Lawrence R. Jacobs and Robert Y. Shapiro, *Politicians Don't Pander: Political Manipulation and the Loss of Democratic Responsiveness* (Chicago: University of Chicago Press, 2000).

delegated a great deal of its own legislative authority to the executive branch. To some extent, this delegation of power has been an almost inescapable consequence of the expansion of governmental activity in the United States since the New Deal. Given the vast range of the federal government's responsibilities, Congress cannot execute and administer all the programs it creates and the laws it enacts. Inevitably Congress must turn to the hundreds of departments and agencies in the executive branch or, when necessary, create new agencies to implement its goals. Thus, for example, in 2002, when Congress sought to protect America from terrorist attacks, it established the Department of Homeland Security and gave it broad powers in the realms of law enforcement, public health, and immigration. Similarly, in 1970, when Congress enacted legislation designed to improve the nation's air and water quality, it assigned the task of implementing its goals to the new Environmental Protection Agency (EPA) created by Nixon's executive order. Congress gave the EPA substantial power to set and enforce air- and water-quality standards.

As they implement congressional legislation, federal agencies collectively develop thousands of rules and regulations and issue thousands of orders and findings every year. Agencies interpret Congress's intent, promulgate rules aimed at implementing that intent, and issue orders to individuals, firms, and organizations throughout the nation designed to impel them to conform to the law. When it establishes an agency, Congress sometimes grants it only limited discretionary authority, providing very specific guidelines and standards that must be followed by the administrators charged with the program's implementation. Take the Internal Revenue Service (IRS), for example. Most Americans view the IRS as a powerful agency whose dictates can have an immediate and sometimes unpleasant effect on their lives. Yet congressional tax legislation is specific and detailed and leaves little to the discretion of IRS administrators.[24] The agency certainly develops numerous rules and procedures to enhance tax collection. It is Congress, however, that establishes the structure of the tax liabilities, tax exemptions, and tax deductions that determine each taxpayer's burdens and responsibilities.

In many instances, however, congressional legislation is not very detailed. Often Congress defines a broad goal or objective and delegates enormous discretionary power to administrators to determine how that goal is to be achieved. For example, the 1970 act creating the Occupational Safety and Health Administration (OSHA) states that Congress's purpose is "to assure so far as is possible every working man and woman in the nation safe and healthful working conditions." The act, however, neither defines such conditions nor suggests how they might be achieved.[25] The result is that agency administrators have enormous discretionary power to draft rules and regulations that have the effect of law.

---

24 Kenneth F. Warren, *Administrative Law*, 3rd ed. (Upper Saddle River, NJ: Prentice-Hall, 1996), p. 250.

25 Theodore J. Lowi, *The End of Liberalism: The Second Republic of the United States,* 2nd ed. (New York: Norton, 1979), pp. 117–8.

Indeed, the courts treat these administrative rules like congressional statutes. For all intents and purposes, when Congress creates an agency such as OSHA or the EPA, giving it a broad mandate to achieve some desirable outcome, it transfers its own legislative power to the executive branch.

In the nineteenth and early twentieth centuries, Congress typically wrote laws that provided fairly clear principles and standards to guide executive implementation. For example, the 1922 Tariff Act empowered the president to increase or decrease duties on certain manufactured goods in order to reduce the difference in cost between products produced domestically and those manufactured abroad. The act authorized the president to make the final determination, but his discretionary authority was quite constrained. The statute listed the criteria the president was to consider, fixed the permissible range of tariff changes, and outlined the procedures to be used to calculate the cost differences between foreign and domestic goods. When an importer challenged a particular executive decision as an abuse of delegated power, the Supreme Court had no difficulty finding that the president was merely acting in accordance with Congress's directives.[26]

At least since the New Deal, however, Congress has tended to give executive agencies broad mandates and draft legislation that offers few clear standards or guidelines for implementation by the executive. For example, the 1933 National Industrial Recovery Act, a major piece of New Deal legislation, gave the president the authority to set rules to bring about fair competition in key sectors of the economy without ever defining what the term meant or how it was to be achieved. This pattern of broad delegation became typical in the ensuing decades. The 1972 Consumer Product Safety Act, for example, authorizes the Consumer Product Safety Commission to reduce unreasonable risk of injury from household products but offers no suggestions to guide the commission's determination of what constitutes reasonable and unreasonable risks or how these are to be reduced.[27]

This shift from the nineteenth-century pattern of issuing relatively well-defined congressional guidelines to administrators to the more contemporary pattern of broadly delegating congressional power to the executive branch is, to be sure, partially a consequence of the great scope and complexity of the tasks that America's contemporary government has undertaken. During much of the nineteenth century, the federal government had relatively few domestic responsibilities, and Congress could pay close attention to details. Today the operation of an enormous executive establishment and thousands of programs under varied and changing circumstances requires that administrators be allowed some considerable measure of discretion to carry out their jobs. Nevertheless, the result is to shift power from Congress to the executive branch.[28]

---

26 *J. W. Hampton & Company. v. United States*, 276 U.S. 394 (1928).

27 Lowi, *The End of Liberalism*, p. 117.

28 It must be noted that, to some extent, the shift in power is illusory. What authority Congress delegates, it can recover. The wise president or executive branch administrator is eminently aware of this and conditions her discretionary decisions with one eye cast over a shoulder at a watchful Congress.

Inherent Powers

A number of presidential powers are neither expressed explicitly in the Constitution nor delegated by congressional statute or resolution. They are "inherent" in the role of the office. The president exercises these powers through his leadership in proposing ideas for legislation to Congress and by broadly employing the means to execute constitutional and statutory authority.

War and Inherent Presidential Power. The Constitution, of course, gives Congress the power to declare war. Presidents, however, have gone a long way toward capturing this power for themselves. Congress has not declared war since December 1941, and yet since then American military forces have engaged in numerous campaigns throughout the world under orders of the president. When North Korean forces invaded South Korea in June 1950, Congress was prepared to declare war, but President Harry S. Truman decided not to ask for congressional action. Instead, Truman asserted the principle that the president, and not Congress, could decide when and where to deploy America's military might. Truman dispatched U.S. forces to Korea without a congressional declaration, and in the face of the emergency Congress felt it had to acquiesce. It passed a resolution approving the president's actions, and this sequence of events became the pattern for future congressional-executive relations in the military realm. The wars in Vietnam, Bosnia, Afghanistan, and Iraq, as well as a host of lesser conflicts, were all fought without declarations of war.

In 1973, Congress responded to presidential unilateralism by passing the **War Powers Resolution**—over President Richard Nixon's veto. This resolution reasserted the principle of Congress's power to declare war, required the president to inform Congress of any planned military campaign, and stipulated that forces must be withdrawn within 60 days in the absence of a specific congressional authorization for their continued deployment. Presidents have generally ignored the War Powers Resolution, however, claiming inherent executive power to defend the nation. Thus, for example, in 1989 President George H. W. Bush ordered an invasion of Panama without consulting Congress. President George W. Bush responded to the 2001 attacks by Islamic terrorists by organizing a major military campaign to overthrow the Taliban regime in Afghanistan, which had sheltered the terrorists. In 2003, Bush ordered a major U.S. campaign against Iraq, which he accused of posing a threat to the United States. In both of these most recent instances, Congress passed resolutions approving the president's actions, but President Bush was careful to assert that he did not need congressional authorization.[29] The War Powers Resolution was barely mentioned on Capitol Hill and was ignored by the White House.

However, the fact that presidents since 1974 have ignored the War Powers Resolution, with virtually no objection from Congress, does not mean that

---

War Powers Resolution

A resolution of Congress declaring that the president can send troops into action abroad only by authorization of Congress or if U.S. troops are already under attack or seriously threatened

---

29 These were, in fact, joint resolutions authorizing the use of military force—PL107-40 for Afghanistan and PL 107-243 for Iraq—thus protecting some role for Congress in the deployment of military forces.

tensions stemming from the separation of powers between the president and Congress have ceased. The powers of the purse and of investigation give Congress levers with which to constrain even the most freewheeling executive. For all these reasons, the president restrains himself, often self-censoring to minimize adverse political consequences.[30] Thus in 2013, with public opinion running against him, President Obama sought authorization from Congress for an airstrike on Syria as punishment for its use of chemical weapons, in part of implicate Congress in the action and thereby share accountability.

Legislative Initiative. Although not explicitly stated, the Constitution provides the president with the power of **legislative initiative**. To initiate means to originate, and in government that can mean power. The framers of the Constitution clearly saw legislative initiative as one of the keys to executive power. Initiative obviously implies the ability to formulate proposals for important policies, and the president, as an individual with a great deal of staff assistance, is able to initiate decisive action more frequently than Congress, with its large assemblies that have to deliberate and debate before taking action. With some important exceptions, Congress banks on the president to set the agenda of public policy. And quite clearly there is power in initiative: there is power in being able to set the terms of discourse in the making of public policy.

For example, during the weeks immediately following September 11, 2001, George W. Bush took many presidential initiatives to Congress, and each was given almost unanimous support: from commitments to pursue Al Qaeda and remove the Taliban in Afghanistan all the way to almost unlimited approval to regulate American civil liberties. Bush faced more difficulty in his second term, however. Growing problems (and casualties) in Iraq, administrative scandals, and a financial crisis plagued the president. As presidential popularity ebbed in the polls, so, too, did Bush's agenda power.

In 2009, soon after taking office, President Obama presented Congress with a record-breaking $3 trillion budget proposal that included a host of new programs in such areas as health and human services, transportation, housing, and education. Obama told Congress that he would soon be requesting several hundred billion more for the financial bailout designed to rescue America's banks and revive the nation's credit markets. Not only was Congress responsive to the president's initiatives but lawmakers also expected the president to take the lead in responding to America's financial emergency and other problems.

Together with the Democratic 111th Congress, President Obama achieved a number of legislative results in his first two years: the Lilly Ledbetter Fair Pay Act, the Children's Health Insurance Program Reauthorization Act of 2009, the American Recovery and Reinvestment Act of 2009, financial reform legislation, and, of course, health care reform legislation. Table 7.2 shows how Congress voted on each of these bills. In working to get these bills passed, Obama's team was strategic

 legislative initiative

The president's inherent power to bring a legislative agenda before Congress

---

30 On this point, see William G. Howell and Jon C. Pevehouse, *While Dangers Gather: Congressional Checks on Presidential Power* (Princeton, NJ: Princeton University Press, 2007).

Table 7.2A

FINAL PASSAGE VOTE TALLIES, 2009–12: HOUSE OF REPRESENTATIVES

LEGISLATION	TOTAL		DEMOCRATS		REPUBLICANS	
	YEAS	NAYS	YEAS	NAYS	YEAS	NAYS
The Lilly Ledbetter Fair Pay Act	250	177	247	5	3	172
The Children's Health Insurance Program Reauthorization Act of 2009	290	135	250	2	40	133
The American Recovery and Reinvestment Act of 2009	246	183	246	7	0	163
The Fraud Enforcement and Recovery Act of 2009	338	52	224	0	114	52
The Helping Families Save Their Homes Act of 2009	367	54	244	3	123	51
The Credit Card Accountability Responsibility and Disclosure Act of 2009	279	147	105	145	174	2
The Dodd-Frank Wall Street Reform and Consumer Protection Act	237	192	234	19	3	173
The Patient Protection and Affordable Care Act	219	212	219	34	0	178
The Middle Class Tax Relief and Job Creation Act of 2012	293	132	147	41	146	91

SOURCE: Library of Congress, http://thomas.loc.gov/home/rollcallvotes.html (accessed 6/25/13).

in how they pursued their goals and mindful of the institutional rules and practices that would affect the outcomes. Despite Obama's efforts to assemble bipartisan support, Republicans mainly opposed the legislation. After Republicans won control of the House in 2010, the president won fewer major legislative successes.[31]

31 During a "lame duck" session after the 2010 elections but before the new 112th Congress was seated, President Obama enjoyed some additional legislative successes, including Senate approval of a new nuclear treaty with Russia, extension of unemployment benefits, the prevention of tax hikes for middle- and upper-class families, and a free-trade agreement with South Korea.

Table 7.2B

FINAL PASSAGE VOTE TALLIES, 2009–12: SENATE

LEGISLATION	TOTAL		DEMOCRATS		REPUBLICANS	
	YEAS	NAYS	YEAS	NAYS	YEAS	NAYS
The Lilly Ledbetter Fair Pay Act	61	36	56	0	5	36
The Children's Health Insurance Program Reauthorization Act of 2009	66	32	57	0	9	32
The American Recovery and Reinvestment Act of 2009	60	38	57	0	3	38
The Fraud Enforcement and Recovery Act of 2009	92	5	56	0	36	4
The Helping Families Save Their Homes Act of 2009	91	5	56	0	35	5
The Credit Card Accountability Responsibility and Disclosure Act of 2009	90	5	55	1	35	4
The Dodd-Frank Wall Street Reform and Consumer Protection Act	60	39	57	1	3	38
The Patient Protection and Affordable Care Act	60	39	60	0	0	39
The Middle Class Tax Relief and Job Creation Act of 2012	60	36	46	5	14	31

SOURCE: Library of Congress, http://thomas.loc.gov/home/rollcallvotes.html (accessed 6/25/13).

There were also legislative disappointments. Obama took on enormous political risks when he staked his presidency on legislative accomplishments. The first risk was that he would fail to accomplish what he had set out to do. For example, President Jimmy Carter's inability to realize his big plans contributed greatly to his defeat in the 1980 election and to the impression that his presidency was "a failure."

The second risk is that the messy and often ugly process of legislation will frustrate a president's efforts to meet these goals. There is a reason that the German statesman Otto von Bismarck said, "Laws are like sausages. It's better not to see them being made." Compromise is at the heart of politics in a democracy. When the president gives special favors to those whose votes might help his legislation pass or when the majority leader tries to pass amendments that favor a particular senator or representative, the seamy side of politics is rearing its head. During the attempt to pass health care reform, critics of bartering political favors for crucial votes had a field day. For example, Nebraska was given a Medicare exemption that no other state received solely to secure the vote of the pivotal Nebraska senator, something the media publicized and Obama opponents took great pains to point out. For a president who campaigned on "changing politics as we know it," it looked an awful lot like old-school politics. The Republicans were free to point out the inconsistencies between Democratic pledges for open, honest government and the closed-door negotiations, proposals, and counterproposals that were taking place. Even worse, elements of the coalitions that supported President Obama in the campaign had to watch as their objectives were sacrificed or ignored in the quest to get *something* done. Compromise is all well and good unless your pet policy is the one that's about to be compromised away, and public legislative bargaining alienated some supporters. In short, the messiness of the political process negatively affected the Democrats and left the Republicans largely unscathed.

Even when the president takes great pains to understand his political situation, he sometimes fails to meet his objectives. Most notably, Obama has not passed significant environmental legislation or comprehensive immigration reform. Both goals were announced at the outset of his presidency. Each was sacrificed as higher priorities dominated (and exhausted) the legislative agenda.[32]

The 112th Congress, created by the 2010 elections, proved to be an altogether different experience for Obama. His party lost majority control of the House and had its large Senate majority trimmed to a bare minimum. The Republicans thus shared legislative initiative with the president, pursuing legislative objectives of their own and blocking numerous presidential initiatives. Notably, the president and Congress failed to solve the problem of the debt ceiling or to negotiate a spending-reduction package. Nevertheless, Obama prevailed in his 2012 re-election bid, at least in part because he did, in fact, deliver on important legislation early in his term and could blame Republican obstructionism for his lack of success later on.

The president's initiative does not end with policy making involving Congress and the making of laws in the ordinary sense of the term. The president has still another legislative role (in all but name) within the executive branch. This is designated as the power to issue **executive orders**. The executive order is foremost a normal tool of management, a power virtually any CEO possesses to make company policy—rules-setting procedures, etiquette, chains of command, functional responsibilities, and so on. But evolving from this normal

executive orders

A rule or regulation issued by the president that has the effect and formal status of legislation

---

32 Immigration reform has re-emerged as a high priority for the Obama administration in the 113th Congress. In June 2013, a significant bill that would strengthen border security and provide a path to citizenship for many illegal immigrants passed the Senate but it made little progress in the House.

management practice is a recognized presidential power to promulgate rules that have the effect and formal status of legislation. Most of the executive orders of the president provide for the reorganization of structures and procedures or otherwise direct the affairs of the executive branch—either to be applied across the board to all agencies or to be applied in some important respect to a single agency or department. The power to issue executive orders illustrates that although reputation and persuasion are typically required in presidential policy making, the practice of issuing executive orders, within limits, allows a president to govern without the necessity to persuade.[33] We take a closer look at how modern presidents have used executive orders later in the chapter.

THE RISE OF PRESIDENTIAL GOVERNMENT

Most of the real influence of the modern presidency derives from the powers granted by the Constitution and the laws made by Congress. Presidential power is institutional. Thus any person properly elected and sworn in as president will possess almost all the power held by the strongest presidents in American history. Even when they are lame ducks, presidents still possess all the power of the office. For example, in 2008, lame-duck president Bush secured the enactment of a major piece of legislation aimed at ameliorating the nation's economic crisis.

What variables account for a president's success in exercising these powers? Why are some presidents considered great successes, others colossal failures, and most somewhere in between? These questions relate broadly to the very concept of presidential power. Is it a reflection of the attributes of the person, or is it more a characteristic of the political situations that a president encounters? The personal view of presidential power dominated political scientists' thinking for several decades,[34] but recently scholars have argued that presidential power should be analyzed in terms of the strategic interactions that a president has with other political actors.[35] With the occasional exception, however, it took more than a century, perhaps as much as a century and a half, before presidents came to be seen as consequential players in these strategic encounters. A bit of historical review will be helpful in understanding how the presidency has risen to its current level of influence.

33 This point is developed in both Kenneth R. Mayer, *With the Stroke of a Pen: Executive Orders and Presidential Power* (Princeton, NJ: Princeton University Press, 2001), and William G. Howell, *Power without Persuasion: The Politics of Direct Presidential Action* (Princeton, NJ: Princeton University Press, 2003).

34 Neustadt, *Presidential Power and the Modern Presidents*.

35 Charles M. Cameron, "Bargaining and Presidential Power," in *Presidential Power: Forging the Presidency for the Twenty-First Century*, Robert Y. Shapiro, Martha Joynt Kumar, and Lawrence R. Jacobs, eds. (New York: Columbia University Press, 2000). See also Samuel Kernell, *Going Public: New Strategies of Presidential Leadership*, 4th ed. (Washington, DC: CQ Press, 2006).

The Legislative Epoch, 1800–1933

In 1885, a then-obscure political science professor named Woodrow Wilson titled his general textbook *Congressional Government* because American government was just that, congressional government. There is ample evidence that Wilson's description of the national government was consistent not only with nineteenth-century reality but also with the intentions of the framers. Within the system of three separate and competing powers, the clear intent of the Constitution was legislative supremacy. In the early nineteenth century, some observers saw the president as little more than America's chief clerk. Indeed, most historians agree that after Thomas Jefferson and until the beginning of the twentieth century, presidents Andrew Jackson and Abraham Lincoln were the only exceptions to a succession of weak presidents. Both Jackson and Lincoln are considered great presidents because they used their power in momentous ways. But it is important in the history of the presidency that neither of them left his powers as an institutional legacy to his successors. That is to say, once Jackson and Lincoln left office, the presidency reverted to the subordinate role that it played during the nineteenth century.

One of the reasons so few great men became president in the nineteenth century is that there was only occasional room for greatness.[36] As Chapter 3 indicated, the national government of that period was not a particularly powerful entity. The presidency of the nineteenth century was also weak because during this period the presidency was not closely linked to major national political and social forces. Indeed, there were few important *national* political or social forces to which presidents could have linked themselves even if they had wanted to. Federalism had taken very good care of this by fragmenting political interests and diverting the energies of interest groups toward the state and local levels of government, where most key decisions were being made.

As discussed earlier in the chapter, the presidency was strengthened in the 1830s when the national convention system of nominating presidential candidates was introduced. However, this additional independence did not change the presidency into the office we see today because the parties disappeared, returning to their states and Congress once the national election was over. In addition, as the national government grew, Congress kept a tight rein on the president's power. For example, when Congress began to make its first efforts to exert power over the economy (beginning in 1887 with the adoption of the Interstate Commerce Act and in 1890 with the adoption of the Sherman Antitrust Act), it sought to keep this power away from the president and the executive branch by placing the new regulatory policies in "independent regulatory commissions" responsible to Congress rather than to the president (see also Chapter 8).

---

36 For related appraisals, see Jeffrey Tulis, *The Rhetorical Presidency* (Princeton, NJ: Princeton University Press, 1987); Stephen Skowronek, *The Politics Presidents Make: Leadership from John Adams to Bill Clinton* (Cambridge, MA: Harvard University Press, 1997); and Robert J. Spitzer, *President and Congress: Executive Hegemony at the Crossroads of American Government* (Philadelphia: Temple University Press, 1993).

The New Deal and the Presidency

As discussed earlier, the key moment in the history of American national government came during Franklin Delano Roosevelt's administration. The Hundred Days at the outset of the Roosevelt administration in 1933 had no parallel in U.S. history. But it was only the beginning. The policies proposed by President Roosevelt and adopted by Congress during the first 100 days of his administration so changed the size and character of the national government that they constitute a moment in American history equivalent to the Founding or the Civil War. The president's constitutional obligation to see "that the laws be faithfully executed" became, during Roosevelt's presidency, virtually a responsibility to shape the laws before executing them.

Many of the New Deal programs were extensions of the traditional national government approach, which was described in Chapter 3. But the New Deal went well beyond the traditional approach, adopting types of policies never before tried on a large scale by the national government; it began intervening in economic life in ways that had hitherto been reserved to the states. For example, during the early days of the New Deal in the throes of the Great Depression, the Roosevelt administration created the Works Progress Administration, seeking to put the able-bodied back to work; the federal government became the nation's largest employer at this time. The Social Security Act, to give another example, sought to improve the economic condition of the most impoverished segment of the population—the elderly. In other words, the national government discovered that it, too, had "police power" and could directly regulate individuals as well as provide roads and other services.

The new programs were such dramatic departures from the traditional policies of the national government that their constitutionality was in doubt. The Supreme Court in fact declared several of them unconstitutional, mainly on the grounds that in regulating the conduct of individuals or their employers, the national government was reaching beyond "*inter*state" and involving itself in "*intra*state"—essentially local—matters. Most of the New Deal remained in constitutional limbo until 1937, five years after Roosevelt was first elected and one year after his landslide 1936 re-election.

The turning point came with *National Labor Relations Board v. Jones and Laughlin Steel Corporation*, a Supreme Court case challenging the federal government's authority over the regulation of labor relations. The Court affirmed a federal role in the regulation of the national economy.[37] After the end of the New Deal, the Court has never again seriously questioned the legitimacy of interventions of the national government in the economy or society.[38]

---

37 *National Labor Relations Board v. Jones and Laughlin Steel Corporation,* 301 U.S. 1 (1937).

38 Some will argue that there are exceptions to this statement. One was *National League of Cities v. Usery,* 426 U.S. 833 (1976), which declared unconstitutional Congress's effort to apply national minimum wage standards to state and local government employees. But the Court reversed itself on this nine years later, in *Garcia v. San Antonio Metropolitan Transit Authority,* 469 U.S. 528 (1985). Cases such as these are few and far between, and they touch on only part of a law, not the constitutionality of an entire program.

The most important constitutional effect of Congress's actions and the Supreme Court's approval of those actions during the New Deal was the enhancement of presidential power. Most major acts of Congress in this period involved significant exercises of control over the economy. But few programs specified the actual controls to be used. Instead, Congress authorized the president or in some cases, a new agency, to determine what the controls would be. Some of the new agencies were independent commissions responsible to Congress. But most of the new agencies and new programs of the New Deal were placed in the executive branch directly under presidential authority. The institutional power of the presidency had been greatly increased.

Technically this form of congressional act, as we noted earlier, is the delegation of power. In theory, the delegation of power works as follows: (1) Congress recognizes a problem; (2) Congress acknowledges that it has neither the time nor the expertise to deal with the problem; and (3) Congress therefore sets the basic policies and then delegates to an agency the power to fill in the details. But in practice, Congress was delegating to the executive branch not merely the power to fill in the details but also real policy-making powers—that is, real legislative powers.

No modern government can avoid the delegation of significant legislative powers to the executive branch. But the fact remains that this delegation produced a fundamental shift in the American constitutional framework. During the 1930s, the growth of the national government through acts delegating legislative power tilted the national structure away from a Congress-centered government toward a president-centered government.[39] Make no mistake, Congress continues to be the constitutional source of policy. Legislative supremacy remains a constitutional fact of life, even in the twenty-first century, because delegations of power are contingent. And not all delegations are the same. A Democratic Congress, for example, is unwilling to empower a Republican president, and vice versa; unified governments are more likely than divided governments to engage in broad delegation.[40] In short, Congress can rescind these delegations of power, restrict them with subsequent amendments, and oversee the exercise of delegated power through congressional hearings, oversight agencies, budget controls, and other administrative tools. However, it is fair to say that presidential government has become an administrative fact of life as government by delegation has expanded greatly over the past century. The world of Woodrow

---

39 The Supreme Court did in fact *dis*approve broad delegations of legislative power by declaring the National Industrial Recovery Act of 1933 unconstitutional on the grounds that Congress did not accompany the broad delegations with sufficient standards or guidelines for presidential discretion (*Panama Refining Co. v. Ryan*, 293 U.S. 388 [1935], and *Schechter Poultry Corporation v. United States*, 295 U.S. 495 [1935]). The Supreme Court has never reversed those two decisions, but neither has it really followed them. Thus broad delegations of legislative power from Congress to the executive branch can be presumed to be constitutional. See Sotirios A. Barber, *The Constitution and the Delegation of Congressional Power* (Chicago: University of Chicago Press, 1975).

40 David Epstein and Sharyn O'Halloran, *Delegating Powers: A Transaction Cost Politics Approach to Policy Making under Separate Powers* (New York: Cambridge University Press, 1999).

Wilson's *Congressional Government* is forever changed. But Congress has many clubs behind its door with which to influence the manner in which the executive branch exercises its newly won power.

PRESIDENTIAL GOVERNMENT

The locus of policy decision making shifted to the executive branch because, as we just noted, Congress made delegations of authority to the president. Congress delegated authority to the executive for instrumental reasons, much as a principal delegates to an agent. An expanded agenda of political demands, necessitated first by economic crisis—the Great Depression—but also by an accumulation of the effects of nearly a century's worth of industrialization, urbanization, and greater integration into the world economy, and finally by World War II, confronted the national government, forcing Congress's hand. The legislature itself was limited in its ability to expand its own capacity to undertake these growing responsibilities, so delegation proved a natural administrative strategy. These acts of delegation gave a far greater role to the president, empowering this "agent" to initiate in his own right.

In the case of Franklin Delano Roosevelt, his New Deal launched an era of presidential government. Congress certainly retained many tools with which to threaten, cajole, encourage, and persuade its executive agent to do its bidding. But presidents in general, and Roosevelt in particular, are not *only* agents of Congress and not *only* dependent on Congress for resources and authority. They are also agents of national constituencies for whom they are eager to demonstrate their capacity for leadership in executing constituency policy agendas.[41]

Likewise, congressional delegations of power are not the only resources available to a president. Presidents have at their disposal a variety of other formal and informal resources that have important implications for their ability to govern. Indeed, without these other resources, presidents would lack the ability—the tools of management and public mobilization—to make much use of the power and responsibility given to them by Congress. Let us first consider the president's formal or official resources and then turn to the more informal resources that affect a president's capacity to govern, in particular the president's base of popular support.

The Formal Resources of Presidential Power

The Cabinet. In the American system of government, the **Cabinet** is the traditional but informal designation for the heads of all the major departments of the federal government (Figure 7.2). The Cabinet has only a limited

← **Cabinet**

The secretaries, or chief administrators, of the major departments of the federal government. Cabinet secretaries are appointed by the president with the consent of the Senate

---

41 See Terry M. Moe, "Presidents, Institutions, and Theory," in *Researching the Presidency: Vital Questions, New Approaches,* George C. Edwards III, John H. Kessel, and Bert A. Rockman, eds. (Pittsburgh, PA: University of Pittsburgh Press, 1993), p. 367.

Figure 7.2
THE INSTITUTIONAL PRESIDENCY, 2013

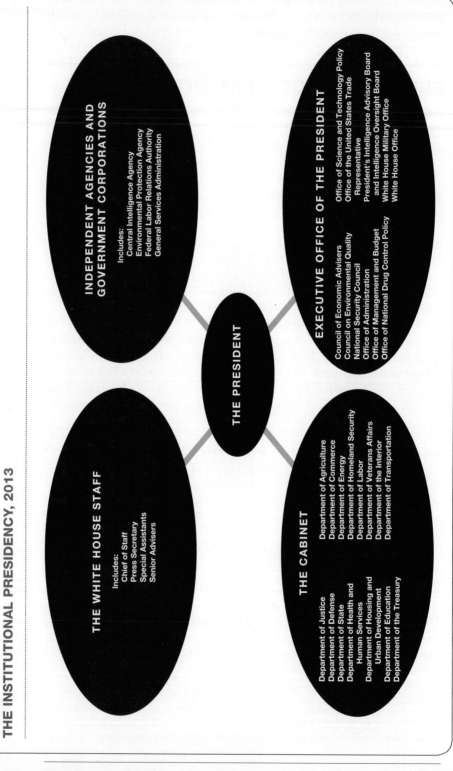

THE INSTITUTIONAL PRESIDENCY, 2013

THE PRESIDENT

INDEPENDENT AGENCIES AND GOVERNMENT CORPORATIONS

Includes:
Central Intelligence Agency
Environmental Protection Agency
Federal Labor Relations Authority
General Services Administration

EXECUTIVE OFFICE OF THE PRESIDENT

Council of Economic Advisers
Council on Environmental Quality
National Security Council
Office of Administration
Office of Management and Budget
Office of National Drug Control Policy

Office of Science and Technology Policy
Office of the United States Trade
  Representative
President's Intelligence Advisory Board
  and Intelligence Oversight Board
White House Military Office
White House Office

THE WHITE HOUSE STAFF

Includes:
Chief of Staff
Press Secretary
Special Assistants
Senior Advisers

THE CABINET

Department of Justice
Department of Defense
Department of State
Department of Health and
  Human Services
Department of Housing and
  Urban Development
Department of Education
Department of the Treasury

Department of Agriculture
Department of Commerce
Department of Energy
Department of Homeland Security
Department of Labor
Department of Veterans Affairs
Department of the Interior
Department of Transportation

constitutional status.[42] In contrast to the United Kingdom and many other parliamentary countries, where the cabinet is the government, the American Cabinet is not a collective body. It meets but makes no decisions as a group. Each appointment must be approved by the Senate, but cabinet members are not responsible to the Senate or to Congress at large. Cabinet appointments help build party and popular support, but the Cabinet is not a party organ. The Cabinet is made up of directors but is not a true board of directors. Because cabinet appointees generally have not shared political careers with the president or with one another and because they may meet each other for the first time after their selection, the formation of an effective governing group out of this motley collection of appointments is unlikely. Although the Cabinet is not always powerful, it does serve an important role in managing policy for the president and his political associations. For instance, members of the Cabinet will travel on the president's behalf, make policy speeches, and negotiate with other political leaders, both at home and abroad.

Some presidents have relied more heavily on an "inner cabinet," the **National Security Council (NSC)**. The NSC, established by law in 1947, is composed of the president, the vice president, the secretary of state, the secretary of defense, and other officials invited by the president. It has its own staff of foreign policy specialists run by the assistant to the president for national security affairs. For these highest appointments, presidents usually turn to people from outside Washington, often longtime associates.

Presidents have obviously been uneven in their reliance on the NSC and other subcabinet bodies because executive management is inherently a personal matter. Despite all the personal variations, however, one generalization can be made: presidents have increasingly preferred the White House staff to the Cabinet as their means of managing the gigantic executive branch.

The White House Staff.

The **White House staff** is composed mainly of analysts and advisers.[43] Although many of the top White House staff members are given the title "special assistant" for a particular task or sector, the types of judgments they are expected to make and the kinds of advice they are supposed to give are a good deal broader and more generally political than those coming from the Executive Office of the President or the cabinet departments. The members of the White House staff also tend to be more closely associated with the president than other presidentially appointed officials. President Obama, in his early months in office, relied heavily on his chief of staff, Rahm Emanuel; his former chief campaign strategist and now senior adviser, David Axelrod; the deputy chief of staff, Jim Messina; and the press secretary, Robert Gibbs. Collectively, this tight-knit group of Obama loyalists was known in Washington as "the boys."

National Security Council (NSC)

A presidential foreign policy advisory council composed of the president, the vice president, the secretaries of state, defense, and the treasury, the attorney general, and other officials invited by the president

White House staff

The analysts and advisers to the president, often given the title "special assistant"

---

42 The Twenty-Fifth Amendment gives the Cabinet a formal role in determining presidential disability.

43 A substantial portion of this section is taken from Lowi, *The Personal President,* pp. 141–50.

kitchen cabinet ➡

An informal group of
advisers to whom the
president turns for
counsel and guidance.
Members of the official
cabinet may or may not
also be members of the
kitchen cabinet

From an informal group of fewer than a dozen people (popularly called the **kitchen cabinet**) and no more than four dozen at the height of Roosevelt's prewar administration, the White House staff has grown substantially with each successive president.[44] Richard Nixon employed 550 people in 1972. President Carter, who found so many of the requirements of presidential power distasteful and publicly vowed to keep his staff small and decentralized, built an even larger and more centralized staff. President Clinton reduced the White House staff by 20 percent, but a large White House staff is still essential and the staff remained large under presidents George W. Bush and Barack Obama.

The White House staff is a crucial information source and management tool for the president. But it may also insulate the president from other sources of information. Managing this trade-off between in-house expertise and access to independent outside opinion is a major challenge for the president. Sometimes it is botched, as when President George W. Bush depended too heavily on his staff for information about weapons of mass destruction (WMD) in Iraq, leading him to erroneous conclusions.[45]

**Executive Office
of the President
(EOP)** ➡

The permanent agencies
that perform defined
management tasks for
the president. Created
in 1939, the EOP
includes the Office
of Management and
Budget, the Council
of Economic Advisers,
the National Security
Council, and other
agencies

The Executive Office of the President. The development of the White House staff can be appreciated only in its relation to the still-larger **Executive Office of the President (EOP)**. Created in 1939, the EOP is a major part of what is often called the institutional presidency—the permanent agencies that perform defined management tasks for the president. The most important and the largest EOP agency is the Office of Management and Budget (OMB). Its roles in preparing the national budget, designing the president's program, reporting on agency activities, and overseeing regulatory proposals make OMB personnel part of virtually every conceivable presidential responsibility. The status and power of the OMB have grown in importance with each successive president. The process of budgeting at one time was a bottom-up procedure, with expenditure and program requests passing from the lowest bureaus through the departments to "clearance" in OMB and hence to Congress, where each agency could be called in to reveal what its original request had been before it was revised by the OMB. Now the budgeting process is top-down: OMB sets the terms of discourse for agencies as well as for Congress. The director of OMB is now one of the most powerful officials in Washington.

The staff of the Council of Economic Advisers (CEA) constantly analyzes the economy and economic trends and attempts to give the president the ability to anticipate events rather than waiting and reacting to events. The Council on

---

44 All the figures since 1967, and probably since 1957, are understated because additional White House staff members have been on "detailed" service, borrowed from the military and various cabinet departments (some secretly assigned) and are not counted here because they were not on the White House payroll.

45 See George Krause, "The Secular Decline in Presidential Domestic Policymaking: An Organizational Perspective," *Presidential Studies Quarterly* 34 (2004): 779–92. On the general issue, see James P. Pfiffner, ed., *The Managerial Presidency,* 2nd ed. (College Station: Texas A&M University Press, 1999).

Environmental Quality was designed to do for environmental issues what the CEA does for economic issues. The members of the National Security Council meet regularly with the president to give advice on the large national security picture. The staff of the NSC assimilates and analyzes data from all intelligence-gathering agencies (the CIA, and so on). Other EOP agencies perform more specialized tasks.

Somewhere between 1,500 and 2,000 highly specialized staffers work for EOP agencies.[46] The importance of each agency in the EOP varies according to the personal orientation of the president. For example, the NSC staff was of immense importance under President Nixon, especially because it served essentially as the personal staff of the presidential assistant Henry Kissinger before his elevation to the office of secretary of state. But it was of less importance to President George H. W. Bush, who looked outside the EOP altogether for military policy matters, turning much more to the Joint Chiefs of Staff and its chair at the time, General Colin Powell.

The Vice Presidency. The vice presidency is a constitutional anomaly, even though the office was created by the Constitution along with the presidency. The vice president exists for two purposes only: to succeed the president in case of death, resignation, or incapacitation and to preside over the Senate, casting a tie-breaking vote when necessary.[47]

The main value of the vice presidency as a political resource for the president is electoral. Traditionally a presidential candidate's most important rule for the choice of a running mate is that she brings the support of at least one state (preferably a large one) not otherwise likely to support the ticket. Another rule holds that the vice-presidential nominee should provide some regional balance and, wherever possible, some balance among various ideological or ethnic subsections of the party. It is very doubtful that John Kennedy would have won in 1960 without his vice-presidential candidate, Lyndon Johnson, and the contribution Johnson made to winning in Texas. George W. Bush's choice of Dick Cheney in 2000 was almost completely devoid of direct electoral value, since Cheney comes from one of our least populous states (Wyoming, which casts only three electoral votes). But given Cheney's stalwart right-wing record both in Congress and as President George H. W. Bush's secretary of defense, coupled with his even more prominently right-wing wife, Lynne Cheney, his inclusion on the Republican ticket was clearly an effort to consolidate the support of the restive right wing of the Republican Party. In 2008, Barack Obama chose Senator Joseph Biden of Delaware as his vice-presidential running mate. Obama had often been criticized for lacking background in the realm of foreign policy.

---

46 The actual number is difficult to estimate because, as with the White House staff, some EOP personnel, especially those in national security work, are detailed to the office from outside agencies.

47 Article I, Section 3, provides that "the Vice President . . . shall be President of the Senate, but shall have no Vote, unless they be equally divided." This is the only vote the vice president is allowed.

Biden, chair of the Senate Foreign Relations Committee, brought considerable foreign policy experience to the ticket. In both 2008 and 2012 the Republican presidential nominees, John McCain and Mitt Romney, respectively, sought to appease conservatives in their respective choices of Sarah Palin and Paul Ryan.

As the institutional presidency has grown in size and complexity, most presidents of the past 25 years have sought to use their vice presidents as management resources after the election. George H. W. Bush, as President Reagan's vice president, was kept within the loop of decision making because Reagan delegated so much power. President Bush did not take such pains to keep Vice President Dan Quayle in the loop, but President Clinton relied greatly on his vice president, Al Gore, and Gore emerged as one of the most trusted and effective figures in the Clinton White House. The presidency of George W. Bush resulted in unprecedented power and responsibility for his vice president, Dick Cheney. Known as a hands-on vice president, Cheney played an active role in cabinet meetings and policy formation, as well as in organizing the war on terror and launching the Iraq War. Cheney was widely viewed as one of the most—if not the most—influential vice presidents in American history. In the Obama administration, Vice President Joe Biden has wielded considerable influence. Drawing on his vast experience in the Senate, he has played an important role as liaison to the Congress. He has also been, as noted, an important sounding board on matters involving foreign affairs, and has taken on some high-profile assignments, for example, chairing the special commission on gun control.

The President and Policy. The president's powers and institutional resources, taken together, give the chief executive a substantial voice in the nation's policy-making processes. Strictly speaking, presidents cannot introduce legislation. Only members of Congress can formally propose new programs and policies. However, presidents often do send proposals to Congress. Congress, in turn, takes up these proposals by referring them to the relevant committee of jurisdiction. Sometimes these proposals are said to be dead on arrival, an indication that presidential preferences are at loggerheads with those in the House or Senate. This is especially common during periods of divided government. In such circumstances, presidents and legislators engage in bargaining, although in the end the status quo may prevail—a situation sometimes termed *gridlock* by pundits and the media. Presidents are typically in a weak position in these circumstances, especially if they have grand plans to change the status quo.[48] During periods of unified government, the president has fellow partisans in charge of each chamber; in these cases, the president may indeed seize the initiative, seeking to coordinate policy initiatives from the White House. The political scientist Charles Cameron suggests that the distinction between unified and divided government is quite consequential for presidential "style": it makes the chief executive either bargainer in chief or coordinator in chief.[49]

---

48 D. Roderick Kiewiet and Mathew D. McCubbins, *The Logic of Delegation: Congressional Parties and the Appropriations Process* (Chicago: University of Chicago Press, 1991).

49 Cameron, "Bargaining and Presidential Power."

Congress has come to expect the president to propose the government's budget, and the nation has come to expect presidential initiatives to deal with major problems. Some of these initiatives have come in the form of huge packages of programs—Franklin Delano Roosevelt's New Deal and Lyndon Johnson's Great Society. Sometimes presidents craft a single program they hope will have a significant effect on both the nation and their political fortunes. For example, George W. Bush made the war on terrorism the centerpiece of his administration. To fight this war, Bush brought about the creation of a new cabinet department, the Department of Homeland Security, and the enactment of such pieces of legislation as the USA PATRIOT Act to give the executive branch more power to deal with the terrorist threat. For President Obama there has been a series of successful legislative initiatives (some listed earlier in Table 7.2), the most important of which is health care.

At one time, historians and journalists liked to debate the question of strong versus weak presidents. Today every president is strong. This strength is not so much a function of personal charisma or political savvy as it is a reflection of the increasing power of the institution of the presidency.

The Contemporary Bases of Presidential Power

In the nineteenth century, when Congress was America's dominant institution of government, its members sometimes treated the president with disdain. Today, however, no one would assert that the presidency is an unimportant institution. Presidents seek to dominate the policy-making process and claim the inherent power to lead the nation in time of war. The expansion of presidential power over the course of the past century has come about not by accident but as the result of an ongoing effort by successive presidents to enlarge the powers of the office. Some of these efforts have succeeded, and others have failed. As the framers of the Constitution predicted, presidential ambition has been a powerful and unrelenting force in American politics.

Generally presidents can expand their power by three means: party, popular mobilization, and administration. In the first instance, presidents may construct or strengthen national partisan institutions with which to exert influence in the legislative process and through which to implement their programs. Alternatively or in addition to the first tactic, presidents may use popular appeals to create a mass base of support that will allow them to subordinate their political foes. This tactic has sometimes been called the strategy of going public, or the "rhetorical" presidency.[50] In the third instance, presidents may seek to bolster their control of established executive agencies or create new administrative institutions and procedures that will reduce their dependence on Congress and give them a more independent governing and policy-making capability. Presidents' use of executive orders to achieve their policy goals in lieu of seeking to persuade Congress to enact legislation is, perhaps, the most obvious example.

---

50 Kernell, *Going Public*; see also Tulis, *The Rhetorical Presidency*.

Party as a Source of Power. All presidents have relied on the members and leaders of their own party to implement their legislative agendas. President George W. Bush, for example, worked closely with congressional GOP leaders on such matters as energy policy and Medicare reform. But the president does not control his own party; party members have considerable autonomy. On immigration policy, for example, the Bush proposals in 2006 were supported in most respects by the Republican-controlled Senate. The Republican-controlled House, however, passed much more punitive policies. The two chambers, despite being controlled by the president's party, were unable to agree on a compromise and ended up settling on elements of the House bill that the president least desired. Nevertheless, he signed the measure in October 2006, noting it was only the first step in comprehensive immigration reform. President Obama made immigration reform one of his priorities, but failed to induce the 111th Congress, controlled by his party, or the 112th, divided between the parties, to take up the issue. Finally, the 113th Congress considered a broad bill that would address a path to citizenship for some illegal immigrants, increase the number of employment-based visas, and enhance border security. The bill passed with bipartisan support in the Democratic-controlled Senate, while the Republican-controlled House was less supportive.

President Obama initially declared that he would seek bipartisan support for all of his programs. Congressional Republicans, however, calculated that they had little to gain from supporting Obama and much to lose if his administration were successful. Hence, the GOP opposed the president's domestic and foreign policy initiatives. With overwhelming Democratic majorities in both houses of Congress in 2009–11, President Obama found that he had no difficulty turning to the Democratic leadership for support. Indeed, Republican opposition helped Democratic leaders unite their fractious followers behind the president's budget proposals in 2009. Indeed, most of Obama's successes (see Table 7.2) involved overwhelming Democratic support prevailing over nearly unanimous Republican opposition in his first two years.

In America's system of separated powers, the president's party may be in the minority in Congress and unable to do much for the chief executive's programs (Figure 7.3). This is because the majority party in a legislative chamber may not only control votes on the floor but also controls *what* is voted on on the floor. When it is the minority, the president's party lacks agenda control. Consequently, although their party is valuable to chief executives, it has not been a fully reliable presidential tool. The more unified the president's party is in supporting his legislative requests, the more unified the opposition party is likely to be. Unless the majority of the president's party is very large, he must also appeal to the opposition to make up for the inevitable defectors within the ranks of his own party. Thus the president often poses as being above partisanship to win "bipartisan" support in Congress. But to the extent that he pursues a bipartisan strategy, he cannot throw himself fully into building the party loyalty and the party discipline that would maximize the value of his own party's support in Congress. This is a dilemma for every president, and is particularly acute with an opposition-controlled Congress.

The role of the filibuster in the Senate should not be underestimated in this context (see Chapter 6). Even a president with a large majority in the House and a good working majority in the Senate may not have the 60 votes needed to shut

Figure 7.3
THE PRESIDENTIAL BATTING AVERAGE,* 1953–2012

*Percentage of congressional votes in which the president took the position supported by Congress.
**In 2001, the government was divided for only part of the year.
NOTE: Percentages are based on votes on which presidents took a position.
SOURCES: *Congressional Quarterly Weekly Report*, January 3, 2011, pp. 18–24, and authors' update.

down debate in the Senate. This is especially apparent in the case of presidential appointments, where individual senators can place a hold on a nomination, putting everyone on notice that the president's pursuit of a particular candidate will trigger a filibuster.[51] Filibuster power was especially prominent in 2005 as President Bush sought Senate confirmation of federal judges and two Supreme Court justices. The Democrats, who were in the minority, were in a position to filibuster nominations they regarded as "extremist," forcing the president (and his majority partisans in the Senate) to negotiate. The Democrats lifted the filibuster threat in exchange for some moderation on the part of the president, and they allowed up-or-down votes on some nominees. Obama encountered similar resistance in the Senate where the powerful "Senator #60" was usually a Republican. Because they cannot always rely on their party in Congress, contemporary

51 A powerful argument that invokes this logic is that of Keith Krehbiel in *Pivotal Politics: A Theory of U.S. Lawmaking* (Chicago: University of Chicago Press, 1998).

presidents are more likely to use two other methods—popular mobilization and executive administration—to achieve their political goals.

Going Public. Popular mobilization as a technique of presidential power has its historical roots in the presidencies of Theodore Roosevelt and Woodrow Wilson and subsequently became a weapon in the political arsenals of most presidents after the mid-twentieth century. During the nineteenth century, it was considered rather inappropriate for presidents to engage in personal campaigning on their own behalf or in support of programs and policies. When Andrew Johnson broke this unwritten rule and made a series of speeches vehemently seeking public support for his Reconstruction program, even some of his most ardent supporters were shocked at what was seen as a lack of decorum and dignity. The president's opponents cited his "inflammatory" speeches in one of the articles of impeachment drafted by Congress pursuant to the first effort in American history to oust an incumbent president.[52]

The president who used public appeals perhaps most effectively was Franklin Delano Roosevelt. The political scientist Sidney Milkis observes that Roosevelt was "firmly persuaded of the need to form a direct link between the executive office and the public."[53] Roosevelt developed a number of tactics aimed at forging such a link. Like his predecessors, he often embarked on speaking trips around the nation to promote his programs. On one such tour, he told a crowd, "I regain strength just by meeting the American people."[54] In addition, Roosevelt made limited but important use of the new electronic medium, radio, to reach millions of Americans. In his famous "fireside chats," the president, or at least his voice, came into living rooms across the country to discuss programs and policies and generally to assure Americans that Roosevelt was aware of their difficulties and working diligently toward solutions.[55] Another executive, Mayor Fiorello La Guardia of New York City, also "went public," using radio to read comic strips to Depression-era city children during a long newspaper strike. A brilliant political ploy, it deeply impressed voting-age citizens while entertaining the young ones.

Roosevelt was also an innovator in the realm of what now might be called press relations. When he entered the White House, he faced a mainly hostile press typically controlled by conservative members of the business establishment. As the president wrote, "All the fat-cat newspapers—85 percent of the

---

52 Tulis, *The Rhetorical Presidency*, p. 91.

53 Quoted in Sidney M. Milkis, *The President and the Parties: The Transformation of the American Party System since the New Deal* (New York: Oxford University Press, 1993), p. 97.

54 Quoted in James MacGregor Burns, *Roosevelt: The Lion and the Fox* (New York: Harcourt, Brace, 1956), p. 317.

55 The distribution of radio ownership in the 1930s was quite uneven, however. Roosevelt reinforced his "going public" radio addresses with a similarly uneven distribution of relief funds during the Depression. Counties with a high concentration of radio ownership received more relief funds, even after controlling for income and unemployment. Popular mobilization and public policy worked hand in hand to burnish the president's reputation. See David Strömberg, "Radio's Impact on Public Spending," *Quarterly Journal of Economics* 119 (2004): 189–221.

whole—have been utterly opposed to everything the Administration is seeking."[56] Roosevelt hoped to be able to use the press to mold public opinion, but to do so he needed to circumvent the editors and publishers who were generally unsympathetic to his goals. To this end, the president worked to cultivate the reporters who covered the White House. Roosevelt made himself available for twice-weekly press conferences, during which he offered candid answers to reporters' questions and made important policy announcements that would provide the reporters with significant stories to file with their papers.[57] Roosevelt was especially effective in designating a press secretary (Stephen Early), who organized the press conferences and made certain that reporters observed the informal rules distinguishing presidential comments that were off the record from those that could be attributed directly to the president.

Every president since Roosevelt has sought to craft a public relations strategy that emphasized his strengths and maximized his popular appeal. One Clinton innovation was to make the White House Communications Office an important institution within the EOP.[58] In a practice continued by George W. Bush, the Communications Office became responsible not only for responding to reporters' queries but also for developing and implementing a coordinated communications strategy: promoting the president's policy goals, developing responses to unflattering news stories, and making certain that a favorable image of the president would, insofar as possible, dominate the news. Consistent with President Obama's successful use of social networking in his 2008 election campaign, the Obama administration's communications office has emphasized social networking techniques, including tweeting, to reach newsmakers and the American people directly. The White House posts several tweets a day on topics as varied as immigration reform, climate change, and the Chicago Blackhawk's Stanley Cup win. Of course, unlike ordinary tweets, presidential tweets must, under the terms of the Presidential Records Act, be recorded and stored for posterity.

In addition to using the media, recent presidents have reached out directly to the American public to gain its approval (Figure 7.4). During his first full month in office, for example, President Obama addressed Congress and the American people on the nation's financial crisis, seeking to reassure the public and to mobilize its support for his policies. During his first year in office, Obama made additional major speeches in the United States and abroad designed to generate both domestic and international support for his programs. In his speeches, the president frequently sought to explain how his approaches would differ from those of the Bush administration. In a nationally televised May 2009 speech on national security, for example, Obama declared that the security policies employed by the Bush administration, including harsh interrogations, indefinite detention of suspects, and other violations of America's customary rule of law, were both inconsistent with American values and ineffective. He promised to

---

56 Burns, *Roosevelt*, p. 317.

57 Kernell, *Going Public*, p. 79.

58 The office had first been established in the Nixon administration and was used very effectively by President Reagan.

Figure 7.4

PUBLIC APPEARANCES BY PRESIDENTS

ANALYZING THE EVIDENCE

In the nineteenth century, presidents seldom made public speeches or other public appearances. By the end of the twentieth century, the number of times presidents went public had increased dramatically. What accounts for the growth in public appearances? What do presidents hope to accomplish through speeches and other public events? What risks do presidents take when they seek to develop and use popular support as a political tool?

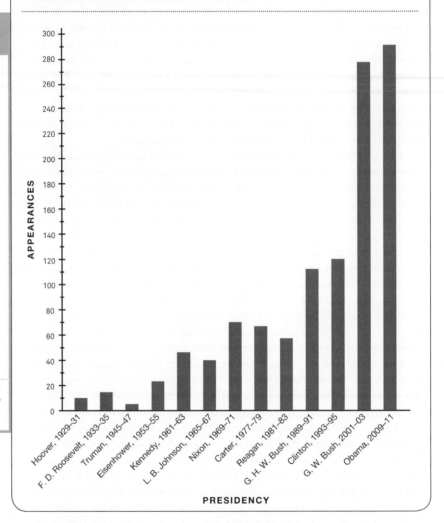

NOTE: Only the first two years of each term are included, because the last two years include many purely political appearances for the president's re-election campaign.

SOURCES: Kernell, *Going Public*, p.118, Lyn Ragsdale, *Vital Statistics on the Presidency*, 3rd ed. (Washington, DC: CQ Press, 2009), Table 4-9, pp. 202–3; POTUS Tracker, *Washington Post*, http://projects.washingtonpost.com/potus-tracker/ (accessed 8/8/11); and authors' updates.

craft an approach that would protect both liberty and the nation's security. In a June 2009 speech delivered in Cairo, Egypt, Obama sought to reassure the Arab world that the United States was not its enemy. Obama began his speech with the traditional Muslim greeting, "Assalamu Alaykum," and made reference in his text to the "holy Koran." The speech was well received, though many listeners wondered if the president's words would be followed by changes in policy.

The Limits of Going Public. Some presidents have been able to make effective use of popular appeals to overcome congressional opposition. Popular support, though, has not been a firm foundation for presidential power. To begin with, it is notoriously fickle. President George W. Bush maintained an approval rating of over 70 percent for more than a year after the September 11 terrorist attacks. By 2003, however, his approval rating had fallen nearly 20 points as American casualties in Iraq mounted; by the end of 2005, it had fallen almost another 20 points, to the high 30s, where it remained through much of 2006. Such declines in popular approval during a president's term in office are nearly inevitable and follow a predictable pattern (Figure 7.5). Presidents generate popular support by promising to undertake important programs that will contribute directly to the well-being of large numbers of Americans. Almost always, presidential performance falls short of those promises and popular expectations, leading to a sharp decline in public support and an ensuing

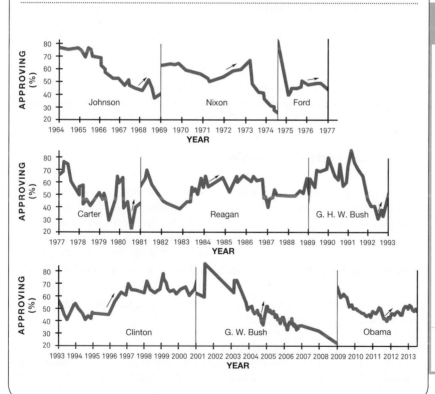

Figure 7.5
PRESIDENTIAL PERFORMANCE RATINGS

ANALYZING THE EVIDENCE

In the presidential performance-rating poll, respondents are asked, "Do you approve of the way the president is handling his job?" The graphs show the percentage of positive responses. What factors help explain changes in presidential approval ratings? Does popular approval really affect presidential power? How can popular feelings about the president affect the president's conduct and influence?

NOTE: Arrows indicate preelection upswings.
SOURCES: Gallup, Presidential Job Approval Center, www.gallup.com/poll/124922/presidential -approval-center.aspx (accessed 6/14/13).

collapse of presidential influence. Reagan and Clinton are the exceptions among modern presidents—leaving office at least as popular as when they arrived.

Presidents certainly have not abandoned the tool of going public, but they have employed institutionalized public and media relations efforts more to create a generally favorable public image than to promote specific policies.[59] Thus in 2002, President George W. Bush made several speeches to boost the proposed creation of the Homeland Security Department. At the same time, however, the White House Communications Office was engaged in a nonstop, seven-day-a-week effort to promote news and feature stories aimed at bolstering the president's more general public image. Stories emphasized the president's empathy for retirees hurt by the downturn of stock prices, the president's anger over corporate abuses, the president's concern for the environment, and so forth. These are all examples of image polishing rather than going public on behalf of specific programs. Confronted with the limitations of a strategy of popular mobilization, presidents have shifted from an offensive strategy to a more defensive mode in this domain.

Technological change has also affected the tactics of going public. The growing heterogeneity of media outlets—cable stations, streamed radio, the blogosphere—and the declining viewership and readership of mainstream outlets has fragmented the public. This has necessitated newly crafted approaches—"narrowcasting" to reach targeted demographic categories rather than broadcasting to reach "the public." Instead of going "capital P" public, new approaches seek to appeal to myriad "small p" publics (plural). Shrinking and fragmented audiences have raised the costs and cast doubt on the effectiveness of presidential efforts to educate and mobilize public opinion. The limitations of going public as a route to presidential power have also led contemporary presidents to make use of a third technique: expanding their administrative capabilities.

The Administrative State

Contemporary presidents have increased the administrative capabilities of their office in two important ways. First, they have sought to increase White House control over the federal bureaucracy. Second, they have expanded the role of executive orders and other instruments of direct presidential governance. Taken together, these components of what might be called the White House administrative strategy have given presidents a capacity to achieve their programmatic and policy goals even when they are unable to secure congressional approval. Indeed, some recent presidents have been able to accomplish quite a bit without much congressional, partisan, or even public support.

regulatory review ⮞

The OMB function of reviewing all agency regulations and other rule making before they become official policy

Appointments and Regulatory Review. Presidents have sought to increase their influence through bureaucratic appointments and **regulatory review**. By appointing loyal supporters to top jobs in the bureaucracy, presidents

---

59 Kernell, *Going Public*, p. 114.

make it more likely that agencies will follow the president's wishes. As the Analyzing the Evidence unit on the following page shows, recent presidents have increased the number of political appointees in the bureaucracy.

Through regulatory review, presidents have tried to control rule making by the agencies of the executive branch (see also Chapter 15). Whenever Congress enacts a statute, its actual implementation requires the promulgation of hundreds of rules by the agency charged with administering the law and giving effect to the will of Congress. Some congressional statutes are quite detailed and leave agencies with relatively little discretion. Typically, however, Congress enacts a relatively broad statement of legislative intent and delegates to the appropriate administrative agency the power to fill in many important details.[60] In other words, Congress typically says to an administrative agency: "Here is the problem. Deal with it."[61]

The discretion Congress delegates to administrative agencies has provided recent presidents with an important avenue for expanding their power. For example, President Clinton believed the president had full authority to order agencies of the executive branch to adopt such rules as the president thought appropriate, and he issued 107 directives to administrators ordering them to propose specific rules and regulations. In some instances, the language of the rule to be proposed was drafted by the White House staff; in other cases, the president asserted a priority but left it to the agency to draft the precise language of the proposal. Presidential rule-making directives covered a wide variety of topics. For example, Clinton ordered the Food and Drug Administration (FDA) to develop rules designed to restrict the marketing of tobacco products to children. White House and FDA staffers then spent several months preparing nearly 1,000 pages of new regulations affecting tobacco manufacturers and vendors.[62] Republicans denounced Clinton's actions as a usurpation of power.[63] After he took office, however, President George W. Bush made no move to surrender the powers Clinton had claimed. Bush continued the Clinton-era practice of issuing presidential directives to agencies to spur them to issue new rules and regulations. When he assumed office, President Obama appointed the Harvard law professor Cass Sunstein to head his regulatory review effort. Sunstein, an expert on the regulatory process, served for three years in the post and made regulatory review an even more important arrow in the president's quiver.

Governing by Decree: Executive Orders. Another mechanism through which contemporary presidents have sought to enhance their power to govern unilaterally is the use of executive orders and other forms of presidential decrees, including executive agreements, national security findings and directives,

---

60 The classic critique of this process is Lowi, *The End of Liberalism*.

61 Kenneth Culp Davis, *Administrative Law Treatise* (St. Paul, MN: West, 1958), p. 9.

62 Elena Kagan, "Presidential Administration," *Harvard Law Review* 114 (2001): 2265.

63 For example, Douglas W. Kmiec, "Expanding Power," in *The Rule of Law in the Wake of Clinton,* Roger Pilon, ed. (Washington, DC: Cato Institute Press, 2000), pp. 47–68.

Presidential Appointees in the Executive Branch

Contributed by
David Lewis
Vanderbilt University

Article II of the Constitution states that "The executive power shall be vested in a President of the United States of America" and details one of the president's most important constitutional roles: leading the executive branch. Today, this means the president must manage 15 cabinet departments and 55–60 independent agencies—and the over 2 million civilian employees who work in the federal government. Given the system of separation of powers, the president often competes with Congress for control of the executive branch. Congress also has a legitimate interest in the actions of executive branch officials since Congress creates programs and agencies and determines their budgets. The stakes of this competition between the branches are increasing. As the scope and complexity of government work have grown, Congress has delegated important policy-making responsibility to government officials working in the executive branch. These officials determine important public policies such as allowable levels of pollutants in the environment, eligibility rules for government benefits like medical care and Social Security, and safety rules in workplaces. Modern presidents have sought to exert more control over these agencies by a number of means, including increasing the number of presidential appointments.

Civil Service Systems

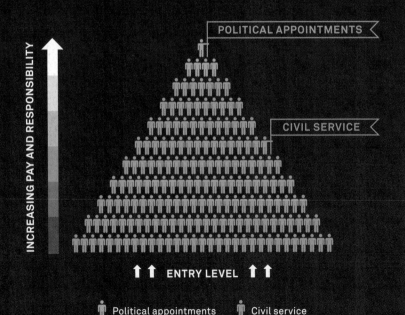

POLITICAL APPOINTMENTS

CIVIL SERVICE

INCREASING PAY AND RESPONSIBILITY

↑ ↑ ENTRY LEVEL ↑ ↑

Political appointments   Civil service

Government agencies are generally staffed by a mix of two types of employees: civil servants and political appointees. Civil servants staff the lower strata of government agencies and are to be hired, fired, promoted, and demoted on the basis of merit, and they cannot be removed without good cause. Political appointees, however, are generally selected from outside the civil service by the president, and most can be removed at the president's discretion.

SOURCE: David E. Lewis, *The Politics of Presidential Appointments* (Princeton, NJ: Princeton University Press, 2008).

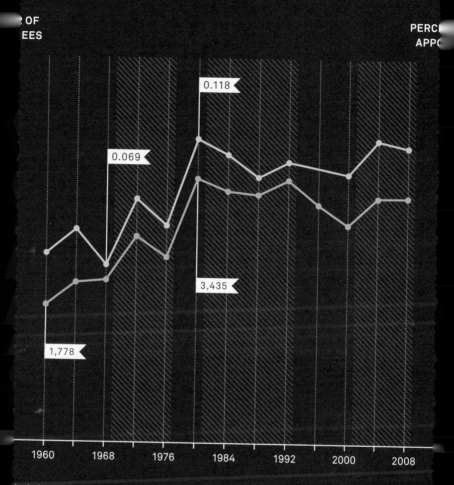

Includes salaried Senate-confirmed appointees and lower-level appointees that do not require Senate confirmation. Excludes ambassadors, U.S. marshals, U.S. attorneys, and advisory positions.

● Percent appointed   ● Number of appointees   ▨ Republican presiden...

...since the middle of the twentieth century have sought to push down the dividing li... ...and civil servants in government agencies. The figure above presents the total... ...appointees as well as the percentage of appointees in the federal government wor... ...decades. First, it should be noted that appointees make up a very small percentage o... ...However, and interestingly, the proportion of federal employees who are appointees... ...ime period, as presidents have tried to exert greater influence over the executive bra...

...id E. Lewis, "Modern Presidents and the Transformation of the Federal Personnel System," *The Foru...*

proclamations, reorganization plans, signing statements, and a host of others.[64] Executive orders have a long history in the United States and, as we saw earlier, have been the vehicles for a number of important government policies. These include the purchase of Louisiana, the annexation of Texas, the emancipation of the slaves, the internment of the Japanese, the desegregation of the military, the initiation of affirmative action, and the creation of important federal agencies, among them the Environmental Protection Agency, the Food and Drug Administration, and the Peace Corps.[65]

Although wars and national emergencies produce the highest volume of executive orders, such presidential actions also occur frequently in peacetime (Figure 7.6). In the realm of foreign policy, unilateral presidential actions in the form of executive agreements have virtually replaced treaties as the nation's chief foreign-policy instruments.[66] Presidential decrees, however, are often issued for purely domestic purposes.

Presidents may not use executive orders to issue whatever commands they please. The use of such decrees is bound by law. If a president issues an executive order, proclamation, directive, or the like, in principle he does so pursuant to the powers granted to him by the Constitution or delegated to him by Congress, usually through a statute. When presidents issue such orders, they generally state the constitutional or statutory basis for their actions. For example, when President Truman ordered the desegregation of the armed services, he did so pursuant to his constitutional powers as commander in chief. In a similar vein, when President Johnson issued Executive Order No. 11246, he asserted that the order was designed to implement the 1964 Civil Rights Act, which prohibited employment discrimination. Where an executive order has no statutory or constitutional basis, the courts have held it to be void. The most important case illustrating this point is *Youngstown Sheet and Tube Company v. Sawyer*, the so-called steel seizure case of 1952.[67] Here the Supreme Court ruled that President Truman's seizure of the nation's steel mills during the Korean War had no statutory or constitutional basis and was thus invalid.

A number of court decisions, though, have established broad boundaries that leave considerable room for presidential action. By illustration, the courts have held that Congress might approve a presidential action after the fact or, in effect, ratify a presidential action through "acquiescence"—for example, by not

---

64 A complete inventory is provided in Harold C. Relyea, *Presidential Directives: Background and Review*, Congressional Research Service Report for Congress, 98–611 GOV, November 9, 2001.

65 Terry M. Moe and William G. Howell, "The Presidential Power of Unilateral Action," *Journal of Law, Economics, and Organization* 15 (1999): 133–4. Also see William G. Howell, *Power without Persuasion*.

66 Moe and Howell, "Unilateral Action," p. 164.

67 *Youngstown Sheet and Tube Company v. Sawyer*, 343 U.S. 579 (1952).

Figure 7.6
SIGNIFICANT EXECUTIVE ORDERS, 1900–95

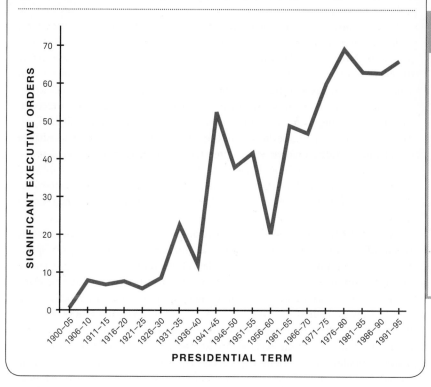

SOURCE: William G. Howell, "The President's Powers of Unilateral Action: The Strategic Advantages of Acting Alone" (Ph.D. diss., Stanford University, 1999).

ANALYZING THE EVIDENCE

During the twentieth century, presidents made increasingly frequent use of executive orders to accomplish their policy goals. What factors explain this development? How have Congress and the courts responded to increased presidential assertiveness?

objecting for long periods of time or by continuing to provide funding for programs established by executive orders. In addition, the courts have indicated that some areas, most notably the realm of military policy, are presidential in character, and they have allowed presidents wide latitude to make policy by executive decree. Thus, within the very broad limits established by the courts, presidential orders can be and have been important policy tools.

President Clinton issued numerous orders designed to promote a coherent set of policy goals: protecting the environment, strengthening federal regulatory power, shifting the focus of America's foreign policy from unilateral to multilateral, expanding affirmative action programs, and helping organized labor in its struggles with employers.[68] Clinton did not issue more executive orders than

68 Todd Gaziano, "The New 'Massive Resistance,'" *Policy Review* (May/June 1998): 283.

his immediate predecessors. His innovation was to take an instrument that had been used sporadically and show that an activist president could develop and implement a significant policy agenda without legislation—a lesson that surely was not lost on his successors.

Indeed, just as he continued the practice of using regulatory review as a policy instrument, President George W. Bush did not hesitate to use executive orders. In November 2001, for example, Bush issued a directive authorizing the creation of military tribunals to try noncitizens accused of involvement in acts of terrorism against the United States. The presidential directive also prohibits defendants from appealing their treatment to any federal or state court. In 2005 and 2006, it came to light that Bush had ordered the National Security Administration to conduct a massive program of domestic surveillance of telephone traffic involving suspected terrorists. In *Hamdan v. Rumsfeld*, the Supreme Court in June 2006 determined that the military tribunals established by Bush's executive order to try detainees at the U.S. naval base at Guantánamo Bay, Cuba, violated both the Uniform Code of Military Justice and the Geneva Conventions.[69]

President Obama signed four executive orders on his second full day in office. With the stroke of a pen, he changed government policy on detention operations at the naval base at Guantánamo Bay; clarified his administration's stance on the use of torture and/or controversial interrogation techniques; reversed the previous administration's ban on certain types of stem-cell research; and reversed the so-called Mexico City gag rule, which restricted federal funding for groups in other countries that performed or advocated abortion as a component of family planning services. In 2012 alone, Obama issued 31 executive orders, including the blocking of property of the government of Iran and its financial institutions; the promotion of international regulatory cooperation; the acceleration of broadband deployment; and the restoration of Gulf Coast ecosystems.

Signing Statements. The signing statement has become another instrument of presidential power. To negate congressional actions to which they objected, recent presidents have made frequent and calculated use of presidential signing statements when signing bills into law.[70] A **signing statement** is an announcement made by the president at the time of signing a congressional enactment into law, sometimes presenting the president's interpretation of the law as well as usually innocuous remarks predicting the many benefits the new law would bring to the nation. Occasionally, presidents have used signing statements to point to sections of the law they deemed improper or even unconstitutional, and to instruct executive branch agencies how they were to execute

signing statement

An announcement made by the president when a bill is signed into law

---

69 *Hamdan v. Rumsfeld*, 548 U.S. 557 (2006).

70 Mark Killenbeck, "A Matter of Mere Approval? The Role of the President in the Creation of Legislative History," 48 *University of Arkansas Law Review* 239 (1995).

the law.[71] President Harry Truman, for example, accompanied his approval of the 1946 Hobbs Anti-Racketeering Act with a message offering his interpretation of ambiguous sections of the statute and indicating how the federal government would implement the new law.[72]

Presidents have made signing statements throughout American history, though many were not recorded and so did not become part of the official legislative record. Ronald Reagan's attorney general, Edwin Meese, is generally credited with transforming the signing statement into a routine tool of presidential direct action.[73] Meese believed that carefully crafted signing statements would provide a basis for action by executive agencies and, perhaps even more important, would become part of the history and context of a piece of legislation if and when judicial interpretation became necessary. Indeed, to make certain that signing statements became part of the legislative history, Meese reached an agreement with the West Publishing Company to include them in its authoritative texts.[74] With the way paved, Reagan proceeded to use detailed and artfully designed signing statements—prepared by the Department of Justice—to attempt to reinterpret congressional enactments. For example, when signing the Safe Drinking Water Amendments of 1986, President Reagan issued a statement that interpreted sections of the act to allow discretionary enforcement when Congress seemed to call for mandatory enforcement.

This strategy, to be sure, is not always successful. When he signed the Competition in Contracting Act in 1984, President Reagan declared that portions of the law were unconstitutional and directed executive branch officials not to comply with them. Subsequently, U.S. District Court judge Harold Ackerman upheld the act and decried the notion that the president had the power to declare acts of Congress unconstitutional.[75] The same conclusion was later reached by the Ninth Circuit Court of Appeals, which declared that the president did not have the authority to "excise or sever provisions of a bill with which he disagrees."[76]

Despite these adverse rulings, however, the same tactic of reinterpreting and nullifying congressional enactments was continued by Reagan's successor, George H. W. Bush. When he signed the 1991 Civil Rights Act, Bush asserted his concern that one of its provisions might be unfairly applied to businesses. By so doing, the president established his own reading to

71 Philip J. Cooper, *By Order of the President: The Use and Abuse of Presidential Direct Action* (Lawrence: University Press of Kansas, 2002), p. 201.

72 Edward S. Corwin, *The President: Office and Powers*, 4th ed. (New York: New York University Press, 1957), p. 283.

73 Cooper, *By Order of the President*, p. 201.

74 Cooper, *By Order of the President*, p. 203.

75 *Ameron, Inc. v. U.S. Army Corps of Engineers*, 610 F.Supp. 750 (D.N.J. 1985).

76 *Lear, Siegler v. Lehman*, 842 F.2nd 1102 (1988).

shape the act's legislative history, provided guidance to administrators regarding the law's implementation, and attempted to influence future court interpretations.[77]

Presidential use of signing statements to challenge legislative provisions and to declare that provisions not favored by the president would not be enforced increased sharply during the George W. Bush years. President Reagan used signing statements to attack 71 legislative provisions, and President Clinton made 105 significant signing statements. Bush challenged more than 800 legislative provisions with his signing statements, including a number of important domestic and security matters, such as a congressional effort, led by Senator John McCain, to ban the use of torture by American interrogators. During the 2008 presidential campaign, Democrats denounced Bush's use of signing statements. In March 2009, however, President Obama made use of the same tactic employed by his predecessors. After he signed a $410 billion budget bill into law, Obama declared five provisions of the act to be unconstitutional and non-binding, including a provision to prevent punishment of whistle-blowers. By the end of his first term, Obama had issued more than two dozen signing statements in which he offered his own interpretation of portions of the bills he signed into law.

Ed Meese's contrivance has become a full-blown instrument of presidential power. Adding to the importance of this power in recent years, as presidents had hoped, courts have begun giving weight to presidential signing statements when interpreting the meaning of statutes.[78] Still, the legal status of signing statements has not been fully resolved.

The Advantages of the Administrative Strategy. Through the course of American history, party leadership and popular appeals have played important roles in presidential efforts to overcome political opposition, and both continue to be instruments of presidential power. Reagan's tax cuts and Clinton's budget victories were achieved with strong partisan support. George W. Bush, lacking the oratorical skills of a Reagan or a Roosevelt, nevertheless made good use of sophisticated communications strategies to promote his agenda. Yet, as we saw, in the modern era, parties have waned in institutional strength, and the effects of popular appeals have often proved evanescent. The limitations of the alternatives have increasingly impelled presidents to try to expand the administrative capabilities of the office and their own capacity for unilateral action as means of achieving their policy goals. And in recent decades, the expansion of the Executive Office,

---

77 Cooper, *By Order of the President*, p. 207.

78 Kristy Carroll, "Whose Statute Is It Anyway? Why and How Courts Should Use Presidential Signing Statements When Interpreting Federal Statutes," 16 *Catholic University Law Review* 475 (1997).

the development of regulatory review, and the use of executive orders, signing statements, and the like have given presidents a substantial capacity to achieve significant policy results despite congressional opposition to their legislative agendas.

To be sure, the administrative strategy does not always succeed. In some instances over the years, as just noted, the federal courts have struck down unilateral actions by the president. And occasionally Congress acts to reverse presidential orders. For example, in 1999, Congress enacted legislation prohibiting the Department of Education from carrying out a presidential directive to administer national tests of reading and mathematics.[79] And before that, in 1996, in response to President Clinton's aggressive regulatory review program, the Republican-controlled Congress moved to strengthen its capacity to block the president's use of administrative directives by enacting the Congressional Review Act (CRA). This piece of legislation requires federal agencies to send all proposed regulations to Congress for review 60 days before they take effect. It also creates a fast-track procedure to allow the House and Senate to enact a joint resolution of disapproval that would not only void the regulation but also prohibit the agency from subsequently issuing any substantially similar rule.

In principle, perhaps, Congress could respond more vigorously than it has to unilateral policy making by the president. Certainly a Congress willing to impeach a president should have the mettle to overturn his administrative directives. But the president has significant advantages in such struggles with Congress. In battles over presidential directives and orders, Congress is on the defensive, reacting to presidential initiatives. The framers of the Constitution saw "energy," or the ability to take the initiative, as a key feature of executive power.[80] When the president takes action by issuing an order or an administrative directive, Congress must initiate the cumbersome and time-consuming lawmaking process, overcome internal divisions, and enact legislation that the president may ultimately veto. Moreover, as the political scientist Terry Moe has argued, in such battles Congress faces a significant collective action problem insofar as members are likely to be more sensitive to the substance of a president's action and its effects on their constituents than to the more general implications of presidential power for the long-term vitality of their institution.[81]

79 Kagan, "Presidential Administration," p. 2351.

80 Alexander Hamilton, James Madison, and John Jay, *The Federalist Papers,* Clinton L. Rossiter, ed. (New York: New American Library, 1961), no. 70, pp. 423–30.

81 Terry M. Moe, "The Presidency and the Bureaucracy: The Presidential Advantage," in *The Presidency and the Political System,* 7th ed., Michael Nelson, ed. (Washington, DC: CQ Press, 2003), pp. 425–57.

PRESIDENTIAL POWER: MYTHS AND REALITIES

We began this chapter by observing that presidents have a distinct institutional advantage vis-à-vis other governmental actors. Presidents are unitary "deciders," whereas other political actors are members of institutions whose decision-making processes are collective, requiring deliberation, debate, compromise, and voting. This institutional difference has contributed to the steady growth of presidential power, which has occasioned an ongoing debate between the advocates of a strong presidency and those who favor America's traditional separation of powers system, with its built-in limitations and constraints on collective action, discussed in Chapter 1.

Emergency Power

Advocates of presidential power have typically advanced three arguments for deferring to the White House. The first, which echoes themes articulated by Alexander Hamilton and others among the nation's Founders, is that executive power is needed to deal with emergencies and to ensure the nation's security.[82] Although no one could argue with this position in the abstract, particularly in an age of global terrorism, the problem is that presidents can sometimes be too anxious to act forcefully in response to what they perceive as security threats. The framers of the Constitution gave Congress, and not the president, the power to make war precisely because they feared that presidents might be altogether too willing to commit the nation to armed conflicts. "The strongest passions and most dangerous weaknesses of the human breast," wrote James Madison, "ambition, avarice, vanity, the honorable or venial love of fame, are all in a conspiracy [within the executive branch] against the desire and duty of peace. Hence it has grown into an axiom that the executive is the department of power most distinguished by its propensity to war."[83]

But if the president is too anxious to go to war, is Congress too reluctant to respond to emergencies? The short answer is no. It would be difficult to

---

82 A contemporary statement of this position is Harvey C. Mansfield, Jr., *Taming the Prince: The Ambivalence of Modern Executive Power* (New York: Free Press, 1989), chap. 1.

83 Richard Loss, ed., *The Letters of Pacificus and Helvidius* (Delmar, NY: Scholars Facsimiles and Reprints, 1976), pp. 91–2. It may be noted that the context in which the framers met was one in which English kings had displayed this same propensity to wage war and pursue foreign adventures, a tendency checked by a more activist Parliament only after centuries of disputation with the monarch.

---

identify an instance of the past half-century in which the nation's security was compromised because Congress refused to act, though in a number of cases, including perhaps the recent Iraq War, the president was, as Madison feared, too quick to take vigorous action. When the nation has faced actual emergencies, Congress has seldom refused to grant appropriate powers to the president. Indeed, the legislative branch has generally been too pliable, granting presidents powers to deal with emergencies of their own making, as in the case of the Gulf of Tonkin Resolution, which President Lyndon Johnson used as the legislative basis for his Vietnam War policies.

Thus, support of presidential power on the grounds of the superior capacity of the executive to respond to emergencies is a false basis on two counts: the legislature is not an obstacle to expeditious responses to emergency and presidents all too frequently use executive power for myriad purposes other than to respond to emergencies. Executive superiority in national emergencies is Myth 1.

The Public Interest

A second argument often made in favor of expanded presidential power is that the president champions the national interest as opposed to the particularistic interests defended by members of Congress, party politicians, bureaucrats, and most other political actors. This notion that the president is above party politics seems reminiscent of the premodern yearning for a wise and beneficent king who would brush aside the selfish claims of manipulative courtiers and rule in the best interests of all his subjects. Perhaps such kings have existed from time to time, but the behavior of the kingly stratum as a whole does not inspire much confidence in the notion that powerful executives are a good antidote to factional selfishness and rent-seeking special interests.

Presidents, to be sure, are unitary actors. As such they may find it more difficult than members of Congress to escape responsibility for their conduct or, through inaction, to become free riders on the efforts of others. And it is certainly the case that presidents are accountable to a larger, more heterogeneous constituency than most House members or senators. To this extent, the presidentialist argument might have some merit. Empirically, however, presidents do not appear much more likely than senators and representatives to set aside personal concerns in favor of some abstract public good. Presidents often enough promote programs designed mainly to reward important political backers and contributors even when such programs clearly do not serve the larger public interest. What public interest was served by President Clinton's decision to pardon the fugitive financier Marc Rich? Why did President Bush block stem-cell research even though such work is important to maintaining America's technological edge? In both instances, personal or political calculations appear to have outweighed presidential concern for the public interest. Hence, Myth 2, with some qualifications, is superior presidential responsiveness to the public interest.

Presidential Power and Democracy

Beyond assertions of the need for a strong presidency and the allegedly superior commitment of the president to the national interest, a third argument is frequently made in support of enhanced presidential power. This is the contention that the presidency is a more democratic institution than Congress.[84] This argument has a certain surface plausibility. The president is, of course, the nation's only elected official who can claim to represent all the people. As a decision-making institution, however, the presidency is perhaps America's least democratic entity.

Presidential decision making generally takes place in private and is often shrouded in secrecy. Recent presidents have vehemently asserted that the secrecy of the processes leading up to their decisions is shielded by executive privilege. This was the Bush administration's claim when it refused to disclose information regarding the composition or deliberations of the task forces with whom Vice President Cheney met in 2001 to plan the administration's energy policies. The Supreme Court supported the administration's position on the grounds that the "energetic performance" of the executive branch's duties required protection from intrusive requests for information.[85] Successive presidents have also disciplined staffers who revealed information to Congress and worked to block legislation that would protect whistle-blowers. Not only are the deliberations leading up to presidential decisions often removed from the public domain, but even the decisions themselves are sometimes not revealed to the public or even to Congress. Many so-called national security directives issued by presidents in recent years have been used to initiate secret missions by intelligence and defense agencies.[86] For many years, too, presidents have signed secret executive agreements with other governments obligating the United States to various forms of action without congressional knowledge, much less approval.

Arguably, the Congress is inherently a more democratic decision-making institution than the presidency. To exert influence, competing factions in Congress must maintain active and ongoing relationships with important groups and forces in civil society. For members of Congress, constituency mobilization and political power are closely connected. Journalists may cluck their tongues at the "senator from Goldman Sachs" or the "congressman from Boeing." But ties to the financial sector, aerospace industry, or a host of other key constituencies help members of Congress exercise influence on

---

84 Grant McConnell, *The Modern Presidency* (New York: St. Martin's, 1976). See also Steven Calabresi, "Some Normative Arguments for the Unitary Executive," 48 *Arkansas Law Review* 23 (1995), p. 58.

85 *Cheney v. U.S. District Court of the District of Columbia*, 542 U.S. 367 (2004).

86 Christopher Simpson, *National Security Directives of the Reagan and Bush Administrations* (Boulder, CO: Westview Press, 1995).

Capitol Hill and strengthen the Congress as a collective body vis-à-vis the executive branch. Today, indeed, Congress must sometimes mobilize constituency pressure just to compel the president to implement its decisions. One of Congress's weaknesses as an institution is that it must depend on the executive to carry out and enforce most of its dictates. As we saw when we discussed presidential signing statements, presidents are increasingly wont to claim that they are not required to implement decisions with which they disagree.

Presidents, of course, can also mobilize supporters and interests. Indeed, some presidents, such as Andrew Jackson and Franklin Delano Roosevelt, worked to expand the scope of political participation in order to overwhelm their political opponents at the polls and in the national legislature. When it comes to the routines of governance, however, presidents usually prefer processes that limit political debate and social mobilization. In an open political struggle, involving contestation among many interests and forces, presidents may win or they may lose. But where decisions are made discreetly if not covertly, in the corridors and offices of the White House with minimal external intervention, then surely the president will prevail. And unlike Congress, the president does not have to rely on an agency outside his sphere of control to implement his decisions. To a far greater extent, presidents control bureaucrats and soldiers and contractors and mercenaries. They view the involvement of other political actors as more likely to hinder their plans than to help them govern. For these reasons, where possible, presidents seek to develop institutions and procedures that restrict the number and range of participants in decision making and limit rather than expand the scope of political debate. These observations would seem entirely inconsistent with the idea that the presidency is somehow a more democratic institution than the Congress. Institutions matter a great deal, and the claim that the presidency is the more democratic branch is Myth 3.

The Limits of Presidential Power

Presidents are powerful political actors and have become increasingly so during the past century. This is the take-home point of this chapter. But we would be remiss if we said nothing about the limits of presidential power. Indeed, presidents have had to resort to institutional and behavioral invention—signing statements, executive orders, public appeals—precisely because their official powers are limited. The separation of powers is a mighty constraint—"the president proposes; the Congress disposes." The president cannot always bend the Congress to his will, though it is an easier task when his party controls the two chambers. On the other hand, the agendas of powerful congressional players must obtain the president's consent, as the presentment clause of the Constitution requires. Through his veto power the president can defeat, but more importantly can influence in advance, congressional aspirations. Presidential power is real but it is tempered by the necessity of bilateral bargaining with the legislature, by his ability to lead the bureaucracy, and by the permissiveness of the federal judiciary. The growth in presidential power of the last hundred years has required the acquiescence if not the outright support of all the other players in the game.

For Further Reading

Selections highlighted in red are included in *Readings in American Politics: Analysis and Perspectives*, Third Edition.

Cameron, Charles M. *Veto Bargaining: Presidents and the Politics of Negative Power.* New York: Cambridge University Press, 2000.

Canes-Wrone, Brandice. *Who Leads Whom? Presidents, Policy, and the Public.* Chicago: University of Chicago Press, 2006.

Crenson, Matthew, and Benjamin Ginsberg. *Presidential Power: Unchecked and Unbalanced.* New York: Norton, 2007.

Deering, Christopher, and Forrest Maltzman. "The Politics of Executive Orders: Legislative Constraints on Presidential Power," *Political Research Quarterly* 52 (1999): 767–83.

Howell, William G. *Power without Persuasion: The Politics of Direct Presidential Action.* Princeton, NJ: Princeton University Press, 2003.

James, Scott C. *Presidents, Parties, and the State: A Party System Perspective on Democratic Regulatory Choice.* New York: Cambridge University Press, 2000.

Krutz, Glen, and Jeffrey Peake. *Presidential-Congressional Governance and the Rise of Executive Agreements.* Ann Arbor: University of Michigan Press, 2009.

Lowi, Theodore J. *The Personal President: Power Invested, Promise Unfulfilled.* Ithaca, NY: Cornell University Press, 1985.

Milkis, Sidney M. *The President and the Parties: The Transformation of the American Party System since the New Deal.* New York: Oxford University Press, 1993.

Nelson, Michael, ed. *The Presidency and the Political System.* 9th ed. Washington, DC: CQ Press, 2009.

Neustadt, Richard E. *Presidential Power and the Modern Presidents: The Politics of Leadership from Roosevelt to Reagan.* 1960. Rev. ed. New York: Free Press, 1990.

Pfiffner, James P. *The Modern Presidency.* 4th ed. Belmont, CA: Wadsworth, 2005.

Skowronek, Stephen. *The Politics Presidents Make: Leadership from John Adams to Bill Clinton.* Cambridge, MA: Harvard University Press, 1997.

The Executive Branch: Bureaucracy in a Democracy

The bureaucracy is the administrative heart and soul of government. It is where the rubber meets the road—where the policies formulated, refined, and passed into law by elected officials are interpreted, implemented, and ultimately delivered to a nation's citizens. Government touches the life of the ordinary citizen most directly in her interactions with bureaucratic agents—at the Department of Motor Vehicles when obtaining a driver's license; in filing one's income tax return with the Internal Revenue Service; at the recruiting center when enlisting in one of the armed services; at the Board of Elections when registering to vote. We examine the federal bureaucracy in this chapter both as an organizational setting within which policies are interpreted and implemented and as a venue in which politicians pursue their own (and sometimes the public's) interests.

As an organizational setting, a bureaucracy is something created by elected politicians. These politicians seek to coordinate governmental effort in order to accomplish public purposes (and private objectives) as well as to solve collective action problems. Sometimes bureaucracies are created in the face of a pressing need, indeed at times of crisis. Consider the case of the Department of Homeland Security (DHS).

On March 1, 2003, 22 federal agencies with responsibilities for combating international terrorism in the United States were combined in the DHS (Table 8.1). By all accounts, this event marked the most dramatic reform of the federal bureaucracy since the establishment of the Department of Defense in 1947. The story begins with the catastrophic events of September 11, 2001. Both Republicans and Democrats realized that the public was going to demand an ongoing response to the terrorist threat (beyond the immediate military response in Afghanistan).[1] A congressional investigation quickly revealed that

---

1 John W. Kingdon calls events that limit and focus our political options "windows of political opportunity." See his *Agendas, Alternatives, and Public Policies* (Boston: Little, Brown, 1984).

serious security lapses and a lack of coordination among the various agencies with responsibility for domestic and foreign intelligence had occurred during the administrations of presidents Bill Clinton and George W. Bush. Both political parties might be blamed if the government did not respond aggressively enough to the terrorist threat. Furthermore, the major alternative solution—the creation of a homeland-security "czar"—was tried and proved inadequate. In the end, Congress decided to create a new cabinet-level department with responsibility for coordinating efforts to protect domestic security in the United States.

Whatever the initial stimulation or inspiration for the creation of a new bureaucracy, such an entity does not drop fully formed from the heavens. It is actively shaped by politicians who come at the problem from a variety of perspectives and must hammer out an agreement (often involving bargaining and compromise) about the size, shape, and authority of the new entity. DHS was an amalgam of 22 major units previously housed in seven cabinet departments and several other independent entities. They were stitched together through intense negotiations between President Bush's White House and legislators on Capitol Hill. Bureaucracies, thus, are administrative in purpose but are born through a political process. Their features are designed by politicians who appreciate, as in our institution principle, that the institutional powers with which they endow a bureaucracy have consequences for the kinds of decisions subsequently made.

CORE OF THE ANALYSIS

 Bureaucratic institutions are created by Congress to achieve policy goals.

 By implementing the laws and policies passed by elected officials, bureaucrats can be seen as agents of Congress and the presidency. As in any principal-agent relationship, the agent (the bureaucracy) is delegated authority and has a certain amount of leeway for independent action.

 Despite the efforts of elected officials (the principals) to check departments and agencies (the agents), bureaucrats have their own goals and thus exercise their own influence on policy.

 Although controlling the growth of bureaucracy has been a concern in American politics, most Americans benefit in some way from government programs and thus are reluctant to cut back on specific programs.

Table 8.1

THE SHAPE OF A DOMESTIC SECURITY DEPARTMENT

DEPARTMENT OF HOMELAND SECURITY	AGENCIES AND DEPARTMENTS NOW PART OF THE MAIN DIVISIONS OF THE DHS	PREVIOUSLY RESPONSIBLE AGENCY OR DEPARTMENT
Border and Transportation Security Directorate	U.S. Customs and Border Protection	Treasury
	U.S. Citizenship and Immigration Services	Justice
	U.S. Immigration and Customs Enforcement	
	Federal Protective Service*	
	Transportation Security Administration	Transportation
	Federal Law Enforcement Training Center	Treasury
	Animal and Plant Health Inspection Service**	Agriculture
	Office for Domestic Preparedness	Justice
Emergency Preparedness and Response Directorate	Federal Emergency Management Agency†	Health and Human Services
	Strategic National Stockpile and the National Disaster Medical System	
	Nuclear Incident Response Team	Energy
	Domestic Emergency Support Teams	Justice
	National Domestic Preparedness Office	FBI
Science and Technology Directorate	CBRN (Chemical, Biological, Radiological and Nuclear) Countermeasures Programs	Energy
	Environmental Measurements Laboratory	Energy
	National BW (Biological Warfare) Defense Analysis Center	Defense
	Plum Island Animal Disease Center	Agriculture
Information Analysis and Infrastructure Protection Directorate††	Federal Computer Incident Response Center	General Services Administration
	National Communications System	Defense
	National Infrastructure Protection Center	FBI
	Energy Security and Assurance Program	Energy
Secret Service		Treasury
Coast Guard		Transportation

*New.

**Only partially under the aegis of DHS; some functions remain elsewhere.

†Previously independent.

††Established to analyze information provided by the CIA, the FBI, the Defense Intelligence Agency, the National Security Agency, and other agencies.

SOURCE: Department of Homeland Security, www.dhs.gov/who-joined-dhs (accessed 7/3/13)

Bureaucracies are also venues in which bureaucratic actors pursue public and private purposes. Bureaucrats are politicians who make decisions, form coalitions, and engage in bargaining; in short, they bring private preferences and values to the table as they engage in various administrative processes—just as our rationality principle suggests. We should no more think of them as automatons or cogs in some giant wheel than we do legislative, executive, or judicial politicians. The private hopes and aspirations they bring to this setting interact with the institutional features with which their bureaucracy has been endowed to produce policies, outcomes, and decisions. And these, as the policy principle tells us, will reflect both the private interests of bureaucratic politicians and the institutional ways in which they conduct their business.

In our focus on the federal bureaucracy—the administrative structure that on a day-by-day basis is the American government—we first define and describe bureaucracy as a social and political phenomenon. Second, we look in detail at American bureaucracy in action by examining the government's major administrative agencies, their role in the governmental process, and their political behavior.

WHY BUREAUCRACY?

Bureaucracies touch nearly every aspect of daily life. Government bureaucracies implement the decisions made by the political process. Bureaucracies are full of routine because routine ensures that services are delivered regularly and that each agency fulfills its mandate. For this reason, students often conclude that bureaucracy is mechanical, routinized, and just plain boring. But that is a mistake. Bureaucracy is not just about collecting garbage, training police, or mailing Social Security checks. It is all these things for sure, but it is much more besides. Mainly, it is a reflection of political deals consummated by elected politicians, turf wars among government agents and private-sector suppliers and contractors, policy-delivery successes and failures in the eyes of the public, and to complete the circle, reactions to these by the very same elected officials who cut the deals in the first place. It is politics through and through.

Public bureaucracies are powerful because legislatures and chief executives—and, indeed, the people—delegate to them vast power to make sure a particular job is done, enabling the rest of us to be freer to pursue our private ends. The public sentiments that emerged after September 11 revealed this underlying appreciation of public bureaucracies. When faced with the challenge of making air travel safe again, the public strongly supported giving the federal government responsibility for airport security even though this meant increasing the size of the federal bureaucracy in order to make the security screeners federal workers. The former House majority whip Tom DeLay sought to forestall this growth in the federal government, declaring that "the last thing we can afford to do is erect a new bureaucracy that is unaccountable and unable to protect the

American public."[2] But the antibureaucratic language that had been so effective before September 11 no longer resonated with a fearful public. Instead, there was a widespread belief that a public bureaucracy would provide more effective protection than the cost-conscious private companies that had been charged with airport security in the past.

We can shed some systematic light on public attitudes toward government bureaucracy by examining one of the standard questions posed in election years by the American National Election Studies (ANES). As part of its survey of the American public, the ANES asks a range of questions, among which is "Do you think that people in the government waste a lot of money we pay in taxes, waste some of it, or don't waste very much of it?" Although not perfect for eliciting from the public a nuanced assessment of bureaucratic performance, the question allows respondents to register a blunt evaluation. Results from the past several decades are given in Figure 8.1. Public unhappiness with bureaucratic inefficiency grew during the 1960s and 1970s and became one of Ronald Reagan's campaign themes in the 1980 election. In recent decades, this unhappiness has declined somewhat from its high in 1980, when nearly 80 percent of the survey respondents believed government "wastes a lot." Between 1984 and 2000, opinion held steady near the low 60 percent range. There was a significant downward tick in 2002, just after September 11. But whatever honeymoon there might have been after the terrorist attacks, it appears that the public is once again increasingly cynical about bureaucratic performance. The poor response of the Federal Emergency Management Agency (FEMA)—part of DHS—to the Hurricane Katrina crisis in the fall of 2005, and domestic terrorist incidents later in the decade that seem to have evaded early detection, contributed to further cynicism.

Bureaucratic Organization Enhances Efficiency

Despite this tendency to criticize bureaucracy, most Americans recognize that maintaining order in a large society is impossible without some sort of large governmental apparatus, staffed by professionals with some expertise in public administration. **Bureaucracy** refers to the actual offices, tasks, and principles of organization that are employed by large institutions to coordinate their work. The core of bureaucracy is the division of labor. The key to bureaucratic effectiveness is the coordination of experts performing complex tasks. If each job is specialized to gain efficiencies, then each worker must depend on the output of other workers, and that dependence requires careful allocation of jobs and resources. Inevitably bureaucracies become hierarchical, often approximating a pyramid in form. At the base of the organization are workers with the fewest skills and specializations; one supervisor can deal with a relatively large number of these workers. At the next level of the organization, where there are more highly specialized

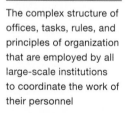

bureaucracy

The complex structure of offices, tasks, rules, and principles of organization that are employed by all large-scale institutions to coordinate the work of their personnel

---

2   Janet Hook, "U.S. Strikes Back: Political Landscape; GOP Bypasses the Bipartisan Truce," *Los Angeles Times*, October 14, 2001, p. A8.

Figure 8.1

PUBLIC OPINION ON WASTE IN GOVERNMENT

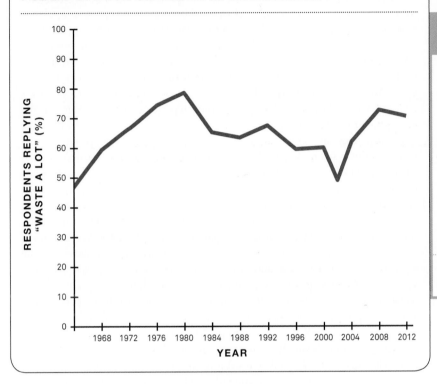

ANALYZING THE EVIDENCE

Survey respondents were asked the following question: "Do you think that people in the government waste a lot of the money we pay in taxes, waste some of it, or don't waste very much of it?" What do you think? Is the public justified in its belief that the government wastes a lot of money?

SOURCES: American National Election Studies, Cumulative Data File, 1958–2008, www.electionstudies.org/nesguide/toptable/tab5a_3.htm (accessed 12/7/11), and www.electionstudies.org/studypages/anes_timeseries_2012/anes2012TS_codebook.pdf (accessed 6/11/13).

workers, the supervision and coordination of work involves fewer workers per supervisor. Toward the top of the organization, a very small number of high-level executives engages in the "management" of the organization, meaning the organization and reorganization of all the tasks and functions, plus the allocation of the appropriate supplies and the distribution of the output of the organization to the market (if it is a private-sector organization) or to the public.

Bureaucracies Allow Governments to Operate

Bureaucracy, when used pejoratively, conjures up images of endless paperwork, red tape, and lazy, uncaring employees. But bureaucracy in fact represents a rather spectacular human achievement. By dividing up tasks, matching tasks to a labor force that develops appropriately specialized skills, routinizing procedure, and providing the incentive structure and oversight arrangements to get large numbers of people to operate in a coordinated, purposeful fashion, bureaucracies accomplish tasks and missions in a manner that would otherwise be unimaginable. The provision of an array of "government goods" as broad as the defense of people, property, and national borders or as narrow as a subsidy to a wheat farmer, a beef rancher, or a manufacturer of specialty steel requires organization, routines, standards, and at the end of the day, the authority that allows for someone to cut a check and put it in the mail. And, of course, delivering the mail is as old as the Republic itself! Bureaucracies are created to do these tasks. Although there are mistakes and miscalculations, a bureaucracy reflects instrumental thinking about how to accomplish particular undertakings; it is the rationality principle at work.

Bureaucracy also consolidates a range of complementary programs and insulates them from the predatory ambitions of out-of-sympathy political forces. Nothing in this world is permanent, but bureaucracies come close. By creating clienteles—in the legislature, the world of interest groups, and public opinion—a bureaucracy establishes a coalition of supporters, some of whom will fight to the end to keep it in place. Clienteles, after all, value consistency, predictability, and durability. It is a well-known rule of thumb that everyone in the political world cares deeply and intensely about a subset of policies and the agencies that produce them and opposes other policies and agencies, but not with nearly the same passion. Opponents, to succeed, must clear many hurdles, while proponents, to maintain the status quo, must marshal their forces only at a few veto points. In the final analysis, opponents typically meet obstacle after obstacle and eventually give up their uphill battles and concentrate on protecting and expanding what they care most deeply about. In a complex political system like that of the United States, it is much easier to do the latter. Politicians appreciate this fact of life. Consequently, both opponents and proponents of a particular set of governmental activities wage the fiercest battles at the time programs are enacted and a bureaucracy is created. Once created, these organizations assume a status of relative permanence, and future developments are shaped, as the history principle suggests, by these "initial conditions."

This raises an interesting dilemma that we only flag here, because we will develop it more systematically in the next section. In principle, bureaucratic agents are "servants" of elected politicians. They are charged with implementing statutes and policies produced by their "masters," the elected politicians in the White House and on Capitol Hill. But the relative permanence enjoyed by bureaucracy is a form of insulation—servants have discretion and masters are limited in their ability to control them. Elected officials who might want to steer a bureaucracy in a different direction often find the obstacles substantial. Only those with intense concern for the jurisdiction of a bureaucracy are likely to persist in their efforts to guide it; others have more important fish to fry in different bureaucratic jurisdictions. Thus bureaucratic agents are most affected by legislators with extraordinary interest in that bureaucracy's mission. Even among these, rational legislators who support the bureaucratic mission are likely to dominate, because those in opposition succumb to the obstacles and move their attention elsewhere.

So in response to the question of how bureaucracy makes government possible, there is an efficiency part to the answer, as well as a credibility part.

The creation of a bureau is a way to deliver government goods efficiently, and it is a device by which to tie one's hands, thereby providing a credible commitment to the long-term existence of a policy.

Bureaucrats Fulfill Important Roles

Bureaucracy conveys to most people a picture of hundreds of office workers shuffling millions of pieces of paper. There is a lot of truth in that image, but we have to look more closely at what papers are being shuffled and why.

Bureaucrats Implement Laws. Bureaucrats, whether in public or in private organizations, communicate with each other to coordinate all the specializations within their organization. This coordination is necessary to carry out the primary task of bureaucracy, which is **implementation**—that is, implementing the objectives of the organization as laid down by its board of directors (if a private company) or by law (if a public agency). In government, the "bosses" are ultimately the legislature and the elected chief executive. As we saw in Chapter 1, in a principal-agent relationship it is the principal who stipulates what he wants done, relying on appropriate incentives and other control mechanisms to secure the agent's compliance with his wishes. Thus we can argue that legislative principals establish bureaucratic agents—in departments, bureaus, agencies, institutes, and commissions of the federal government—to implement the policies promulgated by Congress and the president.

◀ implementation

The efforts of departments and agencies to translate laws into specific bureaucratic routines

Bureaucrats Make and Enforce Rules. When the bosses—Congress, in particular, when it is making the law—are clear in their instructions to bureaucrats, implementation is a fairly straightforward process. Bureaucrats translate the law into specific routines for each employee of an agency. But what happens to routine administrative implementation when there are several bosses who disagree as to what the instructions ought to be? The agent of multiple principals who disagree among themselves often finds himself or herself in a bind. The agent must chart a delicate course, seeking to do the best she can and trying not to offend any of the bosses too much. This requires yet another job for the bureaucrats: interpretation. Interpretation is a form of implementation in that the bureaucrats have to carry out what they believe to be the intentions of their superiors. But when bureaucrats have to interpret a law before implementing it, they are in effect engaging in lawmaking.[3] Congress often deliberately delegates

---

3   When bureaucrats engage in interpretation, the result is what political scientists call bureaucratic drift. Bureaucratic drift occurs because, as we've suggested, the "bosses" (in Congress) and the agents (within the bureaucracy) don't always share the same purposes. Bureaucrats also have their own agendas to fulfill. A vast body of political science literature focuses on the relationship between Congress and the bureaucracy. For a review, see Kenneth A. Shepsle, *Analyzing Politics: Rationality, Behavior, and Institutions*, 2nd ed. (New York: Norton, 2010), pp. 420–40.

to an administrative agency the responsibility of lawmaking. Members of Congress often conclude that some area of industry needs regulating or some area of the environment needs protection, but they are unwilling or unable to specify just how that should be done. In such situations, Congress delegates to the appropriate agency a broad authority within which the bureaucrats have to make law, through the procedures of **rule making** and administrative adjudication.

Rule making is essentially the same as legislation; in fact, it is often referred to as quasi-legislation. The rules issued by government agencies provide more detailed and specific indications of what a policy will actually mean. For example, the Forest Service is charged with making policies that govern the use of national forests. Just before President Clinton left office, the agency issued rules that banned new road building and development in the forests. This was a goal long sought by environmentalists and conservationists. In 2005, the Forest Service relaxed the rules, allowing states to make proposals for building new roads within the national forests. Just as the timber industry opposed the Clinton rule banning road building, environmentalists have challenged the new ruling and have sued the Forest Service in federal court for violating clean-water and endangered-species legislation.

New rules proposed by an agency take effect only after a period of public comment. Reaction from the people or businesses that are subject to the rules may cause an agency to modify the rules they first issue. Public participation takes the form of filing statements and giving testimony in public forums devoted to eliciting public opinion from interested parties. This occurs after a draft rule or regulation is announced but before it becomes official, giving the agency the opportunity to revise its draft. The rule-making process is thus a highly political one. Once rules are approved, they are published in the *Federal Register* and have the force of law.[4]

Bureaucrats Settle Disputes. Administrative adjudication is very similar to what the judiciary ordinarily does: apply rules and precedents to specific cases to settle disputes. In administrative adjudication, the agency charges the person or business suspected of violating the law. The ruling in an adjudication dispute applies only to the specific case being considered. Many regulatory agencies use administrative adjudication to make decisions about specific products or practices. For example, the National Labor Relations Board (NLRB) uses case-by-case administrative adjudication to decide union certification. Groups of workers seek the right to vote on the formation of a union or the right to affiliate with an existing union as their bargaining agent and are opposed by their employers, who assert that relevant provisions of labor law do not apply. The NLRB takes testimony case by case, considers evidence, and makes determinations for one side or the other, acting essentially like a court. The adjudicative

rule making

A quasi-legislative administrative process that produces regulations by government agencies

administrative adjudication

The application of rules and precedents to specific cases to settle disputes with regulated parties

---

4   The *Federal Register* is the daily journal of the U.S. government. It is published every day by the Government Printing Office and contains publications and notices of government agencies.

role of the Federal Communications Commission (FCC) in license renewal challenges is a further illustration. In seeking a renewal, a television or radio station may be challenged in its claims to have met all requirements (mainly technical requirements but also those regarding the adequacy of local public service programming). The FCC determines whether the renewing station or the challenger has made the stronger case.

In sum, bureaucrats in government do essentially the same things that bureaucrats in large private organizations do. But because of the authoritative, coercive nature of government, far more constraints are imposed on public bureaucrats than on private bureaucrats, even when their jobs are the same. Public bureaucrats are required to maintain a far more thorough paper trail. They are also subject to a great deal more access by the public—newspaper reporters, for example, have access to public bureaucrats. And public access has been vastly facilitated in the past half century; the adoption of the Freedom of Information Act (FOIA) in 1966 gave ordinary citizens the right of access to agency files and agency data so that they might determine whether those files (and data) contain derogatory information about them and learn what the agency is doing in general.

Bureaucracies Serve Politicians

We have provided two main answers to the question "Why bureaucracy?": (1) Bureaucracies enhance efficiency, and (2) they are the instruments of policy implementation. We would be remiss if we didn't include a third important answer: legislatures find it valuable to delegate.

In principle, the legislature could make all bureaucratic decisions itself, writing very detailed legislation each year, dotting every *i* and crossing every *t*. In some jurisdictions—tax policy, for example—this is in fact done. Tax policy is promulgated in significant detail by the House Ways and Means Committee, the Senate Finance Committee, and the Joint Committee on Taxation. The Internal Revenue Service, the administrative agency charged with implementation, engages in relatively less discretionary activity than many other regulatory and administrative agencies. But it is the exception.

The norm is for statutory authority to be delegated to the bureaucracy, sometimes with specificity but often in relatively vague terms. The bureaucracy is expected to fill in the gaps. This, however, is not a blank check to exercise unconstrained discretion. The bureaucracy will be held to account by the legislature's oversight of bureaucratic performance. The latter is monitored by the staffs of relevant legislative committees, which also serve as repositories for complaints from affected parties.[5] Poor performance or the exercise of

---

5 See Mathew D. McCubbins and Thomas Schwartz, "Congressional Oversight Overlooked: Police Patrols versus Fire Alarms," *American Journal of Political Science* 28 (1984): 165–79.

discretion inconsistent with the preferences of important legislators invites sanctions ranging from the browbeating of senior bureaucrats to the trimming of budgets and the clipping of authority.

HOW IS THE EXECUTIVE BRANCH ORGANIZED?

Cabinet departments, agencies, and bureaus are the operating parts of the bureaucratic whole. These parts can be separated into four general types: (1) cabinet departments, (2) independent agencies, (3) government corporations, and (4) independent regulatory commissions.

Although Figure 8.2 is an organizational chart of the Department of Agriculture, any other department could have been used as an illustration. At the top is the head of the department, called the secretary of the department. Below the department head and his deputy are several top administrators, such as the general counsel and the chief economist, whose responsibilities cut across the various departmental functions and provide the secretary with the ability to manage the entire organization. Of equal status are the undersecretaries and assistant secretaries, each of whom has management responsibilities for a group of operating agencies, which are arranged vertically below each of the undersecretaries.

The next tier, generally called the bureau level, is the highest level of responsibility for specialized programs. The names of these bureau-level agencies are often very well known to the public: the Forest Service and the Food Safety and Inspection Service are two examples. Sometimes they are officially called bureaus, as in the FBI, which is a bureau in the Department of Justice. Nevertheless, *bureau* is also the generic term for this level of administrative agency. Within the bureaus, there are divisions, offices, services, and units—sometimes designating agencies of the same status, sometimes designating agencies of lesser status.

Not all government agencies are part of cabinet departments. A second type of agency, the independent agency, is set up by Congress outside the departmental structure altogether, even though the president appoints and directs the heads of these types of agencies. Independent agencies usually have broad powers to provide public services that are either too expensive or too important to be left to private initiatives. Some examples of independent agencies are the National Aeronautics and Space Administration (NASA), the Central Intelligence Agency (CIA), and the Environmental Protection Agency (EPA). Government corporations are a third type of government agency but are more like private businesses performing and charging for a market service, such as transporting railroad passengers (Amtrak).

Yet a fourth type of agency is the independent regulatory commission, given broad discretion to make rules. The first regulatory agencies established by Congress, beginning with the Interstate Commerce Commission in 1887, were set up as independent regulatory commissions because Congress recognized that

Figure 8.2

ORGANIZATIONAL CHART OF THE DEPARTMENT OF AGRICULTURE

SOURCE: U.S. Department of Agriculture, www.usda.gov/documents/AgencyWorkflow.pdf

regulatory agencies are mini-legislatures, whose rules and rulings are the same as legislation and legislative interpretation but require the kind of expertise and full-time attention that is beyond the capacity of Congress. Until the 1960s, most of the regulatory agencies that were set up by Congress, such as the Federal Trade Commission (1914) and the Federal Communications Commission (1934), were independent regulatory commissions. But beginning in the late 1960s and early 1970s, all new regulatory programs, with a few exceptions (such as the Federal Election Commission), were placed within existing departments and made directly responsible to the president. Since the 1970s, no new major regulatory programs had been established, independent or otherwise, until the financial crisis of 2008–09. Congress and the president then formulated new regulatory arrangements involving the Federal Reserve System, the Federal Deposit Insurance Corporation, the Treasury, and related agencies. The Dodd-Frank Wall Street Reform and Consumer Protection Act (Public Law no. 111-203), signed into law by President Obama on July 21, 2010, brought major changes to the regulation of banks and other financial institutions. To accomplish a very complex mission, the act created several new regulatory bodies, including the Financial Stability Oversight Council, the Office of Financial Research, and the Bureau of Consumer Financial Protection.

There are too many agencies in the executive branch to identify them all here, so a simple classification of agencies will be helpful. Instead of dividing the bureaucracy into four general types, as we did earlier, an alternative classification organizes each agency by its mission, as defined by its jurisdiction: clientele agencies, agencies for maintenance of the Union, regulatory agencies, and redistributive agencies. We examine each of these types of agencies, focusing on both their formal structure and their place in the political process.

Clientele Agencies

clientele agency

A department or bureau of government whose mission is to promote, serve, or represent a particular interest

The entire Department of Agriculture is an example of a **clientele agency**. So are the departments of the Interior, Labor, and Commerce. Although all administrative agencies have clienteles, certain agencies are singled out and called clientele agencies because they are directed by law to foster and promote the interests of their clientele. For example, the Department of Commerce and Labor was founded in 1903 as a single department "to foster, promote, and develop the foreign and domestic commerce, the mining, the manufacturing, the shipping, and fishing industries, and the transportation facilities of the United States."[6] It remained a single department until 1913, when the law created the separate departments of Commerce and Labor, with each statute providing for the same obligation: to support and foster each agency's respective clientele.[7]

6   *U.S. Statutes at Large* 32 (1903): 825; 15 U.S. Code 1501.

7   For a detailed account of the creation of the Department of Commerce and Labor and its division into separate departments, see Theodore J. Lowi, *The End of Liberalism: The Second Republic of the United States*, 2nd ed. (New York: Norton, 1979), pp. 78–84.

The Department of Agriculture serves the many farming interests that, taken together, are one of the largest economic sectors of the United States.

Most clientele agencies locate a relatively large proportion of their total personnel in field offices dealing directly with their clientele. The Extension Service of the Department of Agriculture is among the most familiar, with its numerous local "extension agents" who consult with farmers on farm productivity. These same agencies also seek to foster the interests of their clientele by providing "functional representation"—that is, they try to learn what their clients' interests and needs are and then operate almost as a lobby in Washington on their behalf. In addition to the departments of Agriculture, the Interior, Labor, and Commerce, other clientele agencies include five of the newest cabinet departments: Housing and Urban Development (HUD), created in 1965; Transportation (DOT), created in 1966; Energy (DOE), created in 1977; Education (ED), created in 1979; and Health and Human Services (HHS), created in 1979.[8]

Agencies for the Maintenance of the Union

The Constitution entrusts many of the vital functions of public order, such as the police, to the state governments. But some agencies vital to maintaining national bonds do exist in the national government, and they can be grouped into three categories: (1) agencies for managing the sources of government revenue, (2) agencies for controlling conduct defined as a threat to internal national security, and (3) agencies for defending American security from external threats. The most powerful departments in these three areas are Treasury, Justice, Defense, State, and Homeland Security.

Revenue Agencies. The Treasury Department's Internal Revenue Service (IRS) is the most important revenue agency. The IRS is also one of the federal government's largest bureaucracies. Over 100,000 employees are spread throughout 4 regions, 63 districts, 10 service centers, and hundreds of local offices. In 2010, more than 140 million individual tax returns and nearly 2.5 million corporate returns were filed. In that same year, the IRS collected nearly $2.3 trillion in taxes from individuals and corporations.

Agencies for Internal Security. As long as the country is not in a state of insurrection, most of the task of maintaining the Union takes the form of legal work, and the main responsibility for that lies with the Department of Justice. It is indeed a luxury, and rare in the world, when national unity can be maintained by routines of civil law rather than imposed by military force. The largest and most important agency in the Justice Department is the Criminal Division, which is responsible for enforcing all the federal criminal laws except a few

---

8 Until 1979, the Department of Education and the Department of Health and Human Services were joined in a single department, Health, Education, and Welfare (HEW), which was established by Congress in 1953.

specifically assigned to other divisions. Criminal litigation is actually conducted by the U.S. attorneys. A presidentially appointed U.S. attorney is assigned to each federal judicial district, and he or she supervises the work of assistant U.S. attorneys. The work or jurisdictions of the Antitrust and Civil Rights Divisions are described by their official names. Although it looms so very large in American folklore, the FBI is simply another bureau of the Department of Justice. The FBI handles no litigation but instead serves as the information-gathering agency for all the other divisions.

In 2002, Congress created the Department of Homeland Security (DHS) to coordinate the nation's defense against the threat of terrorism. The new department is responsible for a number of tasks, including protecting commercial airlines from would-be hijackers. Most visible to the traveling public are the employees of the Transportation Security Administration (TSA). Consisting of 50,000 security officers and employees protecting airports and rail and bus depots, and staffing security screening operations, TSA is the largest unit of the DHS.

Agencies for External National Security. Two departments occupy center stage here, State and Defense. A few key agencies outside State and Defense also have external national-security functions.

Although diplomacy is generally considered the primary task of the State Department, diplomatic missions make up only one of its organizational dimensions. The State Department is also composed of geographic, or regional, bureaus concerned with all problems within that region of the world; "functional" bureaus, which handle such things as economic and business affairs, intelligence, and research; and international organizations and bureaus of internal affairs, which handle such areas as security, finance and management, and legal issues.

Despite the importance of the State Department in foreign affairs, fewer than 20 percent of all U.S. government employees working abroad are directly under its authority. By far the largest number of career government professionals working abroad are under the authority of the Defense Department.

The creation of the Department of Defense by legislation enacted between 1947 and 1949 was an effort to unify the two historic military departments, the War Department and the Navy Department, and integrate them into a new department, the Air Force Department. Real unification did not occur, however. Instead, the Defense Department added more pluralism to national security.

America's primary political problem with its military has been relatively mundane compared to the experience of many other countries, which have struggled to keep their militaries out of the politics of governing. Rather, the American military problem is that of pork-barrel politics: defense contracts are often incredibly lucrative for local districts, so military spending becomes a matter of parochial interests as well as military need. For instance, President Clinton's long list of proposed military-base closings, a major part of his budget-cutting drive for 1993, caused a firestorm of opposition even in his own party, with some of the opposition coming from members of Congress who otherwise prominently favored significant reductions in the Pentagon budget. Emphasis on jobs rather than strategy and policy means pork-barrel use of the military for political purposes. This is a classic way for a bureaucracy to defend itself politically in a democracy. It is the distributive tendency, in which the bureaucracy ensures political support among elected officials by making sure to distribute things—military bases, contracts, facilities, and jobs—to the states and districts that elected the legislators.

Regulatory Agencies

As we saw in Chapter 3, our national government did not even begin to get involved in the regulation of economic and social affairs until the late nineteenth century. Until then, regulation was strictly a state and local affair. The federal **regulatory agencies** are, as a result, relatively new, most dating from the 1930s. But they have come to be extensive and important. In this section, we look at these regulatory agencies as an administrative phenomenon, with its attendant politics.

The United States has many regulatory agencies. Some of these are bureaus within departments, such as the Food and Drug Administration (FDA) in the Department of Health and Human Services, and the Occupational Safety and Health Administration (OSHA) in the Department of Labor. Other regulatory agencies are independent regulatory commissions—for example, the Federal Trade Commission (FTC). But whether departmental or independent, an agency or commission is regulatory if Congress delegates to it relatively broad powers over a sector of the economy or a type of commercial activity and authorizes it to make rules governing the conduct of people and businesses within that jurisdiction. Rules made by regulatory agencies have the force and effect of legislation; indeed, the rules they make are referred to as **administrative legislation**. And when these agencies make decisions or orders settling disputes between parties or between the government and a party, they are acting like courts.

Because regulatory agencies exercise a tremendous amount of influence over the economy and because their rules are a form of legislation, Congress was at first loath to turn them over to the executive branch as ordinary agencies under the control of the president. Consequently, most of the important regulatory programs were delegated to independent commissions with direct responsibility to Congress rather than to the White House. This is the basis of the 1930s reference to them as the "headless fourth branch."[9] With the rise of presidential government, most recent presidents have supported more regulatory programs but have successfully opposed the expansion of regulatory independence. The 1960s and 1970s witnessed the adoption of an unprecedented number of new regulatory programs but only a few new independent commissions.

 regulatory agency

A department, bureau, or independent agency whose primary mission is to eliminate or restrict certain behaviors defined as negative in themselves or negative in their consequences

administrative legislation

Rules made by regulatory agencies and commissions

9 *Final Report of the President's Committee on Administrative Management* (Washington, DC: Government Printing Office, 1937). The term *headless fourth branch* was invented by a member of the committee staff, the Cornell University government professor Robert Cushman.

Agencies of Redistribution

Welfare, fiscal, and monetary agencies are responsible for the transfer of hundreds of billions of dollars annually between the public and the private spheres, and through such transfers these agencies influence how people and corporations spend and invest trillions of dollars annually. We call them agencies of redistribution because they influence the amount of money in the economy and because they directly influence who has money, who has credit, and whether people will want to invest or save their money rather than spend it.

Fiscal and Monetary Policy Agencies. Governmental activity affecting or relating to money may be partitioned into fiscal and monetary policy. **Fiscal policy** includes taxing and spending activities. **Monetary policy** focuses on banks, credit, and currency.

Administration of fiscal policy is primarily performed in the Treasury Department. It is no contradiction to include the Treasury both here and with the agencies for maintenance of the Union. This duplication indicates (1) that the Treasury is a complex department, performing more than one function of government and (2) that traditional controls have had to be adapted to modern economic conditions and new technologies.

Today, in addition to administering and policing income tax and other tax collections, the Treasury is responsible for managing the enormous federal debt. The Treasury Department also prints the currency that we use, a tool of monetary policy, but currency is only a tiny proportion of the entire money economy. Most of the trillions of dollars used in the transactions that make up the private and public sectors of the American economy exist on printed accounts and computers, not in currency.

Another important fiscal and monetary policy agency is the **Federal Reserve System**, headed by the Federal Reserve Board. The Federal Reserve System (the Fed) has authority over the credit rates and lending activities of the nation's most important banks. Established by Congress in 1913, the Fed is responsible for adjusting the supply of money to both the needs of banks in the different regions and the commerce and industry in each. It also ensures that banks do not overextend themselves by adopting lending policies that are too liberal. The basis for this responsibility is the fear that if there is a sudden economic scare, a run on a few banks might be contagious and cause another terrible crash like the one in 1929. The Federal Reserve Board sits at the top of a pyramid of 12 district Federal Reserve banks, which are "bankers' banks," serving the monetary needs of the hundreds of member banks in the national bank system. The subprime mortgage crisis of 2008 and 2009, which resulted after banks and other lenders provided home mortgages that proved unusually risky and led to home foreclosures, reflected gaps and loopholes in the regulation of the banking sector. In the midst of the crisis, the Fed played a major role in coping with the resulting recession by reducing interest rates to lower the price of borrowing and by overseeing support to struggling banks.

---

fiscal policy

Policies that regulate the economy through taxing and spending powers

---

monetary policy

Policies to regulate the economy through manipulation of the supply of money, the price of money (interest rate), and the availability of credit

---

Federal Reserve System (the Fed)

A system of 12 Federal Reserve banks that facilitates exchanges of cash, checks, and credit; regulates member banks; and uses monetary policies to fight inflation and deflation

---

Information and coordination of the nation's finances are provided by the Office of Management and Budget (OMB) in the White House and the Congressional Budget Office (CBO), an arm of the two legislative chambers. OMB organizes the president's budget and plays a coordinating role in clearing spending and regulatory decisions. CBO plays primarily an informational role, providing the legislative chambers and their committees with an assessment of budgetary proposals and conducting long-range forecasts of different budget, spending, and tax policies.

Welfare Agencies. No single government agency is responsible for all the programs making up the "welfare state." The largest agency in the field is the Social Security Administration (SSA), which manages the social insurance aspects of Social Security and Supplemental Security Income (SSI). These include massive expenditures that finance monthly Social Security checks for retirees, as well as payments to the disabled, the unemployed, and some other categories of individuals. They are funded by taxes levied on employees and employers. As the baby-boom generation ages, a growing bloc of voters (and their children) have become concerned about the solvency of this system. Many argue that without some adjustments in benefit schedules, taxes, or retirement age, the present population will begin drawing down the enormous amount of funds in the Social Security Trust Fund in two decades and exhaust it in 40 years (see the Analyzing the Evidence unit in Chapter 16 for a discussion of policy options for Social Security).

Agencies in the Department of Health and Human Services administer Temporary Assistance to Needy Families (TANF) and Medicaid, and the Department of Agriculture is responsible for the Food Stamp Program. With the exception of Social Security, these are *means-tested* programs, requiring applicants to demonstrate that their total annual cash earnings fall below an officially defined poverty line. These public-assistance programs create a large administrative burden. In August 1996, virtually all of the means-tested public-assistance programs were legally abolished as national programs and "devolved" to the states (see also Chapter 3).

THE PROBLEM OF BUREAUCRATIC CONTROL

Two centuries, millions of employees, and trillions of dollars after the Founding, we must return to James Madison's observation that "you must first enable the government to control the governed; and in the next place oblige it to control itself."[10] Today the problem is the same, but the form has changed. The problem

---

10 Alexander Hamilton, James Madison, and John Jay, *The Federalist Papers*, Clinton L. Rossiter, ed. (New York: New American Library, 1961), no. 51.

today is the challenge of keeping the government bureaucracy accountable to elected political authorities.

Motivational Considerations of Bureaucrats

The economist William Niskanen proposed that we regard a bureau or department of government as analogous to a division of a private firm and conceive of the bureaucrat just as we would the manager who runs that division.[11] In particular, Niskanen stipulated that the behavior of a bureau chief or department head be thought of as following the rationality principle. In this view the bureaucrat is a rational maximizer of her budget (just as the private-sector counterpart is a maximizer of his division's profits).

There are quite a number of motivational bases on which bureaucratic budget maximizing might be justified. A cynical (though some would say realistic) basis for budget maximizing is that the bureaucrat's own compensation is often tied to the size of her budget. Not only might bureaus with large budgets have higher-salaried executives with more elaborate fringe benefits but there also may be enhanced opportunities for career advancement, travel, a poshly appointed office, possibly even a chauffeur-driven limousine.

A second, related motivation for large budgets is nonmaterial personal gratification. An individual understandably enjoys the prestige and respect that comes from running a major enterprise. You can't take these things to the bank or put them on your family's dinner table, but your sense of esteem and your stature are surely buoyed by the conspicuous fact that your bureau or division has a large budget. That you are also boss of a large number of subordinates, made possible by a large bureau budget, is another aspect of this sort of ego gratification.

But personal salary, "on-the-job consumption," and power tripping are not the only forces driving a bureaucrat toward gaining as large a budget as possible. Some bureaucrats, perhaps most, actually *care* about their mission.[12] They initially choose to go into public safety, or the military, or health care, or social work, or education—as police officers, soldiers, hospital managers, social workers, and teachers, respectively—because they believe in the importance of helping people in their community. As they rise through the ranks of a public bureaucracy and assume management responsibilities, they take this mission orientation with them. Thus as chief of detectives in a big-city police department,

---

11 William A. Niskanen, Jr., *Bureaucracy and Representative Government* (Chicago: Aldine, 1971).

12 John Brehm and Scott Gates, *Working, Shirking, and Sabotage: Bureaucratic Response to a Democratic Public* (Ann Arbor: University of Michigan Press, 1997). For detailed insight about the motivations for government service combining the personal and the patriotic, consider the case of Henry Paulson, who became George W. Bush's Treasury secretary. Paulson's story is described well in Andrew Ross Sorkin, *Too Big to Fail* (New York: Viking, 2009), chap. 2.

as head of procurement in the air force, as director of nursing services in a public hospital, as supervisor of the social work division in a county welfare department, or as assistant superintendent of a town school system, individuals try to secure as large a budget as they can to succeed in achieving the mission to which they have devoted their professional lives.

Whether for cynical, self-serving motives or for the noblest of public purposes, it is entirely plausible that individual bureaucrats seek to persuade others (typically legislators or taxpayers) to provide them with as many resources as possible. Indeed, it is sometimes difficult to distinguish the saint from the sinner because each sincerely argues that he needs more to do more. This is one nice feature of the rationality principle in general, and Niskanen's assumption of budget maximizing in particular: it doesn't really matter *why* a bureaucrat is interested in a big budget; what matters is simply that she prefers more resources to fewer.

This does not mean that the legislature, which controls the bureau's budget, has to fork over whatever the bureau requests.[13] In making budget allocations, Congress can and often does evaluate a bureau's performance. Legislative committees hold hearings, request documentation on production, assign investigatory staff to various research tasks, and query bureau personnel on the veracity of their data and their use of the lowest-cost technologies (making it more difficult for the bureau to disguise on-the-job consumption). After the fact, the committees engage in oversight, making sure that what the legislature was told at the time when authorization and appropriations were voted actually holds in practice.

This doesn't mean budget maximizing is an implausible hypothesis about bureau motivations; it simply means that bureaus don't always get (all of) what they want. Reinforcing the budget-maximization objective of bureaus is the fact that bureaus are intimately associated with interest groups (their clienteles) and legislative committees and subcommittees whose members count those interest groups among their major supporters. All concur in giving the bureau resources to pursue commonly held goals and policies. These close connections between agency, interest group, and legislative committee are known as "cozy little triangles" and are also given such colorful labels as "policy whirlpools," "unholy trinities," and "policy subgovernments." According to this account, interest groups lobby legislators (and provide election support) for large bureau budgets; legislators deliver in providing authority and appropriations for bureaus; and bureaus, in turn, deliver by implementing favorable policies for interest groups. Interest groups express their appreciation by starting the cycle all over again. What sustains this system of policy making is, as we observed earlier, the weak incentives to oppose it. Legislators appalled by this arrangement in one policy area are often embedded in precisely this kind of arrangement in other areas. The president may try to trim its more outrageous manifestations, but his

---

13 This and other related points are drawn from Gary J. Miller and Terry M. Moe, "Bureaucrats, Legislators, and the Size of Government," *American Political Science Review* 77, no. 2 (June 1983): 297–323.

political capital is limited and he is not always willing to go to the mat to eliminate the practice entirely.

Before leaving motivational considerations, we should remark that budget maximizing is not the only objective that bureaucrats pursue. It needs to be emphasized and reemphasized that career civil servants and high-level political appointees are *politicians*. They spend their professional lives pursuing political goals, bargaining, forming alliances and coalitions, solving cooperation and collective action problems, making policy decisions, operating within and interfacing with political institutions—in short, doing what other politicians do. They do not have elections to win, but even elections affect their conditions of employment by determining the composition of the legislature and the partisan and ideological complexion of the chief executive. Bureaucrats are politicians beholden to other politicians for authority and resources. They are servants of many masters.

As politicians who are subject to the oversight and authority of others, bureaucrats must be strategic and forward thinking. Whichever party wins control of the House, Senate, and presidency, whoever becomes chair of the legislative committee with authorization or appropriation responsibility over their agency, bureau chiefs will have to adjust to the prevailing political winds. To protect and expand authority and resources, bureaucratic politicians seek, in the form of autonomy and discretion, insurance against political change. They don't always succeed in acquiring this freedom, but they do try to insulate themselves from changes in the broader political world.[14] So bureaucratic motivations include budget-maximizing behavior, to be sure, but bureaucrats also seek the autonomy to weather changes in the political atmosphere and the discretion and flexibility to achieve their goals.

Bureaucracy and the Principal-Agent Problem

As we have mentioned already, bureaucrats can be understood as the agents of elected officials (the principals). In any principal-agent relationship, two broad categories of control mechanisms enable a principal to guard against opportunistic or incompetent agent behavior. They can be illustrated by a homeowner (the principal) who seeks out a contractor (the agent) to remodel a kitchen. The first category of control is employed before the fact and depends on the reputation an agent possesses. One guards against selecting an incompetent or corrupt agent by relying on various methods for authenticating the promises made by the agent. These include advice from people you trust (your neighbors who just had their kitchen remodeled), certification by various official boards

---

14 For an expanded view of bureaucratic autonomy and insulation with historical application to the U.S. Department of Agriculture and the Post Office, see Daniel P. Carpenter, *The Forging of Bureaucratic Autonomy: Reputations, Networks, and Policy Innovation in Executive Agencies, 1862–1928* (Princeton, NJ: Princeton University Press, 2001).

(an association of kitchen contractors), credentials (specialized training programs), and interviews. Before-the-fact protection relies on the assumption that an agent's reputation is a valuable asset that she does not want to depreciate.

The second class of control mechanisms operates after the fact. Payment may be made contingent on completion of various tasks by specific dates, so that it may be withheld for nonperformance. Alternatively, financial incentives (for example, bonuses) for early or on-time completion may be part of the arrangement. An inspection process, after the work is completed, may lead to financial penalties, bonuses, or possibly even legal action. Of course, the principal can always seek legal relief for breach of contract, either in the form of an injunction stipulating that the agent comply or in the form of an order demanding that the agent pay damages.

How does the principal-agent problem apply to the president's and Congress's control of the bureaucracy?

Suppose the legislation that created the EPA required that after 10 years new legislation be passed renewing its existence and mandate. The issue facing the House, the Senate, and the president in their consideration of renewal involves how much authority to give this agency and how much money to permit it to spend. Suppose the House is conservative on environmental issues and prefers limited authority and a limited budget. The Senate wants the agency to have wide-ranging authority but is prepared to give it only slightly more resources than the House is (because of its concern with the budget deficit). The president is happy to split the difference between House and Senate on the matter of authority but feels beholden to environmental types and is thus prepared to shower the EPA with resources. Bureaucrats in the EPA want more authority than even the Senate is prepared to grant and more resources than even the president is willing to grant. Eventually relevant majorities in the House and the Senate (including the support of relevant committees) and the president agree on a policy reflecting a compromise among their various points of view.

The bureaucrats are not particularly pleased with this compromise because it gives them considerably less authority and funding than they had hoped for. If they flout the wishes of their principals and implement a policy exactly to their liking, they risk the unified wrath of the House, the Senate, and the president. Undoubtedly the politicians would react with new legislation (and they would also presumably find other political appointees and career bureaucrats at the EPA to replace the current bureaucratic leadership). If, however, the EPA implements some policy located between its own preferences and the preferences of its principals, it might be able to get away with it. That is, at the margin, the bureau tilts policy toward its own preferences, but the tilt is subtle enough so as not to stimulate a legislative response.

Thus we have a principal-agent relationship in which a political principal—a collective principal consisting of the president and coalitions in the House and Senate—formulates policy and creates an implementation agent to execute its details. The agent, however, has policy preferences of its own and, unless subjected to further controls, will inevitably implement a policy that drifts toward its ideal.

bureaucratic drift

The oft-observed phenomenon of bureaucratic implementation that produces policy more to the liking of the bureaucracy than faithful to the original intention of the legislation that created it, but without triggering a political reaction from elected officials

A variety of controls might conceivably restrict this **bureaucratic drift**. Indeed, legislative scholars often point to congressional hearings in which bureaucrats may be publicly humiliated; annual appropriations decisions that may be used to punish out-of-control bureaus; and watchdog agents, such as the Government Accountability Office, that may be used to monitor and scrutinize the bureau's performance. But these all come after the fact and may be only partially credible threats to the agency.[15]

Before-the-Fact Controls. The most powerful before-the-fact political weapon is the appointment process. The adroit control of the political stance of a given bureau by the president and Congress, through their joint powers of nomination and confirmation (especially if they can arrange for appointees who closely share the political consensus on policy), is a self-enforcing mechanism for ensuring reliable agent performance.

A second powerful before-the-fact weapon, following from the institution principle, is procedural controls. The general rules and regulations that direct the manner in which federal agencies conduct their affairs are contained in the Administrative Procedure Act. This act is almost always the boilerplate of legislation creating and renewing federal agencies. It is not uncommon, however, for an agency's procedures to be tailored to suit particular circumstances.

Coalitional Drift as a Collective Action Problem. Not only do politicians want the legislative deals that they strike to be faithfully implemented by the bureaucracy, but they also want those deals to endure. This is especially problematic in American political life, with its shifting alignments and absence of permanent political cleavages. Today's coalition transforms itself overnight. Opponents today are partners tomorrow, and vice versa. A victory today, even one implemented in a favorable manner by the bureaucracy, may unravel tomorrow. What is to be done?

To some extent, legislators are disinclined to undo legislation. If a coalition votes for handsome subsidies to grain farmers, say, it is very hard to reverse this policy without the gatekeeping and agenda-setting assistance of members on the House and Senate Agriculture Committees, yet their members undoubtedly participated in the initial deal and are unlikely to turn against it. But even these structural units are unstable; old politicians depart, and new ones are enlisted. For example, by winning control of the House in the 2010 midterm elections, the Republican majority had opportunities to overturn legislation passed in the Democratic-dominated 111th Congress. In particular, Republicans were eager to reverse the 2010 health care reform. While Democratic control of the Senate

---

15 For the classic statement that, despite before-the-fact and after-the-fact tools available to the political principals, the bureau-agent will "drift" in policy implementation toward its own preferences, see Mathew D. McCubbins, Roger G. Noll, and Barry R. Weingast, "Structure and Process; Politics and Policy: Administrative Arrangements and the Political Control of Agencies," *Virginia Law Review* 75 (1989): 431–82.

and presidency did not allow this to happen, the Republicans in the House retain the possibility of blocking spending measures to implement parts of the health care legislation.

What this means is that legislatively formulated and bureaucratically implemented output is subject to **coalitional drift**.[16] To prevent shifting coalitional patterns among politicians from endangering carefully fashioned policies, one step the legislature might take is insulate the bureaucracy and its implementation activities from legislative interventions. If an enacting coalition makes it difficult for its *own* members to intervene in implementation, then it also makes it difficult for enemies of the policy to disrupt the flow of bureaucratic output. This political insulation can be provided by giving bureaucratic agencies long lives, their political heads long terms of office and wide-ranging administrative authority, and other political appointees overlapping terms of office and secure sources of revenue. This insulation comes at a price, however. The civil servants and political appointees of bureaus insulated from political overseers are thereby empowered to pursue independent courses of action. Protection from coalitional drift comes at the price of an increased potential for bureaucratic drift. It is one of the great trade-offs in the field of intergovernmental relations.

 coalitional drift

The prospect that enacted policy will change because the composition of the enacting coalition is temporary and provisional

The President as Manager-in-Chief

In 1937, President Franklin Delano Roosevelt's Committee on Administrative Management gave official sanction to an idea that had been growing increasingly urgent: "The president needs help." The national government had grown rapidly during the preceding 25 years, but the structures and procedures necessary to manage the burgeoning executive branch had not yet been established. The response to the call for help for the president initially took the form of three management policies: (1) all communications and decisions that related to executive policy decisions must pass through the White House; (2) to cope with such a flow, the White House must have an adequate staff of specialists in research, analysis, legislative and legal writing, and public affairs; and (3) the White House must have additional staff to follow through on presidential decisions—to ensure that those decisions are made, communicated to Congress, and carried out by the appropriate agency.

Establishing a management capacity for the presidency began in earnest with Roosevelt, but it did not stop there. The story of the modern presidency can be told largely as a series of responses to the plea for managerial help.

---

16 This idea, offered as a supplement to the analysis of bureaucratic drift, is found in Murray J. Horn and Kenneth A. Shepsle, "Administrative Process and Organizational Form as Legislative Responses to Agency Costs," *Virginia Law Review* 75 (1989): 499–509. It is further elaborated in Kenneth A. Shepsle, "Bureaucratic Drift, Coalitional Drift, and Time Consistency," *Journal of Law, Economics, and Organization* 8 (1992): 111–8.

Indeed, each expansion of the national government into new policies and programs in the twentieth century was accompanied by a parallel expansion of the president's management authority. This pattern began even before Roosevelt's presidency, with the policy innovations of President Woodrow Wilson between 1913 and 1920. Congress responded to Wilson's policies with the 1921 Budget and Accounting Act, which conferred on the White House agenda-setting power over budgeting. The president, in his annual budget message, transmits comprehensive budgetary recommendations to Congress. Because Congress retains ultimate legislative authority, a president's proposals are sometimes said to be dead on arrival on Capitol Hill. Nevertheless, the power to frame deliberations is potent and constitutes an important management tool. Each successive president has continued this pattern of setting the congressional agenda, creating what we now know as the managerial presidency.

Along with the development of the managerial presidency came expectations of administrative competence. Presidents are now *expected* to be CEOs and are roundly criticized for ineptitude. For example, President Clinton was often disparaged for the way he managed his administration. (Clinton's easygoing approach led critics to liken his management style to college bull sessions.) George W. Bush was the first president with a graduate degree in business. His management strategy followed a standard business-school dictum: select skilled subordinates and delegate responsibility to them. Bush followed this model closely in his appointment of highly experienced officials to cabinet positions. This was no guarantee of policy success as doubts emerged about the conduct of the Iraq War and the administration's mishandling of relief to New Orleans and the Gulf Coast after Hurricane Katrina. Barack Obama's administrative style fell somewhere in between his two predecessors. He selected highly talented and self-assured manager-politicians at the State (Hillary Clinton) and Defense (Robert Gates) departments. Yet he brought a "Chicago crowd" to the White House, led by chief-of-staff Rahm Emmanuel, who choreographed administrative policy from the center.

Congressional Oversight and Incentives

Congress is constitutionally essential to responsible bureaucracy because the key to governmental responsibility is legislation. When a law is passed and its intent is clear, then the president knows what to "faithfully execute," and the responsible agency understands what is expected of it. In our modern age, legislatures rarely make laws directly for citizens; most laws are really instructions to bureaucrats and their agencies. But when Congress enacts vague legislation, agencies must rely on their own interpretations. The president and the federal courts step in to tell them what the legislation intended. And so do intensely interested organized groups. But when everybody—from the president to the courts to interest groups—gets involved in the interpretation of legislative intent, to whom is the agency responsible?

The answer lies in the process of **oversight**. The more legislative power Congress has delegated to the executive bureaucracy, the more it has sought

oversight

The effort by Congress, through hearings, investigations, and other techniques, to exercise control over the activities of executive agencies to get back into the game through committee and subcommittee oversight of the agencies. (See the Analyzing the Evidence unit for a discussion of control of the bureaucracy.) The standing committee system in Congress is well suited for oversight, inasmuch as most of the congressional committees and subcommittees are organized with jurisdictions roughly parallel to one or more executive departments or agencies. Appropriations committees as well as authorization committees have oversight powers, as do their subcommittees. In addition to these, there is a committee on government operations in both the House and the Senate, each with oversight powers not limited by departmental jurisdiction.

The best indication of Congress's oversight efforts is the holding of public hearings, before which bureaucrats and other witnesses are summoned to discuss and defend agency budgets and decisions. Committee or subcommittee hearings in 2012, for example, focused on a wide range of topics including the attack on the U.S. consulate in Benghazi, Libya, the Dodd-Frank financial service act, the impact of Hurricane Sandy, climate change science, and the Freedom of Information Act. Hearings, in short, apply to the full range of government activities. In the case of the U.S. consulate in Benghazi, both the Department of State and the Central Intelligence Agency were aggressively questioned about their respective security failures that led to the deaths of four Americans, including the U.S. ambassador, and the destruction of the facility.

However, often the most effective and the most influential control over bureaucratic accountability is the power of the purse—the ability of the House and Senate committees and subcommittees on appropriations to look at agency performance through the microscope of the annual appropriations process. This process makes bureaucrats attentive to Congress, especially members of the relevant authorizing committee and appropriations subcommittee, because they know that Congress has a chance each year to reduce their authority or funding.[17] This may be another explanation for why there may be some downsizing but almost no terminations of federal agencies.

Oversight can also be carried out by individual members of Congress. Such inquiries addressed to bureaucrats are considered standard congressional "casework" and can turn up significant questions of public responsibility even when the motive is only to meet the demand of an individual constituent. Oversight also very often takes place through communications between congressional staff and agency staff. Congressional staff has grown tremendously since the Legislative Reorganization Act of 1946, and the legislative staff, especially the staff of the committees, is just as professionalized and specialized as the staff of an executive agency. In addition, Congress has created for itself three quite large agencies whose obligations are to engage in constant research on problems taking place in the executive branch: the Government Accountability Office, the Congressional Research Service, and the Congressional Budget Office. Each

---

17 See Aaron Wildavsky, *The New Politics of the Budgetary Process*, 2nd ed. (New York: HarperCollins, 1992), pp. 15−6.

Congressional Design and Control of the Bureaucracy

Contributed by
Sean Gailmard
University of California,
Berkeley

Who controls the bureaucracy? Scholars usually argue that political principals try to make bureaucratic agents responsive to their own direction. For example, Congress tries to make agencies choose policies that Congress prefers through oversight and threat of budget reductions. Paradoxically, however, in some cases the best agent for Congress is not one that is controlled by Congress itself but by some other political principal.

When might this be true? On some issues, the president exercises substantially more authority over the direction of public policy than other issues. This is true of foreign policy and defense. The president sets the agenda for U.S. diplomacy, can commit U.S. troops to battle without the prior approval of Congress, and plays an important role in the use of U.S. armed forces as commander in chief.

In order to use this authority effectively, the president needs advice that he trusts. Congress could try to control the bureaucratic agents that advise the president on foreign and defense policy. But if congressional interests conflict with those of the president, such agents might not be effective or trusted advisers to the president. A better alternative for Congress is to let the president control these agents himself. This will build trust and make the agencies' advice more helpful to the president as he exercises his formidable policy authority in foreign affairs and defense. Ultimately, informed use of this policy authority by the president is good for Congress too.[1]

Congress can influence how much control different political principals exert over agencies in its decision about where the agencies are "located" within the executive branch. The location of an agency within the executive branch is determined in the legislation creating that agency.

Organization of the Executive Branch

- President
- Executive office of the president
- Cabinet departments
- Independent agencies

The president's closest advisers (e.g., national security adviser, budget director) are in the executive office of the president (EOP). Senior members serve at the pleasure of the president and help him formulate policy. In cabinet departments (e.g., Department of State, Department of Agriculture), senior staff also serve at the pleasure of the president, and major policy decisions are reviewed by the EOP. Independent agencies (e.g., Securities and Exchange Commission, Federal Communications Commission) are the furthest removed from presidential control. Senior officers cannot be dismissed by the president simply for disagreements over policy, and major policy decisions are not reviewed by the EOP.

If Congress wishes the president to have relatively more control over agencies involved in foreign policy and defense than over agencies involved primarily in domestic affairs, then it should locate those agencies closer to the president within the executive branch. This expectation is borne out.[2]

Percentage of Agencies in Each Sphere of the Executive Branch

For all agencies created in legislation between 1946 and 2000, Congress was twice as likely to locate foreign and defense policy agencies in the EOP than domestic policy agencies. The reverse is true for independent agencies and commissions. Overall, when Congress designs agencies, it appears to consider the effect of bureaucratic structure on the ease of control by the relevant political principals.

☐ Domestic policy agencies

▨ Foreign/defense policy agencies

1   Sean Gailmard and John W. Patty, *Learning While Governing: Institutions and Accountability in the Executive Branch* (Chicago: University of Chicago Press, 2012).

2   Data are from David E. Lewis, *Presidents and the Politics of Agency Design: Political Insulation in the United States Government Bureaucracy, 1946–1997* (Palo Alto, CA: Stanford University Press, 2003).

is designed to give Congress information independent of the information it can get through hearings and other communications directly with the executive branch.[18]

Congressional Oversight: Abdication or Strategic Delegation?

Congress often grants the executive-branch bureaucracies discretion in determining certain features of a policy during the implementation phase. Although the complexities of governing a modern industrialized democracy make the granting of discretion necessary, some argue that Congress not only gives unelected bureaucrats too much discretion but also delegates too much policy-making authority to them. Congress, they say, has transferred so much power that it has created a "runaway bureaucracy" in which unelected officials accountable neither to the electorate nor to Congress make important policy decisions.[19] By enacting vague statutes that give bureaucrats broad discretion, so the argument goes, members of Congress effectively abdicate their constitutionally designated roles and effectively remove themselves from the policy-making process. Ultimately this extreme delegation has left the legislative branch weak and ineffectual and has dire consequences for the health of our democracy.

Others claim that even though Congress may possess the tools to engage in effective oversight, it fails to use them, as we do not see Congress actively engaging in much oversight activity.[20] However, Mathew McCubbins and Thomas Schwartz argue that these critics have focused on the wrong type of oversight and have missed a type of oversight that benefits members of Congress in their bids for re-election (in accord with the rationality principle).[21] McCubbins and Schwartz distinguish between two types of oversight: police patrol and fire alarm. Under the police-patrol variety, Congress systematically initiates

---

18 Until 1983, there was still another official tool of legislative oversight, the legislative veto. Each executive agency was obliged to submit to Congress proposed decisions or rules. These were to lie before both houses for 30 to 60 days; then, if Congress took no explicit action by a one-house or two-house resolution to veto a proposed measure, it became law. The legislative veto was declared unconstitutional by the Supreme Court in 1983 on the grounds that it violated the separation of powers because the resolutions Congress passed to exercise its veto were not subject to a presidential veto, as required by the Constitution. See *Immigration and Naturalization Service v. Chadha,* 462 U.S. 919 (1983). On the congressional staff more generally, see Robert H. Salisbury and Kenneth A. Shepsle, "Congressman as Enterprise," *Legislative Studies Quarterly* 6 (1981): 559–76. On the role and activities of the Government Accountability Office, see Anne Joseph O'Connell, "Auditing Politics or Political Auditing?" UC Berkeley Public Law Research Paper no. 964656 (2007), http://ssrn.com/abstract=964656 (accessed 12/8/12).

19 Lowi, *The End of Liberalism*; and Lawrence C. Dodd and Richard L. Schott, *Congress and the Administrative State* (New York: Wiley, 1979).

20 Morris S. Ogul, *Congress Oversees the Bureaucracy: Studies in Legislative Supervision* (Pittsburgh, PA: University of Pittsburgh Press, 1976); and Peter Woll, *American Bureaucracy,* 2nd ed. (New York: Norton, 1977).

21 McCubbins and Schwartz, "Congressional Oversight Overlooked."

investigation into the activity of agencies. Under the fire-alarm variety, members of Congress do not initiate investigations but wait for adversely affected citizens or interest groups to bring bureaucratic perversions of legislative intent to the attention of the relevant congressional committee. To make sure that individuals and groups bring these violations to members' attention—to set off the fire alarm, so to speak—Congress passes laws that help individuals and groups make claims against the bureaucracy, granting them legal standing before administrative agencies and federal courts.

McCubbins and Schwartz argue that fire-alarm oversight is more efficient than the police-patrol variety, given costs and the electoral incentives of members of Congress. Why should members spend their scarce resources (mainly time) to initiate investigations without having any evidence that they will reap electoral rewards? Police-patrol oversight can waste taxpayers' dollars too, because many investigations will not turn up any evidence of violations of legislative intent. It is much more cost effective for members to conserve their resources and then claim credit for fixing the problem (and saving the day) after the fire alarms have been sounded.

On the other hand, bureaucratic drift might be contained if Congress spent more of its time clarifying its legislative intent and less of its time on oversight activity. If its original intent in the law were clearer, Congress could then afford to defer to presidential management to maintain bureaucratic responsibility. Bureaucrats are more responsive to clear legislative guidance than to anything else. But when Congress and the president are at odds (or coalitions within Congress are at odds), bureaucrats have an opportunity to evade responsibility by playing one side off against the other.

Policy Implications. Because the bureaucracy finds itself squarely in the middle of the separation of powers between the legislature and the executive, it often manages to elude systematic and comprehensive review and oversight. The institution principle suggests as much. Rational political actors in both branches will pay some attention to the bureaucracy, but as we have just seen, their own goals and objectives may not be well served by obsessive attention. The result is a bureaucracy that retains some discretion—partly because political actors' own specialization and expertise warrant it, but also because political arrangements permit their oversight to fall between the institutional cracks. Bureaus, in turn, perform their missions in ways that aim to maintain this kind of independence. They produce rulings, interpretations, and particular implementations of policy in order to deter after-the-fact oversight, allowing sleeping dogs (potential overseers) to lie.

Rational political adaptations to these institutional arrangements have policy consequences. In particular, bureaucrats will be extraordinarily attentive to the policy needs of those legislators who are in a position to help or harm them. Thus, states and districts represented on the House and Senate authorizing committees, as well as on the relevant appropriations subcommittees, can expect to have government largesse steered their way. Legislative lore points to instances in which, for example, a major weapons system is sustained politically by an implicit agreement between Defense Department agents and private-sector contractors to ensure that subcontracts are distributed, geographically, to politically significant locations.

Repeat this pattern of deals among agency officials, powerful legislators, and private-sector special interests over many projects in many policy areas and we have a "distributive tendency" in which successful play of the political game by legislators and bureaucrats requires the wide distribution of spending. More efficient targeting of spending takes a backseat to the practical politics of making sure the "right" states and districts are taken care of. One classic example of the distributive tendency is found in the attempt by President Lyndon Johnson in the mid-1960s to focus federal assistance on those central cities in direst need of economic stimulus. His Model Cities program identified 10 cities in desperate straits. But 10 was too small a number in a political system with 50 states and 435 legislative districts. By the time Johnson's proposal had worked its way through the legislative process, the relevant bureaucratic entities had been given discretion to spread funds to many distressed cities—numbering in the hundreds when all was said and done—rather than concentrating assistance on the most desperate ones. The policy principle suggests that institutional arrangements (bicameralism and the separation of powers, in this instance) combined with rational political behavior (re-election motivations of legislators and programmatic survival instincts of bureaucrats) produce policy distortions (the wide distribution of funds to sustain programs and to avoid the risk of critical oversight).

REFORMING THE BUREAUCRACY

Americans like to complain about bureaucracy. Americans don't like big government because big government means big bureaucracy, and bureaucracy means the federal service—about 2.8 million civilian and 1.4 million military employees.[22] Promises to cut the bureaucracy are popular campaign appeals; "cutting out the fat," with big reductions in the number of federal employees, is held out as a surefire way of cutting the deficit.

Despite fears of bureaucratic growth's getting out of hand, however, the federal service has hardly grown at all during the past 30 years; it reached its peak post–World War II level in 1968 with 2.9 million civilian employees plus an additional 3.6 million military personnel (a figure swollen by the war in Vietnam). The number of civilian federal executive-branch employees has since remained close to that figure. The growth of the federal service is even less imposing when placed in the context of the total workforce and compared to the size of state and local public employment, which was 16.3 million full- and part-time employees in 2011.[23] Figure 8.3 indicates that since 1950 the ratio of federal service

22 U.S. Bureau of the Census, *Statistical Abstract of the United States, 2011* (Washington, DC: Government Printing Office, 2011), tables 494 and 508.

23 U.S. Bureau of the Census, www.census.gov/govs/.

Figure 8.3

EMPLOYEES IN THE FEDERAL SERVICE: TOTAL NUMBER AS A PERCENTAGE OF THE WORKFORCE

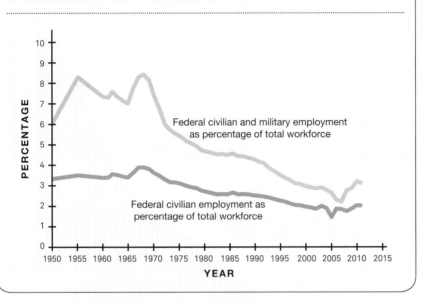

NOTE: Workforce includes unemployed persons.

SOURCES: Tax Foundation, *Facts and Figures on Government Finance* (Baltimore: Johns Hopkins University Press, 1990), pp. 22, 44; Office of Management and Budget, *Budget of the U.S. Government, Fiscal Year 2009*, table 17.5; U.S. Bureau of Labor Statistics, "Employment Status of the Civilian Population by Sex and Age," *Labor Force Statistics from the Current Population Survey*, http://stats.bls.gov/webapps/legacy/cpsatab1.htm, table A1, and U.S. Office of Personnel Management, Historical Federal Workforce Tables.

employment to the total workforce has been fairly steady, declining only slightly in the past 25 years. Another useful comparison is to be found in Figure 8.4: Although the dollar increase in federal spending shown by the bars looks impressive, the orange line indicates that even here the national government has simply kept pace with the growth of the economy. During the Clinton years, federal outlays as a percent of the size of the economy (GDP) actually declined. During the Bush years, this percent steadily grew (from 18.5 percent to over 20 percent). During the first four years of Obama's presidency, outlays rose to 25 percent of GDP, in large part an effect of the great recession and financial crisis (smaller GDP) and the response to it (larger outlays).

In sum, the national government is indeed very large, but the federal service has not been growing any faster than the economy or the society. The same is roughly true of the growth pattern of state and local public personnel. Our bureaucracy keeps pace with our society, despite our seeming dislike for it, because we cannot operate the control towers, the prisons, the Social Security system, and other essential elements of the state without it. And we

Figure 8.4
ANNUAL FEDERAL OUTLAYS

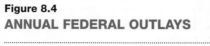
As percentage of GDP (right scale)

In current dollars (left scale)

BILLIONS OF DOLLARS

PERCENTAGE OF GROSS DOMESTIC PRODUCT (GDP)

YEAR

estimate

NOTE: Data for 2012–17 are estimated.
SOURCE: Office of Management and Budget, *Budget of the U.S. Government, Fiscal Year 2013*, Tables 1.1 and 1.2.

certainly could not conduct wars in Iraq and Afghanistan without a gigantic military bureaucracy.

Nevertheless, some Americans continue to argue that bureaucracy is too big and that it should be reduced. In the 1990s, Americans seemed particularly enthusiastic about reducing the federal bureaucracy. However, following the attacks of September 11, 2001, and during the deep economic recession beginning in December 2007, popular sentiment for an enlarged role for government grew.

Termination

The only *certain* way to reduce the size of the bureaucracy is to eliminate programs. But most agencies have a supportive constituency—people and groups that benefit from the programs—that will fight to reinstate any cuts that are made. Termination is the only way to ensure an agency's reduction, and it is a rare occurrence.

The overall lack of success in terminating bureaucracy is a reflection of Americans' love-hate relationship with the national government. As antagonistic as Americans may be toward bureaucracy in general, they grow attached to the services rendered and protections offered by particular bureaucratic agencies—that is, they fiercely defend their favorite agencies while perceiving no inconsistency between that defense and their antagonistic attitude toward the bureaucracy in general. A good case in point was the agonizing problem of closing military bases in the wake of the end of the Cold War, when the United States no longer needed so many bases. Because every base is in some congressional member's district, it proved impossible for Congress to decide to close any of them. Consequently, between 1988 and 1990, Congress established the Defense Base Closure and Realignment Commission to decide on base closings. Even though the matter is now out of Congress's hands altogether, the process has been slow and agonizing.

Elected leaders have come to rely on a more incremental approach to downsizing the bureaucracy. They have done much by budgetary means, reducing the budgets of all agencies across the board by small percentages and cutting some poorly supported agencies by larger amounts. Yet these changes are still incremental, leaving the existence of agencies unaddressed.

An additional approach has been taken to thwart the highly unpopular regulatory agencies, which are so small (relatively) that cutting their budgets contributes virtually nothing to reducing the deficit. This approach is called **deregulation**, simply defined as a reduction in the number of rules promulgated by regulatory agencies. But deregulation by rule reduction is still incremental and has certainly not satisfied the hunger of the American public in general and Washington representatives in particular for a genuine reduction in the size of the bureaucracy.

 deregulation

The policy of reducing or eliminating regulatory restraints on the conduct of individuals or private institutions

Devolution

An alternative to genuine reduction in the size of the bureaucracy is **devolution**—downsizing the federal bureaucracy by delegating the implementation of programs to state and local governments. Indirect evidence for this is seen in Figure 8.5, which shows the increase in state and local government employment against a backdrop of flat or declining federal employment. This evidence suggests a growing share of governmental actions taking place on the state and local levels.

Devolution often alters the pattern of who benefits most from government programs. In the early 1990s, a major devolution in transportation policy sought to open up decisions about transportation to a new set of interests. Since the 1920s, transportation policy had been dominated by road-building interests in the federal and state governments. Many advocates for cities and many environmentalists believed that the emphasis on road building hurt cities and harmed the environment. The 1992 reform, initiated by environmentalists, put more power into the hands of metropolitan planning organizations and lifted

 devolution

The policy of removing a program from one level of government by deregulating it or passing it down to a lower level, such as from the national government to the state and local governments

Figure 8.5
GOVERNMENT EMPLOYMENT

NOTE: Federal government employment figures include civilians only. Military employment figures include only active-duty personnel.
SOURCE: U.S. Bureau of the Census, *Statistical Abstract of the United States*, 2011 and 2012 (Washington, DC: Government Printing Office, 2011).

many federal restrictions on how the money should be spent. Reformers hoped that these changes would open up the decision-making process so that those advocating alternatives to road building, such as mass transit, bike paths, and walkways, would have more influence over how federal transportation dollars were spent. Although the pace of change has been slow, devolution has indeed brought new voices to decisions about transportation spending, and alternatives to highways have received increasing attention.

Often the central aim of devolution is to provide more efficient and more flexible government services. Yet by its very nature, devolution entails variation across the states. In some states, government services may improve as a consequence of devolution. In other states, services may deteriorate as the states use devolution as an opportunity to cut spending and reduce services. This has been the pattern in the implementation of the welfare reform passed in 1996, the most significant devolution of federal social programs in many decades. Some states, such as Wisconsin, have used the flexibility of the reform to design innovative programs that respond to clients' needs; other states, such as Idaho, have virtually dismantled their welfare programs. Because the legislation placed a five-year lifetime limit on receiving welfare, the states will take on an even greater role in the future as existing clients lose their eligibility for federal benefits. Welfare reform has been praised by many for reducing welfare rolls and responding to the public desire that welfare be a temporary program. At the same time, it has placed more low-income women and their children at risk of being left with no form of assistance at all.

Privatization

Privatization, another downsizing option, may seem like a synonym for termination, but that is true only at the extreme. Most of what is called privatization is not termination at all but the provision of government goods and services by private contractors under direct government supervision. Except for top-secret strategic materials, virtually all of the production of military hardware, from boats to bullets, is done on a privatized basis by private contractors. Billions of dollars of research services are bought under contract by government; these private contractors are universities as well as ordinary industrial corporations and private think tanks. **Privatization** simply means that a public purpose is provided under contract by a private company.[24] But such programs are still very much government programs; they are paid for by government and supervised by government. Privatization downsizes the government only in that the workers providing the service are no longer counted as part of the government bureaucracy.

 privatization

The act of moving all or part of a program from the public sector to the private sector

The central aim of privatization is to reduce the cost of government. When private contractors can perform a task as well as a government but for less money, taxpayers win. Government workers are generally unionized and, therefore, receive good pay and generous benefits. Private-sector workers are less likely to be unionized, and private firms often provide lower pay and fewer benefits. For this reason, public-sector unions have been one of the strongest voices arguing against privatization. Other critics of privatization observe that private firms may not be more efficient or less costly than government. This is especially likely when there is little competition among private firms and public bureaucracies are not granted a fair chance to bid in the contracting competition.

---

24 A more general term is *outsourcing*. Privatization is outsourcing to the private sector. Devolution is outsourcing to a lower level of government. A third example of outsourcing is the opposite of devolution, as when a small community contracts with a county for, say, police services.

When private firms have a monopoly on service provision, they may be more expensive than government.

There are important questions about how private contractors can be held accountable. As one analyst of Pentagon spending put it, "The Pentagon is supposed to be representing the taxpayer and the public interest—its national security. So it's really important to have transparency, to be able to see these competitions and hold people accountable."[25] As security has become the nation's paramount concern, new worries about privatization have surfaced. Some Pentagon officials fear that too many tasks vital to national security may have already been contracted out and that national security might best be served by limiting privatization.

The new demands of domestic security have altered the thrust of bureaucratic reform. Despite the strong agreement on the goal of fighting terrorism, the effort to streamline the bureaucracy by focusing on a single purpose is likely to face considerable obstacles along the way. Reform of public bureaucracies is always complex because strong constituencies may attempt to block changes that they believe will harm them. Initiatives that aim to improve coordination among agencies can easily provoke political disputes if the proposed changes threaten to alter the access of groups to the bureaucracy. And groups that oppose bureaucratic changes can appeal to Congress to intervene on their behalf.

CONCLUSION

Bureaucracy is one of humanity's most significant inventions. It is an institutional arrangement that allows for division and specialization of labor, harnesses expertise, and coordinates collective action for social, political, and economic purposes. It enables governments to exist and perform. In this chapter, we have focused on what public bureaucracies do, how they are organized at the national level in the United States, and how they are controlled (or not) by elected politicians.

At a theoretical level, public bureaucracy is the concrete expression of rational, purposeful, political action. Elected politicians have goals—as broad as defending the realm, maintaining public health and safety, or promoting economic growth; as narrow as securing a post office for Possum Hollow, Pennsylvania, or an exit off the interstate highway for Springfield, Massachusetts. Bureaucracy is the instrument by which political objectives, established by elected legislators and executives, are transformed from ideas, concepts, and intentions into the actual "bricks and mortar" of implemented policies.

---

25 Ellen Nakashima, "Defense Balks at Contract Goals: Essential Services Should Not Be Privatized, Pentagon Tells OMB," *Washington Post*, January 30, 2002, p. A21.

At a practical level, this transformation depends upon the motivations of bureaucratic agents and the institutional machinery created when a bureaucratic entity is formed or reformed. Elected politicians engage in institutional design in creating agencies. They have their greatest impact at this point. Once an agency is up and running, elected officials only imperfectly control their bureaucratic agents. Institutional arrangements, and simple human nature, provide a certain amount of insulation to agencies, enabling bureaucrats to march to their own drummers, at least some of the time. Of course, bureaucrats are not entirely free agents. But control is a constant and recurring problem for elected officials.

The policy principle suggests that the combination of bureaucratic arrangements and individual motivations produce evident patterns in policy. Because of its insulation, an agency's policies, once underway, are difficult to reverse. Insulation thwarts only but the most intensely expressed interventions in the affairs of an agency. This has the benefit of commitment—interested parties are reassured about the continued provision of a bureaucratic product or service. The farmer can rely on his subsidy check; the senior citizen can count on her monthly Social Security stipend; truckers and other motorists can be secure in the expectation that the interstate highways will be there for them.

But these commitments have distributive costs. Bureaucrats will be most attentive to the most intense interested parties. As a consequence, policies will come to be skewed in particular ways. The efficiency gains that come from the expertise and coordinating services of bureaucracy are thus dissipated by these political pressures. For example, highway funds will find their way disproportionately to the states and districts of legislators who sit on the public works authorizing and appropriating committees. For the last quarter century, until 2009, Alaska was a major beneficiary of infrastructure expenditures precisely because one of its senators (Ted Stevens) and its lone representative (Don Young) were powerhouses in their respective legislative chambers.

In describing the federal bureaucracy in this chapter, we hope we have made clear the ways in which rationality, institutional processes, and the resulting policy outputs are a consequence of the way in which agencies straddle the divide produced by the separation of powers. Attuned partly to the executive and partly to the legislature, bureaucratic agents tread a careful line between their several masters, protected in part by the natural insulation associated with bureaucracy but vulnerable to intense political pressure. Politics is at the very heart of these organizations and the policies they produce.

For Further Reading

Selections highlighted in red are included in *Readings in American Politics: Analysis and Perspectives,* Third Edition.

Aberbach, Joel, and Bert A. Rockman. *In the Web of Politics: Three Decades of the U.S. Federal Executive.* Washington, DC: Brookings Institution, 2000.

Besley, Timothy. *Principled Agents? Motivations and Incentives in Politics.* Oxford, UK: Oxford University Press, 2006.

Brehm, John, and Scott Gates. *Working, Shirking, and Sabotage: Bureaucratic Response to a Democratic Public.* Ann Arbor: University of Michigan Press, 1997.

Downs, Anthony. *Inside Bureaucracy.* Boston: Little, Brown, 1966.

Fiorina, Morris P. "Legislative Choice of Regulatory Forms: Legal Process or Administrative Process." *Public Choice* 39 (1982): 33–66.

Gailmard, Sean, and John W. Patty. *Learning While Governing: Expertise and Accountability in the Executive Branch.* Chicago: University of Chicago Press, 2013.

Goodsell, Charles. *The Case for Bureaucracy.* 4th ed. Washington, DC: CQ Press, 2003.

Heclo, Hugh. *On Thinking Institutionally.* Boulder, CO: Paradigm, 2007.

Huber, John, and Charles Shipan. *Deliberate Discretion? The Institutional Foundations of Bureaucratic Autonomy.* New York: Cambridge University Press, 2002.

Kerwin, Cornelius M., and Scott R. Furlong. *Rulemaking.* 4th ed. Washington, DC: CQ Press, 2010.

Kettl, Donald F., and James Fesler. *The Politics of the Administrative Process.* 3rd ed. Washington, DC: Brookings Institution, 2005.

Light, Paul C. *The True Size of Government.* Washington, DC: Brookings Institution, 1999.

McCubbins, Mathew, Roger Noll, and Barry Weingast. "Structure and Process; Politics and Policy: Administrative Arrangements and the Political Control of Agencies." *Virginia Law Review* 75 (1989): 431–82.

McCubbins, Mathew, and Thomas Schwartz. "Congressional Oversight Overlooked: Police Patrols versus Fire Alarms." *American Journal of Political Science* 28 (1984): 165–79.

Meier, Kenneth J., and John Bohte. *Politics and the Bureaucracy.* 5th ed. Belmont, CA: Wadsworth, 2006.

Seidman, Harold. *Politics, Position, and Power: The Dynamics of Federal Organization.* 5th ed. New York: Oxford University Press, 1997.

Wilson, James Q. *Bureaucracy: What Government Agencies Do and Why They Do It.* New York: Basic Books, 1989.

9

The Federal Courts

Courts serve an essential and ancient function. When disputes arise, those involved need an impartial arbiter to help settle the matter. When laws must be enforced, justice requires an impartial judge to determine guilt and innocence and, if the accused is found guilty, the appropriate punishment. And when questions arise about the meaning of those laws, we rely on the wisdom of judges to interpret what Congress meant and how that meaning applies in a given circumstance. It is not possible, or even wise, to pass a law to cover every contingency. Thus, nearly every nation today has established a system of courts to satisfy the need for an arbiter and interpreter.

Perhaps the most significant and distinctive feature of the American judiciary is its independence. The Constitution of the United States, as it was written and as it has evolved over time, set up the courts as a separate entity from the legislature, the executive, and the states, and insulated it from electoral politics. As we see in this chapter, four important institutional features of the American judiciary ensure a powerful, independent court system. First, the Constitution establishes the federal courts as a separate branch of government from Congress and the president. Second, authority among the courts is hierarchical, with federal courts able to overturn state courts, and the U.S. Supreme Court as the ultimate authority. Third, the U.S. Supreme Court and other federal courts of appeals can strike down actions of Congress, the president, or the states if the judges deem those acts to be violations of the Constitution. This authority to find government actions unconstitutional is the power of *judicial review*. And fourth, federal judges are appointed for life. Federal judges are not subject to the pressures of running for re-election and need not be highly responsive to changes in public opinion.[1]

---

1   However, judges in many state and local courts are elected.

An independent judiciary has been one of the most successful institutions of our government. It has settled constitutional crises, when Congress and the president are at odds. It has guaranteed that no person is above the law, even members of Congress and the president. It has helped ensure that all people, even noncitizens, enjoy the equal protection of the laws. It has made it possible for small businesses, large corporations, and workers to engage in economic activities and agreements, knowing that their rights will be protected. It has ensured that the democratic branches of government operate in a democratic manner and that every citizen's vote counts equally in the selection of the legislature. The cumulative effect of an independent judiciary has been a stable, successful democracy and economy.

On its face, granting judges lifetime appointments and the power to strike down acts of Congress might seem like the foundation for tyrannical rule by courts. The sources and nature of judicial power in American government are, however, quite subtle and even democratic. Courts lack Congress's power of the purse or the president's ability to move troops or to order other branches of the executive to act or the bureaucracy's power to police. Courts are also passive

CORE OF THE ANALYSIS

➡ Just like presidents and legislators, judges have preferences about what government should do, and they use their powers to shape public policy.

➡ Judicial decisions are highly constrained by the past, in the form of common law and precedents, but every decision also contributes to the evolution of the law.

➡ The courts maintain their independence from the legislature and executive because federal judges are appointed for life and not elected. Independence allows the courts to act as a check on the democratically chosen branches of government.

➡ Courts can block or overturn political decisions of the legislature or executive if those decisions violate the Constitution or conflict with other laws, a power called judicial review.

➡ However, the courts are also constrained by the checks and balances built into the institutional setting within which they operate.

and must wait for people to file lawsuits in order to make any decisions or issue any decree.

The real power of the courts emanates from their ability to interpret the meaning of the laws in a way that society accepts. Courts are powerful to the extent that the people and groups involved accept the decrees that judges issue. In nearly all cases, judges' edicts are ultimately accepted. However, if people ignored the decrees of judges in local courts or if Congress routinely passed legislation contradicting the Supreme Court, the judicial function in our society would vanish. Herein lies the ability of the judiciary not just to interpret but to make law. The decree of any one judge in any single case may not seem very important, but each decision or settlement in a court is an act of lawmaking, a function as important as the passage of a statute by the legislature. Any one decision may serve as a precedent or guide for deciding a future case, and the accumulation of many such decisions, accepted by common practice, eventually becomes the norm.

Common law consists of all past agreements that we accept when we reach any decision. A contract for a real estate sale, for example, consists of many pages of language pertaining to the possible contingencies that might arise, what would happen in each case, and who would bear responsibility. Each clause has been developed through past legal decisions accumulated over centuries, indeed millennia, dating back in some instances to ancient Rome. The Supreme Court is similarly constrained by decisions that it has made in the past. When a majority of justices have issued an opinion interpreting the law a particular way, that opinion has the standing of precedent and constrains future courts. The history principle matters more fundamentally for the judiciary than for the other branches of government and is instrumental to its success. If the judges themselves were to ignore precedent, they would undercut the power of the courts and their own authority.

Precedents limit the power of the independent judiciary, but the past does not render the courts impotent. In any decision, a judge is both constrained by the past and contributing to the future meaning of the law. Usually, the influence of the courts on American politics is incremental and difficult to discern. At times, however, courts have made sweeping changes in the country's law and politics. With industrialization in the late nineteenth century came new ideas about the enforcement of contracts that dominated the thinking of the courts. The New Deal eventually won the support of the Supreme Court and with that a new acceptance of the role of government in the economy and society. During the 1950s and 1960s, the Supreme Court confronted lingering conflicts over racial and gender equality, religious freedoms, police powers, and legislative redistricting. Today, the courts must deal with new questions, many of which stem from rapid changes in information and biological technologies: Who owns your DNA? Do you have a right to privacy when you send an e-mail? As in the past, our society will call on the courts to settle cases that raise such questions, and how the courts address these issues will shape the meaning of the law and the definition of fundamental rights, such as the right to property and privacy.

The place of the judiciary in the American system of government points to a basic lesson about the courts in the United States and throughout the world: they are fundamentally political. Just like presidents and legislators, judges have preferences about what the government should do, and they use their powers to interpret, apply, and review laws to shape public policy. Judges are also constrained by the institutional setting within which they operate. They are mindful that others in the political process may try to alter or undo a court's rulings.

In this chapter, we examine the judicial process first, including the types of cases that the federal courts consider and the types of laws with which they deal. Second, we assess the organization and structure of the federal court system and explain how judges are appointed to the courts. Third, we analyze courts as political institutions and consider their roles in the political system. Fourth, we consider judicial review and how it makes the Supreme Court a lawmaking body. Fifth, we examine the flow of cases through the courts and various influences on the Supreme Court's decisions. Finally, we analyze the process of judicial decision making and the power of the federal courts in the American political process, looking in particular at the growth of judicial power in the United States.

THE JUDICIAL PROCESS

Many centuries ago a court was the place where a sovereign ruled—where a king and his entourage governed. Judging—settling disputes between citizens—was part of governing. Over time the function of settling disputes was slowly separated from the king and the king's court and made into a separate institution of government. Courts have taken over from kings the power to settle controversies by hearing the facts on both sides and deciding which side possesses the greater merit. But because judges are not kings, they must have a basis for their authority. That basis in the United States is the Constitution and the law. Courts decide cases by applying the relevant law or principle to the facts. This approach of applying relevant law lends authority derived from past law and past social compacts. It also provides a basis for continuing judicial independence, as common law and past precedents evolve on their own, often separate from the legislation passed by Congress and the executive. What then are these systems of rules that the judiciary has developed? What are the organizations and institutions of the judiciary, and how do they help carry out the complex function of the administration and interpretation of the law?

Court cases in the United States proceed under two broad categories of law: criminal and civil. One form of civil law, public law, is so important that we consider it as a separate category (Table 9.1).

Cases of **criminal law** are those in which the government charges an individual with violating a statute that has been enacted to protect the public health, safety, morals, or welfare. In criminal cases, the government is always the plaintiff (the party that brings charges) and alleges that a criminal violation has been

 criminal law

The branch of law that deals with disputes or actions involving criminal penalties (as opposed to civil law)

Table 9.1

TYPES OF LAWS AND DISPUTES

TYPE OF LAW	TYPE OF CASE OR DISPUTE	FORM OF CITATION
Criminal law	Cases arising out of actions that violate laws protecting the health, safety, and morals of the community. The government is always the plaintiff.	*U.S. (or state) v. Jones, Jones v. U.S. (or state)* if Jones lost and is appealing
Civil law	Law involving disputes between citizens or between a government and a citizen where no crime is alleged. Two general types are contract law and tort law. Contract cases are disputes that arise over voluntary actions. Tort cases are disputes that arise out of obligations inherent in social life. Negligence and slander are examples of torts.	*Smith v. Jones, New York v. Jones, U.S. v. Jones, Jones v. New York*
Public law	All cases in which the powers of government or the rights of citizens are involved. The government is the defendant. Constitutional law involves judicial review of the basis of a government's action in relation to specific clauses of the Constitution as interpreted in Supreme Court cases. Administrative law involves disputes over the statutory authority, jurisdiction, or procedures of administrative agencies.	*Jones v. U.S. (or state), In re Jones, Smith v. Jones* if a license or statute is at issue in their private dispute

committed by a named defendant. Most criminal cases arise in state and municipal courts and involve matters ranging from traffic offenses to robbery and murder. Although the great bulk of criminal law is still a state matter, a large and growing body of federal criminal law deals with such matters as tax evasion, mail fraud, and the sale of narcotics. Defendants found guilty of criminal violations may be fined or sent to prison.

Cases of **civil law** involve disputes between individuals or between individuals and the government where no criminal violation is charged. Unlike criminal cases, the losers in civil cases cannot be fined or sent to prison, although they may be required to pay monetary damages for their actions. In a civil case, the one who brings a complaint is the plaintiff and the one against whom the complaint is brought is the defendant. The two most common types of civil cases involve contracts and torts. In a typical contract case, an individual or corporation charges that it has suffered because of another's violation of a specific agreement between the two. For example, the Smith Manufacturing Corporation may charge that Jones Distributors failed to honor an agreement to deliver raw materials at a specified time, causing Smith to lose business. Smith asks the court to order Jones to compensate it for the damage allegedly suffered. In a typical tort case, one individual charges that he or she has been injured by another's negligence or malfeasance. Medical malpractice suits are one example of tort cases.

civil law

A system of jurisprudence, including private law and govermental actions, for settling disputes that do not involve criminal penalties

In deciding cases, courts apply statutes (laws) and legal **precedents** (prior decisions). State and federal statutes often govern the conditions under which contracts are and are not legally binding. Jones Distributors might argue that it was not obliged to fulfill its contract with the Smith Corporation because actions by Smith—the failure to make promised payments—constituted fraud under state law. Attorneys for a physician being sued for malpractice, on the other hand, may search for prior instances in which courts ruled that actions similar to those of their client did not constitute negligence. Such precedents are applied under the doctrine of ***stare decisis***, a Latin phrase meaning "let the decision stand."

A case becomes a matter of a third category, **public law**, when a plaintiff or defendant in a civil or criminal case seeks to show that his case involves the powers of government or the rights of citizens as defined under the Constitution or by statute. One major form of public law is constitutional law, under which a court will examine the government's actions to see if they conform to the Constitution as it has been interpreted by the judiciary. Thus what began as an ordinary criminal case may enter the realm of public law if a defendant claims that her constitutional rights were violated by the police. Another important arena of public law is administrative law, which involves disputes over the jurisdiction, procedures, or authority of administrative agencies. Under this type of law, civil litigation between an individual and the government may become a matter of public law if the individual asserts that the government is violating a statute or abusing its power under the Constitution. For example, landowners have asserted that federal and state restrictions on land use constitute violations of the Fifth Amendment's restrictions on the government's ability to confiscate private property. Recently the Supreme Court has been very sympathetic to such claims, which effectively transform an ordinary civil dispute into a major issue of public law.

Most of the Supreme Court cases we examine in this chapter involve judgments concerning the constitutional or statutory basis of the actions of government agencies. As we see, in this arena of public law Court decisions can have significant consequences for American politics and society.

 precedents

Prior cases whose principles are used by judges as the bases for their decisions in present cases

stare decisis

Literally, "let the decision stand." The doctrine whereby a previous decision by a court applies as a precedent in similar cases until that decision is overruled

public law

Cases involving the action of public agencies or officials

THE ORGANIZATION OF THE COURT SYSTEM

Types of Courts

In the United States, systems of courts have been established both by the federal government and by the governments of the individual states. Both systems have several levels, as shown in Figure 9.1. Nearly 99 percent of all court cases in the United States are heard in state courts. The overwhelming majority of criminal cases, for example, involve violations of state laws prohibiting such actions as murder, robbery, fraud, theft, and assault. If such a case is brought to trial, it

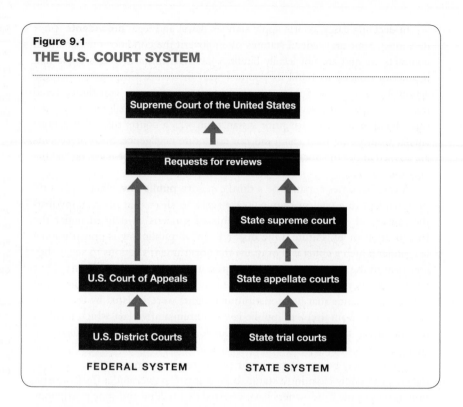

Figure 9.1
THE U.S. COURT SYSTEM

Supreme Court of the United States

Requests for reviews

U.S. Court of Appeals

U.S. District Courts

FEDERAL SYSTEM

State supreme court

State appellate courts

State trial courts

STATE SYSTEM

trial court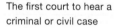

The first court to hear a criminal or civil case

court of appeals (or appellate court)

A court that hears the appeals of trial-court decisions

supreme court

The highest court in a particular state or in the United States. This court primarily serves an appellate function

will be heard in a state **trial court** in front of a judge and sometimes a jury, who will determine whether the defendant violated state law. If the defendant is convicted, he may appeal the conviction to a higher court, such as a state **court of appeals**, and from there to a state's **supreme court**. Similarly, in civil cases, most litigation is brought in the courts established by the state in which the activity in question took place. For example, a patient bringing suit against a physician for malpractice would file the suit in the appropriate court in the state where the alleged malpractice occurred. The judge hearing the case would apply state law and state precedent to the matter at hand. (It should be noted that in both criminal and civil matters, most cases are settled before trial through negotiated agreements between the parties. In criminal cases, these agreements are called plea bargains. Such bargains may affect the severity of the charge and/or the severity of the sentence.)

In addition, the U.S. military operates its own court system under the Uniform Code of Military Justice, which governs the behavior of men and women in the armed services. On rare occasions, the government has constituted special military tribunals to hear cases deemed inappropriate for the civil courts. Such tribunals tried Nazi saboteurs apprehended in the United States during World War II. More recently, President George W. Bush ordered the creation of military tribunals to try individuals suspected of acts of terrorism against the United States.

Federal Jurisdiction

Cases are heard in the federal courts if they involve federal laws, treaties with other nations, or the U.S. Constitution; these areas are the official **jurisdiction** of the federal courts. In addition, any case in which the U.S. government is a party is heard in the federal courts. If, for example, an individual is charged with violating a federal criminal statute, such as evading the payment of income taxes, charges would be brought before a federal judge by a federal prosecutor. Civil cases involving the citizens of more than one state and in which more than $75,000 is at stake may be heard in either the federal or the state courts, usually depending on the preference of the plaintiff.

But even if a matter belongs in federal court, how do we know which federal court should exercise jurisdiction over the case? The answer to this seemingly simple question is somewhat complex. The jurisdiction of each federal court is derived from the U.S. Constitution and federal statutes. Article III of the Constitution gives the Supreme Court **appellate jurisdiction** in all federal cases and **original jurisdiction** in cases involving foreign ambassadors and issues in which a state is a party. Article III assigns original jurisdiction in all other federal cases to the lower courts that Congress was authorized to establish. Over the years, as Congress enacted statutes creating the federal judicial system, it specified the jurisdiction of each type of court it established. For the most part, Congress has assigned jurisdictions on the basis of geography. The nation is currently, by statute, divided into 94 judicial districts, including one court for each of three U.S. territories: Guam, the U.S. Virgin Islands, and the Northern Marianas. Each of the 94 U.S. district courts exercises jurisdiction over federal cases arising within its territorial domain. The judicial districts are, in turn, organized into 11 regional circuits and the District of Columbia circuit (Figure 9.2). Each circuit court exercises appellate jurisdiction over cases heard by the district courts within its region.

Geography is not the only basis for federal court jurisdiction. Congress has also established several specialized courts that have nationwide original jurisdiction in certain types of cases. These include the U.S. Court of International Trade, created to deal with trade and customs issues, and the U.S. Court of Federal Claims, which handles damage suits against the United States. Congress has, in addition, established a court with nationwide appellate jurisdiction. This is the U.S. Court of Appeals for the Federal Circuit, which hears appeals involving patent law and those arising from the decisions of the trade and claims courts. Other federal courts assigned specialized jurisdictions by Congress include the U.S. Court of Appeals for Veterans Claims, which exercises exclusive jurisdiction over cases involving veterans' claims, and the U.S. Court of Appeals for the Armed Forces, which deals with questions of law arising from trials by court martial.

With the exception of the claims court and the Court of Appeals for the Federal Circuit, these specialized courts were created not in accordance with Article III of the Constitution but by Congress on the basis of the powers the legislature exercises under Article I. Article III was designed to protect judges from political pressure by granting them life tenure and prohibiting reduction of their salaries while they serve. The judges of Article I courts, by contrast, are appointed by the president for fixed terms of 15 years and are not protected

jurisdiction

The domain over which an institution or member of an institution has authority

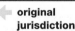

appellate jurisdiction

The class of cases provided in the Constitution and by legislation that may be appealed to a higher court from a lower court

original jurisdiction

The class of cases provided in the Constitution (Article III) that may be taken directly to a federal court

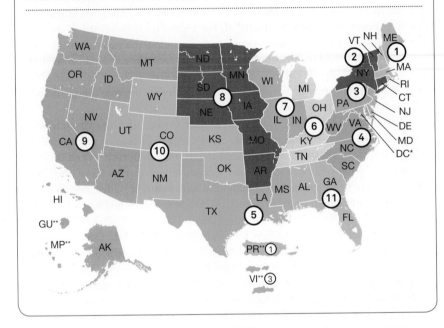

Figure 9.2

GEOGRAPHIC BOUNDARIES OF U.S. COURTS OF APPEALS

* The District of Columbia has its own circuit, called the D.C. Circuit.

** U.S. Postal Service abbreviations for Guam (GU), Northern Mariana Islands (MP), Puerto Rico (PR), and the U.S. Virgin Islands (VI).

SOURCE: Administrative Office of the U.S. Courts, www.uscourts.gov/uscourts/images/CircuitMap .pdf (accessed 4/2/13).

due process

Proceeding according to law and with adequate protection for individual rights

writ of *habeas corpus*

A court order demanding that an individual in custody be brought into court and shown the cause for detention. *Habeas corpus* is guaranteed by the Constitution and can be suspended only in cases of rebellion or invasion

by the Constitution from salary reduction. As a result, these so-called legislative courts are generally viewed as less independent than the courts established under Article III of the Constitution. The three territorial courts were also established under Article I, and their judges are appointed for 10-year terms.

The appellate jurisdiction of the federal courts also extends to cases originating in the state courts. In both civil and criminal cases, a decision of the highest state court can be appealed to the U.S. Supreme Court by raising a federal issue. Appellants might assert, for example, that they were denied the right to counsel or otherwise deprived of the **due process** guaranteed by the federal Constitution, or they might assert that important issues of federal law were at stake in the case. The U.S. Supreme Court is not obligated to accept such appeals and will accept them only if it believes that the matter has considerable national significance. (We return to this topic later in this chapter.) In addition, in criminal cases defendants who have been convicted in a state court may request a **writ of *habeas corpus*** from a federal district court. Sometimes known as the Great Writ, *habeas corpus* is a court order to the authorities to release a prisoner deemed to be held in violation of her legal rights. In 1867, its distrust of southern courts led Congress to authorize federal district judges to issue such writs to prisoners they believed had been deprived of their constitutional rights in state court. Generally speaking, state defendants seeking a federal writ of *habeas corpus* must show that they have exhausted all available state remedies and raise issues not previously raised in their state appeals. Federal courts of appeals and, ultimately, the U.S. Supreme Court have appellate jurisdiction over federal district court *habeas* decisions.

Over the past four decades, the caseload of the federal courts has more than quadrupled, to more than 450,000 cases a year. This has come about because Congress has greatly expanded the number of federal crimes, particularly in the realm of drug possession and sale. Behavior that was once exclusively a state criminal matter has, to some extent, come within the reach of federal law. In 1999, Chief Justice William Rehnquist criticized Congress for federalizing too many offenses and intruding unnecessarily into areas that should be handled by the states.[2] About 80 percent of federal cases end in the district courts, and the remainder are appealed to the circuit courts. In recent years, moreover, approximately 2,000 circuit court decisions per year were appealed to the Supreme Court. Most of the cases filed with the Supreme Court are dismissed without a ruling on their merits. The Court has broad latitude to decide what cases it will hear and generally listens only to those it deems to raise the most important issues. Thus in recent years, fewer than 90 cases per year were given full-dress Supreme Court review (the nine justices actually sitting en banc—in full court—and hearing lawyers argue the case).[3]

Even seemingly unimportant events can raise fundamental questions of law, such as when the First Amendment protects speech. The case of *Morse v. Frederick*, although not the most serious matter facing the nation, exemplifies the appellate process at work in the United States. On January 24, 2002, the Olympic torch relay passed through Juneau, Alaska, on its way to Salt Lake City and the winter games. The parade, to be carried on local television, passed immediately in front of Juneau-Douglas High School. The high school's principal, Deborah Morse, decided to allow staff and students to cheer on the relay as it paraded down the street in front of the high school. As the torch relay passed by the school, Joseph Frederick, a senior, and several of his friends unfurled a 14-foot banner that read *BONG HiTS 4 JESUS*. Principal Morse promptly confiscated the banner and later suspended Frederick for 10 days for promoting illegal drug use at a school-sponsored event. Frederick appealed his suspension to the Juneau School Committee. The expression "BongHits4Jesus," he argued, did not advocate drug use. It was a meaningless phrase that merely attracted the attention of the television cameras. The school committee was not sympathetic.

Frederick felt that his right to free speech under the First Amendment had been violated. He went to court. The federal district court ruled that the school committee had qualified immunity from the First Amendment. Frederick

---

2   Roberto Suro, "Rehnquist: Too Many Offenses Are Becoming Federal Crimes," *Washington Post*, January 1, 1999, p. A2.

3   Administrative Office of the U.S. Courts, 2013, www.uscourts.gov/adminoff.html.

pushed his appeal onward and won. The Ninth Circuit Court of Appeals ruled that "a school cannot censor or punish students' speech merely because the students advocate a position contrary to government policy." The school committee did not let the matter end there. It appealed the circuit court's ruling to the U.S. Supreme Court. The Court agreed to hear the case because it raised significant legal questions about the reach of the First Amendment. Citing a 1969 school speech decision involving antiwar protests, a majority of the justices ruled in favor of Principal Morse and the school committee. "Schools may reasonably take steps to safeguard those entrusted to their care from speech that can reasonably be regarded as encouraging illegal drug use," Chief Justice Roberts wrote for the majority.[4]

Although the federal courts hear only a small fraction of all the civil and criminal cases decided each year in the United States, their decisions are extremely important (Table 9.2). It is in the federal courts that the Constitution and federal laws that govern all Americans are interpreted and their meaning and significance established. Moreover, it is in the federal courts that the powers and limitations of the increasingly powerful national government are tested. Finally, through their power to review the decisions of the state courts, it is ultimately the federal courts that dominate the American judicial system.

Federal Trial Courts

The federal district courts are trial courts of general jurisdiction, and their cases are, in form, indistinguishable from cases in the state trial courts.

There are 89 district courts in the 50 states, one each in the District of Columbia and Puerto Rico, and one in each of three U.S. territories. There are 663 district judgeships. District judges are assigned to district courts according to the workload; the busiest of these courts may have as many as 28 judges. Only one judge is assigned to each case, except where statutes provide for three-judge courts to deal with special issues. The routines and procedures of the federal district courts are essentially the same as those of the lower state courts except that federal procedural requirements tend to be stricter. States, for example, do not have to provide a grand jury, a 12-member trial jury, or a unanimous jury verdict. Federal courts must provide all these things. As we saw earlier, in addition to the district courts, cases are handled by several specialized courts, including the U.S. Tax Court, the Court of Federal Claims, and the Court of International Trade.

Federal Appellate Courts

Roughly 20 percent of all lower-court cases, along with appeals of some federal agency decisions, are subsequently reviewed by a federal appeals court. As already noted, the country is divided into 12 judicial circuits, each with a U.S.

---

4   *Morse v. Frederick*, 551 U.S. 393 (2007).

Table 9.2

LANDMARK SUPREME COURT CASES

Not all cases and decisions are equally important. Landmark cases are decisions that revolutionize an area of law and announce new legal standards or have far-reaching political consequences.

Marbury v. Madison (1803). The Court declared part of the Judiciary Act unconstitutional, establishing judicial review.

McCulloch v. Maryland (1819). The Supreme Court justified the "implied powers" of the government under the Constitution, enabling Congress and the president to assert their authority beyond those activities explicitly mentioned in the Constitution.

Gibbons v. Ogden (1824). This decision establishes the supremacy of the federal government over the states in the regulation of commerce so as to create uniform business law.

Dred Scott v. Sandford (1857). The Court declared that people of African origin brought to the United States as part of the slave trade were not given the rights of citizenship under the Constitution and could, therefore, claim none of the rights and privileges that the Constitution provides.

Plessy v. Ferguson (1896). The Court interpreted the post–Civil War amendments to the Constitution in such a way as to allow segregation, so long as facilities were "separate but equal."

Lochner v. New York (1905). The Court established a general right to enter freely into contracts as part of business, including the right to purchase and sell labor. The decision made it more difficult for unions to form.

Schenck v. United States (1919). The Court declared that the right to free speech does not extend to words that are "used in such circumstances and are of such a nature as to create a clear and present danger."

Korematsu v. United States (1944). The Court allowed the U.S. government to intern Japanese-Americans in concentration camps during World War II as a safeguard against insurrection or spying.

Brown v. Board of Education (1954). The Court ruled that separate educational facilities could not be equal, overturning *Plessy*, and ordered an end to segregation "with all deliberate speed."

Mapp v. Ohio (1961). The Court ruled that all evidence obtained by searches and seizures in violation of the federal Constitution is inadmissible in a court of law.

Baker v. Carr (1962). The justices established that the Court had the authority to hear cases involving legislative districting, even though that is a "political matter," ultimately guaranteeing equal representation in the state legislatures and the U.S. House of Representatives.

Griswold v. Connecticut (1965). The Court struck down a Connecticut law prohibiting counseling on the use of contraceptives and declared that the Bill of Rights implied a right to privacy.

Brandenburg v. Ohio (1969). The Court ruled that inflammatory speech may not be punished by government unless it is likely to incite imminent lawless action.

(Continued)

Table 9.2
(Continued)

> ***Roe v. Wade* (1973).** The Court held that a mother may abort her baby for any reason up to the point that the fetus becomes "viable" and that any law passed by a state or Congress inconsistent with this holding violated the right to privacy and the right to enter freely into contracts.

> ***Kelo v. City of New London* (2005).** The Court upheld the power of local government to seize property for economic development.

> ***Boumediene v. Bush* (2008).** The Court declared that foreign terrorism suspects have the constitutional right to challenge their detention (using the writ of *habeas corpus*) at the Guantánamo Bay naval base in U.S. courts, even though the detainees are not citizens.

Court of Appeals. Every state and the District of Columbia are assigned to the circuit in the continental United States that is closest to it. A thirteenth appellate court, the U.S. Court of Appeals for the Federal Circuit, is defined by subject matter (patent law and decisions of trade and claims courts) rather than geographic jurisdiction.

Except for cases selected for review by the Supreme Court, decisions made by the appeals courts are final. Because of this finality, certain safeguards have been built into the system. The most important is the provision of more than one judge for every appeals case. Each court of appeals has from 3 to 28 permanent judgeships, depending on the workload of the circuit. Although normally three judges hear appealed cases, in some instances a larger number of judges sit together en banc. Another safeguard is provided by the assignment of a Supreme Court justice as the circuit justice for each of the 12 circuits. The circuit justice deals with requests for special action by the Supreme Court. The most frequent and best-known action of circuit justices is that of reviewing requests for stays of execution when the full Court is unable to do so—mainly during the summer, when the Court is in recess.

The Supreme Court

The Supreme Court is America's highest court. Article III of the Constitution vests "the judicial Power of the United States" in the Supreme Court, and this court is supreme in fact as well as form. The Supreme Court is made up of a chief justice and eight associate justices. The **chief justice** presides over the Court's public sessions and conferences. In the Court's actual deliberations and decisions, however, the chief justice has no more authority than his colleagues. Each justice casts one vote. The chief justice, though, is always the first to speak and vote when the justices deliberate; voting then proceeds in order of seniority. In addition, if the chief justice has voted with the majority, he decides which of the justices will write the formal opinion for the Court. To some extent, the influence of the chief justice is a function of his leadership ability. Some chief

chief justice

The justice on the Supreme Court who presides over the Court's public sessions justices, such as Earl Warren, have been able to lead the Court in a new direction. In other instances, a forceful associate justice, such as Felix Frankfurter, is the dominant figure on the Court.

The Constitution does not specify the number of justices who should sit on the Supreme Court; Congress has the authority to change the Court's size. In the early nineteenth century, there were six Supreme Court justices; later there were seven. Congress set the number of justices at nine in 1869, and the Court has remained that size ever since. In 1937, President Franklin Delano Roosevelt, infuriated by several Supreme Court decisions that struck down New Deal programs, asked Congress to enlarge the Court so that he could add sympathetic justices to the bench. Although Congress balked at Roosevelt's "Court-packing" plan, the Court gave in to Roosevelt's pressure and began to take a more favorable view of his policy initiatives. The president, in turn, dropped his efforts to enlarge the Court. The Court's surrender to Roosevelt came to be known as "the switch in time that saved nine."[5]

How Judges Are Appointed

The president appoints federal judges. Nominees are typically prominent or politically active members of the legal profession. Many federal judges previously served as state court judges or state or local prosecutors; some were prominent attorneys; others were highly regarded law professors. Supreme Court justice Thurgood Marshall was the chief counsel for the NAACP and argued *Brown v. Board of Education* before the Court. Felix Frankfurter was a prominent law professor at Harvard University and adviser to Franklin Delano Roosevelt. Still others were prominent elected officials. Prior experience as a judge is not necessary, either for appointment or ultimately success. Many of the greatest Supreme Court justices, including John Marshall, William Rehnquist, Louis Brandeis, Earl Warren, William O. Douglas, Harlan Fiske Stone, Robert Jackson, Felix Frankfurter, Joseph Storey, and Roger Taney, had no prior experience as judges. They were political and intellectual leaders in the country. John Marshall, the longest serving chief justice, was John Adams's secretary of state. Roger Taney, who delivered the *Dred Scott* opinion in 1858, was a trusted adviser of Andrew Jackson and served as attorney general and secretary of treasury. Earl Warren was governor of California. Elena Kagan, appointed in 2010, was dean of Harvard Law School and Barack Obama's first solicitor general.

In general, presidents endeavor to appoint judges who possess legal experience and good character and whose partisan and ideological views are similar to theirs. During the presidencies of Richard Nixon, Ronald Reagan, George H. W. Bush, and George W. Bush, most federal judicial appointees were conservative Republicans. Bill Clinton's and Barack Obama's appointees to the federal bench, on the other hand, tended to be liberal Democrats. Following the example of Jimmy Carter, Clinton also made a major effort to appoint women and African

---

5 For an alternative view, see David R. Mayhew, "Supermajority Rule in the Senate," *PS: Political Science and Politics* 36 (2003): 31–6.

Americans to the federal courts. Nearly half his nominees were drawn from these groups. George W. Bush made a strong effort to appoint Hispanics to the federal bench. (See Figure 9.7 on p. 381 for more information on diversity of court appointees.)

The Constitution calls on the Senate to "advise and consent" to federal judicial nominations. This power gives the upper chamber of the Congress an important check on the president's influence over the judiciary. Before the president formally nominates a candidate for a federal district judgeship, the senators from the nominee's state must indicate that they support her. This is an informal but seldom violated practice called **senatorial courtesy**. If one or both senators from a prospective nominee's home state belong to the president's political party, the president will almost invariably consult them and secure their blessing for the nomination. Because the president's party in the Senate will rarely support a nominee opposed by a home-state senator from their ranks, this arrangement gives these senators virtual veto power over appointments to the federal bench in their own states. Senators often see this power to grant their support as a way to reward important allies and contributors in their states. If the state has no senator from the president's party, the governor or members of the state's House delegation may make suggestions. Senatorial courtesy is less consequential for appellate court appointments and plays no role in Supreme Court nominations.

senatorial courtesy

The practice whereby the president, before formally nominating a person for a federal district judgeship, finds out whether the senators from the candidate's state support the nomination

Once the president has formally nominated an individual, the appointment must be considered by the Senate Judiciary Committee and confirmed by a majority vote in the full Senate. The politics and rules of the Senate determine the fate of a president's judicial nominees and influence the types of people the president selects for judicial positions. Like any piece of legislation, approval of a nomination must be given by the relevant committee and brought to the floor of the Senate, and to be successful, the nomination must receive a majority of votes. What is more, because this takes place in the Senate, there is always the risk of a filibuster, and cloture of debate requires an affirmative vote of three-fifths of the senators. (See Chapter 6 for discussion of these procedures.) The composition of the Senate Judiciary Committee as well as the Senate as a whole, then, is critical in determining whether a particular nominee will succeed.

Before the 1950s, the Senate Judiciary Committee rarely questioned nominees on their judicial views. Instead, committee inquiries would focus exclusively on qualifications. This norm changed in 1954, however, when President Eisenhower nominated John Marshall Harlan II to succeed Robert Jackson on the Supreme Court. The Senate did not act on his nomination, and Eisenhower had to nominate him a second time. The chairman of the Senate Judiciary Committee, Senator James Eastland of Mississippi, and several other southern Democratic senators delayed any hearings fearing that Harlan would support school integration and that he would further strengthen the Court's efforts to desegregate the South. When the committee finally did hold hearings, the senators grilled the normally reticent Harlan about his views on *Plessy v. Ferguson* and other judicial opinions. Every Supreme Court nominee since Harlan has been questioned about his views by the Judiciary Committee.

Since the mid-1950s, then, judicial appointments have become increasingly partisan and, ultimately, ideological. Today, the Judiciary Committee of the

Senate subjects nominees for the federal judiciary to lengthy questioning about a wide range of issues, from gun rights to abortion to federal power under the commerce clause. Senators' support for or opposition to specific nominees turns on the individual's ideological and judicial views as much as on her qualifications.

Trends in Presidential Appointments. For their part, presidents nominate individuals who share their own political philosophy. Presidents Ronald Reagan and George H. W. Bush, for example, appointed five justices whom they believed to have conservative perspectives: Sandra Day O'Connor, Antonin Scalia, Anthony Kennedy, David Souter, and Clarence Thomas. Reagan also elevated William Rehnquist to the position of chief justice. Reagan and George H. W. Bush sought appointees who believed in reducing government intervention in the economy and supported the moral positions taken by the Republican Party in recent years, particularly opposition to abortion. However, not all the Reagan and Bush appointees fulfilled their sponsors' expectations. David Souter, for example, appointed by President George H. W. Bush, was attacked by conservatives as a turncoat for his decisions on school prayer and abortion rights. Nevertheless, through their appointments, Reagan and George H. W. Bush were able to create a far more conservative Supreme Court. For his part, President Clinton endeavored to appoint liberal justices. He named Ruth Bader Ginsburg and Stephen Breyer to the Court, hoping to counteract the influence of the Reagan and Bush appointees.

In 2005, President George W. Bush was given an opportunity to put his own stamp on the Supreme Court after Justice O'Connor announced her decision to retire and Chief Justice Rehnquist died. Bush quickly nominated the federal appeals court judge John Roberts, initially to replace O'Connor and then as chief justice after Rehnquist's death. Roberts, a moderate conservative with an impressive legal record, provoked some Democratic opposition but was confirmed without much difficulty. Bush's next nominee, though, sparked an intense battle within the president's own party. To the surprise of most observers, the president named a longtime associate, White House counsel Harriet Miers, to replace O'Connor. Many Republicans viewed Miers as merely a Bush crony who lacked judicial qualifications and was insufficiently supportive of conservative causes. Opposition to Miers within the Republican Party was so intense that Democrats remained gleefully silent as the president was forced to allow her to withdraw her name from consideration. In the wake of the Miers debacle, President Bush turned to a more conventional nominee, the federal appeals court judge Samuel Alito, who pleased conservative Republicans. Democrats and liberal political forces attempted to block the nomination but ultimately failed, and Alito was confirmed in February 2006. Barack Obama's nominations of Sonia Sotomayor and Elena Kagan to the Court were easily approved, despite Republican criticisms, thanks to a strong Democratic majority in the Senate (Table 9.3).

These struggles over judicial appointments reflect the growing intensity of partisanship in the United States today. They also indicate how much importance competing political forces attach to Supreme Court appointments. Because the contending forces see the outcome as critical, they are willing to engage in a fierce struggle when Supreme Court appointments are at stake.

Table 9.3

SUPREME COURT JUSTICES, 2013

NAME	YEAR OF BIRTH	PRIOR EXPERIENCE	APPOINTED BY	YEAR OF APPOINTMENT
John G. Roberts, Jr., *chief justice*	1955	Federal judge	G. W. Bush	2005
Antonin Scalia	1936	Federal judge	Reagan	1986
Anthony M. Kennedy	1936	Federal judge	Reagan	1988
Clarence Thomas	1948	Federal judge	G. H. W. Bush	1991
Ruth Bader Ginsburg	1933	Federal judge	Clinton	1993
Stephen G. Breyer	1938	Federal judge	Clinton	1994
Samuel A. Alito, Jr.	1950	Federal judge	G. W. Bush	2006
Sonia Sotomayor	1954	Federal judge	Obama	2009
Elena Kagan	1960	Solicitor general	Obama	2010

The increasing role of partisanship or ideology in the nomination process creates a potential danger for the court system. Courts, as we said at the outset, derive much of their authority from their position of political independence, as nonpartisan arbiters in our society. The politics of appointments, which has grown increasingly focused on ideology, risks tainting judges and the judicial process as little more than extensions of the political views of the people who nominated them. Fortunately, the individuals appointed to the federal judiciary tend to have a strong independent sense of themselves and their mission. Throughout the history of the federal courts we find instances of judges who have frustrated the presidents who appointed them.

HOW COURTS WORK AS POLITICAL INSTITUTIONS

Judges are central players in important political institutions, and this role makes them politicians. To understand what animates judicial behavior, we need to place the judge or justice in context by considering the role of the courts in the political system more generally. In doing so, we emphasize the role of the courts as dispute resolvers, coordinators, and interpreters of rules.

Dispute Resolution

Much productive activity occurs in a modern society because its members do not have to devote substantial resources to protecting themselves and their property or monitoring compliance with agreements. For any potential violation of person or property or defection from an agreement, all parties know in advance that an aggrieved party may take an alleged violator to court. The court, in turn, is a venue in which the facts of a case are established, punishment is meted out to violators, and compensation awarded to victims. An employee, for example, may sue his employer for allegedly violating the terms of a privately negotiated employment contract. Or a consumer may sue a producer for violating the terms of a product warranty. The court, then, is an institution that engages in fact-finding and judgment. It provides the service of dispute resolution. In criminal cases, the "aggrieved party" is not only the victim of the crime but also the entire society whose laws have been violated.

Coordination

Dispute resolution occurs after the fact—that is, after a dispute has occurred. We may also think of courts and judges as before-the-fact coordination mechanisms inasmuch as the anticipation of legal consequences allows private parties to form rational expectations and thereby coordinate their actions in advance of possible disputes. A prospective embezzler, estimating the odds of getting caught, prosecuted, and subsequently punished, may think twice about cheating her partner. Conversely, the legal system can work as an incentive: two acquaintances, for example, may confidently entertain the possibility of going into business together, knowing that the sword of justice hangs over their collaboration.

In this sense, the court system is as important for what it doesn't do as for what it does. The system of courts and law coordinates private behavior by providing incentives and disincentives for specific actions. To the extent that these work, there are fewer disputes to resolve and thus less after-the-fact dispute resolution for courts and judges to engage in.

Rule Interpretation

Dispute resolution and coordination affect private behavior and the daily lives of ordinary citizens tremendously. Judges, however, are not entirely free agents. In matching the facts of a specific case to judicial principles and statutory guidelines, judges must engage in interpretive activity: they must determine what particular statutes or judicial principles mean, which of them fit the facts of a particular case, and then, having determined this, ascertain the disposition of the case at hand. Does the statute of 1927 regulating the electronic transmission of radio waves apply to television, cellular phones, ship-to-shore radios, fax machines, and e-mail? Does the law governing the transportation of dangerous substances, passed in 1937, apply to nuclear fuels, infected animals, and artificially created biological hazards? Often the enacting legislative body has not been entirely clear about the scope of the legislation it passed.

Interpreting the rules is probably the single most important activity in which higher courts engage. This is because the court system is hierarchical in the sense that judgments by higher courts constrain the discretion of judges in lower courts. If the Supreme Court rules that nuclear fuels are covered by the 1937 law on transporting dangerous substances, then lower courts must render subsequent judgments in a manner consistent with this ruling.

As we see in the following section, courts and judges engage not only in statutory interpretation but in constitutional interpretation as well. Here they interpret the provisions of the U.S. Constitution, determining their scope and content. In determining, for example, whether the act of Congress regulating the transportation of dangerous substances from one state to another is constitutional, the justices of the Supreme Court might invoke the commerce clause of the Constitution (allowing the federal government to regulate interstate commerce) to justify the constitutionality of the act. On the other hand, a Supreme Court majority might also rule that a shipment of spent fuel rods from a nuclear reactor in Kansas City to a nuclear-waste facility outside St. Louis is not covered by this clause because the shipment took place entirely within the boundaries of a single state and thus did not constitute interstate commerce.

In short, judges and justices are continually engaged in elaborating, embellishing, even rewriting the rules by which private and public life are organized. However, judicial interpretation—elaboration, embellishment, and "redrafting"—of statutes is naturally subject to review. Statutory interpretation, even if it is conducted by the highest court in the land, is exposed to legislative review. If Congress is unhappy with a specific statutory interpretation, then it may amend the legislation so as to overcome the Court's objection. In January 2005, for example, the Supreme Court struck down the mandatory sentencing rules enacted by Congress in 1984.[6] The rules severely limited judicial discretion in the realm of sentencing and had long been resented by the bench. The Court found that mandatory minimum sentences violated the Sixth Amendment, because the latter required that only evidence provided at trial, together with the defendant's previous criminal record, could be used in determining a sentence. Members of Congress vowed to reinstate the guidelines through new legislation. Senator Jeff Sessions (R-Ala.) said, "The challenge will be to . . . re-create the guidelines in a way that will meet the court's test."[7] Since the *Booker* decision, mandatory sentencing guidelines, at both the state and federal levels, remain in flux. For the most part, however, the thrust of

---

6 *United States v. Booker*, 543 U.S. 220 (2005).

7 Quoted in Carl Hulse and Adam Liptak, "New Fight over Controlling Punishments Is Widely Seen," *New York Times*, January 13, 2005, p. A27.

Booker remains in effect, rendering legislatively constructed guidelines essentially advisory (not mandatory). Of course, if the Court makes a constitutional ruling, Congress cannot then abrogate that ruling through new legislation. Congress would need to commence the process of constitutional amendment to overturn a constitutional interpretation with which it disagreed.

THE POWER OF JUDICIAL REVIEW

The phrase **judicial review** refers to the power of the judiciary to examine and, if necessary, invalidate actions undertaken by the legislative and executive branches. The phrase is sometimes also used to describe the scrutiny that appellate courts give to the actions of trial courts, but strictly speaking, that is an improper usage.

The development of judicial review, which is not expressed explicitly in the Constitution, is one of the most powerful expressions of the independent judiciary. In countries without an independent judiciary and without judicial review, the parliament or the executive is the ultimate authority. In English law, for example, the Parliament is sovereign. Judicial review exists only in scrutinizing the administration of the laws. An individual cannot challenge an act of Parliament in the courts and ask that the courts void that law as a violation of the constitution. But in the U.S. system of government the process of judicial review has taken root and is an essential means by which the judiciary checks the legislature and executive.

 judicial review

The power of the courts to declare actions of the legislative and executive branches invalid or unconstitutional. The Supreme Court asserted this power in *Marbury v. Madison* (1803)

Judicial Review of Acts of Congress

Because the Constitution does not give the Supreme Court the power of judicial review of congressional enactments, the Court's exercise of it may be seen as something of a usurpation. Among the proposals debated at the Constitutional Convention was one to create a council composed of the president and the judiciary that would share the veto power over legislation. Another proposal was to route all legislation through both the Court and the president; overruling a veto by either one would have required a two-thirds vote of the House and the Senate. Those and other proposals were rejected by the delegates, and no further effort was made to give the Supreme Court review power over the other branches. This does not prove that the framers of the Constitution opposed judicial review, but it does indicate that "if they intended to provide for it in the Constitution, they did so in a most obscure fashion."[8]

Disputes over the intentions of the framers were settled in 1803 in the case of *Marbury v. Madison.*[9] In that case, William Marbury sued Secretary of State James Madison for Madison's failure to complete Marbury's appointment to a lower

8   C. Herman Pritchett, *The American Constitution* (New York: McGraw-Hill, 1959), p. 138.

9   *Marbury v. Madison*, 1 Cranch 137 (1803).

judgeship that had been initiated by the outgoing administration of President John Adams. Quite apart from the details of the case, Chief Justice John Marshall, speaking on behalf of the Court, used the case to declare a portion of a law unconstitutional. In effect, he stated that although the substance of Marbury's request was not unreasonable, the Court's jurisdiction in the matter was based on a section of the Judiciary Act of 1789, which the Court declared unconstitutional.

Although Congress and the president have often been at odds with the Court, its legal power to review acts of Congress has not been seriously questioned since 1803. One reason is that judicial power has been accepted as natural, if not intended. Another reason is that during the early years of the Republic, the Supreme Court was careful to use its power sparingly, striking down only two pieces of legislation during the first 75 years of its history. One of these decisions was the 1857 *Dred Scott* ruling, which invalidated the Missouri Compromise and helped precipitate the Civil War. In *Dred Scott v. Sandford*, Chief Justice Roger Taney wrote in the Court's majority opinion that the fact that a slave, Dred Scott, had been transported to a free state (Illinois) and a free territory (Wisconsin) before returning to the slave state of Missouri did not alter the fact that he was property.[10] This ruling had the effect of invalidating a portion of the Missouri Compromise of 1820, thus permitting slavery in all the country's territories. In recent years, with the power of judicial review securely accepted, the Court has been more willing to use it. Between 1980 and 2008, the Supreme Court struck down 56 acts of Congress in whole or in part.[11] (See Figure 9.3.)

Judicial Review of State Actions

The power of the Supreme Court to review state legislation or other state action and to determine its constitutionality is neither granted by the Constitution nor inherent in the federal system. But the logic of the **supremacy clause** of Article VI of the Constitution—which declares the Constitution and laws made under its authority to be the supreme law of the land—is very strong. Furthermore, in the Judiciary Act of 1789, Congress conferred on the Supreme Court the power to reverse state constitutions and laws whenever they are clearly in conflict with the U.S. Constitution, federal laws, or treaties.[12] This power gives the Supreme Court jurisdiction over all of the millions of cases handled by American courts each year.

The history of civil rights protections abounds with examples of state laws that were overturned because the statutes violated the guarantees of due process and equal protection contained in the Fourteenth Amendment to the

supremacy clause

A clause of Article VI of the Constitution that states that all laws passed by the national government and all treaties are the supreme laws of the land and superior to all laws adopted by any state or any subdivision

---

10 *Dred Scott v. Sandford,* 60 U.S. 393 (1857).

11 For an analysis of the Court's use of judicial review to nullify acts of Congress, see Ryan Emenaker, "Constitutional Interpretation and Congressional Overrides: Changing Trends in Court–Congress Relations," presented at the annual meeting of the Western Political Science Association, Hollywood, CA, March 28–30, 2013.

12 This review power was affirmed by the Supreme Court in *Martin v. Hunter's Lessee,* 14 U.S. 304 (1816).

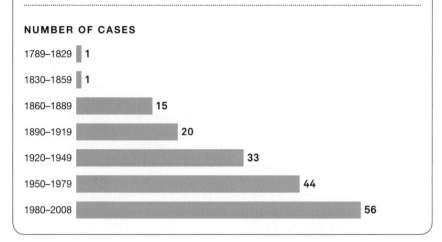

Figure 9.3

SUPREME COURT RULINGS INVALIDATING ACTS OF CONGRESS, 1789–2008

NUMBER OF CASES

Period	Number
1789–1829	1
1830–1859	1
1860–1889	15
1890–1919	20
1920–1949	33
1950–1979	44
1980–2008	56

SOURCE: U.S. Government Printing Office, "The Constitution of the United States of America: Analysis and Interpretation," S. Doc. 108–17 (2002) and S. Doc 110–17 (2008).

Constitution. For example, in the 1954 case of *Brown v. Board of Education*, the Court overturned statutes in Kansas, South Carolina, Virginia, and Delaware that either required or permitted segregated public schools, on the basis that such statutes denied black schoolchildren equal protection of the law.[13] In 1967 in *Loving v. Virginia*, the Court invalidated a Virginia statute prohibiting interracial marriages.[14] State statutes in other areas are equally subject to challenge. In *Griswold v. Connecticut*, the Court invalidated a Connecticut statute prohibiting the general distribution of contraceptives to married couples, on the basis that the statute violated the couples' right to marital privacy.[15] The Court has also overturned state laws that conflict with federal law: in 2012 in *Arizona et al. v. United States* for instance, the Court struck down parts of an Arizona law regulating immigration on the grounds that it was preempted by federal law.[16]

Judicial Review of Federal Agency Actions

Although Congress makes the law, as we saw in Chapters 6 and 8, Congress can hardly administer the thousands of programs it has enacted and must delegate power to the president and to a huge bureaucracy to achieve its purposes. For

---

13 *Brown v. Board of Education*, 347 U.S. 483 (1954).

14 *Loving v. Virginia*, 388 U.S. 1 (1967).

15 *Griswold v. Connecticut*, 381 U.S. 479 (1965).

16 *Arizona et al. v. United States*, 567 U.S. ____ (2012).

example, if Congress wishes to improve air quality, it cannot possibly anticipate all the conditions and circumstances that may arise over the years with respect to its general goal. Inevitably Congress must delegate to the executive substantial discretionary power to make judgments about the best ways to bring about improved air quality in the face of changing circumstances. Thus, over time, almost any congressional program will result in thousands and thousands of pages of administrative regulations developed by executive agencies nominally seeking to implement the will of Congress.

The issue of delegation of power has led to a number of court decisions over the past two centuries, generally involving the question of the scope of the delegation. Courts have also been called on to decide whether the rules and regulations adopted by federal agencies are consistent with Congress's express or implied intent.

As presidential power expanded during the New Deal era, one measure of increased congressional subordination to the executive was the enactment of laws that contained few if any principles limiting executive discretion. Congress enacted legislation, often at the president's behest, that gave the executive virtually unfettered authority to address a particular concern. For example, the Emergency Price Control Act of 1942 authorized the executive to set "fair and equitable" prices without offering any indication of what those terms might mean. Although the Court initially challenged these delegations of power to the president during the New Deal, a confrontation with President Franklin Delano Roosevelt caused the Court to retreat from its position. Perhaps as a result, no congressional delegation of power to the president has been struck down as impermissibly broad since then. In the last two decades in particular, the Supreme Court has found that as long as federal agencies developed rules and regulations "based upon a permissible construction" or "reasonable interpretation" of Congress's statute, the judiciary would accept the views of the executive branch.[17] Generally the courts give considerable deference to administrative agencies as long as those agencies have engaged in a formal rule-making process and can show that they have carried out the conditions prescribed by the various statutes governing agency rule making. These statutes include the 1946 Administrative Procedure Act, which requires agencies to notify parties affected by proposed rules and to allow them ample time to comment on such rules before they go into effect.

Judicial Review and Presidential Power

The federal courts are also called on to review the actions of the president. As we saw in Chapter 7, presidents have increasingly made use of unilateral executive powers rather than relying on congressional legislation to achieve their objectives. On many occasions, presidential orders and actions have been challenged in the federal courts by members of Congress and by individuals and groups opposing

---

17 *Cookman Realty Group, Inc. v. West Virginia Division of Environmental Protection,* no. 30116 (W. Va. S. Ct. App. 2002).

the president's policies. In recent years, assertions of presidential power in such realms as foreign policy, war and emergency powers, legislative power, and administrative authority have, more often than not, been upheld by the federal bench. Indeed, the federal judiciary has sometimes taken extraordinary presidential claims that were made for limited and temporary purposes and rationalized them—that is, the Court has converted them into routine and permanent instruments of presidential government. Take, for example, Richard Nixon's sweeping claims of executive privilege. In *United States v. Nixon*, the Court, to be sure, rejected the president's refusal to turn over tape recordings to congressional investigators. For the first time, though, the justices recognized the validity of the principle of executive privilege and discussed the situations in which such claims might be appropriate.[18] This judicial recognition of executive privilege encouraged presidents Bill Clinton and George W. Bush to base broad claims on that principle during their terms in office.[19] Executive privilege has even been invoked to protect the deliberations of the vice president from congressional scrutiny, in the case of Dick Cheney's consultations with representatives of the energy industry.

This pattern of judicial deference to presidential authority is also manifest in the Supreme Court's decisions regarding President Bush's war on terrorism. In June 2004, the Supreme Court ruled on three cases involving the president's antiterrorism initiatives and claims of executive power and in two of them appeared to place some limits on presidential authority. Although the Court's decisions were widely hailed as reining in the executive branch, they fell far short of stopping presidential power in its tracks.

Perhaps the most important of these cases was *Hamdi v. Rumsfeld*.[20] In June 2004, the Supreme Court ruled that Yaser Esam Hamdi was entitled to a lawyer and "a fair opportunity to rebut the government's factual assertions." However, the Supreme Court affirmed that the president possessed the authority to declare a U.S. citizen an enemy combatant and order that such an individual be held in federal detention. Several of the justices intimated that once designated an enemy combatant, a U.S. citizen might be tried before a military tribunal, with the normal presumption of innocence suspended. In 2006, in *Hamdan v. Rumsfeld*, the Court ruled that the military commissions established to try enemy combatants and other detainees violated both the Uniform Code of Military Justice and the Geneva Conventions.[21] Thus the Supreme Court did assert that presidential actions were subject to judicial scrutiny and placed some constraints on the president's power. But at the same time, the Court affirmed the president's single most important claim: the unilateral power to declare individuals, including U.S. citizens, "enemy combatants" who could be detained by federal authorities under adverse legal circumstances.

---

18 *United States v. Nixon*, 418 U.S. 683 (1974).

19 On Clinton, see Jonathan Turley, "Paradise Lost: The Clinton Administration and the Erosion of Executive Privilege," *Maryland Law Review* 60 (2001): 295. On Bush, see Jeffrey P. Carlin, "*Walker v. Cheney*: Politics, Posturing, and Executive Privilege," *Southern California Law Review* 76 (November 2002): 235.

20 *Hamdi v. Rumsfeld*, 542 U.S. 507 (2004).

21 *Hamdan v. Rumsfeld*, 548 U.S. 557 (2006).

Judicial Review and Lawmaking

Much of the work of the courts involves the application of statutes to a particular case at hand. Over the centuries, however, judges have developed a body of rules and principles of interpretation that are not grounded in specific statutes. This body of judge-made law is called common law.

The appellate courts are in another realm. Their rulings can be considered laws, but they are laws governing only the behavior of the judiciary. They influence citizens' conduct only because, in the words of Justice Oliver Wendell Holmes, Jr. (who served on the Supreme Court from 1902 to 1932), lawyers make "prophecies of what the courts will do in fact."[22]

The written opinion of an appellate court is about halfway between common law and statutory law. It is judge made and draws heavily on the precedents of previous cases. In that it tries to articulate the rule of law controlling the case in question and future cases like it, it is like a statute. But a statute addresses itself to the future conduct of citizens, whereas a written opinion addresses itself mainly to the willingness or ability of courts in the future to take cases and render favorable opinions.

An example may help clarify the distinction. In *Gideon v. Wainwright*, the Supreme Court ordered a new trial for Clarence Earl Gideon, an indigent defendant, because he had been denied the right to legal counsel. This ruling said to all trial judges and prosecutors that henceforth they would be wasting their time if they cut corners in the trials of indigent defendants.[23] The Court was thereby predicting what it would and would not do in future cases of this sort. It also invited thousands of prisoners to appeal their convictions.

Many areas of civil law have been constructed in the same way—by judicial messages to other judges, some of which are codified eventually in legislative enactments. It has become "the law," for example, that employers are liable for injuries in the workplace without regard to negligence. But the law in this instance is simply a series of messages to lawyers that they should advise their corporate clients not to appeal injury decisions.

In the realm of criminal law, almost all the dramatic changes in the treatment of criminals and persons accused of crimes have been made by the appellate courts, especially the Supreme Court. The Supreme Court brought about a veritable revolution in the criminal process with three cases over less than five years. The first, *Gideon v. Wainwright*, in 1963, was just discussed. The second, *Escobedo v. Illinois*, in 1964, gave suspects the right to remain silent and the right to have counsel present during questioning.[24] But the decision left confusion that allowed differing decisions to be made by lower courts. In the third case, *Miranda v. Arizona*, in 1966, the Supreme Court cleared up the confusion by

---

22 Oliver Wendell Holmes, Jr., "The Path of the Law," *Harvard Law Review* 10 (1897): 457.

23 *Gideon v. Wainwright,* 372 U.S. 335 (1963).

24 *Escobedo v. Illinois,* 378 U.S. 478 (1964).

setting forth what is known as the Miranda rule: arrested people have the right to remain silent, the right to be informed that anything they say can be held against them, and the right to counsel before and during police interrogation.[25]

One of the most significant changes brought about by the Supreme Court was the revolution in legislative representation unleashed by the 1962 case of *Baker v. Carr*.[26] In this landmark case, the Supreme Court held that it could no longer avoid reviewing complaints about the apportionment of seats in state legislatures. Following that decision, the federal courts went on to force reapportionment of all state, county, and local legislatures in the country.

As these various cases illustrate, the appellate courts are intimately involved in creating and interpreting laws. Many experts on court history and constitutional law criticize the federal appellate courts for being too willing to introduce radical change, even when the experts agree with the general direction of the changes. Often they are troubled by the willingness of the courts (especially the Supreme Court) to jump into such cases prematurely—before the constitutional issues have been fully clarified by decisions of district and appeals courts in many related cases in various parts of the country.[27] But from the perspective of the appellate judiciary, and especially the Supreme Court, the situation is one of choosing between the lesser of two evils: they must take the cases as they come and then weigh the risks of opening new options against the risks of embracing the status quo.

THE SUPREME COURT IN ACTION

The Supreme Court sits at the pinnacle of the U.S. judiciary. It is the only court expressly mentioned in the Constitution, and it is one of the most distinctive political bodies created by the U.S. system. The Supreme Court is often the focal point for understanding the judiciary both because of its special constitutional status and also because it embodies the many principles of the American court system—its independence, its durability, the collective nature of court decision making, and the delicate balance that judges strike between historical precedent and new interpretation. The Supreme Court plays a vital role in the government as it is part of the structure of checks and balances that prevents the legislative and executive branches from abusing their power. The Court also operates as an institution unto itself, with its own internal rules for decision making. In this way, it has its own version of the policy principle discussed in Chapter 1.

---

25 *Miranda v. Arizona*, 384 U.S. 436 (1966).

26 *Baker v. Carr*, 369 U.S. 186 (1962).

27 See Philip B. Kurland, *Politics, the Constitution, and the Warren Court* (Chicago: University of Chicago Press, 1970).

How Cases Reach the Supreme Court

Given the millions of disputes that arise every year, the job of the Supreme Court would be impossible if it were not able to control the flow of cases and its own caseload. The Supreme Court has original jurisdiction in a limited variety of cases defined by the Constitution. Original jurisdiction includes (1) cases between the United States and one of the 50 states, (2) cases between two or more states, (3) cases involving foreign ambassadors or other ministers, and (4) cases brought by one state against citizens of another state or against a foreign country. The most important of these cases are disputes between states over land, water, or old debts. Generally the Supreme Court deals with these cases by appointing a "special master," usually a retired judge, to hear the case and present a report. The Supreme Court then allows the states involved in the dispute to present arguments for or against the master's opinion.[28]

Rules of Access. Over the years, the courts have developed specific rules that govern which cases within their jurisdiction they will and will not hear. Thus the Court is an institution very much in control of its own agenda, which, according to the institution principle, gives it a great deal of independence to follow the preferences of its members. To have access to the courts, cases must meet certain criteria that are initially applied by the trial court but may be reconsidered by appellate courts. These rules of access can be broken down into three major categories: case or controversy, standing, and mootness.

Both Article III of the Constitution and past Supreme Court decisions define judicial power as extending only to "cases and controversies." This means that the case before a court must be an actual controversy, not a hypothetical one, with two truly adversarial parties (called **ripeness**). The courts have interpreted this language to mean that they do not have the power to render advisory opinions to legislatures or agencies about the constitutionality of proposed laws or regulations. Furthermore, even after a law is enacted, the courts will generally refuse to consider its constitutionality until it is actually applied.

Parties to a case must also have **standing**—that is, they must show that they have a substantial stake in the outcome of the case. The traditional requirement for standing has been that one must show injury to oneself; that injury can be personal, economic, or even aesthetic, for example. In order for a group or class of people to have standing (as in class-action suits), each member must show specific injury. This means that a general interest in the environment, for instance, does not provide a group with a sufficient basis for standing.

The third criterion in determining whether the Supreme Court will hear a case is **mootness**. In theory, this requirement disqualifies cases that are brought too late—after the relevant facts have changed or the problem has been resolved by other means. The criterion of mootness, however, is subject to the discretion

ripeness

A case that is ready for litigation and does not depend upon hypothetical future events

standing

The right of an individual or an organization to initiate a court case

mootness

A criterion used by courts to avoid hearing cases that no longer require resolution

---

28 Walter F. Murphy, "The Supreme Court of the United States," in *Encyclopedia of the American Judicial System: Studies of the Principal Institutions and Processes of Law*, Robert J. Janosik, ed. (New York: Scribner, 1987).

---

of the courts, which have begun to relax the rules pertaining to this criterion, particularly in cases in which a situation that has been resolved is likely to come up again. In the abortion case of *Roe v. Wade*, for example, the Supreme Court rejected the lower court's argument that because the pregnancy had already come to term, the case was moot. The Court agreed to hear the case because no pregnancy was likely to outlast the lengthy appeals process.

Putting aside the formal criteria, the Supreme Court is most likely to accept cases that involve conflicting decisions by the federal circuit courts, cases that present important questions of civil rights or civil liberties, and cases in which the federal government is the appellant.[29] Ultimately, however, the question of which cases are accepted can come down to the preferences and priorities of the justices. If a number of justices believe that the Court should intervene in a particular area of policy or politics, they are likely to look for a case or cases that will be vehicles for judicial intervention. For many years, for example, the Court was not interested in considering challenges to affirmative action or other programs designed to provide particular benefits to minorities. In recent years, however, several of the Court's more conservative justices have been eager to push back the limits of affirmative action and racial preference and have therefore accepted a number of cases that would allow them to do so. In 1995, the Court's decisions in *Adarand Constructors v. Pena*, *Missouri v. Jenkins*, and *Miller v. Johnson* placed new restrictions on federal affirmative action programs, school desegregation efforts, and attempts to increase minority representation in Congress through the creation of "minority districts" (see Chapter 11).[30]

Most cases reach the Supreme Court through a **writ of *certiorari*** (Figure 9.4). *Certiorari* is an order to a lower court to deliver the records of a particular case to be reviewed for legal errors. The term is sometimes shortened to *cert*, and cases deemed to merit *certiorari* are referred to as *certworthy*. An individual who loses in a lower federal court or a state court and wants the Supreme Court to review the decision has 90 days to file a petition for a writ of *certiorari* with the clerk of the Supreme Court. There are two types of petitions: paid petitions and petitions *in forma pauperis* ("in the form of a pauper"). The former requires the payment of filing fees, submission of a certain number of copies, and compliance with a variety of other rules. For *in forma pauperis* petitions, which are usually filed by prison inmates, the Court waives the fees and most other requirements.

Since 1972, most of the justices have participated in a "*certiorari* pool" in which their law clerks work together to evaluate the petitions. Each petition is reviewed by one clerk, who writes a memo summarizing the facts and issues and making a recommendation for all the justices participating in the pool. Clerks for the other justices add their comments to the memo. After the justices have reviewed the memos, any one of them may place any case on the

 writ of *certiorari*

A formal request by an appellant to have the Supreme Court review a decision of a lower court. *Certiorari* is from a Latin word meaning "to make more certain"

---

29 Gregory A. Caldeira and John R. Wright, "Organized Interests and Agenda Setting in the U.S. Supreme Court," *American Political Science Review* 82, no. 4 (December 1988): 1109–27.

30 *Adarand Constructors v. Pena*, 115 U.S. 200 (1995); *Missouri v. Jenkins*, 515 U.S. 70 (1995); *Miller v. Johnson*, 515 U.S. 900 (1995).

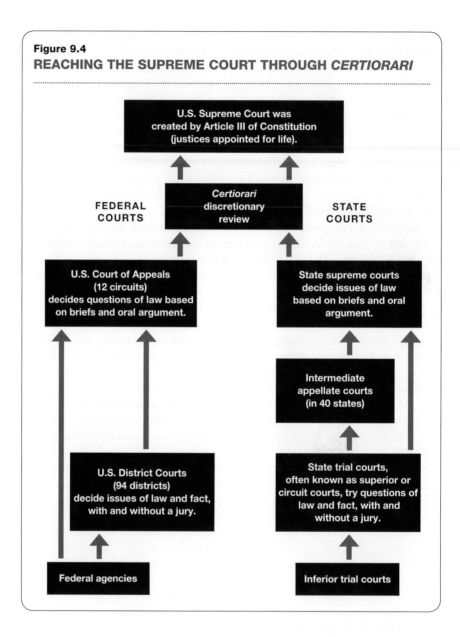

Figure 9.4

REACHING THE SUPREME COURT THROUGH *CERTIORARI*

U.S. Supreme Court was created by Article III of Constitution (justices appointed for life).

Certiorari discretionary review

FEDERAL COURTS

STATE COURTS

U.S. Court of Appeals (12 circuits) decides questions of law based on briefs and oral argument.

State supreme courts decide issues of law based on briefs and oral argument.

Intermediate appellate courts (in 40 states)

U.S. District Courts (94 districts) decide issues of law and fact, with and without a jury.

State trial courts, often known as superior or circuit courts, try questions of law and fact, with and without a jury.

Federal agencies

Inferior trial courts

discuss list, which is circulated by the chief justice. If a case is not placed on the discuss list, it is automatically denied *certiorari*. Cases placed on the discuss list are considered and voted on during the justices' closed-door conference. For *certiorari* to be granted, four justices must be convinced that the case satisfies Rule 10 of the Rules of the U.S. Supreme Court. Rule 10 states that *certiorari* is not a matter of right but is to be granted only when there are special and compelling reasons. These include conflicting decisions by two or more circuit courts, conflicts between circuit courts and state courts of last resort, conflicting decisions by two or more state courts of last resort, decisions by circuit courts on matters of federal law that should be settled by the Supreme Court, and a circuit court decision on an important question that conflicts with a Supreme Court decision. It should be clear from this list that the Court will usually take action under only the most compelling circumstances—when there are conflicts among the lower courts about what the law should be, when an important legal question has been raised in the lower courts and not definitively answered, or when a lower court deviates from the principles and precedents established by the high court. The support of four justices is needed for *certiorari*, and few cases are able to satisfy this requirement. In recent sessions, although thousands of petitions have been filed (Figure 9.5), the Court has granted *certiorari* to fewer than 90 petitioners each year—about 1 percent of those seeking a Supreme Court review.

A handful of cases reach the Supreme Court through avenues other than *certiorari*. One of these is the writ of certification. This writ can be used when a Court of Appeals asks the Supreme Court for instructions on a point of law

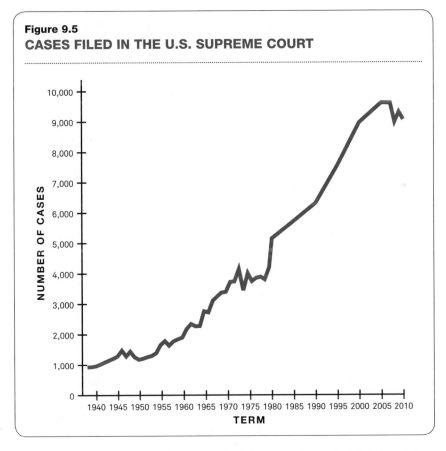

Figure 9.5

CASES FILED IN THE U.S. SUPREME COURT

SOURCES: Years 1938–69: successive volumes of U.S. Bureau of the Census, *Statistical Abstract of the United States* (Washington, DC: Government Printing Office); 1970–79: Office of the Clerk of the Supreme Court; 1980–2010: U.S. Census Bureau, *The 2012 Statistical Abstract*, Table 331, www .census.gov/prod/2011pubs/12statab/law.pdf (accessed 6/11/13).

that has never been decided. A second alternative avenue is the writ of appeal, which is used to appeal the decision of a three-judge district court.

Controlling the Flow of Cases

In addition to the judges themselves, two other actors play an important role in shaping the flow of cases through the federal courts: the solicitor general and the federal law clerks.

The Solicitor General. If any single person has greater influence than the individual justices over the work of the Supreme Court, it is the solicitor general of the United States. The solicitor general is third in status in the Justice Department (below the attorney general and the deputy attorney general), but he is the top government lawyer in virtually all cases before the appellate courts in which the government is a party. Although others can regulate the flow of cases, the solicitor general has the greatest control, with no review of his or her actions by any higher authority in the executive branch. More than half the Supreme Court's total workload consists of cases under the direct charge of the solicitor general.

The solicitor general exercises especially strong influence by screening cases involving the federal government as a party long before they approach the Supreme Court; indeed, the justices rely on the solicitor general to "screen out undeserving litigation and furnish them with an agenda to hear government cases that deserve serious consideration."[31] Typically, more requests for appeals are rejected than are accepted by the solicitor general. Agency heads may lobby the president or otherwise try to circumvent the solicitor general, and a few of the independent agencies have a statutory right to make direct appeals, but without the solicitor general's support these are seldom reviewed by the Court.

amicus curiae

"Friend of the court," an individual or group that is not party to a lawsuit but seeks to assist the court in reaching a decision by presenting an additional brief

By writing an **amicus curiae** ("friend of the court") brief, the solicitor general can enter a case even when the federal government is not a direct litigant. A "friend of the court" is not a direct party to a case but has a vital interest in its outcome. Thus when the government has such an interest, the solicitor general can file as *amicus curiae*, or the Court can invite such a brief because it wants an opinion in writing. Other interested parties may file briefs as well.

In addition to exercising substantial control over the flow of cases, the solicitor general can shape the arguments used before the Court. Indeed, the Court tends to give special attention to the way the solicitor general characterizes the issues. The solicitor general is the person appearing most frequently before the Court and, theoretically at least, the most disinterested. The credibility of the solicitor general

---

31 Robert Scigliano, *The Supreme Court and the Presidency* (New York: Free Press, 1971), p. 162. For an interesting critique of the solicitor general's role during the Reagan administration, see Lincoln Caplan, "Annals of the Law," *New Yorker*, August 17, 1987, pp. 30–62.

372   **Chapter 9:** The Federal Courts

is not hurt when several times each year she comes to the Court to withdraw a case with the admission that the government has made an error.[32]

Law Clerks. Every federal judge employs law clerks to research legal issues and assist with the preparation of opinions. Each Supreme Court justice is assigned four clerks. The clerks are almost always honors graduates of the nation's most prestigious law schools. A clerkship with a Supreme Court justice is a great honor and generally indicates that the fortunate individual is likely to reach the very top of the legal profession. One of the most important roles performed by the clerks is screening the thousands of petitions for writs of *certiorari* that come before the Court.[33] It is also likely that some justices rely heavily on their clerks for advice in writing opinions and deciding whether an individual case ought to be heard by the Court. It is often rumored that certain opinions were actually written by a clerk rather than a justice.[34] Although such rumors are difficult to substantiate, it is clear that at the end of long judicial careers, justices such as William O. Douglas and Thurgood Marshall had become so infirm that they were compelled to rely on the judgments of their law clerks.

The Supreme Court's Procedures

The Preparation. The Supreme Court's decision to accept a case is the beginning of what can be a lengthy and complex process (Figure 9.6). First, the attorneys on both sides must prepare **briefs**—written documents in which the attorneys explain why the Court should rule in favor of their client. The document filed by the individual bringing the case is called the petitioner's brief. It summarizes the facts of the case and presents the legal basis on which the Supreme Court is being asked to overturn the lower court's decision. The document filed by the side that prevailed in the lower court is called the respondent's brief. It explains why the Supreme Court should affirm the lower court's verdict. The petitioners then file a brief answering and attempting to refute the points made in the respondent's brief. This document is called the petitioner's reply brief. Briefs are filled with references to precedents specifically chosen to show that other courts have frequently ruled in the same way that the Supreme Court is being asked to rule.

 brief

A written document in which an attorney explains—using case precedents—why the Court should rule in favor of his or her client

---

32 On the strategic and informational role played by the solicitor general, see Kevin McGuire, "Explaining Executive Success in the U.S. Supreme Court," *Political Research Quarterly* 51 (1998): 505–26. Also see Michael Bailey, Brian Kamoie, and Forrest Maltzman, "Signals from the Tenth Justice: The Political Role of the Solicitor General in Supreme Court Decision Making," *American Journal of Political Science* 49 (2005): 72–85.

33 H. W. Perry, Jr., *Deciding to Decide: Agenda Setting in the United States Supreme Court* (Cambridge, MA: Harvard University Press, 1991).

34 Edward Lazarus, *Closed Chambers: The First Eyewitness Account of the Struggles inside the Supreme Court* (New York: Times Books, 1998).

Figure 9.6

THE SUPREME COURT'S DECISION-MAKING PROCESS

Petitions → *Certiorari* pool → Discuss list → Conference

Briefs | *Amicus curiae* briefs → Oral argument → Conference → Opinions and dissents

As the attorneys prepare their briefs, they often ask sympathetic interest groups for their help by means of *amicus curiae* briefs. In a case involving separation of church and state, for example, liberal groups such as the American Civil Liberties Union (ACLU) and People for the American Way are likely to be asked to file *amicus* briefs in support of strict separation, whereas conservative religious groups, the Family Research Council or Focus on the Family, for example, are likely to file *amicus* briefs advocating increased public support for religious ideas. Often dozens of briefs will be filed on each side of a major case.

oral argument

The stage in Supreme Court proceedings in which attorneys for both sides appear before the Court to present their positions and answer questions posed by the justices

Oral Argument. The next stage of a case is **oral argument**, in which attorneys for both sides appear before the Court to present their positions and answer the justices' questions. Each attorney has only a half hour to present his case, and this time includes interruptions for questions. Certain members of the Court, such as Justice Antonin Scalia, are known to interrupt attorneys dozens of times. Others, such as Justice Clarence Thomas, seldom ask questions. Oral argument can be very important to the outcome of a case. It allows justices to better understand the heart of a case and raise questions that might not have been addressed in the opposing sides' briefs. It is not uncommon for justices to go beyond the strictly legal issues and ask opposing counsel to discuss the implications of the case for the Court and the nation at large.[35] In oral arguments on the constitutionality of the Defense of Marriage Act in 2013, for example, Justice Kennedy returned frequently to the matter of whether the definition of marriage resided with the states rather than with the federal government. Justice Ginsburg took a social perspective, objecting to the fact that the law

---

35 On the consequences of oral argument for decision making, see Timothy R. Johnson, Paul J. Wahlbeck, and James F. Spriggs II, "The Influence of Oral Arguments on the U.S. Supreme Court," *American Political Science Review* 100, no. 1 (February 2006): 99–113.

created "two kinds of marriage: the full marriage, and then this sort of skim milk marriage."[36]

The Conference. After oral argument, the Court discusses the case in its Wednesday or Friday conference. The chief justice presides over the conference and speaks first; the other justices follow in order of seniority. The Court's conferences are secret, and no outsiders are permitted to attend. The justices reach a decision on the basis of a majority vote. As the case is discussed, justices may try to influence or change each other's opinions. At times, this may result in compromise decisions.

Opinion Writing. After a decision has been reached, one of the members of the majority is assigned to write the **opinion**. This assignment is made by the chief justice or the most senior justice in the majority if the chief justice is on the losing side. The assignment of the opinion can make a significant difference to the interpretation of a decision, as its wording and emphasis can have important implications for future litigation. Thus in assigning an opinion, the justices must give serious thought to the impression the case will make on lawyers and the public, as well as to the probability that one justice's opinion will be more widely accepted than another's.[37]

opinion

The written explanation of the Supreme Court's decision in a particular case

One of the more dramatic instances of this tactical consideration occurred in 1944, when Chief Justice Harlan Fiske Stone chose Justice Felix Frankfurter to write the opinion in the "white primary" case *Smith v. Allwright*, which overturned the southern practice of prohibiting black participation in primaries. The day after Stone made the assignment, Justice Robert Jackson wrote a letter to Stone arguing that Frankfurter, a foreign-born Jew from New England, would not win over the South with his opinion, regardless of his brilliance. Stone accepted the advice and substituted Justice Stanley F. Reed, an American-born Protestant from Kentucky and a southern Democrat in good standing.[38]

Once the majority opinion is drafted, it is circulated to the other justices. Some members of the majority may agree with both the outcome and the rationale but wish to emphasize or highlight a particular point and so draft a concurring opinion, called a regular **concurrence**. In other instances, one or more justices may agree with the majority but disagree with the rationale presented in the majority opinion. Then the justices may draft a special concurrence, explaining their disagreements with the majority. The pattern of opinions that emerge on a case ultimately depends on bargaining among the justices, as suggested by the collective action principle.

concurrence

An opinion agreeing with the decision of the majority but not with the rationale provided in the majority opinion

36 Quoted in Adam Liptak and Peter Baker, "Justices Cast Doubt on Benefits Ban in U.S. Marriage Law," *New York Times*, March 27, 2013, p. A1.

37 For this and other strategic aspects of the Court's process, see Forrest Maltzman, James F. Spriggs II, and Paul J. Wahlbeck, *Crafting Law on the Supreme Court: The Collegial Game* (New York: Cambridge University Press, 2001).

38 *Smith v. Allwright*, 321 U.S. 649 (1944).

Dissent. Justices who disagree with the majority decision of the Court may choose to publicize the character of their disagreement in the form of a **dissenting opinion**. The dissenting opinion is generally assigned by the senior justice among the dissenters. Dissents can be used to signal to defeated political forces in the nation that their position is supported by at least some members of the Court. Ironically, the most dependable way an individual justice can exercise a direct and clear influence on the Court is to write a dissent. Because there is no need to please a majority, dissenting opinions can be more eloquent and less guarded than majority opinions. The current Supreme Court often produces 5–4 decisions, with dissenters writing long and detailed opinions that, they hope, will help them convince a swing justice to join their side on the next round of cases dealing with a similar topic. Thus, for example, Justice David Souter wrote a 34-page dissent in a 2002 case upholding the use of government-funded school vouchers to pay for parochial school tuition. Souter called the decision "a dramatic departure from basic Establishment Clause principle" and went on to say that he hoped it would be reconsidered by a future court.[39]

Dissent plays a special role in the work and impact of the Court because it amounts to an appeal to lawyers all over the country to keep bringing cases of the sort at issue. Therefore, an effective dissent influences the flow of cases through the Court as well as the arguments that lawyers will make in later cases.

These rules of collective decision making shape how the Supreme Court addresses cases. But they are just the structure within which judges operate. The rules tell us something about the nature of judicial authority—it is restrained and cautious, it is incremental and rational. But the rules, in the end, tell us little about how judges will deal with the great political and social questions of the day. The same basic appellate system yielded both *Plessy v. Ferguson* and *Brown v. Board of Education*. How the courts ultimately decide matters of law depends on the views and beliefs of those in the judiciary and the nature of the problems they must address and on the relationship of the courts to the other branches of government.

---

dissenting opinion →

A decision written by a justice who voted with the minority opinion in a particular case in which the justice fully explains the reasoning behind his or her opinion

---

JUDICIAL DECISION MAKING

The judiciary is conservative in its procedures, but its effect on society can be radical. That effect depends on a variety of factors, two of which stand out above the rest. The first is the individual members of the Supreme Court, their attitudes and goals, and their relationships with one another. The second is the other branches of government, particularly Congress.

---

39 Warren Richey, "Dissenting Opinions as a Window on Future Rulings," *Christian Science Monitor*, July 1, 2002, p. 1.

The Supreme Court Justices

The Supreme Court explains its decisions in terms of law and precedent. But although law and precedent do have an effect on the Court's deliberations and eventual decisions, it is the Supreme Court that decides what laws mean and what importance precedents will have. Throughout its history, the Court has shaped and reshaped the law. If any individual judges in the country influence the federal judiciary, the Supreme Court justices are the ones who do.

From the 1950s to the 1980s, the Supreme Court took an active role in such areas as civil rights, civil liberties, abortion, voting rights, and police procedures. For example, the Supreme Court was more responsible than any other governmental institution for breaking down America's system of racial segregation. The Supreme Court virtually prohibited states from interfering with the right of a woman to seek an abortion and sharply curtailed state restrictions on voting rights. And it was the Supreme Court that placed restrictions on the behavior of local police and prosecutors in criminal cases. But since the early 1980s, resignations, deaths, and new appointments have led to many shifts in the mix of philosophies and ideologies represented on the Court. In a series of decisions between 1989 and 2001, the conservative justices who had been appointed by Ronald Reagan and George H. W. Bush were able to swing the Court to a more conservative position on civil rights, affirmative action, abortion rights, property rights, criminal procedure, voting rights, desegregation, and the power of the national government.

The importance of ideology was very clear during the Court's 2000–01 term. In important decisions, the Court's most conservative justices—Scalia, Thomas, and Rehnquist, usually joined by Kennedy—generally voted as a bloc.[40] Indeed, Scalia and Thomas voted together in 99 percent of all cases. At the same time, the Court's most liberal justices—Breyer, Ginsburg, Souter, and Stevens—also generally formed a voting bloc.[41] Justice O'Connor, a moderate conservative, was the swing vote in many important cases.[42] This ideological division led to a number of important 5–4 decisions. In the case *Bush v. Gore*, which concerned the recounting of ballots in Florida in the 2000 presidential election, Justice O'Connor joined with the conservative bloc to give Bush a 5–4 victory. Indeed, more than 33 percent of all the cases heard by the Court in its 2000–01 term were decided by a 5–4 vote. In the Court's 2012–13 term, 7 of the 14 most important cases were decided by a 5–4 margin.

However, precisely because the Court was so evenly split during this period, the conservative bloc did not always prevail. On some issues Justice O'Connor or Justice Kennedy sided with the liberal camp, producing a 5–4 and, sometimes, a 6–3 victory for the liberals. In the 2003 case of *Missouri v. Seibert*, for example,

---

40 Linda Greenhouse, "In Year of Florida Vote, Supreme Court Also Did Much Other Work," *New York Times*, July 2, 2001, p. A12.

41 Charles Lane, "Laying Down the Law," *Washington Post*, July 1, 2001, p. A6.

42 For an insightful discussion about identifying the swing justice on the Court, see Andrew D. Martin, Kevin M. Quinn, and Lee Epstein, "The Median Justice on the U.S. Supreme Court," *North Carolina Law Review* 83 (2005): 1275–1322.

Justice Kennedy joined a 5–4 majority to strengthen Miranda rights.[43] Similarly, in *McConnell v. Federal Election Commission*, Justice O'Connor joined the liberal bloc to uphold the validity of the Bipartisan Campaign Reform Act.[44] On abortion, women's rights, and affirmative action, Justice O'Connor often joined the liberal bloc. With the departure of O'Connor and her replacement by Alito in 2006, many anticipated a series of new 5–4 decisions favoring the conservatives under new chief justice John Roberts.[45] In 2007, for example, the Court upheld the Partial Birth Abortion Ban Act—a law favored by conservatives—by a 5–4 majority. The departure of Justice O'Connor shifted the center of the Court (the part that proves pivotal in formulating opinions) to Justice Kennedy, who by many measures does not significantly differ from O'Connor in his jurisprudence. The Court's policies may have drifted rightward since O'Connor's departure, but only from O'Connor's position to Kennedy's, not nearly so dramatic a difference as that between O'Connor and Alito.[46]

It should be noted that, while the pattern of a four-person liberal bloc pitted against a four-person conservative bloc with a centrist justice (O'Connor or Kennedy) swinging between them to create a 5–4 division has prevailed frequently in the last decade or two, this bloc structure is not always predictive, even in important cases. In *National Federation of Independent Business v. Sebelius*, the 2012 case on the constitutionality of Obama's health care law, it was Chief Justice Roberts, a firm member of the conservative bloc, who joined the four liberals to uphold the law.[47]

Finally let us observe that the Court's policy influence comes not from the "horse race" results often trumpeted by the media but from the written opinions providing the constitutional or statutory rationale for policy in the future. These opinions establish the guidelines that govern how federal courts must decide similar cases in the future.

Activism and Restraint. One element of judicial philosophy is the issue of activism versus restraint. Over the years, some justices have believed that courts should interpret the Constitution according to the stated intentions of its framers and defer to the views of Congress when interpreting federal statutes. Justice Felix Frankfurter, for example, advocated judicial deference to legislative bodies and avoidance of the "political thicket," in which the Court would entangle itself by deciding questions that were essentially political rather than legal in character. Advocates of **judicial restraint** are sometimes called strict constructionists because they look strictly to the words of the Constitution in interpreting its meaning.

judicial restraint

The judicial philosophy whose adherents refuse to go beyond the text of the Constitution in interpreting its meaning

---

43 *Missouri v. Seibert,* 542 U.S. 600 (2004).

44 *McConnell v. Federal Election Commission,* 540 U.S. 93 (2003).

45 Adam Liptak, "Entrances and Exits: The New 5-to-4 Supreme Court," *New York Times,* April 22, 2007.

46 For a development of this argument, see David W. Rohde and Kenneth A. Shepsle, "Advising and Consenting in the 60-Vote Senate: Strategic Appointments to the Supreme Court," *Journal of Politics* 69, no. 3 (August 2007): 664–77.

47 Adam Liptak, "Supreme Court Upholds Health Care Law, 5–4 in Victory for Obama," *New York Times,* June 28, 2012, www.nytimes.com/2012/06/29/us/supreme-court-lets -health-law-largely-stand.html?pagewanted=all&_ro (accessed 7/15/13).

The alternative to restraint is **judicial activism**. Activist judges such as Chief Justice Earl Warren believe that the Court should go beyond the words of the Constitution or a statute to consider the broader societal implications of its decisions. Activist judges sometimes strike out in new directions, promulgating new interpretations or inventing new legal and constitutional concepts when they believe them to be socially desirable. For example, Justice Harry Blackmun's opinion in *Roe v. Wade* was based on a constitutional right to privacy that is not found in the words of the Constitution but was, rather, based on the Court's prior decision in *Griswold v. Connecticut*. Blackmun and the other members of the majority in the *Roe* case argued that the right to privacy is implied by other constitutional provisions. In this instance of judicial activism, the Court knew the result it wanted to achieve and was not afraid to make the law conform to the desired outcome.

It is sometimes difficult to discern a difference between restraint and different flavors of activism. The conservative bloc on the Court sometimes does try to rein in the more expansive posture taken by previous activist majorities. In other cases however, it seeks to move "boldly" and "actively" in areas that had previously been regarded as settled. In the *Citizens United* case in 2010, for example, the Court held that corporations and unions could not be restricted from financial participation in elections.[48] It did not reverse previous prohibitions on corporate donations directly to candidates, but it did allow independent expenditures, for example, advertising during a campaign. This seems to fit uncomfortably with a philosophy of restraint.

Political Ideology. The second component of judicial philosophy is political ideology. The liberal or conservative attitudes of justices play an important role in their decisions.[49] The philosophy of activism versus restraint is sometimes a smoke screen for political ideology. In the past, liberal judges have been activists, willing to use the law to achieve social and political change, whereas conservatives have been associated with judicial restraint. Conservative politicians often castigate "liberal activist" judges and call for the appointment of conservative jurists who will refrain from reinterpreting the law. It is interesting, however, that in recent years some conservative justices who have long called for restraint have become activists in seeking to undo some of the work of liberal jurists over the past three decades. To be sure, some liberal jurists are activists and some conservatives have been advocates of restraint, but the relationship is by no means one to one. Indeed, the Rehnquist Court, dominated by conservatives, was among the most activist Supreme Courts in American history, striking out in new directions in areas such as federalism and election law.

In our discussion of congressional politics in Chapter 6, we described legislators as policy oriented. In conceiving of judges as legislators in robes, we are

◀ **judicial activism**

The judicial philosophy that posits that the Court should see beyond the text of the Constitution or a statute to consider broader societal implications for its decisions

---

48 *Citizens United v. Federal Election Commission*, 558 U.S. 310 (2010).

49 C. Herman Pritchett, *The Roosevelt Court: A Study in Judicial Politics and Values* (New York: Macmillan, 1948); Jeffrey A. Segal and Harold J. Spaeth, *The Supreme Court and the Attitudinal Model* (New York: Cambridge University Press, 1993); and by the same authors, *The Supreme Court and Attitudinal Model Revisited* (New York: Cambridge University Press, 2002).

effectively claiming that judges, like other politicians, have policy preferences that they seek to implement. The Analyzing the Evidence unit in this chapter looks at ideology in the Court.

Other Institutions of Government

Congress. At both the national and the state level in the United States, courts and judges are players in the policy game because of the separation of powers. Essentially this means that the legislative branch formulates policy (defined constitutionally and institutionally by a legislative process), the executive branch implements policy (according to well-defined administrative procedures and subject to initial approval by the president or the legislative override of his veto), and the courts, when asked, rule on the faithfulness of the legislated and executed policy, either to the substance of the statute or to the Constitution itself. The courts may strike down an administrative action either because it exceeds the authority granted in the relevant statute (statutory rationale) or because the statute itself exceeds the authority granted the legislature or executive by the Constitution (constitutional rationale).

If the Court declares the administrative agent's act as outside the permissible bounds, the Court's majority opinion can effectively declare whatever policy it wishes. If the legislature is unhappy with this judicial action, then it may either recraft the legislation (if the rationale for striking it down was statutory)[50] or initiate a constitutional amendment that would enable the stricken policy to pass constitutional muster (if the rationale for originally striking it down was constitutional).

In reaching their decisions, Supreme Court justices must anticipate Congress's response. As a result, judges will not always vote according to their true preferences because doing so may provoke Congress to enact legislation that moves the policy further from what the judges prefer. By voting for a lesser preference, the justices can get something they prefer to the status quo without provoking congressional action to overturn their decision. The most famous example of this phenomenon is the "switch in time that saved nine," when two justices voted in favor of New Deal legislation, the constitutionality of which they doubted, in an effort to diminish congressional support for President Franklin Delano Roosevelt's plan to "pack" the Court by increasing the number of justices. In short, the interactions between the Court and Congress are part of a complex strategic game.[51]

The President. The president's most direct influence on the Court is the power to nominate justices. Presidents typically nominate judges who they believe are close to their policy preferences and close enough to the

---

50 William N. Eskridge, Jr., "Overriding Supreme Court Statutory Interpretation Decisions," *Yale Law Journal* 101 (1991): 331–55.

51 A full strategic analysis of the maneuvering among legislative, executive, and judicial branches in the separation-of-powers arrangement choreographed by the U.S. Constitution may be found in William N. Eskridge, Jr., and John Ferejohn, "The Article I, Section 7, Game," *Georgetown Law Review* 80 (1992): 523–65. The entire issue of this journal is devoted to the theme of strategic behavior in American institutional politics.

preferences of a majority of senators, who must confirm the nomination, as discussed earlier.

For example, with a combined total of 12 years in office, Reagan and G. H. W. Bush were able to exercise a good deal of influence on the composition of the federal district and appellate courts. By the end of Bush's term, he and Reagan together had appointed nearly half of all the federal judges, which clearly had a continuing influence on the temperament and behavior of the district and circuit courts. President Clinton promised to appoint more liberal jurists to the district and appellate courts and to increase the number of women and minorities serving on the federal bench. During his years in office, Clinton held to this promise (Figure 9.7).

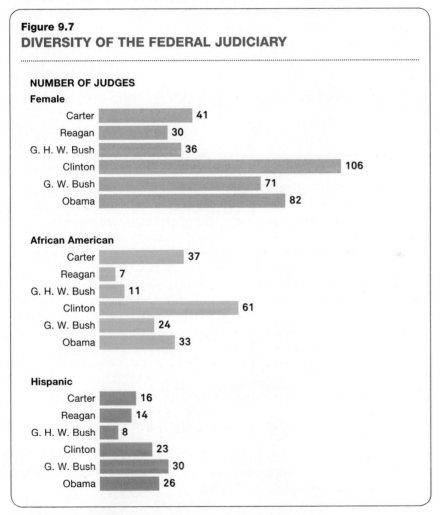

Figure 9.7
DIVERSITY OF THE FEDERAL JUDICIARY

NUMBER OF JUDGES

Female
- Carter: 41
- Reagan: 30
- G. H. W. Bush: 36
- Clinton: 106
- G. W. Bush: 71
- Obama: 82

African American
- Carter: 37
- Reagan: 7
- G. H. W. Bush: 11
- Clinton: 61
- G. W. Bush: 24
- Obama: 33

Hispanic
- Carter: 16
- Reagan: 14
- G. H. W. Bush: 8
- Clinton: 23
- G. W. Bush: 30
- Obama: 26

NOTE: Carter appointed 261 federal judges; Reagan appointed 364; G. H. W. Bush appointed 188; Clinton appointed 372; G. W. Bush appointed 321; and Obama appointed 201 (as of August 2013).

SOURCE: The Federal Judiciary Center, History of the Federal Judiciary, www.fjc.gov/history/home.nsf/page/research_categories.html (accessed 9/5/13).

Ideological Voting on the Supreme Court

Contributed by
Andrew D. Martin
Washington University in St. Louis
Kevin M. Quinn
UC Berkeley School of Law

Do the political preferences of Supreme Court justices influence their behavior? The starting point for the analysis of the behavior of Supreme Court justices is to look at their votes.[1] For non-unanimous cases, we can compute agreement scores—the fraction of cases in which a pair of justices vote the same way. We display these agreement scores for the Court's 2012–13 term in the first figure below. If you examine this figure, you will see that two groups of justices emerge. Within each group, the justices agree with one another a lot, around 70 to 90 percent of the time. Voting is more structured than we would expect by chance.

One way to represent that structure is by arranging the justices on a line as in the diagram below to the right.[2] Justices who agree a lot should be close to one another; justices who disagree a lot should be far apart.

Does the fact that there are patterns of agreement mean that the justices are deciding based on political ideology? Not necessarily. These patterns are consistent with ideological decision making, but other things might explain the patterns as well. However, when we read the cases and see who wins or loses, there is a great deal of support for the idea that political ideology influences how justices vote.[3]

Agreement Scores for the 2012–13 Term

	Ginsburg	Sotomayor	Kagan	Breyer	Kennedy	Scalia	Roberts	Thomas	Alito
Ginsburg	1	.89	.92	.77	.46	.36	.28	.15	.13
Sotomayor	.89	1	.94	.76	.47	.32	.29	.21	.19
Kagan	.92	.94	1	.81	.43	.35	.3	.19	.14
Breyer	.77	.76	.81	1	.54	.23	.46	.33	.37
Kennedy	.46	.47	.43	.54	1	.59	.72	.54	.63
Scalia	.36	.32	.35	.23	.59	1	.72	.74	.55
Roberts	.28	.29	.3	.46	.72	.72	1	.72	.79
Thomas	.15	.21	.19	.33	.54	.74	.72	1	.76
Alito	.13	.19	.14	.37	.63	.55	.79	.76	1

● < 0.35   ● 0.35–0.44   ● 0.45–0.54

● 0.55–0.64   ● 0.65–0.74   ● 0.75–0.99

POSITION

Ginsburg
Sotomayor
Kagan

Breyer

Kennedy

Scalia
Roberts

Thomas
Alito

The figure to the left contains the agreement scores for the 2012–13 term of the U.S. Supreme Court for all non-unanimous cases. These scores are the proportion of cases when each justice agreed with every other justice. Two justices that always disagreed with each other would get a zero; two justices who always agreed would get a one. Red indicates low agreement scores; green indicates high agreement scores. The policy dimension to the right of the figure is one that best represents the patterns in the agreement scores.

0 = Justices always disagreed
1 = Justices always agreed

This type of analysis can be done for any court, but it becomes more difficult if we are interested in comparing justices across time instead of during just one term. What if we are interested in whether the Supreme Court is becoming more ideologically polarized over time? Or whether individual justices have become more liberal or conservative? Martin-Quinn scores based on a statistical model of voting on the Court help solve this problem.[4]

A number of interesting patterns emerge. Consider the case of Justice Harry Blackmun, who often claimed, "I haven't changed; it's the Court that changed under me."[5] The figure below shows that Justice Blackmun's position did in fact change ideologically over the course of his career. This evidence is consistent with some clear changes in Justice Blackmun's behavior, especially in the area of the death penalty.

We can also look at patterns in the positions of chief justices. While the chief's vote counts just the same as the other justices, he or she plays an important role in organizing the court. Justice Rehnquist was the most conservative justice on the court when he arrived in 1971, but as the figure below shows, after he was elevated in 1986 he, too, drifted more toward the middle. This is what we would expect to see of a justice who was working strategically to build coalitions, as any good chief would.

Ideological Trajectories of Selected Justices

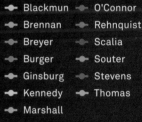

JUSTICES

- Blackmun
- Brennan
- Breyer
- Burger
- Ginsburg
- Kennedy
- Marshall
- O'Connor
- Rehnquist
- Scalia
- Souter
- Stevens
- Thomas

This figure shows the Martin-Quinn score for selected justices serving in the Burger (1969–86) and Rehnquist Courts (1986–2004). Each line represents the trajectory of each justice on the ideological dimension.

1   C. Herman Pritchett, *The Roosevelt Court: A Study in Judicial Politics and Values, 1937–1947* (New York: MacMillan Co., 1948).
2   Glendon A. Schubert, *The Judicial Mind: The Attitudes and Ideologies of Supreme Court Justices, 1946–1963* (Evanston, IL: Northwestern University Press, 1965).
3   Jeffry A. Segal and Harold J. Spaeth, *The Supreme Court and the Attitudinal Model* (New York: Cambridge University Press, 1993).
4   Andrew D. Martin and Kevin M. Quinn, "Dynamic Ideal Point Estimation via Markov Chain Monte Carlo for the U.S. Supreme Court, 1953–1999," *Political Analysis* 10, no. 2, (2002): 134–53, http://mqscores.wustl.edu (accessed 10/18/11).
5   Linda Greenhouse, *Becoming Justice Blackmun* (New York: Times Books, 2005).

The president must also confront Congress in shaping the judiciary. By using the filibuster (see Chapter 6), both parties have blocked judicial nominees: when George W. Bush was president, the Democrats repeatedly blocked nominees, and the Republicans have done so since Obama became president. The acrimony over judicial nominees have prompted both parties to suggest changing Senate rules to allow their preferred nominees through, although these changes have not yet come to pass. In the meantime, the federal judiciary remains understaffed. One high-profile nominee, Goodwin Lin, withdrew his nomination to the Ninth Circuit of Appeals in 2011, after a year and a half wait.

The Implementation of Supreme Court Decisions

The president and the rest of the executive branch, along with Congress, the states, the lower courts, and a variety of private organizations and individuals play key roles in the implementation of Supreme Court decisions. Once the high court has made a decision, a variety of other government agencies must put it into effect. The lower courts must understand and apply to new cases the principles asserted by the Supreme Court. The executive branch must enforce the Court's decision. State legislators and governors must implement the decision in their own jurisdictions. And often individuals and organizations must take action in the courts and in the political arena to demand that the Supreme Court's verdicts be fully implemented. At each of these stages, opposition on the part of the revelant actors may delay full national implementation of a Supreme Court decision, sometimes for years.

For example, if lower-court judges strongly disagree with a Supreme Court decision, they may use a variety of tactics to avoid fully implementing it. Lower-court judges may, for example, avoid applying the case by disposing of similar cases on technical or procedural grounds. Similarly, they may apply the case as narrowly as possible or declare that some portion of the Court's opinion was merely "dicta"—useful as guidance but not binding.

As for executive agencies, most Supreme Court decisions must be implemented by federal, state, and local agencies. If these agencies are unsympathetic to the Court's decision, they may obstruct, delay, or even refuse to accept them. In the nineteenth century, President Andrew Jackson famously refused to obey a Supreme Court decision, declaring, "John Marshall has made his decision. Now let him enforce it." Although few executives or executive agencies have been as overtly defiant as Jackson, many have quietly ignored or sought to circumvent the Court. For example, many local school boards have searched for years for ways to circumvent the Court's various rulings prohibiting religious observance in the public schools.

Strategic Behavior in the Supreme Court

In describing the role and effect of the Supreme Court, we have occasionally referred to the strategic opportunities the Court provides. It is useful to gather some of these insights in one place to stitch together a more consistent strategic interpretation. Let's divide this strategic behavior into three stages. Stage 1 begins with a period of "normal" politics—in (local or national) legislatures, (local or national) executive and regulatory agencies, political processes like elections, and the stuff of everyday life involving interactions among public and private entities (citizens, corporations, nonprofits, voluntary associations, governments). Conflict arises, and interested parties must decide what to do: live with the results, pursue normal political channels using legislatures and agencies to resolve the conflict, or move the conflict into the courts. Stage 2 involves a court responding to its environment, with judges both reacting to demands from the outside and fashioning their own behavioral strategies within the legal process. Stage 3 involves what happens once a court renders a decision and how the actors in stages 1 and 2 anticipate the decision and adjust their behavior to its expectations. Although our discussion could be developed for all courts, we will focus on the Supreme Court. Indeed, we will narrow things even further by devoting the bulk of our remarks to the internal strategic environment of the Supreme Court at stage 2, when it both reacts to developments that have preceded its being drawn into a conflict (stage 1) and anticipates what will happen if it responds in a particular manner (stage 3).

Stage 1. Assume that a conflict has arisen and appeals have been made through normal channels. Administrative and regulatory agencies, for example, often have well-defined procedures for appealing a ruling within the agency, with the opportunity of a subsequent appeal to a court always being available. Dissatisfied with the outcome, one of the parties moves the dispute to the courts, and at some point in the process the option of appeal to the Supreme Court is available. The aggrieved party has a decision to make. It is a calculated, strategic decision in two respects.

First, an appeal will consume resources that might otherwise be redeployed and used for different purposes. A prospective appellant must weigh an appeal against this "opportunity cost." The Sierra Club, for example, might use resources to appeal a lower-court decision on environmental protection to the Supreme Court or, alternatively, devote some of those same resources to lobbying Congress on other issues.

Second, all options are uncertain propositions whose resolution stretches out over time. Regarding uncertainty, a prospective appellant must recognize that the probability of successfully getting to the Court is slim, and even if it succeeds in obtaining *certiorari*, it may not win on the merits of its case. Regarding the time dimension, even if the appellant wins, the process may take years, making the delayed victory bittersweet. Ultimately these strategic calculations revolve around what an appellant can expect in pursuing an appeal—that is, what might happen in stages 2 and 3.[52]

---

52 There are subtleties to the strategies of appellants. They may seek an appeal to the Supreme Court, for example, as a bluff to induce the winner in the lower court to accommodate in advance some of their preferences—in effect, to settle out of court. Why might the lower-court winners be induced to accommodate the losers? There are at least two reasons: first, to avoid the exorbitant costs of fighting an appeal to the Supreme Court and, second, to avoid the prospect that their victory in the lower court may be reversed.

Stage 2. As we have already noted, thousands of cases are appealed to the Supreme Court. The nine justices of the Supreme Court (or, more accurately, their clerks) must sort through these petitions and, according to the **rule of four**, build their docket each session. The Court, in short, has the power to create its own agenda.

In building their docket for the current session of the Court, how do justices think about the available options? They support some cases undoubtedly out of a strong belief that an area is ripe for constitutional clarification. They support others out of an interest in the development of legal principles in a particular area of the law—criminal rights, privacy, First Amendment, abortion, affirmative action, federal-state relations, and so on—or in the belief that contradictory decisions in lower courts need to be sorted out. They may oppose certain appeals because they believe a particular case will not provide a sufficiently clear-cut basis for clarifying a legal issue. That is, even though a case might attract the interest of a justice on substantive grounds or might be perceived by a justice as containing procedural errors that could lead to a reversal, she might not support *certiorari* because of a strategic calculation that it is not a particularly good vehicle or that it would be prudent to wait until a better vehicle comes up through the appeals process in a subsequent session.[53]

Once a case is included on the docket and oral arguments have been delivered by the attorneys for the litigants and *amicus curiae* briefs filed by other interested parties, the case becomes the subject of two decisions.[54] The first takes place after it is discussed by the justices in one of the regularly scheduled conferences during the Court's term. When discussion has concluded and all attempts at persuasion have come to an end, there is a vote on the merits—a vote in favor of the appeal or against it. In principle, this vote affects only the parties to the case, either affirming or reversing the lower-court decision.

It is the second decision that has a wider bearing. Having decided one way or the other, the justices must determine whether there is agreement on the reasons for their decision. This is a highly strategic decision because the Court's impact over and above its effect on the contesting parties depends on the reasons it gives for the decision at hand. The reasons of a Court majority set legal precedent for similar cases in the future, thus influencing litigation in lower courts. If the majority cannot agree among themselves on why they decided as they did, there is no binding effect on other comparable cases. Drafting an opinion that can attract the signatures of at least five justices is therefore of pivotal significance. A justice on the winning side who stakes out an extreme position relative to the others is unlikely to be able to draft such an opinion, so moderate members of the Court usually do the heavy lifting of opinion drafting for especially controversial cases. Of course, in some cases a majority may agree

---

53 An excellent discussion of this facet of Supreme Court decision making is found in Perry, *Deciding to Decide*.

54 On the strategic decisions of *amicus* groups, see Thomas Hansford, "Information Provision, Organizational Constraints, and the Decision to Submit an *Amicus Brief* in a U.S. Supreme Court Case," *Political Research Quarterly* 57 (2004): 219–30.

on the merits of a case but are unable to come to a consensus on the reasons. In such cases, there will be no majority opinion, though each justice is free to write his own opinion (possibly cosigned by others), either supporting or dissenting from the decision on the merits, giving his particular reasons. These opinions have no binding effect on future lower-court cases but may still serve a strategic signaling role, conveying to the lower courts and the legal community where a justice stands on the issues involved in the case at hand.[55]

Stage 3. The Supreme Court is not an island unto itself. It is the top rung of one branch in a separation-of-powers system. Its decisions are not automatically implemented; it must depend on executive agencies for implementation and on lower courts for enforcement of its dicta. In fact, it ultimately depends on the willingness of others, especially ordinary citizens, to conform to its rulings. In some instances, the Court may worry about resistance. Throughout the 1940s and 1950s, for example, there were concerns that issues relating to integration would meet with popular disapproval and defiance in the South. Indeed, in the famous *Brown* decision desegregating public schools in 1954, Chief Justice Earl Warren worried about precisely this. When he wrote the majority opinion for the Court, he strategically softened some of its language in order to attract the signatures of all nine justices. The 9–0 decision and opinion were a signal to a potentially defiant South that the Court was united and that it would take a very long time (the time needed to replace at least five justices) before there would be any prospect of reversal—that is, resistance would not pay off in the near or medium term.

In addition to compliance, enforcement, and resistance, the Court also considers the possibility of reversal. On a decision taken by the Court on a statutory issue—for example, on whether an existing law covers a particular situation—majorities in both houses of Congress and the president may pass a new statute reversing the Court's interpretation. If, for example, the Court rules that the Radio Act of 1927 does not cover transmissions by cellular phones and Congress and the president think otherwise, then Congress may pass legislation, and the president may sign it into law, amending the Radio Act of 1927 to allow for its provisions to govern the regulation of cell phones. The Court may well say "what the law is" (to quote Justice Oliver Wendell Holmes), but Congress and the president are free to change the law.[56] Members of the Court may have no particular stake in being reversed—that is, they may not care whether the "political" branches decide, for example, to allow for cell phones to be covered by the Radio Act of 1927. Indeed, they may feel a certain sense of satisfaction that the act, as originally written, had a narrow scope that only subsequent statutory activity

---

55 For an insightful discussion of the strategic elements influencing how the senior justice in the winning coalitions assigns opinion writing, see David W. Rohde, "Policy Goals, Strategic Choice, and Majority Opinion Assignments in the U.S. Supreme Court," *Midwest Journal of Political Science* 16 (1972): 652–82.

56 On the strategic interaction among the Court, Congress, and the president, see Eskridge and Ferejohn, "The Article I, Section 7, Game."

could broaden. Then again, in order to have impact on politics generally, the Court would not want their decisions questioned, reversed, or defied routinely.

For decisions taken by the Court on constitutional (as opposed to statutory) grounds, no mere revision of existing law is sufficient to reverse the Court; an amendment to the Constitution is required. President George W. Bush, for example, gave his blessing to efforts to amend the Constitution to reverse the *Roe v. Wade* decision permitting a woman to choose an abortion in the first two trimesters of her pregnancy.

In the long run, the Supreme Court is the final legal authority on whether governmental and interpersonal practices satisfy statutory or constitutional scrutiny. But as Yogi Berra put it, "It ain't over till it's over." The other branches of government must be taken into account as justices vote on cases and write legal opinions; the justices are not free agents. Hence strategic calculation can never be far from their thinking.

THE EXPANDING POWER OF THE JUDICIARY

Over the past 50 years, the place of the judiciary in American politics and society has changed dramatically. Demand for legal solutions has increased, and the reach of the judiciary has expanded. Some now call for reining in the power of the courts and discretion of judges in areas ranging from criminal law and sentencing to property rights to liability and torts. How our society deals with these issues will shape the nature of the judiciary—its independence and effectiveness—over the generations to come. All indications now are that even the most conservative justices are reluctant to relinquish their newfound power, authority that, once asserted, has become accepted and thus established.

Let us summarize what we have learned so far: judges enjoy great latitude because they are not subject to electoral pressures. Judges and justices, more than any other politicians in America, can pursue their own goals and preferences concerning what is right, their own ideologies. They are, however, constrained— by institutional rules governing access to the courts, by other courts, by Congress and the president, by their lack of enforcement powers, and, most important, by the past in the form of precedent and common law. For much of its history, the federal judiciary acted very cautiously. The Supreme Court rarely challenged Congress or the president. The justices instead tended to legitimate laws passed by Congress and the actions of the president. The scope of the Court's decisions were limited only to those individuals granted access to the courts.

Three judicial revolutions have expanded the power and reach of the federal judiciary in the decades since World War II. The first of these revolutions brought about the liberalization of a wide range of public policies in the United States. As we saw in Chapters 4 and 5, in certain policy areas—including school desegregation, legislative apportionment, and criminal procedure, as well as obscenity, abortion, and voting rights—the Supreme Court was at the forefront of a series of sweeping changes in the role of the U.S. government and, ultimately, the character of American society. The Court put many of these issues before the public long before Congress or the president were prepared to act.

At the same time that the courts forged these policy innovations, they were bringing about a second, less visible revolution. During the 1960s and 1970s, the Supreme Court and other federal courts began a series of institutional changes in judicial procedures that had major consequences by fundamentally expanding the power of the courts in the United States. First, the federal courts liberalized the concept of standing to permit almost any group seeking to challenge the actions of an administrative agency to bring its case before the federal bench. In 1971, for example, the Supreme Court ruled that public interest groups could invoke the National Environmental Policy Act to challenge the actions of federal agencies by claiming that the agencies' activities might have adverse environmental consequences.[57] Congress helped make it even easier for groups dissatisfied with government policies to bring their cases to the courts by adopting Title 42, Section 1988, of the U.S. Code, which permits the practice of "fee shifting." Section 1988 allows citizens who successfully bring a suit against a public official for violating their constitutional rights to collect their attorneys' fees and costs from the government. Thus Section 1988 encourages individuals and groups to bring their problems to the courts rather than to Congress or the executive branch. These changes have given the courts a far greater role in the administrative process than ever before.

In a second institutional change, the federal courts broadened the scope of relief to permit themselves to act on behalf of broad categories or classes of persons in "class-action" cases, rather than just on behalf of individuals.[58] A **class-action suit** is a procedural device that permits a large number of persons with common interests to join together under a representative party to bring or defend a lawsuit. In 1999, for example, a consortium of several dozen law firms filed a class-action suit against firearms manufacturers on behalf of victims of gun violence. Some of the same law firms had been involved earlier in the decade in a massive class-action suit against cigarette manufacturers on behalf of victims of tobacco-related illnesses. This suit eventually led to a settlement in which the tobacco companies agreed to pay out several billion dollars. The beneficiaries of the settlement included the treasuries of all 50 states, which received compensation for costs allegedly borne by the states in treating illnesses caused by tobacco use.

In the third major judicial change, the federal courts began to employ so-called structural remedies, in effect retaining jurisdiction of cases until a court's mandate had been implemented to its satisfaction.[59] The best known of these

◄ **class-action suit**

A lawsuit in which a large number of persons with common interests join together under a representative party to bring or defend a lawsuit, as when hundreds of workers join together to sue a company

---

57 *Citizens to Preserve Overton Park v. Volpe*, 401 U.S. 402 (1971).

58 See "Developments in the Law—Class Actions," *Harvard Law Review* 89 (1976): 1318.

59 See Donald L. Horowitz, *The Courts and Social Policy* (Washington, DC: Brookings Institution, 1977).

instances was the effort by federal judge W. Arthur Garrity to operate the Boston school system from his bench to ensure its desegregation. Between 1974 and 1985, Judge Garrity issued 14 decisions relating to different aspects of the Boston school desegregation plan that had been developed under his authority and put into effect under his supervision.[60]

Through these three judicial mechanisms, the federal courts paved the way for an unprecedented expansion of national judicial power. In essence, liberalization of the rules of standing and expansion of the scope of judicial relief drew the federal courts to link with important social interests and classes. The introduction of structural remedies enhanced the courts' ability to serve these constituencies. Thus during the 1960s and 1970s the power of the federal courts expanded in the same way the power of the executive expanded during the 1930s: through links with constituencies—such as groups advocating civil rights, consumers' rights, gay rights, women's rights, and environmental issues— that staunchly defended the Supreme Court in its battles with Congress, the executive, or other interest groups.

During the 1980s and 1990s, the Reagan and Bush administrations sought to end the relationship between the Court and liberal political forces. Conservative judges appointed by these Republican presidents modified the Court's position in areas such as abortion, affirmative action, and judicial procedure, though not so completely as some conservative writers and politicians had hoped. Within a one-week window in 2003, for example, the Supreme Court affirmed the validity of affirmative action, reaffirmed abortion rights, strengthened gay rights, offered new protection to individuals facing the death penalty, and issued a ruling in favor of a congressional apportionment plan that dispersed minority voters across several districts—a practice that appeared to favor the Democrats.[61] The Court had made these decisions based on the justices' interpretations of precedent and law, not simply personal belief.

The current Court has not been conservative in another sense. It has not been eager to surrender the expanded powers carved out by earlier Courts, especially in areas that assert the power of the national government over the states. Indeed, the opponents to the U.S. Constitution (the Antifederalists in Chapter 2) feared the assertion of the national interest over the states through the independent judiciary. Over two centuries of U.S. history, the reach and authority of the federal judiciary has expanded greatly, and the judiciary has emerged as a powerful arm of our national politics. Whatever their policy beliefs or partisan orientations, judges and justices understand the newfound importance of the courts among the three branches of American government and act not just to interpret and apply the law but also to maintain the power of the courts.

---

60 *Morgan v. McDonough*, 540 F. 2nd 527 (1 Cir., 1976); *cert.* denied 429 U.S. 1042 (1977).

61 David Van Drehle, "Court That Liberals Savage Proves to Be Less of a Target," *Washington Post*, June 29, 2003, p. A18.

For Further Reading

Selections highlighted in red are included in *Readings in American Politics: Analysis and Perspectives*, Third Edition.

Abraham, Henry J. *The Judicial Process: An Introductory Analysis of the Courts of the United States, England, and France.* 7th ed. New York: Oxford University Press, 1998.

Baum, Lawrence. *The Puzzle of Judicial Behavior.* Ann Arbor: University of Michigan Press, 1997.

Bickel, Alexander M. *The Least Dangerous Branch: The Supreme Court at the Bar of Politics.* Indianapolis, IN: Bobbs-Merrill, 1962.

Epstein, Lee, and Jack Knight. *The Choices Justices Make.* Washington, DC: CQ Press, 1998.

Kahn, Ronald. *The Supreme Court and Constitutional Theory, 1953–1993.* Lawrence: University Press of Kansas, 1994.

Marbury v. Madison, 5 U.S. (1 Cranch) 137, 1803.

O'Brien, David M. *Storm Center: The Supreme Court in American Politics.* 10th ed. New York: Norton, 2014.

Perry, H. W., Jr. *Deciding to Decide: Agenda Setting in the United States Supreme Court.* Cambridge, MA: Harvard University Press, 1991.

Rosenberg, Gerald. *The Hollow Hope: Can Courts Bring About Social Change?* Chicago: University of Chicago Press, 2008.

Segal, Jeffrey A., and Harold J. Spaeth. *The Supreme Court and the Attitudinal Model Revisited.* New York: Cambridge University Press, 2002.

Silverstein, Mark. *Judicious Choices: The New Politics of Supreme Court Confirmations.* New York: Norton, 1994.

Toobin, Jeffrey. *The Nine: Inside the Secret World of the Supreme Court.* New York: Knopf, 2008.

Whittington, Keith. *Political Foundations of Judicial Supremacy: The President, the Supreme Court, and Constitutional Leadership in U.S. History.* Princeton, NJ: Princeton University Press, 2008.

10

Public Opinion

Public support is the coin of the realm in Washington politics. Popular presidents succeed; unpopular presidents struggle. A president who has the backing of a large majority of the public gains leverage in dealing with Congress and the bureaucracy, but a president who lacks public support often meets resistance from members of Congress, even those in his own party. President George W. Bush described a president's popularity as political capital, an asset that must be spent wisely on a few well-chosen issues.[1]

Members of Congress are perhaps even more attuned than the president to the ups and downs of public opinion. Representatives in the U.S. House must run for re-election every two years, a very short election cycle. They cannot afford to make many unpopular decisions for fear of being punished by their constituents in the next election. Members of Congress and party leaders pay close attention to various indicators of public sentiment, including polls, visits to their districts or home states, and letters, phone calls, and e-mails from constituents. A saying among members of Congress goes, "It's okay to be on the losing side of a vote, but you don't want to be on the wrong side."

Even the courts are not immune to the influence of public opinion. Courts lack the power to enforce their decisions; they depend on the compliance of those affected and the cooperation of Congress, the president, and political leaders in the states. That cooperation is not always forthcoming. As we saw in Chapter 5, *Brown v. Board of Education,* perhaps the most important court

---

[1] Chris Suellentrop, "America's New Political Capital," *Slate*, November 30, 2004, www
.slate.com/id/2110256/ (accessed 3/18/09). Also see Richard Neustadt, *Presidential
Power and the Modern Presidents*, 4th ed. (New York: Free Press, 1990); and Brandice
Canes-Wrone, *Who Leads Whom? Presidents, Policy, and the Public* (Chicago: University
of Chicago Press, 2006).

decision of the twentieth century, met with immediate opposition in the southern states, and desegregation occurred slowly. Only after public opinion turned in support of equal rights for all races did Congress and the president act, accelerating the pace of desegregation.[2]

Public opinion is also the standard by which we judge democracy. Ideally, representative democracy approximates what the nation as a whole would choose to do were all 315 million Americans to consider a given matter. Congress and the president are supposed to act as the public's agents, enacting laws that a clear majority of the public wants and rejecting laws that fail to achieve widespread support. If the norms of society shift strongly in one direction for a period of time, so too should the laws of the land. The nature and origins of public opinion are a central concern of modern political science precisely because democratic government is supposed to reflect the will of the people.

Public opinion is, ultimately, the rationale behind democratic government. The public provides democratic government the will to act. The rationality principle applied to the public holds that average people have preferences about what government should and shouldn't do. At stake in many government decisions are individuals' interests and values, and people pursue those goals when voting or engaging in other forms of political action. Democratic politics in its

CORE OF THE ANALYSIS

Public opinion is the aggregation of individuals' views. It expresses the range of attitudes and beliefs and on which side of any question a majority of people fall.

There are a wide range of interests at stake in any question that the government must decide, as well as differing preferences, beliefs, and opinions about what ought to be done.

Politicians follow public opinion as part of the representative process. They take signals from polls and other indicators of public sentiment to gauge whether a particular decision might affect their prospects at the next election.

Politicians, interest groups, the media, and others try to shape public opinion by influencing what issues are debated, what alternatives are offered, and what information is presented.

2 Gerald Rosenberg, *The Hollow Hope* (Chicago: University of Chicago Press, 1991).

various forms aggregates peoples' preferences and beliefs into an expression of what a majority of people want. How individuals' preferences are transformed into electoral decisions and public policies depends on institutions, problems of collective action, and history. These factors will be emphasized in later chapters on elections, interest groups, political parties, and the media. Public opinion operates through these various institutions to determine who serves in government, what problems government must address, and the principles and values that shape public policy. This chapter concerns what people want their government to do and how people understand the political choices and decisions that they confront.

While individuals pursue their own interests and values when making decisions about politics, they do not necessarily understand fully the choices they face. People look for information—facts, labels, cues—that can help simplify their decision making. This is quite a different notion of the electorate than is commonly found in civics books. The civics textbook view presents a highly idealized democratic citizen who is assumed to closely follow the important issues of the day, who is well informed about the decisions of her representatives, who understands the consequences of actions, and who participates actively in public debate, elections, and even in public decision making. That seems like an absurd level of attention to and participation in politics. Were we all that attentive, we would have little time for our education, our jobs, our families, and other aspects of daily life. It is not surprising, then, that individuals fall far short of the civics-book view of the ideal citizen. Survey researchers have long found that most Americans are not highly attentive to the issues before their representatives in their state's capital or in Washington, D.C. Lack of attention to public affairs is a necessary feature of representative democracy, but it also creates a potential problem.

Does public opinion adequately reflect the true preferences of the people? If people do not fully know what the choices are, then there is the possibility that elites might manipulate public decisions or that people may simply make the wrong choices. American history contains numerous examples when politicians, newspaper editors, and other elites misled the public and manipulated public opinion for their own gain.[3] The prospect that elites can readily manipulate the public presents a lingering and difficult problem. The United States continually grapples with this challenge, especially in ongoing struggles to reform electoral rules such as campaign finance. Interestingly enough, the solution to the weaknesses of democracy seems to be more democracy. Most of the legal decisions and electoral laws governing the United States embrace the notion that participation ought to be universal but voluntary and that public discourse ought to be unfettered and wide open. That, so the theory goes, is the best guarantee that government does what society wants.

---

3   William Riker, *The Art of Political Manipulation* (New Haven, CT: Yale University Press, 1986).

WHAT IS PUBLIC OPINION?

Public opinion may be understood on two levels—aggregate and individual. The term *public opinion* itself refers to an aggregate—the public. But, it is the accumulation of millions of individuals' expressions of their opinions, attitudes, and choices.

There are many different procedures for aggregating individual opinion, including voting, town meetings, protests, and other forms of political participation, as well as public-opinion polls. The aggregate expression of the choices that people make or the opinions they offer is rarely unanimous; instead, public opinion is usually shorthand for what most people want or think—in other words, majority rule.

Aggregate opinion may not always appear rational, but there is power in numbers. The basic idea behind democracy holds that the sum of many millions of votes produces a better outcome than the decision of a small number of people. This idea is brilliantly expressed in Condorcet's jury theorem. The Marquis de Condorcet, a French political philosopher of the eighteenth century, argued that the majority of a jury would more likely reach the right decision in a trial than would a single individual who heard the same evidence. Every person would like to make the right decision, but there is some chance that an individual will make a mistake. Adding up the judgments of many separate individuals, however, reduces the probability of a mistake. A majority of a jury of 12 people, then, is less likely to reach the wrong decision than a single individual. And millions of voters are even more likely to produce the right verdict.[4] Democracy works, then, because voting efficiently collects the knowledge widely held in society.

This idea has been rediscovered at the beginning of the twenty-first century, as new information technology has expanded the opportunities and the possibility for millions of people to express their opinions on virtually any matter. Firms such as Amazon.com aggregate the millions of decisions made by consumers to figure out who is likely to buy particular products. There is wisdom in masses, a lesson borne out in markets and democracy.[5]

Public opinion can also be understood at the level of individuals. Votes cast during elections, answers to surveys, letters and e-mails to members of Congress, and other ways that people communicate their opinions reflect how

 public opinion

Citizens' attitudes about political issues, leaders, institutions, and events

---

4 Marquis de Condorcet, "Essai sur l'application de l'analyse à la probabilité des décisions rendues à la pluralité des voix," http://gallica.bnf.fr/ark:/12148/bpt6k417181 (accessed 3/24/09). Condorcet also argued that democracy has a weakness in that it need not always produce a definite majority-rule winner and may be manipulated by a clever agenda setter. This idea was rediscovered in the middle of the twentieth century by the Nobel Prize–winning economist Kenneth Arrow in *Social Choice and Individual Values* (New York: Wiley, 1963).

5 See Cass Sunstein, *Infotopia: How Many Minds Produce Knowledge* (Oxford, UK: Oxford University Press, 2006).

individuals think and behave politically. Aggregate public opinion, after all, is the collection of these many expressions. An individual's political opinion depends on three factors: (1) the individual's basic preferences (what he wants), (2) his beliefs about the current circumstances and the consequences of different courses of action, and (3) the choices presented. A person will make a given political choice among the options presented, say, in an election or on a survey, because she wants a certain outcome (such as higher income or better education) and because she believes that a given political option is the best approach among the alternatives offered. The choices offered in any situation are usually few in number—Democrat or Republican, a proposed bill versus the status quo, vote yes or vote no, get involved or stay at home. The significance of the individual's actions depends on why he chooses one of the alternatives.

Preferences and Beliefs

Preferences and beliefs are complex. Preferences reflect what people want, such as material goods and money, and also people's values, such as justice and morality. Income is often taken as the basis for political preferences. People want to have higher income: other things being equal, people want lower taxes and more government spending on programs that benefit them directly. But it is also the case that moral values, which are shaped by religion, family, and social conscience, influence the way Americans behave.[6] These two factors—economic self-interest and social or moral values—are viewed as the basis for people's preferences in the political or public arena.

Preferences are also characterized by their intensity—how much individuals want a certain outcome or care about a given issue. It is virtually impossible to compare intensity of preferences directly, to say that one person wants something twice as much as someone else. But it is obvious from behavior that some people do have stronger or more intense preferences than others. Those who have strong opinions and attitudes are more likely to express their views and take political action than those who do not. It is also clear that people differ in the strength of their preferences about different issues. Public opinion polls reveal that some people care more about some issues or problems, such as taxes, while others care more about other issues, such as abortion.

Beliefs reflect what people know and how they understand the world and the consequences of their actions. An individual who has developed considerable expertise about a topic usually has clearer beliefs about that subject. He or she will have more certainty about the choices involved and the consequences of different actions. However, strong beliefs about politics are not necessarily based only on fact. Often in politics, one encounters people who have strong convictions about a specific issue that are based on the intensity of their general political views. When the facts don't fit their theories, they may ignore fact and stick with their theory. Thus, Democrats and Republicans may observe the same

---

6   Benjamin Wattenberg, *Values Matter Most* (New York: Simon & Schuster, 1995).

event, such as a political debate, and come to completely opposite conclusions about who won. And public figures may, in the face of strong scientific evidence, reject the science if it does not favor their own political position. As in other aspects of life, people often find it easier to stick to their political beliefs than to change their minds.

Choices

Whether and how individuals' preferences and beliefs are expressed depends, ultimately, on a third component of opinion and that is the choice offered. We never really observe an individual's preferences and beliefs. Rather we observe how she responds to a given situation or issue and the alternatives presented. In a public opinion survey, respondents answer the questions put to them, which usually reflect important issues at a given time. In elections, we choose among a small set of choices: the candidates or parties. Those candidates themselves have taken stands on many different issues—taxes, spending, national defense, welfare, abortion, and so on. However, we can not mix and match the different positions. If one candidate is low tax and antiabortion and another is high tax and prochoice, then the only choices are between those two clusters of policies. If a voter wants low taxes and is prochoice, there is no candidate who reflects the cluster of policies (or perhaps ideology) that the voter prefers. A wider set of candidates might yield someone who reflects the voter's ideology, but it is not an option in the election.

Not only might some ideological positions not be reflected in the choices offered, some issues may not be on the political agenda. Throughout the 1930s and 1940s, the national Democratic leadership did its best to keep race relations out of the Democratic Party platform in order to keep southern Democrats in the party. An issue that is potentially of broad concern but has not yet reached the public arena is called *latent*. Because the issue is not on the agenda, there is no opportunity for people to express their preferences on it. In 1948, Mayor Hubert Humphrey of Minneapolis proposed a plank to the Democratic Party's national platform calling for desegregation. South Carolina governor Strom Thurmond and other southern politicians, unhappy with the change in the racial platform of the party, left the Democrats and formed the Dixiecrats, a short-lived party espousing states' rights and segregation. Thurmond himself ran for president that year as the Dixiecrat candidate against Harry Truman and Thomas Dewey, winning four states. Not only did race rise from a latent national issue to one at the forefront of the national agenda confronting the Democratic and Republican parties but it became an active electoral choice in the form of the Dixiecrat Party.

Some latent issues never rise even to the level of public discourse. Race in the 1930s and 1940s, although off the national agenda, was nonetheless an issue on which most people had well-formed opinions. On the other hand, some issues are so thoroughly removed from public debate that many people would have a hard time formulating a clear opinion because they simply have not thought about the matter. The process through which issues are vetted and debated publicly, then, is also an essential part of the formulation and expression of public opinion. Americans had debated the question of race relations for centuries prior to the 1948 election, and they continue to debate the matter today. Other fundamental issues that could cause contention instead lurk beneath the surface, receiving little public debate. For instance, other countries, such as Spain and Canada, have recently had to grapple with questions of separatism—whether Quebec should remain in Canada or how much independence Catalonia, the Basque Region, and Galicia ought to have in Spain. One might imagine similar independence movements in the United States, but they have not surfaced since the 1870s; nor has there been serious discussion on the topic. One might also imagine significant constitutional reform, such as the creation of a unicameral legislature at the national level. Were separatism or unicameralism put on a public opinion poll today it seems likely that many people would decline to give an opinion. On latent issues such as these, coherent public opinion likely does not exist, or if it does, it takes the form of knee-jerk reactions—"Of course we shouldn't get rid of the U.S. Senate." That is not to say that public opinion could not form on these matters. After extensive debate on such matters, people would eventually discover where their preferences lay.

The choices offered to people in elections, polls, town meetings, and other venues shape how preferences and beliefs are expressed in democratic politics. Public opinion, then, is never the pure expression of preferences but rather revealed preference, the choices people make among a given set of issues and alternatives available. In this chapter we examine the basis for individuals' preferences and the origins of their beliefs, as well as aggregate public opinion.

Variety of Opinion

The term *public opinion* is often bandied about in a way that suggests that all people are of the same mind. As we've noted, that is rarely the case. The term *public opinion* is really a shorthand description of the variety of opinion in society on a given question. One segment of the population supports the president, a second segment opposes him, and a third is unsure. A percentage of people are for a given bill in Congress, and a percentage are against it.

Americans do hold common views on questions vital to governance and society. There is consensus on the legitimacy of the Constitution of the United States and trust in the rule of law, the principle that no one is above the law. There is consensus that we are a democratic society and that the outcomes of elections, whether a person likes the winners or not, determine who governs. These commonly held opinions and values are essential to maintaining a functioning democracy in the United States. They ensure peaceful transitions of government after each election and respect for laws produced by a legitimately chosen government.

There is also wide agreement on fundamental political values, such as equality of opportunity, liberty, and democracy.[7] Nearly all Americans agree that all people

---

7   See Louis Hartz, *The Liberal Tradition in America: An Interpretation of American Political Thought since the Revolution* (New York: Harcourt, Brace, 1955).

should have equal rights, regardless of race, gender, or social standing. Americans hold a common commitment to freedom. People who live in the United States are free to live where they want, travel where they want, work where they want, say what they want, and practice whatever religion they wish, including no religion at all. And Americans have an undying belief in democracy, that whenever possible public officials should be chosen by majority vote.[8] It makes sense to think of the American public as having a single opinion on these elemental questions.

On most matters that come before the government, however, the public does not hold a single view. Usually, opinions are divided between those who support the government or a proposed action and those who do not. Politicians are still attuned to public opinion when it is divided, but what matters most are the balance and direction of opinion. What do the majority of constituents want? Which way is opinion trending? Is it possible to find a popular middle ground?

People express their views to those in power in a variety of ways. Constituents contact their members of Congress directly through letters, phone calls, e-mails, and even personal visits to the representatives' offices. Most questions before Congress elicit little reaction from the public, but some questions start a maelstrom of objections. During the fall of 2008, Congress considered a $700 billion bailout of financial institutions. The volume of e-mail related to this bill was so great that at one point the House of Representatives had to limit incoming e-mail to keep its computers from crashing.[9]

People also express their opinions more publicly, through blogs, letters to newspapers and op-ed pieces, and conversations with others. They express their support for candidates with lawn signs and bumper stickers; by working on campaigns; by giving money to candidates, groups, and party organizations; and, most simply, by voting.

Such expressions of opinions and preferences are not always easy to interpret. If a constituent votes against a member of Congress, did the voter do so because of a controversial decision that the legislator made in Congress or because the voter decided to vote against all politicians from the legislator's party? Or for some other reason?

Political scientists and political consultants try to provide more refined and structured descriptions of public opinion using surveys. On any important issue, the government might pursue any one of a wide variety of policies. Public opinion on a given issue can be thought of as the distribution of opinion across the different options. Likewise, public opinion may represent the division of support for a leader or party. We try to gauge where majority support lies and how intensely or firmly citizens across the spectrum hold their views. More and more, politicians rely on opinion polls to anticipate the effects of their decisions, to identify opportunities, and to develop ways to blunt the objections to

---

8   For a discussion of political beliefs of Americans, see Everett Carl Ladd, *The American Ideology* (Storrs, CT: Roper Center, 1994).

9   Jordy Yeager, "House Limits Constituent E-mail to Prevent Crash," *The Hill*, September 30, 2008, http://thehill.com/leading-the-news/house-limits-constituent-e-mails-to-prevent-crash-2008-09-30.html (accessed 3/24/09).

controversial decisions. Answering a survey, then, can also be a form of political action, because it may influence political decisions.

Public opinion should not be thought of as a single-minded view or consensus on a given matter, but as the variation in the opinion and attitudes across a range of options. A set of exclusive options that capture the range of opinions is called a variable. One might want to know whether people support the president. We can do a survey and count how many people support the president. Support for the president alone does not summarize attitudes toward the president because the category "support" on its own does not carry information about all people in the survey: it is only half of the variable. But we can simply reformulate the question by counting the number of people who support the president, the number of people who do not support the president, and the number of people who have no opinion or neither support nor oppose the president. Such a dichotomy is perhaps the simplest variable, but also the most common: support or oppose, favor or not, yes or no.

Often, however, people think about politics in more subtle terms than just yes and no or support and oppose. Consider, for instance, the debate over the legality of abortion. In the immediate aftermath of the *Roe v. Wade* decision, survey researchers sorted people into two polar positions—prolife and prochoice. Survey researchers at that time measured the percentage of the public that identified as prolife or as prochoice or as having no opinion. As social scientists continued to study the politics of abortion, it became clear that people had more nuanced opinions and saw a much wider range of possible government policies on abortion. As a result, survey researchers developed more refined questions to ascertain the conditions under which people would and would not allow abortion. Would a respondent allow abortion for teenagers if parents did not consent? What about cases of rape or incest? What if the pregnancy endangered the life of the mother? Such refinements have allowed the public to express its preferences more precisely on this issue.

Opinions themselves take a variety of forms, depending on what is at issue. It is helpful to keep in mind a few common examples in thinking about this subject.

- **Evaluations of those in government and other institutions.** Survey researchers use a variety of questions to gauge support for or opposition to the government. They ask about approval of the job that the president is doing, approval of the job that Congress is doing, approval of individual members of Congress, and approval of the job the Supreme Court is doing. At elections, those who vote express their support for and opposition to members of government directly through their votes. In political science as well as other disciplines, similar questions are asked about social and economic institutions and leaders.

- **Assessments of public policies.** Do you support or oppose a given policy? Do you think a problem is important or not? What do you think is the most important problem that the government should address? How people answer such questions depends on the choices that are presented and immediate circumstances. Views on specific issues may follow the same patterns as general political orientations, if they directly affect partisan groups or derive from ongoing political debates between parties or ideological groups. For instance, a bill that would alter wages for public employees affects unions directly and thus touches a core constituency of the Democratic Party. So, we might find that Democrats are more likely to view this issue in a certain way.

- **Assessments of current circumstances.** Is the economy performing well or poorly? Is crime high or low? Is the country headed in the right direction? Such questions might seem to have objective answers, but often there are differences of opinion about the state of the economy and other aspects of our society, depending on each individual's own experiences and what she has read or heard through the media.

- **Political orientations.** The two most important indicators of individuals' general political orientations are party identification and ideology. Do you consider yourself a Democrat, a Republican, of another party, or of no party in particular? Do you consider yourself liberal, moderate, or conservative? These concepts capture general political orientations that are usually quite stable. Researchers have shown that party identifications predict voting preferences very well and correlate strongly with evaluations of those in office. Party identification often acts as a filter for information, a tinted lens that colors the way people view the world and interpret a piece of information. Immediately after an election, members and supporters of the winning party express much greater optimism about the economy, about global affairs, and even about their own personal finances. Often a Democrat and a Republican will offer markedly different views on a presidential debate, with the Democrat concluding that the Democratic candidate clearly won and the Republican concluding that the Republican candidate was victorious.

Political scientists characterize the variation in public opinion by measuring the percentage of people who choose each particular option of a variable. A bar chart provides one way to display the distribution of public opinion. In such a chart the height of each bar is the percentage of people choosing each outcome of a variable, and the sum of these percentages equals 100 percent. Typically, we care about which option receives the most support (a plurality) or the support of a majority. In elections, for example, counties and states tally the votes received by each candidate. The candidate with the largest number of votes (not necessarily a majority) wins. Nationwide in 2012, Barack Obama received 51 percent of all votes cast, Mitt Romney received 47 percent of all votes cast, and all other candidates combined received 2 percent of votes cast. Politicians and political observers view the size of the winner's vote margin as an indication of the breadth and intensity of the support for the policies and ideology of the winner.

Opinion data, such as the information gathered in surveys, provide an even more subtle and varied measure of public attitudes and political orientations. Consider ideology (which we discuss in more detail later in this chapter). According to a survey by the Pew Research Center in June 2012, 35 percent of Americans described themselves as conservative, 34 percent as moderate, and 22 percent as liberal. Another 9 percent do not think of themselves in these terms.[10] For an indicator such as ideology, then, no single camp has a clear majority, but we can say that self-described conservatives outnumber self-described liberals.[11]

Polarization. One particularly important debate about public opinion today concerns ideological polarization. Pundits and other observers have often argued that the public is deeply divided into very conservative and very liberal groups, with relatively few people in the middle. Observers assume that this view of "two Americas" holds true for questions about ideology and across a wide range of issues, such as taxation, health care, education, and foreign affairs. The political scientists Morris Fiorina, Jeremy Pope, and Samuel Abrams tackled this alleged polarization in their 2004 book *Culture War? The Myth of a Polarized America*. Fiorina and his coauthors made simple bar charts to describe the distribution of public opinion in the United States. Rather than a deep divide, they found that on most issues Americans are centrists, meaning either moderate or leaning somewhat to the right or left. This finding has important implications about the ability to reach consensus in public debate. It also raises an even more elusive puzzle. Although most Americans are centrist, most representatives in Congress vote either on the very liberal end of the spectrum or on the very conservative end. The public, then, is not polarized, but Congress is. It is worth pausing to consider why this is the case. Political scientists have suggested that it is the nature of the debate in Washington and the choices put before Congress, or that it is due to institutional factors such as the organization of parties in Congress or to the election process—who votes and who doesn't, primary elections, and campaign contributors. The debate over this question has yet to come to a definitive resolution; as yet a convincing answer has not been found.[12]

Just as we do not think of public opinion as a consensus, nor do we think of the public as monolithic. From the start, American society was conceived to be a

---

10 Pew Research Center for the People and the Press, "Trends in American Values: 1987–2012," June 2012, www.people-press.org/2012/06/04/partisan-polarization -surges-in-bush-obama-years/ (accessed 4/8/13).

11 As an exercise, we recommend (1) writing down several concepts of interest (such as ideology, partisanship, policy preferences on taxes or abortion), (2) finding surveys that have measured public opinion on those topics (for example, at the Roper Center or the Pew Research Center on People and the Press), and (3) making a bar chart showing the percentage of people who chose each category for a given question.

12 For five different views, see Morris Fiorina, Samuel Adams, and Jeremy Pope, *Culture War?* 2nd ed. (New York: Pearson, Longman, 2005); Nolan McCarty, Keith Poole, and Howard Rosenthal, *Polarization in America: The Dance of Ideology and Unequal Riches* (Princeton, NJ: Princeton University Press, 2007); Gary Jacobson, *A Divider, Not a Uniter: George W. Bush, the American People, the 2006 Election, and Beyond* (White Plains, NY: Longman, 2007); Alan Abramowitz, "Constraint, Ideology, and Polarization in the American Electorate," paper presented at the annual meeting of the American Political Science Association, August 30, 2007; and Stephen Ansolabehere, Jonathan Rodden, and James M. Snyder, Jr., "Purple America," *Journal of Economic Perspectives* 20, no. 2 (Spring 2006): 97–118.

large, heterogeneous nation. The guarantees of freedom of religion, the press, and association in the Bill of Rights were meant to protect this diversity of opinion and belief. Indeed, one of the problems the Founders faced was how to maintain a stable democracy in a large heterogeneous society. James Madison famously wrote that "expanding the sphere" of the United States would make it less likely for any single group to achieve a stable majority capable of riding roughshod over other groups. A large heterogeneous nation, then, would cure the "mischief of faction."[13]

Madison's vision of diverse opinions and beliefs has indeed come to pass. American society is a hodgepodge of different ethnic and racial groups; Americans differ greatly in educational attainment, income, and religion. The U.S. census, conducted every 10 years, measures variations in housing, family, employment, and other demographic characteristics. The Census Bureau also conducts monthly surveys measuring such activities as communication, employment, and voting. These data provide a rich picture of the diversity and complexity of American society. For example, 15 percent of Americans claim Hispanic ethnicity, 13 percent are black or African American, 5 percent are Asian, 1 percent are Native American, and 74 percent identify themselves as white. One person of every eight living in the United States today was not born here. Although the large majority of Americans identify with some form of Christianity and most of those are Protestant, the single largest sect is Roman Catholicism. Slightly more than 25 percent of adults in the United States have a college degree; 15 percent did not complete high school. America is one of the richest nations on earth, but approximately 1 in 10 Americans still lives in poverty. The most populous region of the country is the South, with approximately 35 percent of the people. American society can be divided in many other ways. The picture that emerges from the census data is indeed one of a heterogeneous society.[14] In describing and understanding the attitudes, opinions, needs, and wants of the American public, we must be mindful of the fact that the public itself is fractured into many subgroups and interests.[15]

ORIGINS AND NATURE OF OPINION

To understand the meaning and origins of the public's opinions, we must have some sense of the basis for individuals' preferences and beliefs. An individual's opinions are the products of her personality, social characteristics,

---

13 Alexander Hamilton, James Madison, and John Jay, *The Federalist Papers,* Clinton L. Rossiter, ed. (New York: New American Library, 1961), no. 10.

14 U.S. Ceusus Bureau, *The Statistical Abstract of the United States,* 2012.

15 As an exercise, we recommend consulting the *Statistical Abstract of the United States* and constructing bar charts (distributions) for the following demographic variables: (1) household incomes, (2) residency (urban, suburban, and rural), (3) region, (4) race, and (5) religion. Note the largest category for each variable. For income, calculate the level of income such that half of the people have income below that level and half have income above it (the median).

and interests. They mirror who a person is, what she wants, and the manner in which she is embedded in a family and community as well as the broader economy and society. But opinions are also shaped by institutional, political, and governmental forces that make it more likely that an individual will hold some beliefs and less likely that he will hold others.

Foundations of Preferences

Self-Interest. Individuals' preferences about politics and public policy are usually rooted in self-interest. Laws and other governmental actions directly affect people's interests—their disposable income, the quality of public services and goods, and personal safety, to give just a few examples. It is not surprising, then, that when people express their political opinions, they react to the effects that government actions have on them personally.

Economic interests are perhaps the most salient preferences when it comes to people's opinions. Government policies, ranging from export and import rules to regulations to spending and taxes, directly affect individual Americans' personal well-being. Taxes reduce disposable income. The average American family has income of $64,000 before taxes and $50,000 after taxes. Those taxes, of course, pay for government programs like Social Security and Medicare, national defense, and other goods. Not all families and individuals are taxed equally, nor do all benefit equally from government programs. Very low-income families pay little or no taxes because they cannot afford to, and they are net recipients of government assistance. Middle-income families are also direct and indirect beneficiaries of government programs, such as public education for children.

Government regulations also affect people's economic self-interests. Government rules aim to protect people from potentially harmful pollutants, preserve the value of property, protect consumers from potential harm, and even create the property rights necessary to maintain a well-functioning market economy. But they also limit how people use their property and may raise the cost of operating a business.

The government is directly involved in the labor market. Approximately 19 million people, 12 percent of the U.S. civilian labor force, work for federal, state, or local governments; another 1 million people are in the armed services. Government spending comprises a substantial share of the national economy (though less than in most other nations). In the United States, federal government expenditures account for about 20 percent of gross domestic product (GDP).[16] Virtually every American has an interest in the government's role in the nation's economy and strong preferences about tax rates and expenditure priorities. Public opinion about taxes and spending reflect these preferences. Given the enormous influence of the federal government in the economy,

---

16 The gross domestic product consists of the value of all goods and services produced in the United States. It is one measure of the nation's income.

assessments of the president and the party in power often correspond to how well the nation's economy performs.

Individuals' attitudes toward government reflect other forms of self-interest as well. Laws affect families, the status of civic and religious organizations, and communities. Zoning laws and urban redevelopment programs shape the nature of neighborhoods, including the mix of commercial and residential housing and the density of low-income housing in an area. Tax laws treat non-profits, such as universities, religious organizations, and social clubs, differently from for-profit companies, making it easier for nonprofit organizations to exist. Family law affects how easy it is for families to stay together, what happens when they break down, and what rights and responsibilities parents have. Individuals have a personal stake in decisions bearing on their own communities and families. Proposed changes in such laws bring immediate reaction from those affected.

Values. Much of what individuals want from their government is also rooted in values concerning what is right or wrong, or in other words, our philosophies about morality, justice, and ethics. Most of us have values systems—principles of right and wrong that we can apply to new problems and circumstances. Such values systems originate in many places—families, religion, education, groups, and so forth—and they shape what we want. Views of right and wrong are deeply seated and often determine our preferences in particular circumstances. Individuals will often act in ways that defy their economic self-interest because such behavior is guided by their values. For example, many religions call for their adherents to tithe—to give some fraction of their income to those less well off. Such behavior runs strictly against economic self-interest, but it is nonetheless rational behavior to the extent that it is consistent with the individual's values.

Tithing is an example of economic justice. Values of what is right and wrong may determine an individual's preferences about how government and society distributes or redistributes income. Americans generally adhere to a belief in equal opportunity. So long as all people have an equal opportunity, an equal chance to excel, we will have a just society. That idea has driven our society to try to root out discrimination in employment, housing, and education. It has also led us to create a universal public education system. In some states, such as New Hampshire, Ohio, and California, courts have invoked this principle of equality to insist that the states try to equalize public school expenditures per pupil across districts.

Values also shape our notions of what is a crime and what is a suitable punishment. One of the most morally laden debates in American history is the debate over capital punishment. Does the government have the right to take the life of an individual, even if that individual has taken the life of someone else? An ancient sense of justice seems to call for exactly that: an eye for an eye. Other ideas of morality speak against capital punishment. And our values about government and its appropriate powers say that people must be protected against arbitrary and capricious acts of government. The death penalty is irreversible and the possibility of a governmental error has led some to claim that the government can never have the power to take the life of an individual.

In 1972, the U.S. Supreme Court ruled just that in *Furman v. Georgia*, though it validated the death penalty in certain cases four years later.[17]

Our values also reflect established social norms of our community, analogous to common law. What, for example, is marriage? One might argue that marriage is an economic convenience, as defined by laws that tie taxes and inheritance to marital status. Most people, however, express more complex ideas of marriage, and those principles dictate whether they think that same-sex marriages ought to be allowed. Such norms change over time. For example, a century ago interracial marriages were deemed unacceptable by most in American society, and most states adopted laws designed to prevent interracial marriage. It took a Supreme Court decision in 1967, *Loving v. Virginia*, to eliminate the last of these laws.[18] Today, advocates of same-sex marriage draw parallels to this earlier struggle for rights, and they too have made their arguments in the courts. Indeed, it was a challenge to marriage law in Massachusetts, the case of *Goodridge v. Department of Public Health*, that ultimately led the state's Supreme Judicial Council to allow same-sex marriage in the state in May 2004.[19] That decision opened the way for other states to legalize same-sex marriage, which they have done through court decisions, legislation, and popular referenda.

Principles and values guide our notions of what we want government to do. Values, however, often conflict with one another. Many of us struggle with knowing what is right and wrong in various circumstances because a given law or policy touches on different values and in conflicting ways. A question like capital punishment evokes our notions of how much power government ought to have over individuals, even criminals, and our fundamental ideas of justice and vengeance. A person may support capital punishment as a just response to a heinous crime, but that individual might also think that the government should not have the power to kill its citizens. At a societal level, conflicting values are particularly difficult to resolve. Unlike situations involving economic interests, it is hard to bargain over our differences when the differences strike at fundamental principles of right and wrong.

By the same token, there are many values that unite us. Probably no nation and certainly no democracy could survive if its citizens did not share some fundamental beliefs. If Americans had few common values or perspectives, it would be very difficult for them to reach agreement on particular issues. Over the past half-century, political philosophers and political scientists have reflected on what those values are and settled on three important precepts. Americans almost universally agree with (1) the democracy principle (that majority rule is a good decision rule), (2) the importance of equal opportunity, and (3) the idea that that government is best which governs least.

Social Groups. Individuals' preferences about politics and government are rooted in a third source—social groups. We are connected to one another through various social situations and groupings, including family, neighborhood,

---

17 *Furman v. Georgia,* 408 U.S. 238 (1972).

18 *Loving v. Virginia,* 388 U.S. 1 (1967).

19 *Goodridge v. Department of Public Health,* 798 N.E. 2d 941 (Mass. 2003).

language groups, race, and religion. People often describe themselves using such characteristics. These descriptors tap fundamental psychological attachments that go beyond self-interest and values, though they are often reinforced by our interests and values.

Social groups affect political preferences in two ways. First, people have preferences for political decisions that benefit their group and, thus, indirectly them. Social groups change our preferences by virtue of simply being members of those groups. A group or organization, such as a union or a church, helps overcome the collective action problem. When we join a group, each of us usually does so for some private benefit, but the group helps us attain some common benefit through collective action that we could not achieve acting alone. Our preferences, then, shift to maintain the group because of the benefits it gains for us.

Second, social groups can change our values and even our view of ourselves. Take a simple example: a person finishes college and takes a job at a corporation as an employee to earn wages. Upon doing so, the person begins to take on the perspective of that organization. On one level this is a matter of self-interest: as goes the corporation so goes the person's wages. But it often goes much deeper. People often internalize the collective value; they take them on as if their own. When the corporation does well, we feel proud of the contribution to the corporation and that can spur us to work harder still. We identify with our churches, schools, towns and cities, ethnicities, and other groups.

The process through which our social interactions and social groups change our perspectives and preferences is called **socialization**. Most 18-year-olds already have definite political attitudes even though they have not yet voted, and they have learned those opinions and attitudes from their parents and grandparents, their friends, their teachers and religious leaders, and others in their social groups and networks. Of course, socialization does not end upon leaving home. We learn about politics and even what we should think about complex political questions from our family members, coworkers, and others we see and speak with daily.

Socialization works many different ways. One way is simply to provide information. Social groups are one of the main ways that people stay abreast with what is going on in their community and even in national politics. Socialization also takes the form of education or instruction. Parents teach their children how to think about a problem, what is a right or wrong choice or action, and even how to participate in politics. There is nothing wrong with this; indeed, it is how we as humans have learned to survive and adapt. But it does mean that we have, by the time we are adults, already learned much about what we want government to do, what sorts of people we want in government, and even whether it is worth our while to participate. Sometimes, socialization takes the form of outright pressure to think or behave a certain way. If an employer asks her employees to vote a certain way or to work for a candidate, that employer has used a position of power to influence how others in her social group behave. In these and other ways, social groups shape what and how people think and how they behave in politics.

 socialization

A process through which individuals assimilate community preferences and norms through social interactions

Political Ideology

Political decisions, especially those about public policies, are complex. It can be difficult to see how one's interests and values map into a given vote. Political discourse and debate, however, is often simplified as a conflict between different ideologies. An ideology is a comprehensive way of understanding political or cultural situations. It is a set of assumptions about the way the world and society works that helps us to organize our beliefs, information, and new situations. It ascribes values to different alternatives (this is good, that is bad). Ideology is of further importance in political decision making because it helps people balance competing values. Political decisions usually involve tradeoffs between values or interests. Belief systems such as conservatism and liberalism help us think through those tradeoffs. As such, understanding different political ideologies can help us make decisions in a political, social, or cultural setting. Ideologies are very handy simplifications of an otherwise complex world.

In America today, people often describe themselves as liberals or conservatives. Liberalism and conservatism are political ideologies that include beliefs about the role of government, ideas about public policies, and notions about which groups in society should properly exercise power. In earlier times, these terms were defined somewhat differently. As recently as the nineteenth century, a liberal was an individual who favored freedom from state control, whereas a conservative was someone who supported the use of governmental power and favored continuation of the influence of the church and the aristocracy in national life.

Today, in the United States, the term **liberal** has come to imply support for political and social reform; government intervention in the economy; the expansion of federal social services; more vigorous efforts on behalf of the poor, minorities, and women; and greater concern for consumers and the environment. In social and cultural areas, liberals generally support abortion rights and oppose state involvement with religious institutions and religious expression. In international affairs, liberal positions usually include support for arms control, opposition to the development and testing of nuclear weapons, support for aid to poor nations, opposition to the use of American troops to influence the domestic affairs of developing nations, and support for international organizations such as the United Nations. Of course, liberalism is not monolithic. For example, among individuals who view themselves as liberal, many support American military intervention when it is tied to a humanitarian purpose, as in the case of America's military action in Kosovo in 1998–99. Most liberals initially supported President George W. Bush's war on terrorism even when some of the president's actions seemed to curtail civil liberties.

By contrast, the term **conservative** today is used to describe those who generally support the social and economic status quo, favor markets as solutions to social problems, and are suspicious of government involvement in the economy. Conservatives believe that a large and powerful government poses a threat to citizens' freedom. Thus in the domestic arena conservatives generally oppose the expansion of governmental activity, asserting that solutions to social and economic problems can be developed in the private sector. Conservatives in

---

liberal ➡

A liberal today generally supports political and social reform; government intervention in the economy; the expansion of federal social services; more vigorous efforts on behalf of the poor, minorities, and women; and greater concern for consumers and the environment

---

conservative ➡

Today this term refers to those who generally support the social and economic status quo and are suspicious of efforts to introduce new political formulas and economic arrangements. Many conservatives also believe that a large and powerful government poses a threat to citizens' freedoms particular oppose efforts to impose government regulation on business, pointing out that such regulation is frequently economically inefficient and costly and can ultimately lower the entire nation's standard of living. As for social and cultural positions, many conservatives oppose abortion and support school prayer. In international affairs, conservatism has come to mean support for the maintenance of American military power. Like liberalism, conservatism is far from a monolithic ideology. Some conservatives support many government social programs. George W. Bush, a Republican, called himself a compassionate conservative to indicate that he favored programs that assist the poor and the needy. Other conservatives oppose efforts to outlaw abortion, arguing that government intrusion in this area is as misguided as government intervention in the economy. The real political world is far too complex to be seen in terms of a simple struggle between liberals and conservatives.

There are many other ideologies beside liberal and conservative. Some people seek to expand liberty above all other principles and wish to minimize government intervention in the economy and society. Such a position is sometimes called libertarian. Other ideologies seek a particular outcome, such as environmental protection. Such a stance may emphasize certain issues, such as economic growth, and de-emphasize other issues, such as abortion. Communism and fascism are ideologies that involve government control of all aspects of the economy and society. These ideologies dominated politics in many European countries from the 1920s through the 1940s. Political discourse in the United States, however, has revolved around the division between liberals and conservatives for most of the last century.

Liberal and conservative differences manifest themselves in a variety of contexts. For example, the liberal approach to chronically low test scores and high dropout rates at a public high school might be to increase funding for teachers and reduce class sizes. The conservative approach might be to remove administrators or fire teachers from low-performing schools, or even to close such schools. To some extent, contemporary liberalism and conservatism can be seen as blends of the fundamental American political values of liberty and equality. For liberals, equality is often the most important of the core values. Liberals are willing to tolerate government intervention in such areas as college admissions and business decisions to help remedy high levels of race, class, or gender inequality. For conservatives, on the other hand, liberty is the core value. Conservatives oppose most efforts by the government, however well intentioned, to intrude into private life or the marketplace. This simple formula for distinguishing liberalism and conservatism is of course not always accurate because political ideologies seldom lend themselves to neat or logical characterizations. Conservatives, for example, sometimes seek more government intervention in social policy realms involving family, marriage, homosexuality, and abortion, whereas liberals tend to resist government regulation of such social relations.

Political scientists often think of liberal and conservative ideologies as anchors on a spectrum of possible belief systems. Our own values and interests might make us adhere to many of the tenets and policy positions of one of these ideologies but not all. The Pew Center on People and the Press offers just such a classification in its American Values Survey, conducted annually since

1987.[20] The Pew Survey asked respondents about a wide range of political, social, and cultural preferences, behaviors, and beliefs. Many of these beliefs do cluster: for instance, people who believe in the literal truth of the Bible tend to be prolife and tend to favor cuts in taxes. These people also tend to call themselves conservative. However, the more such questions one asks the more finely one may sort people. Classifying people this way, the Pew Center finds that a large plurality of Americans are in fact very moderate—having as many conservative views as liberal views. As discussed earlier, that is essentially what Morris Fiorina and his colleagues concluded about the degree of polarization in the United States—most people are quite moderate. Interestingly, the Pew surveys also document that the number of Americans who choose more liberal policy positions than conservative policy positions is greater than the number of Americans who choose more conservative policy positions than liberal ones. This is true even though the number who choose the conservative label outnumber those who choose the liberal label. Why this is the case is an interesting puzzle.

Identity Politics

Ideology offers one lens through which people can discern where their interests and values lie in political choices. Identity provides an alternative simplification of the political world. Political identities are distinctive characteristics or group associations that individuals carry, reflecting individuals' social connections or common values and interests with others in that group. A harm or benefit to any individual with a given identity is viewed as a harm or benefit to all people of that identity.

Identities are both psychological and sociological. At the psychological level these are attachments felt by individuals, and at the sociological level they function at the collective level, such as racial groups, genders, or language groups. Unlike ideological politics, identities are absolutes, and identity politics are often zero-sum: one group wins and another loses. The term *identity politics* is sometimes used today to refer to groups that have been oppressed and that seek to assert their rights. But the concept is much broader. *Political identity* is not just a term that describes the situation of groups that have suffered some harm; it applies to any collective identity. In fact, political identity often has a very positive side, as the glue that holds society together and as another way to overcome problems of collective action.[21]

Identity politics are quite obvious in the United States today. All citizens of the United States and even many noncitizens identify themselves as Americans. During international sporting competitions we root for athletes representing the United States because we identify with that country, and when those athletes win Americans feel happy and proud. We may feel similarly when an American

20 The American Values Survey is available at www.people-press.org/values-questions/.

21 Rawi Abdelal, Yoshiko M. Herrera, Alastair Iain Johnston, and Rose McDermott, "Identity as a Variable," *Perspectives on Politics* 4, no. 4 (2006): 695–711.

wins a Nobel Prize or makes a significant scientific discovery. The same is true of people from any country: we feel pride in the accomplishments of others from our country.

One of the most salient political identities in the United States is political party. The authors of *The American Voter*, a now classic work of political science research on the social and psychological foundations of electoral behavior in the United States, characterize party identification as a stable psychological attachment usually developed in childhood and carried throughout one's adult life. Party identifications are, of course, shaped by interests and values as well as by current events, but partisanship also has deep roots in family, local culture, and other factors that shape identities. It is common, for example, for people to rely on their partisan identities in filtering information. Partisan identifiers who watch presidential debates overwhelmingly think their candidate won the debate, regardless of what actually transpired. Party also has its own unique hold on our voting behavior. Even after taking into account self-interests, moral values, and other identities, partisanship continues to be one of the best predictors of how someone will vote. (See the discussion of party voting in Chapters 11 and 12.)

An ingenious study showing how identity matters to people's preferences was conducted by Alan Gerber and Gregory Huber of Yale University in 2006. They studied consumption behavior of people following elections and found that people who identified strongly with a particular party and whose party won the election spent much more on durable consumer goods, such as washing machines and other appliances, than did people whose candidates did not win or people who did not identify strongly with a party. Behavioral economists and social psychologists have documented other such phenomena, such as the effect of sports teams' victories on feelings of happiness.[22]

This is not to say that party does not reflect ideological choices or self-interest. It does. But it is certainly also the case that party functions as a social identity.

People who hold a specific identity often express strong affinity for others of the same identity. You might vote for someone of the same national background or ethnicity quite apart from, or in spite of, the sorts of laws that politicians promise to enact. Political scientists call this preference for like types of people "descriptive representation." The preference for people of the same identity is an important subject in the area of race and elections. The Voting Rights Act tries to protect African Americans, Hispanics, and other racial and ethnic groups against discriminatory electoral practices that prevent those voters from electing their preferred candidates. Since the Voting Rights Act was passed in 1965, the percentage of members of Congress who are African American and Hispanic increased from 0 to about 15 to 20 percent. Race, gender, social class, and place—all create strong identities that shape voting behavior.

A little introspection reveals a wide range of social, cultural, and political identities that people have. Gender and race are obvious, especially because of physical characteristics. Religions, regions of the country, sexual orientations,

---

22 Alan Gerber and Gregory Huber, "Partisanship and Economic Behavior," *American Political Science Review* 103 (2009): 407–26.

occupation, and many other distinctive characteristics of people also function as identities. In a provocative essay in the *Atlantic Monthly* following the 2000 election, commentator David Brooks wrote that Americans are divided not so much along the lines of ideologies and interests but along cultural lines.[23] Brooks's assessment gave rise to the argument that there are red (Republican) and blue (Democratic) areas of the nation, but, he also argued, the divisions are not based so much on ideologies and interests. Rather, Americans have identities based on who they are, where they live, and how they live, and these identities can have a large impact on individuals' preferences and political behavior.

Blacks. The practice of slavery in the colonies and early American states created a deep, lasting divide in our society between whites and blacks. That division is reflected in a staggering number of statistics, from wages and education levels to poverty levels to neighborhood integration to political ideals. There are, for example, stark differences between blacks and whites in their beliefs about the basic responsibilities of government for providing shelter, food, and other basic necessities to those in need.[24] Blacks and whites also differ in their views of equality of opportunity in the United States, which can impact their preferences for policies that address perceived disadvantages (Figure 10.1).

More striking still, race seems to affect how other factors, like income and education, shape preferences. Among whites, there is a definite correlation between conservatism and income. Higher-income whites tend to support more conservative policies and are more likely to identify with the Republican Party, while lower-income whites tend to favor more liberal economic policies and align with the Democratic Party. Nearly all African Americans, on the other hand, side with the Democrats and support liberal economic policies, regardless of income. Why are high-income African Americans not as supportive of Republicans as their white counterparts? There are many other such instances, including differences across religious groups, between men and women, and between young and old. Some of these differences may be traced to self-interest, but most cannot. The explanations for differences in opinions and voting behaviors among social groups surely has something to do with the nature of such groups in American society.

Latinos. Latinos are another major American subgroup with distinctive opinions on some public issues. A 2008 survey by the Pew Hispanic Center found that education, followed by immigration, are the top concerns of Hispanic voters, whereas the economy ranked highest among white non-Hispanic voters.[25]

---

23 David Brooks, "One Nation, Slightly Divisible," *Atlantic Monthly,* December 2001, www .theatlantic.com/past/docs/issues/2001/12/brooks.htm (accessed 5/17/13).

24 Pew Research Center for the People and the Press, "The Black and White of Public Opinion," October 31, 2005, http://people-press.org/commentary/?analysisid=121 (accessed 3/24/09).

25 Mark Lopez and Susan Minushkin, "2008 National Survey of Latinos: Hispanic Voter Attitudes," Pew Hispanic Center, July 24, 2008, http://pewhispanic.org/files /reports/90.pdf (accessed 3/24/09).

Figure 10.1
DISAGREEMENT AMONG BLACKS AND WHITES

Do you feel that racial minorities in this country have equal job opportunities as whites, or not?

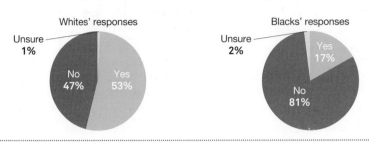

Whites' responses

Unsure 1%
No 47%
Yes 53%

Blacks' responses

Unsure 2%
Yes 17%
No 81%

Although America's system of legally mandated racial segregation ended nearly half a century ago, its effects continue to linger. In contemporary America, blacks and whites have different perspectives on race relations. Do you think that black–white differences have increased or decreased in the past few decades? Are these differences of opinion important?

Do you generally favor or oppose affirmative action programs for racial minorities?

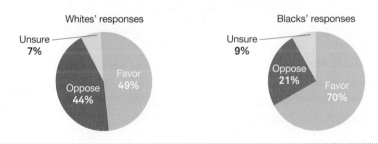

Whites' responses

Unsure 7%
Oppose 44%
Favor 49%

Blacks' responses

Unsure 9%
Oppose 21%
Favor 70%

Do you think racism against blacks is or is not widespread in the United States?

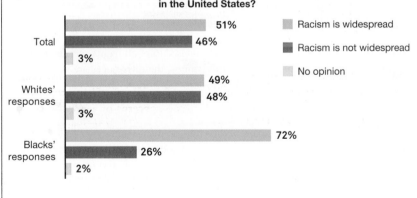

Total
51%
46%
3%

Whites' responses
49%
48%
3%

Blacks' responses
72%
26%
2%

- Racism is widespread
- Racism is not widespread
- No opinion

NOTE: Percentages may not sum to 100 due to rounding.
SOURCES: Gallup polls, June 8–25, 2006, June 12–15, 2003, and October 16–19, 2009, gallup.com.

Table 10.1

CHANGING PARTY AFFILIATION IN THE LATINO COMMUNITY

BACKGROUND	2004		2008	
	DEM. (%)	REP. (%)	DEM. (%)	REP. (%)
Cuban	17	52	53	20
Mexican	47	18	50	18
Puerto Rican	50	17	61	11

SOURCE: Mark Hugo Lopez and Susan Minushkin, "2008 National Survey of Latinos: Hispanic Voter Attitudes," Pew Hispanic Center Report, July 24, 2008, http://pewhispanic.org/files/reports/90.pdf (accessed 4/30/09).

Hispanic political identities have a different character than political identities of blacks. Hispanic and Latino group identities are often rooted in particular immigrant communities, such as Mexican American, Puerto Ricans, and Cubans.[26] And, Hispanic and Latino political identities are strongly tied to particular issues of immigration.[27] These differences have led to heterogeneity in opinion among Latinos on certain issues. Among Latinos, Cuban Americans have long been disproportionately Republican, while those of Mexican, Puerto Rican, and Central American descent identify more often as Democrats (Table 10.1). That difference traces to Cuban Americans' relationship with their homeland and the long-standing policy differences between the Republicans and Democrats over Cuba. Interestingly, that difference had largely vanished by 2008; surveys during the presidential campaign found that Cuban Americans were nearly as Democratic as other Hispanic groups.

As with blacks, Latino identity tempers the way other demographic characteristics translate into political identities and values. Although higher-income Latinos are more Republican than lower-income Latinos, the differences are not as stark as among whites, and low-income Latinos are much more Democratic than low-income whites. Latino identity mutes the political effects of other characteristics.

Gender. Men and women express differing political opinions as well. Women tend to be less militaristic than men on issues of war and peace, more likely than men to favor measures to protect the environment, and more supportive

26 Gabriel R. Sanchez, "The Role of Group Consciousness in Latino Public Opinion," *Political Research Quarterly* 59, no. 3 (2006): 435–46. Pamela Johnston Conover, "The Influence of Group Identifications on Political Perception and Evaluation," *Journal of Politics* 46, no. 3 (1984): 760–85.

27 Taeku Lee, "Race, Immigration, and the Identity-to-Politics Link," *Annual Review of Political Science* 11 (2008): 457–78.

Table 10.2

DISAGREEMENTS AMONG MEN AND WOMEN ON ISSUES OF WAR AND PEACE

	APPROVE OF ACTION (%)	
GOVERNMENT ACTION	**MEN**	**WOMEN**
Support U.S. missile strikes against Syria (2013)	43	30
Use U.S. troops to attack a terrorist camp (2012)	71	55
Support withdrawal of troops from Iraq (2008)	70	52
Use U.S. troops to intervene in a genocide or civil war (2008)	53	42
Go to war against Iraq (2003)	66	50
Broker a cease-fire in Yugoslavia instead of using NATO air strikes (1999)	44	51
End the ban on homosexuals in the military (1993)	34	51
Go to war against Iraq (1991)	72	53

SOURCES: Gallup polls, 1991,1993, and 1999; *Washington Post*, 2003; Cooperative Congressional Election Study, 2008 and 2012; Langer Research, 2013.

than men of government social and health care programs (Table 10.2). Perhaps because of these differences on issues, women are more likely than men to vote for Democratic candidates, whereas men have become increasingly supportive of Republicans.[28] This tendency for men's and women's opinions to differ is called the **gender gap**. The gender gap in voting first emerged quite clearly in the 1980 election and has persisted, averaging about 8 percentage points.

Why the gender gap emerged 30 years ago and persists today is something of a puzzle. Many speculate that reproductive rights and abortion politics lie at the root of this division. Yet surprisingly, the gender gap has virtually vanished

gender gap

A distinctive pattern of voting behavior reflecting the differences in views between women and men

28 For data, see Center for American Women and Politics, Eagleton Institute of Politics, Rutgers, State University of New Jersey, www.cawp.rutgers.edu/fast_facts/voters /turnout.php (accessed 4/30/09).

on the abortion issue. An August 2006 Pew Research Center poll indicated that men and women are nearly identical—52 percent versus 51 percent—on the issue of allowing abortion in general or on a limited basis, and 46 percent of both men and women believe abortion should always or almost always be illegal.[29] Rather, the gender gap appears to be more clearly attributable to wages, inheritance, and other differences between the ways that men and women are treated in the economy and society, and to the sense among women who have a shared objective of ensuring equal treatment for all women.[30]

Religion. Religion shapes peoples' values and beliefs and, thus, political ideologies, but it also serves as a strong identity quite apart from what values are at play. One of the clearest examples was the attachment of Catholics to the Democratic Party. This began in 1924 with the nomination of Al Smith, a Catholic, for president of the United States by the Democratic Party. When Democrat John Kennedy became the country's first Catholic president in 1961, that bond was strengthened.[31] The lesson of the Kennedy election is quite sharp: people are much more likely to vote for candidates of the same religion, even after controlling for ideology, party, and other measures of value. This pattern held true for born-again Christians and Jimmy Carter in 1976 and for Mormons and Mitt Romney in 2012.

Geography. Where we live also molds our sense of identity. People pick up on subtle cues, such as another person's accent or how a person dresses or even wears her hair as an indicator of where that person is from. People from different regions of the country, even from specific states, often have a strong identification with others from that region or state. They are more likely to trust someone of the same region or state as them, and they are more likely to vote for that person. And people often hold negative stereotypes of people from other regions. An unfortunate consequence of the Civil War is a lasting discomfort that many people from the North and South still feel around each other—and that conflict was 150 years ago. Yet to this day Americans contest the symbols of that conflict, such as whether a southern state should have a Confederate battle flag as part of its state's symbol or flying in the statehouse.

Other geographic identities are tied to the type of community one lives in (or prefers to live in). The division between those in urban and rural areas often reflects self-interest—who gets what from the government. For instance, people from states that have predominantly agricultural economies express stronger support for government farm subsidies. But geography also reflects different ways

---

29 Pew Research Center for the People and the Press, "Pragmatic Americans Liberal and Conservative on Social Issues: Most Want Middle Ground on Abortion," August 3, 2006, http://people-press.org/report/283/pragmatic-americans-liberal-and -conservative-on-social-issues (accessed 3/24/09).

30 An outstanding research paper along these lines is Ebonya Washington, "Female Socialization: How Daughters Affect Their Legislator Fathers' Voting on Women's Issues," *American Economic Review* 98 (2008): 311–32.

31 See Angus Campbell, Philip E. Converse, Warren E. Miller, and Donald E. Stokes, *The American Voter* (Chicago: University of Chicago Press, 1960).

of living, and we tend to identify with people who live like us. Such differences are cultural. Where we shop, which restaurants we frequent, what we like to do in our spare time, and so forth—all are aspects of our local culture. They shape our identification with others of like backgrounds, experiences, and ways of living.

Residential segregation can also strengthen other aspects of identity politics. People segregate according to income, which might strengthen social class identities, and race and ethnicity, which reinforces racial and ethnic identities. Those who live in highly segregated neighborhoods have much stronger identities with their own racial groups, and they also express much stronger prejudices against other groups.[32]

Outgroups. Some groups are defined not by who they are but by who they are not; they are the outgroups in society. Discrimination is one manifestation of the treatment of an outgroup. If a group is well organized, it can achieve higher success but usually at the expense of those defined not to be in that group. In some industries, workers who are not members of a union cannot work in that industry. Such "closed shop" rules benefit union members but at the cost of nonunion members. Often an outgroup is clearly identifiable and ostracized, leading to systematic discrimination or persecution. When the discrimination is intense, systematic, and long-held, the outgroup can itself develop a particular psychology. Social psychologist James Sidanius expresses this as a social dominance relationship and argues that more numerous groups in all societies systematically discriminate against less numerous groups. The less numerous groups develop a common identity, and they come to see their own situation in the treatment of others of their group.[33] Writing about the particular psychology of African Americans in the United States, Professor Michael Dawson calls this the "linked fate" of African Americans. It has been found in many other societies as well, such as Albanians in Italy. Discrimination then is the collective bad against which the identity of all in a given group must act. Even high-income African Americans will, thus, be led by the collective needs and identities of their group to support policies that are likely to help large numbers of low-income or underemployed African Americans. Groups that have experienced severe discrimination over very long periods of time are most likely to feel a sense of linked fate, which helps account for the persistence of a sense of common identity that remains strong in some groups.[34]

Political, social, and economic discrimination is not limited to race and ethnicity. As we discussed in Chapter 5, the United States has witnessed struggles

---

32 Rene R. Rocha and Rodolfo Espino, "Racial Threat, Residential Segregation, and the Policy Attitudes of Anglos," *Political Research Quarterly* 62, no. 2 (2009): 415–26.

33 Being a numerical majority is not necessary. For over a century, Blacks in South Africa were oppressed by Afrikkaners, even though the white population accounted for only about 10 percent of all people in the country.

34 Paula D. McClain, Jessica D. Johnson Carew, Eugene Walton, Jr., and Candis S. Watts, "Group Membership, Group Identity, and Group Consciousness: Measures of Racial Identity in American Politics?" *Annual Review of Political Science* 12 (2009): 471–85.

for equity for many different groups, including women, Catholics, Jews, homosexuals, divorced fathers, and even people in urban areas. In all of these cases, people who were part of these groups had to assert themselves politically in order to establish or protect their rights to property, to vote, and to equal protection of the laws. It is exceedingly difficult for those with diminished political rights to work inside the legislative process, and so these people often had to pursue outsider strategies, including protests, propaganda, and litigation. The reason that they had their rights abrogated was because they were treated as a class or group, and their identity was the target of discrimination. That very same identity, however, also served as a source of power, as it ultimately led these groups to organize and to defend their political rights and identities.

Self-interest, values and beliefs, and identities all influence how people make sense of politics, what they want government to do, and what political decisions people make. Interests, values, and identities are the basis of people's preferences.

PUBLIC OPINION AND POLITICAL KNOWLEDGE

When survey researchers do a poll of the public they seek to measure what government action the majority of Americans support, or which political party or faction enjoys the support of most people. But what do those responses really mean? At one level we might take those responses to mean that every individual has weighed all sides of an issue and arrived at a reasoned judgment as to whether one side or the other is more consistent with the individual's interests, values, or identity. Yet, from the advent of public-opinion research, observers have noted the stunning lack of knowledge that most people have about specific issues, even about the major political parties. Learned Hand, one of the most distinguished jurists in American history, described the problem of political knowledge as a collective action problem. People have so many other problems to worry about, and most issues are so complex that simply studying the issues would leave us with little time to do anything else. It is far easier to rely on the wisdom of others.[35] Walter Lippmann, a great American journalist, wrote in the 1920s that this creates the opportunity for a learned class of elites to govern not by winning elections but by shaping how others think.[36]

One of the most troubling questions about American democracy is how is democracy possible when people seem to know so little? We have our own views on this matter, but leave it to the reader to decide where he or she stands. Here we present different perspectives on this matter.

---

35 Learned Hand, "Democracy: Its Presumptions and Realities" in *The Spirit of Liberty: Papers and Addresses of Learned Hand*, Irving Dilliard, ed. (New York: Knopf, 1932).

36 Walter Lippmann, *Public Opinion* (New York: Harcourt, Brace and Company, 1922).

Political Knowledge and Preference Stability

People are constantly confronted with new political events, issues, and personalities as they watch television, surf the web, talk to friends and family, or read the news. In our democracy we expect every citizen to have views about the major problems of the day as well as opinions about who should be entrusted with the nation's leadership, and we expect people to cast informed votes that convey their preferences about what government ought to do. Issues, however, come and go, and people are continually learning about new issues the nation faces.

Some Americans know quite a bit about politics, and many have general views and hold opinions on several issues. Few Americans, though, devote sufficient time, energy, or attention to politics to really understand or evaluate the myriad issues with which they are bombarded on a regular basis. Since the advent of polling in the 1930s, studies have repeatedly found that the average American appears to know little about current events or even basic facts of American government.[37]

Low levels of information lead to instability and incoherence in people's responses to surveys. Professor Philip Converse, in one of the most widely cited pieces of social science research ever, noted that most people do not seem to have clear opinions on important issues. The answers they give to a question one year, he found, correlated poorly to the answers they gave to the same question two years later, and the answers across issues did not seem to form a consistent pattern or system of belief. The incoherence of respondents' opinions was traceable to their level of education. Better-educated people gave more coherent answers and more stable answers over time. This research led social scientists to argue that most people are in fact not capable of expressing meaningful opinions on issues because of their low levels of information or cognitive ability.

Converse's views have represented an important pole in the debate over public knowledge and democracy. More recent research, including new analyses of Converse's own data, have shown a markedly different picture. It is not that people are incapable of reasoning but that surveys are not perfect instruments for measuring what people know and how they think. Vague or difficult questions, it turns out, explain much of the apparent incoherence that Converse's respondents expressed. When the data were reanalyzed and further studies were conducted, researchers found much more stability in people's preferences from year to year and much more coherence from issue to issue. Even people who have less than a high school education or did not know many common facts about the government still have fairly coherent and stable preferences.[38] It was the survey, not the people, that failed the test.

---

37 Philip E. Converse, "The Nature of Belief Systems in Mass Publics," in *Ideology and Discontent*, David E. Apter, ed. (New York: Free Press, 1964).

38 See Christopher Achen, "Mass Political Attitudes and the Survey Response," *American Political Science Review* 69 (1975), p. 1281; and Stephen Ansolabehere, Jonathan Rodden, and James M. Snyder, Jr., "The Strength of Issues," *American Political Science Review* 102 (2008), pp. 215–32.

Even so, there is something compelling about Converse's account. Why do people seem to know so little, and what might be the consequence of low levels of information about current events and political institutions for the long-run health of democracy?

Attending to the day-to-day goings on in Washington or the state capital or city council is costly; it means spending time at the very least, and often money as well, to collect, organize, and digest political information.[39] Balanced against this cost is the very low probability that the individual will take an action based on this costly information, that this new action will make a beneficial difference to her, and that this benefit will exceed the cost of acquiring the information in the first place. Because individuals anticipate that informed actions that they take will rarely make much difference and that the costs of informing oneself are often not trivial, it may be rational to remain ignorant. In other words, the rationality principle suggests that many people should more profitably devote their personal resources—particularly their time—to more narrowly personal matters. This idea is in turn suggested by the collective action principle, in which the bearing of burdens—such as the cost of becoming informed—is not likely to have much impact in a mass political setting. A more moderate version of "rational" ignorance recognizes that some kinds of information are inexpensive to acquire, such as sound bites from the evening news, or can be pleasant, such as reading the front page of the newspaper while drinking a cup of coffee. In such cases, an individual may become partially informed, but usually not in detail.

Precisely because becoming truly knowledgeable about politics requires a substantial investment of time and energy, many Americans seek to acquire political information and to make political decisions on the cheap, using short-cuts, labels, and stereotypes, rather than following current events closely. One "inexpensive" way to become informed is to take cues from trusted others—the local minister, the television commentator or newspaper editorialist, an interest-group leader, friends, or relatives.[40] A common shortcut for political evaluation and decision making is to assess new issues and events through the lenses of one's general beliefs and orientation. Thus if a conservative learns of a plan to expand federal social programs, she might express opposition to the endeavor without needing to pore over the specifics of the proposal.

These shortcuts are handy, but not perfect. Taking cues from others may lead individuals to accept positions that they would not support if they had more information. And general ideological orientations can be coarse guides to decision making on concrete issues. For example, what position should a liberal take on immigration? Should a liberal favor keeping America's borders open to poor people from all over the world, or should he be concerned that America's open borders create a pool of surplus labor that permits giant corporations to

---

39 Anthony Downs, *An Economic Theory of Democracy* (New York: Harper & Row, 1957).

40 For a discussion of the role of information in democratic politics, see Arthur Lupia and Mathew D. McCubbins, *The Democratic Dilemma: Can Citizens Learn What They Need to Know?* (New York: Cambridge University Press, 1998).

drive down the wages of poor American workers? Many other issues defy easy ideological characterization.

Although understandable and perhaps inevitable, widespread inattentiveness to politics weakens American democracy in two ways. First, those who lack political information might not truly understand where their interests lie, and they might not effectively defend their political interests. Second, the presence of large numbers of politically inattentive or ignorant individuals means that the political process can be more easily manipulated by the various institutions and forces that seek to shape public opinion.

As to the first of these problems, in our democracy millions of ordinary citizens take part in political life, at least to the extent of voting in national elections. Those with little knowledge of the election's issues, candidates, or procedures can find themselves acting against their own preferences and interests. One example is U.S. tax policy. Over the past several decades, the United States has substantially reduced the rate of taxation for its wealthiest citizens.[41] Tax cuts signed into law by President Bush in 2001 and mostly maintained throughout the decade provided a tax break mainly for the top 1 percent of the nation's wage earners, and further tax cuts proposed by the president offered additional benefits to this privileged stratum. Polling data showed that millions of middle-class and lower-middle-class Americans who did not stand to benefit from the president's tax cuts seemed to favor them nonetheless.

Their support for these taxes might have been based on principle. As Professor Andrea Campbell argues in her work on the history of public attitudes toward taxes, public opinion toward taxation changed in the 1960s, and since then there has been a consistent, ideological resistance to taxation among political conservatives and most moderates.[42] The support of the 2001 tax cuts among middle- and-lower income people might also have arisen out of ignorance or by following the wrong cue-givers. Professors Larry Bartels, Paul Pierson, and Jacob Hacker, among others, attribute this state of affairs to a lack of political knowledge.[43] Millions of individuals who were unlikely to derive much advantage from President Bush's tax policy thought they would. Bartels has called this phenomenon "misplaced self-interest."[44] Knowledge may not always translate into political power, but lack of knowledge is almost certain to translate into political weakness. And according to the policy principle, the lack of knowledge and concomitant political weakness mean policy disappointment.

---

41 One of the most detailed analyses of the distribution of the tax burden in advanced industrial democracies in the past half-century is Thomas Piketty and Emmanuel Saez, "How Progressive Is the U.S. Federal Tax System? Historical and International Perspectives," working paper 12404, National Bureau of Economic Research, 2006, www.nber.org/papers/w12404 (accessed 3/25/09).

42 Andrea Campbell, *How Americans Think about Taxes.* (Princeton, NJ: Princeton University Press, 2013).

43 Jacob Hacker and Paul Pierson, *Winner Take All Politics* (New York: Simon & Shuster, 2010).

44 Larry M. Bartels, "Homer Gets a Tax Cut: Inequality and Public Policy in the American Mind," *Perspectives on Politics* 3 (2005): 15–31.

Campaigns and other forums for public discourse can change public attitudes on issues by altering the nature of the choices or informing the public about the effects of policies. Continued debate of the tax issue throughout the 2008 and 2012 presidential campaigns brought about changes in public attitudes toward taxes, especially taxes on the wealthiest segment of the population. During the 2008 presidential election campaign, Barack Obama seized on the tax issue at a time when the economy was worsening and people's economic prospects looked bleak. He returned to that theme during the 2012 election, promising to raise taxes on the top 2 percent of income earners, those who make at least $250,000 a year. That promise was instrumental in both of President Obama's successful election campaigns. In January 2013, staring at potential automatic tax increases on all Americans, Obama was able to outmaneuver the Republican leadership in Congress and increase taxes on income over $400,000 per year, a tax increase that affected only 1 percent of the population, yet nearly failed to make it through the Congress.

Stability and the Meaning of Public Opinion

There is a great stability to public opinion in the United States. What people want government to do on specific issues and who people want to have in charge usually changes little from election to election. Benjamin Page and Robert Shapiro's *The Rational Public* traces public attitudes across a wide range of issues since the 1950s and finds that on most issues and political attitudes, aggregate public opinion is quite stable. Consider party identification. Almost all people who identify with a party in one election remain with that party in the next election. Indeed, a large fraction of the American public remains Republican for life or Democrat for life. Such stability is also observed in other aspects of people's political preferences. Individuals' notions of what is right and wrong are often formed in childhood and remain fairly stable throughout their lives. Our racial and ethnic identities, gender identities, and other cultural identities are also formed early in life and are quite stable. Our occupations and educational achievement also shape our economic interests, and those tend to be constant throughout our adult lives. Interests, identities, and values, in turn, influence attitudes about when and how government should act.

One of the most important factors generating stability in public opinion is a fundamental truth about democracy: there is power (and stability) in numbers. Democratic theorists since the Marquis de Condorcet, the great political philosopher of the French Revolution, have understood that aggregation counteracts the effects of political ignorance. When people do not fully know their interests they will make mistakes. Fortunately, those mistakes usually look like "random" errors, and when individuals' opinions and choices are aggregated, in surveys or elections, those errors seem to average out. People may, for example, vote on the basis of how they are doing today, without knowing the macroeconomic indicators, such as the unemployment and inflation rates. Some people are doing well economically, while others are doing poorly. Adding up all of those personal experiences, though, will lead to a collective sense of how the society is doing. A wisdom of the masses thus emerges in public opinion polls, election results, and other aggregates of people's preferences. And, more important, these aggregates are much more stable and even more meaningful than individuals' opinions.

But it is also clear that public opinion is not static. At times in American history, the majority of Americans' opinions have changed dramatically and rapidly. Between 1945 and 1965, public opinion toward federal action to promote racial equality swung from majority opposition to majority support for the Civil Rights Act and the Voting Rights Act, as well as for integration of schools and public conveyances. During the late 1960s, public attitudes about taxation changed. Up until that time, most Americans supported high taxes because they believed they promoted the common good. Since the early 1970s, the nation has been divided over the question of taxes, especially income taxes.[45] And since the mid-1990s there has been a near about-face in public attitudes toward same-sex marriage. In 1996, Congress passed the Defense of Marriage Act, which defined marriage as a union between one man and one woman for the purpose of federal benefits. A CNN/USA Today/Gallup poll in 1996 showed that 68 percent of Americans opposed same-sex marriage and only 27 percent supported it. By 2011, a Gallup poll found than 53 percent of Americans supported same-sex marriage and 45 percent opposed it. (See the Analyzing the Evidence unit.)

In each of these cases, public attitudes changed quickly—within the span of one or two decades. How and why does public opinion change? In part, the answer lies in the evolving positions of the political choices and elite discourse. As party leaders, celebrities, and other elites debate an issue, the public often follows cues and takes sides. The answer also surely lies with public learning. As the public learns about an issue, the implications of government action and inaction become clearer, as does the right thing to do.

In turn, such evolutions in public opinion influence public policy, which is fairly responsive to shifts in public opinion. Professor James Stimson has provided a comprehensive assessment of the link between aggregate public opinion and public policy. His research tracks public opinion on a wide variety of issues from the 1950s to the present. When aggregate public opinion has shifted left, as in the 1960s, or right, as in the 1980s, public policy has generally followed suit. Although it is hard to know whether public policy exactly equaled what a majority of people wanted in each policy area, the high level of responsiveness of policy outcomes to changes in aggregate opinion suggests that the political system follows the general sense of aggregate opinion, or what Stimson calls the policy mood. This result, he argues, strongly suggests that "the magic of aggregation" provides a corrective for the low levels of knowledge that the typical citizen has.[46]

45 See Andrea Louise Campbell, "What Americans Think of Taxes," in *The New Fiscal Sociology: Taxation in Comparative and Historical Perspective,* Isaac William Martin, Ajay K. Mehrotra, and Monica Prasad, eds. (New York: Cambridge University Press, 2009).

46 James Stimson, Robert Erikson, and Michael MacKuen, *The Macro Polity* (Cambridge, UK: Cambridge University Press, 1998).

The Contact Hypothesis and Attitudes about Gay Rights

Contributed by
Patrick J. Egan
New York University

Americans' attitudes toward gay rights have evolved significantly over the past 20 years. In 1996, opponents of gay marriage in the United States greatly outnumbered supporters by 65 to 27 percent. By 2012, Americans favored gay marriage by 49 to 40 percent.

Americans' Attitudes toward Same-Sex Marriage, 1996–2012

SOURCE: Pew Research Center, 2012.

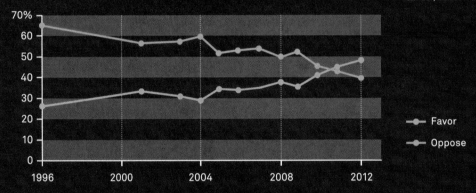

What explains this change in American attitudes? A theory from social psychology known as the *contact hypothesis* holds that contact between in-group and out-group members reduces the stigma directed toward the out-group. In this case, are straight people (the in-group) who know openly gay people (the out-group) more supportive of gay rights? The graphs show that support for gay rights has increased at the same time that growing shares of Americans have reported knowing gays and lesbians.

Americans' Contact with Gays and Lesbians, 1984–2008

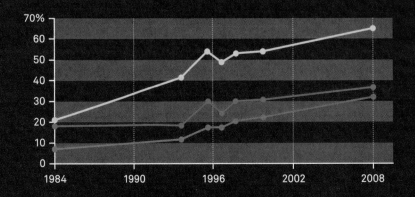

Americans who report having a gay or lesbian:

● Friend or acquaintance
● Coworker
● Family member

SOURCE: Princeton Survey Research Associates/ Newsweek, 2009.

Furthermore, those who report having gay friends are indeed significantly more supportive of gay rights than those who do not. We can see this by creating a composite score for survey respondents based on their opinions on such issues as gay marriage, adoption, and job discrimination. A score of 100 is fully supportive of all gay rights. Those with gay friends score an estimated 43 on the scale; those who report having no gay friends score only 36 (see graph below).

Americans' Contact with Gay People and Support for Gay Rights

NOTE: Bars indicate support for gay rights on a 100-point scale after accounting for demographic and political factors that affect the likelihood of contact as well as attitudes on gay rights.

Has contact

Does not have contact

TYPE OF CONTACT

But can we be sure that contact with gay people is actually *causing* increased support for gay rights? One concern is selection bias. Gay people may be selective about disclosing their identity to those friends whom they already know to be supportive, and straight people who hold more tolerant attitudes may be more likely to select gay people as friends.

To further explore this question, we can examine types of contact that are governed less by selection. While we typically do chose our friends, coworkers and family members are essentially chosen for us. These types of contact thus offer much cleaner tests of the contact hypothesis. As shown in the bar graph above, in these contexts the effect of contact on attitudes is essentially zero (i.e., individuals with gay coworkers or gay family members are no more supportive of gay rights than those without).

This evidence thus runs counter to the contact hypothesis. But it does not entirely settle the question, and some political scientists have presented results in support of the hypothesis. When political scientists find evidence against a hypothesis, they consider different theories. For example, it may be that it is not the *type* but the *quality* of contact that changes attitudes. Definitive answers to these questions await discovery through additional research.

SHAPING OPINION: POLITICAL LEADERS, PRIVATE GROUPS, AND THE MEDIA

The fact that many Americans are inattentive to politics and lack even basic political information means that there is a place for public debate and political discourse. Controversy educates us. Through debate, the average person learns what is important and the information needed to make sensible decisions. The lack of information also creates opportunities to influence how the public thinks. Although direct efforts to manipulate opinion often don't succeed, three forces play especially important roles in shaping opinion. These are the government, private groups, and the news media.

Government and the Shaping of Public Opinion

All governments attempt, to a greater or lesser extent, to influence, manipulate, or manage their citizens' beliefs. But the extent to which public opinion is affected by government public relations efforts is probably limited. The government—despite its size and power—is only one source of information in the United States. Very often government claims are disputed by the media and interest groups, and at times by opposing forces within the government itself. Often, too, government efforts to manipulate public opinion backfire when the public is made aware of the government's tactics. Thus in 1971 the government's efforts to build popular support for the Vietnam War were hurt when CBS News aired its documentary "The Selling of the Pentagon," which purported to reveal the extent and character of government efforts to sway popular sentiment. In this documentary, CBS demonstrated the techniques, including planted news stories and faked film footage, that the government had used to misrepresent its activities in Vietnam. These revelations, of course, undermined popular trust in government claims.

A hallmark of the administration of President Bill Clinton was the steady use of election-campaign-type techniques to bolster popular enthusiasm for White House initiatives. The president established a political "war room" similar to the one that operated in his campaign headquarters. In the presidential version, representatives from all cabinet departments met daily to discuss and coordinate the president's public-relations efforts. Many of the same consultants and pollsters who directed the successful Clinton campaign were also employed in the selling of the president's programs.[47]

After he assumed office in 2001, George W. Bush asserted that political leaders should base their programs on their own conception of the public interest, not on the polls. This did not mean that Bush ignored public opinion, however.

---

47 Gerald F. Seib and Michael K. Frisby, "Selling Sacrifice," *Wall Street Journal*, February 5, 1993, p. 1.

He relied on the pollster Jan van Lohuizen to conduct a low-key operation, sufficiently removed from the limelight to allow the president to renounce polling while continuing to make use of survey data.[48] At the same time, the Bush White House developed an extensive public-relations program, led initially by the former presidential aide Karen Hughes, to bolster popular support for the president's policies. Hughes, working with the conservative TV personality Mary Matalin, coordinated White House efforts to maintain popular support for the administration's war against terrorism. These efforts included presidential speeches, media appearances by administration officials, numerous press conferences, and thousands of press releases presenting the administration's views.[49] The White House also made a substantial effort to sway opinion in foreign countries, even sending officials to present the administration's views on television networks serving the Arab world.

Not all political media strategies work. President Obama, striving to maintain the political momentum from his 2008 election campaign, attempted to use social media to keep up the same buzz about his legislative agenda as his campaign enjoyed. He brought Macon Philips, who developed the campaign's social media strategy, into the White House team to organize the effort. The White House maintains a newsy website, a blog, a YouTube channel, a Facebook page, and a Twitter account. But many have criticized the low level of actual engagement with the people. Each of these new media is being used like the old media—to talk at people rather than with them, to disseminate information to the press rather than respond to reporters' questions. Indeed, many White House reporters feel that the Obama press office is less accessible than its predecessors.[50]

Private Groups and the Shaping of Public Opinion

We have already seen how the government tries to shape public opinion. But the ideas that become prominent in political life are also developed and spread by important economic and political groups searching for issues that will advance their causes. Rational political entrepreneurs pursue strategies that—in an application of the collective action principle—give the groups they lead a decided advantage in the political arena in comparison with latent, unorganized groups. In some instances, in the hope of bringing others over to their side, private groups espouse values they truly believe in. Take, for example, the campaign against so-called partial birth abortion, which resulted in the Partial Birth Abortion Ban Act of 2003. Proponents of the act believed that prohibiting particular sorts of abortions would be a first step toward eliminating all

48 Joshua Green, "The Other War Room," *Washington Monthly,* April 2002.

49 Peter Marks, "Adept in Politics and Advertising, Four Women Shape a Campaign," *New York Times,* November 11, 2001, p. B6.

50 Michael Calderone, "White House News Strategy Causes Concerns about Access," February 15, 2011, http://news.yahoo.com/s/yblog_thecutline/20110215/bs_yblog _thecutline/white-house-media-strategy-causes-concerns-about-access (accessed 8/22/11).

abortions, something they view as a moral imperative.[51] In other cases, however, groups will promote principles designed mainly to further hidden agendas of political and economic interests. One famous example is the campaign against cheap imported handguns—the so-called Saturday-night specials—that was covertly financed by the domestic manufacturers of more expensive firearms. The campaign's organizers claimed that cheap handguns pose a grave risk to the public and should be outlawed. The real goal, though, was not safeguarding the public but protecting the economic well-being of the domestic gun industry. A more recent example is the campaign against the alleged "sweatshop" practices of some American companies manufacturing their products in third world countries. This campaign is mainly financed by U.S. labor unions seeking to protect their members' jobs by discouraging American firms from manufacturing their products abroad.[52]

Typically, ideas are marketed most effectively by groups with access to financial resources, public or private institutional support, and sufficient skill or education to select, develop, and draft ideas that will attract interest and support. Thus the development and promotion of conservative themes and ideas in recent years have been greatly facilitated by the millions of dollars that conservative corporations and business organizations such as the U.S. Chamber of Commerce and the Public Affairs Council spend each year on public information and what is now called in corporate circles "issues management." In addition, conservative business leaders have contributed millions of dollars to such conservative institutions as the Heritage Foundation, the Hoover Institution, and the American Enterprise Institute.[53] Many of the ideas that helped those on the right influence political debate were first developed and articulated by scholars associated with institutions such as these.

Although they do not usually have access to financial assets that match those available to their conservative opponents, liberal intellectuals and professionals have ample organizational skills, access to the media, and practice in creating, communicating, and using ideas. During the past three decades, the chief vehicle through which liberal intellectuals and professionals have advanced their ideas has been the "public interest group," an institution that relies heavily on voluntary contributions of time, effort, and interest on the part of its members. Through groups such as Common Cause, the National Organization for Women, the Sierra Club, Friends of the Earth, and Physicians for Social Responsibility, intellectuals and professionals have been able to use their organizational skills and educational resources to develop and promote ideas.[54] Often research

51 Cynthia Gorney, "Gambling with Abortion," *Harper's Magazine*, November 2004, pp. 33–46.

52 David P. Baron and Daniel Diermeier, "Strategic Activism and Nonmarket Strategy," *Journal of Economics and Management Strategy* (2006).

53 See David Vogel, "The Power of Business in America: A Reappraisal," *British Journal of Political Science* 13 (1983): 19–44.

54 See David Vogel, "The Public Interest Movement and the American Reform Tradition," *Political Science Quarterly* 96 (Winter 1980): 607–27.

conducted at universities and liberal "think tanks" such as the Brookings Institution provides the ideas on which liberal politicians rely. For example, the welfare reform plan introduced by the Clinton administration in 1994 originated with the work of Harvard professor David Ellwood. Ellwood's academic research led him to the conclusion that the nation's welfare system would be improved if services to the poor were expanded in scope but limited in duration. His idea was adopted by the 1992 Clinton presidential campaign, which was searching for a position on welfare that would appeal to both liberal and conservative Democrats. The Ellwood plan seemed perfect: It promised liberals an immediate expansion of welfare benefits, yet it held out to conservatives the idea that welfare recipients would receive benefits for only a limited time. The Clinton welfare reform plan even borrowed phrases from Ellwood's book *Poor Support*.[55]

The Media and Public Opinion

The communications media are among the most powerful forces operating in the marketplace of ideas. Most Americans say that their primary source of information about public affairs is news media—newspapers, broadcast and cable news, radio, and Internet news providers. The alternative sources of political information are direct contact with politics, information provided by groups, and information conveyed by other individuals, such as family members or coworkers. Certainly, few people actually go to Washington to find out what's going on in American politics, and the broad access people have to media outlets dwarfs the number of households that receive direct mail from organizations and elected officials. Personal conversation is also an important source for information, but people tend to avoid controversial political topics in casual conversation.

The mass media, as the term suggests, can be thought of as mediators. They are the conduits through which information flows. Through newspapers, radio and television, magazines, and the Internet we can learn about what's going on in our world and in our government. Providing this opportunity to learn about the world and politics is the most important way the media contribute to public opinion.

People rely on the media, rather than other sources of information, to find out what's going on in politics and public affairs because it is easy to do so. Media outlets are ubiquitous. More households in the United States have television than have indoor plumbing. Nearly every community has a newspaper, with 1,500 daily newspapers published throughout the United States. The number of news programs and the availability of news has also expanded tremendously in recent decades. In the 1960s there were only three television news outlets—CBS, NBC, and ABC. They aired evening and nightly news programs and allowed a half-hour slot for news from local affiliates. The rise of cable television in the 1980s brought a 24-hour news station, CNN; expanded news programming through the Public Broadcasting System (PBS); and a network devoted

---

55 Jason DeParle, "The Clinton Welfare Bill Begins Trek in Congress," *New York Times*, July 15, 1994, p. 1.

exclusively to broadcasting proceedings of Congress and government agencies, C-SPAN. Important competitors to the big three networks emerged, including Fox and the Spanish-language networks Univision and Telemundo. Today there is no shortage of televised news programming available at all hours.[56]

Technological innovations continue to push change in political communication in the United States. Today, more than 75 percent of Americans have Internet access.[57] Conventional media have moved much of their content online, often provided for free. Internet users can gain access not only to U.S. media but also to media from around the world. The Internet has also spawned new forms of communications, most notably blogs and Twitter, which provide platforms for anyone to have their say. Several websites, such as Google News and realclearpolitics .com, are clearinghouses for traditional media, newswire stories, and blogs. This new, highly competitive media environment has put increased financial pressures on the traditional media, and it has radically changed the flow and nature of communication in the United States and the availability of information to the public. In Chapter 14, we discuss the media as a democratic institution at greater length. Our concern here is the media's role in how people learn about politics and public affairs.

Learning through mass media occurs both actively and passively. Active learning occurs when people search for a particular type of program or a particular type of information. If you turn on the nightly news to find out what has happened in national and international affairs or search the web for information about your member of Congress, you are engaged in actively learning. Passive learning may be just as important. Many entertainment programs discuss current affairs and issues, such as social issues or an election. When that occurs, learning takes a passive form: you watch the program for entertainment but gain information about politics. One study of information gain among voters found that people learned as much from Oprah as from the evening news.[58] Political advertising is perhaps the most common form of passive information. During the last month of national political campaigns, it is not uncommon to see three or four political advertisements during one commercial break in a primetime television program.

Mass media are our primary source for information about current affairs. They influence how Americans understand politics not just through the volume of information available but also through what is presented and how. Editors, reporters, and others involved in preparing the content of the news must ultimately decide what topics to cover, what facts to include, and whom to interview. Journalists usually try to present issues fairly, but it is difficult, perhaps impossible, to be perfectly objective.

---

56 See Stephen Ansolabehere, Roy Behr, and Shanto Iynger, *The Media Game* (New York: Macmillian, 1993).

57 These figures are tracked regularly by the Pew Internet and American Life Project, www.pewintemet.org/Static-Pages/Trend-Data/Whos-Online.aspx (accessed 7/14/11).

58 See Matthew Baum, *Soft News Goes to War* (Princeton, NJ: Princeton University Press, 2006).

What the media cover and how news is presented and interpreted can affect public opinion. Psychologists have identified two potential pathways through which media coverage shapes what people think. First, the news sets the public's agenda. Through this **agenda-setting effect**, the media cues people to think about some issues rather than others; it makes some considerations more salient than others. Suppose, for example, that the local news covers crime to the exclusion of all else. When someone who watches the local news regularly thinks about the mayoral election, crime is more likely to be his or her primary consideration, compared with someone who does not watch the local news. Psychologists call this **priming**.

Second, news coverage of an issue frames the way the issue is defined. News coverage of crime, to continue the example, may include a report on every murder that happens in a large city. Such coverage would likely make it seem that murder occurs very often and is much more common than it actually is. This in turn might heighten viewers' sense of insecurity or threat, leading to an exaggerated sense of risk of violent crime and increased support for tough police practices.[59] **Framing** refers to the media's power to influence how events and issues are interpreted.

Priming and framing are often viewed as twin evils. One can distract us from other important problems, and the other can make us think about an issue or a politician in a biased way. The cumulative effects of priming and framing on public opinion depend ultimately on the variety of issues covered and the diversity of perspectives represented. That, after all, is the idea behind the guarantee of a free press in the First Amendment to the Constitution. Free and open communication media allow the greatest likelihood that people will learn about important issues, that they will gain the information they need to distinguish good ideas from bad ones, and that they will learn which political leaders and parties can best represent their interests.

In this regard, the most significant framing effects take the form of the balance in the information available to people. Those in politics—elected officials, candidates, leaders of organized groups—work hard to influence what the news covers. A competitive political environment usually translates into a robust flow of information. However, some political environments are not very competitive, where only one view gets expressed and only one view is reflected in the media. Congressional elections are a case in point. Incumbent politicians today are able to raise much more money than their challengers (an advantage of about $3 to $1). As a result, House elections often have a gross imbalance in the amount of advertising and news coverage between the two campaigns, that of the incumbent member of Congress and that of the challenger. This will likely affect public opinion, because voters hear the incumbent's views and message more often than the challenger's.

A further example of an imbalance in news coverage arises with the president and Congress. Presidential press conferences and events receive much

 agenda-setting effect

The power to bring attention to particular issues and problems

 priming

A process of preparing the public to take a particular view of an event or a political actor

 framing

The power of the media to influence how events and issues are interpreted

---

59 The seminal work on priming and framing in public policy and politics is Shanto Iyengar and Donald Kinder, *News That Matters* (Chicago: University of Chicago Press, 1987).

more coverage than the press events of the leaders of the House or Senate. This gives the president the upper hand in setting the public agenda through the media, because members of the public are more likely to hear the president's arguments for a particular policy. That opportunity and power, of course, must be used wisely. A president who pursues an ill-advised policy can easily squander the advantage that is gained from disproportionate attention from the media. If a policy fails, the president's media advantage can be short-lived. In 2002, for example, President George W. Bush convinced the nation that Iraq was developing weapons of mass destruction and the United States needed to topple the regime of Saddam Hussein immediately. The invasion occurred and Hussein's regime quickly fell, but large caches of chemical and nuclear weapons were never found, and the United States remained in Iraq for a decade. The backlash against these policies cost the Republicans support among the public, contributing to their loss of control of Congress in the 2006 election, and ultimately the presidency in 2008. The power of the president is the power to persuade, but control of information for political aims is a power to be used with caution.

Today, it is easy to learn about public affairs and to hear different opinions—even when we don't want to. Furthermore, it is widely conjectured that the new media have facilitated learning and muted some of the biases that may emerge through priming and framing. No one voice or perspective dominates our multifaceted media environment and competitive political system. And biases in the media often reflect not the lack of outlets or restrictive editorial control but, rather, failures of political competition.

MEASURING PUBLIC OPINION

A century ago, American political leaders gauged public opinion by people's applause and the size of crowds at meetings. This direct exposure to the people's views did not necessarily produce accurate knowledge of public opinion. It did, however, give political leaders confidence in their public support—and therefore confidence in their ability to govern by consent.

Abraham Lincoln and Stephen Douglas debated each other seven times in the summer and autumn of 1858, two years before they became presidential nominees. Their debates took place before audiences in parched cornfields and courthouse squares. A century later most presidential debates, although seen by millions, take place before a few reporters and technicians in television studios that might as well be on the moon. The public's response cannot be experienced firsthand. This distance between leaders and followers is one of the agonizing problems of modern democracy. The media provide information to millions of people, but they are not yet so efficient at providing leaders with feedback from the public. Is government by consent possible when the scale of communication is so large and impersonal? To compensate for the decline in their ability to experience public opinion for themselves, leaders have turned to science, in particular the science of opinion polling.

It is no secret that politicians and public officials make extensive use of **public-opinion polls** to help them decide whether to run for office, what policies to support, how to vote on important legislation, and what types of appeals to make in their campaigns. President Lyndon Johnson was famous for carrying the latest Gallup and Roper poll results in his pocket, and it is widely believed that he began to withdraw from politics because the polls reported losses in public support. All recent presidents and other major political figures work closely with pollsters and consultants who themselves are steeped in the polls.

Constructing Public Opinion from Surveys

The population that we are interested in studying is usually quite large, such as all adults or all voters in the United States. To conduct their polls, survey researchers first identify the relevant population and choose a **sample** of the total population. The selection of this sample is important. Above all, it must be representative: the views of those in the sample must accurately and proportionately reflect the views of the whole. To a large extent, the validity of the poll's results depends on the sampling procedure used.

Sampling Techniques and Selection Bias. The most common techniques for choosing such a sample are probability sampling and random digit dialing. In the case of **probability sampling**, the pollster begins with a list of the population to be surveyed. This list is called the sampling frame. After each member of the population has been assigned a number, a table of random numbers or a computerized random selection process is used to pick those members of the population to be surveyed.

It is important to emphasize, first, that a sample selected in this manner produces a subset of the population that is representative of the population—it is a microcosm, so to speak. It is also important to point out that whatever is learned about this representative sample can also be attributed to the larger population with a high level of assurance. Random sampling helps ensure that the way in which people were chosen for the study is not related to characteristics of the individuals, such as their level of education.

This technique for constructing a sample is appropriate when the entire population can be identified. For example, all students registered at Texas colleges and universities can be identified from college records, and a sample of them can easily be drawn. When the pollster is interested in a national sample of Americans, however, this technique is not feasible, because no complete list of Americans exists.[60]

Exit polls conducted during national elections use areas to construct their sample. The polling organization randomly selects a set of precincts (voting stations) within each state throughout the nation. In most states, the organizations will select between 50 and 150 such locations. The polling organization trains

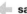

public-opinion poll

A scientific instrument for measuring public opinion

sample

A small group selected by researchers to represent the most important characteristics of an entire population

probability sampling

A method used by pollsters to select a representative sample in which every individual in the population has an equal probability of being selected as a respondent

60 Herbert Asher, *Polling and the Public* (Washington, DC: CQ Press, 2001), p. 64.

individuals to conduct the exit poll on Election Day and deploys those individuals to the voting stations. The pollster approaches people as they leave the voting area and persuades them to fill out the exit poll questionnaire. To guard against biases, the pollster is instructed how many people to choose and which people to approach, such as every seventh person. As the day progresses the pollsters tally the results of the exit poll and report them to the organization, which tallies those figures and distributes them to the media outlets that use them on election night.

For the typical public-opinion poll today, national samples are usually drawn using a technique called **random digit dialing**, in which a computerized random-number generator produces a list of as many 10-digit numbers as the pollster deems necessary. As with exit polls, the pollster is trained how to interview people and record responses. Because there are biases in who answers the phone in a given home, pollsters randomly choose an adult in the house, such as the "oldest female adult," "oldest male adult," "youngest adult male" and so forth. Given that more than 95 percent of American households have telephones, this technique provides very good coverage of all households in the United States. Randomization—of which household is chosen and of which person is to be interviewed in each household—helps guard against potential biases.

In recent years, however, problems have arisen with the traditional phone poll. With the growth in cell phone use and the enactment of "do-not-call" legislation to discourage telemarketers, random digit dialing has become less reliable. Computerized methods of random digit dialing have difficulty reaching households that are registered on the do-not-call list or that only have cell phones. In addition, some people are simply more willing to talk to pollsters. If pollsters could be certain that those who responded to their surveys simply reflected the views of those who refused to respond, there would be no problem. Some studies suggest, however, that the views of respondents and nonrespondents can differ, especially along social-class lines. Middle- and upper-middle-class individuals are more likely to be willing to respond to surveys than their working-class counterparts.[61] The experience with cell phones and random digit dialing phone polls points to a general feature of public-opinion research. It is driven by the ways that people communicate in our society.

Innovations in technology and the spread of new modes of communication create problems for establishing research methods, as we have seen in the case with cell phones. They also create opportunities. These new methods often offer much cheaper ways to contact people and conduct research, but their newness usually means that not everyone uses these modes of communication equally. The challenge for capturing the potential of new technologies is to figure out how to reach as broad a segment of the population using these methods and how to ensure the representativeness of the resulting samples.

Over the past 10 years a new set of firms have emerged that conduct survey research over the Internet. They use a variety of techniques to enlist people into their surveys, such as pop-up ads on websites. However, not everyone uses the

random digit dialing

A poll in which respondents are selected at random from a list of 10-digit telephone numbers, with every effort made to avoid bias in the construction of the sample

---

61 John Goyder, Keith Warriner, and Susan Miller, "Evaluating Socio-Economic Status Bias in Survey Nonresponse," *Journal of Official Statistics* 18, no. 1 (2002): 1–11.

Internet and people respond to pop-ups differently. To correct for such issues, Internet survey firms try different ways of reaching different audiences over the Internet and different sorts of appeals to potential respondents. After they have collected survey responses, Internet survey firms (indeed all polling firms) further adjust their data to correct for segments of the population that they over- or underrepresent.

Although these technical aspects of how surveys are constructed may seem obscure, the importance of sampling was brought home early in the history of political polling. A 1936 *Literary Digest* poll predicted that the Republican presidential candidate, Alf Landon, would defeat the Democrat, Franklin Delano Roosevelt, in that year's election. The election, of course, ended in a Roosevelt landslide. The main problem with the survey was what is called **selection bias** in drawing the sample. The pollsters had relied on telephone directories and automobile registration rosters to produce a sampling frame. During the Great Depression, however, only wealthy Americans owned telephones and automobiles. Thus the millions of working-class Americans who constituted Roosevelt's principal base of support were excluded from the sample.

A more recent instance of polling error caused by selection bias occurred during the 1998 Minnesota gubernatorial election. A poll conducted by the *Minneapolis Star Tribune* just six weeks before the election showed the former professional wrestler Jesse Ventura running a distant third to the Democratic candidate, Hubert Humphrey III (who seemed to have the support of 49 percent of the electorate), and the Republican, Norm Coleman (whose support stood at 29 percent). Only 10 percent of those polled said they were planning to vote for Ventura. On Election Day, Ventura outpolled both Humphrey and Coleman. Analysis of exit poll data showed why the preelection polls had been so wrong. In an effort to be accurate, preelection pollsters' predictions often take account of the likelihood that respondents will actually vote. They do this by polling only people who have voted in the past or by correcting for past frequency of voting. The *Star Tribune* poll was conducted only among individuals who had voted in the previous election. Ventura, however, brought to the polls not only individuals who had not voted in the last election but also many people who had never voted before in their lives. Approximately 12 percent of Minnesota's voters in 1998 said they came to the polls only because Ventura was on the ballot. This surge in turnout was facilitated by the fact that Minnesota permits same-day voter registration. Thus the pollsters were wrong because Ventura changed the composition of voters.[62]

Polling organizations are ever mindful of these fateful stories. Their business depends on producing accurate representations of the American public's opinions and behavior. The challenges are to keep pace with ever-changing ways that people communicate and to anticipate the sometimes surprising nature of the American electorate.

 selection bias

A polling error in which the sample is not representative of the population being studied, so that some opinions are over- or underrepresented

---

62 Carl Cannon, "A Pox on Both Our Parties," in *The Enduring Debate: Classic and Contemporary Readings in American Politics*, 2nd ed., David T. Canon, Anne Khademian, and Kenneth R. Mayer, eds. (New York: Norton, 2000), p. 389.

Sample Size. The degree of reliability in polling is also a function of sample size. For polls of citizens of the United States, the typical size of a sample ranges from 450 to 1,500 respondents. This number reflects a trade-off between cost and degree of precision desired. A larger and hence more costly sample size is associated with greater precision in making generalizations to the full population than is a smaller sample size.

The chance that the sample used does not accurately represent the population from which it is drawn is called the **sampling error**, or *margin of error*. The sampling error measures the range of possibilities for a particular characteristic of a population based on the estimate of that characteristic in the sample drawn. The margin of error acknowledges that any given sample may not be perfectly representative of the full population. A typical survey of 1,500 respondents, for example, will have a sampling error of approximately 3 percent. When a preelection poll indicates that 51 percent of voters surveyed favor the Republican candidate and 49 percent support the Democratic candidate, the outcome is in fact too close to call because it is within the margin of error of the survey. A figure of 51 percent means that between 48 and 54 percent of voters in the population favor the Republicans, whereas a figure of 49 percent indicates that between 46 and 52 percent of all voters support the Democrats. Thus in this example, any outcome ranging from a 54-to-46 Republican victory to a 48-to-52 Republican loss is consistent with the survey evidence. The precision of the poll in this case does not permit a clear prediction of a winner.

Polling organizations conduct surveys in the days leading up to an election in order to predict what will happen on Election Day. Attempts to predict the final outcome allow us to examine whether some survey methods are more accurate than others and which surveys should be viewed as most credible.[63] Figure 10.2 shows the results from 28 different organizations' final preelection poll before the 2012 presidential election. The vertical line is the actual election outcome and each dot is a survey organization's estimate of Obama's margin of victory. The most accurate survey was Democracy Corps, an independent organization founded by former Democratic advisors James Carville and Stanley Greenberg. Interestingly, 26 of the 28 polls underpredicted Obama's margin of victory.

Survey Design. Much of the science of public-opinion research concerns the appropriate way to ask questions. If a question is too vague or confusing or doesn't offer the opinion that the survey respondent would have said, the respondent will skip the question or perhaps answer the question in a confused way. Researchers have also learned to frame questions in a balanced way and to offer people as full a set of options as possible. Leading questions will prompt respondents to give answers that fit with the bias of the question, because many people try to answer questions in ways that they think the surveyor would like

---

sampling error

A polling error that arises on account of the small size of the sample

---

63 For a recent paper on the difficulties with polls, especially in trying to assess the preferences of specific subgroups in the population, see David Leal, Matt Barreto, Jongho Lee, and Rodolfo O. de la Garza, "The Latino Vote in the 2004 Election," *PS: Political Science and Politics* 38 (January 2005): 41–9.

Figure 10.2

ACCURACY OF FINAL PREELECTION POLLS, 2012

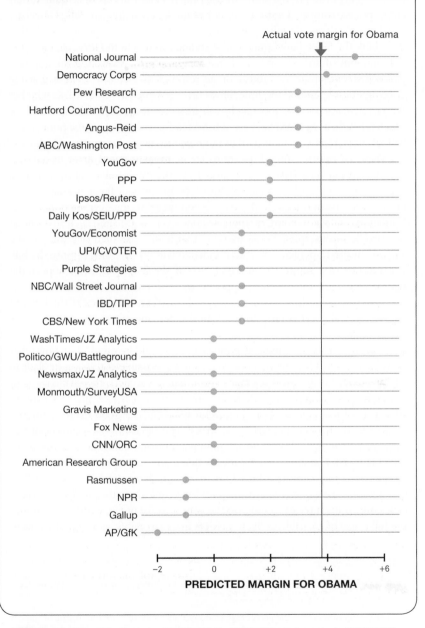

SOURCE: John Sides, "The Accuracy of the Final National Polls," themonkeycage.org/2012/11/07/
the-accuracy-of-the-final-national-polls (accessed 5/28/13). Data from Pollster. Data analysis by
Costas Panagopoulos.

CREDIT: Graph from http://themonkeycage.org/2012/11/07/the-accuracy-of-the-final-national-polls/, by
John Sides. Reprinted with permission.

them to. The challenge is to discover ways of asking questions that allow people to express their own views, without the questions getting in the way.

Sometimes, seemingly minor differences in the wording of a question can convey vastly different meanings to respondents and thus produce quite different response patterns (Figure 10.3). For example, for many years the University of Chicago's National Opinion Research Center has asked respondents whether they think the federal government is spending too much, too little, or about the right amount of money on "assistance for the poor." Answering the question posed this way, about two-thirds of all respondents seem to believe that the government is spending too little. However, the same survey also asks whether the government spends too much, too little, or about the right amount for "welfare." When the word *welfare* is substituted for assistance for the poor, about half of all respondents indicate that too much money is being spent.[64]

measurement error

➡

The failure to identify the true distribution of opinion within a population because of errors such as ambiguous or poorly worded questions

Vague or poorly worded questions create **measurement error** in our surveys, which can skew data analyses away from the true results. Suppose that on a given piece of legislation 75 percent of people in fact favor passage of the bill and 25 percent oppose it. A survey is conducted to measure support for the legislation, but the wording of the question is very confusing, such that one in five people misinterpret the meaning. If that is the case then one-fifth of the 75 percent (or 15 percent of all respondents) will say that they oppose the bill, when in fact they support it, and one-fifth of the 25 percent who oppose the bill (or 5 percent) will say they support it when in fact they do not. As a result only 65 percent of those in the survey will say that they support the bill and 35 percent will say that they do not.[65] In this way measurement error can bias survey results.

You, as a savvy consumer of political data, should be mindful of how what surveys in fact ask of their respondents and of possible confusion or slant in any question. For political scientists and other researchers, the challenge is to ask questions that allow people to express their preferences and that capture what people really think about important issues. It is a good exercise for any student to try her hand at writing a survey. The typical public-opinion survey over the phone lasts about 5 to 10 minutes, and each question takes about 15 seconds to ask and answer. That means that a typical survey consists of 20 to 40 questions that capture a broad set of current issues and events as well as demographic characteristics of people. Each question, then, must be asked efficiently. It must try to summarize the issue at stake in few words and capture the full range of possible or likely answers in a reasonably small set of options.

64 Michael R. Kagay and Janet Elder, "Numbers Are No Problem for Pollsters, Words Are," *New York Times,* August 9, 1992, p. E6.

65 The calculation is that the percentage who say they support it are four-fifths of the 75 percent who really support it (60 percent of all people in the survey) plus one-fifth of the 25 percent (5 percent of all people in the survey) who do not support it but mistakenly say that they do. The total percentage who say they support the bill is 60 percent plus 5 percent.

Figure 10.3
IT DEPENDS ON HOW YOU ASK

THE QUESTION
President Clinton has proposed setting aside approximately two-thirds of an expected budget surplus to fix the Social Security system. What do you think the leaders in Washington should do with the remainder of the surplus?

Variation 1:
Should the money be used for a tax cut, or should it be used to fund new government programs?

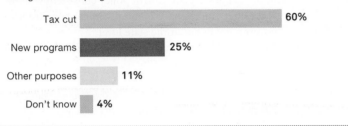

Tax cut	60%
New programs	25%
Other purposes	11%
Don't know	4%

Variation 2:
Should the money be used for a tax cut or should it be spent on programs for education, the environment, health care, crime fighting, and military defense?

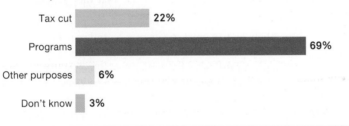

Tax cut	22%
Programs	69%
Other purposes	6%
Don't know	3%

SOURCE: Pew Research Center for the People and the Press, reported in the *New York Times*, January 30, 2000.

ANALYZING THE EVIDENCE

The public's desire for tax cuts can be hard to measure. Pollsters asking what should be done with the nation's budget surplus got different results, depending on the specifics of the question. What differences in the two versions of the question do you think account for the different answers?

An Exercise. Choose a topic of interest to you, such as a current political controversy or support for political figures or institutions. Write a 15-question survey to measure public opinion on this topic and how it is divided among different segments of American society. Express support for or attitudes toward the specific issue, person, or institution as a variable. Write a question that would allow people to express their opinions. Try to write a balanced and clear question. Think about how public opinion on this issue might vary across different segments of American society. Write questions that measure who is in those different groups or segments. Have a friend, roommate, or relative fill out the survey. Ask them for comments. How could you make your survey better?

HOW DOES PUBLIC OPINION INFLUENCE GOVERNMENT POLICY?

In democratic nations, leaders should pay heed to public opinion, and most evidence suggests that they do. In many instances, public policy and public opinion do not coincide, but in general the government's actions are consistent with citizens' preferences. One study, for example, found that between 1935 and 1979, in about two-thirds of all cases, significant changes in public opinion were followed within one year by changes in government policy consistent with the shift in the popular mood.[66] Other studies have come to similar conclusions about public opinion and government policy at the state level.[67]

There are three important ways in which public opinion influences government policy.

Electoral Accountability. The Constitution of the United States gives the public the power to change government. If the public disagrees with what its government has done or if people do not like how their representatives have voted on specific bills or behaved in office, they can simply vote their representatives out of office. Originally this means of popular control extended only to the public for the House of Representatives, but it has since been extended to the U.S. Senate, and there are increasing calls to get rid of the last vestige of indirect representation, the electoral college. We discussed the power that constituents have on their members of Congress in Chapter 6. Today, political scientists see members of Congress as single-mindedly focused on re-election. Legislators who are out of step with the majority in their constituency quickly find themselves out of office. We will discuss how elections work in the next chapter.

Building Coalitions. Legislative politics, however, goes beyond a member's own constituency. In order to pass legislation, it is important that any bill have public support (or at least not have intense public opposition) in a majority of House districts and a majority of states (the constituencies of the Senate) and for a majority of people in the nation (the constituency of the president). It is not enough, then, for a legislator to be attentive to his own constituency. To pass legislation one must be attuned to public opinion nationwide. Likewise no president can push her agenda in Congress without having the support of the public, at least in a majority of states and districts. Some presidents have managed to pass major legislation even in the face of public opposition, but the consequences have usually been disastrous for his party. In January 2010, in the face of stiff public opposition, President Obama pushed through the Affordable Care Act. Ten months later, the Democratic Party was dealt a stunning

---

66 Benjamin I. Page and Robert Y. Shapiro, "Effects of Public Opinion on Policy," *American Political Science Review* 77, no. 1 (March 1983): 175–90.

67 Robert S. Erikson, Gerald C. Wright, and John P. McIver, *Statehouse Democracy: Public Opinion and Policy in the American States* (New York: Cambridge University Press, 1993).

defeat in the House of Representatives and nearly lost its nine-seat majority in the Senate as well.

Input in Rule-Making and Legal Decisions. Some laws explicitly rely on public opinion or social science evidence concerning political behavior. The state and federal governments have various open meeting and sunshine laws, which allow for public commentary on new rules and new laws. Federal Advisory Committees consist of experts and stakeholders, such as scientists, industry representatives, public interest group advocates, and people who are very active and interested in a subject, who advise federal agencies on the likely impact of particular rules or laws. These committees cover an enormous range of subjects and agencies, from approval of drugs by the FDA to space exploration by NASA to licensing of telecommunications under the FCC. The Federal Advisory Committee Act of 1972 requires that such committees operate in an open manner; that they post public notices of any meetings, hearings, or proposed rules; and that they collect public commentary on any proposed rules.

A somewhat different example is the Voting Rights Act, discussed in Chapter 5 and in Chapter 11. The implementation of the Voting Rights Act by the federal courts relies heavily on information about the political preferences of ethnic and racial groups, including electoral and survey data, and on historical patterns of discrimination. Historians and political scientists have been vitally important in conveying what is known about how different racial groups vote in a given state and even county, and how they are viewed and treated in politics and other settings. This information is essential to courts and to the Department of Justice in deciding whether states have discriminated against racial minorities in the administration of election laws.[68]

Shaping Public Opinion

Politicians try to anticipate or even shape what people think, and they try to persuade people to join their particular cause. They do this through a variety of means—speeches and op-eds, political advertising, and working with the media to present the issue the way the politicians want. The reason they have to try to persuade people is that their opponents on a given issue will also try to influence how people think. The public benefits from competition among politicians, as it leads politicians to present the best arguments for and against a given policy or government action. This is the real testament to the power of public opinion.

Politicians take risks when they get out in front of public opinion and try to convince the public to follow them. Political leaders cannot anticipate which way the public will break on an issue; they must gamble and hope that they have chosen issues that people care about and framed policies in ways that will eventually be judged to be consistent with the interests and values of a majority of people. An excellent example is President Clinton's failed attempt to enact health care reform in 1993. Public opinion polls had long shown health care to be among the highest

---

68 David Epstein, Richard Pildes, Rudolfo de la Garza, and Sharyn O'Haloran, eds., *The Future of the Voting Rights Act* (New York: Russell Sage Foundation, 2006).

priorities of the American public, and Clinton saw his victory as a mandate for action to control costs or reform insurance. The resulting national debate ended in a stalemate. Unable to rally public support, Clinton's health care bill failed.[69]

Public opinion and public policy are not always in agreement. Perhaps the most striking example comes from the area of civil liberties and rights. Most Americans are far less concerned with the rights of the accused than the federal courts seem to be. Most Americans would impose restrictions on campaign spending, on violent video games, and on forms of communication, but the federal courts protect those activities under the First Amendment. And most Americans disagree with decisions of local governments and of federal courts on issues involving government takings of private property.[70]

Several factors can contribute to a lack of consistency between opinion and government policy. First, the nominal majority on a particular issue may not be as intensely committed to its preference as the adherents of the minority viewpoint. An intensely committed minority may often be more willing to commit its time, energy, efforts, and resources to the affirmation of its opinions than an apathetic majority, even if it is large. In the case of firearms, for example, although the proponents of gun control are in the majority by a wide margin, most do not regard the issue as being of critical importance to themselves and are not willing to commit much effort to advancing their cause. The opponents of gun control, by contrast, are intensely committed, well organized, and well financed, and as a result are usually able to carry the day. In accordance with the institution principle, the collective action principle, and the policy principle, intense commitment, organization, and financial resources are potent assets in the legislature, the executive bureaucracy, and the courts.

A second important reason why public policy and public opinion may not coincide has to do with the character and structure of the American system of government. The framers of the Constitution, as we saw in Chapter 2, sought to create a system of government that was based on popular consent but did not invariably and automatically translate shifting popular sentiments into public policies. As a result, the American governmental process includes arrangements such as an appointed judiciary that can produce policy decisions that may run contrary to prevailing popular sentiment—at least for a time.

Inconsistencies between opinion and policy might be reduced if the United States used ballot initiatives nationwide, as many states do. This procedure allows propositions to be placed on the ballot and voted into law by the electorate, bypassing most of the normal machinery of representative government. Over the years, ballot measures in the states have been used to restrict property tax increases; ban the use of racial or gender preferences in government employment, contracting, and university admissions; enact environmental regulations including restrictions on greenhouse gas emissions; legalize marijuana;

69 Lawrence R. Jacobs, Eric D. Lawrence, Robert Y. Shapiro, and Steven S. Smith, "Congressional Leadership of Public Opinion," *Political Science Quarterly* 113 (Spring 1998): 21–41.

70 Nathaniel Persily, Jack Citrin, and Patrick Egan, *Public Opinion and Constitutional Controversy* (New York: Oxford University Press, 2008).

limit campaign spending; regulate auto insurance; change the rules governing redistricting; opt out of the Affordable Care Act; and allow same-sex marriage.[71] Some states even use initiatives to pass budget agreements when the legislature does not want to be held responsible for casting unpopular votes.[72] Initiatives such as these seem to provide the public with an opportunity to express its will.

The problem, however, is that government by initiative offers little opportunity for reflection and compromise. Voters are presented with a proposition, usually sponsored by a special interest group, and are asked to take it or leave it. Perhaps the true will of the people lies somewhere between the positions taken by the various interest groups. For example, California voters might have wanted affirmative action programs to be modified but not scrapped altogether, as Proposition 209 mandated. In a representative assembly, as opposed to a referendum campaign, a compromise position might have been achieved that would have been more satisfactory to all the residents of the state. This capacity for compromise is one reason the Founders strongly favored representative government rather than direct democracy.[73]

When all is said and done, however, the actions of the American government do not remain out of line with popular sentiment for long. A major reason for this is, of course, the electoral process.

CONCLUSION

Representative democracy was a novel form of government when the United States created its Constitution. Behind this radical system lies one central idea— that the government reflects the will of the people. People have the opportunity to express their preferences through elections, public meetings and organizations, and free expression and debate. Public deliberations and public choices, it is conjectured, aggregate individuals' preferences and opinions to form the collective "will of the people" that would guide those in office. This chapter has explored the meaning of this idea today.

We no longer speak of the people of the United States as if they were an organic whole with a coherent will. Rather we characterize the "people" as the aggregation of individuals' preferences about the choices presented to them—in a phrase, public opinion. The individual is the foundation of public opinion. Politicians assume that individuals will pursue and express their own preferences and beliefs. They will act in ways to protect and expand their own property and wealth; they will express their own ideologies and ideals about what is right; they will

---

71 David Broder, *Democracy Derailed: Initiative Campaigns and the Power of Money* (New York: Harcourt, 2000).

72 Robert Tomsho, "Liberals Take a Cue from Conservatives: This Election, the Left Tries to Make Policy with Ballot Initiatives," *Wall Street Journal*, November 6, 2000, p. A12.

73 For the classic treatment of take-it-or-leave-it referendums and initiatives, see Thomas Romer and Howard Rosenthal, "Political Resource Allocation, Controlled Agendas, and the Status Quo," *Public Choice* 33 (1978): 27–44.

pursue their own happiness and not sacrifice their own interests for those of the state or the community. When they vote, attend meetings, talk to others, or otherwise engage in democratic politics, people are free to say what they want, meet with whomever they want, and do what they want, so long as they don't harm others. The aggregation of all those activities and actions expresses the public's opinion.

The succeeding chapters will consider how public opinion manifests itself through different institutions of democracy—elections, parties, organized interests, and communications media. As we discuss these institutions, it will be useful to keep in mind how we have described public opinion in this chapter. Specifically, every individual has his own preferences and own beliefs about the right policy or action to pursue. On any particular question or issue, individuals face a range of choices or options. Individuals choose the options that best reflect their preferences as to the outcomes and their beliefs about what is the best way to achieve those outcomes. On many issues, social scientists describe the range of people's preferences along a single dimension, such as ideology (from very liberal to very conservative) or partisanship (from strongly Democratic to strongly Republican). On general economic indicators, such as income, most people in the United States have what may be described as middle-class incomes; a significant percentage are poor, and a very small percentage are wealthy. Preferences about social spending and taxation often reflect these economic differences. On matters of ideology or public policy, social scientists gauge the percentage of people adhering to each of the many possible views. Most people in the United States hold fairly centrist or moderate views on most questions. The tilt, depending on the issue and the choices offered, is slightly right of center or slightly left of center. Neither right nor left nor center, however, commands an outright majority of public support in the United States on any issue of importance. Anyone adhering to one of these views must reach out beyond her particular ideological slant in order to find a coalition large enough to capture the support of a majority.

Democracy in this free and open society is complicated further by the heterogeneity of American society. The nation's political institutions tolerate all manner of religious and political beliefs and all manner of social and economic relations, and the United States has long been a refuge for those from other countries seeking religious or political asylum or just a better way of life. As a result the United States is one of the most diverse societies in the world, with freedom to practice every major religion, with all manner of political and social organizations, and with great concentrations of wealth and poverty. This would seem to be a recipe not for consensus but for disagreement and conflict, even civil conflict.

The open society in the United States, however, has worked for over two centuries, and it works because its members have a strong common commitment to democracy itself. Americans, in essence, agree to disagree. We agree that it is best to have a heterogeneous society and to tolerate many different opinions. We value liberty and restrain the government from imposing itself on how people think or express themselves politically. We further agree to allow the institutions of democracy to help us reach collective decisions about who should govern and how they should govern. The next four chapters examine in detail those institutions—the institutions of elections, of political parties, of interest groups, and of the media and communications technologies.

For Further Reading

Selections highlighted in red are included in *Readings in American Politics: Analysis and Perspectives*, Third Edition.

Althaus, Scott. *Collective Preferences and Democratic Politics*. New York: Cambridge University Press, 2003.

Ansolabehere, Stephen, Jonathan Rodden, and James M. Snyder, Jr. "Purple America." *Journal of Economic Perspectives* 20, no. 2 (Spring 2006): 97–118.

Bartels, Larry. *Unequal Democracy: The Political Economy of the New Gilded Age*. Princeton, NJ: Princeton University Press, 2008.

Berinsky, Adam. *In Time of War: Understanding Public Opinion from World War II to Iraq*. Chicago: University of Chicago Press, 2009.

Erikson, Robert S., and Kent L. Tedin. *American Public Opinion: Its Origins, Content, and Impact*. 8th ed. New York: Pearson, 2010.

Fiorina, Morris, Samuel Abrams, and Jeremy Pope. *Culture War?* 3rd ed. New York: Pearson, 2010.

Ginsberg, Benjamin. *The Captive Public: How Mass Opinion Promotes State Power*. New York: Basic Books, 1986.

Jacobson, Gary. *A Divider, Not a Uniter: George W. Bush, the American People, the 2006 Election, and Beyond*. White Plains, NY: Longman, 2007.

Kinder, Donald, and Cindy Kam. *Us against Them: Ethnocentric Foundations of American Opinion*. Chicago: University of Chicago Press, 2010.

Lee, Taeku. *Mobilizing Public Opinion*. Chicago: University of Chicago Press, 2002.

Lupia, Arthur, and Mathew D. McCubbins. *The Democratic Dilemma: Can Citizens Learn What They Need to Know?* New York: Cambridge University Press, 1998.

McCarty, Nolan, Keith Poole, and Howard Rosenthal. *Polarized America: The Dance of Ideology and Unequal Riches*. Princeton, NJ: Princeton University Press, 2007.

Page, Benjamin I., and Robert Y. Shapiro. *The Rational Public: Fifty Years of Trends in Americans' Policy Preferences*. Chicago: University of Chicago Press, 1992.

Stimson, James A. *Public Opinion in America: Moods, Cycles, and Swings*. 2nd ed. Boulder, CO: Westview Press, 1999.

Zaller, John R. *The Nature and Origins of Mass Opinion*. New York: Cambridge University Press, 1992.

11

Elections

The most profound expression of an individual's political preferences is the vote. It is a blunt but effective instrument for controlling the government. Citizens usually cannot decide directly what laws are enacted, what the tax or interest rates will be, or whether to declare war. Citizens can affirm a commitment to stay the course or to change their government when they think a new direction is needed. It is our way of reining in government and ensuring that elected officials remain attentive to public preferences. Elections have proved a remarkably successful method of bringing about continual renewal of government through peaceful means.

Frequent, regular elections are the hallmark of democracy. The United States embraces this idea to a greater extent than any other democracy. America has elections very frequently, with great regularity, and for all manner of governments. Voters in the United States elect the president, governors, and other executive officers every four years,[1] federal and state legislators every two years, and thousands of local mayors, councilors, and commissioners with similar frequency. All told there are over 88,000 governments at the federal, state, and local levels in the United States, nearly all of them run by elected bodies.[2] In a typical election, a voter may choose candidates for a dozen different offices, as well as deciding bond issues and other local questions put before the voters, and in any given year a typical person in the United States has the opportunity to vote three or four times.

Why do elections work? How is it that elections create a government that reflects and responds to the preferences of the public? The simple idea behind

---

1   Vermont and New Hampshire elect their governors every two years.

2   One federal government, 50 state governments, over 3,000 county governments, about 36,000 municipal and town governments, about 13,500 school districts, and over 35,000 special districts (for example, water or utility). www.census.gov/govs/www /cog2007.html (accessed 3/26/09; site discontinued).

democracy is that there is power, and perhaps even wisdom, in numbers. Voting allows each of us to express our preferences, and election procedures aggregate those votes into a legitimate collective choice. Election laws determine how votes are counted and translate into a government—who wins seats in the legislature, who is elected to the executive, and, in many states, who will serve as judges.

Elections in the United States work by choosing who will govern, not what they should do or what the laws should be. We do not have direct democracy in federal elections, although many states and municipalities allow voting on bonds and a small number of laws. For the most part, elections are, to put the matter in terms introduced in Chapter 1, occasions when multiple principals—the citizens—choose political agents to act on their behalf.

Two problems immediately arise for the principals (the citizens). First, are we selecting the best people for the job? This is a problem of **adverse selection** and stems from hidden information. We want to choose the people who have the necessary competence to write smart legislation or who have our interests at heart, but we may not have the information to judge which candidate possesses those characteristics. Second, once elected, do the politicians do the job as we wish them

 adverse selection

The problem of incomplete information—of choosing alternatives without fully knowing the details of available options

CORE OF THE ANALYSIS

 The United States holds frequent elections as a means of keeping politicians close to the preferences of a majority of the people.

 The United States uses a system of plurality rule in which the candidate with the most votes wins the electoral district. Plurality rule creates a strong pressure toward two-party politics and makes it difficult for third parties to succeed.

 Plurality rule also shapes the incentives facing candidates and parties. It creates strong pressure on the parties or candidates to take centrist policies so as to appeal to the median voter among the electorate as a whole.

 Most voters develop strong attachments to political parties, based on agreement on policy, social pressure, or upbringing. Those who identify with a party, vote with that party nearly all of the time.

 Campaigns try to mobilize their candidate's supporters and persuade undecided voters. In the process, they provide information that helps solve some of the informational problems inherent in representative democracy.

to? This is a problem of **moral hazard** and stems from hidden actions. Once selected, representatives cannot easily be monitored. Political leaders necessarily engage in many acts that do not attract public attention, such as making deals with other politicians to build a winning coalition for a particular bill. In these situations, we need to make sure that the decisions the politicians make are the ones we want them to make. However, voters cannot know everything about the candidates running for office or about politicians' actions once they are elected. In fact, the incentives to be highly knowledgeable are minimal. In a nation of 180 million registered voters or even a district of 700,000 voters, surely one's own ballot is unlikely to make a difference in the outcome and the cost of making a mistake is nil. Why, then, go to great lengths to find out the details of the candidates' backgrounds and personalities or to learn about the goings-on in Congress?

Voters use simple rules to solve these problems. Politicians caught in scandals are usually voted out of office. One need not know the details about the inner workings of government to hold politicians accountable for large-scale malfeasance. Voters also usually take economic downturns as evidence of mismanagement of economic policy, and they vote against the incumbent president's party, as occurred in 2008 and 2010. They will also reward a party for economic good times and express their desire to continue with current economic policies, as occurred in 2004. In other years, like 2012, when economic signals are mixed, elections are quite close. But given the simplicity of these rules, how do we hold politicians accountable for the details of legislation?

Ultimately, elections work through competition. The public relies on competition among politicians, the parties, interest groups, and the media to inform them. This chapter focuses on the politicians; later chapters go into greater detail about parties, interest groups, and the media.

In the United States politicians are central. Rival politicians or teams of politicians (parties) seek to hold elective office—we consider that their primary motivation. They try to formulate positions on important policies that appeal to the greatest number of voters; they develop personal appeals; they advertise their own ability to do the job at hand, their honesty and strength of character, and their fidelity to the public. Likewise, politicians draw attention to the failings of their rivals. Candidates and parties use advertisements, press conferences, speeches, and other modes of reaching the public to highlight policy decisions made by their opponents that are out of step with the wishes of a majority of voters, and they expose scandalous behavior and play up political gaffes. Politicians themselves bear much of the cost of informing the public about their own performance and ideas and those of their opponents. Competition, then, creates strong incentives for those vying for office to reveal information to the electorate.

Competition alone does not cure all. Proponents of electoral reform criticize many features of U.S. election laws, including the campaign finance system, redistricting procedures, the lack of third parties, and the relatively low levels of voter turnout. In this chapter, we look at how the institutional features of American elections shape the way that citizens' goals and preferences are reflected in their government and how voters decide among the candidates and questions put before them on the ballot. Democracy is a work in progress. Americans constantly tinker with the rules to try to make it a better system.

INSTITUTIONS OF ELECTIONS

Elections don't just happen. They are not spontaneous affairs but formal institutions for making collective decisions. As in Congress, the executive branch, and the courts, rules (institutions) determine the operations of elections—who is allowed to vote, how votes are cast and counted, and how we determine who wins office. Election rules consist of a mix of state and federal laws, legal decisions, and local administrative practices. Federal laws regulate the time of congressional and presidential elections, the qualifications for office, the allocation of seats, the structure of electoral districts, and the qualifications and rights of voters. State laws determine a wider range of factors, including how votes are cast and counted, the procedures for registering voters, candidate qualifications for all elected officials other than members of Congress and the president, the procedures for nominating candidates and getting on the ballot, the operations of the parties, and the conduct of all state and local elections. The responsibility for making all of this go smoothly on Election Day falls, in turn, on the roughly 5,000 local election offices in counties and municipalities. Workers in local election offices manage the registration lists, prepare the ballots and voting machinery, set up polling places, recruit and train poll workers, and tally and certify the votes. And at the polling places on Election Day the poll workers, roughly 1 million volunteers across the country, administer the election.

The laws and procedures governing elections have important consequences. They can skew the electorate toward one interest or another; they can create barriers to some sorts of political organizations; and they can create a legislature that reflects the diversity of the population or one in which one segment of society dominates.

Four features of U.S. election laws deserve particular emphasis:

- First, *who*. The United States provides for universal adult suffrage—all citizens over the age of eighteen have the right to vote.[3]

- Second, *how*. Americans vote in secret and choose among candidates for particular office using a form of the ballot called the "Australian ballot."

- Third, *where*. The United States selects almost all elected offices through single-member districts that have equal populations—one person, one vote.

- Fourth, *what* it takes to win. For most offices in the United States, the candidate who wins the most votes among all of those competing for a given seat wins the election.

We consider each matter and its consequences in turn. In short, we will see that in the United States these rules create a two-party system that broadly

---

3 In addition, there is the restriction that those currently serving sentences for felonies cannot vote; some states prohibit ex-felons from voting.

encompasses the entire adult population but that exaggerates the political power of the majority. Other features of American election laws and procedures, including rules governing campaign expenditures and fund-raising, party nominations, and ballot access, further shape political competition in the United States.

Also notable are rules that the United States does not have. Federal and state laws do not limit the amount of television and other forms of advertising, total campaign spending, the activities of groups and parties on behalf of candidates, or how the media cover the campaigns. Most other countries limit the use of television or forbid it altogether, restrict how candidates can campaign and how much they can spend, and tightly regulate the activities of organized interest groups. Compared with other countries, then, the United States has a relatively unregulated electoral system that allows candidates to run on their own, separate from the parties, and allows candidates to spend relatively freely on media and other aspects of their campaigns. We turn to these campaign activities in the next section, especially as they bear on the important question of voter learning through campaigns. The features of election law considered here regulate the nature of the electorate and the choices that voters face.

The rules governing elections are not static. The features of American electoral institutions have evolved over time through legislation, court decisions, administrative rulings of agencies, and public agitation for electoral reform. The nation has gradually converged on our present system of universal suffrage with secret voting and to the use of single-member districts with plurality rule. The future will likely bring further innovations in voting and elections. With waves of immigration, new communication technologies, and other changes reshaping society, the institutions of democracy must change as well. Perhaps the most dramatic changes under way involve the rise of "convenience voting"—voting by mail or voting early at a polling center or town hall. In 1972, approximately 5 percent of all votes nationwide were cast in absentia; in 2012, almost 40 percent of all votes were absentee or early ballots. The rate of absentee and early voting more than doubled over the past decade alone. Both Oregon and Washington State vote entirely by mail. A few states, such as Virginia, accept absentee ballots by e-mail, which is particularly convenient for military personnel. The rise of these new modes of voting presents new questions about secrecy and about the form of the ballot; it also provides new opportunities for reform and modes of voting (such as instant runoff voting). Such changes rarely come about through carefully planned federal legislation. Rather, new election institutions emerge out of the experiences and experiments of local election officials and state laws.

Who Can Vote: Defining the Electorate

Over the course of American history the electorate has expanded greatly. As discussed in Chapter 5, the United States has gradually extended the right to vote, both on paper and in practice. At the beginning of the Republic, voting rights in most states were restricted to white men over 21 years of age, and many states further required that those people own property. Today, all citizens over 18 years of age are allowed to vote, and the courts and Department of Justice and activist organizations actively ferret out discrimination in elections.[4]

While the right to vote is universal, the exercise of this right is not. In a typical U.S. presidential election, approximately 60 percent of those eligible to vote in fact do so. The rate of voting is lower still in midterm elections for Congress, with typically around 45 percent of the eligible electorate voting. And in local elections the percent of people who vote can be quite low: in some locales, city elections conducted in odd years attract only 10 to 20 percent of the eligible electorate. Some of the most basic questions concerning the functioning and health of our democracy concern the exercise of the franchise. Who votes and why? How does nonparticipation affect election outcomes, and would election outcomes be different if everyone voted? Does low voter turnout threaten the legitimacy of government?

It is also important to point out that voting in the United States is a right, not a requirement. Voting, like most other activities in our society, is voluntary. If we do not feel strongly about government, we do not have to participate. If we want to send a message of dissatisfaction, one way to do so is not to vote. Of course, if no one voted, it would be a disaster for American democracy; it would signal the end of Americans' commitment to their form of government. And when large numbers of people do participate in elections, it is evidence of a robust democracy.

Not all nations take the same view of democracy. While most democracies view voting as a right and a voluntary act, some also treat it as a responsibility of citizenship. In Germany and Australia, for example, adult citizens are required to vote in national elections, and if they fail to vote they must either receive a medical exemption or pay a fine. That guarantees turnout rates in the range of 90 percent of the eligible electorate and it makes election results a reflection of the preferences of all people. Universal voting in the United States, however, is not viewed favorably. Those who don't vote don't want to face a potential fine, and those who do vote may not want the "nonvoters" diluting their power. And most Americans simply do not like the notion that the government can compel us to do something. Even without being compelled to participate, the United States is one of the most participatory democracies in the world. There are many other ways that we can participate in electoral politics, such as blogging and speaking with others, joining organizations, giving money, and of course voting. On nearly all of these activities, Americans participate in politics at much higher rates than people in nearly every other country.[5]

That said, levels of voter participation in the latter half of the twentieth century were quite low in the United States, as compared with voter participation

---

4   There are further restrictions in some states that prohibit ex-felons from voting and impose residency requirements.

5   Sidney Verba, Kay Schlozman, and Henry Brady, *Voice and Equality: Civic Volunteerism in America* (Cambridge, MA: Harvard University Press, 1995).

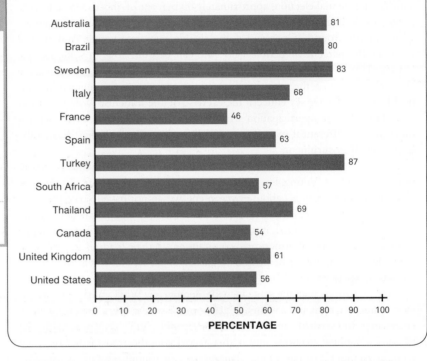

Figure 11.1

VOTER TURNOUT AROUND THE WORLD

ANALYZING THE EVIDENCE

The United States trails many democracies in the rate at which citizens vote. Are Americans simply more apathetic about politics, or do institutional features in the United States produce greater obstacles to participation?

Country	Percentage
Australia	81
Brazil	80
Sweden	83
Italy	68
France	46
Spain	63
Turkey	87
South Africa	57
Thailand	69
Canada	54
United Kingdom	61
United States	56

PERCENTAGE

NOTE: Turnout as a percentage of voting-age population in the most recent national presidential or parliamentary election as of 2012.
SOURCE: International Institute of Democracy and Electoral Assistance, www.idea.int/vt/ (accessed 7/15/13).

in other democracies (Figure 11.1).[6] And voter participation was low compared to earlier eras of American history, especially the late nineteenth century (Figure 11.2).[7] Over the five decades after World War II there was a steady erosion of voter turnout in the United States. Voter participation in presidential elections in the United States fell below 50 percent in 1996. That decline alarmed many observers and even stirred Congress to reform voter registration rules in the mid-1990s. Turnout rates have grown since then, in response to legal

---

6   See Walter Dean Burnham, "The Changing Shape of the American Political Universe," *American Political Science Review* 59, no. 1 (March 1965): 7–28. It should be noted that other democracies, such as India and Switzerland, have even lower turnout rates, as do some of the new democracies in eastern Europe.

7   See statistics of the U.S. Bureau of the Census and the Federal Election Commission. For voting statistics for 1960 to 2004, see "National Voter Turnout in Federal Elections: 1960–2004," at www.infoplease.com/ipa/A0781453.html (accessed 3/26/09).

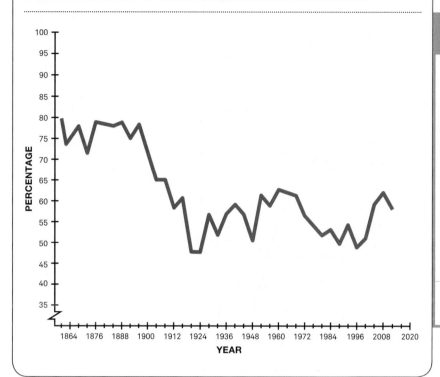

Figure 11.2

VOTER TURNOUT IN U.S. PRESIDENTIAL ELECTIONS

YEAR

ANALYZING THE EVIDENCE

Voter turnout for American presidential elections was significantly higher in the nineteenth century than in the twentieth. What institutional change caused the sharp decline in turnout between 1890 and 1910? Why did this change have such a dramatic effect? Did it have any positive outcomes?

NOTE: Data reflect the population of eligible voters; the percentage of the voting-age population that voted would be smaller.
SOURCES: For 1860–1928, U.S. Bureau of the Census, Historical Statistics of the United States, Colonial Times to 1970, www.census.gov/prod/www/abs/statab.html (accessed 3/26/09); pt. 2, p. 1071; for 1932–92, U.S. Bureau of the Census, Statistical Abstract of the United States, 1993 (Washington, DC: Government Printing Office, 1993), p. 284; for 1996–2012, U.S. Census Bureau data.

changes and in response to the observation by the political parties and candidates that there was an opportunity to influence elections by bringing people back to the polls. In 2012, 56.5 percent of adult citizens in the United States voted.

The question "who votes" is partly explained by the behavior of individuals and partly explained by the laws of democracy, which are the institutions of elections. Later in this chapter we will discuss the correlates of voting to understand who chooses to vote. We discuss here the institutions and how they define and constrain behavior.

It is worth a brief detour to explain one term—the *turnout rate*. That quantity is bandied about quite a bit. It is simple to define, but worth understanding some of the subtleties, especially when making comparisons over time or across countries. The turnout rate is the number of people who vote in a given election divided by the number of people who are allowed to vote. The first part of this ratio is relatively uncontroversial—it is the number of individuals who cast ballots in the election, at polling stations or through absentee ballots.[8] The appropriate baseline in the turnout ratio is more difficult to define. Most commonly, the turnout rate presented for the United States (and other countries) is turnout as a percentage of the voting-age population (all adults). This understates the true turnout rate, because it includes noncitizens and people who are institutionalized or not allowed to vote in some states because they are ex-felons. It is possible to estimate from census reports the numbers of noncitizens and institutionalized populations. Such calculations are somewhat controversial because of difficulties in getting reliable figures on populations of institutionalized people and noncitizens. Following the usual conventions, we focus here on the voting-age population. However, it is worth understanding the size of the eligible electorate and the effects of current restrictions on the franchise.[9]

How big is the U.S. electorate? There are approximately 315 million people in the United States today. But not all of them are allowed to vote. First, children under eighteen are not allowed to vote. Second, noncitizens are not allowed to vote. Third, people in prison are not allowed to vote, and in most states ex-felons are not allowed to vote. The biggest restriction on the size of the electorate is age. There are approximately 75 million people under age eighteen in the United States. Citizenship reduces the eligible electorate further, by about 20 million adults.[10] Finally, the total ineligible prison and felon population is approximately 3 million persons. Hence, the eligible electorate is approximately 217 million persons, or about two-thirds of the people living in the United States.

To put the changes in election laws in perspective, suppose that the restrictive rules of the nineteenth century were in place today, and that only white male citizens over 21 were allowed to vote. If that were the law of the land 2012, the eligible electorate would total only about 70 million people. That is, only about one in four people in the United States today would be eligible to vote if the nineteenth-century restrictions on voting remained in place today. Those restrictions surely would have made for a very different electorate in terms of its interests, values, and preferences; they would have altered the strategies of the political parties; and they would have surely resulted in very different election outcomes.

---

8 Not all states report such figures in their certified tally of the vote. In fact, 11 states do not report the number of ballots cast, and researchers must substitute the total votes for all candidates for the presidency or another office on the top of the ballot. So, for example, if an individual voter in one of these states does not cast a vote for president but does turn out to vote on other questions on the ballot, this voter might not be counted in the total. However, since nearly all voters who turn out do vote on the races at the top of the ticket, counting those totals is a reasonably accurate substitute for official turnout records.

9 Michael McDonald and Samuel Popkin, "The Myth of the Vanishing Voter," *American Political Science Review* 95 (December 2001): 963–74.

10 These figures exclude undocumented, illegal immigrants, of which there are estimated to be another 12 million persons.

Other restrictions on the franchise arise from the ways that local election officials run elections. As Figure 11.2 indicates, voter turnout declined markedly in the United States between 1890 and 1910. These years coincided with two changes in the institutions of elections. First, many states imposed rules such as literacy tests to keep immigrants, blacks, and other groups out of the electorate. Second, many states began to create formal registration systems and lists, so that people had to be on a formal list of eligible voters in order to establish that they were allowed to vote on Election Day. Personal registration was one of several "progressive" reforms of political practices initiated at the beginning of the twentieth century. The ostensible purpose of registration was to discourage fraud and corruption. At that time, "corruption" was also code language that referred to machine politics in large cities, where political parties had organized immigrant and ethnic populations. Election reforms not only tried to reign in corruption but to weaken the power of urban factions within parties and keep immigrant and blacks from voting.

Over the years, voter registration restrictions have been modified somewhat to make registration easier. In 1993, for example, Congress approved and President Bill Clinton signed the "motor voter" bill to ease voter registration by allowing individuals to register when they applied for driver's licenses, as well as in public-assistance and military recruitment offices.[11] In many jurisdictions, casting a vote automatically registers the voter for the next election. In Europe, there is typically no registration burden on the individual voter; voter registration is handled automatically by the government. This is one reason that voter turnout rates in Europe are higher than those in the United States.

The mere requirement that people register in order to vote has a significant effect on turnout rates. Today, we can get reliable counts of the number of persons who are actually registered as well the percentage of registered persons who vote. (In earlier years, the states were not very good at purging their lists of obsolete registrations; today they are much better at this.) Studies of contemporary voter registration lists find that almost 90 percent of registered voters in fact vote, but only about 80 percent of the eligible electorate is currently registered to vote. In other words, the eligible electorate is really only about 180 million people—the number who are actually registered to vote. There are approximately 35 million eligible voters who have not yet registered. They are disproportionately those ages 18–29 (Figure 11.3). Getting those people into the registration system, and keeping them on the rolls, is viewed by many as an important way to increase the turnout rate. If you are not registered to vote, you cannot vote.[12]

Why, then, have a registration system? Registration systems contain a fairly reliable list of all people who are interested in voting. Local election offices and campaigns use the registration lists to communicate with voters about when, where, and how to vote. Campaigns also use these lists to prepare grassroots

---

11 Helen Dewar, "'Motor Voter' Agreement Is Reached," *Washington Post*, April 28, 1993, p. A6.

12 Stephen Ansolabehere and Eitan Hersh, "Validation: What Big Data Tell Us about the Actual Electorate," *Political Analysis* (2012).

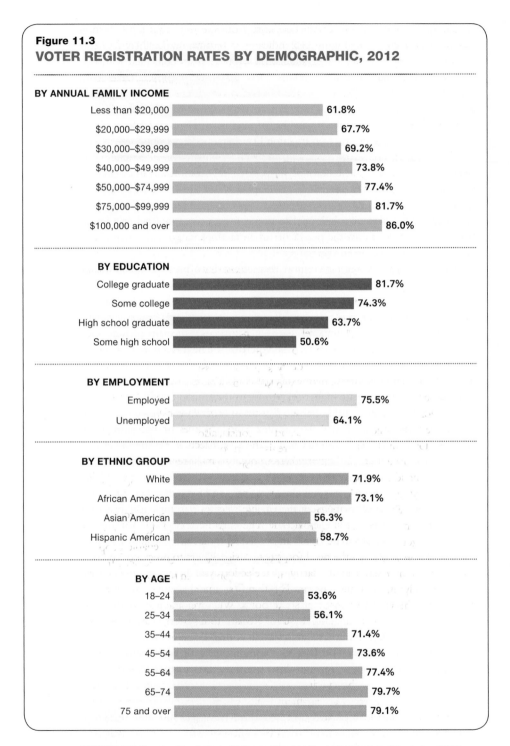

Figure 11.3

VOTER REGISTRATION RATES BY DEMOGRAPHIC, 2012

BY ANNUAL FAMILY INCOME

Less than $20,000	61.8%
$20,000–$29,999	67.7%
$30,000–$39,999	69.2%
$40,000–$49,999	73.8%
$50,000–$74,999	77.4%
$75,000–$99,999	81.7%
$100,000 and over	86.0%

BY EDUCATION

College graduate	81.7%
Some college	74.3%
High school graduate	63.7%
Some high school	50.6%

BY EMPLOYMENT

Employed	75.5%
Unemployed	64.1%

BY ETHNIC GROUP

White	71.9%
African American	73.1%
Asian American	56.3%
Hispanic American	58.7%

BY AGE

18–24	53.6%
25–34	56.1%
35–44	71.4%
45–54	73.6%
55–64	77.4%
65–74	79.7%
75 and over	79.1%

SOURCE: U.S. Bureau of the Census, "Voting and Registration in the Election of November 2012," www.census.gov/hhes/www/socdem/voting/publications/p20/2012/tables.html (accessed 7/15/13).

organizing efforts and direct-mail campaigns. Indeed, the registration system was originally developed in the nineteenth century in cities such as New York so that political organizations could target their supporters and get them to vote.

Today, registration lists serve another very important purpose: they are the basis for administering elections. Local election offices rely on their registration databases to format ballots, set up precincts, determine which voters should vote in which place, and communicate with people. Any given area contains many overlapping election jurisdictions, creating many different combinations of unique sets of offices. For example, one voter might reside in Congressional District 1, State Senate District 7, State Representative District 3, City Council District 1, and so forth. Variations in district boundaries may mean that a few blocks away, another voter lives in Congressional District 2, State Senate District 4, State Representative District 12, City Council District 6, and so forth. Although they live in the same city, these voters live in very different sets of political districts and must vote on different ballots. The first voter is not supposed to vote in Congressional District 2, for instance. Registration lists have become vitally important in sorting out where people should vote. Using the definitions of the boundaries, local election offices determine how many distinct ballots they must prepare. Each distinct ballot is assigned to a precinct: to avoid confusion there is only one ballot constellation per precinct. The local election office then uses the registration list to assign individuals to precincts and to communicate to the voter exactly where he or she is supposed to vote. Without this means of assigning voters to precincts and communicating to voters, there would be considerable confusion and practical difficulty running elections on Election Day. Efforts to get rid of or reform registration requirements must confront this very practical problem.

Some states, such as Minnesota and Wisconsin, allow registration at the polls on Election Day (called same-day registration or Election Day registration). These states have noticeably higher turnout but also must recruit additional poll workers to handle the new registrants in the precincts. Other states, such as Colorado, are trying to get rid of traditional precincts and have experimented with vote centers. Electronic voting equipment now makes it possible to program many different ballots on a single machine. The voter need only key in his or her address to get the appropriate ballot and vote. Such machines enable people to vote anywhere and lessen the need for lists to assign voters to precincts. Innovations such as these may lead ultimately to an election system that does not require or rely heavily on registration before Election Day, but even these mechanisms still require the voter to register at some point. Wherever these innovations in voting may lead in the long term, the United States today relies heavily on registration to run elections, even though it creates a hurdle to voting.

Over the past decade, there has been a push to create new ways of authenticating voters at the polls. Half of all states require that voters provide some form of identification when voting, such as a driver's license. Some states now require that all voters show government-issued photo identification. Such rules have been adopted out of fears of voter fraud. The other half of states either have no such formal requirement or prohibit election officials from asking for photographic identification. Legislators and voters in these states either do not judge the risk of voter fraud as great or they view the potential barrier to voting or potentially discriminatory effects of such laws as greater than any possible fraud. Social scientists have tended to find minimal levels of fraud, minimal effects of such laws on voter turnout, and minimal effects on people's confidence in the electoral system.[13]

Laws alone, however, cannot explain the variations observed in turnout. Perhaps the biggest, systematic differences in turnout are between election years. When the president is on the ticket, which happens every four years, turnout exceeds 60 percent of the eligible electorate. But when the president is not on the ticket, turnout plummets. It drops 15 to 20 points in midterm congressional elections, and as many as 50 points in odd-year local elections. This pattern of surge and decline in turnout is a function of the election calendar, but it is certainly also a function of the activities of the campaigns and the interests of the voters in the outcomes of the elections. These are behavioral matters, which we will discuss later.

How Americans Vote: The Ballot

The way Americans cast their votes reflects some of our most cherished precepts about voting rights. Most people today view voting as a private matter. They may tell others how they voted or choose not to tell them, but that is their prerogative. Polling places provide privacy for voters and keep an individual's vote secret. In some respects, the secret ballot seems incongruous with voting, because elections are a very public matter. Indeed, for the first century of the Republic, voting was conducted in the open. However, public voting led to vote buying and voter intimidation. American history is full of lore involving urban party workers paying poor voters for their support or intimidating members of the opposing party to keep them from voting. The secret ballot became widespread at the end of the nineteenth century in response to such corrupt practices.

The secret ballot has important implications for how people see themselves as voters. The secret ballot is a strong assertion of the individual. The vote is meant to reflect the individual's own mind—what the individual knows about the choices and what his or her own preferences are about government—not the influences of others. In contrast, when voting is public, the choices individuals make reflect the group as well as their own thinking. American elections still have vestiges of public voting, in town meetings in New England states and at party-nominating caucuses, such as in Iowa, Nevada, and Minnesota.

Attend a caucus or town hall meeting and you will appreciate the difference between these events and voting in the seclusion of a voting booth. Town meetings and caucuses often exhibit what social psychologists call groupthink, the tendency of the pack to follow particular individuals or to reflect a public conversation rather than each individual's private information. Public voting

---

13 Stephen Ansolabehere and Nathaniel Persily, "Vote Fraud in the Eye of the Beholder," *Harvard Law Review* 121 (2008): 1737; and Stephen Ansolabehere, "Effects of Identification Requirements on Voting: Evidence from the Experiences of Voters on Election Day," *PS* (January 2009): 127–30.

also demands more of the individual—more time and more attention to the decision-making process. Attending a caucus, for example, is an all-evening affair. As a result, public voting tends to draw in a much smaller and more committed electorate. These two methods can lead to very different results. A good example comes from the Democratic nominating process in Texas during the 2008 election. The Texas Democratic Party allocates one-half of its delegates through a primary election involving secret ballots and the other half through caucuses. Primary voting runs throughout the day; the caucuses begin in the evening immediately after polls close. In 2008, Hillary Rodham Clinton won a decisive victory over Barack Obama in the primary voting in Texas, but Barack Obama won the caucuses by an equally large margin. The caucuses are reminiscent of an older style of democracy in which people took a stand quite publicly for what they believed. Today, secrecy in voting is the norm.

With the secret ballot came another innovation, the **Australian ballot**. The Australian ballot lists the names of all candidates running for a given office and allows the voter to select any candidate for any office. This way of offering choices to voters was first introduced in Australia in 1851, and in the United States today it is universal. Before the 1880s Americans voted in different ways. Some voted in public meetings; others voted on paper ballots printed by the political parties or by slates of candidates distributed to the voters. Voters chose which ballot they wished to submit—a Republican ballot, a Democratic ballot, a Populist ballot, a Greenback ballot, and so forth. The ballots were often printed on different-colored paper so that voters could distinguish among them—and so that the local party workers could observe who cast which ballots. With these party ballots, voters could not choose candidates from different parties for different offices; they had to vote the party line.

In a 10-year period from 1885 to 1895, nearly every state adopted the Australian ballot and, with it, the secret ballot. This new form of voting came about in an era of administrative reform in government throughout the United States. County governments took on the job of formatting and printing ballots, and the conduct of elections became an administrative task of government rather than a political activity of the parties. The move toward this new way of casting votes also reflected the efforts of the state governments to break the hold of local political organizations. All ballots are identical under the Australian form, making it difficult to observe who votes for which party. More importantly, voters could choose any candidate for any office, breaking the hold of parties over the vote. The introduction of the Australian ballot gave rise to the phenomenon of split-ticket voting, in which some voters select candidates from different parties for different offices.[14]

The secret and Australian ballot creates the opportunity for voters to choose candidates as well as parties and, as we discuss in more depth later, created a necessary condition for the rise of the personal vote and the incumbency advantage in American electoral politics. (See the discussion of the incumbency advantage in Congress in Chapter 6.) The party ballot made it impossible to

 Australian ballot

An electoral format that presents the names of all the candidates for any given office on the same ballot. Introduced at the end of the eighteenth century, the Australian ballot replaced the partisan ballot and facilitated split-ticket voting

---

14 Jerold G. Rusk, "The Effect of the Australian Ballot Reform on Split Ticket Voting, 1876–1908," *American Political Science Review* 64, no. 4 (December 1970): 1220–38.

---

choose particular candidates without voting for an entire list of candidates nominated by a party or slate. Voters could not split their tickets, choosing, say, one party's nominee for president and another party's nominee for the House of Representatives. In the absence of a real possibility of split-ticket voting, the electorate could express a desire for change only as a vote against all candidates of the party in power. When the electorate voted to oust those in power at the national level, the election would sweep into power the opposing party or slate at the state and local levels as well. As a result, elections in the United States before 1896 were highly partisan affairs, often producing wholesale changes in control of government at all levels. The Australian ballot allows voters to cast a more sophisticated ballot that reflects both the performance of individual officeholders and assessments of the political parties as a whole.

The possibility of split-ticket voting created greater fragmentation in the control of government in the United States. With the party ballot, an insurgent party could more readily be swept to power at all levels of government in a given election. A strong national tide toward one of the parties in the presidential election would change not just the presidency but also political control of every state and locality that gave a majority of its votes to that presidential candidate's party. The party ballot thus reinforced the effect of elections on party control of government and public policy. In contrast, because the Australian ballot permitted voters to choose for each office separately, it lessened the likelihood that the electorate would sweep an entirely new administration into power. Thus, ticket splitting led to increasingly divided control of government as well as the rise of personal voting.

Where: Electoral Districts

Elected officials in the United States represent places as well as people. Today, the president, representatives, senators, governors, and many other state officers, state legislators, and most local officers are elected by the people through geographic areas called electoral districts. Generally speaking, the United States employs **single-member districts** with equal populations. This means that the U.S. House of Representatives, almost all state legislatures, and almost all local governments have their own districts and elect one representative per district, and all of the districts for a given legislative body must have equal populations.[15]

single-member district ⇨

An electorate that is allowed to elect only one representative from each district—the typical method of representation in the United States

---

15 The exceptions in the state legislatures are Arizona, Idaho, Maryland, New Hampshire, New Jersey, North Dakota, South Dakota, Vermont, Washington, and West Virginia. These states use multimember districts in either their state house of representatives or their state senate. In some cases legislators are elected en bloc: if there are two seats in a district, the top vote getters win the seats, as in both chambers in Vermont and the lower chambers in Arizona, Maryland, New Hampshire, New Jersey, North Dakota, and West Virginia. In some cases, there are multiple posts for each district, candidates must declare which post they are running for, and the top vote getter for a given post wins that seat, as in the lower chambers in Idaho, Maryland (also uses bloc), South Dakota (also uses bloc), and Washington.

Elections for the U.S. Senate and the presidency are the odd cases. In the U.S. Senate, the states are the districts. Senate districts, then, have multiple members and unequal populations. In presidential elections, every state is allocated votes in the **electoral college** equal to its number of U.S. senators (two) plus its number of House members. The states are the districts, and each state chooses all of its electors in a statewide vote. The electors commit to casting their votes for a certain candidate in the electoral college.[16] Within the political parties, the nomination process in most states allocates delegates to the parties' national conventions on the basis of House districts, and thus population. However, some states choose their delegates on a statewide basis, with all districts selecting multiple delegates to the party conventions.

 electoral college

The presidential electors from each state who meet in their respective state capitals after the popular election to cast ballots for president and vice president

The system of single-member districts with equal populations was not part of the Founders' original design. Rather, it evolved over nearly two centuries, from 1790 to 1970. Article II of the Constitution designed the House to represent the people, with the number of seats elected by each state allocated on the basis of population following each decennial census, and the Senate to represent the states. The Constitution originally specified that the state legislatures would choose the U.S. senators, with each state choosing two senators to staggered six-year terms. That system was jettisoned in 1913 with the adoption of the Seventeenth Amendment, providing for direct election of senators.

The Constitution said nothing about the election of individual House members or electors to the electoral college. That task fell to the states, and in early times the states used many different electoral systems for choosing their House delegations. Most of the early state laws adopted single-member districts. The states divided their territory into as many districts as they had House seats, and each district elected one member. Some states created multimember districts, in which a district would elect more than one legislator. This was common in urban counties and cities, where the population exceeded the number required for two or more districts, but the legislature did not want to draw district boundaries. And some states elected all their House members in a single, statewide election (called an at-large election). An even greater hodgepodge of election procedures applied to the state legislatures and local councils.[17]

Congress tried to bring order to the election of House members with the 1842 Apportionment Act. Following the sixth decennial census (of 1840), Congress had to pass a new apportionment bill to assign House seats to the states. Through an amendment from Representative John Campbell of South Carolina, the act included an additional requirement on districts:

> [I]n every case where a State is entitled to more than one Representative, the number to which each State shall be entitled under this apportionment shall be

16 The exceptions are Maine and Nebraska, which choose the House electors in individual House districts and the Senate electors in a statewide vote.

17 For a history of districting politics, see Stephen Ansolabehere and James Snyder, Jr., *The End of Inequality: One Person, One Vote and the Transformation of American Politics* (New York: Norton, 2008).

elected by districts, composed of contiguous territory, equal in number to the number of Representatives to which said State may be entitled; no one district electing more than one Representative.[18]

Most states complied with this provision, even though it placed a new responsibility on the states of creating appropriate districts, especially around urban areas. Some states, however, insisted on using at-large and multimember districts up to the 1960s. Finally, in the 1967 Apportionment Act, Congress forbade the use of anything but single-member districts.

A second important change in the nature of political districts in the United States occurred at that time as well. In a series of decisions beginning with *Baker v. Carr* in 1962, the U.S. Supreme Court ruled that all federal and state legislative districts must have equal populations: one person, one vote. That simple aphorism today rings as the very definition of democracy, but before 1962 state legislative districts often had highly unequal populations, which meant that some votes in effect counted more than others. In the California state senate, Los Angeles County elected as many seats as Alpine County, even though Los Angeles had almost 500 times as many people. As a result, voters in Alpine County had greater representation (500 times greater) relative to their population than did voters in Los Angeles County. Similar inequities reigned in every state legislature, producing a pattern of overrepresentation of rural areas and underrepresentation of most urban areas and, especially, suburban counties. In most states these inequalities arose from neglect. Most state constitutions require redistricting to keep district populations equal, but as urban populations grew, especially in the first half of the twentieth century, those in power realized that redistricting might jeopardize their own re-election. As a result, the legislatures chose to do nothing. With each successive decade, representation in the United States became more unequal, and there seemed to be no way to force the state legislatures to act. Finally, the U.S. Supreme Court ruled, in a series of important cases, that unequal representation violated the Fourteenth Amendment's guarantee of equal protection under the law. By 1971, nearly every legislative district in the United States elected one representative, and the populations of the districts for each legislative chamber were equal. Lawsuits brought by civil rights groups in the 1980s forced school districts and city councils to adopt single-member districts as well. Single-member districts with equal populations have become the rule in the United States, from city councils and school districts to the House of Representatives.[19]

The U.S. Senate and the electoral college remain the two great exceptions to the requirements of single-member districts with equal populations. The apportionment of Senate seats to states makes that chamber inherently unequal. California's 38 million people have the same number of senators as Wyoming's 575,000 people. The allocation of electoral college votes creates a population

---

18 Congressional Globe, 27th Cong., 2d sess., 1842, 11, Part 1:471, 348.

19 The story of this transformation is told in Ansolabehere and Snyder, *The End of Inequality*.

inequity in presidential elections, with larger states selecting fewer electors per capita than smaller states. In the 1960s, the Supreme Court let stand the unequal district populations in the Senate and the electoral college, because the representation of states in the Senate is specified in the Constitution. The reason lies in the politics of the Constitutional Convention (see Chapter 2). That convention consisted of delegations of states, each of which held equal numbers of votes under the Articles of Confederation. In order to create a House of Representatives to reflect the preferences of the population, the large states had to strike a deal with the smaller states, which stood to lose representation with the initial plan of a single chamber that reflected population. That deal, the Connecticut Compromise, created the U.S. Senate to balance representation of people with representation of places and led to a clause in Article V of the Constitution that guarantees equal representation of the states in the Senate.

Nonetheless, the Senate and the electoral college share the salient feature of elections for the House and other elections in the use of districts to select representatives. All elections in the United States and all elected officials are tied to geographically based constituencies rather than to the national electorate as a whole. This is certainly true for the House and Senate. It applies also to presidential elections, in which candidates focus on winning key states in the electoral college rather than on winning a majority of the popular vote.

Electoral Districts and Majority Rule. Electoral districts have a particularly important political consequence: the use of districts tends to magnify the power of the majority. In a system like that of the United States with two parties and single-member districts, the party that wins a majority of the vote nationwide tends to win a disproportionate share of the seats. In 2010, Republicans won 53.5 percent of the two-party vote nationwide for the U.S. House, but 55.6 percent of the seats. As an empirical matter, in the United States, when the election is a tie, the parties win equal shares of the vote, and for every 1 percent of the vote above 50 percent a party gains an additional 2 percent of the seats. This pattern has been observed in data on U.S. House elections over the last 60 years. In 2012, however, Democrats and Republicans finished in a virtual tie for popular votes cast for the two parties in House races, but the GOP won 54 percent of the seats. This anomaly was in part the result of the Republican advantage in redrawing district boundaries. These boundaries are drawn by the state legislatures, and in 2010 the GOP won control of a majority of these bodies. Candidate recruitment, retirements, and reapportionment also played a role. The electoral college tends to magnify the vote majority even more dramatically. In 2012, Barack Obama won 51 percent of the vote nationwide, but he captured nearly 62 percent of the electoral college delegates. Electoral districts, then, create a very strong tendency toward majority rule.

This magnifying effect has been a particular problem for smaller parties and minority groups. Just as districts magnify the number of seats won by the majority party, they shrink the representation of small parties. If a party wins 5 percent of the vote nationwide, it is difficult for it to win any seats or electoral college delegates unless the support for that party is highly concentrated in a particular geographic area. The most successful third party in recent U.S. history was the Reform Party, started by Ross Perot in 1992. Perot won 19 percent of the presidential vote nationwide that year, a very strong third place throughout the country, but he won no electoral college delegates.

The majoritarian tendency of districts also makes it very difficult for racial minorities to gain representation. Blacks and Hispanics constitute roughly a quarter of the population. Districts crafted without regard to race would spread the minority vote across many districts, making it unlikely that those groups would be a sufficiently large segment in any one district to elect proportionate numbers of blacks or Hispanics to the legislature. This problem, compounded by the historic discrimination against blacks and Hispanics, led Congress to amend the Voting Rights Act in 1982 to provide for the creation of legislative districts with sufficient numbers of black and Hispanic voters to elect House members representative of those groups. This law has been interpreted and implemented to mean that the state legislatures must create districts, called majority-minority districts, containing majorities of black or Hispanic people, whenever possible. As we discuss later, that provision has proved highly controversial in each subsequent round of districting, but the Voting Rights Act has been renewed repeatedly by Congress and has withstood legal challenges.[20] It is a direct reaction against the majoritarian pressures created by districts. Even with this rule, blacks and Hispanics make up only 15 percent of members of the Congress, even though they accounted for 26 percent of the vote in 2012.

House districts and state legislative districts are not static. In order to comply with the dictum of equal population representation, they must be remade every decade. Responsibility for drawing new district boundaries rests, in most states, with the state legislatures and the governors, with the supervision of the courts and sometimes with the consultation of commissions (Figure 11.4). Every 10 years, the U.S. census updates the official population figures of the states, as well as population counts, to a fine level of geographical detail. The politicians, their staffs, party consultants, and others with a stake in the outcome use the census data to craft a new district map; ultimately, the legislatures must pass and the governors must sign a law defining new U.S. House and state legislative districts. This job is forced on the legislatures by their constitutions and by the courts. As the history of unequal representation suggests, most legislatures would, if left to their own devices, leave the existing boundaries in place. Periodic redistricting, although it corrects one problem, invites another. Those in charge of redistricting may try to manipulate the new map to increase the likelihood of a particular outcome, such as the election of a majority of seats for one party or social interest. This problem arose with some of the earliest congressional district maps. A particularly egregious map of the 1812 Massachusetts House districts drawn with the imprimatur of Governor Elbridge Gerry prompted an editorial writer in the *Boston Gazette* to dub a very strangely shaped district the "Gerry-Mander."

---

20 In 2013, the Supreme Court struck down Section 4 of the Voting Rights Act, which determined which states were automatically subject to preclearance. The remaining sections, including this one and the prohibition against intentional discrimination (Section 2), were not affected. See *Shelby County, Alabama v. Holder,* 570 U.S. ____ (2013).

Figure 11.4
CONGRESSIONAL REDISTRICTING

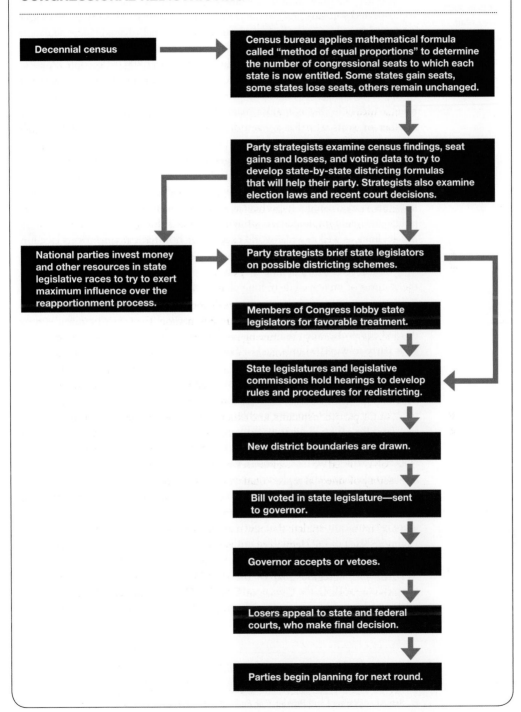

Decennial census

Census bureau applies mathematical formula called "method of equal proportions" to determine the number of congressional seats to which each state is now entitled. Some states gain seats, some states lose seats, others remain unchanged.

Party strategists examine census findings, seat gains and losses, and voting data to try to develop state-by-state districting formulas that will help their party. Strategists also examine election laws and recent court decisions.

National parties invest money and other resources in state legislative races to try to exert maximum influence over the reapportionment process.

Party strategists brief state legislators on possible districting schemes.

Members of Congress lobby state legislators for favorable treatment.

State legislatures and legislative commissions hold hearings to develop rules and procedures for redistricting.

New district boundaries are drawn.

Bill voted in state legislature—sent to governor.

Governor accepts or vetoes.

Losers appeal to state and federal courts, who make final decision.

Parties begin planning for next round.

gerrymandering

The apportionment of voters in districts in such a way as to give unfair advantage to one political party

The term stuck, and **gerrymandering** refers broadly to any attempt at creating electoral districts for political advantage.

It is easy to draw intentionally an unfair electoral map, especially with the sophisticated software and data on local voting patterns and demographics that are available today. To facilitate districting, the Census Bureau divides the nation into very small geographic areas, called census blocks, which typically contain a few dozen people. U.S. House districts contain over 700,000 people. Political mapmakers combine various local areas, down to census blocks, to construct legislative districts. Those seeking political advantage try to make as many districts as possible that contain a majority of their own voters, maximizing the number of seats won for a given division of the vote. There are constraints on political cartography: the district populations must be equal, and all parts of the district must touch (be contiguous). Even with those constraints, the number of possible maps that could be drawn for any one state's legislative districts is extremely large.[21] The Analyzing the Evidence unit on page 468 shows how this works, using a hypothetical state to explain some basic strategies that politicians might implement to influence elections through the manipulation of district lines, as well as a real-world example of how redistricting affects election outcomes.

Political scientists examine the fairness of plans by assessing quantitatively the features of any given districting plan. Such measures are widely used by state legislatures, commissions, and courts in assessing districting plans. Of central importance is the notion of bias. In a hypothetical election where the vote is divided equally between the two major parties, what share of seats do we expect each party to win? An unbiased or fair districting plan would give both parties half of the seats in this hypothetical election. To gauge the magnitude of the bias, political scientists then simulate such hypothetical elections among a state's electorate under a given districting plan. A bias of, say, 5 points means that when the two parties split the vote evenly, one of the parties wins 55 percent of the seats and the other 45 percent. With each round of districting, experts weigh in with their assessments of the bias in the plans. Those who want fair elections will try to achieve no bias. Those who want to gain the upper hand try to inject bias into elections with a cleverly constructed map.

Empirical study of U.S. House and state legislative elections has documented several very important patterns in the bias of electoral districts. First, there is significant evidence of partisan bias in redistricting maps passed today. In the 1990s and 2000s, the bias in the average state legislative district map was approximately 5 points.[22] Second, while bias remains, it is notable that bias has dropped substantially over the past 50 years since the courts became involved in the process. In 1960, the typical state legislative electoral map had approximately a 10- to 12-point bias in favor of one of the parties (depending on who drew

---

21 For definitions of these units, see Bureau of the Census, Geographic Area Reference Manual, www.census.gov/geo/www/garm.html (accessed 3/27/09).

22 See Ansolabehere and Snyder, *The End of Inequality*, chap. 11.

the map). That means that around 1960, a dead-even election would actually produce a large majority for one of the parties in the legislature. Since the 1960s, frequent redistricting and court oversight has forced state legislatures to create districting plans that treat both parties more fairly. Third, the bias is the largest in states where the legislature conducts redistricting and one party controls both chambers of the legislature and the governor's office. When the legislature and executive are controlled by the same party, the legislature can create a map heavily biased toward that party, and the governor will likely sign it. However, when the legislature and executive are controlled by different parties, then the legislature might face a veto from the governor and must create districts that will be acceptable to the other party.[23] This is one of the benefits of divided party control of the legislature and executive.

Politicians can use gerrymandering to dilute the strength not only of a party but also of a group. Until recently, many state legislatures employed gerrymandering to dilute the strength of racial minorities. One of the more common strategies involved redrawing congressional district boundaries in such a way as to divide and disperse a black population that would have constituted a majority within the original district. This form of gerrymandering, sometimes called cracking, was used in Mississippi during the 1960s and 1970s to prevent the election of black candidates to Congress. Historically, the black population of Mississippi was clustered in the western half of the state along the Mississippi River Delta. From 1882 until 1966, the Delta constituted one congressional district. Although blacks were a clear majority within this district, discrimination against them in voter registration and at the polls guaranteed the continual election of white congressmen. With the passage of the Voting Rights Act in 1965, this district would almost surely be won by a black candidate or one favored by the black majority. To prevent that from happening, the Mississippi state legislature drew new House districts in 1965 in order to minimize the voting power of the black population. Rather than a majority of a single district that encompassed the Delta, the black population was split across three districts and constituted a majority in none. Mississippi's gerrymandering scheme was preserved in the state's redistricting plans in 1972 and 1982 and helped prevent the election of any black representative until 1986, when Mike Espy became the first African American since Reconstruction to represent Mississippi in Congress.

Continuing controversies about the legislatures' involvement in drawing their own districts have raised deep concerns about the fairness of the process. Many states have created commissions to draw plans or appointed "special masters" to draw the maps. California and Arizona conducted their redistricting in 2012 using independent commissions. Both of these procedures were adopted via ballot measures, not by the state legislatures. Political scientists' analyses of the underlying electoral bias indicates that these commissions produced very fair maps.

---

23 See Gary King and Robert X. Browning, "Democratic Representation and Partisan Bias in Congressional Elections," *American Political Science Review* 81, no. 4 (December 1987): 1252–73.

The Electoral Impact of Congressional Redistricting

District boundaries can have subtle but significant effects on the partisan division of a legislature. If a party can control the districting process, it may be able to craft the lines in such a way that the party wins more seats for the same number of Republican and Democratic votes.

Drawing District Lines

Consider a hypothetical state where Republicans represent 60 percent of voters and Democrats represent the remaining 40 percent of voters. As a result of population changes during the preceding decade, this state now has five congressional districts. A state legislature controlled by a Republican majority could draw congressional districts in such a way that Republicans are 60 percent of voters in each seat and expected to win every seat.

SCENARIO 1

Now suppose that the Democrats are in control of the state legislature. With the same distribution of voters in the state, they could draw the districts to favor the Democrats as much as possible (with Democratic voters dominating three of the districts).

SCENARIO 2

U.S. House Districts, Texas, 2011

PLAN C185

Consider a real-world example. Reapportionment following the 2010 census allotted Texas four new districts, and the shifting demographics of the state required considerable redrawing of the congressional district lines. The Democrats and Republicans in the Texas state legislature each proposed new district plans. The Republican-controlled legislature passed the Republican plan (Plan C185), and Republican governor Rick Perry signed that plan into law.

In a state of 25 million people, comparing different districting plans is more complicated than in our simple models, but comparing the Republican plan (C185) and the main Democratic plan (C166) in Texas revealed a significant difference. Political scientists started by calculating each party's share of the two-party vote in statewide and federal elections over the decade from 2002 to 2010: the average was 42.3 percent Democratic and 57.7 percent Republican. This average is called the normal vote. Using the normal vote as the measure of the Democratic and Republican strength in each area, Democrats comprise 42.3 percent of the electorate, and they are the majority in 27.8 percent of districts (10 seats) and Republicans the majority 72.2 percent of districts (26 seats).

Political scientists analyzing this case also estimated the bias toward one party or the other. A districting plan is said to be unbiased if when the parties each win 50 percent of the votes statewide, they also each win 50 percent of the legislative seats. A plan is biased in favor of one party if that party wins *more* than half of the seats in an election in which it wins just half of the votes. A plan is biased against the party if it wins *less* than half of the seats when it wins half of the votes. Of course, most elections do not end up with each party winning 50 percent of the vote. More generally, a districting plan is unbiased if a party wins half of its seats by the same margin that it wins the statewide vote, and the plan is biased in favor of a party if it wins more than half of its seats by the margin it wins the statewide vote. Hence, if a party wins 60 percent of the vote statewide, one expects, under an unbiased plan, that the party will win half of its seats with at least 60 percent of the vote. If the map is biased in favor of that party, it will win more than half of its seats by at least 60 percent.

Expected Share of Seats: Democrats

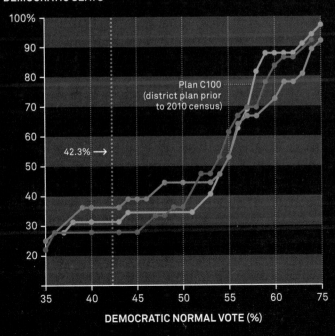

EXPECTED
DEMOCRATIC SEATS

Plan C100
(district plan prior
to 2010 census)

42.3% →

DEMOCRATIC NORMAL VOTE (%)

Plan C185 (Republican)
Plan C166 (Democratic)
Plan C100 (Previous district plan)

The graph shows the expected Democratic share of Texas U.S. House seats won at 42.3 percent and for percentages of the statewide vote above and below that, including at the 50 percent point. We can see the partisan biases of each plan in the graph by looking at the expected Democratic seat share at 50 percent of the vote. The plan passed into law (the red line) has a 13-point bias: under Texas's new districts, Democrats are expected to win 37 percent of seats if they win half of the vote statewide (the difference between 37 and 50 is the partisan bias). Under the Democrats' own plan (the blue line), the bias is just 5 points.

SOURCE: Texas Legislative Council, www.tlc.state.tx.us/redist/redist.html (accessed 10/31/11) and author calculations.

It has proved difficult to find a satisfactory reform for redistricting. Perhaps the most unusual and creative attempt to engage the issue is that proposed by Ohio secretary of state Jennifer Brunner. Working with the League of Women Voters of Ohio, Common Cause, and state representatives Joan Lawrence and Dan Stewart, the Ohio secretary of state created a public contest in 2009 to develop the best districting plan—the Ohio Redistricting Competition. The purpose of the competition was not to produce a new districting law but to show how "a robust public conversation about the process can occur, leading to the development of the best possible redistricting recommendations for consideration by the Ohio General Assembly."[24] This was a way to inform the legislature and courts about what the public wanted in the districting plans and to produce a blueprint to guide those who would draw the official maps.

The Ohio experiment was just the beginning in an important transformation in districting. In 2011, the Public Mapping Project, led by Professor Michael McDonald and Harvard researcher Micah Altman, conducted similar contests in a dozen states. And independent software developer David Bradlee developed Dave's Redistricting App, a powerful tool that is easy to use and free.[25] The State of Texas and the State of Florida made available on their districting website all of the districting tools and data that were available to the legislative committees that drafted the maps. The technology has created a new era of open redistricting.

During the redistricting process in 2010 and 2011, these new tools and public mapping projects generated many different plans that the legislatures and commissions examined as part of their deliberations. Interest groups and the minority party within legislatures now wield the information and technology to propose their own alternative configurations of districts during the legislative process (not just after the fact), and to argue for their interests. Before the 2011 redistricting, the districting committee in the legislature and, even more specifically, the majority party in most states controlled the technology and shaped the political debate in the legislature and afterward. As controversies over district plans moved into the courts, the public mapping projects and open-source districting tools empowered plaintiffs and the courts. The plaintiffs could point to alternative and (arguably) fairer maps. The courts, who traditionally have not had the resources and staff to do their own districting plans, could see the range of possible maps that could have been constructed and contrast those with what the legislatures produced. Such evidence is especially powerful when allegations of racial discrimination are at stake.

For two centuries, the districting process has been closed off to the public, to interest groups, even to members of the minority party within the legislature. Now, new developments in geographic information systems (GIS) software and provision of census data make it possible for anyone to draw credible district

---

24 The contest was available at www.ohioredistricting.org, sponsored by the Ohio secretary of state (accessed 8/31/11; site discontinued).

25 Dave's Redistricting, http://gardow.com/davebradlee/redistricting (accessed 8/31/11); Public Mapping Project, www.publicmapping.org (accessed 8/31/11).

maps. Opening up the process, it is hoped, will lessen the extent and effect of gerrymandering.

What It Takes to Win: Plurality Rule

The fourth prominent feature of U.S. electoral law is the criterion for winning. Americans often embrace majority rule as a defining characteristic of democracy. However, that is not quite right. The real standard is **plurality rule**. The candidate who receives the most votes in the relevant district or constituency wins the election, even if that candidate doesn't receive a majority of votes. Suppose, for example, three parties nominate candidates for a seat and divide the vote such that one wins 34 percent and the other two each receive 33 percent of the vote. Under plurality rule, the candidate with 34 percent wins the seat, even though he did not win a majority of votes (more than 50 percent). There are different types of plurality systems. The system currently used in the United States combines plurality rule with single-member districts and is called *first past the post.* The electoral college is a plurality system in which the candidate who receives the most votes wins all of the delegates: winner take all.[26] Some states set an even higher standard and require a candidate to receive at least 50 percent of all votes in order to win. This is **majority rule**. Louisiana and Georgia, for instance, require a candidate to receive an outright majority in an election in order to be declared the winner. If no candidate receives a majority in an election, a runoff election is held about one month later between the two candidates who received the most votes in the first round. Other systems also use plurality- and majority-rule criteria. For instance, some city councils still have multimember districts. The top vote getters win the seats. If there are, say, seven seats to fill, the seven candidates who win the most votes each win a seat.

Plurality rule is often criticized for yielding electoral results that do not reflect the public's preferences. The votes for the losing candidates seem wasted, because they do not translate directly into representation. Indeed, as the example of the three-candidate race above suggests, it is possible that a majority of voters wanted someone other than the winner. In the aggregate, plurality rule with single-member districts tends to inflate the share of seats won by the largest party and deflate the others' shares. A striking example of the effects comes from Great Britain. In 2005, the British Labour Party won 35 percent of the vote and 55 percent of the seats; the Conservatives finished second, with 31 percent of the vote and 31 percent of the seats; the Liberal Democrats garnered 22 percent of the popular vote, but won just 8 percent of the seats. Nevertheless, plurality rule offers certain advantages. It gives voters the ability to choose individuals to represent them personally, not just political parties, and it picks a definite winner without the need for runoff elections.

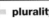

plurality rule

A type of electoral system in which victory goes to the individual who gets the most votes in an election, but not necessarily a majority of the votes cast

majority rule

A type of electoral system in which, to win a seat in a representative body, a candidate must receive a majority (50 percent plus one) of all the votes cast in the relevant district

---

26 Over the centuries, many systems for voting and determining electoral outcomes have been devised. For an excellent analysis of voting systems and a complete classification see Gary Cox, *Making Votes Count* (New York: Cambridge University Press, 1997).

Among the democracies of the world, the main alternative to plurality rule is proportional representation, also called PR for short. Under proportional representation, competing parties win legislative seats in proportion to their share of the popular vote. For example, if three parties running for seats in the legislature divide the vote such that one wins 34 percent and the other two receive 33 percent of the vote, the first party receives 34 percent of the seats and the other two receive 33 percent of the seats.

PR is used rarely in the United States. The most substantial elections in which it is employed are the Democratic presidential primary elections. During the 1988 primary season, Jesse Jackson routinely won 20 percent of the vote in the primaries but ended up with only about 5 percent of the delegates. To make the Democratic National Convention and the party more representative of its disparate voting groups, Jackson negotiated with other party leaders to change the delegate allocation rules so that delegates within congressional districts would be assigned on a proportional basis. If a district elects five delegates, a candidate wins a delegate if the candidate receives at least 20 percent of the vote in the district, two delegates if the candidate wins at least 40 percent of the vote, and so forth. Prior to this rule change the Democratic Party awarded all delegates from a given congressional district to the candidate who won a plurality of the vote. Like any districted system with plurality rule, this created a strong majoritarian tendency.

Plurality rule in single-member districts has a very important consequence. It is the reason for two-party politics in the United States. Around the world, countries with plurality rule in single-member districts have far fewer political parties than other nations. Typically, elections under plurality rule boil down to just two major parties that routinely compete for power, with one of them winning a majority of legislative seats outright. Proportional representation systems, on the other hand, tend to have many more than two parties. Rarely does a single party win a majority of seats. Governments form as coalitions of many different parties. The political scientist Maurice Duverger described that pattern in a pathbreaking book, *Party Politics*, first published in 1951. Duverger formalized his law of politics quite simply: plurality rule creates two-party politics; proportional representation encourages more than two parties.

The rationale behind Duverger's Law has two components, the strategic behavior of politicians and the behavior of voters. Consider, first, how politicians would think about the prospects of forming a new party. Suppose that there already are two parties, a center-right party and a center-left party. A politician from the far right, for example, might be unhappy that the parties do not represent the ideals she espouses. She wants a far-right policy most, a center-right policy less, and least of all a center-left policy. One solution for the far-right politician is to leave the center-right party and form a far-right party. The problem with doing that is that it helps the center-left party. A far-right party in this circumstance splits the vote of those on the right without affecting the vote for the center-left party. Under plurality rule, the center-left party would almost certainly win, an outcome that the far-right politician likes even less.

Thus, politicians on the extremes cannot gain by forming a new party. A politician with a centrist orientation also cannot win the election if the center-right and center-left parties are not too extreme. The center-right party would win all votes of voters on the right and on the center right. The same is true for the center-left party. That would leave only a small segment of true centrists for a potential centrist party. Hence, if the current parties are not too extreme, there is no incentive for a third party to enter a two-party system when plurality rule is the criterion for winning.

Voters follow a similar logic. They do not want to waste their votes. If voters understand that the extremist party or candidate cannot win, they will vote for the more moderate alternative. Although second best for extremist voters, the moderate has a better chance of winning. This logic leads the extremist voters to choose the moderate party or candidate in order to have a better chance of selecting a candidate more to their liking. Extremist parties and candidates, then, have little incentive to enter a race, and when they do they usually attract few votes.

Such sophisticated voting occurs often in U.S. primary elections. John McCain was significantly more moderate than Mike Huckabee and Mitt Romney in the 2008 Republican presidential primaries, and he was more moderate than the typical Republican voter. Nevertheless, he won the nomination easily because many Republicans understood that McCain represented their best chance in the general election. Mitt Romney was the most moderate candidate in the 2012 field and, again, the most moderate candidate prevailed.

Proportional representation (PR), in contrast, creates an incentive for more parties and candidates to enter, because they will win seats in proportion to their support among the national electorate. PR systems often have a multitude of parties, none of which represents a decisive majority. Elections in PR systems rarely decide which party will lead the government and often lead to coalition governments, because no one party wins enough seats to govern. In the Democratic Party, proportional representation has the further effect of stretching out the nominating season. If a candidate wins a plurality of 40 percent of the vote in a state's Democratic primary, he wins roughly 40 percent of the delegates. As a result, it takes many more victories in the Democratic primaries to accumulate sufficient delegates to lock the nomination. In 2008, Obama and Clinton split the votes and delegates almost equally, and Obama won by the barest of majorities. By contrast, plurality rule and winner take all in the Republican primaries means that even when there are many candidates, as in 2008 and 2012, the primary elections are decided rather quickly. John McCain had won a smaller share of the vote in the primary elections through March 5, 2008, than either of the two main Democratic contestants, Hillary Clinton and Barack Obama, but by the beginning of March, McCain had virtually sewn up the Republican nomination.

How votes are cast and counted, and what it takes to win a seat, then, have very substantial consequences for American politics. Plurality rule with single-member districts creates strong pressures toward two-party politics and majority rule in the legislature.

Direct Democracy: The Referendum and the Recall

referendum

A measure proposed or passed by a legislature that is referred to the vote of the electorate for approval or rejection

In addition to voting for candidates, 24 states also provide for referendum voting. The **referendum** process allows citizens to vote directly on proposed laws or other governmental actions. Referendums may come about two ways. First, some state constitutions and laws require that certain types of legislation (such as bonds or property tax increases) be approved by popular vote. Second, people may get a measure put on the ballot by obtaining enough signatures of registered voters to a petition. In recent years, voters in several states have voted to set limits on tax rates, block state and local spending proposals, define marriage, and prohibit social services for illegal immigrants. Although it involves voting, a referendum is not an election. The election is an institution of representative government. Through an election, voters choose officials to act for them. The referendum process, by contrast, is an institution of direct democracy; it allows voters to govern directly without intervention by government officials. The validity of referendum results, however, are subject to judicial action. If a court finds that a referendum outcome violates the state or national constitution, it can overturn the result. For example, in 2008 California voters passed Proposition 8, which stated, "Only marriage between a man and a woman is valid and recognized in California." A federal district court in California ruled Proposition 8 unconstitutional in 2010, and the Supreme Court let stand the district court's ruling in 2013.[27]

Referendums are by far the most common way that issues are placed on the ballot for public consideration, but there are other means as well. Twenty-four states also permit various forms of the initiative. Whereas the referendum process described above allows citizens to affirm or reject a policy produced by legislative action, the **initiative** provides citizens with a way forward in the face of legislative inaction. This is done by placing a policy proposal (legislation or a state constitutional amendment) on the ballot to be approved or rejected by the electorate. To have a place on the ballot, a petition must be accompanied by a minimum number of voters' signatures—a requirement that varies from state to state—that have been certified by the state's secretary of state.

initiative

A process by which citizens may petition to place a policy proposal on the ballot for public vote

The initiative process has both potential advantages and disadvantages. Ballot propositions involve policies that the state legislature cannot (or does not want to) resolve. Like referendum issues, these are often highly emotional and, consequently, not always well suited to resolution in the electoral arena. On the other hand, one of the "virtues" of the initiative is that it may force action. That is, leaders in the legislature may induce recalcitrant legislators to move on controversial issues by using as a threat the possibility that a worse outcome will result from inaction.[28]

recall

The removal of a public official by popular vote

Legal provisions for **recall elections** exist in 18 states. The recall is an electoral device that was introduced by early twentieth-century Populists to allow

---

27 *Hollingsworth et. al. v. Perry et. al.,* 570 U.S. ____ (2013).

28 This point is developed in Morton Bennedsen and Sven Feldmann, "Lobbying Legislatures," *Journal of Political Economy* 110 (2002): 919–46.

voters to remove governors and other state officials from office before the expiration of their term. Federal officials such as the president and members of Congress are not subject to recall. Generally speaking, a recall effort begins with a petition campaign. For example, in California—the site of a tumultuous recall battle in 2003—if 12 percent of those who voted in the last general election sign petitions demanding a special recall election, one must be scheduled by the state board of elections. Such petition campaigns are relatively common, but most fail to garner enough signatures to bring the matter to a statewide vote. In California in 2003, however, a conservative Republican member of Congress, Darrell Issa, led a successful effort to recall Governor Gray Davis, a Democrat. Voters were unhappy about the state's economy and dissatisfied with Davis's performance: they blamed him for the state's $38 billion budget deficit. Issa and his followers secured enough signatures to force a vote, and in October 2003 Davis became the second governor in American history to be recalled by his state's electorate (the first was North Dakota governor Lynn Frazier, who was recalled in 1921). Under California law, voters in a special recall election are also asked to choose a replacement for the official whom they dismiss. Californians elected the movie star Arnold Schwarzenegger to be their governor. Although critics charged that the Davis recall had been a "political circus," the campaign had the effect of greatly increasing voter interest and involvement in the political process. More than 400,000 new voters registered in California in 2003, many drawn into the political arena by the opportunity to participate in the recall campaign. More recently, labor unions campaigned to recall Wisconsin governor Robert Walker following cuts in state employee benefits and collective bargaining rights of unions. In the June 2012 special election, Governor Walker managed to fend off the challenge from Milwaukee mayor Tom Barrett.

Direct democracy, even if it is not used aggressively, can change legislative, executive, and even judicial decision making. The referendum, initiative, and recall all entail shifts in agenda-setting power. The referendum gives an impassioned electoral majority the opportunity to reverse legislation that displeases it, thus affecting the initial strategic calculations of institutional agenda setters (who want to get as much of what they want without its being subsequently reversed). The initiative has a similar effect on institutional agenda setters, but here it inclines them toward action rather than inaction. Combining the two, an institutional agenda setter is caught on the two horns of an institutional dilemma: Do I act, risking a reversal via referendum, or do I maintain the status quo, risking an overturn via initiative? The recall complements both of these choices, keeping institutional agenda setters on their toes to avoid being ousted. As the institution principle implies, these arrangements do not just provide citizens with governance tools. They also affect the strategic calculations of institutional politicians—legislators and governors.

While initiatives and referendums are often pointed to as a means of making sure that the legislature represents the public's preferences, they are also criticized for being expensive, for slowing down government action, and for making bad laws. The issues brought before the public are often emotional matters, which require deliberation and reflection, and many more complicated questions, such as public spending, might be better dealt with in a legislative setting where it is necessary to make tradeoffs in order to maintain balance in the overall policy area (such as the budget). Many critics of direct democracy point to the fiscal problems that confront California, where a long history of ballot measures restrict how California can raise revenue and how it must distribute expenditures. This leaves the legislature and governor little flexibility when facing an economic downturn.

HOW VOTERS DECIDE

An election expresses the preferences of millions of individuals about whom they want as their representatives and leaders. Electoral rules and laws—the institutional side of elections—impose order on that process, but ultimately, elections are a reflection of the people, the aggregation of many millions of individuals' expressions of their preferences about politics.

The voter's decision can be understood as really two linked decisions: whether to vote and for whom to vote. Social scientists have examined both facets of the electoral decision by studying election returns, survey data, and experiments conducted in laboratories as well as field experiments conducted during actual elections. Out of generations of research into these questions, a broad picture emerges of how voters decide. First, the decision to vote or not to vote correlates very strongly with the social characteristics of individuals, especially age and education, but it also depends on the electoral choices and context. An individual who does not know anything about the candidates or dislikes all of the choices is unlikely to vote. Second, which candidates or party voters choose depends primarily on three factors: partisan loyalties, issues, and candidate characteristics. Partisan loyalties have been found to be the strongest single predictor of the vote, though party attachments also reflect issues and experience with candidates. Party, issues, and candidates act together to shape vote choice.

Voters and Nonvoters

As we saw earlier in the chapter, turnout in modern American presidential elections ranges from 50 to 60 percent of the voting-age population. The Census Bureau's Current Population Survey provides the most comprehensive and trusted data about the demographics of voting. According to that survey, 65 percent of adults were registered voters in 2012, and 57 percent of adults voted that year. Excluding noncitizens, who are ineligible to vote in federal elections, 80 percent of the adult citizen population is registered, and 62 percent of citizens of voting age turned out in 2012. Thus, almost 40 percent of those who could have voted did not. Why do so many people not vote?

This phenomenon has long puzzled social scientists and motivated reformers. A general explanation is elusive, but what social scientists do know about this phenomenon is that a few demographic characteristics routinely prove to be strong predictors of who votes. The most important of these characteristics are age, education, and residential mobility. Other factors, such as gender, income, and race also matter, but to a much smaller degree. According to the 2012 Current Population Survey, only 41 percent of those under age 25 voted that year, fully 20 points below the population average. By comparison, 71 percent of those over 65 years of age voted. The difference between these groups was 30 percentage points, and the effect of age on voting surely translated into an electoral difference. The interests of retirees are much more likely to receive attention by the government than are the interests of those in college or just entering the labor force.

Education shows similarly large differences. Those without a high school degree voted at half the rate of those with a college education. More than three in four people with a college education voted, and the rate was 81 percent among those with a professional degree. In contrast, slightly fewer than 40 percent of those without a high school diploma voted, and 52 percent of those with only a high school degree voted. Finally, consider residency and mobility. Only 51 percent of people who had lived in their current residence less than a year report voting, compared with 76 percent of people who lived in their residence at least five years. Those who own their home or apartment vote at a 67 percent rate, but only 49 percent of those who rent vote.[29] Politicians listen to those who vote, and those who vote are disproportionately older, better educated, and more rooted in their communities.

As discussed earlier, election laws have historically had a large effect on the size and character of the electorate. Those interested in encouraging greater participation today have focused on voter registration requirements, which are thought to create an unnecessary hurdle and thus to depress turnout. The decision to vote itself consists of two steps: registration and turnout. In 2012, 87 percent of those who reported that they registered said they voted. Weakening registration requirements may increase participation. One approach to minimizing such requirements is Election Day registration. As of 2013, 10 states plus the District of Columbia allow people to register on Election Day at the polls or at a government office. The three states with the longest experience with same-day registration—Minnesota, Wisconsin, and Maine—do have higher turnout than most other states, and most studies suggest that in a typical state adopting such a law would increase turnout by about 3 to 5 percent.[30]

---

29 The most reliable source of information about the demographics of voting is the Current Population Survey, conducted by the Census Bureau. For these and other statistics see U.S. Census Bureau, "Voting and Registration in the Election of November 2012," www.census.gov/hhes/www/socdemo/voting/publications/p20/2012/tables.html (accessed 7/17/13).

30 The classic study in this area is Raymond Wolfinger and Steven Rosenstone, *Who Votes?* (New Haven, CT: Yale University Press, 1978). See also Steven Rosenstone and John Mark Hansen, *Participation, Mobilization and American Democracy* (New York: Macmillan, 1993).

Demographics and laws are only part of what accounts for voting and non-voting. The choices presented to the voters are also quite important. The problem is not that many people have a hard time making up their minds but that many people do not feel engaged by current elections or dislike politics altogether. People who are disinterested, "too busy to vote," or do not like the candidates tend not to vote. The Census Bureau survey asks registered nonvoters why they did not vote. The top four reasons are "too busy," "sick or disabled," "not interested," and "did not like the choices."

Not voting may also stem partly from a sense that the election does not hinge on how any individual votes. As advanced by Anthony Downs in *An Economic Theory of Democracy*,[31] rational citizens may decide whether to participate in voting based on the calculation of potential benefits and costs of voting plus their personal sense of civic duty or psychological compunction to vote.

There are, however, strong differences across demographic groups in their voting rates, and these might have political consequences. One hypothetical to consider is, what if everyone voted? In some specific domains, universal voting would certainly alter government policy. Increasing the voting rate of younger cohorts would probably affect government policy on Social Security, for instance. But would 100 percent turnout lead the country to elect a different person for president or put a different party in control of Congress? Interestingly, the answer seems to be no. Voters and nonvoters, for all of their demographic and political differences, hold fairly similar partisan views, ideological orientations, and preferences about the candidates.[32] Voters are somewhat more conservative and more Republican than nonvoters, as a result of the higher income levels and higher home ownership incidence of voters, but the median voter would be only slightly more liberal if everyone voted.

Partisan Loyalty

The single strongest predictor of how a person will vote is that individual's attachment to a political party. The American National Election Study (ANES), exit polls, and media polls have found that even in times of great political change in the United States, the overwhelming majority of Americans identifies with one of the two major political parties and votes almost entirely in accordance with that identity. Survey researchers ascertain **party identification** with simple questions along the following lines: Generally speaking, do you consider yourself to be a Democrat, a Republican, an Independent, or what?[33] Survey researchers further classify people by asking of those who choose a party

party identification

An individual's attachment to a particular political party, which might be based on issues, ideology, past experience, or upbringing

31 Anthony Downs, *An Economic Theory of Democracy* (New York: Harper & Row, 1957).

32 See, for instance, Sidney Verba, Kay Schlozman, and Henry Brady, *Voice and Equality* (Cambridge, MA: Harvard University Press, 1995).

33 This is the wording used by the Gallup Poll. Others ask "In politics today . . ." or offer "or another party" instead of "or what."

whether they identify strongly or weakly with that party, and by asking independents whether they lean toward one party or another.

Over the past three decades party identifications have broken evenly between the Democrats and Republicans. Figure 12.2, in the next chapter on political parties, shows the historical fluctuations in party identifications. From the 1930s to the 1970s, Democratic identifiers outnumbered Republican identifiers, sometimes by a sizable margin. In the 1980s, the parties reached parity in identifications, especially because younger Americans at that time identified very heavily with the Republican Party. The balance in party identifications remained fairly stable through 2000, even though from 1992 to 2004 those ages 18 to 25 chose the Democrats by a sizable margin. From 2002 through the summer of 2009, Democrats steadily gained in overall party identification and Republicans lost ground, because of generational changes and the backlash against the Iraq War. By July 2009, 50 percent of Americans identified as Democrats or leaned toward the Democratic Party, while 42 percent of Americans identified as Republicans or leaned toward the Republican Party.[34] In Obama's first term, however, the partisan battles over health care and other legislative initiatives, the continuing wars in Iraq and Afghanistan, and unemployment ranging from 8 to 10 percent dragged down public support for the Democrats. Today, public support for the parties is evenly split, approximately 45 to 45, with some variation depending on sampling. Interestingly, over a 50-year period there has been little change in the percentage of people calling themselves independents and leaning toward neither party. Only 10 to 15 percent consider themselves pure independents.[35]

Party identifications capture the voters' predisposition toward their party's candidates. Many of these predispositions are rooted in public policies, such as the parties' positions on taxes or abortion or civil rights. Those long-standing policy positions lead to divisions in party identifications and voting patterns among different demographic groups. Large majorities of African Americans and Hispanics, for example, identify and vote with the Democratic Party. Since 1980 there has been a clear gender gap in voting. Women tend to identify more and vote more with the Democrats than men do. In 1980, Ronald Reagan won 55 percent of the vote of men and 47 percent of the vote of women. That gap was novel in 1980, but it has persisted, averaging 7 percentage points over the past three decades. In the 2012 election, the gender gap jumped to 10 points: Barack Obama received 55 percent of the vote of women, but only 45 percent of the vote among men. That difference is not as large as the difference across racial groups, but it is no less significant because women now comprise a majority (53 percent) of voters.

---

34 Jeffrey M. Jones, "More Independents Lean GOP; Smallest Gap since '05," September 30, 2009, www.gallup.com/poll/123362/independents-lean-gop-party-gap-smallest -since-05.aspx (accessed 8/30/11).

35 Marc Hetherington, "Resurgent Mass Partisanship: The Role of Elite Polarization," *American Political Science Review* 95, no. 3 (September 2001): 619–31. Pew Research Center for the People and the Press, "Obama Leads McCain 52% to 46% in Campaign's Final Days," November 2, 2008, http://pewresearch.org/pubs/1020/pew-final-pre -election-poll (accessed 3/31/09).

It is a subject of considerable debate as to why the gender gap arose in the late 1970s and early 1980s and why it has persisted. The timing of the emergence of the gender gap is consistent with the alignment of the two political parties on a range of civil rights issues that affect women. On issues such as pay equity, divorce law, abortion, and women's health, the Democratic administrations and Congress have pursued policies much more favorable to the interests of women. Barack Obama's first major piece of legislation in 2009 was the Lilly Leadbetter Fair Pay Act. Abortion and other issues of women's health have also separated the party's platforms and legislative agendas. During the 2012 Republican presidential primaries, the candidates debated whether to restrict birth control, an issue that had been seen as settled in the 1960s. The very fact that this was openly considered alienated many women voters and likely contributed to the increase in the gender gap in the fall election. It is, however, hard to pin down the exact causes of the shifts as so many of these issues emerged at the same time (the 1970s) and shifts in party attachments tend to be subtle and complex.[36] Issues played some part in the rise of the gender gap, but cultural, racial, and regional differences might also explain some of this phenomenon.

Although specific features of the choices and context matter as well, party identifications express how the voter would likely vote in a "neutral" election. Party identifications are extremely good predictors of voting behavior in less prominent elections, such as for state legislatures or lower-level statewide offices, about which voters may know relatively little. Even in presidential elections, with their extensive advertising and very thorough news coverage, party predispositions predict individual voting behavior. Figure 11.5 displays the percentages of Democratic identifiers, Republican identifiers, and self-described independents who voted for Romney, Obama, or someone else in 2012. Approximately 92 percent of party identifiers voted for their own party's standard bearer. Independents (including independents who lean toward either party) broke 50 to 45 for Romney. The 2012 election was typical in that partisan loyalty is usually in the range of 90 percent. Sometimes, the independent vote decides the election. However, because more Americans are Democrats than Republicans, in this case Obama still won even though more independents voted for Romney.

Since the discovery of its importance in the 1950s, party identification has raised deeper questions about its origins and meaning. There are three distinct views about what party identification is. They are not necessarily exclusive of each other, but they point to very different understandings of the nature of party identification and its effect on elections.[37] Debate over the meaning of party identification cuts to the heart of the meaning of elections.

---

36 Christina Wohlbrecht, *The Politics of Women's Rights* (Princeton, NJ: Princeton University Press, 2000).

37 For an excellent treatment of the meanings of party identification and analysis of the implications of different theories, see Donald Green, Bradley Palmquist, and Eric Schickler, *Partisan Hearts and Minds* (New Haven, CT: Yale University Press, 2003).

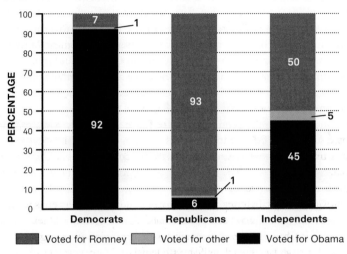

Figure 11.5

THE EFFECT OF PARTY IDENTIFICATION ON THE VOTE FOR PRESIDENT, 2012

Party Identification as Psychological Attachment. First, party identification is a psychological attachment that individuals hold, often throughout their adulthood, to one of the parties. Individuals learn as children and adolescents from parents, other adults, and even peers about politics, and as part of that socialization they develop attachments to a party, not unlike religion and community. Party identifications continue to form into early adulthood. The first few presidential elections that an individual experiences as an adult are thought to have particularly profound influence on that individual's understanding of the parties and politics. And as different cohorts come into politics, their experiences carry forward throughout their lives. Those who were 18 to 24 years old in 1984, for example, identify overwhelmingly with the Republican Party, because those elections marked the triumph of Ronald Reagan's presidency and political philosophy, the rise of a revitalized Republican Party, and the beginning of the end of the Cold War. Those 18 to 24 years old in 2008, on the other hand, identify disproportionately with the Democratic Party, because the Obama campaign galvanized young voters around a new vision for the future. However it is developed, an individual's psychological affinity for a party makes that person want that party to win and want to support that party, even when she disagrees with the party on important policies or disapproves of the party's nominees for office.

Party Identification as Ideological Affinity. Of course, the Democratic and Republican parties are quite different entities today than they were 40 years ago or 80 years ago. On matters of race relations, for example, the

Democratic Party has moved over the past century from supporting segregation to spearheading civil rights. The Republican Party, once a bastion of economic protectionism, now champions free trade. However strong generational transmission of party identifications may be, the dissonance between identities and issues must surely weaken the pull of party, which suggests a second theory of party. This second idea is that party identification reflects underlying ideologies of voters and policy positions of parties. Parties in government, as we discussed in Chapter 6, are meaningful organizations for producing public policies. The relatively high degree of party loyalty in Congress and other branches of government means that voters can reasonably anticipate how politicians will act in office. Citizens identify with parties that pursue public policies more to their liking. For example, a union worker will feel a stronger attachment to the Democratic Party because the Democrats have historically protected union interests. A high-income earner may feel a strong pull toward the Republican Party because that party pushes lower taxes overall, whereas the Democrats promote higher tax rates for higher-income households. As mentioned in the introduction to this chapter, elections present an informational problem of adverse selection. The party labels act as brand names and help voters choose the candidates that will best match their preferences. Voters need not know the details of an individual candidate's voting record or campaign promises in order to understand how that politician will likely behave on important matters. As such, party labels provide an informational shortcut for voters. Party identification means, in part, that a voter feels that party represents his interests better than other parties; hence, an identifier is highly likely to vote for that party.[38]

Over the past two decades, the ideological alignments of voters and parties have shifted. Republicans have lost many of their moderate identifiers, especially in the Northeast, and conservative Southerners, who a generation ago would have called themselves Democrats, now overwhelmingly identify with the Republican Party. This shift reflects long-term changes in the ideological orientations of the parties at the elite level and thus their brand names. The 1994 election was critically important in establishing a new label for the Republicans, because that election swept into office large numbers of Republican members of Congress in the South and eliminated much of the conservative wing of the Democratic Party. The parties, then, became more distinctive, presenting a much clearer choice to voters.[39]

Not all people fit neatly into one ideological camp or another. Some people do not think about politics in ideological or policy terms. Others are indifferent to the parties ideologically. A significant portion of Americans consider themselves to be centrists and feel that the Democrats are somewhat too liberal

38 For a detailed assessment of the political use of information-economizing devices such as party labels, see Arthur Lupia and Mathew D. McCubbins, *The Democratic Dilemma: Can Citizens Learn What They Need to Know?* (New York: Cambridge University Press, 1998).

39 See Hetherington, "Resurgent Mass Partisanship."

and the Republicans somewhat too conservative. They may turn one way or the other, but they do not have a strong affinity for either party. Other people feel pulled in different directions by different issues and concerns. A union member who strongly opposes abortion, for example, is drawn to the Democrats' labor policies and the Republicans' abortion policies. Campaigns target such cross-pressured voters, who are often pivotal in elections.[40]

Party Identification as Tally of Experiences. A third explanation is that party identification reflects experiences with political leaders and representatives, especially the presidents from each of the parties. As the political scientist Morris Fiorina put it, party identifications are running tallies of experience. Americans hold their presidents, and to a lesser extent Congress, accountable for the economic performance of the country and success in foreign affairs. A bad economy or a disastrous military intervention will lead voters to disapprove of the president and to lower their assessment of the president's party's ability to govern. Parties are, by this account, teams seeking to run the government. They consist of policy experts, managers, and leaders who will conduct foreign policy, economic policy, and domestic policies (such as environmental protection and health care). When things go well, voters infer that the incumbent party has a good approach to running national affairs, but when things go badly, they learn that the party lacks the people needed to run the government competently or the approach needed to produce economic prosperity, international peace, and other outcomes desired by the public. With each successive presidency and their experience of it, individuals update their beliefs about which party is better able to govern.

Psychological attachments, ideological affinities, and past experiences add up to form an individual's current party identification. But party is not the only factor in voting. Some partisans do defect, especially in elections when voters are dissatisfied with the incumbent party or are especially drawn to a particular candidate. Even in 2012, when 90 percent of partisans voted with their party's presidential candidate, significant defections occurred down the ticket. Republican nominee Mitt Romney handily carried Montana, North Dakota, and West Virginia by 15, 20, and 26 percentage points, respectively. But the Democratic Senate candidates in these states managed victories. Most strikingly, Joe Manchin won the West Virginia contest for U.S. Senate by 25 points, while Romney racked up an equally large victory in the state. The issues at stake and the characteristics of the candidates overrode party attachments in these races and drew large numbers of independents to the Democratic Senate candidates in otherwise Republican territory. We consider next how issues and candidates shape voting behavior.

---

40 For a more in-depth discussion of independent voters, policy indifference, and cross pressure, see Sunshine Hillygus and Todd Shields, *The Persuadable Voter: Wedge Issues in Presidential Campaigns* (Princeton, NJ: Princeton University Press, 2008).

Issues

Issues and policy preferences constitute a second factor influencing voters' decisions. Voting on issues and policies cuts to the core of our understanding of democratic accountability and electoral control over government. A simple, idealized account of **issue voting** goes as follows. Governments make policies and laws on a variety of issues that affect the public. Voters who disagree with those policies and laws on principle or who think those policies have failed will vote against those who made the decisions. Voters who support the policies or like the outcomes that government has produced will support the incumbent legislatures or party. It is important to note that policies are not taken as constants or fixed attributes of the candidates or parties. Rather, politicians choose what kinds of laws to enact and what kinds of administrative actions to take with the express aim of attracting electoral support. Voters, as we discussed in the previous chapter, have preferences about what policies the government pursues or what outcomes result, and they choose the candidates and parties that produce the best results or most preferred laws. Even party identifications, as we have noted, reflect the policy preferences of the voters and the policies pursued by the parties and candidates.

Voters' choice of issues usually involves a mix of their judgments about the past behavior of competing parties and candidates and their hopes and fears about candidates' future behavior. Political scientists call choices that focus on future behavior **prospective voting** and those based on past performance **retrospective voting**. To some extent, whether prospective or retrospective evaluation is more important in a particular election depends on the strategies of the competing candidates. Candidates always endeavor to define the issues of an election in terms that will serve their interests. Incumbents running during a period of prosperity will seek to take credit for the economy's happy state and define the election as revolving around their record of success. This strategy encourages voters to make retrospective judgments. By contrast, an insurgent running during a period of economic uncertainty will tell voters it is time for a change and ask them to make prospective judgments. Thus Barack Obama focused on the need for change in 2008, but the White House repeatedly stressed the need to stay the course in 2010 and 2012.

Not all issues, however, are alike. There are, as discussed in the previous chapter, different sorts of issues and dimensions to politics, such as economic concerns, moral questions, and foreign affairs. Voters may hold different views on each. Some voters might favor low taxes and no government restrictions on abortion (a libertarian perspective), while others want low taxes and a prohibition on abortion; still others may see a need for high taxes and no restrictions on abortion; and so on. And voters differ according to how important they judge each issue to be. Some voters weigh economics more heavily; others give the greatest weight to social issues; still others are national security voters. According to 2012 exit polls, the economy was viewed as the most important issue facing the country. An Edison Research poll that presented voters with four issues—foreign policy, federal budget deficit, the economy, and health care—found that 75 percent of those who identified health care as most important

---

issue voting

An individual's propensity to select candidates or parties based on the extent to which the individual agrees with one candidate more than others on specific issues

prospective voting

Voting based on the imagined future performance of a candidate

retrospective voting

Voting based on the past performance of a candidate

---

voted for Obama, while 65 percent who identified the budget deficit as most important voted for Romney. Among those who identified the economy as most important, the vote was close, with 47 percent for Obama and 51 percent for Romney.[41]

Issues differ politically in another important respect, and that is the extent to which the policy principle is invoked. Broadly speaking, issues may be distinguished as spatial issues and valence issues. **Spatial issues** are issues on which voters have preferences over what policy is pursued. On many issues voters have beliefs about which policies will lead to the best outcomes, or they have moral convictions that lead them to value the means, not just the ends. Valence issues are issues on which voters do not care about the means (the policy) only the ends (the outcome). Voters care about having peaceful and prosperous lives, quite apart from how they are achieved.

Spatial Issues. Many issues are characterized by a range of different policies and conflicting preferences over policies and outcomes. We call these spatial preferences because the choices can be mapped along a continuum or line, such as tax rates or size of government. Minimum wages offer an excellent example. Low-wage workers and unions favor minimum wages because they benefit from them. Low-wage workers will earn higher wages, and union members expect all wages to be pushed up with the minimum wage. Employers and investors tend not to like the minimum wage because it increases labor costs and reduces profit margins. Abortion rights provide another often-discussed example of a spatial issue. At one extreme are those who defend the legality of abortion under all circumstances; at the other extreme are those who want to ban the procedure under all circumstances. Between those two poles lie a range of policy alternatives, from putting some restrictions on access, to regulations on the time during pregnancy and procedures used, to allowing the practice only when the life of the mother is threatened. Public-opinion research (as discussed in Chapter 10) has demonstrated that public preferences are distributed across such policy options, with many people favoring a moderate approach of placing some restrictions on the practice. Minimum-wage laws and abortion laws exemplify the features of spatial issues—a range of policy options and a lack of consensus on the right policy.

Politicians compete for voters by pursuing particular policies that they think will attract the most voters. Romney promised to cut taxes and reduce government expenditures and regulations in order to stimulate economic growth. Obama proposed to increase taxes on those making over $250,000 a year but cut taxes on all others. On health care, the choice was starker still. President Obama touted the Patient Protection and Affordable Care Act as essential for containing health care costs in the United States over the long term. Mitt Romney promised to repeal the Patient Protection and Affordable Care Act, and Republican-oriented Super

 spatial issue

An issue for which a range of possible options or policies can be ordered, say, from liberal to conservative or from most expensive to least expensive

---

41 "Exit Polls: Casting Ballots in 2012," *Wall Street Journal,* November 7, 2012, http://online.wsj.com/article/SB10001424127887324894104578103850653249588.html (accessed 3/13/13).

PACs that aligned with the Romney campaign hammered away at the Patient Protection and Affordable Care Act as a government takeover of the health care industry. Voters made judgments based on a head-to-head comparison of many of these issues and the overall ideologies of these candidates.

Spatial voting is one way that voters solve the adverse selection problem. Adverse selection arises if we choose people for office who do not fit with our interests, due to a lack of information about the candidates. Party identities might lead us to vote for people with whom we fundamentally disagree or who will act contrary to our interests. The "one price fits all" label of the parties may not correctly reflect how an individual candidate will vote on legislation. If voters choose candidates on the basis of what policies those candidates represent or promise to support, then voters can choose the right people to represent their interests and values. Spatial voting also helps correct for moral hazard. Moral hazard arises if there is no accountability for legislative decisions made by legislators or executives. However, politicians must run for re-election. If people are attentive to what laws the politicians supported and opposed, then people can vote against politicians with whom they disagree. Recent research on congressional roll-call voting suggests that this is a strong factor in U.S. House elections and accounts for a significant portion of party identification.[42]

When voters engage in issue voting, competition between two candidates has the effect of pushing the candidates' issue positions toward the middle of the distribution of voters' preferences. This is known as the **median-voter theorem**, made famous by Duncan Black and Anthony Downs.[43] (Chapter 6 discussed the median-voter theorem in the context of congressional committees.) To see the logic of this claim in the context of elections, imagine a series of possible stances on a policy issue as points along a line, stretching from 0 to 100 (Figure 11.6). A voter is represented by an "ideal" policy and preferences, which decline as policy moves away from this ideal. Thus voters in group 1 prefer policy X_1 most, and their preference declines as the policy moves to the left or right of X_1. Voters whose ideal policy lies between, say, 0 and 25 are said to be liberal on this policy (groups 1 and 2), those whose ideal lies between 75 and 100 are conservative (groups 4 and 5), and those whose favorite policy is between 25 and 75 are moderate (group 3). An issue voter cares only about issue positions, not partisan loyalty or candidates' characteristics, and would, therefore, vote for the candidate whose announced policy is closest to his or her own most preferred policy.

Consider now an electorate of 125 voters evenly distributed among the five groups shown in Figure 11.6.[44] The middle group contains the median voter

median-voter theorem

A proposition predicting that when policy options can be arrayed along a single dimension, majority rule will pick the policy most preferred by the voter whose ideal policy is to the left of half of the voters and to the right of exactly half of the voters (see Chapter 6 for further discussion)

---

42 See Stephen Ansolabehere and Philip Jones, "Constituents' Responses to Congressional Roll-Call Voting," *American Journal of Political Science* 54 (July 2010): 583–97.

43 See Duncan Black, *The Theory of Committees and Elections*, 2nd ed. (Boston: Kluwer, 1998); and Anthony Downs, *An Economic Theory of Democracy* (New York: Harper & Row, 1957). A general, accessible treatment of this subject is found in Shepsle and Bonchek, *Analyzing Politics*, chap. 5.

44 For the sake of this illustration, 25 voters have been included in each group. This argument holds true with any distribution of voters among the groups.

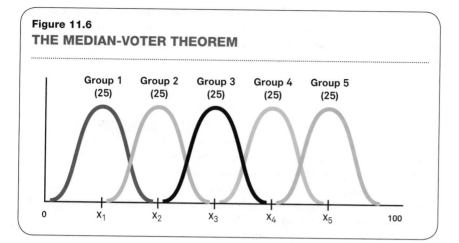

Figure 11.6

THE MEDIAN-VOTER THEOREM

because half or more of this electorate has an ideal policy at or to the left of X_3 (groups 1, 2, and 3), and half or more has an ideal policy at or to the right of X_3 (groups 3, 4, and 5). Group 3 is in the driver's seat, as the following reasoning suggests. If a candidate announces X_3 as her policy—the most preferred alternative of the median voter—and if her opponent picks any point to the right, then the median voter and all those with ideal policies to the left of the median voter's (groups 1–3) will support the first candidate. They constitute a majority, by definition of the median, so this candidate will win. Suppose instead that the opponent chose as his policy some point to the left of the median ideal policy. Then the median voter and all those with ideal policies to the right of the median voter's (groups 3–5) will support the first candidate—and she wins, again. In short, the median-voter theorem says that the candidate whose policy position is closest to the ideal policy of the median voter will defeat the other candidate in a majority contest. We can conclude from this brief analysis that issue voting encourages candidate convergence (in which both candidates move to cozy up to the position of the median voter). Even when voters are not exclusively issue voters, two-candidate competition still encourages a tendency toward convergence, although it may not fully run its course.[45]

Valence Issues. Some issues lack conflict: all people want the same outcome. All people want less crime, more prosperity and less poverty, less inflation, better health, peace, and security. They may have different beliefs about what to do to attain those objectives, but they don't really care about the means; they care about the outcome.

---

45 This convergence will also be a moderating force as candidates move toward what they believe will appeal to voters in the middle. But if the middle of the voter distribution of preferences tilts toward the right or the left, it may not be very moderate. If X_3, for example, were barely to the left of X_4, then the median voter would be fairly right wing rather than in the middle of the issue dimension.

In the context of elections, economic conditions are the most important **valence issue**. If voters are satisfied with their economic prospects, they tend to support the party in power, while voters' unease about the economy tends to favor the opposition. Richard Nixon, Ronald Reagan, Bill Clinton, and George W. Bush won re-election easily in the midst of favorable economies. Jimmy Carter in 1980 and George H. W. Bush in 1992 ran for re-election in the midst of economic downturns, and both lost.

How bad must the economy be in order for the incumbent to get turned out of office? Social scientists have developed several rules of thumb based on historical correlations between economic performance and the vote. A common sort of empirical analysis uses economic growth (annual percentage changes in gross domestic product) to predict the vote. The idea is that large numbers of voters decide to vote against the incumbent party in bad times and with the incumbent party in good times. Every individual may have a different sense of the economy, but adding up the 100 million or so votes will aggregate every individual's experiences and reflect roughly what is going on in the economy and how the economy affects his voting. Although the fit between economic growth and votes for the incumbent party is hardly perfect, correlation is sufficient to allow statistically minded political scientists to make forecasts. Roughly speaking, every additional 1 percent growth in GDP corresponds to a 1 percentage point increase in the incumbent president's party's vote.[46]

Another approach relies on the Consumer Confidence Index, which has been calculated over the past quarter-century by the Conference Board, a business research group. The Consumer Confidence Index is based on a public opinion survey that administers a simple battery of questions about people's sense of the economy in their area and their expectations over the coming months. A score above 100 means that most people are optimistic about the economy and that growth is strong. A score below 100 means that most people are pessimistic about the economy and job growth is weak. It has proven a fairly accurate predictor of presidential outcomes. A generally rosy view, indicated by a score greater than 100, augurs well for the party in power. An index score of less than 100, suggesting that voters are pessimistic about the economy's trend, suggests that incumbents should worry about their job prospects (Figure 11.7). In 2008, when the Republican Party held the White House, the Consumer Confidence Index fell below 30 in the months before the election, and the Republican candidate for president lost. In 2012, the Consumer Confidence Index was still below 100, but had risen considerably since 2008, to roughly 70, and Obama won re-election.

Economic voting is one way that voters solve the moral hazard problems inherent in representative democracy. They cannot monitor every policy that the government initiates. They do, however, have a rudimentary way to hold the government accountable—staying the course when times are good, and voting for change when the economy sours.

---

46 Perhaps the most comprehensive study of the responsiveness of elections to fluctuations in the U.S. economy is Robert Erikson, Michael MacKuen, and James Stimson, *The Macro-Polity* (New York: Cambridge University Press, 2002).

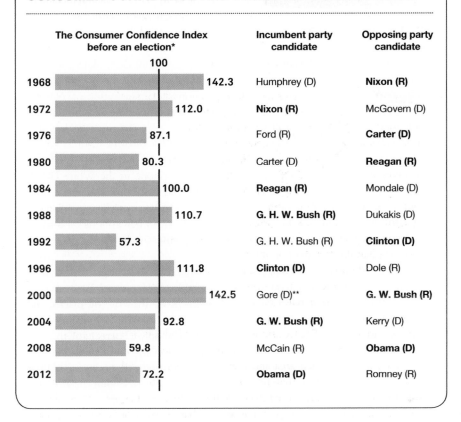

Figure 11.7

CONSUMER CONFIDENCE AND PRESIDENTIAL ELECTIONS

The Consumer Confidence Index before an election*	Incumbent party candidate	Opposing party candidate
1968 — 142.3	Humphrey (D)	**Nixon (R)**
1972 — 112.0	**Nixon (R)**	McGovern (D)
1976 — 87.1	Ford (R)	**Carter (D)**
1980 — 80.3	Carter (D)	**Reagan (R)**
1984 — 100.0	**Reagan (R)**	Mondale (D)
1988 — 110.7	**G. H. W. Bush (R)**	Dukakis (D)
1992 — 57.3	G. H. W. Bush (R)	**Clinton (D)**
1996 — 111.8	**Clinton (D)**	Dole (R)
2000 — 142.5	Gore (D)**	**G. W. Bush (R)**
2004 — 92.8	**G. W. Bush (R)**	Kerry (D)
2008 — 59.8	McCain (R)	**Obama (D)**
2012 — 72.2	**Obama (D)**	Romney (R)

*Survey was bimonthly before 1977, so figures for 1968, 1972, and 1976 are for October; from 1980 on, they are for September.
**Gore won the popular vote, but Bush was elected by the electoral college.
NOTE: A score above 100 means most people are optimistic about the economy. A score below 100 means most people are pessimistic about the economy. The candidate who won the election appears in bold.
SOURCE: *Bloomberg Markets.*

Candidate Characteristics

Candidates' personal attributes always influence voters' decisions. The more important characteristics that affect voters' choices are race, ethnicity, religion, gender, geography, and social background. In general, voters prefer candidates who are closer to themselves in terms of these categories. Voters presume that such candidates are likely to have views and perspectives close to their own. Moreover, they may be proud to see someone of their ethnic, religious, or geographic background in a position of leadership. This is why, for many years, politicians sought to "balance the ticket," making certain that their party's ticket included members of as many important groups as possible.

Just as a candidate's personal characteristics may attract some voters, so they may repel others. Many voters are prejudiced against candidates of certain ethnic, racial, or religious groups. And for many years, voters were reluctant to support the political candidacy of women, although this tendency appears to be changing.

Voters also pay attention to candidates' personality characteristics, such as their "competence," "honesty," and "vigor." Voters want these skills and attributes because the politicians who have them are more likely to produce good outcomes, such as laws that work, fair and honest administration of government, and ability to address crises. Candidates will emphasize certain qualities that they think all voters will value. An excellent example arose in the 2008 primary election between Hillary Clinton and Barack Obama. Clinton ran an ad that intended to show her experience and ability to solve crises. "It's 3 A.M. and your children are safely asleep. But there's a phone in the White House and it's ringing. Something's happening in the world. Your vote will decide who answers that call. . . . Whether it's someone tested and ready to lead in a dangerous world. . . ." Whether this ad had a lasting effect on perceptions of Obama is impossible to know, but it was designed to tap voters' belief in the need for a certain set of competencies in the White House.

Other personal characteristics of candidates are quite important as well. Obama's race weighed heavily for many voters. In 2004, George W. Bush won 43 percent of the vote of Hispanics, 12 percent of the vote of blacks, and 58 percent of the vote of whites. In 2012, Mitt Romney won 59 percent of the vote of whites (nearly the same as Bush), but he won only 27 percent of the vote of Hispanics and 6 percent of the vote of blacks. Obama's race raised the support for the Democrats among Hispanics and black voters. It also increased their turnout. Blacks were 8 percent of voters in 2004; they were 13 percent of voters in 2012. Gender, religion, and other characteristics also matter.

One of the most distinctive features of American politics is the apparent advantage that incumbents have, as we saw in Chapter 6. Why the incumbency advantage has emerged and grown remains something of a puzzle. Redistricting is almost certainly not the explanation: incumbency effects are as large in gubernatorial elections, where there are no districts, as in House elections. It is thought that about half of the incumbency advantage reflects the activities of the legislator in office; it is the result of voters rewarding incumbents for their performance. The other half of the incumbency advantage evidently reflects not the incumbents but their opponents.[47] The typical challenger in U.S. elections may not have the personal appeal of the typical incumbent; after all, the

---

47 The partitioning of the incumbency effect into officeholder advantages and challenger qualities begins with the important work of Gary C. Jacobson. See, for example, his text *The Politics of Congressional Elections*, 7th ed. (White Plains, NY: Longman, 2008). Estimating exactly what fraction of the incumbency effect is due to officeholder benefits is tricky. See Stephen Ansolabehere, James M. Snyder, Jr., and Charles H. Stewart III, "Old Voters, New Voters, and the Personal Vote: Using Redistricting to Measure the Incumbency Advantage," *American Journal of Political Science* 44, no. 1 (January 2000): 17–34.

typical incumbent has already won office once. Moreover, challengers usually lack the experience and resources that the incumbent has for running a campaign. This is critical. The ability to communicate with the voters can give a politician the edge in close elections.

Although party, issues, and candidate characteristics are perhaps the three most important factors shaping voting decisions, there is much debate among political scientists as to the relative importance of each. Problems of measurement and the limitations of research methods have made it exceedingly difficult to parse the relative importance of these factors in voters' thinking. Recent scholarship suggests that they have roughly equal weight in explaining the division of the vote in national elections.[48] Part of the difficulty in understanding their importance is that the extent to which these factors matter depends on the information levels of the electorate. In the absence of much information, most voters rely almost exclusively on party cues. A highly informed electorate relies more heavily on issues and candidate characteristics.[49]

CAMPAIGNS: MONEY, MEDIA, AND GRASS ROOTS

American political campaigns are freewheeling events with few restrictions on what candidates may say or do. Candidates in hotly contested House and Senate races spend millions of dollars to advertise on television and radio, as well as direct mail and door-to-door canvassing. Those seeking office are in a race to become as well known and as well liked as possible and to get more of their supporters to vote. Federal laws limit how much an individual or organization may give to a candidate, but with the exception of presidential campaigns, place no restrictions on how much a candidate or party committee may spend.

Adding to the freewheeling nature of campaigns is their organizational structure. Most political campaigns are temporary organizations. They form for the sole purpose of winning the coming elections and disband shortly afterward. To be sure, political parties in the United States have a set of permanent, professional campaign organizations that raise money, strategize, recruit candidates, and distribute resources. These are, on the Republican side, the Republican National Committee, the National Republican Senatorial Committee, and the National Republican Congressional Committee. On the Democratic side are the Democratic National Committee, the Democratic Senatorial Campaign Committee, and the Democratic Congressional Campaign Committee. They account

---

48 See Stephen Ansolabehere, Jonathan Rodden, and James M. Snyder, Jr., "Issue Voting," *American Political Science Review* (May 2008).

49 The classic study showing this is Philip Converse, "The Nature of Belief Systems in Mass Publics," in *Ideology and Discontent*, David Apter, ed. (New York: Free Press, 1964).

for roughly one-third of the money in politics and have considerable expertise. But most campaigns are formed by and around individual candidates, who often put up the initial cash to get the campaign rolling and rely heavily on family and friends as volunteers. Thousands of such organizations are at work during an election. The two presidential campaigns operate 50 different state-level operations, with other campaigns competing for 34 Senate seats, 435 House seats, dozens of gubernatorial and other statewide offices, and thousands of state legislative seats. There is relatively little coordination among these myriad campaigns, though they all simultaneously work toward the same end—persuading as many people as possible to vote for their candidate on Election Day.

What It Takes to Win

All campaigns, big and small, face similar challenges—how to bring people in, how to raise money, how to coordinate activities, what messages to run, and how to communicate with the public. There is no single best way to run a campaign. There are many tried-and-true approaches, especially building up a campaign from many local connections, from the grass roots. Candidates have to meet as many people as possible and get their friends and their friends' friends to support them. In-person campaigning becomes increasingly difficult in larger constituencies. Candidates continually experiment with new ways of communicating with the public and new ways of organizing in order to more efficiently reach large segments of the electorate. In the 1920s, radio advertising eclipsed handbills and door-to-door canvassing, as broadcasting captured economies of scale. In the 1960s, television began to eclipse radio. In the 1980s and 1990s, cable television and innovations in marketing (especially phone polling and focus groups) allowed candidates to target very specific demographic groups through the media. The great innovation of the Obama campaign was to meld Internet networking tools with old-style organizing methods to develop a massive communications and fund-raising network, what came to be called a "netroots" campaign.

However they are organized, campaigns play an essential role in American democracy. They are the opportunity for the politicians to present themselves to the public to explain who they are, what they have accomplished, and what they will do in office. Television advertisements, get-out-the-vote activities, direct mail, and the like provide voters with factual information about the personal characteristics and ideologies of the candidates, about the meaning of the party labels, and about what issues distinguish the politicians.

Campaigns are also a time when the foibles and failures of those in office may be revealed. Challengers must make the case that a new direction is needed, and that case rests on showing that the incumbent is the wrong person to represent the constituency (a case of adverse selection) or has failed to do the job as constituents wanted (a case of moral hazard). Incumbents, for their part, try to appeal to voters on the basis of their ideological fit with their constituents and their performance in office. It has become an assumption of American elections and election law that candidates and parties will mount competitive campaigns to win office. They will spend millions, even billions of dollars, to persuade people to vote and how to vote. And because of those efforts voters will understand better the choices they face in the elections. In short, campaigns inform voters, and they do so through competition.

In addition to being costly, American political campaigns are long, often spanning years. Campaigns for the presidency officially launch a year and a half to two years in advance of Election Day. Serious campaigns for the U.S. House of Representatives begin at least a year ahead of the general election date and often span the better part of two years. To use the term of the Federal Election Commission, an election is a two-year *cycle*, not a single day or even the period between Labor Day and Election Day loosely referred to as "the general election."

The long campaigns in the United States are due in large part to the effort required to mount a campaign. There are roughly 315 million people in the United States, and the voting-age population exceeds 240 million people. Communicating with all of those people is an expensive and time-consuming enterprise. A simple calculation reveals the challenge. Suppose you ran for president of the United States. Sending one piece of mail to each household in the United States would cost approximately $100 million dollars. That is probably the minimum imaginable campaign effort. How long would it take to raise $100 million and mobilize such an effort to communicate with the American people? In the 2012 election cycle, the Barack Obama campaign and allied committees spent $1.20 billion; Mitt Romney's campaign and allied committees spent $1.25 billion—almost $2.5 billion total. Approximately half of that sum was spent to purchase airtime for television advertisements. That money was raised through personal and political networks that the campaigns built up over months, even years of effort. It takes extensive operations to reach out to so many people and to raise such vast sums. Simply putting such an organization in place takes months.

The campaign season is further extended by the election calendar. American elections proceed in two steps: the party primary elections and the general election. General elections for federal offices are set by the U.S. Constitution to take place on the first Tuesday after the first Monday in November. The first presidential caucuses and primaries come early in January and last through the beginning of June. State and congressional primaries do not follow the same calendar, but most occur in the spring and early summer, with a handful of some states waiting to hold their nominating elections until September of the election year. The immediate result of this yearlong calendar of elections is to stretch the campaigns over the entire election year.

American electoral campaigns contrast starkly with those in other democracies, such as Germany, France, Japan, and even the United Kingdom. Parliamentary systems have short campaigns. Once the government calls for an election, the campaign proceeds for a few months, and an election is held. The yearslong gestation of an American election is unheard of and even considered unseemly in most other democracies. Most democracies also limit candidates' campaign expenditures and fund-raising activities, constraining the ability of individual politicians to develop personal campaign organizations and appeals. Money and other resources in other democracies flow through party organizations, often with little government oversight. Most democracies also regulate how candidates and parties campaign. Very few countries permit television advertising, phone banks, or door-to-door canvassing. Posters and billboards are commonplace in other democracies, as are public campaign forums. These restrictions on campaign communications make the campaigns themselves less important and make media coverage of the parties, the candidates, and the government more prominent.

Campaign Finance

The expense, duration, and chaos of American campaigns have prompted many efforts at reform, including attempts to limit campaign spending, shorten the campaign season, and restrict what candidates and organizations can say in advertisements. The most sweeping campaign reforms came in 1971, when Congress passed the Federal Elections Campaign Act (FECA). It limited the amounts that a single individual could contribute to a candidate or party to $1,000 per election for individuals and $5,000 for organizations (these limits have since been increased, as Table 11.1 indicates). It further regulated how business firms, unions, and other organizations could give money, prohibiting donations directly from the organization's treasury and requiring the establishment of a separate, segregated fund—a **political action committee (PAC)**. It established public funding for presidential campaigns and tied those funds to expenditure limits. And it set up the Federal Election Commission (FEC) to oversee public disclosure of information and to enforce the laws.[50] Congress has amended the act several times, most importantly in the Bipartisan Campaign Reform Act of 2002 (BCRA, also called the McCain-Feingold Act, after senators John McCain and Russell Feingold, its primary sponsors in the Senate). The McCain-Feingold Act prohibited unlimited party spending (called soft money) and banned certain sorts of political attack advertisements from interest groups in the last weeks of a campaign. See Table 11.1 for a summary of some of the rules governing campaign finance in federal elections.

FECA also established public funding for presidential campaigns. If a candidate agrees to abide by spending limits, that candidate's campaign is eligible for matching funds in primary elections and full public funding in the general election. The general election amount was set at $20 million in 1974 and allowed to increase with inflation. Until 2000, nearly all candidates bought into the system. George W. Bush chose to fund his 2000 primary election campaign outside this system and spent $500 million to win the Republican nomination. Barack Obama and Hillary Clinton ignored the public financing system in their 2008 primary contest, and Obama opted out of the public system in the general election as well, allowing him to spend several hundred million more dollars than the Republican nominee, John McCain. In 2012, neither Obama nor the Republican candidates for president used public funding.

---

political action committee (PAC)

A private group that raises and distributes funds for use in election campaigns

---

50 The FEC's website is an excellent resource for those interested in U.S. campaign finance (www.fec.gov).

Table 11.1

FEDERAL CAMPAIGN FINANCE CONTRIBUTION LIMITS

	To each candidate or candidate committee per election	To national party committee per calendar year	To state, district, and local party committee per calendar year	To any other political committee per calendar year
Individual may give	$2,600*	$32,400*	$10,000 (combined limit)	$5,000
National party committee may give	$5,000	No limit	No limit	$5,000
State, district, and local party committee may give	$5,000 (combined limit)	No limit	No limit	$5,000 (combined limit)
PAC (multicandidate) may give	$5,000	$15,000	$5,000 (combined limit)	$5,000
PAC (not multicandidate) may give	$2,600*	$32,400*	$10,000 (combined limit)	$5,000
Authorized campaign committee may give	$2,000†	No limit	No limit	$5,000

*These contribution limits are increased for inflation in odd-numbered years.
**A multicandidate committee is a political committee with more than 50 contributors that has been registered for at least six months and, with the exception of state party committees, has made contributions to five or more candidates for federal office.
†A federal candidate's authorized committee(s) may contribute no more than $2,000 per election to another federal candidate's authorized committee(s).
SOURCE: Federal Election Commission, www.fec.gov/pages/brochures/contriblimits.shtml (accessed 7/17/13).

FECA originally went much further than the law that survives today. Congress originally passed mandatory caps on spending by House and Senate candidates and prohibited organizations from running their own independent campaigns on behalf of or in opposition to a candidate (and not coordinated with any candidate). James Buckley, a candidate for U.S. Senate in New York, challenged the law, arguing that the restrictions on spending and contributions limited his rights to free speech and that FEC had excessive administrative power. In the 1976 landmark case *Buckley v. Valeo*, the U.S. Supreme Court agreed in part.[51] The Court ruled that "money is speech," but the government also has a compelling interest in protecting elections from corrupt practices, such as bribery through large campaign donations. The justices declared the limits on candidate spending unconstitutional because they violated free speech rights of candidates and groups. However, the need to protect the integrity of the electoral process led the justices to leave contribution limits in place. The presidential public-funding system was also validated because it is voluntary. Candidates can opt into the system, but they are not required to; hence, there is no violation of free speech. What survived *Buckley* is a system in which candidates, groups, and parties may spend as much as they like to win office, but donations must come in small amounts. In an expensive election, campaigns must accumulate their resources from large numbers of individuals and groups. This is a more democratic process of campaign finance, but it increases the effort and time needed to construct a campaign.

The Supreme Court's decision in *Buckley*, though highly controversial, rests on an essential truth of American democracy and elections. The First Amendment right to free speech amounts to a "profound national commitment to the principle that debate on public issues should be uninhibited, robust, and wide-open."[52] "In a republic where the people are sovereign," the Court continued, "the ability of the citizenry to make informed choices among candidates for office is essential, for the identities of those who are elected will inevitably shape the course that we follow as a nation. . . . It can hardly be doubted that the constitutional guarantee has its fullest and most urgent application precisely to the conduct of campaigns for political office."[53] Without competitive political campaigns, voters would lack the information to make electoral decisions. Most of us might not even know when or how to vote; we would certainly lack basic information about the choices before us.

In 2010, the Supreme Court reinforced its reasoning in *Buckley v. Valeo* in the case *Citizens United v. Federal Election Commission*.[54] In *Citizens United* the justices ruled that the BCRA of 2002 had erred in imposing restrictions on independent spending by corporations. It overturned key components of the BCRA and reversed its ruling in the case that had upheld BCRA, *McConnell v. Federal Election Commission*.[55] The majority opinion struck down limits on independent expenditures from corporate treasuries but kept in place limits on direct contributions from corporations and other organizations to candidates. The majority opinion went further than past decisions, however, in solidifying corporations' right to free political speech, on par with the right to free speech of individuals. In the wake of this decision, two sorts of organizations formed—501c(4) organizations,

---

51 *Buckley v. Valeo*, 424 U.S. 1 (1976).

52 The majority opinion in *Buckley* quotes an earlier landmark case, *New York Times Co. v. Sullivan*, 376 U.S. 254 (1964).

53 *Buckley v. Valeo*, 424 U.S. 1 (1976).

54 *Citizens United v. Federal Election Commission*, 558 U.S. 310 (2010).

55 *McConnell v. Federal Election Commission*, 540 U.S. 93 (2003).

---

which derive their title from the section of the tax code that allows such entities, and Super PACs. Each can raise and spend unlimited amounts on campaigns, though Super PACs are subject to more disclosure laws. Super PACs spent a total of approximately $546.5 million in 2012, most of that on the presidential election. However, independent expenditures from other organizations decreased, so the increase in total independent spending was on the order of $300 million from 2008 to 2012. That is a hefty sum, but amounts to only $2 per voter.

Congressional Campaigns

Congressional campaigns share a number of important features with presidential campaigns, but they are also distinctive. One of the salient features of congressional campaigns is the incumbent advantage. While there is an incumbent advantage for sitting presidents, the two-term limit on the president means that incumbency is a more important feature for congressional representatives, who have no term limits. Beginning around 1970, political scientists noted a peculiar change overtaking electoral politics, especially in congressional elections. Incumbents were winning re-election at higher rates than in previous generations and by wider margins. Closer examination of the election results revealed that this phenomenon appeared due to incumbency itself. As a simple natural experiment, Professor Robert Erikson compared the same politician running for election not as an incumbent and as an incumbent. In the first sort of election, the politician ran for a seat left vacant by an incumbent's retirement or against an incumbent and won. In the second sort of election, the politician had just won the previous election and had to defend the seat in the next election as a "sophomore." Erikson called the increase in the politician's vote share from the first election to the second the "sophomore surge." It is the increase in the vote attributable solely to the fact that the politician ran as an incumbent rather than as a non-incumbent. Erikson found an incumbency effect of approximately 5 percentage points around 1970. If the party division of the vote in a congressional district without an incumbent is, say, 50–50, then in a race where one candidate is the incumbent, that same district would vote for the incumbent with 55 percent to 45 percent.

The incumbency advantage has increased both in magnitude and in importance in U.S. elections. Incumbency advantages in House elections grew rapidly beginning in the mid-1950s, when they were worth only 1 to 2 percentage points, to 5 or 6 percentage points by the end of the 1960s. They have continued to inch upward, and today, almost every elective office at the state and federal level exhibits an incumbency advantage. Those advantages have ranged from about 5 percent in state legislative elections to 10 percent for U.S. House, U.S. Senate, and governor. A 10 percent incumbency advantage is a massive electoral edge. It turns a competitive race into a blowout for the incumbent.[56]

---

56 See Stephen Ansolabehere and James M. Snyder, Jr., "The Incumbency Advantage in U.S. Elections: An Analysis of State and Federal Offices, 1942–2000," *Election Law Journal* 1 (2002): 315–38.

Congressional incumbents' advantages arise in campaign spending as well as votes. Like presidential campaigns, congressional campaigns have witnessed increasing amounts of spending over time. The average U.S. House incumbent in 2012 spent $1.6 million, to the $260,000 spent by the typical challenger. Once a campaign has enough money to initiate operations, it begins to communicate with the voters, often starting small by attending meetings with various groups. A successful campaign builds on early successes, bringing in more supporters and volunteers and culminating with intensive advertising campaigns in the final months or weeks before Election Day. Although the Democratic and Republican parties may help campaigns that have a good shot of succeeding, they typically come in late. Every campaign for Congress or president is built by the individual candidates and their close friends and associates from the ground up. The personal style of political campaigning that Americans have come to appreciate reflects an enormous investment of time and resources, an investment that takes the better part of a year to grow. Incumbent members of Congress have particular advantages in campaign fund-raising. They have already been tested, they have their campaign organizations in place, and they have connections in their constituencies, as well as in Washington, D.C.

Effectiveness of Campaigns

Campaigns address the information problems discussed at the beginning of this chapter. In mass elections, individual voters have little incentive or opportunity to find information about the many candidates and ballot measures at issue. This situation creates an opportunity for candidates and parties. Through advertising, get-out-the-vote activities, and other campaign efforts, politicians try to shape the electorate and the outcome of the election. Candidates and parties bear much of the responsibility and costs for gathering and disseminating electoral information and for creating an informed electorate. Through their campaigns, parties and candidates spend money in order to present voters with the information they need to make a decision come Election Day—what the candidates and parties have done and what they promise to do, who they are, and which person is right for the job and the challenges the country faces.

Political scientists have long wondered how much that money matters. After all, the high rates of party loyalty among most people would suggest that there is only so much that campaigns can do. Research on the effectiveness of campaign spending and advertising began in earnest in the 1970s with the pathbreaking studies of Professor Gary Jacobson. Jacobson found that challengers did better in races in which they spent more money, holding constant the underlying partisan division of the district, but that incumbents who spent higher amounts did no better. Part of the explanation, Jacobson reasoned, was that vulnerable incumbents would have to raise and spend more money, so the observation of high spending reflected the eventual outcome as much as it influenced it. It was impossible to tell how much money influenced votes and how much votes influenced money.[57] A decades-long debate over how to measure the effectiveness of campaign spending has ensued, most of it focusing on the same sort of aggregate data that Jacobson used.

In the 1990s, political scientists turned to experiments. Rather than look at the correlation between how many votes candidates received and how much they spent, we could manipulate who sees TV commercials or receives mailers and then measure their attitudes toward the candidates, whether they vote, and how they vote. The first such study was conducted by Stephen Ansolabehere and Shanto Iyengar, who found that seeing a single TV commercial from a candidate in the context of a news program increased support for that candidate by, on average, 7 percentage points. Importantly, that holds constant how much the other candidate spends and other important features of the electoral context. Interestingly, the effect of advertising was found to vary across people. Those who were ideologically hostile to a candidate could not be persuaded to change their opinions and cross party lines. TV ads from Democrats had very little effects on Republican viewers, and ads from Republicans had very little effect on Democrats. Rather, the ads affected independent voters and people of the same party or ideological orientation as the candidate who aired the ad. This finding echoes a much older argument owing to the social psychologist Paul Lazarsfeld. Lazarsfeld studied communications among people in the 1940s and found that political messages and conversations tended not to *convert* people but to *reinforce* their beliefs. Such is the case today. TV ads strengthen support for a candidate among that candidate's partisans and among independents.[58]

Following on this project, Alan Gerber and Donald Green initiated a new research program to measure the effectiveness of canvassing, direct mail, and other means of voter mobilization. Working with political campaigns, they conducted dozens of field experiments in which some households and precincts received get-out-the-vote messages and some did not. They then measured the participation rates and vote shares of households and precincts of those who received the messages and those who did not. Although the effects were somewhat smaller than the TV advertising studies, they too found significant effects of campaign advertising on rates of participation and candidates' vote shares.[59] These research projects provide clear and strong evidence of the effectiveness of campaigns, a conclusion masked by studies of aggregate election patterns.

Elections, of course, fail to serve the important function of informing the electorate when competition is weak or lacking all together. At times in our history, there have been prolonged outages of electoral competition. Perhaps the most infamous example took the form of Democratic dominance in the South

---

57 Gary C. Jacobson, *Money in Congressional Elections* (New Haven, CT: Yale University Press, 1980).

58 Stephen Ansolabehere and Shanto Iyengar, *Going Negative* (New York: Free Press, 1996).

59 Alan Gerber and Donald Green, *Get Out the Vote*, 2nd ed. (Washington, DC: Brookings Institution, 2008).

from the 1890s through 1960s—a political arrangement termed the Solid South. During this period, election laws were employed to exclude blacks and many poor whites from primary elections, and Republicans comprised a relatively small part of the electorate. As a result, Democrats won nearly every House seat, Senate seat, and gubernatorial race in the South from the end of Reconstruction through the passage of the Voting Rights Act in 1965. Shifting political alignments in the South during the 1960s and 1970s brought a rapid rise in Republican fortunes in the South and with that the benefits of electoral competition.

Today, some observers fear that the incumbency advantage stifles electoral competition. As we noted earlier, incumbents enjoy a sizable electoral advantage, a bonus of roughly 5 to 10 percentage points. Some of that advantage reflects the voters' reward of the incumbents' performance in office, but some of it may also reflect an imbalance in campaign politics. That imbalance is most obvious in campaign funds. The average House challenger in 2012 raised and spent a little over $260,000; the typical incumbent raised and spent more than six times as much, approximately $1.6 million. To put matters another way, incumbents could spend roughly $2.30 per voting-age person in the district; the typical challenger could spend only $0.38 per voting-age person. Incumbents' funding advantages allow them to communicate more extensively with constituents than their opponents.

THE 2012 ELECTION

In the fall of 2012, more than 132 million Americans went to the polls to select a president, members of Congress, governors, and numerous other officials. Voters re-elected Barack Obama to the presidency and confirmed the Democratic Party's control of the Senate and the Republican Party's majority in the House of Representatives. Obama won 65 million votes, roughly 51 percent, while his Republican challenger, Mitt Romney, received about 61 million votes, or 47 percent. Though the president's margin of victory was about 5 percentage points less than in 2008, it was enough to give him 332 electoral votes, 62 more than the 270 needed to win a majority in the electoral college (Figure 11.8). The president's margin of victory was built on a coalition of women, working-class voters, and minority voters in several key battleground states. Despite the billions of dollars spent by candidates and the hoopla of the campaign, the 2012 election was decided more by demographic realities than political rhetoric.

Generally speaking, incumbent presidents have a substantial advantage when they seek re-election to a second term. During the course of American history, incumbent presidents standing for re-election have won about 70 percent of the time. Despite this advantage of incumbency, the re-election of President Obama in 2012 was never a foregone conclusion. Although Obama scored major legislative successes early in his first term, these accomplishments, especially the Affordable Care Act, were controversial. To make matters worse, unemployment remained high throughout Obama's first four years. The

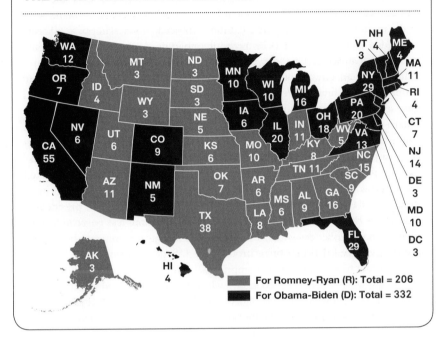

Figure 11.8

DISTRIBUTION OF ELECTORAL VOTES IN THE 2012 PRESIDENTIAL ELECTION

For Romney-Ryan (R): Total = 206	
For Obama-Biden (D): Total = 332	

combination of controversial legislation and a weak economic record made the incumbent vulnerable coming into the 2012 election season.

In his 2008 campaign, Obama energized legions of young supporters who saw in the senator from Illinois a charismatic and energetic politician who would pursue a progressive social agenda and bring an end to America's wars in the Middle East. Many liberal voters had also been eager to elect America's first black president and thus make a break with the nation's long and unhappy history of racial oppression and discrimination. Once in office, Obama was keen to make good on his promise of change. He worked to bring an end to the war in Iraq and to wind down the war in Afghanistan, partly in order to shift the nation's spending priorities from the military to domestic social needs. In the realm of domestic policy, between 2008 and 2010, with both chambers of Congress controlled by the Democrats, the president succeeded in passing a $700 billion economic stimulus bill, a law that guaranteed equal pay for women, new financial regulations, and an extensive overhaul of the nation's health care laws. President Obama also appointed two women to the U.S. Supreme Court. The Affordable Care Act, which came to be known as "Obamacare," became a flashpoint for the 2010 and 2012 elections. The law sought to make access to health care universal: it required individuals without insurance to purchase insurance, it required businesses to provide insurance, it set up insurance pools to allow those without care to purchase inexpensive insurance, it required states to extend their Medicaid coverage, and it forbade insurance companies from excluding people from coverage for preexisting conditions.

These successes came at a cost. The president appeared to push aggressively a liberal legislative agenda, and the opportunity for a corrective came at the 2010 midterm election. It is often the case that the president's party loses some seats in the midterm elections, but in 2010 the Democrats lost a whopping 60 seats and ceded control of the House to the Republicans. A majority of Americans opposed Obamacare. They saw it as a costly government takeover of a major industry and an unwarranted intrusion into the lives of all Americans. Many people also saw financial reform and economic stimulus as policies that would impose too much regulation or create mounting debt problems. The backlash against Obama's early legislative successes took the form of a loose but broad conservative movement called the Tea Party, whose organizations sponsored rallies and protests and recruited candidates to run for office. Against this background of dissatisfaction and dissent, Republican challengers in 2010 defeated numerous Democratic members of Congress and left the president with a Republican House of Representatives that vowed to block any new presidential initiatives. Over the next two years, the president and Congress engaged in acrimonious battles over the federal budget and the federal government's borrowing power (the debt limit) that twice brought the U.S. government to the brink of financial ruin before last-minute compromises temporarily averted disaster.

All the while, the nation's economy, which had been battered by recession in 2007 and 2008, showed only tepid signs of recovery throughout Obama's first four years in office. For much of the president's first term, unemployment remained in the uncomfortably high 8 to 9 percent range, with hundreds of thousands of recent college graduates finding themselves unemployed or underemployed; the housing market was weak; and a number of major financial institutions seemed to totter on the edge of failure. As a result, President Obama's re-election hardly seemed assured. However, the Republicans needed to find a candidate who could defeat the president and appeal to the various factions of their party.

Political Parties in 2012: Unity and Division

The American political landscape experienced a national realignment of political forces in the 1960s and 1970s, as we will discuss in Chapter 12. Over time, the Democrats became a much more liberal party and the Republicans a much more conservative political force. This ideological realignment of the two parties is one reason that partisan struggles in Congress—and between Congress and the White House when party control of the two branches is divided—have become especially intense in recent years.

The growing ideological split between the two parties has not meant that each party is ideologically uniform, however. Rather, disputes among the various liberal groups within the Democratic Party and among the disparate conservative groups in the GOP have also been quite heated. In 2012, the divisions among the Democrats were relatively inconsequential for the simple reason that the party's presidential nominee was a given. Like it or not, all the party's factions had to line up behind President Obama, or risk losing the White House altogether. The divisions in the GOP, however, did matter, and the Republican nomination battle took place among candidates representing different factions within the party. Former Massachusetts governor and successful financier Mitt Romney spoke for the party's fiscal conservatives, who feel excessive taxation and regulation are the major issues facing the country. Former Pennsylvania senator Rick Santorum and Minnesota congresswoman Michele Bachmann were the champions of the social conservatives, who seek to end abortion and prevent same-sex marriage. Former House Speaker Newt Gingrich represented neoconservatives who favor a robust military policy, and former Texas congressman Ron Paul spoke for the libertarians and isolationists. Several other candidates, who lacked significant bases of support, including business executive Herman Cain, Texas governor Rick Perry, former Utah governor and ambassador Jon Huntsman, former New Mexico governor Gary Johnson, and former Minnesota governor Tim Pawlenty, sought to stake out positions that might attract supporters if the front-runners faltered.

Between May 2011 and February 2012, Republican hopefuls engaged in a series of televised debates where each argued that he or she would be best able to defeat the Democrats. The candidates were generally polite to one another and saved their criticisms for Obama and the Democrats. Gradually, candidates who found themselves unable to attract much support dropped out of the race, and by February 2012, only four remained: Gingrich, Paul, Romney, and Santorum. Over the next several months, these four candidates faced one another in a series of Republican primaries and caucuses, competing for the votes of 2,286 Republican convention delegates, with 1,144 needed to win the nomination.

From the beginning, Romney's superior organization and financial base made him the front-runner. The GOP's social and religious conservatives, though, were unenthusiastic about the former Massachusetts governor. Some saw him as a liberal in Republican clothing while others, particularly evangelical Protestants, were unhappy about the idea of a member of the Mormon faith leading the party. These groups gave their support to Rick Santorum, who eventually carried 11 states and more than 20 percent of the primary vote. By April 2012, though, Romney had clearly won the delegate votes needed for the nomination, and Santorum suspended his campaign.

Having won the Republican nomination, Romney moved to reassure the party's social conservatives that he was worthy of their enthusiastic support in the general election. One of the biggest challenges facing candidates is motivating putative supporters to actually *vote* come Election Day. Conservatives would not jump to the Obama camp, but anything less than enthusiastic participation in the campaign by social conservatives would doom the GOP's ticket. Accordingly, Romney endorsed a party platform that would appeal to this group. Its provisions included a constitutional amendment to ban abortion; elimination of government-funded family planning programs, with the exception of abstinence-only education; and a program of detention for "dangerous" aliens. Other provisions included repealing the Affordable Care Act and reducing taxes. As icing on the conservative cake, Romney chose as his vice-presidential running mate Congressman Paul Ryan of Wisconsin. Ryan had vigorously opposed Democratic fiscal and social policies and was enthusiastically supported by the GOP's social and fiscal conservatives.

The General Election

U.S. presidential elections are shaped by fundamental forces: the economy, foreign conflicts, the underlying partisanship and composition of the electorate, and the approval rating of the incumbent president. The election in 2012 proved to be no exception. But the fundamentals in 2012 pointed in conflicting directions. Barack Obama was a fairly popular incumbent who boasted significant foreign policy successes; however, he also had to defend a record of four years of slow economic growth and, in some parts of the country, economic stagnation. No president has been re-elected with an unemployment rate exceeding 8 percent, but no president with an approval rating of 50 percent has failed to win re-election. Political scientists' and economists' forecasts based on these fundamentals predicted a very tight election, with a slight edge to the president. The average of many forecasting models predicted that President Obama would win 50.3 percent of the vote, but there was considerable uncertainty associated with that forecast.

Table 11.2A
CONGRESSIONAL ELECTION RESULTS, 1994–2012

HOUSE OF REPRESENTATIVES					
YEAR	TURNOUT	PARTY RATIO	SEAT SHIFT	DEMOCRATS RE-ELECTED	REPUBLICANS RE-ELECTED
1994	41.1%	204 D, 230 R	+54 R	89.3%	99.4%
1996	51.7	207 D, 227 R	+3 D	98.3	91.4
1998	38.1	211 D, 223 R	+4 D	99.5	97.2
2000	54.2	212 D, 222 R	+1 D	98.0	97.5
2002	39.5	205 D, 229 R	+8 R	97.4	97.5
2004	60.3	201 D, 232 R	+3 R	97.4	99.0
2006	40.2	233 D, 202 R	+30 D	100.0	89.6
2008	61.0	257 D, 178 R	+24 D	97.9	92.1
2010	37.8	193 D, 242 R	+64 R	78.8	98.7
2012	54.0	201 D, 234 R	+8 D	89.0	90.0

SOURCE: Michael McDonald, United States Election Project, http://elections.gmu.edu/ (accessed 7/15/13).

In recent years, the bedrock base of GOP support has consisted of reasonably affluent, educated, middle-aged, middle-class white men living in suburban and rural areas. The Democrats, on the other hand, have been able to rely on the votes of a majority of women, less affluent Americans, urban residents, younger voters, African Americans, and, increasingly, Hispanic voters. While there are certainly poor Republicans and affluent Democrats, this split approaches a classic division between the "have mores" and "have lesses." Mitt Romney alluded to this division when he said, in what he thought to be a closed-door meeting with Republican donors, that 47 percent of Americans paid few taxes, depended on government handouts, and would never vote for him. When news of Romney's comments leaked, Republicans sought to contain the damage but did not necessarily dispute the accuracy of Romney's analysis.

The division of the electorate into "have mores" and "have lesses" also dictated a major struggle in the campaign. In a number of states, Republican governors and legislatures enacted voter ID laws requiring prospective voters to present valid, government-issued photo identification cards at the polls. Republicans said such laws were needed to prevent fraudulent voting. The GOP's calculus, though,

Table 11.2B

CONGRESSIONAL ELECTION RESULTS, 1994–2012

			SENATE		
YEAR	TURNOUT	PARTY RATIO	SEAT SHIFT	DEMOCRATS RE-ELECTED	REPUBLICANS RE-ELECTED
1994	41.1%	47 D, 53 R	+10 R	87.5%	80.0%
1996	51.7	45 D, 55 R	–	100.0	85.7
1998	38.1	45 D, 55 R	–	92.3	87.5
2000	54.2	50 D, 50 R	+5 D	93.3	64.3
2002	39.5	48 D, 51 R	+1 R	83.3	93.3
2004	60.3	44 D, 55 R	+4 R	92.9	100.0
2006	40.2	50 D, 49 R	+6 D	100.0	57.1
2008	61.0	59 D, 41 R	+8 D	100.0	66.7
2010	37.8	53 D, 47 R	+6 R	76.9	100.0
2012	54.0	55 D*, 45 R	+2 D	100.0	71.0

* Includes two Independents who caucus with the Democrats.

was that less-educated and minority voters (who tend to vote Democratic) were less likely to be able to produce valid ID at the polls and would thus be barred from voting. Two dozen states enacted voter ID laws, and though Democrats mounted court challenges, many of these laws were in effect on Election Day.

While America, of course, consists of 50 states, presidential elections are usually fought in only a handful of "battleground" states. This is so because some states are solidly Republican (sometimes called the red states), while others are solidly Democratic (known as the blue states). The states of the Deep South and mountain West, for example, are so securely in the Republican camp that Democratic presidential candidates hardly bother to campaign there. Most of the states of the Northeast and West Coast, on the other hand, are heavily committed to the Democrats and receive little attention from the GOP. In 2012 opinion polls indicated that only 8 of the 50 states were actually toss-ups. These were Colorado, Florida, Iowa, Nevada, New Hampshire, Ohio, Virginia, and Wisconsin. A handful of other states, including Michigan, Minnesota, New Mexico, and Pennsylvania, were seen as leaning toward Obama, while Arizona, Indiana, and North Carolina were viewed as leaning toward Romney. The remaining 35 states seemed to be solidly in either the Democratic or the Republican camp.

Thus, the 2012 presidential race was waged in 8 to 10 battleground states. Here the Obama and Romney campaigns and their various supporters matched each other dollar for dollar in an unprecedented amount of political advertising. All told, Team Obama and allied groups spent over $400 million on televised advertising across the United States, and Team Romney and allied groups spent almost $500 million on television advertising. Nearly all of it was concentrated in the battleground states. In places like Las Vegas, Nevada; Denver, Colorado; Columbus, Ohio; and Charlotte, North Carolina, the campaigns bought over 30,000 TV ads. In places like Los Angeles, California, and New York, New York, they bought none. While voters in many states would hardly have reason to notice the presidential contest, voters in the battleground states could hardly turn on their television sets or answer their phones without being urged to support Obama or Romney.

The Debates

The candidates faced each other in one major set of national forums: three nationally televised presidential debates along with the one vice-presidential debate. The first presidential debate, which was watched by 67 million people, was more remarkable for style than substance. In terms of substance, the candidates discussed the economy, the federal deficit, Social Security, and the Affordable Care Act, with Romney criticizing Obama's record and the president defending his accomplishments. Though both candidates made mistakes and factual errors, both seemed to possess a thorough knowledge of the details of major American domestic policies. In terms of style, however, Obama and Romney differed sharply. Governor Romney seemed alert and aggressive, making points assertively and methodically as he accused the president of increasing the nation's debt, failing to bolster the economy, and undermining the private sector in favor of government-run programs. The president, for his part, appeared disengaged and listless. In the wake of the first debate, the national polls, which had consistently shown Obama with a slim lead over his Republican opponent, now suggested that the race was neck and neck. Republicans were elated and Democrats dismayed by the debate and its results.

The president improved his performance in the next two debates and was generally judged to have been the winner, as was Vice President Biden in his confrontation with Republican vice-presidential candidate Paul Ryan. However, in the 34 states that allowed early voting in 2012, hundreds of thousands of voters had cast their ballots after the first debate but before the other debates. With the damage done, Obama had two weeks after the debates to slow his opponent's growing momentum.

Obama responded by redoubling his efforts in battleground states, with speeches and campaign commercials labeling Romney a multimillionaire who was out of touch with ordinary Americans and who sent American jobs overseas. The Obama campaign argued that Romney had favored allowing Detroit to go bankrupt, despite the potential loss of hundreds of thousands of jobs. These efforts succeeded in shoring up Obama's support among working-class Americans. According to exit polls, the president won 63 percent of the votes of those whose family incomes were less than $30,000 per year and 57 percent of those who earned between $30,000 and $49,000 per year. Among more affluent voters, by contrast, Romney was the winner, taking 52 percent of the votes of those who earned between $50,000 and $100,000 per year and about 54 percent of the votes of those whose annual family incomes exceeded $100,000.

The Obama campaign also redoubled its efforts among women voters. In recent years, women have tended to give a majority of their votes to the Democrats, producing a so-called gender gap in the electoral arena. Democratic ads reminded women that it was the Democratic Party that supported such issues as equal pay. Foolish remarks on rape and abortion by GOP senatorial candidates in Indiana and Missouri were highlighted by the Democrats to underscore Republican insensitivity to women. On Election Day, 55 percent of women voters supported Obama, while Obama received the votes of only 45 percent of America's men. That is a gender gap of 10 percentage points. This is one of the largest gaps between men and women ever measured; it was up 3 points from 2008, and it was bad news for Romney because women comprise about 53 percent of the voters, while men comprise about 47 percent.

Finally, Obama campaign workers were determined to ensure high levels of turnout among minority voters, who potentially could be decisive in several battleground states. African American voters were a loyal Democratic constituency and could be counted on to turn out for the president. But the Democrats had been making enormous efforts to bring Asian and, especially, Latino voters into their camp, too. Latinos are the most rapidly growing group in the American population and were responsible for about 10 percent of the votes cast in 2012. The Democratic Party had made a major effort to court Latinos on such issues as immigration and, in 2012, Democrats had pushed for ballot initiatives in a number of states that offered undocumented young Latinos who had been raised in the United States the opportunity to attend public colleges at the in-state tuition rate. This strategy proved extremely successful. Not only did Obama capture 93 percent of the African American vote, but he also won approximately 71 percent of the Latino vote across the country. While African Americans usually vote at a very high rate for Democrats, Obama had a particularly strong showing among Hispanics. Four years earlier, Obama won 67 percent of the Latino vote, and in 2004 Democrat John Kerry won only 54 percent of the Latino vote. Among whites, by contrast, Romney received 59 percent of the vote (Figure 11.9).

Taken together, working-class voters, women, and minority constituents gave Obama the votes he needed for victory. Astonishingly, President Obama carried the eight toss-up battleground states, and in each one, exit polls suggested that the critical margin was provided by low-income groups, minorities, and women.

Looking toward the Future

As they surveyed the results, Republicans consoled themselves that 2012 had not been a complete disaster. To be sure, in Senate races, Democrats increased their majority by a net gain of two, from 51 to 53 seats. In addition, two Independents promised to work with the Democrats in the Senate, effectively making the Democrats' margin 55 to 45 seats. Nevertheless, the GOP had successfully defended its bastion in the House of Representatives. In House races, the Republicans lost a net of eight seats, and maintained their majority, albeit with a somewhat smaller margin. After machine recounts in several very close elections, Republicans had won 234 seats to the Democrats 201. Republicans also picked up one gubernatorial seat, North Carolina, that had previously been held by a Democrat. (See Tables 11.2A and 11.2B.)

The 2012 House results provided a silver lining to an otherwise difficult night for Republican candidates. The loss of the presidential election and the Democrats' surprising gains in the Senate led many Republicans to question whether their party must change, reaching out to women, to Latinos and Asians, and to other groups that seem to have been driven further away from the GOP during the 2012 election. Not only did Republicans struggle to win the support of these groups, but these groups are a growing portion of the electorate. If the GOP remained merely the party of affluent white men, particularly as the U.S. population became less white, demographics would doom it to the status of a permanent minority. Thus, if it hoped to become a party capable of winning majorities in 2016 and beyond, the GOP would need to find a way to broaden its appeal to women and to racial and ethnic minorities, especially Hispanics.

CONCLUSION: ELECTIONS AND ACCOUNTABILITY

Elections should stir wonder in even the most jaded person. In an election, no one person matters much, and each person acts in apparent isolation, indeed secrecy. The individual voter's decisions reflect diverse experiences, opinions,

Figure 11.9
VOTE SHIFTS BETWEEN 2008 AND 2012

% Voted for Obama

% Voted for McCain (2008) Romney (2012)

+100 | +50 | 0 | +50 | +100

2008
2012

GENDER

Male — 49% / 48% (2008), 45% / 52% (2012)

Female — 56% / 43% (2008), 55% / 44% (2012)

AGE

18–29 — 66% / 32% (2008), 60% / 37% (2012)

30–44 — 52% / 46% (2008), 52% / 45% (2012)

45–64 — 50% / 49% (2008), 47% / 51% (2012)

65+ — 45% / 53% (2008), 44% / 56% (2012)

PARTY

Democrat — 89% / 10% (2008), 92% / 7% (2012)

Republican — 9% / 90% (2008), 6% / 93% (2012)

Independent or something else — 52% / 44% (2008), 45% / 50% (2012)

RACE

White — 43% / 55% (2008), 39% / 59% (2012)

Black — 95% / 4% (2008), 93% / 6% (2012)

Hispanic — 67% / 31% (2008), 71% / 27% (2012)

Asian — 62% / 35% (2008), 73% / 26% (2012)

Figure 11.9
(Continued)

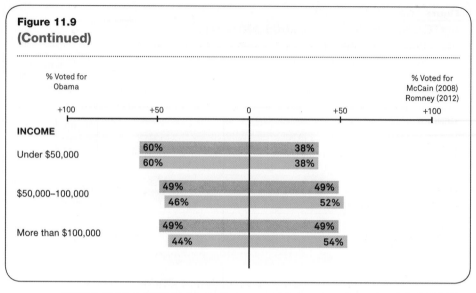

SOURCE: "Exit Polls 2012." *Washington Post*, www.washingtonpost.com/wp-srv/special/politics/2012 -exit-polls/table.html (accessed 11/28/12).

and preferences about government and public policy. And the millions of votes cumulate into an expression of whom the majority wants to have as its representatives in state government, in Congress, and in the presidency.

The design of the institutions of American elections facilitate majority rule. Single-member districts and plurality rule create strong pressures toward a two-party system and majoritarianism. Even in elections in which one party wins a plurality but not a majority, that party typically wins an outright majority of legislative seats. The election itself, then, determines the government. Other systems often produce multiparty outcomes, resulting in a period of negotiation and coalition formation among the parties in order to determine who will govern.

The significance of elections derives not so much from the laws as from the preferences of voters. Voting behavior depends in no small part on habit and the tendency to vote for a given party as a matter of ingrained personal identity. If that were all there is to voting behavior, then it is not clear that elections would provide a meaningful way of governing. Elections would be reduced to little more than a sporting event, in which people merely rooted for their own team. However, voters' preferences are as strongly rooted in the issues at hand as in the choices themselves, the candidates. Voting decisions reflect individuals' assessments about whether it makes sense to keep public policies on the same track or to change direction, whether those in office have done a good job and deserve to be re-elected, or whether they have failed and it is time for new representation. The aggregation of all voters' preferences responds collectively to fluctuations in the economy, to differences in the ideological and policy orientations of the parties, and to the personal abilities of the candidates.

For Further Reading

Selections highlighted in red are included in *Readings in American Politics: Analysis and Perspectives,* Third Edition.

Ansolabehere, Stephen, and James M. Snyder, Jr. *The End of Inequality: One Person, One Vote and the Transformation of American Politics.* New York: Norton, 2008.

Brady, David W. *Critical Elections and Congressional Policy Making.* Palo Alto, CA: Stanford University Press, 1988.

Carmines, Edward G., and James A. Stimson. *Issue Evolution: Race and the Transformation of American Politics.* Princeton, NJ: Princeton University Press, 1989.

Conway, M. Margaret. *Political Participation in the United States.* 3rd ed. Washington, DC: CQ Press, 2000.

Fowler, Linda L. *Candidates, Congress, and the American Democracy.* Ann Arbor: University of Michigan Press, 1994.

Gelman, Andrew. *Red State, Blue State, Rich State, Poor State: Why Americans Vote the Way They Do.* Princeton, NJ: Princeton University Press, 2008.

Ginsberg, Benjamin, and Martin Shefter. *Politics by Other Means: Politicians, Prosecutors, and the Press from Watergate to Whitewater.* 3rd ed. New York: Norton, 2002.

Green, Donald, and Alan Gerber. *Get Out the Vote: How to Increase Voter Turnout.* Washington, DC: Brookings Institution, 2008.

Jacobson, Gary, C. *The Politics of Congressional Elections.* 8th ed. Boston: Pearson, 2013.

McCarty, Nolan, Keith Poole, and Howard Rosenthal. *Polarized America: The Dance of Ideology and Unequal Riches.* Cambridge, MA: MIT Press, 2006.

Morton, Rebecca B. *Analyzing Elections.* New York: Norton, 2006.

Reichley, A. James, ed. *Elections American Style.* Washington, DC: Brookings Institution, 1987.

Rosenstone, Steven, and John Mark Hansen. *Mobilization, Participation, and Democracy in America.* New York: Macmillan, 1993.

Witt, Linda, Karen M. Paget, and Glenna Matthews. *Running as a Woman: Gender and Power in American Politics.* New York: Free Press, 1994.

12

Political Parties

Political parties are defined as teams of politicians, activists, and voters whose goal is to win control of government. They do so by recruiting and nominating candidates to run for office; by accumulating the resources needed to run political campaigns, especially manpower and money; and by pursuing a policy agenda that can appeal to large numbers of voters and secure electoral majorities. As we saw in Chapter 6, once in office, parties organize the legislature and attempt to put their stamp on the laws passed by Congress and the president. Their potential political power is immense.

The prospect of "party rule" has long made Americans suspicious of these organizations. Indeed, the separation of powers into different branches was meant to blunt any attempts by a "faction" or party to gain control of government, as might more readily occur in a parliament.[1] Divided government, in which one party controls the presidency and the other has a majority in at least one chamber of the legislature, has been the norm in American national and state politics, especially over the past 50 years. In some elections, as in 1980, one party wins a landslide victory for the presidency but still fails to capture control of Congress. And, in some midterm elections, as in 1994, 2006, and 2010, the public decides to give control of Congress to the party opposing the president in order to rein in the executive. Our political system intentionally makes it difficult for any party or organized interest to gain complete control of American government, and when one does, unified government is often short-lived. Separation of powers and divided government have not, however, put the parties out of business. Quite the contrary.

The Democratic and Republican parties remain essential to the day-to-day operation of the legislature and the conduct of elections. It is difficult to imagine how candidates would emerge and how individuals would vote without

---

1   James Madison famously made this argument in *Federalist 51* during the campaign to ratify the Constitution of the United States. Alexander Hamilton, James Madison, and John Jay, *The Federalist Papers*, Clinton Rossiter, ed. (New York: New American Library, 1961), no. 51.

political parties to organize the electoral system. Our inability to conceive of democracy without parties is not a failure of our imaginations or an accident of American history. Rather, it reflects a law of democratic politics. Parties form to solve key problems of rationality and collective action in a democracy. They are not unlike businesses providing a service that consumers need. Parties offer clear choices to voters, lowering the costs of collecting information about the candidates and making it easier for voters to hold government accountable. Parties also ease the transition from elections to government. They bear the costs of bringing together representatives of disparate constituencies into coherent coalitions that can act collectively in government. Thus, parties link elections to governing. Throughout this chapter we highlight some of the general functions of parties in any democracy, but we are especially attentive to party politics in the United States.

The simplest observation about American parties is also perhaps the most important: the United States has just two major parties, the Democrats and the Republicans. The American two-party system is impressive in its durability and

CORE OF THE ANALYSIS

➡️ Political parties are teams of politicians, activists, and interest groups organized to win control of government.

➡️ The United States has a two-party system in which Democrats and Republicans compete for most offices. This two-party system is a consequence of the form of government (presidential-congressional as opposed to parliamentary) and election laws, especially the use of single-member legislative districts.

➡️ Parties offer distinctive views about how government ought to operate and what laws ought to be enacted. They often serve distinct interests and communities.

➡️ Parties help solve an important informational problem for voters. By offering distinctive "brands," the parties simplify the choices that voters must make and reduce the costs of gathering information about how to vote.

➡️ The legislative and executive branches of the U.S. government are organized by the parties, with the party that won a majority of seats controlling most of the key positions and levers of power, especially congressional committees, the congressional agenda, and the appointment of agency heads.

flexibility. Sustained third parties have not been able to compete with the Democrats and Republicans since the 1850s. The Democratic and Republican parties have, for the past 150 years, elected every president and nearly every member of Congress and governor and state legislator in the United States. Occasionally, a governor or legislator decides to run as a third-party candidate, but those independent candidacies usually fail unless the person eventually attaches him- or herself to one of the parties. When a faction breaks from one of the parties, as occurred with the Progressive Republicans in the 1920s and the Southern Democrats in 1948 and again in 1968, those factions eventually return to the fold or move into the other party. The parties have not remained static, however. For instance, the parties have shifted their regional bases of support, with Democrats moving from a southern base to a northern one and the Republicans' base moving increasingly from the Northeast and Midwest to the South. And the two major parties have adapted to radical changes in the ideologies and social structure of American society.

The institutions of a two-party system, combined with majority rule, mean that the choice between the parties translates into the choice of government. Whichever party wins a majority of seats in House or Senate elections wins control of that chamber. Whichever party wins a majority of electoral votes wins the presidency. At election time, we choose between those who are in power and those who would like to be; those who are on the side of the president or the ruling coalition in the legislature, and those who oppose them. Choosing to change the government means voting against the party that currently holds the presidency and Congress.

In contrast, most parliamentary systems, especially those that allocate seats to parties based on the proportion of votes won nationwide, have more than two parties. In such systems, no party regularly wins a majority, and governments consist of coalitions of several parties. It is difficult to anticipate which coalitions might form, and it is hard to assign blame to any one party in a coalition government. There is a great simplicity in having a two-party system.

The Democratic and Republican parties have proved remarkably adept at accommodating diverse sets of interests and ideas while still presenting distinctive visions for governing. They each capture a range of ideological views while keeping successful third parties at bay. This situation arises in large measure because of the electoral and governmental institutions of the United States and the strategic skills of the party leaders. The opportunity for a third party to enter races and win large numbers of congressional seats or the presidency is very limited.

The French political scientist Maurice Duverger laid out the reason for this state of affairs in his classic book *Political Parties*. Duverger relied on both the institution principle and the rationality principle. As we discussed briefly in Chapter 11, any third-party movement that attempts to enter the American party system would likely fail to win, or worse, would improve the electoral fortunes of the party it most opposes. Also, any voter would not want to waste a vote on a losing cause. Hence, the number of successful parties is two.

U.S. government institutions and electoral rules create strong pressures to maintain just two parties, distinctive in their plans for governing but expansive in the interests and ideas that they encompass. This simplifies politics inside governing institutions, because one party will have a majority and control that institution (the presidency or one or both chambers of Congress). It also simplifies vote choice, because voters can readily sort into one of the two major party camps or use the party labels to figure out the most effective way to vote.

Parties, however, are not benevolent. They don't solve the rationality and collective action problem simply to make democracy work. Those in the party recognize that these problems represent opportunities to secure elected office, to influence public policy, even to make a profit. For the politicians inside these organizations, the parties provide a clear path to office through the nominating system and to power through the party organization. For its activists, the party is a potential way to pull the policies of government in a direction more favorable to the party's views. For interest groups that sustain the parties, the parties offer the potential benefits of being closer to power and influencing what government does. At times, the influence of activists, party leaders, organized interests, and local bosses becomes too great. Regulations on campaign contributions and government contracting, sunshine laws and federal advisory rules, even civil-service reforms, have all come about through efforts to prevent party bosses and interest groups from taking advantage of their power. Party organizations have been weakened by these reforms, but they have invariably found new resources to draw on. As a result of these actions and reactions, American history has witnessed eras of very strong party organization and periods of relative party weakness.

Today, American politics is characterized by relatively strong party organizations and disciplined legislative parties. They offer the American voter meaningful electoral choices and a simple strategy for changing the direction of government.

WHY DO POLITICAL PARTIES FORM?

Political parties, like interest groups, are organizations seeking influence over government. Ordinarily, they can be distinguished from interest groups on the basis of their orientation. A party seeks to control the entire government by electing its members to office, thereby controlling the government's personnel. Interest groups, through campaign contributions and other forms of electoral assistance, are also concerned with electing politicians—in particular, those who are inclined in their policy direction. But interest groups ordinarily do not sponsor candidates directly, and between elections they usually accept government and its personnel as givens and try to influence government policies through them. They are benefit seekers, whereas parties are composed mainly of office seekers.[2]

 political party

An organized group that attempts to influence government by electing its members to office

---

2 This distinction is from John H. Aldrich, *Why Parties? The Origin and Transformation of Party Politics in America* (Chicago: University of Chicago Press, 1995).

Political parties form to solve three problems with which politicians and other political activists must cope. The first is the problem of collective action. This is chiefly an outgrowth of elections in which a candidate for office must attract campaign funds, assemble a group of activists and workers, mobilize prospective voters, and persuade them to vote for her. The second problem is the collective choice of policy.[3] The give-and-take within a legislature and between the legislature and the executive can make or break policy success and subsequent electoral success. The third problem is power sharing and competition among politicians. Politicians, like members of any organization, seek success simultaneously for the organization and for themselves. In seeking to further their own ambitions, politicians can act in ways that serve their own interests but that can undermine the collective aspirations of fellow partisans unless astutely managed. We briefly examine each of these problems below.

Ultimately, each is a problem faced by politicians, especially those already in office. This fact reveals an important reason that parties form—to serve the interests of politicians. The political parties in the United States were, ultimately, formed by politicians to serve their aims. Politicians do not need to form or join political parties, and some don't. But parties make easier the basic tasks of political life—running for office, organizing one's supporters, and forming a government.

To Facilitate Collective Action in the Electoral Process

Political parties as we know them today developed along with the expansion of suffrage and can be understood only in the context of elections. Parties and elections are so intertwined that American parties actually take their structure from the electoral process. The shape of party organization in the United States has followed a simple rule: for every district where an election is held, there should be some kind of party unit. These units provide the brand name, the resources (both human and financial), the "buzz," and the link to the larger national organization, which all help the party's candidates arouse interest in their candidacy and stimulate commitment by voters. All of these activities facilitate collective action as they make it easier for voters to understand the choice of candidates and ultimately overcome the free riding that diminishes turnout in general elections.

Party organization also enables and encourages electoral competition by groups. The Republican Party has long been the party of business interests (among other groups), especially small business and peak associations

---

3   A slight variation on this theme is emphasized by Gary W. Cox and Mathew D. McCubbins in *Legislative Leviathan: Party Government in the House* (Berkeley: University of California Press, 1993). They suggest that parties in the legislature are electoral machines whose purpose is to preserve and enhance party reputation, thereby giving meaning to the party labels when elections are contested. By keeping order within their ranks, parties make certain that individual actions by members do not discredit the party label. This is an especially challenging task for party leaders when there is diversity within each party, as has often been the case in American political history.

(organizations of organizations) such as the Chamber of Commerce and the National Association of Manufacturers. The Democratic Party has been aligned with labor unions and reformers that want to regulate the economy since the 1930s. Often, groups with significant numbers but lacking substantial economic and institutional resources find their voice in the party system. Women's organizations worked closely with the Progressive faction inside the Republican Party in the 1900s and 1910s in the struggle to gain the right to vote for women. By the 1970s, changing social issues and changed strategies by the parties led many newer women's groups, such as the National Organization for Women, to align with the Democratic Party. Throughout American history, immigrant groups have also aligned themselves with the parties. Irish immigrants attached themselves to the Democrats, whose urban political organizations helped those immigrants find jobs and negotiate the immigration system; Italian immigrants tended toward Republicans; most Hispanic groups have gravitated to the Democrats because of the party's immigration policies; and Cubans aligned with the Republicans because that party took a harder line against the Castro regime. In the 1970s, disaffection with liberal policies concerning school prayer, funding of religious schools, abortion, and other social issues led fundamentalist church leaders to align with the Republican Party. Fundamentalist and born-again Christians became an essential and enduring part of the Republican electoral coalition that Ronald Reagan constructed leading up to the 1980 election.

The relationship between collective action by groups and party electoral strategy is clearly a two-way street. Groups that align with a party provide that party with essential electoral resources, including a reliable voting bloc, money, personnel, and even candidates. When the party they support wins, these interests gain influence over public policy. Of course, there are risks as well: an organized interest may suffer if the party it supports loses the election.

To Resolve Problems of Collective Choice in Government

Political parties are also essential elements in the process of making policy. Within the government, parties are coalitions of individuals with shared or overlapping interests who, as a rule, will support one another's programs and initiatives. Even though there may be areas of disagreement within each party, a common party label in and of itself gives party members a reason to cooperate. Because they are permanent coalitions, parties greatly facilitate the policy-making process. If alliances had to be formed from scratch for each legislative proposal, the business of government would slow to a crawl or halt altogether. Parties create a basis for coalition and thus sharply reduce the time, energy, and effort needed to advance a legislative proposal. Every president works closely with his party's leadership in the House and Senate, even if the party is in the minority, in order to make sure that the executive's agenda will be introduced into Congress and supported. Without the support of a party, the president would be compelled to undertake the daunting and probably impossible task of forming a completely new coalition for every policy proposal.

Party cohesion is not a given, however, and sometimes breaks down because of fundamental conflict between the public philosophy of the party and the need for action on a crucial issue. For instance, in September 2008, facing a collapse of the financial industry, President George W. Bush proposed a $700 billion intervention to unlock frozen credit markets. The government needed to act quickly. Democratic leaders in the House twisted enough arms to produce a sizable majority of Democratic votes in favor of the Republican president's plan. The competing presidential nominees, Barack Obama and John McCain, both called for colleagues in their respective parties to back the bill. But Republican leadership in the House failed to produce enough Republican votes to pass the measure. Those voting against the bill argued that the plan would increase the size of government, that it rewarded irresponsible investors, and that it violated the free-market principles that lie at the heart of the Republican policy agenda. The failure of the president and his party to come to agreement on this plan in advance doomed the president's proposal. The following day the Dow Jones Industrial Index dropped 777 points, losing almost one-tenth of its value.[4]

To Deal with the Problem of Ambition

Parties are important vehicles that enable individual politicians to achieve their ambitions. The very "brand names" they provide are often a significant electoral asset. Moreover, once their candidates are elected, parties provide these politicians, who share principles, causes, and constituencies, with a basis for coordination, common cause, cooperation, and joint enterprise. But individual ambition, sometimes in the background but often in the foreground, constantly threatens to undermine any bases for cooperation. Political parties, by regulating career advancement, providing for the orderly resolution of ambitious competition, and attending to the post-career care of elected and appointed party officials, do much to rescue coordination and cooperation and permit fellow partisans to pursue common causes where feasible. Simple devices such as primaries, for example, provide a context in which clashing electoral ambitions can be resolved. Representative partisan bodies, like the Democratic Committee on Committees in the House (with comparable bodies for the Republicans and for both parties in the Senate), resolve competing claims for power positions. In short, politics consists not of foot soldiers walking in lockstep but, rather, of ambitious and autonomous individuals seeking power. The unchecked and unregulated burnishing of individual careers is a formula for chaos and destructive competition in which the dividends of cooperation are rarely reaped. Political parties constitute organizations of relatively kindred spirits who try to capture some of those dividends by providing a structure in which ambition is not suppressed altogether but is not so destructive either.

---

4   Carl Hulse and David M. Herszenhorn, "Defiant House Rejects Huge Bailout; Next Step Is Uncertain," New York Times, September 29, 2008, www.nytimes.com/2008/09/30 /business/30cong.html (accessed 4/3/09).

WHAT FUNCTIONS DO PARTIES PERFORM?

Parties are mainly involved in nominations and elections—recruiting the candidates for office, getting out the vote, and facilitating mass electoral choice. That is, they help solve the problems of collective action and ambition that we described earlier. They also influence the institutions of government—providing leadership as well as organization of the various congressional committees and activities on the floor in each chamber. That is, they help solve the problem of collective choice concerning institutional arrangements and policy formulation that we also noted earlier.

Recruiting Candidates

One of the most important but least noticed party activities is the recruitment of candidates for local, state, and national office. Each election year, candidates must be found for thousands of state and local offices as well as for congressional seats. Where an incumbent is not running for re-election or where an incumbent in the opposing party appears vulnerable, party leaders attempt to identify strong candidates and interest them in entering the campaign. The recruiting season begins early, because the dates by which candidates must file for office come as early as January of the election year, though in some states they are as late at June. Candidate recruitment in the spring shapes the parties' message and fortunes in the November general election. In 2006 and 2008, Democrats recruited a number of Iraq War veterans, who became the spokespeople for opposition to the war and helped the party capitalize on public frustration with the conduct of the war after 2005. In 2010 and 2012, Republicans capitalized on public anger and opposition to President Obama's health care law, which contributed to the emergence of the Tea Party movement, and managed to recruit a very strong class of candidates.[5] The biggest challenge for parties is when they fail to recruit anyone to run for a seat. You can't beat somebody with nobody.

An ideal candidate will be charismatic, organized, knowledgeable, an excellent debater; have an unblemished record; and possess the ability and wherewithal to raise enough money to mount a serious campaign. Party leaders are usually not willing to provide financial backing to candidates who are unable to raise substantial funds on their own. For a House seat, this can mean between $500,000 and $1 million; for a Senate seat, a serious candidate must be able to raise several million dollars. Often party leaders have difficulty finding attractive candidates and persuading them to run. In recent years, party leaders in several states have reported that many potential congressional candidates declined the

---

5   See Adam Nagourney, "Eyeing '08: Democrats Nurse Freshmen at Risk," *New York Times*, December 22, 2006.

opportunity to run for office, saying they were reluctant to leave their homes and families for the hectic life of a member of Congress. Candidate recruitment has become particularly difficult in an era when political campaigns often involve mudslinging and candidates must assume that their personal lives will be intensely scrutinized in the press.[6]

Nominating Candidates

Article I, Section 4, of the Constitution makes only a few provisions for elections. It delegates to the states the power to set the "Times, Places and Manner of holding Elections," even those for U.S. senators and representatives. It does, however, reserve to Congress the power to make such laws if it chooses to do so. The Constitution has been amended from time to time to expand the right to participate in elections. Congress has also occasionally passed laws regulating elections, congressional districting, and campaign practices. But the Constitution and the laws are almost completely silent on nominations, setting only citizenship and age requirements for candidates. The president must be at least 35 years of age, a natural-born citizen, and a resident of the United States for 14 years. A senator must be at least age 30, a U.S. citizen for at least nine years, and a resident of the state he or she represents. A member of the House must be at least age 25, a U.S. citizen for seven years, and a resident of the state he or she represents.

nomination

The process by which political parties select their candidates for election to public office

Nomination is the process by which a party selects a single candidate to run for each elective office. Nomination is the parties' most serious and difficult business. The nominating process can precede the election by many months (Figure 12.1), as it does when the many candidates for the presidency are eliminated from consideration through a grueling series of debates and state primaries until there is only one survivor in each party—that party's nominee.

Nomination by Convention. A nominating convention is a formal caucus bound by a number of rules that govern participation and nominating procedures. Conventions are meetings of delegates elected by party members from the relevant county (a county convention) or state (a state convention). Delegates to each party's national convention (which nominates the party's presidential candidate) are chosen by party members on a state-by-state basis; there is no single national delegate selection process.

Nomination by Primary Election. In primary elections, party members select the party's nominees directly rather than selecting convention delegates who then select the nominees. Primaries are far from perfect replacements for conventions because it is rare that more than 25 percent of the enrolled voters

6   For an excellent analysis of the parties' role in recruitment, see Paul S. Herrnson, *Congressional Elections: Campaigning at Home and in Washington* (Washington, DC: CQ Press, 1995).

Figure 12.1
TYPES OF NOMINATION PROCESSES

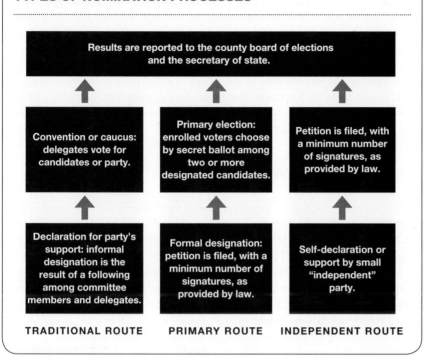

Results are reported to the county board of elections and the secretary of state.

| Convention or caucus: delegates vote for candidates or party. | Primary election: enrolled voters choose by secret ballot among two or more designated candidates. | Petition is filed, with a minimum number of signatures, as provided by law. |

| Declaration for party's support: informal designation is the result of a following among committee members and delegates. | Formal designation: petition is filed, with a minimum number of signatures, as provided by law. | Self-declaration or support by small "independent" party. |

TRADITIONAL ROUTE　　**PRIMARY ROUTE**　　**INDEPENDENT ROUTE**

participate.[7] Nevertheless, they have replaced conventions as the dominant method of nomination.[8]

Primary elections fall mainly into two categories—closed and open. In a **closed primary**, participation is limited to individuals who have previously declared their affiliation by registering with the party. In an **open primary**, individuals declare their party affiliation on the day of the primary election. To do so, they simply go to the polling place and ask for the ballot of a particular party. The open primary allows each voter to consider candidates and issues before deciding whether to participate and in which party's contest to participate. Open primaries, therefore, are less conducive to strong political parties. But in either case, primaries are more open than conventions or caucuses to new issues and new types of candidates.

Most states adopted primary elections for Congress and state offices at the beginning of the twentieth century, and from the 1950s through the 1970s states

 closed primary

A primary election in which only those voters who registered with the party a specified period before the primary election day can participate

 open primary

A primary election in which voters can choose on the primary election day itself which party's primary to vote in

---

7　Anthony King, *Running Scared: Why America's Politicians Campaign Too Much and Govern Too Little* (New York: Martin Kessler Books, 1997).

8　At the present time, only a small number of states, including Connecticut, Delaware, and Utah, provide for state conventions to nominate candidates for statewide offices, and even those states also use primaries whenever a substantial minority of delegates has voted for one of the defeated aspirants.

gradually adopted primaries as a means of nominating presidential candidates. The shift from party conventions to primary elections creates an additional screen that selects candidates who are particularly good at campaigning. Candidates must now win not one election, but two—the primary and the general election—in order to hold office. As a result the introduction of primary elections are thought to have contributed to the rise of candidate-centered politics by creating advantages to politicians who are particularly strong campaigners, but who may be less effective at governing.[9] Thus there is a "selection" effect that results from the particular institutional arrangement a state employs. Institutions matter in this case because they encourage or discourage particular types of candidates, as the institution principle suggests.

Getting Out the Vote

The election period begins immediately after the nominations. Historically, this has been a time of glory for the political parties, whose popular base of support is fully displayed. All the paraphernalia of party committees and all the committee members are activated in the form of local party workforces.

The first step in the electoral process involves voter registration. This aspect of the process takes place all year round. There was a time when party workers were responsible for virtually all of this kind of electoral activity, but they have been supplemented (and in many states virtually displaced) by civic groups such as the League of Women Voters, unions, and chambers of commerce.

Those who have registered have to decide on Election Day whether to go to the polling place, stand in line, and vote for the various candidates and referendums on the ballot. Political parties, candidates, and campaigning can make a big difference in persuading eligible voters to vote. Because it is costly for voters to participate in elections and because many of the benefits that winning parties bestow are public goods (that is, parties cannot exclude any individual from enjoying them), people will often free ride by enjoying the benefits without incurring the costs of electing the party that provided the benefits. This is the free-rider problem (see Chapter 1), and parties are important because they help overcome it by mobilizing the voters to support the candidates.

In recent years, the parties themselves and not-for-profit groups have registered and mobilized large numbers of people to vote and raised millions of dollars to devote to election organizing and advertising. Legions of workers, often volunteers, have proved especially effective at using new technologies to build networks of supporters and communicate through those networks. They are the "netroots" organizations of politics. To comply with federal election and tax law, groups must maintain their independence from the political parties, although they have the same objectives as the parties and work very hard to elect politicians from a particular party. Such organizations act as shadow appendages

---

9 Matthew Crenson and Benjamin Ginsberg, *Presidential Power: Unchecked and Unbalanced* (New York: Norton, 2007).

of the two parties, with some groups mobilizing Democratic supporters and others mobilizing Republicans. The netroots have become integral to campaign organizations, and with the advent of these new forms of direct campaigning, there has been a noticeable uptick in turnout in the United States.

Facilitating Electoral Choice

Parties make the electoral choice much easier for voters. It is often argued that we should vote for the best person regardless of party affiliation. But on any general-election ballot, there are likely to be only a handful of candidates who are well known to the voters, namely, some of the candidates for president, U.S. Senate, U.S. House, and governor. As one moves down the ballot, voters' familiarity with the candidates declines. Without party labels, voters would be constantly confronted by a bewildering array of new names and new choices and might have considerable difficulty making informed decisions. Without a doubt, candidates' party affiliations help voters make reasonable choices.

Parties lower the information costs of participating in elections by providing a recognizable "brand name." Without knowing a great deal about a candidate for office, voters can infer from party labels how the candidate will likely behave once elected. Individuals know about the parties through their past experience with those parties in state and federal office and from the actions of prominent political leaders from both parties. In the United States, the Democratic Party is associated with a commitment to more extensive government regulation of the economy and a larger public sector; the Republican Party favors a limited government role in the economy and reduced government spending paired with tax reductions. The Democrats favor aggressive protection of civil rights and a secular approach to religion in public life. The Republicans want to ban abortion and favor government participation in expanding the role of religious organizations in civil society. The parties' positions on the economy were cemented in the 1930s, and their division over civil society emerged during the 1960s and 1970s. The Democratic positions are loosely labeled liberal and those of the Republicans conservative.

Most Americans personally identify with one of the two parties. When asked in surveys whether they think of themselves as Democrats, as Republicans, or neither, large majorities pick one of the two major parties. When voting, those who identify with a party are extremely likely to vote with that party (usually about 90 percent of the time). For these individuals, party simplifies the electoral decision. Except in rare circumstances, they vote with their team.

Even those who do not identify with one of the major parties derive value from the party labels. Nonpartisan voters are more conflicted about which party or candidate best represents their interests and ideals. But it would be the height of folly to try to learn about every politician running for every office. A voter would spend an enormous amount of time tracking down the information about dozens of different people. And if the entire electorate behaved this way, the advertising costs to politicians would be tremendous. So party labels simplify the decision making of nonpartisan voters by reducing the choice to an evaluation of two competing policy positions or to the evaluation of the performance of those in office. The independent voter may ask, "Which of the two parties will better represent my ideals and interests?" The voter will choose the party that offers the best option today. Or the voter may ask, "Am I better off now than four years ago?" If not, she will vote against the president's party up and down the ballot. If yes, she will vote to keep the president and his party in power. Whichever strategy the independent voter uses, parties are essential for simplifying what is otherwise a bewildering choice.

For all voters, partisans and independents alike, the parties make it easier to hold government accountable. People can vote against the party in power in bad times and for the party in power in good times. They can vote against the party in power if that party enacts very unpopular or irresponsible legislation. Thus political parties solve one of the most important collective action problems facing American democracy, the problem of collective responsibility. If every politician ran on her own, without regard to other candidates or districts or what was happening in the nation at large, each race for legislator or executive would become an isolated event. In such a setting it would be exceedingly difficult for voters to send a message to the government that they want government to go in a different direction. Parties, then, lend coherence to government and meaning to elections.[10]

Party labels also benefit the politicians. By having simple, recognizable labels, candidates running in most districts and states are spared the great expense of educating voters about what they stand for. The labels Democrat and Republican are usually sufficient. The content of the labels is sustained because like-minded people sort themselves into the respective organizations. People who broadly share the principles espoused by a party and who wish to participate on a high level in politics will attend party meetings, run for leadership positions in local and state party organizations, attend state and national conventions, and even run for elected office.[11] Each party, then, draws on a distinct pool for activists and candidates. Each successive election reinforces the existing division between the parties.

Influencing National Government

One of the most familiar observations about American politics is that the two major parties are "big tents." They position themselves to bring in as many groups and ideas as possible. The parties make such broad coalitions as a matter of strategy, much as businesses purchase other companies to expand their market share. Positioning themselves as broad coalitions prevents effective national

---

10 Morris Fiorina, "The Decline of Collective Responsibility in American Politics," *Daedalus* 109, no. 3 (Summer 1980): 25–45.

11 Comprehensive studies of delegates were conducted by Walter J. Stone and Ronald B. Rapoport from 1980 through 1996. See Ronald B. Rapoport and Walter J. Stone, *Three's a Crowd: The Dynamic of Third Parties, Ross Perot, and Republican Resurgence* (Ann Arbor: University of Michigan Press, 1999). Surveys of candidates find similar sorting.

third parties from emerging and guarantees that the Democrats and Republicans vie for control of Congress.

The coalitions that come together in the Democratic and Republican parties shape the parties' platforms on public policy. The political coalitions that party leaders assemble determine what interests and social groups align with the parties and also what sorts of issues can emerge. The Democratic Party today embraces a philosophy of active government intervention in the economy, based on the premise that regulation is necessary to ensure orderly economic growth, to prevent the emergence of monopolies, and to address certain costs of economic activity, such as pollution, poverty, and unemployment. In addition, the Democratic Party pushes for aggressive expansion and protection of civil rights, especially for women and racial minorities. The Republican Party espouses a philosophy of laissez-faire economics and a minimal government role in the economy. The coalition that Ronald Reagan built in the late 1970s paired this vision of limited government intervention in the economy with an expanded role for religion in society and strong opposition to immigration, affirmative action, and abortion.

To many European observers, the American parties appear as odd amalgams of contradictory ideas. Liberalism, as it developed as a political philosophy in Europe, naturally pairs laissez-faire economics with liberal views on civil rights. Conservatism, which maintains a respect for social and political order, would speak for a stronger role for social organizations in society, especially religions; a greater respect for existing social hierarchies, most notably social classes and higher-educated elites; and government power in the economy. The American parties, partly because of their histories, have scrambled these traditional views and developed their own political philosophies. In the Republican Party today, laissez-faire economics goes hand in hand with conservative views on civil rights and religion in society. In the Democratic Party today, liberal views on civil rights are tied to an expansive view of government in the economy. The American parties have mixed and matched different ideas as new issues have emerged and as leaders within the parties have seized opportunities. The New Deal coalition that President Franklin Delano Roosevelt assembled consisted of Progressive Republicans, who favored greater economic regulation; old-line Democrats, especially in the South; and urban political machines in northern and midwestern cities. This peculiar coalition gave rise to the political philosophy and public policies pursued under the New Deal. It also constrained what Roosevelt could do on some issues. Most important, he could not push for expanding civil rights for blacks without losing the support of southerners. The meaning of Democratic liberalism in the United States, then, was very much a function of the history of the parties.

Even though American liberalism and conservatism do not coincide neatly with their European counterparts, they still represent distinct views about how government ought to act, and they appeal to distinctly different core constituencies. The Democratic Party at the national level seeks to unite organized labor, the poor, members of racial minorities, and liberal upper-middle-class professionals. The Republicans, by contrast, appeal to business, upper-middle-class and upper-class groups in the private sector, and social conservatives. Often party leaders will seek to develop issues that they hope will add new groups to their party's constituent base. During the 1980s, for example, under the leadership of President Reagan, the Republicans devised a series of "social issues," including support for school prayer, opposition to abortion, and opposition to affirmative action, designed to cultivate the support of white southerners. This effort was extremely successful in increasing Republican strength in the once solidly Democratic South. In the 1990s, under the leadership of President Clinton, who called himself a "new Democrat," the Democratic Party sought to develop social programs designed to solidify the party's base among working-class and poor voters and somewhat conservative economic programs aimed at attracting the votes of middle-class and upper-middle-class voters.

As these examples suggest, parties do not always support policies because they are favored by their constituents. Instead, party leaders can play the role of policy entrepreneurs, seeking ideas and programs that will expand their party's base of support while eroding that of the opposition. In recent years, for example, leaders of both major political parties have sought to develop ideas and programs they hoped would appeal to America's most rapidly growing electoral bloc: Latino voters. President George W. Bush recommended a number of proposals designed to help Latinos secure U.S. residence and employment. Democrats, for their part, have proposed education, social service programs, and immigration reform designed to appeal to the needs of Latino families. Latino votes split nearly evenly between the parties in the 2004 presidential election. But, since 2005, many Republican leaders at the local, state, and federal levels began to take a hard line on immigration, especially from Latin America. Those policies were very popular among the Republican party base and worked well in Republican primaries, but they alienated many Latino voters in general elections. Exit polls revealed that Obama won 66 percent of the Latino vote in 2008, a huge swing from 2004, and he added to that margin in 2012, winning 70 percent of Latino votes.

Both parties translate their general goals into concrete policies through the members they elect to office. Republicans, for example, implemented tax cuts, increased defense spending, cut social spending, and enacted restrictions on abortion during the 1980s and 1990s. Democrats were able to defend consumer and environmental programs against Republican attacks and sought to expand domestic social programs in the late 1990s. In 2009, President Obama and a Democratic-controlled Congress created a national health insurance system that guarantees all people access to health care, a key item on the Democratic Party's platform since the 1940s.

PARTIES IN GOVERNMENT

Parties operate in three spheres: elections, political institutions, and government. The ultimate test of a political party is its influence on the institutions of government and the policy-making process. We begin there.

Most parties originate inside the government. Political parties form as those who support the actions of the government and those who do not; in the United Kingdom, these groups are called Government and Opposition.[12] In the American context, parties vie to control and to oppose those who control both Congress and the presidency.

The Parties and Congress. The two major political parties have a profound influence on the organization and day-to-day operation of Congress. The Speaker of the House, perhaps the most powerful person in Congress, is essentially a party officer. All the members of the House take part in the election of the Speaker, but the actual selection is made by the **majority party**. When the majority party caucus presents a nominee to the entire House, its choice is invariably ratified in a straight party-line vote.

majority party

The party that holds the majority of legislative seats in either the House or the Senate

The committee system of both houses of Congress is also organized by the parties. Although the rules organizing committees and the rules defining the jurisdiction of each committee are adopted like ordinary legislation by the whole membership, all other features of the committees are shaped by the party leadership and caucuses. For example, each party is assigned a quota of members for each committee, depending on the percentage of total seats held by the party. On the rare occasions when an independent or third-party candidate is elected, the leaders of the two parties must agree against whose quota this member's committee assignments will count. Presumably, the member will not be able to serve on any committee until the question of quota is settled.[13] As we saw in Chapter 6, the assignment of individual members to congressional committees is a party decision. Each party has a committee on committees to make such decisions. Moreover, who advances up the committee ladder toward the chair is a party decision. Since the late nineteenth century, most advancements have been automatic, based on the length of continuous service on the committee. This seniority system has survived only because of the support of the two parties, and each party can depart from it by a simple vote. During the 1970s, both parties reinstituted the practice of reviewing each chairmanship, voting anew every two years on whether each chair would be continued. In 2001, Republicans lived up to their 1995 pledge to limit House committee chairs to three terms. Existing chairs were forced to step down but were generally replaced by the next most senior Republican member of each committee.

President and Party. The presidency is, in many ways, the focal point of the party system in the United States. As we saw earlier, the president carries the mantle of leader of his party, and the electoral fortunes of the parties rise and fall with the success of the president. During midterm congressional elections, when the president is not on the ballot, voters hold the president's party accountable for current problems. When the economy does poorly, Americans will punish the party of the president, even when the opposing party controls Congress.

12 Maurice Duverger, *Political Parties* (New York: John Wiley and Sons, 1951).

13 Scott A. Frisch and Sean Q. Kelly, *Committee Assignment Politics in the U.S. House of Representatives* (Norman: University of Oklahoma Press, 2006).

The president of the United States also relies heavily on fellow party members in organizing the executive and passing legislation. Unlike parliamentary governments, such as in the United Kingdom, the heads of executive departments are not sitting members of the legislature. With few exceptions, heads of the executive departments and other key presidential appointments are people loyal to the president and his political party. Most are politicians who have served as governors of states or members of Congress or are close advisers who have worked with the president on political campaigns or in offices the president previously held.

The president and White House staff also work closely with congressional party leaders to shepherd legislation through Congress. The president cannot introduce legislation and must rely on members of Congress to do so. (There are a few exceptions such as nominations and treaties.) Nearly all of the president's legislative initiatives are proposed as bills by fellow party members in the U.S. House and Senate. As discussed in Chapter 7, when the president's party controls both chambers of Congress, there is the opportunity to get the large majority of the president's legislative agenda passed. The leadership of the president's party also helps to negotiate with individual members of Congress to construct a majority behind a White House–sponsored bill. Sometimes the president will reach out to individual legislators to try to persuade the member of Congress to support a particular bill.

The president's ability to prevail in Congress depends strongly on which party controls the House and Senate. When the president's party enjoys majorities in the House and Senate, the president's legislative agenda succeeds most of the time. A typical president will win in excess of 80 percent of the time on bills if his party controls the House and Senate. Barack Obama, during his first year in office, had the highest degree of support for a president since World War II, with a majority of Congress supporting his position 96 percent of the time.[14] When another party controls at least one chamber of Congress, however, the White House has a much more difficult time getting new laws passed. After Republicans took control of the House in 2011, a majority of the House voted in support of the position President Barack Obama had taken on legislation only 32 percent of the time. In the Senate, by contrast, Democrats retained control after the 2010 and the 2012 elections, and a majority of the Senate voted in line with Obama's preferred outcome 85 percent of the time.

PARTIES IN THE ELECTORATE

Political parties are more than just political leaders; they are made up of millions of people and organizations, such as labor unions, corporations, and other interest groups.

---

14 Don Gonyea, "CQ: Obama's Winning Streak on Hill Unprecedented," NPR, January 11, 2010, www.npr.org/templates/story/story.php?storyId=122436116 (accessed 5/28/13).

Party Identification

As we saw in Chapter 11's discussion of elections, individual voters tend to develop **party identification** with one of the political parties. Party identification partly reflects a psychological attachment developed in childhood or adolescence and carried throughout life. Party identification also has a rational component, rooted in evaluations of the performance of the parties in government, the policies they will pursue, and an individual's interest and ideology.[15] Voters generally form attachments to parties that reflect their views and interests. Once those attachments are formed, however, they are likely to persist and even be handed down to children, unless some very strong factors convince individuals that their party is no longer an appropriate object of their affections. In some sense, party identification is similar to brand loyalty in the marketplace: consumers choose a brand of automobile for its appearance or mechanical characteristics and stick with it out of loyalty, habit, and unwillingness to reexamine their choices constantly, but they may eventually switch if the old brand no longer serves their interests.

Although the strength of partisan ties in the United States seems to have declined in the 1960s and 1970s, most Americans continue to identify with either the Republican Party or the Democratic Party (Figure 12.2). Party identification gives citizens a stake in election outcomes that goes beyond the race at hand. This is why strong party identifiers (that is, people who identify strongly with one party) are more likely than other Americans to go to the polls and, of course, are more likely than others to support the party with which they identify. **Party activists** are drawn from the ranks of the strong identifiers. Activists are those who not only vote but also contribute their time, energy, and effort to party affairs. Activists ring doorbells, stuff envelopes, attend meetings, and contribute money to the party cause. No party could succeed without the thousands of volunteers who undertake the mundane tasks needed to keep the organization going. It is worth noting that attachment to a party does not guarantee voting for that party's candidates, though it does reflect a tendency. Strong identifiers do so almost always, and weak identifiers do so most of the time.

 party identification

An individual's attachment to a particular political party, which might be based on issues, ideology, past experience, or upbringing

party activist

A partisan who contributes time, energy, and effort to support a party and its candidates

Group Basis of Parties

The Democratic and Republican parties are America's only national parties. They are the only political organizations that draw support from most regions of the country and from Americans of every racial, economic, religious, and

---

15 For what is perhaps still the best discussion of the bases of party identification, see Arthur S. Goldberg, "Social Determinism and Rationality as Bases of Party Identification," *American Political Science Review* 63, no. 1 (March 1969): 5–25. For a more recent article weighing in on economic versus social determinants of party attachments, see Larry M. Bartels, "What's the Matter with *What's the Matter with Kansas?*" *Quarterly Journal of Political Science* 1 (2006): 201–26.

Figure 12.2
AMERICANS' PARTY IDENTIFICATION

ANALYZING THE EVIDENCE

In 1952, Democrats outnumbered Republicans significantly. Today, the two parties appear to have similar numbers of loyalists. What factors might account for this partisan transformation?

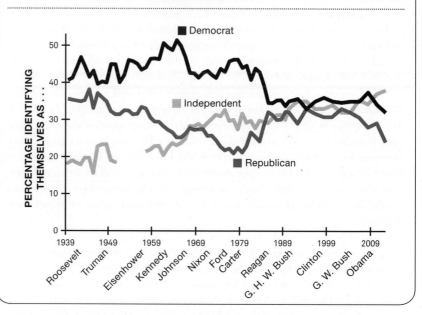

NOTE: Independent data not available for 1951–56.

SOURCES: Pew Research Center for the People & the Press, "Trend in Party Identification," www .people-press.org/2012/06/01/trend-in-party-identification-1939–2012/ (accessed 5/28/13).

ethnic group. The two parties do not draw equal support from members of every social stratum, however. When we refer to the Democratic or Republican coalition, we mean the groups that generally support one or the other party.

One view of political parties, a Pluralist view, is that they consist of coalitions of many organized groups. The leaders of organizations such as the American Federation of Labor or Christian Coalition may choose to side with a party to try to influence what government does by influencing the policy orientation of one of the major parties. A group can offer resources to the party, such as campaign workers, contributions, and votes, and the party, in exchange, can pursue policies in line with what the groups want. Once aligned with a party, a group's leaders can then signal to members for whom they should vote. The more disciplined the group and the more resources it can offer, the more power it will have in the party. Party leaders try to build coalitions consisting of many different groups, each of which wants a distinct policy or political benefit. The Reagan Coalition consisted of quite disparate groups including corporate political leaders, who wanted to minimize taxes; the Christian Coalition and other fundamental Christian groups that wanted changes in various social policies; and activists in western states who wanted open access to land (called the Sage Brush Rebellion). The challenge for political parties is how to build coalitions that can win majorities in elections and that do not create too many conflicting demands.[16]

Unorganized social groups are equally important. Parties can appeal to different types of voters through distinct policy promises. A person with a particularly strong social group attachment might find one of the parties appealing because that party aligns well on the group's pet issue. For instance, the Republican Party's hard line toward Cuba and Communism meant most Cuban Americans identified as Republican, even while other Hispanic and Latino groups lined up with Democrats over issues such as immigration and education. In the United States today, a variety of group characteristics are associated with party identification. These include race and ethnicity, gender, religion, class, region, and age.

Race and Ethnicity. Since the 1930s and Franklin Delano Roosevelt's New Deal, African Americans have been overwhelmingly Democratic in their party identification. More than 90 percent of African Americans describe themselves as Democrats and support Democratic candidates in national, state, and local elections. Approximately 25 percent of the Democratic Party's support in presidential races comes from African American voters.

Latino and Hispanic voters consist of people whose ancestors came from many different countries, with disparate political orientations. Mexican Americans are the single largest group. They have historically aligned with the Democratic Party, as have Puerto Ricans and Central Americans. Historically, Cuban Americans have voted heavily and identified as Republican. Over the past five years, however, Cubans have exhibited a rapid shift toward the Democratic Party. This trend appears to reflect generational differences, as younger Cuban Americans look to be as Democratic as other Hispanic and Latino groups. Asian Americans tend to be divided as well. Japanese, Chinese, Filipino, and Korean communities have been long established in the United States and have influential business communities. Higher-income Asians tend to be as Republican as higher-income whites. It is not clear whether newer Asian immigrant groups, such as the Hmong, the Vietnamese, Thais, and Indians, will follow the same trajectory as the Japanese and Chinese communities.

Gender. Women are somewhat more likely to support Democrats, and men are somewhat more likely to support Republicans, in surveys of party identification and voting. This difference is known as the **gender gap**. It is somewhat new in American politics. Early studies of the women's vote in the 1920s, shortly after the extension of the franchise, found little difference in voting behavior between men and women. If anything, women tended to be slightly more Republican, and they more strongly favored the prohibition of alcohol than men did. The modern gender gap emerged full-fledged in the 1980 presidential

◀ **gender gap**

A distinctive pattern of voting behavior reflecting the differences in views between women and men

---

16 A recent formulation of the Pluralist model of parties is Kathleen Bawn, Martin Cohen, David Karol, Seth Masket, Hans Noel, and John Zaller, "A Theory of Political Parties: Groups, Policy Demands, and Nominations in American Politics," *Perspectives on Politics* 10 (2012): 571–97.

election and has ranged from a difference of 4 percentage points in how men and women voted in 1992 to a high of 11 percentage points in 1996.[17] In the 2012 election, Barack Obama won 55 percent of the women's vote and 45 percent of the men's vote, a 10-point gap.

Religion. Jews are among the Democratic Party's most loyal constituent groups and have been since the New Deal. Nearly 90 percent of all Jewish Americans describe themselves as Democrats, although the percentage is declining among younger Jews. Catholics were once a strongly pro-Democratic group as well but have been shifting toward the Republican Party since the 1970s, when the Republicans began to focus on abortion and other social issues deemed important to Catholics. More religiously conservative Protestant denominations tend to identify with the Republicans, while Protestants who are religiously liberal, such as Unitarians and Episcopalians, tend to identify as Democrats. Protestant fundamentalists, in particular, have been drawn to the Republicans' conservative stands on social issues, such as school prayer and abortion. (See the Analyzing the Evidence unit for a discussion of candidate religion and partisan voting.)

Class. Upper-income Americans are considerably more likely to affiliate with the Republicans, whereas very lower-income Americans are far more likely to identify with the Democrats. Middle-class voters tend to split evenly between Democrats and Republicans. This divide reflects the differences between the two parties on economic issues. In general, the Republicans support cutting taxes and social spending—positions that reflect the interests of the wealthy. The Democrats, however, favor increased social spending, even if this requires increasing taxes—a position consistent with the interests of less-affluent Americans. One important exception to this principle is that relatively affluent individuals who work in the public sector or such related institutions as foundations and universities also tend to affiliate with the Democrats. Such individuals are likely to appreciate the Democratic Party's support for an expanded role of government and high levels of public spending. White voters with less than a college education (a measure of class) have become less strongly affiliated with the Democrats over time, but this trend is restricted almost entirely to the South. (Outside the South, voters with less than a college education have declined in their support of Democratic presidential candidates by only 1 percentage point in the last 50 years.)[18]

Region. Between the Civil War and the 1960s, the "Solid South" was a Democratic bastion. Today much of the South has become solidly Republican in national elections, although it is more divided in state elections. The area of greatest Democratic Party strength is the Northeast and the Far West (especially

---

17 Susan Carroll, *Women and American Politics: New Questions, New Directions* (Oxford, UK: Oxford University Press, 2003).

18 Andrew Gelman et al., *Red State, Blue State, Rich State, Poor State: Why Americans Vote the Way They Do* (Princeton, NJ: Princeton University Press, 2008).

California, Washington, Oregon, and Hawaii). The Midwest is a battleground, more or less evenly divided between the two parties.

The explanations for these regional variations are complex. The legislative agendas of the two parties certainly play differently in the two regions, with the Republican agenda of social conservatism, low taxes, and high military spending appealing more to voters in the South and Mountain West and the Democratic agenda of social liberalism, high domestic spending (especially on Medicare and Social Security) appealing more in urban areas and in the Northeast and Far West. Republican strength in the South and Mountain West is related to the weakness of organized labor in these regions, as well as to the dependence of the two regions on military programs supported by the Republicans. Democratic strength in the Northeast is a function of the continuing influence of organized labor in the large cities of this region, as well as the region's large population of minority and elderly voters, who benefit from Democratic social programs.

Age. Age is another factor associated with partisanship. There is nothing about a particular numerical age that leads to a particular party loyalty. Instead, individuals from the same age cohort are likely to have experienced a similar set of events during the period when they formed their party loyalties. Thus Americans between the ages of 50 and 64 came of political age during the Cold War, the Vietnam War, and the civil rights movement, and those older than 65 are the product of the Great Depression and World War II. Apparently among voters whose initial perceptions of politics were shaped during these periods, more responded favorably to the role played by the Democrats than to the actions of the Republicans. It is interesting that among the youngest group of Americans, a group that came of age during an era of political scandals that tainted both parties, the plurality describe themselves as independents.

Figure 12.3 indicates the relationship between party identification and a number of social criteria. Race, religion, income, and ideology seem to have the greatest influence on Americans' party affiliations. None of these social characteristics is inevitably linked to partisan identification, however. There are union Republicans and business Democrats, Democrats in Utah, and Republicans in Rhode Island. The general party identifications just discussed are broad tendencies that both reflect and reinforce the issue and policy positions the two parties take in the national and local political arenas. They reflect the general tendency of groups—organized and unorganized—to sort into partisan camps.

PARTIES AS INSTITUTIONS

Political parties in the United States today are not tightly disciplined, hierarchical organizations. Indeed, they never have been. Rather, the American parties consist of extensive networks of politicians, interest groups, activists and donors, consultants, and, ultimately, voters. Some of these pieces of the parties, such as the party caucuses in Congress, seem to have more influence over the policies

Candidate Religion and Partisan Voting

CHAPTER | 12

Contributed by

Geoffrey C. Layman
University of Notre Dame

John C. Green
University of Akron

David E. Campbell
University of Notre Dame

Jeremiah J. Castle
University of Notre Dame

Individuals identify with a political party for many reasons, one of which is their own social group memberships as well as their feelings toward other social groups.[1] To what extent do the social group characteristics of political candidates affect the connection between citizens' party identifications and their support for those candidates? One important social group for many people is religion. In recent decades, the American public has come to view the Republican Party as the party of religious people and the Democratic Party as the party of nonreligious people.[2]

Public Perception of Religious Groups' Party Ties

We asked survey respondents whether they considered Evangelical Christians, religious people, and nonreligious people to be "mainly Republicans, mainly Democrats, or a pretty even mix of both." Americans overwhelmingly view Evangelicals as Republican, tend to view religious people as Republican, and generally perceive nonreligious people as Democrats.

SOURCE: 2007 Candidate Religion Survey (conducted online by YouGov/Polimetrix).

Respondents who answered:
Mainly Republicans   Even mix of both   Mainly Democrats

1 Angus Campbell, Philip E. Converse, Warren E. Miller, and Donald E. Stokes, *The American Voter* (Chicago: University of Chicago Press); Donald Green, Bradley Palmquist, and Eric Schickler, *Partisan Hearts and Minds* (New Haven, CT: Yale University Press, 2002).

2 Geoffrey Layman, *The Great Divide: Religious and Cultural Conflict in American Party Politics* (New York: Columbia University Press, 2001); John C. Green, *The Faith Factor: How Religion Influences American Elections* (Westport, CT: Praeger, 2007).

How does the public's perception of political parties' social group profiles affect the connection between individuals' party ties and their voting decisions? To find out, we presented survey respondents with descriptions of candidates that were identical except for what they said about the candidate's religion.[3] We found that the support of Republican and Democratic identifiers for the candidate changed markedly with the candidate's religious profile. Our findings suggest that because voters make assumptions about candidates' political orientations based on their social characteristics, these characteristics are quite important for electoral behavior.

The Electoral Impact of Candidate Religiosity

PERCENTAGE "VERY LIKELY"
TO SUPPORT CANDIDATE

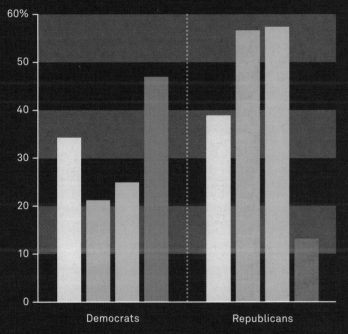

RESPONDENT PARTY IDENTIFICATION

Candidate religiosity treatment

Baseline   Moderately religious

Strongly religious   Secular

We randomly varied what we told survey respondents about the religiosity of a hypothetical state legislative candidate with a nonpartisan issue profile (focusing on goals such as good jobs, a strong economy, and efficient government) and no identified party affiliation. In the baseline (or control) condition, no mention was made of the candidate's religious orientation. When we told respondents that the candidate was moderately religious ("a man of faith") or strongly religious (a "deeply religious" person with a "personal relationship with God"), support decreased among Democrats and increased among Republicans. When we described the candidate as a secular critic of religion in public life (a "man of science" belonging to Americans United for the Separation of Church and State), support strongly increased among Democrats and strongly decreased among Republicans.

SOURCE: 2009 Cooperative Congressional Election Study (conducted online by YouGov/Polimetrix).

3   David E. Campell, John C. Green, and Geoffrey C. Layman, "The Party Faithful: Partisan Images, Candidate Religion, and the Electoral Impact of Party Identification," *American Journal of Political Science* 55, no. 1 (2011): 42–58; and Jeremiah J. Castle, Geoffrey C. Layman, David E. Campbell, and John C. Green, "Candidate Religiosity and Electoral Support: An Experimental Assessment," 2012. Presented at the Annual Meeting of the Southern Political Science Association, New Orleans.

Figure 12.3
PARTY IDENTIFICATION BY SOCIAL GROUP, 2012

SEX

	Republican	Independent	Democrat
Men	29%	38%	29%
Women	27%	29%	40%

AGE

	Republican	Independent	Democrat
18–29	23%	38%	36%
30–49	27%	38%	32%
50–64	29%	31%	36%
65 and over	34%	26%	36%

RACE AND RELIGION

	Republican	Independent	Democrat
White Evangelical Protestant	52%	27%	17%
White Mainline Protestant	34%	35%	28%
Jewish	19%	28%	49%
Unaffiliated	13%	45%	39%

RACE OR ETHNICITY

	Republican	Independent	Democrat
White, non-Hispanic	34%	35%	28%
Black, non-Hispanic	5%	16%	76%
Hispanic	16%	37%	42%

EDUCATION

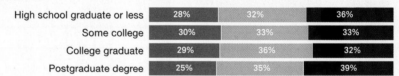

	Republican	Independent	Democrat
High school graduate or less	28%	32%	36%
Some college	30%	33%	33%
College graduate	29%	36%	32%
Postgraduate degree	25%	35%	39%

INCOME

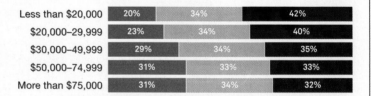

	Republican	Independent	Democrat
Less than $20,000	20%	34%	42%
$20,000–29,999	23%	34%	40%
$30,000–49,999	29%	34%	35%
$50,000–74,999	31%	33%	33%
More than $75,000	31%	34%	32%

IDEOLOGY

	Republican	Independent	Democrat
Conservative	51%	28%	18%
Moderate	18%	42%	36%
Liberal	5%	29%	64%

■ Republican ■ Independent ■ Democrat

and political strategies pursued by the parties than others, but each of these political players shapes the ability of the party to influence what government does. Party campaign finance committees may, for example, work with the congressional caucus to maximize the party's appeal to donors. National party leaders must work with state and local party officials and activists to try to coordinate the many campaign activities in presidential and congressional elections. If parties are such wide-flung networks, how do they make decisions about their most momentous decisions, nominating candidates for offices and choosing a policy or ideological platform? Such decisions are made at every level of government in party committees, conventions, and primary elections, and it is through these institutions that the parties truly come together to make collective decisions.

Contemporary Party Organizations

In the United States, party organizations exist at virtually every level of government (Figure 12.4). These organizations are usually committees made up of a number of active party members. State law and party rules prescribe how such committees are constituted. Usually, committee members are elected at a local party meeting—called a **political caucus**—or as part of the regular primary election. The best-known examples of these committees are at the national level: the Democratic National Committee and the Republican National Committee.

The National Convention. At the national level, the party's most important institution is the national convention. The convention is attended by delegates from each of the states; as a group, they nominate the party's presidential and vice-presidential candidates, draft the party's campaign platform for the presidential race, and approve changes in the rules and regulations governing party procedures. Before World War II, presidential nominations occupied most of the time, energy, and effort expended at the national convention. The nomination process required days of negotiation and compromise among state party leaders and often required many ballots before a nominee was selected. In recent years, however, presidential candidates have essentially nominated themselves by winning enough delegate support in primary elections to win the official nomination on the first ballot. The convention itself has played little or no role in selecting the candidates.

The convention's other two tasks, establishing the party's rules and establishing its platform, remain important. Party rules can determine the relative influence of competing factions within the party and can increase or decrease the party's chances for electoral success. In 1972, for example, the Democratic National Convention adopted a new set of rules favored by the party's liberal wing, according to which state delegations to the Democratic convention are required to include women and members of minority groups in rough proportion to those groups' representation among the party's membership in their state. The convention also approves the party platform. Platforms are often

 political caucus

A normally closed meeting of a political or legislative group to select candidates, plan strategy, or make decisions regarding legislative matters

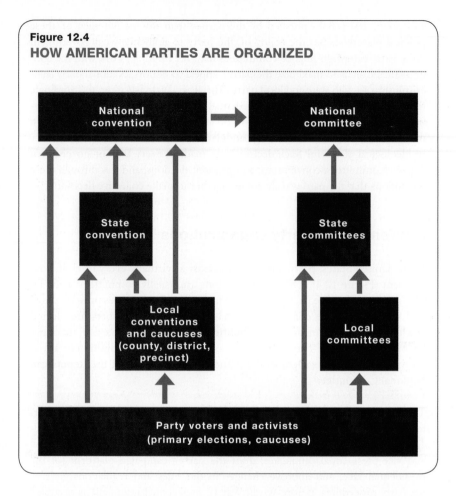

Figure 12.4

HOW AMERICAN PARTIES ARE ORGANIZED

dismissed as platitude-laden documents that are seldom read by voters. Furthermore, the parties' presidential candidates make little use of the platforms in their campaigns; usually they prefer to develop and promote their own themes. Nonetheless, the platform should be understood as a "treaty" in which the various party factions attending the convention state their terms for supporting the ticket.

The National Committee. Between conventions, each national political party is technically headed by its national committee. For the Democrats and Republicans, these are called the Democratic National Committee (DNC) and the Republican National Committee (RNC), respectively. These national committees raise campaign funds, head off factional disputes within the party, and endeavor to enhance the party's media image. Since 1972, the size of staff and the amount of money raised have increased substantially for both national committees. The actual work of each committee is overseen by its chairperson. Other committee members are generally major party contributors or fundraisers and serve in a largely ceremonial capacity.

For the party that controls the White House, the national committee chair is appointed by the president. Typically, this means that that party's national committee becomes little more than an adjunct to the White House staff. For a first-term president, the committee devotes the bulk of its energy to the re-election campaign. The national committee chair of the party that is not in control of the White House is selected by the committee itself and usually takes a broader view of the party's needs, raising money and performing other activities on behalf of the party's members in Congress and in the state legislatures. In 2006, the DNC was headed by Howard Dean, whose failed but impressive presidential bid in 2004 launched him onto the national scene. Dean crafted a 50-state strategy for the 2006 midterm elections in an effort to build party strength and recruit quality candidates in all 50 states. Barack Obama's 2008 and 2012 presidential campaigns capitalized on Dean's 50-state strategy. Obama developed extensive grassroots organizations in every state, which registered many new Democratic voters in traditionally Republican areas, a change that will likely benefit the Democrats for years to come.

Congressional Campaign Committees. Each party forms House and Senate campaign committees to raise funds for the House and Senate election campaigns. The Republicans call their House and Senate committees the National Republican Campaign Committee (NRCC) and the National Republican Senatorial Committee (NRSC). The Democrats call their House and Senate committees the Democratic Congressional Campaign Committee (DCCC) and the Democratic Senatorial Campaign Committee (DSCC). These organizations also have professional staff devoted to raising and distributing funds, developing strategies, recruiting candidates, and conducting on-the-ground campaigns. These organizations, however, are accountable to the caucuses inside the House and Senate. The chairs of these committees come from within their respective chambers and rank high in the party leadership hierarchy. The current chairs are Representative Steve Israel (D-N.Y.) and Senator Michael Bennett (D-Colo.) on the Democratic side and Representative Greg Walden (R-Ore.) and Senator Jerry Moran (D-Kans.) on the Republican side. The national committees and the congressional committees are sometimes rivals. Both groups seek donations from the same pool of people but for different candidates: the national committee seeks funds primarily for the presidential race, whereas the congressional campaign committees focus on House and Senate seats.

State and Local Party Organizations. Each of the two major parties has a central committee in each state. The parties traditionally also have county committees and, in some instances, state senate district committees, judicial district committees, and in larger cities, citywide party committees and local assembly district "ward" committees as well. Congressional districts may also have party committees. Some cities also have precinct committees.[19]

---

19 Well-organized political parties—especially the famous old machines of New York, Chicago, and Boston—provided for "precinct captains" and a fairly tight group of party members around them. Precinct captains were usually members of long standing in neighborhood party clubhouses.

State and local party organizations are very active in recruiting candidates, conducting voter registration drives, and providing financial assistance to candidates. In many respects, federal election law has given state and local party organizations new life, permitting them to spend unlimited amounts of money on "party-building" activities such as voter registration and get-out-the-vote drives. As a result, the national party organizations, which have enormous fund-raising abilities but are limited by law in the amount of money they can spend on candidates, transfer millions of dollars each year to the state and local organizations. The state and local parties, in turn, spend these funds, sometimes called soft money, to promote the candidacies of national, state, and local candidates. In this process, as local organizations have become linked financially to the national parties, American political parties have become somewhat more integrated and nationalized than ever before. At the same time, the state and local party organizations have come to control large financial resources and play important roles in elections despite the collapse of the old patronage machines.

The Contemporary Party as Service Provider to Candidates

Party leaders have adapted parties to the modern age. Parties as organizations are more professional, better financed, and better organized than ever before.[20] Political parties have evolved into "service organizations," which, although they no longer hold a monopoly over campaigns, still provide services to candidates, without which it would be extremely difficult for them to win and hold office. For example, the national organizations of the political parties collect information, ranging from lists of likely supporters and donors in local areas to public opinion polls in states and legislative districts, and they provide this information directly to their candidates for state and federal offices. They also have teams of experienced campaign organizers and managers who provide assistance to local candidates who are in tight races but are understaffed.

Parties provide assistance to candidates in tight races. The national parties' campaign committees today target the closest 50 or so House races and the closest 5 to 10 Senate races. In these contests the parties spend large sums on advertising and other campaign activities. In 2012, party committees' expenditures for and against congressional candidates exceeded $125 million and almost all of that was concentrated in 40 to 50 races. The parties provide tactical support for the candidates' campaign organizations. Consultants from the DCCC, NRCC, NRSC, and DSCC are often deployed to specific campaigns to assist with get-out-the-vote efforts, direct mail, and the like. The party organizations also maintain voter contact lists for the entire nation and can provide candidates with access to such information. Occasionally the party organizations put in place an entire campaign operation if there is the prospect of pulling off an upset.

---

20 See Aldrich, *Why Parties?*, chap. 8.

The rise of party campaign organizations is fairly new. In the 1970s, the organizations (at least nationally) were extremely weak and underfunded, and not capable of providing candidates with such support on a large scale. Congressional campaigns in the 1970s and 1980s were built entirely from the ground up by each individual candidate. Those who were unusually good at raising money, organizing volunteers, and attracting media attention prevailed. In the late 1980s this began to change as the party leaders in Congress and in their national organizations saw that they could do better in national elections if they could somehow redistribute campaign resources to close races and away from safe seats.

The rise of party campaign organizations over the past two decades has altered the politics of swing districts. In the 1970s and 1980s, incumbents in the swing districts built up personal electoral advantages based on prior elections and their prowess as fund-raisers. This allowed these incumbents to vote in Congress less with their party and more with their districts.[21] The independence of legislators in swing districts frustrated party leaders in Congress as they could not rely on the votes of conservative Democrats and liberal Republicans, who might very well cross party lines on important votes. Since the early 1990s, the parties have poured resources into the most competitive seats in order to improve their chances of winning control of the legislature. The winners in these competitive House and Senate races became more beholden to their party, as their electoral fortunes have come to depend more heavily on support from the national party organizations and congressional leadership.

PARTY SYSTEMS

Our understanding of political parties would be incomplete if we considered only their composition and roles. America's political parties compete with each other for offices, policies, and power. The struggle between the major parties for control of government shapes the policies that the parties put forth, the coalitions of interests that they represent, and the ability of the parties, indeed the government, to respond to the demands of the time and age. In short, the fate of each party is inextricably linked to that of its major rival.

Political scientists often call the constellation of parties that are important at any given moment a nation's party system. The most obvious feature of a party system is the number of major parties competing for power. Usually the United States has had a two-party system, meaning that only two parties have a serious chance to win national elections.

21 This argument is developed in great detail in David W. Rohde, *Parties and Leaders in the Post-Reform House* (Chicago: University of Chicago Press, 1991), and in the two books by Gary W. Cox and Mathew D. McCubbins, *Legislative Leviathan* and *Setting the Agenda: Responsible Party Government in the U.S. House of Representatives* (New York: Cambridge University Press, 2005).

There are both institutional and psychological reasons why the United States has just two parties. The American electoral system is winner take all. Whoever gets the most votes wins the congressional seat. Whoever gets the most electoral votes wins the presidency. The Democratic and Republican parties have positioned themselves as center-left and center-right parties, respectively, neither extremely liberal nor extremely conservative. The ideological positions they have chosen maintain their policy distinctiveness and still divide the electorate about equally. If, for example, a far-left party (such as the Green Party) decided to make a strong play to win the presidency, it would split votes with the Democratic Party. It would not decrease votes of the Republican Party but would divide the votes of left-leaning voters between the Democrats and the Greens, effectively guaranteeing a Republican victory. A third party that entered in the middle, on the other hand, would be squeezed between the two parties and would have no hope of gaining sufficient support to win. Understanding this situation, most third parties decide to stay out. Getting on the ballot, recruiting candidates, building an organization—all create tremendous costs. The best that the party could do would be to come in a distant third. Even worse, it could cause the major party it likes less to win. Voters also appear to understand this situation. Voters who would normally want to vote for the third party see that by doing so, they end up boosting the electoral prospects of the major party that they favor less.

The same forces are less likely to influence elections in parliamentary systems, or systems that allocate seats in the legislature to parties in proportion to their share of the national vote. In parliaments, if no party wins a majority, the smaller parties can join with larger parties in a coalition. Systems that divvy up power based on the percentage of the vote won, rather than winner take all, occasionally have to form coalitions in order to form a government. That creates an incentive for small parties to fracture off larger parties or to form de novo.

We have not always had the same two parties, and minor parties often put forward candidates. The term *party system* refers to more than just the number of parties competing for power. It also connotes the organization of the parties, the balance of power between and within party coalitions, the parties' social and institutional bases, and the issues and policies around which party competition is organized.

Implicit in the idea of a party system is a sense of stability, of equilibrium. Voters can reliably expect that the Democrats and Republicans will be the main parties in the next election, that Democrats will tend to be ideologically liberal and Republicans ideologically conservative, that Democrats will align with unions and urban interests while Republicans will align more closely with corporations and rural areas.

That equilibrium is itself an outcome of the political system. It reflects the policies that those in office choose to pursue and the coalitions of interests that they represent. The stability of the party system in the United States does not mean that the system is static. Within each party there exists a tension between its more moderate interests and politicians and its more extreme interests and politicians. Moderates within the parties would like the parties to pursue more centrist policies, as that would increase the support of the party among more moderate voters and groups. The conflicts among the factions within the parties are worked out in state and national conventions, in the caucuses inside

Congress and the state legislatures, and in primary elections. Those involved in the political struggle inside the parties, however, always have an ultimate goal to control government, to gain the upper hand in the struggle with their opposing parties. The party system reflects the balance of the political struggles within parties and the political struggles between them.

Seen from this perspective, one may appreciate both the apparent stability of the party system and its historical evolution. From year to year, the alignment between the parties changes, but only a little. As we discussed earlier, those who have the greatest influence over party policy making are those already in office—the president and members of Congress, especially congressional leaders. They rose to power from within party ranks. They represent the core principles and ideology of the party and have relied on the primary interest groups within the party in their ascent to power. They are reluctant to embrace new principles or alter in any fundamental way the party coalitions, as such radical changes would likely harm their own political position.

The character of a nation's party system changes as the parties realign their electoral coalitions and alter their public philosophies. Such realignment sometimes comes subtly and sometimes suddenly. Today's American party system is very different from the party system of 1950, even though the Democrats and the Republicans continue to be the major competing forces (Figure 12.5). Half a century ago, the Democrats' political strength lay in the South and the Republicans in the North. Democrats favored racial desegregation in the South, and Republicans wanted protectionist trade policies and dismantling of Social Security. Over the past 60 years, gradual social and economic changes in the United States forced the parties to shift their policy orientations and to encompass different political coalitions. Political scientists have referred to this era of gradual change in the party system as a creeping realignment. One of the central issues driving the most recent realignment of the political parties was race. Democratic leaders of the 1940s, such as Harry Truman and Hubert Humphrey, pulled their party to embrace a new platform to end racial desegregation. That change in policy redefined the Democratic party and took the better part of a generation.[22]

Change has also come suddenly to the party system in the United States in response to historical events beyond the control of "political entrepreneurs." The American Civil War and the economic depressions of the 1890s and 1930s brought dramatic and lasting changes to the balance of power between the parties and to the principles and policies that the parties represent. The parties in power and their response to those events redefined their image among the electorate.

Over the course of American history, changes in political forces and alignments have produced six party systems, each with distinctive political institutions, issues, and patterns of political power and participation. Of course, some political phenomena have persisted across party systems. Conflicts over the distribution of wealth, for example, are an enduring feature of American political life. But even such phenomena manifest themselves in different ways during different political eras.

---

22 Edward Carmines and James Stimson, *Issue Evolution* (Princeton, NJ: Princeton University Press, 1989).

Figure 12.5
HOW THE PARTY SYSTEM EVOLVED

Major Parties

Third Parties* and Independents

Year		
1788	Federalist	
1790	Democratic-Republicans	
1804		
1812		
1816		
1820		
1824	National Republicans	
1828	Democrats	
1832		Anti-Masonic**
1836	Whigs	
1840		Liberty
1844		
1848		Free-Soil
1852		
1856	Republicans (GOP)	American
1860		Constitutional Union
1864		
1868		
1872	Prohibition (1869)	
1876		
1880		Greenback Labor
1884		
1888		Union Labor
1892		Populist
1896		
1900		
1904	Socialist	
1908		
1912		T. Roosevelt's Progressive (Bull Moose)
1916		
1920		
1924		Progressive
1928		
1932		
1936		
1940		
1944		
1948		States' Rights (Dixiecrats)
1952		
1956		
1960		
1964		
1968		Wallace's American Indepedent
1972		
1976		
1980		Anderson's National Unity
1984		
1988		
1992		Perot's United We Stand
1996		Perot's Reform Party
2000		Green Party
2004		Nader's Indepedence Party
2008		Green Party, Libertarian Party, Constitution Party
2012		

*In some cases, there was even a fourth party. Most of the parties listed here existed for only one term.
** The Anti-Masonics not only had the distinction of being the first third party but also were the first party to hold a national nominating convention and the first to announce a party platform.

The First Party System: Federalists and Democratic-Republicans

Although George Washington and, in fact, many other leaders of the time deplored partisan politics, the two-party system emerged early in the history of the new Republic. Competition in Congress between northeastern mercantile and southern agrarian factions led Alexander Hamilton and the northeasterners to form a cohesive voting bloc within Congress. The southerners, led by Thomas Jefferson and James Madison, responded by attempting to organize a popular following to change the balance of power within Congress. When the northeasterners replied to this southern strategy, the result was the birth of America's first national parties—the Democratic-Republicans, whose primary base was in the South, and the Federalists, whose strength was greatest in the New England states. The Federalists spoke mainly for New England mercantile groups and supported protective tariffs to encourage manufacturers, the assumption of the states' Revolutionary War debts, the creation of a national bank, and resumption of commercial ties with England. The Democratic-Republicans opposed these policies, favoring instead free trade, the promotion of agrarian over commercial interests, and friendship with France.

The rationale behind the formation of both parties was primarily that they would be a means by which to institutionalize existing voting blocs in Congress around a cohesive policy agenda. Although the Federalists and the Democratic-Republicans competed in elections, their ties to the electorate were loose. In 1800, the American electorate was small, and deference was an important political factor, with voters generally expected to follow the lead of local political and religious leaders and community notables. Nominations were informal, without rules or regulations. Local party leaders would simply gather the party elites, and they would agree on the person, usually one of them, who would be the candidate. The meetings where candidates were nominated were generally called caucuses. In this era, before the introduction of the secret ballot, many voters were reluctant publicly to defy the views of influential members of their community. In this context, the Democratic-Republicans and the Federalists organized political clubs and developed newspapers and newsletters designed to mobilize elite opinion and relied on local elites to bring along their followers. In the election of 1800, Jefferson defeated the incumbent Federalist president, John Adams, and led the Democratic-Republicans to power. Over the ensuing years, the Federalists gradually weakened. The party disappeared altogether after the pro-British sympathies of some Federalist leaders during the War of 1812 led to charges that the party was guilty of treason.

The Second Party System: Democrats and Whigs

From the collapse of the Federalists until the 1830s, America had only one political party, the Democratic-Republicans. This period of one-party politics is sometimes known as the Era of Good Feeling, to indicate the absence of party competition. Throughout this period, however, there was intense factional conflict within the Democratic-Republican Party, particularly between the supporters and opponents of General Andrew Jackson, America's great military hero of the War of 1812. Jackson was one of five significant candidates for president in 1824 and won the most popular and electoral votes but a majority of neither, throwing the election into the House of Representatives. Jackson's opponents united to deny him the presidency, but Jackson won election in 1828 and again in 1832.

Jackson was greatly admired by millions of ordinary Americans living on the nation's farms and in its villages, and the Jacksonians made the most of the general's appeal to the common people by embarking on a program of suffrage expansion that would give Jackson's impecunious but numerous supporters the right to vote. To bring growing numbers of voters to the polls, the Jacksonians built political clubs and held mass rallies and parades, laying the groundwork for a new and more popular politics. Jackson's vice president and eventual successor, Martin Van Buren, was the organizational genius behind the Jacksonian movement, establishing a central party committee, state party organizations, and party newspapers. In response to widespread complaints about cliques of party leaders dominating the nominations at party caucuses and leaving no place for other party members who wanted to participate, the Jacksonians also established the state and national party conventions as the forums for nominating presidential candidates. The conventions gave control of the presidential nominating process to the new state party organizations that the Jacksonians had created and expected to control. As the political scientist John Aldrich has argued, unlike any political leader before him, Van Buren appreciated the possibilities for mass mobilization and the necessity of a well-oiled national organization to overcome free riding and other collective action problems.[23] With a keen sense of what it took to organize a party for electoral competition, Van Buren produced institutional solutions to collective action problems, leaving as a historical legacy the blueprint for the modern mass-based political party.

The Jacksonians, whose party came to be known as the Democratic Party, were not without opponents, however, especially in the New England states. During the 1830s, groups opposing Jackson for reasons of personality and politics united to form a new political force—the Whig Party—thus giving rise to the second American party system. During the 1830s and 1840s, the Democrats and the Whigs built party organizations throughout the nation, and both sought to enlarge their bases of support by expanding the suffrage through the elimination of property restrictions and other barriers to voting—although voting was still restricted to white men. This would not be the last time that party competition paved the way for expansion of the electorate. Support for the new Whig Party was stronger in the Northeast than in the South and the West and stronger among mercantile groups than among small farmers. Hence to some extent the Whigs were the successors of the Federalists. Many, though not all, Whigs favored a national bank, a protective tariff, and federally sponsored internal improvements. The Jacksonians opposed all three policies. Yet conflict between the two parties revolved around personalities as much as policies. The Whigs were a diverse group, united more by opposition to the Democrats than by agreement on programs. In 1840, the Whigs won their first presidential election

---

23 See Aldrich, *Why Parties?*, chap. 4.

under the leadership of General William Henry Harrison, a military hero known as Old Tippecanoe. The 1840 election marked the first time in American history that two parties competed for the presidency in every state in the Union. The Whig campaign carefully avoided issues—because different party factions disagreed on most matters—and emphasized the personal qualities and heroism of the candidate. The Whigs also invested heavily in campaign rallies and entertainment to win the hearts, if not exactly the minds, of the voters. The 1840 campaign came to be called the hard-cider campaign to denote the then-common practice of using food and, especially, drink to elicit electoral favor.

In the late 1840s and early 1850s, conflicts over slavery produced sharp divisions within both the Whig and the Democratic parties, despite the efforts of party leaders such as Henry Clay and Stephen A. Douglas to develop sectional compromises that would bridge the widening gulf between the North and the South. By 1856, the Whig Party had all but disintegrated under the strain. The 1854 Kansas-Nebraska Act overturned the Missouri Compromise of 1820 and the Compromise of 1850, which together had hindered the expansion of slavery in the American territories. The Kansas-Nebraska Act gave each territory the right to decide whether to permit slavery. Opposition to this policy led to the formation of a number of antislavery parties, with the Republicans emerging as the strongest of the new forces.[24] They drew their membership from existing political groups—former Whigs, Know-Nothings of the American Party, free soilers, and antislavery Democrats. In 1856, the party's first presidential candidate, John C. Frémont, won one-third of the popular vote and carried 11 states.

The early Republican platforms appealed to commercial as well as antislavery interests. The Republicans favored homesteading, internal improvements, the construction of a transcontinental railroad, and protective tariffs, as well as the containment of slavery. In 1858, the Republican Party won control of the House of Representatives; in 1860, the Republican presidential candidate, Abraham Lincoln, was victorious. Lincoln's victory strengthened southern calls for secession from the Union and led, soon thereafter, to all-out civil war.

The Third Party System: Republicans and Democrats, 1860–96

During the course of the war, President Lincoln depended heavily on Republican governors and state legislatures to raise troops, provide funding, and maintain popular support for a long and bloody military conflict. The secession of the South had stripped the Democratic Party of many of its leaders and supporters, but the Democrats nevertheless remained politically competitive throughout the war and nearly won the 1864 presidential election due to war weariness on the part of the northern public. With the defeat of the Confederacy in 1865, some congressional Republicans sought to convert the South into a Republican bastion through Reconstruction, a program that enfranchised newly freed slaves while disenfranchising many white voters and disqualifying many

24 See William E. Gienapp, *The Origins of the Republican Party, 1852–1856* (New York: Oxford University Press, 1994).

white politicians from seeking office. Reconstruction collapsed in the 1870s as a result of divisions within the Republican Party in Congress and violent resistance to the program by southern whites. With the end of Reconstruction, the former Confederate states regained full membership in the Union and full control of their internal affairs. Throughout the South, African Americans were deprived of political rights, including the right to vote, despite post–Civil War constitutional guarantees to the contrary. The post–Civil War South was solidly Democratic in its political affiliation, and with a firm southern base, the national Democratic Party was able to confront the Republicans on a more or less equal basis. From the end of the Civil War to the 1890s, the Republican Party remained the party of the North, with strong business and middle-class support, while the Democratic Party was the party of the South, with support from working-class and immigrant groups in the North. Republican candidates campaigned by waving the "bloody shirt" of the Civil War and urging their supporters to "vote the way you shot." Democrats emphasized the issue of the tariff, which they claimed was ruinous to agricultural interests.

Party Machines as a Strategic Innovation.
It was during the third party system that party entrepreneurs were most successful at turning party organizations into well-oiled machines. In the nineteenth and early twentieth centuries, many cities and counties, and even a few states on occasion, had such well-organized parties that they were called **party machines** and their leaders were called bosses. Party machines depended heavily on the patronage of the spoils system, the party's power to control government jobs. Patronage worked as a selective benefit for anyone the party wished to attract to its side. With thousands of jobs to dispense to the party faithful, party bosses were able to recruit armies of political workers, who in turn mobilized millions of voters. During the height of the party machines, party and government were virtually interchangeable. Just as the creation of mass parties by Van Buren and other political entrepreneurs of the second party system solved a collective action problem, the well-oiled machines used the selective incentives of patronage and nomination to maintain their organizations and diminish free riding. Many organizational aspects of party politics, in short, involve the ingenuity of rational politicians and leaders grappling with problems of coordination and collective action, as the rationality principle and the collective action principle suggest.

Many critics condemned party machines as antidemocratic and corrupt. They argued that machines served the interests of powerful businesses and did not help the working people who voted for them. But one of the most notorious machine leaders in American political history, George Washington Plunkitt of New York City's Tammany Hall, considered machine politics and the spoils system to be "patriotic." Plunkitt grasped a simple, central fact about purposeful behavior and overcoming the collective action problem. To create and retain political influence and power, "you must study human nature and act accordin'." He argued with some acumen that the country was built by political parties, that the parties needed such patronage to operate and thrive, and that if patronage was withdrawn, the parties would "go to pieces." As we see shortly, Plunkitt was somewhat prescient in making this observation.

---

party machine

In the late nineteenth and early twentieth centuries, the local party organization that controlled local politics through patronage and the nomination process

Institutional Reforms of the Progressives. As the nineteenth century gave way to the twentieth, the excessive powers and abuses of party machines and their bosses led to one of the great reform movements in American history, the so-called Progressive Era. Many Progressive reformers were undoubtedly motivated by a sincere desire to rid politics of corruption and improve the quality and efficiency of government in the United States. But simultaneously, from the perspective of middle- and upper-class Progressives and the financial, commercial, and industrial elites with whom they were often associated, the weakening or elimination of party organization would also mean that power could more readily be acquired and retained by the "best men"—that is, those with wealth, position, and education.

The list of antiparty reforms of the Progressive Era is a familiar one. As we saw in Chapter 11, the introduction of voter registration laws required eligible voters to register in person well before an election. The Australian-ballot reform took away the parties' privilege of printing and distributing ballots and thus introduced the possibility of split-ticket voting (see also Chapter 11). The introduction of nonpartisan local elections eroded grassroots party organization. The extension of "merit systems" for administrative appointments stripped party organizations of their vitally important access to patronage and thus reduced party leaders' capacity to control the nomination of candidates. These reforms obviously did not destroy political parties as entities, but taken together they did substantially weaken party organizations in the United States. After the beginning of the twentieth century, the strength of American political parties gradually diminished, and voter turnout declined precipitously. Between the two world wars, organization remained the major tool available to contending electoral forces, but in most areas of the country the "reformed" state and local parties that survived the Progressive Era gradually lost their organizational vitality and coherence and became less effective campaign tools. Although most areas of the nation continued to boast Democratic and Republican Party groupings, reform did mean the elimination of the permanent mass organizations that had been the parties' principal campaign weapons.

The Fourth Party System, 1896–1932

During the 1890s, profound and rapid social and economic changes led to the emergence of a variety of protest parties, including the Populist Party, which won the support of hundreds of thousands of voters in the South and the West. The Populists appealed mainly to small farmers but also attracted western mining interests and urban workers. In the 1892 presidential election, the Populist Party carried four states and elected governors in eight states. In 1896, the Democrats in effect adopted the Populist Party platform and nominated William Jennings Bryan, a Democratic senator with pronounced Populist sympathies, for the presidency. The Republicans nominated the conservative senator William McKinley. In the ensuing campaign, northern and midwestern business made an all-out effort to defeat what it saw as a radical threat from the Populist-Democratic alliance. When the dust settled, the Republicans had won a resounding victory. In the nation's metropolitan regions, especially in the Northeast and upper Midwest, workers became convinced that the Populist-Democratic alliance threatened the industries that provided their jobs, while immigrants were frightened by the nativist rhetoric employed by some Populist orators and writers. The Republicans had carried the northern and midwestern states and confined the Democrats to their bastions in the South and the Far West. For the next 36 years, the Republicans were the nation's majority party, carrying 7 of 9 presidential elections and controlling both houses of Congress in 15 of 18 contests. The Republican Party of this era was very much the party of American business, advocating low taxes, high tariffs, and a minimum of government regulation. The Democrats were far too weak to offer much opposition. Southern Democrats, moreover, were more concerned with maintaining the region's autonomy on issues of race to challenge the Republicans on other fronts.

The Fifth Party System: The New Deal Coalition, 1932–68

Soon after the Republican candidate Herbert Hoover won the 1928 presidential election, the nation's economy collapsed. The Great Depression, which produced unprecedented economic hardship, stemmed from a variety of causes, but from the perspective of millions of Americans the Republican Party had not done enough to promote economic recovery. In 1932, Americans elected Franklin Delano Roosevelt and a solidly Democratic Congress. Roosevelt developed a program for economic recovery that he dubbed the New Deal, under the auspices of which the size and reach of America's national government was substantially increased. The federal government took responsibility for economic management and social welfare to an extent that was unprecedented in American history. Roosevelt designed many of his programs specifically to expand the political base of the Democratic Party. He rebuilt the party around a nucleus of unionized workers, upper-middle-class intellectuals and professionals, southern farmers, Jews, Catholics, and northern African Americans (few blacks in the South could vote) that made the Democrats the nation's majority party for 36 years. Republicans groped for a response to the New Deal but often wound up supporting popular New Deal programs such as Social Security in what was sometimes derided as "me-too" Republicanism.

The New Deal coalition was severely strained during the 1960s by conflicts over President Lyndon Johnson's Great Society initiative, civil rights, and the Vietnam War. A number of Johnson's Great Society programs, designed to fight poverty and racial discrimination, involved the empowerment of local groups that were often at odds with established city and county governments. These programs touched off battles between local Democratic political machines and the national administration that split the Democratic coalition. For its part, the struggle over civil rights initially divided northern Democrats, who supported the civil rights cause, and white southern Democrats, who defended the system of racial segregation. Subsequently, as the civil rights movement launched a northern campaign aimed at securing access to jobs and education and an end to racial discrimination in such realms as housing, northern Democrats also experienced a split, often along class lines, with blue-collar workers tending to vote

Republican. The struggle over the Vietnam War further divided the Democrats, with upper-income liberal Democrats strongly opposing the Johnson administration's decision to send U.S. forces to fight in Southeast Asia. These schisms within the Democratic Party provided an opportunity for the Republican Party to return to power, which it did in 1968 under the leadership of Richard Nixon.

The Sixth Party System

In the 1960s, conservative Republicans argued that me-tooism was a recipe for continual failure and sought to reposition the party as a genuine alternative to the Democrats. In 1964, for example, the Republican presidential candidate, Barry Goldwater, author of a book titled *The Conscience of a Conservative*, argued in favor of substantially reduced levels of taxation and spending, less government regulation of the economy, and the elimination of many federal social programs. Although Goldwater was defeated by Lyndon Johnson, the ideas he espoused continue to be major themes of the Republican Party. The Goldwater message, however, was not enough to lead Republicans to victory. As discussed in Chapter 11, it took Richard Nixon's "southern strategy" to give the Republicans the votes it needed to end Democratic dominance of the political process. Nixon appealed strongly to disaffected white southerners and, with the help of the independent candidate and former Alabama governor George Wallace, sparked the shift of voters that eventually gave the once-hated "party of Lincoln" a strong position in all the states of the former Confederacy. In the 1980s, under the leadership of Ronald Reagan, Republicans added another important group to their coalition: religious conservatives who were offended by Democratic support of abortion rights as well as alleged Democratic disdain for traditional cultural and religious values.

While Republicans built a political base with economic and social conservatives and white southerners, the Democratic Party maintained its support among unionized workers and upper-middle-class intellectuals and professionals. Democrats also appealed strongly to racial minorities. The 1965 Voting Rights Act had greatly increased the participation of black voters in the South and helped the Democratic Party retain some congressional and Senate seats in the South. And while the GOP appealed to social conservatives, the Democrats appealed strongly to Americans concerned about abortion rights, gay rights, feminism, environmentalism, and other progressive social causes. The results have been something of a draw. Democrats have won the presidency 5 out of the 12 elections since the passage of the Voting Rights Act and held at least one chamber of Congress for most of that time. That apparent stalemate masked dramatic changes in the regional bases of the parties. Republicans surged in the south, making the southern states the foundation of their presidential and congressional victories. Those gains came at the expense of the old-line Republicans in the northeast. New England, once the bedrock of the party, had not one Republican U.S. House member after the 2008 election.

 Ideology and Parties. The shift of much of the South from the Democratic to the Republican camp, along with the other developments mentioned earlier, meant that each political party became ideologically more homogeneous after the 1980s. Today as we've noted before, there are few liberal Republicans or conservative Democrats. One consequence of this development is that party loyalty in Congress, which had been weak between the 1950s and the 1970s, became a more potent force. The 1990s witnessed a dramatic resurgence of party-line voting in Congress. A simple measure of party developed by Professor Stuart Rice in the 1920s and tracked by *Congressional Quarterly* since the 1950s is the party unity score. This is the percentage of bills on which a majority of one party votes against a majority of the other party. Between the 1950s and the 1970s, unity hovered around 70 percent. Since the 1980s it has regularly exceeded 90 percent.[25]

To some extent, ideology has replaced organization as the glue holding together each party's coalition. But in the long run, ideology is often an unreliable basis for party unity. Although the activists within each party grouping are united by some beliefs, ideological divisions also plague both camps. Within the Republican coalition, social conservatives are often at odds with economic conservatives, whereas among Democrats proponents of regulatory reform and economic internationalism are frequently at odds with traditional liberals, who favor big government and protecting American workers from foreign competition. The party workers of yesteryear supported the leadership almost no matter what. Today's more ideologically motivated party activists give their leaders only very conditional backing and feel free to withhold support if they disagree with the leadership's goals and plans. Because of internal divisions in the Republican Party, for example, Republican congressional leaders have adopted a strategy of avoiding votes on the many issues that might split the party.[26] The price of unity based on ideology can be the inability to act.

The ideological gap between the two parties has been exacerbated by two other factors: each party's dependence on ideologically motivated activists and the changes in the presidential nominating system that were introduced during the 1970s. As for the first of these, Democratic political candidates depend heavily on the support of liberal activists—such as feminists, environmentalists, and civil libertarians—to organize and finance their campaigns, while Republican political candidates depend equally on the support of conservative activists, including religious fundamentalists. In the nineteenth century, political activists were motivated more by party loyalty and political patronage than by programmatic concerns. Today's issue-oriented activists, by contrast, demand that politicians demonstrate strong commitments to moral principles and political causes in exchange for their support. The demands of party activists have tended to push Democrats further to the political left and Republicans further to the political right. Often efforts by politicians to reach compromises on key issues are attacked by party activists as "sellouts," leading to stalemates on such matters as the budget and judicial appointments.

---

25 The classic statement of the connection between cohesive legislative parties and ideological homogeneity within party ranks is found in Rohde, *Parties and Leaders in the Post-Reform House*. An elaboration of this argument is presented in Cox and McCubbins, *Setting the Agenda*. See also Nolan McCarty, Keith Poole, and Howard Rosenthal, *Polarized America: The Dance of Inequality and Unequal Riches* (Cambridge, MA: MIT Press, 2006).

26 Isaiah J. Poole, "Votes Echo Electoral Themes," *Congressional Quarterly Weekly Report*, December 11, 2004, pp. 2906–8.

The second factor exacerbating the parties' ideological split, the changes in the presidential nominating system, took place in response to the Democratic Party's defeat in 1968. Liberal forces, guided by the so-called McGovern-Fraser Commission on party reform, succeeded in changing the rules governing Democratic presidential nominations to reduce the power of party officials and party professionals while increasing the role of issue-oriented activists. Among other changes, the new rules required national convention delegates to be chosen in primaries and caucuses rather than by each state party's central committee, as had previously been the practice in many states. Subsequently, Republican activists were able to bring about similar changes in the Republicans' rules, so that today in both parties presidential nominating processes are strongly influenced by precisely the sorts of grassroots activists who are often inclined to oppose centrist or pragmatic politicians in favor of those appearing to manifest ideological purity. As a result, elections have tended to pit liberal Democrats against conservative Republicans. Observers of post–World War II American political parties often dubbed them Tweedledum and Tweedledee, but the two parties today differ sharply on social, economic, and foreign policy issues and are deeply divided over questions concerning taxation and government spending.

Finally, the parties have been sorted out along cultural and regional lines. As discussed earlier, Republicans now win most of the House and Senate seats in the South, while Democrats tend to dominate in the Northeast and Pacific West.

American Third Parties

Although the United States is said to possess a two-party system, we have always had more than two parties. Typically, **third parties** in the United States have represented social and economic protests that, for one or another reason, were not given voice by the two major parties.[27] Such parties have had a good deal of influence on ideas and elections in the United States. The Populists, a party centered in the rural areas of the West and the Midwest during the late nineteenth century, and the Progressives, spokesmen for the urban middle classes in the late nineteenth and early twentieth centuries, are among the most important examples. More recently, Ross Perot, who ran in 1992 and 1996 as an independent, impressed some voters with his folksy style in the presidential debates and garnered almost 19 percent of the votes cast in the 1992 presidential election. Earlier, the independent candidate George Wallace received almost 10 percent of the vote in 1968, and John Anderson received about 5 percent in 1980.

Table 12.1 lists the parties that offered candidates in one or more states in the presidential election of 2012, as well as independent candidates. The third-party and independent candidates together polled only 2,250,000 votes, and they gained no electoral votes for president. Third-party candidacies also arise at the state and local levels. In New York, the Liberal and Conservative parties have been on the ballot for decades. In 1998, Minnesota elected a third-party

 third party

A party that organizes to compete against the two major American political parties

---

27 For a discussion of third parties in the United States, see Daniel A. Mazmanian, *Third Parties in Presidential Elections* (Washington, DC: Brookings Institution, 1974).

Table 12.1

PARTIES AND CANDIDATES, 2012

ANALYZING THE EVIDENCE

Though the Democrats and the Republicans are America's dominant political forces, many minor parties nominate candidates for the presidency. Why are there so many minor parties? Why don't these parties represent much of a threat to the major parties?

CANDIDATE	PARTY	VOTE TOTAL	PERCENT OF VOTE
Barack Obama	Democrat	65,907,213	51.06
Mitt Romney	Republican	60,931,767	47.21
Gary Johnson	Libertarian	1,275,804	0.99
Jill Stein	Green	469,501	0.36
Virgil Goode	Constitution	122,001	0.09
Roseanne Barr	Independent	67,278	0.05
Rocky Anderson	Justice Party	43,111	0.03
Tom Hoefling	America's Party	40,586	0.03
Richard Duncan	Independent	12,557	0.01
Others		217,669	0.17

SOURCE: Federal Election Commission, www.fec.gov.

governor, the former professional wrestler Jesse Ventura. And, two Independents currently serve in the U.S. Senate, Senator Bernie Sanders of Vermont and Senator Angus King of Maine.

Although it is difficult for third parties to survive, it is worth noting that the two major parties today themselves started as third parties. The Democrats emerged at the beginning of the nineteenth century as an alternative to the Federalists and their opponents, loosely, the Anti-Federalists. The Federalist Party, a party organized largely around the ideas and policies of Alexander Hamilton, itself gave way to the Whig Party, which was replaced by the Republicans. In some sense, then, the two major parties today started as alternative parties, as third parties. They have reinvented themselves ideologically to change with the times and to co-opt supporters of emerging parties. The Democratic Party, for example, became a great deal more liberal when it adopted most of the Progressive program early in the twentieth century. Many socialists felt that President Franklin Delano Roosevelt's New Deal had adopted most of their party's program, including old-age pensions, unemployment compensation, an agricultural marketing program, and laws guaranteeing workers the right to organize into unions.

The ability of the major parties to evolve is one explanation for the short lives of third parties. Their causes are usually eliminated by the ability of the major parties to absorb their programs and draw their supporters into the mainstream. There are, of course, additional reasons for the short duration of most third parties. One is the typical limitation of their electoral support to one or two regions. Populist support, for example, was primarily midwestern. The 1948 Progressive Party, with Henry Wallace as its candidate, drew nearly half its votes from the state of New York. The American Independent Party polled nearly 10 million popular votes and 45 electoral votes for George Wallace in 1968—the most electoral votes ever polled by a third-party candidate. But all of Wallace's electoral votes and the majority of his popular vote came from the states of the Deep South. Americans usually assume that only the candidates nominated by one of the two major parties have any chance of winning an election. Thus a vote cast for a third-party or an independent candidate is often seen as a wasted vote. For instance, there is evidence in the 2000 race between Al Gore, the Democrat, and George W. Bush, the Republican, that the third-party candidate Ralph Nader did better in those states where either Bush or Gore was nearly certain of winning, whereas his support dwindled in more closely contested states. Third-party candidates must struggle—usually without success—to overcome the perception that they cannot win.

As many scholars have pointed out, third-party prospects are also hampered by America's single-member-district plurality election system. In many other nations, several individuals can be elected to represent each legislative district. This is called a system of multiple-member districts. With this type of system, the candidates of weaker parties have a better chance of winning at least some seats. For their part, voters are less concerned about wasting ballots and usually more willing to support minor-party candidates.

Reinforcing the effects of the single-member district (as noted in Chapter 11), plurality voting rules generally have the effect of setting what could be called a high threshold for victory. To win a plurality race, candidates usually must secure many more votes than they would need under most European systems of proportional representation. For example, to win an American plurality election in a single-member district with only two candidates, a politician must win more than 50 percent of the votes cast. To win a seat in a European multimember district under proportional-representation rules, a candidate may need to win only 15 or 20 percent of the votes cast. This high threshold in American elections discourages minor parties and encourages the various political factions that might otherwise form minor parties to minimize their differences and remain within the major-party coalitions.[28]

It would nevertheless be incorrect to assert (as some scholars have maintained) that America's single-member plurality election system guarantees that only two parties will compete for power in all regions of the country. All that can be said is that American election law depresses the number of parties likely to survive over long periods of time in the United States. There is nothing magical about two.

28 See Maurice Duverger, *Political Parties: Their Organization and Activity in the Modern State,* trans. Barbara North and Robert North (New York: Wiley, 1954).

CONCLUSION: PARTIES AND DEMOCRACY

Political parties help make democracy work. We often do not appreciate that democratic government is a contradiction in terms. Government implies policies, programs, and decisive action. Democracy, on the other hand, implies an opportunity for all citizens to participate fully in the governmental process. Full participation by everyone is inconsistent with getting things done in an efficient and timely manner. How can we balance the ideals of democracy and efficiency in government? How can we make certain that popular participation will result in a government capable of making decisions and developing needed policies? At what point should participation stop and government begin? Strong political parties are a partial antidote to the inherent contradiction between participation and governance. Strong parties can both encourage popular involvement and convert participation into effective government.

As we've seen, parties simplify the electoral process. They set the electoral agenda by laying out party platforms, recruit candidates, accumulate and distribute campaign resources, and register and mobilize people to vote. Party control of the nominating process and the pressures toward two-party politics in the United States mean that most voters must decide between just two meaningful or plausible choices in any election. Parties, thus, serve as sort of an informal institution in elections and government. They structure electoral choices and manage the legislative agenda, and they serve as a bridge between elections and government.

This, in turn, facilitates voters' decision making. Voters can reasonably expect what sorts of policies a candidate who has a party's endorsement will represent if elected. Even before a given candidate has received the nomination, most voters have already sorted themselves into one of the two competing camps, Democratic or Republican. They know for whom they will vote before the election begins. This may seem like a gross simplification of politics. It reduces the many complex interests in our society to just two competing teams, whose policy platforms must be watered down to accommodate the many subtle differences or ideological nuances among the groups inside the party. It further reduces politics into warring factions that have little hope of finding compromise or common ground. However, what the two-party system does accomplish is that it gives meaning to the vote. It empowers the voter to say, "I want to stay the course with the party in power," or, "I want to go in a new direction."

But, there is a downside. Simplification of the choices leaves some voters without a party that approximates what they would like government to do and without an effective voice. Parties also try to monopolize politics. They are often viewed as coalitions or teams seeking to control government for their own purposes, and not necessarily the interests of the whole. And the competition for control of government between just two parties in a system with separation of powers can lead to gridlock and stalemate. George Washington, James Madison, John Adams, and Thomas Jefferson all viewed parties with disdain. Washington's farewell address warned "against the baneful effects of the spirit of party." Jefferson wrote "If I could not go to Heaven but with a party, I would not go there at all." Nonetheless all of the Founding Fathers ended up in one way or another involved with the founding of the political parties: Washington, Adams, and Hamilton, the Federalists; Jefferson and Madison, the Democrat-Republicans. They could not help but fall into parties because of the nature of politics and the need for an organization to solve the problems of selecting candidates, organizing elections, and simplifying electoral choice.

For Further Reading

Selections highlighted in red are included in *Readings in American Politics: Analysis and Perspectives*, Third Edition.

Aldrich, John H. *Why Parties? A Second Look.* Chicago: University of Chicago Press, 2011.

Campbell, Angus, Philip E. Converse, Warren E. Miller, and Donald E. Stokes. *The American Voter.* Chicago: University of Chicago Press, 1980.

Chambers, William N., and Walter Dean Burnham, eds. *The American Party Systems: Stages of Political Development.* 2nd ed. New York: Oxford University Press, 1975.

Coleman, John J. *Party Decline in America: Policy, Politics, and the Fiscal State.* Princeton, NJ: Princeton University Press, 1996.

Cox, Gary W., and Mathew D. McCubbins. *Legislative Leviathan: Party Government in the House.* Berkeley: University of California Press, 1993.

Cox, Gary W., and Mathew D. McCubbins. *Setting the Agenda: Responsible Party Government in the U.S. House of Representatives.* New York: Cambridge University Press, 2005.

Hershey, Marjorie Randon. *Party Politics in America.* 15th ed. New York: Pearson, 2013.

Hofstadter, Richard. *The Idea of a Party System: The Rise of Legitimate Opposition in the United States, 1780–1840.* Berkeley: University of California Press, 1969.

Mayhew, David. *Electoral Realignments: A Critique of an American Genre.* New Haven, CT: Yale University Press, 2007.

Rohde, David W. *Parties and Leaders in the Post-Reform House.* Chicago: University of Chicago Press, 1991.

Wattenberg, Martin P. *The Decline of American Political Parties, 1952–1996.* Cambridge, MA: Harvard University Press, 1998.

13

Groups and Interests

Democratic politics in the United States does not end with elections. Federal, state, and local governments provide many additional avenues through which individuals and organizations can express their preferences. People may, for example, contact elected officials, their staff, and bureaucrats directly about a particular decision or problem. They may participate in public meetings about legislation or administrative rulings; some private citizens are even selected to serve on special government commissions because of their expertise or particular concerns. People may file lawsuits to request that a government agency take a particular action or to prevent it from doing so. They may express their opinions in newspapers, on television, and the Internet, or through other venues, and hold public protests, all without fear of persecution. Individuals, organizations, and even governments make frequent use of these many points of access. Many of these encounters with government are episodic, as when an individual contacts an agency to solve a particular problem. But a substantial amount of political activity in the United States occurs through enduring, organized efforts that bring together many individuals into collective action to seek a common goal.

Both a pull and a push drive organized political activity in the United States. The pull comes from the government's need to collect information about the impact of decisions on various constituencies or sectors of society. A responsive government needs subtle and refined information about how a decision will affect people or society or about the best way to implement a law. Legislators, judges, and bureaucrats typically do not have the time or resources to study all potential problems. Instead they rely on information from individuals and organizations to gauge the importance of a given problem and to learn about the consequences of particular decisions. The solution in American government is to allow, and indeed encourage, an open government with many points of access for competing views.

The push comes from the willingness and ability of people to contact government. Individuals and organizations bring their concerns to the government with some purpose in mind, to gain some benefit. Those benefits often take the form of simply better understanding government regulations and actions. When a commission or department issues a new regulation, firms that are potentially affected must figure out whether the regulation applies to them, how to comply if they are affected, and the exact interpretation of the regulations. Firms frequently hire representation in Washington or the state capital just to stay on top of such matters. But many of those involved in direct political action want more than information; they want to change laws and public policies to favor their particular interests. They want targeted appropriations or favorable regulatory rulings, potentially worth millions, even billions of dollars. One influential study discovered that half of the activities and efforts of businesspeople who contacted the government consisted of gathering information and half consisted of advocacy for a particular policy or action.[1]

Interest group politics in the United States involves thousands of organizations and individuals competing for the attention of elected representatives

CORE OF THE ANALYSIS

 Individuals, firms, and other organizations engage in a wide variety of political activities, including contacting elected officials, attending government meetings, engaging in campaign activities, and contributing money in order to shape how those in office make and implement laws.

 These activities help government solve an important problem—the problem of how to learn about what problems are important to society and how government actions might affect society.

 There is a clear orientation of interest groups toward those segments of society with better education or more economic resources, and those most directly affected by government actions, especially corporations.

 Collective organization of interests is difficult, as there are strong incentives for any single individual to free ride. As a result, interests in society, especially very broad interests such as "all consumers" or "the middle class," often lack effective organizations that can express their preferences.

---

1 Raymond Bauer, Ithiel de Sola Pool, and Lewis Dexter, *American Business and Public Policy* (Chicago: Atherton Press, 1972).

and government officials and, once they have that attention, competing with other groups and individuals to influence particular government decisions. There are roughly 13,000 registered lobbyists in Washington, D.C., and many more in state capitals and city governments. In the din of day-to-day politics, it can be hard to get a particular concern before Congress or the bureaucracy, and one group's "special interest" may not seem so special in comparison with the demands of many other groups. The institutions of American government further shape the political outcomes that interest groups can achieve. Groups strategically seek out institutional venues they believe will be most hospitable to their goals and interests, but the system of American government often means that one must win in many different domains in order to change public policy. A group may succeed in one domain, such as a House committee, only to find itself blocked elsewhere, such as in the analogous Senate committee.

This is pluralism at work. It is messy and often disliked by the public at large, but it is an essential feature of American government. The U.S. Constitution embraces this idea fully. The more competition there is among many different interests, the less likely it is that any one will triumph and the more likely it is that representatives and government officials will learn what they need to know.[2] There is always the risk, however, that organized interests will have excessive influence over the government. Regulation of lobbying and campaign contributions, as well as ethics rules in government, are designed to prevent government from serving particular interests to the detriment of the common good.

One of the most difficult and profound questions about the U.S. system of government is whether the separation of powers and free and open political competition provide sufficient safeguards against excessive influence by certain groups. How much should American governments limit what individuals and organizations say and do in order to prevent particular interests from having too much influence? In short, how should we manage the trade-off between free speech and the potential corrupting influence of groups? Other countries severely limit lobbying and campaign spending. Should the United States do so as well? Or does open political competition limit the power of special interests? The answers to these questions are continually examined and debated in American government, from city councils to the Supreme Court.

In this chapter we analyze the social basis of organizations, the problems inherent in collective action, and some solutions to these problems. We discuss the character and balance of the interests promoted through the pluralistic political system in the United States. We further examine the tremendous growth of interest groups in their number, resources, and activity in recent decades. Finally, we examine the strategies that groups use to influence politics and whether their influence in the political process has become excessive.

---

2   This sentiment is expressed most eloquently in Alexander Hamilton, James Madison, and John Jay, *The Federalist Papers*, Clinton L. Rossiter, ed. (New York: New American Library, 1961), no. 10.

WHAT ARE THE CHARACTERISTICS OF INTEREST GROUPS?

An **interest group** is an organized group of individuals or organizations that makes policy-related appeals to government. Individuals form groups and engage in collective action to increase the chances that their views will be heard and their interests treated favorably by the government. Interest groups are organized to influence governmental decisions; they are sometimes referred to as lobbies.

Interest groups are sometimes confused with political action committees (see Chapter 11). The difference is that PACs focus on helping their favored candidates win elections, and interest groups focus on influencing elected officials. Another distinction we should make is that interest groups differ from political parties: interest groups tend to concern themselves primarily with the policies of government; parties tend to concern themselves primarily with the personnel of government.

← **interest group**

An organized group of individuals or organizations that makes policy-related appeals to government

Interest Groups Not Only Enhance Democracy . . .

There are an enormous number of interest groups in the United States, and millions of Americans are members of one or more groups, at least to the extent of paying dues or attending an occasional meeting. By representing the interests of such large numbers of people and encouraging political participation, organized groups can and do enhance American democracy. Organized groups educate their members about issues that affect them. Groups lobby members of Congress and the executive branch, engage in litigation, and generally represent their members' interests in the political arena. Groups mobilize their members for elections and grassroots lobbying efforts, thus encouraging participation. Interest groups also monitor government programs to make certain that they do not adversely affect their members. In all these ways, organized interests can be said to promote democratic politics.

But Also Represent the Evils of Faction

The framers of the U.S. Constitution feared the power that could be wielded by organized interests. James Madison wrote:

> The public good is disregarded in the conflict of rival [factions], . . . citizens . . . who are united and actuated by some common impulse of passion, or of interest, adverse to the rights of other citizens, or to the permanent and aggregate interests of the community.[3]

3   *The Federalist,* no. 10, p. 78.

Yet the Founders believed that interest groups thrived because of freedom—the freedom, enjoyed by all Americans, to organize and express their views. To the framers, this problem presented a dilemma. If the government were given the power to regulate or in any way forbid efforts by organized interests to interfere in the political process, it would in effect have the power to suppress freedom. The solution to this dilemma was presented by Madison:

> Take in a greater variety of parties and interest [and] you make it less probable that a majority of the whole will have a common motive to invade the rights of other citizens. . . .[Hence the advantage] enjoyed by a large over a small republic.[4]

According to the Madisonian theory, a good constitution encourages multitudes of interests so that no single interest can ever tyrannize the others. The basic assumption is that competition among interests will produce balance and compromise, with all the interests regulating one another.[5] Today this Madisonian principle of regulation is called **pluralism.** According to pluralist theory, all interests are and should be free to compete for influence in the United States. Moreover, according to pluralist doctrine, the outcome of this competition is compromise and moderation, because no group is likely to be able to achieve any of its goals without accommodating some of the views of its many competitors.[6]

pluralism

The theory that all interests are and should be free to compete for influence in the government. The outcome of this competition is compromise and moderation

There are tens of thousands of organized groups in the United States today, but the huge number of interest groups competing for influence does not mean that all interests are fully and equally represented in the American political process. The political deck is heavily stacked in favor of those interests that are able to organize and that wield substantial economic, social, and institutional resources on behalf of their cause. This means that within the universe of interest group politics, it is political power—not some abstract conception of the public good—that is likely to prevail. Moreover, this means that interest group politics, taken as a whole, works more to the advantage of some types of interests than others. In general, a politics in which interest groups predominate is a politics with a distinctly upper-class bias.

Organized Interests Are Predominantly Economic

When most people think about interest groups, they immediately think of groups with a direct and private economic interest in governmental actions, and, indeed, economic interest is one of the main purposes for which individuals and groups

---

4 *The Federalist*, no. 10, p. 83.

5 *The Federalist*, no. 10.

6 The best statement of the pluralist view is in David B. Truman, *The Governmental Process: Political Interests and Public Opinion* (New York: Knopf, 1951), chap. 2.

engage in political action. Interest groups are generally supported by groups of producers or manufacturers in a particular economic sector. Examples of this type of group include the National Petrochemical Refiners Association, the American Farm Bureau Federation, and the National Federation of Independent Business, which represents small-business owners. At the same time that broadly representative groups such as these are active in Washington, specific companies—such as Disney, Shell, Microsoft, and General Motors—may be active on certain issues that are of particular concern to them.

Labor organizations, although fewer in number and more limited in their financial resources, are extremely active lobbyists. The AFL-CIO, the United Mine Workers, and the International Brotherhood of Teamsters are examples of groups that lobby on behalf of organized labor. In recent years, lobbies have arisen to further the interests of public employees, the most significant among these being the American Federation of State, County, and Municipal Employees.

Professional lobbies such as the American Bar Association and the American Medical Association have been particularly successful in furthering their interests in state and federal legislatures. The "gun lobby," composed of the representatives of firearms manufacturers and dealers as well as gun owners, is represented by the National Rifle Association (NRA). The NRA mobilized furiously in 2012 and 2013 to thwart gun control efforts introduced in Congress in the wake of the December 2012 shooting of 20 first graders in a Connecticut elementary school. Financial institutions, represented by organizations such as the American Bankers Association and America's Community Bankers, although often less visible than other lobbies, also play an important role in shaping legislative policy.

Recent decades have witnessed the growth of a powerful "public interest" lobby purporting to represent interests whose concerns are not addressed by traditional lobbies. These groups have been most visible in the consumer protection and environmental policy areas, although public interest groups cover a broad range of issues, from nuclear disarmament to civil rights to abortion. The Natural Resources Defense Council, the Union of Concerned Scientists, the National Association for the Advancement of Colored People, the Christian Coalition of America, and Common Cause are all examples of public interest groups.

The perceived need for representation on Capitol Hill has generated a public-sector lobby, including the National League of Cities, and the "research" lobby. The latter group comprises universities and think tanks, such as Harvard University, the Brookings Institution, and the American Enterprise Institute, that have an interest in obtaining government funds for research and support. Indeed, universities have expanded their lobbying efforts even as they have reduced faculty positions and course offerings and increased tuition.[7] Even with the great expansion in the number of interests, the lion's share of organizations

---

7   Betsy Wagner and David Bowermaster, "B.S. Economics," *Washington Monthly* (November 1992): 19–21.

involved in politics in Washington, D.C., and in the state capitals represent economic interests.

Most Groups Require Members, Money, and Leadership

Although there are many kinds of interest groups, most share certain key organizational components. First, most groups must attract and keep members. Usually, groups appeal to members not only by promoting political goals or policies that they favor but also by providing them with direct economic or social benefits. Thus, for example, AARP (formerly the American Association for Retired Persons), which promotes the interests of senior citizens, at the same time offers members a variety of insurance benefits and commercial discounts. Similarly, many groups whose goals are chiefly economic or political also seek to attract members through social interaction and good fellowship. Thus the local chapters of many national groups provide their members with a congenial social environment while collecting dues that finance the national office's political efforts.

Second, every group must build a financial structure capable of sustaining an organization and funding the group's activities. Most interest groups rely on yearly membership dues and voluntary contributions from sympathizers. Many also sell members some ancillary services, such as insurance and vacation tours. Third, every group must have a leadership and decision-making structure. For some groups, this structure is very simple. For others, it can involve hundreds of local chapters that are melded into a national apparatus. Finally, most groups include an agency that actually carries out the group's tasks. This may be a research organization, a public relations office, or a lobbying office in Washington or a state capital.

Group Membership Has an Upper-Class Bias

Membership in interest groups is not randomly distributed in the population. People with higher incomes, higher levels of education, and management or professional occupations are much more likely to become members of groups than are those who occupy the lower rungs on the socioeconomic ladder.[8] Well-educated upper-income professionals are more likely to have the time and the money, and to have acquired through the educational process the concerns and skills, needed to play a role in a group or association. Moreover, for business and professional people, group membership may provide personal contacts and access to information that can help advance their careers. At the same time, corporate entities—businesses and trade associations—usually have ample resources to form or participate in groups that seek to advance their causes.

8   Kay Lehman Schlozman and John T. Tierney, *Organized Interests and American Democracy* (New York: Harper & Row, 1986), p. 60.

The result is that interest group politics in the United States tends to have a pronounced upper-class bias. Certainly, many interest groups and political associations have a working-class or lower-class membership—labor organizations or welfare-rights organizations, for example—but the great majority of interest groups and their members are drawn from the middle and upper-middle classes. In general, the "interests" served by interest groups are the interests of society's haves. Even when interest groups take opposing positions on issues and policies, the conflicting positions they espouse usually reflect divisions among upper-income strata rather than conflicts between upper and lower classes.

Even groups associated with a progressive political agenda and support for the rights of the poor tend, in their own membership, to reflect the interests of the middle and upper-middle classes. Take, for example, the National Association for the Advancement of Colored People (NAACP) and the National Organization for Women (NOW). Both the NAACP and NOW advocate for the rights of the poor, but both have a middle-class membership and both groups tend to focus on issues relevant to that membership. The NAACP is concerned with minority access to the universities and professions, a topic primarily of concern to its middle-class supporters. For its part, NOW seeks gender equality in education and access to positions in business and the professions, again, matters mainly of interest to its largely middle and upper-middle-class membership. (See the Analyzing the Evidence unit in chapter 5 for research on interest group advocacy of marginalized groups.)

In general, to obtain adequate political representation, forces from the bottom rungs of the socioeconomic ladder must be organized on the massive scale associated with political parties. Parties can organize and mobilize the collective energies of large numbers of people who, as individuals, may have very limited resources. Interest groups, on the other hand, generally organize smaller numbers of the better-to-do. Thus the relative importance of political parties and interest groups in American politics has far-ranging implications for the distribution of political power in the United States. As we saw in Chapter 12, after a period of relative weakness in the 1970s, political parties have witnessed a resurgence over the past 25 years, especially in Congress. Interest groups have also become more numerous, more active, and more influential in American politics. To use the language of the 2012 campaign, active interest groups generally empower the "one percent." Strong political parties give the "ninety-nine" percent a chance as well.

Groups Reflect Changes in the Political Environment

If interest groups and the concerns about them were a new phenomenon, we would not have begun this chapter with James Madison. As long as there is government, as long as government makes policies that add value or impose costs, and as long as there is liberty to organize, interest groups will abound. And if government expands, so will interest groups. For example, a spurt of growth in the national government occurred during the 1880s and 1890s, arising largely from the first government efforts at economic intervention to fight large monopolies and regulate some aspects of interstate commerce. In the latter decade, a parallel spurt of growth occurred in national interest groups, including the imposing National Association of Manufacturers and numerous other trade associations. Many groups organized around specific agricultural commodities as well. This period also marked the beginning of the expansion of trade unions as interest groups. Later, in the 1930s, interest groups with headquarters and representation in Washington began to grow significantly, concurrent with that decade's expansion of the national government.

Over the past 50 years, there has been an enormous increase both in the number of interest groups seeking to play a role in the American political process and in the extent of their opportunity to influence that process. The total number of interest groups in the United States today is not known. There are certainly tens of thousands of groups at the national, state, and local levels. One indication of the proliferation of such groups' activity is the growth over time in the number of political action committees (PACs) attempting to influence U.S. elections. PACs are how most interest group money is spent to influence elections. Nearly 10 times as many PACs operated in 2012 as in the 1970s, increasing from fewer than 500 to more than 5,000. A *New York Times* report, for example, noted that during the 1970s, expanded federal regulation of the automobile, oil, gas, education, and health care industries impelled each of these interests to increase substantially its efforts to influence the government's behavior. These efforts, in turn, had the effect of spurring the organization of other groups to augment or counter the activities of the first.[9] The rise of PACs exhibits one of the most common features of business political activity: businesses are reactive. They are usually drawn into politics in response to regulations, rather than to create a new program.

Similarly, federal social programs have occasionally sparked political organization and action on the part of clientele groups seeking to influence the distribution of benefits and, in turn, the organization of groups opposed to the programs or their cost. AARP, perhaps the largest membership organization in the United States, owes its emergence to the creation and expansion of Social Security and Medicare. Once older Americans had guaranteed retirement income and health insurance, they had a clear stake in protecting and even expanding these benefits. AARP formed and grew in response to attempts to pare back the program.[10]

Another factor accounting for the explosion of interest group activity in recent decades was the emergence of new social and political movements. The civil rights and antiwar movements of the 1960s and the reactions against them

---

9 John Herbers, "Special Interests Gaining Power as Voter Disillusionment Grows," *New York Times*, November 14, 1978.

10 Andrea Campbell, *How Policies Make Citizens: Senior Citizen Activism and the American Welfare State* (Princeton, NJ: Princeton University Press, 2003).

created a generation of upper-middle-class professionals and intellectuals who have seen themselves as a political force in opposition to the public policies and politicians associated with the nation's postwar regime. Following close on the heels of these movements came the decade-long debate over the Equal Rights Amendment, the Sagebrush Rebellion (concerning land use in the West), the nuclear disarmament movement, and the antiabortion movement. More recent social movements include the antitax Tea Party movement and the Occupy movement of 2011–12 protesting corporate power in the United States. Such groups sought to make changes in social behavior and public policy, usually through civil disobedience.

Members of these movements—collectively known as the new politics movement—constructed or strengthened public interest groups such as Common Cause, the Sierra Club, the Environmental Defense Fund, Physicians for Social Responsibility, the National Organization for Women, and the various organizations formed by the consumer activist Ralph Nader. These groups were able to influence the media, Congress, and even the judiciary and enjoyed a remarkable degree of success during the late 1960s and early 1970s in securing the enactment of policies they favored. Activist groups also played a major role in promoting the enactment of environmental, consumer, and occupational health and safety legislation.

Among the factors contributing to the rise and success of public interest groups is technology. Computerized direct-mail campaigns in the 1980s were perhaps the first big innovation that allowed organizations to identify and reach out to potential members efficiently and effectively. Today, e-mail, Facebook, Twitter, and other new media have allowed public interest groups to reach hundreds of thousands of potential sympathizers and contributors. Relatively small groups can now efficiently identify and mobilize their adherents throughout the nation. Individuals with perspectives that might be in a small, anonymous minority can become conscious of each other and mobilize for national political action through social networking tools that were unheard of even 30 years ago.

Latent Groups

Of course, many individuals who share a common interest do not form interest groups. For example, college students could be said to share an interest in the cost and quality of education, but they have not organized to demand lower tuition, better facilities, or a more effective faculty. Students could be called a "latent group." American society is filled with such latent groups. In many instances, the failure of a latent group to organize reflects the ability of individuals to achieve their goals without participating in an organized effort. Individual students, for example, are free to choose among colleges that, in turn, force colleges to compete for patronage. Where the market or other mechanisms allow individuals to achieve their goals without joining groups, they are less likely to do so.

HOW AND WHY DO INTEREST GROUPS FORM?

Pluralist theory argues that because individuals in the United States are free to join or form groups that reflect their common interests, interest groups should easily form whenever a change in the political environment warrants their formation. If this argument is correct, groups should form roughly in proportion to people's interests. We should find a greater number of organizations around interests shared by a greater number of people. The evidence for this pluralist hypothesis is weak, however. In the 1980s, the political scientists Kay Schlozman and John Tierney examined interest groups that represent people's occupations and economic roles.[11] Using census data and lists of interest groups, they compared how many people in the United States have particular economic roles with how many organizations represent those roles in Washington. For example, they found that (in the mid-1980s) 4 percent of the population was looking for work, but only a handful of organizations represented the unemployed in Washington, making up 0.1 percent of total organizations.[12] There is a considerable disparity in Washington representation across categories of individuals in the population, as Table 13.1 suggests. Schlozman and Tierney note, for example, that there are at least a dozen groups representing senior citizens, but none for the middle-aged. Although their study has not been repeated since the 1980s, a perusal of the Directory of Washington Representatives—the lobbyists' phonebook—reveals that little has changed.

The observation that groups form around some interests and not others creates a problem for the pluralist notion of democracy. If there is a bias in the sorts of groups that form, such as only wealthy groups, then political decisions may reflect the bias in who is organized and who is not. Mancur Olson's work, discussed later in this chapter, is the most well-known challenge to pluralist theory. It is in Olson's insights that we find the basis for interest group formation.

Interest Groups Facilitate Cooperation

Groups of individuals pursuing some common interest or shared objective—maintenance of a hunting and fishing habitat, creation of a network for sharing computer software, lobbying for favorable legislation, playing a Beethoven symphony, and so on—consist of individuals who bear some cost or make some contribution on behalf of the joint goal. Each member of the Possum Hollow

---

11 Schlozman and Tierney, *Organized Interests and American Democracy*.

12 Of course, the number of organizations is at best only a rough measure of the extent to which various categories of citizens are represented in the interest group world of Washington.

Table 13.1

WHO IS REPRESENTED BY ORGANIZED INTERESTS?

ECONOMIC ROLE OF THE INDIVIDUAL	U.S. ADULTS (%)	ORGS. (%)	TYPE OF ORG. IN WASHINGTON	NUMBER OF ORGS. PER ADULT
Managerial/administrative	7	71.0	Business association	10.10
Professional/technical	9	17.0	Professional association	1.90
Student/teacher	4	4.0	Educational organization	1.00
Farmworker	2	1.5	Agricultural workers' organization	0.75
Unable to work	2	0.6	Organization for the handicapped	0.30
Other nonfarm workers	41	4.0	Union	0.10
Homemaker	19	1.8	Women's organization	0.09
Retired	12	0.8	Senior citizens' organization	0.07
Looking for work	4	0.1	Unemployment organization	0.03

SOURCE: Kay Lehman Schlozman and John T. Tierney, *Organized Interests and American Democracy.* (New York: Harper & Row, 1986).

ANALYZING THE EVIDENCE

What types of interests are most likely to be represented by interest groups? If interest group politics is biased in favor of the wealthy and the powerful, should we curb group politics? What was James Madison's answer? Do you agree with Madison?

Rod and Gun Club may, for example, pay annual dues and devote one weekend a year to cleaning up the rivers and forests of the club-owned game preserve.

We can think of this in an analytic fashion as an instance of two-person cooperation writ large. Accordingly, each one of a very large number of individuals has, in the simplest situation, two options in his behavioral repertoire: "contribute" or "don't contribute" to achieving the jointly shared objective. If the number of contributors to the group enterprise is sufficiently large, a group goal is achieved. However, there is a twist. If the group goal is achieved, then every member of the group enjoys its benefits, whether she contributed to its achievement or not.

The Prisoner's Dilemma and Free Riding. Researchers often rely on the metaphor of the prisoner's dilemma when theorizing about social situations of collective action. The prisoner's dilemma is a famous hypothetical problem from game theory as it is used to discuss why people will rationally take actions that may not be optimal or in the best interests of all. This is similar to the fence-mending example in Chapter 1's discussion of bargaining failure.

In the prisoner's dilemma, two prisoners (call them A and B) are accused of jointly committing a crime. They are kept in separate interview rooms. The police have only minimal evidence, however, so they want (at least) one prisoner to roll on the other so that the prosecutor's case becomes a slam dunk. Each prisoner is offered the same plea bargain: "Testify against the other prisoner in exchange for your freedom, provided that your accomplice does not also testify against you. Remain silent, and you will possibly get the maximum sentence if your accomplice testifies against you." Figure 13.1 displays the options Prisoner A faces along the rows and that Prisoner B faces along the columns, and in each cell are the sentences (incentives) that each person receives for each combination of actions. If neither "snitches," each gets one year; if both snitch each gets three years, and so on. Importantly, the outcome of the plea bargain depends on what the other person does. Before reading on, it is worth studying the table and asking what you would do if you were Prisoner A.

The prisoners face an unpleasant choice. They are self-interested, rational actors, who, given the choice between the two alternatives, will choose the one that offers the best deal. They prefer less jail time to more, and the police, understanding their motivations, have structured the choice so that each prisoner will rat on the other. Notice that in Figure 13.1, Prisoner A is better off choosing to snitch no matter what Prisoner B does. If B chooses to snitch, then A's choice to snitch gets A a three-year jail term, but a don't-snitch choice by A results in six years for A—clearly worse. On the other hand, if B chooses not to snitch, then A gets no jail time if he snitches instead of one year if he also chooses not to snitch. In short, A is always better off snitching. But this situation is symmetrical, so it follows that B is better off snitching, too. If both prisoners snitch,

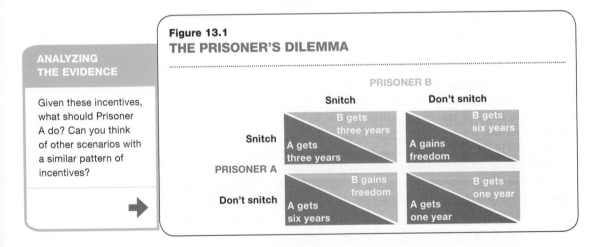

ANALYZING THE EVIDENCE

Given these incentives, what should Prisoner A do? Can you think of other scenarios with a similar pattern of incentives?

Figure 13.1
THE PRISONER'S DILEMMA

PRISONER B

	Snitch	Don't snitch
Snitch	B gets three years / A gets three years	B gets six years / A gains freedom
Don't snitch	B gains freedom / A gets six years	B gets one year / A gets one year

PRISONER A

the prosecutor is able to convict both of them, and each serves three years. If they had both kept silent, they would have gotten only one year each. In terms of game theory (from which the prisoner's dilemma is drawn), each player has a dominant strategy—snitching is best no matter what the other player does—and this leads paradoxically to an outcome in which each player is worse off.

The prisoner's dilemma provides the insight that rational individual behavior does not always lead to the best collective results. The logic is compelling—if A appreciates the dilemma and realizes that B appreciates the dilemma, then A will still be drawn to the choice of snitching. The reasons for this are the temptation to get off scot free (if he testifies and his accomplice doesn't) and the fear of being suckered (if his accomplice testifies and he doesn't). The prisoner's dilemma carries a brilliant if troubling insight about collective decision making. People often have difficulty achieving objectives that are in the collective good because the incentive to shirk, to defect, to free ride is just too strong.

Consider the swamp-clearing example described in Chapter 1, in which each person benefits from a drained swamp even if she does not provide the required effort. As long as enough other people do so, any individual can ride free on the efforts of the others. This is a multiperson prisoner's dilemma because not providing effort, like snitching, is a dominant strategy, yet if everyone avails himself or herself of it, it leads to an unwanted outcome: a mosquito-infested swamp. The prospect of free riding, as we see next, is the bane of collective action.

The Logic of Collective Action. The economist Mancur Olson, writing in 1965, essentially took on the political science establishment by noting that the pluralist assumption of the time—that common interests among individuals are automatically transformed into group organization and collective action—was problematic. Individuals wishing to engage in collective action face the prisoner's dilemma. They are tempted to free ride on the efforts of others, making it exceedingly difficult to achieve outcomes that are best for all.

Olson was at his most persuasive when talking about large groups and mass collective action, such as the antiwar and civil rights movements of the 1960s. Although these groups mobilized large rallies, most individuals who sympathized with the causes failed to participate. In these circumstances, the world of politics is a bit like the swamp-clearing example, where each individual has a rational strategy of not contributing. The logic of collective action makes it difficult to induce participation in and contribution to collective goals.

Olson claimed that this difficulty is most severe in large groups for three reasons. First, large groups tend to be anonymous. Each household in a city is a tax-paying unit and may share the wish to see property taxes lowered. It is difficult, however, to forge a group identity or induce households to contribute effort or activity for the cause of lower taxes on such a basis. Second, in the anonymity of the large-group context, it is especially plausible to claim that no one individual's contribution makes much difference. Should an individual citizen kill the better part of a morning writing a letter to his city council member in support of lower property taxes? Will it make much difference? If hardly anyone else writes, then the council member is unlikely to pay much heed to this one letter; on the other hand, if the council member is inundated with letters, would one more have a significant additional effect? Finally, there is the problem of enforcement. In a large group, are other group members going to punish a slacker? By definition, they cannot prevent the slacker from receiving the benefits of collective action should those benefits materialize. (Every property owner's taxes will be lowered if anyone's are.) But more to the point, in a large, anonymous group it is often hard to know who has and who has not contributed, and because there is only the most limited sort of group identity, it is hard for contributors to identify, much less take action against, slackers. As a consequence, many large groups that share common interests fail to mobilize at all—they remain latent.

This same problem plagues small groups, too, as the swamp-clearing problem in Chapter 1 reveals. But Olson argued that small groups manage to overcome the problem of collective action more frequently and to a greater extent than their larger counterparts. Small groups are more personal, and their members are therefore more vulnerable to interpersonal persuasion. In small groups, individual contributions may make a more noticeable difference, so that individuals feel that their contributions are more essential. Contributors in small groups, moreover, often know who they are and who the slackers are. Thus punishment, ranging from subtle judgmental pressure to social ostracism, is easier to effect.

Contrasting large groups that often remain latent to smaller ones, Olson called these small groups privileged, because of their advantage in overcoming the free-riding, coordination, and conflict-of-interest problems of collective action. It is for these perhaps counterintuitive reasons that small groups often prevail over, or enjoy greater privileges relative to, larger groups. These reasons, therefore, help explain why we so often see producers win out over consumers, owners of capital win out over labor, and a party's elite win out over its mass members.

Selective Benefits: A Solution to the Collective Action Problem

selective benefits

Benefits that do not go to everyone but, rather, are distributed selectively—only to those who contribute to the group enterprise

Despite the free-rider problem, interest groups offer numerous incentives to join. Most important, as Olson shrewdly noted, they make various "**selective benefits**" available only to group members. This removes the free-riding option for certain benefits, which makes participation more attractive for the individual. These benefits can be informational, material, solidary, or purposive. Table 13.2 gives some examples of the range of benefits in each of these categories.

Informational benefits are the most widespread and important category of selective benefits offered to group members. Information is provided through conferences, training programs, and newsletters and other periodicals sent automatically to those who have paid membership dues. Material benefits include anything that can be measured monetarily, such as special services, goods, and even money. A broad range of material benefits can be offered by groups to attract members. These benefits often include discount purchasing, shared advertising, and perhaps most valuable of all, health and retirement insurance.

Another category identified in Table 13.2 is that of solidary benefits. The most notable of this class of benefits are the friendship and "networking" opportunities that membership provides. Another benefit that has been

Table 13.2

SELECTIVE BENEFITS OF INTEREST GROUP MEMBERSHIP

CATEGORY	BENEFITS
Informational benefits	Conferences and publications
	Professional contacts
	Training programs
	Coordination among organizations
	Research
	Legal help
	Professional codes
	Collective bargaining
Material benefits	Travel packages
	Insurance
	Discounts on consumer goods
Solidary benefits	Friendship
	Networking opportunities
Purposive benefits	Advocacy
	Representation before government
	Participation in public affairs

SOURCE: Adapted from Jack L. Walker, Jr., *Mobilizing Interest Groups in America: Patrons, Professions, and Social Movements* (Ann Arbor: University of Michigan Press, 1991), p. 86.

important to many nonprofit and citizens' groups is consciousness-raising. One example of this can be seen in the claims of many women's organizations that active participation conveys to each member an enhanced sense of her own value and a stronger ability to advance individual as well as collective civil rights.

A fourth type of benefit involves the appeal of the purpose of an interest group. The benefits of religious interest groups provide us with good examples of such purposive benefits. The Christian right is a powerful movement made up of a number of interest groups that offer virtually no material benefits to their members. The growth and the success of these groups depend on the religious identification and affirmation of their members. Many such religiously based interest groups have arisen, especially at state and local levels, throughout American history. For example, both the abolition and the prohibition movements were driven by religious interest groups whose main attractions were nonmaterial benefits. Ideology itself, or the sharing of a commonly developed ideology, is another important nonmaterial benefit. Many of the most successful interest groups of the past 20 years have been citizens' groups or public interest groups whose members are brought together largely around shared ideological goals, including government reform, election and campaign reform, civil rights, economic equality, "family values," or even opposition to government itself.

Of course, some groups have employed coercion in addition to selective benefits to deal with the collective action problem. Labor unions, for example, call workers who refuse to join a strike "scabs." At one time, unions employed violence and intimidation against scabs.

Political Entrepreneurs Organize and Maintain Groups

In a review of Olson's book, the economist Richard Wagner noticed that Olson's arguments about groups and politics in general, and his theory of selective incentives in particular, had very little to say about the internal workings of groups.[13] In Wagner's experience, however, groups often came into being and then were maintained in good working order, not only because of selective incentives but also because of the extraordinary efforts of specific individuals—leaders, in ordinary language, or "political entrepreneurs" in Wagner's more colorful expression.

Wagner was motivated to raise the issue of group leaders because, in his view, Olson's theory was too pessimistic. Mass organizations in the real world— labor unions, consumer associations, senior citizens' groups, environmental organizations—all exist, some persisting and prospering over long periods. Contrary to Olson's suggestions, they seem somehow to get jump-started in the real world. Wagner suggests that a special kind of theory of selective incentives is called for. Specifically, he argues that certain selective benefits may accrue to those who organize and maintain otherwise latent groups.

Senator Robert Wagner (no relation) in the 1930s and Congressman Claude Pepper in the 1970s each had private reasons—electoral incentives—to try to organize laborers and the elderly, respectively. Wagner, a Democrat from New York, had a large constituency of working men and women who would reward him by re-electing him if he bore the cost of organizing workers (or at least bore the cost of facilitating their organization). And this he did. The law that bears his name, the Wagner Act of 1935, made it much easier for unions to organize in the industrial North.[14] Likewise, Claude Pepper, a Democratic congressman

---

13 Richard Wagner, "Pressure Groups and Political Entrepreneurs," *Papers on Non-Market Decision Making* 1 (1966): 161–70.

14 The Wagner Act made it possible for unions to organize by legalizing the so-called closed shop. If a worker took a job in a closed shop or plant, she was required to join the union there. "Do not contribute" was no longer an option, so that workers in closed shops could not free ride on the efforts made by others to improve wages and working conditions.

---

with a large number of elderly constituents in his South Miami district, saw it as serving his own electoral interests to provide the initial investment of effort to organize the elderly as a political force.

In general, a political entrepreneur is someone who sees a prospective dividend from facilitating cooperation. This is another way of saying that there is a latent group that, if it were to become manifest, would enjoy the fruits of collective action. For a price, whether in votes (as in the cases of Wagner and Pepper), a percentage of the dividend, nonmaterial glory, or other perks, the entrepreneur bears the costs of organizing, expends effort to monitor individuals for slacker behavior, and sometimes even imposes punishment on slackers (such as expelling them from the group and denying them any of its selective benefits).

Thus political entrepreneurs may be thought of as complements to Olsonian selective incentives in that both provide ways of motivating groups to accomplish collective objectives. Indeed, if selective incentives resolve the paradox of collective action, then political entrepreneurs dissolve the paradox. Both are helpful and sometimes both are needed to initiate and maintain collective action. Groups that manage, perhaps on their own, to get themselves organized with a low level of activity often take the next step of creating leaders and leadership institutions to increase the activity level and the resulting cooperation dividends. Richard Wagner, in other words, took Olson's theory of selective incentives and suggested an alternative explanation, one that made room for institutional solutions to the problem of collective action.

HOW DO INTEREST GROUPS INFLUENCE POLICY?

Interest groups work to improve the probability that they and their policy interests will be heard and treated favorably by all branches and levels of the government. The quest for political influence of power takes many forms. We can roughly divide these strategies into "insider strategies" and "outsider strategies."

Insider strategies include gaining access to key decision makers and using the courts. Influencing policy through traditional political institutions, of course, requires understanding how those institutions work. A lobbyist who wishes to have Congress address a problem with legislation will try to find a sympathetic member of Congress, preferably on a committee with jurisdiction over the problem, and will work directly with the member's staff. If an organization decides to bring suit in the courts, it may want to sue in a jurisdiction where it has a good chance of getting a judge favorable to the case or where the immediate appellate courts are likely to support the case. Gaining access is not easy. Legislators and bureaucrats have little time and many requests to juggle; courts have full dockets. Interest groups themselves have limited budgets and staff. They must choose their battles well and map out the strategy most likely to succeed.

Outsider strategies include going public and using electoral tactics. Just as politicians can gain an electoral edge by informing voters, so too can groups. A well-planned public information campaign or targeted campaign activities and contributions can have as much influence as working the corridors of Congress.

Many groups employ a mix of insider and outsider strategies. For example, environmental groups such as the Sierra Club lobby members of Congress and key congressional staff members, participate in bureaucratic rule making by offering comments and suggestions to agencies on new environmental rules, and bring lawsuits under various environmental acts, such as the Endangered Species Act, which authorizes groups and citizens to come to court if they believe the act is being violated. At the same time, the Sierra Club attempts to influence public opinion through media campaigns and to influence electoral politics by supporting candidates who they believe share their environmental views and by opposing candidates who they view as foes of environmentalism. The Analyzing the Evidence unit on page 582 considers the relative influence of different groups.

Direct Lobbying

lobbying

An attempt by a group to influence the policy process through persuasion of government officials

Lobbying is an attempt by a group to influence the policy process through persuasion of government officials. Most Americans tend to believe that interest groups exert their influence through direct contact with members of Congress, but lobbying encompasses a broad range of activities that groups engage in with all sorts of government officials and the public as a whole.

Organized advocacy of political interests, commonly known as lobbying, is a multibillion-dollar-a-year industry in Washington, D.C., alone, involving 13,000 individuals, firms, and other organizations. Who is a lobbyist? The 1946 Federal Regulation of Lobbying Act defined a lobbyist as "any person who shall engage himself for pay or any consideration for the purpose of attempting to influence the passage or defeat of any legislation of the Congress of the United States." According to the 1995 Federal Lobbying Disclosure Act, any person who makes at least one lobbying contact with either the legislative or executive branch in a year, any individual who spends 20 percent of his time in support of such activities, or any firm that devotes 10 percent of its budget to such activities must register as a lobbyist. They must report what topics they discussed with the government, though not which particular individuals or offices they contacted. The industry that spent by far the most on lobbying over the past decade was pharmaceuticals and health products, which together spent a whopping $5 billion over the course of the decade. In addition, insurance, electric utilities, business associations, computer and Internet, oil and gas, agribusiness, and defense each spent at least a billion on lobbying between 1998 and 2012.[15] Table 13.3 presents the top spenders on lobbying in 2012.

---

15 Data compiled from federal reports by the Center for Responsive Politics, www .opensecrets.org/lobby/top.php?indexType=i (accessed 12/24/12).

Table 13.3

TOP SPENDERS ON LOBBYING, 2012

LOBBYING CLIENT	TOTAL ($)
U.S. Chamber of Commerce	966,955,680
General Electric	284,040,000
American Medical Association	281,282,500
American Hospital Association	235,219,136
Pharmaceutical Research and Manufacturers of America	232,583,920
AARP	222,822,064
National Association of Realtors	219,817,423
Blue Cross/Blue Shield	202,740,052
Northrop Grumman	189,485,253
Exxon Mobil	182,392,742
Edison Electric Institute	172,936,789
Verizon Communications	172,427,933
Boeing Co.	171,972,310
Business Roundtable	171,400,000
Lockheed Martin	166,366,488
AT&T Inc.	152,419,336
Southern Co.	146,280,694
National Cable and Telecommunications Association	142,380,000
General Motors	134,534,170
National Association of Broadcasters	132,890,000

ANALYZING THE EVIDENCE

Some groups spend more on lobbying than others. What patterns are there in this list of top spenders? Why are some groups willing to spend millions of dollars on lobbying? What groups are absent from the list?

SOURCE: Center for Responsive Politics, www.opensecrets.org/lobby/top.php?indexType=s (accessed 3/14/13).
CREDIT: Table from http://www.opensecrets.org/lobby/top.php?indexType=s. Reprinted with permission from the Center for Responsive Politics (opensecrets.org).

The federal figures do not include campaign contributions or lobbying at the state and local levels, but the amount spent to influence state legislatures is also substantial. For example, in 2005, according to the Center for Public Integrity, lobbyists spent $240 million to influence California lawmakers, $175 million in Texas, $150 million in New York, $130 million in Pennsylvania, and more than $50 million apiece in Massachusetts and Minnesota. All told, $1.16 billion was spent in 42 states that require lobbyists to report their expenditures. The total resources devoted to lobbying at the state and federal level, then, is approximately $4 billion a year.[16]

Lobbying involves a great deal of activity on the part of someone speaking for an interest. Lobbyists badger and buttonhole legislators, administrators, and committee staff members with facts about pertinent issues and facts or claims about public support of them.[17] Lobbyists can serve a useful purpose in the legislative and administrative process by providing this kind of information.

However, within each industry, there are a great many different individuals and organizations involved in government advocacy, and they usually do not speak with a common voice. Rather each advocates for and defends its own particular interests, often in conflict with other firms in the same industry. What the leading organization or peak association of an industry may advocate may be undercut by the activities of individual firms. The Entertainment Software Association, which spent roughly $3.5 million on lobbying in 2010, likely wants a different set of regulations than Microsoft or Google.

Lobbying Members of Congress. Interest groups have substantial influence in setting the legislative agenda and in helping craft the language of legislation (Figure 13.2). Today sophisticated lobbyists win influence by providing information about policies to busy members of Congress. As one lobbyist noted, "You can't get access without knowledge. . . . I can go in to see John Dingell [former chairman of the House Committee on Energy and Commerce], but if I have nothing to offer or nothing to say, he's not going to want to see me."[18]

Providing access is only one of the many services lobbyists perform. Lobbyists often testify on behalf of their clients at congressional committee and agency hearings; lobbyists sometimes help their clients identify potential allies with whom to construct coalitions; lobbyists provide research and information to government officials; lobbyists often draft proposed legislation or regulations to be introduced by friendly lawmakers; lobbyists talk to reporters, place ads in newspapers, and organize letter-writing, e-mail, and telegram campaigns. Lobbyists also play an important role in fund-raising, helping to direct clients' contributions to members of Congress and presidential candidates. In recent years, interest groups have also begun to build broader coalitions and comprehensive campaigns around particular policy issues.[19] Lobbyists, seeing an opportunity

---

16 Sarah Laskow, "State Lobbying Becomes Billion-Dollar Business," The Center for Public Integrity, December 20, 2006, www.iwatchnews.org/2006/12/20/5896/state-lobbying-becomes-billion-dollar-business (accessed 11/11/11).

17 For discussions of lobbying, see Jeffrey M. Berry, *Lobbying for the People: The Political Behavior of Public Interest Groups* (Princeton, NJ: Princeton University Press, 1977); and John R. Wright, *Interest Groups and Congress: Lobbying, Contributions, and Influence* (Boston: Allyn & Bacon, 1996).

18 Daniel Franklin, "Tommy Boggs and the Death of Health Care Reform," *Washington Monthly* (April 1995): 36.

19 Marie Hojnacki, "Interest Groups' Decisions to Join Alliances or Work Alone," *American Journal of Political Science* 41 (1997): 61–87; Kevin W. Hula, *Lobbying Together: Interest Group Coalitions in Legislative Politics* (Washington, DC: Georgetown University Press, 1999).

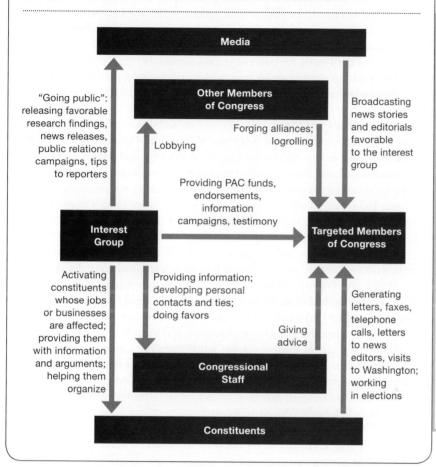

Figure 13.2

HOW INTEREST GROUPS INFLUENCE CONGRESS

Media

Other Members of Congress

"Going public": releasing favorable research findings, news releases, public relations campaigns, tips to reporters

Lobbying

Forging alliances; logrolling

Broadcasting news stories and editorials favorable to the interest group

Providing PAC funds, endorsements, information campaigns, testimony

Interest Group

Targeted Members of Congress

Activating constituents whose jobs or businesses are affected; providing them with information and arguments; helping them organize

Providing information; developing personal contacts and ties; doing favors

Giving advice

Generating letters, faxes, telephone calls, letters to news editors, visits to Washington; working in elections

Congressional Staff

Constituents

ANALYZING THE EVIDENCE

Interest groups can influence members of Congress in a variety of ways. They may seek to mobilize popular support in the form of grassroots campaigns; they may try to generate publicity favorable to their cause; they may work through congressional staffers; or they may seek to lobby members of Congress directly. How might these various strategies work together? What pitfalls might an interest group encounter in trying to influence members of Congress?

to harness the enthusiasm of political amateurs, now organize and even launch comprehensive campaigns that combine simulated grassroots activity with information and campaign funding for members of Congress.[20]

Some interest groups go still further. They develop strong ties to individual politicians or policy communities within Congress by hiring ex-staffers, ex-members of Congress, or even relatives of sitting members of Congress. The rotation of those in positions of power into lobbying jobs has become sufficiently common as to have its own term in Washington circles: revolving-door

20 An excellent example is the mobilization of corporate executives in the tax reform efforts in the mid-1980s. See Jeff Birnbaum and Alan S. Murray, *Showdown at Gucci Gulch: Lawmakers, Lobbyists, and the Unlikely Triumph of Tax Reform* (Westminster, MD: Random House, 1987).

politics. The revolving door of congressional and executive staff joining the ranks of lobbying firms is driven by the continual turnover of staff, of lobbyists, and even of the political parties in Washington. Lobbying firms must stay current and connected to Congress in order to offer the best service to their clients. This means that most of the larger lobbying firms in Washington have strong ties to both the Democrats and the Republicans on the Hill. This revolving door has been cause for concern among some policy makers, and a number of states have put restrictions on how quickly ex-lawmakers can return as lobbyists. Seventeen states have one-year restrictions, and seven have two-year bans.[21]

Lobbying the President. All these efforts and more are needed when the target of a lobbying campaign is the president of the United States. So many individuals and groups clamor for the president's time and attention that only the most skilled and well-connected members of the lobbying community can hope to influence presidential decisions. When running for president, Barack Obama laid down a bold promise to "free the executive branch from special-interest influence." No political appointee, the Obama team promised, "will be permitted to work on regulations or contracts directly and substantially related to their prior employer for two years." That promise proved exceedingly difficult to keep as many in the Obama transition team, including the nominee for Health and Human Services secretary and former Senate majority leader Thomas Daschle, had close ties to lobbyists or had worked for lobbying firms.[22] One of President Obama's first executive orders created an ethics standard and pledge for all executive branch appointments, and the administration imposed further restrictions on those receiving funds from the Emergency Economic Stabilization Act and the American Recovery and Reinvestment Act. Anyone wishing to receive funds from the $700 billion authorized for the economic stimulus bills had to show that they did not have conflicting interests and were not involved in lobbying the government.[23]

Lobbying the Executive Branch. Even when an interest group is very successful at getting its bill passed by Congress and signed by the president, the prospect of full and faithful implementation of that law is not guaranteed. Often a group and its allies do not pack up and go home as soon as the president turns their lobbied-for law over to the appropriate agency. On average, 40 percent of interest group representatives regularly contact both legislative

---

21 Peggy Kerns, "Revolving Door Laws," National Conference of State Legislators, www .ncsl.org/legislatures-elections/ethicshome/legisbrief-revolving-door.aspx (accessed 3/4/13).

22 Chris Frates, "Daschle Lobby Ties Bump Obama Vow," *Politico*, November 30, 2008, www.politico.com/news/stories/1108/16015.html (accessed 4/7/09); David Kirkpatrick, "In Transition, Ties to Lobbying," *New York Times*, November 15, 2008, www.nytimes .com/2008/11/15/us/politics/15transition.html (accessed 4/7/09).

23 Jacob Straus, *Lobbying the Executive Branch: Current Practices and Options for Change.* Congressional Research Service, December 6, 2010. Report 7-5700, pages 3 and 4.

and executive branch organizations, whereas 13 percent contact only the legislative branch and 16 percent contact only the executive branch.[24]

In some respects, interest group access to the executive branch is promoted by federal law. The Administrative Procedure Act, first enacted in 1946 and frequently amended, requires most federal agencies to provide notice and an opportunity for comment before implementing proposed rules and regulations. So-called notice-and-comment rule making is designed to allow interests an opportunity to make their views known and participate in the implementation of federal legislation that affects them. In 1990, Congress enacted the Negotiated Rulemaking Act to encourage administrative agencies to engage in direct and open negotiations with affected interests when developing new regulations. These two pieces of legislation, which have been strongly enforced by the federal courts, have played an important role in opening the bureaucratic process to interest group influence. Today few federal agencies would consider attempting to implement a new rule without consulting affected interests, which are known as "stakeholders."[25]

Regulation of Lobbying. As a result of the constant access to important decision makers that lobbyists seek out and require, stricter guidelines regulating the actions of lobbyists have been adopted in the last two decades. For example, as of 1993, businesses may no longer deduct from their taxes the cost of lobbying. Trade associations must report to members the proportion of their dues that goes to lobbying, and that proportion may not be reported as a business expense. The most important attempt to limit the influence of lobbyists was the 1995 Lobbying Disclosure Act, which significantly broadened the definition of people and organizations that must register as lobbyists. According to the filings under this act, almost 13,000 lobbyists were working the halls of Congress in 2010.

Congress also chose to restrict interest group influence by passing legislation in 1996 that limited gifts from a single source to $50 and no more than $100 annually. It also banned the practice of honoraria, which had been used by special interests to supplement congressional salaries. But Congress did not limit the travel of representatives, senators, their spouses, or congressional staff members. Interest groups can pay for congressional travel as long as a trip is related to legislative business and is disclosed on congressional reports within 30 days. On these trips, meals and entertainment expenses are not limited to $50 per event and $100 annually. The rules of Congress allow its members to travel on corporate jets as long as they pay an amount equal to first-class airfare.

In 2007, congressional Democrats secured the enactment of a package of ethics rules designed to fulfill their 2006 campaign promise to bring an end

24 John P. Heinz, Edward O. Laumann, Robert L. Nelson, and Robert H. Salisbury, *The Hollow Core: Private Interests in National Policy Making* (Cambridge, MA: Harvard University Press, 1993).

25 For an excellent discussion of the political origins of the Administrative Procedure Act, see Martin Shapiro, "APA: Past, Present, Future," *Virginia Law Review* 72 (1986): 447–92.

Interest Group Influence

Contributed by
Beth L. Leech
Rutgers University

Which interest groups have the most influence over political outcomes? It is generally accepted among those who study interest groups that business and economic interests predominate. Economic interests are more likely to form organized groups, are more likely to be active, and on average spend more money and more time on political issues than are noneconomic interests like citizen groups or "public interest" groups. When we look at interest groups' involvement in the policy-making process, however, the sheer number of groups or dollars may not directly equal the amount of influence that those groups have. While numbers and dollars are important indicators of which interests are represented, it would be preferable to try to measure which groups actually were influential in politics. To address this question, the political scientist Frank Baumgartner and his colleagues interviewed 315 lobbyists and government officials about 98 randomly selected policy issues. Citizen groups were more likely to be mentioned as being important in the debates than any other type of group, despite the fact that they spent less and they made up a smaller part of the overall group population.

Why were citizen groups seen as so influential despite their relative lack of resources? It may be that those groups have important ties to constituents, granting them greater legitimacy in the eyes of members of Congress, or it could be that some members of Congress already supported the policies that the citizen groups were advocating. Whatever the reason, it is clear that citizen groups have greater voice in Washington than the dollar counts might suggest.

Types of Interest Groups Registered to Lobby

41%
Businesses

22%
Trade associations

14%
Citizen groups

12%
Other*

9%
Professional associations

2%
Unions

These data from the federal Lobbying Disclosure Reports show the dominance of business organizations in Washington. Businesses make up 41 percent of those registered to lobby, and trade associations, which represent groups of businesses, comprise another 22 percent. Citizen groups, professional associations, and unions make up a much smaller portion, and it is especially striking to note that unions are only 2 percent of the total.

*Includes governmental groups, think tanks, universities, and hospitals.

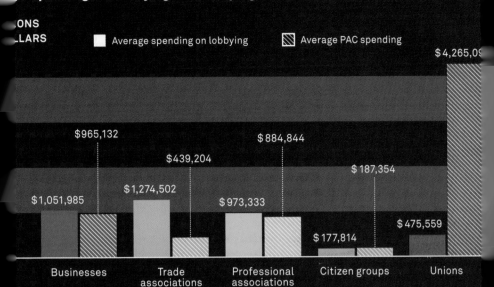

...e Spending on Lobbying and Campaign Contributions

...ONS
...LLARS

■ Average spending on lobbying   ▨ Average PAC spending

$4,265,0...

$965,132

$884,844

$439,204

$187,354

$1,274,502

$1,051,985 $973,333

$475,559

$177,814

| Businesses | Trade associations | Professional associations | Citizen groups | Unions |

...h above shows the average amounts spent on lobbying or campaign contributions by interest grou...
...major role in 98 randomly selected issues studied by Baumgartner et al. Citizen groups on average spen...
...obbying and campaign contributions than other types of groups. Unions on average spent more on ca...
...ions than any other type of group, but that spending is tempered by the fact that there are fewer union...

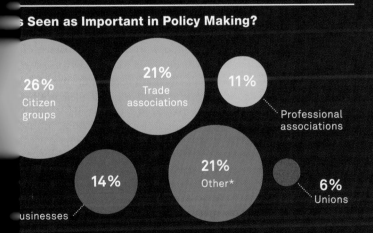

...s Seen as Important in Policy Making?

26%
Citizen groups

21%
Trade associations

11%
Professional associations

14%
...usinesses

21%
Other*

6%
Unions

...s coalitions, governmental associations, and think tanks.

SOURCES:

Frank R. Baumgartner and ...
L. Leech, "Issue Niches an...
Policy Bandwagons: Patte...
Interest Group Involvemen...
National Politics," *Journal ...*
Politics 63, no. 4 (2001):
1191–1213.

Frank B. Baumgartner, Jef...
Berry, Marie Hojnacki, Dav...
Kimball, and Beth L. Leech...
Lobbying and Policy Chan...
Who Wins, Who Loses, an...
(Chicago: Chicago Univers...
Press, 2009).

...n the overall population of interest groups has fewer citizen groups than business groups, as seen in the
...eft, not all groups are equally influential. Baumgartner and his colleagues interviewed 315 lobbyist...
...ent officials about 98 randomly selected policy issues. Citizen groups were more likely to be mentior...
...portant in the debate than any other type of group. More than a quarter of the interest groups seen as
...al were citizen groups.

to lobbying abuses. The new rules prohibited lobbyists from paying for most meals, trips, parties, and gifts for members of Congress. Lobbyists were also required to disclose the amounts and sources of small campaign contributions they collected from clients and "bundled" into large contributions. And interest groups were required to disclose the funds they used to rally voters to support or oppose legislative proposals. As soon as these new rules were enacted, lobbyists and politicians hurried to find ways to circumvent them, and these reforms have had little impact. Executive rulings and memoranda issued by President Obama in 2009 have further strengthened these rules and made it much more difficult for lobbying firms to influence executive decision making either through direct lobbying or indirectly by hiring people with direct access to decision makers.

Using the Courts

Interest groups sometimes turn to the courts to augment other avenues of access. They can use the courts to affect public policy in at least three ways: (1) by bringing suit directly on behalf of the group itself, (2) by financing suits brought by individuals, and (3) by filing a companion brief as amicus curiae (literally, "friend of the court") to an existing court case.

Among the most significant modern illustrations of the use of the courts as a strategy for political influence are those that accompanied the "sexual revolution" of the 1960s and the emergence of the movement for women's rights. Beginning in the mid-1960s, a series of cases was brought into the federal courts in an effort to force the definition of a right to privacy in sexual matters. The effort began with a challenge to state restrictions on obtaining contraceptives for nonmedical purposes, a challenge that was effectively made in *Griswold v. Connecticut*, in which the Supreme Court held that states could neither prohibit the dissemination of information about, nor prohibit the actual use of, contraceptives by married couples. That case was soon followed by *Eisenstadt v. Baird*, in which the Court held that the states could not prohibit the use of contraceptives by single persons any more than it could prohibit their use by married couples. One year later, in the 1973 case of *Roe v. Wade*, the Court held that states could not impose an absolute ban on voluntary abortions. Each of these cases, as well as others, were part of the Court's enunciation of a constitutional doctrine of privacy.[26]

The 1973 abortion case sparked a controversy that brought conservatives to the fore on a national level. Conservative groups then made extensive use of the courts to whittle away the scope of the privacy doctrine. They obtained rulings, for example, that prohibit the use of federal funds to pay for voluntary abortions. And in 1989, right-to-life groups were able to use a strategy of litigation that significantly undermined the *Roe v. Wade* decision—namely, in the case of

---

26 *Griswold v. Connecticut*, 381 U.S. 479 (1965); *Eisenstadt v. Baird*, 405 U.S. 438 (1972); *Roe v. Wade*, 410 U.S. 113 (1973).

Webster v. Reproductive Health Services, which restored the right of states to place restrictions on abortion.[27]

Another extremely significant set of contemporary illustrations of the use of the courts as a strategy for political influence are those found in the history of the National Association for the Advancement of Colored People. The most important of these court cases was *Brown v. Board of Education*, in which the Supreme Court held that legal segregation of the schools was unconstitutional.[28]

Business groups are also frequent users of the courts, because of the number of government programs that apply to them. Litigation involving large businesses is most mountainous in such areas as taxation, antitrust issues, interstate transportation, patents, and product quality and standardization. Often a business is brought to litigation against its will by virtue of initiatives taken against it by other businesses or by government agencies. But many individual businesses bring suit themselves to influence government policy. Major corporations and their trade associations pay tremendous amounts of money each year in fees to the most prestigious Washington law firms. Some of this money is expended in gaining access. A great proportion of it, however, is used to keep the best and most experienced lawyers prepared to represent the corporations in court or before administrative agencies when necessary.

The forces of the new politics movement made significant use of the courts during the 1970s and 1980s, and judicial decisions were instrumental in advancing their goals. Facilitated by changes in the rules governing access to the courts (the rules of standing are discussed in Chapter 9), the new politics agenda was clearly visible in court decisions handed down in several key policy areas. In environmental policy, new politics groups were able to force federal agencies to pay attention to environmental issues even when the agencies were not directly involved in activities related to environmental quality. By the 2000s, the courts often were the battleground on which those in the new political movements waged their fights. Perhaps the most dramatic were a string of lawsuits spanning 20 years (from 1986 to 2006) in which antiabortion protest organizations, such as Pro-Life Action Network and Operation Rescue, and the National Organization of Women repeatedly took each other to court to establish the rules governing clinic protests. Ultimately, the U.S. Supreme Court sided with the antiabortion organizations, but not before deciding three separate cases on the matter, at extremely high cost to both sides.[29]

Mobilizing Public Opinion

Organizations try to bring pressure to bear on politicians through a variety of methods designed to mobilize public opinion. This strategy is known as **going public**. When groups go public, they use their various resources to try to

 going public

The act of launching a media campaign to build popular support

---

27 *Webster v. Reproductive Health Services*, 492 U.S. 490 (1989).

28 *Brown v. Board of Education*, 347 U.S. 483 (1954).

29 *Scheidler v. National Organization of Women et al.*, 547 U.S. 9 (2006).

persuade large numbers of people to pay attention to their concerns. They hope that greater visibility and public support will help underline the importance of such issues to those in power. Advertising campaigns, protests, and grassroots lobbying efforts are all examples of going public. An increased use of this kind of strategy is traced to the rise of modern advertising at the beginning of the twentieth century. As early as the 1930s, political analysts distinguished between the "old lobby" of direct group representation before Congress and the "new lobby" of public-relations professionals addressing the public at large in order to reach Congress indirectly.[30] Going public, then, differs from other strategies that interest groups use to influence public policy. The "new lobby" techniques are designed to change the way people think, rather than just changing the actions of insiders.

Advertising. One way of going public that groups often use is conventional advertising. For example, a casual scan of major newspapers, magazines, and websites will often reveal examples of expensive, well-designed ads by major companies and industry associations, such as those from oil and gas, automobile, and health and pharmaceutical companies. Such ads are frequently intended to show what the firms do for the country, not merely the products they develop. Their purpose is to create and maintain a strongly positive association between the organization and the community at large in the hope that the community's favorable feelings can be drawn on as needed in specific political controversies later.

Sometimes groups advertise expressly to shift public opinion on a question. One of the most famous such advertising campaigns was run by the Health Insurance Association of America in 1993 and 1994 in opposition to President Bill Clinton's proposed national health insurance plan. These ads featured a middle-class couple, Harry and Louise (played by the actors Harry Johnson and Louise Caire Clark), sitting at their kitchen table disparaging the excessive red tape and bureaucratic problems that they would face under Clinton's plan. The Harry and Louise ads are widely attributed with turning public opinion against Clinton's plan, which never even got off the ground in Congress. A decade later, when President Barack Obama proposed an extensive overhaul of the health insurance industry in the United States, a trade group representing drug makers brought the same actors back and remade the Harry and Louise spot, but this time fully supporting the administration's plan. In the new advertisements, Harry and Louise are once again in their kitchen, and Louise pores over medical bills and forms. "Having choices we don't like," says a worried Louise, "is no choice at all." Louise concludes the ad saying "A little more cooperation, a little less politics, and we can get the job done this time."[31]

30 Pendleton Herring, *Group Representation before Congress* (1928; repr.: New York: Russell & Russell, 1967). See also Kenneth W. Kollman, *Outside Lobbying: Public Opinion and Interests Group Strategies* (Princeton, NJ: Princeton University Press, 1998).

31 Natasha Singer, "Harry and Louise Return, with a New Message," *New York Times*, July 16, 2009, www.nytimes.com/2009/07/17/business/media/17adco.html?_r=1&ref=media (accessed 10/3/11).

Grassroots Lobbying. A second strategy that groups use to bring public pressure to bear is grassroots lobbying. Grassroots lobbyists use many of the same organizing methods we see in political campaigns—developing lists of supporters and urging those supporters to voice their concern with an issue and to recruit others to do so. It is common today to send direct mail that includes a draft letter that the recipient can adapt and then send to her representative in Congress or to send e-mails urging people to contact their member of Congress regarding a particular bill or controversy. A grassroots campaign can cost anywhere from $40,000 to attempt to sway the votes of one or two crucial members of a committee or subcommittee to millions of dollars to mount a national effort aimed at Congress as a whole. Such grassroots campaigns are often organized around controversial, prominent legislation or appointments, such as nominees to the U.S. Supreme Court.

Grassroots lobbying has become more prevalent in Washington over the last couple of decades because the adoption of congressional rules limiting gifts to members has made traditional lobbying more difficult. This circumstance makes all the more compelling the question of whether grassroots campaigning has reached an intolerable extreme. One case in particular illustrates the extremes of "Astroturf" lobbying (a play on the brand name of an artificial grass used on many sports fields). In 1992, 10 giant companies in the financial services, manufacturing, and high-tech industries began a grassroots campaign and spent millions of dollars to influence a decision in Congress to limit the ability of investors to sue for fraud. Retaining an expensive consulting firm, these corporations paid for the use of specialized computer software to persuade Congress that there was "an outpouring of popular support for the proposal." Thousands of letters from individuals flooded Capitol Hill. Many of the letters were written and sent by people who sincerely believed that investor lawsuits are often frivolous and should be curtailed. But much of the mail was phony, generated by the Washington-based campaign consultants; the letters came from people who had no strong feelings, or even no opinion at all, about the issue. More and more people, including leading members of Congress, are questioning such methods, charging that these are not genuine grassroots campaigns but instead are Astroturf lobbying. Such Astroturf campaigns have increased in frequency in recent years as members of Congress grow more and more skeptical of Washington lobbyists and far more concerned about demonstrations of support for a particular issue by their constituents. But after the firms spent millions of dollars and generated thousands of letters to members of Congress in their attempt to influence legislation affecting investors' ability to sue for fraud, they came to the somber conclusion that "it's more effective to have 100 letters from your district where constituents took the time to write and understand the issue," because "Congress is sophisticated enough to know the difference."[32]

Protest. Finally, groups often organize protests as a means of bringing attention to an issue or pressure on the government. Protests, in fact, are the oldest means of going public. Those who lack other resources, such as money, contacts,

---

32 Jane Fritsch, "The Grass Roots, Just a Free Phone Call Away," *New York Times*, June 23, 1995, pp. A1 and A22.

and expertise, can always resort to protest as a means of making their concerns public. Indeed, the right to assembly is protected in the First Amendment of the U.S. Constitution. Protests may have many different consequences, depending on how they are managed. One basic consequence of a well-run protest is that it attracts attention. Peaceful demonstrations at city hall, the state legislature, Congress, the Supreme Court, or some other location typically involve people holding signs and chanting slogans. Passersby certainly notice, and occasionally news outlets cover the event in newspapers or on television, and the larger the protest the more likely it is to attract attention. By getting on the news, the protesters hope to attract attention to their issue and possibly raise the sympathies of others and bring them into their movement.

Organized protests also create a sense of community and common interest among those involved and raise the consciousness of people outside the protest. Civil rights protests during the 1960s brought hundreds of thousands of people to march in the nation's capitol. Newspapers and television news programs across the country carried images of Martin Luther King, Jr., and other civil rights leaders speaking to an audience that stretched from the Lincoln Memorial across the Washington Mall and surrounded the Reflecting Pool. That image wrapped the civil rights movement in the symbolism of the nation; it was not a violent confrontation between protesters and police but a peaceful plea for equal voting and civil rights. Forty years later, similar marches mobilized protesters for immigrants' rights. In spring 2006, hundreds of thousands of people, organized mainly by Hispanic and Latino groups, as well as unions and local churches, marched in Washington, D.C., and in several state capitals to protest anti-immigration policies. That movement drew attention to immigrants' concerns in a political environment that was increasingly hostile, and it influenced the political debate over the issue. It also engaged large numbers of Hispanics and Latinos. According to the Pew Hispanic Center, one in four Hispanics in the United States participated in these protests.[33] More recently, the encampments organized by the Occupy Wall Street movement were specifically designed to promote solidarity and community among the protestors.

Finally, protests often attempt to impose costs on others by disrupting traffic or commerce, thereby forcing people to bargain with protesters. Labor strikes are a form of political action against companies, industries, or the government. Workers in a labor strike refuse to work, costing the company the revenue it would have gained from services rendered. In an industry such as automotives, the companies may have enough existing stock of cars and parts to allow for weeks or maybe months of negotiations without disrupting sales. However, in an industry such as education or the airlines, once the teachers or pilots go on strike, all service stops. On rare occasions labor organizations can instigate a general strike—all workers in the entire industry, a city, or a nation stay home from work, bringing all commerce to a stop. Such strikes have a significant effect

---

33 Pew Hispanic Center and Pew Forum on Religion & Public Life, "Changing Faiths: Latinos and the Transformation of American Religion," 2007, http://pewhispanic.org /files/reports/75.pdf (accessed 4/7/09).

on businesses and the larger economy and are called to remind the government and industry leaders of the political pull of labor.

Unions aren't the only groups that organize protests designed to disrupt normal activities. One impressive demonstration occurred during the winter of 1977–78. American farmers were frustrated with federal agricultural policies and increasing failures of family farms. The farmers' frustration culminated in the organization of a convoy of 600 tractors and other farm vehicles to Washington, D.C. The tractor procession was peaceful but highly disruptive. It snarled traffic for weeks and tore up the grass mall running between the Lincoln Memorial and the Capitol. The protest made for compelling news photographs and was covered extensively in national newsmagazines and newspapers. The farmers did not get a revision of the 1977 Farm Bill, but they did get a promise from the Federal Housing Administration (FHA) temporarily to cease seizures of land and equipment of farmers who could not repay loans.[34] Farmers' protests, teachers' strikes, and other activities disrupt government and business activity in order to force negotiation of a better deal.

Protests may spill over and become riots or even civil conflict, or they may be confronted by counterprotests. Companies affected by protests and the government have an interest in containing or breaking up demonstrations and strikes. However, the First Amendment is generally interpreted as protecting free expression through protests and strikes so long as they do not erupt into open rioting. Courts are often asked to rule on whether a protest is lawful or unlawful. For example, during George W. Bush's second inauguration, on January 20, 2005, about 250 to 300 people conducted a protest against the war in Iraq by marching through the streets of the Adams Morgan neighborhood in Washington, D.C. Police broke up the march with mass arrests. Some of the protesters sued to overturn their convictions and complained of alleged damages from police actions. The district court agreed with the protesters, reasoning that they were engaged in a peaceful protest, but had they been involved in riotous behavior, police actions may have been justified.[35]

Using Electoral Politics

In addition to attempting to influence members of Congress and other government officials, interest groups seek to use the electoral process to elect the right legislators in the first place and ensure that those who are elected will owe them a debt of gratitude for their support. To put matters into perspective, groups invest far more resources in lobbying than in electoral politics. Nevertheless, financial support and campaign activism can be important tools for organized interests.

---

34 "Furious Farmers," *Time*, December 19, 1977, www.time.com/time/magazine /article/0,9171,945836,00.html (accessed 4/7/09); Marty Strange, *Family Farming: A New Economic Vision* (Lincoln: University of Nebraska Press, 1988).

35 *Carr et al. v. District of Columbia*, U.S. District Court of the District of Columbia, Civil Action, No. 2006-0098, July 15, 2008, https://ecf.dcd.uscourts.gov/cgi-bin/show _public_doc?2006cv0098-69 (accessed 4/7/09).

Political Action Committees. By far, the most common electoral strategy employed by interest groups is that of giving financial support to the parties or to particular candidates. But such support can easily cross the threshold into outright bribery. Therefore, Congress has occasionally made an effort to regulate this strategy. For example, the Federal Election Campaign Act of 1971 (amended in 1974) limits campaign contributions and requires each candidate or campaign committee to provide the full name and address, occupation, and principal business of each person who contributes more than $100. The FECA requires that any organization that wishes to contribute to a candidate must do so through a "separate and segregated fund"—a political action committee.

These provisions have been effective up to a point, considering the rather large number of embarrassments, indictments, resignations, and criminal convictions in the aftermath of the Watergate scandal. The Watergate scandal itself was triggered when Republican "dirty tricksters" were caught breaking into the office of the Democratic National Committee in the Watergate complex in Washington. An investigation revealed numerous violations of campaign finance laws, involving millions of dollars that were passed from corporate executives to President Nixon's re-election committee.

Reaction to Watergate produced further legislation on campaign finance in 1974 and 1976, but the effect has been to restrict individual rather than interest-group campaign activity. Individuals may now contribute no more than $2,600 to any candidate for federal office in any primary or general election. A political action committee, however, can contribute $5,000, provided it contributes to at least five different federal candidates each year.[36] Beyond this, the laws permit corporations, unions, and other interest groups to form PACs and pay the costs of soliciting funds from private citizens for the PACs.

Electoral spending by interest groups has increased steadily despite the campaign finance reforms that followed the Watergate scandal: total PAC contributions increased from nearly $260 million in 2000 to over $1 billion in the 2012 election cycle. Interest groups focus their direct contributions on Congress, especially the U.S. House. Given the enormous cost of running modern political campaigns (see Chapter 11), most politicians are eager to receive PAC contributions. A typical U.S. House incumbent receives half of his campaign funds from interest groups. There is little evidence that interest groups buy roll-call votes or other favors from members of Congress with their donations. Group donations do, however, help to keep those who are sympathetic to groups' interests and views in office.[37]

The potential influence of interest group campaign donations over the legislature has prompted frequent calls from reformers to abolish PACs or limit their activities. The challenge is how to regulate the participation of groups without violating their members' rights to free speech and free association. In 1976, the U.S. Supreme Court weighed in on this matter in the case *Buckley v. Valeo*, which

---

36 Federal Election Commission, "Contribution Limits 2013–14," www.fec.gov/pages /brochures/contriblimits.shtml (accessed 3/4/13).

37 See Stephen Ansolabehere, John de Figueiredo, and James M. Snyder, Jr., "Why Is There So Little Money in U.S. Politics?" *Journal of Economic Perspectives* 17 (2006): 105–30.

questioned the constitutionality of the 1974 Federal Elections Campaign Act.[38] In its decision to let the act stand, the majority on the Court ruled that donors' rights of expression are at stake, but that these must be weighed against the government's interest in limiting corruption, or the perception of corruption. The Court has repeatedly upheld the key tenets of its 1976 decision: (1) That money is a form of speech but (2) that speech rights must be weighed against concerns about corruption. The balance between the rights to free speech and the need to protect against corruption lie at the heart of not just campaign finance law but how Americans think about the representation of interests in our government. We value both the right of people and organizations to say freely what they want government to do and the quality and integrity of representation provided to the people through the electoral and legislative process.

Independent Expenditures. The balance between free speech and corruption has led to a system of limitations on direct campaign contributions to candidates and parties through political action committees. For many groups, however, the limits are not adequate. They would like to communicate directly with voters about the election and advocate for one candidate or party.

As we saw in Chapter 11, Congress in 2002 sought to impose significant limits on independent campaign expenditures via the Bipartisan Campaign Reform Act (BCRA). BCRA restricted donations to nonfederal (for example, state party) accounts as a necessary reform to limit corruption, and it imposed limits on the types of campaign commercials that could be aired by groups within 60 days of an election. It also raised the limits on direct campaign contributions for the first time since 1976, as inflation had seriously squeezed the value of contributions.

In 2010, the Supreme Court struck down the restrictions on independent advertising.[39] The case involved a political movie critical of then-senator and presidential candidate Hillary Clinton and created by an organization called Citizens United. The movie aired on cable television inside the blackout date for independent political advertising stipulated by the BCRA. A 5–4 majority on the Court ruled that such blackout dates imposed by BCRA restricted the rights to free speech of corporations and other associations. This decision firmly established the right of business corporations and labor unions to engage in political advocacy and opened the gates to a flood of money in the political arena.

This flood was evident during the 2012 national elections, in which independent expenditures amounted to some $1.1 billion (Figure 13.3). A significant portion of this money was raised by independent expenditure committees that the media dubbed "Super PACs," which are allowed to raise unlimited amounts of money from any source—individuals, businesses, or other associations. There are some restrictions on Super PACs, however: they must report donors to the Federal Election Commission, and they are not allowed to directly coordinate their activities with political candidates. However, they are allowed to advertise for and against candidates. The top two Super PACs in the 2012 election

---

38 *Buckley v. Valeo*, 424 U.S. 1 (1976).

39 *Citizens United v. Federal Election Commission*, 558 U.S. 310 (2010).

Figure 13.3
INDEPENDENT EXPENDITURES PER ELECTION CYCLE

NOTE: The years 1992, 1996, 2000, 2004, 2008, and 2012 were presidential election years.
SOURCE: Center for Responsive Politics, www.opensecrets.org/outsidespending/cycle_tots.php
(accessed 7/27/13).

were Restore Our Future and American Crossroads, both of which had a conservative bent. Together they raised close to $300 million. The primary spending of all Super PACs, both liberal and conservative, was on negative advertising.

Campaign Activism. Financial support is not the only way in which organized groups seek influence through the electoral process. Sometimes activism can be even more important than campaign contributions.

Perhaps the most notable instance of such activism occurs on behalf of the Democratic Party and candidates through unions. Labor unions regularly engage in massive get-out-the-vote drives during political campaigns. The largest such activities come from the Service Employees International Union (SEIU), which represents workers ranging from hotel and restaurant workers to clerical staff, and the United Auto Workers (UAW). SEIU, for instance, spent in excess of $14.4 million to support Democratic candidates in 2012. Other sorts of groups routinely line up behind the Democratic and Republican campaigns. The National Rifle Association, for example, spent $9.5 million in the 2012 election cycle, and all but $7,000 was in support of Republican candidates.

The cumulative effect of such independent campaign activism is difficult to judge. One important research initiative within political science seeks to measure systematically the marginal effectiveness of campaign contact. Professors Alan Gerber and Donald Green have developed a program of field experiments in which campaigns agree to randomly assign direct campaign activity to some neighborhoods but not others. They have been able to measure the marginal effect of an additional piece of mail, direct canvasser, or phone call. In a typical election context, it costs about $40 to get an additional voter to the polls. Professors Gerber and Green further find that campaign activism initially can have a large impact, but after six or so attempted contacts the effects of campaign contact diminish dramatically. This important empirical research has given campaigns and reformers some sense of the effectiveness of campaign activism in stimulating turnout and possibly influencing elections. Especially in low-turnout elections, such as for city council or state legislature, interest groups' get-out-the-vote activities can have very large effects on who wins, but as other money enters the scene, especially candidates' own campaign expenditures, the effects of interest groups' direct campaign activities become muted.[40]

The Initiative. Another political tactic sometimes used by interest groups is sponsorship of ballot initiatives at the state level. The **initiative**, a device adopted by a number of states around 1900, allows proposed laws to be placed on the general election ballot and submitted directly to the state's voters. This procedure bypasses the state legislature and governor. The initiative was originally promoted by late nineteenth-century Populists as a mechanism that allows the people to govern directly. Populists saw the initiative as an antidote to interest group influence in the legislative process.

Ironically, many studies have suggested that most initiative campaigns today are sponsored by interest groups seeking to circumvent legislative opposition to their goals. In recent years, for example, initiative campaigns have been sponsored by the insurance industry, trial lawyers' associations, and tobacco companies. The role of interest groups in initiative campaigns should come as no surprise, since such campaigns can cost millions of dollars.

 initiative

A process by which citizens may petition to place a policy proposal on the ballot for public vote

Are Interest Groups Effective?

Do interest groups have an effect on government and policy? A clear answer is difficult to find among the mountains of research on this question. A survey of dozens of studies of campaign contributions and legislative decision making found that in only about 1 in 10 cases was there evidence of a correlation between contributors' interests and legislators' roll-call voting.[41]

Earmarks are a good case in point. Earmarks are expenditures on particular projects in specific districts or states, and they are usually included in a bill late in the legislative process to help secure enough votes for passage. Millions of dollars in earmarks are written into law every year. John de Figueiredo of UCLA and Brian Silverman of the University of Toronto examined the effectiveness of lobbyists to obtain "earmarks" for colleges and universities on whose behalf they are working.[42]

40 Donald Green and Alan Gerber, *Get Out the Vote: How to Increase Voter Turnout*, 2nd ed. (Washington DC: Brookings Institution Press, 2008).

41 Ansolabehere, de Figueiredo, and Snyder, "Why Is There So Little Money in U.S. Politics?"

42 John M. de Figueiredo and Brian S. Silverman, "Academic Earmarks and the Returns to Lobbying" working paper 9064, National Bureau of Economic Research, 2002; substantially rev., 2003, http://web.mit.edu/jdefig/www/papers/academic_earmarks .pdf (accessed 4/7/09).

The authors discovered that lobbying had a limited impact. The more money schools spent on lobbying activities, the larger the total quantity of earmarked funds they received; however, the magnitude of the effect depended greatly on institutional factors. For most schools, every $1 spent on representation gained about $1 more on earmarks—hardly worth it. In a handful of cases, though, there appear to be exceedingly high returns. Schools in states with a senator on the Senate Appropriations Committee received $18 to $29 in earmarks for every $1 spent on lobbying. Schools in congressional districts whose representative served on the House Appropriations Committee received between $49 and $55 for every $1 spent on lobbying. Having a legislator on the relevant committee then is a precursor to having influence and explains most of the observed influence.[43]

These results suggest, as is so often the case, that institutions and politics are profoundly related. Schools without access to members of Congress in positions to help them cannot gain much from lobbying. Schools with such access still need to lobby to take advantage of the potential that representation on the Senate and House Appropriations Committees can give them. But if they do so, the potential return from lobbying is substantial.

Perhaps the largest challenge to the claim that interest group politics drive American democracy arises when we consider how much political advocacy occurs. The usual argument about the power and influence of lobbyists and campaign contributions suggests that any dollar spent by a corporation or other organization on political activity is a dollar well spent. One can turn that thinking on its head. If it is a dollar well spent, then groups should spend as much as possible on politics, and total spending on politics should reflect the value of political action to firms and organizations, relative to other sorts of investments. In other words, view the political actions of any firm—and most organizations involved in politics are firms—not as a political decision but as a business decision. What insight comes from that perspective?

Those engaged in lobbying provide a valued service for the firms that they represent by helping to shape legislation, influence administrative decisions, and advocate in court. There are, however, other investments one can make: buy new machines, purchase another company, hire additional employees. How do lobbying and campaign contributing compare with those sorts of bottom-line decisions made by firms?

As a business and economic matter, the amount of money spent on political activity by firms is small. The value of goods purchased in a market is approximately equal to the amount of money someone is willing to pay for them. The total U.S. economy is valued at $15.8 trillion; government expenditures are over $5 trillion; corporate profits alone exceed $1.7 trillion. As a fraction of total government expenditures, total lobbying expenditures equal less than one-tenth of 1 percent, and lobbying is only a trace amount of the total revenue of firms' total expenses. This simple calculation suggests that the total influence of

---

43 John M. de Figueiredo and Brian S. Silverman, "Academic Earmarks and the Returns to Lobbying," *Journal of Law and Economics* 42 (October 2006): 597–626.

groups cannot be substantial.[44] If the returns on political investment were high, then we ought to see large firms like Microsoft, General Electric, and Wal-Mart spending much more (and getting much more) on politics.

Why isn't there more money in politics? One answer is suggested by Mancur Olson—groups are simply free riding. But that still suggests there is an opportunity for influence for those who are engaged, and they should spend even more money to get even greater returns. The pluralist line of thinking points to a more compelling answer. The United States has a wide-open political system, with many points of access and many points of influence. By allowing more political activity and discourse, no one group is able to have much influence. There is not much money in politics because the separation of powers and other features of the U.S. political system make it exceedingly difficult to have much immediate influence over the legislative and executive branches of government. The pluralist argument is wrong in asserting that all interests will find expression through political organization, but it is perhaps right that a system of divided political authority, such as in the United States, will make it exceedingly hard for particular interests to dominate in the political arena.

CONCLUSION

The institutions of American government embrace an open and democratic process in order to ensure that government is responsive to the public's preferences and needs. The Bill of Rights provides for the rights of free speech, freedom of the press, and freedom of assembly. The laws of the land have only further cemented this commitment, providing for open meetings, citizen advisory commissions, lobbying, direct contact from constituents, contributions from interested individuals and groups, an open legal system, protests, and many other routes through which individuals and groups may advocate for their interests. Through these many points of access, representatives and government officials learn how their decisions affect groups and individuals. Politics, then, becomes the arena in which these many interests compete for the attention and support of the government.

Such a system creates an opportunity for those who have the willingness and capacity to use their resources to represent their interests before the government. Problems of collective action and free riding prevent many latent interests from developing permanent political organizations capable of bringing concerted pressure on the government. Businesses, unions, and professional and industry associations usually have less trouble overcoming the obstacles to organization and group maintenance that many volunteer associations may face. Interest group politics in Washington and state legislatures, consequently, tends to reflect the interests of and conflicts among those engaged in economic activity in the country.

---

44 See Ansolabehere, de Figueiredo, and Snyder, "Why Is There So Little Money in U.S. Politics?"

Although firms, unions, and other organizations can solve the collective action problem, they do not necessarily succeed in the political arena. They often find politics unfamiliar, even hostile, terrain in which to pursue organizational goals. Unlike economic activity, politics involves power derived from the ability to vote on measures, to introduce legislation or rules, or to block actions from happening. Interest groups are necessarily outsiders that can do none of these things directly. Nonetheless, these organizations seek out support in the appropriate institutions, such as a court with a sympathetic judge or a subcommittee of Congress where the chair holds views similar to those of the group. And the way to success is usually quite subtle. Often, groups succeed not by bringing pressure but by providing expertise to the government and by learning from those in office about the impact of new rules and regulations.

Over the past 30 to 40 years, interest groups have increasingly found that the best route to power is through public action and public opinion. It is not enough for a group to hire a lobbyist to advocate on its behalf in the halls of government. Real pressure may be brought to bear on politicians by shaping what others think. Through advertising, protests, and grassroots networks, interest groups have increasingly brought their issues to the attention of the public. Tens of thousands of organizations now compete in the political sphere.

Interest group politics at the beginning of the twenty-first century does not fit stereotypical notions clearly. There are certainly as many lobbyists as ever, but the backroom dealings of the "old lobby" are an anachronism. Interest group politics is diffuse, spread across all branches of government and involving many different interests vying for the attention of politicians in an increasingly crowded and active interest group ecology. Those who are organized gain the advantages of pooling resources, but an interest group's political action today constitutes only one aspect of the debate over any given political issue or decision. Other interests and voices making competing claims may very well cancel out a given organization's efforts. And the activities of all groups amount to just one facet of legislators', judges', and executives' deliberations. Those who must ultimately make political decisions and be held accountable for those decisions consider other voices as well, especially the opinions and preferences of their constituents. Perhaps a better contemporary characterization is that the organized and disorganized interests participating in politics today are really contributing to a much broader sphere of political discourse and debate. That debate takes place inside the institutions of government—Congress, courts, executives, and elections. It also takes place in another arena, the media. That forum is the final leg of our discussion of democracy in America, and to that subject we turn in the next chapter.

For Further Reading

Selections highlighted in red are included in *Readings in American Politics: Analysis and Perspectives*, Third Edition.

Abramoff, Jack. *Capitol Punishment: The Hard Truth about Washington Corruption from America's Most Notorious Lobbyist*. New York: WND Books, 2011.

Ainsworth, Scott. *Analyzing Interest Groups*. New York: Norton, 2002.

Alexander, Robert, ed. *The Classics of Interest Group Behavior*. New York: Wadsworth, 2005.

Ansolabehere, Stephen, John M. de Figueiredo, and James M. Snyder, Jr. "Why Is There So Little Money in U.S. Politics?" *Journal of Economic Perspectives* 17, no. 1 (Winter 2003): 105–30.

Baumgartner, Frank, Jeffrey M. Berry, Beth L. Leech, David C. Kimball, and Marie Hojnacki. *Lobbying and Policy Change: Who Wins, Who Loses, and Why*. Chicago: University of Chicago Press, 2009.

Cigler, Allan, and Burdett A. Loomis. *Interest Group Politics*. 8th ed. Washington, DC: CQ Press, 2011.

Esterling, Kevin. *The Political Economy of Expertise*. Ann Arbor: University of Michigan Press, 2004.

Galanter, Marc. "Why the 'Haves' Come Out Ahead: Spectulations on the Limits of Legal Change." *Law and Society Review* 9, no. 1 (1974): 95–160.

Gilens, Martin. *Affluence and Influence: Economic Inequality and Political Power in America*. New York and Princeton, NJ: Russell Sage Foundation and Princeton University Press, 2012.

Harrison, Paul, Christopher Deering, and Clyde Wilcox. *Interest Groups Unleashed*. Washington, DC: CQ Press, 2012.

Lowi, Theodore J. *The End of Liberalism: The Second Republic of the United States*. 2nd ed. New York: Norton, 1979.

Moe, Terry M. *The Organization of Interests: Incentives and the Internal Dynamics of Political Interest Groups*. Chicago: University of Chicago Press, 1980.

Nownes, Anthony. *Total Lobbying: What Lobbyists Want and How They Try to Get It*. New York: Cambridge University Press, 2006.

Olson, Mancur, Jr. *The Logic of Collective Action: Public Goods and the Theory of Groups*. 1965. Reprinted with new preface and appendix. Cambridge, MA: Harvard University Press, 1965.

Rosenthal, Alan. *The Third House: Lobbyists and Lobbying in the States*. Washington, DC: CQ Press, 2001.

Strolovitch, Dara. *Affirmative Advocacy: Race, Class, and Gender in Interest Group Politics*. Chicago: University of Chicago Press, 2007.

14

The Media

The media make up one of the most unusual institutions of American democracy. They are not a singular institution, such as the Congress or the presidency. Rather, the media comprise an industry that exists primarily for communication and entertainment. The main business model is simple enough. Using communication technologies such as the printing press and Internet, media firms develop and distribute content—news articles, TV shows, websites, and the like—to attract an audience. The audience pays for access to content by purchasing subscriptions, paying cover prices and access charges, and buying computers, televisions, and radios. More significant still, other businesses, organizations, and individuals want access to that audience, and they will pay media firms to advertise their messages. Most media revenue derives from advertising, from selling access to the audience attracted by television and radio, newspapers and magazines, and the Internet.[1] And the audience is huge. Nearly every household in the United States has at least one television; three-quarters have Internet access. The typical American adult watches four hours of television a day.

Politics and public affairs are an important part of the content produced by the media. People are willing to pay for information about politics and public affairs, and politicians and organized interests are willing to pay to reach that audience through advertisements or events that will attract news coverage. Most major media outlets offer news coverage and analysis as a way to attract readers and listeners. The major television networks—ABC, CBS, NBC, and Fox—offer approximately six hours of news programming every day, and some media organizations are devoted exclusively to politics and public affairs. The cost of news programs to consumers is minimal, even free, and the content is presented in a widely accessible manner. In this way, the media offer most people an easy

---

1   Roughly 75 percent of newspaper revenue comes from advertising, and 20 percent
    from subscriptions. See Laura Houston Santhanam and Tom Rosenstiel, "Why
    U.S. Newspapers Suffer More Than Others," *The State of the News Media, 2011,* Pew
    Research Center's Project for Excellence in Journalism, http://stateofthemedia
    .org/2011/mobile-survey/international-newspaper-economics/ (accessed 10/3/11).

way to learn about the important actions of the government, the state of the nation, and the choices in an election.

The media, then, address one of the most important problems of democracy—how to create an informed electorate. As we discussed in Chapters 10 and 11, democratic politics assumes some awareness among the electorate about who is in power, what problems the nation faces, and what actions and policies the government has taken. The news media make information about politics and public affairs readily and widely accessible, even entertaining. Most Americans learn about government and politics not through firsthand experience but from media sources and through the lenses of those who report the news or comment on important issues and events.

The challenge for every democracy is how to foster the development of media that will allow for robust discourse and dissent. The United States, from its inception, has embraced the principle that a free press allows people to speak freely and to make reasoned electoral decisions. The First Amendment to the Constitution states that "Congress shall make no law . . . abridging the freedom of speech, or the press." Over time the Supreme Court has expanded that idea to cover all forms of communication and has interpreted that restraint to apply to all levels and branches of government, not just Congress.

A free, open, and largely unregulated media environment is the engine of American democracy. It is the great marketplace of ideas. Collectively the media present a vast range of ideas, opinions, and information and make it easily accessible to everyone. Any consumer may choose to watch, read, or listen to what

CORE OF THE ANALYSIS

 The primary objective of the American media is to make profits, which they do by charging fees to access their content and by selling advertising.

 The market for news is extremely large, as most Americans rely on the media to find out about issues, government activities, and electoral choices. This makes the private media industry into an important part of the public sphere.

 Politicians, bureaucrats, organized interests, and private citizens can shape how the media portray public issues by providing information to journalists.

 The U.S. government takes a light hand in regulating media ownership and operation, relying on the marketplace to produce a robust flow of information about politics and government affairs.

she wants. Those media that do not attract consumers fail, whereas those that offer people what they want succeed. This system does not always provide the ideal outcome, but, at least in theory, it is considered the best way to guarantee an adequately informed public.[2] The First Amendment, wrote Judge Learned Hand at the height of World War II, "presupposes that right conclusions are more likely to be gathered out of a multitude of tongues, than through any kind of authoritative selection. To many this is, and always will be, folly; but we have staked upon it our all."[3]

An alternate view holds that journalists and owners of media firms hold a privileged and powerful position in any society, and with that privilege comes responsibilities that can only be ensured through regulation. Most countries regulate political speech by limiting advertising; they require a minimum amount of public affairs programming; and they regulate what is and is not said by reporters. Slander and libel laws apply to American journalists as do restrictions owing to national security, but there is far less regulation of reporting in the United States than in just about every other country. Most other countries underwrite or own their main broadcast media outlets, such as the Canadian or British Broadcasting Corporations. In the United States, media firms succeed or fail as businesses and rely on their ability to attract audiences and revenue, not on whether they provide a public service or good.

How and how well does the marketplace of ideas work? Is there enough competition? Today, for example, very few cities are served by more than one local newspaper. Local news monopolies may give owners, editors, and journalists excessive political power in their local markets. Or is there too much competition? The emergence of the Internet has cut into the profit margins of traditional media, forcing newspapers and television and radio companies to cut their more expensive staff, often the very reporters who produce the content on the news. Media firms, Congress, and executive agencies (especially the Federal Communications Commission [FCC]) must deal with these and other complex questions over the coming decades as new communications technologies transform the media industry in the United States and the ways that people become informed about and engage in politics.

THE MEDIA AS A POLITICAL INSTITUTION

Perhaps the most salient feature of the American media—as an industry and as a political institution—is the diversity of sources, firms, and technologies. There are approximately 1,400 daily newspapers in the United States and 1,500 television stations affiliated with seven major broadcasting networks. Hundreds

---

2 This idea is most elegantly expressed in the majority opinion in the Supreme Court case *New York Times v. Sullivan,* 376 U.S. 254 (1964).

3 *United States v. Associated Press,* 52 F. Supp. 362, 372 (D. C. S. D. N. Y. 1943).

of weekly magazines, independent television stations, and affiliates of smaller networks are devoted to national politics. Countless websites stream news from sources throughout the world. These media reach every community in the United States and provide information in every language.

Types of Media

There is some order to the apparent chaos. The American media are organized into three categories—print, broadcast, and Internet. Regulations of the media follow these lines. Print media, such as newspapers and magazines, have long enjoyed strong First Amendment protections and provide a good example of the "marketplace of ideas." The technology of printing presses and digital reproduction makes it quite easy for new papers to enter local markets, and that fact has led the courts to stay the hand of those pushing for regulation of print media.

Broadcast and cablecast media, by contrast, have historically faced technological limits that have led to restrictions on ownership, distribution, and at times content. With the advent of radio in the 1920s, the need for regulation immediately became evident. Broadcasters would vary the strength of their signal and the part of the radio-frequency spectrum over which they broadcast to find audiences and squelch other broadcasters. That behavior threatened to ruin the medium, because consumers could not reliably find the programming that they wanted. In 1927, Commerce Secretary Herbert Hoover introduced the first regulations of broadcast media, requiring every broadcaster to secure a license from the U.S. government and to agree to send its signal only over a narrow band of the spectrum (which would be allocated to that station within a certain region). The U.S. government could revoke that license for failure to comply with spectrum regulations. In the late 1940s, concern about the use of the spectrum in emerging television technology led the federal government to freeze the development of that nascent industry for four years while the Federal Communications Commission worked out a distribution and ownership plan. Regulation of the broadcast spectrum continues to dictate federal communications policy to this day. Because spectrum is limited, broadcasting and cablecasting firms serve a public trust and bear responsibility for their actions.[4] Of course, spectrum is not very limited any more. Rather, this view exhibits the history principle at work. When broadcasting and cable were developed the technology was not as good as today, and the technology limited the number of stations possible, with only some firms having access—hence, the public responsibility. Today, broadcasting and cable technology permit hundreds of channels. Nonetheless the

---

4 Perhaps the best account of these developments is Erik Barnouw's excellent three-volume history *A Tower in Babel: A History of Broadcasting in the United States to 1933; The Golden Web: A History of Broadcasting in the United States, 1933 to 1953;* and *The Image Empire: A History of Broadcasting in the United States from 1953* (New York: Oxford University Press, 1966, 1968, and 1970).

rules developed in the 1920s persist, and those firms that have flourished under the rules fight to keep their control over the airwaves.

Since the mid-1990s, a third media sector has arisen, one driven by Internet technology. Internet technology blurs the line between the other two media sectors. It requires governance for the assignment of web domains, but it otherwise operates as perhaps the most open and competitive of the three sectors. The Internet sector is still developing its distinctive identity as a mode of communication, especially political communication. For the first two decades of its existence, the traditional media dominated the Internet provision of content, as print and broadcast firms moved their content online. But since 2000 an increasingly unique and distinctive form of web-based political communication has emerged, including blogs and citizen journalism, which many fear is supplanting traditional media and the norms of professional journalism.[5] The 2008 election marked the true arrival of the Internet as one of the three pillars of "the media." In 2008, for the first time, more people reported that they got news from a digital platform, including websites, social networking, and mobile devices, than from newspapers. By 2012, Internet and mobile technologies had far surpassed radio and newspapers: 50 percent of the public reported that they got some of their news through the web or a mobile device, compared with just 29 percent by newspaper with another 33 percent from radio (Table 14.1).

Table 14.1
TRENDS IN NEWS CONSUMPTION, 1994–2012

	1994 (%)	1996 (%)	1998 (%)	2000 (%)	2002 (%)	2004 (%)	2006 (%)	2008 (%)	2010 (%)	2012 (%)
Watched news on TV	72	59	59	56	54	60	57	57	58	55
Read a daily newspaper	49	50	49	47	41	42	40	34	31	29
Listened to news on radio	47	44	48	43	41	40	36	35	34	33
Got news online	—	—	—	—	—	24	23	29	34	39
Got news from any digital platform	—	—	—	—	—	—	—	—	42	50

SOURCE: Pew Research Center for People and the Press, "In Changing News Landscape, Even Television Is Vulnerable," September 27, 2012, www.people-press.org/2012/09/27/section-1 -watching-reading-and-listening-to-the-news-3 (accessed 12/10/12).

5 Cass R. Sunstein, *Republic.com 2.0* (Princeton, NJ: Princeton University Press, 2007).

Broadcast Media. Television news reaches more Americans than any other single news source. Tens of millions of individuals watch national and local news programs every day. Television news, however, covers relatively few topics and provides little depth of coverage. Television news is more like a series of newspaper headlines connected to pictures. It serves the important function of alerting viewers to issues and events but provides little else.

The 24-hour news stations such as Cable News Network (CNN) offer more detail and commentary than the networks' half-hour evening news shows. In 2003, at the start of the war in Iraq, CNN, Fox News, and MSNBC provided 24-hour-a-day coverage of the war, including on-the-scene reports from embedded reporters, expert commentary, and interviews with government officials. In this instance, these networks' depth of coverage rivaled that of the print media. Normally, however, CNN and the others offer more headlines than analysis, especially during their prime-time broadcasts. Nevertheless, in recent years, cable has been growing in importance as a news source.

Radio news is essentially a headline service without pictures. In the short time that they devote to news (usually five minutes per hour), radio stations announce the day's major events without providing much detail. All-news stations such as WTOP (Washington, D.C.) and WCBS (New York City) assume that most listeners are in their cars and that, as a result, the people who constitute the audience change markedly throughout the day as they reach their destinations. Thus, rather than use their time to flesh out a given set of stories, these stations repeat the same stories each hour to present them to new listeners. In recent years, radio talk shows have become important sources of commentary and opinion. A number of conservative radio hosts, such as Rush Limbaugh, have huge audiences and have helped mobilize support for conservative political causes and candidates. Liberals have had less success in the world of talk radio and have complained that biased coverage over radio has hurt them in elections.

In recent years, much of the content of the news, especially local news, has shifted away from politics and public affairs toward "soft news"— coverage focusing on celebrities, health tips, advice to consumers, and other topics more likely to provide entertainment than enlightenment. Even a good deal of political coverage is soft. For example, articles about the Obamas' choice of their dog Bo outnumbered stories about the Iraq War by 3 to 2 during April 2009.[6]

Another category of programming is sometimes called *infotainment*. This term refers to material that purports to combine information with entertainment. *The Daily Show with Jon Stewart* on Comedy Central calls itself America's "most trusted name in fake news," yet a significant fraction of people under 35 years of age report this show as one of their main sources of political information and news. The news on *The Daily Show* is not fake but a comedic twist on current events and on the media itself, especially CNN and Fox News.

---

6   Project for Excellence in Journalism, "The Dog Days of Spring," April 22, 2009, http://journalism.org/TheDogDaysofSpring+ (accessed 5/7/09).

Print Media. Newspapers remain an important source of news even though they are not the primary news source for most Americans. The print media are important for at least three reasons. First, as we see later in this chapter, the broadcast media rely on leading newspapers such as the *New York Times* and the *Washington Post* to set their news agenda. The broadcast media engage in very little actual reporting; they primarily cover stories that have been "broken," or initially reported, by the print media. For example, sensational charges that President Bill Clinton had an affair with a White House intern were reported first by the *Washington Post* and *Newsweek* before being trumpeted around the world by the broadcast media. It is only a slight exaggeration to observe that if an event is not covered in the *New York Times*, it is not likely to appear on the *CBS Evening News*. One important exception, obviously, is the case of "breaking" news, which can be carried by the broadcast media as it unfolds or soon after, whereas the print media are forced to catch up later in the day. For example, dramatic real-time videos of the collapsing World Trade Center towers were seen by tens of millions of Americans on September 11, 2001. Second, the print media provide more detailed and more complete information, offering a better context for analysis. Third, the print media are also important because they are the prime source of news for educated and influential individuals. The nation's economic, social, and political elites rely on the detailed coverage provided by the print media to inform and influence their views about important public matters. The print media may have a smaller audience than their cousins in broadcasting, but they have an audience that matters.

Today, however, the newspaper industry is in serious economic trouble. The rise of websites advertising jobs, items for sale, and personal ads has dramatically reduced newspapers' revenues from traditional advertising, such as "help wanted" and personal ads. The *Rocky Mountain News* in Denver closed in 2008, and in 2009 the *Seattle Post-Intelligencer* announced it would adopt an online format only. Major newspapers serving dozens of large U.S. cities and metropolitan areas confirmed in 2008 and 2009 that they faced serious financial difficulties that might end in closure, including the *Philadelphia Inquirer*, the *Minneapolis Star Tribune*, the *Miami Herald*, the *Boston Globe*, and the *San Francisco Chronicle*. Such closures would leave many cities with one or possibly no daily print newspapers. And in 2013, the Graham family, which had owned the *Washington Post* for three generations, surprised the industry by announcing the sale of the paper to Jeffrey Bezos, founder and CEO of Amazon.com. It is widely believed that the troubles experienced by these papers are the beginning of a wider transformation of the print media in the United States that may leave the country with few or no print newspapers—the traditional "press"—in the future. The great unknown is whether other venues, such as the Internet, can adequately replace newspapers, especially in the provision of news about local area politics and public affairs.[7]

The possible demise of major city newspapers raises important questions. Since the beginning of the Republic, newspapers have been ingrained in the way we think about political communication. The First Amendment specifically

---

7 24/7 Wall Street, "The 10 Most Endangered Newspapers in America," *Time*, March 9, 2009, www.time.com/time/business/article/0,8599,1883785,00.html (accessed 5/7/09).

protects a "free press," and legal doctrines and laws concerning political communication in the United States have evolved around the idea of a robust press serving every community. Many cities now face the prospect of no significant press, in the conventional sense. These changes will likely force a rethinking of the laws governing many aspects of political communication in this country, from campaign finance laws to obscenity standards to ownership guidelines. So far, the U.S. Supreme Court has not extended the same set of free press protections to broadcasters.[8]

This transformation of print media may change the extent to which people are informed about politics and public affairs. The media that will replace newspapers may raise the overall level of information among the mass public or create further differences between those in the know and those who decide to tune out politics. The Internet, television, radio, and other outlets that replace newspapers may reach more people with similar content, or they may segment the audience further, reducing the number of people aware of public affairs. Social science research so far suggests that the decline of newspapers is changing news-gathering behavior. Rather than rely on a single source—the daily paper—Americans are sampling many different sources, a practice known as "grazing" according to a recent study by the Pew Research Center. And that behavior is facilitated by the Internet.[9]

The Internet. The Internet emerged as a major form of communication in the mid-1990s. As with radio in the 1920s and television in the 1950s, over the span of a decade the Internet grew from a curiosity into one of the dominant modes of communication. Internet news providers now stand as a significant competitor to traditional media outlets. Every day tens of millions of Americans scan one of many news sites on the Internet for coverage of current events. Websites such as craigslist have taken away one of the most important sources of revenue for newspapers—classified advertising. As classified advertising has moved online, newspapers have seen an important line of revenue dry up. At one of many recent forums on the changing media world, an editor at the *Boston Globe* said, "Who knew that the problem we would face would be one of too much competition rather than too little."

In many ways, the Internet as a medium parallels newspapers, television, radio, and magazines. The main newspapers and television outlets—such as the *Wall Street Journal* and the *New York Times*, Reuters and the Associated Press, CNN and Fox News—are mainstays of the Internet. All have websites that they use to attract audiences to their traditional media and that they use to sell advertising. The Internet, however, has revolutionized how content is provided and what content is accessible to audiences. The Internet captures the strengths of the traditional media. It combines the depth of newspaper coverage with the

8   *Red Lion Broadcasting Company v. Federal Communications Commission*, 395 U.S. 367 (1969).

9   "Key News Audience Now Blend Online and Traditional Sources," Pew Research Center for the People and the Press, August 17, 2008, http://people-press.org/report/444 /news-media (accessed 5/7/09).

timeliness of television and radio, but it goes much further. Look at the website of one of the traditional media outlets, such as the *New York Times* or CNN. There you will see a reproduction of the content on the newspaper or headline news from television that resembles a traditional newspaper, but there is also streaming video like a television report or audio like a radio program, and you will also find commentary from many different sources, like an opinion magazine or news journal, such as *Time* magazine.

Unlike a newspaper, which is wholly new every day, a website, such as for the *New York Times*, can keep important stories up for many days. Most news websites contain easily searchable archives of past stories, which allows persistent readers to follow the thread of the news. Many websites now function as aggregators, accumulating news on a given topic from many different sources. Perhaps the most powerful such aggregator is Google, whose news service accumulates and organizes information from news organizations as different as the *Wall Street Journal* and Al Jazeera, Reuters and the Associated Press, and the *Lebanon Daily Star* and *Shanghai Daily*. In addition to traditional news sites, there have emerged more specialized sites. Some focus on commentary, such as Slate; others on investigative reporting, such as the Drudge Report; others provide polling and other analytics, such as Cook Political Report; and still others offer a roundup of news, commentary, and analytics, most notably RealClearPolitics and Politico.

In many ways, the Internet most closely approximates the marketplace of ideas mentioned in this chapter's introduction. There is an unparalleled amount of information and commentary available on any one news site, let alone on one of the aggregator sites.

The Internet differs from traditional outlets in another important way: it allows people to get involved directly. Individual citizens can more easily help create the news and interpret it. Public-access television and radio has always been a source of citizen journalism, but the World Wide Web has expanded greatly the space available for news, commentary, and debate. Most news sites provide space for people to post their own photos, video, and blogs of important events. Individuals who are at the scene of a natural disaster or important political event can provide more (and sometimes even better) coverage of a story and more quickly than a reporter.

The ability to connect with others through the Internet—through e-mail, blogs, Facebook, Twitter, and other social media venues—makes the new media a two-way street. The traditional media firms can distribute information and citizens can contribute to journalism, and people can also connect with one another directly. The power of these new media is not lost on political organizers and campaigns. Political entrepreneurs within social movements and the political parties have sought to organize online advocacy groups to raise money, make their positions known through e-mail and letter campaigns, and provide support for politicians who accept their views. One of the most successful of these enterprises is MoveOn.org, founded by two liberal Silicon Valley entrepreneurs. MoveOn seeks to build electronic advocacy groups, allowing members to propose issues and strategies and then acting on behalf of those that appear to have the highest level of member support. Reflecting the importance of the

Internet, two days after announcing her bid for the 2008 Democratic presidential nomination, Senator Hillary Rodham Clinton fielded questions from voters in an online chat. Speaking into a webcam, Clinton discussed health care, energy policy, and even her favorite movies with a group of preselected voters. President Obama's Press Office developed White House Live, a service that streams video of events live and keeps an archive of past events. A typical day will have live video of two or three events, such as the president touring a natural disaster, holding a press conference, or meeting with other world leaders. As the 2012 presidential campaign unfolded, the Internet had become the medium of choice. Governor Tim Pawlenty announced his bid for the presidency on Facebook. Obama restarted his presidential campaign with an online video. And Mitt Romney kicked off his campaign with a tweet.[10]

Regulation of the Broadcast and Electronic Media

In most countries, the government controls media content and owns the largest media outlets. In the United States, the government neither owns nor controls the communications networks, but it does regulate the content and ownership of the broadcast media.

The print media in the United States are essentially free from government interference. The broadcast media, on the other hand, are subject to federal regulation. American radio and television are regulated by the FCC, an independent regulatory agency established in 1934. Radio and TV stations must renew their FCC licenses every five years. Licensing provides a mechanism for allocating radio and TV frequencies in such a way as to prevent broadcasts from interfering with and garbling one another. License renewals are almost always granted automatically by the FCC. Indeed, renewal requests are now filed online.

Through regulations prohibiting obscenity, indecency, and profanity, the FCC has also sought to prohibit radio and television stations from airing explicit sexual and excretory references between 6 A.M. and 10 P.M., the hours when children are most likely to be in the audience. The FCC has enforced these rules haphazardly. Since 1990, nearly half the $5 million in fines levied by the agency have involved Howard Stern, the shock jock whose programs are built around sexually explicit material. In 2004, after another set of FCC fines, Stern's program was dropped by a major outlet, Clear Channel Communications. Stern charged that the Bush administration had singled him out for censure because of his known opposition to the president. To avoid FCC regulations, he relaunched his show on Sirius Satellite Radio in 2006.

For more than 60 years, the FCC also sought to regulate and promote competition in the broadcast industry, but in 1996 Congress passed the

---

10 Beth Fouhy, "Elections 2012: The Social Network, Presidential Campaign Edition," *The Huffington Post,* April 17, 2011, www.huffingtonpost.com/2011/04/17 /elections-2012-social-media_n_850172.html (accessed 10/4/11).

Telecommunications Act, a broad effort to do away with most regulations in effect since 1934. The act loosened restrictions on media ownership and allowed for telephone companies, cable television providers, and broadcasters to compete with one another for the provision of telecommunication services. Following the passage of the act, several mergers between telephone and cable companies and between different segments of the entertainment media produced an even greater concentration of media ownership.

The Telecommunications Act of 1996 also included an attempt to regulate the content of material transmitted via the Internet. This law, known as the Communications Decency Act, made it illegal to make "indecent" sexual material on the Internet accessible to anyone under 18 years of age. The act was immediately denounced by civil libertarians and brought to court as an infringement of free speech. The case reached the Supreme Court in 1997, and the act was ruled an unconstitutional infringement of the First Amendment's guarantee of freedom of speech.

Although the government's ability to regulate the content of the electronic media on the Internet has been questioned, the federal government has used its licensing power to impose several regulations that can affect the political content of radio and TV broadcasts. The first of these is the **equal time rule**, under which broadcasters must provide candidates for the same political office equal opportunities to communicate their messages to the public. If, for example, a television station sells commercial time to a state's Republican gubernatorial candidate, it may not refuse to sell time to the Democratic candidate for the same position.

The second regulation affecting the content of broadcasts is the **right of rebuttal**, which requires that individuals be given the opportunity to respond to personal attacks. In the 1969 case of *Red Lion Broadcasting Company v. Federal Communications Commission*, for example, the U.S. Supreme Court upheld the FCC's determination that a radio station was required to provide a liberal author with an opportunity to respond to an attack by a conservative commentator that the station had aired.[11]

For many years, a third important federal regulation was the **fairness doctrine**, under which broadcasters that aired programs on controversial issues were required to provide air time for opposing views. In 1985, the FCC stopped enforcing the fairness doctrine on the grounds that there were so many radio and television stations—to say nothing of newspapers and newsmagazines—that in all likelihood many different viewpoints were being presented even without the requirement that each station present all sides of an argument. Critics of this FCC decision charge that in many media markets the number of competing viewpoints is small. Nevertheless, a congressional effort to require the FCC to enforce the fairness doctrine was blocked by the administration of President Ronald Reagan in 1987, and the doctrine died.

---

equal time rule

The requirement that broadcasters provide candidates for the same political office an equal opportunity to communicate their messages to the public

---

right of rebuttal

An FCC regulation giving individuals the right to have the opportunity to respond to personal attacks made on a radio or TV broadcast

---

fairness doctrine

An FCC requirement that broadcasters that air programs on controversial issues provide time for opposing views

---

11 *Red Lion Broadcasting Company v. Federal Communications Commission*, 395 U.S. 367 (1969).

The emergence of the Internet has presented two substantial regulatory challenges: (1) protecting intellectual property and (2) setting standards to create a rational system of domains and websites. The first issue concerned whether the Internet could function as a profitable means of distributing content. In *A&M Records v. Napster*, the Ninth Circuit court sided with record companies against firms that offered free Internet distribution of copyrighted content.[12] The second sort of challenge is how to organize and govern the Internet. In the 1990s, Tim Berners-Lee organized researchers, firms, and government agencies involved in the development of the Internet in the international World Wide Web Consortium.[13] The Consortium is a form of self-regulation by corporations and organizations that has led to the development of new concepts of intellectual property and new concepts of communication wholly different from traditional print and broadcast media. The philosophy of the Consortium calls for much less government regulation and a much more communal flavor than the notion of competitive markets that lies behind America's conception of print media.

Freedom of the Press

Unlike the broadcast media, the print media are not subject to federal regulation. Indeed, the great principle underlying the federal government's relationship with the press is the doctrine against **prior restraint**. Beginning with the landmark 1931 case of *Near v. Minnesota*, the U.S. Supreme Court has held that, except under the most extraordinary circumstances, the First Amendment of the Constitution prohibits government agencies from seeking to prevent newspapers or magazines from publishing whatever they wish.[14] Indeed, in the case of *New York Times v. United States*, the so-called Pentagon Papers case, the Supreme Court ruled that the government could not even block publication of secret Defense Department documents furnished to the *New York Times* by an opponent of the Vietnam War who had obtained the documents illegally.[15] In 1990, however, the Supreme Court upheld a lower-court order restraining CNN from broadcasting tapes of conversations between the former Panamanian leader Manuel Noriega and his lawyer, supposedly recorded by the U.S. government. By a vote of 7–2, the Court held that CNN could be restrained from broadcasting the tapes until the trial court in the Noriega case had listened to them and decided whether their broadcast would violate Noriega's right to a fair trial. This case would seem to weaken the no-prior-restraint doctrine. But in later decisions, the Supreme Court ruled that cable television

 prior restraint

An effort by a government agency to block the publication of material it deems libelous or harmful in some other way: censorship. In the United States, the courts forbid prior restraint except under the most extraordinary circumstances

---

12 *A&M Records v. Napster*, 239 F.3d 104 (9th Circuit 2001).

13 Tim Berners-Lee with Mark Fischetti, *Weaving the Web: The Original Design and Ultimate Destiny of the World Wide Web by Its Inventor* (New York: HarperBusiness, 1999).

14 *Near v. Minnesota ex rel.*, 283 U.S. 697 (1931).

15 *New York Times v. United States*, 403 U.S. 713 (1971).

systems were entitled to essentially the same First Amendment protections as the print media.[16]

Even though newspapers may not be restrained from publishing whatever they want, they may be subject to sanctions after the fact. Historically, newspapers have been subject to the law of libel, which provides that newspapers that print false and malicious stories can be compelled to pay damages to those they defame. In recent years, however, American courts have greatly narrowed the meaning of libel and made it extremely difficult, particularly for politicians and other public figures, to win a libel case against a newspaper. The most important case on this topic is the 1964 Supreme Court case of *New York Times v. Sullivan*, in which the Court held that to be deemed libelous, a story about a public official not only had to be untrue but also had to result from "actual malice" or "reckless disregard" for the truth.[17] In other words, the newspaper had to deliberately print false and malicious material. In practice, it is nearly impossible to prove that a paper deliberately printed false and damaging information, and as conservatives discovered in the 1980s, it is very difficult for a politician or other public figure to win a libel case. Libel suits against CBS News by General William Westmoreland and against *Time* magazine by Ariel Sharon of Israel, both financed by conservative legal foundations that hoped to embarrass the media, were defeated in court because they failed to show "actual malice." In the 1991 case of *Masson v. New Yorker Magazine*, this tradition was again affirmed by the Court's opinion that fabricated quotations attributed to a public figure were libelous only if the fabricated account "materially changed" the meaning of what the person said.[18] To all intents and purposes, the print media can publish almost anything they want about a public figure.

Organization and Ownership of the Media

The scope and breadth of the media industry in the United States are impressive: more than 2,000 television stations, approximately 1,400 daily newspapers, and more than 13,000 radio stations. There are 20 major television networks, up from just 3 in the 1970s, as well as an extensive system of public television and radio stations.

The media environment since the 1980s has opened considerably, and wholly new networks devoted to news have emerged and succeeded. CNN became a major news source in the late 1980s and gained a substantial market share during the first Gulf war in 1991. At one point, CNN was able to provide live coverage of American bombing raids on Baghdad after the major networks' correspondents had been forced to flee to bomb shelters. In the 2000s, a competitor news

---

16 *Cable News Network v. Noriega*, 498 U.S. 976 (1990); *Turner Broadcasting v. Federal Communications Commission*, 512 U.S. 622 (1994).

17 *New York Times v. Sullivan*, 376 U.S. 254 (1964).

18 *Masson v. New Yorker Magazine, Inc.*, 501 U.S. 496 (1991).

---

channel emerged: Fox News. By 2003, Fox had displaced CNN as the nation's primary cable news source, and by 2010 Fox News was the fourth most highly rated cable channel, trailing USA, TNT, and ESPN. The rise of Fox News has had important political implications because its coverage and commentators are considerably more conservative than CNN's. The emergence of Fox News also demonstrates the importance of the existence of more and varied news sources. When there are few sources of news, each is likely to appeal to the same broad national audience and, accordingly, to maintain a middle-of-the-road stance. When there are more sources, each is likely to position itself within a discrete ideological or partisan niche, increasing the diversity of viewpoints presented to listeners and viewers.

News Concentration. Nonetheless, there is a very real concern that these trends mask considerable concentration in the industry. The problem is most evident in the wire services, which provide a steady stream of stories and images. There is now just one American wire service, the Associated Press (AP). United Press International (UPI) went bankrupt in the 1980s and has since failed to reemerge as a competitor. In Europe, Reuters offers wire service and has the dominant market position similar to AP. Interestingly, CNN may make a run at offering its own competing service, especially for graphics and images.

Concentration of ownership of media outlets raises further concerns about the robustness of the marketplace of ideas. The 1996 Telecommunications Act opened the way for additional consolidation in the media industry, and a wave of mergers and consolidations has further reduced the field of independent media across the country. Since that time, among the major news networks ABC was bought by the Walt Disney Company; CNN was bought by Time Warner; and NBC, which was owned by General Electric from 1986 until 2011, is now owned by Comcast. The Australian press baron Rupert Murdoch owns Fox plus a host of radio, television, and newspaper properties around the world. Murdoch's entry into the American market was of considerable importance because it required changes in U.S. laws prohibiting foreign ownership of U.S. broadcasting firms.[19] As a result of these consolidations, a relatively small number of giant corporations now control a wide swath of media holdings, including television networks, movie studios, record companies, cable channels and local cable providers, book publishers, magazines, and newspapers. This development has prompted questions about whether enough competition exists among the media to produce a diverse set of views on political and corporate matters or whether the United States has become the prisoner of media monopolies (Figure 14.1).[20]

In June 2003, the FCC announced a set of new rules that seemed to pave the way for even more concentration in the media industry. The rules mandated that the major networks could own television stations that collectively reached

---

19 Columbia Journalism Review provides regular updates on media ownership. See www.cjr.org/resources/index.php (accessed 9/17/11).

20 For a criticism of the increasing consolidation of the media, see the essays in Erik Barnouw et al., *Conglomerates and the Media* (New York: New Press, 1997).

After several years of mergers and acquisitions, a small number of corporations have come to dominate the print, broadcast, cable, and Internet industries. What factors precipitated this media consolidation? What effects, if any, does media consolidation have on news reporting?

Figure 14.1

NUMBER OF CORPORATIONS THAT CONTROL THE MAJORITY OF U.S. MEDIA

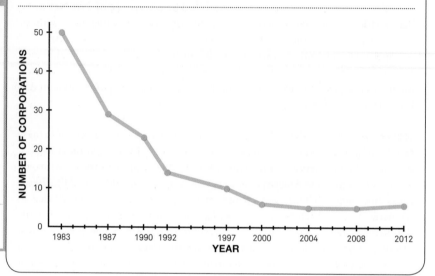

NOTE: Included are newspapers, magazines, TV and radio stations, books, music, movies, videos, wire services, and photo agencies.

SOURCE: Media Reform Information Center. www.corporations.org/media, and Ashley Lutz, "These 6 Corporations Control 90% of the Media in America," *Business Insider*, June 14, 2012, www .businessinsider.com/these-6-corporations-control-90-of-the-media-in-america-2012-6 (accessed 6/6/13).

45 percent of all viewers, up from 35 percent under the old rules. The new FCC rules also permitted a single company to own the leading newspaper, as well as multiple television and radio outlets, in a single market. In the largest cities, this could include a newspaper, three television stations, and as many as eight radio stations.[21] Major media companies, which had long lobbied for the right to expand their activities, welcomed the new FCC rules. Critics, however, expressed grave concern that a decision would result in a narrowing of the range of views and issues presented to the general public. Congressional opponents of the FCC's action sought to overturn the rules but were stymied by opposition from the House Republican leadership as well as a threatened presidential veto. However, a federal appeals court placed the new regulations on hold, and in January 2005 the Bush administration decided not to appeal the case to the Supreme Court. The FCC debuted new rules in 2007 to comply with the federal appeals court's ruling. In November 2012, a proposal to streamline the cross-ownership rules was introduced on to the FCC's agenda for the third time in a decade. The cross-ownership

21 David Lieberman, "How Will FCC's Action Affect Consumers?" *USA Today*, June 4, 2003, p. 48.

rule, however, might outlive the printed newspaper itself. The fight over the cross-ownership rule shows the power of institutions and regulations even when it comes to the flow of information in our democracy.

Distribution of news over the Internet goes against the trend toward increased concentration of media ownership. From the audience's perspective, the problem of increased concentration is that it will lead to less variety in the news and fewer voices heard. The Internet has made people less dependent on a single local newspaper to get information, however. Using websites that aggregate news from many different sources, a consumer can readily get many views on the same event. And people can easily search official websites to find out local information, such as meeting times of city councils and school committees.

One important question is whether there will become increased concentration of news distribution through the Internet as well. Google has emerged as the dominant search firm. Its position allows it the power to block out certain sites and effectively censor the news. This problem arose recently in China. Google China, a subsidiary of Google, was forced by the government to censor many websites, especially those of dissidents. In order to maintain access to the enormous China market, Google complied, effectively blocking non-Chinese media from those users and conversely blocking Chinese media websites from others, including users in the United States. Eventually, Google directed traffic to those websites through its Hong Kong subsidiary, but the tense negotiations over access to the web and to the Chinese market continue between Google and the Chinese government. While censorship in China might seem like a faraway problem, an American firm (Google) is at its center. Google was sufficiently powerful to negotiate access to censored websites, but it also had the market power to restrict access of U.S. users to China.

WHAT AFFECTS NEWS COVERAGE?

Because of the important role the media can play in national politics, it is essential to understand the factors that affect media coverage.[22] What accounts for the media's agenda of issues and topics? What explains the character of coverage? In other words, why does a politician receive good or bad press? What factors determine the interpretation, or spin, that a particular story will receive? Although a host of minor factors play a role, there are three major factors: (1) journalists or producers of the news, (2) politicians or other sources of the news, and (3) consumers.

22 See the discussions in Michael Parenti, *Inventing Reality: The Politics of the Mass Media* (New York: St. Martin's Press, 1986); Herbert Gans, *Deciding What's News: A Study of CBS Evening News, NBC Nightly News, Newsweek, and Time* (New York: Vintage, 1980); and W. Lance Bennett, *News: The Politics of Illusion*, 5th ed. (New York: Longman, 2002).

Journalists

The character of the news is shaped by the people who produce it. The people who seek out, write, and produce the news have their own perspectives, passions, interests, and biases. Although a strong norm of objectivity and unbiasedness pervades the journalism profession, it is impossible to expect that reporters, editors, and media owners will always set aside their personal views. What motivates those who produce the news, and how do their personal beliefs and interests shape what we see and hear?

The marketplace of ideas sets out a single objective for the owners of media organizations: making a profit. Owners seek to maintain a successful business, and if their personal political beliefs endanger that business, then those beliefs will quickly be pushed aside by the internal organization in the newspaper or broadcasting station. This has not always been the case. At one time, newspaper publishers exercised a great deal of influence over their papers' news content. Publishers such as William Randolph Hearst and Joseph Pulitzer became political powers through their manipulation of news coverage. Hearst, for example, almost single-handedly pushed the United States into war with Spain in 1898 through his newspapers' relentless coverage of the alleged brutality employed by Spain in its efforts to suppress a rebellion in Cuba, then a Spanish colony. The sinking of the American battleship *Maine* in Havana Harbor under mysterious circumstances gave Hearst the ammunition he needed to force a reluctant President William McKinley to lead the nation into war. Today, few publishers have that kind of power. The business end dominates the editorial content of papers, although a few continue to impose their interests and tastes on the news.

Individual reporters and editors have far more influence today over what is presented in the news day in and day out. They also pursue their interests and professional objectives. The goals and incentives of journalists are varied, but they often include considerations of ratings, career success and professional prestige, and political influence. For all of these reasons, journalists seek not only to report the news but also to interpret it. Journalists' goals have a good deal of influence on what is created and reported as news.

Those journalists who cover the news for the national media generally have considerable discretion or freedom to interpret stories and, as a result, have an opportunity to interject their own views and ideals into news stories. For example, some reporters' personal friendship with and respect for Franklin Delano Roosevelt and John F. Kennedy helped generate more favorable news coverage for those presidents. On the other hand, many reporters' dislike of and distrust for Richard Nixon was also communicated to the public. In the case of Ronald Reagan, the disdain that many journalists felt for the president was communicated in stories suggesting that he was often asleep or inattentive when important decisions were made.

Do Journalists Bias the News? From the perspective of the marketplace of ideas, perhaps the most troubling concern is the possibility that journalism on the whole is biased heavily in favor of one party or another or one set of ideals or another. Journalists lean decidedly to the left in their personal political beliefs. Surveys of reporters and editors at major media outlets have repeatedly found that those who produce the news are overwhelmingly liberal and Democratic. Surveys of journalists sponsored by the Pew Center for Excellence and by the Knight Foundation have found repeatedly that Democrats and liberals outnumber Republicans and conservatives by about 2 to 1 among journalists. A Knight Foundation survey conducted by Professor Dan Weaver of Indiana University found that 36 percent of journalists (across all media) identify as Democrats, while 18 percent identify as Republicans; 33 percent say that they do not identify with any party and 13 percent identify with another party.[23] The Pew survey found that most journalists identify themselves as moderates, but those who do claim an ideological orientation are decidedly more liberal than conservative. Of national reporters, 34 percent state that they are liberal and 7 percent say they are conservative, while 54 percent say they are moderates. Of local reporters, 23 percent are liberal and 12 percent are conservative, while 61 percent say they are moderates.[24] Even among the radio talk-show hosts, Democrats outnumber Republicans by a wide margin: of 112 hosts surveyed, 39 percent had voted for the Democrat in the most recent presidential election, and only 23 percent had supported the Republican.[25] Generally speaking, reporters for major national news outlets tend to be more liberal than their local counterparts, who often profess moderate or even conservative views.

Do these political biases color the news? A classic study by Michael Robinson and Margaret Sheehan of CBS and the *New York Times* in the 1980s suggested that there was little evidence of political favoritism or bias.[26] Subsequent studies by the Pew Project for Excellence in Journalism echo that conclusion. Comparing the press coverage of the first 100 days of presidents Bill Clinton and George W. Bush, the Pew Project found nearly identical patterns of coverage. About half of printed stories were neutral toward the new presidents; a quarter were positive and a quarter negative. Interestingly, Barack Obama received a much different welcome from the press. Using the same methodology, the Pew Project for Excellence in Journalism found that Obama's coverage was considerably more positive. Obama received positive coverage in 42 percent of stories, neutral coverage in 38 percent of stories, and negative coverage in 20 percent of stories.[27]

23 Dan Weaver, *The American Journalist of the 21st Century: U.S. News People at the Dawn of a New Millennium* (Mahwah, NJ: Erlbaum, 2007).

24 Pew Center on Press and Politics, "How Journalists See Journalists," Washington, DC, 2004, www.people-press.org/http://people-press.org/files/legacy-pdf/214.pdf (accessed 9/17/11).

25 Michael Kinsley, "Bias and Baloney," *Washington Post*, November 26, 1992, p. A29; and John H. Fund, "Why Clinton Shouldn't Be Steamed at Talk Radio," *Wall Street Journal*, July 7, 1994, p. A12.

26 Michael J. Robinson and Margaret A. Sheehan, *Over the Wire and on TV: CBS and UPI in Campaign '80* (New York: Russell Sage Foundation, 1983).

27 Pew Research Center's Project for Excellence in Journalism, "Obama's First 100 Days: How the President Fared in the Press vs. Clinton and Bush," April 28, 2009, http://journalism.org/files/100%20DAYS.pdf (accessed 5/7/09).

More subtle biases do exist, usually arising from the nature of the language used. A 2005 academic study by the political economists Timothy Groseclose and Jeffrey Milyo found that reporters use ideologically loaded terms when referring to some politicians but not others. Press reports typically mention both parties in a story, but they do so with no small degree of editorializing, using words like *radical* or *extreme conservative* to describe one politician or another. Analysis of such language revealed that most major media outlets slanted their reporting to the left, with three important exceptions. The *Wall Street Journal* and Fox News leaned to the right. Only PBS—the publicly owned and licensed network—presented balanced and evenhanded reporting of politics, government, and current events.[28]

Editorial endorsements of papers offer further evidence of political leanings of news organizations. *Editor and Publisher*, a trade journal of the media business, tracks endorsements of newspapers across the United States. Before the 1960s, the editorial endorsements and political leanings of the editors of most newspapers were overwhelmingly Republican. Since the 1960s, however, newspaper endorsements for president, the U.S. Senate, the U.S. House, and statewide offices have on average balanced out between the Democrats and Republicans. George W. Bush received a solid majority (192 of 344) of endorsements in 2000; John Kerry edged Bush out in 2004; in 2008, Barack Obama received nearly 70 percent of the endorsements over John McCain; and in 2012, Mitt Romney just edged out Obama (Figure 14.2). The papers endorsing Obama had a circulation totaling tens of millions more than the papers that endorsed Romney, however.[29] To the extent that there is a partisan bias to editorials and endorsements, it is toward those already in office.[30]

Journalism, as a profession, has attempted to rise above personal motivations and biases. Most journalists adhere to strong norms of fairness and balance in reporting. They attempt to get the perspectives of both sides of a controversy. Even coverage of popular presidents still attempts to maintain balance. Indeed, one of the values of treating journalism as a profession is that doing so forces norms of behavior and ethics that help reduce political biases. But that important ethos of objectivity and fairness appears to be changing.

Two shifts in journalism are eroding the professional standards of objectivity. The first of these shifts is the blurring of the line between editorializing and reporting in traditional media. Over the past decade, the emergence of Fox News, MSNBC, and the *Huffington Post* have attempted to change that ethos of objectivity by presenting more ideological and partisan versions of the news, with Fox News on the right and MSNBC on the left. Many traditional journalists have been tempted to follow suit. Among professional journalists much

---

28 Timothy Groseclose and Tom Milyo, "A Measure of Media Bias," *Quarterly Journal of Economics* 120 (2005): 1191–1237.

29 "Final Tally of Newspaper Endorsements—Obama Landslide at 287–159," *Editor and Publisher*, November 9, 2008, www.editorandpublisher.com.

30 Stephen Ansolabehere, Rebecca Lessem, and James M. Snyder, Jr., "The Orientation of Newspaper Endorsements 1940–2002," *Quarterly Journal of Political Science* 1, no. 4 (October 2006): 393–404, http://dx.doi.org/10.1561/100.00000009 (accessed 5/8/09).

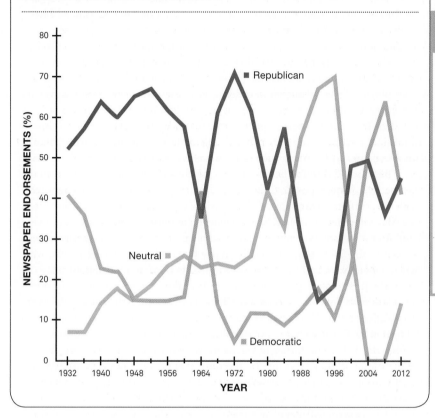

Figure 14.2
NEWSPAPER ENDORSEMENTS

NEWSPAPER ENDORSEMENTS (%)

■ Republican

Neutral ■

■ Democratic

YEAR

ANALYZING THE EVIDENCE

What can the pattern of newspaper endorsements from 1932 through 2012 tell us regarding the biases of the print media? What other indicators might be used to evaluate media bias? What would an "unbiased" media look like?

is made of the battle among the cable networks to divide the audience along partisan lines. In a widely read opinion piece, Tom Edsall, a long-time journalist with four decades of experience covering every level of American government, wrote that it was time for all journalists to throw off the norm of nonpartisanship and fairness.[31] Edsall, now a regular columnist for the *Huffington Post*, argues that Fox News and its large audience had changed the old norms. The gloves are off, and, at least from Edsall's corner, it is time for traditional journalists, most of whom have a liberal orientation, to take on the challenge from the conservatives directly.

31 Thomas Edsall, "Journalism Should Own Its Liberalism: And Then Manage It, Challenge It, and Account for It," *Columbia Journalism Review*, October 8, 2009, www.cjr.org/campaign_desk/journalism_should_own_its_libe.php?page=all (accessed 10/4/11).

Citizen Journalism. The second shift in journalism is more profound and may perhaps be more far-reaching. That is the emergence of citizen journalism. New technologies such as smartphones, powerful laptop computers, and the Internet now make it possible for anyone to report on events. CNN has a regular feature called i-Reporter that feeds video sent by people at events, such as natural disasters, campaigns and other political events, and political protests and rebellions. Needless to say, this is a huge threat to traditional journalism, which relies on highly trained professionals. A newspaper or television station does not need a large bureau in order to get instant recordings of events, and journalists cost money to keep on staff and to deploy to faraway places such as China or Iraq. By the same token, these technologies have allowed journalism to flourish in countries with very little existing media or tight government controls on television and the press, such as those in central Africa and the Middle East.

The subtle revolution behind the rise of citizen journalism comes from the perspective of the reporter. Citizen journalism replaces the "objective reporter" with the "subjective participant." A traditional reporter from the *New York Times*, the AP, or another agency will try to get different perspectives on the same event and offer a investigative report that attempts to answer the key questions (also known as the 5 Ws and 1H) taught on day one of Journalism 101: what, who, when, where, why, and how? Citizen journalists become reporters of an event precisely because they are in the event. A protestor who sends a video of a violent clash with police in Damascus or Tripoli or London is "in the event," as are a legislative staffer who tweets about the goings-on in a committee meeting or a campaign worker who texts about a rally. There is no attempt to rise above and answer the 5 Ws. The texts and videos from such communications are raw and in the moment; they are some of the most compelling journalism today. This represents a sea change in journalism. It will not replace the old style, which has been around for centuries and survived many a technological revolution. Rather, citizen journalism will augment traditional journalism and even change it somewhat. It gives traditional journalists license to also be "in the moment," in other words, to be more subjective.

News Sources

News Leaks. A news leak is the disclosure of confidential information to the news media. Leaks may emanate from a variety of sources, including whistle-blowers, lower-level officials who hope to publicize what they view as their bosses' improper activities. In 1971, for example, a minor Defense Department staffer named Daniel Ellsberg sought to discredit official justifications for America's involvement in Vietnam by leaking top-secret documents to the press. The *New York Times* and the *Washington Post* published these classified documents, the so-called Pentagon Papers, after the U.S. Supreme Court ruled that the government could not block release of the documents. In a similar vein, President George W. Bush was infuriated in 2005 when he learned that a still-unidentified source, presumed to be a whistler-blower, had leaked information concerning the president's secret orders authorizing the National Security

Agency to conduct clandestine surveillance of suspected terrorists without obtaining authorization from the special federal tribunal created for that purpose. Bush ordered the Justice Department to launch a probe of the leak. In 2006, a still-unidentified source leaked to the press part of a secret intelligence summary that seemed to contradict the administration's claims of progress in the war in Iraq. The president claimed the leaked portion of the report did not accurately reflect the full report. The administration proceeded to declassify other portions of the report, which seemed to support its claims about the war. President Barack Obama pursued an even stronger line against press leaks in his administration. The Obama administration aggressively and successfully prosecuted one Defense Department worker and one FBI analyst who had leaked information to the press in 2009.

Most leaks, though, originate not with low-level whistle-blowers but rather with senior government officials and prominent politicians and political activists. Such persons often cultivate long-term relationships with journalists, to whom they regularly leak confidential information, knowing that it is likely to be published on a priority basis in a form acceptable to them. Their confidence is based on the fact that journalists are likely to regard high-level sources of confidential information as valuable assets whose favor must be retained. For example, I. Lewis "Scooter" Libby, former vice president Dick Cheney's chief of staff, was apparently such a valuable source of leaks to so many prominent journalists that his name was seldom mentioned in the newspapers despite his prominence in Washington and his importance as a decision maker.[32] And the more recipients of leaked information strive to keep their sources secret, the more difficulty other journalists will have in checking the validity of the information.

Through such tacit alliances with journalists, prominent figures can manipulate news coverage and secure the publication of stories that serve their purposes. The Valerie Plame affair, which was ultimately the undoing of Scooter Libby, exposed the complexities of the culture of leaks in Washington, D.C. Plame was an undercover CIA analyst married to Joseph Wilson, a prominent career diplomat. Wilson had angered the Bush White House by making a number of statements that were critical of the president's policies in Iraq. In an apparent effort to discredit Wilson, one or more administration officials informed prominent journalists that Plame had improperly used her position to help Wilson. In so doing, these officials may have violated a federal statute prohibiting the disclosure of the identities of covert intelligence operatives. The subsequent investigation revealed that the story had been leaked to several journalists, including the *Washington Post*'s Bob Woodward, who did not use it, and the *New York Times*'s Judith Miller, who did. Miller spent several months in jail for contempt of court after initially refusing to testify before a federal grand jury looking into the leak. After Miller finally testified, Libby was charged and convicted of lying and obstruction for his role in the affair, although it later emerged that the information was actually leaked by a former State Department official, Richard Armitage. The leak

---

32 Michael Massing, "The Press: The Enemy Within," *New York Review of Books*, December 15, 2005, p. 36.

in the Plame case came to light only because it might have been illegal. Thousands of other leaks each year are quietly and seamlessly incorporated into the news.

The Press Release. Also seamlessly incorporated into daily news reports each year are thousands of press releases. The press release, sometimes called a news release, is a story written by an advocate or publicist and distributed to the media in the hope that journalists will publish it under their own bylines with little or no revision. The inventor of the press release was a New York public relations consultant named Ivy Lee. In 1906, a train operated by one of Lee's clients, the Pennsylvania Railroad, was involved in a serious wreck. Lee quickly wrote a story about the accident that presented the railroad in a favorable light and distributed the account to reporters. Many papers published Lee's slanted story as their own objective account of events, and the railroad's reputation for quality and safety remained intact.

Consistent with Lee's example, today's press release presents facts and perspectives that serve an advocate's interests but is written in a way that mimics the factual news style of the paper, periodical, or television news program to which it has been sent. It is quite difficult for the audience to distinguish a well-designed press release from a news story. For example, a recent posting by PharmaWatch, a blog monitoring the pharmaceutical industry, identified an article published in the *New York Times* "Science Times" section that rehashed a news release issued by Pfizer, the giant pharmaceutical corporation. "A lawyer in New York has had to deal with what is politely referred to as 'bladder control' for as long as she can remember," the article began. Thanks to the press release it copied, the article was able to propose a solution. "Urge incontinence is often treated with drugs like tolterodine, sold as Detrol."[33] Not surprisingly, the drug touted in this news story is sold by Pfizer.

To take another example, an article sent to thousands of newspapers by the AP was headlined "Fed Unveils Financial Education Website." Apparently written by an AP reporter, the article discussed the various ways in which a new website developed by the Federal Reserve could help consumers make informed decisions. The article did not mention that the information was basically a slight revision of a press release that could be found on the Federal Reserve's website.[34] And what about the June 2005 *Los Angeles Times* story "County Homeless Number 90,000"? This article claimed, without offering an explanation, that the number of homeless individuals in Los Angeles County had quintupled since the previous year. In presenting this shocking news of the increase in homelessness, though, the reporter neglected to mention that the data came from a press release issued by the Los Angeles Homeless Services Authority (LAHSA), whose budget is tied to the number of clients it serves. For the LAHSA, more homelessness equals more money and more staff.

---

33 Martica Heaner, "Enduring Incontinence in Silence," *New York Times*, October 25, 2005, www.nytimes.com/2005/10/25/health/25inco.html?_r=1 (accessed 5/8/09).

34 Brian Montopoli, "Press Release Journalism," *Columbia Journalism Review Daily*, April 18, 2005.

Indeed, on its own website, it indicated that it had undertaken its new count of homeless individuals in part to "increase funding for homeless services in our community."[35] These should not be seen as isolated examples. According to some experts, more than 50 percent of the articles in a newspaper on any given day are based on press releases. Indeed, more than 75 percent of the journalists responding to a recent survey acknowledged using press releases for their stories.[36]

Journalists are certainly aware of the fact that the authors of press releases have their own agendas and are hardly unbiased reporters of the news. Nevertheless, the economics of publishing and broadcasting dictate that large numbers of stories will always be based on press releases. Newspapers and television stations are businesses, and for many the financial bottom line is more important than journalistic integrity.[37] The use of press releases allows a newspaper or a broadcast network to present more stories without paying more staff or incurring the other costs associated with investigating and writing the news. As one newspaper executive said, the public relations people who generally write news releases are our "unpaid reporters."[38]

In recent years, the simple printed press release has been joined by the video news release, which is designed especially for television stations. The video release is a taped report, usually about 90 seconds long, the typical length of a television news story, designed to look and sound like any other broadcast news segment. In exchange for airing material that serves the interests of some advocate, the television station airing the video release is relieved of the considerable expense and bother of identifying and filming its own news story. The audience is usually unaware that the "news" it is watching is someone's canned publicity footage.

One example of a video news release was a pair of 90-second segments funded by the U.S. Department of Health and Human Services (HHS). After Congress enacted legislation adding a prescription drug benefit to the Medicare program, HHS sent a video release designed to look like a news report to local TV stations around the nation. Forty television stations aired the report without indicating that it had come from the government or that the "reporter" identified in the report was an employee of the ad agency hired by the government to create the video release. In response to criticism, an HHS spokesperson pointed out that the same sort of video news releases had often been used by

---

35 "LA Times: County Homeless Population Tops Two Kazillion, No Further Reporting Required," *IndependentSources*, June 16, 2005, http://independentsources .com/2005/06/16/la-times-county-homeless-population-tops-two-kazillion-no -further-reporting-required (accessed 4/9/09).

36 Dennis L. Wilcox and Glen T. Cameron, *Public Relations: Strategy and Tactics*, 8th ed. (Boston: Allyn & Bacon, 2006), p. 357.

37 See, for example, Davis Merritt, *Knightfall: Knight Ridder and How the Erosion of Newspaper Journalism Is Putting Democracy at Risk* (New York: Amacom Books, 2005).

38 Quoted in Wilcox and Cameron, *Public Relations*, p. 357.

the Clinton administration and was commonly used by a number of firms and interest groups. "The use of video news releases is a common, routine practice in government and the private sector," he said. "Anyone who has questions about this practice needs to do some research on modern public information tools."[39]

Hiring Reporters. From creating phony reporters to reading make-believe news stories, it is but a small step to hiring real reporters to present sham accounts. A number of cases have come to light in recent years in which the government or a private concern has paid journalists to write favorable accounts of its activities and efforts. Late in 2005, for example, the U.S. military acknowledged that contractors in its employ had regularly paid Iraqi newspapers to carry positive news about American efforts in that nation. The Washington-based Lincoln Group, a public-relations firm working under contract for the federal government, says it placed more than 1,000 news stories in the Arab press since 2001.[40] Iraqis reading the articles would have had no way of knowing that the material presented was produced at the behest of the American authorities.

The government's practice of hiring journalists is not limited to operations abroad. In recent years, federal agencies have paid several journalists and commentators to report favorably on government initiatives and programs in the United States. The Department of Education, for example, paid the commentator Armstrong Williams $241,000 to promote President George W. Bush's No Child Left Behind Act. Williams wrote favorably about the law in his newspaper column, commented positively about it during his cable television appearances, and urged other commentators to interview Education Secretary Roderick Paige.[41] Williams did not disclose his financial relationship with the agency whose programs he was touting. Similarly, the Department of Health and Human Services paid the syndicated columnist Maggie Gallagher $20,000 to promote the administration's views on marriage. Gallagher wrote several columns on the topic without revealing her financial relationship with the administration.

As local newspaper budgets have shrunk, some local governments have hired reporters or paid newspapers for reporters to cover local government. The Metropolitan Government of Portland, Oregon, hires a local reporter to cover goings-on in the government, including council meetings, events, and changes in policies and laws. The Los Angeles Kings hockey franchise, a Los Angeles County Supervisor, and a California trial lawyers group all hire journalists to follow their activities. The list goes on.

One group especially noted for paying writers and reporters for favorable coverage is the pharmaceutical industry. As the Detrol example suggests, many

---

39 Quoted in Ben Fritz, Bryan Keefer, and Brendan Nyhan, *All the President's Spin* (New York: Touchstone Books, 2004), pp. 252–3, 357.

40 Jeff Gerth, "Military's Information War Is Vast and Often Secretive," *New York Times*, December 11, 2005, p. 1.

41 Howard Kurtz, "Administration Paid Commentator," *Washington Post*, January 8, 2005, p. 1.

---

of the articles that appear in popular—and even scientific—journals reporting favorably on particular drugs are written by the drug companies themselves. In some cases, the writers are actually paid by the drug companies; in other reported instances, the writer cited in the story's byline is not the actual author of the account. Often a ghostwriter employed by a drug company writes the story while the nominal author is paid for the use of his name.[42]

All of these practices—hiring of reporters, press leaks, and planted news stories—offend our sensibilities about what the news is because we expect a degree of objectivity from reporters. They are our main source of information, and fair and balanced reporting helps us sort out sometimes complex issues. The media also play an important watchdog role. They are there to make noise when something is amiss. That becomes increasingly difficult if the main revenues for the news come from the firm or government agency being covered. Of course, although politicians try to use the media for their purposes, reporters often have their own agenda. Often enough, hostile or merely determined journalists will break through the smoke screens thrown up by the politicians and report annoying truths.

Consumers

The print and broadcast media are businesses that, in general, seek to show a profit. This means that like any other business they must cater to the preferences of consumers. Their doing so has very important consequences for the content and character of the news media. The long-term health and success of the media as a political institution depends on their ability to find a sizable audience. The Analyzing the Evidence unit considers how market-level factors have influenced consumers' interest in following the news.

Catering to the Upscale Audience. In general and especially in the political realm, the print and broadcast media and the publishing industry are not only responsive to the interests of consumers generally but are also particularly responsive to the interests and views of the better-educated and more affluent segments of the audience. The preferences of these segments have a profound effect on the content and orientation of the press, radio and television programming, and books, especially in the areas of news and public affairs.[43]

Affluent and well-educated consumers are the core audience of newsmagazines, journals of opinion, books dealing with public affairs, serious newspapers such as the *New York Times* and the *Washington Post*, broadcast news, and evening

42 Anna Wilde Matthews, "At Medical Journals, Writers Paid by Industry Play Big Role," *Wall Street Journal*, December 13, 2005, p. 1.

43 See Tom Burnes, "The Organization of Public Opinion," in *Mass Communication and Society*, James Curran, Michael Gurevitch, and Janet Woollacott, eds. (Beverly Hills, CA: Sage, 1979), pp. 44–230. See also David L. Altheide, *Creating Reality: How TV News Distorts Events* (Beverly Hills, CA: Sage, 1976).

Where Does Interest in the News Come From?

Contributed by

Scott Althaus
University of Illinois, Urbana-Champaign

James Gimpel
University of Maryland, College Park

The audiences for newspaper, television, and radio news have been shrinking. If an informed citizenry is important to democracy, this decline might be alarming. What explains people's choices to follow the news, and can this trend be reversed? Previous research has assumed that the choice to follow news is largely a function of individual-level factors: those who regularly follow the news tend to be older, more educated, and more knowledgeable about politics than those who rarely follow the news. To the extent that these factors matter, news audiences should be evenly distributed around the country, and recent losses in the size of audiences for traditional news sources may be difficult to reverse.

However, market-level factors might also play a role in the choice to follow news. There are more than 200 media markets in the United States, each offering its own local news coverage. Larger markets surrounding major cities tend to have a wider variety of choices than smaller markets and are able to satisfy a broader range of audience demands. Within each market, people talk to one another about what they learn from the news and where they've learned it from. To the extent that these market-level factors drive the choice to follow news, audiences for different types of news should be distributed unevenly around the country and changes in the structure of media markets could potentially reverse the shrinking audiences for news.

As the following maps make clear, there is a geographic pattern to news interest. Cable news viewing is more common in the southeastern United States than in the northwestern states, and newspaper reading is more common in northern states than in southern states.

Average Days per Week Watching Cable News Channels by Media Market

● 2.10–2.92   ● 2.93–5.50

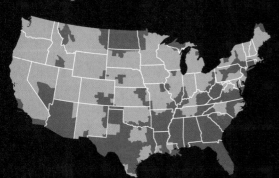

Cable news programming is more popular in southeastern states than in northwestern states.

Average Days per Week Reading Newspapers by Media Market

● 2.86–3.82   ● 3.83–5.00

Newspapers are more widely read in northern states than in southern states.

Research assessing the relative contribution of individual- and market-level factors shows that while both matter, market-level factors such as the number of local television stations and the amount of advertising revenue available to support news programming tend to explain more variation in news consumption than individual-level factors. This chart summarizes research that predicts how often people follow different types of news. Only for online news and talk radio consumption do individual-level factors explain as much variance as market-level factors. Between half and two-thirds of the variation in how frequently people follow news on television and newspapers can be explained by market-level factors alone.

Thus the choice to follow news tends to be influenced less by individual characteristics than by the programming choices available, which can be affected by the market and by policy regulation. As a result, the development of new technologies for accessing news content online could bring about important changes in levels of news consumption.

Explaining Variation in News Consumption

SOURCE:
Scott L. Althaus, Anne M. Cizmar, and James G. Gimpel, "Media Supply, Audience Demand, and the Geography of News Media Consumption in the United States." *Political Communication* 26, no. 3 (2009): 249–77.

■ Individual-level factors

■ Market-level factors

and weekend public affairs programming. Of course, other segments of the public also read newspapers and watch the television news. Overall, however, level of interest in "hard news" (world events, national political issues, and the like) is closely related to level of education (Table 14.2). As a result, upscale Americans are overrepresented in the news and public affairs audience. The concentration of these strata in the audience makes news, politics, and public affairs potentially very attractive topics to advertisers, publishers, radio broadcasters, and television executives.

As a result, entire categories of events, issues, and phenomena of interest to lower-, middle-, and working-class Americans receive scant attention from the national print and broadcast media. For example, trade union news and events are discussed only in the context of major strikes or revelations of corruption. No network or national periodical routinely covers labor organizations. Religious and church affairs receive little coverage unless scandal is involved. The activities of veterans', fraternal, ethnic, and patriotic organizations are also generally ignored.

The rise of new media sources has not altered this picture. For example, a recent study by Markus Prior of the rise of cable television shows that the restructuring of television from three networks to a vast range of cable venues during the 1980s and 1990s actually increased the knowledge gap among different groups in the electorate. Further, Professor Gary Jacobson's research found that viewers of different cable news channels (for example, Fox News,

Table 14.2
EDUCATION AND ATTENTION TO THE NEWS

LEVEL OF EDUCATION	LEVEL OF ATTENTION TO HARD NEWS*		
	HIGH (%)	MEDIUM (%)	LOW (%)
College graduate	36	59	6
Some college	30	59	11
High school graduate	23	59	18
Not a high school graduate	12	60	28

*People with high levels of attention to hard news follow international, national, local, and business news closely; those with low levels do not follow the news.
SOURCES: Compiled by authors from the Pew Research Center for the People and the Press, "Audience Segments in a Changing News Environment," Pew Research Center Biennial News Consumption Survey, August 17, 2008, http://people-press.org/reports/pdf/444.pdf (accessed 5/8/09).

MSNBC, and CNN) held widely varying beliefs about basic facts concerning public affairs. Professor Jacobson's research contrasts sharply with research in the 1970s on CBS, NBC, and ABC, which found that the three main networks tended to present the news from similar perspectives. The three networks would provide the same information in the same way as each other and as print media.[44]

The Media and Conflict.

Although the media respond most to the upscale audience, groups that cannot afford the services of media consultants and issues managers can publicize their views and interests through protest. Frequently, the media are accused of encouraging conflict and even violence in response to the fact that their audiences mostly watch news for the entertainment value that conflict can provide. Clearly, conflict can be an important vehicle for attracting the attention and interest of the media and thus may provide an opportunity for media attention to groups otherwise lacking the financial or organizational resources to broadcast their views. But although conflict and protest can succeed in drawing media attention, these methods ultimately do not allow groups from the bottom of the social ladder to compete effectively in the media.

The chief problem with protest as a media technique is that, in general, the media on which the protesters depend have considerable discretion in reporting and interpreting the events they cover. For example, should the media focus on the conflict itself, rather than on the issues or concerns created by the conflict? The answer to this question is typically determined by the media, not by the protesters. Therefore, media interpretation of protest activities is more a reflection of the views of the groups and forces to which the media are responsive—which, as we have seen, are usually segments of the upper middle class—than it is a function of the wishes of the protesters themselves. It is worth noting that civil rights protesters received their most favorable media coverage when a segment of the white upper middle class saw blacks as potential political allies in the Democratic Party.

Typically, upper-middle-class protesters—student demonstrators and the like—have little difficulty securing favorable publicity for themselves and their causes. They are often more skilled than their lower-class counterparts in the techniques of media manipulation. That is, they typically have a better sense—often as a result of formal courses on the subject—of how to package messages for media consumption. For example, it is important to know what time of day a protest should occur if it is to be carried on the evening news. Similarly, the setting, definition of the issues, character of the rhetoric used, and so on all help determine whether a protest will receive favorable media coverage, unfavorable

---

44 Markus Prior, *Post-Broadcast Democracy: How Media Choice Increases Inequality in Political Involvement and Polarizes Elections*, New York: Cambridge University Press. 2007; Gary C. Jacobson, "How the Economy and Partisanship Shaped the 2012 Presidential and Congressional Elections," *Political Science Quarterly*, vol. 128, no. 1, Spring 2013. On TV and newspaper reporting in the 1970s, see Michael J. Robinson and Margaret A. Sheehan, *Over the Wire and On TV* (New York: Russell Sage Foundation, 1983).

coverage, or no coverage at all. Moreover, upper-middle-class protesters can often produce their own media coverage through "underground" newspapers, college papers, student radio and television stations, and the Internet. The same resources and skills that generally allow upper-middle-class people to publicize their ideas are usually not left behind when segments of this class choose to engage in disruptive forms of political action. Note the media attention given antiwar protesters in 2003 even though polls indicated that such groups were a minor force in American politics.

CONCLUSION: MEDIA POWER AND RESPONSIBILITY

The content and character of news and public affairs programming—what the media choose to present and how they present it—can have far-reaching political consequences. Media disclosures can greatly enhance or fatally damage the careers of public officials. Media coverage can rally support for or intensify opposition to national policies. The media choose what issues to cover and how and, as discussed in Chapter 9, set the national political agenda and frame political discourse.

The media have played a central role in shaping some of the most significant events in recent American political history. News media were critically important in the civil rights movement of the 1950s and 1960s. Television footage and photographs of civil rights marchers attacked by club-swinging police galvanized public support for the civil rights movement among northern whites and greatly increased pressure on Congress to bring an end to segregation.[45] The media were also central actors in the Watergate affair, which ultimately forced President Richard Nixon, the landslide victor in the 1972 presidential election, to resign from office in disgrace. The relentless series of investigations launched by the *Washington Post*, the *New York Times*, and the television networks led to the disclosure of various abuses of power by those in the White House, ultimately forcing Nixon to resign.[46]

Mass media have been central to every election of the past century. They cover the emergence and activities of the candidates, political debates and conventions, and election-night returns. They are the vehicles for political advertising. They even generate their own campaign news, especially by conducting public-opinion polls and reporting who is ahead and who is behind, who is gaining momentum and who is fading.

45 David J. Garrow, *Protest at Selma: Martin Luther King, Jr., and the Voting Rights Act of 1965* (New Haven, CT: Yale University Press, 1978).

46 Todd Gitlin, *The Whole World Is Watching: Mass Media in the Making and Unmaking of the New Left* (Berkeley: University of California Press, 2003).

And the media go to war along with the U.S. military. Since the American Civil War, news reporting and photography have brought wars home. Graphic depictions of the atrocities in Vietnam, including the My Lai massacre, and of American war dead and wounded helped turn popular sentiment against the war, which compelled the government to negotiate an end to the conflict.[47] Video of precision bombs destroying targets in Baghdad and of the rout of Saddam Hussein's army in 1991 pushed up President George H. W. Bush's popularity and solidified his reputation as commander in chief.[48] News coverage of the Iraq War in 2003 portrayed the toppling of Saddam Hussein's statue in Baghdad, and President George W. Bush's announcement of "Mission Accomplished" at the end of combat in 2003 would later be used against the president as the military struggled for years to restore a modicum of stability in Iraq.

The tremendous power that reporters and editors sometimes wield emanates from the free hand that the press has in American politics. So long as they do not overstep the bounds of libel, journalists can (and often do) criticize the American government openly. Given the diversity of media outlets today, especially after the rise of cable television and the Internet, it is not uncommon to find defenders and critics of the government or of particular political decisions, and often those on either side of the debate argue their positions side by side. The rise of the new media has brought more voices to the fore and a broader potential debate over public policy. Wide-open debate and criticism of public officials is essential, but it sometimes exacts a social cost.

Free media are essential to democratic government. We depend on the media to investigate wrongdoing, publicize and explain governmental actions, evaluate programs and politicians, and bring to light matters that might otherwise be known only to a handful of government insiders. In short, without free and active media, popular government would be virtually impossible. Citizens would have few means of knowing or assessing the government's actions, other than the claims or pronouncements of the government itself. Moreover, without active—indeed, aggressive—media, citizens would be hard-pressed to make informed choices among competing candidates at the polls. Often enough, the media reveal discrepancies between candidates' claims and their records and between the images that candidates seek to project and the underlying realities.

At the same time, politicians have become ever more reliant on news coverage, especially favorable coverage. National political leaders and journalists have had symbiotic relationships, at least since Franklin Delano Roosevelt's presidency. Initially, politicians were the senior partners. Thus, for example, reporters did not publicize potentially embarrassing information, widely known in Washington, D.C., about the personal lives of such figures as Roosevelt and John F. Kennedy. Today, the balance has shifted. Often it seems the journalists have the upper hand. Now that individual politicians have become heavily dependent

---

47 William M. Hammond, *Reporting Vietnam: Media and Military at War* (Lawrence: University of Kansas Press, 1998).

48 Jon Krosnik and L. A. Brannon, "The Impact of the Gulf War on the Ingredients of Presidential Evaluations," *American Political Science Review* 87 (1993): 963–75.

on media to reach their constituents, journalists no longer need fear that their access to information can be restricted in retaliation for negative coverage. It is not uncommon today to hear the White House press corps challenge the president's press liaison or even the president himself.

Freedom gives the media enormous power. The media can make or break reputations, help launch or destroy political careers, and build support for or rally opposition against programs and institutions.[49] Wherever there is so much power, at least the potential for its abuse or overly zealous use exists. All things considered, free media are so critically important to the maintenance of a democratic society that we may be willing to take the risk that the media will occasionally abuse their power. The forms of government control that would prevent the media from misusing their power would also certainly pose a serious risk to our freedom.

For Further Reading

Selections highlighted in red are included in *Readings in American Politics: Analysis and Perspectives*, Third Edition.

Ansolabehere, Stephen, Roy Behr, and Shanto Iyengar. *The Media Game: American Politics in the Television Age.* New York: Macmillan, 1993.

Arnold, R. Douglas. *Congress, the Press, and Political Accountability.* Princeton, NJ: Princeton University Press, 2004.

Bagdikian, Ben. *The New Media Monopoly.* Boston: Beacon Press, 2004.

Baum, Matthew, A. *Soft News Goes to War: Public Opinion and American Foreign Policy in the New Media Age.* Princeton, NJ: Princeton University Press, 2003.

Cook, Timothy. *Governing with the News: The News Media as a Political Institution.* Chicago: University of Chicago Press, 1997.

Groseclose, Timothy, and Jeffrey Milyo. "A Measure of Media Bias." *Quarterly Journal of Economics* 120, no. 4 (November 2005): 1191–1237.

Hamilton, James T. *All the News That's Fit to Sell: How the Market Transforms Information into News.* Princeton, NJ: Princeton University Press, 2003.

Iyengar, Shanto. *Media Politics: A Citizen's Guide.* 2nd ed. New York: Norton, 2011.

Kellner, Douglas. *Media Spectacle and the Crisis of Democracy: Terrorism, War, and Election Battles.* Boulder, CO: Paradigm, 2005.

---

49 See Martin Linsky, *Impact: How the Press Affects Federal Policy Making* (New York: Norton, 1991).

Merritt, Davis. *Knightfall: Knight Ridder and How the Erosion of Newspaper Journalism Is Putting Democracy at Risk.* New York: Amacom Books, 2005.

Norris, Pippa, Montague Kern, and Marion R. Just, eds. *Framing Terrorism: The News Media, the Government, and the Public.* New York: Routledge, 2003.

Schudson, Michael. "The News Media as Political Institutions." *Annual Review of Political Science* 5 (June 2002): 249–69.

Starr, Paul. *The Creation of the Media.* New York: Basic Books, 2004.

15

Economic Policy

Few Americans realize how much their economic freedom owes to government action. Americans often point with pride to their "free-market" economy and view governmental institutions and policies as intrusions on the freedom of the marketplace. Yet the very existence of what we regard as a free market depends heavily on public policies and institutions. Ironically, without ongoing collective action coordinated by the government, individual market freedom would be difficult to exercise and might be limited to small-scale barter and trade. America's huge free-market economy could not exist without the government. Even our increasingly global economy depends on international economic institutions and cooperation among national governments. In the economic realm, maintaining individual freedom ultimately rests on our capacity for collective action. In the 2012 presidential debates, both candidates agreed with this principle.

The importance of collective action and the role of government in the economy were evident in the response to the Great Recession of 2008–09 and the economic crisis it spawned—a crisis that may extend well into the future.[1] The magnitude of this crisis has been profound.

In the first several years of the twenty-first century, the American economy was propelled by massive amounts of borrowing, both by government and consumers. These were boom times as the federal government ran enormous deficits (that is, spending that exceeded the revenue it was collecting) and consumers went on a spending spree far exceeding their incomes, running up debt on their credit cards and taking on further debt with excessive home mortgages. By the latter part of the decade, the boom had ended, the economy was in a tailspin, and most of the financial gains made during the early part of the decade had been wiped out. The unemployment rate approached 10 percent—meaning that 1 in every 10 people looking for full-time employment was unable to find work. The housing market collapsed, with home prices dropping by about one-third

---

1   See Menzie Chinn and Jeffry Frieden, *Lost Decades* (New York: Norton, 2011) for an
    excellent analysis and narrative development of the events surrounding the financial
    crisis, its causes, and its possible long-run effects.

nationally. Almost one-fourth of all homeowners held mortgage debt (what they owed on their houses) that exceeded the market value of those homes. The stock market collapsed, losing more than half its value as measured by most stock indexes. Nearly everyone—businesses, nonprofits, universities, foundations, state and local governments, and individuals rich and poor—suffered losses of income and revenues, savings, pensions, endowments, and other forms of wealth. To sum up the massive effect on the overall economy, one set of expert observers noted that "the U.S. economy's growth rate over the decade was barely one-quarter that of the 1990s (6 percent as opposed to 24 percent)."[2] And, during the darkest days of the crisis, there was the fear that things could grow worse, that the recession could turn into a long depression or, worse still, that the foundations of the entire economy could be severely, perhaps permanently, damaged.

The immediate challenge for economic policy makers was to shake the economy out of its downward spiral by stimulating spending. More spending would translate into more demand for goods and services, which would mean jobs and other economic activity that would, in turn, generate even more spending and jobs. The biggest sticking point was credit—what banks lend to businesses and consumers to facilitate that spending. Banks were hesitant to lend since they were not certain borrowers could repay. Government action was required. In order to generate that first round of spending, banks would need an injection of capital and relief from the bad loans they were carrying on their books—what were called *toxic assets*. The Bush administration, through its

CORE OF THE ANALYSIS

 Public policies create incentives for people to alter their behavior.

 In economic policy, government can play an important role in establishing the rules and institutions that allow a market economy to function.

 Government has numerous tools with which to affect the economy, but there is considerable political conflict over which tools to use, how to use them, and when to use them.

 Historical events such as the Great Depression can spur government officials to make significant changes in economic policies.

2 Chinn and Frieden, *Lost Decades*, p. 148. The growth rate is measured by the change in the value of goods and services produced by the economy, or gross domestic product (GDP).

Troubled Assets Relief Program (TARP), the Federal Reserve System, and its mighty efforts to pump capital into the banking system, managed to keep the financial system from total collapse.

But the country was not out of the woods yet. Following that first-order piece of business, government intervened in the economy in numerous other ways. The government injected capital into a giant insurance company, AIG, whose failure would have brought down many other enterprises with it. It bought stock in General Motors and Chrysler, becoming their largest stockholders, to prevent them from going bankrupt, with the expectation that they would emerge from the crisis leaner but financially more sound. It helped broker merger deals by which weaker banks and investment houses were absorbed by stronger ones. In 2009 the new Obama administration proposed, and induced Congress to pass, a massive $787 billion stimulus package—a potpourri of projects and programs to pump money into the economy and, in 2010, the Dodd-Frank Wall Street Reform Act sought to impose new requirements on financial firms that would reduce the chance of massive failures.

The complexities of American political institutions—including a partisan executive (controlled by the Republicans 2007–09 and the Democrats thereafter), the separation of executive from legislature, the bicameral legislative setting (with both chambers controlled by the Democrats 2007–10, but the Republicans controlling the House after the 2010 election), administrative agencies including some (like the Federal Reserve) that were at least nominally independent of elected officials—all of these facets, as the institution principle implies, made the response to the crisis complicated, sluggish, and imperfect.

Government action in the economy is highlighted during a crisis. But in the United States today government is engaged in the economy all the time. The present chapter examines the complementary roles played by politics and economics in the shaping of economic policy. The job of this and the succeeding two chapters of this book is to look at the purposive actions of government—the policies it makes. **Public policy** can be defined simply as an officially expressed intention backed by a sanction, which can be a reward or a punishment. Thus a public policy is a law, a rule, a statute, an edict, a regulation, or an order. Its purpose is to provide incentives, whether carrotlike rewards or sticklike punishments, to induce people to change what they are currently doing and do something else or to do more or less of what they are currently doing. In the first section of this chapter, we discuss the rationale for government's involvement in the economy. In the next sections, we look at the goals and tools of U.S. economic policy.

public policy ➡

A law, rule, statute, or edict that expresses the government's goals for rewards and punishments to promote their attainment

HOW DOES GOVERNMENT MAKE A MARKET ECONOMY POSSIBLE?

There are myriad ways in which governments at all levels in our federal system undergird, manage, protect, and sometimes undermine markets. Indeed, as our experience with the recent financial crisis dramatically revealed, government provided both the context that allowed the crisis to emerge and the responses that kept the market system from failing altogether. In this section, we explore the conditions required for a functioning market economy and the role of government in providing them.

Conditions Required for a Market Economy

A market economy does not just happen. It is a complex set of arrangements that is fostered by political provisions that both nourish and protect. We discuss the conditions constituting this support system below.

Establishing Law and Order. The first condition necessary for a market economy is inherent in the very idea of government. There must be a minimal degree of predictability about the basic rules of social interaction. In other words, there must be a system of law and order. Participants in the market must be able to assume not only that they can get to the market safely—that they won't be robbed on the way—but also that, having arrived, the people with whom they are dealing will behave predictably and will be bound by some number of calculable laws.

Defining Rules of Property and Its Exchange. The second condition that encourages people to participate in the market has to do with defining and dealing with property. If the market involves exchanges of ownership, there must be clear laws about what constitutes property. Property may be many things—your labor or your ideas or the bed you sleep in—but the very concept of property is inconceivable without laws that define what you can call your own.

The existence of property ownership means that we can exercise dominion over something that we have declared our own, and it is defined by laws that enable us to exercise that dominion. Something is not our own unless we can be reasonably certain that someone else cannot walk away with it. Trespass laws, for example, give concrete meaning to what constitutes property: a trespass law confers on us a legal right to keep others away from certain kinds of property. Other laws, to give another example, confer title to property. The possessor of title may use the property but also may transfer it to someone else. It is clear, then, that laws or rules that define property are an essential part of the political economy. Before we can enter a market and participate in an exchange, we must be able to expect not only that we can lay claim to something but also that those around us will respect that claim. In this sense, private property has a public component. The probability of enjoying property would be remote without laws that were widely enforced and accepted.

A related prerequisite for the emergence or creation of a market economy is closely tied to the contract requirement. A market exists only when exchanges occur, and there must be rules governing exchange itself. Laws of exchange structure how, when, and under what conditions you can sell your property. You might think that once the laws of property have defined what you own, you ought to be able to transfer it, but that transfer is surrounded by rules that govern the transfer itself. Certain kinds of exchanges are deemed off limits altogether. For example, you own your own body, but under what conditions can you sell it? Laws about prostitution limit the selling or renting of one's body.

Enforcing Contracts.

A third condition that must be met before a market economy can operate involves rules governing the enforcement of contracts. There are societies that do not have a recognizable concept of contract, but our economy is highly dependent on such notions.

Contracts are closely related to property in that they facilitate exchanges of property, broadly construed. A contract is a voluntary agreement between two or more private persons that governs future conduct. And although the agreement may be private, it has a distinctively public component: a contract must be enforceable, or it is meaningless. If contracts were meaningless, the economy would grind to a halt. Businesses would not sell goods to one another if they could not count on the other's promise to provide the agreed-upon good, service, or payment. Similarly, lenders would not offer loans to home buyers without a legally binding promise to repay the loan. What makes these contracts "enforceable" is the role of the courts in arbitrating disputes between parties in a contract. If a homeowner fails to repay her home loan, for instance, the lending institution can follow a legal procedure to demand payment or take possession of the house.

Setting Market Standards.

The fourth condition necessary for the emergence of the modern free market is related to defining property and the conditions for its exchange. When people engage in exchanges that are not face to face—where they can't point to a good and say, "I want that tomato" or "that fish"—both parties must have some way of understanding what the goods are that they are bargaining over. To do that, terminology must be standardized, and one of the essential acts of any government is to establish standard weights and measures.

With modern products, the standards must go beyond weights and measures; buyers and sellers must be able to specify both the quantity and the quality of goods before they enter into their contracts. These buyers and sellers must know, for example, what is meant by long- and short-staple cotton and everything in between; they must know what they are getting when they order automobile tires of a particular quality. Many of these standards today are developed by private-sector trade associations, of course, but those standards are often incorporated into government regulations, and so they acquire governmental status—or, more important, they are protected by governmental action through the courts. If a member of the porcelain enamel association, for example, agrees to produce a certain type of enamel according to the trade association's specifications, the member can be sued if he cuts corners and evades those standards.

Providing Public Goods and Ameliorating Externalities.

A fifth condition necessary to the operation of a market economy involves the provision of **public goods**. As we saw in Chapter 1, *public good* refers to facilities that

public good

A good that, first, may be enjoyed by anyone if it is provided and, second, may not be denied to anyone once it has been provided the government may provide because no single participant can afford or is willing to provide herself. The provision of public goods extends from supplying the physical marketplace itself—like the common in New England towns, the agora in ancient Greece, or the suk in North Africa and the Middle East—to building and maintaining an interstate highway system to stimulate development and, in the modern era, support for the automobile and trucking industries. The provision of public goods is essential to market operation, and the manner in which the government provides those goods affects the market's character. The classic example of a public good is the system of lighthouses established by the U.S. government in the nineteenth century. Before modern electronics, lighthouses were essential for the safety of seagoing vessels including the transport of goods and people. No individual shipping company, however, would be willing to pay on its own to build a system of lighthouses because its rivals would be able to take advantage of the system free of charge.

In the United States, public goods related to transportation have been particularly important in promoting economic development. From the first canal systems that spread commerce into the interior of the country to the contemporary public role in supporting and regulating air transportation, government has created the conditions for reliable and efficient business activity. In some cases, government will supply a public good to stimulate the economy and then allow private companies to take over. The federal government brought electricity to rural areas in the 1930s to promote economic development, but over time the provision of electricity has been taken over by private companies. Government often supplies public goods that are too big or too risky for private actors to tackle. Major dams and hydroelectric projects are an example. By bringing water and energy to new areas, such public projects transformed the American West. More recently, government-supplied public goods have enhanced public security through such measures as the federal takeover of airport security, the creation of a pharmaceutical stockpile to protect against bioterrorism and epidemics, and the support for research to develop new vaccines.

Closely related to providing public goods, another condition for a market economy is a system for allocating responsibility when the social cost of some behavior far exceeds the private cost. For instance, the total cost of driving a gas-guzzling car may be more than the total of the monthly payments, insurance, and gasoline, because the social cost also includes the widely distributed impact of smog and carbon monoxide emissions. External effects, such as pollution, that can result from market activities are called **externalities**. When individuals or firms engage in private behavior that has broad social consequences, these externalities provide government with an additional rationale for regulating the economy.

 externalities

The differences between the private cost and the social cost of economic behavior

Creating a Labor Force.
A sixth condition necessary for the emergence of a market economy is the creation of a labor force. Every society has provisions that enable and encourage, or sometimes force, people to work. One example of an enabling provision is the requirement for universal compulsory education: in the United States, people are educated so that they can learn the skills

necessary to function in the market. Long before education laws, however, we had poorhouses, vagrancy laws, and other more police-oriented means of forcing people to work; these rules meant that people might starve or suffer punishment if they failed to earn their own keep. Our welfare system today includes provisions that serve the same purpose: the government adjusts the welfare system in cycles to be sure that the support given is uncomfortable enough that people will prefer work to the low income they get from welfare.

Promoting Competition. Finally, once markets emerge, they must be maintained. This means that it should be reasonably easy for a producer to enter and freely compete in the market. If this is not the case, as when one company has established a **monopoly**, the efficiency of the market and the equitable distribution of its benefits are threatened. Decreased competition provides government with another reason for getting involved in the economy: to function as a watchdog over potential monopoly control.

Market Failures and Collective Responses

Satisfying the prerequisites for a free market does not guarantee that the market will always operate smoothly and effectively. Markets sometimes fail to deliver the efficient allocation of society's economic resources because of imperfections of various sorts. For example, a seller may possess information about his product of which a prospective buyer is unaware. This is a problem of incomplete information. This lack of information may lead to more or fewer transactions than might have taken place under conditions of full and complete information. In this instance of **market failure**, the market has misallocated resources because incomplete information has misled market participants.

Another and often devastating form of market failure occurs when speculative buying drives the price of major commodities such as real estate or natural resources to levels far exceeding their intrinsic value. This situation can be referred to as a *bubble*. As the bubble grows, more and more capital is misallocated and eventually wiped out in the crash that almost inevitably follows the "bursting" of the bubble. Occasional bubbles seem to be inherent features of market economies—unfortunate by-products of unfettered individual choices.[3] The collapse of a major bubble almost always leads to demands for government intervention to alleviate the economic distress left in the bubble's wake. In the recent financial crisis, homeowners left with homes worth less than the mortgages they owed and lenders holding mortgages unlikely to be repaid were two groups that sought relief from government. Figure 15.1 shows America's housing bubble and its collapse in 2008.

monopoly

The existence in a market of a single firm that provides all the goods and services of that market; the absence of competition

market failure

An instance when the market fails to produce an efficient outcome

---

3   Vernon L. Smith, Gerry Suchanek, and Arlington W. Williams, "Bubbles, Crashes, and Endogenous Expectations in Experimental Spot Asset Markets," *Econometrica* 56, no. 5 (September 1988): 1119–51.

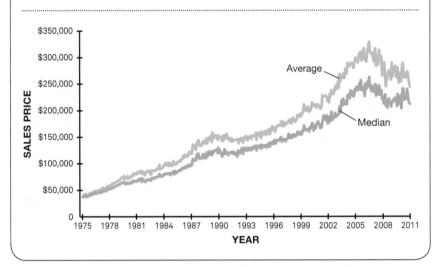

Figure 15.1

MEDIAN AND AVERAGE SALES PRICES OF NEW HOMES SOLD IN THE UNITED STATES

NOTE: The sales price includes the land.

SOURCE: U.S. Census Bureau, www.census.gov/const/uspricemon.pdf (accessed 7/29/13).

Markets fail when individually rational behavior fails to produce efficient market outcomes. Imperfect information and speculative behavior have already been mentioned as sources of market failure. Insecure property rights are another source. For example, since no one "owns" the environment, we over-utilize it as a place to dump pollutants. We drive automobiles, burn coal and oil, and employ chemical-rich fertilizers without taking account of the damage we do to the "global commons" we call our environment. The optimal amount of pollution may not be zero—for life without any pollution would hardly allow for human civilization—but excessive pollution is a problem, too.

Externalities are still another source of market failure. Pollution is one example of an externality, but there are many others. Most towns and cities have noise ordinances, for example, to reduce those negative externalities; likewise, local, state, and national laws regulating speed on roads and highways are designed to reduce safety externalities. In all these cases, the rationality principle describes the fact that individuals do not always take account of the external effects their actions have on others. These individual failures, when widespread, may constitute a market failure. Governments are often tasked with correcting for these with carrots and sticks. A subsidy for using green technology, for example, is a carrot that reduces externalities associated with pollution. Taxes on pollution and fines for speeding or making excessive noise are sticks. These are some of the tools with which governments engage in a collective response to market failures.

In the following section, we will examine the fundamental goals that the government seeks to achieve through its role in the economy.

THE GOALS OF ECONOMIC POLICY

The last section surveyed some prerequisites for establishing a market economy and avoiding market failures. These prerequisites are necessary components—means to an end, so to speak. But to what end? It is not enough simply to say that a well-functioning market economy is the end in mind. The economic policies of government require more concrete objectives. And while "enforcing contracts" or "ameliorating externalities" seem uncontroversial as means for promoting public well-being, there is often vigorous disagreement about the extent to which government should intervene in the economy to promote the public welfare or the form such intervention should take.

Government intervenes in the economy not only to buttress the conditions for a market economy but also to achieve other concrete goals. These goals once were themselves controversial but by the mid-twentieth century had become part of a broad consensus. The first goal is to promote economic stability, the second is to stimulate economic growth, the third is to promote business development, and the fourth is to protect employees and consumers.

Promoting Stable Markets

One of the central reasons for government involvement in the economy is to protect the welfare and property of individuals and businesses. Because the threats to welfare and property change as the economy grows and new technologies emerge, government actions are constantly being updated and adapted to meet new conditions. Generally, governments seek to maintain a measure of stability and predictability in the marketplace so that investors, lenders, and consumers will feel confident in engaging in economic activity.

Maintenance of law and order is one of the most important ways that government can protect welfare and property. The federal government has also enacted laws designed to protect individuals and businesses in economic transactions. Federal antiracketeering laws, for example, aim to end criminal efforts to control businesses through such illegal means as extortion and kickbacks.

Another way in which the government promotes economic stability is by regulating competition. Beginning in the nineteenth century, as many sectors of the national economy flourished, certain companies began to exert monopolistic control over those sectors. Decreased competition threatened the efficiency of the market and the equitable distribution of its benefits. As a result, the national government stepped in to "level the playing field."

Another major reason that Congress began to adopt national business regulatory policies was that the regulated companies themselves felt burdened by the inconsistencies among the states. These companies often preferred a single, national regulatory authority, no matter how burdensome, because it would ensure consistency throughout the United States; the companies could thereby treat the nation as a single market.[4]

Political shifts and advances in technology make the regulation of competition a moving target. In 1913, when telephone service was becoming widely available, the federal government sanctioned AT&T's status as a publicly regulated monopoly. It believed that a single company—publicly regulated—could provide the best service in this industry. By the 1980s, views about the necessity and effectiveness of such monopoly control had changed, and the federal government moved to break up AT&T and open the field to new competitors. Creating competition in the telephone industry, the government hoped, would reduce prices and make the industry more responsive to consumers. And indeed, although consumers still have complaints about telephone companies, prices dropped dramatically as competitors arose. In the late 1990s, there was considerable concern about emerging monopolies in high technology. A federal lawsuit charged that Microsoft Corporation's monopoly position would stifle future innovation in software. The subsequent settlement did little initially to alter Microsoft's market dominance. In the subsequent two decades, however, the public has enjoyed massive innovation of new technologies by new market entrants, such as Google, Facebook, and Twitter. So, while this first goal surely involves providing a stable framework, governments also promote stable market opportunities. And this might involve, from time to time, markets being shaken up by a new technology or new entrant.

Promoting Economic Prosperity

In addition to setting the basic conditions that allow markets to function, governments may actively intervene in the economy to promote economic growth. Although the idea that government should stimulate economic growth can be traced back to Alexander Hamilton's views about promoting industry, it was not until the twentieth century that the federal government assumed a central role in promoting economic growth. There had long been a suspicion of centralized political power, and this persistent suspicion tended to privilege state and local governments in engaging with the private economy. By the end of the nineteenth century, circumstances began to change as states found themselves unable to deal with the massive growth in interstate economic activity.

Measuring Economic Growth. Since the 1930s, the federal government has carefully tracked national economic growth. Economic growth is measured in several different ways. The two most important measures are the gross national product (GNP), which is the market value of the goods and services produced in the economy, and the **gross domestic product (GDP)**, the same measure but excluding income from foreign investments. In the late 1990s, the

 gross domestic product (GDP)

The total value of goods and services produced within a country

4   Compare with Gabriel Kolko, *The Triumph of Conservatism* (New York: Free Press, 1963), chap. 6.

American economy grew at a rate of over 4 percent a year, a rate considered high by modern standards (Figure 15.2). Growth fell to 0.5 percent during the recession in 2001. It briefly rose but began to fall again, rising to a modest 2.2 percent in 2007. During 2008 and 2009—crisis years—the economy experienced meager growth. Growth was again positive in 2010, 2011, and 2012, hovering between 2 and 2.5 percent a year.

The engine of American economic growth has shifted over the centuries. In the 1800s, our nation's rich endowment of natural resources was especially important in propelling growth. Manufacturing industries became the driving force of economic growth during the late nineteenth century as mass production made it possible to manufacture goods at a pace that was once unimaginable. In more recent times, the high-technology boom fostered unanticipated and vigorous economic growth that made the United States the envy of the world. Despite these very different economic engines, the basic prerequisites of growth are similar in each case: strong investment, technological innovation, and a productive workforce. Throughout the nation's history, the federal government has adopted policies to promote each of these conditions needed to sustain economic growth.

Figure 15.2

CHANGES IN REAL GROSS DOMESTIC PRODUCT, 1960–2012

The rates of growth in gross domestic product have varied over time. They were particularly volatile during the 1980s as the economy first plunged into recession and then rapidly recovered with high rates of growth. In 2008, growth slowed as the economy went into recession. What was the pattern of growth during the last five presidential election years?

SOURCE: U.S. Department of Commerce, www.bea.gov/national (accessed 7/12/13).

Tools for Promoting Growth. The most fundamental way that government affects investment is by promoting business, investor, and consumer confidence. When businesses fear political instability, unpredictable government action, or widespread disregard of the law, they are unlikely to invest. When consumers are insecure about the future, they are unlikely to spend. Government officials monitor surveys of business and consumer confidence as they devise economic policy. After the terrorist attacks of 2001, the federal government moved quickly to reassure the financial markets, businesses, and consumers. The Federal Reserve responded with interest-rate cuts aimed at promoting spending and investment. In 2008, the federal government enacted a $700 billion rescue plan in order to restore investor confidence after several large banks failed. As was mentioned in the introduction, this was followed in 2009 with a $787 billion stimulus package and financial support to Chrysler and General Motors to allow them the breathing room to reorganize as profitable enterprises.

Businesses also need access to new sources of capital in order to grow. The federal government promotes reliable access to new investment through its regulation of financial markets. The most important federal agency in this regard is the **Securities and Exchange Commission (SEC)**, created after the stock market crash of 1929. The SEC requires companies to disclose information about the stocks and bonds they are selling, inform buyers of the investment risks, and protect investors against fraud. In this way, the SEC helps to maintain investor confidence and a strong supply of capital for American business. The SEC came in for harsh criticism during the financial crisis in 2008 and 2009. Analysts pointed to weak SEC oversight and regulation as an important factor in driving the financial sector to the brink of collapse. Congressional critics called for tougher SEC regulation of Wall Street in the future. In 2010 the Democratic Congress passed, and President Obama signed, the Dodd-Frank Wall Street Reform and Consumer Protection Act aimed at doing precisely this.

Public investment is a third important source of growth in the American economy. In the 1930s and again in the late 1970s, the federal government promoted public investment as a means to spark economic growth. Some kinds of public investment promote growth as a by-product of other more central objectives. One of the most important of these is military spending. Many analysts credited the rise in military spending associated with the war in Iraq with helping to spur economic growth in 2003.

The fourth important condition for economic growth is innovation. The federal government has sought to support innovation in a variety of ways. One of the most important is through the National Science Foundation. Created in 1950, the National Science Foundation supports basic research across a range of scientific fields. The aim is to advance fundamental knowledge that may be useful in many different applications.[5] Federal government sponsorship of health research began in the late 1800s. Today, the National Institutes of Health

 Securities and Exchange Commission (SEC)

Agency charged with regulating the U.S. securities industry and stock exchanges

5   See David M. Hart, *Forged Consensus: Science, Technology and Economic Policy in the United States, 1921–1953* (Princeton, NJ: Princeton University Press, 1998).

(NIH) conduct basic and applied research in biomedicine. The Human Genome Project—the effort to map the basic genetic structure of human life—was initiated by government researchers and only later taken up by private corporations. Recently, the NIH has taken the lead in basic research to counter bioterrorism. Its efforts to understand the biology of various infectious agents and to develop vaccines are expected to produce important new knowledge about the human immune system. Research sponsored by the military has long been an important source of innovation for the American economy. Such key twentieth-century innovations as radar and nuclear power stemmed from military research. Military research also created the technology for the twenty-first century with ARPANET, the precursor of the Internet.

A fifth fundamental condition for economic growth is workforce productivity. Federal immigration policy has played a key role in ensuring an adequate supply of labor throughout American history, giving special priority to workers who have skills that are in demand among American employers. Immigrants with nursing degrees, for example, have long received special priority.

Today, a productive workforce is a highly educated workforce. Education, as we see in Chapter 16, is primarily the responsibility of state and local governments, though the federal government has taken an increasing role. The federal government supports the development of a productive workforce with a variety of programs to support higher education, such as educational grants, tax breaks, and loans. The federal government also sponsors a limited array of job-training programs that focus primarily on low-skilled workers. Some analysts argue that the federal government must do much more to support the development of a highly skilled workforce if the United States is to sustain economic growth in the future.

Full Employment. Before the 1930s, neither the federal nor the state governments sought to promote full employment. Unemployment was widely viewed as an unfortunate occurrence that government could do little to alter. The New Deal response to the prolonged and massive unemployment of the Great Depression changed that view. The federal government put millions of people back to work on public projects sponsored by such programs as the Works Progress Administration (WPA). The bridges, walkways, and buildings they constructed can still be seen across the United States today. The federal government viewed these programs as temporary measures, however. As the buildup for World War II boosted the economy and unemployment melted away, the employment programs were dismantled.

The New Deal and government wartime spending, however, showed that government could help ensure full employment. Public expectations changed as well: Americans looked to the federal government to reduce unemployment after the war. Moreover, economic theory now supported their expectations. The British economist John Maynard Keynes's theories that government could boost employment by stimulating demand had become very influential.

Federal policy placed the most emphasis on achieving full employment during the 1960s. Keynesian economists in the Council of Economic Advisers convinced President Kennedy to enact the first tax cut designed to stimulate the economy and promote full employment.[6] The policy was widely seen as a success, and unemployment declined to a low of 3.4 percent in 1968.

Favorable economic conditions in the 1990s reduced unemployment to record lows once again. But when the economy fell into recession in 2001, it was apparent that the boom of the 1990s—and many of the economic speculations it generated—were only temporary. The new economic worry was the "jobless recovery." Throughout 2003, as economic growth surged, job creation lagged far behind. Economists and politicians alike remained puzzled by the sluggish job market, speculating about the impact of foreign trade and growing productivity on limiting new hires. Not until the middle of 2005 did the number of private-sector jobs surpass the level in March 2001, the peak of the last economic expansion.

As the economy fell into recession in 2008, unemployment began once again to climb. It remained stuck in the 9–10 percent range for 2009 and most of 2010. It finally seemed to start coming down in 2012. But since the unemployment rate measures those looking for full-time work as a percentage of those employed in or looking for full-time work, it is unclear whether the decline measured a genuine increase in full-time employment or, instead, a decline in those looking for work at all or an increase in those who have settled for part-time employment.

Low Inflation. During the 1970s and early 1980s, **inflation**, a consistent increase in the general level of prices, was one of America's most vexing problems. There was much disagreement over what to do about it—which public policies were most appropriate and effective. The first effort, beginning in 1971, was the adoption of strict controls over wages, prices, dividends, and rents—that is, authorizing an agency in the executive branch to place limits on what wage people could be paid for their work, what rent their real estate could bring, and what interest they could get on their money. After two years of effort, these particular policies were fairly well discredited, and the search resumed for one or more other policies to fight inflation. Since oil prices had become so clearly a major source of inflation in the late 1970s, President Carter experimented with the licensing of imports of oil from the Middle East, with tariffs and excise taxes on unusually large oil profits made by producers, and with sales taxes on gasoline at the pump to discourage all casual consumption of gasoline. President Carter also attempted to reduce consumer spending in general by raising income taxes, especially Social Security taxes on employees.

The continuing high rate of inflation paved the way to an entirely different approach by President Reagan in the early 1980s. In place of oil import licensing and selective tax increases, President Reagan proposed and got a general tax cut. The Reagan theory was that if tax cuts were deep enough and were guaranteed to endure, although they would increase the supply of money, they would also change people's psychology from pessimism to optimism, thereby encouraging

 inflation

A consistent increase in the general level of prices

6 See Margaret Weir, *Politics and Jobs: The Boundaries of Employment Policy in the United States* (Princeton, NJ: Princeton University Press, 1992).

individuals and corporations to invest enough and produce more goods and services to get the country out of an inflationary period. At the same time, President Reagan supported the continuation of the high Social Security taxes enacted during the Carter administration, which probably went further than any other method to fight inflation by discouraging consumption. Inflation is caused by too many dollars chasing too few goods, bidding up prices. Any tax will take dollars out of consumption, but since the Social Security tax hits middle- and lower-middle-income people the hardest, and since these middle-income people are the heaviest consumers, such a tax reduces consumer dollars. Another policy supported by the Reagan administration was restraining the amount of credit in the economy by pushing up interest rates.

Inflation was finally reduced from its historic highs of over 10 percent down toward 2 or 3 percent each year. Noting that the 1970s were America's only "peacetime inflation," the economist Bradford DeLong contends that it wasn't until inflation had risen to dizzying heights late in the decade that the Federal Reserve truly had a mandate to reduce inflation.[7] Once it had full political support for reducing inflation in 1979, the Federal Reserve raised interest rates sharply and brought inflation rates down, provoking a sharp recession at the same time.

Promoting Business Development

During the nineteenth century, the national government was a promoter of markets. National roads and canals were built to tie states and regions together. National tariff policies promoted domestic markets by restricting imported goods; a tax on an import raised its price and weakened its ability to compete with similar domestic products. The national government also heavily subsidized the railroad system. Subsidies promote business by making it cheaper for firms to produce their goods. Until the 1840s, railroads were thought to be of limited commercial value. But between 1850 and 1872, Congress granted over 100 million acres of public-domain land to railroad interests, and state and local governments pitched in an estimated $280 million in cash and credit. Before the end of the century, 35,000 miles of track had been built—almost half the world's total at the time.

Railroads were not the only clients of federal support for the private markets. Many sectors of agriculture began receiving federal subsidies during the nineteenth century. Agriculture remains highly subsidized. In 2001, an environmental group caused a stir by putting the exact amounts of subsidies received by individual farmers on a widely publicized website. In 2005, 40 percent of farms in the United States received subsidies; by 2006 the total subsidy was estimated at more than $20 billion. One of the many criticisms of the farm-subsidy program

---

7 Bradford DeLong, "America's Only Peacetime Inflation: The 1970s," National Bureau of Economic Research, working paper no. h0084 (May 1996). Available at http://ssrn .com/abstract-225048 (accessed 4/15/11).

is that it disproportionately supports large-scale farmers rather than small family farmers. The list of farm-subsidy recipients includes many large corporations.

The national government also promotes business development indirectly through **categorical grants-in-aid** (see Chapter 3), whereby the national government offers grants to states on the condition that the state (or local) government undertake a particular activity. Thus, in order to use motor transportation to improve national markets, a 900,000-mile national highway system was built during the 1930s, based on a formula whereby the national government would pay 50 percent of the cost if the states would provide the other 50 percent. Over 20 years, beginning in the late 1950s, the federal government constructed an additional 45,000 miles of interstate highways. In this program, the national government agreed to pay 90 percent of the construction costs on the condition that each state provide 10 percent of the costs of any portion of a highway built within its boundaries.[8] The tremendous growth of highways was, as noted earlier, a major boon to the automobile and trucking industries.

The federal government supports specific business sectors with direct subsidies, loans, and tax breaks. In 1953, the Small Business Administration (SBA) was created to offer loans, loan guarantees, and disaster assistance to small businesses. Recognizing that such businesses often find it harder to obtain financing and to recover from unexpected events such as fires, the federal government has provided assistance where the market would not.

Since September 11, 2001, the federal government has taken on a major role in promoting technological innovation related to national security. With defense and homeland security at the top of the national agenda, military spending increased during the George W. Bush administration. A new emphasis on technological innovation accompanied the increase in spending. As a way to promote its access to the latest technology, the Department of Defense runs a $1.1 billion program and its own venture-capital firm that funds the early stages of research and development for innovative small firms and high-tech start-ups.

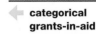

categorical grants-in-aid

Funds given by Congress to states and localities that are earmarked by law for specific categories, such as education or crime prevention

Protecting Employees and Consumers

Stable relations between business and labor are important elements of a productive economy. During the latter half of the nineteenth century, strikes over low wages or working conditions became a standard feature of American economic life. In fact, the United States has one of the most violent histories of labor relations in the world. Yet for most of American history, the federal government did little to regulate relations between business and labor. Local governments and courts often weighed in on the side of business by prohibiting strikes and arresting strikers.

8   The act of 1955 officially designated the interstate highways as the National System of Interstate and Defense Highways. It was indirectly a major part of President Dwight Eisenhower's defense program. But it was just as obviously a "pork-barrel" policy as any rivers-and-harbors legislation.

As the economic depression enveloped the United States in the 1930s, plummeting wages and massive strikes for union recognition prompted the federal government to take action. Congress passed the 1935 National Labor Relations Act, which set up a new framework for industrial relations. The new law created a permanent agency, the National Labor Relations Board (NLRB), charged with overseeing union elections and collective bargaining between labor and industry. The federal government weighed in further on the side of organized labor in 1938, when it passed the Fair Labor Standards Act, which created the minimum wage. Because it is not indexed to inflation, the value of the minimum wage declines if it is not raised periodically. Since 1938, conflicts over increasing the minimum wage have been a regular feature of American politics.

During the 1950s and 1960s, the federal government played an active role in industrial relations. The Department of Labor and occasionally even the president directly intervened in labor-management disputes to ensure peaceful industrial relations. Although Democrats were generally seen as more supportive of labor, both parties sought to achieve a balance between business and labor that would promote a strong, stable economy. More recently, politicians have been unlikely to intervene in labor relations, although President Reagan's firing of striking air traffic controllers in 1981 is a notable exception.

Economic policies also protect consumers. The idea that the federal government should protect consumers emerged in the first decade of the 1900s. Upton Sinclair's graphic exposé about the unsanitary practices of the meat-packing industry, *The Jungle*, published in 1906, galvanized public concern about unsanitary food processing. These concerns prompted the U.S. Department of Agriculture to inspect packing plants and the meat they produced, stamping approved meats with the now familiar "USDA" certification. Similar concern about food and drug safety led to the creation of the Food and Drug Administration in 1927. Today, the FDA regulates many areas of food and drug production, though gaps in consumer protection sometimes emerge. In 2012, for example, a number of deaths caused by a rare fungal meningitis were traced to contaminated steroids sold by a Massachusetts "compounding" pharmacy. Such enterprises are not covered by FDA regulations.

The movement for consumer protection experienced new momentum in the 1960s. The consumer advocate Ralph Nader's 1965 book *Unsafe at Any Speed* helped spark new demands for federal action. Nader's book showed that design flaws in the Corvair, a popular car model, had caused deaths that could have been prevented. Nader's book not only led to the demise of the Corvair but also galvanized calls for more federal action to protect consumers. The first response was the 1966 National Traffic and Motor Vehicle Safety Act, which gave the Department of Transportation responsibility for ensuring vehicle safety. Federal responsibility for consumer safety expanded in 1972 when Congress created the Consumer Product Safety Commission. The commission, which is an independent agency, informs consumers about hazards associated with products and works with industry to set product standards. In cases where safety concerns are severe, it will see that such products are recalled. Through the Consumer Product Safety Commission, the Department of Transportation, and the Food and Drug Administration (which regulates food, drugs, and cosmetics), the federal government continues to play an active role in protecting the public from unsafe products. Other federal statutes aimed at consumer protection include the Fair Credit Reporting Act and the Truth in Lending Act, designed to discourage rapacious lending practices. In 2010, as part of the Dodd-Frank Act, Congress created the Consumer Financial Protection Bureau to regulate financial products and services, such as credit cards, used by Americans on a daily basis.

THE TOOLS OF ECONOMIC POLICY

The current state and structure of the U.S. economy is no accident; it is the result of specific policies that have expanded American markets and sustained massive economic growth. As it works to meet the multiple goals of economic policy outlined above, the federal government relies on a broad set of tools that has evolved over time. Let us now turn to the actual tools designed to accomplish the goals of economic policy.

Monetary Policies

Monetary policies manipulate the growth of the entire economy by controlling the availability of money to banks. With a very few exceptions, banks in the United States are privately owned and locally operated. Until well into the twentieth century, banks were regulated, if at all, by state legislatures. Each bank was granted a charter, giving it permission to make loans, hold deposits, and make investments within that state. Although more than 25,000 banks continue to be state-chartered banks, they are less important than they used to be in the overall financial picture, as the most important banks now are members of the federal banking system.

But banks did not become the core of American capitalism without intense political controversy. The Federalist majority in Congress, led by Alexander Hamilton, did in fact establish a Bank of the United States in 1791, but it was vigorously opposed by agrarian interests led by Thomas Jefferson, who feared that the interests of urban, industrial capitalism would dominate such a bank. The Bank of the United States was terminated during the administration of Andrew Jackson, but the fear of a central, public bank lingered eight decades later, when Congress in 1913 established an institution—the **Federal Reserve System**—to integrate private banks into a single national system. The Federal Reserve System did not become a central bank in the European tradition but rather comprises 12 Federal Reserve banks, each located in a major commercial city. The Federal Reserve banks are not ordinary banks; they are banker's banks that make loans to other banks, clear checks, and supply the economy with currency and coins. They also play a regulatory role over the member banks. Every national bank must be a member of the Federal Reserve System and must follow national banking rules. State banks and savings and loan associations may also

 monetary policy

Policies to regulate the economy through the manipulation of the supply of money, the price of money (interest rate), and the availability of credit

 Federal Reserve System

A system of 12 Federal Reserve banks that facilitates exchanges of cash, checks, and credit; regulates member banks; and uses monetary policies to fight inflation and deflation

join if they accept national rules. At the top of the system is the Federal Reserve Board—"the Fed"—comprising seven members appointed by the president (with Senate confirmation) for 14-year terms. The chairman of the Fed is selected by the president from among the seven members of the board for a four-year term. In all other concerns the Fed is an independent agency inasmuch as its members cannot be removed during their terms except "for cause," and the president's executive power does not extend to them or their policies. Nonetheless, in recent years the Fed chairman has been a politically visible figure. For example, observers charged the longtime Federal Reserve chairman, Alan Greenspan, with being attentive to politics in his endorsement of President George W. Bush's tax cuts. In his 2005 confirmation hearings to head the Fed, economist Ben Bernanke promised Congress that he would be "strictly independent of all political influences."[9] Nevertheless, a few short years later he played a significant, visible role during the financial crisis, often photographed in close consultation with Bush's last treasury secretary, Henry Paulson, and Obama's first treasury secretary, Timothy Geithner.

The major advantage that a bank gains from being in the Federal Reserve System is that it can borrow from the system. This enables banks to expand their loan operations continually, as long as there is demand for loans in the economy. On the other hand, it is this very access of member banks to the Federal Reserve System that gives the Fed its power: the ability to expand and contract the *amount of credit* available in the United States.

The Fed can affect the total amount of credit through the interest it charges (called the discount rate) on the loans it extends to member banks. If the Fed significantly decreases the discount rate, it can give a boost to a sagging economy. During 2001, the Fed cut interest rates 11 times to combat the combined effects of recession and the terrorist attacks. As the economy began to sag in late 2007, all eyes were on the Fed to reduce interest rates. By March 2008, the Fed had cut rates six times from their high in September 2007. By 2009 the discount rate had been pushed down nearly to zero in an effort to stimulate recovery from the deepest recession since the Great Depression of the 1930s; it has remained there for several years. If the Fed raises the discount rate, it can put a brake on the economy because the higher discount rate also increases the general interest rates charged by leading private banks to their customers.

Although the Federal Reserve is responsible for ensuring high employment as well as price stability, it has been particularly important in fighting inflation. During the late 1970s and early 1980s, with inflation at record high levels, Federal Reserve Chairman Paul Volcker aggressively raised interest rates in order to dampen inflation. Although his actions provoked a sharp recession, they raised the stature of the Fed, demonstrating its ability to manage the economy. Because the Fed is so closely associated with inflation fighting, Senate Democrats pressed Ben Bernanke, President Bush's nominee to head the Fed, to indicate that he would view maximum employment as a goal of equal importance to that of fighting inflation. As late as 2012, Bernanke, who was reappointed as Fed

---

9 Kevin G. Hall, "Bernanke to Stay on Greenspan Path, but Not All the Way," *Seattle Times*, November 16, 2005, p. C1.

chair by President Obama in 2010, has kept interests rates low, allowing inflation to creep up (to 3.2 percent in 2011 and 2.1 percent in 2012), in order to promote economic activity that might bring down unemployment.[10]

A second power of the Fed is control over the **reserve requirement**—the amount of cash and negotiable securities every bank must hold readily available to cover withdrawals and checks written by its depositors. When the Fed decides to increase the reserve requirement, it can decrease significantly the amount of money banks have to lend; conversely, if the Fed lowers the reserve requirement, banks can be more liberal in extending more loans.[11] As noted earlier, during the crisis of 2008–09, banks balked at lending because of nervousness that borrowers would default on loan payments. Indeed, many homeowners did precisely this, leading to a wave of property foreclosures with banks taking ownership. Bank hesitancy to lend, called the "credit crunch," forced the Fed to remove a variety of constraints on lending to stimulate more of it.

A third power of the Fed is called **open-market operations**, whereby the Fed buys and sells government securities to increase or decrease the supply of money in the economy. When the Fed buys government securities in the open market, it increases the amount of money available to consumers to spend or invest; when it sells securities, it is reducing the money supply.

Finally, a fourth power is derived from one of the important services the Federal Reserve System renders, which is the opportunity for member banks to borrow from one another. One of the original reasons for creating a Federal Reserve System was to balance regions of the country that might be vigorously expanding with other areas that might be fairly dormant: the national system would enable the banks in a growing region, facing great demand for credit, to borrow money from banks in regions of the country where the demand for credit is much lower. This exchange is called the "federal funds market," and the interest rate charged by one bank to another, the **federal funds rate**, can be manipulated just like the discount rate, to expand or contract credit.[12]

The federal government also provides insurance to foster credit and encourage private capital investment. The Federal Deposit Insurance Corporation

reserve requirement

The amount of liquid assets and ready cash that the Federal Reserve requires banks to hold to meet depositors' demands for their money

open-market operations

The process whereby the Open Market Committee of the Federal Reserve buys and sells government securities, and so on, to help finance government operations and to reduce or increase the total amount of money circulating in the economy

federal funds rate

The interest rate on loans among banks that the Federal Reserve Board influences by affecting the supply of money available

---

10 The Federal Reserve Bank of Minneapolis, Consumer Price Index 1913–2013, www.minneapolisfed.org/community_education/teacher/calc/hist1913.cfm? (accessed 3/28/13).

11 As a general rule, in a growing economy where there is demand for credit, and assuming a reserve requirement of 20 percent, a deposit of $100 will create nearly $500 of new credit. This is called the "multiplier effect," because the bank can lend out $80 of the original $100 deposit to a new borrower; that becomes another $80 deposit, 20 percent of which ($64) can be lent to another borrower, and so on until the original $100 grows to approximately $500 of new credit.

12 Good treatments of the Federal Reserve System and monetary policy can be found in Donald Kettl, *Leadership at the Fed* (New Haven, CT: Yale University Press, 1986); and Albert T. Sommers, *The U.S. Economy Demystified* (Lexington, MA: Lexington Books, 1988), especially chap. 5. In the context of the recent financial crisis, see Nolan McCarty, Keith T. Poole, Thomas Romer, and Howard Rosenthal, "Political Fortunes: On Finance and Its Regulation," *Daedalus* 139 (Fall 2010): 61–73.

(FDIC) insures bank deposits up to $250,000. Another important promoter of investment is the federal insurance of home mortgages through the Department of Housing and Urban Development (HUD). By guaranteeing mortgages, the government can reduce the risks that banks run in making such loans, thus allowing banks to lower their interest rates and make such loans more affordable to middle- and lower-income families. Such programs have enabled millions of families that could not have otherwise afforded it to finance the purchase of a home.

Housing Crisis. This system began to unravel in the first decade of the 2000s with the growth of the subprime market for lending. This market made home loans available to people who could not otherwise afford to buy a home. At the same time, however, it created new instabilities in the market by offering risky loans that would become more costly due to adjustable interest rates. The slowing housing market in 2007 set off a wave of foreclosures as many homeowners discovered that they could not pay back their loans.[13]

The foreclosure crisis in turn sent shock waves through the financial system, as investment banks found themselves holding worthless loans. One casualty of the home loan meltdown was the Wall Street investment bank Bear Stearns, which faced bankruptcy early in March 2008. Seeking to limit the harm to the broader economy that such a bankruptcy would cause, Fed chair Ben Bernanke arranged for Bear Stearns to be bought—at a bargain-basement price—by JP Morgan Chase, another investment bank. In making this move, Bernanke was exercising powers of the Federal Reserve Act that had not been used since the 1930s.[14] By the fall of 2008 several other investment banks and insurance companies were close to insolvency. In September 2008, the Treasury and the Federal Reserve announced a rescue package in which the federal government made up to $700 billion in emergency credit and capital available.

The government's actions are an excellent illustration of the policy principle from Chapter 1. Just as President Bush had done in September 2001, President Obama used the power of his office to respond forcefully to a crisis. Like Bush, Obama knew that he would be judged by his ability to deal with the threat facing the nation—in this case an economic threat. Accordingly, President Obama mobilized the relevant institutions, including Congress, the Treasury Department, and the Federal Reserve to craft a response to the threatened collapse of

---

13 Majority Staff of the Joint Economic Committee, Senator Charles E. Schumer, Chairman, Rep. Carolyn B. Maloney, Vice Chair, *The Subprime Lending Crisis: The Economic Impact on Wealth, Property Values and Tax Revenues, and How We Got Here*, Report and Recommendations, October 2007, p. 1, www.jec.senate.gov/index .cfm?FuseAction=Reports.Reports&ContentRecord_id=c6627bb2-7e9c-9af9-7ac7 -32b94d398d27&Region_id=&Issue_id= (accessed 4/20/09). A definitive academic study is Atif Mian, Amir Sufi, and Francesco Trebbi, "The Political Economy of the US Mortgage Default Crisis," *American Economic Review* 100 (2010): 1967–98.

14 Steven R. Weisman, "Bernanke Faces Bear Stearns Queries," *New York Times*, April 2, 2008, p. C1.

the nation's economy. The resulting programs could well be described by our principle: ambition plus institutions equals policy.

The Fed in action also illustrates the rationality and institution principles. The Fed is a bureaucracy with goals and objectives of its own on the one hand, and constraints and threats in its environment on the other. Perhaps the most important thing to know about the Fed is that its independence—something extremely consequential for a modern economy—is conditional. It is eager to protect its capacity for independent action by making certain its political principals do not move to trim its sails. It does this by taking its role as agent seriously. Its willingness to elevate the goal of reducing unemployment, alongside keeping inflation at a moderate level, is a response to congressional preferences in order to quell attacks on its independence. Likewise, Bernanke's willingness in 2011 to meet with the press and to render Fed decision making more transparent was a further accommodation of congressional preferences.

Fiscal Policies

Fiscal policy includes the government's taxing and spending powers. On the tax side of the ledger, personal and corporate income taxes raise most of the U.S. government's revenues. Although the direct purpose of a tax is to raise revenue, each tax has a different impact on the economy, and government can attempt to plan for that impact. After passing major tax cuts in 2001, President George W. Bush proposed and Congress passed a sweeping new round of cuts in 2003. Bush's plan was intended to promote investment by reducing taxes on most stock dividends, to spur business activity by offering tax breaks to small businesses, and to stimulate the economy by reducing the tax rates for all taxpayers. In 2006, Congress extended the rate reductions on dividends and capital gains. The Bush administration tax cuts were criticized on several grounds. Many Democrats argued that the tax cuts were simply a giveaway to the wealthy and to corporations and that they did nothing to promote growth. There has been concern that the tax cuts are partly responsible for the large federal deficits: the federal budget moved from running surpluses in 2000 to steep deficits throughout the next decade.

The administration of the revenue side of fiscal policy occurs primarily in the Treasury Department. In addition to collecting income, corporate, and other taxes, the Treasury also manages the enormous national debt—$16 trillion in 2012.[15] (The national debt was a mere $710 billion in 1980.) Debt is not simply something the country owes; it is something the country has to manage and administer. The debt is also a fiscal instrument in the hands of the

 fiscal policy

The government's use of taxing and spending powers to manipulate the economy

---

15 About 60 percent of the debt is held by the public, corporations, foreign governments, and other creditors. About 40 percent of the debt consists of "intragovernmental holdings." These are funds borrowed by the Treasury from other government agencies, in particular the Social Security and Medicare trust funds, which serve as a large source of funding for the federal government's major expenditures.

federal government that can be used—through manipulation of interest rates and through the buying and selling of government bonds—to slow down or to speed up the activity of the entire national economy, as well as to defend the value of the dollar in international trade.

Taxation. During the nineteenth century, the federal government received most of its revenue from a single tax, the **tariff**. It also relied on excise taxes, which are taxes levied on specific products, such as tobacco and alcohol. As federal activities expanded in the 1900s, the federal government added new sources of tax revenue. The most important was the income tax, proposed by Congress in 1909, ratified by the states, and added to the Constitution in 1913 as the Sixteenth Amendment. The income tax is levied on individuals as well as corporations. With the creation of the Social Security system in 1935, social insurance taxes became an additional source of federal revenue.

Before World War II, individual income taxes accounted for only 14 percent of federal revenues.[16] The need to raise revenue for World War II made the income tax much more important. Congress expanded the base of the income tax so that most Americans paid income taxes after World War II. Table 15.1 shows several notable shifts that have occurred in taxes since 1960. Social insurance taxes now make up a much greater share of federal revenues, rising from 15.9 percent of revenues in 1960 to more than 30 percent since 1980. Receipts from corporate income taxes have declined over the same time period, dropping from 23.2 percent of receipts in 1960 to barely 10 percent since 2004. The share of the federal individual income tax has remained fairly stable; it was 44 percent in 1960 and about 47 percent currently.

One of the most important features of the American income tax is that it is a progressive, or graduated, tax, with the heaviest burden carried by those most able to pay. A tax is called **progressive** if the rate of taxation goes up with each higher income bracket. A tax is called **regressive** if people in lower income brackets pay a higher proportion of their income toward the tax than people in higher income brackets. For example, a sales tax is deemed regressive because everybody pays at the same rate, so that the proportion of total income paid in sales tax goes down as the total income goes up (assuming, as is generally the case, that as total income goes up the amount spent on sales-taxable purchases increases at a slower rate).

Although the primary purpose of the graduated income tax is, of course, to raise revenue, an important second objective may be to collect revenue in such a way as to reduce the disparities of wealth between the lowest and the highest income brackets. We call this a policy of **redistribution**. Another policy objective of the income tax is the encouragement of the capitalist economy by rewarding investment. The tax laws allow individuals or companies to deduct from their taxable

tariff

A tax on imported goods

progressive taxation

Taxation that hits the upper income brackets more heavily

regressive taxation

Taxation that hits the lower income brackets more heavily

redistribution

A policy whose objective is to tax or spend in such a way as to reduce the disparities of wealth between the lowest and the highest income brackets

---

16 Executive Office of the President of the United States, GPO Access, "Budget of the United States Government Historical Tables Fiscal Year 2011," table 2.2—Percentage Composition of Receipts by Source: 1934–2013, http://origin.www.gpoaccess.gov /usbudget/fy11/hist.html (accessed 4/19/11).

Table 15.1

FEDERAL REVENUES BY TYPE OF TAX AS PERCENTAGE OF TOTAL RECEIPTS, 1960–2012

FISCAL YEAR	INDIVIDUAL INCOME TAXES	CORPORATION INCOME TAXES	SOCIAL INSURANCE AND RETIREMENT RECEIPTS	EXCISE TAXES	OTHER
1960	44.0	23.2	15.9	12.6	4.2
1970	46.9	17.0	23.0	8.1	4.9
1980	47.2	12.5	30.5	4.7	5.1
1990	45.2	9.1	36.8	3.4	5.4
2000	49.6	10.2	32.2	3.4	4.5
2001	49.9	7.6	34.9	3.3	4.3
2002	46.3	8.0	37.8	3.6	4.3
2003	44.5	7.4	40.0	3.8	4.3
2004	43.0	10.1	39.0	3.7	4.2
2005	43.1	12.9	36.9	3.4	3.8
2006	43.4	14.7	34.8	3.1	4.0
2007	45.3	14.4	33.9	2.5	3.9
2008	45.4	12.1	35.7	2.7	4.2
2009	43.5	6.6	45.3	3.0	4.7
2010	41.5	8.9	40.0	3.1	6.5
2011	47.4	7.9	35.5	3.1	6.1
2012*	47.2	9.6	34.1	3.2	6.0

*Estimated

SOURCE: Office of Management and Budget, table 2.2, www.whitehouse.gov/omb/budget/Historicals (accessed 12/10/12).

income any money they can justify as an investment or a "business expense"; this gives an incentive to individuals and companies to spend money to expand their production, their advertising, or their staff, and reduces the income taxes businesses have to pay. These kinds of deductions are called incentives or "equity" by those who support them; others call them "loopholes." The tax laws of the 1980s actually closed a number of important loopholes in U.S. tax laws. But others still exist—on home mortgages and on business expenses, for example—and others will return, because there is a strong consensus among members of Congress, both Democrats and Republicans, that businesses often need such incentives. The differences between the two parties focus largely on which incentives are justifiable.[17]

As we noted earlier, taxes were a controversial issue during the George W. Bush administration. President Bush made tax reduction the centerpiece of his administration and enacted major tax cuts.[18] These tax breaks were scheduled to expire in 2010. As the economy dipped into recession in early 2008, Bush urged making the cuts permanent: "The smartest thing we can do is to keep taxes low. In a time of economic uncertainty, we don't need to be taking money out of your pocket."[19] Democratic politicians, on the other hand, argued that the tax cuts benefited the rich too much, exacerbating income inequality (see the Analyzing the Evidence unit on page 658). They argued that moving back to higher tax rates on the wealthy would help fund crucial public programs, such as improving the health care system.

In 2010, as the clock ticked on the expiring Bush rates and would revert to the higher pre-2001 rates if nothing were done, the Republicans sought to make all the rates permanent, while the Democrats wanted only lower- and middle-class tax rates protected. In a last-minute compromise, all rates were protected but only for two more years. Thus the issue surfaced again in 2012, requiring more negotiations and another compromise in which the GOP agreed to a rate increase for the wealthiest taxpayers.

Spending and Budgeting. The federal government's power to spend is one of the most important tools of economic policy. Decisions about how much to spend affect the overall health of the economy. They also affect every aspect of American life from the distribution of income to the availability of different modes of transportation to the level of education in society. Not surprisingly, the fight for control over spending is one of the most contentious in Washington, as interest groups and politicians strive to determine the priorities and appropriate levels of spending. Decisions about spending are made as part of the annual budget process. During the 1990s, when the federal **budget deficit**

budget deficit

The amount by which government spending exceeds government revenue in a fiscal year

---

17 For a systematic account of the role of government in providing incentives and inducements to business, see C. E. Lindblom, *Politics and Markets* (New York: Basic Books, 1977), chap. 13. For a detailed account of the dramatic Reagan tax cuts and reforms, see Jeffrey Birnbaum and Alan Murray, *Showdown at Gucci Gulch: Lawmakers, Lobbyists, and the Unlikely Triumph of Tax Reform* (New York: Random House, 1987).

18 Center on Budget and Policy Priorities, "Tax Cuts: Myths and Realities," updated May 9, 2008, www.cbpp.org/cms/?fa=view&id=692 (accessed 4/20/09).

19 "Bush Urges Permanent Tax Cuts Amid 'Economic Uncertainty,'" *New York Times,* January 8, 2008.

first became a major political issue and when parties were deeply split on spending, the budget process became the focal point of the entire policy-making process. Even though the budget deficit disappeared in the late 1990s, the budget continued to dominate the attention of policy makers (Figure 15.3). With the rapid swing from budget surpluses in 2000 to record deficits by 2003, deficits once again emerged as a political issue. This time, however, Republican leaders, who had made deficits the focal point of politics in the mid-1990s, largely dismissed their importance. As then House Republican majority leader Tom DeLay put it, "The Soviet Union had a balanced budget. Well, you can raise taxes until you balance it, but the economy will go into the toilet."[20]

Deficits persisted throughout Bush's second term, a result of both the earlier massive tax cuts and spending increases. The Bush administration and Republican congressional leadership continued to push the view that lower taxes would stimulate the economy and thereby generate more revenue. Government revenues did rise during this period, but so did spending—from $2.47 trillion in the last fiscal year of Bush's first term to $2.66 trillion, $2.73 trillion, $2.98 trillion, and $3.52 trillion in the four years of Bush's second term.[21] As Figure 15.3 displays, deficits diminished for several years but then dramatically increased. Thus, despite a revenue dividend, political leaders could not agree on where in the budget to restrain spending, so they didn't, exacerbating the deficit.

In 2011, the nation's growing budget deficit produced a political crisis. The newly elected Republican Congress declared that it would not allow an increase in the debt ceiling—the amount the government is permitted to borrow. Republicans demanded that President Obama slash spending instead. Without an increase in the debt ceiling, the United States could default on its securities, producing a financial calamity. After months of negotiations, the president and Congress reached an agreement that raised the debt ceiling and reduced increases in future expenditures. The resulting Budget Control Act of 2011 (BCA) provided that if Congress and the president could not agree on a deficit reduction formula by 2013, automatic spending cuts would be imposed on most categories of federal outlays. These would be split evenly between defense and nondefense spending with some programs such as Social Security, Medicaid, and veterans' benefits exempted. The Joint Select Committee on Deficit Reduction failed to reach an agreement, thus the automatic cuts, called "sequestration," began in March 2013 with an $85 billion reduction in the government's spending authority scheduled for the fiscal year. Unless a budget agreement is reached, similar cuts will be made in fiscal years 2014 through 2021.

Despite sequestration, it is unlikely that political preferences for spending in states and districts will diminish. Everyone wants to reduce the deficit, but also says, "don't cut my project." From our rationality principle, the

20 Andrew Taylor, "With Half-Trillion in Red Ink, U.S. Inc. Looks Bad on Paper," *Congressional Quarterly Weekly*, January 17, 2004, p. 132.

21 Office of Management and Budget, http://origin.www.gpoaccess.gov/usbudget/fy11/hist.html (accessed 4/20/2011).

The Income Gap

Examined carefully, data often raise more questions than they answer. When viewing a table or figure, especially in the context of policy debates, it is usually prudent to make a list of the questions raised by the data presented rather than to accept as a given the interpretation offered by the analyst presenting the data. Take, for example, the so-called income gap that has become a major issue in contemporary American politics. As indicated by the graph below, in the last several years the share of America's income going to the richest Americans has increased, and the share going to the poorest segments of the population has decreased. Many Democrats blame Republican tax cuts for making the rich richer and the poor poorer and assert that major changes in tax policy are needed to restore a measure of equality to American society.

The Portion of Money Income Going to Each Fifth of the Population, 1929–2010*

PORTION OF INCOME
(CUMULATIVE)

● Highest fifth
● Fourth fifth
● Third fifth
● Second fifth
● Lowest fifth

These data may indicate an emergent social problem in the United States, but at least two questions would have to be answered before we can draw any meaningful conclusions from them and certainly before we can make policy recommendations. First, the data deal with portions among income groups. They do not show the absolute income of any group. It is possible that all income groups are better off today than they were in prior years.

* Data for 1929–44 are not strictly comparable to later data because of differences in calculating procedures.

...e in Constant (2010) Dollars, 1950–2010

...NDS OF
...ARS

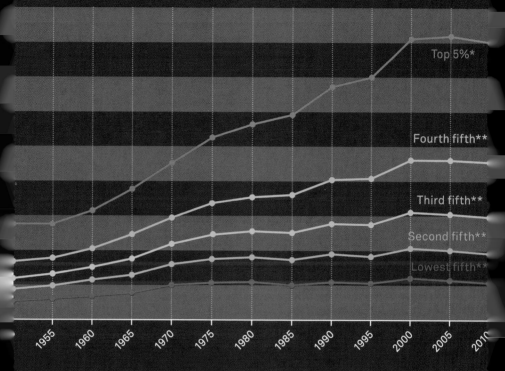

1955   1960   1965   1970   1975   1980   1985   1990   1995   2000   2005   2010

Top 5%*

Fourth fifth**

Third fifth**

Second fifth**

Lowest fifth**

*Average income   ** Income at upper limit of each fifth

...ne is better off, perhaps we do not want to change our tax policies even if they tend to incre... ...nequality. This possibility is at least partially borne out by census data. Since 1950, the aver... ...of every income group increased—though the incomes of the wealthiest Americans increased m... ...han those of any others.

...cond consideration is that the data showing a growing income gap deal with aggregates, ...ls. We cannot know from the data presented whether families are generally locked in to a partic... ...uartile or are likely to move from year to year. If the latter, then the apparent increase in inequa... ...the first table is at least mitigated by social mobility. Thus in considering the income gap, we ...onsider whether policies designed to reduce inequality might also interfere with social mobility...

:
...29–44, Allan Rosenbaum "State Government, Political Power, and Public Policy" (PhD diss., University of Chicago ...10–11; data for 1950, 2010, U.S. Census Bureau, Historical Income Tables, Table F-2, U.S. Census Bureau, Histo...

The federal deficit grew during the 1980s under President Ronald Reagan. During the 1990s, the budget deficit declined significantly but then grew dramatically in the 2000s. When was the last time that the federal budget showed a surplus? Why did the budget deficit grow so much after 2001 and after 2007?

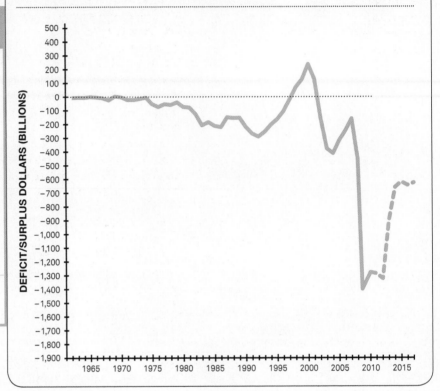

Figure 15.3

U.S. BUDGET DEFICITS AND SURPLUSES, 1962–2017*

*2012–2017 deficits are estimates (indicated with a dashed line).
SOURCE: Office of Management and Budget, table 1.1, www.whitehouse.gov/omb/budget/Historicals (accessed 2/18/13).

re-election imperative means politicians will continue to advocate on behalf of their constituents. This predilection is amplified by the ways we arrive at taxing and spending decisions (institutional principle). The first-order institutional problem is that we separate the two. Tax policy falls to the Senate Finance and House Ways and Means committees, and is administered by the Department of Treasury. Spending decisions are made by authorizing and appropriating committees in the two chambers and are administered by line agencies in the federal bureaucracy. A budget process, initiated in the 1970s to coordinate these far-flung activities, has had only limited success. In all likelihood only a massive fiscal crisis will force elected officials to broker an agreement, and this will require institutional change—major surgery, not just a Band-Aid. A harbinger of such a crisis arose in 2013, when House Republicans refused to allow a budget resolution to be brought to the floor unless it cut social spending, particularly for Obama's new health care program. This forced many federal agencies to shut down when the government's spending authority expired in October 2013. Republicans also renewed their threat to prevent an increase in the nation's debt limit, potentially producing a default. After two weeks of political struggle, however, GOP leaders calculated that public opinion had turned against them and agreed to a bill reopening the government and increasing the debt limit. In the next part of this chapter, we look more carefully at the present institutional features that affect taxing and spending.

Institutions and Policies

The budget process involves both the president and Congress. Each branch has created institutions and procedures designed to fulfill its budgetary responsibilities and to assert control over the budget process. Each branch has sought to expand the jurisdiction of its budgetary institution and to use its institution to enhance its own agenda and veto power over the budget. As we noted in Chapter 1, institutions provide political actors with authority for their policy preferences. The president and Congress use their budget institutions to promote their own budgetary preferences and priorities. The Office of Management and Budget (OMB) in the Executive Office of the President is responsible for preparing the president's budget. This budget contains the president's spending priorities and the estimated costs of the president's policy proposals. It is viewed as the starting point for the annual debate over the budget. When different parties control the presidency and Congress, the president's budget may have little influence on the budget that is ultimately adopted. Members of the president's own party also may have different priorities. The clash of objectives—between the parties and within them—happens every year.

Congress has its own budget institutions. Congress created the Congressional Budget Office (CBO) in 1974 so that it could have reliable information about the costs and economic impact of the policies it considers. At the same time, Congress created a budget process designed to establish spending priorities and to consider individual expenditures in light of the entire budget. A key element of the process is the annual budget resolution, which designates broad targets for spending. By estimating the costs of policy proposals, Congress hoped to control spending and to reduce deficits. When the congressional budget process proved unable to hold down deficits in the 1980s, Congress established stricter measures to control spending, including spending caps that limit spending on some types of programs. Even these stricter restrictions have proven ineffective. For one thing, when actual spending bills arrive on the legislative floor in violation of spending caps, appropriators seek, and often are granted, waivers of the restriction, permitting the out-of-compliance measure to be taken up. It is evident that small tweaks to the spending process are not up to the task. Whether legislators have the internal fortitude to entertain more dramatic reform is an open question.

A very large and growing proportion of the annual federal budget is **mandatory spending**, expenditures that are, in the words of the OMB, "relatively uncontrollable." Interest payments on the national debt, for example, are determined by the actual size of the national debt. Legislation has mandated payment rates for such programs as retirement under Social Security, retirement for federal employees, unemployment assistance, Medicare, and farm price supports

 mandatory spending

Federal spending that is made up of "uncontrollables," budget items that cannot be controlled through the regular budget process. Some uncontrollables, such as interest on the debt, are beyond the power of Congress because the terms of payments are set in contracts

ANALYZING
THE EVIDENCE

Spending on mandatory
programs has grown
considerably over the
past four decades. By
2022, these popular
programs are expected
to make up almost 70
percent of government
expenditures. What
drives the increase
in spending on these
programs? What are
the consequences of
mandatory spending for
government attempts to
control its budget and
budget deficit?

Figure 15.4

COMPONENTS OF MANDATORY SPENDING AS A PERCENTAGE OF FEDERAL SPENDING, 1970–2022

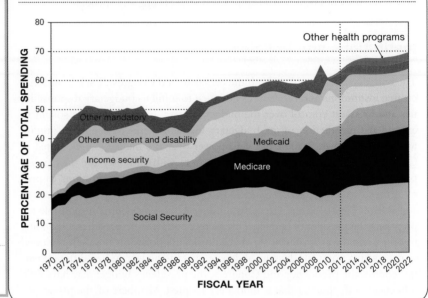

NOTE: Data for 2012–22 are estimates.
SOURCE: D. Andrew Austin and Mindy R. Levit, "Mandatory Spending since 1962," Congressional Research Service, 7-5700, March 23, 2012.

(see Figures 15.4 and 15.5). These payments increase with the cost of living; they increase as the average age of the population goes up; they increase as national and world agricultural surpluses go up. In 1970, 38.5 percent of the total federal budget was made up of these uncontrollables; in 1975, 52.5 percent fell into that category; and by 2012, around 65 percent was in the uncontrollable category. This means that the national government now has very little **discretionary spending**, which would allow it to counteract fluctuations in the business cycle.

Government spending as a fiscal policy works fairly well when deliberate deficit spending is used to stop a recession and to speed up the recovery period, as we have witnessed during the financial crisis of 2008–10. But it does not work very well in fighting inflation or deficits, because elected politicians are politically unable to make the drastic expenditure cuts necessary to balance the budget, much less to produce a budgetary surplus.

discretionary spending

Federal spending on programs that are controlled through the regular budget process

Regulation and Antitrust Policy

Americans have long been suspicious of concentrations of economic power. Federal economic regulation aims to protect the public against potential abuses

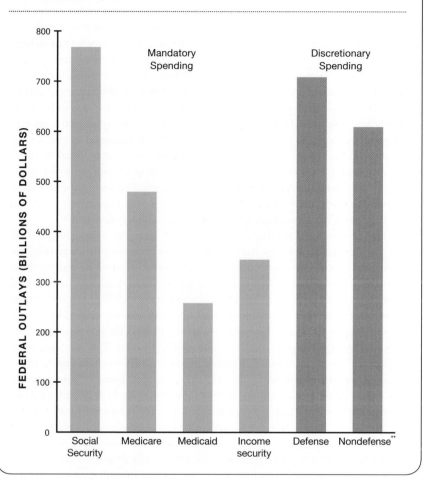

Figure 15.5

BUDGET OUTLAYS OF THE FEDERAL GOVERNMENT BY FUNCTION, 2012*

*Estimate in 2005 dollars.

**Includes appropriations for all domestic programs, for example, agriculture, transportation, labor, interior, health and human services, education, housing, and homeland security.

SOURCE: Office of Management and Budget, www.whitehouse.gov/omb/budget/Historicals (accessed 10/5/12), and D. Andrew Austin and Mindy R. Levit, "Mandatory Spending since 1962," Congressional Research Service, 7-5700, March 23, 2012.

by concentrated economic power in two ways. First, the federal government can establish conditions that govern the operation of big businesses to ensure fair competition. For example, it can require business to make information about its activities and account books available to the public. Second, the federal government can force a large business to break up into smaller companies if it finds that the company has established a monopoly. This is called **antitrust policy**. In addition to economic regulation, the federal government engages in social regulation.

 antitrust policy

Government regulation of large businesses that have established monopolies

Social regulation establishes conditions on businesses in order to protect workers, the environment, and consumers.

Federal regulatory policy was a reaction to public demands. As the American economy prospered throughout the nineteenth century, some companies grew so large that they were recognized as possessing "market power." This meant that they were powerful enough to eliminate competitors and to impose conditions on consumers rather than catering to consumer demand. The growth of billion-dollar corporations led to collusion among companies to control prices, much to the dismay of smaller businesses and ordinary consumers. Small businesses, laborers, farmers, and consumers all began to clamor for protective regulation. They faced problems in organizing, however, as the collective action principle asserts, and thus were always at a disadvantage against better-organized corporate interests. Nevertheless the states had been regulating businesses in one way or another all along, since in these geographically more concentrated locales, collective action problems were less severe. Local interest groups turned to Washington and national political entrepreneurs as economic problems appeared to be beyond the reach of the individual state governments. If markets were national and commerce interstate, there would have to be national regulation.

The first national regulatory policy was the Interstate Commerce Act of 1887, which created the first national independent regulatory commission, the Interstate Commerce Commission (ICC), designed to control the monopolistic practices of the railroads. Two years later, the Sherman Antitrust Act extended regulatory power to cover all monopolistic practices, including "trusts" or any other agreement between companies to eliminate competition. These were strengthened in 1914 with the enactment of the Federal Trade Act (creating the Federal Trade Commission, or FTC) and the Clayton Act. The only significant addition of economic regulatory policy beyond regulation of interstate trade, however, was the establishment in 1913 of the Federal Reserve System, which was given powers to regulate the banking industry along with its general monetary powers. At the same time, public demands for consumer protection led the federal government to enact a more limited number of social regulations. As mentioned earlier, Upton Sinclair's best-seller about the meatpacking industry, *The Jungle*, led to the federal meat inspection program in 1906. Two decades later, the Food and Drug Administration was set up to test and regulate products viewed as essential to public health.

The modern epoch of comprehensive national regulation began in the 1930s. Most of the regulatory programs of the 1930s were established to regulate the conduct of companies within specifically designated sectors of American industry. For example, the jurisdiction of one agency was the securities industry; the jurisdiction of another was the radio (and eventually television) industry. Another was banking. Another was coal mining; still another was agriculture. At this time, Congress also set the basic framework of American labor regulation, including the rules for collective bargaining and the minimum wage.

When Congress turned once again to regulatory policies in the 1970s, it became still bolder, moving beyond the effort to regulate specific sectors of industry toward regulating some aspect of the entire economy. The scope or jurisdiction of such agencies as the Occupational Safety and Health

Administration (OSHA), the Consumer Product Safety Commission (CPSC), and the Environmental Protection Agency (EPA) is as broad and as wide as the entire economy, indeed the entire society.

Despite occasional high-profile regulatory cases, the trend in the late 1970s was against regulation. Businesses complained about the burden of the new regulations they confronted, and many economists began to argue that excessive regulation was hurting the economy. Congress and the president responded with a wave of **deregulation**. For example, President Reagan went about the task of changing the direction of regulation by way of "presidential oversight." Shortly after taking office, he gave the OMB authority to review all executive-branch proposals for new regulations. By this means, Reagan reduced the total number of regulations issued by federal agencies, dropping the number of pages in the *Federal Register* from 74,000 in 1980 to 49,600 in 1987.[22]

However, calls for more regulation, especially for the financial services industry, surged in 2008, when weaknesses in the subprime mortgage business triggered a worldwide crisis of confidence. Banks and other companies had devised new ways of bundling individual mortgage loans into complex securities known as derivatives. Since mortgages were thought to be solid investments, the investment banks borrowed capital to purchase and resell them in high volume. As some homeowners started finding it difficult to keep up with their payments, however, the banks suddenly appeared overextended. Other investors became reluctant to lend. Congress decided it had little choice but to approve the massive rescue plan proposed by the Treasury and the Federal Reserve. But an unmistakable movement had by then taken shape for a thorough overhaul of the country's regulatory architecture of the financial system. Such an overhaul, the Dodd-Frank Act, was enacted by Congress and signed into law by President Obama in 2010, subjecting banks to tighter regulation and prohibiting them from engaging in a number of risky activities. The new law also established a consumer protection agency to oversee consumer lending and the practices of credit card issuers.

 deregulation

The policy of reducing or eliminating regulatory restraints on the conduct of individuals or private institutions

Subsidies and Contracting

Subsidies and contracting are the carrots of economic policy. Their purpose is to encourage people to do something they might not otherwise do or to get people to do more of what they are already doing. Sometimes the purpose is merely to compensate people for something done in the past.

Subsidies. **Subsidies** are simply government grants of cash or other valuable commodities, such as land. Although subsidies are often denounced as "giveaways," they have played a fundamental role in the history of government in the United States. Subsidies were the dominant form of public policy of the

subsidy

A government grant of cash or other valuable commodities, such as land, to an individual or an organization; used to promote activities desired by the government, to reward political support, or to buy off political opposition

---

22 The *Federal Register* is the daily publication of all official acts of Congress, the president, and the administrative agencies. A law or executive order is not legally binding until it is published in the *Federal Register*.

national government and the state and local governments throughout the nineteenth century. They continue to be an important category of public policy at all levels of government. The first planning document ever written for the national government, Alexander Hamilton's *Report on Manufactures*, was based almost entirely on Hamilton's assumption that American industry could be encouraged by federal subsidies and that these were not only desirable but constitutional.

The thrust of Hamilton's plan was not lost on later policy makers. Subsidies in the form of land grants were given to farmers and to railroad companies to encourage western settlement. Substantial cash subsidies have traditionally been given to shipbuilders to help build the commercial fleet and to guarantee the use of their ships as military personnel carriers in time of war. Policies using the subsidy technique continued to be plentiful in the twentieth century, despite widespread public and official hostility toward subsidies. Crop subsidies for farmers, for example, from all levels of government amounted to more than $240 billion in 2012. Of this total between $10 billion and $30 billion was distributed to more than 800,000 farmers by the U.S. Department of Agriculture. An additional $5 billion comes as an indirect subsidy in the form of federally sponsored agricultural research and collection of production data.

Politicians have always favored subsidies because subsidies can be treated as benefits that can be spread widely in response to many demands that might otherwise produce profound political conflict. Subsidies can, in other words, be used to buy off the opposition.

Contracting. Like any corporation, a government agency must purchase goods and services by contract. The law requires open bidding for a substantial proportion of these contracts because government contracts are extremely valuable to businesses in the private sector and because the opportunities and incentives for abuse surrounding contracting are very great. But contracting is more than a method of buying goods and services. Contracting is also an important technique of policy because government agencies are often authorized to use their **contracting power** as a means of encouraging corporations to improve themselves, as a means of helping to build up whole sectors of the economy, and as a means of encouraging certain desirable goals or behavior, such as equal employment opportunity. For example, the infant airline industry of the 1930s was nurtured by the national government's lucrative contracts to carry airmail. A more recent example is the use of government contracting to encourage industries, universities, and other organizations to engage in research and development on a wide range of issues in basic and applied science.

Military contracting has long been a major element in government spending. So tight was the connection between defense contractors and the federal government during the Cold War that as he was leaving office, President Eisenhower warned the nation to beware of the powerful "military-industrial complex." After the Cold War, as military spending and production declined, major defense contractors began to look for alternative business activities to supplement the reduced demand for weapons. For example, Lockheed Martin, the nation's largest defense contractor, began to bid on contracts related to welfare reform. After the terrorist attacks of 2001, however, the military budget was awash in new funds: President

---

contracting power

The power of government to set conditions on companies seeking to sell goods or services to government agencies

Bush increased the Pentagon budget by more than 7 percent a year, requesting so many weapons systems that one observer called the budget a "weapons smorgasbord."[23] Military contractors geared up to produce not only weapons for foreign warfare but also surveillance systems to enhance domestic security.

During the recent financial crisis the Obama administration, as part of its stimulus package to fight the recession, invited businesses, state and local governments, universities, and laboratories to submit "shovel-ready" and "beaker-ready" project proposals. These were funded on an expedited basis in order to generate economic activity in a timely fashion. Tens of billions of dollars were pumped into the economy in the form of contracts to repair roads and bridges, National Institutes of Health grants for research projects, Army Corps of Engineers and Reclamation Bureau activities, and so on.

The government's growing use of contractors can sometimes illustrate what we called the dark side of the principal-agent relationship. Recall that when we create institutions to solve collective action problems, we are delegating decision-making power to them. We are the principals, and our governmental institutions are the agents. Inherent in all such delegations is the possibility that the agent will not act in the interest of the principal. Legislative institutions, for example, may enact laws desired by lobbyists rather than programs demanded by public opinion. Our system of government includes numerous checks—such as frequent elections—to compel agents to pay attention to the wishes of the principals.

The principal-agent problem is compounded in the case of government contracting. Here, our agent—the U.S. Congress—has delegated power to a secondary agent, a government bureaucracy, which has, in turn, delegated power to a tertiary agent—a private contractor. Thus, the agent of the agent of our agent undertakes actions on behalf of the citizens of the United States. We often discover that these tertiary agents are hardly controlled by the bureaucracies that employ them, much less by Congress or the citizenry. Military contractors, for example, were responsible for a number of acts of violence against Iraqi civilians that helped to turn Arab opinion against the United States. President Obama has declared that the government will rely less on contractors and more on civil servants to carry out its responsibilities. The government's dependence on contractors is so great, however, that it seems unlikely that the role of these agents of our agents' agents will truly be diminished.

THE ENVIRONMENT AND THE ECONOMY

Federal interest in environmental conservation stretches back to the early 1900s, with the creation of the National Park Service and other efforts to preserve natural beauty. But it was not until the 1970s that environmental policy emerged as a major component of federal action, with the passage of new laws reaching into many aspects of the economy.

23 James Dao, "The Nation; Big Bucks Trip Up the Lean New Army," *New York Times,* February 10, 2002, sec. 4, p. 5.

Protecting the environment presents policy makers with difficult trade-offs. Compliance with environmental regulations can be very costly. Moreover, critics maintain that federal standards are sometimes too high. How clean should the air be? What is the difference between pure drinking water and safe drinking water? Who should bear the costs of providing environmental benefits? Not only do citizens, consumers, and businesses take different perspectives on these questions but the goals themselves often present a moving target. As new scientific evidence shows (or fails to find evidence for) new or suspected environmental hazards, conflicts over the proper government role emerge. And, as the collective action principle warns us, the playing field is not always level. Political entrepreneurs and public opinion are often pitted against organized interests that will bear the burdens of regulatory interventions. The balance between the competing sides is not always obvious.

Nowhere have these conflicts been more acute, and the collective action obstacles more apparent, than in the debate over climate change. A large and growing body of scientific evidence suggests that greenhouse gas emissions from cars, power plants, and other human-made sources are causing temperatures on earth to rise.[24] The projected environmental consequences are dire: melting polar ice caps, extreme weather, droughts, fire, rising sea levels, and disease. All would have profound economic consequences. Yet these projections come with considerable uncertainty: How likely are most catastrophic scenarios? Should we prepare for the most damaging outcomes or only the most likely outcomes of climate change?[25] These questions are important because the costs of transforming the world's carbon-based technologies through lower energy use and newer green technologies are enormous. These questions are especially salient for the United States, which has the world's largest economy and is responsible for 25 percent of the world's greenhouse gas emissions but has only 5 percent of the world's population.[26] And because the United States relies so heavily on fossil fuels for its energy sources, the effort to reduce carbon emission requires a major shift in how we obtain and use energy.

As scientists have learned more about the effects of human activity on the climate, the issue of climate change has risen on the national agenda. The issue attracted broad attention in 2006 with the success of former vice president Al Gore's film *An Inconvenient Truth*. In 2007, the film won an Academy Award, and Gore, along with the UN's International Panel on Climate Change, received the Nobel Peace Prize for arousing public awareness about the dangers of climate change. American public opinion reflected the growing salience of climate change as a policy issue. For example, in 2007, 84 percent of Americans reported believing

---

24 Pew Center on Global Climate Change, "Climate Change 101: The Science and Impacts," www.pewclimate.org/docUploads/101_Science_Impacts.pdf (accessed 4/20/09).

25 See the discussion in Peter R. Orszag, "Issues in Climate Change," Congressional Budget Office, November 16, 2007, www.cbo.gov/ftpdocs/88xx/doc8819/11-16 -ClimateChangeConf.pdf (accessed 4/20/09).

26 Energy Information Administration, "Greenhouse Gases, Climate Change, and Energy," www.eia.doe.gov/bookshelf/brochures/greenhouse/Chapter1.htm (accessed 4/20/09).

that human activity was at least a contributing factor in climate change.[27] In the same survey, just over half of the public said that they would support protecting the environment over stimulating the economy, while 36 percent chose the economy.[28]

When he campaigned for office in 2008, Barack Obama emphasized the need to protect the environment, backing legislation to cut greenhouse gas emissions, and called for more rapid development of renewable energy sources such as wind, solar, and geothermal. During his first months in office, Obama directed billions of dollars to the Department of Energy for a number of renewable-energy projects.

The financial crisis changed this priority. The Obama administration's fiscal support of renewable-energy projects was as much a response to economic as to environmental conditions. The administration put major environmental initiatives on a back burner. On top of that, public opinion on climate change does not rise very high on a list of environmental concerns. As a Gallup poll of early March 2011 put it, global warming is "dead last" (Table 15.2).

Table 15.2

DEGREE TO WHICH AMERICANS WORRY ABOUT ENVIRONMENTAL PROBLEMS

	GREAT DEAL/ FAIR AMOUNT (%)	NOT MUCH/ NOT AT ALL (%)
Contamination of soil and water by toxic waste	79	20
Pollution of rivers, lakes, and reservoirs	79	22
Pollution of drinking water	77	23
Air pollution	72	28
Extinction of plant and animal species	64	36
Urban sprawl and loss of open spaces	57	42
Global warming	51	48

SOURCE: http://wattsupwiththat.com/2011/gallups-public-opinion-on-global-warming-dead-last /March 3–6, 2011 (accessed 4/20/11).

27 John M. Broder and Marjorie Connelly, "Public Says Warming Is a Problem, but Remains Split on Response," *New York Times,* April 27, 2007, p. 20.

28 Broder and Connelly, "Public Says Warming Is a Problem."

Climate change action is not only a domestic collective action problem, in which proactive environmental groups must face well-organized industrial and labor groups less inclined to sacrifice their welfare for this cause; it is a *global* collective action problem as well. International efforts to combat climate change, from the Kyoto Protocol of 1997 (amended in 2012) to the failed meeting in Copenhagen, Denmark, in December 2009,[29] suffer from conflicts—between rich and poor nations, higher and lower carbon-producing nations, developing and developed nations—as well as from free-riding inclinations—nations unwilling to shoulder the burdens of reducing their carbon production while benefiting from reductions made by others.

THE POLITICS OF ECONOMIC POLICY MAKING

Addressing economic challenges and maintaining a healthy economy are extremely important to political leaders. As presidents from Herbert Hoover (who presided over the beginning of the Great Depression of the 1930s) to Jimmy Carter (who faced double-digit inflation alongside a stagnant economy—what is known as *stagflation*) discovered, voters will punish politicians for poor economic performance. Yet even though all politicians want a healthy economy, they often differ in their views about how to attain it. Moreover, politicians disagree about what the priorities of economic policy should be. Democrats and Republicans alike want to promote economic growth, but Democrats are generally more concerned about equality and unemployment than are Republicans. Republicans stress the importance of economic freedom for maintaining a healthy economy, whereas Democrats are often more willing to support economic regulation to attain social objectives. Such differences along party lines are not hard and fast divisions, however. The politics of economic policy making are also greatly influenced by economic ideas.

Until 1929, most Americans believed that government had little to do with actively managing the economy. The world was guided by the theory that the economy, if left to its own devices, would produce full employment and maximum production. This traditional view of the relationship between government and the economy crumbled in 1929 before the stark reality of the Great Depression. Some misfortune befell nearly everyone. Around 20 percent of the workforce became unemployed, and few of these individuals had any monetary resources or the old family farm to fall back on. Banks failed, wiping out the savings of millions who had been prudent enough or fortunate enough to have any. Thousands of

29 See Peter N. Spotts, "Copenhagen Global Warming Talks Suspended over Rich-Poor Divide," *Christian Science Monitor*, December 14, 2009, found at www.csmonitor.com /World/2009/1214/Copenhagen-global-warming-talks-suspended-over-rich-poor -divide (accessed 4/22/11).

businesses failed, throwing middle-class Americans on to the bread lines alongside unemployed laborers and dispossessed farmers. The Great Depression proved to Americans that imperfections in the economic system could exist.

Demands grew for the federal government to act. In Congress, some Democrats proposed that the federal government finance public works to aid the economy and put people back to work. Other members introduced legislation to provide federal grants to the states to assist their relief efforts.

When President Franklin Delano Roosevelt took office in 1933, he energetically threw the federal government into the business of fighting the Depression. He proposed a variety of temporary measures to provide federal relief and work programs. Most of the programs he proposed were to be financed by the federal government but administered by the states. In addition to these temporary measures, Roosevelt presided over the creation of several important federal programs designed to provide future economic security for Americans. The experience of the 1930s transformed public expectations about federal government involvement in the economy. Since that time, the public has held the government—and the president in particular—responsible for ensuring a healthy economy.

Presidents who preside over periods of economic downturn are generally punished by the electorate. In 1992, economic recession and relatively high levels of unemployment greatly improved the challenger Bill Clinton's presidential prospects, even though he was not widely known when he started campaigning. Clinton's campaign took as a central theme the unofficial slogan, "It's the economy, stupid." The uncertain direction of the economy made it an issue again in the 2004 presidential campaign. Anxious not to repeat his father's experience in 1992, President George W. Bush claimed in 2004 that his policies were creating new jobs and touted the benefits of his tax cuts for middle-income families. Democrats countered that Bush's policies benefited the wealthy but left most Americans economically worse off. By 2008 the economy was in a shambles, giving the Republicans little chance against Democratic challenger Obama. Despite a still-sluggish economy, President Obama was re-elected in 2012.

The groups that influence decisions about economic policy are as wide ranging as the objectives of policy. Consumer groups, environmentalists, businesses, and labor all attempt to shape economic policy. Of these groups, organized labor and business are the most consistent actors that weigh in across the spectrum of policies. In the past, organized labor was much more important in influencing economic policy than it is today. At the height of their strength in the 1950s, unions represented some 35 percent of the labor force. Today, labor unions, representing 12.5 percent of the labor force, are much less powerful in influencing economic policy. Democratic presidents continue to court labor because unions control resources and votes important to Democratic politicians, but labor's overall power has waned. On particular issues, organized labor can still exercise significant influence. For example, labor played a key role in Congress's decision to increase the minimum wage in 1996. Labor has recently sought to boost its political profile and has particularly sought to influence trade policy. The greatest growth in labor-force unionization has been among public-sector employees. They have become reliable Democratic allies, and are currently under assault by Republican governors in a number of states.

Business organizations are the most consistently powerful actors in economic policy. Business groups are most united around the goal of reducing government regulation. Organizations such as the U.S. Chamber of Commerce, which represents small business, and the Business Roundtable and the National Association of Manufacturers, which represent big business, actively worked to roll back government regulation in the 1970s and 1980s.

Making economic policy requires leaders to balance all of these competing interests as well as their own ideas about the role of government and the best solutions.

CONCLUSION: HISTORY AND OPPORTUNITY IN ECONOMIC POLICY

Increased government intervention in the economy is often brought about by the economic crises engendered by market failures such as bursting "bubbles." Such crises often are opportunities for the introduction of new programs and policies that had been rejected as misguided or too radical in normal times. During times of crisis, the iron hand of historical precedent is relaxed, and policy makers are offered opportunities to try new approaches. Thus, during the Great Depression of the 1930s, the Roosevelt administration experimented with new forms of economic policy, such as wage and price controls, that had previously been seen as inconsistent with American peacetime tradition.

As Obama took office in 2009, his chief of staff, Rahm Emanuel, called the economic crisis "an opportunity to do things you could not do before." Emanuel observed that, "You never want a serious crisis to go to waste."[30] History always matters, but at some times it matters less than at other times.

Obama's policies have been highly interventionist in dealing with the economy during a crisis. He and his predecessor, George W. Bush, have taken major ownership positions for the government in banks, insurance companies, investment houses, and automobile manufacturers. These exercises in "applied socialism" have been supported, at the end of the day, by both political parties but not without serious opposition from the Democratic left and the Republican right. In moving to protect large enterprises, either by buying their stock or taking toxic assets off their balance sheets, in order to preserve jobs or to prevent negative spillovers into the larger economy, these massive, novel undertakings have given truth to the belief that some enterprises are "too big to fail."[31] The Obama administration, Congress, and the Fed have given much attention to the

---

30 Jonathan Weisman, "Wider U.S. Interventions Would Yield Winners, Losers as Industries Realign," *Wall Street Journal*, November 20, 2008, p. A6.

31 For excellent descriptions and analysis, see Chinn and Frieden, *Lost Decades*; and Andrew Ross Sarkin, *Too Big to Fail* (New York: Viking, 2009).

matter of systemic *risk*—actions taken by a firm that might have major effects on the larger economic system—and the best ways to identify and regulate it.

For Further Reading

Selections highlighted in red are included in *Readings in American Politics: Analysis and Perspectives*, Third Edition.

Barth, James, Gerard Caprio, and Ross Levine. *Rethinking Bank Regulation*. New York: Cambridge University Press, 2005.

Chinn, Menzie, and Jeffry Frieden. *Lost Decades*. New York: Norton, 2011.

Farrier, Jasmine. *Passing the Buck: Congress, the Budget, and Deficits*. Lexington: University Press of Kentucky, 2004.

Friedman, Milton. *Capitalism and Freedom*. Chicago: University of Chicago Press, 1962.

Keynes, John Maynard. *The General Theory of Employment, Interest, and Money*. Boston: Harcourt, 1965.

Madrick, Jeff. *The Case for Big Government*. Princeton, NJ: Princeton University Press, 2008.

Meyers, Annette. *Evolution of United States Budgeting*. New York: Praeger, 2002.

Schick, Alan. *The Federal Budget*. 3rd ed. Washington, DC: Brookings Institution, 2007.

Sorkin, Andrew Ross. *Too Big to Fail*. New York: Viking, 2009.

Stanton, Thomas. *Why Some Firms Thrive While Others Fail: Governance and Management Lessons from the Crisis*. New York: Oxford University Press, 2012.

Stiglitz, Joseph. *Making Globalization Work*. New York: Norton, 2006.

Wells, Donald. *The Federal Reserve System*. Jefferson, NC: McFarland, 2004.

Wessell, David. *Red Ink: Inside the High-Stakes Politics of the Federal Budget*. New York: Crown, 2012.

16

Social Policy

In his January 2013 inaugural address, which launched his second term in office, President Barack Obama declared that the beneficiaries of social programs were not "takers" who weakened the nation by undermining Americans' sense of initiative. Instead, said Obama, social programs like Social Security, Medicare, and Medicaid "strengthen us," by making certain that all have an opportunity to share in America's prosperity.

This assertion presents a view of social policy that is at odds with the traditional American perspective. Unlike people in many other Western democracies, Americans do not have a long history of taking public responsibility for economic inequality. The United States was, in fact, one of the last Western democracies to enter this realm of social policy, for a number of reasons. First, Americans' faith in individualism was extremely strong. Second, that faith was long fed by the existence of the frontier, which was so enticing that poverty was seen as a temporary condition that could be alleviated by moving westward. Third, Americans conceived of poverty as belonging in two separate classes: the "deserving poor" and the "undeserving poor." The deserving poor were the widows, orphans, and others rendered dependent by some misfortune beyond their control, such as national disaster, injury in the course of honest labor, or the effects of war. The undeserving poor were able-bodied persons unwilling to work, transients, or others of whom, for various reasons, the community did not approve.

Until the end of the nineteenth century, government involvement in charitable activities, or what we today call *welfare*, was slight, not only because of Americans' preference for individual endeavors and private, voluntary approaches to charity but also because Americans believed that all the deserving poor would be taken care of by private efforts. Congress did enact pensions for Civil War veterans and their dependents, and for its day this was considered a generous social policy. But those pension policies were badly undercut by a patronage-ridden administration responsible for the benefits, thus damaging the system and depriving a large segment of American citizens of federal aid.[1] Congress also attempted to reach lower-income groups with policies that would eliminate child labor, and a number of states joined in with attempts to eliminate the most dangerous and unsanitary working conditions. But these efforts were soon declared unconstitutional by the Supreme Court. Other efforts, such as the experiment with mothers' pensions and additional protective labor policies, were adopted by a few progressive states. But even as late as 1928, only 11.6 percent of all relief granted in 15 of the largest cities came from public funds.[2]

The traditional approach, dominated by the private sector, with its severe distinction between deserving and undeserving poor, crumbled in 1929 in the face of the stark reality of the Great Depression. During the Depression, misfortune became widespread and private wealth shrank so drastically that private charity was out of the question. The Great Depression proved to Americans that poverty could be a result of imperfections in the economic system rather than a result of individual irresponsibility. Americans held to their distinction between the deserving and the undeserving poor but significantly altered their standard of who was deserving and who was not.

CORE OF THE ANALYSIS

 After the Great Depression and the New Deal, the national government assumed greater responsibility for social policies related to broadening opportunity and addressing poverty.

 However, because social policies are often redistributive, it can be difficult to get social issues on the government's agenda.

 Critics of social welfare policies have argued that these policies create a moral hazard by providing the wrong incentives to recipients.

 Reducing or changing the social welfare system is difficult, given the size and strength of the groups that benefit from contributory programs like Social Security and could oppose any attempt to eliminate such programs.

---

1   See Suzanne Mettler, *Divided Citizens: Gender and Federalism in New Deal Public Policy* (Ithaca, NY: Cornell University Press, 1998), p. 2. See also Theda Skocpol, *Protecting Soldiers and Mothers: The Political Origins of Social Policy in the United States* (Cambridge, MA: Harvard University Press, 1992).

2   Merle Fainsod, Lincoln Gordon, and Joseph C. Palamountain, Jr., *Government and the American Economy*, 3rd ed. (New York: Norton, 1959), p. 769, based on a WPA study by Ann E. Geddes.

Once poverty and dependency were accepted as problems inherent in the economy, a large-scale public policy approach became practical. Indeed, there was no longer any real question about whether the national government would assume a major responsibility for poverty; from that time forward, it was a question of how generous or restrictive the government was going to be about the welfare of the poor.

In 1935, Congress adopted the historic Social Security Act, which provided old-age pensions and other benefits for retired workers. As expanded over the years, Social Security programs covered the vast majority of Americans: all wage earners, temporarily unemployed workers seeking work, survivors of eligible workers, the elderly, and disabled persons. Later, Congress enacted many other social programs, most recently the massive 2010 health care act.

The grip of history and Americans' traditional views about individual responsibility and poverty were relaxed but never released by the Great Depression. As in the realm of economic policy, a crisis created opportunities for new policy directions. However, America never truly lost its historic discomfort with social policy, and the United States still spends a far lower percentage of its wealth on social programs than do other Western governments. In the United States, social spending amounts to less than 20 percent of the nation's gross domestic product (GDP). In most of the European Union, social spending accounts for nearly 30 percent of national GDPs.

WHAT IS SOCIAL POLICY?

The term *social policy* refers to programs promoting a range of public goals. The first is to protect against the risks and insecurities that most people face over the course of their lives. These include illness, disability, temporary unemployment, and the reduced earning capability that comes with old age. Most spending on social welfare in the United States goes to programs for the elderly that serve these purposes, such as Social Security and medical insurance. These are widely regarded as successful and popular programs. They are the least controversial areas of social spending, although the debates about funding Social Security reveal that even widely agreed-on policies can generate conflict.

equality of opportunity →

A universally shared American ideal, according to which all people have the freedom to use whatever talents and wealth they possess to reach their full potential

More controversial have been the other two goals of social policy: promoting **equality of opportunity** and assisting the poor. Although Americans admire the ideal of equal opportunity, there is no general agreement about what government should do to address inequalities: groups that have suffered from past inequality generally support much more extensive governmental action to promote equality of opportunity than do others. Yet most Americans favor some governmental action, especially in the area of education.

The third goal of social policy—to alleviate poverty—has long generated controversy in the United States. Americans take pride in their strong work ethic and prize the value of self-sufficiency. As a result, the majority of Americans seem to suspect that the able-bodied poor will not try to support themselves if they are offered "too much" assistance or if they receive the wrong kind. Yet there is also recognition that poverty may be the product of past inequality of opportunity. Since the 1960s, a variety of educational programs and income-assistance policies have sought to end poverty and promote equal opportunity. Much progress has been made toward these goals. However, the disproportionate rates of poverty among minorities suggest that our policies have not solved the problem of unequal opportunity. Likewise, the high rates of poverty among children challenge us to find new ways to assist the poor.

There is no way to know precisely when the government ought to be called on and what the government ought to do to help individuals secure the right to pursue their own happiness. Economic and social transformations pose new challenges and often alter public views about what government should do. In the 1930s, a deep and widespread economic depression created broad public support for new federal programs such as unemployment insurance. Today the increased number of women in the labor force and the growth in single-parent households have prompted calls for more government assistance to help people combine work and family responsibilities more effectively. At the same time growing budget deficits have led to demands for cuts in social spending. There is no agreement on how much the government should do. Likewise, as the economy has changed, inequality among working people has grown. Should the government address such inequality? If so, with what measures? When patterns of risk and opportunity are shifted, citizens make new demands, thereby placing social policy issues at the center of national politics.

The first section of this chapter deals with the politics of social policy. The second section examines policies concerned with increasing security by reducing the risk of poverty and dependence. Most of these policies come under the conventional label of "social security" or "social insurance," which concerns the *contributory* part of the welfare state. The third section of the chapter focuses on welfare or the welfare system, which is also concerned with the alleviation of poverty and dependence but is the *noncontributory*, or "means-tested" dimension—eligibility to receive benefits is based on demonstrated need. The two dimensions together—contributory and noncontributory—make up the "welfare state." This section concludes with a consideration of recent efforts to reform the system. The fourth section deals with social policies that fall outside the realm of civil rights policies but are nevertheless concerned primarily with increasing opportunities for the poor and the underprivileged. The final section is a dialogue on the welfare state, including a discussion of efforts at reform by its supporters and opponents throughout its history.

THE POLITICS OF SOCIAL POLICY

The process of forging social policy sounds like the usual noise of democratic politics: interest groups, mass opinions, political parties, and public appeals interact at all levels with representative institutions, culminating in legislation that passes into the agencies of the executive branch for implementation. However, it is important to note that many social policies are redistributive. Redistributive policies tend to be especially controversial because even small changes can have enormous consequences for large numbers of citizens. For example, a tiny increase in the tax liability of the top income earners or a tiny increase in Social Security benefits for those with the lowest incomes can result in a significant transfer of income from the upper-income brackets to the lower. Or a tiny boost or reduction in interest rates can redistribute economic opportunities, as well as hard cash, shifting them between the investing classes and the working classes. Because of their potential redistributive effect, it is extremely difficult to get social policies on the agenda of the president and Congress, who fear the wrath of negatively affected groups. For the same reason, once a social policy is adopted, it tends to remain on the statute books as though it were untouchable. This is why in recent years, despite budget deficits, social policies have often been referred to as the "third rail" of American politics. In 2011, the Republican leadership vowed to cut social spending but many of the party's legislators were reluctant to go along, fearing electoral reprisals, and by 2013 the GOP had muted its demand for such cuts.

Care should be taken here not to let the *politics* of policy making overshadow the significance of *agenda*. Policy making is the end of a long process. Chapter 6 lays out how a bill becomes a law, but before that, and just as important, is how a bill becomes a bill. Any member of Congress can propose a bill. It is read once by the presiding officer and then referred to a committee, where it can die after a long waiting period. To survive, it has to be moved up to a higher priority, the real agenda of Congress. An agenda is simply a list of things to be done. Getting on the policy agenda of a legislature or a president is difficult—and probably the most creative phase of the entire policy-making process. In this institutional context, the agenda can be seen as the current list of agreements on what to discuss and debate.

Lacking the capacity to agree on what to debate, a legislative assembly is doomed. The popular picture of representative government presents a legislature made up of representatives, all equal in having been elected from a "constituency," who debate for as long as necessary, then call for a vote on the bill. But if the legislature is to be what the name implies, a giver of the laws, it must depart from that ideal of equality among representatives and organize itself in a way that allows it to control the order of the items to be considered—which comes first, second, and third; the rules of debate and amendment; and the terms of when the debate will be closed and the vote taken. Moreover, the yea-or-nay vote after formal debate is the end process; important issues are not born in a simple two-part debate format. It is a prime function of the two major parties, probably their most important function, to compose the agenda, enforce the order of priority, control the time allotted, and provide and police the procedures governing debate and passage. None of this has anything to do with which side of the issue one is on. The two major parties have to operate in virtual unanimity to make the legislative process work, largely because the agenda requires nonpartisan, bipartisan, virtual unanimous agreement.

We may oversimplify politics and make bad judgments about political power by adding up who got what in the policies produced by government. We also have to take into account what kinds of issues are kept off the agenda and never come up for any attention whatsoever.[3] For example, it took the 1954 Supreme Court decision and 10 years of mass movements coupled with the assassination of John F. Kennedy to get the first serious civil rights bill on Congress's agenda. For another, more complex example, it takes a majority of members to get an issue of any sort assigned to a congressional committee agenda and then placed on Congress's formal agenda (the Calendar), but given the filibuster rule in the Senate, it takes a three-fifths vote (60 senators) to get it on the *real* agenda for debate and an up-or-down roll-call vote. Republicans kept many of President Bill Clinton's judicial nominees off the agenda by bottling up their names in the Senate Judiciary Committee. Democrats paid them back, keeping a number of President George W. Bush's judicial nominees off the agenda by threatening to filibuster any nominee reported from the Republican-controlled Judiciary Committee to the Senate. A lot of power is at stake in that workaday word: *agenda*.

The government's agenda is equally a presidential concern. The president's party and indeed the entire membership of Congress depend on the president to mobilize the public in support of key issues. This is part of what is sometimes called presidential initiative. As President Obama began his second term in 2013, for example, he declared that social policy would be at the top of his agenda. This declaration virtually guaranteed that the politics of social policy would become important in the coming years.

Presidential initiative is most important when the policy at issue is a redistributive social policy. This is because mass support on either side of such an issue is so much more difficult to mobilize than the support that is already mobilized and well organized by the interest groups that dominate in the regulatory and promotion field of public policy. An entire class of people is too large and too diffuse to become suddenly organized when an issue arises. This is why issues such as Social Security and welfare and income tax structure get on the national agenda only once in 10 or 20 years.

We turn now to the most important of those policies that seek to change the rules regarding (1) who shall be poor; (2) how poor the government will allow them to be; and (3) who will be provided for because they cannot work or otherwise find the means to provide for themselves. These policies together make up what we have come to call the welfare state.

---

3   A classic argument on this point is Peter Bachrach and M. S. Baratz, "Two Faces of Power," *American Political Science Review* 56, no. 4 (December 1962): 947–52. On the basis of their research, Bachrach and Baratz conclude that pluralism is not very democratic because, despite vigorous competition among interest groups and the universalization of suffrage, groups representing lower or less-respected classes do not have power because their demands rarely get on the agenda at all.

THE FOUNDATIONS OF THE SOCIAL WELFARE SYSTEM

The foundations of the American welfare system were established by the Social Security Act of 1935. Table 16.1 presents an outline of the key programs in the social welfare system.

Social Security

contributory program

A social program financed in whole or in part by taxation or other mandatory contributions by its present or future recipients. The most important example is Social Security, which is financed by a payroll tax

Social Security

A contributory welfare program into which working Americans place a percentage of their wages and from which they receive cash benefits after retirement

indexing

The process of periodically adjusting social benefits or wages to account for increases in the cost of living

Contributory programs are financed by taxation, which justifiably can be called forced savings. These contributory programs are what most people have in mind when they refer to **Social Security**, or social insurance. Under the original retirement program, Old-Age Insurance, the employer and the employee were required to pay equal amounts, which in 1937 was set at 1 percent of the first $3,000 of wages, to be deducted from the paycheck of each employee and matched by the employer. This percentage has increased over the years; the total employee contribution is now 6.2 percent on the first $113,700 of income for Social Security benefits, plus 1.45 percent on all earnings for Medicare. Individuals must pay an additional 0.9 percent on earnings over 200,000 for Medicare. Employers pay another 6.2 percent for Social Security and 1.45 percent for Medicare.[4]

Social Security is a rather conservative approach to welfare. In effect, the Federal Insurance Contributions Act (FICA) tax, as Social Security is formally known, sends a message that people cannot be trusted to save voluntarily to take care of their retirement needs. But in another sense, it is quite radical. Social Security is not real insurance: workers' contributions do not accumulate in a personal account as an annuity does. Consequently, contributors do not receive benefits in proportion to their contributions, and this means that there is a redistribution of wealth. In brief, contributory Social Security mildly redistributes wealth from higher- to lower-income people, and it significantly redistributes wealth from younger workers to older retirees. Since 1972, Social Security benefits and costs have been adjusted through **indexing**, whereby benefits paid out under contributory programs are modified annually by cost-of-living adjustments (COLAs) based on changes in the consumer price index, so that benefits increase automatically as the cost of living rises. And to pay for these automatic adjustments, Social Security taxes (contributions) also increased. These changes made Social Security, in the words of one observer, "a politically ideal program. It bridged partisan conflict by providing liberal benefits under conservative financial auspices."[5] In other words, conservatives could more

4 Social Security Administration, "OASDI and SSI Program Rates & Limits, 2013," www.socialsecurity.gov/policy/docs/quickfacts/prog_highlights/ (accessed 7/30/13).

5 Edward J. Harpham, "Fiscal Crisis and the Politics of Social Security Reform," in *The Attack on the Welfare State*, Anthony Champagne and Edward J. Harpham, eds. (Prospect Heights, IL: Waveland Press, 1984), p. 13.

Table 16.1

PUBLIC WELFARE PROGRAMS

	YEAR ENACTED	FEDERAL OUTLAYS, 2012 (IN BILLIONS OF DOLLARS)	FEDERAL OUTLAYS, 2013 ESTIMATE (IN BILLIONS OF DOLLARS)	FEDERAL OUTLAYS, 2015 ESTIMATE (IN BILLIONS OF DOLLARS)
CONTRIBUTORY				
Old-Age and Survivors Insurance; Disability Insurance (Social Security)	1935	767	811	910
Medicare	1965	549	690	647
Unemployment compensation	1935	92	80	45
NONCONTRIBUTORY				
Medicaid	1965	251	267	327
Food Stamps	1964	80	82	72
Supplemental Security Income	1974	44	51	56
National School Lunch Program (listed as Child Nutrition and Special Milk Programs)	1946	18	21	21
Temporary Assistance for Needy Families (TANF, listed as Family Support Payments to States)	1996	20	21	22

SOURCE: Office of Management and Budget, *Budget of the U.S. Government, Fiscal Year 2013, Historical Tables*, Table 11.3 www.whitehouse.gov/sites/default/files/omb/budget/fy2013/assets/hist .pdf (accessed 9/23/13).

readily yield to the demands of the well-organized and expanding constituency of elderly voters if benefit increases were guaranteed and automatic, and liberals could cement conservative support by agreeing to finance the expanded benefits through increases in the regressive Social Security tax rather than through general revenues from the more progressive income tax.

The Politics of Reforming Social Security. In 2011, nearly 55 million Americans received almost $700 billion in Social Security benefits. For more than half of all American workers, Social Security is their only pension plan. And if there were no Social Security, half of all senior citizens would be living below the poverty line.

Clearly, then, the Social Security program makes a real difference to many people's lives. The program, however, faces demographic pressure as the ratio between contributing workers and retirees has declined, from a comfortable 16 contributors to one retiree in the 1950s downward toward three contributors to one retiree today. With the record-breaking retirement of the baby boomers beginning around 2010, the ratio of contributors to workers is expected to drop even further in coming years. Fear is therefore growing in all circles that contributions today will not pay for the retirements of tomorrow. Up to now, the system has run with a surplus. But the low ratio of contributors to retirees coupled with projected higher life expectancies could stress the system—that is, without reform (see the Analyzing the Evidence unit on page 684).

Bankruptcy of Social Security will never be permitted, not only because it would be a national moment of shame but also because retired persons are already too large a class to permit it, and their political clout will be greater still as baby boomers retire. All contributions are deposited in a Social Security Trust Fund, which officially earns interest at the average level for U.S. government securities. But that is a myth. The U.S. Treasury regularly borrows money from the trust fund and leaves IOUs to hide—or soften the impression of—the true national debt in the country. Thus the Social Security system, through no fault of its own but due to the irresponsibility of successive Democratic and Republican administrations, turned out to be a pay-as-you-go program in which today's youth take care of today's aged. That is what we mean when we say that Social Security provides for the redistribution of some wealth from the young to the elderly.

Reforms to safeguard Social Security funds have been proposed but tossed aside. One idea—going back to the 1940s, when the system was just beginning to take hold—was to safeguard the reserve (the trust fund) by having the Treasury invest the contributions in *private* securities, earning interest and at the same time keeping the reserve safely away from politics and government. A more recent reform, on which Al Gore staked his 2000 presidential campaign, was simply to respect the trust fund by keeping it in interest-bearing government securities but in a "locked box," unavailable to serve as a hidden part of the national debt. Gore's position was ridiculed.

Most experts believe that social security taxes must be increased and the retirement age raised to maintain the program's solvency. When Social Security was first introduced in 1935, a retirement age of 60 seemed reasonable. Indeed, the average life expectancy for American workers was barely 60. Today, Americans can expect to live longer and healthier lives than their forebears. Rather than view increasing the national retirement age as some sort of national failure we should see it as a sign of our success.

Medicare

In February 2005, the ordinarily restrained *Congressional Quarterly* led off its cover story with this headline: "The Real Crisis Waits Its Turn: Looming Medicare Crunch Dwarfs the . . . Social Security Shortfall."[6]

Medicare was the biggest expansion in contributory programs after 1935. Established in 1965, it was set up to provide substantial medical services to elderly persons who are already eligible to receive Old-Age, Survivors, and Disability Insurance through their contributions under the original Social Security system. Like Social Security, Medicare is not means tested. (Means-tested non-contributory programs are discussed in the next section.) Medicare provides hospital insurance and allows beneficiaries to choose whether or not to participate in the government-assisted program to cover doctors' fees. A major role is given to the private health care industry by essentially limiting Medicare to the role of third-party payer. In other words, program recipients purchase all their health services in the free market, and then they or their doctors and hospitals are reimbursed by Medicare. As a result, there is little government control over the quality of the services and the level of fees that health care providers charge. That is a major reason that Medicare costs have expanded to such a great degree.

Medicare

National health insurance for the elderly and the disabled

Today, more than 45 million senior citizens are covered by Medicare. However, the spectacular increase in the cost of Medicare is only partly attributable to the growing number of participants; much of the increase is because of the rising cost of health care, whose rate has risen much more sharply than inflation. Another more recent boost in Medicare costs resulted from the 2003 drug benefit championed by the Bush administration, adding billions every year to the government's outlays (Figure 16.1).

"Obamacare." In 2010, the Obama administration brought about a major expansion of federal health care policy. The Patient Protection and Affordable Care Act, popularly known as "Obamacare," was designed to ensure that tens of millions of Americans who could not afford health insurance would have access to at least basic coverage. Among other things, the act requires individuals to maintain health insurance—the so-called individual mandate—and requires the states to establish insurance exchanges through which individuals and small employers can obtain low-cost and in some cases federally subsidized health insurance policies. The act also expands Medicaid and children's health insurance programs and imposes a number of regulations upon health care providers aimed at cutting health care costs. Indeed, the administration claimed that the new law would ultimately lower health care costs by imposing greater efficiencies on providers and reducing fraud.

The act passed despite vehement Republican opposition in Congress, who charged that Obamacare would be enormously expensive and would

---

6 "The Real Crisis Waits Its Turn," *Congressional Quarterly*, February 21, 2005, p. 446.

Fixing Social Security?

Since Franklin Delano Roosevelt signed the Social Security Act into law in 1935, millions of Americans have come to depend on monthly Social Security checks as their chief source of retirement income. Benefits are based on the number of years an individual worked and the amount of income he or she earned prior to retirement. Individuals can retire as early as age 62 and be eligible for Social Security benefits. However, the amount they receive each month increases if they delay retirement for several years. The Social Security program is funded through payroll taxes called FICA (after the Federal Insurance Contributions Act), which are collected through payroll withholding from most wage earners in the United States and matched by their employers.

As of 2011, revenues collected by FICA exceed program expenditures by nearly $50 billion per year. However, government projections indicated that by 2019 Social Security expenditures will exceed revenues and the system will gradually become unable to meet its obligations to retirees. Social Security, according to some analysts, will be "bankrupt," relegating millions of retirees to poverty.

The idea, however, that Social Security can go bankrupt is based on the mistaken assumption that Social Security is an insurance program whose revenues must meet or exceed its expenditures. Social Security is in fact a spending program funded by tax revenues. In that sense, it is the equivalent of the defense program, the farm program, or the space program. If tax revenues become inadequate to fund Social Security, Congress can increase taxes, cut spending, or shift money from other programs. Roughly speaking, it has been estimated that within 75 years the difference between Social Security revenues and expenditures will be 1 percent of the nation's GDP (perhaps $100 billion). The figure to the right looks at the impact that various policy options to address the shortfall would have.

The fact that there are so many possible options for fixing Social Security suggests that, as in so many cases, the issues are political rather than economic. Current beneficiaries and those nearing retirement firmly believe that their Social Security benefits should be untouchable and would certainly be prepared to oppose any politician or political party that dared question them. When it comes to future beneficiaries, Democrats favor approaches that reduce the benefits received by wealthier recipients such as increased taxation of benefits. Republicans, on the other hand, favor means-neutral approaches such as raising the retirement age. Some Republicans support privatizing the entire system in the form of investment accounts whose value would be linked to the market. Many of the nation's policy problems are political problems. This means that there is no neutral solution. Some would win and some would lose from one or another policy approach.

The Effect of Policy Options on Social Security Finances

POLICY OPTIONS	CHANGE IN ANNUAL BALANCE (% OF GDP) COMPARED TO CURRENT LAW			
CHANGE THE TAXATION OF EARNINGS	2020	2040	2060	2080
01. Increase the payroll tax rate by 1% in 2012	0.4			0.4
02. Increase the payroll tax rate by 2% over 20 years	0.3			0.8
03. Increase the payroll tax rate by 3% over 60 years	0.2			1.1
04. Eliminate the taxable maximum	0.8			0.4
05. Raise the taxable maximum to cover 90% of earnings	0.3			0.2
CHANGE THE BENEFIT FORMULA	2020	2040	2060	2080
06. Raise from 35 to 38 the years of earnings included in the AIME	0.1			0.1
07. Index earnings in the AIME formula to prices	0.1			0.5
08. Reduce all PIA factors by 15%	0.2			0.8
09. Reduce the top two PIA factors by roughly one-third	0.2			1.1
10. Reduce the top PIA factor by one-third	0.1			0.1
INCREASE BENEFITS FOR LOW EARNERS	2020	2040	2060	2080
11. Introduce a new poverty-related minimum benefit	−0.1			−0.5
12. Enhance low-earners' benefits on the basis of years worked	−0.2			−0.4
RAISE THE FULL RETIREMENT AGE	2020	2040	2060	2080
13. Raise the FRA to 70	0			0.6
14. Index the FRA to changes in longevity	0			0.5
REDUCE COST-OF-LIVING ADJUSTMENTS	2020	2040	2060	2080
15. Reduce COLAs by 0.5%	0.2			0.4
16. Base colas on the chained CPI-U	0.1			0.2

There are any number of ways that Social Security revenues and expenditures can be reconciled: increases in revenues (taxation), cuts in benefits, or a mix of the two. In the area graphs, an increase over time indicates that the proposed policy increases Social Security revenue (or decreases benefits) compared to current law. A decrease over time indicates that the proposed policy would decrease revenue (or increase benefits) compared to current law.

Each approach is favored by some interests and fiercely opposed by others. Thus, we see that the problem with "fixing" Social Security is political, not economic.

NOTES:
FRA = full retirement age
AIME = average indexed monthly earnings
PIA = primary insurance amount (the basic Social Security benefit)
COLA = cost of living adjustment (adjusted to account for inflation)
CPI-U = consumer price index for all urban consumers (a measure of inflation)

SOURCE:
Congressional Budget Office, *Social Security Policy Options*, July 2010.

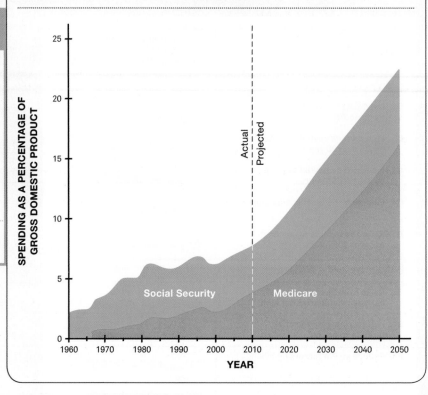

Figure 16.1

THE INCREASING COST OF ENTITLEMENT PROGRAMS

ANALYZING THE EVIDENCE

Under current eligibility requirements, federal spending on entitlement programs, particularly Medicare, will grow enormously in the future. What accounts for this growth? What are the arguments for and against the welfare state?

SPENDING AS A PERCENTAGE OF GROSS DOMESTIC PRODUCT

Actual | Projected

Social Security

Medicare

YEAR

SOURCE: Congressional Budget Office, Budget and Economic Outlook (2013).

noncontributory program

A social program that assists people based on demonstrated need rather than contributions they have made; also known as a public assistance program

Temporary Assistance for Needy Families (TANF)

Federal funds for children in families that fall below state standards of need

represent a huge expansion of the federal government's power over the lives of Americans. Republicans also feared that an enormous new entitlement program might substantially expand the Democratic Party's base of support as Social Security had in the 1930s. If millions of Americans came to depend upon government-sponsored health insurance, they would also have reason to support the political party—the Democrats—that backed the policy. And Republicans feared an expansion of the power of federal social agencies, such as the Department of Health and Human Services (HHS), they saw as bastions of Democratic influence in Washington.

Though enacted by Congress, Obamacare continues to be challenged. In 2012, the Supreme Court upheld major provisions the act, but Republicans have vowed to abolish or amend it. In 2013, the Obama administration, citing various problems, delayed implementation of a key provision of the act—the requirement that employers provide health insurance—to 2015. Republicans cited this delay as further proof that the act was unworkable, and they continued their efforts to dismantle Obamacare by stripping it of government funding.

Welfare: Means-Tested Public-Assistance Policy

Programs to which beneficiaries do not have to contribute—**noncontributory programs**—are also known as public-assistance programs, or welfare. Until 1996, the most important noncontributory program was Aid to Families with Dependent Children (AFDC, originally called Aid to Dependent Children, or ADC), which was founded in 1935 by the original Social Security Act. In 1996, Congress abolished AFDC and replaced it with the **Temporary Assistance for Needy Families (TANF)** block grant. Eligibility for public assistance is determined by **means testing**, a procedure that requires applicants to show a financial need for assistance. Between 1935 and 1965, the government created programs to provide housing assistance, school lunches, and food stamps to other needy Americans.

Like contributory programs, the noncontributory public-assistance programs made their most significant advances in the 1960s and 1970s. The largest single category of expansion was the establishment in 1965 of **Medicaid**, a program that provides extended medical services to all low-income persons who have already established eligibility through means testing under TANF. Noncontributory programs underwent another major transformation in the 1970s in the level of benefits they provided. Besides being means tested, noncontributory programs are federal rather than national; grants-in-aid are provided by the national government to the states as incentives to establish the programs (see Chapter 3). Thus from the beginning, there were considerable disparities in benefits from state to state. The national government sought to rectify the disparities in levels of old-age benefits in 1974 by creating **Supplemental Security Income (SSI)** to augment benefits for the aged, the blind, and the disabled. SSI provides uniform minimum benefits across the entire nation and includes mandatory COLAs. States are allowed to be more generous if they wish, but no state is permitted to provide benefits below the minimum level set by the national government. As a result, 25 states increased their SSI benefits to the mandated level.

The TANF program is also administered by the states, and like the old-age benefits just discussed, benefit levels vary widely from state to state. For example, in 2012 the states' monthly TANF benefits for a family varied from $216 in South Carolina to more than $1,400 in Alaska. Even the most generous TANF payments fall well below the federal poverty line, however. In 2012, the poverty level for a family of three was set at $19,090, or $1,590 a month.[7]

The number of people receiving AFDC benefits expanded in the 1970s, in part because new welfare programs had been established in the mid-1960s: Medicaid (discussed earlier) and **food stamps** (now called Supplemental Nutrition Assistance Program, or SNAP), which are now debit cards that are used to buy food at most grocery stores. These programs provide what are called

means testing

A procedure that determines eligibility for government public-assistance programs. A potential beneficiary must show a need and an inability to provide for that need

Medicaid

A federally financed, state-operated program for medical services to low-income people

Supplemental Security Income (SSI)

A program providing a minimum monthly income to people who pass a means test and are 65 years old or older, blind, or disabled. SSI is financed from general revenues that are not Social Security contributions

food stamps

The largest in-kind benefits program, administered by the Department of Agriculture, for individuals and families who satisfy a means test. Food stamps can be used to buy food at most grocery stores

---

7   David Kassabian, Anne Whitesell, and Erika Huber, "Welfare Rules Databook: State TANF Policies as of July 2011," *The Urban Institute*, August 2010, http://anfdata.urban .org/databooks/Databook%202008%20FINAL.pdf (accessed 6/10/13).

in-kind benefits

Goods and services provided to needy individuals and families by the federal government, as contrasted with cash benefits. The largest in-kind federal welfare program is food stamps

entitlement

The eligibility for benefits by virtue of a category defined by law. Categories can be changed only by legislation; deprivation of individual benefits can be determined only through due process in court

in-kind benefits—noncash goods and services that would otherwise have to be paid for in cash by the beneficiary. The possibility of receiving Medicaid benefits provided an incentive for many poor Americans to establish their eligibility for AFDC, which also established their eligibility to receive Medicaid. At the same time, the government significantly expanded its publicity efforts to encourage the dependent unemployed to establish their eligibility for these programs.

Another, more complex reason for the growth of AFDC in the 1970s was that it became more difficult for the government to terminate AFDC benefits for lack of eligibility. In the 1970 case of *Goldberg v. Kelly*, the Supreme Court held that the financial benefits of AFDC could not be revoked without due process—that is, a hearing at which evidence is presented.[8] This ruling inaugurated the concept of **entitlement**, a class of government benefits with a status similar to that of property (which, according to the Fourteenth Amendment, cannot be taken from people "without due process of law"). *Goldberg v. Kelly* did not provide that the beneficiary had a "right" to government benefits; it provided that once a person's eligibility for AFDC was established, and as long as the program was in effect, that person could not be denied benefits without due process. The decision left open the possibility that Congress could terminate the program and its benefits by passing legislation. If the welfare benefit were truly a property right, Congress would have no authority to deny it by a mere majority vote.

Thus the establishment of in-kind benefit programs and the legal obstacles involved in terminating benefits contributed to the growth of the welfare state. Together, these programs have significantly increased the security of the poor and the vulnerable and must be included in a genuine assessment of the redistributive influence and the cost of the welfare system today. It is also important to note that real federal spending on AFDC did not rise after the mid-1970s. Unlike Social Security, AFDC was not indexed to inflation; without COLAs, the value of AFDC benefits fell by more than one-third. Moreover, the largest noncontributory welfare program, Medicaid (see Table 16.1), actually devotes less than one-third of its expenditures to poor families; the rest goes to the disabled and the elderly in nursing homes.[9]

The Politics of Welfare Reform. The unpopularity of welfare led to widespread calls for reform as early as the 1960s. Public-opinion polls consistently showed that Americans disliked welfare more than any other government program. Although a series of modest reforms were implemented starting in the late 1960s, it took 30 years for Congress to enact a major transformation in the program. Why did welfare become so unpopular, and why was it so hard to reform? How has the 1996 law that replaced AFDC with TANF changed welfare?

From the 1960s to the 1990s, opinion polls consistently showed that the public viewed welfare beneficiaries as "undeserving."[10] Underlying that judgment was the belief that welfare recipients did not want to work. The Progressive

---

8 *Goldberg v. Kelly,* 397 U.S. 254 (1970).

9 See U.S. House of Representatives, Committee on Ways and Means, *Where Your Money Goes: The 1994–95 Greenbook* (Washington, DC: Brassey's, 1994), pp. 325, 802.

10 See Martin Gilens, *Why Americans Hate Welfare: Race, Media, and the Politics of Antipoverty Policy* (Chicago: University of Chicago Press, 1999), chaps. 3–4.

Era reformers who first designed AFDC wanted single mothers to stay at home with their children. Motivated by horror stories of children killed in accidents while their mothers were off working or of children tied up at home all day to keep them safe, these reformers believed that it was better for the child if the mother did not work. By the 1960s, as more women were entering the labor force and welfare rolls were rising, welfare recipients appeared in a more unfavorable light. Common criticisms charged that welfare recipients were taking advantage of the system, that they were irresponsible people who refused to work. These negative assessments were amplified by racial stereotypes. By 1973, approximately 46 percent of welfare recipients were African American. Although the majority of recipients were white, media portrayals helped create the widespread perception that the vast majority of welfare recipients were black. A careful study by Martin Gilens has shown how racial stereotypes of blacks as uncommitted to the work ethic reinforced public opposition to welfare.[11]

Despite public opposition, it proved difficult to reform welfare. Congress added modest work requirements in 1967, but little changed in the administration of welfare. A more significant reform in 1988 imposed stricter work requirements but also provided additional support services, such as child care and transportation assistance. This compromise legislation reflected a growing consensus that effective reform entailed a combination of sticks (work requirements) and carrots (extra services to make work possible). The 1988 reform also created a new system to identify absent parents (usually fathers) and enforce child-support payments.

These reforms were barely implemented when welfare rolls rose again with the recession of the early 1990s, reaching an all-time high in 1994. Sensing continuing public frustration with welfare, presidential candidate Bill Clinton vowed "to end welfare as we know it," an unusual promise for a Democrat. Once in office, Clinton found it difficult to design a plan that would provide an adequate safety net for recipients who were unable to find work. One possibility—to provide government jobs as a last resort—was rejected as too expensive. Clinton's major achievement in the welfare field was to increase the earned income tax credit. This credit allows working parents whose annual income falls below approximately $45,000 to file through their income tax return for an income supplement of up to $5,000, depending on the size of the family. It was a first step toward realizing Clinton's campaign promise to ensure that "if you work, you shouldn't be poor."

Congressional Republicans proposed a much more dramatic reform of welfare, and Clinton, faced with re-election in 1996, signed the legislation. The Personal Responsibility and Work Opportunity Reconciliation Act repealed AFDC. In place of the individual entitlement to assistance, the new law created block grants to the states and allowed states much more discretion in designing their cash-assistance programs to needy families. The new law also established time limits, restricting recipients to two years of assistance and creating a lifetime limit of five years. It imposed new work requirements on those receiving welfare, and it kept most legal immigrants from receiving benefits. The aim of the new law was to reduce welfare caseloads, promote work, and reduce out-of-wedlock births. Notably, reducing poverty was not one of its stated objectives.

---

11 Gilens, *Why Americans Hate Welfare.*

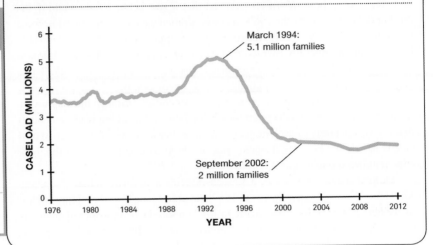

Figure 16.2

AVERAGE MONTHLY AFDC/TANF CASELOAD

ANALYZING THE EVIDENCE

Welfare caseloads dropped dramatically after 1994. What accounted for this? What are the positive and negative consequences of the policy change that reduced welfare rolls?

March 1994: 5.1 million families

September 2002: 2 million families

CASELOAD (MILLIONS)

YEAR

SOURCE: Congressional Research Service, based on data from U.S. Department of Health and Human Services.

After this law was enacted, the number of families receiving assistance dropped by 61 percent nationwide (Figure 16.2). The sharp decline in the number of recipients was widely hailed as a sign that welfare reform was working. Indeed, former welfare recipients have been more successful at finding and keeping jobs than many critics of the law predicted. The law has been less successful in other respects: researchers have found no evidence that it has helped reduce out-of-wedlock births. And critics point out that most former welfare recipients are not paid enough to pull their families out of poverty. Moreover, many families eligible for food stamps and Medicaid stopped receiving these benefits when they left the welfare rolls. The law has helped reduce welfare caseloads, but it has done little to reduce poverty.[12]

As Congress prepared to reauthorize the welfare law in 2002, two perspectives emerged. Democrats proposed changes that would make the welfare law "an antipoverty weapon."[13] They sought to increase spending on child care, allow more education and training, and relax time limits for those working and receiving welfare benefits. Republicans, by contrast, proposed stricter work requirements and advocated programs designed to promote marriage among welfare recipients.[14]

12 See the discussion of the law and the data presented in U.S. House of Representatives, Ways and Means Committee, 2000 *Greenbook*, www.gpoaccess.gov/wmprints /green/2000.html (accessed 4/16/09).

13 Robert Pear, "House Democrats Propose Making the '96 Welfare Law an Antipoverty Weapon," *New York Times*, January 24, 2002, p. A22.

14 Robin Toner, "Welfare Chief Is Hoping to Promote Marriage," *New York Times*, February 19, 2002, p. A1.

Neither party challenged the basic features of the 1996 reform. Nonetheless, as caseloads began to rise again in 2001 as a result of a recession, both sides were attentive to new problems. Because of the nation's economic downturn, welfare rolls surged in 2009, straining many state welfare budgets. To cope with the crisis, the federal government made $5 billion in stimulus funds available to the states to help meet welfare needs and extended unemployment benefits. In 2011, President Obama proposed making welfare benefits available to a larger number of poor Americans, but analysts are divided over the effects of the president's efforts.

ANALYZING THE WELFARE SYSTEM

Arguments against State Welfare

America's welfare programs have always been controversial. Let us examine some of the arguments presented by opponents and proponents of social programs:

1. The first argument is the simplest: the welfare state costs too much. The contributory programs will sooner (say the Republicans) or later (say the Democrats) come into their second or third financial crisis. But both parties agree that the crisis will come because too little account has been taken of demographic factors, with a ratio of workers to retirees approaching two to one. And that does not take into account increased life expectancy. Another factor affecting cost is the indexing of benefits to the cost-of-living index, which reflects inflation and in fact contributes to inflation.

2. A major factor contributing to cost escalation, especially in health care benefits paid by Medicare and Medicaid, was the adoption of a third-party structure of repayment. The systems that allowed doctors and patients to establish a relationship, with the fees being paid by the government, relieved doctors and patients of almost any concern about the cost of services.

3. The welfare state is too paternalistic. The contributory programs are based on forced savings, leaving all individuals with some degree of concern for their future. The noncontributory programs are also paternalistic even though it is true that people in poverty usually have no chance to save.

4. The welfare state is an example of moral hazard—the danger that a policy will encourage the behavior or bring about the problem that it is supposed to ward off. For example, many people whose cars are insured will take less care than those whose cars are uninsured to prevent their cars from being damaged or stolen. The safety net might be a moral hazard if it can be shown to weaken self-reliance and individual responsibility. That is why the sponsors of the 1996 welfare reform included "personal responsibility" in the title of the legislation. A second argument is that entitlement to benefits weakens the work incentive. Even the strong supporters of noncontributory public assistance agree that care has to be taken to keep the benefits high

enough for subsistence but not so high that people will prefer receiving benefits to taking a job. Finally, entitlement to child support, so the argument goes, "brings more babies into the world."[15]

5. The welfare system lays most of the blame for society's woes on "the system." Consequently, it removes the morality (or immorality) from poverty and relieves employers of a large part of their traditional responsibility to take care of their employees. Meanwhile, the employees to a large extent are relieved of personal responsibility.

These critiques are not subject to scientific proof or disproof. Like a good lawyer preparing a case for court, the critic of the welfare state is summoning up the best examples and the best logic available in the hopes that "the preponderance of evidence" will convince the jury—that is, the public and the policy makers. But the strength of those arguments is that they are based more on moral principles than on science and empirical demonstration.

Arguments for State Welfare

1. The welfare system is good fiscal policy. When the economy is declining, welfare payments go up enough to help maintain consumer demand. In contrast, during inflationary periods, welfare taxes take an extra bite out of consumers' dollars, thereby dampening inflation somewhat.

2. The welfare system is paternalistic. A vice to the critics of welfare, paternalism is a virtue to its supporters because it is a notorious fact that Americans don't save enough. Welfare taxation has produced a system of universal saving, which is a safety net for employers just as much as for employees. Social Security, unemployment compensation, disability benefits, and other features of contributory and noncontributory welfare have cushioned employers, especially those operating on narrow profit margins in our globalizing economy. It is no paradox that the employers who at first opposed the welfare state quickly accepted it once it was established.

3. As a consequence of the first and second arguments, many believe that the welfare system is the savior of capitalism. Every title in the original Social Security Act creating the welfare system identified a particular imperfection of capitalism and sought to cope with it: age, unemployment, widowhood, disability for injury, illness, birth defects, inadequate education or training, and so on. The welfare system is not anticapitalist. It recognizes that capitalism is neither perfect nor self-perfecting and therefore needs various deliberate, public means of dealing with its imperfections.

---

15 The strongest arguments for all these points may be those of Charles Murray, *Losing Ground: American Social Policy, 1950–1980*, 2nd ed. (New York: Basic Books, 1994); and "Does Welfare Bring More Babies?" 2nd ed. *Public Interest* 114 (Spring 1994): 17–31. Another influential critic of the welfare state is George Guilder. See his *Wealth and Poverty* (New York: Basic Books, 1981), chap. 10.

4. The welfare system lays most of the blame for society's woes on the system. In other words, it removes the morality (or immorality) from poverty and relieves employers of a large part of their traditional responsibility to take care of their employees. This is the brighter side of the "personal responsibility" complaint covered by the critics' arguments 2 and 3. Welfare-system proponents have to agree that there are many chiselers and abusers in the contributory and noncontributory parts of the system, but cheating abounds in the private sector as well and need not discredit welfare any more than it discredits business. Roughly half the people on welfare at any one time are off it within one year. It should also be noted that a large proportion of recipients of the more respectable Social Security retirement system receive far more in benefits than they contribute in taxes, especially if they live 10 or more years beyond their retirement. This gives rise to an interesting question: Which of us isn't taking welfare?[16]

5. The welfare system is politically essential. As the pro-welfare-system conservative George Will put the case:

> Two conservatives (Disraeli and Bismarck) pioneered the welfare state, and did so for impeccably conservative reasons: to reconcile the masses to the vicissitudes and hazards of a dynamic and hierarchical industrial economy. They acted on the principle of "economy of exertion," using government power judiciously to prevent less discriminating, more disruptive uses of power.[17]

In Otto von Bismarck's own words, in a speech to the Reichstag in 1899:

> I will consider it a great advantage when we have 700,000 small pensioners drawing their annuities from the state, especially if they belong to those classes who otherwise do not have much to lose by an upheaval and erroneously believe they can actually gain much by it.[18]

If this appears to be cynical, so be it. It may be difficult to sympathize in this epoch of relative prosperity and stability, but the likelihood of great social and political disorder, if not revolution, was very much on the minds of American political leaders in 1933–35, the years leading up to the passage of the Social Security Act. In the spring of 1933, for example, Secretary of Labor Frances

---

16 Ruth Rosen, "Which of Us Isn't Taking 'Welfare'?" *Los Angeles Times,* December 27, 1994, p. B5; source of data: Jan Tin, "Who Gets Assistance?" *Current Population Reports,* Household Economic Studies, series P70–58, U.S. Bureau of the Census, July 1996, www.census.gov/prod/2/pop/p70/p70–58.pdf (accessed 4/16/09).

17 George F. Will, *Statecraft as Soulcraft: What Government Does* (New York: Simon & Schuster, 1983), p. 126.

18 Quoted in Gaston V. Rimlinger, *Welfare Policy and Industrialization in Europe, America, and Russia* (New York: Wiley, 1971), p. 121.

Perkins was urged by an influential friend to leave Washington for the summer if she possibly could because of expectations of widespread violence.[19]

There is obviously no simple solution to the welfare system. Most critics and defenders make cogent arguments for their side largely because they emphasize different aspects of the beast.[20] The welfare system was not a solution in the first place. It was a series of improvisations to some challenges that every nation faces when it tries, in George Will's words, "to reconcile the masses to the . . . hazards of . . . industrial economy," especially when those come to a head as quickly as they did in the early 1930s.[21] The welfare state is an institution of many parts, and it seems no single approach to the whole will work.

HOW CAN GOVERNMENT CREATE OPPORTUNITY?

America's social programs not only supply a measure of economic security but also seek to broaden opportunity. The American belief in equality of opportunity makes such programs particularly important. Programs that provide opportunity keep people from falling into poverty, and they offer a hand up to those who are poor. At their best, opportunity policies allow all individuals to rise as high as their talents will take them. One of the most important ways the government opens opportunity is through education policies. With education, individuals from the most impoverished backgrounds can hope to improve their life chances and achieve the American dream of material success and social acceptance. Thus, education can be profoundly redistributive in its impact on society. Some programs, such as Head Start, have been specifically designed to enhance educational opportunities for poor and minority children.

Education Policies and Their Politics

Most education programs in the United States are provided by the public policies of state and local governments. What may be less obvious is that these education policies—especially the policy of universal compulsory public education—

---

19 Episode reported in Theodore J. Lowi, *The End of Liberalism: Ideology, Policy, and the Crisis of Public Authority* (New York: Norton, 1969), p. 200. For an entirely different view of the same political phenomenon, see Frances Fox Piven and Richard A. Cloward, *The New Class War: Reagan's Attack on the Welfare State and Its Consequences* (New York: Pantheon Books, 1982).

20 From the Right, one serious academic critique is Lawrence M. Mead, *The New Politics of Poverty: The Nonworking Poor in America* (New York: Basic Books, 1992). A defense of the welfare system is John E. Schwarz and Thomas J. Volgy, *The Forgotten Americans: Thirty Million Working Poor in the Land of Opportunity* (New York: Norton, 1993).

21 Will, *Statecraft as Soulcraft.*

are the most important single force in the distribution and redistribution of opportunity in America.

Compared with state and local efforts, national education policy pales. With just a few exceptions, the national government did not involve itself at all in education for the first century of its existence as an independent republic (Table 16.2). The first two of these exceptions preceded the Constitution—the Land Ordinance of 1785, followed by the Northwest Ordinance of 1787. These provided for a survey of all the public lands in the Northwest Territory and required that four of the 36 sections in each township be reserved for public schools and their maintenance. It was not until 1862, with the adoption of the Morrill Act, that Congress took a third step, establishing the land-grant colleges and universities. Later in the nineteenth century, more federal programs were created for the education of farmers and other rural residents. But the most important national education policies did not come until after World War II: the GI Bill

Table 16.2
GROWTH OF THE WELFARE SYSTEM

WELFARE	EDUCATION	HEALTH AND HOUSING
STATE ERA (1789–1935)		
Private and local charity	Northwest Ordinance (1787, federal)	Local public health ordinances
State child labor laws	Local academies	
State unemployment and injury compensation	Local public schools	
State mothers' pensions	State compulsory education laws	
	Morrill Act (1862) for land-grant colleges (federal)	
FEDERAL ERA (1935–PRESENT)		
Social Security Disability Insurance	GI Bill of Rights	Public housing
Volunteers in Service to America, Office of Economic Opportunity	National Defense Education Act (1958)	Hospital construction
	Elementary and Secondary Education Act (1965)	School lunch program
Supplemental Security Income		Food stamps
	School desegregation	Medicare
Cost-of-living adjustment (indexing)	Head Start	Medicaid
	No Child Left Behind Act (2001)	Patient Protection and Affordable Care Act

of Rights of 1944, the National Defense Education Act (NDEA) of 1958, the Elementary and Secondary Education Act (ESEA) of 1965, and various youth and adult vocational training acts since 1958. Note, however, that since the GI Bill was aimed almost entirely at postsecondary schooling, the national government did not really enter the field of elementary education until after 1957.[22]

What finally brought the national government into elementary education was embarrassment over the Soviets' beating us into space with the launching of *Sputnik*. The national policy under the NDEA was aimed specifically at improving education in science and mathematics. General federal aid for education did not come until 1965, with ESEA, which allocated funds to school districts with a substantial number of children whose families were unemployed or earning less than $2,000 a year.

President Ronald Reagan's administration signaled a new focus for federal education policy: the pursuit of higher standards. In 1983, the Department of Education issued *A Nation at Risk*, an influential report that identified low educational standards as the cause of America's declining international economic competitiveness. The report did not suggest any changes in federal policy, but it urged states to make excellence in education their primary goal. This theme was picked up again by President George H. W. Bush. Calling himself the "education president," Bush convened the nation's governors for a highly publicized retreat designed to promote the development of state educational standards. Because Republicans have historically opposed a strong federal role in education, the initiatives of Reagan and Bush remained primarily advisory. But they were influential in focusing educational reform on standards and testing, now widely practiced across the states.

Bill Clinton and George W. Bush further energized the movement for educational achievement. The standards remained voluntary, however; the federal government restricted its role to providing grants to states that developed standards programs.[23] The federal role was substantially increased by President George W. Bush's signature education act, the No Child Left Behind Act, signed in 2002, which created stronger federal requirements for testing and school accountability. It requires that every child in grades 3 through 8 be tested yearly for proficiency in math and reading. Individual schools are judged on the basis of how well their students perform on these tests. Parents whose child is in a failing school have the right to transfer the child to a better school. Students in failing schools can also get access to special funds for tutoring and summer programs. Because there was strong congressional opposition to creating a national test, the states are responsible for setting standards and devising appropriate tests.

Although there was strong bipartisan support for the program, the act was difficult to implement. Many states were unable to move to a new system of standards and testing. In addition, many education experts contend that

---

22 There were a couple of minor precedents. First was the Smith-Hughes Act of 1917, which made federal funds available to the states for vocational education at the elementary and secondary levels. Second, the Lanham Act of 1940 made federal funds available to schools in "federally impacted areas"—that is, areas with an unusually large number of government employees and/or areas where the local tax base was reduced by a large amount of government-owned property.

23 See Diane Ravitch, *National Standards in American Education: A Citizen's Guide* (Washington, DC: Brookings Institution, 1995).

yearly test results are too volatile to provide a good measure of school performance and that failing schools have been made weaker as motivated parents transferred their children out of them.[24] But the big problem was that the federal government was demanding major improvements without providing sufficient funding to pay for them. There was some embarrassment in Republican Party circles because for years Republicans had complained about "unfunded mandates" that Democratic Congresses were imposing on the states. Now they found themselves doing the same thing in the area of education.

Despite the compromises and confusions in the new program, federal money aimed at the poorest students did increase by one-third. Local educators argue it is not enough to meet the high standard the law requires, but money is at least forthcoming.

In 2011, President Obama introduced revisions in the program's testing requirements that would show fewer schools failing under the law and gave the states more leeway in the law's implementation. Critics charged that the proficiency requirement had been essentially nullified by the president.

Education: The Policy Principle in Action

In Chapter 1 we presented the policy principle, which suggests that policy is a result of political goals and ambitions played out in a context of institutional processes (ambition + institutions = policies). In the case of education, former president Bush was eager to make his mark by improving the performance of America's schoolchildren. Initially, Bush was an advocate of national testing for schoolchildren. However, there was strong opposition in the Republican Party to the idea of the national government's taking over what had traditionally been a state responsibility. As a result, Bush's signature No Child Left Behind Act required the states to set standards and develop tests of educational performance.

Initially, the states favored the new law. But soon they objected to the expensive new obligations the law placed upon their schools. Under the law, the states were required to improve student performance by providing such new services as supplemental tutoring, longer school days, and additional summer schools. By 2004, several states were refusing to implement No Child Left Behind, claiming that they could not afford to comply with the law's provisions. Several states, along with the National Education Association, sued the federal government on the grounds that Congress had not provided enough money to pay for the testing and other services required by the law, and, as noted above, the Obama administration gradually allowed the states to opt out of the requirements.

No Child Left Behind is a case in which the institutional context worked against a policy maker's ambitions. Ambition and institutions undermined policy because the institutions chosen to implement the president's program, namely the states, were not fully convinced of the value of the effort and certainly were not willing to spend their own funds to achieve the president's goals. It remains to be seen whether the Obama administration will abandon the program or

---

24 For a critique of the act's provisions, see Thomas Toch, "Bush's Big Test," *Washington Monthly,* November 2001, pp. 12–18.

will, instead, endeavor to change the program's institutional context either by providing the states with incentives to carry out federal mandates or shifting the program's administration to a federal bureaucracy.

Another controversial topic in education policy is the issue of school choice. Here again the political cleavages occur within and between the major parties, as well as within the well-established ideological groups. One issue of school choice is the simple one of permitting parents to move their children from a local public school that has been defined as failing to a public school in another district anywhere in the area. A far more controversial issue is the school-voucher movement, which calls for parents to be given vouchers to enroll their children in the school of their choice, whether public or private. The vouchers could be used to help defray the cost of tuition at a chosen private school. Supporters of vouchers claim that the public education system is too bureaucratic to provide quality education and does not give parents enough control over the education of their children. After several years of trial use, vouchers remain fairly popular in principle, but the data on their comparative success are not clear enough to provide a verdict.

Finally, there is the issue of the charter school. Charter schools are publicly funded schools that are free from the bureaucratic rules and regulations of the school district in which they are located. They are called charter schools because there must be an organization to form one, it must present its proposal to state authorities, and it must receive a charter as a kind of corporation that gives it the legal opportunity to operate. Charter schools are free to design specialized curricula and use resources in ways that their administrators think most effective. Since the creation of the first charter schools in Minnesota in 1990, states across the country have passed legislation to allow such schools. But here again, there are many charges against charter schools, as there are against vouchers, as being class biased. The fear persists that the opportunity for school choice will skim off the best students in the problem schools and thus doom those schools to continued mediocrity or failure.

We can safely predict that the politics of education policy will continue to be heated as long as the technological revolutions and globalized markets in the new economy push ahead of the education and training that schools are providing. (U.S. policy makers had a similar national curriculum crisis after World War I and yet another one after World War II, when policy makers finally got serious about equal education opportunities for minorities.) And like the politics of the welfare state, the politics of education has a redistributive component.

WHO IS POOR? WHAT CAN GOVERNMENT DO?

The federal government defines poverty as the lack of goods and services that are taken for granted by most Americans. The so-called poverty line below which individuals are seen as impoverished is annually adjusted for inflation; in 2013, the threshold was set at $19,530 for a family of three and $23,550 for a family of four. Using this criteria, nearly 50 million Americans live in poverty. These include 10 percent of the white population, 26 percent of the Hispanic population, and

27 percent of the African American population. Nearly 20 percent of America's children live in poverty. Generally, the data show that minorities, women, and children are disproportionately poor. Much of this poverty is the result of disadvantages that stem from the position of these groups in the labor market. African Americans and Latinos tend to be economically less well off than the rest of the American population. Much of this economic inequality stems from the fact that minority workers tend to have low-wage jobs. Minorities are also more likely to become unemployed and remain unemployed for longer periods of time than are white Americans. African Americans, for example, typically have experienced twice as much unemployment as other Americans. The combination of low-wage jobs and unemployment often means that minorities are less likely to have jobs that give them access to the shadow welfare state. They are more likely to fall into the precarious categories of the working poor or the nonworking poor.

In the past several decades, policy analysts have begun to talk about the "feminization of poverty," or the fact that women are more likely to be poor than men are. This problem is particularly acute for single mothers, who are more than twice as likely as the average American to fall below the poverty line. When the Social Security Act was passed in 1935, the main programs for poor women were ADC and Survivors Insurance for widows. The framers of the act believed that ADC would gradually disappear as more women became eligible for Survivors Insurance. The social model behind the Social Security Act was that of a male breadwinner with a wife and children. Women were not expected to work, and if a woman's husband died, ADC or Survivors Insurance would help her stay at home and raise her children. The framers of Social Security did not envision today's large number of single women heading families. Nor did they envision that so many women with children would be working. This combination of changes helped make AFDC (the successor to ADC) more controversial. Many people ask "Why shouldn't welfare recipients work if the majority of women who are not on welfare work?"

Controversies over the welfare state have led to adaptations in welfare policy in recent years. Similar controversies over affirmative action policies—those that partially determine "who shall be poor"—have led to gradual changes in civil rights policies. But although the problems of rights in America are agonizing, we can look at them optimistically. The United States has a long way to go before it constructs a truly just, "equally protected" society. But it has also come very far in a relatively short time. Groups pressing for equality have been able to use government to change a variety of discriminatory practices. The federal government has become an active partner in ensuring civil rights and political equality. All explicit de jure barriers to minorities have been dismantled. Many de facto barriers have also been dismantled, and thousands upon thousands of new opportunities have been created.

James Madison set the tone for this chapter in *Federalist 51*, in prose that has more the character of poetry:

> Justice is the end of government
> It is the end of civil society
> It ever has been and ever will be pursued
> Until it be obtained,
> Or until liberty be lost in the pursuit.

Equality of opportunity has produced unequal results, and the unequal results of one generation can be visited upon later generations. Considerable inequality is accepted unless the advantages are maintained through laws and rules that favor those already in positions of power and through prejudices that tend to develop against any group that has long been on the lower rungs of society. Yet efforts to reduce the inequalities or eliminate the consequences of prejudice can produce their own injustices if government intervention is poorly planned or too heavy-handed.

CONCLUSION: HISTORY VERSUS COLLECTIVE ACTION IN SOCIAL POLICY

Social policy is a realm in which history and collective action are frequently at odds with one another. Alleviation, or even amelioration, of poverty in the United States would require an enormous collective effort to expand welfare, educational, health care, and other programs. Americans, though, have qualms about the desirability of such an effort. Although we certainly do not want our fellow citizens to be poor, hungry, and uneducated, our history and traditional views tell us that poverty is alleviated through individual rather than collective effort. The story of impoverished immigrants rising "from rags to riches" is deeply ingrained in our psyches. The notion of America as a land of opportunity where any hard-working and deserving individual can succeed implies that those who do not succeed are neither hardworking nor deserving. Even as President Barack Obama avers that we should do more in the realm of social policy, his own family history signals to millions of Americans that individual self-help is still the key to success in America. Thus, history and collective action are often at war in America's social policy arena. Our history tells us that anyone can succeed in America. Our eyes and ears tell us that many do not succeed on their own and require the rest of us to help them, but what kind and how much help should government provide?

The severe economic recession that began with the collapse of the housing bubble in 2008 and continued with a financial crisis and the bankruptcy of a number of major corporations such as the venerable Chrysler, has led more and more Americans to turn to the national government for help. The Obama administration has launched new initiatives in health care and other arenas of social policy that expand the welfare state. Americans continue to be inspired by the idea of rugged individualism, but when they lose their jobs and their health insurance they turn to the government. Just as there are no atheists in foxholes, there are no rugged individualists in the unemployment line.

For Further Reading

Selections highlighted in red are included in *Readings in American Politics: Analysis and Perspectives*, Third Edition.

Bartels, Larry M. *Unequal Democracy: The Political Economy of the New Gilded Age*. Princeton, NJ: Princeton University Press, 2008.

Baumgartner, Frank R., and Bryan D. Jones. *Agendas and Instability in American Politics*. 2nd ed. Chicago: University of Chicago Press, 2009.

Collins, Jane L., and Victoria Mayes. *Both Hands Tied: Welfare Reform and the Race to the Bottom in the Low-Wage Labor Market*. Chicago: University of Chicago Press, 2010.

Gilbert, Neil. *Transformation of the Welfare State*. New York: Oxford University Press, 2004.

Hacker, Jacob. *The Divided Welfare State: The Battle over Public and Private Social Benefits in the United States*. New York: Cambridge University Press, 2002.

Levi, Margaret. "Organizing Power: The Prospects for an American Labor Movement." *Perspectives on Politics* (March 2003): 45–68.

McCarty, Nolan, Keith Poole, and Howard Rosenthal. *Polarized America: The Dance of Unequal Riches*. Cambridge, MA: MIT Press, 2006.

Mettler, Suzanne. *The Submerged State: How Invisible Government Policies Undermine American Democracy*. Chicago: University of Chicago Press, 2011.

Murray, Charles. *In Our Hands: A Plan to Remake the Welfare State*. Washington, DC: American Enterprise Institute Press, 2006.

Ravitch, Diane. *The Death and Life of the Great American School System*. New York: Basic Books, 2011.

Shipler, David. *The Working Poor*. New York: Vintage, 2005.

Skocpol, Theda. *The Missing Middle: Working Families and the Future of American Social-Policy*. New York: Norton, 2000.

Starr, Paul. *Remedy and Reaction: The Peculiar American Struggle over Health Care Reform*. New Haven, CT: Yale University Press, 2011.

Trattner, Walter. *From Poor Law to Welfare State*. 6th ed. New York: Free Press, 1998.

Weir, Margaret, ed. *The Social Divide: Political Parties and the Future of Activist Government*. Washington, DC: Brookings Institution, 1998.

17

Foreign Policy

Accomplishing any policy goal requires collective action, but in the arena of foreign policy, in particular, we expect Americans to accept the need for collective effort on behalf of the "national interest." Questions of the collective or national interest figure more prominently in the foreign policy arena than in most domestic policy debates. For instance, Americans are expected to shoulder the enormous tax burdens associated with our nation's huge military forces. To be sure, advocates of competing social and economic policies argue that their preferred programs promote the interests of the nation as a whole. Yet such pronouncements are usually taken with a grain of salt, as the preferred economic or social policies advocated by particular groups usually turn out to serve discrete constituencies rather than the entire nation.

In the realm of foreign policy, though, the collective interest looms larger. In a world where entities ranging from rival nation states to shadowy terrorist groups present genuine threats to the security of the entire nation, advocates of particular foreign policies are more likely than their domestic counterparts to be asked to demonstrate that the policies they espouse serve broad national interests. In foreign policy, unlike, say, health care reform, advocates can and do accuse each other of threatening the nation's security and demonstrating outright disloyalty.

An old American adage asserts that "politics stops at the water's edge." The point of this saying is that if we fail to work together to protect our nation's political, economic, and security interests in the wider world, we will all suffer. However, this does not mean that collective action problems don't arise in the foreign policy realm. All Americans benefit from policies that effectively safeguard the nation's security. But Americans may not all agree on the most effective national security programs—or who should pay for them. Indeed, national security is the quintessential public good. If the nation is safe, we all benefit, and each individual's contribution to the nation's security is slight. Hence, many Americans hope that someone else will shoulder the tax burdens and make the other sacrifices needed to maintain the nation's security.

Also, as in other policy areas, when it comes to foreign policy, history matters. Foreign policy is often influenced by historical events, experiences, and commitments. Debates over foreign policy tend to be strongly affected by competing historical perceptions. For example, those who argue in favor of confronting Iran, North Korea, and other potentially hostile powers often refer to the disastrous consequences of pre–World War II efforts by Britain and France to appease Nazi Germany. On the other hand, those who favored quickly withdrawing American forces from Iraq following the war launched in 2003 cited the parallels to America's failed efforts in Vietnam. Each group's view of the present is strongly shaped by its understanding of the past.

The foreign policy arena is also affected by America's historic wariness of foreign commitments and the difficulties of making and justifying what are often cold, harsh, calculating foreign policy decisions in the context of America's historic commitment to liberal democracy. Ever since George Washington, in his Farewell Address, warned the American people "to have . . . as little political connection as possible" to foreign nations and to "steer clear of permanent alliances," Americans have been distrustful of foreign policy. Though America has been a great world power for more than 60 years, many Americans continue to agree with Washington that we should tend to our own affairs and leave other nations to their own devices. Doubt about ongoing foreign commitments may be one reason why many Americans question U.S. participation in the United Nations.[1]

The term *foreign policy* refers to the programs and policies that determine America's relations with other nations and foreign entities. Foreign policy includes diplomacy, military and security policy, international human rights policies, and various forms of economic policy, such as trade policy and international energy policy. Of course, foreign policy and domestic policy are not completely separate

CORE OF THE ANALYSIS

 The goals of American foreign policy include security, economic prosperity, and—to a lesser extent—humanitarian objectives.

 Foreign policy is shaped by domestic actors—including the president, the bureaucracy, Congress, and interest groups—and through strategic interactions with foreign actors.

 The instruments that the government uses to implement foreign policy may include economic, diplomatic, institutional, or military means. These instruments are deployed strategically to serve the interests of the United States.

---

1 Alynna Lyon, "Rejecting One's Protégé? American Media, Public Opinion and the United Nations" (paper presented to the annual meeting of the International Studies Association, San Francisco, March 26, 2008).

categories but are instead closely intertwined. Take security policy, for example. Defending the nation requires the design and manufacture of tens of billions of dollars worth of military hardware. The manufacture and procurement of this military equipment involves a host of economic policies, and paying for it shapes America's fiscal policies. In 2013 an unexpected link between foreign and domestic policy came to light. Leaks revealed that in its efforts to thwart foreign terrorists, the National Security Agency (NSA) had eavesdropped on millions of communications by ordinary American citizens. This revelation sparked a debate on the proper balance between privacy and security.

Many of the basic contours of the foreign policy arena are similar to those of America's other policy domains. The nation's chief foreign policy makers are the president, Congress, and the bureaucracy. Just as in economic and social policy, battles over foreign policy often erupt among and within these institutions as competing politicians and a variety of organized groups and rival political forces pursue their own versions of the national interest or their own narrower purposes, which they seek to present as the national interest.

In this chapter, we first examine the main goals and purposes of American foreign policy. We then discuss the actors and institutions that shape foreign policy. Next, we analyze the instruments that policy makers have at their disposal to implement foreign policy.

THE GOALS OF FOREIGN POLICY

Although U.S. foreign policy has a number of purposes, three main goals stand out. These are security, prosperity, and the creation of a better world. These goals are, of course, closely intertwined and can never be pursued fully in isolation from one another.

Security

To many Americans, the chief purpose of the nation's foreign policy is protection of America's security in an often hostile world. Traditionally, the United States has been concerned about threats that might emanate from other nations, such as Nazi Germany during the 1940s and then Soviet Russia until the Soviet Union's collapse in the late 1980s. Today, American security policy is concerned not only with the actions of other nations but also with the activities of terrorist groups and other hostile **non-state actors**.[2] To protect the nation's security from foreign threats, the United States has built an enormous military apparatus and a complex array of intelligence-gathering institutions, such as the Central

non-state actor

A group other than a nation-state that attempts to play a role in the international system. Terrorist groups are one type of non-state actor

---

2 Rupert Smith, *The Utility of Force: The Art of War in the Modern World* (New York: Vintage, 2008).

Intelligence Agency (CIA), charged with evaluating and anticipating challenges from abroad.[3] While all nations are concerned with security, American power and global commitments give U.S. foreign policy a unique focus on security issues.

Security is, of course, a broad term. Policy makers must be concerned with Americans' physical security. The September 11 terrorist attacks killed and injured thousands of Americans, and the government constantly fears that new attacks could be even more catastrophic. Policy makers must also be concerned with such matters as the security of America's food supplies, transportation infrastructure, and energy supplies. Many of our foreign policy efforts in the Middle East, for example, are aimed at ensuring continuing American access to vital oil fields. In recent years, cyberspace has become a new security concern. The nation's dependence on computers means that the government must be alert to efforts by hostile governments, groups, or even individual "hackers" to damage computer networks.

During the eighteenth and nineteenth centuries, the United States believed that its security was based on its geographic isolation. We were separated by two oceans from European and Asian powers, and many Americans thought that our security would be best preserved by remaining aloof from international power struggles. This policy was known as **isolationism**. In his 1796 farewell address, President George Washington warned Americans to avoid permanent alliances with foreign powers, and in 1823, President James Monroe warned foreign powers not to meddle in the Western Hemisphere. Washington's warning and what came to be called the Monroe Doctrine were the cornerstones of U.S. foreign policy of isolationism until the end of the nineteenth century. The United States saw itself as the dominant power in the Western Hemisphere and, indeed, believed that its "manifest destiny" was to expand from sea to sea. The rest of the world, however, should remain at arm's length.

In the twentieth century, technology made oceans less of a barrier to foreign threats, and the world's growing economic interdependence meant that the United States could no longer ignore events abroad. At the beginning of the twentieth century, despite its isolationist sentiments, the United States entered World War I on the side of Great Britain and France when the Wilson administration concluded that America's economic and security interests would be adversely affected by a German victory. In 1941, America was drawn into World War II when Japan attacked the U.S. Pacific fleet anchored at Pearl Harbor, Hawaii. Even before the Japanese attack forced America to fight, the Roosevelt administration had already concluded that the United States must act to prevent a victory by the German-Japanese-Italian Axis alliance. Until the Japanese attack, however, President Franklin Delano Roosevelt had not been able to overcome proponents of American isolationism, who declared that our security was best served by leaving foreigners to their own devices. With their attack, the Japanese proved that the Pacific Ocean could not protect the United States from foreign foes and effectively discredited isolationism as a security policy.

 isolationism

The desire to avoid involvement in the affairs of other nations

---

3   D. Robert Worley, *Shaping U.S. Military Forces: Revolution or Relevance in a Post–Cold War World* (Westport, CT: Praeger Security International, 2006).

Containment and Deterrence during the Cold War.

In the aftermath of World War II, the United States developed a new security policy known as **containment** to check the growing power of the Soviet Union. This policy was articulated by George F. Kennan, Director of Policy Planning at the State Department, who said the United States must contain the Soviet Union's expansionist tendencies with the patient application of counter-pressure where the Soviets sought to expand their geopolitical sphere.

By the end of the 1940s, the Soviets had built a huge empire and enormous military forces. Most threatening of all, the Soviet Union had built nuclear weapons and intercontinental bombers capable of attacking the United States. The United States was committed to maintaining its own military might as a means of **deterrence**, to discourage the Soviets from attacking the United States or its allies. Containment and deterrence remained the cornerstone of American policy towards the Soviet Union for the duration of the Cold War. Some Americans argued that we should attack the Soviets before it was too late. This policy is known as **preventive war**. Others said that we should show our peaceful intentions and attempt to placate the Soviets. This policy is called **appeasement**.

The policies that the United States actually adopted, deterrence and containment, could be seen as midway between preventive war and appeasement. A nation pursuing a policy of deterrence, on the one hand, signals its peaceful intentions, but on the other hand indicates its willingness and ability to fight if attacked. Thus, during the era of confrontation with the Soviet Union, known as the **Cold War**, the United States frequently asserted that it had no intention of attacking the Soviet Union. At the same time, however, the United States built a huge military force, including an arsenal of nuclear weapons and intercontinental missiles, and frequently asserted that in the event of a Soviet attack, it had the ability and will to respond with overwhelming force. The Soviet Union announced that its nuclear weapons were also intended for deterrent purposes. Eventually the two sides possessed such enormous arsenals of nuclear missiles that each potentially had the ability to destroy the other in the event of war. This heavily armed standoff came to be called a posture of mutually assured destruction. During the 1962 "Cuban missile crisis," the United States and the USSR came to the brink of war when President Kennedy declared that the Soviet Union must remove its nuclear missiles from Cuba and threatened to use force if the Soviets refused. After an extremely intense several weeks, the crisis was defused by a negotiated compromise in which the Soviets agreed to remove their missiles in exchange for a U.S. guarantee that it would not invade Cuba. The two superpowers had come so close to nuclear war that the leaders of both nations sought ways of reducing tensions. This effort led to a period of détente in which a number of arms control agreements were signed and the threat of war was reduced.

A policy of deterrence not only requires the possession of large military forces but also requires that the nation pursuing such a policy convince potential adversaries that it is willing to fight. France had a large army in the 1930s, but Nazi Germany was not deterred from pursuing its expansionist goals in Europe because the German chancellor, Adolf Hitler, did not believe that the French were actually willing to fight. Thus, as part of its policy of deterrence, the United States engaged in wars in Korea, Vietnam, and elsewhere in response

---

containment ⇨

A policy designed to curtail the political and military expansion of a hostile power

deterrence ⇨

The development and maintenance of military strength as a means of discouraging attack

preventive war ⇨

The policy of striking first when a nation fears that a foreign foe is contemplating hostile action

appeasement ⇨

The effort to forestall war by giving in to the demands of a hostile power

Cold War ⇨

The period of struggle between the United States and the former Soviet Union between the late 1940s and about 1990 to what it believed to be Soviet aggression. Though the United States had no particular interests in Korea or Vietnam, American policy makers believed that if the United States did not fight in these areas, the Soviets would be emboldened to pursue an expansionist policy elsewhere, thinking that the Americans would not respond. Interventions in Korea and Vietnam were also justified by the so-called Truman Doctrine, which called for American assistance to any nation threatened by the Soviet Union and its allies.

The dissolution of the Soviet Union began in 1985, and the final collapse occurred in 1991, partly because its huge military expenditures undermined its creaky and inefficient centrally planned economy. The new Russia, though still a formidable and sometimes unfriendly power, seemed to pose less of a threat to the United States. Americans celebrated the end of the Cold War and believed that the enormous expense of America's own military forces might be reduced. Within a few years of the Soviet collapse, however, a new set of security threats emerged, requiring new policy responses. The September 11 terrorist attacks demonstrated a threat against which some security scholars had long warned. The threat was that non-state actors and so-called rogue states might acquire significant military capabilities, including nuclear weapons, and would not be affected by America's deterrent capabilities.

New Security Threats. A policy of deterrence assumes certainty and rationality. Certainty means that a potential adversary must know for sure that the United States will reply with force if attacked. Rationality means that, to be deterred, a potential adversary must be capable of rationally assessing the risks and costs of aggression against the United States. These two assumptions, which were valid when we faced the Soviet Union, may not be appropriate in the face of contemporary security threats. Unlike **nation-states**, countries with governments and fixed borders, terrorist groups are non-state actors having no fixed geographic location that can be attacked. Terrorists may believe that they can attack and melt away, leaving the United States with no one against whom to retaliate. Hence, the threat of massive retaliation does not deter them. Rogue states are nations with unstable and erratic leaders who seem to pursue policies driven by ideological or religious fervor rather than careful consideration of economic or human costs. The United States considers North Korea and Iran to be rogue states.

To counter these new security threats, the George W. Bush administration shifted from a policy of deterrence to one of **preemption**. Preemption is often used as another name for preventive war or willingness to strike first in order to prevent an enemy attack. The United States declared that it would not wait to be attacked but would, if necessary, take action to disable terrorist groups and rogue states before they could do us harm. The Bush administration's "global war on terror" is an expression of this notion of preemption, as was the U.S. invasion of Iraq. The United States has also refused to rule out the possibility that it would attack North Korea or Iran if it deemed those nations' nuclear programs to be an imminent threat to American security interests. Accompanying this shift in military doctrines has been an enormous increase in overall U.S. military spending (see the Analyzing the Evidence unit on the following page).

 nation-state

A political entity consisting of a people with some common cultural experience (nation) who also share a common political authority (state), recognized by other sovereignties (nation-states)

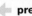 **preemption**

The willingness to strike first in order to prevent an enemy attack

Cutting Defense Spending?

Contributed by
Kenneth Mayer
University of Wisconsin

What will happen to the defense budget in the next decade? With the war in Iraq over and most troops in Afghanistan scheduled to come home by the end of 2014, defense spending will come down from the levels seen at the height of the "war on terror." That height reached $705 billion in 2011, which was twice what the United States spent on defense in 2001.

In addition, further cuts may occur as a result of the budget agreement reached during the summer of 2011, when President Obama and Congress committed to automatic cuts (sequestration) if they could not agree on long-term deficit reduction strategies. Those cuts, which are to be split between defense and nondefense discretionary spending, went into effect in 2013, and if they stay in place will require cuts of about $55 billion in the defense budget each year for the next decade.

In his 2014 budget, President Obama proposed overall defense spending of $627 billion, with declining spending through 2018, when the defense budget is projected to be $592 billion. Some of these savings will come from the continued drawdown of U.S. forces in Afghanistan, although funding for some ongoing activities in Iraq and Afghanistan (Overseas Contingency Operations) will likely continue.

Long-range defense planning is inherently uncertain, as it is difficult to identify concrete threats and to predict the likelihood of action by potential adversaries. Critics of the planned reductions (and sequester cuts) argue that the cuts will jeopardize defense capabilities. A number of expensive programs (the F-35 aircraft and ballistic missile defense especially) will put pressure on defense budgets for years to come.

U.S. Budget, 2012 (in billions of dollars)

SOURCE: Bipartisan Policy Center and Congressional Budget Office.

$252
Interest

$617
Nondefense

$2,052
Mandatory

$684
Defense

$1,301
Discretionary

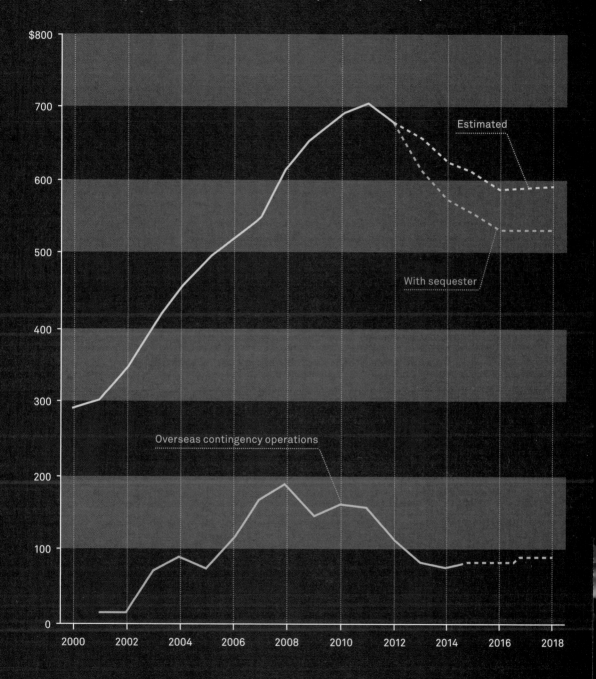

U.S. Defense Spending Fiscal Years 2000–18 (in billions of dollars)

Estimated

With sequester

Overseas contingency operations

SOURCE: FY 2014 Budget, Historical Perspectives table 3-1, Spending by Function and Subfunction; Congressional Budget Office, *Final Sequestration Report for Fiscal Year 2013* (March 2013); Congressional Budget Office, *Updated Budget Projections: Fiscal Years 2013–23* (May 2013).

After Obama was elected in 2008, his administration took a different tone, declaring that it would endeavor to establish constructive dialogues with North Korea, Iran, and other hostile states. However, Obama did not necessarily renounce the **Bush Doctrine** for those states that declined to become constructively engaged. Furthermore, President Obama did not immediately hasten the departure of American troops from Iraq and Afghanistan, as many Democrats had expected. Instead, Obama initially chose to step up America's military effort in Afghanistan and keep U.S. forces in Iraq. This policy was finally reversed, and by 2012 the United States had withdrawn all combat forces from Iraq and was bringing an end to armed engagement in Afghanistan.

Though U.S. involvement in the conflicts in Iraq and Afghanistan is finally coming to an end, U.S. foreign policy makers continue to express concern over Iran and North Korea. In 2013, the North Korean regime continued to test missiles that might soon be able to reach U.S. shores. The Obama administration responded by positioning additional antimissile batteries to protect America's west coast. For its part, Iran continued to work toward the development of a nuclear weapon, despite global economic sanctions and President Obama's repeated demands that Iranian nuclear work be halted.

Economic Prosperity

A second major goal of U.S. foreign policy is promoting American prosperity. America's international economic policies are intended to expand employment opportunities in the United States, to maintain access to foreign energy supplies at a reasonable cost, to promote foreign investment in the United States, and to lower the prices Americans pay for goods and services.

Among the most visible and important elements of U.S. international economic policy is trade policy. The promotion and advertising of American goods and services abroad is a long-standing goal of U.S. trade policy, and it is one of the major obligations of the Department of Commerce. Yet modern trade policy involves a complex arrangement of treaties, tariffs, and other mechanisms of policy formation. For example, the United States has a long-standing policy of granting **most favored nation status** to certain countries—that is, the United States offers to another country the same tariff rate it already gives to its most favored trading partner, in return for trade (and sometimes other) concessions. In 1998, to avoid any suggestion that "most favored nation" implied some special relationship with an undemocratic country (China, for example), President Clinton changed the term from "most favored nation" to "normal trade relations."[4]

The most important international organization for promoting trade is the **World Trade Organization (WTO)**, which officially came into being in 1995.

Bush Doctrine

Foreign policy based on the idea that the United States should take preemptive action against threats to its national security

most favored nation status

An agreement to offer a trading partner the lowest tariff rate offered to other trading partners

World Trade Organization (WTO)

An international group promoting free trade that grew out of the General Agreement on Tariffs and Trade

4 This was done quietly in an amendment to the Internal Revenue Service Reform Act (PL 105–206), June 22, 1998. But it was not accomplished easily. See Bob Gravely, "Normal Trade with China Wins Approval," *Congressional Quarterly Weekly Report*, July 25, 1998; and Richard Dunham, "MFN by Any Other Name Is . . . NTR?," *Business Week* online news flash, June 19, 1997.

The WTO grew out of the **General Agreement on Tariffs and Trade (GATT)**. Since World War II, the GATT has brought together a wide range of nations for regular negotiations designed to reduce barriers to trade. Such barriers, many believed, contributed to the breakdown of the world economy in the 1930s and helped to cause World War II. The WTO has 159 members worldwide, including the United States. Similar policy goals are pursued in regional arrangements, such as the **North American Free Trade Agreement (NAFTA)**, a trade treaty among the United States, Canada, and Mexico.

Working toward freer trade has been an important goal of each presidential administration since World War II. Yet as globalization has advanced, concerns about free trade and about the operation of the WTO, in particular, have grown. Critics believe that the WTO does not pay sufficient attention to the concerns of developing nations and to such issues as environmental degradation, human rights, and labor practices, including the use of child labor in many countries. In recent years, the major problem in WTO negotiations has been conflicts between poor, developing nations and rich, developed countries. Countries in the developing world as well as some critics in the developed world accuse the United States and Europe of hypocrisy, preaching free trade but then using patents and subsidies to protect their own markets. There have been some successes on these issues, notably new WTO guidelines that allow poor countries to override expensive patents. Such patents make desperately needed drugs unavailable to most of the developing world. It has been more difficult to reach agreement on agricultural subsidies. Both the United States and Europe provide massive subsidies to their own agricultural industries. The prospects for resolving this issue are dim. The developed world has been reluctant to confront the economic dislocations and political costs of reducing the subsidies.

For over a half-century, the United States has led the world in supporting free trade as the best route to growth and prosperity. Yet the American government, too, has sought to protect domestic industry when it is politically necessary. Subsidies, as we have seen, have long boosted American agriculture, artificially lowering the price of American products on world markets. In 2002, President George W. Bush, a vocal advocate of free trade, angered the rest of the world when he imposed protective tariffs on imported steel. Accused of hypocrisy and faced with retaliation from trading partners, the administration defended its actions by pointing to the damage that imports were doing to the domestic steel industry. When the WTO ruled that the steel tariffs violated WTO rules, Bush faced an unhappy choice. He could allow the European Union to retaliate by imposing tariffs, many of them on goods produced in politically important states, or he could lift the tariffs, thus angering steel producers and workers. The president chose to lift the steel tariffs.

Trade was also an issue in the 2012 election. Throughout the campaign, the Republican candidate, Mitt Romney, accused President Obama of remaining silent as hundreds of thousands of American factory jobs disappeared in the face of what he called China's unfair trade practices. "It's time to stand up to the cheaters," Romney campaign ads declared. For its part, the Obama campaign charged that Romney had run a private equity firm that invested in a Chinese firm that exploited low-wage labor and cost Americans their jobs.

 General Agreement on Tariffs and Trade (GATT)

An international trade organization, in existence from 1947 to 1995, that set many of the rules governing international trade

 North American Free Trade Agreement (NAFTA)

A trade treaty among the United States, Canada, and Mexico to lower and eliminate tariffs among the three countries

International Humanitarian Policies

A third goal of American policy is to make the world a better place for all its inhabitants. The main forms of policy that address this goal are international environmental policy, international human rights policy, and international peacekeeping. America's wealth often makes the United States the major source of funding for such endeavors. The United States also contributes to international organizations such as the World Health Organization that work for global health and against hunger. These policies are often seen as secondary to the other goals of American foreign policy, forced to give way if they interfere with security or foreign economic policy. Moreover, although the United States spends billions annually on security policy and hundreds of millions on trade policy, we spend relatively little on environmental, human rights, and peacekeeping efforts. Some critics charge that America has the wrong priorities, spending far more to make war than to protect human rights and the global environment. Nevertheless, a number of important American foreign policy efforts are, at least in part, designed to make the world a better place.

In the realm of international environmental policy, the United States supports a number of international efforts to protect the environment. These include the United Nations Framework Convention on Climate Change, an international agreement to study and ameliorate harmful changes in the global environment, and the Montreal Protocol, an agreement signed by more than 150 countries to limit the production of substances potentially harmful to the world's ozone layer. Other nations have severely criticized the United States for withdrawing from the 1997 Kyoto Protocol, an agreement setting limits on emissions of greenhouse gases from industrial countries. The United States has asserted that the Kyoto Protocol would be harmful to American economic interests. Although the United States is concerned with the global environment, national economic interests took precedence in this case. In preparation for the expiration of the Kyoto agreement at the end of 2012, world leaders gathered in Copenhagen, Denmark, in 2009 to begin the process of negotiating a new climate treaty. The Copenhagen climate summit, however, failed to produce a binding international agreement and ended with the United States, Europe, and China blaming one another for the lack of concrete results.

The same national priorities seem apparent in the area of human rights policy. The United States has a long-standing commitment to human rights and is a signatory to many major international agreements concerning human rights. These include the International Covenant on Civil and Political Rights, the International Convention against Torture, the Convention on the Elimination of All Forms of Racial Discrimination, and various agreements to protect children. The State Department's Bureau of Democracy, Human Rights, and Labor works cooperatively with international organizations to investigate and focus attention on human rights abuses. In 1998, the United States enacted the International Religious Freedom Act, which calls on all governments to respect religious freedom. The act lists a number of sanctions that the United States and other signatories may employ to punish nations found to be in violation.

Although the United States is committed to promoting human rights, this commitment has a lower priority in American foreign policy than the nation's security concerns and economic interests. Thus, the United States is likely to overlook human rights violations by its major trading partners, such as China, and remain silent in the face of human rights violations by such allies as Saudi Arabia. Nevertheless, human rights concerns do play a role in American foreign policy. For example, beginning in 2007, the United States has made available several million dollars annually in small grants to pay medical and legal expenses incurred by individuals who have been the victims of retaliation in their own countries for working against their governments' repressive practices. In this small way, the United States is backing its often-asserted principles.

Another form of U.S. policy designed to improve the condition of the world is support for international peacekeeping efforts. At any point in time, a number of border wars, civil wars, and guerrilla conflicts flare somewhere in the world, usually in its poorer regions. These wars often generate humanitarian crises in the form of casualties, disease, and refugees. In cooperation with international agencies and other nations, the United States funds a number of efforts to keep the peace in volatile regions and to deal with the health care and refugee problems associated with conflict. In 2007, the United States provided more than $1 billion in funding for United Nations peacekeeping operations in Bosnia, Kosovo, Sierra Leone, Lebanon, the Democratic Republic of Congo, and East Timor. As the world's wealthiest nation, the United States also recognizes an obligation to render assistance to nations facing crises and emergencies. In 2010, for example, the United States sent medical aid, food relief, and rescue teams to Haiti when that impoverished island nation was struck by a devastating earthquake. In 2011, the United States backed a NATO effort to support rebel forces seeking to overthrow Libyan leader Mu'ammar Qaddafi. In 2012, the United States offered sympathy, but not support, to antigovernment forces in Syria. As the civil war in Syria dragged on and the world learned that the Syrian government had used chemical weapons, constituencies in the United States took different views as to whether and how the United States should intervene.

America's humanitarian policies are important. Without American efforts and funding, many international humanitarian programs would be far less successful than they are today. In general, though, security and economic interests take precedence in the eyes of U.S. policy makers over humanitarian concerns. The U.S. government is far more likely to decry abuses of religious freedom in Iran—an adversary—than in Saudi Arabia—an ally.

WHO MAKES AMERICAN FOREIGN POLICY?

As we have seen, domestic policies are made by governmental institutions and influenced by a variety of interest groups, political movements, and even the mass media. The same is true in the realm of foreign policy. The president and his chief advisers are the principal architects of U.S. foreign policy. However, Congress, the bureaucracy, the courts, political parties, interest groups, and trade associations also play important roles in this realm. Let us examine the major institutions and forces shaping American foreign policy.

The President

The president is the dominant actor in the realm of American foreign policy. The president exercises substantial control over the nation's diplomatic and military institutions and, as a result, is in a position to decide with whom, when, and how the United States will engage in the international arena. Since World War II, for example, American military forces have fought numerous engagements throughout the world—Korea, Indo-China, the Middle East, Kosovo, Panama, and others. In every instance, the decision to commit troops to battle was made by the president, often with little or no consultation with the Congress. When, following the September 11 terrorist attacks, President Bush ordered American troops into Iraq and Afghanistan, Congress voiced its approval but the president made it clear that he did not believe he needed Congress's permission. In 2011, when President Obama ordered American warplanes into action against Libyan rebels, he made no effort to consult with Congress. And when Obama ordered special operations soldiers to attack Osama bin Laden's compound in Pakistan, members of Congress learned of the operation and bin Laden's death from news broadcasts—just like other Americans.

The president's foreign policy powers, particularly in the military realm, are far greater than the Constitution's framers had thought wise. The framers gave the power to declare war to Congress and made the president the nation's top military commander if and when Congress chose to go to war.[5] Today, presidents command the troops and decide when to go to war.

The Bureaucracy

The major foreign policy actors in the bureaucracy are the secretaries of the departments of State, Defense, and the Treasury; the joint chiefs of staff (JCS), especially the chair of the JCS; and the director of the Central Intelligence Agency (CIA). Since 1947, a separate unit in the White House has overseen the vast foreign policy establishment for the purpose of synthesizing all the messages arising out of the bureaucracy and helping the president make his own foreign policy. This is the National Security Council (NSC). It is a "sub-cabinet" made up of the president, the vice president, the secretary of defense, and the secretary of state, plus others each president was given the authority to add. Since the profound shake-up of September 11, two additional key players have been added. The first of these was the secretary of the new Department of Homeland Security (DHS), comprising 22 existing agencies relocated from

---

5   Alexander Hamilton and James Madison, *Letters of Pacificus and Helvidius* (New York: Scholars Facsimiles and Reprints, 1999).

all over the executive branch on the theory that their expertise could be better coordinated, more rational, and more efficient in a single organization designed to fight international terrorism and domestic natural disasters. The second was imposed during the war in Iraq: a director of national intelligence, to collate and coordinate intelligence coming in from multiple sources and to report a synthesis of all this to the president on a daily basis.

Since the creation of the CIA and the Department of Defense in 1947, the secretary of defense and the director of the CIA have often been rivals engaged in power struggles for control of the intelligence community.[6] For the most part, secretaries of defense have prevailed in these battles, and the Defense Department today controls more than 80 percent of the nation's intelligence capabilities and funds. The creation of the position of director of national intelligence in 2005 to coordinate all intelligence activities set off new Washington power struggles as the "intelligence czar" faced opposition from both the CIA and the Department of Defense. As of 2012, the Defense Department has continued to resist cooperating with civilian intelligence agencies and moved to expand its own intelligence capabilities at their expense.

In addition to these top cabinet-level officials, key lower-level staff members have policy-making influence as strong as that of the Cabinet secretaries. Some may occasionally exceed Cabinet influence. These include the two or three specialized national security advisers in the White House, the staff of the NSC (headed by the national security adviser), and a few other career bureaucrats in the departments of State and Defense whose influence varies according to their specialty and to the foreign policy issue at hand. A few civilian intelligence agencies are also involved in foreign policy and national security, the most important of which are the Federal Bureau of Investigation (FBI), the U.S. Citizenship and Immigration Services, and the Internal Revenue Service (IRS).

In the wake of September 11, military and law enforcement agencies have increased their role in America's foreign-policy making.[7] To a significant extent, American foreign policy is driven by military and antiterrorist concerns, and the agencies deemed capable of addressing these concerns are coming to play a larger and larger role in American foreign policy. For example, in recent years, American ambassadors have complained that they have been relegated to secondary status as the White House has looked to military commanders for information, advice, and policy implementation. For every region of the world, the U.S. military has assigned a "combatant commander," usually a senior general or admiral, to take charge of operations in that area. In many instances, these combatant commanders, who control troops, equipment, and intelligence capabilities, have become the real eyes, ears, and spokespersons for American foreign policy in their designated regions.

---

6   Benjamin Ginsberg, *The American Lie: Government by the People and Other Political Fables* (Boulder, CO: Paradigm, 2007).

7   Paul R. Pillar, *Terrorism and American Foreign Policy* (Washington, DC: Brookings Institution, 2003).

Congress

Although the Constitution gives Congress the power to declare war (Table 17.1), Congress has exercised this power on only five occasions: the War of 1812, the Mexican War (1846), the Spanish-American War (1898), World War I (1917), and World War II (1941). For the first 150 years of American history, Congress's role was limited because the United States' role in world affairs was limited. During this time, the Senate was the only important congressional foreign policy player because of its constitutional role in reviewing and approving treaties. The treaty power is still the primary entrée of the Senate into foreign policy making. But since World War II and the continual involvement of the United States in international security and foreign aid while the president has been the dominant actor, Congress as a whole has continued to exercise influence because most modern foreign policies require financing, which requires action by both the House of Representatives and the Senate. For example, Congress's first act after September 11 was to authorize the president to use "all necessary and appropriate force," coupled with a $40 billion emergency appropriations bill for homeland defense.

Table 17.1

PRINCIPAL FOREIGN POLICY PROVISIONS OF THE CONSTITUTION

	POWERS GRANTED	
	PRESIDENT	**CONGRESS**
War power	Commander in chief of armed forces	Provide for the common defense; declare war
Treaties	Negotiate treaties	Ratification of treaties by two-thirds majority (Senate)
Appointments	Nominate high-level government officials	Confirm president's appointments (Senate)
Foreign commerce	No explicit powers, but treaty negotiation and appointment powers pertain	Explicit power "to regulate foreign commerce"
General powers	Executive power; veto	Legislative power; power of the purse; oversight and investigation

Not only does the president need Congress to provide funding for foreign and military policy initiatives but, under the Constitution, many presidential agreements with foreign nations also have to be approved by Congress. Article II, Section 2, of the Constitution declares that proposed treaties with other nations must be submitted by the president to the Senate and approved by a two-thirds vote. Because this "supermajority" is usually difficult to achieve, presidents generally prefer a different type of agreement with other nations called an **executive agreement**. An executive agreement is similar to a treaty and has the force of law but usually requires only a plurality vote (that is, 50 percent plus one) in both houses of Congress for approval.

Another aspect of Congress's role in foreign policy is the Senate's power to confirm the president's nominations of Cabinet members, ambassadors, and other high-ranking officials (such as the director of the CIA, but not the director of the NSC). A final constitutional power of Congress is the regulation of "commerce with foreign nations."

Other congressional players are the foreign policy, military policy, and intelligence committees: in the Senate, these are the Foreign Relations Committee, the Armed Services Committee, and the Homeland Security and Governmental Affairs Committee; in the House, these are the Foreign Affairs and Homeland Security Committee and the Armed Services Committee. Usually, a few members of these committees who have spent years specializing in foreign affairs become trusted members of the foreign policy establishment and are influential makers of foreign policy. In fact, several members of Congress have left the legislature to become key foreign-affairs cabinet members, including current secretary of state John Kerry. After September 11, congressional committees conducted hearings on the failure of the intelligence agencies, but at the time most members of Congress were reluctant to take on these agencies or a popular president. In 2007, though, with Congress under Democratic control and the president's popularity fading, a number of congressional committees launched inquiries into the conduct of the war in Iraq and the more general operations of the intelligence and defense communities. Within weeks, congressional testimony revealed flaws in military procurement procedures, military planning, and other aspects of the administration's programs and policies. Congressional investigations and the publicity they generate are weapons Congress frequently uses to blunt presidential power.

executive agreement

An agreement between the president and another country that has the force of a treaty but does not require the Senate's "advice and consent"

Interest Groups

Although the president, the executive-branch "bureaucracy," and Congress are the true makers of foreign policy, the "foreign policy establishment" is a much larger arena, including what can properly be called the shapers of foreign policy—a host of unofficial, informal players, people who possess varying degrees of influence, depending on their prestige, their reputation, their socioeconomic standing, and—most important—the party and ideology that are dominant at a given moment.

By far the most important category of nonofficial player is the interest group—that is, the interest group to which one or more foreign policy issues are of long-standing and vital relevance. The type of interest group with the reputation for the most influence is the economic interest group. Yet the myths about its influence far outnumber and outweigh the realities. The actual influence of organized economic interest groups in foreign policy varies enormously from issue to issue and year to year. Most of these groups are "single-issue" groups and are therefore most active when their particular issue is on the agenda. On many of the broader and more sustained policy issues—such as the North American Free Trade Agreement (NAFTA) or the general question of American involvement in international trade—the larger interest groups, sometimes called peak associations, find it difficult to maintain tight enough control of their many members to speak with a single voice. The most systematic study of international trade policies and their interest groups concluded that the leaders of these large economic interest groups spend more time maintaining consensus among their members than they do lobbying Congress or pressuring major players in the executive branch.[8] The more successful economic interest groups, in terms of influencing foreign policy, are the narrower, single-issue groups such as the tobacco industry, which over the years has successfully kept American foreign policy from putting heavy restrictions on international trade in and advertising of tobacco products; and the computer hardware and software industries, which have successfully hardened the American attitude toward Chinese piracy of intellectual property rights.

Another type of interest group with a well-founded reputation for influence in foreign policy is made up of people with strong attachments to and identification with their country of national origin. The interest group with the reputation for the greatest influence is Jewish Americans, whose family and emotional ties to Israel make them one of the most alert and active interest groups in the whole field of foreign policy. In 2010, a dispute between Israel and the Obama administration over Israel's construction of new Jewish housing in Jerusalem led to an intense effort by American Jews to generate congressional support for Israel's position. In 2012, many American Jews criticized Obama for not doing enough to thwart Iran's nuclear program, which they said was a threat to both Israel and the United States. Similarly, Americans of Irish heritage, despite having lived in the United States for two, three, or four generations, still maintain vigilance about American policies toward Ireland and Northern Ireland; some even contribute to the Irish Republican Army. Many other ethnic and national interest groups wield similar influence over American foreign policy.

These ethnic or national-origin interest groups are more influential than their counterparts in other democratic countries. This is a kind of dual loyalty that Americans generally welcome as a worthy sentiment. But there are limits, especially when national origin is coupled with or tied to countries in which a single religion is dominant. For example, Jews with strong ties to Israel and Catholics with connections to Ireland have on occasion been blocked from group influence on foreign policy because "dual loyalty" can be taken by other

---

8   Raymond A. Bauer, Ithiel de Sola Pool, and Lewis Anthony Dexter, *American Business and Public Policy: The Politics of Foreign Trade*, 2nd ed. (Chicago: Aldine-Atherton, 1972).

groups as "doubtful loyalty."[9] Nevertheless, Irish and Jewish groups, as well as a variety of other ethnic American interest groups, are vigorously involved in salient aspects of foreign policy, and it is an irrational or nonrational elected politician who disregards their signals. It is quite possible that the "electoral connection"[10] and the politics of representation in Congress (and the White House) are at their most intense when national origin is linked to a foreign policy issue. Many will argue that the rationality principle "need not . . . be equated with such narrowly self-serving actions."[11] However, the nationality interest is often the strongest electoral connection.

A third type of interest group, one with a reputation that has been growing in the past two decades, is devoted to human rights. Such groups are made up of people who, instead of having self-serving economic or ethnic interests in foreign policy, are genuinely concerned about the welfare and treatment of people throughout the world—particularly those who suffer under harsh political regimes. A relatively small but often quite influential example is Amnesty International, whose exposés of human rights abuses have altered the practices of many regimes around the world. In recent years, the Christian right has been a vocal advocate for the human rights of Christians who are persecuted in other parts of the world, most notably in China, for their religious beliefs. For example, the Christian Coalition joined groups such as Amnesty International in lobbying Congress to restrict trade with countries that permit attacks against religious believers.

A related type of group with rapidly growing influence is the ecological or environmental group, sometimes collectively called "greens." Groups of this nature often depend more on demonstrations than on the usual forms and strategies of influence in Washington, such as lobbying and using electoral politics, for example. In recent years environmental activists staged major protests, at the 2009 London and 2010 Toronto international economic summits.

Putting It Together

What can we say about who really makes American foreign policy? First, except for the president, whose influence is felt in virtually every area of foreign policy, the influence of players and shapers varies from case to case—this is a good reason to look with some care at each example of foreign policy in

---

9 For a good treatment of this in regard to Irish Catholics and Catholics in general, see Timothy Byrnes, *Catholic Bishops and American Politics* (Princeton, NJ: Princeton University Press, 1991). For a (controversial) discussion of the role of Jewish groups, see John J. Mearsheimer and Stephen M. Walt, *The Israel Lobby and U.S. Foreign Policy* (New York: Farrar, Straus & Giroux, 2007).

10 This felicitous term is from David R. Mayhew, *Congress: The Electoral Connection* (New Haven, CT: Yale University Press, 1974).

11 John H. Aldrich, *Why Parties? The Origin and Transformation of Political Parties in America* (Chicago: University of Chicago Press, 1995), p. 278.

this chapter. Second, because the one constant influence is the centrality of the president in foreign policy making, it is useful to evaluate other actors and factors as they interact with the president.[12] Third, the reason influence varies from case to case is that each case arises under different conditions and with vastly different time constraints: for issues that arise and are resolved quickly, the opportunity for influence is limited. Fourth, foreign policy experts often disagree about the level of influence any player or type of player has on policy making.

But just to get started, let's make a few tentative generalizations. When an important foreign policy decision has to be made under conditions of crisis—where time is of the essence—the influence of the presidency is at its strongest. Within those time constraints, access to the decision is limited almost exclusively to the narrowest definition of the foreign policy establishment. The arena for participation is tiny; any discussion at all is limited to the officially and constitutionally designated players. To put this another way, in a crisis the foreign policy establishment works as it is supposed to.[13] As time becomes less restricted, even when the decision to be made is of great importance, the arena of participation expands to include more government players and more nonofficial, informal players—the most concerned interest groups and the most important journalists. In other words, the arena becomes more pluralistic and, therefore, less distinguishable from the politics of domestic policy making.

However, because there are so many other countries with power and interests on any given issue, there are severe limits on the choices the United States can make. That is, in sharp contrast to domestic politics, U.S. policy makers in the foreign policy realm are engaged not only in infighting but also in strategic interaction with policy makers in other nations; their choices are made both in reaction to and in anticipation of these strategic interactions. As one author concludes, in foreign affairs, "policy takes precedence over politics."[14] Thus, even though foreign policy making in noncrisis situations may closely resemble the pluralistic politics of domestic policy making, foreign policy making is still a narrower arena with fewer participants.

---

12 A very good brief outline of the centrality of the president in foreign policy is found in Paul E. Peterson, "The President's Dominance in Foreign Policy Making," *Political Science Quarterly* 109 (Summer 1994): 215–34.

13 One confirmation of this is found in Theodore Lowi, *The End of Liberalism: The Second Republic of the United States,* 2nd ed. (New York: Norton, 1979), pp. 127–30; another is found in Stephen Krasner, "Are Bureaucracies Important?" *Foreign Policy* 7 (Summer 1972): 159–79. However, it should be noted that Krasner was writing his article in disagreement with Graham T. Allison, "Conceptual Models and the Cuban Missile Crisis," *American Political Science Review* 63, no. 3 (September 1969): 689–718.

14 Peterson, "The President's Dominance in Foreign Policy Making," p. 232.

THE INSTRUMENTS OF MODERN AMERICAN FOREIGN POLICY

Any government has at hand certain instruments, or tools, to use in implementing its foreign policy. An instrument is neutral, capable of serving many goals. There have been many instruments of American foreign policy, and we can deal here only with those instruments we deem to be most important in the modern epoch: diplomacy, the United Nations, the international monetary structure, economic aid, collective security, and military deterrence. Each of these instruments will be evaluated in this section for its role in the conduct of American foreign policy, including its place in the history and development of American values.

Diplomacy

We begin this treatment of instruments with diplomacy because it is the instrument to which all other instruments should be subordinated, although they seldom are. **Diplomacy** is the representation of a government to other foreign governments. Its purpose is to promote national values or interests by peaceful means. According to Hans Morgenthau, "a diplomacy that ends in war has failed in its primary objective."[15] (See Table 17.2 for an overview of the budget of the U.S. Department of State, which is responsible for carrying out much of U.S. diplomacy.)

 diplomacy

The representation of a government to other governments

The first effort to create a modern diplomatic service in the United States was made through the Rogers Act of 1924, which established the initial framework for a professional foreign-service staff. But it took World War II and the Foreign Service Act of 1946 to forge the foreign service into a fully professional diplomatic corps.

Although diplomacy is a powerful tool of foreign policy, by its very nature it is overshadowed by spectacular international events and dramatic initiatives. The traditional American distrust of diplomacy continues today, albeit in weaker form. Impatience with or downright distrust of diplomacy has been built not only into all the other instruments of foreign policy but also into the modern presidential system itself.[16] So much personal responsibility has been heaped on the presidency that it is difficult for presidents to entrust any of their authority or responsibility in foreign policy to professional diplomats in the State Department and other bureaucracies.

---

15 Hans Morgenthau, *Politics among Nations*, 2nd ed. (New York: Knopf, 1956), p. 505.

16 See Theodore Lowi, *The Personal President: Power Invested, Promise Unfulfilled* (Ithaca, NY: Cornell University Press, 1985), pp. 167–9.

Table 17.2

U.S. DEPARTMENT OF STATE BUDGET, SELECTED EXPENDITURES, 2012

OPERATION	BUDGET (BILLIONS $)
Diplomatic and consular programs	**10.9**
Embassy security, construction, and maintenance	**1.6**
Educational and cultural exchange programs	**0.6**
Contributions to international organizations	**1.5**
Contributions to international peacekeeping operations	**1.8**
U.S. Agency for International Development	**1.5**
Bilateral economic assistance	**20.8**
International narcotics and law enforcement	**1.6**
International financial institutions	**2.6**
Total Department of State budget = $50.8 billion	
Total U.S. federal budget = $3.7 trillion	

SOURCE: Department of State, "Executive Budget Summary," April 10, 2013, www.state.gov /documents/organization/207305.pdf (accessed 5/13/13).

In 2008, both parties' presidential candidates criticized the Bush administration for having failed to use diplomacy to secure greater international support for the Iraq War. Both promised to revitalize American diplomacy. President Obama appointed Hillary Clinton secretary of state in part to underline the importance he attached to diplomacy by choosing such a prominent figure as America's chief diplomat. Obama and Clinton worked to improve America's relations with the nation's European allies who had become disenchanted with what they saw as American unilateralism during the Bush years. They also worked to "restart" America's relationship with Russia, to find diplomatic solutions to the threat of Iranian nuclear weapons development, to identify possible approaches to resolving the seemingly intractable dispute between Israelis and Palestinians and, in a variety of others ways, to advance American interests by peaceful means.

In 2013, Obama appointed former senators John Kerry as secretary of state and Chuck Hagel as secretary of defense. Both promised continuity with their predecessors' policies. Obama also promised to work to develop a better relationship with China. Though China is America's chief trading partner outside of North America, the two nations are deeply suspicious of each other. The United States views China as a growing threat, while China believes that the United States wants to undermine its influence. Both, unfortunately, are correct.

The United Nations

The utility of the **United Nations (UN)** to the United States as an instrument of foreign policy can be too easily underestimated because the United Nations is a very large and unwieldy institution with few powers and no armed forces to implement its rules and resolutions. Its supreme body is the UN General Assembly, comprising one representative of each of the 192 member states; each member representative has one vote, regardless of the size of the country. Important issues require a two-thirds majority vote, and the annual session of the General Assembly runs only from September to December (although it can call extra sessions). It has little organization that can make it an effective decision-making body, with only six standing committees, few tight rules of procedure, and no political parties to provide priorities and discipline. Its defenders are quick to add that although it lacks armed forces, it relies on the power of world opinion—and this is not to be taken lightly.

The powers of the United Nations devolve mainly to its "executive committee," the UN Security Council, which alone has the real power to make decisions and rulings that member states are obligated by the UN Charter to implement. The Security Council may be called into session at any time, and each member (or a designated alternate) must be present at UN Headquarters in New York at all times. It is composed of 15 members: 5 are permanent (the victors of World War II), and 10 are elected by the General Assembly for two-year, nonrepeatable terms. The 5 permanent members are China, France, Russia, the United Kingdom, and the United States. Each of the 15 members has only one vote, and a 9-vote majority of the 15 is required on all substantive matters. But each of the 5 permanent members also has a negative vote, a "veto," and one veto is sufficient to reject any substantive proposal.

The UN can serve as a useful forum for international discussions and an instrument for multilateral action. Most peacekeeping efforts to which the United States contributes, for example, are undertaken under UN auspices. Though the United States generally finds the UN useful, it sometimes objects to the policies of UN agencies. For example, for several years, the United States boycotted the United Nations Educational, Scientific and Cultural Organization (UNESCO) over UNESCO's support for Palestinian groups.

The International Monetary Structure

Fear of a repeat of the economic devastation that followed World War I brought the United States together with its allies (except the USSR) to Bretton Woods,

 United Nations (UN)

An organization of nations founded in 1945 to be a channel for negotiation and a means of settling international disputes peaceably. The UN has had frequent successes in providing a forum for negotiation and on some occasions a means of preventing international conflicts from spreading. On a number of occasions, the UN has been a convenient cover for U.S. foreign policy goals

New Hampshire, in 1944 to create a new international economic structure for the postwar world. The result was two institutions: the International Bank for Reconstruction and Development (commonly called the World Bank) and the International Monetary Fund.

The World Bank was set up to finance long-term capital. Leading nations took on the obligation of contributing funds to enable the World Bank to make loans to capital-hungry countries. (The U.S. quota has been about one-third of the total.)

The **International Monetary Fund (IMF)** was set up to provide for the short-term flow of money. After the war, the U.S. dollar replaced gold as the chief means by which the currencies of one country would be "changed into" currencies of another country for purposes of making international transactions. To permit debtor countries with no international balances to make purchases and investments, the IMF was set up to lend dollars or other appropriate currencies to needy member countries to help them overcome temporary trade deficits. For many years after World War II, the IMF, along with U.S. foreign aid, in effect constituted the only international medium of exchange.

During the 1990s, the IMF returned to a position of enhanced importance through its efforts to reform some of the largest debtor nations and formerly communist countries, to bring them more fully into the global capitalist economy. For example, in the early 1990s, Russia and 13 other former Soviet republics were invited to join the IMF and the World Bank with the expectation of receiving $10.5 billion from these two agencies, primarily for a currency-stabilization fund. Each republic was to get a permanent IMF representative, and the IMF increased its staff by at least 10 percent to provide the expertise necessary to cope with the problems of these emerging capitalist economies.[17]

The IMF, with tens of billions of dollars contributed by its members, has more money to lend poor countries than does the United States, Europe, or Japan (the three leading IMF shareholders) individually. It makes its policy decisions in ways that are generally consonant with the interests of the leading shareholders.[18] For example, two weeks after September 11, 2001, the IMF had approved a $135 million loan to economically troubled Pakistan, a key player in the war against the Taliban government of Afghanistan because of its strategic location. Turkey, also because of its strategic location in the Middle East, was likewise put back in the IMF pipeline.[19] In 2010, the IMF organized a $40 billion

----

17 "IMF: Sleeve-Rolling Time," *Economist*, May 2, 1992, pp. 98–9.

18 James Dao and Patrick E. Tyler, "U.S. Says Military Strikes Are Just a Part of Big Plan," *The Alliance*, September 27, 2001; and Joseph Kahn, "A Nation Challenged: Global Dollars," *New York Times*, September 20, 2001, p. B1.

19 Turkey was desperate for help to extricate its economy from its worst recession since 1945. The Afghanistan crisis was going to hurt Turkey all the more; its strategic location helped its case with IMF. "Official Says Turkey Is Advancing in Drive for I.M.F. Financing," *New York Times*, October 6, 2001, p. A7.

loan package to rescue the Greek government, which faced the threat of default on its debt. The United States and major European governments feared that a Greek default might spark a worldwide economic crisis. The future of the IMF, the World Bank, and all other private sources of international investment will depend in part on extension of more credit to the Third World and other developing countries, because credit means investment and productivity. But the future may depend even more on reducing the debt that is already there from previous extensions of credit.

Economic Aid and Sanctions

Every year, the United States provides nearly $30 billion in economic assistance to other nations. Some aid has a humanitarian purpose, such as helping to provide health care, shelter for refugees, or famine relief. A good deal of American aid, however, is designed to promote American security interests or economic concerns. For example, the United States provides military assistance to a number of its allies in the form of advanced weapons or loans to help them purchase advanced weapons. Such loans generally stipulate that the recipient must purchase the designated weapons from American firms. In this way, the United States hopes to bolster its security and economic interests with one grant. For years, the two largest recipients of American military assistance have been Israel and Egypt, American allies that fought two wars against one another. The United States believes that its military assistance allows both to feel sufficiently secure to remain at peace with each other.

Aid is an economic carrot. Sanctions are an economic stick. Economic sanctions that the United States employs against other nations include trade embargoes, bans on investment, and efforts to prevent the World Bank or other international institutions from extending credit to a nation against which the United States has a grievance. Sanctions are most often employed when the United States seeks to weaken what it considers a hostile regime or when it is attempting to compel some particular action by another regime. Thus, for example, in order to weaken the Castro government, the United States has long prohibited American firms from doing business with Cuba. In recent years, the United States has maintained economic sanctions against Iran and North Korea in an effort to prevent those nations from pursuing nuclear-weapons programs.

Unilateral sanctions by the United States usually have little effect, since the target can likely trade elsewhere, sometimes even with foreign affiliates of U.S. firms. If, however, the United States is able to convince its allies to cooperate, sanctions have a better chance of success. International sanctions that were applied to Libya, for example, played a role in the regime's decision to enter into negotiations with the United States over Libyan responsibility for a number of terrorist attacks. Similarly, international sanctions applied to Iran weakened that nation's economy and slowed its nuclear weapon project.

Collective Security

In 1947, most Americans hoped that the United States could meet its world obligations through the United Nations and economic structures alone. But most foreign policy makers recognized that was a vain hope even as they were permitting and encouraging Americans to believe it. They had anticipated the need for military entanglements at the time of drafting the original UN Charter by insisting on language that recognized the right of all nations to provide for their mutual defense independent of the United Nations. And almost immediately after enactment of the Marshall Plan, designed to promote European economic recovery, the White House and a parade of State and Defense Department officials followed up with an urgent request to the Senate to ratify, and to both houses of Congress to finance, mutual defense alliances.

At first quite reluctant to approve treaties providing for national security alliances, the Senate ultimately agreed with the executive branch. The first collective security agreement was the Rio Treaty (ratified by the Senate in September 1947), which created the Organization of American States (OAS). This was the model treaty, anticipating all succeeding collective security treaties by providing that an armed attack against any of its members "shall be considered as an attack against all the American States," including the United States. A more significant break with U.S. tradition against peacetime entanglements came with the North Atlantic Treaty (signed in April 1949), which created the **North Atlantic Treaty Organization (NATO)**. ANZUS, a treaty tying Australia and New Zealand to the United States, was signed in September 1951. Three years later, the Southeast Asia Treaty created the Southeast Asia Treaty Organization (SEATO). In addition to these multilateral treaties, the United States entered into a number of **bilateral treaties**—treaties between two countries.

As one author has observed, the United States has been a *producer* of security, whereas most of its allies have been *consumers* of security.[20] This pattern has continued in the post–Cold War era, and its best illustration is in the Persian Gulf War, where the United States provided the initiative, the leadership, and most of the armed forces, even though its allies were obliged to reimburse over 90 percent of the cost.

It is difficult to evaluate collective security and its treaties, because the purpose of collective security as an instrument of foreign policy is prevention, and success of this kind has to be measured in terms of what did *not* happen. Critics have argued that U.S. collective security treaties posed a threat of encirclement to the Soviet Union, forcing it to produce its own collective security, particularly the Warsaw Pact.[21] Nevertheless, no one can

North Atlantic Treaty Organization (NATO)

A treaty organization comprising the United States, Canada, and most of Western Europe, formed in 1949 to counter the perceived threat from the Soviet Union

bilateral treaty

A treaty made between two nations

---

20 George Quester, *The Continuing Problem of International Politics* (Hinsdale, IL: Dryden Press, 1974), p. 229.

21 The Warsaw Pact was signed in 1955 by the Soviet Union, the German Democratic Republic (East Germany), Poland, Hungary, Czechoslovakia, Romania, Bulgaria, and Albania. Albania later dropped out. The Warsaw Pact was terminated in 1991.

deny the counterargument that more than 60 years have passed without a world war.

In 1998, the expansion of NATO took its first steps toward former Warsaw Pact members, extending membership to Poland, Hungary, and the Czech Republic. Most of Washington embraced this expansion as the true and fitting end of the Cold War, and the U.S. Senate echoed this with a resounding 80-to-19 vote to induct these three former Soviet satellites into NATO. The expansion was also welcomed among European member nations, which quickly approved the move, hailing it as the final closing of the book on Yalta, the 1945 treaty that divided Europe into Western and Soviet spheres of influence after the defeat of Germany. Expanded membership seems to have made NATO less threatening and more acceptable to Russia. Russia became a partner when the NATO-Russia Council was formed in 2002. Finally, although the expanded NATO membership (28 countries in 2013) reduces the threat to Russia, it also reduces the utility of NATO as a military alliance. The September 11 attack on the United States was the first time in its more than 50-year history that Article 5 of the North Atlantic Treaty had to be invoked; it provides that an attack on one country is an attack on all the member countries. In fighting the war on terror, the Bush administration recognized that no matter how preponderant American power was, some aspects of its foreign policy could not be achieved without multilateral cooperation. On the other hand, the United States did not want to be constrained by its alliances. The global coalition initially forged after September 11 numbered over 170 countries. Not all joined the war effort in Afghanistan, but most if not all provided some form of support for some aspect of the war on terrorism, such as economic sanctions and intelligence. The war in Iraq, however, put the "coalition of the willing" to a test. The Bush administration was determined not to make its decision to go to war subject to the UN or NATO or any other international organization. The breadth of the United States' coalition was deemed secondary to its being nonconstraining. As a result, other than the British government, no major power supported the United States' actions.

Military Force

The most visible instrument of foreign policy is, of course, military force. The United States has built the world's most imposing military, with army, navy, marine, and air force units stationed across the globe. The United States spends nearly as much on military might as the rest of the world combined (Figure 17.1). The famous Prussian military strategist Carl von Clausewitz called war "politics by other means." By this he meant that nations used force not simply to demonstrate their capacity for violence. Rather, force or the threat of force is a tool nations must sometimes use to achieve their foreign policy goals. Military force may be needed to protect a nation's security interests and economic concerns. Ironically, force may also be needed to achieve humanitarian

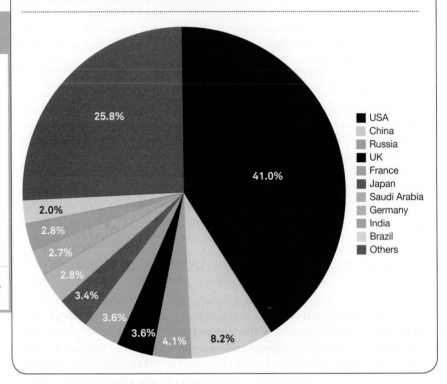

Figure 17.1

SHARES OF WORLD MILITARY EXPENDITURES BY TEN LARGEST SPENDERS, 2011

NOTE: Total world military spending in 2011: $1.7 trillion
SOURCE: Stockholm International Peace Research Institute, "Background Paper on SIPRI Military Expenditure Data, 2011," www.sipri.org/research/armaments/milex/sipri-factsheet-on-military -expenditure-2011.pdf (accessed 3/31/13).

ANALYZING THE EVIDENCE

Although U.S. military spending is much greater than that of any other country, the United States also has the world's biggest economy. Why does the United States spend so much on its military? What roles do external security concerns and domestic political factors play in the budget process?

goals. For example, without international military protection, the Africans who took refuge in Darfur refugee camps would have been at the mercy of the violent Sudanese regime.

Though force is sometimes necessary, military force is generally seen as a last resort and avoided if possible because of a number of problems commonly associated with its use. First, the use of military force is extremely costly in both human and financial terms. In the past 50 years, tens of thousands of Americans have been killed and hundreds of billions of dollars spent in America's military operations. Before they employ military force to achieve national goals, policy makers must be certain that achieving these goals is essential and that other means are unlikely to succeed.

Second, the use of military force is inherently fraught with risk. However, carefully policy makers and generals plan for military operations, results can seldom be fully anticipated. Variables ranging from the weather to unexpected weapons and tactics deployed by opponents may upset the most careful calculations and turn military operations into costly disasters or convert maneuvers that were expected to be quick and decisive into long, drawn-out, expensive struggles. For example, American policy makers expected to defeat the Iraqi army quickly and easily in 2003—and they did. Policy makers did not anticipate, however, that American forces would still be struggling years later to defeat the insurgency that arose in the war's aftermath.

Finally, in a democracy, any government that chooses to address policy problems through military means is almost certain to encounter political difficulties. Generally speaking, the American public will support relatively short and decisive military engagements. If, however, a conflict drags on, producing casualties and expenses with no clear outcome, the public loses patience and opposition politicians point to the government's lies and ineptitude. Korea, Vietnam, and Iraq are all examples of protracted conflicts whose domestic political repercussions included dissipating public support.

Thus, military force remains a major foreign policy tool, and the United States currently possesses a more powerful and effective set of military forces than any other nation. Nevertheless, even for the United States, the use of military force is fraught with risk and is not to be undertaken lightly.

Arbitration

The final foreign policy tool we shall consider is dispute arbitration. Arbitration means referring an international disagreement to a neutral third party for resolution. Arbitration is sometimes seen as a form of "soft power" as distinguished from military force, economic sanctions, and other coercive foreign policy instruments. The United States will occasionally turn to international tribunals to resolve disputes with other countries. For example, in February 2008, the U.S. government asked the **International Court of Justice** to resolve a long-standing dispute with Italy over American property confiscated by the Italian government more than 40 years ago. To take another example, in 1981 the United States and Iran established an arbitral tribunal to deal with claims arising from Iran's seizure of the U.S. embassy in Tehran in 1979.

 International Court of Justice (ICJ)

The UN's chief judicial agency. Located in The Hague, Netherlands, the ICJ settles legal disputes submitted by UN member states

More important, the United States relies heavily on the work of arbitral panels to maintain the flow of international trade on which America's economy depends. American firms would be reluctant to do business abroad if they could not be certain that their property and contractual rights would be honored by other nations. Arbitration helps produce that certainty. Almost every international contract contains an arbitration clause requiring that disputes between the parties will be resolved not by foreign governments but by impartial arbitral panels accepted by both sides. By the terms of the New York Convention, virtually every nation in the world has agreed to accept and enforce arbitral verdicts. The United States has incorporated the terms of the New York Convention into federal law, and U.S. courts vigorously enforce arbitral judgments. The United States may not be happy with the outcome of every proceeding, but the arbitral system is essential to America's economic interests.

THINKING CRITICALLY ABOUT AMERICA'S ROLE IN THE WORLD TODAY

The nineteenth-century British statesman Lord Palmerston famously said, "Nations have no permanent friends or allies; they only have permanent interests." Palmerston's comment illustrates what is sometimes known as the "realist" view of foreign policy. The realist school holds that foreign policies should be guided by the national interest—mainly security and economic interest—and that policy makers should steel themselves to the necessity of making decisions that might be viewed from the outside as cold and ruthless, as long as those decisions serve the nation's interests. Although many public officials have denounced such views in public—especially if they were running for office—many have become realists once in power. Every one of America's post–World War II presidents, liberals and conservatives, Democrats and Republicans alike, have been willing to order young Americans into battle and to visit death and destruction on the citizens of foreign states if they believed the national interest required it.

The harsh rationality of foreign policy often clashes with America's history and ideals. Our democratic and liberal traditions lead us to hope for a world in which ideals rather than naked interests govern foreign policy and in which our leaders pay heed to ideals. The ideals that Americans have historically espoused (though not always lived by) assert that our foreign policies should have a higher purpose than the pursuit of interest and that America is to use force only as a last resort. Since the realities of our foreign policy often clash with these historic ideals, our policy makers often struggle to explain their actions and avoid admitting to motivations that don't embody those ideals.

"I have previously stated and I repeat now that the United States plans no military intervention in Cuba," said President John F. Kennedy in 1961 as he planned military action in Cuba. "As president, it is my duty to the American people to report that renewed hostile actions against United States ships on the high seas in the Gulf of Tonkin have today required me to order the military forces of the United States to take action in reply," said President Lyndon Johnson in 1964 referring to a fabricated incident used to justify expansion of American involvement in Vietnam. "We did not, I repeat, did not trade weapons or anything else [to Iran] for hostages, nor will we," said President Ronald Reagan in November 1986, four months before admitting that U.S. arms had been traded to Iran in exchange for Americans being held hostage there. "Simply stated, there is no doubt that Saddam Hussein now has weapons of mass destruction," said Vice President Dick Cheney in 2002. When it turned out that these weapons did not exist, Assistant Defense Secretary Paul Wolfowitz explained that the administration focused on weapons of mass destruction as the justification for invading Iraq because it was one everyone could agree on. These false statements may hide discrepancies between our historic ideals and rationality, but they do not resolve them.

The ever-present conflicts between ideals and harsh realities manifested themselves again in 2009. As a candidate for the presidency, Barack Obama was praised for denouncing the Bush administration's treatment of enemy combatants. Obama was especially critical of the Guantánamo detention facility, where some alleged enemy combatants were incarcerated, and the creation of military tribunals, outside the regular court system, to hear their cases. Once in office, however, Obama did not rush to close the Guantánamo facility—though he continued to plan for the facility's eventual closure. As for the tribunals, the Obama administration indicated in 2010 that it might employ them in some cases after all, not wishing to bring the most important enemy combatant cases to the regular courts. Ideals seemed to have given way to interests again. In 2011, the United States watched from the sidelines as a popular revolution ousted Egyptian president Hosni Mubarak. On the one hand, Americans sympathized with the democratic aspirations of the Egyptian people. On the other hand, Mubarak was a long-time and useful American ally. American policy makers seemed frozen by indecision as they watched events unfold, and in 2012 scurried to mend fences with the new Egyptian government.

Must America always choose between its ideals and its interests? The founders of the republic believed that America would be different from other nations. They believed that its ideals would be its source of power; that its ideals would allow it to inspire and lead others as a "shining beacon." If, in the interest of national power and security, our political leaders always choose narrow interests over transcendent ideals, might they be robbing America of its true source of international power and global security?

For Further Reading

Selections highlighted in red are included in *Readings in American Politics: Analysis and Perspectives*, Third Edition.

Bacevich, Andrew. *The Limits of Power: The End of American Exceptionalism*. New York: Metropolitan Books, 2008.

Bacevich, Andrew. *The New American Militarism: How Americans Are Seduced by War*. New York: Oxford University Press, 2006.

Berman, Paul. *Terror and Liberalism*. New York: Norton, 2004.

Drezner, Daniel. "The Realist Tradition in American Public Opinion." *Perspectives on Politics* (March 2008): 51–70.

Gaddis, John L. *The Cold War: A New History*. New York: Penguin, 2005.

Herring, George. *From Colony to Superpower*. New York: Oxford University Press, 2011.

Ikenberry, John, Thomas Knock, Anne-Marie Slaughter, and Tony Smith. *The Crisis of American Foreign Policy*. Princeton, NJ: Princeton University Press, 2011.

Jentleson, Bruce. *American Foreign Policy—The Dynamics of Choice in the Twenty-First Century*. New York: Norton, 2013.

Johnson, Chalmers. *The Sorrows of Empire*. New York: Holt, 2004.

Kagan, Robert. *Dangerous Nation*. New York: Knopf, 2006.

Kaufman, Joyce. *A Concise History of U.S. Foreign Policy*. New York: Rowman & Littlefield, 2010.

Kennan, George F. *Around the Cragged Hill: A Personal and Political Philosophy*. New York: Norton, 1993.

Maddow, Rachel. *Drift: The Unmooring of American Military Power*. New York: Crown, 2012.

Mandelbaum, Michael. *The Case for Goliath: How America Acts as the World's Government in the Twenty-First Century*. Washington, DC: PublicAffairs Press, 2005.

Mayer, Jane. *The Dark Side: The Inside Story of How the War on Terror Turned into a War on American Ideals*. New York: Doubleday, 2008.

Mayhew, David. "Wars and American Politics." *Perspectives on Politics* (September 2005): 473–93.

Mead, Walter Russell. *Special Providence: American Foreign Policy and How It Changed the World*. New York: Routledge, 2002.

Reid, T. R. *The United States of Europe—The New Superpower and the End of American Supremacy*. New York: Penguin, 2004.

Renshon, Stanley. *National Security in the Obama Administration*. New York: Routledge, 2009.

Appendix

The Declaration of Independence

In Congress, July 4, 1776

When in the course of human events, it becomes necessary for one people to dissolve the political bands which have connected them with another, and to assume among the Powers of the earth, the separate and equal station to which the Laws of Nature and of Nature's God entitle them, a decent respect to the opinions of mankind requires that they should declare the causes which impel them to the separation.

We hold these truths to be self-evident, that all men are created equal, that they are endowed by their Creator with certain unalienable rights, that among these are Life, Liberty, and the pursuit of Happiness. That to secure these rights, Governments are instituted among Men, deriving their just powers from the consent of the governed. That whenever any Form of Government becomes destructive of these ends, it is the Right of the People to alter or to abolish it, and to institute new Government, laying its foundation on such principles and organizing its powers in such form, as to them shall seem most likely to effect their Safety and Happiness. Prudence, indeed, will dictate that Governments long established should not be changed for light and transient causes; and accordingly all experience hath shown, that mankind are more disposed to suffer, while evils are sufferable, than to right themselves by abolishing the forms to which they are accustomed. But when a long train of abuses and usurpations, pursuing invariably the same Object evinces a design to reduce them under absolute Despotism, it is their right, it is their duty, to throw off such Government, and to provide new Guards for their future security.—Such has been the patient sufferance of these Colonies; and such is now the necessity which constrains them to alter their former Systems of Government. The history of the present King of Great Britain is a history of repeated injuries and usurpations, all having in direct object the establishment of an absolute Tyranny over these States. To prove this, let Facts be submitted to a candid world.

He has refused his Assent to Laws, the most wholesome and necessary for the public good.

He has forbidden his Governors to pass Laws of immediate and pressing importance, unless suspended in their operation till his Assent should be obtained; and when so suspended, he has utterly neglected to attend to them.

He has refused to pass other Laws for the accommodation of large districts of people, unless those people would relinquish the right of Representation in the Legislature, a right inestimable to them and formidable to tyrants only.

He has called together legislative bodies at places unusual, uncomfortable, and distant from the depository of their public Records, for the sole purpose of fatiguing them into compliance with his measures.

He has dissolved Representative Houses repeatedly, for opposing with manly firmness his invasions on the rights of the people.

He has refused for a long time, after such dissolutions, to cause others to be elected; whereby the Legislative powers, incapable of Annihilation, have returned to the People at large for their exercise; the State remaining in the mean time exposed to all dangers of invasion from without, and convulsions within.

He has endeavored to prevent the population of these States; for that purpose obstructing the Laws of Naturalization of Foreigners; refusing to pass others to encourage their migrations hither, and raising the conditions of new Appropriations of Lands.

He has obstructed the Administration of Justice, by refusing his Assent to Laws for establishing Judiciary powers.

He has made Judges dependent on his Will alone, for the tenure of their offices, and the amount and payment of their salaries.

He has erected a multitude of New Offices, and sent hither swarms of Officers to harass our People, and eat out their substance.

He has kept among us, in times of peace, Standing Armies without the Consent of our legislature.

He has affected to render the Military independent of and superior to the Civil Power.

He has combined with others to subject us to a jurisdiction foreign to our constitution, and unacknowledged by our laws; giving his Assent to their Acts of pretended Legislation:

For quartering large bodies of armed troops among us:

For protecting them, by a mock Trial, from Punishment for any Murders which they should commit on the Inhabitants of these States:

For cutting off our Trade with all parts of the world:

For imposing taxes on us without our Consent:

For depriving us in many cases, of the benefits of Trial by jury:

For transporting us beyond Seas to be tried for pretended offences:

For abolishing the free System of English Laws in a neighboring Province, establishing therein an Arbitrary government, and enlarging its Boundaries so as to render it at once an example and fit instrument for introducing the same absolute rule into these Colonies:

For taking away our Charters, abolishing our most valuable Laws, and altering fundamentally the Forms of our Governments:

For suspending our own Legislatures, and declaring themselves invested with Power to legislate for us in all cases whatsoever.

He has abdicated Government here, by declaring us out of his Protection and waging War against us.

He has plundered our seas, ravaged our Coasts, burnt our towns, and destroyed the lives of our people.

He is at this time transporting large armies of foreign mercenaries to compleat the works of death, desolation, and tyranny, already begun with circumstances of Cruelty & perfidy scarcely paralleled in the most barbarous ages, and totally unworthy the Head of a civilized nation.

He has constrained our fellow Citizens taken Captive on the high Seas to bear Arms against their Country, to become the executioners of their friends and Brethren, or to fall themselves by their Hands.

He has excited domestic insurrections amongst us, and has endeavored to bring on the inhabitants of our frontiers, the merciless Indian Savages, whose known rule of warfare, is an undistinguished destruction of all ages, sexes, and conditions.

In every stage of these Oppressions We have Petitioned for Redress in the most humble terms: Our repeated Petitions have been answered only by repeated injury. A Prince, whose character is thus marked by every act which may define a Tyrant, is unfit to be the ruler of a free people.

Nor have We been wanting in attention to our British brethren. We have warned them from time to time of attempts by their legislature to extend an unwarrantable jurisdiction over us. We have reminded them of the circumstances of our emigration and settlement here. We have appealed to their native justice and magnanimity, and we have conjured them by the ties of our common kindred to disavow these usurpations, which, would inevitably interrupt our connections and correspondence. They too must have been deaf to the voice of justice and of consanguinity. We must, therefore, acquiesce in the necessity, which denounces our Separation, and hold them, as we hold the rest of mankind, Enemies in War, in Peace Friends.

WE, THEREFORE, the Representatives of the UNITED STATES OF AMERICA, in General Congress, Assembled, appealing to the Supreme Judge of the world for the rectitude of our intentions, do, in the Name, and by Authority of the good People of these Colonies, solemnly publish and declare, That these United Colonies are, and of Right ought to be FREE AND INDEPENDENT STATES; that they are Absolved from all Allegiance to the British Crown, and that all political connection between them and the State of Great Britain, is and ought to be totally dissolved; and that as Free and Independent States, they have full Power to levy War, conclude Peace, contract Alliances, establish Commerce, and to do all other Acts and Things which Independent States may of right do. And for the support of this Declaration, with a firm reliance on the Protection of Divine Providence, we mutually pledge to each other our Lives, our Fortunes, and our sacred Honor.

The foregoing Declaration was, by order of Congress, engrossed, and signed by the following members:

John Hancock

NEW HAMPSHIRE
Josiah Bartlett
William Whipple
Matthew Thornton

MASSACHUSETTS BAY
Samuel Adams
John Adams
Robert Treat Paine
Elbridge Gerry

RHODE ISLAND
Stephen Hopkins
William Ellery

CONNECTICUT
Roger Sherman
Samuel Huntington
William Williams
Oliver Wolcott

NEW YORK
William Floyd
Philip Livingston
Francis Lewis
Lewis Morris

NEW JERSEY
Richard Stockton
John Witherspoon
Francis Hopkinson
John Hart
Abraham Clark

PENNSYLVANIA
Robert Morris
Benjamin Rush
Benjamin Franklin
John Morton
George Clymer
James Smith
George Taylor
James Wilson
George Ross

DELAWARE
Caesar Rodney
George Read
Thomas M'Kean

MARYLAND
Samuel Chase
William Paca
Thomas Stone
Charles Carroll,
of Carrollton

VIRGINIA
George Wythe
Richard Henry Lee
Thomas Jefferson
Benjamin Harrison
Thomas Nelson, Jr.
Francis Lightfoot Lee
Carter Braxton

NORTH CAROLINA
William Hooper
Joseph Hewes
John Penn

SOUTH CAROLINA
Edward Rutledge
Thomas Heyward, Jr.
Thomas Lynch, Jr.
Arthur Middleton

GEORGIA
Button Gwinnett
Lyman Hall
George Walton

Resolved, That copies of the Declaration be sent to the several assemblies, conventions, and committees, or councils of safety, and to the several commanding officers of the continental troops; that it be proclaimed in each of the United States, at the head of the army.

The Articles of Confederation

Agreed to by Congress November 15, 1777;
ratified and in force March 1, 1781

To all whom these Presents shall come, we the undersigned Delegates of the States affixed to our Names send greeting. Whereas the Delegates of the United States of America in Congress assembled did on the fifteenth day of November in the Year of our Lord One Thousand Seven Hundred and Seventy seven, and in the Second Year of the Independence of America agree to certain articles of Confederation and perpetual Union between the States of Newhampshire, Massachusetts-bay, Rhodeisland and Providence Plantations, Connecticut, New-York, New-Jersey, Pennsylvania, Delaware, Maryland, Virginia, North-Carolina, South-Carolina and Georgia in the Words following, viz. "Articles of Confederation and perpetual Union between the states of Newhampshire, Massachusetts-bay, Rhodeisland and Providence Plantations, Connecticut, New-York, New-Jersey, Pennsylvania, Delaware, Maryland, Virginia, North-Carolina, South-Carolina and Georgia.

Art. I. The Stile of this confederacy shall be "The United States of America."

Art. II. Each state retains its sovereignty, freedom and independence, and every Power, Jurisdiction and right, which is not by this confederation expressly delegated to the United States, in Congress assembled.

Art. III. The said states hereby severally enter into a firm league of friendship with each other, for their common defence, the security of their Liberties, and their mutual and general welfare, binding themselves to assist each other, against all force offered to, or attacks made upon them, or any of them, on account of religion, sovereignty, trade, or any other pretence whatever.

Art. IV. The better to secure and perpetuate mutual friendship and intercourse among the people of the different states in this union, the free inhabitants of each of these states, paupers, vagabonds and fugitives from Justice excepted, shall be entitled to all privileges and immunities of free citizens in the several states; and the people of each state shall have free ingress and regress to and from any other state, and shall enjoy therein all the privileges of trade and commerce, subject to the same duties, impositions and restrictions as the inhabitants thereof respectively, provided that such restriction shall not extend so far as to prevent the removal of property imported into any state, to any other state of which the Owner is an inhabitant; provided also that no imposition, duties or restriction shall be laid by any state, on the property of the united states, or either of them.

If any Person guilty of, or charged with treason, felony, or other high misdemeanor in any state, shall flee from Justice, and be found in any of the united states, he shall upon demand of the Governor or executive power, of the state from which he fled, be delivered up and removed to the state having jurisdiction of his offence.

Full faith and credit shall be given in each of these states to the records, acts and judicial proceedings of the courts and magistrates of every other state.

Art. V. For the more convenient management of the general interests of the united states, delegates shall be annually appointed in such manner as the legislature of each state shall direct, to meet in Congress on the first Monday in November, in every year, with a power reserved to each state, to recall its delegates, or any of them, at any time within the year, and to send others in their stead, for the remainder of the Year.

No state shall be represented in Congress by less than two, nor by more than seven Members; and no person shall be capable of being a delegate for more than three years in any term of six years; nor shall any person, being a delegate, be capable of holding any office under the united states, for which he, or another for his benefit receives any salary, fees or emolument of any kind.

Each state shall maintain its own delegates in a meeting of the states, and while they act as members of the committee of the states.

In determining questions in the united states, in Congress assembled, each state shall have one vote.

Freedom of speech and debate in Congress shall not be impeached or questioned in any Court, or place out of Congress, and the members of congress shall be protected in their persons from arrests and imprisonments, during the time of their going to and from, and attendance on congress, except for treason, felony, or breach of the peace.

Art. VI. No state without the Consent of the united states in congress assembled, shall send any embassy to, or receive any embassy from, or enter into any conference, agreement, or alliance or treaty with any King, prince or state; nor shall any person holding any office or profit or trust under the united states, or any of them, accept of any present, emolument, office or title of any kind whatever from any king, prince or foreign state; nor shall the united states in congress assembled, or any of them, grant any title of nobility.

No two or more states shall enter into any treaty, confederation or alliance whatever between them, without the consent of the united states in congress assembled, specifying accurately the purposes for which the same is to be entered into, and how long it shall continue.

No state shall lay any imposts or duties, which may interfere with any stipulations in treaties, entered into by the united states in congress assembled, with any king, prince or state, in pursuance of any treaties already proposed by congress, to the courts of France and Spain.

No vessels of war shall be kept up in time of peace by any state, except such number only, as shall be deemed necessary by the united states in congress assembled, for the defence of such state, or its trade; nor shall any body of forces be kept up by any state, in time of peace, except such number only, as in the judgment of the united states, in congress assembled, shall be deemed requisite to garrison the forts necessary for the defence of such state; but every state shall always keep up a well regulated and disciplined militia, sufficiently armed and accoutred, and shall provide and constantly have ready for use, in public stores, a due number of field pieces and tents, and a proper quantity of arms, ammunition and camp equipage.

No state shall engage in any war without the consent of the united states in congress assembled, unless such state be actually invaded by enemies, or shall have received certain advice of a resolution being formed by some nation of Indians to invade such state, and the danger is so imminent as not to admit of a delay, till the united states in congress asssembled can be consulted; nor shall any state grant commissions to any ships or vessels of war, nor letters of marque or reprisal, except it be after a declaration of war by the united states in congress assembled, and then only against the kingdom or state and the subjects thereof, against which war has been so declared, and under such regulations as shall be established by the united states in congress assembled, unless such state be infested by pirates; in which case vessels of war may be fitted out for that occasion, and kept so long as the danger shall continue, or until the united states in congress assembled shall determine otherwise.

Art. VII. When land-forces are raised by any state for the common defence, all officers of or under the rank of colonel, shall be appointed by the legislature of each state respectively by whom such forces shall be raised, or in such manner as such state shall direct, and all vacancies shall be filled up by the state which first made the appointment.

Art. VIII. All charges of war, and all other expences that shall be incurred for the common defence or general welfare, and allowed by the united states in congress assembled, shall be defrayed out of a common treasury, which shall be supplied by the several states, in proportion to the value of all land within each state, granted to or surveyed for any Person, as such land and the buildings and improvements thereon shall be estimated according to such mode as the united states in congress assembled, shall from time to time direct and appoint. The taxes for paying that proportion shall be laid and levied by the authority and direction of the legislatures of the several states within the time agreed upon by the united states in congress assembled.

Art. IX. The united states in congress assembled, shall have the sole and exclusive right and power of determining on peace and war, except in the cases mentioned in the sixth article—of sending and receiving ambassadors—entering into treaties and alliances, provided that no treaty of commerce shall be made whereby the legislative power of the respective states shall be restrained from imposing such imposts and duties on foreigners, as their own people are subjected to, or from prohibiting the exportation of any species of goods or commodities whatsoever—of establishing rules for deciding in all cases, what captures on land or water shall be legal, and in what manner prizes taken by land or naval forces in the service of the united states shall be divided or appropriated—of granting letters of marque and reprisal in times of peace—appointing courts for the trial of piracies and felonies committed on the high seas and establishing courts for receiving and determining finally appeals in all cases of captures, provided that no member of congress shall be appointed a judge of any of the said courts.

The united states in congress assembled shall also be the last resort on appeal in all disputes and differences now subsisting or that hereafter may arise between two or more states concerning boundary, jurisdiction or any other cause whatever; which authority shall always be exercised in the manner following. Whenever the legislative or executive authority or lawful agent of any state in controversy with another shall present a petition to congress stating the matter in question and praying for a hearing, notice thereof shall be given by order of congress to the legislative or executive authority of the other state in controversy, and a day assigned for the appearance of the parties by their lawful agents, who shall then be directed to appoint by joint consent, commissioners or judges to constitute a court for hearing and determining the matter in question: but if they cannot agree, congress shall name three persons out of each of the united states, and from the list of such persons each party shall alternately strike out one, the petitioners beginning, until the number shall be reduced to thirteen; and from that number not less than seven, nor more than nine names as congress shall direct, shall in the presence of congress be drawn out by lot, and the persons whose names shall be so drawn or any five of them, shall be commissioners or judges, to hear and finally determine the controversy, so always as a major part of the judges who shall hear the cause shall agree in the determination: and if either party shall neglect to attend at the day appointed, without shewing reasons, which congress shall judge sufficient, or being present shall refuse to strike, the congress shall proceed to nominate three persons out of each state, and the secretary of congress shall strike in behalf of such party absent or refusing; and the judgment and sentence of the court to be appointed, in the manner before prescribed, shall be final and conclusive; and if any of the parties shall refuse to submit to the authority of such court, or to appear to defend their claim or cause, the court shall nevertheless proceed to pronounce sentence, or judgment, which shall in like manner be final and decisive, the judgment or sentence and other proceedings being in either case transmitted to congress, and lodged among the acts of congress for the security of the parties concerned: provided that every commissioner, before he sits in judgment, shall take an oath to be administered by one of the judges of the supreme or superior court of the state, where the cause shall be tried, "well and truly to hear and determine the matter in question, according to the best of his judgment, without favour, affection or hope of reward:" provided also that no state shall be deprived of territory for the benefit of the united states.

All controversies concerning the private right of soil claimed under different grants of two or more states, whose jurisdictions as they may respect such lands, and the states which passed such grants are adjusted, the said grants or either of them being at the same time claimed to have originated antecedent to such settlement of jurisdiction, shall on the petition of either party to the congress of the united states, be finally determined as near as may be in the same manner as is before prescribed for deciding disputes respecting territorial jurisdiction between different states.

The united states in congress assembled shall also have the sole and exclusive right and power of regulating the alloy and value of coin struck by their own authority, or by that of the respective states—fixing the standard of weights and measures throughout the united states—regulating the trade and managing all affairs with the Indians, not members of any of the states, provided that the legislative right of any state within its own limits be not infringed or violated—establishing and regulating post-offices from one state to another, throughout all the united states, and exacting such postage on the papers passing thro' the same as may be requisite to defray the expences of the said office—appointing all officers of the land forces, in the service of the united states, except regimental officers—appointing all the officers of the united states—making rules for the government and regulation of the said land and naval forces, and directing their operations.

The united states in congress assembled shall have the authority to appoint a committee, to sit in the recess of congress, to be denominated "A Committee of the States," and to consist of one delegate from each state; and to appoint such other committees and civil officers as may be necessary for managing the general affairs of the united states under their direction—to appoint one of their number to preside, provided that no person be allowed to serve in the office of president more than one year in any term of three years; to ascertain the necessary sums of Money to be raised for the service of the united states, and to appropriate and apply the same for defraying the public expences—to borrow money, or emit bills on the credit of the united states, transmitting every half year to the respective states an account of the sums of money so borrowed or emitted,—to build and equip a navy—to agree upon the number of land forces, and to make requisitions from each state for its quota, in proportion to the number of white inhabitants in such state; which requisition shall be binding, and thereupon the legislature of each state shall appoint the regimental officers, raise the men and cloath, arm and equip them in a soldier like manner, at the expence of the united states, and the officers and men so cloathed, armed and equipped shall march to the place appointed, and within the time agreed on by the united states in congress assembled: But if the united states in congress assembled shall, on consideration of circumstances judge proper that any state should not raise men, or should raise a smaller number than its quota, and that any other state should raise a greater number of men than the quota thereof, such extra number shall be raised, officered, cloathed, armed and equipped in the same manner as the quota of such state, unless the legislature of such state shall judge that such extra number cannot be safely spared out of the same, in which case they shall raise, officer, cloath, arm and equip as many of such extra number as they judge can be safely spared. And the officers and men so cloathed, armed and equipped, shall march to the place appointed, and within the time agreed on by the united states in congress assembled.

The united states in congress assembled shall never engage in a war, nor grant letters of marque and reprisal in time of peace, nor enter into any treaties or alliances, nor coin money, nor regulate the value thereof, nor ascertain the sums and expences necessary for the defence and welfare of the united states, or any of them, nor emit bills, nor borrow money on the credit of the united states, nor appropriate money, nor agree upon the number of vessels of war, to be built or purchased, or the number of land or sea forces to be raised, nor appoint a commander in chief of the army or navy, unless nine states assent to the same: nor shall a question on any other point, except for adjourning from day to day be determined, unless by the votes of a majority of the united states in congress assembled.

The congress of the united states shall have power to adjourn to any time within the year, and to any place within the united states, so that no period of adjournment be for a longer duration than the space of six Months, and shall publish the Journal of their proceedings monthly, except such parts thereof relating to treaties, alliances or military operations as in their judgment require secresy; and the yeas and nays of the delegates of each state on any question shall be entered on the Journal, when it is desired by any delegate; and the delegates of a state, or any of them, at his or their request shall be furnished with a transcript of the said Journal, except such parts as are above excepted to lay before the legislatures of the several states.

Art. X. The committee of the states, or any nine of them, shall be authorised to execute, in the recess of congress, such of the powers of congress as the united states in congress assembled, by the consent of nine states, shall from time to time think expedient to vest them with; provided that no power be delegated to the said committee, for the exercise of which, by the articles of confederation, the voice of nine states in the congress of the united states assembled is requisite.

Art. XI. Canada acceding to this confederation, and joining in the measures of the united states, shall be admitted into, and entitled to all the advantages of this union: but no other colony shall be admitted into the same, unless such admission be agreed to by nine states.

Art. XII. All bills of credit emitted, monies borrowed and debts contracted by, or under the authority of congress, before the assembling of the united states, in pursuance of the present confederation, shall be deemed and considered as a charge against the united states, for payment and satisfaction whereof the said united states and the public faith are hereby solemnly pledged.

Art. XIII. Every state shall abide by the determinations of the united states in congress assembled, on all questions which by this confederation are submitted to them. And the Articles of this confederation shall be inviolably observed by every state, and the union shall be perpetual; nor shall any alteration at any time hereafter be made in any of them; unless such alteration be agreed to in a congress of the united states, and be afterwards confirmed by the legislatures of every state.

AND WHEREAS it hath pleased the Great Governor of the World to incline the hearts of the legislatures we respectively represent in congress, to approve of, and to authorize us to ratify the said articles of confederation and perpetual union. KNOW YE that we the undersigned delegates, by virtue of the power and authority to us given for that purpose, do by these presents, in the name and in behalf of our respective constituents, fully and entirely ratify and confirm each and every of the said articles of confederation and perpetual union, and all and singular the matters and things therein contained: And we do further solemnly plight and engage the faith of our respective constituents, that they shall abide by the determination of the united states in congress assembled, on all questions, which by the said confederation are submitted to them. And that the articles thereof shall be inviolably observed by the states we respectively represent, and that the union shall be perpetual. In Witness whereof we have hereunto set our hands in Congress. Done at Philadelphia in the state of Pennsylvania the ninth Day of July in the Year of our Lord one Thousand seven Hundred and Seventy-eight and in the third year of the independence of America.

The Constitution of the United States of America

Annotated with references to *The Federalist Papers*

Federalist Paper
Number (Author)

[PREAMBLE]

We the People of the United States, in Order to form a more perfect Union, establish Justice, insure domestic Tranquility, provide for the common defence, promote the general Welfare, and secure the Blessings of Liberty to ourselves and our Posterity, do ordain and establish this Constitution for the United States of America.

84 (Hamilton)

ARTICLE I

Section 1
[LEGISLATIVE POWERS]

All legislative Powers herein granted shall be vested in a Congress of the United States, which shall consist of a Senate and House of Representatives.

10, 45 (Madison)

Section 2
[HOUSE OF REPRESENTATIVES, HOW CONSTITUTED, POWER OF IMPEACHMENT]

The House of Representatives shall be composed of Members chosen every second Year by the People of the several States, and the Electors in each State shall have the Qualifications requisite for Electors of the most numerous Branch of the State Legislature.

39, 45, 52–53, 57 (Madison)

No Person shall be a Representative who shall not have attained to the Age of twenty-five Years, and been seven Years a Citizen of the United States, and who shall not, when elected, be an inhabitant of that State in which he shall be chosen.

52 (Madison)

Representatives and *direct Taxes*[1] shall be apportioned among the several States which may be included within this Union, according to their respective Numbers, *which shall be determined by adding to the whole Number of free Persons, including those bound to Service for a Term of Years,* and excluding Indians not taxed, *three-fifths of all other Persons.*[2] The actual Enumeration shall be made within three Years after the first Meeting of the Congress of the United States, and within every subsequent Term of ten Years, in such Manner as they shall by Law direct. The Number of Representatives shall not exceed one for every thirty Thousand, but each State shall have at Least one Representative; *and until such enumeration shall be made, the State of New*

60 (Hamilton)
54, 58 (Madison)

55–56 (Madison)

---

1 Modified by Sixteenth Amendment.

2 Modified by Fourteenth Amendment.

Hampshire shall be entitled to chuse three, Massachusetts eight, Rhode-Island and Providence Plantations one, Connecticut five, New-York six, New Jersey four, Pennsylvania eight, Delaware one, Maryland six, Virginia ten, North Carolina five, South Carolina five, and Georgia three.[3]

When vacancies happen in the Representation from any State, the Executive Authority thereof shall issue Writs of Election to fill such Vacancies.

79 (Hamilton)

The House of Representatives shall chuse their Speaker and other Officers; and shall have the sole Power of Impeachment.

Section 3
[THE SENATE, HOW CONSTITUTED, IMPEACHMENT TRIALS]

39, 45 (Madison)
60 (Hamilton)

The Senate of the United States shall be composed of two Senators from each State, *chosen by the Legislature thereof,*[4] for six Years; and each Senator shall have one Vote.

62–63 (Madison)
59, 68 (Hamilton)

Immediately after they shall be assembled in Consequence of the first Election, they shall be divided as equally as may be into three Classes. The Seats of the Senators of the first Class shall be vacated at the Expiration of the second Year, of the second Class at the Expiration of the fourth Year, and of the third Class at the Expiration of the sixth Year, so that one third may be chosen every second Year: *and if vacancies happen by Resignation, or otherwise, during the Recess of the Legislature of any State, the Executive thereof may make temporary Appointments until the next Meeting of the Legislature, which shall then fill such Vacancies.*[5]

62 (Madison)
64 (Jay)

No person shall be a Senator who shall not have attained to the Age of thirty Years, and been nine Years a Citizen of the United States, and who shall not, when elected, be an Inhabitant of that State for which he shall be chosen.

The Vice-President of the United States shall be President of the Senate, but shall have no Vote, unless they be equally divided.

The Senate shall chuse their other Officers, and also a President pro tempore, in the Absence of the Vice-President, or when he shall exercise the Office of President of the United States.

39 (Madison)
65–67, 79 (Hamilton)

The Senate shall have the sole Power to try all Impeachments. When sitting for that Purpose, they shall be on Oath or Affirmation. When the President of the United States is tried, the Chief Justice shall preside: And no Person shall be convicted without the Concurrence of two-thirds of the Members present.

84 (Hamilton)

Judgment in Cases of Impeachment shall not extend further than to removal from Office, and disqualification to hold and enjoy any Office of honor, Trust or Profit under the United States: but the Party convicted shall nevertheless be liable and subject to Indictment, Trial, Judgment and Punishment, according to Law.

Section 4
[ELECTION OF SENATORS AND REPRESENTATIVES]

59–61 (Hamilton)

The Times, Places and Manner of holding Elections for Senators and Representatives, shall be prescribed in each State by the Legislature thereof; but the

---

3 Temporary provision.

4 Modified by Seventeenth Amendment.

5 Modified by Seventeenth Amendment.

Congress may at any time by Law make or alter such Regulations, except as to the Places of chusing Senators.

The Congress shall assemble at least once in every Year, and such Meeting shall be on the first Monday in December, unless they shall by Law appoint a different Day.[6]

Section 5
[QUORUM, JOURNALS, MEETINGS, ADJOURNMENTS]

Each House shall be the Judge of the Elections, Returns and Qualifications of its own Members, and a Majority of each shall constitute a Quorum to do Business; but a smaller Number may adjourn from day to day, and may be authorized to compel the Attendance of absent Members, in such Manner, and under the Penalties as each House may provide.

Each House may determine the Rules of its Proceedings, punish its Members for disorderly Behavior, and, with the Concurrence of two-thirds, expel a Member.

Each House shall keep a Journal of its Proceedings, and from time to time publish the same, excepting such Parts as may in their Judgment require Secrecy; and the Yeas and Nays of the Members of either House on any questions shall, at the Desire of one-fifth of the present, be entered on the Journal.

Neither House, during the Session of Congress, shall, without the Consent of the other, adjourn for more than three days, nor to any other Place than that in which the two Houses shall be sitting.

Section 6
[COMPENSATION, PRIVILEGES, DISABILITIES]

The Senators and Representatives shall receive a Compensation for their Services, to be ascertained by Law, and paid out of the Treasury of the United States. They shall in all Cases, except Treason, Felony and Breach of the Peace, be privileged from Arrest during their Attendance at the Session of their respective Houses, and in going to and returning from the same; and for any Speech or Debate in either House, they shall not be questioned in any other Place.

No Senator or Representative shall, during the time for which he was elected, be appointed to any civil Office under the authority of the United States, which shall have been created, or the Emoluments whereof shall have been encreased during such time; and no Person holding any Office under the United States, shall be a Member of either House during his Continuance in Office.

55 (Madison)
76 (Hamilton)

Section 7
[PROCEDURE IN PASSING BILLS AND RESOLUTIONS]

All Bills for raising Revenue shall originate in the House of Representatives; but the Senate may propose or concur with Amendments as on other Bills.

66 (Hamilton)

Every Bill which shall have passed the House of Representatives and the Senate, shall, before it become a Law, be presented to the President of the United States; if he approve he shall sign it, but if not he shall return it, with his Objections to that House in which it shall have originated, who shall enter the Objections at large on their Journal, and proceed to reconsider it. If after such Reconsideration

69, 73 (Hamilton)

---

6 Modified by Twentieth Amendment.

two-thirds of that House shall agree to pass the Bill, it shall be sent, together with the Objections, to the other House, by which it shall likewise be reconsidered, and if approved by two-thirds of that House it shall become a Law. But in all such Cases the Votes of both Houses shall be determined by Yeas and Nays, and the Names of the Persons voting for and against the Bill shall be entered on the Journal of each House respectively. If any Bill shall not be returned by the President within ten Days (Sundays excepted) after it shall have been presented to him, the Same shall be a Law, in like Manner as if he had signed it, unless the Congress by their Adjournment prevent its Return, in which Case it shall not be a Law.

69, 73 (Hamilton)

Every Order, Resolution, or Vote to which the Concurrence of the Senate and House of Representatives may be necessary (except on a question of Adjournment) shall be presented to the President of the United States; and before the Same shall take Effect, shall be approved by him, or being disapproved by him, shall be repassed by two-thirds of the Senate and House of Representatives, according to the Rules and Limitations prescribed in the Case of a Bill.

Section 8
[POWERS OF CONGRESS]

The Congress shall have Power

To lay and collect Taxes, Duties, Imposts and Excises, to pay the Debts and

30–36 (Hamilton)
41 (Madison)

provide for the common Defence and general Welfare of the United States; but all Duties, Imposts and excises shall be uniform throughout the United States;

To borrow Money on the Credit of the United States;

56 (Madison)
42, 45, 56
(Madison)

To regulate Commerce with foreign Nations, and among the several States, and with the Indian Tribes;

32 (Hamilton)

To establish an uniform Rule of Naturalization, and uniform Laws on the subject of Bankruptcies throughout the United States;

42 (Madison)

To coin Money, regulate the Value thereof, and of foreign Coin, and fix the Standard of Weights and Measures;

42 (Madison)

To provide for the Punishment of counterfeiting the Securities and current Coin of the United States;

42 (Madison)

To establish Post Offices and post Roads;

42 (Madison)
42, 43 (Madison)

To promote the Progress of Science and useful Arts, by securing for limited Times to Authors and Inventors the exclusive Right to their respective Writings and Discoveries;

81 (Hamilton)

To constitute Tribunals inferior to the supreme Court;

42 (Madison)

To define and Punish Piracies and Felonies committed on the high Seas, and Offences against the Law of Nations;

41 (Madison)

To declare War, grant Letters of Marque and Reprisal, and make Rules concerning Captures on Land and Water;

23, 24, 26 (Hamilton)

To raise and support Armies, but no Appropriation of Money to that Use shall be for a longer Term than two Years;

41 (Madison)

To provide and maintain a Navy;

To make Rules for the Government and Regulation of the land and naval forces;

29 (Hamilton)

To provide for calling for the Militia to execute the Laws of the Union, suppress Insurrections and repel Invasions;

To provide for organizing, arming, and disciplining, the Militia, and for governing such Part of them as may be employed in the Service of the United States, reserving to the States respectively, the Appointment of the Officers, and the Authority of training the Militia according to the discipline prescribed by Congress;

29 (Hamilton)
56 (Madison)

To exercise exclusive Legislation in all Cases whatsoever, over such District (not exceeding ten Miles square) as may, by Cession of particular States, and the Acceptance of Congress, become the Seat of the Government of the United States, and to exercise like Authority over all Places purchased by the Consent of the Legislature of the State in which the Same shall be, for the Erection of Forts, Magazines, Arsenals, dock-Yards, and other needful Buildings;—And

32 (Hamilton)
43 (Madison)

To make all Laws which shall be necessary and proper for carrying into Execution the foregoing Powers, and all other Powers vested by this Constitution in the Government of the United States, or in any Department or Officer thereof.

29, 33 (Hamilton)
44 (Madison)

Section 9
[SOME RESTRICTIONS ON FEDERAL POWER]

The Migration or Importation of such Persons as any of the States now existing shall think proper to admit, shall not be prohibited by the Congress prior to the Year one thousand eight hundred and eight, but a Tax or Duty may be imposed on such Importation, not exceeding ten dollars for each Person.[7]

42 (Madison)

The privilege of the Writ of *Habeas Corpus* shall not be suspended, unless when in Cases of Rebellion or Invasion the public Safety may require it.

83, 84 (Hamilton)

No Bill of Attainder or ex post facto Law shall be passed.

84 (Hamilton)

No Capitation, or other direct, Tax shall be laid, unless in Proportion to the Census or Enumeration herein before directed to be taken.[8]

No Tax or Duty shall be laid on Articles exported from any State.

No Preference shall be given by any Regulation of Commerce or Revenue to the Ports of one State over those of another; nor shall vessels bound to, or from, one State, be obliged to enter, clear, or pay Duties in another.

32 (Hamilton)

No Money shall be drawn from the Treasury, but in Consequence of Appropriations made by Law; and a regular Statement and Account of the Receipts and Expenditures of all public Money shall be published from time to time.

No Title of Nobility shall be granted by the United States: And no Person holding any Office of Profit or Trust under them, shall, without the Consent of the Congress, accept of any present, Emolument, Office or Title, of any kind whatever, from any King, Prince, or foreign State.

39 (Madison)
84 (Hamilton)

Section 10
[RESTRICTIONS UPON POWERS OF STATES]

No State shall enter into any Treaty, Alliance, or Confederation; grant Letters of Marque and Reprisal; coin Money; emit Bills of Credit; make any Thing but gold and silver Coin a Tender in Payment of Debts; pass any Bill of Attainder, ex post facto Law, or Law impairing the Obligation of Contracts, or grant any Title of Nobility.

33 (Hamilton)
44 (Madison)

---

7   Temporary provision.

8   Modified by Sixteenth Amendment.

No State shall, without the Consent of the Congress, lay any Imposts or Duties on Imports or Exports, except what may be absolutely necessary for executing its inspection Laws: and the net Produce of all Duties and Imposts, laid by any State on Imports or Exports, shall be for the Use of the Treasury of the United States; and all such Laws shall be subject to the Revision and Control of the Congress.

No State shall, without the Consent of Congress, lay any Duty of Tonnage, keep Troops, or Ships of War in time of Peace, enter into any Agreement or Compact with another State, or with a foreign Power, or engage in War, unless actually invaded, or in such imminent Danger as will not admit of Delay.

ARTICLE II

Section 1
[EXECUTIVE POWER, ELECTION, QUALIFICATIONS OF THE PRESIDENT]

The executive Power shall be vested in a President of the United States of America. *He shall hold his Office during the Term of four years and, together with the Vice-President, chosen for the same Term, be elected, as follows:*[9]

Each State shall appoint, in such Manner as the Legislature thereof may direct, a Number of Electors, equal to the whole Number of Senators and Representatives to which the State may be entitled in the Congress: but no Senator or Representative, or Person holding an Office of Trust or Profit under the United States, shall be appointed an Elector.

The electors shall meet in their respective States, and vote by ballot for two Persons, of whom one at least shall not be an Inhabitant of the same State with themselves. And they shall make a List of all the Persons voted for, and of the Number of Votes for each; which List they shall sign and certify, and transmit sealed to the Seat of the Government of the United States, directed to the President of the Senate. The President of the Senate shall, in the Presence of the Senate and House of Representatives, open all the Certificates, and the Votes shall then be counted. The Person having the greatest Number of Votes shall be the President, if such Number be a Majority of the whole Number of Electors appointed; and if there be more than one who have such Majority and have an equal Number of Votes, then the House of Representatives shall immediately chuse by Ballot one of them for President; and if no person have a Majority, then from the five highest on the List the said House shall in like Manner chuse the President. But in chusing the President, the Votes shall be taken by States, the Representation from each State having one Vote; A quorum for this Purpose shall consist of a Member or Members from two-thirds of the States, and a Majority of all the States shall be necessary to a Choice. In every Case, after the Choice of the President, the person having the greatest Number of Votes of the Electors shall be the Vice-President. But if there should remain two or more who have equal vote, the Senate shall chuse from them by Ballot the Vice-President.[10]

The Congress may determine the Time of chusing the Electors, and the Day on which they shall give their Votes; which Day shall be the same throughout the United States.

32 (Hamilton)
44 (Madison)

39 (Madison)
70, 71, 84
(Hamilton)
68, 69, 71, 77
(Hamilton)
39, 45 (Madison)

66 (Hamilton)

---

9 Number of terms limited to two by Twenty-Second Amendment.

10 Modified by Twelfth and Twentieth Amendments.

No Person except a natural born Citizen, or a Citizen of the United States, at the time of the Adoption of this Constitution, shall be eligible to the Office of President; neither shall any Person be eligible to that Office who shall not have attained to the Age of thirty-five Years, and been fourteen Years a Resident within the United States.

64 (Jay)

In Case of the Removal of the President from Office, or his Death, Resignation, or Inability to discharge the Powers and Duties of the said Office, the same shall devolve on the Vice-President, and the Congress may by Law provide for the Case of Removal, Death, Resignation, or Inability, both of the President and Vice-President, declaring what Officer shall then act as President, and such Officer shall act accordingly, until the Disability be removed, or a President shall be elected.

The President shall, at stated Times, receive for his Services, a Compensation, which shall neither be encreased nor diminished during the Period for which he shall have been elected, and he shall not receive within that Period any other Emolument from the United States, or any of them.

73, 79 (Hamilton)

Before he enter on the Execution of his Office, he shall take the following Oath or Affirmation:—"I do solemnly swear (or affirm) that I will faithfully execute the Office of President of the United States, and will to the best of my Ability, preserve, protect and defend the Constitution of the United States."

Section 2
[POWERS OF THE PRESIDENT]

The President shall be Commander in Chief of the Army and Navy of the United States, and of the Militia of the several States, when called into the actual Service of the United States; he may require the Opinion, in writing, of the principal Officer in each of the executive Departments, upon any Subject relating to the Duties of their respective Offices, and he shall have Power to grant Reprieves and Pardons for Offences against the United States, except in Cases of Impeachment.

69, 74 (Hamilton)

He shall have Power, by and with the Advice and Consent of the Senate, to make Treaties, provided two-thirds of the Senators present concur; and he shall nominate, and by and with the Advice and Consent of the Senate, shall appoint Ambassadors, other public Ministers and Consuls, Judges of the Supreme Court, and all other Officers of the United States, whose Appointments are not herein otherwise provided for, and which shall be established by Law: but the Congress may by Law vest the Appointment of such inferior Officers, as they think proper, in the President alone, in the Courts of Law, or in the Heads of Departments.

42 (Madison)
64 (Jay)
66, 69, 76, 77
(Hamilton)

The President shall have Power to fill up all Vacancies that may happen during the Recess of the Senate, by granting Commissions which shall expire at the End of their next Session.

67, 76
(Hamilton)

Section 3
[POWERS AND DUTIES OF THE PRESIDENT]

He shall from time to time give to the Congress Information of the State of the Union, and recommend to their Consideration such Measures as he shall judge necessary and expedient; he may, on extraordinary Occasions, convene both Houses, or either of them, and in Case of Disagreement between them, with Respect to the Time of Adjournment, he may adjourn them to such Time

69, 77, 78
(Hamilton)
42 (Madison)

as he shall think proper; he shall receive Ambassadors and other public Ministers; he shall take Care that the Laws be faithfully executed, and shall Commission all the Officers of the United States.

Section 4
[IMPEACHMENT]

39 (Madison)
69 (Hamilton)

The President, Vice-President and all civil Officers of the United States shall be removed from Office on Impeachment for, and Conviction of, Treason, Bribery, or other high Crimes and Misdemeanors.

ARTICLE III

Section 1
[JUDICIAL POWER, TENURE OF OFFICE]

65, 78, 79, 81, 82
(Hamilton)

The judicial Power of the United States, shall be vested in one supreme Court, and in such inferior Courts as the Congress may from time to time ordain and establish. The Judges, both of the supreme and inferior Courts, shall hold their Offices during good Behavior, and shall, at stated Times, receive for their Services, a Compensation, which shall not be diminished during their Continuance in Office.

Section 2
[JURISDICTION]

80 (Hamilton)

The judicial Power shall extend to all Cases, in Law and Equity, arising under this Constitution, the Laws of the United States, and Treaties made, or which shall be made, under their Authority;—to all Cases affecting Ambassadors, other public Ministers and Consuls;—to all Cases of admiralty and maritime Jurisdiction;—to Controversies to which the United States shall be a party;—to Controversies between two or more States;—*between a State and Citizens of another State;*—between Citizens of different States,—between Citizens of the same State claiming Lands under Grants of different States, *and between a State,* or the Citizens thereof, *and foreign States, Citizens or Subjects.*[11]

81 (Hamilton)

In all Cases affecting Ambassadors, other public Ministers and Consuls, and those in which a State shall be Party, the supreme Court shall have original Jurisdiction. In all the other Cases before mentioned, the supreme Court shall have appellate Jurisdiction, both as to Law and Fact, with such Exceptions, and under such Regulations as Congress shall make.

83, 84 (Hamilton)

The Trial of all Crimes, except in Cases of Impeachment, shall be by Jury; and such Trial shall be held in the State where the said Crimes shall have been committed; but when not committed within any State, the Trial shall be at such Place or Places as the Congress may by Law have directed.

---

11 Modified by Eleventh Amendment.

Section 3
[TREASON, PROOF, AND PUNISHMENT]

Treason against the United States, shall consist only in levying War against them, or in adhering to their Enemies, giving them Aid and Comfort. No Person shall be convicted of Treason unless on the Testimony of two Witnesses to the same overt Act, or on Confession in open Court.

43 (Madison)
84 (Hamilton)

The Congress shall have Power to declare the Punishment of Treason, but no Attainder of Treason shall work Corruption of Blood, or Forfeiture except during the Life of the Person attained.

43 (Madison)
84 (Hamilton)

ARTICLE IV

Section 1
[FAITH AND CREDIT AMONG STATES]

Full Faith and Credit shall be given in each State to the public Acts, Records, and judicial Proceedings of every other State. And the Congress may by general Laws prescribe the Manner in which such Acts, Records and Proceedings shall be proved, and the Effect thereof.

42 (Madison)

Section 2
[PRIVILEGES AND IMMUNITIES, FUGITIVES]

The Citizens of each State shall be entitled to all Privileges and Immunities of Citizens in the several States.

80 (Hamilton)

A person charged in any State with Treason, Felony or other Crime, who shall flee from Justice, and be found in another State, shall on Demand of the executive Authority of the State from which he fled, be delivered up to be removed to the State having Jurisdiction of the Crime.

No person held to Service or Labour in one State, under the Laws thereof, escaping into another, shall, in Consequence of any Law or Regulation therein, be discharged from such Service or Labour, but shall be delivered up on Claim of the Party to whom such Service or Labour may be due.[12]

Section 3
[ADMISSION OF NEW STATES]

New States may be admitted by the Congress into this Union; but no new State shall be formed or erected within the Jurisdiction of any other State; nor any State be formed by the Junction of two or more States, or Parts of States, without the Consent of the Legislatures of the States concerned as well as of the Congress.

43 (Madison)

The Congress shall have Power to dispose of and make all needful Rules and Regulations respecting the Territory or other Property belonging to the United States; and nothing in this Constitution shall be so construed as to Prejudice any Claims of the United States, or of any particular State.

43 (Madison)

---

12 Repealed by Thirteenth Amendment.

Section 4

[GUARANTEE OF REPUBLICAN GOVERNMENT]

39, 43
(Madison)

The United States shall guarantee to every State in this Union a Republican Form of Government, and shall protect each of them against Invasion; and on Application of the Legislature, or of the Executive (when the Legislature cannot be convened) against domestic Violence.

ARTICLE V

[AMENDMENT OF THE CONSTITUTION]

39, 43 (Madison)
85 (Hamilton)

The Congress, whenever two-thirds of both Houses shall deem it necessary, shall propose Amendments to this Constitution, or, on the Application of the Legislatures of two-thirds of the several States, shall call a Convention for proposing Amendments, which, in either Case, shall be valid to all Intents and Purposes, as Part of this Constitution, when ratified by the Legislatures of three-fourths of the several States, or by Conventions in three-fourths thereof, as the one or the other Mode of Ratification may be proposed by the Congress; *Provided that no Amendment which may be made prior to the Year One thousand eight hundred and eight shall in any Manner affect the first and fourth Clauses in the Ninth Section of the first Article;*[13] and that no State, without its Consent, shall be deprived of its equal Suffrage in the Senate.

ARTICLE VI

[DEBTS, SUPREMACY, OATH]

43 (Madison)

All Debts contracted and Engagements entered into, before the Adoption of this Constitution, shall be as valid against the United States under this Constitution, as under the Confederation.

27, 33 (Hamilton)
39, 44 (Madison)

This Constitution, and the Laws of the United States which shall be made in Pursuance thereof; and all Treaties made, or which shall be made, under the Authority of the United States, shall be the supreme Law of the Land; and the Judges in every State shall be bound thereby, any Thing in the Constitution or Laws of any State to the Contrary notwithstanding.

27 (Hamilton)
44 (Madison)

The Senators and Representatives before mentioned, and the Members of the several State Legislatures, and all executive and judicial Officers, both of the United States and of the several States, shall be bound by Oath or Affirmation, to support this Constitution; but no religious Test shall be required as a Qualification to any Office or public Trust under the United States.

ARTICLE VII

[RATIFICATION AND ESTABLISHMENT]

39, 40, 43
(Madison)

The Ratification of the Conventions of nine States, shall be sufficient for the Establishment of this Constitution between the States so ratifying the Same.[14]

---

13 Temporary provision.

14 The Constitution was submitted on September 17, 1787, by the Constitutional Convention, was ratified by the conventions of several states at various dates up to May 29, 1790, and became effective on March 4, 1789.

Done in Convention by the Unanimous Consent of the States present the Seventeenth Day of September in the Year of our Lord one thousand seven hundred and Eighty seven and of the Independence of the United States of America the Twelfth. *In Witness* whereof We have hereunto subscribed our Names,

G:^{0} WASHINGTON—
Presidt, and Deputy
from Virginia

NEW HAMPSHIRE
John Langdon
Nicholas Gilman

MASSACHUSETTS
Nathaniel Gorham
Rufus King

CONNECTICUT
Wm Saml Johnson
Roger Sherman

NEW YORK
Alexander Hamilton

NEW JERSEY
Wil: Livingston
David Brearley
Wm Paterson
Jona: Dayton

PENNSYLVANIA
B Franklin
Thomas Mifflin
Robt Morris
Geo. Clymer
Thos. FitzSimons
Jared Ingersoll
James Wilson
Gouv Morris

DELAWARE
Geo Read
Gunning Bedfor Jun
John Dickinson
Richard Bassett
Jaco: Broom

MARYLAND
James McHenry
Dan of St Thos Jenifer
Danl Carroll

VIRGINIA
John Blair—
James Madison Jr.

NORTH CAROLINA
Wm Blount
Richd Dobbs Spaight
Hu Williamson

SOUTH CAROLINA
J. Rutledge
Charles Cotesworth Pinckney
Charles Pinckney
Pierce Butler

GEORGIA
William Few
Abr Baldwin

Amendments to the Constitution

Proposed by Congress and Ratified by the Legislatures of the Several States, Pursuant to Article V of the Original Constitution

Amendments I–X, known as the Bill of Rights, were proposed by Congress on September 25, 1789, and ratified on December 15, 1791. *The Federalist Papers* comments, mainly in opposition to a Bill of Rights, can be found in number 84 (Hamilton).

AMENDMENT I
[FREEDOM OF RELIGION, OF SPEECH, AND OF THE PRESS]

Congress shall make no law respecting an establishment of religion, or prohibiting the free exercise thereof; or abridging the freedom of speech, or of the press; or the right of the people peaceably to assemble, and to petition the Government for a redress of grievances.

AMENDMENT II
[RIGHT TO KEEP AND BEAR ARMS]

A well regulated Militia, being necessary to the security of a free State, the right of the people to keep and bear Arms, shall not be infringed.

AMENDMENT III
[QUARTERING OF SOLDIERS]

No Soldier shall, in time of peace be quartered in any house, without the consent of the Owner, nor in time of war, but in a manner to be prescribed by law.

AMENDMENT IV
[SECURITY FROM UNWARRANTABLE SEARCH AND SEIZURE]

The right of the people to be secure in their persons, houses, papers, and effects, against unreasonable searches and seizures, shall not be violated, and no Warrants shall issue, but upon probable cause, supported by Oath or affirmation, and particularly describing the place to be searched, and the persons or things to be seized.

AMENDMENT V
[RIGHTS OF ACCUSED PERSONS IN CRIMINAL PROCEEDINGS]

No person shall be held to answer for a capital, or otherwise infamous crime, unless on a presentment or indictment of a Grand Jury, except in cases arising in the land or naval forces, or in the Militia, when in actual service in time of

War or in public danger; nor shall any person be subject for the same offence to be twice put in jeopardy of life or limb; nor shall be compelled in any Criminal Case to be a witness against himself, nor be deprived of life, liberty, or property, without due process of law; nor shall private property be taken for public use, without just compensation.

AMENDMENT VI
[RIGHT TO SPEEDY TRIAL, WITNESSES, ETC.]

In all criminal prosecutions, the accused shall enjoy the right to a speedy and public trial, by an impartial jury of the State and district wherein the crime shall have been committed, which district shall have been previously ascertained by law, and to be informed of the nature and cause of the accusation; to be confronted with the witnesses against him; to have compulsory process for obtaining Witnesses in his favor, and to have the Assistance of Counsel for his defence.

AMENDMENT VII
[TRIAL BY JURY IN CIVIL CASES]

In suits at common law, where the value in controversy shall exceed twenty dollars, the right of trial by jury shall be preserved, and no fact tried by a jury shall be otherwise re-examined in any Court of the United States, than according to the rules of the common law.

AMENDMENT VIII
[BAILS, FINES, PUNISHMENTS]

Excessive bail shall not be required, nor excessive fines imposed, nor cruel and unusual punishments inflicted.

AMENDMENT IX
[RESERVATION OF RIGHTS OF PEOPLE]

The enumeration in the Constitution, of certain rights, shall not be construed to deny or disparage others retained by the people.

AMENDMENT X
[POWERS RESERVED TO STATES OR PEOPLE]

The powers not delegated to the United States by the Constitution, nor prohibited by it to the States, are reserved to the States respectively, or to the people.

AMENDMENT XI
[Proposed by Congress on March 4, 1794; declared ratified on January 8, 1798]
[RESTRICTION OF JUDICIAL POWER]

The Judicial power of the United States shall not be construed to extend to any suit in law or equity, commenced or prosecuted against one of the United States by Citizens of another State, or by Citizens or Subjects of any Foreign State.

AMENDMENT XII

[Proposed by Congress on December 9, 1803; declared ratified on September 25, 1804.]

[ELECTION OF PRESIDENT AND VICE-PRESIDENT]

The Electors shall meet in their respective states, and vote by ballot for President and Vice-President, one of whom, at least, shall not be an inhabitant of the same state with themselves; they shall name in their ballots the person voted for as President, and in distinct ballots the person voted for as Vice-President, and they shall make distinct lists of all persons voted for as President, and of all persons voted for as Vice-President, and of the number of votes for each, which lists they shall sign and certify, and transmit sealed to the seat of the government of the United States, directed to the President of the Senate;—The President of the Senate shall, in presence of the Senate and House of Representatives, open all the certificates and the votes shall then be counted;—The person having the greatest number of votes for President, shall be the President, if such number be a majority of the whole number of Electors appointed; and if no person have such majority, then from the persons having the highest numbers not exceeding three on the list of those voted for as President, the House of Representatives shall choose immediately, by ballot, the President. But in choosing the President, the votes shall be taken by states, the representation from each state having one vote; a quorum for this purpose shall consist of a member or members from two-thirds of the states, and a majority of all states shall be necessary to a choice. And if the House of Representatives shall not choose a President whenever the right of choice shall devolve upon them, before the fourth day of March next following, then the Vice-President, shall act as President, as in the case of the death or other constitutional disability of the President. The person having the greatest number of votes as Vice-President, shall be the Vice-President, if such a number be a majority of the whole number of Electors appointed, and if no person have a majority, then from the two highest numbers on the list, the Senate shall choose the Vice-President; a quorum for the purpose shall consist of two-thirds of the whole number of Senators, and a majority of the whole number shall be necessary to a choice. But no person constitutionally ineligible to the office of President shall be eligible to that of Vice-President of the United States.

AMENDMENT XIII

[Proposed by Congress on January 31, 1865; declared ratified on December 18, 1865]

Section 1

[ABOLITION OF SLAVERY]

Neither slavery nor involuntary servitude, except as a punishment for crime whereof the party shall have been duly convicted, shall exist within the United States, or any place subject to their jurisdiction.

Section 2

[POWER TO ENFORCE THIS ARTICLE]

Congress shall have power to enforce this article by appropriate legislation.

AMENDMENT XIV

[Proposed by Congress on June 13, 1866; declared ratified on July 28, 1868]

Section 1
[CITIZENSHIP RIGHTS NOT TO BE ABRIDGED BY STATES]

All persons born or naturalized in the United States, and subject to the jurisdiction thereof, are citizens of the United States and of the State wherein they reside. No state shall make or enforce any law which shall abridge the privileges or immunities of citizens of the United States; nor shall any State deprive any person of life, liberty, or property, without due process of law; nor deny to any person within its jurisdiction the equal protection of the laws.

Section 2
[APPORTIONMENT OF REPRESENTATIVES IN CONGRESS]

Representatives shall be apportioned among the several States according to their respective numbers, counting the whole number of persons in each State, excluding Indians not taxed. But when the right to vote at any election for the choice of electors for President and Vice-President of the United States, Representatives in Congress, the Executive and Judicial officers of a State, or the members of the Legislature thereof, is denied to any of the male inhabitants of such State, being twenty-one years of age, and citizens of the United States, or in any way abridged, except for participation in rebellion, or other crime, the basis of representation therein shall be reduced in the proportion which the number of such male citizens shall bear to the whole number of male citizens twenty-one years of age in such State.

Section 3
[PERSONS DISQUALIFIED FROM HOLDING OFFICE]

No person shall be a Senator or Representative in Congress, or elector of President and Vice-President, or hold any office, civil or military, under the United States, or under any State, who, having previously taken an oath, as a member of Congress, or as an officer of the United States, or as a member of any State legislature, or as an executive or judicial officer of any State, to support the Constitution of the United States, shall have engaged in insurrection or rebellion against the same, or given aid or comfort to the enemies thereof. But Congress may by a vote of two-thirds of each House, remove such disability.

Section 4
[WHAT PUBLIC DEBTS ARE VALID]

The validity of the public debt of the United States, authorized by law, including debts incurred for payment of pensions and bounties for services in suppressing insurrection or rebellion, shall not be questioned. But neither the United States nor any State shall assume or pay any debt or obligation incurred in aid of insurrection or rebellion against the United States, or any claim for the loss or emancipation of any slave; but all such debts, obligations and claims shall be held illegal and void.

Section 5
[POWER TO ENFORCE THIS ARTICLE]

The Congress shall have power to enforce, by appropriate legislation, the provisions of this article.

AMENDMENT XV
[Proposed by Congress on February 26, 1869; declared ratified on March 30, 1870]

Section 1
[NEGRO SUFFRAGE]

The right of citizens of the United States to vote shall not be denied or abridged by the United States or by any State on account of race, color, or previous condition of servitude.

Section 2
[POWER TO ENFORCE THIS ARTICLE]

The Congress shall have power to enforce this article by appropriate legislation.

AMENDMENT XVI
[Proposed by Congress on July 12, 1909; declared ratified on February 25, 1913]
[AUTHORIZING INCOME TAXES]

The Congress shall have power to lay and collect taxes on incomes, from whatever source derived, without apportionment among the several States, and without regard to any census or enumeration.

AMENDMENT XVII
[Proposed by Congress on May 13, 1912; declared ratified on May 31, 1913]
[POPULAR ELECTION OF SENATORS]

The Senate of the United States shall be composed of two Senators from each State, elected by the people thereof, for six years; and each Senator shall have one vote. The electors in each State shall have the qualifications requisite for electors of the most numerous branch of the State Legislature.

When vacancies happen in the representation of any State in the Senate, the executive authority of such State shall issue writs of election to fill such vacancies: Provided, That the Legislature of any State may empower the executive thereof to make temporary appointment until the people fill the vacancies by election as the Legislature may direct.

This amendment shall not be so construed as to affect the election or term of any Senator chosen before it becomes valid as part of the Constitution.

AMENDMENT XVIII

[Proposed by Congress December 18, 1917; declared ratified on January 29, 1919]

Section 1
[NATIONAL LIQUOR PROHIBITION]

After one year from the ratification of this article the manufacture, sale, or transportation of intoxicating liquors within, the importation thereof into, or the exportation thereof from the United States and all territory subject to the jurisdiction thereof for beverage purposes is hereby prohibited.

Section 2
[POWER TO ENFORCE THIS ARTICLE]

The Congress and the several states shall have concurrent power to enforce this article by appropriate legislation.

Section 3
[RATIFICATION WITHIN SEVEN YEARS]

This article shall be inoperative unless it shall have been ratified as an amendment to the Constitution by the legislatures of the several states, as provided in the Constitution, within seven years from the date of the submission hereof to the states by the Congress.[15]

AMENDMENT XIX

[Proposed by Congress on June 4, 1919; declared ratified on August 26, 1920]
[WOMAN SUFFRAGE]

The right of the citizens of the United States to vote shall not be denied or abridged by the United States or by any state on account of sex.

Congress shall have power to enforce this article by appropriate legislation.

AMENDMENT XX

[Proposed by Congress on March 2, 1932; declared ratified on February 6, 1933]

Section 1
[TERMS OF OFFICE]

The terms of the President and Vice-President shall end at noon on the 20th day of January, and the terms of the Senators and Representatives at noon on the 3rd day of January, of the years in which such terms would have ended if this article had not been ratified; and the terms of their successors shall then begin.

Section 2
[TIME OF CONVENING CONGRESS]

The Congress shall assemble at least once in every year, and such meeting shall begin at noon on the 3rd day of January, unless they shall by law appoint a different day.

---

15 Repealed by Twenty-First Amendment.

Section 3

[DEATH OF PRESIDENT-ELECT]

If, at the time fixed for the beginning of the term of the President, the President-elect shall have died, the Vice-President-elect shall become President. If a President shall not have been chosen before the time fixed for the beginning of his term, or if the President-elect shall have failed to qualify, then the Vice-President-elect shall act as President until a President shall have qualified; and the Congress may by law provide for the case wherein neither a President-elect nor a Vice-President-elect shall have qualified, declaring who shall then act as President, or the manner in which one who is to act shall be selected, and such person shall act accordingly until a President or Vice President shall have qualified.

Section 4

[ELECTION OF THE PRESIDENT]

The Congress may by law provide for the case of the death of any of the persons from whom the House of Representatives may choose a President whenever the right of choice shall have devolved upon them, and for the case of the death of any of the persons from whom the Senate may choose a Vice-President whenever the right of choice shall have devolved upon them.

Section 5

[AMENDMENT TAKES EFFECT]

Sections 1 and 2 shall take effect on the 15th day of October following ratification of this article.

Section 6

[RATIFICATION WITHIN SEVEN YEARS]

This article shall be inoperative unless it shall have been ratified as an amendment to the Constitution by the legislatures of three-fourths of the several States within seven years from the date of its submission.

AMENDMENT XXI

[Proposed by Congress on February 20, 1933; declared ratified on December 5, 1933]

Section 1

[NATIONAL LIQUOR PROHIBITION REPEALED]

The eighteenth article of amendment to the Constitution of the United States is hereby repealed.

Section 2

[TRANSPORTATION OF LIQUOR INTO "DRY" STATES]

The transportation or importation into any State, Territory, or Possession of the United States for delivery or use therein of intoxicating liquors, in violation of the laws thereof, is hereby prohibited.

Section 3

[RATIFICATION WITHIN SEVEN YEARS]

This article shall be inoperative unless it shall have been ratified as an amendment to the Constitution by conventions in the several States, as provided in the Constitution, within seven years from the date of the submission hereof to the States by the Congress.

AMENDMENT XXII

[Proposed by Congress on March 21, 1947; declared ratified on February 26, 1951]

Section 1

[TENURE OF PRESIDENT LIMITED]

No person shall be elected to the office of President more than twice, and no person who has held the office of President or acted as President for more than two years of a term to which some other person was elected President shall be elected to the Office of the President more than once. But this Article shall not apply to any person holding the office of President when this Article was proposed by the Congress, and shall not prevent any person who may be holding the office of President, or acting as President, during the term within which this Article becomes operative from holding the office of President or acting as President during the remainder of such term.

Section 2

[RATIFICATION WITHIN SEVEN YEARS]

This Article shall be inoperative unless it shall have been ratified as an amendment to the Constitution by the legislatures of three-fourths of the several states within seven years from the date of its submission to the States by the Congress.

AMENDMENT XXIII

[Proposed by Congress on June 21, 1960; declared ratified on March 29, 1961]

Section 1

[ELECTORAL COLLEGE VOTES FOR THE DISTRICT OF COLUMBIA]

The District constituting the seat of Government of the United States shall appoint in such manner as the Congress may direct:

A number of electors of President and Vice-President equal to the whole number of Senators and Representatives in Congress to which the District would be entitled if it were a State, but in no event more than the least populous State; they shall be in addition to those appointed by the States, but they shall be considered, for the purposes of the election of President and Vice-President, to be electors appointed by a State; and they shall meet in the District and perform such duties as provided by the twelfth article of amendment.

Section 2

[POWER TO ENFORCE THIS ARTICLE]

The Congress shall have power to enforce this article by appropriate legislation.

AMENDMENT XXIV

[Proposed by Congress on August 27, 1963; declared ratified on January 23, 1964]

Section 1

[ANTI-POLL TAX]

The right of citizens of the United States to vote in any primary or other election for President or Vice-President, for electors for President or Vice-President, or for Senator or Representative of Congress, shall not be denied or abridged by the United States or any State by reasons of failure to pay any poll tax or other tax.

Section 2

[POWER TO ENFORCE THIS ARTICLE]

The Congress shall have power to enforce this article by appropriate legislation.

AMENDMENT XXV

[Proposed by Congress on July 7, 1965; declared ratified on February 10, 1967]

Section 1

[VICE-PRESIDENT TO BECOME PRESIDENT]

In case of the removal of the President from office or his death or resignation, the Vice-President shall become President.

Section 2

[CHOICE OF A NEW VICE-PRESIDENT]

Whenever there is a vacancy in the office of the Vice-President, the President shall nominate a Vice-President who shall take the office upon confirmation by a majority vote of both houses of Congress.

Section 3

[PRESIDENT MAY DECLARE OWN DISABILITY]

Whenever the President transmits to the President pro tempore of the Senate and the Speaker of the House of Representatives his written declaration that he is unable to discharge the powers and duties of his office, and until he transmits to them a written declaration to the contrary, such powers and duties shall be discharged by the Vice-President as Acting President.

Section 4

[ALTERNATE PROCEDURES TO DECLARE AND TO END PRESIDENTIAL DISABILITY]

Whenever the Vice-President and a majority of either the principal officers of the executive departments, or of such other body as Congress may by law provide, transmit to the President pro tempore of the Senate and the Speaker of the House of Representatives their written declaration that the President is unable to discharge the powers and duties of his office, the Vice-President shall immediately assume the powers and duties of the office as Acting President.

Thereafter, when the President transmits to the President pro tempore of the Senate and the Speaker of the House of Representatives his written declaration that no inability exists, he shall resume the powers and duties of his office unless the Vice-President and a majority of either the principal officers of the executive departments, or of such other body as Congress may by law provide, transmit within four days to the President pro tempore of the Senate and the Speaker of the House of Representatives their written declaration that the President is unable to discharge the powers and duties of his office. Thereupon Congress shall decide the issue, assembling within 48 hours for that purpose if not in session. If the Congress, within 21 days after receipt of the latter written declaration, or, if Congress is not in session, within 21 days after Congress is required to assemble, determines by two-thirds vote of both houses that the President is unable to discharge the powers and duties of his office, the Vice-President shall continue to discharge the same as Acting President; otherwise, the President shall resume the powers and duties of his office.

AMENDMENT XXVI

[Proposed by Congress on March 23, 1971; declared ratified on June 30, 1971]

Section 1

[EIGHTEEN-YEAR-OLD VOTE]

The right of citizens of the United States, who are eighteen years of age or older, to vote shall not be denied or abridged by the United States or by any State on account of age.

Section 2

[POWER TO ENFORCE THIS ARTICLE]

The Congress shall have power to enforce this article by appropriate legislation.

AMENDMENT XXVII

[Proposed by Congress on September 25, 1789; ratified on May 7, 1992]

No law varying the compensation for the services of the Senators and Representatives shall take effect until an election of Representatives shall have intervened.

NO. 10: MADISON

Among the numerous advantages promised by a well-constructed Union, none deserves to be more accurately developed than its tendency to break and control the violence of faction. The friend of popular governments never finds himself so much alarmed for their character and fate as when he contemplates their propensity to this dangerous vice. He will not fail, therefore, to set a due value on any plan which, without violating the principles to which he is attached, provides a proper cure for it. The instability, injustice, and confusion introduced into the public councils have, in truth, been the mortal diseases under which popular governments have everywhere perished, as they continue to be the favorite and fruitful topics from which the adversaries to liberty derive their most specious declamations. The valuable improvements made by the American constitutions on the popular models, both ancient and modern, cannot certainly be too much admired; but it would be an unwarrantable partiality to contend that they have as effectually obviated the danger on this side, as was wished and expected. Complaints are everywhere heard from our most considerate and virtuous citizens, equally the friends of public and private faith and of public and personal liberty, that our governments are too unstable, that the public good is disregarded in the conflicts of rival parties, and that measures are too often decided, not according to the rules of justice and the rights of the minor party, but by the superior force of an interested and overbearing majority. However anxiously we may wish that these complaints had no foundation, the evidence of known facts will not permit us to deny that they are in some degree true. It will be found, indeed, on a candid review of our situation, that some of the distresses under which we labor have been erroneously charged on the operation of our governments; but it will be found, at the same time, that other causes will not alone account for many of our heaviest misfortunes; and, particularly, for that prevailing and increasing distrust of public engagements and alarm for private rights which are echoed from one end of the continent to the other. These must be chiefly, if not wholly, effects of the unsteadiness and injustice with which a factious spirit has tainted our public administration.

By a faction I understand a number of citizens, whether amounting to a majority or minority of the whole, who are united and actuated by some common impulse of passion, or of interest, adverse to the rights of other citizens, or to the permanent and aggregate interests of the community.

There are two methods of curing the mischiefs of faction: the one, by removing its causes; the other, by controlling its effects.

There are again two methods of removing the causes of faction: the one, by destroying the liberty which is essential to its existence; the other, by giving to every citizen the same opinions, the same passions, and the same interests.

It could never be more truly said than of the first remedy that it was worse than the disease. Liberty is to faction what air is to fire, an aliment without which it instantly expires. But it could not be a less folly to abolish liberty, which is essential to political life, because it nourishes faction than it would be to wish the annihilation of air, which is essential to animal life, because it imparts to fire its destructive agency.

The second expedient is as impracticable as the first would be unwise. As long as the reason of man continues fallible, and he is at liberty to exercise it, different opinions will be formed. As long as the connection subsists between his reason and his self-love, his opinions and his passions will have a reciprocal influence on each other; and the former will be objects to which the latter will attach themselves. The diversity in the faculties of men, from which the rights of property originate, is not less an insuperable obstacle to a uniformity of interests. The protection of these faculties is the first object of government. From the protection of different and unequal faculties of acquiring property, the possession of different degrees and kinds of property immediately results; and from the influence of these on the sentiments and views of the respective proprietors ensues a division of the society into different interests and parties.

The latent causes of faction are thus sown in the nature of man; and we see them everywhere brought into different degrees of activity, according to the different circumstances of civil society. A zeal for different opinions concerning religion, concerning government, and many other points, as well of speculation as of practice; an attachment to different leaders ambitiously contending for pre-eminence and power; or to persons of other descriptions whose fortunes have been interesting to the human passions, have, in turn, divided mankind into parties, inflamed them with mutual animosity, and rendered them much more disposed to vex and oppress each other than to co-operate for their common good. So strong is this propensity of mankind to fall into mutual animosities that where no substantial occasion presents itself the most frivolous and fanciful distinctions have been sufficient to kindle their unfriendly passions and excite their most violent conflicts. But the most common and durable source of factions has been the various and unequal distribution of property. Those who hold and those who are without property have ever formed distinct interests in society. Those who are creditors, and those who are debtors, fall under a like discrimination. A landed interest, a manufacturing interest, a mercantile interest, a moneyed interest, with many lesser interests, grow up of necessity in civilized nations, and divide them into different classes, actuated by different sentiments and views. The regulation of these various and interfering interests forms the principal task of modern legislation and involves the spirit of party and faction in the necessary and ordinary operations of government.

No man is allowed to be judge in his own cause, because his interest would certainly bias his judgment and, not improbably, corrupt his integrity. With equal, nay with greater reason, a body of men are unfit to be both judges and parties at the same time; yet what are many of the most important acts of legislation but so many judicial determinations, not indeed concerning the rights of single persons, but concerning the rights of large bodies of citizens? And what are the different classes of legislators but advocates and parties to the causes which they determine? Is a law proposed concerning private debts? It is a question to which the creditors are parties on one side and the debtors on the other. Justice ought to hold the balance between them. Yet the parties are, and must be, themselves the judges; and the most numerous party, or in other words, the most powerful faction must be expected to prevail. Shall domestic manufacturers be encouraged, and in what degree, by restrictions on foreign manufacturers? are questions which would be differently decided by the landed and the manufacturing classes, and probably by neither with a sole regard to justice and the public good. The apportionment of taxes on the various descriptions of property is an act which seems to require the most exact impartiality; yet there is, perhaps, no legislative act in which greater opportunity and temptation are given to a predominant party to trample on the rules of justice. Every shilling with which they overburden the inferior number is a shilling saved to their own pockets.

It is in vain to say that enlightened statesmen will be able to adjust these clashing interests and render them all subservient to the public good. Enlightened statesmen will not always be at the helm. Nor, in many cases, can such an adjustment be made at all without taking into view indirect and remote considerations, which will rarely prevail over the immediate interest which one party may find in disregarding the rights of another or the good of the whole.

The inference to which we are brought is that the *causes* of faction cannot be removed and that relief is only to be sought in the means of controlling its *effects*.

If a faction consists of less than a majority, relief is supplied by the republican principle, which enables the majority to defeat its sinister views by regular vote. It may clog the administration, it may convulse the society; but it will be unable to execute and mask its violence under the forms of the Constitution. When a majority is included in a faction, the form of popular government, on the other hand, enables it to sacrifice to its ruling passion or interest both the public good and the rights of other citizens. To secure the public good and private rights against the danger of such a faction, and at the same time to preserve the spirit and the form of popular government, is then the great object to which our inquiries are directed. Let me add that it is the great desideratum by which alone this form of government can be rescued from the opprobrium under which it has so long labored and be recommended to the esteem and adoption of mankind.

By what means is this object attainable? Evidently by one of two only. Either the existence of the same passion or interest in a majority at the same time must be prevented, or the majority, having such coexistent passion or interest, must be rendered, by their number and local situation, unable to concert and carry into effect schemes of oppression. If the impulse and the opportunity be suffered to coincide, we well know that neither moral nor religious motives can be relied on as an adequate control. They are not found to be such on the injustice and violence of individuals, and lose their efficacy in proportion to the number combined together, that is, in proportion as their efficacy becomes needful.

From this view of the subject it may be concluded that a pure democracy, by which I mean a society consisting of a small number of citizens, who assemble and administer the government in person, can admit of no cure for the mischiefs of faction. A common passion or interest will, in almost every case, be felt by a majority of the whole; a communication and concert results from the form of government itself; and there is nothing to check the inducements to sacrifice the weaker party or an obnoxious individual. Hence it is that such democracies have ever been spectacles of turbulence and contention; have ever been found incompatible with personal security or the rights of property; and have in general been as short in their lives as they have been violent in their deaths. Theoretic politicians, who have patronized this species of government, have erroneously supposed that by reducing mankind to a perfect equality in their political rights, they would at the same time be perfectly equalized and assimilated in their possessions, their opinions, and their passions.

A republic, by which I mean a government in which the scheme of representation takes place, opens a different prospect and promises the cure for which we are seeking. Let us examine the points in which it varies from pure democracy, and we shall comprehend both the nature of the cure and the efficacy which it must derive from the Union.

The two great points of difference between a democracy and a republic are: first, the delegation of the government, in the latter, to a small number of citizens elected by the rest; secondly, the greater number of citizens and greater sphere of country over which the latter may be extended.

The effect of the first difference is, on the one hand, to refine and enlarge the public views by passing them through the medium of a chosen body of citizens, whose wisdom may best discern the true interest of their country and whose patriotism and love of justice will be least likely to sacrifice it to temporary or partial considerations. Under such a regulation it may well happen that the public voice, pronounced by the representatives of the people, will be more consonant to the public good than if pronounced by the people themselves, convened for the purpose. On the other hand, the effect may be inverted. Men of factious tempers, of local prejudices, or of sinister designs, may, by intrigue, by corruption, or by other means, first obtain the suffrages, and then betray the interests of the people. The question resulting is, whether small or extensive republics are most favorable to the election of proper guardians of the public weal; and it is clearly decided in favor of the latter by two obvious considerations.

In the first place it is to be remarked that however small the republic may be the representatives must be raised to a certain number in order to guard against the cabals of a few; and that however large it may be they must be limited to a certain number in order to guard against the confusion of a multitude. Hence, the number of representatives in the two cases not being in proportion to that of the constituents, and being proportionally greatest in the small republic, it follows that if the proportion of fit characters be not less in the large than in the small republic, the former will present a greater option, and consequently a greater probability of a fit choice.

In the next place, as each representative will be chosen by a greater number of citizens in the large than in the small republic, it will be more difficult for unworthy candidates to practise with success the vicious arts by which elections are too often carried; and the suffrages of the people being more free, will be more likely to center on men who possess the most attractive merit and the most diffusive and established characters.

It must be confessed that in this, as in most other cases, there is a mean, on both sides of which inconveniencies will be found to lie. By enlarging too much the number of electors, you render the representative too little acquainted with all their local circumstances and lesser interests; as by reducing it too much, you render him unduly attached to these, and too little fit to comprehend and pursue great and national objects. The federal Constitution forms a happy combination in this respect; the great and aggregate interests being referred to the national, the local and particular to the State legislatures.

The other point of difference is the greater number of citizens and extent of territory which may be brought within the compass of republican than of democratic government; and it is this circumstance principally which renders factious combinations less to be dreaded in the former than in the latter. The smaller the society, the fewer probably will be the distinct parties and interests composing it; the fewer the distinct parties and interests, the more frequently will a majority be found of the same party; and the smaller the number of individuals composing a majority, and the smaller the compass within which they are placed, the more easily will they concert and execute their plans of oppression. Extend the sphere and you take in a greater variety of parties and interests; you make it less probable that a majority of the whole will have a common motive to invade the rights of other citizens; or if such a common motive exists, it will be more difficult for all who feel it to discover their own strength and to act in unison with each other. Besides other impediments, it may be remarked that, where there is a consciousness of unjust or dishonorable purposes, communication is always checked by distrust in proportion to the number whose concurrence is necessary.

Hence, it clearly appears that the same advantage which a republic has over a democracy in controlling the effects of faction is enjoyed by a large over a small republic—is enjoyed by the Union over the States composing it. Does this advantage consist in the substitution of representatives whose enlightened views and virtuous sentiments render them superior to local prejudices and to schemes of injustice? It will not be denied that the representation of the Union will be most likely to possess these requisite endowments. Does it consist in the greater security afforded by a greater variety of parties, against the event of any one party being able to outnumber and oppress the rest? In an equal degree does the increased variety of parties comprised within the Union increase this security? Does it, in fine, consist in the greater obstacles opposed to the concert and accomplishment of the secret wishes of an unjust and interested majority? Here again the extent of the Union gives it the most palpable advantage.

The influence of factious leaders may kindle a flame within their particular States but will be unable to spread a general conflagration through the other

States. A religious sect may degenerate into a political faction in a part of the Confederacy; but the variety of sects dispersed over the entire face of it must secure the national councils against any danger from that source. A rage for paper money, for an abolition of debts, for an equal division of property, or for any other improper or wicked project, will be less apt to pervade the whole body of the Union than a particular member of it, in the same proportion as such a malady is more likely to taint a particular county or district than an entire State.

In the extent and proper structure of the Union, therefore, we behold a republican remedy for the diseases most incident to republican government. And according to the degree of pleasure and pride we feel in being republicans ought to be our zeal in cherishing the spirit and supporting the character of federalist.

PUBLIUS

NO. 51: MADISON

To what expedient, then, shall we finally resort, for maintaining in practice the necessary partition of power among the several departments as laid down in the Constitution? The only answer that can be given is that as all these exterior provisions are found to be inadequate the defect must be supplied, by so contriving the interior structure of the government as that its several constituent parts may, by their mutual relations, be the means of keeping each other in their proper places. Without presuming to undertake a full development of this important idea I will hazard a few general observations which may perhaps place it in a clearer light, and enable us to form a more correct judgment of the principles and structure of the government planned by the convention.

In order to lay a due foundation for that separate and distinct exercise of the different powers of government, which to a certain extent is admitted on all hands to be essential to the preservation of liberty, it is evident that each department should have a will of its own; and consequently should be so constituted that the members of each should have as little agency as possible in the appointment of the members of the others. Were this principle rigorously adhered to, it would require that all the appointments for the supreme executive, legislative, and judiciary magistracies should be drawn from the same fountain of authority, the people, through channels having no communication whatever with one another. Perhaps such a plan of constructing the several departments would be less difficult in practice than it may in contemplation appear. Some difficulties, however, and some additional expense would attend the execution of it. Some deviations, therefore, from the principle must be admitted. In the constitution of the judiciary department in particular, it might be inexpedient to insist rigorously on the principle: first, because peculiar qualifications being essential in the members, the primary consideration ought to be to select that mode of choice which best secures these qualifications; second, because the permanent tenure by which the appointments are held in that department must soon destroy all sense of dependence on the authority conferring them.

It is equally evident that the members of each department should be as little dependent as possible on those of the others for the emoluments annexed to their offices. Were the executive magistrate, or the judges, not independent of the legislature in this particular, their independence in every other would be merely nominal.

But the great security against a gradual concentration of the several powers in the same department consists in giving to those who administer each department the necessary constitutional means and personal motives to resist encroachments of the others. The provision for defense must in this, as in all other cases, be made commensurate to the danger of attack. Ambition must be made to counteract ambition. The interest of the man must be connected with the constitutional rights of the place. It may be a reflection on human nature that such devices should be necessary to control the abuses of government. But what is government itself but the greatest of all reflections on human nature? If men were angels, no government would be necessary. If angels were to govern men, neither external nor internal controls on government would be necessary. In framing a government which is to be administered by men over men, the great difficulty lies in this: you must first enable the government to control the governed; and in the next place oblige it to control itself. A dependence on the people is, no doubt, the primary control on the government; but experience has taught mankind the necessity of auxiliary precautions.

This policy of supplying, by opposite and rival interests, the defect of better motives, might be traced through the whole system of human affairs, private as well as public. We see it particularly displayed in all the subordinate distributions of power, where the constant aim is to divide and arrange the several offices in such a manner as that each may be a check on the other—that the private interest of every individual may be a sentinel over the public rights. These inventions of prudence cannot be less requisite in the distribution of the supreme powers of the State.

But it is not possible to give to each department an equal power of self-defense. In republican government, the legislative authority necessarily predominates. The remedy for this inconveniency is to divide the legislature into different branches; and to render them, by different modes of election and different principles of action, as little connected with each other as the nature of their common functions and their common dependence on the society will admit. It may even be necessary to guard against dangerous encroachments by still further precautions. As the weight of the legislative authority requires that it should be thus divided, the weakness of the executive may require, on the other hand, that it should be fortified. An absolute negative on the legislature appears, at first view, to be the natural defense with which the executive magistrate should be armed. But perhaps it would be neither altogether safe nor alone sufficient. On ordinary occasions it might not be exerted with the requisite firmness, and on extraordinary occasions it might be perfidiously abused. May not this defect of an absolute negative be supplied by some qualified connection between this weaker branch of the stronger department, by which the latter may be led to support the constitutional rights of the former, without being too much detached from the rights of its own department?

If the principles on which these observations are founded be just, as I persuade myself they are, and they be applied as a criterion to the several State constitutions, and to the federal Constitution, it will be found that if the latter does not perfectly correspond with them, the former are infinitely less able to bear such a test.

There are, moreover, two considerations particularly applicable to the federal system of America, which place that system in a very interesting point of view.

First. In a single republic, all the power surrendered by the people is submitted to the administration of a single government; and the usurpations are guarded against by a division of the government into distinct and separate departments. In the compound republic of America, the power surrendered by the people is first divided between two distinct governments, and then the portion allotted to each subdivided among distinct and separate departments. Hence a double security arises to the rights of the people. The different governments will control each other, at the same time that each will be controlled by itself.

Second. It is of great importance in a republic not only to guard the society against the oppression of its rulers, but to guard one part of the society against the injustice of the other part. Different interests necessarily exist in different classes of citizens. If a majority be united by a common interest, the rights of the minority will be insecure. There are but two methods of providing against this evil: the one by creating a will in the community independent of the majority—that is, of the society itself; the other, by comprehending in the society so many separate descriptions of citizens as will render an unjust combination of a majority of the whole very improbable, if not impracticable. The first method prevails in all governments possessing an hereditary or self-appointed authority. This, at best, is but a precarious security; because a power independent of the society may as well espouse the unjust views of the major as the rightful interests of the minor party, and may possibly be turned against both parties. The second method will be exemplified in the federal republic of the United States. Whilst all authority in it will be derived from and dependent on the society, the society itself will be broken into so many parts, interests and classes of citizens, that the rights of individuals, or of the minority, will be in little danger from interested combinations of the majority. In a free government the security for civil rights must be the same as that for religious rights. It consists in the one case in the multiplicity of interests, and in the other in the multiplicity of sects. The degree of security in both cases will depend on the number of interests and sects; and this may be presumed to depend on the extent of country and number of people comprehended under the same government. This view of the subject must particularly recommend a proper federal system to all the sincere and considerate friends of republican government, since it shows that in exact proportion as the territory of the Union may be formed into more circumscribed Confederacies, or States, oppressive combinations of a majority will be facilitated; the best security, under the republican forms, for the rights of every class of citizen, will be diminished; and consequently the stability and independence of some member of the government, the only other security, must be proportionally increased. Justice is the end of government. It is the end of civil society. It ever has been and ever will be pursued until it be obtained, or until liberty be lost in the pursuit. In a society under the forms of which the stronger faction can readily unite and oppress the weaker, anarchy may as truly be said to reign as in a state of nature, where the weaker individual is not secured against the violence of the stronger; and as, in the latter state, even the stronger individuals are prompted, by the uncertainty of their condition, to submit to a government which may protect the weak as well as themselves; so, in the former state, will the more powerful factions or parties be gradually induced, by a like motive, to wish for a government which will protect all parties, the weaker as well as the more powerful. It can be little doubted that if the State of Rhode Island was separated from the Confederacy and left to itself, the insecurity of rights under the popular form of government within such narrow limits would be displayed by such reiterated oppressions of factious majorities that some power altogether independent of the people would soon be called for by the voice of the very factions whose misrule had proved the necessity of it. In the extended republic of the United States, and among the great variety of interests, parties, and sects which it embraces, a coalition of a majority of the whole society could seldom take place on any other principles than those of justice and the general good; whilst there being thus less danger to a minor from the will of a major party, there must be less pretext, also, to provide for the security of the former, by introducing into the government a will not dependent on the latter, or, in other words, a will independent of the society itself. It is no less certain than it is important, notwithstanding the contrary opinions which have been entertained, that the larger the society, provided it lie within a practicable sphere, the more duly capable it will be of self-government. And happily for the *republican cause,* the practicable sphere may be carried to a very great extent by a judicious modification and mixture of the *federal principle.*

PUBLIUS

Glossary

administrative adjudication The application of rules and precedents to specific cases to settle disputes with regulated parties

administrative legislation Rules made by regulatory agencies and commissions

adverse selection The problem of incomplete information—of choosing alternatives without fully knowing the details of available options

affirmative action A policy or program designed to redress historic injustices committed against specific groups by making special efforts to provide members of these groups with access to educational and employment opportunities

after-the-fact authority The authority to follow up on the fate of a proposal once it has been approved by the full chamber

agency loss The difference between what a principal would like an agent to do and the agent's performance

agency representation The type of representation according to which representatives are held accountable to their constituents if they fail to represent them properly. That is, constituents have the power to hire and fire their representatives

agenda power The control over what a group will consider for discussion

agenda-setting effect The power to bring attention to particular issues and problems

amicus curiae "Friend of the court," an individual or group that is not party to a lawsuit but seeks to assist the court in reaching a decision by presenting an additional brief

amnesty A pardon extended to a group of persons

antitrust policy Government regulation of large businesses that have established monopolies

appeasement The effort to forestall war by giving in to the demands of a hostile power

appellate jurisdiction The class of cases provided in the Constitution and by legislation that may be appealed to a higher court from a lower court

Articles of Confederation and Perpetual Union America's first written constitution. Adopted by the Continental Congress in 1777, the Articles of Confederation and Perpetual Union were the formal basis for America's national government until 1789, when they were superseded by the Constitution

Australian ballot An electoral format that presents the names of all the candidates for any given office on the same ballot. Introduced at the end of the eighteenth century, the Australian ballot replaced the partisan ballot and facilitated split-ticket voting

authoritarian government A system of rule in which the government recognizes no formal limits but may nevertheless be restrained by the power of other social institutions

autocracy A form of government in which a single individual rules

bicameral legislature A legislative assembly composed of two chambers, or houses

bicameralism The division of a legislative assembly into two chambers, or houses

bilateral treaty A treaty made between two nations

Bill of Rights The first 10 amendments to the U.S. Constitution, adopted in 1791. The Bill of Rights ensures certain rights and liberties to the people

block grants Federal funds given to state governments to pay for goods, services, or programs, with relatively few restrictions on how the funds may be spent

brief A written document in which an attorney explains—using case precedents—why the Court should rule in favor of his or her client

budget deficit The amount by which government spending exceeds government revenue in a fiscal year

bureaucracy The complex structure of offices, tasks, rules, and principles of organization that are employed by all large-scale institutions to coordinate the work of their personnel

bureaucratic drift The oft-observed phenomenon of bureaucratic implementation that produces policy more to the liking of the bureaucracy than faithful to the original intention of the legislation that created it, but without triggering a political reaction from elected officials

Bush Doctrine Foreign policy based on the idea that the United States should take preemptive action against threats to its national security

Cabinet The secretaries, or chief administrators, of the major departments of the federal government. Cabinet secretaries are appointed by the president with the consent of the Senate

casework An effort by members of Congress to gain the trust and support of constituents by providing personal services. One important type of casework consists of helping constituents obtain favorable treatment from the federal bureaucracy

categorical grants-in-aid Funds given by Congress to states and localities and that are earmarked by law for specific categories, such as education or crime prevention

causation A relationship or association between two variables such that one causes the other

census A comprehensive enumeration of all individuals in a population

checks and balances The mechanisms through which each branch of government is able to participate in and influence the activities of the other branches

chief justice The justice on the Supreme Court who presides over the Court's public sessions

civil law A system of jurisprudence, including private law and govermental actions, for settling disputes that do not involve criminal penalties

civil liberties The protections of citizens from improper governmental action

civil rights The legal or moral claims that citizens are entitled to make on the government

class-action suit A lawsuit in which a large number of persons with common interests join together under a representative party to bring or defend a lawsuit, as when hundreds of workers join together to sue a company

clear and present danger The criterion formerly used to determine whether speech is protected or unprotected, based on its capacity to present a "clear and present danger" to society

clientele agency A department or bureau of government whose mission is to promote, serve, or represent a particular interest

closed primary A primary election in which only those voters who registered with the party a specified period before the primary election day can participate

closed rule The provision by the House Rules Committee that prohibits the introduction of amendments during debate

cloture A rule allowing a supermajority of the members of a legislative body to set a time limit on debate over a given bill

coalitional drift The prospect that enacted policy will change because the composition of the enacting coalition is temporary and provisional

Cold War The period of struggle between the United States and the former Soviet Union between the late 1940s and about 1990

collective action The pooling of resources and the coordination of effort and activity by a group of people (often a large one) to achieve common goals

commander in chief The power of the president as commander of the national military and the state national guard units (when called into service)

commerce clause The clause found in Article I, Section 8, of the Constitution, which delegates to Congress the power "to regulate Commerce with foreign Nations, and among the several States, and with the Indian Tribes." This clause was interpreted by the Supreme Court to favor national power over the economy

concurrence An opinion agreeing with the decision of the majority but not with the rationale provided in the majority opinion

concurrent powers The authority possessed by *both* state and national governments, such as the power to levy taxes

conference committee A joint committee created to work out a compromise for House and Senate versions of a piece of legislation

congressional caucus An association of members of Congress based on party, interest, or social characteristics such as gender or race

conservative Today this term refers to those who generally support the social and economic status quo and are suspicious of efforts to introduce new political formulas and economic arrangements. Many conservatives also believe that a large and powerful government poses a threat to citizens' freedoms

constituency The district making up the area from which an official is elected

constitutional government A system of rule in which formal and effective limits are placed on the powers of the government

containment A policy designed to curtail the political and military expansion of a hostile power

contracting power The power of government to set conditions on companies seeking to sell goods or services to government agencies

contributory program A social program financed in whole or in part by taxation or other mandatory contributions by its present or future recipients. The most important example is Social Security, which is financed by a payroll tax

cooperative federalism A type of federalism existing since the New Deal era, in which grants-in-aid have been used strategically to encourage states and localities (without commanding them) to pursue nationally defined goals. Also known as intergovernmental cooperation

correlation A relationship or association between two variables

court of appeals (or appellate court) A court that hears the appeals of trial-court decisions

criminal law The branch of law that deals with disputes or actions involving criminal penalties (as opposed to civil law)

de facto segregation Racial segregation that is not a direct result of law or government policy but is, instead, a reflection of residential patterns, income distributions, or other social factors

de jure segregation Racial segregation that is a direct result of law or official policy

decisiveness rules A specification of when a vote may be taken, the sequence in which votes on amendments occur, and how many supporters determine whether a motion passes or fails

delegate A representative who votes according to the preferences of his or her constituency

delegated powers Constitutional powers assigned to one government agency but exercised by another agency with the express permission of the first

delegation The transmission of authority to some other official or body for the latter's use (though often with the right of review and revision)

democracy A system of rule that permits citizens to play a significant part in the governmental process, usually through the selection of key public officials

deregulation The policy of reducing or eliminating regulatory restraints on the conduct of individuals or private institutions

deterrence The development and maintenance of military strength as a means of discouraging attack

devolution The policy of removing a program from one level of government by deregulating it or passing it down to a lower level, such as from the national government to the state and local governments

diplomacy The representation of a government to other governments

discretionary spending Federal spending on programs that are controlled through the regular budget process

dissenting opinion A decision written by a justice who voted with the minority opinion in a particular case in which the justice fully explains the reasoning behind his or her opinion

distributive tendency The tendency of Congress to spread the benefits of a policy over a wide range of members' districts

divided government The condition in American government in which the presidency is controlled by one party while the opposing party controls one or both houses of Congress

double jeopardy The Fifth Amendment right providing that a person cannot be tried twice for the same crime

dual federalism The system of government that prevailed in the United States from 1789 to 1937 in which fundamental governmental powers were shared between the federal and state governments, with the states exercising the most important powers

due process Proceeding according to law and with adequate protection for individual rights

Duverger's Law Law of politics, formalized by Maurice Duverger, stating that plurality-rule electoral systems will tend to have two political parties

electoral college The presidential electors from each state who meet in their respective state capitals after the popular election to cast ballots for president and vice president

eminent domain The right of the government to take private property for public use, with reasonable compensation awarded for the property

entitlement The eligibility for benefits by virtue of a category defined by law. Categories can be changed only by legislation; deprivation of individual benefits can be determined only through due process in court

equal protection clause The provision of the Fourteenth Amendment guaranteeing citizens "the equal protection of the laws." This clause has been the basis for the civil rights of African Americans, women, and other groups

equal time rule The requirement that broadcasters provide candidates for the same political office an equal opportunity to communicate their messages to the public

equality of opportunity A universally shared American ideal, according to which all people have the freedom to use whatever talents and wealth they possess to reach their full potential

establishment clause The First Amendment clause that says, "Congress shall make no law

respecting an establishment of religion." This law means that a wall of separation exists between church and state

exclusionary rule The ability of courts to exclude evidence obtained in violation of the Fourth Amendment

executive agreement An agreement between the president and another country that has the force of a treaty but does not require the Senate's "advice and consent"

Executive Office of the President (EOP) The permanent agencies that perform defined management tasks for the president. Created in 1939, the EOP includes the Office of Management and Budget, the Council of Economic Advisers, the National Security Council, and other agencies

executive orders A rule or regulation issued by the president that has the effect and formal status of legislation

executive privilege The claim that confidential communications between the president and the president's close advisers should not be revealed without the consent of the president

expressed powers The powers enumerated in the Constitution that are granted to the federal government

externalities The differences between the private cost and the social cost of economic behavior

fairness doctrine An FCC requirement that broadcasters that air programs on controversial issues provide time for opposing views

federal funds rate The interest rate on loans among banks that the Federal Reserve Board influences by affecting the supply of money available

Federal Reserve System (the Fed) A system of 12 Federal Reserve banks that facilitates exchanges of cash, checks, and credit; regulates member banks; and uses monetary policies to fight inflation and deflation

federalism The system of government in which a constitution divides power between a central government and regional governments

fighting words Speech that directly incites damaging conduct

filibuster A tactic used by members of the Senate to prevent action on legislation they oppose by continuously holding the floor and speaking until the majority backs down. Once given the floor, senators have unlimited time to speak, and it requires a cloture vote of three-fifths of the Senate to end a filibuster

fiscal policy Policies to regulate the economy through taxing and spending powers

food stamps The largest in-kind benefits program, administered by the Department of Agriculture, for individuals and families who satisfy a means test. Food stamps can used to buy food at most grocery stores

formula grants Grants-in-aid in which a formula is used to determine the amount of federal funds a state or local government will receive

framing The power of the media to influence how events and issues are interpreted

free exercise clause The First Amendment clause that protects a citizen's right to believe and practice whatever religion he or she chooses

free riding Enjoying the benefits of some good or action while letting others bear the costs

frequency In statistics and probability, the number of times a specific behavior or value of a variable occurs or the percent of the observations in which it occurs

full faith and credit clause The provision in Article IV, Section 1, of the Constitution requiring that each state normally honors the public acts and judicial decisions that take place in another state

gatekeeping authority The right and power to decide if a change in policy will be considered

gender gap A distinctive pattern of voting behavior reflecting the differences in views between women and men

General Agreement on Tariffs and Trade (GATT) An international trade organization, in existence from 1947 to 1995, that set many of the rules governing international trade

gerrymandering The apportionment of voters in districts in such a way as to give unfair advantage to one political party

going public The act of launching a media campaign to build popular support

government The institutions and procedures through which a land and its people are ruled

grand jury A jury that determines whether sufficient evidence is available to justify a trial. Grand juries do not rule on the accused's guilt or innocence

grants-in-aid A general term for funds given by Congress to state and local governments

Great Compromise An agreement reached at the Constitutional Convention of 1787 that gave each state an equal number of senators regardless of its population but linked representation in the House of Representatives to population

gross domestic product (GDP) The total value of goods and services produced within a country

home rule The power delegated by the state to a local unit of government to manage its own affairs

impeachment The charging of a government official (president or otherwise) with "Treason, Bribery, or other high Crimes and Misdemeanors" and bringing him or her before Congress to determine guilt

implementation The efforts of departments and agencies to translate laws into specific bureaucratic routines

implied powers Powers derived from the necessary and proper clause (Article I, Section 8) of the Constitution. Such powers are not specifically expressed but are implied through the expansive interpretation of delegated powers

incumbency Holding the political office for which one is running

indexing The process of periodically adjusting social benefits or wages to account for increases in the cost of living

inflation A consistent increase in the general level of prices

inherent powers Powers claimed by a president that are not expressed in the Constitution but are inferred from it

initiative A process by which citizens may petition to place a policy proposal on the ballot for public vote

in-kind benefits Goods and services provided to needy individuals and families by the federal government, as contrasted with cash benefits. The largest in-kind federal welfare program is food stamps

institutions The rules and procedures that provide incentives for political behavior, thereby shaping politics

instrumental Done with purpose, sometimes with forethought, and even with calculation

interest group An organized group of individuals or organizations that makes policy-related appeals to government

intermediate scrutiny The test used by the Supreme Court in gender discrimination cases. Intermediate scrutiny places the burden of proof partially on the government and partially on the challengers to show that the law in question is constitutional

International Court of Justice (ICJ) The UN's chief judicial agency. Located in The Hague, Netherlands, the ICJ settles legal disputes submitted by UN member states

International Monetary Fund (IMF) An institution established in 1944 that provides loans and facilitates international monetary exchange

isolationism The desire to avoid involvement in the affairs of other nations

issue voting An individual's propensity to select candidates or parties based on the extent to which the individual agrees with one candidate more than others on specific issues

judicial activism The judicial philosophy that posits that the Court should see beyond the text of the Constitution or a statute to consider broader societal implications for its decisions

judicial restraint The judicial philosophy whose adherents refuse to go beyond the text of the Constitution in interpreting its meaning

judicial review The power of the courts to declare actions of the legislative and executive branches invalid or unconstitutional. The Supreme Court asserted this power in *Marbury v. Madison* (1803)

jurisdiction The domain over which an institution or member of an institution has authority

kitchen cabinet An informal group of advisers to whom the president turns for counsel and guidance. Members of the official cabinet may or may not also be members of the kitchen cabinet

legislative initiative The president's inherent power to bring a legislative agenda before Congress

legislative supremacy The preeminent position assigned to Congress by the Constitution

Lemon test Rule articulated in *Lemon v. Kurtzman* according to which governmental action in respect to religion is permissible if it is secular in purpose, does not lead to "excessive entanglement" with religion, and neither promotes nor inhibits the practice of religion

libel A written statement made in "reckless disregard of the truth" and considered damaging to a victim because it is "malicious, scandalous, and defamatory"

liberal A liberal today generally supports political and social reform; government intervention in the economy; the expansion of federal social services; more vigorous efforts on behalf of the poor, minorities, and women; and greater concern for consumers and the environment

line-item veto The power of the executive to veto specific provisions (lines) of a bill passed by the legislature

lobbying An attempt by a group to influence the policy process through persuasion of government officials

logrolling A legislative practice wherein reciprocal agreements are made between legislators, usually in voting for or against a bill. In contrast to bargaining, logrolling unites parties that have nothing in common but their desire to exchange support

majority leader The elected leader of the party holding a majority of the seats in the House of Representatives or the Senate. In the House, the majority leader is subordinate in the party hierarchy to the Speaker

majority party The party that holds the majority of legislative seats in either the House or the Senate

majority rule A type of electoral system in which, to win a seat in a representative body, a candidate must receive a majority (50 percent plus one) of all the votes cast in the relevant district

mandatory spending Federal spending that is made up of "uncontrollables," budget items that cannot be controlled through the regular budget process. Some uncontrollables, such as interest on the debt, are beyond the power of Congress because the terms of payments are set in contracts

market failure An instance when the market fails to produce an efficient outcome

mean The average value of a variable

means testing A procedure that determines eligibility for government public-assistance programs. A potential beneficiary must show a need and an inability to provide for that need

measurement error The failure to identify the true distribution of opinion within a population because of errors such as ambiguous or poorly worded questions

median The numerical value separating the higher half of a sample or population from the lower half; also called the fiftieth percentile

median-voter theorem A proposition predicting that when policy options can be arrayed along a single dimension, majority rule will pick the policy most preferred by the voter whose ideal policy is to the left of half of the voters and to the right of exactly half of the voters

Medicaid A federally financed, state-operated program for medical services to low-income people

Medicare National health insurance for the elderly and the disabled

minority leader The elected leader of the party holding less than a majority of the seats in the House or Senate

Miranda rule The convention derived from the Supreme Court's 1966 ruling in the case of *Miranda v. Arizona* whereby persons under arrest must be informed of their legal rights, including their right to counsel, before undergoing police interrogation

monetary policy Policies to regulate the economy through the manipulation of the supply of money, the price of money (interest rate), and the availability of credit

money bill A bill concerned solely with taxation or government spending

monopoly The existence in a market of a single firm that provides all the goods and services of that market; the absence of competition

mootness A criterion used by courts to avoid hearing cases that no longer require resolution

moral hazard The problem of not knowing all aspects of the actions taken by an agent (nominally on behalf of the principal but potentially at the principal's expense)

most favored nation status An agreement to offer a trading partner the lowest tariff rate offered to other trading partners

National Security Council (NSC) A presidential foreign policy advisory council composed of the president; the vice president; the secretaries of state, defense, and the treasury; the attorney general; and other officials invited by the president

nation-state A political entity consisting of a people with some common cultural experience (nation) who also share a common political authority (state), recognized by other sovereignties (nation-states)

necessary and proper clause Article I, Section 8, of the Constitution, which enumerates the powers of Congress and provides Congress with the authority to make all laws "necessary and proper" to carry them out; also referred to as the elastic clause

nomination The process by which political parties select their candidates for election to public office

noncontributory program A social program that assists people based on demonstrated need rather than contributions they have made; also known as a public assistance program

non-state actor A group other than a nation-state that attempts to play a role in the international system. Terrorist groups are one type of non-state actor

North American Free Trade Agreement (NAFTA) A trade treaty among the United States, Canada, and Mexico to lower and eliminate tariffs among the three countries

North Atlantic Treaty Organization (NATO) A treaty organization comprising the United States, Canada, and most of Western Europe, formed in 1949 to counter the perceived threat from the Soviet Union

oligarchy A form of government in which a small group of landowners, military officers, or wealthy merchants controls most of the governing decisions

open primary A primary election in which voters can choose on the primary election day itself which party's primary to vote in

open rule The provision by the House Rules Committee that permits floor debate and the addition of amendments to a bill

open-market operations The process whereby the Open Market Committee of the Federal Reserve buys and sells government securities, and so on, to help finance government operations and to reduce or increase the total amount of money circulating in the economy

opinion The written explanation of the Supreme Court's decision in a particular case

oral argument The stage in Supreme Court proceedings in which attorneys for both sides appear before the Court to present their positions and answer questions posed by the justices

original jurisdiction The class of cases provided in the Constitution (Article III) that may be taken directly to a federal court

oversight The effort by Congress, through hearings, investigations, and other techniques, to exercise control over the activities of executive agencies

pardon Forgiveness of a crime and cancellation of relevant penalty

party activist A partisan who contributes time, energy, and effort to support a party and its candidates

party caucus, or party conference A normally closed meeting of a political or legislative group to select candidates or leaders, plan strategy, or make decisions regarding legislative matters

party identification An individual's attachment to a particular political party, which might be based on issues, ideology, past experience, or upbringing

party machine In the late nineteenth and early twentieth centuries, the local party organization that controlled local politics through patronage and the nomination process

party vote A roll-call vote in the House or Senate in which at least 50 percent of the members of one party take a particular position and are opposed by at least 50 percent of the members of the other party. Party votes are less common today than they were in the nineteenth century

path dependency The idea that certain possibilities are made more or less likely because of the historical path taken

patronage The resources available to higher officials, usually opportunities to make partisan appointments to offices and confer grants, licenses, or special favors to supporters

pluralism The theory that all interests are and should be free to compete for influence in the government. The outcome of this competition is compromise and moderation

plurality rule A type of electoral system in which victory goes to the individual who gets the most votes in an election, but not necessarily a majority of the votes cast

pocket veto A veto that is effected when Congress adjourns during the time a president has to approve a bill and the president takes no action on it

police power The power reserved to the government to regulate the health, safety, and morals of its citizens

political action committee (PAC) A private group that raises and distributes funds for use in election campaigns

political caucus A normally closed meeting of a political or legislative group to select candidates, plan strategy, or make decisions regarding legislative matters

political party An organized group that attempts to influence government by electing its members to office

politics Conflict, struggle, cooperation, and collaboration over the leadership, structure, and policies of government

pork-barrel legislation The appropriations made by legislative bodies for local projects that often are not needed but are created so that local representatives can carry their home district in the next election

precedents Prior cases whose principles are used by judges as the bases for their decisions in present cases

preemption The willingness to strike first in order to prevent an enemy attack

preventive war The policy of striking first when a nation fears that a foreign foe is contemplating hostile action

priming A process of preparing the public to take a particular view of an event or a political actor

principal-agent relationship The relationship between a principal and his or her agent. This relationship may be affected by the fact that each is motivated by self-interest, yet their interests may not be well aligned

prior restraint An effort by a government agency to block the publication of material it deems libelous or harmful in some other way: censorship. In the United States, the courts forbid prior restraint except under the most extraordinary circumstances

privatization The act of moving all or part of a program from the public sector to the private sector

privileges and immunities The provision in Article IV, Section 2, of the Constitution stating that a state cannot discriminate against someone from another state or give its own residents special privileges

probability sampling A method used by pollsters to select a representative sample in which every individual in the population has an equal probability of being selected as a respondent

progressive taxation Taxation that hits the upper income brackets more heavily

project grants Grant programs in which state and local governments submit proposals to federal agencies and for which funding is provided on a competitive basis

proportional representation (PR) A multiple-member district system that allows each political party representation in proportion to its percentage of the vote

proposal power The capacity to bring a proposal before the full legislature

prospective voting Voting based on the imagined future performance of a candidate

public good A good that, first, may be enjoyed by anyone if it is provided and, second, may not be denied to anyone once it has been provided

public law Cases involving the action of public agencies or officials

public opinion Citizens' attitudes about political issues, leaders, institutions, and events

public policy A law, rule, statute, or edict that expresses the government's goals for rewards and punishments to promote their attainment

public-opinion poll A scientific instrument for measuring public opinion

random digit dialing A poll in which respondents are selected at random from a list of 10-digit telephone numbers, with every effort made to avoid bias in the construction of the sample

recall The removal of a public official by popular vote

redistribution A policy whose objective is to tax or spend in such a way as to reduce the disparities of wealth between the lowest and the highest income brackets

referendum A measure proposed or passed by a legislature that is referred to the vote of the electorate for approval or rejection

regressive taxation Taxation that hits the lower income brackets more heavily

regulatory agency A department, bureau, or independent agency whose primary mission is to eliminate or restrict certain behaviors defined as negative in themselves or negative in their consequences

regulatory review The Office of Management and Budget function of reviewing all agency regulations and other rule making before they become official policy

reprieve Cancellation or postponement of a punishment

reserve requirement The amount of liquid assets and ready cash that the Federal Reserve requires banks to hold to meet depositors' demands for their money

reserved powers Powers, derived from the Tenth Amendment to the Constitution, that are not specifically delegated to the national government or denied to the states; these powers are reserved to the states

retrospective voting Voting based on the past performance of a candidate

right of rebuttal A Federal Communications Commission regulation giving individuals the right to have the opportunity to respond to personal attacks made on a radio or TV broadcast

right to privacy The right to be left alone, which has been interpreted by the Supreme Court to entail individual access to birth control and abortions

ripeness A case that is ready for litigation and does not depend upon hypothetical future events

roll-call votes Votes in which each legislator's yes or no vote is recorded

rule making A quasi-legislative administrative process that produces regulations by government agencies

rule of four The rule that *certiorari* will be granted only if four justices vote in favor of the petition

sample A small group selected by researchers to represent the most important characteristics of an entire population

sampling error A polling error that arises on account of the small size of the sample

Securities and Exchange Commission (SEC) Agency charged with regulating the U.S. securities industry and stock exchanges

selection bias A polling error in which the sample is not representative of the population being studied, so that some opinions are over- or underrepresented

selective benefits Benefits that do not go to everyone but, rather, are distributed selectively—only to those who contribute to the group enterprise

senatorial courtesy The practice whereby the president, before formally nominating a person for a federal district judgeship, finds out whether the senators from the candidate's state support the nomination

seniority The priority or status ranking given to an individual on the basis of length of continuous service on a congressional committee

"separate but equal" rule The doctrine that public accommodations could be segregated by race but still be equal

separation of powers The division of governmental power among several institutions that must cooperate in decision making

signing statement An announcement made by the president when a bill is signed into law

single-member district An electorate that is allowed to elect only one representative from each district—the typical method of representation in the United States

slander An oral statement made in "reckless disregard of the truth" and considered damaging to a victim because it is "malicious, scandalous, and defamatory"

Social Security A contributory welfare program into which working Americans place a percentage of their wages and from which they receive cash benefits after retirement

socialization A process through which individuals assimilate community preferences and norms through social interactions

sovereignty Supreme and independent political authority

spatial issue An issue for which a range of possible options or policies can be ordered, say, from liberal to conservative or from most expensive to least expensive

Speaker of the House The chief presiding officer of the House of Representatives. The Speaker is elected at the beginning of every Congress on a straight party vote. He or she is the most important party and House leader

speech plus Speech accompanied by activities such as sit-ins, picketing, and demonstrations. Protection of this form of speech under the First Amendment is conditional, and restrictions imposed by state or local authorities are acceptable if properly balanced by considerations of public order

staff agencies The agencies responsible for providing Congress with independent expertise, administration, and oversight capability

standing The right of an individual or an organization to initiate a court case

standing committee A permanent legislative committee that considers legislation within its designated subject area; the basic unit of deliberation in the House and Senate

stare decisis Literally, "let the decision stand." The doctrine whereby a previous decision by a court applies as a precedent in similar cases until that decision is overruled

state sovereign immunity A legal doctrine holding that states cannot be sued for violating an act of Congress

states' rights The principle that states should oppose increases in the authority of the national government. This view was most popular before the Civil War

strict scrutiny The most stringent standard of judicial review of a government's actions in which the government must show that the law serves a "compelling state interest"

subsidy A government grant of cash or other valuable commodities, such as land, to an individual or an organization; used to promote activities desired by the government, to reward political support, or to buy off political opposition

Supplemental Security Income (SSI) A program providing a minimum monthly income to people who pass a means test and are 65 years old or older, blind, or disabled. SSI is financed from general revenues that are not Social Security contributions

supremacy clause A clause of Article VI of the Constitution that states that all laws passed by the national government and all treaties are the supreme laws of the land and superior to all laws adopted by any state or any subdivision

supreme court The highest court in a particular state or in the United States. This court primarily serves an appellate function

survey A study of a relatively small subset of individuals that is used to make inferences about an entire population

tariff A tax on imported goods

Temporary Assistance for Needy Families (TANF) Federal funds for children in families that fall below state standards of need

third party A party that organizes to compete against the two major American political parties

Three-Fifths Compromise An agreement reached at the Constitutional Convention of 1787 stipulating that for purposes of the apportionment of congressional seats, every slave would be counted as three-fifths of a person

totalitarian government A system of rule in which the government recognizes no formal limits on its power and seeks to absorb or eliminate other social institutions that might challenge it

tragedy of the commons The idea that a common-access facility, owned by no one because it is available to everyone, will be overutilized

transaction costs The cost of clarifying each aspect of a principal-agent relationship and monitoring it to make sure arrangements are complied with

trial court The first court to hear a criminal or civil case

trustee A representative who votes based on what he or she thinks is best for his or her constituency

tyranny Oppressive government that employs the cruel and unjust use of power and authority

unfunded mandates National standards or programs imposed on state and local governments by the federal government without accompanying funding or reimbursement

United Nations (UN) An organization of nations founded in 1945 to be a channel for negotiation and a means of settling international disputes peaceably. The UN has had frequent successes in providing a forum for negotiation and on some occasions a means of preventing international conflicts from spreading. On a number of occasions, the UN has been a convenient cover for U.S. foreign policy goals

valence issue An issue or aspect of a choice for which all voters prefer a higher value, in contrast to a spatial issue. For example, voters prefer their politicians to be honest, and honesty is a valence issue

variable A categorization or numerical representation of all values of a given characteristic

veto The president's constitutional power to turn down acts of Congress within 10 days of their passage while Congress is in session. A presidential veto may be overridden by a two-thirds vote of each house of Congress

veto power The ability to defeat something even if it has made it on to the agenda of an institution

War Powers Resolution A resolution of Congress declaring that the president can send troops into action abroad only by authorization of Congress or if U.S. troops are already under attack or seriously threatened

whip system A communications network in each house of Congress. Whips poll the membership to learn their intentions on specific legislative issues and assist the majority and minority leaders in various tasks

White House staff The analysts and advisers to the president, often given the title "special assistant"

World Trade Organization (WTO) An international group promoting free trade that grew out of the General Agreement on Tariffs and Trade

writ of *certiorari* A formal request by an appellant to have the Supreme Court review a decision of a lower court. *Certiorari* is from a Latin word meaning "to make more certain"

writ of *habeas corpus* A court order demanding that an individual in custody be brought into court and shown the cause for detention. *Habeas corpus* is guaranteed by the Constitution and can be suspended only in cases of rebellion or invasion

Index

coordination mechanisms, courts as, 359
"Copenhagen climate summit," 712
Corzine, Jon, 195
cost-of-living adjustments (COLAs), 680, 687, 688, 691
Council of Economic Advisers (CEA), 276–77, 644
Council on Environmental Quality, 276–77
Court of Appeals, U.S., 352–54, 371
Fifth Circuit, 180–81
Court of Appeals for the Armed Forces, U.S., 349
Court of Appeals for the Federal Circuit, U.S., 349
Court of Appeals for Veterans Claims, U.S., 349
Court of Federal Claims, U.S., 349, 352
Court of International Trade, U.S., 349, 352
court packing plan, FDR's, 355
courts, 342–91
    appellate, 348, 350–51, 352–54, 366–67
    as coordination mechanisms, 359
    dispute resolution and, 359
    interest groups and, 584–85
    organization of, 347–48, 348
    politics and, 4–5, 358–61
    rule interpretation and, 359–61
    see also judicial branch; Supreme Court, U.S.
Cox, Gary W., 516n3
CRA (Congressional Review Act; 1996), 295
Craig's List, 605
credit, 650
Criminal Division, of Justice Department, 315–16
criminal law, 345–46, 346, 377
criminally accused, rights of, 130–31
"cruel and unusual punishment," 137–40
Crystal City, Tex., 173
C-SPAN, 430
Cuba, 414, 531, 614, 706, 725, 730
Cuban Americans, 22, 414, 531
Cuban missile crisis, 706
Culture War? The Myth of a Polarized America (Fiorina), 402
Czech Republic, 727

Daily Show with Jon Stewart, The, 603
Darfur, 728
Daschle, Tom, 195, 211, 580
data, 26–31
Dave's Redistricting App, 470
Davis, Gray, 475
Davis v. Federal Election Commission, 122
Dawson, Michael, 417
Dean, Howard, 539
death penalty, 137–40, 138, 139, 405–6
debates, presidential, 506–8
debt, 653–54
debt ceiling, 101, 657, 661
debt relief, 725
decentralization, 12
decisiveness, 11–12, 13, 218
    see also dispersion of decision
Declaration of Independence, 38–39
    equality and, 151
Declaration of Sentiments and Resolutions, 155
Deep South, 164, 506
Deepwater Horizon oil spill, 255
de facto segregation, 161, 166
defendants, 346
defense, 728
    spending on, 708–9
Defense Base Closure and Realignment Commission, 335
Defense Department, U.S., 124, 315, 316–17, 331, 609, 618, 619, 647, 715, 726
    creation of, 302
    gays in military and, 178
    women in military and, 178
Defense of Marriage Act (DOMA; 1996), 77, 177, 178–79, 374, 423
de jure segregation, 161, 165
Delaware:
    school segregation in, 159, 363
    Virginia Plan opposition of, 45
DeLay, Tom, 236, 305, 657
delegated powers, 252, 261–63
delegates, 188
delegation, 12–13
DeLong, Bradford, 646
democracy, 6
    freedom of the press and, 599
    representative, 12–13
    as weakened by political inattentiveness, 421
Democracy Corps, 436

Democratic Committee on Committees, 518
Democratic Congressional Campaign Committee (DCCC), 491, 539, 540
Democratic Forum, 222
Democratic National Committee (DNC), 491, 537, 538, 590
Democratic National Convention, of 1972, 538
Democratic Party, 210, 212–13, 634
    African Americans and, 412, 479, 490, 500, 627
    Bill Clinton's impeachment and, 193
    "blue states," 506
    California gerrymandering and, 204
    civil rights movement and, 550
    on contributory programs, 691
    divisions within, 550
    economic policy and, 670–71
    filibuster threat and, 281
    Great Depression and, 550
    gun laws and, 15
    G. W. Bush's judicial appointments and, 357, 384
    history of, 545–53
    Jackson's founding of, 546
    Jews and, 22
    Latino support for, 414, 490
    legislative priorities of, 553
    liberalism in, 551, 553
    members of, 234, 235
    New Deal and, 550
    "new Democrats" in, 526
    1968 election and, 553
    1988 national convention of, 472
    partisanship and, 234–35, 236
    primary elections, 472, 473
    reporters in, 615
    Republicans' differences with, 481–83, 523, 524–26, 542
    Social Security and, 682
    South and, 499–500, 543
    Southern Democrats and, 397, 514, 526, 550
    tax cuts and, 656
    Texas gerrymandering and, 204–5
    2006 election victories of, 210, 211
    2010 elections and, 500–501
    2012 elections and, 506–8
    two-party system and, 513–15
    war and, 730

Democratic Party (*continued*)
welfare reform and, 689–91
white southerners in, 548, 550
Democratic-Republican party,
see Republican party
(Jeffersonian)
Democratic Republic of Congo,
713
Democratic Senatorial Campaign
Committee (DSCC), 491,
539, 540
Democratic Study Group, 222
Depression, Great, 271, 273, 435,
550, 644, 650, 670–71, 672,
675–76, 677
deregulation, 335, 665
see also regulation
desegregation, 163–67, *165*, 393,
397, 543
school busing and, 164–66
see also racial discrimination;
racism; segregation
"deserving poor," 674
détente, 706
deterrence, 706–7
definition of, 706
rationality and, 707
Detrol, 620, 622
devolution, 89, 335–37
Dewey, Thomas, 397
Dickerson v. United States, 135
Diet, Japanese, 186
Dingell, John, 221, 578
diplomacy, 255, 721–23
definition of, 721
Disability Rights Education and
Defense Fund, 176
discharge petition, 220
discount rate, 650
discretionary spending, 662
discrimination, 156–61, 417
Disney, 563
dispersion of decision, 72–74
see also decisiveness
dispute resolution, 359
Disraeli, Benjamin, 693
dissenting opinion, 376
distributive tendency, 230–31, 245,
332
District of Columbia, 79
District of Columbia v. Heller, 130
divided government, 96–97
division of labor, 306
Dixiecrat Party, 397
DNC (Democratic National
Committee), 491, 537, 538, 590

Dodd-Frank Wall Street Reform
and Consumer Protection Act
(2010), 314, 327, 634, 643, 649
Dole, Bob, 89
DOMA, *see* Defense of Marriage
Act
Don't Ask, Don't Tell policy, 177,
178
double jeopardy, 112, 114, 134
Douglas, Stephen, 432, 547
Douglas, William O., 141, 355, 373
Douglass, Frederick, 155
Dow Jones Industrial Index, 518
Downs, Anthony, 478
draft card burning, 122
Dred Scott v. Sandford, 98, 147, 355,
362
Drudge Report, 606
drug testing, mandatory, 132–33
dual citizenship, 108–9
dual federalism, 79–83
dual loyalty, 718
due process of the law, 112, 131,
350, 362
Fifth Amendment and, 151
Duke Power Company, 170
Duncan v. Louisiana, 114*n*14
duties, 186–87
Duverger, Maurice, 472, 514
Duverger's Law, 472–73

Early, Stephen, 283
earmarks, 197–98, 593–94
earned income tax credit (EITC),
689
East India Company, 37
Eastland, James, 357
East Timor, 713
economic aid, 725
economic class, in party identity,
532, 533
economics, economy, 543,
632–73
automobile industry and, 642
banks and, 649–50, 651, 665
Bill Clinton and, 671
"bubbles" in market, 638, 672
business development and,
646–47
civil rights and, 151
Congress and, 272, 653
credit and, 650
debt and, 653–54
election outcomes affected by,
488
employees and, 647–49

environment and, 639, 667–70
executive branch and, 272
Federal Reserve and, 646
financial crisis (2008–2009) and,
632–34, 643, 645, 651,
652–53, 667, 671, 672
fiscal policies and, 653–61
foreign policy and, 725
"free market" and, 632
full employment and, 644–45
as global, 632
goals, 640–49
government spending and, 632,
656–61
G. W. Bush and, 633–34, 657,
671, 672
immigration and, 644
individualism and, 632
industrial policy and, 68
inflation and, 645–46
interest groups and, 562–64
Keynesian, 644
laissez-faire principle and, 525
market, *see* market economy
market power and, 664
market stability and, 640–41
military spending and, 643, 647,
666–67, 707
minimum wages and, 648, 671
monetary policies and, 649–53
monopolies and, 640–41, 664
Obama and, 643
oil production and, 645
policy, 640–49
politics and, 670–72
prosperity and, 641–46,
710–11
public order and, 640
recession and, 645
sequestration and, 660
stimulus package and, 501, 502,
643, 667
stock market crash (1929) and,
643
subprime market and, 652
taxation and, 645, 654–56
technology and, 641, 642, 647
toxic assets and, 633
unemployment and, 632,
644–45, 651
wage and price controls and,
672
women's rights and, 155
see also Federal Reserve System;
taxes
economic sanctions, 725

Economic Theory of Democracy, An
(Downs), 478
Edison Research, 484
Editor and Publisher, 616
Edsall, Tom, 617
education, 405, 407, 428, 644,
694–98, 700
bilingual, 174–75
equality in, 162–63
and equality of opportunity,
676
higher, women and, 166–67
labor force and, 637–38, 644
lobbying and, 593–94
media and, 623–26, *626*
social policy and, 697–98
universal access to, 163
voting and, 477
vouchers for, 698
see also No Child Left Behind Act
Education Act (1972), 166
Title IX of, 166
Education Department, U.S., 295,
315, 622, 696
Office for Civil Rights, 167
EEOC (Equal Employment
Opportunity Commission),
171, 176
Egypt, 725, 731
Eighteenth Amendment, 63, 66
Eighth Amendment, 64, 131,
137–40
Eisenhower, Dwight D., 164, 254,
357
on "military-industrial complex,"
666
Eisenstadt v. Baird, 584
EITC (earned income tax credit),
689
elastic clause, 51, 80
see also necessary and proper
clause
elected office:
citizenship and, 150
requirements for, 150
Election Day, 522
Election Day registration, 477
see also voter registration, same
day
election outcomes, candidates'
personal attributes and,
489–91
election reform, 574
elections:
at-large, 461
campaign finance in, 448

parliamentary governments and,
493
elections, U.S., 3–4, 8–9, 277–78,
446–511, *504*, *505*, 519, 527
of 1800, 545
of 1824, 546
of 1828, 546
of 1832, 546
of 1840, 547
of 1856, 547
of 1858, 547
of 1860, 547
of 1892, 549
of 1896, 549–50
of 1928, 550
of 1932, 550
of 1936, 435
of 1948, 555
of 1964, 551
of 1968, 551, 553
of 1972, 628
of 1980, 479, 512, 531
of 1984, 481
of 1992, 201, 234, 532, 553
of 1994, 201, 239, 482, 512
of 1996, 532, 553
of 2006, 201, 210, 211,
432, 512
activism in, 592–93
campaign finance and, 506, *587*
caucuses in, 493, 545
criteria for victory in, 471–73
issues, 484–88
laws governing, 448
nominations for, 520–22, 553
partisan loyalty in, 516–17,
516*n*3
presidential debates in 2012,
506–8
primary, 473, 493, 500, 520–22
runoff, 471
turnout of, 448
voters decisions in, 476–91
elections, U.S., of 2004, 228, 448,
490, 508
Daschle's loss in, 211
Nader in, 555
elections, U.S., of 2008, 448, 484,
490, 500, 501, 507, *509–10*
Internet and, 602
elections, U.S., of 2010, 5,
198–99, 201, 211, 448, 463,
512, 634
campaign finance in, 493
caucuses in, 459
laws governing, 449–50

organization of, 449
partisan loyalty in, 478–83
primary, 473
turnout of, *452*
see also voting rights
elections, U.S., of 2012, *26*, *27*, *30*,
198, 211, 401, 448, 463, 479,
480, *481*, 490, 493, 500–501,
509–10, 532, 607, 671, 711
caucuses in, 503
partisan loyalty in, *481*
electoral college, 48, 251, 440,
461–63, 471, 500, *501*,
514, 542
electoral connection, 9
electoral districts:
bias and, 466–67
Congress and, 460–71
majority-minority, 464
redistricting and, 463–71, *465*
electoral system, 194–206
Elementary and Secondary
Education Act (ESEA; 1965),
696
Eleventh Amendment, 66, 89–92
Ellis, Joseph, 43
Ellsberg, Daniel, 618
Ellsworth, Oliver, 45
Ellwood, David, 429
e-mail voting, 450
Emanuel, Rahm, 275, 672
Emergency Economic Stabilization
Act (2008), 580
emergency power, presidential,
296–97
Emergency Price Control Act
(1942), 364
eminent domain, 76, 110, 135
Emmanuel, Rahm, 326
employment:
discrimination in, 170–71
economics and, 648
full, 644–45
see also unemployment
encroachments, 96–97, 101
Endangered Species Act (1973),
576
Energy Department, U.S., 315,
669
England, 32–33
Magna Carta and, 150–51
see also United Kingdom
Entertainment Software
Association, 578
entitlement, 688, 691–92
rising cost of, *686*

federal jurisdiction, 349–52
Federal Lobbying Disclosure Act (1995), 576
Federal Register, 665
Federal Regulation of Lobbying Act (1946), 576
Federal Reserve Act (1913), 652
Federal Reserve banks, 318
Federal Reserve Board, 318, 650, 652, 665
Federal Reserve System, 314, 318, 620, 634, 646, 649–53, 664
  interest rates and, 643, 646
federal service, 332, *333, 336*
Federal Trade Act (1914), 664
Federal Trade Commission (FTC), 129, 314, 317, 664
federal trial courts, 352
Feingold, Russell, 494
FEMA (Federal Emergency Management Agency), 306
FHA (Federal Housing Administration), 589
FICA tax, 680
  see also Social Security tax
Fifteenth Amendment, 148, 156, 159, 179
Fifth Amendment, 64, 108, 110, 131, 133–35, 141, 146, 347
  due process of the law and, 151
  homosexuals' rights protected under, 179
fifty-state strategy, 539
fighting words, 127–28
Figueiredo, John de, 593
filibuster, 224, 229, 280–81, 384, 679
Financial Stability Oversight Council, 314
Fiorina, Morris, 402, 410, 483
fire alarm oversight, 330–31
fireside chats, FDR and, 282
First Amendment, 64, 112, 114, 115–30, 351–52, 386, 431, 442, 496, 588, 589, 599–600, 601, 604, 609
  establishment clause of, 115–18, 119
  freedom of speech and, 119–30
  freedom of the press and, 599–600, 609–10
  free exercise clause of, 118
  national government and, 107–8
  nationalization of, 112, 114
  religious ideas and, 115–19
First Continental Congress, 38

First Hundred Days, 271
fiscal policies, 653–61
Fisher, Louis, 129
501c(4) organizations, 496
flag-burning:
  amendment banning, 123
  as protected speech, 122–23
Flag Protection Act (1989), 123
Florida, 92, 470
  House seats gained by, 204
Focus on the Family, 374
FOIA (Freedom of Information Act; 1966), 311, 327
Food and Drug Administration (FDA), 287, 290, 317, 441, 648, 664
Food Safety and Inspection Service, 312
food stamps, 687, 690
Food Stamps Program, 319
Force Act, *see* Civil Rights Act (1875)
Ford, Gerald, 248, 256
foreign policy, 187, 702–32
  architects of, 713–20
  bureaucracy and, 704, 714–15, 717, 721
  child labor and, 711
  collective security and, 726–27
  Congress and, 716–17, *716*
  Constitution and, 714, 717
  definition of, 703
  deterrence and, 706, 707
  diplomacy and, 721–23
  economic aid and, 725
  environment and, 711
  goals of, 704–13
  and humanitarianism, 712–13, 725
  human rights and, 711
  instruments of, 721–30
  interest groups and, 717–19
  isolationism and, 705
  military and, 717, 725
  most favored nation status and, 710
  national interest and, 702
  national security and, 702, 704–10
  Obama and, 710, 711, 714
  president and, 704, 714, 716, *716*, 717, 719–20, 721
  protectionism and, 711
  rogue states and, 707
  sanctions and, 725
  tariffs and, 710

trade and, 710–11
  World Bank and, 725
Foreign Service Act (1946), 721
Forest Service, U.S., 310, 312
formal bargaining, 15–16
formula grants, 85
Fourteenth Amendment, 65, 66, 109–14, *111*, 147–48, 151, 157, 158, 159–61, 179, 362, 462, 688
  Bill of Rights and, 65, 107–14, *111*
  Brown v. Board of Education and, 159–61
  Plessy v. Ferguson and, 158
Fourth Amendment, 64, 114, 131–33, 141
Fox News, 598, 603, 605, 611, 616, 626
framing, 431
France, 32, 78, 256, 705
  American Revolution and, 39
  elections in, 493
  Nazi Germany and, 703, 706
  in UN, 723
Frankfurter, Felix, 355, 375, 378
Franklin, Benjamin, 38, 69
Franklin v. Gwinnett County Public Schools, 166–67
Frazier, Lynn, 475
Frederick, Joseph, 128, 351
freedom of assembly, 122–23
  Supreme Court and, 112
Freedom of Information Act (FOIA; 1966), 311, 327
freedom of petition, 122–23
freedom of religion, 112, 115–19
freedom of speech, 119–30, 599, 608
  Supreme Court and, 112, 599
  see also First Amendment
freedom of the press, 119–30, 609–10
  Supreme Court and, 112
free exercise clause, 118
"free market" economy, 632
free riding, 17–18, 548, 570–71, 572, 595
Free-Soilers, 547
free trade, 711
  G. W. Bush and, 711
Frémont, John C., 547
French and Indian Wars, 35
frequency, 27
Friends of the Earth, 428
Frist, Bill, 211, 229

voting rights, 48, 153–57, 173, 175, 377, 467
  African Americans and, 455
  civil rights and, 146–47
  ex-felons and, 454
  institutionalized and, 454
  Justice Department and, 451
  Latino Americans and, 156–57
  New York State constitution and, 152–53
  Protestants and, 154
  Vietnam War and, 150
  women and, 155–56
Voting Rights Act (1965), 155, 156, 167, 175, 205, 411, 423, 441, 467, 500, 551
Voting Rights Act (1982), 464
vouchers, for education, 376, 698

Wabash, St. Louis, and Pacific Railway Company v. Illinois, 82n14
wage and price controls, 672
Wagner, Richard, 574, 575
Wagner, Robert, 574, 575
Wagner Act, *see* National Labor Relations Act
Walden, Greg, 539
Walker, Robert, 475
Wallace, George, 551, 553, 555
Wallace, Henry, 555
wall of separation, 116
Wall Street Journal, 605, 606, 616
Wal-Mart, 595
Walt Disney Company, 611
war:
  in Constitution, 50, 76
  declaration of, 76, 187
  see also specific wars
War Department, U.S., 316
  see also Defense Department, U.S.
wards, 539
Wards Cove v. Atonio, 180
War of 1812, 242, 243, 546, 716
war on terrorism, 279, 365, 408, 727
  see also Afghanistan war; Iraq war
War Powers Act (1973), 97
War Powers Resolution (1973), 264
Warren, Earl, 134, 355, 379, 387
Warsaw Pact, 726–27
Washington, D.C., *see* District of Columbia
Washington, George, 42, 69, 106, 556–57
  farewell address of, 703, 705
  Genet received by, 256

House request refused by, 256
  political parties deplored by, 545
Washington Metropolitan Transit Authority, 79
Washington Post, 604, 618, 619, 623, 628
Washington State, 450
Watergate scandal, 96, 121, 242, 248, 257, 590, 628
Water Resources Development Act (2007), 227
Waxman, Henry, 221
WCBS (radio station), 603
Wealth of Nations (Smith), 12–13
weapons, 725
weapons of mass destruction (WMDs), 276, 432, 730
Weaver, Dan, 615
Web logs (blogs), 430, 602, 606
Webster v. Reproductive Health Services, 142, 585
welfare, 318, 319, 429, 438, 638, 674–76, *681*, 687–94, 700
  arguments against, 691–92
  arguments for, 692–94
  decrease of, *690*
  foundations of, 680–91
  growth of, *695*
  history of, 674–76
  immigrants and, 689
  in polls, 438
  as "welfare state," 83, 677, 679, 688, 700
  see also Personal Responsibility and Work Opportunity Reconciliation Act
welfare reform, 337, 666, 688–91, *690*
Westmoreland, William, 610
West Publishing Company, 293
West Virginia State Board of Education v. Barnette, 118
Whig party, 546–47, 554
whips, whip system, 210–11, 237
White House Communications Office, 283, 286
White House Live, 607
White House Office of Management and Budget (OMB), 276, 319, 661, 665
White House staff, 275–76
white primaries, 156, 158
whites, 412, *413*
  voting among poor, *413*, 500
"wholesale" politics, 9

Wickard v Filburn, 82
Will, George, 693, 694
Williams, Armstrong, 622
Wilson, James, 45, 48
Wilson, Joseph, 619
Wilson, Pete, 183
Wilson, Woodrow, 270, 272–73, 326, 705
  popular mobilization and, 282
Windsor, Edith, 179
Winfrey, Oprah, 430
wiretapping, 257
Wisconsin, 129, 337, 457, 477
Wisconsin v. Mitchell, 129
WMDs (weapons of mass destruction), 276, 432, 730–31
Wolfowitz, Paul, 730
women:
  in Congress, 155, 202–3
  economic rights for, 155
  Education Act and, 166
  higher education and, 166–67
  in labor force, 677
  in military, 178
  party identity and, 479, 517, 531–32
  in post–World War II U.S., 677
  poverty and, 699
  voting rights and, 155–56
  see also gender discrimination; gender gap; League of Women Voters
women's movement, 172
women's rights, 171–73
Woodward, Bob, 619
working conditions, 675
Works Progress Administration (WPA), 271, 644
World Bank, 724–25
World Health Organization, 712
World Trade Center, 604
  see also September 11, 2001, terrorist attacks of; terrorism
World Trade Organization (WTO), 710–11
World War I, 698, 705, 716, 723
  as presidential war, 243
World War II, 23, 677, 698, 703, 705, 706, 711, 716, 721, 723, 724, 140
  grants-in-aid and, 84
  as presidential war, 243
World Wide Web, 606
  see also Internet